Policing America's Empire

New Perspectives in Southeast Asian Studies

Policing America's Empire

The United States, the Philippines, and the Rise of the Surveillance State

Alfred W. McCoy

The University of Wisconsin Press

Publication of this volume has been made possible, in part, through support from the Evjue Foundation, Inc., the charitable arm of *The Capital Times*,
and,
at the University of Wisconsin–Madison,
the Anonymous Fund of the College of Letters and Science, the Center for Southeast Asian Studies, the Graduate School, and the International Institute.

The University of Wisconsin Press
1930 Monroe Street, 3rd Floor
Madison, Wisconsin 53711-2059

uwpress.wisc.edu

3 Henrietta Street
London WC2E 8LU, England

1 3 5 4 2

Printed in the United States of America

Library of Congress Cataloging-in-Publication Data
McCoy, Alfred W.
Policing America's empire : the United States, the Philippines, and the rise of the surveillance state / Alfred W. McCoy.
p. cm.—(New perspectives in Southeast Asian studies)
Includes bibliographical references and index.
ISBN 978-0-299-23414-0 (pbk.: alk. paper)
ISBN 978-0-299-23413-3 (e-book)
1. Espionage, American—Philippines—History—20th century.
2. Philippines—History—Philippine American War, 1899–1902—Secret service.
3. Philippines—History—Autonomy and independence movements.
I. Title. II. Series.
DS685.M343 2009
959.9′031—dc22
2009010253

For friends met on a long journey into the Philippine past

Dr. Brian Fegan

Dr. Doreen G. Fernandez

Dr. Helen Mendoza

Contents

Acknowledgments

The intellectual debts I have accrued during my decade of work on this book begin and end in the Philippines. I started this project as a Fulbright-Hays fellow at the Ateneo de Manila University in 1998 – 99, where my work was hosted by Fr. Bienvenido Nebres, SJ, Antonette Palma-Angeles, and Fr. Jose Cruz, SJ. During my daily commutes across Quezon City through hours of gridlocked traffic to the Ateneo campus, countless taxi drivers regaled me with tales of police corruption and offered insight into the city's endless law enforcement intrigues.

As these conversations led me to launch this research into the history of Philippine police, other observers shared knowledge hard won from a lifetime's immersion in Manila's politics. Attorney Arno Sanidad of the Free Legal Assistance Group (FLAG) arranged for access to case records, as did ex-senator Jovito Salonga, whose assessment of the landmark *Aberca v. Ver* case is reflected in chapter 12. At the Philippine Center for Investigative Journalism, Sheila Coronel, now a professor at Columbia University's School of Journalism, was generous in sharing her wealth of insight and contacts. In each of my periodic visits to Manila over the past thirty-five years, I have learned a great deal from conversations with Edilberto de Jesus about the country's politics and from Melinda de Jesus about the workings of its media. During these research trips, Teresita Deles was enormously helpful in facilitating access to senior officials in the Philippine National Police and the National Bureau of Investigation.

As the project reached back in time to cover two centuries of Philippine policing, Rose Mendoza retrieved Spanish colonial documents at the Philippine National Archives. At Ateneo's wonderful Rizal Library, Mel Lopez and his daughter Miko Lopez assisted my research into postcolonial developments. At the city's journal of record, *The Philippine Daily Inquirer*, the library staff was always accommodating, columnist Amando Doronila insightful about the country's politics, and the paper's founding publisher, Mrs. Eggy Apostol, inspirational in her unflinching integrity. More broadly, I am grateful to dedicated staff at research institutions across Manila—the Lopez Museum, the Philippine National Archives, the Laurel Presidential Library, and the Philippine National Library.

In my Philippine research, I also incurred some more general intellectual debts. In particular, I am thankful to Rey Ileto for his friendship in years past, once driving me through the rural towns that ring Laguna de Bay and teaching me to read the subtle symbols of anticolonial resistance encoded in church iconography—lessons that I tried to keep in mind as I focused on the other side of the colonial equation.

Back in the United States, this project became, at times, more detective work than broad historical research, forcing me to find some very particular data. In these painstaking searches, I was well served by dedicated research associates at the University of Wisconsin–Madison. Ellen Jarosz compiled the data on career patterns in chapter 2. Joshua Gedacht made periodic research forays to Washington, using his impressive investigative skills to locate elusive archival documents. Yosef Djakababa reviewed the sources throughout with extraordinary assiduousness. Ruth de Llobet took time from her own research in Spain to find documents on the Spanish colonial police. A graduate student in Southeast Asian studies, Maj. Christopher O'Brien, a veteran of Operation Enduring Freedom–Philippines, gave chapter 16 a critical reading that forced me to both clarify and correct my analysis. History graduate student Melissa Anderson took time from her parallel study of French colonial police in Vietnam to give the near final manuscript a thoughtful review.

At the University of Wisconsin–Madison, where I did much of this research, I have also benefited from the professionalism and generous support of many dedicated librarians, including Nancy Mulhern, documents specialist at the venerable Wisconsin Historical Society; Judy Tuohy in Inter-Library Loan at Memorial Library; and the Southeast Asian bibliographer at Memorial, Larry Ashmun. Elsewhere in the United States, a history graduate student, Jose Amiel Angeles, did painstaking research into the Philippines Constabulary papers at University of Oregon Library, while another young scholar, Chris Bray, spent a week in close study of Senator Jack Tenney's voluminous oral history at the UCLA Library. At the Special Collections Library, University of Michigan, librarian Kathryn Beam was enormously helpful, assuring maximum yield from several short visits to Ann Arbor squeezed between teaching days in Madison. Elsewhere in Michigan, the editors of *Critical Asian Studies*, Tom Fenton and Mary Heffron, did some painstaking proofing of the final draft, imposing order on a complex manuscript.

At both the University of Wisconsin and campuses elsewhere, the community of Southeast Asia specialists was a supportive and critical audience for papers and drafts presented during the decade of work on this project. I am grateful to them all for their many contributions. To Michael Cullinane for a careful reading of part one, using his expertise to critique and correct my assessment of the extent of U.S. policing's impact on Philippine society. To Florentino Rodao at Universidad Complutense de Madrid, for encouraging my work on the Spanish period. To Gregory Bankoff, University of Hull, for sources and suggestions on Spanish colonial police. To Dan Doeppers, for insights about the way Manila's distinctive geography and settlement patterns impacted upon U.S. colonial policing and for a careful reading of chapter 9. To Michael Onorato, for sharing his verbatim notes of an interview with former Manila mayor Ramon Fernandez nearly forty years ago. To Anna Leah Fidelis Castañeda, for her judicious analysis of the Springer decision and her sharp, informed reading of chapter 8. And to Eric Haanstad, for an engaged analysis of the work's penultimate draft.

This book would not have evolved without the attention of audiences at conferences and seminars that heard various drafts of this study over the past ten years. Most important, Ms. Peggy Choy invited me to present periodic work-in-progress papers at the Center for Southeast Asian Studies, University of Wisconsin–Madison, before an audience of specialists who could engage the project in all its multifaceted dimensions. Beyond Madison, the quadrennial International Conference on Philippine Studies (ICOPHIL) gave me an audience of specialists from five continents at three key points in this project's genesis. The Quezon City ICOPHIL in 2000 heard a tentative first paper that elicited encouraging comments from Paul Hutchcroft and Patricio Abinales; a second, more venturesome paper at the 2004 gathering in Leiden, organized by Otto van den Muizenberg and Rosanne Rutten, received useful comments from Greg Bankoff, Jim Warren, and Glenn May; and the most recent 2008 assembly in Quezon City heard a near-final draft of chapter 1 that brought probing questions from Jim Rush and Esther Pacheco. Over dinner after hearing this last paper, Resil Mojares cautioned me against the inherent arrogance of analyzing the Philippines, even critically, from an U.S. imperial perspective, a positionality that might militate against seeing how Filipino agency mediated foreign controls.

In that same 2008 visit to the Philippines, other audiences offered an engaged response to two near-final chapters from this book. At the University of the Philippines (UP) Diliman campus, Third World Studies hosted a seminar—organized by Maria Ela L. Atienza, Teresa Tadem, and Aries Arugay—that produced thoughtful questions by Vina Lanzona of University of Hawaii and Professor Rico Jose of the UP History Department that forced me to deepen my analysis of U.S. policing as a response to Filipino resistance. Later that week, an afternoon forum at the UP's Manila campus, chaired by Dean Reynaldo Imperial and Professor Bernard Karganilla, provided an audience of students and faculty who stayed for hours to question my early inclination to privilege the imperial state, pressing me to identify social sectors, such as the labor movement, that had eluded the full force of colonial police controls.

Among the many lectures and papers presented elsewhere during this decade of research and writing, three were particularly memorable and helpful. In

September 2005, James C. Scott hosted a lecture at the Yale Southeast Asian Center that gave me a critical hearing to my work on colonial policing. A year later, Melbourne University Law School hosted a conference on para-politics under Tim Lindsey and Eric Wilson that drew scholars from four continents to reflect on the invisible influence of state security and criminal syndicates upon modern political life, allowing me to develop more fully the theoretical dimension of this work found in chapter 1. In November 2006, a conference on "Transitions and Transformations in the U.S. Imperial State" at the University of Wisconsin–Madison gave a thoughtful hearing to an early draft of chapter 9 on the repatriation of the colonial model, as did a second round of this conference at Sydney University two years later. In these latter gatherings, my Wisconsin colleagues Francisco Scarano, Courtney Johnson, and Warwick Anderson offered insight and an outlet to test the broader implications of these ideas.

I have been fortunate in my choice of publishers. Were it not for the constant support of staff at the University of Wisconsin Press, this work would have taken another five years and missed its historical moment. I am particularly indebted to the book's editor, Dr. Gwen Walker. In an age when editors no longer edit, she gave this entire manuscript two careful readings. In the last round of revisions, she cut an ungainly manuscript by nearly half—inserting editorial notes at the start of each chapter to suggest larger themes that could encapsulate masses of detail, bracketing passages for possible excision, and deftly rearranging sections to tighten the chapter's focus. The two anonymous readers retained by the press also gave the book a close reading, identifying implicit themes that helped the work's two parts cohere. Now that the work is in press and they have identified themselves, I can thank these readers, John Sidel of the University of London and Chris Capozzola of the Massachusetts Institute of Technology, for the extraordinary care and creativity that they invested in their reviews, offering suggestions that played a critical role in realizing the analytical potential of this project. Though some of their comments were so brief as to be almost cryptic, they contained a spark of insight that transformed my study of the postwar period in part two into a broader exploration of U.S. global power. As the volume moved into production, Jan Opdyke proved, as always, an assiduous copy editor and Adam Mehring an efficient and encouraging managing editor. The press director, Sheila Leary, believed in the promise of this work and authorized investment of the time and resources necessary for its realization.

Throughout the decade of research and writing needed to complete this project, my wife Mary McCoy was my most important audience for the ideas that took form in these pages. Her support made these endless hours of work sustainable and even enjoyable. In the last months when these chapters reached final form, she took time from her own writing on Indonesia to review the manuscript, identifying passages that lacked clarity and cogency. My mother, Margarita P. McCoy, took time away from her busy retirement career as an urban planner to make very helpful suggestions about the shape of chapter 9. If every scholar is shaped by just one or two teachers during those long years of schooling, then I remain deeply indebted to my high school English teacher Robert Cluett, now retired from the English Department at York University, who introduced me to the craft of writing and nurtured my first essays into a lifelong vocation. Even now, nearly fifty years after he marked my first essays with such care, his lessons and his passion still guide my fingers across this keyboard.

Finally, there are some special debts of a personal nature. As young graduate students back in the 1970s, Doreen Fernandez and I traveled together through the slums and villages of Iloilo Province in the central Philippines, sharing insights, notes, and sources. When I ventured across the Guimaras Strait into her home province of Negros Occidental, her family was protective of my presence, even when they disagreed fundamentally with much of my writing. Her passing has left me feeling diminished. During the whole of my forty-year career writing about the Philippines, Brian Fegan of Sydney was a close friend and a constant source of inspiration, lending a sense of intellectual excitement to the study of the country's volatile social history. His recent death has deprived me of a good friend, a mentor to my sons, and an unflinchingly honest assessment of my work. Above all, I am indebted to Helen Mendoza of Quezon City, an activist researcher who has lent her formidable skills, for over a quarter century, to the development of Philippine democracy. Whenever I have needed elusive documents, personal contacts, or research support, she has reached into her vast political network to accomplish what would otherwise have been impossible. Throughout my ten years of work on this project, Tita Helen was my imagined audience, the person I hoped would read and approve. To these three friends who have accompanied me on this lifelong journey into the Philippine past, this book is dedicated with affection and gratitude.

Abbreviations

ABB	Alex Boncayao Brigade (New People's Army, Philippines)
ABS-CBN	Alto Broadcasting System-Chronicle Broadcasting Network (Philippines)
ACLU	American Civil Liberties Union (United States)
AEF	American Expeditionary Forces
AFP	Armed Forces of the Philippines
AP	Associated Press (United States)
ASSO	Arrest Search and Seizure Order (Philippines)
APL	American Protective League
AT&T	American Telephone and Telegraph
ASAC	Anti-Smuggling Action Center (Philippines)
BI	Bureau of Investigation (later FBI, United States)
BCT	Battalion Combat Team (Philippines)
BPP	Border Patrol Police (Thailand)
BW	Best World Resources Corporation (Philippines)
CAFGU	Citizens Armed Force Geographical Unit (Philippines)
CANU	Constabulary Anti-Narcotics Unit (Philippines)
CIA	Central Intelligence Agency (United States)
CIC	Counter Intelligence Corps (U.S. Army)
CIO	Congress of Industrial Organizations (United States)
CMRF	Consequent Management Response Force (United States)
COINTELPRO	Counterintelligence Program (FBI, United States)
CP	Communist Party (United States)
CPP	Communist Party of the Philippines
CSU	Constabulary Security Unit (Philippines)
DEA	Drug Enforcement Administration (United States)
DI	Division of Investigation (later NBI, Philippines)

DILG	Department of Interior and Local Government (Philippines)
DMI	Division of Military Information (United States)
DOD	Department of Defense (United States)
DPA	deep penetration agent (Philippines)
EDSA	Epifanio de los Santos Avenue (Manila, Philippines)
FBI	Federal Bureau of Investigation (United States)
FLAG	Free Legal Assistance Group (Philippines)
HUAC	House Committee on Un-American Activities (United States)
G-2	Military Intelligence Branch (U.S. Army)
Huk	Hukbalahap, Hukbong Mapagpalaya ng Bayan (People's Liberation Army, Philippines)
IBM	International Business Machines (United States)
ICHDF	Integrated Civilian Home Defense Force (Philippines)
IFI	Iglesia Filipina Independiente
INP	Integrated National Police (Philippines)
IPA	International Police Academy (United States)
ISAFP	Intelligence Service Armed Forces of the Philippines
IWW	International Workers of the World (United States)
JI	*Jemmah Islamiyah* (Indonesia)
JSOC	Joint Special Operations Command (United States)
JSOTF-P	Joint Special Operations Task-Force-Philippines (United States)
JUSMAG	Joint U.S. Military Advisory Group
KGB	Komitjet Gosudarstvjennoj Bjezopasnosti (Committee of Public Safety, USSR)
KKK	Kristiano Kontra Komunismo (Philippines)
KMU	Kilusang Mayo Uno (May Day Movement, Philippines)
LIC	Low Intensity Conflict (U.S. Army)
Meralco	Manila Electric Railroad and Light Company
Metrocom	Metropolitan Command (Philippines Constabulary)
MID	Military Information Division (United States)
MIG	Military Intelligence Group (ISAFP, Philippines)
MIG-15	Military Intelligence Group 15 (ISAFP, Philippines).
MISG	Metrocom Intelligence Service Group (Philippines Constabulary)
MILF	Moro Islamic Liberation Front (Philippines)
MNLF	Moro National Liberation Front (Philippines)
MP	Military Police (U.S. Army)
MPC	Military Police Command (Philippines)
NAACP	National Association for the Advancement of Colored People (United States)
NAIA	Ninoy Aquino International Airport (Manila, Philippines)
Napolcom	National Police Commission (Philippines)

NBI	National Bureau of Investigation (Philippines)
NFSW	National Federation of Sugar Workers (Philippines)
NGO	nongovernmental organization
NICA	National Intelligence Coordinating Agency (Philippines)
NISA	National Intelligence and Security Authority (Philippines)
NISF	Naval Intelligence and Security Force (Philippines)
NPA	New People's Army (Philippines)
NSA	National Security Agency (United States)
NSC	National Security Council (United States)
NUSP	National Union of Students in the Philippines
NPA	New People's Army (Philippines)
ONI	Office of Naval Intelligence (United States)
OPS	Office of Public Safety (United States)
₱	Philippine peso
PACC	Presidential Anti-Crime Commission (Philippines)
Pagcor	Philippine Amusement and Gaming Corporation
PAOCTF	Presidential Anti-Organized Crime Task Force (Philippines)
PARGO	President's Agency for the Reform of Government Operations (Philippines)
PC	Philippines Constabulary
PCIB	Philippine Commercial International Bank
PC-INP	Philippines Constabulary-Integrated National Police
PCSO	Philippine Charity Sweepstakes Office
PCO	Presidential Commitment Order (Philippines)
PD	Presidential Decree (Philippines)
PDP-Laban	Pilipino Democratic Party–Lakas ng Bayan
PMA	Philippine Military Academy
PNB	Philippine National Bank
PNP	Philippine National Police
RAM	Reform the Armed Forces Movement (Philippines)
ROTC	Reserve Officers' Training Corps (Philippines, United States)
RSU-4	Regional Security Unit-4 (formerly 5th CSU, Philippines Constabulary)
SAF	Special Action Force (Philippine National Police)
SAP	Special Action Program (United States)
SD-X	Special Directorate X (PAOCTF, Philippine National Police)
SEALs	Sea, Air and Land Forces (U.S. Navy)
SOT	Special Operations Team (Philippines)
SP	Special Police (Philippines)
SWIFT	Society for Worldwide Interbank Financial Telecommunication
TFAG	Task Force Anti-Gambling (Philippines)
TFD	Task Force Detainees (Philippines)

TIPS	Terrorism Information and Prevention System (United States)
UMW	United Mine Workers (United States)
UN	United Nations
UP	University of the Philippines
USAID	United States Agency for International Development
USIS	United States Information Service
WACL	World Anti-Communist League
ZOTO	Zone One Tondo Organization (Manila, Philippines)
ZTE	Zhong Xing Telecommunications Equipment Corporation (China)

Policing America's Empire

During a search for insurgents in April 2007, American soldiers photograph the eye of an Iraqi in Mansour District, Baghdad, to check his identity in a military database of a million retina scans and fingerprints. (Bob Strong, Reuters)

Prologue

Analogies of Empire

In October 2003, as Baghdad bathed in blood from bombs detonated in opposition to the U.S. occupation, President George W. Bush flew toward Manila aboard Air Force One on a mission of historical affirmation. Over the Pacific the president's entourage recast the past for reporters with a briefing paper explaining that U.S. colonial rule over the Philippines "was always declared to be temporary and aimed to develop institutions that would . . . encourage the eventual establishment of a free and independent government." The formal reason for this Manila visit was, of course, to assure the Philippines' continuing participation in the "Coalition of the Willing," that curious mélange of middling and small states cobbled together for the war in Iraq when most of Washington's major European allies remained aloof. This colonial past, the memo continued, confirmed the correctness of the Bush administration's current mission to bring "institutions of democracy to Iraq."[1]

Repeating these themes in an address to the Philippine Congress, President Bush's words erased the years of brutal pacification that had followed the U.S. occupation in 1898. "America," he said, "is proud of its part in the great story of the Filipino people. Together our soldiers liberated the Philippines from colonial rule." Those who questioned the wisdom of his current course in Iraq should, the president chided, be mindful of history's lessons. "The same doubts," he explained, "were once expressed about the culture of Asia. These doubts were proven wrong nearly six decades ago, when the Republic of the Philippines became the first democratic nation in Asia."[2]

Analogy is arguably the lowest form of history, stripping both cases of nuance to make some tendentious political point. But the war in Iraq has produced a succession of parallels with this Philippine past too numerous to dismiss as merely incidental or ironic. Despite all that has changed in the intervening century, close comparison of these two conflicts reveals some striking similarities, though not those the Bush administration imagined. Indeed, anyone who has followed the Iraq War even casually in the press will be struck, as they read the chapters that follow, by deep resonances from this Philippine past in our Iraqi present.

This study shares the Bush administration's conviction that the Philippines reveals a great deal about America as a world power, albeit from a critical rather than celebratory perspective. At first glance, this book seems a study of Philippine policing, both colonial and national, throughout the twentieth century. At a deeper level, however, this is an essay on the exercise of American power, from imperial rule over a string of scattered islands in 1898 to today's worldwide dominion. By focusing on the actual mechanisms of Washington's global reach, both conventional and covert operations, this study explores the nature of U.S. force projection and its long-term consequences for both the nations within America's ambit and America itself.

The growing relevance of this book's subject, the U.S. pacification and policing of the colonial Philippines, was an unintended, even unwelcome result of spending a decade on its research and writing. Yet this relevance cannot be denied. In the midst of this protracted crisis over Iraq, it would be, in my view, irresponsible to leave these lessons to political partisans whose aims are exculpatory rather than explanatory. Indeed, the U.S. Army has a long tradition of studying military history closely, carefully, to mine the past for prescriptions to guide future operations. Frankly, I would be gratified if in some small way this book could contribute to mitigating some future foreign policy disaster like that of Iraq. Instead of saving these lessons for the book's final chapter, let me offer them here at the outset in part to serve the needs of the political present and in part to move on, unencumbered, to the broader problems of colonial rule and state formation central to this study. For those who prefer their history pointed and pragmatic, this prologue offers a quick review of Philippine-Iraq parallels followed by a summary of their implications for contemporary U.S. policy. In reading this redacted history the reader should be aware that contrasts are often more revealing than similarities.

From a strategic perspective the U.S. invasions of the Philippines and Iraq began as secondary theaters in larger global conflicts: the Spanish-American War and the global war on terror. Just as President William McKinley used the sinking of the battleship *Maine* in Havana as a pretext to invade the Philippines half a world away, so President Bush invoked the attack on New York's Twin Towers by Saudi terrorists trained in Afghanistan to justify the invasion of Iraq. In both cases Republican Party visionaries launched these invasions as modest military operations that would catalyze major geopolitical change. Just as McKinley tried to make America a Pacific power by colonizing the Philippines in 1898, so Bush hoped to transform the modern Middle East by occupying Iraq in 2003 or, as one senior Central Intelligence Agency analyst put it, to "use regime change in Iraq as a stimulus for regime change . . . elsewhere in the region."[3] Both invasions also began with strong support from similar political coalitions of Republican partisans, imperial ideologues, corporate contractors, middle-class patriots, and working-class soldiers.

In the first months of both wars the U.S. Army soon routed the ill-trained Filipino and Iraqi armies. But as guerrilla resistance persisted the American public grew bitter about the ensuing quagmire. The level of U.S. casualties—4,200 killed among 70,000 troops in the Philippines by 1902 and 4,200 killed among 130,000 troops in Iraq by late 2008—were not high compared to the far heavier bloodshed incurred in major conventional conflicts such as the Civil War and World War II. But these losses seem unjustified in wars waged against such weak enemies. And in both cases they were amplified by the bloody aura of high civilian casualties: some 200,000 dead in the Philippines and comparable estimates for Iraq ranging from 97,000 to 601,000 by late 2008.[4] As losses mounted, both interventions were opposed by a diverse group of critics, social progressives and some Democratic Party partisans, who felt that these presidential wars threatened American democracy.

In both cases combat continued long after the White House declared "mission accomplished," first in July 1902 and later in May 2003. In the long pacifications that followed, the U.S. Army descended, directly or through local surrogates, into what the French colonial military once called "la guerre sale," a dirty war marked by clandestine penetration, psychological warfare, disinformation, media manipulation, assassination, and torture. As early combat victories gave way to brutal counterinsurgencies, American domestic critics were increasingly incensed by the wholesale violence and periodic atrocities. After intervening in Cuba in 1898 to stop General Valeriano Weyler's "reconcentrations" of civilians, the U.S. Army soon found itself using similar methods in the Philippines.[5] After invading Iraq in March 2003 to end Saddam Hussein's brutality, the army was soon abusing Iraqis inside the former dictator's most notorious prison, Abu Ghraib. Without accurate intelligence to identify insurgents, both operations employed torture to extract information from hostile populations, via the "water cure" on Filipino insurgents and "water boarding" on Afghani and Iraqi terrorists.[6] Revelations about both practices fueled rising domestic disquiet then and now over such brutality.

In both wars electoral politics played a central role at home and abroad. The presidential campaign of 1900 became a debate over McKinley's imperialism, just as the 2004 and 2006 elections were a referendum on Bush's doctrine of preemptive warfare. Within the occupied territories American officials tried to use local elections to staunch rising resistance. The convening of the first Philippine Assembly in 1907 forged an effective colonial alliance between Americans and conservative Filipino elites, just as the 2005 Iraqi parliamentary elections won qualified support from the majority Shiite population. These elections also provided some legitimation for the controversial military occupations back in the United States, quieting for a time partisan calls for rapid withdrawal.

The real significance of this comparison may lie not in these many similarities but in a few critical contrasts. The spectacular capture of the defeated heads of state, Emilio Aguinaldo in 1901 and Saddam Hussein in 2003, were both successful covert operations that momentarily stilled U.S. domestic dissent. There the similarities end. In Manila, the American commander, Gen. Arthur MacArthur, granted Aguinaldo an immediate pardon and rewarded his officers with positions under colonial rule. As we will see, these Filipino veterans played a critical role in building the political parties and colonial police forces responsible for the ultimate success of the American pacification campaign. In Baghdad, by contrast, General MacArthur's latter-day counterparts punished Saddam Hussein with a show trial, humiliated him with a brutal execution, and barred his officers from any role in the new democratic regime. In 2003 the head of the Coalition Provisional Authority, L. Paul Bremer, dissolved the Iraqi army without pay or pensions, sparking an underground resistance that unleashed a wave of well-planned bombings.[7] "Now you have a couple hundred thousand people who are armed—because they took their weapons home with them—who know how to use the weapons, who have no future, who have a reason to be angry at you," said Col. Thomas X. Hammes of the Marines when he was asked to explain the reasons for the tenacious Iraqi resistance in late 2006.[8]

As the British learned in Burma in the 1880s and the Japanese in Korea a quarter century later, this is perhaps the most important historical lesson for any military occupation: the forced demobilization of a defeated army without conciliation or compensation may well be the key factor in promoting protracted resistance.[9]

Starting in 2007, the fifth year of the war, the U.S. military reversed this disastrous policy and began to tame the resistance by putting ninety-four thousand Sunnis, many of them ex-insurgents, on its payroll as members of local militias—in the face of smoldering opposition from its allies in the Shiite-dominated government. In late 2008, when U.S. commanders finally completed the pacification of Anbar Province, once the site of bloody fighting that resulted in a thousand American deaths, Iraqi leaders pointed out that such violence could have been avoided. "Paul Bremer disbanded the army, the government, the police," said one Sunni tribal leader. "We had no choice but to resist." As the U.S. command began transferring these militia forces, called the Awakening Councils, to Iraqi government jurisdiction in September 2008, the transition was troubled. Key militia commanders were assassinated by Islamic insurgents. There were also tensions with Shia sectarian rivals in the government forces who were still pursuing 650 Awakening commanders as enemies. "The American forces put us in a dilemma," said Sheik Salah al-Egaidi, a militia commander in Baghdad's Dora area. "The Awakening is the reason for the security improvement in Baghdad . . . but they have sold us now. Our choices now are either to be killed or to be arrested or to leave Iraq." Within six months these words proved prophetic, as the Awakening's commanders, numbering some five hundred in Baghdad and nearby provinces, found themselves caught in a vise jaws between assassination by terrorists or arrest by government troops.[10]

As a result of the midcourse policy correction associated with the "surge" in U.S. troop strength in 2007–8, American policy in Iraq finally focused, after five years of failure, on the formation of local army and police forces as the basis for an exit strategy other than retreat. There seems to be a certain parallel between this surge strategy and the U.S. colonial policy that transferred pacification after 1901 to the paramilitary Philippines Constabulary, whose ranks were filled with former Filipino insurgents. Indeed, the army's formation of indigenous forces in the colonial Philippines, the constabulary and the Philippine Scouts, was its first experience training an allied security force, a precursor to the postcolonial strategy of force projection among third world allies through bilateral security agreements, military aid, and training missions.

There are, of course, some deeper structural contrasts. In Iraq the United States has inserted itself into an ongoing civil war between sectarian enemies, Sunni versus Shia. By the time the U.S. Army landed at Manila in 1898, almost all Filipino factions shared common aspirations for independence after two generations of nationalist agitation. To an extent not fully grasped by many historians, the U.S. occupation of the Philippines succeeded because it co-opted this revolutionary nationalism, making an American presence seem a vehicle for the realization of Filipino aspirations. Moderate Filipino collaborators were rewarded with a degree of access to colonial offices unparalleled in an imperial age when colonial office was a white man's privilege. By contrast, Filipino radicals who resisted were punished with exile, imprisonment, and relentless police surveillance, a combination that soon contained Philippine politics within colonial bounds. A century later, by contrast, Washington intervened in a struggle among Iraqi religious factions so bitter that even the formidable firepower of the U.S. military initially failed to restrain a cycle of revenge that ripped this fragile nation apart at its sectarian seams.

More narrowly there are key differences in the effectiveness of the two military occupations, particularly in the realm of policing. In both the Philippines and Iraq the military soon realized that pacification required effective local police and armed forces to identify guerrillas. In the Philippines seasoned U.S. Army officers worked for fifteen years to make the Philippines Constabulary and Manila Police exemplars of imperial efficiency. A century later the Iraqi police grew rapidly into an ill-disciplined force infiltrated by rogue militia and immersed in sectarian slaughters, which soon made them a key factor in the failed

U.S. war effort. Despite American expenditures of over $12 billion on Iraqi security forces by late 2006, Iraq's president, Jalal Talabani, offered a sharply critical assessment shared by American experts: "What have they done so far in training the army and police? What they have done is move from failure to failure."[11] Thus, it seems a second policy prescription can be drawn from this historical comparison: an efficient local police force is critical to the success of any peacekeeping operation.

This comparison also produces some broad cautionary lessons about the domestic costs of these overseas occupations. In both the Philippines and Iraq, the U.S. military, thrust into these crucibles of counterinsurgency, developed innovative methods of social control that had a decidedly negative impact on civil liberties back home. As the military plunged into a fifteen-year pacification campaign in the Philippines, its colonial security agencies fused domestic data management with foreign police techniques to forge a new weapon—a powerful intelligence apparatus that first contained and then crushed Filipino resistance. In the aftermath of this successful pacification, some of these clandestine innovations migrated homeward, silently and invisibly, to change the face of American internal security. During the country's rapid mobilization for World War I, these colonial precedents provided a template for domestic counterintelligence marked by massive surveillance, vigilante violence, and the formation of a permanent internal security apparatus.

Empire thus proved mutually transformative in ways that have arguably damaged democracy in both the Philippines and the United States. In retrospect, this Philippine past is hardly the harbinger of Arab democracy that President Bush hoped to build in Iraq. To break resistance to foreign rule, U.S. colonial police subjected Filipino nationalists to constant surveillance, subverted religious reform, harassed the emerging labor movement, and reinforced entitled elites. After nearly two decades of colonial governance, the U.S. state repatriated these coercive innovations, in the years surrounding World War I, for domestic legislation that curtailed civil liberties: notably, the criminalization of drug use under the Harrison Narcotics Act of 1914, arbitrary arrests of dissidents under the 1917 Espionage Act, widespread wartime surveillance by military intelligence, and the postwar Palmer raids on suspected subversives.

Although at this writing the global war on terror is still far from over, its impact on American civil liberties is already showing some disconcerting parallels with this earlier Philippine pacification. In the five years after 9/11, the Bush administration expanded domestic surveillance with the USA Patriot Act, monitored domestic communications in defiance of U.S. law, and legalized CIA psychological torture under the Military Commissions Act of 2006. And there may well be long-term legacies of our Iraqi occupation that will not become manifest for decades to come. After all, it has taken us nearly a century to grasp the impact of Philippine colonial rule on American democracy. For the time being, it appears that the Iraq War, like the Philippine War of 1899–1902, might prove to be a fiery crucible that recasts the American polity through circumscribed civil liberties and pervasive internal security.

There are slender but significant signs that the Iraqi occupation may in fact become a second such crucible, developing new surveillance technologies with possible domestic applications. In April 2007 the *New York Times* published a photograph showing two American soldiers scanning a retina "to identify an Iraqi after the search of his house in Mansour, a western Baghdad neighborhood, that has been torn apart by sectarian violence." Without any data beyond that terse caption, we can infer the technological ramifications of this single retinal scan: sophisticated digital cameras for each U.S. patrol, wireless data transfer to a mainframe computer, and a comprehensive database for all the adult eyes in Baghdad. Eight months after the cryptic photo appeared, the *Washington Post* reported that the Pentagon had collected over a million Iraqi fingerprints and retinal scans to prepare for the deployment in early 2008 of collapsible labs, called joint expeditionary forensic facilities, each linked by satellite to a biometric database in West Virginia. "A war fighter needs to know one of three things," explained the Pentagon's inventor of this lab in a box. "Do I let him go? Keep him? Or shoot him on the spot?" In the next model the Pentagon planned a portable backpack-sized laboratory, possibly allowing some future U.S. sniper to sight the eyeball of a suspected terrorist, pause for a nanosecond transmission of the target's retina to West Virginia, and then a second later pull the trigger, terrorizing the terrorists and breaking their resistance.[12]

Lest this all seem a bit too fanciful, we should remember that in late 2008 the veteran *Washington Post* reporter Bob Woodward revealed that much of the success of President Bush's troop surge in suppressing the Iraqi resistance was due not to boots on the ground but to bullets in the head. Starting in May 2006 American intelligence agencies launched a series of Special Action Programs (SAPs) using "the most highly classified techniques and information in the U.S. government" in a successful effort "to locate, target and kill key individuals in extremist groups such as al Quaeda, the Sunni insurgency and renegade Shia militias." Under the leadership of Gen. Stanley McChrystal, the Joint Special Operations Command (JSOC) used "every tool available simultaneously, from signals intercepts to human intelligence," for "lightning quick" strikes. One intelligence officer said the techniques were so effective that they gave him "orgasms." President Bush called them "awesome." In a television interview, Woodward said, "I would somewhat compare it to the Manhattan Project in World War II," adding that cutting Iraq's violence in half within a matter of months "isn't going to happen with the bunch of joint security stations or the surge."[13] These operations were part of a broader authority that Defense Secretary Donald Rumsfeld gave JSOC in early 2004 to "kill or capture al-Qaeda terrorists" in twenty countries across the Middle East, producing dozens of lethal operations, including an AC-130 air strike on Somalia in January 2007, a special forces raid in Pakistan's tribal areas that killed twenty in September 2008, and a CIA-directed assault in Syria in October 2008 that left eight dead. Throughout 2008, as well, Predator drones operated inside Pakistan with lethal efficiency, killing nine of the twenty top-priority al-Qaeda targets identified by the U.S. intelligence community.[14]

Just as Philippine colonial police methods percolated homeward in the security crisis surrounding World War I, so in the aftermath of some future terrorist attack on America enhanced retinal recognition could be married to omnipresent security cameras for routine surveillance of public space across America. The same equipment, tempered to a technological cutting edge in the forge of Iraqi counterinsurgency, could be readily adapted to scan every passenger at U.S. airports, every pedestrian on a Manhattan street, and every visitor to a federal facility—matching retinal scans to a national computer database and sending antisubversion teams scrambling for an arrest. In time we may add routine retinal scans to the National Security Agency's constant sweeps of domestic electronic communications to lay the technological foundations for a digital surveillance state. By the time the global war on terror is over, the Iraqi crucible, like its Philippine predecessor, may yet form security doctrines that will increasingly curtail civil liberties inside the United States.

There are some possible explanations for this striking continuity in U.S. policy across the span of a century. Most important, the occupation of the Philippines from 1898 to 1935 transformed the character of the American state, leaving a lasting imprint on its security apparatus and imbuing it with underlying attributes that can recur in any subsequent occupation, even one that comes a century later.

If these similarities are anything more than historical ironies, then this Philippine past may provide some clues about the outcome of the U.S. intervention in Iraq, offering lessons that President Bush ignored during his visit to Manila. From a more critical reading of this colonial history, here is the bottom line. After the U.S. Army destroyed the conventional Philippine forces by November 1899, the complete subjugation of just six million Filipinos living in an impoverished island nation and isolated from any source of arms or ammunition required fifteen years of continuous combat and covert operations. To achieve this hard-won victory, Washington needed a permanent colonial garrison of forty-seven thousand troops led by regular officers who dedicated much of their careers to building the most modern police forces found anywhere under an American flag. Increasing the chances of success, these security forces were backed by a colonial government that claimed full sovereignty and enacted whatever draconian laws were needed for pacification. Even after granting the Philippines independence in 1946, the United States retained massive military bases there for the next half century. In each postcolonial decade, Washington has intervened to revitalize the country's security forces with massive infusions of aid and advisory support, a process that continues today.

Circumstances in the Middle East are even less favorable. Iraq's insurgents have vast supplies of weapons, permeable borders through which to import more, and endless extralegal financing through oil smuggling and kidnapping. Further complicating the chances for long-term success in building a viable democracy, Baghdad's client government is crippled by corruption, ethnic divisions, and a simmering civil war.[15] Yet, with its national prestige at stake, Washington may yet invest sufficient manpower and material resources to reduce the insurgency to manageable levels, transfer power to a viable coalition, and withdraw to fortified bases inside Iraq for another half century, intervening periodically with aid and advisers, much as we are still doing in the Philippines, to shore up a corrupt client state and its secret police whenever it is shaken by coups or insurgency. As Ahmad Chalabi, once America's favored Iraqi ally, observed so acutely at end of the Bush era in late 2008, many in official Washington still wished to make Iraq a "puppet state . . . governed through a corrosive mix of covert intelligence and military support spoon-fed to a permanent oligarchy."[16]

If we wish to understand the future of America's adventures in Iraq and Afghanistan, then this parallel Philippine experience offers some cautionary reminders about the costs of conquest at home and abroad. At this historical moment of America's untrammeled global dominion, it seems timely to look backward and explore the impact of the long-forgotten Philippine pacification, particularly the critical role of colonial policing in the formation of two modern states, America and the Philippines.

From a personal perspective, this study draws together two strands of my research that have remained quite separate. Over the past forty years, for reasons that still elude me, I never quite found a way to fuse my conventional scholarship on Philippine history with my unconventional writing on the demimonde of crime and drugs. Looking back, it seems that I needed several decades of research on Southeast Asia to make sense of all those details and grasp something of a larger design and its implications for the study of history. Simply put, it has taken me half a lifetime to know what I know.

Considering the role of police and crime in shaping the Philippine state has produced some unexpected insights. Through juxtaposition of the formal and informal, legal and illegal, the study of a seemingly small problem—policing in the twentieth-century Philippines—quickly grew into an exploration of larger issues. Arbitrary separations between colonizer and colonized, home and abroad, gritty crime scene details and abstract constitutional principles, dissolved, and there emerged a perspective that should encourage some revisions in the national narratives of the Philippines and the United States. Both modern states were forged after 1898 in the same crucible of colonial conquest that unleashed powerful forces of mutual transformation, particularly in the sub rosa realm of internal security. As a first step toward such a revisionist history, the chapters that follow offer some correctives to our current, overly formal understanding of the modern state.

If the fruits of this fusion are so rich, one might ask why scholars have been so slow to incorporate the criminal and covert margins of society into the history of modern nation-states. Here we can only speculate. Most fundamentally, historians need sources to study. History is thus shaped to a surprising degree by the randomness of the documents that survive war and revolution, fire and flood. Armies usually preserve their papers for posterity while police and secret services tend to conceal or destroy their records. Military histories can quote first-person sources, battlefield dispatches, and staff studies while the far fewer police histories often rely on secondary sources, many of a critical or even adversarial provenance such as court cases or commissions of inquiry.[17] Military history, with its heroism and accessible archives, fills academic journals and library shelves with tens of thousands of volumes; the police, with their sordid aura and sealed dossiers, are thus much less studied.

By ignoring the substantial role of criminal syndicates and clandestine services in modern political life, academic historians have often relegated these unseemly matters, by default, to the lower registers of vocational education or popular entertainment in film, pulp fiction, or tabloid exposé.[18] Soldiers and sailors are integral to national narratives; police, prison guards, syndicate bosses, informers, and spies are much less so. Workers who strike are carefully studied, but the private detectives and secret services that plot their defeat and even their deaths receive brief mention at best. In the writing of national history, society's shadowy interstices and those who inhabit them often remain obscure.

Certainly, there are serious scholarly studies of the criminal and clandestine milieu. In recent years, as the study of globalization and its borderlands has drawn social scientists to the transnational trafficking in illicit goods, their insights have been hampered by what the editors of a seminal volume call "the difficulty of thinking outside the conceptual and material grasp of the modern state."[19] Even this research is still, at this writing, overwhelmed by the sheer mass of dissertations, monographs, histories, textbooks, documentaries, monuments, and museums whose unstated, unwitting aim is to affirm state authority. Through the sum of these endeavors, historians have encircled the nation-state with a sacral barrier that precludes cognizance of its profane margins: systemic violence, institutional corruption, extralegal security operations, and, most important, syndicated vice. Many social historians have escaped the nation-state's hegemony through studies of popular movements among workers, women, or minorities. But few have looked at the state long and hard from its sordid underside—an interstice that is the sum of addiction, avarice, blackmail, cowardice, scandal, torture, venality, and violence. As acolytes of the nation-state, conventional historians turn away from such a disconcerting dimension and often adopt a positive, at times celebratory view of their polity that discourages consideration of the influence of the informal on the formal, the criminal on the powerful, or, in some cases, the colonized on the colonizer.

Understanding how the state operates is a problem of critical import for ordinary citizens who have to function in a social rather than represented reality. These topics omitted from formal scholarship have become subjects of endless popular fascination in fiction and films, from D. W. Griffith's racist epic *Birth of a Nation* to Francis Ford Coppola's *The Godfather.* Academic historians usually find their carefully crafted monographs read in graduate seminars with perhaps a dozen students, while historical films about America's dark underside have become a revisionist curriculum for a worldwide audience of millions.

Clearly some correction is in order. As a discipline that hews closely to primary sources, history is best engaged not in the ether of theoretical abstraction but in its empirical application to particular problems. Thus, to tease out the full significance of the Philippine pacification for American state formation we can mine the mass of archival documents from a half century of U.S. colonial rule, incorporating the police and security services into a revised historical narrative for a new approach to America's imperial past.

To probe the mutually transformative impact of empire, part one of this book examines the origins of U.S. policing in the Philippines. By exploring a range of terrain and topics, these eight chapters show how America's antecedent information revolution created a colonial surveillance state that transformed the character of Philippine politics by repressing radical nationalism and replacing it with conservative patronage politics. On the other side of the Pacific, Washington repatriated the personnel and policies of colonial rule during World War I and used them to conduct what may have been the most systematic surveillance of its citizens ever undertaken by a modern government, producing institutional innovations that helped establish a nascent national security state.

Part two of the book explores the legacy of colonial policing in the postcolonial Philippines with two aims: understanding how the security apparatus embedded inside the Philippine state during U.S. colonial rule remained a potent instrument of executive power; and, of equal import, analyzing how postcolonial American involvement in Philippine security reforms was a manifestation of Washington's global reach. While the book's first half tracks the flow of intelligence innovations from Manila to Washington, the second emphasizes the reverse flow of security doctrines through the periodic dispatch of U.S. military aid and advisory teams to support the Philippine state against internal threats, from counterinsurgency against communist-led peasant guerrillas in the 1950s through the antiterrorist campaign against Islamic insurgents since 2001.

Each chapter in part two explores a distinctive facet of a colonial legacy that has proved deep and lasting. By forming a secret police to serve executive power and then prohibiting vice in ways that encouraged political corruption, the American colonial government set in motion contradictory forces, powerful security and syndicated vice, that continued to shape the Philippine polity after independence in 1946. The new Philippine Republic's reliance on police controls and its citizens' sensitivity to issues of order have made policing a potent source of political legitimacy. As crime and violence roiled Manila in the early 1970s, President Ferdinand Marcos played on this disorder to abolish the Republic and establish an authoritarian regime that ruled for fourteen years through centralized police controls.

After Marcos's fall in 1986 his democratic successors expanded this now pervasive system of police power. While President Corazon Aquino deployed the national police to quash popular protests, her successor, Fidel Ramos, used his long years in command of the constabulary to make police service a new path to the presidency. Two succeeding presidents, Joseph Estrada and Gloria Arroyo, employed their police powers to expropriate a share of the jueteng lottery's illegal profits and thereby finance their political operations—schemes made possible by the colonial and national legal prohibitions that sustained this vast illicit industry.

The continuing influence of U.S. colonial policing was clearly manifest by the late 1990s when mastery of the criminal netherworld became a prerequisite for an effective Filipino president. Just as patronage machines once dominated Philippine elections in the middle decades of the twentieth century, so the nexus of police, crime, and covert operations now shapes the character of Philippine electoral politics. The police powers created under U.S. colonial rule have thus become a central facet of the modern Philippine state in the half century since independence.

Clearly, colonial policing has left a persistent, problematic legacy for the postcolonial Philippines. Whether Filipino presidents exploit their extraordinary police powers, try to limit them, or attempt something in between, each is implicated in the system and is in some way forced to engage this netherworld of secret services and criminal syndicates. At a wider, more abstract level, this study attempts to explore the hidden costs of this march to modernity in both America and the Philippines, arguing that progress toward democracy has also unleashed countervailing forces: a strong state security apparatus, intrusive surveillance, and an empowered executive inclined to use both.

1

Capillaries of Empire

At the dawn of the twentieth century, Commodore George Dewey of the U.S. Navy arrayed his squadron of steel-hulled warships at the edge of Asia. Steaming across Manila Bay at first light on May 1, 1898, his rapid-fire guns sank the aging Spanish fleet and cleared the way for an attack on Manila. After transports arrived three months later, U.S. Army troops stormed Manila's massive battlements and seized a city Spain had ruled for 350 years. At the cost of just 121 casualties in a single day of sporadic fighting, the United States had become, for the first time in its history, an imperial power.[1]

Yet even in this hour of glory, the U.S. Army faced the immediate threat of a second and far more violent war. Only hours after occupying the city, the Provost Guard was charged with maintaining order in what its commander called "this revolutionary and insurrectionary city of . . . 250,000 inhabitants of the most diverse nationality and . . . [with] an unusually large proportion of the criminal classes . . . , gamblers and speculators, toughs and the blackguards." And ringing the city were trench works bristling with the guns of fifteen thousand Filipino soldiers, the army of a revolutionary republic poised to rise in revolt.[2]

At the dawn of the twenty-first century, Chief Superintendent Florencio Fianza of the Philippine National Police (PNP) arrayed his squads of helmeted riot police before the gates of Manila's presidential palace. Fighting desperately from first light on May 1, 2001, police armed with shotguns and water cannons scattered a mob of fifty thousand urban poor, their bodies marked with gang tattoos and fortified with drugs. At the cost of just 117 civilian casualties in six hours of hand-to-hand fighting, Philippine police had saved the presidency of Gloria Arroyo.

Yet even in its hour of victory the Arroyo administration faced volatile instability. Millions of urban poor filled the fetid slums that ringed Manila, ready to spill into the streets in anger over miserable lives plagued by endemic disease and endless unemployment. Armed with special powers, Arroyo's police would struggle to prevent a recurrence of mass violence by "hoodlums and criminals" hidden in the back alleys of a metropolis swollen to some twenty million inhabitants.[3]

The juxtaposition of these two battles separated by a century reveals the Philippines as the site of a protracted social experiment in the use of police as an instrument of state power. In the late nineteenth century at this edge of empire, freed of the constraints of constitution, courts, and civil society, the U.S. regime deployed its information technologies to form what was arguably the world's first surveillance state.[4] True, British imperial rule relied on the Indian Police Service, which grew after 1860 into a repressive "Police Raj" with omnipresent spies and brutal paramilitary squads. The Dutch organized a political police for the Netherlands Indies in 1921 with a blanket surveillance that smothered Indonesian nationalist agitation for nearly twenty years. The French formed "intelligence states" that were "over-stretched and outflanked" in their North African colonies; and, after 1917, created a centralized Sûreté for Indochina that engaged in "the relentless acquisition of information" and became "skilled at forecasting threats to French authority." The famed Paris police, though a "laboratory of police modernity," still suffered "marked shortcomings" throughout the nineteenth century. The czarist secret police was legendary during its long history from 1827 to 1917 for agile agent provocateur tactics, though it, too, was hampered by "technological inadequacy" and as late as 1910 had only forty-nine employees reading mail for the entire empire.[5] Despite certain strengths, none of these could match the synthesis of legal repression, incessant patrolling, and suffocating surveillance found in the colonial Philippines. During the first decade of U.S. rule, the colonial security services, particularly the multifaceted Philippines Constabulary, succeeded in demobilizing a deeply rooted national revolution and advancing a conservative elite to fill the political void. Hence this study's first substantive conclusion: the creation of sophisticated modern policing was crucial to the U.S. pacification of the Philippines.

After creating a formidable counterinsurgency force, the U.S. regime installed this coercive apparatus within the Philippine colonial state, making the constabulary central to both its administration and popular perception. With strong links to the executive and minimal checks and balances, the police quickly emerged as a major factor in the country's politics. Moreover, by enacting stringent laws against personal vices such as gambling and drugs, the colonial government inadvertently amplified the role of police as would-be guardians of public morality. After Philippine independence in 1946, the national police remained as a key instrument of both legal and extralegal presidential power. Simultaneously, a symbiosis of police power, political corruption, and vice prohibition soon metastasized into something akin to a social cancer that persisted long after colonial rule, fomenting iconic incidents of abuse and violence. Through corruption and excessive force, the police became the source of the country's recurring legitimation crises, from the electoral violence of the early 1950s through the latest "people power" uprising of 2001. In a nation with countless sources of social conflict, it seems significant that police scandals, often petty or even sordid, should raise such profound issues of political legitimacy. Thus a second major conclusion: the U.S. colonial regime's reliance on police for pacification and political control embedded this security apparatus within an emerging Philippine state, contributing ultimately to an unstable excess of executive power after independence.

Not only did colonial policing influence Philippine state formation, but it also helped transform the U.S. federal government. Indeed, security techniques bred in the tropical hothouse of colonial governance were not contained at this periphery of American power. Through the invisible capillaries of empire, these innovations percolated homeward to implant both personnel and policies inside the Federal bureaucracy for the formation of a new internal security apparatus. During the social crisis surrounding World War I, a small cadre of colonial police veterans created a clandestine capacity within the U.S. Army, establishing Military Police for the occupation of a war-torn Europe as well as Military Intelligence for both surveillance at home and espionage abroad. Once established under the pressures of wartime mobilization, this federal surveillance effort persisted in various forms for the next fifty years, as a sub rosa matrix that honeycombed U.S. society with active informers, secretive civilian organizations, and government counterintelligence agencies.

This exploration of colonial policing thus reveals an important facet of state formation not only in the Philippines but also in the United States. Though generally ignored by U.S. historians as a regrettable, even forgettable episode in the course of American progress, when viewed through the prism of policing the conquest of the Philippines emerges as an event of seminal import. Viewed conservatively, it was a bellwether, a significant manifestation of the repressive potential of America's first information revolution, discussed below.[6] Viewed more boldly, it arguably accelerated these changes, making the Philippine Islands a social laboratory at a critical juncture in U.S. history and producing a virtual blueprint for the perfection of American state power. From the time its troops landed at Manila in 1898, the U.S. Army applied the nation's advanced information technology for combat operations and colonial pacification, merging Spanish police structures with its own data management to create powerful new security agencies. Unchecked by constitutional constraints, American colonials developed innovative counterintelligence techniques that expanded the state's ability to monitor its Filipino subjects. Indeed, the first U.S. federal agency with a fully developed covert capacity was not the Federal Bureau of Investigation (FBI) or the Office of Naval Intelligence (ONI) but the Philippines Constabulary (PC).

These colonial origins were no mere catalyst for a process that might have produced the same preordained outcome; instead, through a congruence of motive and opportunity, this imperial influence left a distinctive imprint on the character of America's domestic security apparatus. These secret service methods, whether broad information systems or specific interrogation techniques, have a specific institutional genealogy, a gestational continuity, that requires the historian to track personnel, policies, and precedents, not assuming that they somehow arrive axiomatically with the advent of modernity. While Europe's highly evolved state security services, colonial and national, contributed obliquely to the development of U.S. intelligence doctrines, the occupation of the Philippines provided a particularly favorable environment for cultivating covert techniques, institutional networks, and systematic surveillance. These security procedures, bred like tropical hybrids, were antithetical to American political traditions. But empire provided a vehicle for introducing them into a deeply democratic society. Hence a third conclusion: innovative colonial policing in the Philippines influenced the formation of the American state, contributing to the development of a sophisticated internal security apparatus.

The flow of security personnel and practices coursing through these capillaries of empire was neither unilateral nor confined to a particular period. Once their roots were planted in the first decade of colonial rule, the circulation of ideas would continue unabated for another century, first westward from Manila to Washington, where they shaped U.S. internal security operations during World War I, and then eastward back across the Pacific, where they strengthened the repressive capacities of the postcolonial Philippine state. Whenever the Philippines has been shaken by insurgency in the last sixty years, Washington has intervened to shore up its security services with an infusion of military aid, first under the Republic (1946–72), then under President Marcos's martial law regime (1972–86), and most recently through President Arroyo's role in the global war on terror (2001–9). Viewed from Manila, these recurring contacts with U.S. security agencies have made police power a key facet of the Philippine state. The Philippines has become a major battleground in the war on terror—another protracted foreign adventure whose security innovations are slowly migrating homeward silently to spread surveillance and curtail civil liberties inside the United States. Thus a fourth conclusion: by collaborating in the refinement of covert techniques for internal security, these two states have forged powerful instruments to fortify themselves against the processes of political change, slowing progress toward civil rights in America and social justice in the Philippines.

The study of U.S.-Philippine security relations also serves as a microcosm for America's changing role in international affairs. No other nation has felt the force of American power so closely, so constantly throughout Washington's century-long rise to world leadership. No other nation can reveal so much about the character of America's international influence, both direct colonial rule and diffuse global hegemony. At the high tide of European empires circa 1898, the Philippines became the jewel in an American diadem of island colonies that stretched halfway around the world from Cuba through the Canal Zone to Manila Bay. During World War II the Philippines was the site of America's greatest military defeat and greatest naval victory. In the postcolonial era that followed, the constant U.S. presence in the Philippines exemplified Washington's global reach through overseas bases, military alliances, and CIA covert operations whose sum has been the integration of this and other sovereign nations into a nonterritorial American imperium. For nearly half a century, from 1947 to 1992, the massive air and naval bases near Manila were the largest among hundreds of U.S. military facilities in operation overseas. While nuclear armadas contained communist armies behind the Iron Curtain, a mix of covert intervention and counterinsurgency suppressed any dissidence inside the allied nations that lay on America's side of this global divide. At the dawn of the cold war during the 1950s, the CIA tested new counterinsurgency doctrines against peasant guerrillas in the Philippines. A decade later, as Washington trained anticommunist police worldwide, American advisers helped build a massive antiriot force for metropolitan Manila, laying the foundations for martial rule. When Washington embraced third-world dictators during the 1970s, President Marcos and his first lady were toasted at a White House state dinner. After the United States reversed its policy and began advocating democracy worldwide, the Philippines again led the way with its famed 1986 "people power" revolution against Marcos, a televised uprising that inspired imitation along the Iron Curtain from Beijing to Berlin. Its newly elected president, Corazon Aquino, addressed the U.S. Congress to thunderous applause and graced the cover of *Time* as the magazine's woman of the year. Since September 2001, President Bush has spoken before the Philippine Congress and U.S. Special Forces have become a constant presence in the Islamic isles of the southern Philippines. Thus, the study of the twentieth-century Philippines reveals much about the changing character of U.S. global power.

There is an obvious yet overlooked international dimension to the U.S. colonial legacy. By embedding a paramilitary apparatus inside the Philippine executive, the United States installed a point of entry for later intrusions into the internal affairs of a sovereign state. In the half century since independence, the United States has intervened almost every decade, working through its natural allies in the Philippine police and military to introduce aid, advisers, security doctrines, and covert operations, thereby curbing local threats to the U.S. global order posed by communist guerillas, student demonstrators, or Islamic insurgents. Yet the U.S. influence goes beyond strengthening a bureaucratic apparatus of repression. Building on the institutional foundations laid during colonial rule, U.S. advisers have fostered an extralegal dimension in Philippine security operations through the introduction of macabre psychological warfare tactics in the 1950s, training in sophisticated torture techniques during the 1970s, violent vigilante operations in the 1980s, and tacit approval of widespread extrajudicial killings since September 2001.

Though long treated as a peripheral chapter in U.S. history, the pacification and policing of the Philippines after 1898 is a small topic with larger implications. Methodologically, the study of national history via policing's netherworld breaches the analytical barriers that separate high politics from low, colony from metropole, allowing a fuller view of the past and its politics. Empirically, it demands revisions to the political history of two nations. From the U.S. perspective, this is a book about America's exercise of global power, its character and consequences; viewed from Manila, it is an inquiry into America's role, as both a colonial and postcolonial power, in shaping the contemporary Philippine plight of endless poverty and mass desperation contained by efficient police repression. Theoretically, the investigation of Philippine policing can help us move beyond the concept of colonialism as a unilateral process that only affects the far-off periphery toward an awareness of the pervasive, mutually transformative power of empire, changing the character of governance in both colony and metropole. Ultimately, this inquiry invites a reconsideration of the character of the modern state, both its internal security operations and its integration into larger global systems.

Thinking about the State

At the theoretical level, this study of Philippine policing challenges the most venerable axiom about the character of the modern state. "What is a 'state'?" political theorist Max Weber asked an audience at Munich University in 1918. "Today," he famously answered, "we have to say that a state is a human community that (successfully) claims the *monopoly of the legitimate use of physical force* within a given territory."[7] Although this maxim has long resonated for its striking clarity, Weber said surprisingly little about the ways a state might exercise such raw power. By emphasizing physical force, admittedly an important attribute, he overlooked a subtle yet significant facet of political power—the modern state's use of coercion not to enforce brute compliance but to extract information for heightened levels of social control.

Indeed, the modern state seems to be distinguished from its medieval antecedents by an advance beyond exemplary physical punishment of the few to systematic social control over the many. By the eighteenth century the early modern state had sufficient coercive capacities to press-gang peasants or punish enemies in what E. P. Thompson called "the ritual of public execution" with "the corpse rotting on the gibbet beside the highway." The aim of such grisly executions was nothing less than political control through what Michel Foucault styled the "exercise of 'terror.'"[8] But the state still lacked the means for systematic social regulation. The slow perfection of state power in Europe and its colonies was, as the political scientist Benedict Anderson reminds us, "impossible without the kind of financial and technological resources that high-industrial capitalism made possible."[9]

Over the past two centuries the state has been modernized through the deepening penetration of private space for the accumulation of ever more diverse and detailed information. In his provocative study of the first, post-Enlightenment phase of this modernization, James C. Scott suggests that we study the state not by gazing down from its lofty ramparts like Weber but by looking up from its encircling forests and furrows. Viewed from below, the modern state's defining attribute is its imposition of "legibility" on man and nature through a series of "state simplifications." Just as cadastral maps, first adopted by the Netherlands in 1807, transformed a peasant patchwork into a precisely quantified array of taxable land, so Napoleon decreed that all French citizens would have patronyms, distinctive last names, to inscribe them for tax, census, and conscription.[10] Legibility came to Europe's empires somewhat later, with Britain's Colonial Office trying to manage its far-flung territories after 1820 by collecting long lists of loosely aggregated data on taxes, duties, exports, and imports.[11] Yet all this information was passive, statistically, even socially useful but not politically actionable. The bureaucracy was still "blind," unable to read deeply into its endless lists of property and people to detect deviants or subversives.

America's Information Revolution

After this European rationalization played itself out in the mid-nineteenth century, the United States became the site of an information revolution whose synergies were a second, significant phase in the perfection of state power. In an extraordinary burst of human ingenuity, American inventors created new products and processes for the rapid compilation, codification, transmission, storage, and retrieval of information. Moving beyond simple enumeration of land or human bodies, this information revolution allowed the manipulation of raw data that was limitless in its capacity for quantification, swift in its retrieval of significant detail, and agile in its analysis. Among its many applications, such data management invested the state with the potential for mass surveillance, allowing for the first time an advance beyond punishment of the few to control over the many—a critical, defining attribute of the modern state. Instead of compiling mute lists for purposes of taxation and conscription, the state now had the political intelligence with which to identify individuals and surveil groups deemed subversive, amassing incriminating information and monitoring movements. Clearly, the character of this American innovation merits closer examination.

In the late nineteenth century America's information revolution erupted, during two extraordinary decades, the 1870s to the 1880s, from a concatenation of inventions in the management of textual, statistical, and visual data. Let us listen as these dates sing, a cappella, a song of progress. In just a few years, the combination of Thomas A. Edison's quadruplex telegraph (1874), Philo Remington's commercial typewriter (1874), and Alexander Graham Bell's telephone (1876) allowed the transmission and recording of textual data of unprecedented quality, at unequaled speeds, and with unsurpassed accuracy.[12] After completion of the transcontinental telegraph line (1861) and the transatlantic cable (1866), the Western

Union Corporation imposed a monopoly over the nation's fragmented telegraph industry, expanding its wired network tenfold from just 76,000 miles in 1866 to 769,000 by 1893. Through contracts with Western Union, the Associated Press grew with equal speed, leasing its first direct telegraph wire (1875), using the Edison quadruplex for simultaneous transmission of multiple messages (1875), and adopting the typewriter for rapid, accurate transcription (1885). The integration of these innovations allowed the sending of dispatches from around the globe to newsrooms across the nation at forty typed words per minute, the international standard for another century.[13] Fifteen years after the *New York Herald*'s first publication of a transatlantic telegraphic dispatch (1866), over 100,000 miles of oceanic cables, largely British, crisscrossed the globe, making the international wire services, particularly the Reuters-Havas cartel (established 1870), a dominant force in news media. By 1881 America's Bell system had a network of 123,000 telephones, by far the world's largest, and was incorporated four years later as American Telephone and Telegraph (AT&T).[14] The fusion of these innovations fostered a global information regime that allowed fast transmission and accurate processing of almost limitless quantities of textual information.

This dynamic era saw parallel progress in statistical and visual data management. In the business world Dorr E. Felt's development of a key-driven adding machine (1885) accelerated the spread of cost accounting, producing, arguably, the first quantum advance since the development of double-entry bookkeeping in the fifteenth century. After the engineer Herman Hollerith patented the punch card (1889) with the distinctive elongated dimensions used for the next century, the federal government quickly adopted his inventions, first in the Surgeon General's Office to track thousands of military patients and then in the U.S. Census Bureau (1890). With Hollerith's Electrical Tabulating machine clerks could process up to twenty thousand cards per day, counting two hundred tons of census records in just six weeks to announce that the U.S. population was 62,622,250—a speed that stunned the American public and a success that later led its inventor to help found International Business Machines (IBM).[15] Almost simultaneously the development of photoengraving (1881) and George Eastman's roll film (1889) extended this information revolution to visual data, culminating in the construction of the Automatic Photograph Factory in New York with a heretofore unimaginable output of 147,000 prints daily (1895).[16]

Parallel innovations in data storage allowed reliable encoding and rapid retrieval from this swelling torrent of information. At opposite ends of same small state in the mid-1870s, two American librarians solved the ancient riddle of classification. While cataloging the Amherst College Library, Melvil Dewey published his famed *Decimal Classification* (1876), which reduced the complexity of human knowledge to a set of Arabic numerals. At Boston's Athenaeum Library, Charles A. Cutter, finding that this decimal system did not allow close classification, added letters to Dewey's numbers for a system with thirty-six divisions, described in his *Rules for a Dictionary Catalogue* (1875) and *Expansive Classification* (1891). When the new Library of Congress opened in 1897 with 950,000 volumes, many unclassified, its chief cataloger refined Cutter's method to produce a system, striking in its "simplicity and elasticity," which became an international standard. The sum of these innovations was the "smart number," which signified not just mute order but actual content.[17]

Within a decade of Cutter's and Dewey's first publications, U.S. libraries, hospitals, and armed forces applied the smart number to systems that reduced otherwise unmanageable masses of books, persons, and reports to numerical codes, unique and categorical, for rapid filing, retrieval, and cross-referencing. In quick succession the Office of Naval Intelligence created a file card method for recording intelligence (1882) and the U.S. Army's Military Information Division (MID) adopted a similar system at its founding three years later (1885). Indicative of the intense tempo of this information revolution, MID's intelligence cards grew from just four thousand in 1892 to over three hundred thousand a decade later.[18] In its quest for quantification, the army used a short test, developed by the psychologist Lewis M. Terman, to measure the "intelligence quotient" (IQ) of the nearly two million males conscripted at the start of World War I, collecting data that seemed to show marked ethnic differences in intelligence.[19] These synergies in statistical, textual, and visual data represented nothing less than a modern information revolution.

Yet the impact of these innovations on domestic security was surprisingly slow. Gilded Age law enforcement was controlled by urban political machines that used police for patronage, inhibiting both innovation and professionalism. Consequently, change came to U.S. crime control from a mix of foreign and domestic sources.[20] At the Paris police headquarters in 1884 Alphonse Bertillon developed the world's first scientific criminal identification system based on four key elements: eleven precise cranial and corporeal measurements, two facial photographs (front and profile), twenty-seven biometric divisions for accurate filing, and a single six-inch-square card for recording both physical description and criminal history. At Chicago in 1896 the National Association of Chiefs of Police established a central bureau of identification based on Bertillon's method.[21] Just as Bertillonage was winning acceptance, however, the senior inspector for British India, Sir Edward R. Henry, developed a fingerprint classification system so accurate that it was adopted by his colonial police in 1897 and Scotland Yard just four years later. After a British officer demonstrated the speed of the Henry system to American police chiefs at the Saint Louis World's Fair in 1904, New York and other major cities soon adopted fingerprinting as their sole standard for criminal identification. Although the Bureau of Investigation (later the FBI) did not follow suit until 1924, its files passed the six million mark within a decade and its director was soon urging compulsory fingerprinting for all citizens. Only months after a young J. Edgar Hoover became head of the bureau's Radical

Division in 1919, he could boast of eighty thousand file cards "covering the activities of not only the extreme anarchists but also the more moderate radicals."[22] Indeed, Henry's fingerprints and Bertillon's file cards merged into the standard U.S. criminal identification format still seen on the FBI wanted posters displayed at every post office, with physical description, criminal record, and facial photos arrayed much as they were on Bertillon's original card back in 1884. Though long superseded, Bertillonage established the fundamentals for all subsequent biometric systems, even the most recent innovations in retinal identification: precise measurement, reliable taxonomic indices for data retrieval, and visual confirmation.[23]

While it was an imitator in criminal identification, the United States was an innovator in police and fire communications. In 1852, Dr. William F. Channing installed the world's first electric fire-alarm system in Boston using forty cast-iron alarm boxes to transmit signals through telegraph wires to the city's Central Fire Alarm Station. After patenting his invention in 1854, Channing sold the rights to an entrepreneur, John N. Gamewell, who soon made this system the world standard with installations in over five hundred American cities.[24] In 1880, just four years after the invention of the telephone, Gamewell pioneered an integrated police telegraph/telephone call-box system. "With the advent of this service," said the company's commemorative volume, "a police department became . . . a compact unit, quickly responsive to conditions, and controlled and directed as one man by a central authority."[25] In 1890, for example, the city of Brooklyn installed a Gamewell network in nine police precincts with two-way messaging for foot patrols via 189 signal boxes, which were soon handling an annual volume of 143,411 hourly reports and 2,375 patrol wagon calls in a single precinct.[26] By 1900, American cities had a total of 912 municipal security networks transmitting forty-one million messages annually.[27]

In the space of a few decades America had changed from a society with fragmentary records and local constables into a nation with centralized criminal files, wired cities, nascent intelligence services, and systematic social indices. European states, of course, had long maintained libraries, ledgers, and legions of spies that made their capitals nests of espionage and imperial intrigue.[28] But it was the American genius to rationalize data management inside these same institutions, producing innovations whose sum was a modern information infrastructure. For the first time, state security services had the capacity to identify every individual with a unique number, allowing accurate encoding, filing, and retrieval of data on countless millions, whether citizens or colonial subjects.

But application of these innovations inside America itself was blocked by a strong tradition of civil liberties. From the perspective of even a half century later, Washington's reach circa 1898 was faint, its grip on citizens' lives light, and its role in crime control still surprisingly limited. Between 1877 and 1900 the United States experienced what Stephen Skowronek calls a "patchwork" pattern of state building without anything akin to "a concentrated governing capacity." After 1900, however, urbanization, industrialization, and overseas expansion "raised demands for national governmental capacities that were foreign to the existing state structure," unleashing a process of bureaucratic modernization in these imperial decades.[29] The twinned forces of centralization and modernization also influenced federal crime control and domestic security, topics often overlooked in this burgeoning literature on U.S. state formation.[30]

Indeed, policing exemplifies the processes of U.S. state formation through its shift, circa 1900 to 1930, from localized law enforcement, which was mired in patronage, to a modern, centralized administration. As cities grew beyond the early citizen "watch forces," New York formed the nation's first "full-time police force" in 1845, and others soon followed. Between 1865 and 1905 metropolitan police forces grew rapidly, with Chicago's, for example, expanding tenfold to 2,196 officers by century's turn. City fathers, determined to avoid the militarized European model, compromised by creating uniformed police forces under local civilian control. With the start of civil service protection in 1884 at Brooklyn and Milwaukee, police became more professional, but paradoxically, as Americans discovered to their dismay in the 1890s, "they also became more corrupt." For readers of New York City's penny press, these problems were personified by Alexander "Clubber" Williams, a pathologically violent officer with a thirty-year career (1866–95) marked by 350 formal complaints against him in a single year and a tidy $100,000 in graft from his command of the Tenderloin vice district. "There is more law in the end of a policeman's nightstick," he said defiantly, "than in a decision of the Supreme Court." Throughout 1894 the New York legislature's Lexow committee conducted a sensational probe of the city's police, showing how officers purchased promotions, their commanders served as agents of the Democratic machine, and both protected the vice trades. When the committee pressed police chief Thomas F. Byrnes to explain how his annual salary of $5,000 built a real estate fortune that included a Fifth Avenue property worth $550,000, he denied any personal corruption but admitted that his officers took bribes from brothels. The city's subsequent attempt at reform did not last much beyond Theodore Roosevelt's brief tenure as police commissioner, and his most lasting achievement was easing Clubber Williams and Chief Byrnes gently into retirement—with full pensions. Parallel investigations from Baltimore (1895) to Los Angeles (1900) found the same corrupt alliance between precinct captains and powerful ward bosses. Fighting against these big city machines for the next thirty years, middle-class reformers would campaign for centralization under an empowered police chief and rationalization through modern communications. As a counterweight to these urban problems, states such as Pennsylvania (1902) and New York (1917) established paramilitary state police. Moreover, the federal role in local law enforcement grew as the Bureau of Investigation formed a Criminal Division (1919), launched the country's Uniform Crime Reports system (1930), and opened its National Division of Identification (1930), which amassed, over the next quarter century, 141 million fingerprints.[31]

There were, of course, important European innovations in intelligence and counterintelligence that could have had a significant influence on the U.S. federal government but, for complex reasons, did not. Russia's Okhrana state police, established in 1881, proved deft at agent provocateur and penetration operations. Britain's Special Branch started its political surveillance in 1884. Italy established a centralized fingerprint bureau in 1908. Germany excelled in scientific detection and resident registration, with twelve million cards filed by two hundred clerks for Berlin alone by 1914. But many of these advances came too late, their data management was too labor-intensive, and, above all, their clandestine operations were too carefully concealed to have any real impact on America. In the 1880s European armies invited American military attachés to observe their maneuvers. European police regularly exchanged criminal identification procedures and information. But all state security agencies, civil and military, concealed every aspect of their clandestine operations: names, procedures, even their very existence. Starting in 1883, for example, the czarist Okhrana operated in Paris for a full quarter century—with a stunning counterintelligence coup as early as 1890—but its presence was unknown until a press exposé in 1909, and its tradecraft went unstudied until the records were unsealed in 1957.[32]

Whatever lessons the Europeans might have offered, the U.S. Army's Military Information Division remained oblivious to the study of intelligence until the advent of empire in 1898 created an undeniable need for information. Only months before the Spanish-American War, the U.S. military attaché at Saint Petersburg, Lt. Henry T. Allen, compiled a comprehensive report for MID on the Swedish military that ignored only one major area: intelligence.[33] This oversight also appears in an analysis of Europe's 1895 maneuvers by an officer who would soon command MID, Capt. Arthur L Wagner, and recurred in its review of the world's armies for 1896, with just four sentences on intelligence in a twenty-one-page survey of the German army.[34] Indeed, Wagner's own treatise, *The Service of Security and Information,* published in 1893 and revised a decade later, devoted most of its 250 pages to sentry posts and cavalry patrols, seemingly oblivious to the modern craft of intelligence and counterintelligence.[35]

Thus, on the eve of empire in 1898 the United States still had a national bureaucracy with surprisingly limited coercive and covert capacities. During its first century the federal government had created a few small enforcement units, each restricted to a narrow investigative ambit: the U.S. Marshals Service (1789) to support the federal courts; the Postal Service's special agents (1801) to investigate mail fraud; and the Secret Service (1865) to prevent counterfeiting. For most of the Gilded Age Washington left policing to the cities and private detectives. When the Justice Department was first established in 1870, Congress denied it an enforcement arm but allocated funds for investigations the attorney general used to hire the Pinkerton Agency's private detectives. After Pinkerton's armed agents attacked workers during the violent Homestead Steel strike in 1892, Congress barred the federal government from using even these services. Indeed, after President McKinley's assassination in 1901 the treasury secretary reported that "no provision exists for the investigation of the secret organizations which are maintained in all centers of industrial activity" and are filled with members "who preach assassination and anarchy." Absent an adequate federal force, the big three among security firms—Burns, Pinkerton, and Thiel—grew by the end of the "golden age of private detective work" in 1920 to a combined total of 135,000 employees and 10,000 local offices.[36]

Thus, by 1900 U.S. state security was still restricted to revenue investigations by a small Secret Service Division in Treasury and the Special Agency Service in Customs.[37] Recognizing that the government had little investigative reach beyond the customs barrier, the Justice Department, on orders from President Theodore Roosevelt, established the Bureau of Investigation in July 1908. This fledgling force, with just twenty-three agents and limited authority, would slowly grow into the modern FBI.[38] At century's turn, however, Washington still remained, in the clandestine realm, a tabula rasa on which empire could inscribe its writ.

Imperial Army

During its first three years in the Philippine Islands (1898–1901) the U.S. Army combined combat operations, innovative policing, and civil reforms to crush the Filipino revolutionary army, creating an occupation government that it bequeathed to its civilian successor and thereby casting the new colonial state in its coercive mold. Most important, the army also carried a template from America's new information technology that would soon shape the character of the U.S. colonial police. In the years before the outbreak of the Spanish-American War in 1898, the army's fledgling Military Information Division had amassed substantial resources for library research, including a data set of three hundred thousand cards, a collection of six thousand maps, a military monograph series, and a photographic unit. As a result, the Spanish-American War was the first to be fought with real-time telegraph communications and war planning based on MID's intelligence. In the protracted pacification of the Philippines that followed, three among MID's slender cadre of veterans—Gen. Arthur MacArthur, Capt. Henry T. Allen, and Capt. Ralph Van Deman—would expand these rudimentary military methods into an elaborate system of surveillance and counterintelligence.[39]

Although the translation of these innovations into effective military practice was slow, fitful, and surprisingly painful, a protracted counterguerrilla campaign made accurate intelligence an imperative.[40] After its repeating rifles, field artillery, and rapid maneuvers destroyed the regular Filipino formations in the first months of the war (February to November 1899), the U.S. Army spent the next three years mired in demoralizing counterinsurgency operations for which it was ill-prepared. Landing without maps, language, or intelligence, the army soon became, as a senior intelligence officer put it, "a blind giant" that was "more than able to annihilate, to completely smash" anything it faced but found it "impossible to get any information" about where or when to unleash this lethal force. Complicating the army's intelligence efforts, Filipino officers, despite their generally poor combat performance, were surprisingly skilled at espionage, developing codes to conceal their identities and using disinformation to implicate fellow countrymen disloyal to their cause.[41]

In one of history's accidents, the Filipino flair for counterintelligence and the American appetite for information combined to create an advanced form of military espionage that fused combat intelligence and political surveillance. The U.S. Army applied its advanced data management techniques to counterinsurgency through a complex of new security forces: the Manila Metropolitan Police, the Philippines Constabulary, and its own Division of Military Information.[42]

During the four years of combat operations, Manila became the battleground for a new form of information warfare that left an important impress on the subsequent colonial regime. Unlike their European counterparts in New Delhi, Batavia, or Saigon, American expatriates inherited an established city without a segregated colonial cantonment that could insulate them from the crime and disease of the native quarters, compelling the colonial government to impose its police and public health regime on the entire city.[43] Consequently, during its occupation of Manila from 1898 to 1901, the army combined military intelligence and modern data management to lay the institutional foundations for a modern metropolitan police force. When foot patrols and archival analysis failed to destroy the revolution's urban underground, the U.S. Provost Guard Special Brigade developed covert techniques of surveillance and penetration to fight a counterguerrilla war in Manila's maze of bricks and bamboo. After the capital was transferred to American civil officials in 1901, the army bestowed its innovative military procedures on the new civilian police, notably, typed reports, numbered files, specialized intelligence units, and sophisticated clandestine methods.

To these systems, Manila's new police force added, between 1901 and 1906, advanced American crime-control technologies, including a centralized phone network, Gamewell's police and fire alarms, Bertillon's photo identification system, and fingerprinting. Within twenty years the Metropolitan Police would amass an extraordinary "all embracing index" of alphabetized file cards for two hundred thousand Filipinos—the equivalent of 70 percent of Manila's entire population.[44] In an age when most U.S. police still relied on foot patrols and practiced what New York City's commissioner called "systematic and organized blackmail," Manila's Metropolitans had, by 1906, a cadre of clerks trained in data management and photographic identification, bilingual patrolmen who circulated the city with clockwork regularity, and detectives skilled in undercover operations.[45]

Inside the colonial capital five separate secret services—Army, Constabulary, Police, Customs, and Internal Revenue—deployed spies and agents in a ceaseless surveillance of Filipino leaders and their private lives. The paramilitary Philippines Constabulary was a particularly supple force, combining long-arm patrols in the countryside and secret-service operations in the capital. Within five years of its founding in 1901, the constabulary had developed a covert capacity that included media monitoring, psychological profiling, surveillance, disinformation, penetration, manipulation, and, when required, assassination. In their covert operations and information systems, the U.S. colonial police quickly advanced far beyond both their Spanish antecedents and their American counterparts.

In the first decade of civil rule the colonial government covered the archipelago with a coercive apparatus that was invisible in its covert penetrations, omnivorous in its appetite for information, and enveloping in its omnipresence. Regular regiments stood ready near the capital to quell any disturbance, constabulary companies crisscrossed remote hinterlands, and municipal police guarded town plazas and city streets. Armed resistance was met with mass slaughter as artillery and repeating rifles covered the ground with corpses. Nationalist agitation was contained through a suffocating surveillance. Labor agitation was crushed by arbitrary arrests and agent provocateur operations. Within a decade this total information regime had pacified the Philippines.

Spanish Imprint

At this remote periphery of empire, the conjuncture of conquest and colonial rule made the Philippines the site of an informal experiment in policing that revealed the full potential of the new U.S. information infrastructure. Yet the American experience was not altogether unique. With unchecked power over their colonial subjects, imperial regimes worldwide were conducting similar, albeit less successful experiments in social control. Indeed, after 1898 the U.S. colonial police in the Philippines drew heavily on the structure and staff of the defeated Spanish imperial state. In the decades just prior to the U.S. conquest, Spanish officials in Manila and San Juan, Puerto Rico, had applied scientific methods to create modernizing states markedly more effective and empowered than the governments in either Madrid or Washington. Despite their dismissive rhetoric about degenerate Iberian rule, American officials in Manila were heirs to a Spanish colonial apparatus that had participated directly in Europe's liberal application of science to governance, creating in its remaining island colonies intrusive law enforcement, modernized prisons, and centralized police forces.

During its last half century in the Philippine Islands, the Spanish regime slowly built a tripartite structure for modern law enforcement through three broad phases that culminated during the 1890s in the creation of centralized policing in the European mold. After the loss of its Latin American empire and a local revolt by Filipino Creoles in the 1820s, the Spanish established a new police force for Manila and its surrounding provinces with the aim of "protecting the public safety and the property of honorable and pacific men," ordering its agents to "pursue without ceasing those who disturb the public order" with "gambling, vagrancy, and robbery." Reflecting the colony's larger transition from a patrimonial royal domain to the sovereign territory of a modern state, Manila's police were a hybrid force headed by a chief with cavalry and infantry at his disposition yet still relying on local officials to monitor their residents.[46]

In a second, more rigorous centralization during the 1860s, the Manila authorities separated the police from the long-dominant military, creating special paramilitary forces for both capital and countryside. To contain rising unrest in Philippine provinces, Spain introduced the European model of rural police as a mounted force armed with short-barrel carbines, called the Gendarmerie Nationale in France (established 1793), the Carabinieri in Italy (1814), and the Guardia Civil in Spain (1844). In the three decades after its founding in 1868, the colonial version of the Guardia Civil grew rapidly to cover the entire Philippine archipelago with 156 officers and 3,342 men. To discharge its prime responsibility of "determining the loyalty and disloyalty of individuals," its troopers could arrest anyone on the basis of mere suspicion and enjoyed a de facto authority for "the use of force to extort confessions."[47] While the Philippine Guardia Civil secured the countryside, a parallel organization, the Guardia Civil Veterana, policed the streets of Manila, maintaining order and arresting prostitutes, thieves, and drunkards. In 1882 this urban force underwent a substantial modernization. Its regulations for regular mounted and foot patrols were made "military in their essence"; its arms upgraded; and its ranks expanded to four hundred men, including fifty European-born Spaniards of "good antecedents."[48] By the mid-1890s, daily reports filed by the Guardia Civil Veterana depict an organization that had devolved from an elite security squad into a conventional city police force devoted mainly to directing horse cart traffic, enforcing tax payments, and stopping the unsanitary slaughter of pigs and chickens.[49] As Manila grew into a city of 350,000 policing failed to keep pace, dropping from a ratio of one officer per 844 residents in 1872 to one per 912 by 1896.[50]

In its last years the Spanish regime struggled to modernize law enforcement by introducing less obvious components of urban security: fire control, forensic science, telegraph service, telephones, public illumination, and prisons. In a decree of January 1870, the government ordered the Guardia Civil to organize Manila's first firefighting service, which grew, over the next quarter century, into a separate brigade with 276 employees. Following a royal order from Madrid that applied to the entire Spanish empire, the colonial government granted an exclusive franchise to the Manila Telephone Company in 1889 conditional on the provision of free service to government departments. To promote public safety, the Spanish regime also chartered Manila's La Electricista as a joint stock company in

1892, granting it a twenty-year contract for the city's public lighting. Within a few years the city had replaced its faint kerosene street lamps with 1,140 electrical lights along 104,280 meters of public streets, pushing back the shadows where criminals and subversives took refuge.[51] Telegraphy also grew steadily from a single Manila-Cavite line in 1872 to an archipelago-wide system that extended north to Ilocos by 1875, to Hong Kong by 1880, and south to the Visayan Islands after 1881.[52] In 1866 the Spanish government built a prison, the Cárcel de Bilibid, as a model Benthamite *edificio panóptico* with a central tower from which guards could see inside all the radiating cell blocks. Seventeen years later it made this complex the capstone of a three-tiered carceral regime with central prisons, provincial jails, and local work brigades.[53] By the 1890s, the colonial courts were staffed with trained lawyers on both sides of the bar, the colony had a respectable ratio of one constable for each 205 inhabitants, and the prison system was robust enough to hold nearly one percent of the Filipino population behind bars.[54] There was also a qualitative shift toward modern law enforcement exemplified by the opening of the Laboratorio Médico Legal de Manila in late 1894. Following a royal order from the Ministerio de Ultramar in Madrid that a scientific laboratory be built to assist in criminal investigations, Manila's facility imported lab equipment from Paris, established tight technical procedures, and was providing chemical evidence in opium-smuggling cases by 1895.[55] Despite marked limitations, by the end of their rule in 1898 the Spanish had laid the rough foundations for metropolitan security in Manila.

As dissidence rose in the last decade of its rule, the Spanish regime focused not on the broad institutional infrastructure but on specialist operations to maintain order and check subversion. In 1889, the Guardia Civil command in Pampanga Province just north of Manila compiled systematic tabular data on suspected subversives (*filibusteros*), recording residence, race, and profession.[56] Moreover, in July 1895 the Spanish regime announced the formation of the Cuerpo de Vigilancia de Manila, an elite force of forty-five men with eight first-class agents, mainly Spaniards, and thirty-two second-class agents, almost all Filipinos with military experience. Although it was subordinate to Guardia Civil Veterana, its agents wore normal civilian clothes (*vestidos de paisano*).[57] A year later, when revolution erupted in Manila, the Spanish governor authorized these officers to work undercover in "ordinary . . . clothing in order to enter, unnoticed and without causing anyone to suspect them, the anti-Spanish meetings or conspiracies."[58] At the end of Spanish rule in 1898, Manila had 983 police in five units: 413 Veterana, 356 Carabineros, 134 Guardia Municipal, 35 port police, and 45 secret agents of the Cuerpo de Vigilancia.[59]

Like the larger Spanish police apparatus, the Cuerpo de Vigilancia generally failed in its mission to penetrate subversive groups and preempt sedition. During the months before and after the August 1896 revolution, many of the Cuerpo's second-class agents submitted daily reports of uneventful rambles along city streets. A Spanish judge in Cavite Province, the heart of the national revolution just south of Manila, noted that the security services had "contemplated separatist ideas with stoic passivity without placing any obstacle in their way."[60] Only weeks after the outbreak of armed violence, the Cuerpo's chief claimed that his force had been aware of the impending revolt but the movement was so large that it overwhelmed the finite resources of the security forces. As the prisons filled with subversives, there had been "neither force, nor time, nor men sufficient for this task," forcing the Cuerpo to parole prisoners who soon rejoined the rebel forces. Complicating matters further, the Cuerpo soon gathered convincing evidence that the revolution had penetrated and compromised municipal police in the Manila area.[61] This undercover force did have its successes, notably a secret mission by a second-class agent, a Filipino named Toribio Gatbonton, who entered Gen. Emilio Aguinaldo's revolutionary encampment in July 1897. The agent had extensive conversations with the general himself and returned to make a detailed report of the rebel army's weapons, defenses, and morale.[62] Other missions were disastrous, including an undercover reconnaissance of Diliman, due east of Manila, by second-class agent Gregorio Enriquez, who was chased by thirty men armed with bolo knives and only escaped after jumping into a river.[63] In the end the sheer size of the revolutionary movement, the impossibility of monitoring the entire population, and the deeply rooted Spanish accommodation with local elites prevented the colonial security forces from crushing the revolution.

Among Filipinos there was strong antipathy toward the colonial police, particularly in the provinces near Manila where nationalist agitation was strongest. Patrolling the countryside to extirpate banditry, the Guardia Civil harassed thousands of ordinary Filipinos with petty charges of illegal gambling, improper papers, or late taxes.[64] In the last years of Spanish rule, a foreign observer noted that Filipinos "accuse the Guardia Civil . . . with practicing extortion upon defenseless natives [and] torturing witnesses to extort evidence."[65] The U.S. colonial official Dean C. Worcester reported that many dissidents had suffered summary arrest, "which was followed either by their complete disappearance or by the subsequent discovery of their dead bodies." Not surprisingly, he added, the "guardia civil were regarded with detestation and terror by the people."[66]

In retrospect the excesses of Spanish law enforcement may have helped erode the legitimacy of its colonial state. Reflecting this deep Filipino antipathy, the national martyr Jose Rizal broke the narrative of his famed 1886 novel, *Noli Me Tangere,* for a chapter-length indictment. "Go from town to town, from house to house, listen to the silent sighs of families," the outlaw Elias tells the novel's wealthy protagonist, Ibarra, and "you will be convinced that the evils the Guardia Civil correct are . . . less than the evils they continually cause." As the voice of the voiceless poor, Elias asks rhetorically whether the "terrorism" of the Guardia Civil will "be able to put out the fire on which it pours more fuel?"[67] As Rizal predicted, such repression seemed to encourage rather than restrain the rise of a national consciousness. In August 1896 a small revolt erupted on the outskirts of Manila and soon spread south to nearby Cavite Province, where a local landholder named Emilio Aguinaldo quickly assembled a revolutionary army of 5,400 regulars and 15,000 reserves. After some stunning victories against the Spanish forces, General Aguinaldo's troops launched a fitful campaign that, by the time the U.S. Army landed in 1898, had swept Spaniards from the provinces and laid siege to their capital, Manila.[68]

Although underfunded and overwhelmed right to the end, the Spanish forged a surprisingly resilient bureaucratic template for subsequent security operations that would persist for a century after their departure—a modern metropolitan force to secure the capital, mobile constabulary for the countryside, and local police for scattered rural municipalities. More broadly, Spanish colonial police defined a lasting set of missions for any state that would rule these volatile islands: maintaining public order, regulating vice, and suppressing subversion.[69]

Colonial Laboratory

Like some imperial palimpsest, U.S. colonial policing bore the invisible but indelible imprint of Spain's antecedent empire. Facing implacable Filipino resistance from the beginning, American colonials married the technologies of their own information revolution to the centralized Spanish police structure, producing a potent hybrid called the Philippines Constabulary. Lacking a tradition of national police, these accidental American colonials also mimed the tripartite Spanish enforcement structure: the Manila Metropolitans, rural constabulary, and municipal police. Without language skills or local knowledge, American colonial police initially relied on skilled subalterns recruited from the ranks of their former enemies, both mestizo veterans of the Spanish forces and defeated Filipino officers hardened in a decade of revolutionary warfare. The U.S. governor-generals who created and commanded these police were influenced by what one colonial called "the historic continuity of the office under Spain," which soon overcame, in this colonial context, an ingrained "American prejudice . . . against conferring centralized administrative control upon a single executive head."[70] Through this tropical hybridization, executive power, information management, and imperial police were combined into a powerful coercive apparatus that soon became central to U.S. rule.

Despite differences in scale, Great Britain's reliance on colonial police to govern its global empire provides the closest analogy to the American experience in the Philippines. Colonial police were central to both British imperial rule worldwide and modernization of the London metropolitan force at home. Indeed, a recent survey of the British Empire from 1830 to 1940 called its police "the most visible symbol of colonial rule" and "the cutting edge of colonial authority."[71] In Egypt, India, and Central Africa surveillance was essential not just for law enforcement but for political control of native nationalists, leading C. A. Bayly to argue that all European empires found "military and political intelligence . . . a critical determinant of their success."[72] Through a "cross-fertilization of imperial policing" across the British Empire, innovations in India influenced the Royal Irish Constabulary and both later shaped the Palestine police.[73] In this high imperial age the ongoing modernization of London's Metropolitan Police was strongly influenced by colonial innovations, first from Ireland, which between 1780 and 1830 served as "the experiment station" for Britain's own "projects of centralization," and later from a more disparate "colonial experimentation" that introduced "quasi-military practices" to Victorian England.[74] During the empire's protracted, painful decolonization, control over the police force and its "ubiquitous" Special Branch enabled British officials to navigate the transition and shape the new national governments. Across that quarter of the globe once ruled by Great Britain, colonialism left a lasting legacy as newly independent states from India to Ghana inherited a police apparatus that remained, apart from a turnover in senior personnel, surprisingly unchanged.[75]

Though useful, these observations about Great Britain must be amplified in ways that take the United States far beyond the limits of this literature. As a late imperial power America occupied the Philippines in the midst of Asia's first national revolution and soon found a colonial police force critical for both pacification and political control. In a sprawling empire of Western plains and tropical islands, only the Philippines stretched Washington's coercive capacities to the breaking point during a fifteen-year succession of insurgencies by a revolutionary army, guerrilla remnants, an urban underground, messianic peasants, tribal warriors, and Muslim separatists. So strong was this resistance, and so sophisticated Filipino counterintelligence, that the U.S. pacification campaign was pushed beyond the limits of contemporary knowledge. The Americans were forced to develop techniques for which there were no names: psychological profiling before psychology was an academic discipline and disinformation before information warfare was a military doctrine. In an American republic with a tradition of local law enforcement, the creation of a centralized colonial police did not simply influence the nature of metropolitan policing as it had the United Kingdom. Instead, it transformed Washington's nascent national security apparatus.

To contain this Filipino insurgency, U.S. colonial forces fused military intelligence with civilian technologies to create a modern surveillance state. In contrast to Spain's reliance on mass deportations, exemplary executions, and omnipresent police, the American regime achieved political control over the Philippines primarily through a synergy of information technologies: the telegraph, telephone, typewriter, photograph, and numbered file. Not only did the U.S. Army lay ten thousand miles of telegraph lines in just three years and staff its stations with clerk-typists who could pound out text at a rate of up to ninety-five words per minute—six times the speed of the quickest Spanish scribe—but the colonial regime drew these technologies into an integrated system of information-based police controls.[76] In its first decade the colonial state censored public discourse, infiltrated civil society, penetrated households, and placed individual leaders under incessant surveillance. Armed with authority unimagined in America, these colonials conducted an ad hoc experiment in police-state controls, fostering innovations in both data management and shoe-leather surveillance whose sum was a modern police panopticon.[77]

Even at the level of physical coercion American colonials embraced the modern symbolically. In place of Spain's iron garrote, which crushed neck vertebrae slowly in gruesome public executions, the U.S. regime installed an electric chair deep inside Manila's Bilibid Prison in 1924 for quick, closeted dispatch.[78] This combination of information and coercion telescoped time for the Philippines, carrying the archipelago through two centuries of technological change in less than two decades.

In the most fundamental sense, the hostile foreign environment heightened the impact of these operations on the U.S. military, forcing rapid innovation that might not have occurred in a more benign domestic context. While bilingual American police could walk a beat on Manila's streets, they were useless for undercover work, forcing the constabulary to recruit a corps of Filipino civilian agents for infiltration and surveillance. Inside the constabulary's Information Division, Filipino file clerks handled confidential reports from Filipino agents about Filipino leaders, forcing the introduction of numerical identification codes that prevented the otherwise inevitable leaks. Both methods, civilian auxiliaries for penetration and coded identification for security, would become standard procedure for U.S. Army intelligence from 1917 onward.

This centralized information apparatus was dedicated first to the suppression of subversion and later to the moral reformation of Filipino society. After America's first civil governors, William H. Taft and Luke Wright, imposed a rough colonial order through draconian laws and harsh repression, their successors collaborated with both colonial missionaries and educated Filipinos in using police to restrict or prohibit personal vices, which were deemed a threat to the eugenics of the body social—alcohol abuse, gambling, prostitution, and opium smoking. In the second decade of U.S. rule after 1908, the colonial regime thus shifted from simple repression to the inculcation of democratic values through education, elections, public health initiatives, amateur sports, and civic rituals whose totality was an ambitious attempt at "social engineering."[79]

America's invention of the surveillance state was an accidental, almost coincidental confluence of long-term trends and ephemeral events. Washington's conquest of Spain's dying empire brought the U.S. Army to the gates of Manila at the very moment when Philippine revolutionary forces had encircled the city's walls. In their pacification of Asia's first national revolution, American colonials were attempting nothing less than a complete reversal of a deeply rooted national awakening. The Philippine revolution represented two generations of political transformation, starting with the invention of a Filipino national identity, articulation of a political program for its realization, and mobilization of an army in its defense. Washington's decision to colonize the country plunged its soldiers into a sustained campaign to reverse these revolutionary processes: first, a short, bloody war against the Philippine Army; next, a harsh counterinsurgency to crush its guerrilla forces; and, finally, a protracted secret-police operation to demoralize the radical leaders and discredit the nationalist ideals that had been their inspiration. For over a century scholars have focused on the initial, conventional phase of U.S. Army combat operations, which seems, in retrospect, to be of secondary importance in the resolution of what was fundamentally a political conflict. Indeed, the final, most challenging sub rosa phase of this pacification campaign entailed a new form of policing that relied on information, not simple coercion, to break the Philippine nationalist movement from within, recasting both the concept of nationhood and the conduct of politics in more conservative terms.

Under the relentless pressure of covert and counterguerrilla operations, American officers trained as engineers, doctors, and combat soldiers created an entire clandestine tradecraft complete with individual surveillance, covert infiltration, political manipulation, psychological profiling, comprehensive data collection, and strategic disinformation. With little precedent or principle to guide them, this small cadre mobilized the full repertoire of their nation's advanced information systems and then pushed beyond these bounds, experimenting with methods at the very edge of technological capacity. In sum, colonial pacification, with its diverse arenas of conflict, proved an ideal laboratory for innovation in the realm of intelligence and counterintelligence.

Imperial Mimesis

At the high tide of empire, the U.S. colonial police shaped the Philippine polity, creating an interlocking regime of vice prohibition and paramilitary policing whose effect is still evident more than a half century after independence. Since police were central to the colonial regime, the succeeding Philippine Republic inherited a state apparatus reliant on formal and informal police powers. Above all, the American colonial regime, by creating the constabulary as a political and paramilitary force, embedded a powerful security apparatus within the Philippine executive that has been employed by almost every Filipino president from Quezon in 1936 to Arroyo in 2006. Moreover, the covert doctrines developed under U.S. rule persisted inside the Philippines Constabulary and its successor, the Philippine National Police, allowing state control over a volatile society through clandestine methods such as surveillance, infiltration, disinformation, and assassination.

During the 1950s the Armed Forces of the Philippines (AFP) had a mixed record in countering the Hukbalahap (Huk) communist rebels with regular combat, but was quite sophisticated in the use of covert operations. In more recent years the AFP has used these unconventional methods against revolts that challenged its limited conventional capacities. With the end of the Marcos dictatorship in 1986, the AFP's "intelligence projects," which were directed primarily against the Maoist New People's Army (NPA) and the Moro Islamic Liberation Front (MILF), created countergroups that were initially successful but soon spun out of control, devolving into criminal gangs expert in robbery and kidnapping. Of equal import the state's reliance on police repression has prompted periodic mass protests, from the nationalist demonstrations of 1911 through the student marches of 1971 and the two "people power" uprisings of February 1986 and January 2001. As a direct result of the country's long colonial experience, police have played a defining role in shaping the character of the Philippine polity and the conduct of its politics.

If imperial rule had such a profound influence on the colonized, we might well ask whether it had an equally significant impact on the colonizer. Through decades of careful study historians have delineated the transformative impact of U.S. rule on the Philippines, showing how it created a modern civil service, prosperous middle class, and mass education system. After a century of this unilateral approach it is time to press this inquiry further and ask a more elusive question: was the experience of empire mutually transformative, with lasting consequences for both the postcolonial Philippines and the United States?

Such an inquiry demands if not circumspection then a modicum of caution. The formation of the U.S. state was, of course, influenced by its own internal development as well as by multiple processes of expansion: conquest of the western frontier, global commercial reach as a second-tier power, and a formal overseas empire. Yet there seems to have been a uniquely catalytic quality to colonial rule, making it a Promethean fire of institutional change. Through conquest and pacification colonialism pushed the capacities of an occupying power's statecraft to the breaking point while at the same time creating opportunities for experimentation not possible at home—making empire a crucible for forging new state forms and functions. Empire, any empire, makes its metropole more self-conscious, more calculating in the application of power. Just as war transforms technology and industry, so colonialism plays a comparable role for government, producing innovations, particularly in the use of coercive controls, with a profound impact on its bureaucracies both home and abroad. In an age of limited, laissez-faire governance circa 1898, America's activist colonial states, from Puerto Rico through Panama to the Philippines, conducted bold experiments whose lessons were later repatriated through policies and personnel.

Focusing on colonial policing reveals how empire simultaneously formed a modern Philippine polity and transformed the American state, fostering both a coercive capacity and the inclination to apply it. Above all, empire empowered the U.S. presidency, investing the executive branch with broad powers over subject territories and fostering an extraordinary authority akin to what the president had heretofore enjoyed only in wartime. At a more mundane level empire formed an extraconstitutional circuit among the president's colonial appointees, corporate allies, and political cronies. Colonization expanded federal patronage, linking Republican Party machines in powerful states such as Ohio and Michigan to the colonial civil service.[80] More visibly, colonial expansion created a new path to the presidency taken by Theodore Roosevelt and William H. Taft but not by Leonard Wood, making empire a dominant, even decisive influence in four presidential campaigns between 1900 and 1912.

Colonial rule also fostered long-term institutional change in Washington's national security apparatus. The colonial regime in Manila developed a comprehensive internal security doctrine, drawing information technologies from the U.S. metropole, merging them with imperial innovations, and then repatriating these novel procedures, tempered and tested. When high imperial rule over the Philippines ended in 1916, colonial veterans came home to play a key role in the development of the U.S. Army's expanded intelligence operations during World War I. As Washington mobilized for war a year later, the contradiction between its worldwide empire and coastal defenses snapped with a vengeance. After two decades of playing the global game on the cheap, the United States suddenly found itself caught up in the clash of empires with military forces that paled before Great Britain's navy and Germany's army, a lack of preparedness that produced real concerns in Washington and reverberated as xenophobic hysteria across the country. In this hour of crisis Washington relied on its colonial veterans to establish a national security apparatus for both domestic surveillance and foreign espionage, founding the army's Military Intelligence Division and later its Military Police.[81]

The U.S. Army's overall commander in Europe, Gen. John Pershing, had built his military career in the Philippines, first as a celebrated captain fighting Muslim rebels on the southern island of Mindanao and later as military governor of its Moro Province. In selecting his senior officers for the European campaign, General Pershing drew on Philippine veterans for key staff and field positions, particularly in less conventional commands. The former chief of the constabulary, Harry Bandholtz, became Pershing's provost marshal general and at the close of war founded the Military Police (MP) to manage the chaos of occupation and demobilization in Europe. In the lower echelons of this new service, Philippine veterans were also prominent, notably the former chief of Manila's Secret Service and a former senior officer in the Philippine Scouts, both of whom trained MPs for the postwar occupation of Europe.[82]

The influence of these imperial veterans was even more marked on the domestic front. As fear of enemy espionage grew in the first months of war, empire provided Washington with the requisites for greatly expanded state security operations. Just as repressive colonial sedition and libel laws had silenced Filipino radicals by 1907, so parallel U.S. legislation under the Espionage Act of 1917 allowed the jailing of antiwar dissidents such as Eugene V. Debs.[83] Lacking any intelligence capacity whatsoever at the start of this global war, the U.S. Army relied on Col. Ralph H. Van Deman, the former chief of army intelligence in the Philippines, to establish its Military Intelligence Division. Applying colonial lessons from data management to operational doctrines, Van Deman built the MID from a staff of one—himself—into a division of seventeen hundred and within weeks designed a complete intelligence and counterintelligence doctrine.

Yet even in this domestic iteration U.S. military intelligence showed signs of its imperial origins. Just as colonial security had relied on hundreds of Filipino agents, so Van Deman forged close alliances with American civilian auxiliaries for the counterintelligence work that became his division's main wartime mission. To search for suspected subversives among German Americans, the colonel collaborated with a nationwide vigilante group, the American Protective League, to launch the largest mass surveillance yet conducted by any modern state, domestic or otherwise. As an index of its pervasiveness, the league's legion of 350,000 citizen-spies used its extralegal powers to amass, with allied groups, an archive of over a million pages of surveillance reports in just eighteen months of war.[84] Looking back on the spread of internal security, a senior official of the American Civil Liberties Union (ACLU) called Van Deman "the single most important figure in shaping this civilian mission and consolidating its base," using "military intelligence . . . to curb movements for change."[85] Indeed, Van Deman himself was a product of empire, transformed by his Philippine experience from a military mediocrity into the "father of U.S. military intelligence." Hardened in this crucible of colonial pacification, he returned home in 1902 to spend the next half century working tirelessly, obsessively, breaking laws and bending bureaucracies to build almost singlehandedly an intrusive internal security apparatus.

In the tumultuous, anti-Bolshevik aftermath of war known as the "red scare," MID continued its covert campaign against radical unions while senior U.S. Army commanders applied lessons from the colonial Philippines to crush a radical miners' revolt in the West Virginia coalfields—the only armed uprising against the American state in the twentieth century. This alliance between federal agencies and civilian adjuncts forged during World War I would remain a defining feature of U.S. internal security operations for the next half century. Empire also invested U.S. intelligence doctrine with a problematic racial paradigm for the perception of threat. Viewing the Philippines through a filter of social Darwinism that bred both superiority and insecurity, American colonial police acted as racial exemplars ruling over supposedly lesser breeds: Chinese, Filipinos, Spanish mestizos, Muslims, and highland tribes. Indeed, a parallel study of British and French intelligence in the Middle East mandates found that their "threat assessment was inherently politicized by the dominant ideology of imperialism with its coded hierarchies of racial difference."[86] Back home, these colonial veterans imbued the new U.S. domestic intelligence apparatus with an imperious dominion over those deemed other, and thus lesser, whether ethnic communities, political dissidents, or ordinary workers.

These security operations in the years surrounding World War I introduced a recurring tension between America's eighteenth-century constitution and its twentieth-century surveillance. Two decades after America's information revolution had created a capacity for mass surveillance, empire became the means for transforming technological potential into state practice. Once it had adopted the colonial model for its internal security, the federal government cultivated a repressive capability manifest during periodic political crises throughout much of the twentieth century. From the anti-German hysteria of World War I through the anticommunist purges of the early cold war, there were clear signs of fundamental conflict between the constitutional protections of individual liberty and growing state surveillance.

Inspired by their experience of social engineering in colonized societies, American leaders would apply similarly coercive methods to shape their own polity, acculturating immigrants, banning drugs and alcohol, barring aliens, policing subversives, rehabilitating addicts, and rebuilding cities. Just six years after Manila prohibited opium smoking in 1908, for example, the U.S. Congress passed the Harrison Narcotics Act of 1914, the start of American drug prohibition and the first federal law restricting individual rights over the body. Similarly, the U.S. public health service at both the state and federal levels drew on a militarized imperial model, introduced in Cuba and perfected in the Philippines, for domestic control of epidemic disease.[87] Colonialism was thus mutually transformative, forming a modernized Philippine polity and transforming the United States into an activist state with powerful internal security agencies.

For sixty years after its independence in 1946, the Philippines would continue to serve as a laboratory for the perfection of American power, collaborating in the development of new military doctrines to meet a succession of challenges to U.S. global hegemony. During the 1950s, American advisers pioneered unconventional tactics to defeat Filipino peasant guerrillas, creating a novel counterinsurgency later applied throughout the third world. A decade later, as student demonstrations roiled democracies worldwide, Manila's university belt became Washington's testing ground for police riot-control techniques. During the 1980s, as America recoiled from its demoralizing Vietnam defeat, the Philippines, along with Central America, served as a proving ground for a reinvigorated counterguerrilla doctrine called "low intensity conflict." After the September 2001 terrorist attacks, the Pentagon developed a distinctive concept of "population centric warfare" in the southern Philippines that it applied, starting in mid-2009, to an intensified pacification of Afghanistan. In a latter-day iteration of imperial mimesis, the global war on terror also produced innovations in electronic surveillance and biometric identification that are, once again, migrating homeward to circumscribe civil liberties in America.

An Exceptional Empire

As the source of these seminal changes, this distinctive U.S. colonial state merits closer analysis. Recent scholarship on American rule in the Philippines, confusing political rhetoric with imperial reality, has often described its policies through colonial catchphrases such as "benevolent assimilation," "imperialism of suasion," or "tutelary" democracy. Whatever his stated aims might have been, the first colonial governor, William H. Taft, imposed rigid controls over information, using draconian laws to restrict public debate and secret police to monitor private communications.[88] Under a series of U.S. Supreme Court decisions that made Filipinos subjects of the United States but not its citizens, Taft exercised far greater powers over colonized Filipinos than any stateside official did over his fellow citizens.[89] When harsh libel and sedition laws failed to silence Filipino militants, the colonial government used its police powers, including the selective release of incriminating information, to punish its critics. Through this mix of law and police, surveillance and scandal, the U.S. regime slowly stifled political dissidence and constrained Filipino public discourse within colonial bounds.

The underlying character of this U.S. colonial administration has long eluded scholars. To cite a recent example, a leading Filipino historian has argued in essays on American "orientalism" that early U.S. scholar-officials used "colonial knowledge" to create "a certain model of Philippine society in order to facilitate and justify the pacification of Filipinos." Like the European orientalists famously dissected by Edward Said, this American colonial scholarship supposedly created a similarly resilient paradigm that shaped the American perception of the Philippines in the long aftermath of colonial rule.[90]

Whatever its merits might be, this argument does raise some larger questions. While American colonial officials in Manila had little time for the classical studies of language and culture that obsessed European orientalists, clearly there must have been some conceptual framework for rule over an island empire that stretched halfway around the world from Puerto Rico through the Panama Canal to Hawaii and the Philippines. Like all imperialists, Americans needed information. But they seem to have valued a different kind of knowledge. At what is perhaps midpoint in this American century of global dominion, it seems timely to inquire into the character of what scholars, conservative and liberal alike, now regard as history's most powerful empire.[91] Is there some attribute that distinguishes this U.S. imperium from the seventy empires that have preceded it in world history? If Washington has not relied on an orientalist paradigm, was there another intellectual architecture, a deeper design, that informed its overseas occupations, from the Philippines in 1898 to Afghanistan and Iraq since 2001? Simply put, how does Washington exercise its power, and what impact does it have upon the nations subject to its global reach? American historians have spent so many decades in denial about the reality of U.S. global empire that we still understand surprisingly little about its character.[92] Ironically, we can see the essential epistemologic of the American state most clearly not at its epicenter in Washington but at the edge of empire some ten thousand miles away.

The historical record provides little evidence for an American orientalism—if by orientalism we mean a historically specific field of study akin to that which served European imperial expansion into Asia and North Africa. To begin with the basics, there was a striking contrast between European and American educational standards for colonial service. Over 90 percent of the 362 British officials selected for the Sudan Political Service from 1899 to 1952 were graduates of elite private schools and leading universities such as Oxford and Cambridge. Most American officials in the Philippines were discharged soldiers, accidental colonials who soon rose far beyond their formal qualifications. "Corporals became capitalists," recalled one American old-timer of the first years of U.S. rule in Manila, "sergeants became school superintendents, . . . company clerks operated restaurants and bars." Among the 509 schoolteachers who arrived at Manila aboard the U.S. Transport *Thomas* in 1901, arguably the most carefully selected of all American officials, 31 had high school diplomas, 121 normal school training, and the rest "some college," a far cry from England's erudite empire builders.[93] In 1919 French trainees for the Moroccan native affairs directorate took 140 hours of Arabic, studied Arab ethnography, and contributed to the scholarly *Revue du Monde Musulman.* Comparable American recruits for the Philippines Constabulary were cadets plucked from private military schools with little training beyond drill and discipline.[94]

Consequently, American rule in the Philippines was distinguished by its inherently superficial character, by the absence of anything akin to an American orientalism—that is, of anything approaching a deep study of archeology and philology to inform colonial rule. With their schoolboy lessons in Latin and Greek, English colonials emerged from Oxford and Cambridge with a classical approach to imperial rule, heading east of Suez to probe textual and archaeological remains for a timeless cultural essence.[95] In colonizing India during the nineteenth century, the British "believed they could explore and conquer . . . through translation" by learning languages, both classical and vernacular, which they "understood to be the prerequisite form of knowledge for all others."[96] Exemplifying this approach, Britain's famed Arab Bureau, an intelligence unit that operated from Cairo's Savoy Hotel during World War I, was a scholarly coterie with extraordinary cultural expertise. Its chief, David George Hogarth, was an eminent Oxford archaeologist of Arab antiquities; his deputy, Capt. Kinahan Cornwallis, had read Arabic at Oxford; and their agents included two first-class Oxford honors graduates, T. E. Lawrence, adviser to the Arab revolt against the Ottoman Empire, and the archaeologist Gertrude Bell, one of the architects of modern Iraq.[97]

With his Harvard education and affinity for British imperialism, Governor-General W. Cameron Forbes was one of the few American officials to embrace this English cultural emphasis. On his arrival at Manila in 1904, he made a stab at studying the Tagalog language with the famed Filipino socialist Lope K. Santos. But even Forbes soon confessed in his private diary that the local language was "fearfully and wonderfully made most difficult," with pronouns so impossible and syntax so "confusing" that he soon abandoned the effort.[98] Few Americans bothered to learn Filipino languages; instead thousands taught Filipinos to read English.

Through private subscription, a Cleveland publisher issued fifty-two volumes of early Spanish documents on the Philippines edited by Emma H. Blair and James A. Robertson. Although launched by Dr. Robertson, the founding editor of the *Hispanic American Historical Review,* as a scholarly endeavor in the European style, the series was dominated after volume five by James LeRoy, the private secretary to senior colonials Taft and Worcester, who transformed it into a pragmatic vehicle for anti-Spanish, pro-American propaganda. But the project was a financial failure and there is little evidence that U.S. officials made serious use of these weighty tomes, making them not foundational texts for an American orientalism but fifty-two signposts to a road not taken.[99]

While European empires operated under a costly command-style bureaucracy, American colonialism employed a decentralized market model, responding to problems by mobilizing a cadre of contractors for quick, cost-effective solutions. Rather than expanding the federal bureaucracy with a large colonial ministry, Washington created a surprisingly small agency in the bowels of the War Department, the Bureau of Insular Affairs, and then outsourced overseas rule to low-cost surrogate states in the Philippines and Puerto Rico. Instead of career colonials such as the legendary British or Dutch savants who gave their lives to empire, American overseas rule relied on the short-term secondment of consultants and contractors—rotating military officers between continental and colonial service, and dispatching experts such as urban planner Daniel K. Burnham and forester Gifford Pinchot to frame templates for colonial policy. Within a few years of the landing at Manila in 1898, the colonial state had mobilized a transitory A-to-Z army of technical consultants in administration, agronomy, entomology, ethnography, economics, meteorology, plant biology, public health, urban planning, and zoology.[100]

This stark contrast needs some qualification. The British also attempted, through archeology and cartography, to reduce "India to orderly blocks of empirical information that could be rendered in maps, charts, and glossaries." But these remained "micro-knowledges" subordinated to a "generalized body of knowledge organized at the state level" around orientalist conceptions from the study of language and culture. There were, moreover, a few accidental American scholars such as Roy F. Barton or Dr. Najeeb M. Saleeby in the Mountain and Moro provinces, respectively. But they were isolated at the periphery of colonial power, generally ignored in their day, and respected for their scholarship largely in retrospect. On a spectrum of imperial information systems, the British subordinated technical data to cultural models, while the Americans, by contrast, did not temper their empiricism with significant study of language or culture.[101]

If the Europeans prized erudition, the Americans preferred information, accessible and succinct. If European imperialists emphasized deep cultural knowledge of oriental societies for their manipulation from within, American colonials amassed contemporary data for control from without. Instead of immersion in a Philippine past informed by archaeology or philology, it was an American innovation to adapt its new information technologies for hasty, inherently superficial surveys of the Philippine present through cadastral mapping, census taking, geography, photography, police surveillance, and scientific reconnaissance. As a lightly populated archipelago at the edge of Asia, the Philippine Islands had no history of ancient empires that left literary fragments or royal ruins such as Angkor and Borobudur to detain archaeologists or philologists. As products of a utilitarian education system, American colonials favored research for pragmatic or political applications, with all data reduced to compact handbooks for ready reference. Ignoring language and culture, the U.S. colonial government commissioned a Spanish Jesuit, Fr. José Algué of the Manila Observatory, to reduce three centuries of Spanish natural and social science to a handy two-volume summary titled *El Archipiélago Filipino*.[102]

In the first decade of U.S. rule, colonial bureaus thus produced a series of practical guides such as *A Preliminary Check List of the Principal Commercial Timbers* and *Handbook on the Sugar Industry of the Philippine Islands*. Exemplifying this effort was the encyclopedic *Pronouncing Gazetteer and Geographical Dictionary of the Philippine Islands*, a 933-page "compendium of such information [that] would be practically useful to the American people," all arranged alphabetically from Aanosa ("village on W. shore of Talim I") to Zumarraga ("pueblo in Samar, 9 m. from Catabalogan").[103] Building on this base, the U.S. regime's Bureau of Science maintained an impressive library of useful data and published hundreds of pragmatic how-to reports on the mundane details of agriculture, fishery, and handicrafts.[104]

The paragon of this American imperial knowledge was Elmer D. Merrill, the famed botanist who collected a million herbarium specimens as director of the Philippine Bureau of Science, the New York Botanical Garden, and Harvard's Arnold Arboretum. He was known throughout his long, distinguished career, half of it spent in the colonial Philippines from 1902 to 1923, for never going "far below the surface" and for an "ability to deal superficially with extraordinarily large numbers of plants." The rigorous taxonomy that propelled Dr. Merrill's voracious collection, reducing the archipelago's green riot of tropical jungle to just 2,136 pages in his *Enumeration of Philippine Flowering Plants*, also infused the epistemology of America's empire, particularly the army's early intelligence operations. Significantly, the pioneers of military intelligence in the Philippines all had advanced training in the biological sciences in an age when Linnaean taxonomy was ascendant. The army's earliest analysts, Dean C. Worcester and Dr. Frank Bourns, had first come to the Philippines as zoologists on collecting expeditions, while the founder of its field intelligence, Capt. Ralph Van Deman, was a qualified medical doctor. Whether through these specific personalities or the broader ethos of America's information revolution, U.S. intelligence in the Philippines was quintessentially taxonomic in its insatiable appetite for data, punctilious classification, and thin, even superficial treatment.[105]

If the prime aim of the modern state is, as James Scott argues, to establish metrics for rendering "a social hieroglyph into a legible and administratively more convenient format," then U.S. imperial rule was unrivaled in its ability to "read" alien terrains through such surface reconnaissance.[106] European scholars of empire such as Niall Ferguson who fault the contemporary American aversion to foreign languages and deep cultural knowledge in the exercise of its global dominion fail to grasp the guiding genius of a distinctive U.S. imperial style grounded in short-term service and serviceable information.[107] Yet shallowness should not be mistaken for a want of seriousness. For embedded within this seemingly surface engagement was a relentless drive for omniscience, even omnipotence, imbued with the capacity, if challenged, for a lethal response unchecked by any of the empathy that might have come from a deeper cultural engagement.

From this perspective, U.S. colonial rule over the Philippines was a transitional regime, moving its global governance from Europe's older territorial colonialism of plantations, police, and bolt-action repression to a postcolonial, supranational regime of military bases, electronic surveillance, and psychological warfare. Just as the United States conducted cartographic, demographic, and photographic surveys in its quest for colonial legibility in the Philippines after 1901, so a century later it would deploy airpower and satellite imagery for the pacification of Afghanistan and Iraq, seeking to elevate its military controls into an ether beyond either cultural nuance or political complexity. For the present, before the perfection of a future electronic battlefield, the U.S. military still relies on applied social science to aid its earthbound troops. So pronounced is this empirical emphasis that in 2008 when the army found itself adrift in Afghanistan's dense cultural terrain, with Taliban insurgency spreading and American casualties rising, it integrated academic anthropologists into Human Terrain Teams. These contract scholars were assigned to each combat brigade and tasked to reduce social complexities to "ethnographic intelligence" or pithy how-to maxims. According to a leading advocate, Assistant Deputy Under Secretary of Defense John Wilcox, such human terrain mapping "enables the entire kill chain."[108]

Political Scandal

The illiberal character of American colonial rule over the Philippines was evident in its reliance on innovative forms of information and disinformation for political control. Through relentless surveillance and centralized intelligence, U.S. colonial police penetrated private social space to collect derogatory data on Filipino political leaders, whether radical or conservative, revolutionary or collaborator. By the systematic collection and selective release of such incriminating information, the colonial government protected its allies from gossip and damaged or destroyed its critics with scandal. To suppress countervailing criticism, the regime enacted harsh punishments for subversion or libel of its public officials, relying on the colonial courts to punish erring newspaper editors harshly. As this mix of police pressure and political co-optation turned Filipino activists into spies and collaborators, the militant nationalist movement imploded by 1912 amid suspicion and betrayal, leaving conservative politicians in control of public space through patronage politics.

Through their deft manipulation of information, these U.S. colonial police offer us a rare opportunity to explore the elusive role of scandal in modern societies. Historians generally do a poor job with scandal. For history itself, the very process of recovering and recapitulating past events, robs scandal of its central source of fascination: revelation. The petty derelictions of the powerful over sex or money that seem so riveting during their unfolding lose their power immediately upon disclosure. No scandal, no matter how lurid, is as absorbing in the retelling as it was in the heat of discovery. No raconteur, no matter how skilled, can replicate the enthrallment everyone feels as a scandal unfolds. For over two centuries a stream of scandals has fascinated modern publics, yet historians have found surprisingly few are worth recounting. Similarly, for political scientists "engaged in the weighty study of 'real' conflicts," says a scholarly treatise, "scandals rarely reach the level of fluff" and "are best left to the prurient pages of the yellow press." More recently, however, British sociologist John Thompson has argued that, "in this modern age of mediated visibility," political scandals are "social struggles fought out in the symbolic realm," revealing much "about the nature of power and its fragility."[109]

In thus treating scandal as serious politics, fiction succeeds where history usually fails. As George Orwell reminds us in his novel *Burmese Days* (New York, 1934), there is a subtle, unexamined dimension to the colonial state's coercion beyond our contemporary focus on repression and resistance. Inspired by his own service as a British colonial policeman during the 1920s, Orwell's story about a lowly Burmese bureaucrat's use of sexual scandal to best a British rival contains a vision—indeed, a theory—about the subtle interplay of imperial politics. Through secret police the colonial state invaded the privacy of native elites, collecting incriminating information that allowed an almost invisible control over aspiring nationalists. Native politicians responded in kind, as Orwell observed, collecting local gossip about the sexual dalliances of European colonials that served as something of a political counterweight. At moments when circulation of rumor or confidential documents sparked public controversy, the consequent political crisis could disgrace individuals, topple governments, or threaten the legitimacy of entire colonial regimes. Ultimately, we cannot understand the interaction between colonizer and colonized without considering the intertwined roles of secret police and political scandal.

By ignoring the political role of colonial police, particularly their secret services, we historians have produced a one-dimensional portrait of imperial politics that overlooks the constant, high-stakes contestation in the intimate realm of personal privacy mediated by police detectives, special agents, and native spies. Indeed, scandal, often arising from seamy, even sordid cases, influenced high colonial politics—everything from competition for office to issues of political legitimacy. By this oversight we have neglected the fusion of information and coercion central to the rise of the modern state, both its colonial progenitor and its metropolitan successor.

Using the rich U.S. records, study of the Philippines can take us beyond the view of the colonial police as a blunt instrument for physical coercion to a more nuanced understanding of its role as a panopticon, sweeping the shadows for sensitive information with spies or surveillance and then selectively releasing, or threatening to release, scandal to shape the course of Filipino political careers. Though long ignored, such deft control over information was a key facet of colonial control over elites beyond coercion or manipulation. Just as the threat of fusillades from repeating rifles restrained striking workers or rebellious peasants, so the possibility of public humiliation constrained native political elites within the colonial state's tight bounds.

Through their formal repression and informal information controls, colonial police were a significant force in the formation of the modern Philippine state. Apart from the formalities of regular elections and representative government, the U.S. colonial regime fostered a freewheeling system that made newspaper exposés and public scandals integral to the political process. Not only did American rule establish a formal institutional infrastructure of legislature, executive, and judiciary, but it encouraged the informal interplay of courts, press, politicians, and public that helped make Philippine politics so characteristically contentious. As oligarchic families and political elites swapped favors, a crusading press aroused the middle-class public with scandalous exposés, sparking pressure for reform. Through their dominant role in the maintenance of social order, the police became both actor and accused in these grand scandals. By exploring this intersection of high and low, public and private, we can see more clearly how periodic scandals and political crises were central to the conduct of an emerging Philippine democracy.

Covert Netherworld

The study of police and scandal takes us beneath the visible surface of politics into a murky realm between the formal and informal, licit and illicit, that we call, for want of better words, the "covert netherworld." By looking beyond formalities of elections and legislation, we can better understand the riddle that is the Philippine state, weak yet strong, centralized yet localized. To better grasp its colonial origins and postcolonial character, we need to probe this netherworld of secret services and criminal syndicates to see how their commingling has created a supple nexus of control.

At its core this covert netherworld is an invisible interstice, within both individual nations and the international system, inhabited by criminal and clandestine actors with both the means and the need to operate outside conventional channels. Among all the institutions of modern society, only intelligence agencies and crime syndicates can carry out complex financial or political operations that leave no visible trace. While the illegality of their commerce forces criminal syndicates into elaborate concealment of their membership, activities, and profits, political necessity dictates that secret services practice a parallel tradecraft of untraceable finances, concealed identities, and covert operations. The CIA, "like any other professional criminal organization," explained a former covert operative, "lived according to a strict code of secrecy. . . . Cryptonyms replaced the names of agents. Even geographical places were renamed. . . . It was as if the CIA lived in a parallel universe." In sum, both criminal and covert actors are practitioners of what another CIA officer, Lucien Conein, called "the clandestine arts," that is, the shared skill of operating outside the normal channels of civil society.[110]

This vast, complex, and uncharted terrain operates at three distinct yet intersecting levels: the transnational, the national, and the local. Taking a leaf from recent United Nations (UN) documents, its *transnational dimension* is an elusive, largely nonterritorial sector of the global economy created by national and international prohibitions. As an index of scale, consider illicit drug trafficking, which, according to the 1997 edition of the UN's *World Drugs Report,* is a $400 billion industry with 180 million users and 8 percent of world trade—larger than textiles, steel, or automobiles.[111] Although its clandestine character often denies it a spatial manifestation, this illicit international trade occasionally touches ground, thereby creating a *local dimension* of free ports or outlaw zones, epicenters of contraband commerce that are detached from nation-state controls and known by evocative place-names such as the Golden Triangle, Golden Crescent, or Triborder area. Inside *individual nations* the interaction between the state's secret services and outlaw elements, whether rural warlords or urban gangsters, can define the character of an entire polity. During tempestuous times in their respective national histories, nominally nonstate actors such as the Italian Mafia, Indonesian Preman, or Japanese Yakuza have become mechanisms of social control integral to the functioning of the legitimate state. Just as E. H. Norman and Maruyama Masao once argued that the prewar Japanese empire used crime syndicates for political control and Tim Lindsey has recently reached parallel conclusions about contemporary Indonesia, so we need to explore how similar influences may have shaped the Philippine polity.[112]

In searching for appropriate analysis of such a multifocal Philippine state, we can peel the academic onion, stripping away the scholarly layers to reach its core characteristics. For decades historians and political scientists have tried to explain the country's politics by arguing that Manila had married the formal structures of electoral democracy developed under U.S. colonial rule with extrasystemic elements such as clientelism, bossism, and social protest. But this literature, while capturing important dimensions of the process, ignores the influence of the coercive apparatus and its criminal netherworld. Comparing American colonial policing in the Philippines to the Dutch panopticon on Java, for example, the distinguished historian Theodore Friend dismissed U.S. political surveillance as "inexact and unsystematic" and its constabulary as "light-fingered with others' possessions, heavy-handed with their liberties, and sometimes trigger-happy."[113] Such conventional political history cannot explain the country's recurring extrasystemic crises and complex politics.

Among the American specialists in Philippine politics, only one, John T. Sidel, has merged the formal and informal to produce an analysis appropriate to this enigmatic polity. In his study of bossism, he argues that the Philippine state is a "complex set of predatory mechanisms for private exploitation and accumulation of the archipelago's human, natural, and monetary resources" mediated by a constant electoral competition that makes the Philippine state "essentially a multi-tiered racket."[114] Beyond the state's bureaucracy, regular elections foster a system of bossism that rests on an "electorate susceptible to clientelist, coercive, and monetary inducements and pressures."[115] With elections every two years, the periodic mobilization of these voters rests on diverse actors, including elected officials, warlords, militia chiefs, and crime bosses. By delegating its authority to these fragments of the Philippine state, Manila grants them a series of informal immunities that inevitably shape the character of the country's politics, fostering an array of nonstate actors and localized systems of social control. In his biographies of two Cebuano criminals, for example, Sidel argues that the state used them "as subcontracted law enforcement agents" to control the poor of a major city, "bearing witness not to the state's supposed weakness but to its strength."[116]

In the end, however, not even Sidel takes the next step by inverting this analytical framework to show not just the center's influence on these criminal and provincial peripheries but their role in shaping both political processes and actual administration at the epicenter of state power. If we flip his analytical telescope for a microscopic scrutiny of crime, police, and political crisis, we can see the Philippine polity as a union of center and periphery, formal and informal, licit and illicit.

Reaching out from the epicenter, Manila exercises a supple influence over its sprawling archipelago despite seemingly weak central controls. To contain the centrifugal pull of both local and transnational forces, the Republic has deputized a panoply of parastatal elements: bandits, warlords, smugglers, gambling bosses, militia chiefs, special agents, forest concessionaires, planters, industrialists, and vigilantes. Although many are, at best, quasi-legal and some are outlaws, these surrogates of the state serve as agents integral to the Philippine polity. Instead of relying solely on the formal coercive instruments of bureaucracy, military, and police, Manila controls its disparate archipelago by delegating informal authority to this array of de facto state actors whom it invests with legal immunity and local autonomy. This extralegal devolution of coercive authority also allows these Philippine variants of Max Weber's "autonomous functionaries" to privatize police power, producing recurring incidents of spectacular abuse that have periodically culminated in crises of legitimacy for administrations or entire regimes.[117] Yet beneath this untidy, seemingly chaotic spectacle of political violence, rural revolt, and secessionist struggle, the state apparatus stretches or strains but never breaks. Through these surrogate leaders it retains effective control of even its most remote and troubled regions. In sum, by investing these informal deputies with delegated police powers the Philippine state has become decentralized or even diffuse yet resilient and paradoxically powerful.

The application of this covert paradigm to the United States allows new insight into the role of clandestine services in shaping U.S. history throughout the twentieth century. After using this model to write the first fourteen of this book's chapters about U.S. colonial policing in the Philippines, I then applied it, very tentatively, to America, hypothesizing that colonial innovations might have had some influence on the formation of a U.S. internal security apparatus. Processing documents through this paradigm led to some unexpected findings. The first was the extraordinary career of Ralph Van Deman, from his central role in Philippine pacification as a young captain in 1901 through his obsessive compilation of secret files on a quarter million suspected communists as a retired major general by 1952. The second discovery was of other, lower-level figures in the history of the Philippine-American War generally ignored by historians yet central to this history, both its immediate conduct and its long-term consequences. Following these leads through years of additional research led to the realization that a distinctively American fusion of state agencies and civilian adjuncts, first developed in the colonial Philippines, forged a resilient state-civil apparatus as a defining feature of U.S. internal security operations—indeed, of its national political life—for much of the twentieth century. Finally, the analysis of this distinctive covert apparatus revealed a strong skein of institutional continuity through seemingly separate periods across a half century of U.S. history, from the anti-German hysteria of 1917 to the Japanese American incarcerations of 1942 and the anticommunist blacklisting of the 1950s.

Thus, from the historian's perspective police are an apt point of entry into an invisible interstice otherwise beyond the limits of conventional scholarship. In modern states police signify much more than car chases, kickbacks, and shootouts. Although their records are less tidy and more closely held than those of their military counterparts, police are nonetheless a state agency and leave their bureaucratic fingerprints on history's vessels. In many modern societies police are not simply guardians of an impregnable social frontier that keeps moral outcasts at a safe remove from polite society but serve instead as informal gatekeepers between the state and its social margins, patrolling the boundaries of parallel social systems, civil society and its criminal netherworld. This hidden sector of commercial vice—gambling, prostitution, and addictive drugs—is not simply the realm of derelicts and deviants. It is the meeting ground of high and low, a leveling marketplace where the privileged and underprivileged exchange goods and services otherwise prohibited by moral and legal sanctions. Through methods legal and extralegal, police regulate this informal marketplace where high caste and outcast trade illicit goods and illegal services, where society's formal laws and informal imperatives are discreetly mediated.

Although deceptively out of sight at society's margins, this demimonde is an important zone of clandestine political contestation that can, depending on time and circumstance, either amplify or challenge state power. Throughout the modern age, secret police in the strong states of Europe, Asia, and the Americas have used this netherworld as a covert adjunct, conducting extralegal operations to marginalize dissidents, contain restive workers, control the dangerous classes, and even expand empires. Often in weaker third-world polities this netherworld can also serve as a sanctuary for rebels, subversives, and social marginals who challenge entrenched elites.

Whenever conflicts erupt from the netherworld into a *grande scandale d'état,* they usually obsess modern publics for a few weeks or months and then subside to become at best a footnote to national history. Neither the journalists who report these lurid details nor the historians who later ignore them seem to consider whether these periodic scandals might be part of some invisible social substratum, some political dimension worthy of more sustained notice. Breaking through this social barrier and merging these separate realms—police and politics, scandal and legitimacy, plebeian and patrician—allows us a fuller, three-dimensional view of the past and its politics.

Syndicated Vice

In conducting such an unconventional analysis, it is important to place this netherworld and its illicit economy squarely at the intersection of politics and police, supply and demand. Stripped of the usual rhetoric, public morality plays a paramount role by prohibiting specific goods and services, thus forcing them from the legal into the illicit economy. Indeed, legal prohibitions are the necessary precondition for a vice economy and all that it entails: criminal syndicates, police corruption, political collusion, and periodic crisis.

Once banned, illegal goods and services such as gambling or commercial sex are no longer the object of the usual taxation and market regulation but are instead subjected to legal and extralegal police control. Instead of eradicating such activity law enforcement often acts as an informal regulator, controlling the volume of vice trading and setting the level of syndication. Aggressive, uncorrupted enforcement can, in theory, crush powerful syndicates and curb illicit activity. Conversely, a symbiosis of politicians, police, and vice entrepreneurs can foster powerful syndicates and a high volume of illicit activity. Wherever a particular vice sector might fall on this spectrum from license to prohibition, any analysis of the criminal netherworld should be mindful of four strategic actors: law in setting the parameters of the illicit market, police in regulating both the volume of vice trading and the level of syndication, political leadership in either protecting or attacking such collusion, and criminal entrepreneurs in exploiting legal immunities and market opportunities.

In the Philippine case the U.S. colonial regime, with the support of the Filipino political elite, banned opium and most forms of gambling between 1906 and 1908, creating the regulatory preconditions for the rise of a thriving vice economy. Although the opium ban was moderately effective, parallel gambling restrictions were an ill-advised attempt to transform popular culture through police coercion. Officers raided gambling dens endlessly, but physical force could not change a social practice that made betting an abiding Filipino passion. After independence in 1946 a conservative moral consensus preserved these prohibitions on personal vice. Apart from a periodic recurrence of illegal drugs—heroin in the 1960s and amphetamines since the 1980s—illegal gambling, above all a daily lottery called jueteng, has shaped the Philippine vice economy through its resilience, sheer size, and political ramifications.

In retrospect, illegal jueteng gambling seems an extraordinary social phenomenon shaped by an unforeseen convergence of state policy, elections, police, and public morality. In the back alleys of the nation's slums, hidden from public scrutiny and academic analysis, this illegal lottery has become one of the Philippines' largest industries, generating much of the cash that sustains the country's costly machine politics and lavish election campaigns. President Marcos, for example, emptied the national treasury to spend an unprecedented $50 million on his 1969 reelection campaign, far more than the $34 million Richard Nixon needed to capture the U.S. presidency in 1968.[118] A 1999 survey found that 28 percent of all adult Filipinos bet on jueteng. A few months later the Philippine legislature estimated the annual gross from gambling syndicates on the main island of Luzon at nearly a billion U.S. dollars. This illegal lottery was also one of the country's largest employers, with an estimated 400,000 workers—far more than the 280,000 then employed in the country's largest export industry, silicon chip manufacturing. If we add this $1 billion in illegal gambling to the $5 billion in illicit drug sales, the Philippine vice economy is a vast underground industry with gross revenues equivalent to nearly half the government's annual budget and a commensurate power to corrupt.[119] "It's the drug lords and the gambling lords . . . who finance the candidates," said House Speaker Jose de Venecia with disarming frankness in October 2007. "So from Day One, they become corrupt. So the whole political process is rotten."[120]

After the restoration of Philippine democracy in 1986, jueteng emerged from the margins of provincial politics to become a major force in national elections and a potent source of political crisis. As national politics and popular fantasy joined in a latter-day moral economy, political parties competed for a floating mass of predominantly urban voters with cash handouts and celebrity candidates: film stars, television personalities, and sports heroes. Through four successive administrations from 1987 to 2007, jueteng's grip on the country's political system tightened. Confronted with a succession of military coups after taking office, the Aquino administration (1986–92), desperate for cash to build a private army and a bloc of loyal legislators, forged the first explicit alliance between the national executive and provincial jueteng bosses. Under the Estrada administration (1998–2001), an unexpected exposé of the president's alliance with leading "gambling lords" prompted mass demonstrations that soon drove him from the palace. Although his successor, President Gloria Arroyo, took her oath of office before a crowd that cheered her promises of reform, she was soon mired in a strikingly similar scandal that came perilously close to evicting her from the palace as well.

If political patronage, police corruption, and illegal gambling have become the interlocking gears in the machinery of electoral politics, then jueteng was the oil that lubricated a patronage system otherwise unsustainable in such an impoverished society. Throughout the twentieth century jueteng has closed the gap between the Philippines' persistent poverty and the high cost of what a one newspaper columnist called "the most expensive elections among the democracies of the free world."[121] Clearly, ignoring policing and the illicit industries it protects affords but a partial view of Philippine political life.

Legitimation Crisis

Apart from their informal role in regulating the illicit economy, uniformed police also remain the most visible symbols of state power. While military forces are isolated inside remote barracks, police are omnipresent in local precincts or mobile patrols, daily reminders of the nation's armed authority. "The police, in any society," argues David H. Bayley, "helps in the formation of attitudes and values undergirding political life, respect for law, acceptance of government authority. . . . In whatever they do, policemen are teachers of the streets."[122] On a similar note, John Kleinig argues that law enforcement agencies "represent for many citizens the most immediate and visible expression of governmental authority and power."[123] If we accept that legitimacy is somehow grounded in actual political performance, then policing, as the most visible manifestation of the state's majesty, involves matters far beyond mere law enforcement, particularly when it is directed by national rather than local authorities.

Throughout the twentieth century, each of the six regimes that ruled the Philippines found that police played a critical role in both winning and losing legitimacy. After its bloody defeat of the revolutionary Philippine Republic in 1902, the U.S. colonial regime courted first acceptance and later won legitimacy from its Filipino subjects by its performance in three critical areas: education, health, and justice. Indeed, these three priorities consumed nearly half the 1912 colonial budget of ₱17.4 million, with education first (₱3.6 million) followed closely by the constabulary (₱2.5 million) and public health (₱1.4 million).[124] The U.S. regime and its apologists have long emphasized the centrality of public education in building legitimacy, and more recent scholarship has rediscovered public health, but police performance played an even more critical role in a colonial rule founded not on the consent of the governed but on coercion and compliance.

In contrast to their Western counterparts, Filipino analysts have long recognized the paramount importance of police in their country's governance. "There is no institution or branch of government which can be demoralized with a greater direct harm to the people's interest than the police," explained Maj. Emanuel Bajá in his landmark study of Philippine police published near the end of colonial rule.[125] A half century later the leading law enforcement expert of his generation, Gen. Cicero C. Campos, found in a comparative survey of Asia and Africa that the police role in representing and legitimating the state was particularly "extensive" in the Philippines.[126]

If police are a potent source of political legitimacy, then by implication they can also cause their nation's most divisive convulsions. "In the Philippines," observed General Campos, "police . . . corruption is chronic; scandals are discovered perennially."[127] Most are unremarkable, a passing flurry of newspaper headlines that might produce pressure for some sort of investigation. But the scandals that implicate national officials can prompt key social sectors to withdraw obedience and thereby serve as catalyst for a major crisis of legitimacy. As Jürgen Habermas reminds us, when a state's legitimacy collapses the existing order can either unleash its "latent force," a momentary solution, or seek long-term stability by expanding the "scope for participation"—in effect, a choice between repression and reform.[128] When confronted with legitimation crises, Philippine officials, like their counterparts elsewhere, have either reformed or risked losing power.

Indeed, throughout the twentieth century all the crises serious enough to threaten the legitimacy of Philippine governments or regimes have somehow revolved around policing, either corruption from syndicated vice or the illegitimate use of lethal force. During its four decades, the U.S. colonial regime faced only two serious crises of legitimacy and both involved policing, the first in 1905 during a harsh rural pacification campaign and another in 1923 over Manila police corruption. After independence a few spectacular instances of police abuse soon did considerable damage to the Republic's legitimacy, but the problem was eventually corrected through major reforms. In the early 1970s, however, well-publicized police abuse in the countryside and the collapse of public order in the capital created an opening for President Marcos to declare martial law, closing Congress and abolishing the Republic. Similarly, a succession of spectacular controversies over illegal gambling in 2001 and 2005 destroyed one presidency and seriously damaged another. Looking back on these events, it seems both surprising and significant that such petty scandals could spark a crisis of legitimacy at the highest levels of the Philippine state.

Of equal import, a focus on police and legitimacy highlights an issue often overlooked in scholarship on the country's political culture: the popular need for order. With its inherently conservative view of mass politics, an emphasis on order contravenes the thrust of Philippine nationalist scholarship, which generally emphasizes the popular struggle for freedom, implicitly depicting the masses as innately revolutionary and willing to sacrifice in the struggle against oppression. Studies of legitimacy and order, by contrast, incline toward a portrayal of the people as innately conservative, willing to accept any government—colonial or national, authoritarian or democratic—that offers peace and prosperity.[129]

Since by definition the colonial state was an alien imposition, it could not win acceptance through indigenous religious or cultural symbols, the domain of anticolonial nationalists. Instead it courted mass compliance through a rhetoric of modernity, efficiency, and order. Alien imperial regimes sought acceptance by invoking a narrow form of performance legitimacy that gave colonial police forces such as the Philippines Constabulary both substantial and symbolic roles. Through the coercive nature of the colonial state, the perception of order as synonymous with legitimacy has apparently persisted within popular consciousness after independence, fostering a key facet of the country's popular political culture that has survived far beyond the imperial age.

As heirs to the antecedent colonial state apparatus, newly independent nations such as the Philippines have found that their legitimacy also derives to a significant degree from their success in maintaining order. In the latter decades of the twentieth century, as the rise of a mass Filipino electorate erased the personalist ties of clientelism, Philippine presidential politics were increasingly dominated by the symbolic rhetoric of public order. In the half century since independence, a succession of Philippine presidents have appealed to this need for a strong leader.[130]

In postcolonial societies like that of the Philippines, police serve as both surrogates and symbols for the state's promise of order. If police are compromised through corruption or partisan influence, people can see—in a visible, even visceral manner—that their hopes for a just social order have suffered a crippling blow. Beyond their capacity for physical coercion, police are thus powerfully symbolic. Few governments lose legitimacy due to potholes or poor schools. But failures in policing can produce iconic incidents that ramify rapidly into serious political crises. When police scandals erupt, as we will see in the chapters that follow, individual leaders, governments, or even entire regimes can be shaken to their constitutional foundations and tremble on the brink of collapse.

Over the past century police have thus played a significant role in the formation of the Philippine polity, both its structure and its symbolism. Just as a history of the Soviet Union without the KGB or the German Democratic Republic without the Stasi is almost unthinkable, so ignoring the influence of the police on the formation of the Philippine polity and the transformation of the American state risks an analysis that is not only incomplete but inaccurate.

Part One

U.S. Colonial Police

Lt. Edward Y. Miller of the U.S. Army, governor of Palawan Province, Philippines, from 1905 until his drowning there in 1910, posing with the grandson of Sultan Harun. (Field Museum of Natural History, CSA23497)

2

Colonial Coercion

JUST AFTER 8:00 A.M. ON APRIL 30, 1903, the Pacific Mail steamship carrying one of America's most influential imperialists dropped anchor into the mud of Manila Bay. After five years of U.S. colonial rule, the capital was ready for his return. Thousands of American flags fluttered from city spires in the brisk morning breeze. Over a hundred ships sounded their steam whistles to hail the returning colonial hero. Towering above the Filipino and American reporters who clambered up the gangway to catch his first words, the American vice-governor, Luke E. Wright, said simply, in the drawl of his native Tennessee, "This seems like home."

After his launch steamed across the bay past a line of Coast Guard cutters, the vice-governor stepped ashore beneath Manila's massive stone battlements. The guns of Fort Santiago roared. The Philippines Constabulary band struck up the "Star-Spangled Banner." Sabers gleaming, the U.S. Thirteenth Cavalry escorted Wright's open carriage down the mile-long Malecon Drive, washed by a morning rain and lined with thousands of brightly dressed Filipino spectators.

From a reviewing stand wrapped in American flags, Wright gazed approvingly as representatives of the U.S. colony's social hierarchy and military might passed in review. First came the parade's grand marshal, Chief Henry T. Allen, leading his paramilitary constabulary. The U.S. Army's Thirtieth Infantry, two Philippine Scouts companies, and two batteries of light artillery followed. Next was Manila's police chief, John E. Harding, leading a detachment of first-class police, all Americans, and another of second-class police, some of them Filipinos. Then, with a clatter of hooves, the city Fire Department's spirited horses and gleaming engines rolled past. Last of all, just ahead of the street sweepers, trailed hundreds of Manila workers carrying union banners and twenty-five carriages filled with Filipino politicians, the leaders of the rival Nacionalista and Federalista parties.

At the parade's close Wright swept through the walled city of Intramuros to the seat of colonial government, the grand Ayuntamiento building, and up its marble staircase to the waiting crowd. There colonial commissioner James Smith hailed the legislation that Wright had won from the U.S. Congress, saying, "Public order has you to thank for the Constabulary Bill, business prosperity is grateful for the Currency Bill." After Smith's statements were translated into Spanish for the Filipinos, Wright rose to warm applause, assuring the audience, "There is no doubt but that the great heart of the American people beats warmly for the Philippine people . . . Knowing this, I think that all . . . Americans and Filipinos may touch shoulders and work without ceasing for the betterment of these islands." In its lead editorial, the *Manila Times,* voice of the American colony, praised Wright's Constabulary Bill, saying it would increase security by making U.S. Army troops "available for police duty."[1]

With every footfall, every hoofbeat, this procession showed the centrality of coercion to U.S. colonial rule over the Philippines. From its start in 1898, the American regime had been shaped by the imperatives of crushing a national revolution and then containing the dreams that had been its inspiration. During its first, formative years in these islands, the United States devoted an extraordinary effort to pacification, starting with open warfare and then eliding into a counterinsurgency campaign that would drag on fitfully for another decade. Throughout these years of turmoil, the U.S. regime met any challenge with a mailed fist to crush the resistance and political concessions to co-opt its leadership. The first civil governor, William Howard Taft, erected a comprehensive apparatus for colonial repression, with harsh laws and an efficient police network that gave him the means to suppress both armed resistance and political dissent. In the months that followed its founding in July 1901, Taft's civil government drew on military precedents to form a three-tiered security structure that would persist for nearly a century: a lightly armed Filipino force for each of several hundred municipalities; a binational unit, the Manila Metropolitan Police, to contain radical nationalists and militant workers in the capital; and the Philippines Constabulary, a paramilitary police of Filipino soldiers and U.S. officers, to patrol the countryside. Supporting the constabulary in its pacification efforts were the Philippine Scouts, a Filipino infantry integrated into the U.S. Army and led by white American officers.

These formal structures were the core of a security apparatus that imposed overlapping grids of control across the archipelago. Operating first under conditions of martial law and then under a colonial government that denied Filipinos full civil liberties, the U.S. regime deployed police surveillance to track suspected subversives, both Filipino and foreign. In this tropical hothouse of institutional hybridization, the colonial police fused military intelligence methods with the latest in civilian law enforcement to achieve an exemplary efficiency. The Philippines Constabulary created a secret service, the Information Division, that became the first U.S. agency with a fully developed covert capacity. The Manila

Metropolitan Police, equipped with a Secret Service Bureau of its own, soon became the most modern police force anywhere under the American flag. At the apex of this colonial intelligence community, the U.S. Army's Division of Military Information conducted intelligence, counterintelligence, and foreign espionage. Any crowd that formed in Manila was soon thick with spies from these three secret services.

With a complexity and coherence that belied the speed of its formation, this nascent U.S. security state combined uniformed forces for raw coercion and secret services for covert control. Battle hardened in a dirty war against Filipino nationalists and ardent in their embrace of empire, these American colonial police and their native auxiliaries soon mastered techniques of surveillance, intelligence, and penetration. Most important, the U.S. Army's application of military science to municipal administration created something of a revolution in policing. Combining militarized coercion, information management, and covert operations, the army created a police force far more advanced than either its Spanish antecedents or its American contemporaries.[2]

Colonial Infrastructure

From the very start of the U.S. occupation, aggressive colonial policing was a response to tenacious Filipino resistance. In 1898 the Americans landed at Manila in the midst of a revolution that had, in three years of armed struggle, mobilized an army, destroyed an entrenched colonial regime, and created a national government. "We of the Eighth Army Corps," General Arthur MacArthur told the U.S. Senate in 1902, "did not know what a complete structure the Philippine Republic of 1898–9 was until, having shot it to pieces, we had abundant leisure to examine the ruins."[3] Destruction accomplished, it was now the task of the American regime to create a new administration to legitimate its occupation and substantiate its claims of superior governance.

In the capital the colonial regime laid the groundwork for an intricate security system by forming three complementary networks: sanitary inspectors, who enforced a rigid public health code; the fire department's electrical grid; and the U.S. Army's telecommunications. By 1903 Manila's fire department, staffed largely by Americans, operated a telephone system and network of 153 Gamewell cast-iron police and fire alarm boxes, linked by 291 kilometers of copper wire, which dispatched steam pumpers or patrol wagons to any section of the city within minutes. To deny subversives and criminals the shadows of the long tropical night, firemen also installed 11,897 incandescent streetlights in 1903 alone.[4] From its headquarters the U.S. Army operated a telephone system with a central exchange connecting the 176 receivers in the homes of senior officials to fourteen provincial circuits "radiating from Manila." Beyond the city walls the Signal Corps integrated Manila into a nationwide telegraph network that allowed the rapid dispatch of military forces and the instantaneous transmission of intelligence. In just five years, the corps laid 5,355 miles of landlines and 1,615 miles of undersea cable that connected 297 signal stations and carried, in 1903, 3.1 million messages with a total of 100 million words, producing what General Adna Chaffee called "a very potent factor in . . . the maintenance of peace and order."[5]

Simultaneously, American colonials built a government that they trumpeted as both an improvement on the Spanish administration and the foundation for a future Philippine state, seeking first acceptance and then, over the long term, legitimacy in the eyes of their Filipino subjects. In official and unofficial propaganda the U.S. regime emphasized its reforms in three critical areas of colonial administration: education, health, and justice. Visible advances in education and health, both hallmarks of colonial order, helped to legitimate the occupation in the eyes of ordinary Filipinos.[6] But reforms in these areas, though important, were arguably less pressing for Filipino subjects who had long been denied the civil rights of citizenship and subjected to arbitrary, at times capricious Spanish coercion. In the late nineteenth century the Spanish regime had pushed the Filipino elite to revolt by building a quasi-modern complex of courts, police, and prisons that was both abusive and corrupt.[7] Among their self-conscious corrections to Spanish rule, the Americans reformed this troubled colonial justice system, modernizing prisons, appointing qualified judges, and, above all, building a reputable security force. After a century of rough Spanish justice and a decade of revolutionary chaos, Filipino acceptance of American rule rested, to an extent historians have not recognized, on efficient policing and a stable social order.

During nearly two decades of direct U.S. rule over the islands, 1898–1916, police were a vital component of the colonial state, imposing order on a restive populace and administering remote provinces. Numbers can only begin to communicate the enormity of this security effort. By 1903, a year after the end of major combat operations, the American regime was allocating nearly a quarter of its 7,109 civil service posts to security personnel—including 795 Manila police, 287 constabulary officers, 153 customs agents, 81 prison staff, 74 Manila firemen, 65 coast guard officers, and 13 Manila sheriffs.[8] These civil officials were just one arm of a massive security apparatus of 47,000 men, including 18,000 U.S. Army soldiers and 22,000 Filipino troops, or one security officer for every 170 Filipinos.[9] While the British ruled Ceylon quite effectively with just 1,600 police for 3.5 million people, the Americans required a far denser proportion of 10,400 police for 7 million Filipinos.[10]

This concentrated effort produced measurable results. In its first three years, the U.S. regime confiscated over 25,000 military rifles scattered by six years of war and revolution.[11] After taking charge of pacification in 1902, the constabulary pursued these leftover firearms relentlessly while enforcing regulations that in 1909, for example, allowed only 2,766 licenses for revolvers and hunting rifles.[12] Between 1903 and 1908 Manila's police arrested 60,117 residents for minor violations and charged 3,462 more with major crimes, meaning that in just five years a full 30 percent of the city's population felt the grip of colonial law.[13] In 1923 the constabulary's 5,743 troopers, based in 150 posts, mounted 14,042 patrols covering 1,134,613 kilometers; 844 separate municipal police forces with 6,385 officers patrolled town plazas armed with 4,684 revolvers; and Manila's 797 police made 19,580 arrests, most for violations of public order.[14]

This success was due less to brute force than to innovative law enforcement. Under U.S. rule manpower fell markedly from Spain's 27,000 police in the 1880s to just 10,000 in 1902, thus reducing the ratio from one officer per 200 Filipinos to one per 700.[15] While convictions remained steady at 42 percent of all accused, arrests dropped from 13 per 10,000 inhabitants under Spain (1870–87) to just 9.6 under the United States (1903–8). After a close study of these statistics in 1909, Attorney General Ignacio Villamor concluded that there had been "an unquestionable decrease in the number of criminals" and an overall "decrease of criminality" under American rule.[16] If the U.S. regime achieved more control with less coercion, then its methods may well have been more subtle and effective.

Colonial Capital

From the moment the U.S. Army landed at Manila on August 13, 1898, the city became the site of the longest, most complex battle of the Philippine-American War. Arriving with cavalry and light artillery for a rapid advance into the countryside, the army found itself bottled up inside Manila by sixteen miles of revolutionary trench works, facing the constant threat of uprising from within and attack from without. Isolated inside the capital, the army was forced into an impromptu experiment in civil administration. Within weeks it established a city government complete with public health and sanitation programs, schools, tax collectors, animal control officers, courts, and, above all, innovative policing. Throughout four years of war, the U.S. military mounted ceaseless operations inside Manila to suppress what it called the "numerous insurgent agencies . . . in this city for . . . recruiting for their army and securing and forwarding funds and information to the field."[17] Through this combination of city administration and urban pacification, the U.S. Army laid the foundations for a colonial surveillance state that survived long after the end of its military rule.

At the outset, the U.S. occupation of Manila was a fragile venture, a secondary theater in a small war fought at the furthest reach of American power against two weakened but still formidable armies. Looking back on these events a century later the American conquest of the Philippines seems preordained, even inevitable. But at the time, particularly during its first dangerous months, America's colonial adventure flirted with failure. After destroying the Spanish fleet effortlessly in May 1898, Admiral Dewey's fleet patrolled Manila Bay for the next three months while a succession of U.S. troop transports steamed in from San Francisco. By early August the Eighth Army Corps had 10,900 troops on ships in

Manila Bay facing 13,000 Spanish soldiers behind Manila's massive stone battlements and 15,000 armed Filipino revolutionaries in trenches ringing the city.[18]

On August 13, 1898, just hours after Spanish and American diplomats signed a truce in Washington, U.S. troops rushed through the gates of the old walled city, Intramuros. Filipino forces followed in their wake to occupy the southern suburbs just outside the city walls. In a day of desultory combat with light casualties, the U.S. Army captured a colonial capital with 250,000 residents, 22,000 firearms, and nearly $900,000 in cash.[19]

After his troops secured the walled city, the U.S. Army's interim commander, Gen. Wesley Merritt, accepted the surrender of the Spanish forces and seized their seat of government, the grand Ayuntamiento building, where he proclaimed "a military government of occupancy." As the American flag rose over the city, the acting provost marshal general, a colonel of the Oregon Volunteers, occupied the government offices: the Treasury vaults with $750,000 in cash, arsenals with three million rounds of ammunition, stables with 350 horses, and batteries with fifty artillery pieces. Two days later General Merritt appointed his "very efficient brigade commander," Gen. Arthur MacArthur, as provost marshal general and military governor of the city, relieving the Spanish mayor, Don Eugenio del Saz-Orazco, of "offices, clerks, and all municipal machinery."[20]

With his characteristic decisiveness, General MacArthur quickly imposed surface order on the city by cleaning the streets and mounting police patrols that numbered three thousand troops supported by sixty Filipino veterans of the Spanish Guardia Civil. A week later, sensing Filipino hostility toward their former guardians, he ordered the veterans of Manila's now superseded Guardia Civil Veterana and Guardia Municipal to "deposit their arms" at the Ayuntamiento. In early October, the army's new provost marshal general, Gen. Robert P. Hughes, was designated both chief of police and commander of the Provost Guard Separate Brigade, granting him the power, under the U.S. Articles of War, to convene a general court-martial for both soldiers and civilians. With 3,200 troops drawn from three regiments, this brigade became a unique unit for maintaining order in a city of 250,000 with both a criminal underworld and a revolutionary underground.[21]

From the start Manila presented daunting problems, requiring, as the provost marshal general put it, "administrative ability of a high order and . . . very delicate manipulation." Situated in an estuary only three to four feet above high tide, Manila lacked bridges to facilitate congested traffic or rapid police movement. Its "floating population" of migrants from south China and the surrounding Philippine countryside was large and "difficult to keep in check," particularly the great numbers of "vicious classes and the dissolute of both sexes." Spain had distributed alcohol licenses freely, creating an irrepressible "liquor traffic" in native *vino* among American soldiers that the military police tried to control by "a stringent license law." With unrestricted migration from southern China, Spain had also presided over a fluid Chinese population active in commerce, crafts, and vice with licensed opium dens, legalized gambling, and illegal brothels. From the first days of the U.S. occupation Manila also became a garrison city with thousands of "disorderly soldiers" arriving, departing, recuperating, and carousing. Confidence men and racketeers from across Asia and the Pacific flooded in. Compounding all these problems, the Spanish administration had left an inadequate infrastructure for a crowded city of a quarter million, particularly in the areas of finance, public health, sewage, flood control, electricity, water, and fire prevention.[22]

To address these problems, the military governor made his provost marshal general responsible for both Manila's security and administration. This position, occupied by a succession of talented officers—Arthur MacArthur, Robert Hughes, J. Franklin Bell, and George Davis—became the linchpin of the new military government, laying the foundations for a modern metropolitan administration and its police.[23]

The sudden departure of Manila's Spanish administrators created both the need and opportunity for innovation. Fortuitously for Washington, the army had two commanders who proved to be skilled civil administrators: Gen. Ewell S. Otis, a Harvard Law graduate and shrewd bureaucrat; and Gen. Arthur MacArthur, who adroitly blended raw coercion and civic action.[24] As General Otis noted, "[N]early all the city high officials were Spaniards" but soon very "few persons of prominence of the Spanish race remained," leaving behind Filipinos who "had no previous experience in government, save in a very minor degree." On August 19, the provost marshal general's troops had occupied the Custom House "almost at the point of bayonets" and used similarly forceful tactics in taking over the Treasury, mint, and internal revenue offices.[25] Two days later, when U.S. troops entered Manila's Hacienda Pública, the Spanish clerks refused their requests for information and walked out with all the relevant tax regulations. When the soldiers finally located the city's charter and tax codes, they found, according to Otis, "a system so complex that after the study of months it is not yet fully understood." The general considered the "reestablishment of this so-called city government . . . an impossibility" and placed "not only the police of the city but of all its municipal affairs" under his empowered provost marshal general.[26]

In reforming this antiquated administration the U.S. military introduced a novel synthesis of Spanish antecedents and American innovations. For expanded street illumination the provost marshal general installed hundreds of new arc and incandescent lights with power provided by the Spanish licensee, La Electricista. To provide clean water the military simply repaired and reopened the famed Carriedo waterworks, the Spanish regime's greatest contribution to the city's public health. To assure safe food in city markets the provost marshal's Bureau of Licenses cleaned the fetid stalls, required veterinary inspection of slaughtered animals, and imposed "a strict espionage of the street vendors." To check fires the bureau banned the construction of flammable bamboo houses in the inner city. Similarly, on September 1 the military reopened the Spanish system of thirty-nine primary schools, serving five thousand children, and slowly introduced English-language instruction.[27]

To establish a working judicial system, the army balanced continuity and innovation, reviving the local courts while relying on its own military tribunals. Only a day after his forces occupied Manila, the U.S. commander decreed that all laws compatible with American supremacy would remain in effect, and just a week later he opened military tribunals and provost marshal courts. After protracted negotiations the city's Spanish judges resumed civil, though not criminal, proceedings on October 7. They operated for four months until Spain, as a part of its withdrawal, transferred their functions to the U.S. Army on January 31, 1899.[28]

The military courts soon communicated the new regime's capacity for repression. In November 1898, for example, a military commission found the editor of *La Voz Española,* the Spaniard Antonio Hidalgo, guilty of "circulating seditious newspaper articles in violation of the laws of war" and ordered that the press and "all appurtenances of the printing office" be sold to pay a five hundred dollar fine. To counter such anti-Americanism, General Otis hired a propagandist to produce sympathetic articles on "the theory of government" for the city's Filipino and Spanish newspapers.[29] From these rapid-fire innovations the provost marshal general's administration grew into a comprehensive city government, both restoring basic services and planning Manila's future. By mid-1900, the military government was investigating details of urban life and preparing to draft a city charter that would guide Manila's administration for the next half century.[30]

Battle for Manila

Despite its early successes in Manila, the U.S. Army still faced formidable problems of political subversion and common crime. Its commander, Gen. Ewell S. Otis, ordered constant vigilance against "the radical element in the insurgent councils . . . who were then organizing . . . for revolutionary purposes." Without effective intelligence to attack the rebel underground, Otis saturated the city with military police, assigning three thousand troops to the Provost Guard Separate Brigade, nearly a third of his total strength and three times the superseded Spanish force. Apart from sheer numbers, the provost marshal general had the advantage of a "special signal telephone system, putting him in direct communication with his police about town" dispersed in eight precinct stations.[31]

The army was reacting to the very real threats of lawlessness and insurgency when it put its military police on the streets of Manila. Indeed, the situation was more serious than General Otis had imagined. Although the initial occupation of the city in August 1898 had caught Filipino commander Gen. Emilio Aguinaldo unprepared, several of his officers soon formed a revolutionary underground beneath unseeing American eyes. Within weeks Aguinaldo's influence inside the city had grown to the point that his undercover city governor, Ambrosio Flores, intervened to block strikes deemed disruptive of the revolution by workers in La Insular's tobacco factory, the tramway, and the railway. Two months later Aguinaldo was able to conclude a contract with three of the city's Chinese for opium sales in the Bikol provinces for twelve hundred pesos per month.[32] Teodoro Sandiko, a radical nationalist who had studied law in Madrid, even organized a clandestine militia inside the city. Hired as an interpreter by the U.S. provost marshal general, he cultivated American friends and convinced them to release members of the revolutionary society, the Katipunan, who had been jailed by the Spanish. Simultaneously, Sandiko was organizing a network of social clubs as a cover for a spreading revolutionary network inside Manila.[33] After it grew to some ten thousand members, this network became "the subject of grave apprehension," particularly when the military police learned that the group was distributing arms and training fighters.[34]

General Aguinaldo's plans for an urban uprising were accelerated by unexpected events that pushed both sides to war. On January 4, 1899, General Otis released the text of President McKinley's proclamation of "the conquest of the Philippine Islands" and his promise that "the mission of the United States is benevolent assimilation."[35] Outraged, Aguinaldo replied the next day with a declaration that "my government is disposed to open hostilities." Over the next two weeks some fifty thousand Filipinos, a quarter of Manila's population, fled the city, crowding the streets with wagons full of household goods and filling outbound railway cars "to their utmost capacity."[36] On January 9 Aguinaldo issued detailed instructions to the city's guerrilla underground, the "brave soldiers of the *Santadahan*," for an uprising that would massacre the Americans in their homes, murder their sentinels at the barrack gates, and launch a military assault while the city erupted in arson. Over the next three weeks Sandiko worked tirelessly to organize some 6,330 men into guerrilla companies that took their oath to the Philippine flag on February 2 at Caloocan, just north of the city.[37] But before he could complete his preparations sentries at the city's outskirts exchanged shots on the night February 4. Within hours the U.S. Army launched a devastating attack that, at the cost of forty-four American dead, smashed the Filipino lines, killed some five hundred in their trenches, and pushed Aguinaldo's main force north beyond the city's outskirts.[38]

After reforming his lines north of the capital, General Aguinaldo ordered an attack on Manila to counter the initial American advance. On the evening of February 22, two red Bengal flares pierced the darkness over the city, signaling the attack. Over a thousand Filipino troops, led by Gen. Pantaleon Garcia, had already slipped silently into the city's northern Tondo slums for a night-into-day battle. Once inside the city, this Filipino force could only be saved from slaughter through an attack by General Aguinaldo's main force on the American lines and a mass uprising in Manila. But Aguinaldo's troops disobeyed orders to attack and the Manila underground was already weakened by the U.S. Provost Guard, leaving General

Garcia's troops to fight alone. Within twenty-one hours their gamble would fail, with half the Filipino troops dead and whole city blocks reduced to smoking ruins from abortive arson attempts.[39]

Though victorious, the U.S. army was traumatized by this unexpected immersion in urban warfare with its mix of arson, night fighting, and the specter of mass uprising. Emerging from these battles obsessive about security, the U.S. command launched a campaign to pacify Manila through a combination of liberal reforms and harsh repression. General Otis reopened the local courts, starting in May with the Audiencia Territorial, a supreme court for both civil and criminal cases, under three American and four Filipino justices.[40] Despite their political significance, these civil courts could not meet the military's immediate need for drumhead justice to enforce martial rule.[41] Consequently, the army's Inferior Provost Courts continued to operate, trying 10,511 defendants in the year ending June 30, 1900, including 2,111 for curfew violations.[42] During the three years of military rule, army tribunals prosecuted thirty-seven thousand Filipino defendants, over a quarter of Manila's adult population.[43]

The threat of urban uprising forced simultaneous innovations in military policing. Although its first attacks were soundly defeated, the revolutionary underground remained, in the words of the provost marshal general, "almost constantly . . . conspiring . . . to destroy the city." For two years, starting in February 1899, the provost marshal maintained a strict 7:00 p.m. "curfew order" on the capital. Adding to this sense of danger, in late December the military police detected a plot by Gen. Artemio Ricarte, revolutionary commander for Manila, "to dynamite the escort of honor attending the funeral of the late General [Henry] Lawton."[44] To contain incendiary revolutionary rhetoric, the provost marshal general was similarly vigilant in monitoring the Manila press. When several newspapers became "outspoken in their policy of aiding and abetting the insurrection" in mid-1899, the military government moved quickly to "suppress certain of them and discipline others," silencing any criticism of the U.S. regime.[45]

In the months following the attempted bombing, the provost marshal general moved beyond military police patrols, experimenting with new surveillance techniques. "Insurgent agents, some with fair social standing, if not prominence," General Otis complained, "are continually plotting in our midst, and Manila . . . has its accredited insurgent governor." With regular military patrols insufficient to combat this underground, the army was forced to develop new methods that married secret service operations, expanded intelligence, and joint Filipino-American policing. In March 1899 the provost marshal general assigned a combat veteran from the Eleventh Cavalry, Lt. Charles Trowbridge, to command the city's Bureau of Information, a new secret service tasked with tracking subversives. In its first four months this small squad of four Americans and several Filipino agents "succeeded in breaking up many of the active insurgent organizations in the city of Manila," discovering a "secret organization" among the waterworks employees and arresting Col. Lucio Lucas, leader of the Armas Blancas underground with fifteen hundred followers inside the city.[46]

To supplement his military police, General Otis formed a segregated force of 246 native civil police in August 1899, soon discovering that they were "feared by the criminals and disloyal element of the population much more than our soldiers . . . because they are known to and closely watched by them."[47] Despite some difficulties, within a year this binational police force largely succeeded in its main mission of imposing a rough colonial order on the capital. In the year ending June 30, 1900, the U.S. military police and its Native Civil Police made 15,927 arrests, including numerous revolutionary officers operating secretly inside Manila.[48]

The Bureau of Information under Lieutenant Trowbridge was ordered "to be on the 'lookout' for insurgent meetings . . . and people who are actively engaged in working against the Government." In October 1899, this secret service found a "seditious pamphlet" titled "Abajo Caretas" circulating in the city and raided the printing office, seizing two hundred copies and arresting "one Aurelio Tolintino [*sic*], the person who had them printed." In June 1900 its agents located "a recruiting station" for the "Vibora Katam" regiment under General Ricarte, the "director of operations in Manila." In this year of dirty war, the new secret service captured thirty-five insurgent officers at the cost of five of its twelve agents killed or captured, including one "Ludwig Windall, found dead in the street."[49]

Arriving in June 1900, the secretary of the civilian Philippine Commission, the nascent civil regime, described the city as "a huge military camp swarming with khaki-clad soldiers. They patrol the streets, guard the public buildings, and perform all the functions of government. . . . We go to bed to the sound of taps and wake to hear the bugles sounding reveille. Military authority is supreme—omnipotent. To be on the street after ten at night is presumptive evidence of treason; any one found abroad after that hour without a pass is hustled to the guard house."[50] A young Filipino nationalist named Manuel Quezon who visited Manila branded its government "the American Military Dictatorship."[51] In September, when the president ordered the military governor to cede control of many localities to the Philippine Commission, Manila was still deemed "infested with insurgents who were continually plotting for its destruction" and remained under martial rule.[52]

In December 1900 the U.S. commander, General MacArthur, issued a draconian decree warning that all guerrillas would be tried "as war traitors against the United States." These strictures, the general ordered, would "apply with special force to the city of Manila . . . from which an extensive correspondence is distributed to all parts of the archipelago by sympathizers . . . of the insurrection." In effect, the capital was under the "rigid restraints of martial law" and anyone giving "aid, support, encouragement, or comfort to the armed opposition in the field" would be "tried for felonious crimes." The decree, derived from the army's General Order 100 of 1863, warned the Manila press that "any article . . . which, by any construction, can be classed as seditious" would subject "all connected . . . to such punitive action as may be determined by the undersigned."[53] After signaling his seriousness by banishing recalcitrants to Guam, MacArthur felt that his decree had stifled resistance. "Rarely in war," he said grandly, "has a single document been so instrumental in influencing ultimate results."[54]

To aid in the destruction of Manila's revolutionary underground, the provost marshal general appointed a new police superintendent, Lt. Col. W. E. Wilder, to shake up the city's force. After taking command in September 1900, Wilder had found the city's police administration chaotic and lacking leadership for the 618 Filipinos in the segregated native police. "It was quite evident," Wilder reported, "that the police department was not equipped to do the work . . . against either the insurgent or criminal classes." Recognizing the "inability of Americans to get reliable information," Chief Wilder felt that the situation could be salvaged "if only a small percentage of the 618 native police . . . could be honestly and earnestly engaged" through "the intelligent supervision of Americans." Consequently, he arranged the transfer of volunteer officers who in the coming months led the Filipino police in the arrest of eight hundred revolutionary officers and the "circumvention of . . . their plans and conspiracies in this capital."[55]

In these effective police operations, the city's Bureau of Information played a key role, introducing modern methods by collecting "500 photographs of the most noted criminals of Manila," which proved to be of "great value in the successful tracing of those accused of crime." Its chief, Lieutenant Trowbridge, recruited thirty former insurgents to "ferret out the leaders" of the revolutionary underground. This produced some six hundred arrests in four months, which, after freeing the "many persons . . . falsely denounced," resulted in the capture of 250 "bona fide officers of the insurgent army." Apart from these targeted operations, the military police swept the city, making a remarkable 19,200 arrests during its last year, about 20 percent of Manila's adult population.[56] By early 1901 the capital was largely secured against insurrection.

Metropolitan Police

As counterguerrilla warfare wound down in Manila, the U.S. Army worked with the incoming civil government, the Philippine Commission, in a seamless transfer of control over the capital and its police. The civil authorities authorized the army's provost marshal general, under Act 70 of January 1901, "to raise and to properly equip, a police force for the city of Manila." The roster of fifty-seven officers and three hundred privates shall, the commission directed, "be selected from the American Volunteer soldiery now serving in these Islands . . . and shall be known as the Metropolitan Police Force of Manila."[57] An Associated Press correspondent reported, a bit hyperbolically, that this rigorous selection produced "a fine, able-bodied, strong, healthy-looking lot of men, accustomed to discipline" and credited its first chief, Capt. George W. Curry, a former New Mexico sheriff and veteran of the Rough Riders, with "having organized a police force, the white portion of which is the peer of any police force in the world."[58] In March and April these new police units relieved the army patrols, and detectives in the military's Bureau of Information were integrated into the city police as its new Secret Service.[59] By the time military rule ended formally in July, Manila's police force had grown to 1,900 men, including 696 Americans selected from the army for "possessing the best physical and mental qualities" and 1,204 "native police," the core of a future Filipino force.[60]

In planning this transition the army's provost marshal general, George Davis, left a lasting mark on Manila's government by drafting its city charter, forming its bureaucracy, and staffing the new Metropolitan Police with his veterans. On June 13, two months before the city's transfer to civil rule, General Davis delivered a detailed report, with operating budget and draft charter, granting far less self-rule for Manila than for rural municipalities. Although the president's instructions of April 1900 specified that Filipinos should "be afforded the opportunity to manage their own local affairs," Davis felt that granting self-rule to Manila "would prove to be vastly more unwise or even more disastrous than such delegation of power proved to be in the District of Columbia." Hence, the general recommended that Manila, like Washington, DC, be governed by a three-man appointive commission authorized to enact local ordinances for police, health, fire, and public works. Manileños, like Washingtonians, would be denied the vote, but as a concession to local self-rule one of the commissioners would be Filipino, as would most city employees except the police.[61]

Under General Davis's plan, nearly a third of Manila's $1.6 million budget, three times the amount allocated to its schools, would be dedicated to the new Metropolitan Police. With law enforcement consuming nearly 20 percent of the city's tax revenues, Filipino "native police" would be paid $144 annually and American patrolmen $780, the latter salary approaching the $900 paid police in Washington, DC. Noting that the "wide differences in the rate of wages . . . are the subject of adverse comment by the natives," the general defended his policy, arguing that Americans faced "the increased expense of personal maintenance peculiar to this city." Under the proposed charter the city's appointive executive would deploy these American police, under an all-powerful city marshal, with wide powers of warrantless arrest. Taken together, the general's charter and budget meant that Manila householders would face a 500 percent tax increase, from $37.50 to $200 annually, in return for the privilege of arbitrary arrest by foreign police who answered to a city government they did not elect.[62] As the provost marshal general had planned, this structure subjected Manila to strict central oversight and limited the autonomy of its police administration, a pattern that would continue for much of the century.[63] After the city police passed to civil control in August 1901, racial segregation within the department became politically untenable. In November the Philippine Commission ended this division to create, under Act No. 286, a unified metropolitan force of 875 men, including a Secret Service with 24 detectives, 300 first-class American patrolmen paid $900 annually, and 360 third-class Filipino patrolmen paid $240.[64]

The full integration of the metropolitan and native police proved difficult. At first "many full-fledged insurrectos managed to enlist to further the cause of Aguinaldo," but most of these were "weeded out," leaving a residue of suspicion. Over the long term many "prominent ex-insurgents," former lieutenants and captains, served the Manila force as corporals and sergeants and made a strong contribution to "the effectiveness of the native police." All American officers were veterans who had been "actively fighting the Filipinos" and thus "evinced no great desire to work with the native police." Initially, it was necessary to segregate these former enemies into "separate districts" until they could be slowly merged through the mediation of a small cadre of Spanish Filipino officers. For example, the commander of Precinct 5, Capt. Jose de Crame, was a Spanish mestizo and a veteran of the Spanish secret service who had served the U.S. native police since its inception.[65] To facilitate communication the police offered Filipinos night classes in English and expected Americans to be bilingual. Among the expatriate officers, 207 demonstrated a working knowledge of Spanish, 79 of Tagalog, and 47 of both.[66]

In contrast to the constabulary's color bar between white officers and native troops, by 1902 the Manila Police was a binational force of 798 men—with 382 American and 416 Filipino patrolmen led by 33 American and 32 Filipino officers. Within these broad cohorts, however, there was a marked racial disparity since Americans represented 87 percent of the high-ranking patrolmen. More broadly, the Manila Police offered little opportunity for advancement to either race, and a striking 71 percent of Americans and 83 percent of Filipinos who served between 1902 and 1911 went a full decade without a promotion. With low salaries and little opportunity to advance, corruption was common, as evidenced by an unbroken succession of police scandals.[67] Once appointed, American officers clung to their posts in the face of constant fiscal pressures to cut the high-cost colonials. Although the proportion of Filipinos on the force rose gradually through expatriate attrition, the Manila Americans fought a running media battle to retain white officers in the name of efficiency.[68] The *Manila Times,* the voice of the American community, often denigrated the capacity of Filipino patrolmen. "Native Police Take to Heels: Ran Away from Fight in Gordon's Saloon in Pasay," read a typical headline in January 1908.[69] Through such political maneuvering the Manila police remained one of the largest concentrations of Americans in the islands until 1917. And even then it was Filipinized later and less completely than other sectors of the colonial service. Only after a sharp rise in American repatriation, accelerated by World War I and reinforced by pension incentives, did Filipino representation within the Manila force increase from 64 percent in 1911 to 93 percent in 1921.[70]

Despite budgetary constraints, the new civil government moved quickly to build a modern city police force. To secure the city streets, armed foot patrols walked regular beats, using a system of telephones and alarms to summon reinforcements. To overcome the "great difficulty" of communication, the police first stationed three officers at the central telephone office; finding this inadequate, they imported the Gamewell Police and Fire Alarm System to "put this city on an equal footing with any in the United States." After its installation in 1903, the city's police chief reported that "this system prevents loitering on beat by patrolmen, . . . renders the work of men more systematic and thorough . . . and in fact, keeps the station in touch at all times with every part of the Precinct."[71] By 1903, moreover, the Metropolitans were uniformed in olive drab with cork helmets and armed with eight hundred new .38 caliber pistols and three hundred Winchester repeating shotguns called "riot guns."[72]

While uniformed patrols made regular rounds, the plainclothes detectives of the Secret Service Bureau had more specialist beats: boarding all steamships, inspecting every pawnshop daily, and photographing discharged prisoners. Working in a city without any system of criminal identification, in its first year the Secret Service compiled "about 3,000 photographs of convicted criminals of all classes and nationalities" with physical, political, and professional descriptions. To improve the speed and accuracy of identification, in 1905 the bureau sent its top detective, John W. Green, to the United States for a course in dacyloscopy (fingerprinting) and "an exhaustive study of the Bertillon System of identification by anthrometrical system." Inside the new police Identification Department, established in 1907, Green discarded "the bulky system of record-filing" and introduced "an entirely new system" based on Bertillon's model, which reduced a criminal's career to a single page that was, in the words of another Manila detective, "numbered consecutively and bound in book form, each book containing 500 pages, each page a complete and concise record of the offender."[73] In 1909, when the system was fully operational, the Identification Department processed 3,314 suspects, including 836 "measured and photographed," 400 measurement verifications, and 464 confirmations of "old criminals," exposing many who were using false names.[74]

Green was promoted to Secret Service chief in 1913 and spent several years refining this criminal identification system by establishing a police photo laboratory and making Henry fingerprinting a standard police procedure. Above all, he refined his filing system by creating three intersecting records stored in steel cabinets by "modus operandi" for ready retrieval: a file card for every offender, a numbered sheet for habitual criminals, and a rogues' gallery of selected identification photos. Where "system is the motto" and "science is the watchword," wrote a reporter after a 1918 visit to the Secret Service's Luneta headquarters, "few criminals escape the all embracing index." By the mid-1920s the department had amassed 30,870 numbered photographs and 200,000 alphabetized identification cards for the city's 285,000 people, 70 percent of Manila's population.[75] Through his seminal role in scientific detection, Green would rise from patrolman in 1901 to police chief in 1922, retiring seven years later to accolades for his modernization of the force.[76]

The Secret Service Bureau's confidential duties included surveillance of suspected subversives, monitoring prominent Filipinos, and "private and secret investigations of officials and employees, many of whom have had to be shadowed to prevent their leaving the islands." In 1902–3, for example, the Secret Service "cleaned out" gambling houses in Binondo, assisted in prosecuting the labor radical Dr. Dominador Gomez, and took "the initial steps to suppress this evil . . . of the seditious dramas." To maintain the aura of American superiority, detectives also delivered a "body blow" to a gang of the "worthless American element . . . of gamblers, confidence men, ex-Alaska adventurers, and ex-convicts," forcing them to flee the colony. At the broadest level, the bureau's founding chief, Charles Trowbridge, tried "to keep the finger of the bureau at all times upon the pulse of Manila's populace."[77] In these operations the Secret Service collaborated so closely with the Philippines Constabulary's Information Division that within a few years "business of a confidential nature between the two departments" required installation of a direct phone line from the desk of the Secret Service chief to his constabulary counterpart.[78]

Only two years after the founding of the Manila force, U.S. officials would praise "the high character" of American patrolmen and claim that their work could be "favorably compared with that of any police department in the world."[79] By its innovations in communication and criminal identification, the Manila police had become an integral component of America's colonial panopticon.

Municipal Police

In marked contrast to the efficient Manila Metropolitans, the hundreds of municipal police forces spread across the countryside remained the most problematic facet of colonial security. While the Manila police benefited from incessant innovation, the municipal police were an almost accidental mixture of Spanish precedent and U.S. military priorities. Appointed by town mayors and embedded in local politics, municipal police were a perpetual problem not only for the U.S. colonial regime but for its successor, the Philippine Commonwealth. Implementation of serious reforms would have required a degree of oversight that compromised municipal autonomy, a central tenet of American colonial rule. Rather than addressing this contradiction, a succession of U.S. administrations generally ignored local police unless some particularly egregious incident prompted short-term intervention.

As the U.S. Army broke out of Manila and began its march across Central Luzon in early 1899, it soon found that reviving local governments and arming their police were necessary adjuncts to pacification. After occupying the Republic's capital at Malolos in March, the commander of the Third Artillery, Maj. W. A. Kobbé, organized civil governments in four nearby towns with native police to enforce regulations over gambling, intoxication, and any disorder.[80]

Impressed with this model, the U.S. commander, General Otis, used these rudimentary regulations as the basis for his General Order 43 of August 1899, which urged the formation of similar local governments across Luzon. Under these regulations each town would have a municipal council whose president would establish a police force with "the senior headman" as lieutenant of police empowered to "arrest or order the arrest of persons violating a city ordinance." Police could only hold prisoners for twenty-four hours before releasing or transferring them to the U.S. Army's provost court for trial.[81] In March 1900 the general introduced a municipal code under General Order 40, confidently proclaiming a "genuinely liberal spirit" that would soon put the Philippine people on "the path to true progress" through "a really autonomous and decentralized government." The code decreed that all municipalities except Manila would hold elections for a mayor and town councilors who would establish a police department to suppress "games of chance, gambling houses, disorderly houses . . . , and all kinds of vice and immorality," including prostitution and opium smoking. To enforce such local ordinances, the council had the authority to impose jail terms of up to fifteen days without appeal, giving the mayors and their policemen almost unchecked judicial powers.[82]

To transform this nominal authority into armed reality, General MacArthur, who succeeded Otis as commander in May 1899, provided both funds and regulations for local police. Confronted with a surge of guerrilla activity in June 1900, the general authorized his department commanders to arm municipal police with Colt .45 revolvers, thereby encouraging "the idea of self-protection against robbers and roving bands of criminals, with which the country abounds." With a grant of U.S. $150,000 from the Philippine Commission to supplement municipal budgets, MacArthur quickly mobilized, in just eight months, a force of 6,150 municipal police, with 2,500 carrying firearms and the rest short swords called bolos.[83]

In January 1901, during the transition to civilian rule, the incoming Philippine Commission enacted a municipal code that preserved much of the original design, requiring that councils establish a police force to maintain order and prohibit personal vice.[84] When military rule ended in July, the new civil administration inherited a fragmented force of thousands of heavily armed, poorly trained, local police dispersed across the countryside without effective supervision. This was an oversight the commission soon tried to correct by charging the Philippines Constabulary with "frequent inspections . . . of the police force of each and every municipality."[85] Despite its overall efficiency, the constabulary's supervision of local police was a failure. When the governor-general visited Iloilo Province,

Mayor Benito Lopez voiced the concerns of many by condemning the local police as "badly disciplined, badly organized" and called for the creation of "a unified municipal police force . . . drilled and instructed by intelligent officers." To contain the damage, the constabulary reduced the total number of municipal police from nearly ten thousand in 1903 to six thousand two years later and replaced their rifles and shotguns with revolvers and short swords.[86]

Nonetheless, colonial criticism of local police mounted with each passing year. "The entire force of a town goes out of office with the presidente [mayor]," the secretary of commerce and police reported in 1908, "and the appointment of the new policemen is the perquisite of the incoming official, so that they are rather servants of the presidente than law officers of the town."[87] For the next eighty years, countless Filipino and foreign observers would echo these criticisms with varying degrees of vehemence.

Division of Military Information

While the experiment with municipal police was a failure, the army's field intelligence unit, the first in its hundred-year history, was an unqualified success. As it struggled to uproot guerrillas immersed in rugged terrain and hostile populations, the army established the Division of Military Information (DMI) to serve as a central intelligence clearinghouse for the half-dozen civil and military agencies engaged in political warfare.

In the first years of fighting General Otis had assigned intelligence to his divisional commanders, producing a diffuse, decentralized effort and an inconclusive counterinsurgency. In 1899, however, he established the Bureau of Insurgent Records to catalog the masses of documents captured from Filipino forces, who were, in the words of one intelligence officer, "prone to put into writing all their official acts . . . but . . . seem generally not to have taken proper precautions to keep these records from failing into our hands."[88] This Filipino practice of punctilious documentation and the voracious American appetite for information collided to create an effective field intelligence unit within the U.S. Army.

After taking command of the Philippine Division in May 1900, General MacArthur soon recognized the critical role of intelligence. In his systematic search for a winning strategy, the general found that Lt. W. T. Johnson's analysis of the invisible guerrilla influence over towns in La Union Province was "the best description . . . of the insurgent method" while Capt. Henry Allen's use of accurate information for the aggressive pursuit of rebels on Leyte Island exemplified the most appropriate tactics. Consequently, when MacArthur unleashed an intensified counterinsurgency in December 1900, his adjutant general instructed the chief of insurgent records, Capt. John R. M. Taylor, to expand his small bureau into the Division of Military Information with the mission of "collecting and disseminating information that is of great value . . . in fixing the identity" of the insurgents. As the army's first combat intelligence force, the new division lacked the experience or expertise to balance the needs for careful research and timely intelligence. Initially, it seemed to mime the Military Information Division in Washington, using its archival methods to collect and catalog the two hundred thousand insurgent documents captured between 1899 and 1901. From these three tons of paper Captain Taylor eventually selected some fifteen hundred documents for publication in his five-volume *The Philippine Insurrection against the United States,* a boon for later historians but of limited immediate use in pacification. After about three months of operations, the unit began to develop procedures for "the collection and dissemination of military intelligence data" that assisted in the arrest of 600 suspected subversives, including 250 insurgent officers in the Manila area.[89]

When Taylor returned home in early 1901, Capt. Ralph Van Deman, later known as the "father of U.S. military intelligence," assumed command of an embryonic intelligence unit that was still far from meeting the army's needs. Juxtaposing his mediocre military record prior to this post and his remarkable achievements afterward, it seems that imperial warfare proved a transformative experience for both this officer and his army. Educated at Harvard and trained as a medical doctor in Cincinnati, Van Deman had joined the service in 1893 as a surgeon before switching to the infantry for several years of undistinguished duty. The outbreak of the Spanish-American War in 1898 found him working in Washington, DC, as a staff officer at the Military Information Division. There he was relegated to the map section, overshadowed by the division's brilliant commander, Maj. Arthur L. Wagner, and its intrepid operative Lt. Andrew S. Rowan. The lieutenant had been recalled from Arctic explorations for dispatch to Cuba with the famed "message to Garcia," the Cuban insurgent leader. Angry at being passed over for these missions, Van Deman quit MID in early 1899 and transferred to the Philippines where, ill-suited for combat because of bad eyes and ungainly body, he served as a general's aide and mapped terrain for two years. In an era when his peers fought on the frontier and won medals for courage under fire, his was an undistinguished record that showed little hint of the exceptional achievements to come over the next eighteen months.[90]

After taking command of DMI at Manila in February 1901, Captain Van Deman worked tirelessly to raise its intelligence and counterintelligence capacity to unprecedented levels, developing policies and procedures that would shape intelligence operations for the entire U.S. Army fifteen years later. While the heroes of this imperial age won acclaim exploring remote arctic and tropical terrains, Van Deman was quietly discovering an invisible interstice just beneath society's surface and would devote the rest of his life to probing this covert netherworld. Working within a military whose intelligence capacity was at best rudimentary, Van Deman quickly developed innovative doctrines for the DMI by collecting, categorizing, and operationalizing what soon became encyclopedic information on every aspect of the Filipino resistance: active guerrillas, civilian supporters, finances, firearms, ideology, propaganda, communications, movement, and terrain. Instead of passively filing documents and compiling monographs like the Military Information Division in Washington, Van Deman's Manila command combined reports from the army's 450 post information officers with data from the colony's civil police to produce actionable field intelligence. With telegraph lines knitting nets around guerrilla zones and the captain pressing subordinates for fast, accurate information, DMI's field units proved agile in tracking rebel movements and identifying their locations for timely raids.[91]

Exemplifying its voracious appetite for raw data, DMI launched a "confidential" project in March 1901 to map the entire guerilla infrastructure by compiling information cards for every influential Filipino. "In order to facilitate the interchange of information, with reference to insurgents and sympathizers," read the orders, "the Division Commander directs that . . . all posts . . . be called upon to supply the data as indicated on information cards . . . limited to the following persons: (a) Insurgents . . . above the rank of lieutenant (b) priests (c) Presidentes [mayors] or other important officers (d) Active civilian sympathizers of means and standing in the community." Data was to be "supplied from every possible source," duplicate copies would be filed at each echelon, and new names would be added quarterly.[92] From across Luzon hundreds of army posts sent Van Deman one to two dozen "Descriptive Cards of Inhabitants" for each municipality, many revealing extraordinarily detailed local knowledge. On May 1, for example, Captain Harry Nichols submitted twenty-two cards for the town of Malolos, Bulacan, including one (see facing page) with a typically precise knowledge of the subject's physical appearance, personal finances, political loyalties, and kinship networks.

For rapid retrieval, DMI's clerks transcribed these cards into indexed, alphabetical rosters for each military zone, including over two hundred initial entries for the Central Luzon region alone. Systematizing this process six months later, army headquarters ordered each post to appoint a full-time "Intelligence Officer" who "will be expected to avail himself of every opportunity to obtain information," starting with a detailed description of the local infrastructure for insurgency.[93] In DMI's Manila office, Van Deman was assiduous in checking submissions, asking the post intelligence officer at Pila, Laguna, for example, why "the barrios you mention under 'cross roads and trails' do not appear on the one inch map."[94]

To operationalize this information, Van Deman's unit disseminated intelligence among military echelons and the civil police via products ranging from a daily summary for headquarters to operational bulletins for field commands. The mass of data from the army's 450 posts was, as Van Deman later recalled, distilled into "reports on the topography . . . and the Filipino personnel . . . made available to the Commanding General and his staff."[95] Through selection and summary of diverse sources, Van Deman's daily intelligence brief provided headquarters with information on both broad political trends and immediate threats. His report on October 30, 1901, for example, contained warnings from an army detachment in Dasmarinas about three hundred "natives with arms" in the nearby mountains,

DESCRIPTIVE CARD OF INHABITANTS

(To be forwarded through District Headquarters. No letter of Transmittal Necessary.)

Station Reported From: *Mallolos, P.I.* **Date:** *May 1st 1901*
Officer Making Report: *Capt. Maury Nichols 3rd Inf.*
Name of Person Reported upon: *Juanito Reyes,* **M.** ~~**F.**~~
Residence: *Sarioncillo* **Barrio** *Malolos* **Pueblo** *Bulacan* **Province** *Luzon Island*
Description: Height *5–6½* **Weight** *140* **Age** *26* **Married,** ~~**Single**~~
Where Born: *Pueblo Barasoain*
Tribe or nationality: *Tagalog-Pampanganese*
Distinguishing marks: *Bright appearance—neat dresser*
Blood Connections [of prominence only]: *Connected with Tiongson family of Malolos by marriage and closely related to Panlilo family Mexico, Pampanga. Increasing influence.*
Attitude toward U.S.: *Presumably treacherous.*
Oath of Allegiance, where and when recorded: *Not known . . . to have accepted oath at Manila.*
Occupation: *Lawyer*
Ever held as prisoner: *Known to have held important rank as adjutant to Gen. Torres during late insurrection.*
Financial Condition—real and personal property: *Heir presumptive to $20,000 Mex. in farm property.*
Remarks: *Studied the law. Late conduct neutral. Has not been in active service for 2 years . . . His brother was insurgent president [mayor] of Barasoain during American Occupation.*[96]

from a scouts officer in Quingua, Bulacan, about unrest caused by agitators, and from a constabulary inspector in Laoag, Ilocos Norte, who was tracking agents of the dissident Bishop Gregorio Aglipay.[97] Indicative of close interservice cooperation, Van Deman also reported that, to uncover insurgent agents inside Manila, "an exceedingly close watch is being kept on all suspected persons . . . by the Police Department, the Constabulary and ourselves, all of us working together."[98]

While the army and police provided useful information on civilians, operational intelligence about guerillas had to come from Filipino spies, turncoats, or captives, creating an espionage that was both difficult and dangerous. In February 1902, for example, the detachment commander at Boac, Marinduque, tried to recover a cache of some seventy rifles but hit a wall of subtle resistance from the governor, prosecutor, and municipal mayors. When the captain pressed an ex-guerrilla into service as a guide, the man preferred "suicide by jumping off a high cliff."[99] Similarly, as the army intensified its pressure on active guerrillas south of Manila in late 1901 the American captain in command at Tanauan, Batangas, reported that his local informant, Alvaro Narareth, had been butchered with bolos near the town market just before noon. Although "the man's blood was spattered over the counters," proprietors of all thirteen shops fronting the crime scene remained stubbornly silent. After giving them the night to think it over, the captain took decisive albeit counterproductive action: "No information was forthcoming and the 13 places were burned."[100]

When the U.S. Army mobilized to crush Luzon's last pockets of armed resistance in the revolution's heartland just south of Manila, both the strengths and weakness of this intelligence effort soon became evident. Assessing popular sentiments in the provinces of Batangas, Cavite, and Laguna, one officer reported that "the great majority of the people are violently opposed to American rule, and both hate and fear the Americans." With permissive orders that removed restrictions on the treatment of civilians, army patrols began burning crops and villages in July 1900, forcing the surrender of the commander for Cavite Province, Gen. Mariano Trias, with two hundred soldiers in March 1901. After troops captured the correspondence of Laguna's Gen. Juan Cailles in January, DMI quickly reduced this mass of paperwork to a "comprehensive list" of all 560 of his guerrillas. Four months later the capture of another cache of documents revealed "the whereabouts of arms and the names of prominent people associated with him." As troops raided his camps and arrested his supporters, General Cailles marched into the town of Santa Cruz with six hundred troops to surrender his arms and accept his reward, five thousand dollars in cash and an appointment as Laguna's provincial governor.[101]

Farther south in Batangas, the charismatic commander Gen. Miguel Malvar eluded capture through his mastery of the terrain, strong local support, and disciplined guerrilla operations. In August 1901 the U.S. Army's regional commander, Gen. Samuel S. Sumner, reported that his operations against these insurgents were "paralyzed for want of accurate information."[102] A month later the general wrote to army headquarters announcing the formation of a Bureau of Information in his command since it was the only means of defeating the guerrillas "unless we burn the barrios, destroy the food, and subject them to personal torture which is inhuman and unwise."[103] Within weeks, this new bureau's chief, Lt. Emory S. West, issued orders for special intelligence officers to compile lists of insurgents and for the allocation of Secret Service funds to pay Filipino informants.[104]

The search for General Malvar ultimately revealed the limits of intelligence or at least the limits of the army's patience in waiting for it. As army posts sent in captured documents and interrogation reports, DMI's Manila headquarters evaluated each for significance, coded it for filing, and sent a summary to the appropriate commands. After receiving the text of an interrogation from Tanauan dated November 7, for example, DMI clerks cataloged the message with a unique identification number and within twenty-four hours Van Deman himself dispatched it to General Sumner's headquarters, which forwarded it to a cavalry unit that was tracking these guerrillas.[105] Since time-sensitive messages could be sent by telegraph, Van Deman needed only minutes to forward a detailed description of Malvar's messenger to the post at Binan, Laguna: "Forty years of age, poor and barefooted. Has lost all fingers of right hand and habitually carries right hand bent right angles close to body."[106] Beyond individual reports, DMI reduced a mass of detail to a roster of ten "Insurgent Officers still in the field in Batangas and Tayabas Province" with precise physical descriptions, known residences, and recent activities.[107]

When both superiors and subordinates grew tired of General Sumner's slow, incremental progress, the division assigned the search for Malvar to another commander, the hardnosed Gen. J. Franklin Bell. With a ruthlessness that troubled even his superiors, Bell ratcheted up the pressure by degrees from drumhead prosecution of any rebel sympathizer to systematic devastation of the countryside. With a force of 7,600 men, Bell's brigade ravaged Malvar's main refuge, the Lobo Mountains of eastern Batangas, destroying in just one of these forays a million tons of rice, six thousand houses, and nearly nine hundred draft animals. After such wholesale destruction of farming villages and a "reconcentration" of the province's entire population into miserable compounds that caused some eleven thousand civilian deaths, Malvar, stripped of his followers and his family wracked with fever, finally surrendered in April 1902.[108]

Under Van Deman's command, DMI's covert operations also revealed a potential pitfall of intelligence: the capacity to weave discrete strands of data into a dark tapestry of threat. At a time when most accounts suggested that insurgent activity was on the decline, his team was pursuing rumors of "an active plot . . . for the proposed assassination of all . . . important military officers in the city" by an "attacking force . . . concealed in certain swamp land." A visit by a single Japanese military attaché prompted Van Deman to assign scarce staff to unearth a possible "Asiatic" conspiracy.[109] This perception of the Philippines as a bubbling cauldron of insurrection was so deeply ingrained in the colonial intelligence community by the end of formal hostilities in July 1902 that it defied a changing reality. The former revolutionary commander for the Bikol region, Vito Belarmino, was blind, deaf, and defeated, but American security officers still saw him as a dangerous incendiary who could fan the embers of a dying revolution. In January 1902, for example, Manila's Secret Service reported that the ex-general was hosting meetings of "a very suspicious appearance" at his home on Calle Jolo that were "being watched by this Department." In Bikol an army intelligence officer reported that "he pretends to be very feeble" and "pretends to be friendly" to Americans," but he was supposedly "planning in secret" to take to the hills with his troops, a fear shared by Captain Van Deman. These alarmist reports notwithstanding, at his surrender in 1901 Belarmino encouraged a recalcitrant rebel comrade to capitulate and thenceforth remained just what he seemed: blind, deaf, and defeated.[110]

On balance, Captain Van Deman's maiden Philippine effort exhibited the same contradictory elements that would later trouble his expanded intelligence operations during World War I. With few military precedents to guide him, he developed comprehensive doctrines for both intelligence and counterintelligence. Most fundamentally, he instituted new procedures for systematic data collection, accurate coding, and rapid dissemination. Through its central role in coordinating an otherwise fragmented colonial intelligence effort, DMI also promoted institutional cross-fertilization, distilling innovations by, and distributing information from, the half-dozen civil and military agencies fighting this underground war. But this exhaustive effort was also married to a problematic paradigm, marked by the indelible imprint of this imperial age, which equated threat with ethnicity. As we will see in a later chapter, Van Deman would become the vehicle for domesticating these colonial lessons, both their larger design and their operational details, when the U.S. Army established its Military Intelligence command during World War I and put him in charge of its domestic counterintelligence.

U.S. Colonial Constabulary

The Philippines Constabulary (PC) was an almost accidental creation born of a brutal colonial pacification that could not succeed without an adaptable force of Filipino soldiers under American leadership. As the fighting shifted from conventional combat to counterinsurgency, the U.S. Army discovered the utility of "native troops" and recruited Filipinos to serve as guides and interpreters. Drawing on this experience in late 1900, the incoming civil administration, the Philippine Commission, recommended that "a comprehensive scheme of police organization be put in force as rapidly as possible, [and] that it be separated and distinct from the army."[111] In sum, the constabulary's mission was twofold: first, disarm the countryside using paramilitary patrols to capture both guerrillas and their rifles strewn by the revolution; and, second, secure the capital using intelligence operatives to round up subversives and monitor radical nationalists. In carrying out this mission, the constabulary would become a Janus-faced organization, serving as both the long arm of the colonial executive and as a vehicle for Filipino aspirations. During the early years of its operations, the color bar was palpable, presenting significant hurdles to Filipino advancement. But by placing guns in the hands of "natives" and replacing American soldiers with Filipino constables, the constabulary eventually became a force for the realization of Governor-General Taft's goal of building a "Philippines for the Filipinos."[112]

With the inauguration of the U.S. civil government in July 1901, the Philippine Commission recognized the need for a national police force to complete the army's pacification. General Aguinaldo's revolutionary army had been broken, but guerrilla bands, bandits, and messianic rebels were still active across the archipelago. Civilian rule also coincided with departure of all U.S. volunteer soldiers, adding pressure for the recruitment of native auxiliaries to assist the remaining army regulars. Under the commission's legislation of that same July, a new Insular Constabulary was authorized to recruit 162 soldiers for every province. As civil law officers, constables were empowered to "make arrests upon reasonable suspicion without warrant for breaches of the peace" provided that suspects appeared before a judge within twenty-four hours "if reasonably practicable." Accordingly, in August the commission established the Philippines Constabulary and just three months later, reflecting the centrality of intelligence to U.S. rule, added an Information Bureau staffed by a superintendent, three inspectors, two special detectives, a clerk, and a draftsman.[113]

For implementation of these acts Governor Taft turned to his good friend and secretary for police, the former Confederate war hero Luke E. Wright. To this daunting task Wright brought a wealth of experience: four years with the Confederate Army during the American Civil War; eight more as attorney general of Tennessee; and several decades of creative, sometimes courageous civic leadership in Memphis, building the city's banks, press, public health service, and mass transit system.[114] Unlike many of his peers, he soon recognized the need for an alternative to regular U.S. soldiers, whom he felt "had neither the will nor the organization to do police duty."[115] In effect, as Wright designed it, the constabulary became a hybrid force, deployed in localized units like police but armed with rifles like soldiers. So arrayed, its troopers would pursue bandit and revolutionary remnants with considerable success and bring colonial order to the countryside.

In a parallel move some months later the U.S. Army inducted its Filipino irregulars into a unified force called the Philippine Scouts or "Native Scouts," which was periodically mobilized to supplement the constabulary in its pacification efforts. Under General Order 293 of September 1901, the army formed fifty scout companies of 104 men each organized by "tribe" or language group, armed with Springfield rifles, and paid by the U.S. government. Though often criticized by American officers, a Filipino scout cost the army just 36 percent of the expense of an American soldier, suffered half the sick days, and fought with what the army called the "dash and grit" of "racial courage." By July 1902 there were only 15,500 U.S. Army troops left in the islands, concentrated in cantonments for external defense—a deployment that forced the 11,000 Filipino soldiers in the scouts and constabulary to take over the rural pacification campaign.[116] Three years later, when the commission's three-tiered security system was fully developed, the colony's "native" security forces totaled twenty-one thousand men—including seven thousand constabulary, five thousand scouts, and nine thousand municipal police.[117]

Both the constabulary and scouts began with similar colonial profiles—white officers and native soldiers—but they soon developed distinctive institutional cultures. The scouts were infantry units concentrated in a half-dozen major bases for external defense, while the constabulary was a police force dispersed in hundreds of small posts to maintain internal order. The scout regiments remained regular units of the U.S. Army until their abolition in 1949, while the constabulary was a colonial police force subordinate to both Filipino and American civil officials. Whenever electoral fraud, official venality, or police abuse became excessive, the colonial state imposed central control over remote localities through the constabulary, which in the four decades of U.S. rule averaged only 325 officers and 4,700 constables. Whenever peasant or tribal revolts strained the limits of these lightly armed police, the colonial governor could call on the scout infantry, which was, as mandated by Congress in 1903, subordinate to constabulary field officers in these operations[118]

Relations between these colonial forces were complicated by a formal separation of civil and military authority. Unlike European empires, the United States divided colonial power in the Philippines between a civilian executive (the civil governor) and a senior military officer (the general commanding the Philippine Division). Each controlled his own native troops, constabulary or scouts. Each reported to different authorities in Washington, the governor to the president and the general to the army's chief of staff. On the spot in Manila, moreover, there was no formal mechanism to coordinate these two distinct colonial regimes and mediate their inevitable conflicts. Later the army conducted a study, which found that this complete division of civil and military authority had fostered "friction between the Governor-General and the [Philippine] Division commander." Rather than creating a department of colonies to mediate this conflict, Washington administered its overseas possessions through the War Department's Bureau of Insular Affairs, an arrangement that gave "greater prestige to the Division commander."[119]

Though awkward and often inefficient, this dyarchy was a correction to a historical process that had invested the army with unchecked civil and military power over the Philippines for three full years. By the time the fighting was largely over in early 1901, the War Department in Washington realized that a viable civil government required restraints on this military power. "We intend to discontinue the military governor of the Philippine Islands and to establish a civil government which will be supreme there," Secretary of War Elihu Root wrote to his new Philippine commander, Gen. Adna Chaffee. "We are very desirous to have this accomplished . . . because we wish to avoid the prejudice which always arises when military government is too long continued."[120]

Unconvinced, General Chaffee remained suspicious of Filipinos and reluctant to cede authority to American civil officials. After Filipino guerrillas massacred a group of U.S. Marines at Balangiga, Samar, in September 1901, the general concluded that "we are dealing with a treacherous, lying, half-civilized community, that the natural instinct is hatred of the white race, and . . . constant suspicion must be the watchword of our men."[121] A month later he refused to recognize the authority of the new civil courts, arguing that "it is very necessary to maintain here the influence of the army on the mind of the people—That they shall fear it." Despite presidential directives to the contrary, the general felt that the Philippine Supreme Court "has no right I believe to demand the presence of a prisoner held by the Military Authority."[122]

From the outset this unresolved civil-military conflict complicated the work of the constabulary. According to Mrs. Helen Taft's memoir, her husband's "pet project" of forming "a force of several thousand Filipinos, trained and commanded by American Army officers" met firm opposition from General Chaffee. "I am opposed to the whole business," the general announced in mid-1901 when Secretary Wright called to discuss his draft constabulary bill. "It seems to me that you are trying to introduce something to take the place of my Army." "Why, so we are," Wright replied. "We are trying to create a civil police force to do the police work which we understood the army was anxious to be relieved of. . . . We consider it necessary to have a constabulary . . . in a country where the natives take naturally to ladronism [banditry]."[123]

Although he was a regular army officer, the constabulary's first chief, Capt. Henry T. Allen, championed its cause. As his companies took the field, Allen quickly devised an ambitious plan to shift the entire pacification campaign from the U.S. Army to his insular police. By January 1902 Governor Taft had independently concluded that American soldiers were no longer effective for pacification, so he accepted Allen's argument that five thousand constabulary spread across the islands could both guarantee order and allow a rapid reduction of army forces to just fifteen thousand "white soldiers" and five thousand "native troops." Predictably, this proposal aroused heated opposition from the Philippine Division, notably Major General Lloyd Wheaton, who favored a force of forty thousand American troops, and his regular officers, who still felt the best Filipino was a dead one.[124]

The army retaliated by restricting the constabulary's access to modern arms. Originally, Washington had allocated 1,372 Krag-Jorgensen repeating rifles for the new colonial police. But the army's commander, General Chaffee, objected to placing its most advanced weaponry in native hands, warning that "50, 100, or 200 men, with hostile intent, armed with rifle or carbine, constitute a force that takes thousands of troops and months of time to overcome." Consequently, the constabulary wound up with pistols, shotguns, and antiquated Springfield rifles to fight rebels armed with rapid-fire Mausers or razor-sharp fighting bolos, the latter surprisingly lethal in close combat. After General Chaffee delivered five hundred Springfields in early 1902, Captain Allen hailed it as "the weapon for the Constabulary" even though its single-shot magazine was inferior to that of the Mauser, many bores were so worn that their accuracy suffered, and many were not equipped with bayonets, which were essential for close combat against the bolo.[125] Operating outside the army hierarchy further complicated constabulary procurements. As a civil agency, it had to route its orders through the War

Department's Bureau of Insular Affairs in Washington where it joined the awful "confusion here of a Tom, Dick, and Harry order from Tom, Dick and Harry in the Philippines." This confusion was exemplified by errors in delivery of the correct rifle cartridges and problems with an "outrageous" trigger pull on a special order of Colt .45 pistols. These difficulties would not be resolved for another four years until the army adopted the Model 1903 rifle and finally agreed to turn over its superseded, six-shot Krag-Jorgensens to the constabulary.[126]

The army also resisted the transition from martial rule to civil law. In October 1901, after several heated civil-military disputes, the Philippine Commission passed Act No. 272 exempting army officers in just six troubled provinces from the requirement of habeas corpus for military prisoners.[127] Implementation of this accord proved difficult, particularly during the final phase of pacification in 1902. When the army's Manila garrison arrested three former revolutionary officers for sedition, Acting Governor Wright protested to General Chaffee, citing this act to insist "that if he really had any proof against these men the civil authorities would be glad to proceed against them in the courts." After Wright presented evidence that one was a victim of a false report by "political rivals," another had already sworn loyalty to the United States, and the third had no evidence against him, the army released them all. Even so, Wright was concerned that "these continued arbitrary arrests have a tendency to frighten the people."[128]

After the "Philippine Insurrection" formally ended in July 1902, these civil-military conflicts intensified. With primary responsibility for pacification and inadequate forces for the task, the constabulary struggled to contain the insurgency. To address the need for additional manpower, Congress responded to Wright's personal appeal by passing a law in January 1903 that authorized the civil government to mobilize the army's native troops, the Philippine Scouts, "to assist the Philippines Constabulary in the maintenance of order." Since the law effectively placed these regular military forces under the civilian police, the legislation also provided that five regular army officers would be detailed to the constabulary as assistant chiefs or chief, the latter with a brevet rank of brigadier general.[129] In effect, this law meant that for the next decade half a dozen U.S. Army officers would command the constabulary.[130] In spite of this concession to military control, the army's new Philippine Division commander, Gen. George Davis, complained bitterly that the new law placed his officers in "the mortifying position" of being "forbidden to lead into action the troops of their commands whom they had organized, instructed for years, brought to a high state of efficiency, and whose material wants . . . they must still supply."[131] But Taft, continuing to pursue his goal of "Philippines for the Filipinos," asserted that the new act had "worked extremely well," allowing the civil government to restore order with native troops, the constabulary and scouts, rather than white regulars. "In this country," Taft stressed, "it is politically most important that Filipinos should suppress Filipino disturbances and arrest Filipino outlaws."[132]

Despite incessant wrangling over details, the civil and military authorities agreed about the constabulary's overall mission and composition. "With the close of active campaigning," wrote General Davis in early 1902, "the [U.S. Army] troops are assembled into large camps, and the constabulary is day by day showing its capacity to over-awe the evil minded. The Filipinos have at last been disarmed and we must prevent their re-armament."[133] His superior, General Chaffee, also felt that as the army withdrew from pacified areas "the Civil Government is required to install a considerable force of constabulary" to meet what he called "this manifest necessity for military surveillance."[134]

These goals demanded exceptional skills from both the Filipino soldiers and the American officers who led them. In contrast to the civilian carpetbaggers who flocked to Manila in search of patronage posts, the army regulars who commanded the constabulary were educated engineers and military careerists insulated from the colony's pervasive cronyism. "These places require soldiers of no mean qualifications," wrote Chief Allen of his officers. In addition to language proficiency, they "must have special administrative talent, must understand dealing with natives, and must possess sufficient tact to secure the cooperation of both Insular and Provincial officials. A knowledge of Spanish and judgment of character are essential."[135] Indeed, the key attribute of these American officers was their ability to cooperate with Filipinos. "The requisites of a good officer of native troops," Allen explained in 1904, "are a liberal education, tact, and versatility. Above all he should not be . . . a *nigger hater* or one who considers the Filipino question as a *second Indian proposition*."[136] Successful officers needed to have what PC colonel Harry Bandholtz called "a special knack" for understanding the "native character" and for gaining "the confidence of the people." Finding regular officers with such empathy was difficult since, as the colonel noted, army personnel do "not as a rule admit Filipinos even of the highest class to social equality."[137]

When he formed the Philippines Constabulary in 1901, Secretary Wright made colonial race theory his organizing principle, albeit with some unusual twists to the usual imperial practice. Although he was a former Confederate Army officer, Wright had more nuanced views about race, exemplified by his public defense of black soldiers who had fired on white looters in Memphis during the city's devastating yellow fever epidemic of 1878.[138] Instead of exploiting "tribal prejudices" as the Spanish had done and British were doing, Wright insisted that each constabulary unit should be recruited in its home province, eliminating the usual "disposition to abuse and oppression . . . when native military . . . forces were operating among . . . hereditary enemies."[139] During their fifteen years in command, American officers assigned to these ethnically segregated units were encouraged to master the language of their native troops for this was considered critical to effective command in an archipelago without any common language, either colonial or national. By 1913 a total of 36 American officers, among the 261 then in service, were formally qualified in a range of local languages: sixteen in

Visayan, nine in Tagalog, five in Ifugao, two in Bicol, two in Ilocano, one in Natonin Bontoc, and one in Maguindanao.[140] The prevalence of highland languages, Ifugao and Bontoc, is but one indication that American officers, like the British before them, had developed the colonials' natural affinity for "martial tribes" and thus favored Luzon highlanders for their loyalty and marksmanship.[141] For native officers English fluency was a requirement, and early reports by Filipino lieutenants exhibit a mastery of both its grammar and idiom.[142]

It was the task of Captain Allen, as the constabulary's first chief, to translate Secretary Wright's colonial principles into military practice. Born into an antebellum Kentucky household with eleven slaves, Allen graduated from West Point in 1882 ranked twenty in a class of thirty-seven. But with the charm and connections that graced his career Allen was able to join the cavalry, then considered the army's fast track to command. His first assignments took him to garrison duty in Montana and exploration in Alaska where, as a young lieutenant, he won early renown for his intrepid exploration of the Copper River basin. Realizing that the American West was the army's past and the world its future, he left the cavalry to study Russian in Saint Petersburg and later joined the army's new Military Information Division as military attaché in the czarist capital. During his four years abroad Allen gained competence in three languages and filed reports on topics ranging from strategic analysis to thinly disguised espionage. Although his superior in the Information Division often faulted his reports as "too political," this proved an ideal preparation for his future work with the constabulary. When the Spanish-American War broke out, he left a post in Berlin for combat in Cuba and was transferred to the Philippines in January 1899.[143]

Assigned to Leyte and Samar with the Forty-third Volunteer Infantry in 1900, Allen plunged into the fastness of these sprawling, uncharted islands to pursue the country's most elusive guerrillas. During his eighteen months in the eastern Visayas, Allen learned what sort of tactics would not work. After insurgents slaughtered the U.S. troops at Balangiga, Samar, in 1901, Gen. Jacob Smith ordered a punitive campaign, saying, "I want no prisoners. . . . I wish you to kill and burn. . . . The interior of Samar must be made a howling wildness." Privately, the general told Allen that "he never talked with one of the —, — 'niggers'; that he never wanted to see one of the — ,—, s—s of b—s, and that if Leyte were turned back to him for two months he would kill a large number." In a report to Governor Taft, Allen described the general as "a disgrace to the army" who had "done his best to make an insurgent situation in order that he might be able to say that he pacified it." This judgment was confirmed four months later when Smith was court-martialed for ordering his soldiers to kill everyone on Samar over the age of ten.[144]

Unlike many Manila Americans or army officers, Chief Allen felt that Filipinos had the makings of soldiers and citizens. When the arch-imperialist senator Albert J. Beveridge wrote that the Filipinos were "Orientals and Malays" incapable of self-rule, Allen respectfully disagreed. "I fully recognize the defects of the Filipino character, especially the absence of integrity," he wrote, "but over three hundred years of Christian rule, however bad it may have been, accrues enormously to our advantage."[145] When drilled and disciplined by "a goodly number of white officers," Allen advised the War Department, Filipino soldiers were capable of "giving a good account of themselves in battle."[146]

Allen was not immune to fears of a "yellow peril," and like many colonials he viewed the geopolitics of his era in racially inflected terms. To solve the colony's chronic labor shortage he recommended selective immigration to stiffen Filipinos' racial fiber. "Half a million Chinamen put into the fields would work wonders in the harbor of Manila," he wrote in 1904, "and set an example that would be of great value to the Filipinos themselves."[147] When the Russo-Japanese War began in early 1904, Allen analyzed the conflict as a racial struggle against a "gigantic Oriental human wave" that could also become a "menace to Aryan civilization."[148] After Russia's defeat two years later, Allen advised merchants in his native Kentucky that the United States must continue its "highly human and philanthropic" rule over the Philippines "until the people are fit for independent government." Until that day came the United States must hold its "present coaling stations" in the Islands so "we can properly compete in the aggressive commercial rivalry."[149]

Although he was less extreme in his opinions than many in Manila's expatriate community, Chief Allen still believed in countering Filipino opposition with brute force. In April 1902 controversy erupted in the U.S. Congress over a report by the civil governor of Tayabas Province, Maj. Cornelius Gardener, accusing the army of abuses in its pacification campaign. "Of late by reason of the conduct of troops," the major stated, "such as the extensive burning of the barrios in trying to lay waste the country . . . , the torturing of natives by so-called water cure and other methods, . . . a deep hatred toward U.S. . . . is being fast . . . engendered."[150] While conceding the truth of the charges, Allen lobbied hard to have the matter swept aside in the interests of the larger imperial enterprise. In a confidential letter to a War Department officer, he admitted that he had received credible reports of torture, of soldiers raping women in a Tayabas town, and of troops that had worked two Catholic priests to death on a road crew. If investigated these charges would, he said, "scandalize the army in the eyes of all decent Americans," putting "a considerable weapon in the hands . . . of people who apparently would be glad to see the Philippine problem a failure."[151] Rural Filipinos, Allen felt, suffered from "intense ignorance" and the "fanatical tendencies characteristic of semi-savagery" for which, regrettably, "the only immediate remedy is killing and for the same reason that a rabid dog must be disposed of."[152] When he was confronted with persistent resistance by messianic rebels on Samar, Allen wrote West Point's commandant in 1903 that "the only rational policy is to kill off the leaders and enlighten the masses."[153]

Despite his prejudices, Allen supported Secretary Wright, who believed that properly trained Filipinos could "produce an effective military police body at about one third the cost (or less) of Americans."[154] Although Wright aroused antagonism in the army and the Manila American community by arming Filipinos, he tempered this innovation by stipulating that "Americans should . . . be in command" and Filipinos should be "non-commissioned officers and privates." Under these guidelines, Allen personally selected sixty-eight American officers from U.S. volunteer regiments and recruited Filipinos as ordinary soldiers, creating a de facto color line that only slowly faded.[155] Two years later, in 1903, the constabulary officer corps consisted of 212 Americans and 71 Filipinos. Over the longer term the percentage of American officers declined steadily from a peak of 86 percent in 1902 to 54 percent under the Filipinization program in 1916 and then to only 2 percent by the time the Philippine Commonwealth was inaugurated in 1935. As with the Manila Police, American resignations, accelerating after 1917, cleared the way for Filipino recruitment and rapid promotion. While no Filipino ranked higher than first lieutenant in 1905, thirty years later seventy-seven Filipinos held ranks from captain to colonel.[156]

At the apex of this hierarchy, the seventeen U.S. Army regulars who held most of the constabulary's top commands from 1901 to 1917 were among the most talented officers of their generation. Thirteen of the seventeen retired at star rank, a degree of success unequalled by any other army cohort. The constabulary's founder and first chief, Captain Allen, later led the Ninetieth Division "with credit" during the fighting in France and succeeded Gen. John Pershing as U.S. commander for Europe at the end of World War I. His successor as PC chief, Harry H. Bandholtz, later served as wartime provost marshal general in France where he founded the U.S. Army's Military Police (MPs).[157] The constabulary's third commander, James G. Harbord, joined the army as a private in 1889 and rose through the ranks to serve as General Pershing's chief of staff during the war. Later, as president and board chairman of the Radio Corporation of America (RCA) from 1923 to 1947, he led this fledging firm to the first rank among the world's communications companies.[158]

Under U.S. rule, two generations of middle-ranking Filipino officers also served the constabulary, ultimately defining its legacy for the Philippines. The first generation, often recruited from the ranks of the revolutionary army, rarely advanced beyond lieutenant, while the second, trained at the Constabulary School, rose to command by the early 1930s. The decision to include Filipinos in the constabulary had its critics. In 1902 the Associated Press correspondent Edgar Bellairs reported that the PC was "largely composed, as to the rank and file, of the former Filipino soldiers" and "many of the native inspectors . . . were former insurgent officers," raising the "grave possibility" that that they would "rise and massacre every white officer."[159] But the constabulary had taken the precaution of requiring that every Filipino inspector be, in Chief Allen's words, "recommended almost solely by officers of the Regular [U.S.] Army." Allen himself had appointed Licerio Geronimo, a revolutionary notorious among Americans for killing their hero, General Henry Lawton, after several U.S. officers declared him "the most honest, straightforward native that they have ever known."[160] Similarly, Colonel Pedro Guevara, a graduate of the elite Colegio de San Juan de Letran, fought against the Americans as revolutionary officer in his native Laguna Province. He then served the constabulary for three years, becoming one of its first Filipino lieutenants before going on to a distinguished career as a senator and Philippine resident commissioner in Washington, DC.[161]

Another of these long-serving Filipino officers, Maximo Meimban, joined the constabulary as a twenty-two-year-old private in 1901 and five years later won promotion to subinspector. Assigned to tribal highlands alien to the ecology and culture of his native Pampanga Province, Lieutenant Meimban showed real skill in dealing with both his American superiors and Ifugao soldiers. For seven years he served in a small force of sixty tribal constables that established PC control over forty thousand Ifugao who had long resisted Spanish colonial rule. There he led patrols to suppress head-taking, winning over suspicious elders and gathering detailed intelligence about tribal leaders. After this demanding duty, he followed his American commander up the Cordillera to pacify the warlike Kalinga and Apayao before retiring in 1919, still only a captain after eighteen years of exemplary service.[162]

Further down the hierarchy, Filipino sergeants advanced through the ranks even more slowly, often serving for decades in remote frontier outposts where they played a critical role in establishing constabulary control over the countryside. Magno Fruto, for example, enlisted at Iloilo in 1902 and remained a private until his "exceptional ability" finally won him promotion to sergeant in 1912. During ten years spent leading patrols along the upper Agusan River in central Mindanao, he was "known as the terror to the wild Manobos who were living without the reach of law" and fought in eight major engagements before he was killed by a Manobo warrior in 1922.[163]

At the bottom of the hierarchy the ordinary Filipino constables varied widely in ability, from illiterate privates conditioned to colonial deference through educated corporals and sergeants who had been revolutionary officers. Indeed, educational requirements for early recruits were minimal, and in some constabulary companies literacy in any language was as low as 33 percent.[164] Regardless of ability, Americans viewed these armed Filipinos guardedly. "The enlisted natives," reported Police Secretary W. Cameron Forbes in 1904, "need constant and rigorous supervision by competent officers to prevent [them from] using their newly acquired authority to oppress the people."[165] But statistics provide less biased testimony about the quality of Filipino service. During the constabulary's thirty-four years as a U.S. colonial police force, just fifty-nine American officers were killed compared to 2,107 Filipino soldiers, a high mortality rate for a force that averaged only four thousand troops.[166]

The second generation of Filipino recruits followed a more conventional career path. For a few years after 1907, the constabulary found recruitment of qualified "native officers" difficult since the American presence slowed promotion and educated Filipinos found better opportunities in the civil service. Indeed, the PC chief complained in 1909 of "an exceptionally large shortage of officers" compounded by a rash of Filipino resignations and a "marked falling off in Filipino applications since the character of our examinations has become known."[167] Gradually, however, the Filipinization policy adopted in 1913 and the mass resignation of American officers during World War I made rapid promotion possible, attracting a second cohort of educated Filipinos.

On the constabulary's thirtieth anniversary in 1931, its journal, *Khaki and Red,* published photobiographies of the Southern Luzon District's officer corps, providing a tableau of the overall Filipinization of its officer corps. Seventy-three Filipino officers were arrayed in a clear age-grade hierarchy that indicates steady improvement in recruitment, training, and retention. Reflecting early difficulties, the district's six majors, all born between 1881 and 1890, were largely college graduates and all were from the greater Manila area. Indicating wider recruitment, the district's fourteen captains, born between 1889 and 1894, came from towns across Luzon. Most had finished high school, and all had graduated from the Constabulary Academy, the majority in 1915–16. Beneath these captains the district's junior officers, divided into three lieutenant grades, had benefited from the expansion of the academy to a nine-month curriculum by 1916 and the rapid repatriation of Americans a year later. Officers in each of these echelons would later rise to command their nation's military. In addition to Maj. Alejo Valdes, who later headed the PC Intelligence Division (1934–35), Capt. Rafael Jalandoni would serve as Armed Forces chief of staff (1945–48), as would 3d Lt. Jesus Vargas (1953–56).[168]

Yet Filipinization of the constabulary's command came only gradually. In that same 1931 anniversary issue of *Khaki and Red,* the headquarters staff posed for a formal portrait. It was a veritable snapshot of colonial tenacity as five of the seven senior officers seated in the front row, all attired in riding boots and campaign hats, were Americans. At their center was the "old tiger," Gen. Charles E. Nathorst, a sixty-nine-year-old Swedish aristocrat who had come to the islands as a private with the Thirteenth Minnesota Infantry in 1898, joined the constabulary as a lieutenant in 1901, and served with distinction in the Cordillera, negotiating peace agreements among warring highlanders. After the death of the incumbent chief in 1927, Nathorst, famed for knowing the names of all four hundred of his Filipino officers—and, frankly, little else—served as chief for five years. He retired just before his seventieth birthday in 1932, exceptional longevity for any soldier.[169]

Conclusion

During three years of military rule the U.S. Army played a central, even defining role in the formation of the Philippine colonial police, leaving a legacy that persisted for decades. At the end of martial rule in 1901, the U.S. civil administration, following military precedents, left the municipal police under local control, thus avoiding direct responsibility for this political miasma. Again following the army's model, the colonial regime maintained close supervision over Manila's police and formed the Philippines Constabulary as a paramilitary force to control the countryside. Through this contradictory policy of simultaneously centralizing and decentralizing its security forces, the American regime balanced the need for a mobile paramilitary police inherited from its Spanish predecessors with its own national tradition of "maintaining police as a responsibility of local government."[170] Along with the tripartite division into national, metropolitan, and municipal police, this central-local tension would remain a feature of Philippine policing for the rest of the century.

In creating this colonial security apparatus, the military government also developed covert techniques, discussed in the next chapter, that would remain a defining attribute of Philippine policing. Though initiated to protect the new state from insurrection, this systematic surveillance also swept up sensitive intelligence about the moral derelictions of prominent Filipinos and Americans, producing incriminating information whose selective release soon became a key instrument of colonial control. In the transition from military to civil rule, Washington had denied the Filipinos constitutional guarantees that could have restrained the colonial government from this relentless violation of their privacy. The new civil regime and its constabulary, unhindered by concerns about civil liberties, would use this intelligence as a subtle but surprisingly potent weapon of political control, deftly manipulating both Filipino politicians and American colonials.

3

Surveillance and Scandal

ON JULY 2, 1902, fifty American colonials gathered at the Army-Navy Club for "the most sumptuous banquet ever given in Manila," a farewell dinner for the local Associated Press (AP) correspondent, the dashing English gentleman Capt. Edgar G. Bellairs. Led by Gen. Adna Chaffee, the U.S. Army commander in these islands, this distinguished crowd of officers, bankers, editors, and judges raised their glasses to an intrepid reporter who had chronicled every chapter in America's rise to empire.

For four years Captain Bellairs had followed the U.S. Army halfway round the globe. From Cuba, where he reported on Gen. Leonard Wood's rule as American military governor. To China, where he marched with General Chaffee's expedition against the messianic Boxer rebels. All the way to the Philippines, where he covered the army's bloody pacification campaign. Now this roomful of empire builders wished him good luck and Godspeed on his greatest adventure yet—a trip across the Pacific to New York City for the publication of a sensational book, an exposé that would surely oust William Howard Taft as civil governor of the Philippine Islands and install General Wood as his successor, putting the hero of San Juan Hill on a path to the U.S. presidency in 1908.[1]

Matters did not quite go as planned, of course. Governor Taft, not General Wood, won the presidential election of 1908. Instead of putting Wood in the White House, the bid to discredit Taft backfired, producing press attacks and Senate investigations that exiled Wood to a secondary command in the southern Philippines and sent Bellairs to the Arizona Territory in search of a new career.

Although his name has been erased from the collective memory, Edgar G. Bellairs was an important actor in the history of America's early empire.[2] In the story of U.S. imperial expansion dominated by presidents, senators, and generals, this con man, ex-convict, and alleged pederast, born Charles Ballentine, played a surprisingly central role. Spinning a web of deception after his parole from a Florida prison farm in 1896, Ballentine borrowed the name of an English gentry family to baptize himself Edgar Bellairs. With this new persona he wangled an appointment as an AP correspondent in Cuba during the Spanish-American War. In mid-1898 Bellairs arrived at Santiago de Cuba where he befriended another adventurer whose ambitions equaled his own, General Wood, an army doctor who would be president.[3] From this colonial periphery, criminal and general set out to shape America's destiny through skillful media manipulation that made Wood governor-general of Cuba in 1899 and aspired to make him president of the United States within a decade.

As a foreign correspondent for the Associated Press, Bellairs wrote wire service dispatches carried by 90 percent of U.S. newspapers, shaping the views of millions of Americans about their expanding empire. Although he ultimately failed, his scheming to advance General Wood from Havana via Manila to the White House got surprisingly far. More significantly, Captain Bellairs personifies, in both his success and his failure, the imperceptible historical process that allows criminal and colonial peripheries to shape politics at the center of modern empires. Indeed, his uncommon career shows how U.S. national politics became entwined with colonial intrigues in this imperial age, seamlessly weaving together Manila intrigues, Ohio machine politics, New York media, and Washington policy.

Most important, in his dual roles as correspondent and ad hoc press agent for Wood, Bellairs exemplifies the importance of information and its control in the politics of empire. Without discounting his charm and cunning, it was his access to the AP wire service, the most powerful news network in America's first information age, that elevated Bellairs from ex-convict to colonial power broker. If he rose rapidly by means of his brilliant manipulations of the new information regime, he was destroyed just as quickly because he underestimated its capacities and mistook Governor Taft for a mere proconsul instead of a fellow player.

As the first civil governor of the Philippines, William Howard Taft was constructing a new kind of state based not on physical coercion but on control over information. Through a unique convergence of historical forces, he had the autonomy to establish himself as an imperial plenipotentiary with unchecked civil powers. Under his instructions from Secretary of War Elihu Root dated June 1901, Taft was to "exercise the executive authority in all civil affairs . . . heretofore exercised . . . by the military governor of the Philippines." Until the new Philippine Assembly convened in 1907, the governor could, on his own authority, promulgate laws, impose taxes, proclaim martial law, dismiss officials, grant pardons, and order exile or deportation.[4] Moreover, the U.S. Supreme Court had created a special colonial status for the islands by ruling, in the famed Insular Cases, that the Philippines, as Taft himself later explained, was not "incorporated into the Union . . . over which the Constitution extends with all its provisions." As residents of unincorporated American territories, Filipinos could enjoy natural human liberties such as freedom of the press but were denied full citizenship rights such as suffrage and trial by jury. With Filipino civil rights so circumscribed, Taft could enact draconian libel and sedition laws that one U.S. senator called "the harshest . . . known to human statute books," giving himself powerful control over all forms of expression.[5]

Among the many security services formed in the early years of U.S. rule, it was a Taft creation, the Philippines Constabulary, that most fully realized the potential of police to facilitate state control over information. In the constabulary Taft created a new kind of centralized security force that simultaneously monitored public discourse and penetrated private space. Officially, the constabulary's mission was to help with the pacification of the Philippines. But limitations on civil liberties at this edge of empire emboldened the colonial regime to deploy this paramilitary police in ways unforeseen at the time of its formation in August 1901. Of course, intelligence gathered by its agents aided in the prosecution of crimes against the state. In many cases, however, such relentless surveillance uncovered incriminating information that proved more potent when either suppressed or released outside formal judicial bounds. Under such circumstances Americans and Filipinos vied with one another to acquire damaging information, secreting damning documents in private safes as insurance against political reprisals or as currency in future political maneuvers. But American officials had the upper hand as they used the constabulary's clandestine Information Division to compile files on derelictions committed by Filipino leaders and exploited this intelligence to shape the character of Philippine politics during the early years of U.S. rule, 1901 to 1913. Americans also used scandalous intelligence against each other, seeking to advance themselves within the colonial regime or win higher office in Washington.

Through its secret police operations the constabulary demoralized the radical nationalists who had led the revolution, demobilized their followers, and cultivated a cohort of collaborators that included politicians such as the future Philippine president Manuel Quezon. The system protected cooperative Filipino politicians by suppressing rumors that could damage their careers and persecuted uncompromising nationalists by releasing information selected and timed to destroy their reputations. To survive under alien rule ambitious Filipino politicians often served the constabulary as informants, paid spies, or political operatives. Such service could also assist in their rise. Yet even at the apex of power these collaborators, fearful of being exposed as spies or traitors, continued to operate within circumscribed colonial bounds, moderating their rhetoric and calibrating their resistance. Through the constabulary's systematic infiltration of radical circles and skillful co-optation of prominent Filipino leaders, the idealistic nationalist movement imploded within a decade amid suspicion and betrayal, leaving more conservative politicians to lead the nationalist movement by means of a materialist patronage system.

The combination of strict surveillance and repressive laws fostered a pervasive politics of scandal that has generally been ignored by a postcolonial scholarship that until recently was focused on the grander themes of empire and resistance.[6] While the colonial state could use its firepower against peasant rebels, more subtle methods were needed to keep collaborating elites within acceptable limits. Whether exposed by the press, shared with a select audience, or secreted for future use, scandal had the potential to ramify far beyond the private realm, at times determining the fate of senior officials or the future of entire administrations.

Politics of Scandal

Scandal was not just gossip. It was a constant force in the diurnal jostling for colonial patronage and power. It could erupt into serious political controversy, threatening the fragile accommodations whose sum was the colonial order. Across the archipelago ordinary Filipinos toiled and most Americans fought tedium in barracks or classrooms. But in Manila educated Filipino elites and ambitious American expatriates competed for patronage from the colonial state. Within the confines of this tutelary colonialism, both American officials and Filipino leaders were held to high moral standards whose transgression could have devastating consequences. As exemplars of a higher "breed," American officials, often single males, risked dismissal for extramarital liaisons, the colonial crime of concubinage, and lesser sanctions for infractions such as graft, debt, or drunkenness. Under the rigid racial segregation of this period, even an American who married a Filipina risked mockery from colonial superiors and mistrust from Filipino officials.[7] Educated Filipinos, as exemplars of their "race," could be tainted by gambling, a vice deemed a barrier to "racial progress" by nationalists and colonials alike. Within Manila's tight social strictures, everyone collected gossip about everyone: Americans about Filipinos and fellow Americans, Filipinos about local rivals and colonial enemies. Since Americans philandered, Filipinos gambled, and everyone embezzled, all faced the constant threat of political death by scandal.

Americans were the prefects of this school for scandal, using law and the police to make both public discourse and private gossip powerful instruments of colonial control. The progenitors of this system, its senior prefects so to speak, were the two Americans most synonymous with the first decade of U.S. colonial rule: Governor Taft, the legal architect of the new information order; and his interior secretary, Dean C. Worcester, the master of its dark underside. As colonial governor, secretary of war, and eventually president, Taft dominated and defined U.S. policy toward the Philippines from 1900 to 1913, creating the legal framework for this information regime while sharing colonial power with landed, educated Filipinos. As the colony's long-serving secretary of the interior,

Worcester shaped much of the regime's internal administration, using his vast local knowledge to pioneer the extralegal uses of defamatory information. Worcester was a social Darwinist who equated race with civilization in ways that made him a determined imperialist and a fiery opponent of Filipino self-rule. Even their contrasts were complementary: Taft obese and deskbound, Worcester energetic and peripatetic; Taft aristocratic and charming, Worcester hardscrabble and aggressive; Taft focused on imperial design, Worcester obsessive about detail. Despite their differences, a common commitment to America's imperial adventure made them if not fast friends at least close political comrades.

Throughout their long alliance, Taft and Worcester made information essential to both colonial politics and state power. Setting aside their society's tradition of free speech, these two proconsuls made a determined effort to control the flow of information by every means at their disposal, passing punitive laws, forming a powerful colonial police force, prosecuting editors for criminal libel, exiling radicals, and jailing dissidents. At a less formal level they used secret police to compile files on Filipino failings such as gambling, corruption, and "caciquism." When legal means failed they could reach into these files for malicious revelations about the sexual or financial failings of their enemies, both Filipino and American. Through these colonial practices Governor Taft presided over a total information regime.

Behind his Saint Nicholas demeanor of jovial smiles and three-hundred-pound girth, William Taft was personally vindictive and politically astute with an almost intuitive feel for power. Reared in Ohio when that state was the powerhouse of American politics, he apprenticed in a political machine that produced half a dozen presidents in half a century, from Hayes (1879–82) to Harding (1921–23). Taft's family were lead players in a rough Cincinnati politics in which both parties had the same guiding principles: "Stay in office if possible and get all the graft available while in office." Under the tutelage of the legendary Republican boss George B. Cox, the young Taft served the machine in the violent city elections of the mid-1880s before patronage launched him on a judicial career that would include service as U.S. solicitor general and eight years on the federal bench. In the great split of 1888 among Ohio Republicans, Taft distanced himself from Boss Cox by forging ties to the rising Hanna-McKinley machine. It was a judicious move, for eight years later Marcus A. Hanna, a wealthy Cleveland industrialist, would take control of the Republican National Committee and begin building the country's first modern political party. With millions in corporate contributions and fourteen hundred paid campaign workers for the epochal 1896 elections, the Republicans crushed the Democrats' seemingly unstoppable silver crusade and put Ohio's favorite son, William McKinley, in the White House. After the president appointed Taft Philippine governor in 1901, he swapped patronage with Hanna, by then Ohio's junior senator, while deftly maintaining good relations with Joseph Foraker, the state's senior senator and Hanna's bitter rival.[8]

From this long political apprenticeship Taft learned several precepts that guided him through his decade of leadership in Philippine affairs. Above all he equated human progress with corporate profits. He believed in the innate superiority of Anglo-Saxon society, its laws, culture, and civilization. Though committed to training Filipinos for eventual self-rule, he felt, as he wrote in 1907, that it would be a "disaster . . . giving the Philippines independence short of two generations or probably a century." Years later, out of the political fray as chief justice of the U.S. Supreme Court, he still felt that "[Sergio] Osmeña and [Manuel] Quezon represent the standard of [Filipino] civilization . . . , and it isn't a high one." Ethically, Taft believed passionately in loyalty and reciprocity, and he reviled anyone who failed to follow this clubby gentleman's code.[9] He fused ardent imperialism with patronage politics in ways that made him tolerant of cronyism among his Republican allies whether in Cincinnati, Manila, or Washington.

With his mastery of constitutional law and machine politics, Governor Taft pulled the levers of state power to construct a colonial information regime via severe legislation and secret police.[10] Confronted with political and press criticism in the first months of his rule, he enacted punitive libel and sedition laws to curb Manila newspapers, which he privately condemned as "very vicious and venomous little American sheets that delight to revile the [Philippine] Commission in every way."[11] In October 1901 Taft's Civil Commission, which functioned as his executive council, passed a tough Libel Law (Act No. 277) prescribing a year's imprisonment for print or speech that exposed anyone to "public hatred, contempt or ridicule" with the exception of "a fair and true report of any . . . public official proceedings." Significantly, the law also provided that a "publication is presumed to have been malicious" unless its publisher could prove both truth and public good, in effect imposing a presumption of guilt for "malicious defamation" on every edition. Just a week later the commission enacted the complementary Sedition Law (Act No. 292), which severely punished any political activity deemed subversive, notably, death for treason, seven years in prison for failing to report it, two years for uttering "seditious words or . . . scurrilous libels against the Government," and one year for advocating "the independence of the Philippine Islands."[12]

These laws were but one element in a larger legal architecture that gave the colonial government expansive powers over the press and political opposition. Despite his image as a pro-Filipino governor, Taft reversed much of the early recognition of native rights stipulated in President McKinley's formal instructions of April 1900. He used his broad executive authority in ways that rendered moot even the nominal rights the U.S. Supreme Court conferred on Filipinos in the Insular Cases. In addition to the Sedition Act, he enacted a series of authoritarian laws to enforce his rule, including the Bandolerismo Statute (Act No. 518) of November 1902, which allowed the execution of brigands without the need to "adduce evidence that any member of the band has in fact committed robbery," and the Reconcentration Act (No. 781) of June 1903, which permitted the governor-general to order mass incarcerations in any province infested with "*ladrones* or outlaws." Reversing the military regime's policy of favoring native judges, Taft packed the courts with American colonials, reducing Filipinos to a minority on the Supreme Court and to just six of the country's sixteen district court judges. To increase his leverage over the courts, he proclaimed Act No. 396 of May 1902, which allowed him to transfer judges at will and without cause, powers he used to banish those deemed insufficiently punitive to remote provinces at reduced salaries. The fruit of these controls was soon manifest in frequent convictions for political crimes by lower courts and in the landmark 1905 Philippine Supreme Court decision *Barcelon v. Baker*, which exempted the governor-general's suspension of habeas corpus from judicial review, a precedent that would empower colonial and national executives for the next seventy years.[13] With a pliable executive commission to enact his laws and compliant courts to enforce them, Taft soon transformed a relatively liberal colonial regime into a repressive one.

But it was the formation of the Philippines Constabulary, Taft's "pet project," that enabled him to both enforce these laws and, when convenient, circumvent them. While invoking the new legislation to brand editors and correspondents as "anarchists," "agitators," and "liars," he also used sensitive information, much of it constabulary intelligence, to combat political foes and promote political favorites.[14] In 1903, for example, Taft wrote a longtime patron, Ohio senator Joseph B. Foraker, to seek his support for the promotion of district judge E. Finley Johnson to the Philippine high court. The judge was, Taft said, "a pure man, and an honest man and a fearless man" whose nomination might be blocked by local enemies circulating "an unfounded libel that he had improper relations with a woman, a stenographer." Showing his mastery of colonial scandal, Taft then rattled off a catalog of similarly salacious gossip about each of the judge's critics among local lawyers. An American attorney named Terrell was "a thoroughly disreputable man" who rigged local prizefights; another was found "guilty of embezzlement and . . . accepting a retainer to enable a client . . . to evade the gambling laws"; and a prominent Filipino opponent, Felipe Calderon, had been "charged with unprofessional conduct and brought to trial." As befits a loyal patron, Senator Foraker assured his former protégé that patronage would always trump propriety, saying, "It will afford me pleasure to give every assistance I can to secure the confirmation of Judge Johnson."[15]

With even greater ease Dean Worcester evolved from an academic zoologist into a master of colonial intrigue. Along with his University of Michigan schoolmate Dr. Frank S. Bourns, Worcester was one of America's very few Philippine experts when the United States invaded the islands in 1898. As students these two had joined their university's zoological expeditions to the archipelago in 1887–88 and 1890–91, acquiring local knowledge they later used during the Philippine-American War. Finding that his intelligence service lacked linguists, the U.S.

commander, Gen. Elwell S. Otis, had turned to Major Bourns, then Manila's chief medical officer, to develop a "spy system" inside the enemy's ranks and advise him about political dealings with Filipinos. After the doctor went home on leave in July 1899, Worcester took "charge of his spies" to supplement his work as a member of the first Philippine Commission. "Each morning, if there was news," he recalled, "I myself laboriously thumped out my notes on the typewriter," a habit of information collection, recording, and filing that he maintained for the rest of his colonial career. Tall, domineering, and vindictive, Worcester was the embodiment of American empire. He was also its most ardent advocate, believing firmly in racial evolution and telling his Michigan zoology classes that Filipino tribal "savages" were the "lowest of living men," the first step in man's cultural evolution from "the gorilla and the orang-utan."[16] To illustrate these theories, Worcester liked to pose—frame stiffly erect, body fully covered in colonial costume—towering above diminutive forest Negritos, their dark, wiry frames clad only in loincloths.

Worcester's only Filipino friends were a coterie of wealthy, well-educated, fair-skinned Spanish mestizos: Benito Legarda, T. H. Pardo de Tavera, and Cayetano Arellano. While they provided him with intelligence on their fellow Filipinos, Worcester reciprocated by rewarding these "intimate friends of mine" with high offices when Taft's second Philippine Commission formed a civil government after 1900.[17] His bitterest enemies belonged to a circle of radical Tagalog-speaking intellectuals that included Fernando Ma. Guerrero, Rafael Palma, and Mariano Ocampo. When their newspaper, *El Renacimiento,* mocked his racial theories in a famous "Aves de Rapiña" (Birds of Prey) editorial in 1908, Worcester sued for libel, winning both a criminal conviction and a civil suit that bankrupted the journal.[18]

As interior secretary in the first years of U.S. rule, Worcester searched the constabulary's confidential files and compiled, with his formidable taxonomic skills, detailed dossiers on the failings of Filipino leaders. "Possession of such information gave Worcester extraordinary power," wrote a biographer, Peter Stanley, "and he used it cunningly . . . to enhance his own authority and dominate others."[19] But Worcester was not simply a dirty player in a rough colonial game. He was the progenitor of a new system of state power. During his twelve years as a colonial official, he used scurrilous information systematically culled from court and constabulary records to manipulate Filipino politics.

When the first Philippine Assembly took office in 1907, for example, Worcester drafted a twenty-one-page register of the new Filipino legislators, detailing alleged derelictions large and small. He noted, for example, that Representative Manuel Quezon had been "charged with shooting prisoners while a major in the *insurrecto* army" and was later investigated for "charges of attempted rape, abduction, and various acts of abuse as *fiscal* of Mindoro." Other entries noted that many legislators had faced criminal charges, including Jose Altavas of Capiz for "tampering with government witnesses," Dominador Gomez for "highway robbery, brigandage and . . . diverting funds of Union Obrera," and Jose Lerma of Bataan for blackmailing "a woman into paying $600 by threatening to have her son hanged."[20] In an updated dossier for a later session, Worcester noted, with a disdain Filipinos found repellant, that the legislature was full of "vicious criminals."[21]

Worcester was equally aggressive in attacking his fellow Americans. In 1911 the opening of the Philippine General Hospital brought a myriad of problems compounded by his own maladministration. When minor scandals broke in the press and the governor-general ordered an investigation, Worcester compiled a two-hundred-page report that shifted the blame to subordinates, meted out penalties, and absolved any who bent to his will. But the chief surgeon, Dr. John R. McDill, backed by allies in the governor's office, proved insufficiently penitent. "I'm going to get McDill," Worcester told another physician, "and if they attempt to use the Big Stick on me and to interfere in my department . . . [I will] stand them all on their heads." In his final report he distilled reams of stenographic notes into a 110-page indictment of Dr. McDill as a "trouble maker" whose mix of "brain fag" and greed for private gain had "led him into very grave error." Using his trademark method of slander by sexual innuendo, Worcester charged that the doctor had violated regulations by sending emergency room staff to the city's Gardenia "red light district for the purpose of administering morphine to uproarious, drunken, or hysterical prostitutes," creating "circumstances of the most improper and inexcusable sort." Worcester then sealed the report as confidential, denying the doctor redress or reply. He shared salacious passages with allies in the Philippine Assembly and circulated rumors that the doctor had been "forced to resign" for pocketing a hefty two thousand pesos in private fees when the actual amount was an inconsequential seventy-five pesos. By the time Worcester was done with him, Dr. McDill was back in Milwaukee with "my professional reputation . . . under grave suspicion and my future career . . . jeopardized."[22]

Sensitive information sealed in dossiers or released for scandal was thus central to U.S. colonial control, both its policing and its politics. Although none could equal Worcester, a cache of damaging documents was an asset to any colonial official. The threat of exposé imposed discretion on daily life and careful calculation on major political moves. When controversy erupted, partisans on both sides of the imperial divide rushed to open files or dictate sworn affidavits with disparaging revelations about rivals. As a result the Philippine courts heard 703 cases for "offenses against reputation" (slander, calumny, libel) from 1903 to 1908, numbers approaching those for more conventional crimes such as rape or murder.[23]

Rather than precipitate a public scandal with an uncertain outcome, most political actors collected scurrilous documents that were filed carefully but released infrequently. Scandal was most effective when threatened rather than released.

During a bitter battle between Governor Wood and Senator Quezon in 1924, for example, the writer Katherine Mayo discovered a sensational document in "the governor general's archive" that could have silenced his Filipino rival. When she asked why he did not release it, Wood, a master practitioner of this dark art, replied with unintended frankness, "You weaken your position if you do it, even working from under the surface."[24] Beneath this surface of colonial politics, with its rhetoric of nationalism or imperial uplift, events thus turned, to an extent that scholars have not appreciated, on the use of slanderous information held in private papers accessible only with the passage of many decades.

In this school for scandal the anonymous letter was also feared. When Harry Bandholtz, then constabulary chief, wrote Capt. Julius C. Buttner criticizing his performance as a PC inspector at Capiz in 1907, the officer replied that he had been the innocent victim of a poison pen letter from a Filipino police sergeant who had made similar anonymous attacks on at least four officials.[25] During the 1906 gubernatorial elections Manuel Quezon was forced to collect character references from American colonials after an anonymous writer circulated accusations of drunkenness.[26] Correspondence intercepted en route posed another threat. Mindful of his security in the age of the telegraph, Quezon preferred to send his confidential communications in sealed envelopes since "telegrams are always read by other persons," a reference to the operators at both ends of the line who coded and decoded every message.[27] In 1921 Worcester would complain that "there is no privacy obtainable for telegraphic messages" and "private letters frequently show evidence of having been tampered with."[28]

Paradoxically, American colonials were more vulnerable to scandal than their Filipino wards. As supposed exemplars of a higher race, U.S. officials were sensitive to rumor and quick to ostracize any who violated community norms of moral rectitude. Upset by the presence of so many "dissolute, drunken . . . truculent and dishonest" U.S. veterans, the Philippine Commission passed a sweeping vagrancy law in 1903, offering suspended sentences for those who accepted free transportation home and agreed not to return for ten years. The incentive resulted in the de facto deportation of 223 Americans in 1906 alone.[29] In 1902 the head of the constabulary's Information Section, Capt. E. G. Currey, was forced to resign when his wife, a woman of "the most shady type," was caught using a Chinese detective to extort protection money from Manila's Chinese merchants. Although the captain's work had been excellent, he was deemed "responsible for his wife's actions" and dismissed.[30]

While petty scandal could be fatal to a colonial career, serious crimes were covered up to protect the American aura. When a scouts commander in Palawan, Capt. Boss Reese, raped a dozen of his Filipino soldiers in a series of drunken rages, the U.S. Army tried first to silence the subordinate who complained and then to hush the matter up with his hasty resignation. Headquarters convened a formal inquiry only when news of the scandal threatened to leak.[31]

Crime statistics bear out this anecdotal evidence about the paradoxical nature of the U.S. moral regime. Even as political crimes such as sedition accounted for 40 percent of the eleven thousand cases before U.S. colonial courts, prosecution of offenses such as concubinage and prostitution fell from 46 percent of all charges under Spain in 1885 to just 6 percent under the United States in 1903.[32] But the drop in morals violations was misleading. Instead of formally charging suspected perpetrators of adultery, bigamy, abduction, and seduction, as called for under U.S. law, colonial police unofficially collected intelligence about sexual dalliance for later use, both legal and extralegal. Such surveillance, combined with modern police methods, allowed the U.S. regime to increase its secretive controls while reducing overt coercion.

The few American observers who crossed the Pacific were often surprised to discover a police state quite unlike anything back home. Arriving at Manila in early 1904 for a few months' research, Dr. H. Parker Willis, an economist who later served as secretary of the U.S. Federal Reserve, found himself living in "a reign of terror." Pulpit, stage, and public meeting were "subjected either to official or unofficial surveillance." Filipino leaders feared that their servants were "in the employ of the secret service bureau, and even wholly innocent remarks, either oral or by letter, were likely to be seized upon and distorted by detectives." Philippine society was "literally honeycombed by the secret service," whose activities were above the law since "constabulary abuses are always investigated . . . by constabulary officers."[33] Dr. Willis had found a surveillance state that used its information controls to terrorize Filipinos, intimidate Americans, and deny the U.S. Congress news about the policies implemented in its name.

Constabulary Surveillance

The constabulary was, as Dr. Willis had discovered, vital to U.S. political control over these islands. Indeed, the real achievements of its founder and first chief, Henry Allen, lay not in his storied combat operations but in the less visible realm of political intelligence. From his years of prior service in the Military Information Division and as a military attaché in czarist Russia, Allen had gained the experience needed to make the constabulary's Information Section an effective secret police.

At the broadest level Chief Allen faced the daunting task of shifting intelligence collection from the U.S. Army's controversial coercive methods to the less visible surveillance appropriate to a civil administration. Writing a brother officer in 1902 about the earlier use of torture to obtain field intelligence, Allen observed that during combat "the 'watercure' and other inquisitorial methods will be resorted to in spite of the strictest instructions. I have heard that under me, although against my orders, the 'watercure' and other methods as bad, or worse, were adopted, and probably under you the same."[34] While the army had often used torture to extract intelligence from hostile civilians, Allen's constabulary planned to avoid it by cultivating hundreds of paid Filipino agents. Writing President Theodore Roosevelt after just two months of police operations, Allen asserted that "had we known the people and the country upon arrival as we now do, the insurrection could have been put down at half the cost in half the time."[35] Only three months later Allen would claim that "it is scarcely possible for any seditionary measures of importance to be hatched without our knowledge" since "I have secret agents in every province."[36]

Starting with just six officers, a draftsman, and a mission to draw maps, the constabulary's Information Section quickly grew into a multifaceted political intelligence unit. During its first year the section did 672 major translations, compiled 2,034 identification photos, and processed 7,620 reports from twenty-two secret "operators."[37] Over the next two years this fledgling unit grew from a modest-sized "section" into the Information Division, a powerful covert espionage agency with hundreds of spies in nationalist groups across the archipelago. By late 1904 the original 22 Filipino operators had increased to 118, rendering "ready, intelligent, and very valuable advice as detectives and secret-service agents." Indicative of its self-consciously covert ethos, the constabulary's report for that year noted, in appropriately convoluted language, that the division was "more effective in securing results of certain kinds, difficult to officials or agents without special training and aptitude, than any other element."[38] In the constabulary's annual report for 1905, totaling 115 pages, the Information Division's presence shrank to a single table showing 1,589 cases investigated. In subsequent years as the division's net grew ever wider, it disappeared from published reports altogether, becoming fully and formally clandestine.[39]

Constabulary field officers quickly discovered the superiority of covert operations over conventional military force. After posting to Sorsogon at Luzon's southern tip in August 1901, the local PC company began pursuing "a fanatical organization known as 'Anting Anting' " (amulet), led by a peasant named Antonio Colache, that swept villages "like an epidemic" until it had four hundred fighters armed with bolo swords. After leading forty constabulary troops and local militia on patrols for six weeks without result, Inspector Harvey P. Nevill "decided to . . . bring about the capture of Colache by the use of spies." Only four days later one of these spies led local militia into Colache's camp, seizing the movement's entire leadership and ending the revolt.[40] This experience, repeated countless times, soon taught the constabulary the primacy of intelligence for pacification.

While the constabulary's patrols pursued peasant rebels in the countryside, its Information Division monitored and manipulated radical intellectuals in the capital. With the end of military rule in July 1901, Filipinos were nominally free to form nationalist political parties, something Governor Taft circumscribed with both formal legislation and informal manipulation. Working through his top operatives, Dean Worcester and Frank Bourns, the governor encouraged some

125 members of the capital's wealthy elite to form the Partido Federal, a conservative party that advocated U.S. annexation. Throughout 1901 Taft lavished patronage on this party, appointing its leaders to senior posts.[41] As the Federalista advocacy of American statehood produced a steady erosion of the party's popular support throughout 1902, Taft looked for alternative allies among Manila's educated elite. Finding the call for political autonomy by a new party, the Partido Liberal, acceptable, he hosted its leaders at a Malacañang Palace banquet in honor of its leader, Pedro Paterno.[42]

Taft was disturbed, however, by a sudden resurgence of nationalist rhetoric at the start of civil rule in mid-1901. Most threatening from his perspective was a nationalist newspaper publisher, Pascual Poblete, who formed the Partido Nacionalista to advocate independence. The party soon attracted a group of talented young writers: Lope K. Santos, Aurelio Tolentino, and Isabelo de los Reyes. Determined to curb their influence, the colonial regime subjected these nationalists to close surveillance that intensified after the Philippine Commission enacted the Sedition Law in November.[43] In March 1902 the constabulary summoned Poblete, together with ex-general Santiago Alvarez, for questioning about a rumored revival of the Katipunan, the famed secret society that had led the revolution against Spain in 1896. Poblete assured his inquisitors that since the Sedition Law had passed he had required every member of his Nacionalista Party to sign an oath of allegiance to the United States. He was also holding his followers "ready for service to the United States Government at any time, whether as soldiers or as civilians." After this interrogation these two radicals renounced even this modest challenge to the colonial state, and their nationalist party soon dissolved.[44]

Bishop Aglipay

Such raw repression could not long restrain the rising nationalist movement, forcing the constabulary to seek alternative methods, notably scandal. The critical role of petty scandal in the high colonial politics of this period becomes clear through closer study of two key cases: the use of scurrilous intelligence about Bishop Gregorio Aglipay to attack his nationalist church and the suppression of damaging revelations about Representative Manuel Quezon to assist his political career. During the first, formative decade of U.S. rule, such clandestine manipulations allowed the colonial regime to set the tenor of Philippine politics, constraining the influence of radical nationalists such as Aglipay and advancing conservative collaborators such as Quezon.

Bishop Aglipay's nationalist church traced its origins to the work of his close ally, Isabelo de los Reyes, a socialist intellectual arrested in 1902 for leading workers in a series of militant strikes. Emerging from a long trial and imprisonment, de los Reyes transferred his boundless energies to an area that should have been exempt from colonial surveillance, the establishment of a new nationalist church.

Ironically, his success would provide the constabulary with both a unique challenge and a secret victory.[45] Even at the height of his labor activism, de los Reyes had been intrigued by the idea of a national church that could liberate the nation from Catholicism, long an instrument of Spanish control. After returning from Europe in late 1901, he contacted a town mate, Gregorio Aglipay, an excommunicated Catholic priest who had been chaplain-general of the revolutionary army, "advising him to organize an independent Filipino church, arguing that that was the only way to save the dignity . . . of the Filipino clergy." Seeking support for his schism, de los Reyes met with Protestant missionaries at the American Bible Society in November, expressing fears that the Spanish friars "would probably accuse this church of being an enemy of the government." Consequently, the Methodist missionary Dr. Homer C. Stuntz arranged for de los Reyes to meet Chief Allen, who offered assurances that the "authorities would not interfere with him unless the public order was disturbed." After another year of preparatory work, Father Aglipay inaugurated the Iglesia Filipina Independiente (IFI) with a high pontifical mass on the pavement of Tondo's Paseo de Azcarraga before thousands of urban poor. Two months later at a nearby chapel twelve IFI priests and bishops laid their hands on Aglipay to consecrate him as archbishop of the new church—a sudden rupture in the unbroken line of apostolic succession dating back two millennia to Saint Peter, the first Bishop of Rome. From this humble mass the IFI grew quickly into a denomination with twenty bishops, 250 priests, and four million followers, producing an almost seismic shift in a Philippine religious landscape that had been dominated by Catholicism for over three centuries.[46]

With over a third of the population under the spiritual leadership of two radical nationalists, Chief Allen began to monitor the IFI, intervening at strategic moments to slow the growth of a church deemed threatening to colonial order. On the general's direct orders, the Information Division's superintendent, Capt. Winfield S. Grove, interviewed "various prominent residents of the Islands" to compile a detailed, damning set of "Biographical Notes" on Archbishop Aglipay, portraying him as cruel, lecherous, and power hungry. Presenting rumor as fact, the report alleged that during the revolution Aglipay had once ordered three hundred lashes for a jailed Spanish bishop to avenge humiliations he had suffered during his seminary days. Miraculously surviving this lashing, the bishop appointed Aglipay the ecclesiastical governor of his own northern diocese, a promotion Aglipay celebrated with unseemly pomp and ceremony. Armed with his new authority, he allegedly began lurking about the local convent in Vigan looking for opportunities to molest Dominican nuns and their young female charges. Later, when the U.S. Army marched north from Manila in 1899, Aglipay had cast off his cassock and, armed with baton and saber, led Filipino guerrilla forces. Succumbing at last to U.S. authority, he changed sides for a third time, courting Governor Taft by persuading his former comrades to lay down their arms.[47]

If it were released this catalog of Aglipay's alleged sins would dishonor him in all circles. To the American colony the details of Aglipay's combat role would be deeply disturbing. To U.S. missionaries, the report's charges of arrogance, lust, cruelty, and opportunism would make him seem nothing less than despicable. Many of the biography's most demeaning statements—particularly the fable about the three hundred lashes, a number that no human could survive—were so improbable that one must suspect the constabulary of distributing disinformation. Nonetheless, the report had an authoritative aura that would probably have convinced any unsuspecting American reader.[48]

As a devout Protestant and nominal Episcopalian, Chief Allen understood the legitimating force of apostolic succession and used this secret document to deny the IFI access to consecration from its most likely source, the Episcopal Church. By mid-1904 Aglipay was negotiating with the Episcopal missionary Bishop Charles H. Brent for an affiliation that would grant the IFI bishops sacral legitimacy, that is, a proper consecration with a laying on of hands by three Episcopal bishops who could trace their apostolic succession back to Saint Peter.[49] In support of this union Brent wrote a twenty-three-page report, "Religious Conditions in the Philippine Islands," criticizing the Catholic propagation of "coarse blasphemy" and tacit tolerance of its clergy's immorality, particularly concubinage, the "besetting sin of the Filipino." By contrast Brent portrayed Aglipay's IFI as a church of considerable promise that showed a surprising "cohesion," a charter with "a sane view of ecclesiastical polity, Catholic doctrine and moral living," and, above all, a massive membership "in the neighborhood of 3,000,000."[50] When this report reached Bishop Daniel S. Tuttle in New York, the Episcopal prelate pronounced it "excellent and admirable" and forwarded it to his church executive for consideration at its upcoming convention in Boston.[51]

At this critical juncture, when Aglipay seemed assured of winning the apostolic succession that would make him a real bishop, Chief Allen intervened. In July 1904, while steaming across the Indian Ocean en route to Boston, Bishop Brent, though still hopeful of a union between their churches, wrote Aglipay expressing some disappointment that his recent letters about affiliation were "too vague to justify any official action on my part." Brent also forwarded a carbon copy of his letter to Chief Allen. Apparently seeing an opening, the PC chief promptly mailed Brent "a short history of Aglipay compiled in the Division of Information." When the Episcopal bishops gathered in Boston a few months later, Brent acknowledged receipt, saying, in a markedly changed tone, "I am afraid the man is too slippery to do anything with."[52] During the Episcopalian convocation, Bishop Brent expressed his sudden hostility toward Aglipay in a hastily written confidential report, "For Bishops Only," that echoed the constabulary's biography in describing Aglipay as a "selfishly ambitious man" who would not easily "surrender any of his despotic prerogatives." Under its current leadership the IFI was, Brent concluded, such "a sham" that it was better that "the whole disaffected mass should be reabsorbed into the Roman communion than it should continue its present course."[53]

Although the circulation of the constabulary's spurious biography no doubt damaged Aglipay's relationship with the Episcopal Church, this was just one shot in a sustained attack on his schism. After four years of stunning growth that won about half the Filipino faithful, the IFI plunged into a sharp decline after 1906 due to a combination of factors: fading of the nationalist passions that had been its driving force; a court decision restoring all churches to the Catholic hierarchy; and, thanks in part to Allen's letter, the failure to secure apostolic succession. Behind a façade of impartiality, the U.S. regime was instrumental in this decline, enacting a law in 1905 that elevated such church property disputes to the local Supreme Court where the colonial justices, often responsive to political direction, ruled definitively in favor of Rome.[54] In the covert realm Allen dismissed Bishop Aglipay, in a July 1906 report to then Secretary of War Taft, as lacking in "integrity, uprightness, and intellectuality" while also describing a recent meeting with the papal nuncio, Rome's ambassador, that exemplified the constabulary's close ties to the Catholic hierarchy. "The best bureau of information and secret service the world has ever known is organized and at your service—the Church," the nuncio had proclaimed, prompting Allen to affirm their amity.[55]

For the price of a postage stamp, at a critical turning point in the IFI's history Allen was able to transform Bishop Brent from Aglipay's advocate into his implacable enemy, denying his schism the sacral authority of apostolic succession. This breach also blocked a formal affiliation with the Episcopal Church and its influential laity that could have restrained the colonial regime's alliance with the Catholic hierarchy. In this sub rosa alliance of church and state, the constabulary's secretive methods were essential to preempting any backlash in Washington, where such a policy was anathema under the U.S. Constitution. Indeed, the secrecy was so complete that Allen's role eluded both Bishop Aglipay, who continued to treat the PC chief as his protector, and later historians, who would remain unaware of the constabulary's role for another century.[56]

This success indicates that after just six years of operation the constabulary had penetrated the deepest recesses of Philippine society, even the sacral mysteries of apostolic succession. In terms of intelligence tradecraft the Information Division had moved beyond its basic mission of gathering objective information to fabricating misinformation or even disinformation. In other words it had entered the realm of psychological warfare, where the aim is not to defeat the enemy but to demoralize him to the point where he defeats himself.

Representative Quezon

Just as Chief Allen had circulated a derogatory report to discredit a religious leader who seemed to threaten the colonial order, so, just a few years later, he would suppress compromising information about a close ally of the U.S. regime. As it turned out, this was a small decision with lasting implications for Philippine politics. Titled the "Family History of M.Q.," this report, compiled by Captain Frank L. Pyle, a scouts officer attached to the Division of Military Information, began by documenting the murky origins of Representative Manuel Quezon. "A certain Padre in Baler, Tayabas had a *querida* [mistress], whom he put in a family way," reads the report's fable-like opening. "During this period he did the same thing with her sister, from whom was born M.Q." In the fifth month of the second sister's pregnancy, the "padre," who was Manuel Quezon's biological father, paid a carpenter from Manila eight hundred pesos to marry her, thus assuring that his son would be born in wedlock. By the first sister the padre also fathered Emilia, Ampara, and Aurora, "three girls M.Q. always called his cousins; they were, in fact, his half-sisters."

The captain's report offered similarly lurid allegations about Quezon's role in the revolution that many readers, Filipino or foreign, might have found unpalatable. In the first months of the Philippine-American War when insurgents ambushed a U.S. Army patrol, Quezon, then a major in General Aguinaldo's army, ordered that two American prisoners weak with fever be "buried alive," a crime for which he was later tried and acquitted before a Filipino revolutionary tribunal. An American mess boy was also wounded in the attack, but Ampara and Aurora nursed him back to health, teaching him fluent Tagalog and making him a favorite of the Quezon household. A year later, when a U.S. Army column approached Baler, Major Quezon, fearing trouble if the boy were found in his household, had him killed, "some say by head hunters, others by hired men of the family."

Once the war was over, the report continued, Quezon had relations with his half-sister Ampara and the fruit of that union "died at the age of a year and a half and is now buried in Paco cemetery, Manila." He then turned his attention to another half sister, Aurora, and she, too, became pregnant. Although he would marry her years later, at this early stage of his career he arranged an abortion "by certain old woman methods," which left Aurora dangerously weak.

After finishing law school in Manila and opening a practice in Tayabas Province, Quezon accepted a retainer of three hundred pesos from the wife of one Segundo Samonte to file a civil suit against the Church. But "Q." took five hundred pesos from the defendant to throw the case, prompting an angry Samonte to file a malpractice suit. Quezon, when he was later elected provincial governor, "had the former arrested and tried for attempted murder." Although the conviction was reversed on appeal to the Supreme Court of the Philippines, Samonte "through fear, refused further to prosecute Q."

At the bottom of the report's last page, Chief Allen added, in his own hand, a detailed paragraph that reveals his close attention to the later scandals that had marked Quezon's career. "Charged by Gov. Offley with rape," the chief wrote, referring to an official inquiry into Quezon's abuse of authority on Mindoro, and accused of "knocking down a *consejal* with the butt of a gun because he would not let him have his daughter."[57]

Since Allen never had occasion to use this dossier against Quezon—who remained, unlike Bishop Aglipay, a loyal constabulary asset—we can only speculate about why the chief carried it with him for the next quarter century, from Manila to Washington and into retirement. Clearly, secreting this report kept it ready for release should its subject transgress. It may have infused the constabulary chief with the sense of superiority essential for the exercise of colonial dominion. More disturbingly, Allen's apparent belief these sordid stories of assault, murder, rape, and incest were true indicates that Quezon's supposedly weak character may have increased his appeal to the constabulary as an ally and asset.

Despite these disturbing findings, Allen's subordinates, Harry Bandholtz and James Harbord, were determined to protect their protégé from such scandal. In March 1907, with legislative elections on the horizon, Harbord suppressed the "horrible story" that Quezon had impregnated his "cousin" Ampara since local rivals were beginning to circulate that rumor at the behest of powerful Manila politicians. Quezon seemed "genuinely horrified at the yarn," and promised to prove his innocence by sending the still slender Ampara to see Bandholtz and then murdering the source of the gossip. To avert this disaster Harbord urged Bandholtz to have the governor-general prevent the rival Federalista Party leader, Dr. T. H. Pardo de Tavera, the suspected source of this scandal, "from carrying on that kind of campaign."[58] With the rumors somehow quashed, Quezon unified local factions behind his candidacy and cultivated strategic alliances with Manila politicians to triumph in the legislative elections, leaving him well positioned to contend for leadership of the majority Nacionalista Party when the Assembly opened in October.[59]

In retrospect, Chief Allen and Colonel Bandholtz backed Quezon' s political advance confident that their secret dossiers could destroy him should he prove to be too independent. But their relations, grounded in mutual need and genuine affection, held firm. Quezon never gave his American patrons any reason to reveal what was in Allen's file. If necessary, the Americans could have brought him down in 1912 over his questionable role in the Manila Railroad scandal (see chapter 6). Quezon also knew a great deal about dubious dealings by Colonel Bandholtz since they were partners in several get-rich-quick schemes. In sum, Quezon and his constabulary patrons were so tightly bound together that secret documents were mere insurance. The greatest political impact of these secret dossiers may have been the confidence they gave Americans to enter into political alliances with Filipino leaders, wheeling and dealing in a foreign culture where they might otherwise have hesitated to venture, thereby fostering a political system that bound Filipino nationalists and American colonials in a relationship of interdependence.

Taming the Colonial Press

Just as its political maneuvers were supple, so the Information Division's analysis of Filipino politics was nuanced and its monitoring of the Manila press assiduous.[60] Staffed mostly by nationalist intellectuals, the Filipino press reveled in its newfound freedom by criticizing the personnel and policies of the colonial regime. But the civil government suffered even sharper attacks from the city's four American newspapers. Three of these—the *Manila American, Manila Freedom,* and *Cablenews*—were written and edited largely by military veterans, ardent imperialists all. The *Manila Times,* founded by the Englishman Thomas Cowan, was the sole paper without a marked promilitary bias.[61]

In the weeks before Governor Taft signed the libel and sedition laws in October 1901, press criticism of the two Filipinos on the Philippine Commission, Benito Legarda and Dr. T. H. Pardo de Tavera, reached a crescendo of vituperation. In September the editor of the Spanish satirical weekly *Miau,* Vicente Garcia Valdez, charged Pardo de Tavera with both political opportunism and personal cowardice by detailing an incident ten years earlier in which his sister had been fatally shot in Paris by her enraged husband, the famed artist Juan Luna.

> And Pardo, who was in the house, instead of defending his sister and his unfortunate mother, flees like one of those rats for which the Board of Health pays two and one-half cents . . .
>
> [The Philippine Republic] at Malolos is constituted and . . . he . . . is made Minister of State, and, as such, sits side by the side of that Luna, the slayer of his sister and mother . . .
>
> We are sorry not to be able to congratulate the American government for selecting one of such transient loyalties.[62]

With even greater venom, *Miau* published a separate attack on Commissioner Legarda, portraying him as a shameless opportunist who had risen from lowly clerk in the prosperous J. M. Tuason trading company by marrying the chief executive's widow, a woman twelve years his senior, and after she died seducing her young daughter Teresa. Complicating the tangled politics of this exposé, the paper's editor, Vicente Valdez, was the estranged husband of Maria Tuason, the alleged victim's younger sister and Commissioner Legarda's stepdaughter, making this accuser the accused's son-in-law. Whatever its motivations, *Miau* repeated the scurrilous charges against the commissioners for months. When Legarda and Pardo de Tavera finally sued under the old Spanish libel law, the *Manila Times* chided them, arguing that "their honorable name is at stake until they can give the lie to the statements of *Miau.*"[63]

After private meetings in early 1902 failed to dissuade American editors from further attacks, Acting Governor Wright launched a campaign against the city's press under the stringent libel legislation enacted the previous fall.[64] In early April *Manila Freedom* provided grounds for action with an editorial titled "A Few Hard Facts" listing a litany of complaints against the Commission, including its appointment of "Filipinos who are . . . notoriously corrupt and rascally."[65] Just three days later Wright, with the support of both Governor Taft and Secretary of War Elihu Root, ordered the attorney general to indict *Freedom*'s staff for criminal libel.[66]

Within hours the Manila Press Club telegrammed President Theodore Roosevelt complaining about the police "arresting newspaper men virtually lese majeste under sedition law for criticizing civil government." Privately, *Freedom*'s staff signaled the governor that unless the libel charges were dropped it would implicate an American commissioner, Judge Henry C. Ide, "in a nasty scandal, averring . . . he has been too intimate with Eva, the servant in the family, and that she had given him venereal disease which forced him . . . to send her back to the States." Wright shot back that this charge was "disgusting and ridiculous" because it was he, Wright, who had deported "this foolish girl" after a full investigation. He warned *Freedom*'s staff members that should they "attempt to make their threat good they may receive a dose they will never forget."[67]

Despite such pressures, the American press persisted in its lurid coverage of Commissioner Legarda's libel suit against *Miau*. Under the headline "Calls Legarda Seducer Perjurer, and Traitor," the *Manila Times* described the "sensational" courtroom drama that ensued when *Miau*'s American defense attorney, Edward H. Lamme, tried to prove the truth of his client's allegations. "As in a measured and solemn tone," the *Times* reported, the paper's lawyer "read his list of accusations, Benito Legarda paled, his black shifting eyes became as balls of fire and his whole frame shook with emotion." As the attorney finished each sentence of his spellbinding brief, Legarda's lawyer, Felipe Calderon, would "spring to his feet, a torrent of objections pouring from his lips."[68]

Although the *Manila Times* followed this dramatic description with vivid extracts from the defense brief, its editors were not charged with libel, perhaps because Taft considered it a "conservative" paper that had "done very good work for the cause of good government."[69] On the same day, however, the government's bête noir, *Manila Freedom,* though more cautious in its actual coverage, carried the same story beneath a bold headline that made it the target of new libel charges.

TRAITOR, SEDUCER AND PERJURER
Sensational Allegations against Commissioner Legarda
Made of Record and Read in English.
Spanish Reading Waived
Wife Would Have Killed Him.
Legarda Pale and Nervous

In contrast to the colorful account in the *Manila Times, Freedom* simply quoted verbatim from the defense attorney's allegations that Legarda had seduced his young stepdaughter, Teresa Eriberta Tuason. In the words of this statement, his wife, the aging Tuason heiress, "became so enraged at the lewd, lascivious and licentious conduct of her husband . . . that she made a desperate but futile attempt upon his life." During the revolution, the defense brief continued, Legarda "voluntarily took the oath of allegiance to three, separate, distinct and hostile governments within the period of eighteen months." Denying any malicious intent, its lawyer argued that *Miau* was simply informing the American and Filipino people of Legarda's "total unfitness for the official position he was then, and is now, occupying." Governor Wright saw malign motives all around and expressed them in a detailed account he prepared for Taft. Calling Lamme a "swashbuckler" who had "twice failed the bar exam," Wright accused him of delivering "a long string of libels against Legarda." Consequently, on May 23 the attorney general, on Wright's orders, filed new charges of criminal libel under Act No. 277 against *Manila Freedom*'s proprietor, Fred L. Dorr, and its editor, Edward F. O'Brien.[70]

Writing Taft in Washington, Commissioner Legarda recounted his humiliation as *Miau*'s lawyer "read to the Court before a gathering of newspapermen and scandal-mongers who had been previously advised to be present, a filthy and despicable libel . . . , calling me seducer, traitor, and perjurer." To attest to his innocence, Legarda enclosed a recent, front-page retraction from the *Manila Times,* which reported the Tuason heir's denial that "his sister had been seduced by her stepfather," explaining that "Mr. Legarda made every honorable effort to marry Miss Teresa," even visiting Rome in 1893 to petition, unsuccessfully, for a dispensation from Pope Leo XIII.[71]

A month later an angry Taft replied to Legarda, his closest friend among the Federalista leaders, assuring him that "the outrageous libels upon you by the vicious, irresponsible American press of Manila have been the source of the greatest grief to me." To punish these papers Taft had recruited a tough attorney from Michigan who would "prosecute the circulation of such a libel in such a mean contemptible way." That same day Taft wrote Wright that the Manila judge who admitted the evidence of incest against Legarda, Arthur Odlin, had "proved utterly recreant to his trust" and ordered his rustication to a provincial bench. The judge accepted his transfer without protest, and his successor proved more responsive to government wishes. "If we could only land one of these newspaper editors in Bilibid and keep him there for six months," Taft suggested, "I do not think we should have any more trouble."[72]

The government pressed its campaign on all fronts, scoring victories that pummeled the colonial press into submission. In the case against *Freedom* for libeling Legarda, the new judge handed down heavy sentences of six months' imprisonment, just as Taft had dictated. In separate charges under the tougher Sedition Law, the lower court also found the paper's staff guilty for its "Few Hard Facts" editorial. In the original *Miau* libel case Legarda appealed to the Philippine Supreme Court, which multiplied the modest penalties Judge Odlin had imposed on the editor Valdez tenfold, upping them to a heavy fine of ₱6,250 and a severe six years' banishment 250 kilometers from Manila. The high court also affirmed Valdez's conviction for libel against Commissioner Pardo de Tavera, adding four more years' banishment from Manila for a total of ten years. In all this litigation the government suffered but one modest reverse. When *Freedom*'s staff appealed its convictions, the Philippine Supreme Court, in rare defiance of the colonial executive, reversed the paper's second conviction under the Sedition Law (Act No. 292), finding that the "Hard Facts" editorial had not shown any "seditious tendency."[73]

In the wake of these tough penalties, the American colonial press became more circumspect in its coverage of the civil government, henceforth pursuing only the most vulnerable targets. While Commissioner Pardo de Tavera was too austere for further attacks, Legarda's looser lifestyle still made him fair game. In early 1903 a young woman, Tomasa Fidelino, filed a civil claim against Legarda for twenty thousand dollars, claiming that three years earlier he had entered her bedroom, "caught her by the throat," and violated "her virginity." Trusting his promises of marriage, she had agreed to "continue illicit relations" until a child was born. Although he successfully fought her damage claim all the way to the Supreme Court, Legarda admitted to making payments for both sexual liberties and paternity, sparking a sustained attack by the American colony and its press. In December the moderate *Manila Times*, invoking "inexorable principles of morality . . . as broad as civilization," called on the Philippine Commission "to rebuke the libertine and cast him from their midst."[74] But the controversy waned when Taft hailed "my very dear friend, Benito Legarda" at his farewell banquet in December 1903.[75]

In his campaign against Manila's newspapers, Governor Taft had set aside the constitutional principle of press freedom in favor of the colonial state's power to control information. By prosecuting editors for reporting adverse statements made in open court, Taft punished the press not simply for libeling a fellow commissioner but for challenging his control over information. Armed with his libel and sedition laws, Taft alone would decide who would and would not be the target of scandal. Anyone who challenged his control over information would feel the force of the courts and constabulary.

L'Affaire Bellairs

In the midst of all this pressure on Manila's colonial press, Taft singled out one reporter for a sustained vendetta that grew into the *grand scandale d'état* of America's early empire. By the time this controversy had run its course, the U.S. Senate would devote weeks to hearings that ran to a thousand printed pages, leaving the most powerful man in America dead and destroying the presidential ambitions of its greatest war hero.

Landing at San Francisco on medical leave in January 1902, Governor Taft inflamed smoldering resentments among the military and its press allies by announcing that U.S. Army forces in the islands could be reduced from the current forty thousand troops to an "ample force" of just fifteen thousand by transferring pacification to his "native constabulary." Taft's statement "provoked a great deal of adverse criticism" among officers at Philippine Division headquarters in Manila who were, according to Acting Governor Luke Wright, "inclined to adhere to their contention . . . that the only good Filipino is a dead one." Unable to criticize civil officials directly, the division commander, General Chaffee, hit back through his allies in the Manila press. As mere "echoes of military sentiments," the local papers, *Manila Freedom* and the *Manila American,* soon published editorials critical of what the latter called "Governor Taft's Mistaken Hallucination."[76] In mid-January Wright wrote Taft that the military was encouraging these virulent press attacks and buying up large numbers of *Freedom* and the *Manila American* for local distribution.[77]

A few days after Taft's troop announcement, Chief Allen forwarded to him detailed reports on the hostile press, including a front-page article in the *Manila American* blasting his promotion of Filipinos to senior posts under a hyperbolic headline that read "Blood-Thirsty Natives, Who Intimidated, Robbed and Abused the Confidence of the Government."[78] Through unnamed yet "unquestioned sources," Allen traced these inflammatory stories to the flamboyant Associated Press correspondent Capt. Edgar Bellairs, who was ringleader of "a small coterie here in Manila . . . doing everything that can possibly prejudice Civil Government." *Freedom* was "roasting" the constabulary, while the *Manila American,* the chief told Taft, was insinuating that "your mind was influenced by your tropical service." He urged Taft to use his leave in Washington to work for Bellairs's dismissal, saying it "would strike terror into this disaffected element."[79] In graver tones Wright wrote Taft that Bellairs's dispatches were meant to "produce the impression in the United States that we are sitting on a volcano liable to erupt at any moment" and to convince Congress that "a large military force must be maintained here."[80]

Gradually the civil government concluded that Bellairs was part of a plot to oust the ailing Taft as governor-general and replace him with General Wood, who was stepping down as governor-general of Cuba. From local gossip, Wright had gleaned the reporter's two-part strategy. First, Bellairs would float rumors "that General Wood is to be sent out as Governor to take charge of both civil and military affairs," and then he would promote a local victory celebration to "boost" General Chaffee as a candidate for command in Washington, clearing the way for General Wood in Manila. Livid at "the evident effect . . . in the United States" of this press coverage, Wright had summoned Bellairs to rage against his report of "the so called uprising" in nearby Rizal Province and accuse him of "magnifying trifles and sending half truths as descriptive of conditions in these Islands."[81]

Within weeks Bellairs was unmasked and undone. In response to pressure from Taft and other powerful Republicans the AP wire service finally investigated the reporter's background and finding it scandalous quietly dismissed him in March 1902. After that celebratory banquet at the Army-Navy Club, Bellairs sailed for New York in July, leaving behind twelve thousand pesos in bad debts. Clearly "humiliated at having such a man," the AP's New York chief sent carefully screened replacements to Washington for Taft's approval. He found the first, William Dinwiddie, to be "free from the prejudice which we have so often found in previous correspondents" and pronounced the next, Martin Egan, to be possessed of "fairness of spirit." For the balance of the Taft era, the AP would select Manila correspondents sympathetic to his civil government.[82]

Meanwhile, Bellairs gamely continued his public relations campaign from the nation's media hub, New York City. There, trading on his status as a former AP correspondent, he soon published an accusatory book with Scribner's, *As It Is in the Philippines,* indicting Taft, his civil government, and its press controls. Though seemingly "a smiling, courteous, suave gentleman," Governor Taft was, Bellairs charged, duplicitous, autocratic, and manipulative, with a record in Manila that compared poorly with General Wood's in Havana. Taft's Civil Commission was "rotten and corrupt," riddled with "evidences of carpetbagging and rumors of graft," while Wood had developed a "successful form of government in Cuba . . . not duplicated in the Philippines." If only "such a man as Leonard Wood will succeed Taft," Bellairs concluded, the Philippine situation might still be saved.[83] In an age when print was still the medium of politics, this book, with its prestigious Scribner's imprimatur, could have damaged Taft's presidential ambitions. In response the Ohio Republican machine mounted a sustained smear campaign against Bellairs and his backer, General Wood.

The machine's first move came in Manila in January 1903. As word of the book's charges spread, a veteran operative named Frank S. Cairns, then Manila's customs surveyor, called at constabulary headquarters to deliver the dirt on Bellairs. Cairns was the former chief of special agents for U.S. military customs in Cuba, a post that gave him a wealth of sensitive information. Although he refused to speak on the record before a stenographer, he told a tale of his years on the trail of a man known variously as "Captain E.G. Bellairs of Havana," "Mr. E.G. Bellairs of Baltimore," or "Sheridan," lately of the Florida State Penitentiary. At the close of the Spanish-American War in 1898, Bellairs had turned up in the city of Santiago de Cuba as an AP correspondent and quickly befriended the local military governor, General Wood. When Wood was promoted to governor of Cuba, Bellairs presented him to Havana society with a grand banquet at one of the city's most exclusive clubs. Through such diplomacy the reporter, his calling card now sporting an imaginary commission as "Captain E. G. Bellairs," also grew close to

General Chaffee, using his military contacts for wire-service scoops. Other reporters, perhaps envious of his access, began to spread rumors "implicating him in unnatural crimes with a Puerto Rican boy fifteen years of age." Next a "typical specimen of a Florida man" named Charles Johnson hit town. Spotting Bellairs at the Havana race track, he addressed him as "Sheridan," prompting the reply "that he was not Sheridan in Havana, but was Bellairs, and mum was the word." Johnson later told Cairns that the two had served time together at the Florida Penitentiary, he for murder and Bellairs for fraud. Bellairs had been flogged twice, once for "an unnatural crime with one of the inmates." Governor-General Wood, anxious to preserve Bellairs as an ally, ordered the story suppressed. Meanwhile, Bellairs, changing his calling card to read "E. G. Bellairs, Baltimore, Md.," shipped out of Havana as an AP correspondent with the China expedition under General Chaffee.[84]

Only days after Cairns filed this report, the constabulary delivered the document to Governor Taft to be used in a renewed vendetta against Bellairs. Outraged at "the audacity of the man in printing a book like this," Taft fired off a barrage of long letters to New York newspaper editors, citing the report from Cairns, who he described as the former "secret agent of Wood in Cuba."[85] In April 1903, two months after Taft had sought his help, William Laffan, editor of the influential New York *Sun,* published the results of the newspaper's investigation of Bellairs as a dramatic, two-part editorial attacking the reporter's book as part of a crude move to oust Governor Taft and install Wood in his place. "Who is Bellairs," the *Sun* asked, "the defamer of William H. Taft and the eulogist of Leonard Wood?"[86] To answer this question, the *Sun*'s next edition turned to another book, *Professional Criminals of America,* a bound Bertillon-like rogues' gallery illustrated with mug shots compiled by New York's former police chief, Thomas Byrnes. Bellairs, the paper said, bore a striking likeness to photo 346, identified therein as Charles Ballentine, "alias Ernest Allaine Cheiriton, forger and swindler," a clergyman's son from Norfolk County, England, who had gone from fleecing school chums at Cheltenham College to conning "the best families in England, France, Australia, and Canada." Using its global wire service, Laffan's *Sun* had tracked Bellairs across the globe, from Manila, Havana, and Tampa all the way back to his native Norwich, where he was not connected to the distinguished Bellairs family.[87] Picking up the story the next day, the New York *Evening Post* lent its prestige to the attack. "We have before us an attractive menu of a 'farewell' dinner given in Manila on July 2, 1902," it wrote in a withering exposé. "There were toasts to Bellairs in Cuba, Bellairs in China, Bellairs in the Philippines. . . . Only one was lacking—Bellairs on the chain gang in Florida."[88]

Taft was delighted with these attacks on Bellairs. "I hope that the disclosures," he wrote the War Department, "will result in driving him out of America and into some other field than that in which he has wrought so much damage for the last three or four years." Indeed, the exposés discredited Bellairs's book and dispatched its author to the Arizona Territory for new adventures. More significant, as the scandal shifted from the New York press to the U.S. Senate these editorials may have helped send Wood into an extended exile in far-off Zamboanga as military governor of Mindanao, a distinctly secondary colonial post.[89]

Nearly a year later, more reliable evidence about Bellairs surfaced during dramatic Senate hearings into General Wood's rule over Cuba, an inquiry convened by the most powerful kingmaker in America, Marcus A. Hanna, the junior senator from Ohio and chairman of the Republican National Committee. For raising McKinley to the White House in 1896, Hanna had been rewarded with control over the party's patronage appointments. After 1898, as empire opened new paths to the presidency via Havana and Manila, Senator Hanna had been careful to secure prime postings for his protégés: Havana's post office for Estes G. Rathbone, a party stalwart who had bribed Ohio legislators to win Hanna his Senate seat; and Manila's Malacañang Palace for Taft.[90]

Now, in 1903, President Roosevelt's bid to win a second star for Wood, his good friend and Taft's rival, would set the stage for a bitter confirmation battle with the ultimate prize nothing less than the American presidency. Since Roosevelt and Wood were famously former comrades in the Rough Riders, Senator Hanna's attack on the general could weaken the president in 1904 and eliminate Wood as a candidate in 1908. If empire were to raise a proconsul to the presidency in 1908, Hanna seemed determined that it should be his man Taft via Manila not his enemy Wood via Havana. When this nomination for major general reached the Senate in December 1903, Hanna turned the pro forma proceedings into a full-blown investigation of Wood's rule in Cuba that churned out over a thousand printed pages of transcript rich in seamy allegations and vehement denials. With Senator Hanna leading the attack, his longtime Ohio rival, Senator Foraker, served as Wood's impassioned defender. While these Buckeye bosses exchanged verbal shots across the committee room floor, the hearings became a political duel to the death that ended with Hanna's health broken and Wood's reputation irreparably damaged.[91]

The sordid Bellairs scandal became Senator Hanna's secret weapon in this war against General Wood. Testifying under oath, witnesses told the senators how Wood had manipulated the press, through Bellairs, in his extraordinary eighteen-month ascent from army surgeon to governor-general of Cuba. Assisted by Bellairs, Wood solicited hagiographic coverage of his rule over Santiago de Cuba and encouraged criticism of his superior, General John R. Brooke, the military governor of the island. Writing in 1899 in *McClure's* magazine, the famed muckraker Ray Stannard Baker celebrated Wood's transformation of Santiago from "reeking filth" into a "clean, healthy, orderly city." Baker also collaborated with Wood in placing an article in the *North American Review* that condemned General Brooke's rule in Cuba as a "record of error and neglect."[92] After Wood succeeded the hapless Brooke in late 1899, Bellairs, now the AP's Cuba correspondent, acted as the new governor's main booster. "In the year 1908 Leonard A. Wood will be elected president of the United States," he announced at a luncheon for the visiting secretary of war, "and I will put him there. You know what I have done for him in the past; mark my words and watch the future." Governor Wood, Hanna's witnesses revealed, had repaid these political debts with interest. When Bellairs ran into his old cellmate Johnson in May 1900, the governor sent an intermediary to offer the ex-convict hush money and a free ticket home. Four months later, when the *Havana Post*'s editor, Dr. C. L. Fisher, told Wood that Bellairs had engaged in "sodomy" with two Cuban boys and served a prison term in Florida, the governor insisted that the paper suppress the story. Wood later called personally at AP's New York headquarters to scotch these rumors as "stories . . . evolved by known convicts."[93]

In testimony before the Senate, AP's general manager, Melville Stone, explained the reason for his sudden dismissal of Bellairs in March 1902. He stated that Secretary of War Elihu Root had called him to the War Department "very much incensed at the obvious attempt on the part of Bellairs to build up the glory of the Army at the expense of the civil government of the Philippines." Not long after that meeting, Stone was "very much startled" to receive a letter from Senator Hanna himself forwarding a "personal, confidential letter" from a Florida correspondent alleging that Bellairs was "an ex-convict." Disturbed by this news, Stone headed downtown to the Pinkerton Detective Agency at 57 Broadway in lower Manhattan. There Robert A. Pinkerton personally escorted the AP chief into his agency's confidential "records room" where the clerks needed only "a moment" to identify Bellairs as a notorious forger who had once used the alias Cheiriton.[94]

Only fate saved General Wood from a humiliating Senate defeat in his bid for a second star. President Roosevelt, seeing his own prestige at stake in the attacks on Wood, threw the full weight of his office behind the promotion to major general. These high-pressure hearings exhausted Hanna, who in the words of Senator Foraker suffered "great anxiety during the progress of the investigation," which "no doubt did much to precipitate his last illness." Hanna died in early 1904 just before the final vote reached the Senate floor, allowing Wood's confirmation by a comfortable majority.[95]

Although they had failed to stop Wood's promotion, the dexterous use of scandal by Hanna and Taft derailed Bellairs's journalistic career and damaged, perhaps fatally, Wood's presidential ambitions. "I think that Dr. Wood's . . . spurious medals," Mark Twain wrote mockingly of Wood's nomination as major general, "and furtive insubordinations, and clandestine libels, and frank falsehoods, and pimpings for gambling hells, and destitution of honor and dignity . . . have earned it for him and entitled him to it, and that he ought now to be lifted to that lofty summit and permanently left there, . . . for the laughter of a thousand generations!" Before the start of this contentious confirmation process in mid-1903, President Roosevelt sent Wood off to a secondary posting as a regional governor in the southern Philippines, a marked demotion. Even after the Senate approved his second star, the scandals kept Wood on the remote colonial frontier not for the six-month tour the president had planned but for a six-year exile that did not end until well after the 1908 presidential elections. Meanwhile, Governor Taft would return to Washington to become secretary of war in 1904 and the Republican presidential candidate in 1908.[96]

These Senate hearings also help us to place Taft in the context of his times, making his passionate hatred of Bellairs seem understandable, even logical. Flimflam artists like Bellairs, who flitted across oceans and continents with a trail of bad paper and broken lives, seem to have been the raison d'être for Bertillon's biometrics, the Pinkerton record room, and the larger system of criminal identification that Taft and his Victorian peers were building worldwide. Taft the proconsul had good reason to despise and destroy Bellairs, but Taft the leader in a society of laws had no firm basis for his original allegations against an AP reporter whose only verifiable crime had been criticism.

Secret Service Intrigues

After the Manila press had been constrained within Taft's tight strictures, the government's undercover operations continued unabated, making incriminating information vital to many colonial careers. It seems to have been no accident that three of the most avid practitioners of scandal learned their dark craft in colonial customs houses, the gateway through which all mail passed, even the most confidential correspondence. Manila's was a cesspit of corruption, swirling with what the *Manila Times* called "rumors of scandals and irregularities."[97]

In the aftermath of the Bellairs-Wood controversy of 1903–4, Taft, now promoted to secretary of war and well-positioned for the presidency, retained the Manila customs surveyor Frank Cairns to conduct private investigations "of a confidential character," charging him to probe for scandal about his enemies and preempt any about himself. To serve his powerful patron Cairns moved tirelessly across the arc of America's empire, from Manila to New York and Havana, filing confidential reports at every stop. At Manila in 1905, Cairns investigated petty "graft" in procurements by army officers, compiling a list for Taft of persons implicated in this "crookedness," including "generals Chaffee, Humphrey, and Corbin."[98] When Cairns visited New York on home leave in June 1906, Taft asked him to investigate "the author of certain articles which have appeared during the past few weeks in the *New York Daily News*, signed by one W.A. Lewis." Indeed, this tabloid had just published a three-part series beneath the headlines "Dictator Taft and the Scandal of the Benguet Road" and "Taft Gave the Philippine Railroad into Trust Hands." As he later wrote to Taft, Cairns, "pretending to be a disgruntled employee of the Philippines, and without revealing my identity," interviewed the offending editor at his home on 930 West End Avenue. There Lewis had freely admitted that his aim was "to discredit your administration as Governor." Although the *Daily News* editor would not name his source, Cairns emerged "quite satisfied that Mr. Herbert Ross, lately of Manila, whose record I sent you through Captain [Frank] McIntyre [of the War Department], is in part responsible for these attacks."[99] En route to Manila a few months later, Cairns passed through Havana to report on the "repressive and coercive measures," marked by assassination and terror, that the corrupt Moderate Party had used to win the last Cuban election.[100]

By January 1907 Cairns was back in his post as Manila's customs surveyor where he soon was locked in mortal combat with a combine led by his old enemy General Wood, now commander of the Philippine Division of the army, and a longtime local rival, acting customs chief H. B. McCoy. As Cairns explained in a letter to Taft, Wood still felt an "implacable hatred" because of his "connection . . . to the Bellairs investigation."[101] In pursuit of his quarry, the general had forged a working alliance with McCoy, who was now competing with Cairns to succeed the outgoing customs chief, W. Morgan Shuster.[102]

As this bureaucratic vendetta continued, acting customs chief McCoy ordered his secret service to investigate Cairns for possible charges of stealing letters from the mail. Going beyond the usual shoe leather surveillance, the customs security chief deployed some inspired innovations, assigning an agent to compact himself in a cabinet inside Cairns's office to eavesdrop, later emerging to record conversations in sworn affidavits. To secure the combination to Cairns's office safe, another operative drilled a small hole in the ceiling and, suspended from a specially constructed catwalk, used binoculars to peer for hours on end until the target finally turned the tumbler. With the safe's combination secured, agents removed Cairns's private letters for photographic copying.[103] Secret agents thus used human assets to effect the equivalent of audio and visual surveillance, which would not become technologically feasible for another quarter century.

Over the next fourteen months these intrigues culminated in two trials with a typically colonial brew of intrigue, scandal, and purloined letters. In the first trial two of McCoy's secret agents were found guilty of fraud in connection with the theft of confidential documents from the safe in Cairns's office. At the second McCoy was convicted for his role in this same fraud. But before anyone spent a day in prison, all three conspirators were granted full pardons by their patron and protector, Governor-General James Smith. Bitter over the outcome, Morgan Shuster, now a member of the Philippine Commission, encouraged his Filipino allies in the opposition Progresista Party to pass "a resolution condemning the Governor-General for having pardoned McCoy," a move that may have damaged Shuster more than his enemy.[104]

After his inauguration in March 1909, President Taft overlooked Colonel McCoy's criminal conviction and rewarded his years of partisan loyalty with a permanent appointment to the top customs post. Within days McCoy packed

Cairns off to the provinces as customs collector in Iloilo City.[105] Higher on the colonial hierarchy, McCoy's ally, W. Cameron Forbes, bested Shuster in their protracted competition for promotion to governor-general. Apart from his maladroit maneuvers in the Customs House litigation, Shuster was tied to the fading Federalista/Progresista party boss, T. H. Pardo de Tavera, while Forbes had allied himself with leaders of the rising Nacionalista Party, Sergio Osmeña and Manuel Quezon.[106] Most important, the incumbent secretary of war, former governor-general Luke Wright, still nursed a "grudge against Shuster" from an earlier controversy over constabulary operations in Cavite. Now, with president-elect Taft's support, Wright forced Shuster off the commission in January 1909. With his rival eliminated, Forbes became acting governor-general in May, the first step toward a permanent appointment six months later.[107]

Despite their defeat, Shuster and Cairns were by no means amateur players in these imperial intrigues. Though momentarily eclipsed, Shuster returned to his native Washington, DC, where he worked for two years as a lawyer and lobbyist until President Taft was "delighted" to back his appointment as treasurer general of the Persian empire. After overthrowing Shah Mohammad Ali Qajar, whom Shuster called "the most perverted, cowardly, and vice-sodden monster that had disgraced the throne of Persia," the new parliament and its middle-class liberals apparently hoped that a neutral American could bring fiscal reforms to extricate Persia from a British-Russian imperium. With broad powers from the parliament, Shuster picked three protégés from the Philippine Customs House for senior treasury posts in Tehran, including the irrepressible Frank Cairns, who was appointed chief tax collector for an empire of eleven million people.[108]

During their year in Persia, this American contingent plunged into a form of power politics far more ruthless than anything Havana or Manila could offer. On his arrival in Tehran in May 1911, Shuster saw himself as the defender of Persia's recent "bloodless revolution," which had imposed "constitutional forms" on the "centuries-old absolutism of the Persian Monarchs." To lay the fiscal foundations for a modern state, Shuster formed a Treasury Gendarmerie of fifteen thousand troops to collect taxes from recalcitrant provinces. But his attempt to appoint a British attaché, Maj. C. B. Stokes, as its commander precipitated a crisis with Russia, which was jealous of its exclusive sphere of influence in the country's north. Trying the media manipulation so effective in Manila, Shuster wrote the London *Times* denouncing Russia's "hostility to the regeneration of Persia." Rather than endorsing Shuster's views, the British press reacted with skepticism, even hostility. In December Russia demanded the American's ouster, backing its ultimatum by sending thousands of Cossacks across the border to attack two northern cities and advance on Tehran while attempting to assassinate Shuster with several bombs.[109]

After weeks spent as a virtual prisoner inside his lavish Tehran estate, Shuster, now abandoned by both London and Washington, resigned his post and caught a steamer across the Caspian Sea, leaving Cairns to wrap up their mission's work with "his thirteen American associates." Landing at New York to a hero's welcome in early 1912, Shuster spoke to a cheering crowd of two thousand at Carnegie Hall and later published a memoir to laudatory American reviews. The Persian government rejected Cairns as Shuster's successor, and after a few months he left for Manila with his small entourage of American gendarmes, ending this Yankee imperial interlude.[110]

Conclusion

In retrospect the principals in these relentless intrigues—Cairns and McCoy, Shuster and Forbes—were colonials who used scandal in the cutthroat competition for position and power. Yet there was something distinctly American about the way they played the press in these imperial intrigues. Their use of media exposés may have been common to colonial politics in Manila and Washington, but it proved disastrous in London and Saint Petersburg, as Shuster found to his peril. Even as Shuster's press statements prompted British censure and Russian outrage, they also aroused American adulation and brought him home a hero. For there was in this brief Persian adventure and the more protracted Philippine colonization a distinctive strain of American idealism, an aspiration for the democratic transformation of these subject societies mocked abroad yet deeply admired at home.

This same American synthesis of press and politics had its seamier side in the use of scandal to destroy reputations and severe colonial laws to suppress dissent. Through legal restraints and police pressure, the U.S. colonial regime shaped the character of Philippine politics and political culture. By the time Taft left Manila in late 1903, his regime had influenced the formation of key Filipino institutions—church, press, and political parties—that were the seedbeds of social change. In the first decade of colonial rule, prosecutions and sedulous media manipulation curbed the feisty Manila press, leaving just a few independent papers, notably *El Renacimiento* and the *Philippines Free Press*.[111] In 1907 Taft's colonial protégé, the secretary of commerce and police W. Cameron Forbes, noted in his diary that "the newspaper situation is much better in hand. Each month some black-leg is weeded out, and we shall have a respectable news service some day." When Taft moved on to the White House two years later, Forbes added that Martin Egan, Bellairs's successor as AP correspondent and now editor of the *Manila Times*, was "close to the President, with whom he is great friends," enjoying open access to the Oval Office during home visits.[112]

In the first ten years of U.S. rule, 1898 to 1907, the colonial regime redirected the country's political trajectory from confrontation to collaboration, from revolutionary mobilization to electoral participation, and from nationalist idealism to material realism. Such sudden change was necessarily a multifaceted colonial project requiring every available means from attraction to coercion. To court support the U.S. regime offered Filipino nationalists access to policy formation, legislative oversight, and judicial authority. As this emerging Filipino political elite closed ranks with American colonials in a joint nation-building effort after 1907, they also collaborated in curtailing resistance by irreconcilable nationalists, ardent revolutionaries, and messianic peasant rebels. Severe laws enforced by the colonial courts silenced dissent; military forces rounded up the rebels and disarmed the countryside, denying Filipinos any means of armed resistance; and a ubiquitous secret police wrapped the society in surveillance, monitoring elite loyalties and stifling political dissent. In this complex process of political change, reform and repression were inextricably intertwined.

That said, one should be cautious, in this focus on colonial police, about privileging state authority, about assuming imperial omnipotence of the sort that strips the subjugated society of agency, of its ability to shape its own destiny. On balance, this police system may have had a more profound impact on American colonial politics and metropolitan policies than it did on their seemingly powerless Filipino subjects.

To study secret police operations is to enter a house of mental mirrors. As their omnipresent police apparatus infiltrated Philippine society, American colonials amassed files on their Filipino subjects rich in the most intimate details. But the possession and even the release of confidential information takes us into a maze of image and illusion, perception and deception. Possessing such information about Filipinos, even if it was never used, no doubt empowered American colonials to maneuver with magisterial authority, advancing native clients and conceding them power and position confident in the knowledge that they had weapons to destroy their creations. But was this sense of empowerment illusory? While scandals about fiscal or sexual delinquency would have been devastating in late Victorian America, Filipinos moved in a colonized society where scurrilous information in the form of rumor and gossip could be both retailed and discounted.

As this first, formative decade of U.S. colonial rule drew to a close, the constabulary shifted its focus from controlling the elite to containing lower class dissidence. Starting in 1905 and continuing for nearly a decade, the second phase in the constabulary's history was focused on paramilitary pacification of the countryside, both lowland messianic peasants and highland tribes, as well as sub rosa penetration of the city slums, breaking militant unions, mutual aid societies, and radical conspiracies. While Philippine elections extended from the municipal in 1901 to the legislative in 1907, the colonial regime and its constabulary moved beyond shaping the broad structure of political parties and focused instead on the individuals who were forming a new political elite. As we will see in the next two chapters, the constabulary's clandestine operations would play a seminal role in shaping the character of the country's politics, crushing armed resistance, curbing radical conspiracies, and advancing conservative allies.

4

Paramilitary Pacification

ON MARCH 16, 1905, General Henry T. Allen, chief of the Philippines Constabulary, paused during combat against peasant rebels in the central Philippines to record an angry entry in his private diary. For the past three months he had been leading his troops along Samar Island's muddy trails, which were booby-trapped with spike-filled pits and deadly spring spears. Hacking their way up steep ridges and hiking through trackless terrain pushed his men to exhaustion. Then without warning, hundreds of Filipino *pulajan* fanatics would erupt from the underbrush to charge through constabulary rifle volleys. In the hand-to-hand fighting that followed, Allen's men were using their rifle butts to fend off the short, razor-sharp native swords called bolos. This same morning the general had visited a field hospital where one of his lieutenants was recuperating from a bolo charge that killed thirteen of his soldiers. Surprisingly, Allen's anger this day was directed not at these Filipino rebels but at Stanley Portal Hyatt, an English reporter for the *Manila Times.*

"The last numbers of the Manila papers just received," Chief Allen dictated to his aide on the banks of the remote Catubig River, "contain articles . . . antagonistic to the Constabulary" and tending "to prejudice the public against the officers and men." He closed with an intimation of the criminal charges he would soon file against the Manila press: "In some instances, a wholesale perversion of the truth of affairs has resulted in statements so near the libel mark that it is hard to discern the dividing line."[1]

Even while he was steaming upriver into this heavily forested interior, Allen's eye was on Manila. The enemies he dreamed of defeating were not the province's illiterate peasants but the capital's politicians, reporters, and editors—a political sensibility that reflects the centrality of the constabulary in U.S. colonial rule. Indeed, this force was the core of the colonial state. Formed hastily for pacification in 1901, this paramilitary police apparatus included, at its peak in 1905, a central intelligence office, a transport unit with 172 wagons, a fleet of 65 boats, a medical service with 10 hospitals, 230 police posts staffed by 7,300 troops, and a network of 400 telegraph and telephone offices sending 1.7 million messages annually over 4,200 miles of copper wire. Its diverse duties, which one officer called "analogous to [those of] the Indian Civil Service," included administration of tribal territories, supervision of municipal police, surveillance of elite politicians, law enforcement, and rural pacification.[2]

Through these diverse missions, this police force soon came to symbolize the colonial state and its political legitimacy for both Americans and Filipinos. Even as the constabulary's botched counterinsurgency in Samar shook the confidence of the colony's American community, allegations about its abuses in Cavite Province that same year angered Filipinos and sparked the first serious legitimation crisis for U.S. colonial rule. Coverage of the Samar campaign in Manila's American press no doubt enraged Chief Allen. But it was the exposés of constabulary excesses in Cavite published by Filipino newspapers that served as the catalyst for major political change.

Despite Allen's confrontational stance, the U.S. pacification of the Philippines would ultimately rest on the regime's relations with Filipino political elites, first through alliances with a few wealthy, well-educated Manileños and later through the cultivation of rising provincial politicians. In its early years the U.S. regime tried to rule by co-opting the small Spanish mestizo elite in the capital while crushing mass resistance in the countryside. Between 1902 and 1904, the colonial state and its constabulary forced rural Filipinos into crowded "reconcentration" camps, including 451,000 peasants relocated on Luzon and Samar, over 10 percent of the population of those islands.[3] During these same years the constabulary also waged its own informal war on municipal officials in insurgent provinces just south of the capital, producing abuses that outraged Manila's middle-class intelligentsia. After Washington relaxed its punitive policy in 1906 and broadened Filipino participation via provincial and legislative elections, the constabulary allied with Manila intelligentsia and provincial politicians to pacify most rural revolts within a year, in the process forging a political entente with Filipino elites that lasted to the end of U.S. rule. Whether antagonism or alliance, the constabulary's relations with Filipino leaders were thus critical to the success of U.S. colonial rule. Ending these widespread revolts was impossible without the collaboration of Filipino elites, and these leaders would not cooperate unless colonial coercion yielded to political concessions. In the largest sense, therefore, the structure of Philippine society, with its tight, reciprocal ties between elite and mass, forced an unintended fusion of democratization and pacification in U.S. colonial policy. Even the most visible hallmarks of U.S. rule, provincial and legislative elections, were shaped by the imperatives of colonial policing.

Though quick to recognize the value of alliances with wealthy, well-educated Manileños, U.S. officials were slower to appreciate how much damage constabulary excesses in insurgent provinces could inflict on the regime's standing with these influential leaders back in the capital. It took a press campaign and a public relations crisis in 1905 to force the issue and thereby transform U.S. colonial policy. By broadening Filipino participation via legislative elections and emphasizing nation building over military operations, the U.S. regime reaped immediate benefits when its Filipino allies reciprocated by furnishing the support critical in crushing a series of messianic peasant uprisings.

Thus, after trial and costly error American colonials learned that military success rested not on raw coercion but on a supple cooperation with the country's established and emerging political leadership. Indeed, Chief Allen's continuing reliance on paramilitary repression despite growing Filipino political authority made the constabulary the catalyst for a major crisis of legitimacy in 1905–6, forcing a shake-up in the government and its police. Simultaneously, younger constabulary officers, with long service in the provinces where they interacted with and learned from Filipinos, were developing an alternative strategy that balanced politics and pacification. After Allen and his allies were cashiered, Harry Bandholtz, Rafael Crame, and James Harbord assumed command and, understanding that capital and countryside were intertwined, quickly moved the constabulary from antagonism to alliance with Filipino political leaders.

Pacifying Manila

In the intense political conflict that marked the early years of U.S. rule, the constabulary's aptly named Information Division tracked radical nationalists in Manila and nearby provinces, using the colonial courts to jail any deemed subversive. Although most guerrillas had surrendered by July 1902, revolutionary ideals remained strong among both the elite and the masses. Poor workers and rich landowners were, as the wealthy Manila lawyer Felipe Calderon told the Philippine Commission, "weary of the state of anarchy." But Manila also had an intermediate element "made up of clerks and writers, who have the habit of stirring up the town" and "do not want peace under any circumstances because . . . they also have these wrong impressions of Americans."[4] In the war's uneasy aftermath, Manila, from a police perspective, had all the elements for a revival of armed resistance: a militant working class, a fiery local press, radical intellectuals, and charismatic speakers who could rouse the crowds.

To contain this ferment the PC Information Division combined U.S. Army intelligence protocols with innovative secret police methods to conduct a relentless surveillance. Working with the Metropolitan Police, the constabulary watched the homes of suspected radicals. The clerks and analysts of its Information Division also monitored the local press, studying articles translated from

Spanish and Tagalog for signs of subversion. Through its network of secret Filipino agents, the division penetrated nationalist groups and planted spies at the sides of their leaders.

Such espionage helped shape the character of an emerging Filipino political leadership. In the capital's narrow political circles of 1902–3, with just three or four staff persons to manage Filipino political parties and leading newspapers, we can only imagine the full impact of some two hundred paid Filipino spies, circulating incessantly about this small city monitoring and manipulating.[5] With their identities concealed by numeric codes, it is possible that many of the agitators at any Manila meeting were spies maneuvering for both popular leadership and PC rewards. Even more speculatively, prominent leaders on the constabulary's payroll may have used its cash and protection as a cover for nationalist agitation antithetical to American aims. Such possibilities will remain hypothetical until a list of code numbers and their corresponding names surfaces. Despite their many limitations, these covert operations succeeded in containing and then crippling the radical left, advancing collaborating elites and shifting the center of political gravity from militant nationalism to patronage politics.

Among Manila's many agitators, Gen. Artemio Ricarte remained the Information Division's top target for over a decade, the object of intense surveillance for his untiring efforts to arouse a mass uprising. While commanding Manila's underground during the revolution, Ricarte had been captured and exiled to Guam. After his release in early 1903, he refused to take a loyalty oath to America and was deported to Hong Kong where he reestablished the revolutionary government-in-exile. As his agitators began moving throughout Manila to form a new secret society called the Third Zone, the Information Division was able to insert "four spies acting as officers" in his organization.[6]

After slipping into Manila aboard a steamer in December 1903, Ricarte moved about the capital region meeting secretly with nationalist leaders to spark an armed revolt. But Governor William Taft's concessions had already won wide support from prominent Filipinos, and his most likely allies—Gen. Emilio Aguinaldo, Dr. Dominador Gomez, and Isabelo de los Reyes—saw no reason to rebel. Although the playwright Aurelio Tolentino thought his plans for a rebellion with bamboo lances were "absurd," he agreed to join Ricarte, and the two tried, without success, to organize armed resistance in the nearby hills of the Bataan Peninsula. By May 1904 Ricarte, isolated and hungry, had come down from the mountains and worked as a court clerk until he was betrayed to the constabulary. With ample intelligence from its spies, the constabulary soon arrested forty-two of his followers. During his interrogation by the colony's secret service chiefs, the general proved surprisingly cooperative and gave them a detailed confession. Convicted of subversion, he would spend the next six years in solitary confinement.[7]

In this tense political climate, even Filipinos who advocated independence by legal means were also subject to surveillance. With the onset of civil government in July 1901, a half dozen new political parties and a dozen newspapers suddenly appeared in Manila. Ranging from the radical Partido Nacionalista to the reactionary Partido Federal, each claimed a handful of educated leaders, nationalist aims, a Spanish-language newspaper, and a following that narrowed as the party program moved to the right. Still threatened by the specter of revolution, the colonial state and its constabulary struggled to control any manifestation, harassing the radical nationalists, monitoring the moderates, and cultivating the conservatives.

The regime soon attacked the radicals with the full force of law and police, starting with the indomitable Dr. Gomez. Through his infectious charisma and spellbinding oratory, Gomez aroused deep loyalty among Manila's workers, who elected him to every available office, and bitter antipathy from colonial Americans, who were determined to destroy him by every possible means. As a tireless organizer, he expanded the city's main union, revived the Nacionalista Party in July 1902, and launched a militant newspaper, *Los Obreros*. Within months, however, the courts and constabulary moved against him, sentencing him to four years' imprisonment for forming an illegal association, a decision eventually overturned on appeal. Ground down by relentless prosecution, Gomez eventually capitulated and worked with the constabulary in 1906 to negotiate the surrender of the very outlaws he had once been accused of aiding. A year later he won a seat in the National Assembly representing Manila.[8] Indicative of the constabulary's success in restraining this fiery radical within colonial confines, Col. Harry Bandholtz recommended that "it would pay to keep him in our employ" even though he was "a deep-dyed villain."[9]

Samar Campaign

While civil officials struggled to control politics in Manila, the constabulary was equally challenged in pacifying the provinces, producing a resonance between order in capital and countryside. The limitations of this reliance on raw force was most evident on remote Samar Island where messianic pulajan rebels used terrain and tenacity to evade capture, creating a colonial crisis that would soon peak in the harsh pacification of Cavite Province just south of Manila.

Starting in mid-1904, the small pulajan bands swelled into a mass movement along Samar's northeast coast when a new leader, an educated nationalist named Andres Villasis, known locally as "Dagohob" (thunder), became the first to fight with a real strategy. Combining the fervent pulajan faith with revolutionary terror, this "very shrewd individual" burned whole towns and forced their populations into the island's interior. There, as Chief Allen reported, he "soon made himself master of that region by reason of his cruelties, his arms, and his power of organization." Carrying older single-shot Springfield rifles without bayonets, Allen's constables were helpless against the hard-charging pulajan who could erupt suddenly from the brush swinging razor-sharp bolos.[10] After hundreds of bolomen slaughtered twenty scouts soldiers in November and massacred forty-seven more in December, Allen landed on Samar to find the island in crisis with towns burned, villages empty, and fields abandoned.[11]

Allen soon discovered that his main enemy was geography. Samar was a wilderness of dense forests and rugged mountains. The rebels had lined the island's few trails with lethal traps and snares: sharp bamboo spikes (*carang-carang*) concealed in the grass to puncture a soldier's boot; deep, spear-spiked pits (*liong*) hidden beneath hemp leaves; and sprung saplings (*balatic*) triggered by vines and laced with sharp stakes that could cut a man in half. As the troops wound their way up the steep slopes, rebel sentries sounded conch shells or beat hollow logs, sending a signal three or four miles to allow their comrades ample time to escape.[12] Using this terrain and its impassable trails to his advantage, Dagohob proved adept at shifting his force of some eight hundred followers back and forth across the mountains to elude the U.S. forces.[13] From January to March 1905, Allen led three combat patrols that plunged blindly into the island's vast interior for endless days of arduous hiking spiked with a few unpredictable minutes of hand-to-hand combat.[14]

In the midst of this campaign, the constabulary suffered a humiliating defeat. In late March Capt. William Green and scouts lieutenant Emil Speth led their column on an all-night march from Catubig on the north coast to surprise the main pulajan camp on a hilltop at Bongon. As the troops approached up a steep trail, Dagohob unleashed a lethal counterattack. Pulajan riflemen rained volleys from prepared positions. At their bugle's sound, the firing ceased and bolomen surged out of the jungle in a ferocious charge from both sides that split the constabulary column, sending the separated detachments fleeing in panic. As the soldiers straggled out of the jungle with their wounded, rumors about the constabulary's flight under fire reached regular army officers, feeding what Allen called "the well known antagonism of the army toward the organization."[15]

In a bold effort to save his failing campaign, Chief Allen joined Capt. Cary I. Crockett, a descendant of the famed American frontiersman, to lead another column of 115 men up the Gamay River and into the jungles of the Maslog mountains. Without warning, the rebels erupted from the dense foliage, firing a few shots and charging the column's left flank, swinging their bolos with "fanatical courage." One of those shots went right through Crockett's forearm, forcing him to fall back firing. "I therefore got into it with both feet," Allen later wrote Governor Wright, "and I might add with my pumping Winchester also. This effective short range weapon brought down three most gaudily bedecked pulajans, of whom two were officers."[16] A week later Allen emerged from the Gandara Valley, which he called "the cradle of *pulajanism,*" to report that the rebels were "surrendering in great numbers" and the revolt had been contained.[17]

The capital's press did not share his optimism. In March the *Manila Times* carried dispatches from a British adventurer, Stanley Hyatt, under headlines such as "Constabulary Reported Beleaguered in Maslog" and commentary demanding a "Military Governor for Samar." In his concluding report on March 16, Hyatt complained that "the civil government has not the machinery to deal with the revolt" and recommended army rule to end the "curse" of divided civil-military authority. Although Hyatt wrote these dispatches after weeks of hacking through the jungle with Captain Crockett, Allen dismissed them as unreliable.[18]

In the end the reporter's judgment proved sounder than the chief's. After three exhausting months, the constabulary found that "the continuous strain of the campaign had proved too much."[19] When the pulajan mounted a devastating attack on a PC stockade in mid-May, Governor Wright, clearly losing confidence in his constabulary chief, cabled Allen questioning his reports of "pulajan disintegration" and urging that Samar be turned over to the military.[20] From PC headquarters in Manila, the assistant chief, Col. William S. Scott, telegrammed Allen that Samar had "given the Constabulary a black eye" in the press and strained its resources to the breaking point, making it advisable to transfer operations to the army's "unlimited troops."[21]

Under such pressure Chief Allen capitulated. In a May 25 cable to Governor Wright, he relinquished troubled eastern Samar to the army and added, almost spitefully, that they would soon "learn that capturing . . . criminal bands in Samar . . . is more difficult than criticism."[22] But just ten days later army troops surprised the main pulajan camp, killing Dagohob and ninety-three followers, a stunning victory that had "an immediate effect upon the whole region" by returning villagers to government control. With a certain smugness, the Philippine Division's commander, Gen. Henry C. Corbin, claimed Samar "demonstrates that the Constabulary organization is not suitable for extensive punitive expeditions" and should not be used in future campaigns, criticism that soon reverberated in Manila's American press.[23]

Other American journalists chimed in, amplifying the concerns raised in Hyatt's dispatches. The *Army and Navy Journal* of New York, noting that Samar had "become extremely serious," branded the constabulary a "failure" and urged its abolition.[24] A few days later, *Cablenews,* quoting a telegram from the army's regional commander, reported that "the Constabulary had fled before the Pulajanes at Magtaon" on Samar. As Hyatt would later recall, the "plucky" American press had succeeded in making the constabulary and its Samar policy "the laughing stock of Manila."[25]

Cavite Controversy

Still seething from colonial press coverage of his disastrous Samar campaign, Chief Allen returned to Manila where he found the constabulary under even sharper attack by Filipino nationalist newspapers. These two press communities had different, even diametric politics. The Filipino editors, many of them former revolutionaries, were still fighting for independence, whereas the Americans, mostly U.S. Army veterans, favored a restoration of military rule. While the American papers' call for army intervention on Samar implicitly endorsed a punitive approach to pacification, it was the severity of the abuses in Cavite and Batangas provinces on Luzon that drew even sharper criticism from the Filipino press. Led by officers detailed from the army, the constabulary patrolled Luzon's countryside like an occupation force and persisted in the merciless tactics used at the peak of the Philippine-American War—burning crops, maltreating civilians, and torturing suspects. When these methods began to target local elites, the result was a crisis that would challenge the legitimacy of the colonial state and ultimately force the U.S. regime to change its political strategy in the Philippines.

For nearly a decade, 1896 to 1905, a succession of Spanish and American campaigns had failed to pacify the mountainous provinces south of Manila, making this region the heart of the Philippine revolution. When the U.S. Army first marched into Cavite and Batangas in early 1900, it faced "the cream of the rebel army" and a hostile population that "precluded the formation of a spy and scout system"—circumstances that encouraged a recourse to brute force.[26] When the constabulary joined these operations, it took a cue from the army and used the same severe tactics. In November 1901 Chief Allen wrote President Theodore Roosevelt that the punitive Sedition Law should be followed by a "vigorous campaign" in Batangas "until we are complete masters, and one and all of the Philipinos [*sic*] recognize themselves not merely as surrendered but as whipped."[27] The army's commander, Gen. Adna Chaffee, similarly vowed to "bring under surveillance a large proportion of the inhabitants."[28] In practice this uncompromising rhetoric soon translated into torture, including the notorious "water cure" and other extreme measures that according to one officer produced "a deep hatred toward us."[29] In February 1903, however, U.S. civil officials on the Philippine Commission, concerned about Filipino reaction to such repression, passed Act No. 619, which imposed heavy penalties on any constabulary officer "who whips, maltreats, abuses, subjects to physical violences, or tortures by the so-called 'water cure' or otherwise, any native of the Philippine Islands."[30]

Although the army's six-month campaign of fire and sword across Batangas forced the surrender of the last revolutionary general in 1902, just two years later there was a resurgence of guerrilla resistance. South of the capital in these same rugged mountains, Macario Sakay, a former revolutionary officer, proclaimed himself "Supreme President of the Tagalog Isles." Invoking the revolution's rhetoric, Sakay mobilized hundreds of guerrillas by awarding lofty titles to local leaders who combined banditry with resistance. After several months of low-level guerrilla operations, the rebels assaulted the scouts barracks at Laguna in November 1904 and a constabulary post in Parañaque a month later. This latter raid was particularly dramatic, with Cornelio Felizardo, a former revolutionary captain, leading seventy-five guerrillas in a surprise attack just after dark, making off with seventeen firearms and over a thousand rounds of ammunition.[31]

As the insurgency intensified, colonial Manila responded with aggressive tactics, flooding the region with 2,300 constabulary, nearly a third of its forces, and 1,800 scouts.[32] The newly arrived secretary of police, W. Cameron Forbes, "tipped backward in his swivel chair, . . . in his hands a map of Cavite," while PC officers, as one colorfully recalled, explained that this small province, just twenty-five miles square, "could easily be divided by roads, rivers, and ridges into checker board squares; a detachment of twenty constabulary men could be placed in each to comb its cañons and bivouac its bushes, and that within thirty days, certainly within ninety, the work in hand would be finished." Consequently, in September 1904 the constabulary divided Cavite into seventeen operational districts for sweeps by fifty-man detachments.[33]

Simultaneously, the PC's Information Division expanded its "secret service bureau" at Imus, Cavite, under Lt. Rafael Crame, issuing orders that field officers deliver all prisoners who "can be utilized in obtaining information by confessions." With methods deemed "intelligent, conservative, and thorough," Crame released captured *ladrones* (bandits), "as spies to hunt for other ladrones." These spies also proved useful during "dragnet performances" when troops would "round up the male inhabitants of certain barrios and have these ex-ladrones . . . identify any of their former companions." In one such exercise near San Francisco de Malabon, Capt. R. B. Kavanagh observed as fifteen hundred residents "were corraled" and then "required to pass in review" as "our judge eyed them closely," picking out fourteen for trial as subversives. "The ex-governor of the province, the justice of the peace, and the *presidente* walked by," the captain was pleased to report, "with hat in hand as humbly as the 'rice paddy *tao*.'" In a society with a refined sense of status, such humiliation of proud leaders carried a high price. Although the captain believed that the rebel bands had "largely been broken up," the aggrieved Cavite political elite was withholding their cooperation and the revolt was steadily spreading.[34] By October rising resentment led to the murder and mutilation of eight constabulary secret agents, 10 percent of the Information Division, including a Detective Ponce, who was knifed and shot; agent Juan Figueroa, body burned; and agent Alejandro de Jesus, hanged in a Cavite barrio.[35]

In January 1905 hundreds of rebels marched into the town of Taal in Batangas, disarming local police, seizing fifteen thousand pesos from its treasury, and fleeing with twenty-five rifles. The constabulary, increasingly suspicious of local leaders, arrested all the municipal officials and charged them with sedition. Just two weeks later some three hundred guerrillas, disguised as constables and aided by "some prominent men of the province," attacked the town of San Francisco de Malabon, hoping to capture the provincial governor, Mariano Trias, who was working closely with the constabulary. When he jumped out of a window and hid in the river, the rebels kidnapped his family. During three weeks of captivity, they serially raped his wife in the presence of her children and broke her ribs with a rifle butt.[36] Chief Allen wrote Taft that "the leading politicos of Cavite . . . had connived with the ladrones and induced them to attack Malabon for the purpose of literally destroying Trias," now reviled by radicals who were desperate to derail his chances for reelection.[37]

The constabulary met elite resistance with relentless repression. To free the military from legal restraints, Governor Wright suspended habeas corpus in late January 1905 and created a militarized Provisional District for the four affected provinces, moves the *Manila Cablenews* hailed as imperative, dismissing possible hardships as mere "inconvenience or annoyance." Armed with these broad powers, Col. David Baker, the constabulary's leading advocate of the mailed fist, led both PC constables and scout regulars in an unrestrained pacification campaign that combined combat patrols with an untenable social strategy.[38] In Baker's analysis of southern Tagalog society, a group of landed oligarchs called *principales* controlled these four provinces and backed the bandit groups "for their own protection, profit, or both." To gain the "cooperation of these *principales,*" the colonel launched "a campaign of education," hoping to gain accurate local intelligence and "do away with a secret service against which there were many complaints."[39] This perceptive yet prejudiced sociology launched the colonel on a fateful confrontation with the Cavite elite.

To implement his plans, Colonel Baker flooded the district with three thousand troops, including fifty Bontoc constables from the north and fifty Muslims from the south who excelled in tracking Christian Filipinos.[40] After a month of mixed success, he decided that extreme measures were required. "Ladronism must cease," the colonel declared flatly in early March, ordering the "reconcentration" of the population of the Provisional District. In areas suspected of harboring rebels, constabulary troops herded rural residents into concentration camps and unleashed terror to discourage contact with the guerrillas. Observers estimated that a third of the population of Cavite and Batangas was hastily relocated inside military cordons and another third was "partially relocated." Whole towns were deserted, and Cavite Province became "a green desert."[41]

Although he admitted that reconcentration "sounds awful," Secretary Forbes felt that it was "the best thing . . . to handle certain situations here" and praised Colonel Baker for taking what he called "active measures."[42] Governor Wright defended the tactics as humane, claiming that the soldiers had allowed people to bring "food supplies of every sort, together with their cattle and household property." The constabulary's policy, he argued, denied outlaws food, protected prominent citizens, and encouraged residents to provide information. Under these pressures, he claimed, "larger bands began to disintegrate."[43]

When the rebels still refused to surrender, Colonel Baker applied his social theory about the root causes of the revolt by arresting prominent landlords and local officials. In April the colonel inadvertently created a cause célèbre by detaining a wealthy Batangas planter, Pedro A. Roxas, on charges of rebellion. At the trial, the family's plantation manager, Francisco Olivas, retracted a sworn statement about Roxas's alleged contact with the rebels, claiming that it "was extorted by the constabulary under torture." This testimony was, said Forbes, "the foundation of a good deal of that torture talk which those who don't like our being here lap up so greedily and repeat."[44]

The constabulary's coercive methods finally broke the revolt. By June 1905 the last major guerrilla group had surrendered with just nineteen men left, finally completing the pacification of Batangas. A month later the Philippine Scouts withdrew from the special zone, leaving the constabulary to mop up.[45] Colonel Baker reported that his campaign had captured 518 firearms and 422 rebels were killed, captured, or surrendered.[46]

With rebel bands reduced to a handful of fighters, the constabulary shifted from combat to covert operations in pursuit of the few leaders who had fled to the hills beyond Batangas. After taking command of this constabulary district in late 1905, Colonel Bandholtz, convinced that regular patrols were too cumbersome, applied his distinctive mix of political attraction and covert penetration. By courting the Filipino governors, the colonel soon won control of all their secret operational funds for what he called a "nasty campaign" to contain and then destroy the rebel leadership.[47]

In 1905 these covert operations scored what at first report seemed to be a stunning success against the Cavite rebel Cornelio Felizardo, who had become a prize second only to Sakay himself. For nearly three years Lieutenant Crame's Subdivision of Information at Imus had been pursuing this guerrilla leader by watching his cousin and protector Mariano Noriel, a former revolutionary general who was now an influential cacique in the town of Bacoor. On the well-founded theory that their power was intertwined—with the cacique protecting the rebel's "haunts near Bacoor" and the rebel's reputation for "revenge" empowering the cacique—Crame filed three criminal cases against Noriel. But Noriel commanded a loyal local following and the prosecutions all failed.[48] Then, in September 1905, a PC patrol was in hot pursuit of the rebel chief through Cavite's rugged ravines when, according to a banner headline in the *Manila Times*, "Felizardo Leaps 300 Feet to His Death." Reveling in this triumph, Col. David Baker and the head of the constabulary's Information Division, Maj. William Baker, identified the mangled body as Felizardo's.[49]

But this breakthrough soon proved to be a major bungle. In February 1906, five months after Felizardo's supposed death, a PC spy named Gregorio de Guia, a bitter rival of the cacique Noriel, "informed the Constabulary that Felizardo . . . was hidden in the barrios of Bacoor under the protection of Noriel." Acting on this intelligence, Colonel Bandholtz, working through the provincial governor, recruited a PC private who had served under the rebel chief during the revolution and was now willing to "either capture or kill Felizardo." After an elaborate charade to feign desertion, two troopers, Bernardino Carpio and Gregorio Buendia, made contact with the guerrilla leader. At his camp they soon persuaded Felizardo of their sincerity and urged him to attack their garrison, Camp Hayson, to capture arms and kill its commander. When Felizardo paused to urinate during a reconnaissance of the camp, the two attacked him from behind, hacking his neck with a bolo so forcefully that it was nearly severed. After identification of the body by both Crame and Bandholtz, the constabulary, determined to convince a skeptical public, distributed photos of Felizardo's naked corpse to the press.[50]

Other successes soon followed. In April the rebel leader Leon Villafuerte surrendered to Colonel Bandholtz with information that led to the arrest of Sakay's chief Manila agent, Melencio Makapugay, just three days later.[51] In mid-June the colonel used these covert methods to bag Sakay himself. Using the impending legislative elections as a "club" to win cooperation, Bandholtz told politicians from the affected area that "unless Bandolerismo [banditry] was extinct in Cavite and Batangas those provinces would undoubtedly be cut off from representation in the assembly and the assembly jeopardized." In a controversial move, the colonel recruited "the most influential native in the Islands today," Dr. Dominador Gomez, to persuade Sakay to surrender on the promise of a fair trial. After eluding countless PC patrols for over four years, Sakay and five of his followers now walked off a lake steamer and into the constabulary's Manila headquarters. From Washington, Secretary of War Taft sent a celebratory telegram, published on page one of the *Manila Times*, crediting this success to "the persistence and skill of Harry H. Bandholtz." With supreme confidence, the colonel then released Sakay to bring in his remaining followers, a task the rebel chief accomplished in just a month. At their trial Sakay and his commanders tried to plead not guilty. But Captain Crame's evidence was compelling and Dr. Gomez denied making any promises of amnesty, forcing them to plead guilty in hopes of leniency. In the end all were convicted and executed, the culmination of an exemplary campaign that marked Bandholtz as the progenitor of a new politico-military strategy for the constabulary based on close collaboration with local leaders.[52]

As the pacification campaign scored gains throughout 1905, the severity of the American violence alienated many Filipino politicians, who instead of celebrating these successes began to charge the constabulary with abuse, sparking a serious political crisis. With the strong support of his superiors, Wright and Forbes, Colonel Baker had been relentless in pursuit of the rebels and brutal in his treatment of prisoners.[53] With his punitive policy toward the Cavite principales, the colonel had angered landholders and local officials who had close ties to prominent Manileños through proximity and kinship. "Rich residents of Manila are buzzing like a hornet's nest," Police Secretary Forbes noted in April, adding dismissively, "They can't understand why wealth does not give men immunity to do anything."[54]

By the time this crisis erupted in mid-1905, Filipino political leaders were already chafing from seven years of militarized colonial administration. American veterans filled the ranks of the civil regime, staffing its police, courts, and executive bureaus. Compounding the problem, Governor Taft's cordiality had given way, after his departure in late 1903, to Governor Luke Wright's aloof, even racist administration. Instead of welcoming prominent Filipinos to Malacañang Palace as Taft had done, Wright found allies among the Manila Americans who populated the racially exclusive Army-Navy Club.[55] In such a tinder-dry political climate, the constabulary's brutal Cavite pacification soon sparked a clash between American and Filipino leaders.

In March 1905 Dr. T. H. Pardo de Tavera, a Federalista Party leader with family ties to Cavite, wrote Secretary Taft in Washington that "abuses committed by certain officers of the Constabulary . . . have become intolerable and have created enormous feelings of hostility." But Wright insisted that Colonel Baker and his officers "are men of the highest character and would not for a moment . . . tolerate any abuse." At meetings of the Philippine Commission in May, Pardo de Tavera, the leading Filipino member, objected when the governor expressed his "utmost confidence" in the constabulary, insisting that "some of its members merited my most profound contempt."[56] Another Filipino commissioner, Benito Legarda, also wrote Wright protesting the "police methods, the secrecy observed, and the lengthy detention." But the governor replied that the revolt had left the constabulary no choice but to use "reconcentration with its consequent hardship and suffering" and to employ secret agents in a way that "carries with it the possibility of abuse."[57]

Crisis of Legitimacy

Almost from the start of the Cavite campaign, the nationalist newspaper *El Renacimiento* had featured emotive exposés of constabulary brutality, stoking outrage among educated Manileños. After the rebels raided Taal in January 1905, the paper reported that many of the town's "distinguished persons" had been taken by PC's secret service "in the middle of the night without the knowledge of their families." The municipal president was fined two thousand pesos for allegedly aiding the rebels while his vice president and police chief were sentenced to eighteen months' imprisonment.[58] "How can anyone defend," the paper wrote angrily in May 1905, referring to PC troopers, "a sergeant who shoots an elderly man in San Francisco de Malabon; a Strong who strangled the president of Santa Rosa; . . . a Ramos who ordered a witness whipped; . . . a Sims who violated the honor of a married woman in Montalban?"[59]

Then on June 7 *El Renacimiento* published a front-page exposé accusing the constabulary command of systematic cruelty in the municipality of Bacoor, Cavite. "Business is paralyzed," a reporter wrote after visiting the town. "The country people cannot till their lands in view of the fact that Colonel Baker and Inspector [Lorenzo] Ramos consider the well-to-do as persons of suspicion in the pueblo and compel them to take to the field in search of [the rebel] Felizardo." When one Nicolas Gonzales refused, these officers beat and tied him tightly "elbow to elbow" as he cried out, pleading, "Don't maltreat me; I am a man, not an animal." When another of Bacoor's leading citizens, Felix Cuenca, ventured into the bush and brought back just one prisoner instead of the expected thirteen, "Baker became furious" and threw Cuenca into "their pig sty" prison where he slept "in the midst of decaying matter, among human excrement." Poor peasants were reconcentrated on a barren shore, scrounging mollusks from the sea and sleeping "mixed together in motley heaps, men, women, and children exposed night and day to the inclemency of the weather." Smitten by a local beauty in town on her wedding day, Lieutenant Ramos threw her groom in jail and "took the young woman for himself."[60]

Just two days later the *Manila Times* reported that PC headquarters was, in fact, investigating this now notorious Lieutenant Ramos for torturing a Batangas barrio chief, allegedly applying a burning ember "to his stomach, his groin and other portions of his body." In its front-page coverage, the paper noted that the lieutenant had faced many similar complaints of "cruelty and torture," adding in an editorial that "compulsion in the form of physical violence" was standard practice in constabulary interrogations and many officers "take what might be called a professional pride in the form of coercion or torture they impose."[61]

Three weeks later Colonel Baker, calling *El Renacimiento*'s reportage "bitter and reckless," counterattacked by filing charges of criminal libel against the paper's three editors to give "constabulary officers a chance to defend themselves." On June 23 Manila police arrested editor Fernando Guerrero, publisher Martin Ocampo, and writer Lope K. Santos and arraigned them before Judge John C. Sweeney. In the recital of facts, the colonel called the paper's articles "most cunningly contrived lies."[62] In support of this action, Chief Allen wrote a brother officer, almost smugly, that "action is being taken against 'El Renacimiento' for its numerous libelous articles, and undoubtedly 'La Democracia' will enjoy the same treatment."[63]

The trial was high political drama, arguably the most significant litigation in the forty years of U.S. colonial rule, attracting three months of close coverage in the Manila press. Since the Libel Law placed the burden of proof on the accused, most of July and August were devoted to corroborating the paper's reports of constabulary abuses, sensational allegations that were repeated on page one of every Manila newspaper beneath banner headlines. Much of the trial revolved around events in Bacoor, both internment in its reconcentration camps and interrogations conducted during the hunt for the rebel leader Felizardo. One former prisoner, Francisco Garcia, for example, recounted how Lieutenant Ramos had dripped hot candle wax into his eyes during one of these interrogations.

In one of the trial's high points, ex-president Emilio Aguinaldo recalled how he was summoned before Colonel Baker at Bacoor and threatened when he refused to assist in the capture of Felizardo. A prominent resident, Luis Landas, described how Lieutenant Ramos threw him in jail when he failed to return from the bush with any rebels and there witnessed a PC corporal kicking a bound prisoner.[64]

In late August the prosecution presented its witnesses to rebut the defense's sensational allegations. The most persuasive evidence came from Capt. Rafael Crame of the Information Division who testified that from the time he arrived in 1902 Bacoor had been a hotbed of rebel sympathizers. Insurgent chief Felizardo rode freely through the town's main streets, attending cockfights under the protection of the municipal police.[65] In defense of Colonel Baker's extreme measures, the assistant prosecutor, Jesse George, argued, "There is such a thing as a whole community being responsible for the existence of an outlaw and I want to say that Bacoor is responsible for . . . Felizardo." In his summation chief prosecutor Charles A. Smith added that the court's failure to convict would reflect badly on both Colonel Baker and Captain Crame.[66]

At midpoint in the trial, Taft, now secretary of war, returned to Manila with a delegation of U.S. congressmen, a coincidence that inserted these proceedings into a larger process of political change. A few days in the city convinced James Leroy, a colonial scholar with the party, that Filipinos had "genuine grievances," and that the "fundamental cause of the entire trouble" was the rising "race prejudice" of Manila Americans. During a breakfast meeting at the Metropole Hotel between Filipino provincial governors and American congressmen, Manila's mayor, Arsenio Cruz Herrera, ruptured colonial protocol with a stinging attack on Governor-General Wright for constabulary abuses in Cavite, adding pointedly that the governor "did not sympathize with Filipinos" and "considered them an inferior race." The mayor had, he said, accepted U.S. sovereignty "because he believed it was for the best interests of the Filipinos." But he now doubted "the wisdom of ever ceasing the hopeless struggle" for independence. Amid a storm of outrage from the local American press, the mayor resigned on September 18.[67]

Gradually, Filipino nationalists began to win this political showdown in the courts, on the commission, and even in the constabulary. On the eve of Taft's arrival, Chief Allen drew up a thirty-page force review attributing the "libelous, false, and almost seditious" press criticism of the constabulary to Manila politicians trying to stir up the "incitable masses" and create disturbances that "will disgust America in its philanthropic Oriental experiment to the point of renouncing it." But, sensing change in the wind, Allen did a quick about-face after Taft's departure on August 31, writing his American officers that "the military phase of our work [will] be less pronounced" and henceforth "your first consideration" is to convince Filipino officials that the constabulary is "a loyal and actually interested element of Civil Government." After a mass firing of fifty-two officers in mid-1905, Allen tried to replace them with "university men . . . with more solid training" than the usual military school graduates he had been recruiting.[68] The general also admitted that the use of secret agents had "done great harm," and he ordered that "armed *secretos* should be sent out only with the greatest of care." These words were the precursor to a major purge.[69]

Just days after issuing these orders, Chief Allen sailed homeward for nine months' vacation furlough, leaving Colonel Baker as acting chief to implement these changes, which began with a reduction in force from seven thousand to five thousand troops. In November PC headquarters dismissed all thirty officers in the Information Division, now tainted by the Cavite campaign and the indictment of their comrade, Lieutenant Ramos. In a parallel action Baker removed the military eagle from constabulary epaulets and adopted uniforms that resembled the less martial style of the Manila police. The number of scouts companies serving with the constabulary dropped from thirty-one in mid-1905 to just one a year later. By May of 1906, Colonel Harbord could report that he had drilled his Second District subordinates through "inquiry and admonition" in the idea that they should cultivate "friendly relations, social and official, with the Filipino people." The few officers who "failed to see the dawning light" had been dismissed.[70]

To promote long-term change, the constabulary also established a service academy to train its officers for their new civil mission. One of the commanders in the Cavite campaign, Col. W. S. Scott, felt that it was no longer enough for officers to "handle his men and shoot," but they now needed "sufficient education" for the "far more varied and delicate duties" of assisting Filipinos "to become good citizens."[71] To "weed out . . . men not adapted to the service," in mid-September the Philippine Commission required that all PC officers attend a training course focused specifically on "the duties of peace officers, the laws with reference to crime . . . , the rules of evidence, and other procedures in the lower courts." All American trainees would study both Spanish and "one of the native dialects."[72] Within a year, two classes of forty-two officers had completed the required three-month course.[73]

The political climate had changed during the long libel trial, and the courts, once reliable instruments of colonial repression, began to show greater independence. In January 1906 a judge sentenced Lieutenant Ramos, the focus of *El Renacimiento*'s torture charges, to a year's imprisonment for killing a prisoner who was leading him to the rebel Felizardo. Then, in February, Manileños crowded the court for the long-awaited decision in the *El Renacimiento* case. "All of the allegations [in] the articles complained of are clearly proven by the witnesses of the defense," ruled Judge Manuel Araullo, exonerating editor Fernando Guerrero and reporter Lope K. Santos. The judge praised the paper for upholding "the sacred duty of the press to correct abuses and secure good government" and condemned the constabulary for its brutality. When he finished his five-hour reading of the entire decision, the Filipino crowd erupted with euphoria, launching a sustained celebration of their victory over Governor Wright and his constabulary. Even the jingoistic *Cablenews* conceded that Judge Araullo "went by the evidence," chided the government for letting the constabulary "run wild," and called for reforms to restore its "moral fiber." This "sensational outcome," said the conservative *Manila Times,* had a chastening effect on the American colony, leading many to admit that repression and press censorship had been "a mistake."[74]

To regain legitimacy in the eyes of its Filipino subjects, Washington was forced to remove all the colonial officials tainted by the crisis and then, over the longer term, to share power with the Filipino elite. Responding to the *Renacimiento* decision, Secretary of War Taft started a slow purge in March 1906 by removing Governor Wright and assigning him to a lesser post as ambassador to Japan. Apart from his role in this controversy, Taft faulted Wright for being "so contemptuous of Tavera, Legarda, and those old friends of ours" and for that "inborn lack of confidence that a Southerner has in a race of any different color."[75] In October the *Manila Times* reported the dismissal of Colonel Baker and his two ranking constabulary officers. Saddened, Secretary Forbes noted in his journal that Baker "nearly killed himself," adding that "it's all a pro-Filipino doctrine now." By the following May, Chief Allen had been sent home at the reduced rank of major to lead mounted patrols around Yellowstone National Park, making a clean sweep of those responsible for the constabulary's Cavite campaign.[76] All his civilian superiors—Taft, Wright, and Forbes—replied to his request for references with blunt criticism.[77]

In his study of this period, the historian Peter W. Stanley found that the constabulary abuses in Cavite had created a major crisis of legitimacy, alienating the educated Manila politicians who had formed the Federalista Party and begun to accept American rule. To the Federalista leader Pardo de Tavera, the "Constabulary was behaving like the Guardia Civil," unleashing a "centripetal press of forces" like those that had driven the revolution against Spain.[78] Setting a pattern for later legitimation crises, police abuse linked to the chief executive could and did become a virtual lightning rod for broader public dissatisfaction. The resolution of such a serious crisis required not just reform but a broadening of political participation.

Cultivating Political Allies

The constabulary's new leaders, Colonel Bandholtz, a regular army officer, and Captain Crame, a Spanish mestizo, were selected for their ability to work effectively with Filipino politicians. In reporting the first of these changes, the hyperpatriotic *Manila American* noted the "striking comparison" in the Cavite campaign, "where Major Baker failed [and] Captain Crame succeeded in the very essential feat of retaining the esteem of the people." As a "square, frank, level" officer and an "*ilustrado* among his race . . . knowing those with whom he deals,"

Crame, the paper opined, was the ideal choice to head the Information Division.[79] Even the ousted Colonel Baker, writing to congratulate Bandholtz on his promotion to PC chief, said that it was fortunate that the force, with the new Philippine Assembly in the offing, had "at its head one so conversant with and skillful in dealing with natives as yourself."[80] Indeed, Secretary Forbes told Bandholtz that he had been chosen because he had "learned how to deal with the Filipino people, how to win their confidence." Instead of punishing Filipinos under the harsh penal code, Forbes said the constabulary's new mission would be to support the shift "to a modern and civilized system with equal rights to all."[81]

Chief Bandholtz, in turn, began promoting officers who showed a flair for cooperation and reprimanding any who complained about Filipinos.[82] More broadly, Bandholtz started a long-term shift from military pacification to civil policing that in a few months would relieve all scouts companies from service with the civil government.[83] These reforms soon restored the constabulary's rapport with the Filipino leaders. "When I was here more than two years ago," Secretary Taft wrote after a visit in late 1907, complaints against the constabulary "were numerous, emphatic and bitter." Now he was happy to report that "there is a thorough spirit of cooperation between the . . . men of the Constabulary and the local authorities."[84] Indeed, Chief Bandholtz was, Secretary Forbes told Taft, being "very severe in weeding out undesirable officers" to make sure that "the whole organization now understands the absolute necessity of harmonious relations with local officials."[85]

Like the constabulary itself, Bandholtz had learned the imperative of close political collaboration, almost by accident, from his first days in the Philippines. In 1901 a young Major Bandholtz had been assigned to Tayabas as an army intelligence officer and there confronted the challenge of pacifying the province's rugged Pacific coast. While Gen. J. Franklin Bell's seven thousand troops were cutting a fiery swath across nearby Batangas in pursuit of a guerrilla general, Bandholtz captured one of his rebel captains with a small detachment of local volunteers. "All the Filipinos who accompanied me did excellent work," Bandholtz explained, "and it would have been impossible to succeed without them."[86] With fluent Spanish and keen political instincts, the major soon grew close to local officials, becoming convinced that a policy of attraction would win over the guerrillas. Indicative of his success, the province's municipal councilors elected him as their governor in 1902, a post in which he served for a year before resigning to accept a constabulary commission.[87]

These mountains and their messianic traditions provided a test for Governor Bandholtz's emerging strategy of using Filipino leaders for pacification. In mid-1902 a former revolutionary soldier named Ruperto Rios ascended sacred Mount Cristobal to proclaim himself "King of the Philippines," promising that once independence was won "there would be no more labor, no taxes, no jails, and no constabulary." Believing Rios a "direct descendant of God," some two hundred peasants armed with rifles and bolos attacked the town of Laguimanoc in September. Instead of using regular forces, Bandholtz mobilized his municipal police and village militia to support the constabulary, an effort that soon drove Rios into neighboring Laguna where he was captured in March. Five months later this would-be king was tried in Tayabas at Bandholtz's behest and hung before a crowd in his hometown of Antimonan.[88]

After joining the constabulary as commander of this region in April 1903, Colonel Bandholtz applied this same strategy to an uprising farther down the Pacific coast. In Albay Province a former revolutionary major, Simeon Ola, had been driven into the hills "by the persecutions of . . . municipal officials" and there attracted nearly a thousand peasant followers. On taking command of the operation in June, Bandholtz found elite support critical to his strategy of reconcentrating some 150,000 peasants across the province. Several weeks after the reconcentrations commenced in June, the colonel invited Commissioner Pardo de Tavera for a tour, producing "a marked difference in the attitude of the more influential people." Finally, in September Bandholtz worked through the municipal mayor of Guinobatan to arrange General Ola's surrender, thus ending the revolt with a minimum of bloodshed on both sides.[89]

With these same keen political sensibilities, Colonel Bandholtz realized that long-term stability required close alliances with the rising generation of Filipino politicians. When a young lawyer named Manuel Quezon returned home to Tayabas in 1903, Bandholtz recognized his talents and, in Quezon's words, "immediately befriended me." As a former revolutionary officer, Quezon recalled: "[I was] proud of the fact that I knew nothing of English," had not yet "reconciled to American regime," and thought its Filipino collaborators "contemptible." Over the next two years, the colonel opened his home to the ambitious young Filipino, gave him his first English lessons, and backed his appointment as provincial prosecutor, or *fiscal,* first in Mindoro and then in Tayabas. "Despite his faults," Bandholtz later said of Quezon, "I love the little rascal and know he likes me."[90]

As the provincial prosecutor for Tayabas, Quezon won national notice when he indicted Francis J. Berry, the publisher of the influential *Manila American,* for fraudulent land transactions and won a conviction before an American judge, Paul W. Linebarger. In the words of Quezon's biographer, the judge's "sincerity" did much to change the young lawyer's "anti-American feelings." After Bandholtz moved on to command the constabulary's First District at Manila, his successor in Tayabas, Colonel Harbord, formed an even closer friendship with Quezon and backed his successful campaign for provincial governor in 1906. "I must say no American in those early days . . . gave me a better idea of American manhood than the then Colonel Harbord," Quezon later wrote.[91]

If we are to believe Quezon's own celebratory account, constabulary officers, through their inspiring example, persuaded this young Filipino nationalist of America's altruism and launched him on a path to the Philippine presidency. In confidential documents and diaries, however, Quezon's relationship with the U.S. surveillance state and its agents appears more complex and corrupting. To promote Quezon's political career, Bandholtz, Harbord, and other American patrons used their influence to shield their protégé from rumors of abduction, assault, and witness tampering even though Chief Allen apparently believed the allegations credible. To spare Quezon from financial pressures, Bandholtz also gave him interest-free personal loans and made him a partner in two disastrous ventures, the Baler Hemp Company and the Polillo Coal Company, the latter a carbon El Dorado that eventually collapsed with heavy losses for all.[92] Undeterred, Bandholtz likewise concocted the ill-fated Baler Hemp plantation in Quezon's hometown, leaving the Filipino leader with a loss of ten thousand pesos and a potential scandal over the unpaid wages handled by his half brother, Teodorico Molina.[93]

After the new Philippine Assembly convened in August 1907, all of these investments in Quezon's future repaid handsome political dividends, allowing the constabulary continuing influence when the legislature emerged as a coequal branch of the colonial government. All tax and budgetary legislation now required the Philippine Assembly's approval. When Manila nationalists began agitating for Filipinization of the constabulary in mid-1907, Bandholtz, as acting chief, silenced the Filipino papers by calling in political debts from Fernando Guerrero at *El Renacimiento,* Macario Adriatico at *La Independencia,* and Dr. Pardo de Tavera at *La Democracia*. "I also got Quezon up here," Bandholtz wrote Allen, "and for a few moments they are quiet again." Even before the Assembly convened, Quezon and his Nacionalista Party ally Sergio Osmeña assured Bandholtz that "no radical propositions will emanate from them." Throughout the legislature's first session, these two, as speaker and majority whip, blocked any debate over "immediate independence," first by gagging and then expelling the radical Dr. Gomez.[94] As Colonel Harbord noted during the 1908 deliberations over the constabulary's budget, the Assembly "cut us very badly for political effect," but the commission "would not stand for it" and defaulted to the 1907 appropriation, which left the force "in better shape today than ever before."[95] Once the colonial regime invested the legislature with fiscal control, it was clear that the constabulary and the colonial government had to reach a modus vivendi with legislators such as Quezon.

By late 1909, when Quezon left for Washington as Philippine resident commissioner, the highest office then open to a Filipino, American officials viewed him as a useful but problematic ally. Although possessed of "the most brilliant mind of any Filipino," Quezon had, Governor-General W. Cameron Forbes told President Taft, a deeply flawed personality. As *fiscal* of Mindoro he had been "extremely loose morally" in his relations with women and more recently, in Paris for the Navigation Congress "was foolish with money and extravagant in his dissipation." Even so, Quezon "has really been, without exception the most useful man to the Government. . . . He was head and shoulders the leader on the floor of the Assembly, and was my agent for getting everything through which I set out for."[96] With similar ambiguity, Chief Bandholtz described him as "one of the best assets of the Government" and a "loyal friend" who nonetheless "is volatile and needs watching."[97] The colonial police, recognizing both his brilliance and his unstable temperament, played to Quezon's strengths by assisting his rapid ascent, but also played on his weaknesses to keep him within bounds.

Messianic Movements

In the aftermath of the Cavite controversy, the constabulary reforms and the broadening of political participation produced a reconciliation with the Filipino politicians that had measurable results, helping, almost immediately, to quash a series of peasant messianic revolts that had defied the constabulary for nearly five years. In their mix of folk religion and populist nationalism, these magically endowed, messianic leaders had an astonishing capacity to mobilize hundreds, sometimes thousands of bolo-wielding peasants to rush with surprising courage into the constabulary's fusillades. When reinforced by scouts regulars, constables could grind down these peasant rebels with sheer force. But winning the support of Filipino politicians proved far more effective. If properly cultivated, these legislators and local officials could provide accurate intelligence, mobilize militia, and negotiate surrenders—effecting pacification with a surprising economy of blood and treasure.

In the twelve months before the Assembly opened, these essentially political tactics, exemplified by the collaboration between Colonel Bandholtz and Dr. Gomez that had brought about Sakay's surrender, were replicated in operations that swept the last guerrillas from Luzon's Pacific coast. In July 1906 the famed rebel Pataleon Villafuerte, who had been hiding in the extreme north of Tayabas Province since the end of the Philippine-American War, suddenly surfaced to raid the town of Palanan. Governor Quezon joined Maj. Peter Borseth's constabulary forces in an operation that "succeeded in killing Villafuerte and capturing all his followers with their arms." A year later, the governor again worked with the PC, this time joining Colonel Harbord to break up a "religious-military organization," the Ejército Libertador Nacional, that had been active in the hills above the town of Antimonan for nearly three years.[98] After steaming down the coast at night in a darkened launch, the colonel's detachment surprised the guerrillas' sleeping camp at 1:00 a.m., flushing them "like a flock of quail" and capturing several leaders. When Harbord decided to release these prisoners to bring in their leaders, Quezon "did the talking and made the bloody threats of what would be done to them and their relatives if the thing did not result well." Moving on to Antimonan proper, Governor Quezon fired the town officials and called a mass meeting to explain "how they were hurting their own people . . . and not

Americans" by supporting the guerrillas. By May 1907 this extraordinary alliance had effected the capture or surrender of nineteen rebel leaders.[99]

Across a broad swath of the Visayan Islands from Negros to Leyte, the constabulary sought similar alliances with local leaders to defuse another wave of messianic revolts. Eager to court colonial support, provincial politicians worked effectively with constabulary to encourage the surrender of these peasant rebels. In the steep, treeless hills of Cebu Island, the formidable Tabal brothers, Anatolio and Quintin, led some five thousand followers in a successful guerrilla campaign until mid-1906 when they decided to surrender after meeting with Governor Sergio Osmeña, whom the constabulary praised as "untiring in his efforts for peace."[100] Even though the largest and longest of these revolts had ravaged the sugar districts of Negros Island for over a decade, the rebels agreed to surrender in August 1907 after the constabulary enlisted the help of a local mayor, Gil Montilla, whose family had once employed the revolt's leader "Papa Isio."[101]

By contrast, in the eastern Visayas, particularly on Samar Island, where poor local economies denied municipal officials effective control, the U.S. regime was forced to rely on brute force in breaking these messianic revolts.[102] On Leyte Island, the constabulary enjoyed support from relatively affluent elites in the coastal trading towns and was able to contain the local pulajan movement more easily than on Samar. After several years of fitful insurgency, a sharp rise in rebel strength in 1905 inflicted heavy casualties on the constabulary, including fourteen constables hacked to death in an encounter with some two hundred bolomen in July.[103] Gradually, however, combined constabulary and army patrols backed by five thousand "volunteers" mobilized from Leyte's coastal towns forced the rebels out of the hills where they could be more readily tracked and killed. Finally, in June 1907 these forces captured Faustino Albin—a "famous leader," known as "Papa Faustino"—a blow that broke the Leyte revolt.[104] By contrast, on Samar, where local leaders had little influence with the pulajan rebels in the hills, the constabulary pursued the island's surviving leader, Otoy, for another four years. A patrol killed him in November 1911, eliminating the last messianic leader in the central Philippines.[105]

By late 1907 the removal of the region's top rebels—the Tabal brothers on Cebu, Papa Isio on Negros, and Papa Faustino on Leyte—had brought peace "throughout the Visayas." With the exception of insurgent pockets in Samar and Central Luzon, conditions across the archipelago were, General Bandholtz reported, "the very best in my recollection."[106] Although the revolts sprang from diverse causes and persisted for up to eleven years, all ended with a surprising simultaneity between July 1906 and July 1907, just in time for the first Assembly elections on July 30. Clearly, the political accommodation with Filipino elites, exemplified by the provincial and legislative elections, was central to the pacification of half a dozen disparate regions. Above all, effective colonial policing required collaboration between constabulary officers and local officials. Men such as Quezon,

Osmeña, and Bandholtz, who grasped this new imperative, rose to power. Men such as Baker and Wright, who defied it, were disgraced and destroyed.

Policing Morality

Once the countryside was pacified through this ad hoc alliance, American officials and Filipino leaders agreed that the constabulary should undertake a new mission of national rejuvenation by suppressing personal vice. The results of this second phase in colonial police efforts—ambiguous success in stamping out opium use, the failure to stop gambling, and a symbiosis of law enforcement with syndicated vice—suggest both the possibilities and the limits of what colonial policing could achieve.

Only two years after the Cavite controversy, the opening of the legislature in 1907 brought a stable separation of police powers with the colonial executive commanding the constabulary and the Philippine Assembly controlling its budget. As part of this political entente between colonizer and colonized, the constabulary's overarching objective shifted from subjugation to nation building. Instead of paramilitary pacification, it would enforce a prohibition on personal vice that was seen by American colonials and Filipino leaders alike as the foundation for national regeneration. As the missionary Bishop Charles Brent explained, the "constitutional fault of the Filipinos, a fault common to all Orientals, is sensuality," which, he said, manifests itself in laziness, concubinage, and gambling.[107] With the exception of prostitution, which the regime decided to regulate rather than suppress, the colonial government adopted a hard line on matters of personal vice, placing the police on a collision course with two deeply embedded cultures: opium smoking among overseas Chinese workers and gambling among Filipinos of all classes. Ultimately, efforts to extinguish these habits demonstrated the limitations of coercive policing in the realms of public morality and popular culture.

Through the convergence of high imperial politics in Washington and Manila, opium prohibition emerged unexpectedly as the foundation for this new colonial morals regime. After purchasing the Philippines from Spain in 1899, Washington soon discovered that it had acquired, along with these seven thousand islands, hundreds of state-licensed opium dens generating a substantial $500,000 in tax revenues from opium auctions open only to Chinese.[108] Amid a volatile interplay of opium traders, addicts, and their evangelical opponents, colonial officials were frustrated in their attempts to find a satisfactory solution. After attempting a laissez-faire approach, they finally settled for the mailed fist of all-out prohibition and the heavy policing it entailed.

Without any legal basis for doing otherwise, at first the U.S. military regime accepted the Spanish system, with modifications, by abandoning the retail licenses and raising the customs duty to an onerous 45 percent on imported opium, an apparent attempt to reduce demand while maintaining revenue. In 1902 the new civil government found that this ad hoc accommodation had led to substantial growth in drug addiction, with 130 tons of opium sold that year through 190 retail dens to twenty thousand smokers, most of them Chinese. Realizing that high tariffs encouraged smuggling without discouraging use, the Philippine Commission lifted the ban on opium imports and drafted what it styled a "carefully prepared bill" resuming the Spanish auctions for state-licensed Chinese smoking dens. The proposal brought "considerable opposition" from Evangelical Union missionaries, notably Dr. Homer Stuntz, who argued, based on his experience elsewhere in Asia, that licensing would "stimulate the consumption of opium." As Protestant leaders bombarded the White House with cables and cards, President Roosevelt decreed that any opium law would require his approval.[109] Chastened, the Philippine Commission decided to "table the bill," grumbling that much of the agitation against the proposed law, particularly the barrage of cablegrams "arousing the moral sentiment" in America, "were paid for by the importers of and dealers in opium in Manila."[110]

Under such pressure from Washington, Governor Taft formed an Opium Commission to explore alternatives to legalized sales, creating a policy paralysis that allowed an unrestricted opium trade for the first five years of U.S. civil rule. In this legal limbo, powerful Chinese merchants took control of the lucrative traffic, soon raising the number of Manila's "filthy and unsanitary" opium divans, all unlicensed and many selling a pipe for just twenty cents. As legal opium imports increased to a hefty 134 tons in 1905, retail sales rose to an impressive $2.5 million, or ₱5 million, and smokers reached an unprecedented peak of forty thousand.[111]

Meanwhile, the Opium Commission, led by Bishop Brent and a Manila physician, Jose Albert, spent nearly two years traveling across Asia in search of solutions, slowly forming a consensus that equated tolerance with iniquity. In Indochina Brent found that French officials, many of them opium addicts, placed "no restriction whatever . . . upon the free use of the drug by the natives," making Saigon "one of the wickedest cities in the Orient." China's utter lack of controls had subjected it to "the horrors of opium." But in Japan "the prohibitory law is absolutely effective." By the close of the tour, Brent had concluded that prohibition "seemed to be the only hopeful" solution.[112]

As the inquiry proceeded, Bishop Brent's opinions became the Opium Commission's official findings. Surveying the Philippines, the commission found that a half century of licensed sales had fostered three concentrations of serious addiction—527 Chinese smokers in Iloilo, 509 in Cebu, and an estimated eight thousand in Manila. Above all, the commission feared the spread of addiction to Filipinos, a concern corroborated in the Cagayan Valley where the constabulary reported that "nearly two-thirds of the natives of . . . Echague are slaves to this [opium] habit." Through questionnaires sent to nineteen provincial residents, the commission found that educated Filipinos saw addiction as a serious social problem. To control the "alarming" spread of addiction among natives, in its 1905 report the Opium Commission recommended a balanced response involving a state monopoly over imports, limited sales to registered smokers, and free treatment for addicts at government hospitals.[113]

But in March 1905 the U.S. Congress, under strong pressure from Protestant moralists, used its tariff powers to set a three-year deadline for the end of Philippine opium imports and a mandatory ban on all nonmedicinal sales. Suddenly stripped of its discretion, the colonial government prepared for the ban with a three-step plan leading to full prohibition. Adapting the recommendations of the Opium Commission for its first step in March 1906, the regime issued temporary licenses to 289 "retail opium establishments," restricted sales to 12,600 registered Chinese smokers, and offered free hospital treatment. As its next step a year later the regime passed Act No. 1761 requiring a 15 percent reduction in the amount of opium allowed each smoker. Significantly, the act also imposed five years' imprisonment on any who "use or permit to be used in or on his body any opium, except for medicinal purposes." By January 1908 these measures had reduced the trade to thirty "opium dispensaries patronized by about 2,675 registered users."[114]

Finally, with strong support from Manila's clergy and Chinese community, the government banned all narcotics sales on March 1, 1908. This " 'black' Sunday for opium habitués" hit hard, forcing hundreds to flood San Juan de Dios Hospital "in sheer desperation" until staff could no longer restrain "so large a number of frenzied patients" and suspended treatment. In response to this emergency, the government opened its mental wards at San Lazaro Hospital for some 250 addicts who "fought, screamed, threatened, and sulked" for opium until they finally accepted detoxification. As the number of patients at San Lazaro dropped from four hundred in 1908 to just one hundred a year later, an elaborate illicit traffic quickly emerged to supply the thousands of untreated addicts. With drugs smuggled in from Hong Kong, some fifty illegal "opium joints" opened in Manila's Chinese districts of Binondo and San Nicholas, many neutralizing police raids by "barricading the doors with heavy lattice work, barbed wire, ice box doors and iron bars." In May 1909 the government tried "to make the prohibition effective" by imposing penalties of three hundred pesos and three-months' imprisonment for opium use. The price of illicit opium soared, discouraging the poorer stratum of Filipino smokers and encouraging Chinese dealers. Calling them the "world's most adept smugglers," the public health chief, Dr. Victor Heiser, was impressed by ingenious Chinese traffickers who sealed the drug in jam tins or injected liquefied opium into a few fresh eggs concealed among the countless thousands arriving weekly on ships from Hong Kong.[115]

Although drug abuse soon declined markedly compared to neighboring colonies, smuggled opium still met much of Manila's illicit demand and created a major law enforcement problem.[116] In the five years following the 1908 prohibition, colonial police made 7,869 arrests for drug violations, but the number of "habitual users among the Chinese" was still estimated at a substantial five thousand.[117] All the secret services charged with stemming the traffic—the Customs House, Internal Revenue Service, and Manila police—were soon tainted by systemic corruption. In April 1910, for example, when customs scored a record opium seizure of three hundred kilograms valued at ninety thousand pesos, several of its Filipino employees were "implicated in . . . smuggling the opium through the bodega" for an "influential Chinese commercial firm." The five-hundred-peso bribe paid to two customs employees represented a full month's salary for each.[118] A year later, prosecutors charged three Manila detectives with taking bribes to protect several Chinatown opium dens operated by a criminal named Sy Boco. In the sensational trial Sy Boco himself testified that to avoid being raided he had made weekly payments to the police. One of the accused detectives claimed that he had advised his secret service chief, Charles Trowbridge, that "these houses existed and that Detective [Eugenio] Samio was receiving bribes for their protection." In his own testimony, Trowbridge denied any corruption, insisting that he had passed information about these dens to the internal revenue's secret service, which had jurisdiction in opium cases.[119] These charges and countercharges show that in just three years opium traffic had survived in Manila through a symbiosis with systemic corruption in the city's police force.

The illicit traffic was so lucrative that it also corrupted elements of the political elite. After the 1908 opium ban, the wife of Assembly Speaker Sergio Osmeña, Estefania Chiong Veloso, boldly, even brazenly used her husband's influence to continue the family business of supplying Cebu's opium addicts. In the last years of Spanish rule, her Chinese father, Nicasio Veloso Chiong Tuico, had won a three-year contract for opium sales in Cebu and Bohol, bidding an impressive ₱116,280 to beat out fourteen competitors. "She was quite a woman, an amazing businesswoman, deeply involved in opium and other smuggling operations," recalled her grandson John "Sonny" H. Osmeña in a 1974 interview. "She usually picked up the smuggled goods in Talisay and would personally ride in the trucks to San Nicolas, where there was a constabulary checkpoint for traffic coming from the south. When approached by the PC soldiers, she would threaten them with the loss of their jobs if they attempted to search her trucks; if it is was night, she would hold the lantern of the truck up to her face to be sure that they recognized who she was." For nearly a decade, the Speaker's wife remained an active trafficker, using the profits to purchase substantial amounts of land in northern Cebu until she died in 1918 delivering her thirteenth child.[120]

Enforcement of the opium ban remained episodic until 1919 when Governor-General F. B. Harrison, concerned that "the habit will spread its debauching effects" from Chinese to Filipino, ordered a nationwide assault on "the opium evil." With inspectors patrolling Manila's waterfront and launches cruising the southern sea frontier, customs was supposed to interdict opium smuggling whether by Chinese merchants or Muslims in "fast-sailing vintas." The constabulary also "broke up barricaded and labyrinthed Chinese opium joints" across the archipelago.[121] Sustained police pressure on Manila's Chinatown gradually reduced the city's thirty "opium joints" to sixteen by the end of 1919. The surviving smoking dens were concealed inside barricaded houses and protected by diffident city prosecution of arrested smokers. In mid-1921, however, Manila's Municipal Board barred construction of such barricades inside any house that the courts had ruled an "opium joint." Under intensified police pressure, exemplified by 1,443 arrests in 1921–22, what was supposed to be the city's last opium den was closed by late 1922, reducing use inside Manila to a level the police deemed "negligible."[122]

As these suppression campaigns faded, the local equilibrium of illicit drugs and police corruption resumed. In the last decade of direct U.S. rule, the constabulary launched sufficient opium raids across the country to reduce but not eliminate the problem. In 1926 customs reported that due to "strict vigilance" over the past ten years "the opium traffic has been gradually decreasing to a degree that . . . the opium smoking habit is practically confined within the Chinese community."[123] In ending the threat of addiction among Filipinos, the opium campaign had met the aims of the colonial regime's moral alliance with the country's political leaders. Yet it had done so not by eradicating the problem but by confining it within its original core area, Manila's Chinatown, an ambiguous success for colonial policing.

But gambling was the real nemesis in this colonial antivice crusade. After nearly a century of formal prohibition and informal promotion, the Spanish colonial state had left a legacy that would survive a century beyond its demise. In 1838 the Spanish governor-general had called gambling "a consuming cancer that destroys the fortune of many families, encourages sloth, hinders the sources of public wealth, perverts good faith, corrupts the people's morals, and leads them to degradation and misery." The regime prohibited most forms of gambling and applied the force of law to their eradication. In March 1881, for example, Manila police arrested 411 gambling violators, 36 percent of them Chinese, a disproportionate number that reflected their prominence as both promoters and players. Although in time games such as *panguingue* and fan-tan were overtaken by the Spanish *monte,* the low-cost lottery known as jueteng proved remarkably resilient, as did horse racing and the age-old blood sport of cockfighting.[124]

In the last decades of their rule, the Spanish had fostered an irrepressible gambling culture through limited licensing and failed policing. As with opium these practices fortified the state budget while placing serious strains on the wider society. Between 1788 and 1880 tax revenues from cockpits rose from ₱6,000 to ₱118,500, providing nearly one percent of the government budget.[125] By the 1890s gambling had become a significant source of income for many members of the emerging Filipino elite. At the Santa Mesa racetrack, members of the exclusive Manila Jockey Club entered mounts in high-stakes races that paid out over 51,500 Mexican silver dollars during a four-day meet in March 1896.[126] In his memoirs the *ilustrado* Victor Buencamino described how his grandmother, "Lola Ninay," known more formally as Doña Saturnina Salazar, lifted their family into "the flashiest of circles" through money lending and gambling operations, both monte and jueteng. But even Lola Ninay's success paled before the grandeur of Capitan Joaquin Arnedo's casino in Barrio Sulipan, Apalait, the heart of the Pampanga sugar district, where wealthy planters staked "the season's sales from cane sugar and rice and tobacco" on the turn of a single card. Looking back on this Spanish era glitter from a stricter postindependence perspective, Buencamino concluded that "our colonial rulers had tolerated gambling, first, to get the minds of the masses off their misery and, second, the easier to rule the idle rich in their state of degeneration."[127]

When the U.S. Army occupied Manila in 1898, its military government soon found both lively legal gambling, notably high-stakes horse racing, and thriving illegal gambling among the city's Chinese. In Binondo's Chinatown fan-tan card parlors and a jueteng lottery with a jackpot of five hundred Mexican dollars clustered along Calle San Jacinto.[128] As with opium the regime did not initially prohibit gambling. Instead, needing legal diversions for its off-duty soldiers, the colonial government loosened the few restraints left by the Spanish regime. By 1906 Manila's racetracks were operating 220 days a year, up sharply from just eight days under Spain, with wagers totaling an impressive eight million pesos.[129] In October 1902 the colonial government banned cockfighting to extirpate this pervasive Filipino vice, but it relented in response to protests and permitted contests in municipal *gallerias* on public holidays.[130] A year later, during the Philippine Commission's debate over morals legislation, Vice-Governor Luke Wright, the secretary of police, called gambling "one of the greatest curses," but he also expressed strong reservations about using the police to suppress such a popular vice. "If you give to all your policemen," he warned, "the right to rush into a house and see if gambling is not going on, . . . you practically destroy the privacy of a man's home."[131] Reflecting Victorian laissez-faire sensibilities about the limits of government, the U.S. regime at first seemed wary of using coercion to suppress gambling.

But as military pacification faded into moral reconstruction, concerns about gambling intensified among both Americans and Filipinos. In the latter decades of Spanish rule, Filipino nationalists had identified gambling and opium as barriers to national progress. In his influential 1886 novel *Noli Me Tangere,* famed propagandist Jose Rizal broke his narrative with a full chapter condemning cockfighting as "one of the people's vices, more transcendental than opium among the Chinese." Against Spanish claims that "magnificent schools rise, bridges and highways are built" from gambling taxes, Rizal juxtaposed the poor Filipino who returns from the cockpit "awaited by his anxious wife and ragged children, without his little capital and without his cock."[132] Now, as they allied with America to realize their reformist agenda, Filipino leaders pressed the new colonial regime to promote moral reform.

After its initial experiments with deregulation, American colonials came to agree that gambling was, as Protestant missionaries put it, "the curse of the Islands" and would deprive Filipino society of "the vital forces" needed for development.[133] "The Filipinos are born gamblers," wrote Commissioner Dean C. Worcester, adding, "Gambling is their besetting sin."[134] An American justice, George A. Malcolm, concurred, saying, "The evil of gambling infects all classes. The Filipino is an inveterate gambler, for thus he varies a rather monotonous existence."[135]

In its first years the constabulary had found gambling both pervasive and protected. In 1902–3, for example, constables arrested 250 gamblers in Batangas Province but found it "very difficult to convict this class of offenders before the courts, owing to the disinclination of witnesses to testify." From southern Luzon, Colonel Bandholtz reported that local officials "are addicted to the vice" and local police were complicit in the corruption. After several years of probing this illicit alliance, constabulary officials recommended that the Philippine Commission pass "stringent and specific laws" stripping municipal officials of any role in gambling enforcement.[136]

Even when relations were still raw, Filipino nationalists supported the regime's coercive approach to morality. Though often critical of the constabulary, the nationalist newspaper *El Renacimiento* also encouraged police campaigns against the gambling scourge with celebratory headlines such as "Formidable Campaign in Batangas—Brilliant Report of Lipa Police." This coverage struck a responsive chord among readers. "The energetic campaign launched by *El Renacimiento* against gaming in Rizal Province," wrote a resident of Nabutas, "deserves the congratulations of all who care for the good of the Philippines." When an American judge, William A. Kincaid, rejected the idea that Filipinos are "a race of gamblers," a Filipino correspondent from Cebu disagreed vehemently, telling the *Manila Times* that the way to eradicate this "injurious and immoral" vice was "by passing and enforcing laws prohibiting it and not by trying to whitewash a racial fault."[137]

As with opium, American missionaries catalyzed the colonial regime's determination to prohibit gambling. In a six-part essay written for the *Manila American* in February 1906, the Episcopal missionary Mercer G. Johnston branded gambling "an unmitigated evil" and urged a "progressive prohibition" on the model of the opium campaign. As a first step the *Manila Times* suggested that the American community "drop our pharisaical licensing of the race track, which cannot be justified without recourse to casuistry of the worst type." When the regime did not respond, Mercer joined the Methodists in forming the Moral Progress League and staging a mass meeting at the Zorilla Theater with support from both the Catholic archbishop and General Aguinaldo. After Bishop Brent weighed in with an influential sermon damning gambling as "contemptible," the league drafted a restrictive horse-racing bill and sent it to the government for action.[138]

Under pressure, Governor-General James F. Smith, a conservative Catholic moralist, soon changed the libertine laws that had made Manila a wide-open soldiers' town. Starting in mid-1906, the Philippine Commission adopted the Moral Progress League's bill reducing horse racing from 220 days annually to public holidays and one Sunday a month.[139] Then, in October 1907, the regime suddenly adopted a string of legal prohibitions: Act No. 1761 restricting and then banning opium; Act No. 1773 making adultery, along with rape and abduction, "public crimes" exempt from private settlement; and, most ambitious, Act No. 1757 prohibiting most forms of gambling.[140] Under the latter law, the commission replaced the modest Spanish gaming ban of 1887 with a blanket prohibition on all gambling, broadly defined as "the playing of any game for money," except periodic cockfights and horse racing. Gamblers would be fined between ten and five hundred pesos, and any "peace officer . . . who knowingly permits gambling" faced penalties up to a thousand pesos or a year's imprisonment.[141]

As their legislative power grew after 1907, emerging Filipino leaders, with mass support, embraced this coercive approach to morality and equated gambling with racial degeneration.[142] Even after winning full legislative autonomy in 1916, Filipino senators and representatives did not undo the colonial gambling bans. The country's Supreme Court joined this moral majority, writing a dozen decisions between 1912 and 1919 that granted police wide latitude in pursuit of illegal gambling. In a majority decision in *United States v. Salaveria,* Justice Malcolm ruled that local governments "afflicted by this evil" needed adequate authority under "what is called the police power" for the fight against "an act beyond the pale of good morals, which, for the welfare of the Filipino people, should be exterminated."[143]

Under U.S. rule, Filipino educators developed a complementary critique of gambling's social costs. When Reverend Johnston denounced the first Manila Carnival's cockpit concession in 1908 as "A Covenant with Death, Agreement with Hell," the four-hundred-strong Philippine Teachers' Association backed him.[144] "People who gamble are moral degenerates," argued Dr. Serafin Macaraig in his 1933 high school civics text, "for they use trickery and cheating to make a living." Gamblers are "parasites," he said, and gambling, along with usury and caciquism, was one of three "social diseases" that had slowed the nation's progress.[145] In another high school civics text (1940), the famed educator Camilo Osias celebrated Filipino virtue and condemned just one vice. "The blind trust of people in getting something for nothing; their perverted view of amusement or games being uninteresting unless there is something at stake," he wrote, "are qualities and practices that sap the vitality of the Philippines and bring shame to our life."[146]

Reflecting this moral consensus, between 1907 and 1932 the constabulary combined constant local pressure and periodic national campaigns in a largely futile attempt to stem the spread of illegal gambling. In 1917 Interior Secretary

Rafael Palma, a prominent nationalist, called for a "campaign for the speedy and complete eradication of the gambling vice," and the constabulary responded with 296 raids nationwide. In 1925 constables conducted 745 raids, arresting 4,245 suspects and confiscating ₱25,273 in wagers. As always, however, the Manila police carried the weight of this antigambling battle, making 10,845 arrests that same year, more than double the constabulary's figure. As the leading Filipino police expert, Maj. Emanuel A. Bajá, explained, the main aim of these operations lay not in the arrests per se but "in their moral influence . . . on the public mind."[147]

In response to such suppression, criminal syndicates, protected by politicians, emerged to service an unmet popular demand for gambling. By 1912, after several years of aggressive enforcement, the constabulary reported widespread gambling and political corruption in provinces across Central Luzon. Only ten years after the first local elections, gambling was integrated, top-to-bottom, into provincial politics. Cavite's governor attended illegal monte games at the Binacayan cockpit while municipal police guarded the door. Similarly, Bulacan's Governor Teodoro Sandiko protected Marilao's gaming houses and financed his faction's campaigns by taking a peseta from every peso bet that Polo's mayor, his campaign leader, collected from three ongoing jueteng lotteries.[148]

Card games and illegal casinos entertained the rich, but it was jueteng that enticed the poor. Since workers could win up to ten pesos, a week's wages, on a one-centavo bet, it was irrepressibly popular. Bettors won by picking two numbers between one and thirty-seven. This seemingly generous gesture of allowing bets on two numbers instead of one raised the odds, through mathematical sleight of hand, from one chance in thirty-seven to one in 1,332.[149] Through this illusion of easy winnings, the game tapped into lower-class aspirations and made this illegal lottery a central facet of Filipino popular culture that has persisted long beyond the colonial era. These odds also produced ample profits for its promoters and protectors. In the early 1930s Major Bajá expressed the opinion that jueteng had "nourished the gambling spirit of the people more than all the other prohibited games put together" and was prevalent in "99% of our cities and towns." While cockfighting and card games such as monte were a male-only activity, women worked as jueteng collectors and often outnumbered male bettors, effectively doubling this racket's working-class clientele.[150] Moreover, the intimacy that developed between jueteng runners and poor bettors fostered social networks that could be mobilized during elections. Through its unique integration into the fabric of Filipino mores and mass politics, jueteng fused illicit profits, police corruption, and political patronage into a resilient nexus that defied state controls.[151]

While raiding monte clubs was difficult, stopping jueteng was impossible. Its powerful Chinese operators usually bribed local police and politicians for protection. In 1926, for example, jueteng bankers met an informal weekly payroll: provincial governors two hundred pesos, municipal mayors one hundred, police chiefs fifty, and patrolmen five. Three years later Manila's mayor gave his police "strict instructions to eradicate this vice within the city limits," but the operators simply moved their base to the nearby suburbs of Pasay and Malabon. Whenever the police made an arrest, the lowly *cobradores* (runners) went to prison on full pay, sparing the principals, who hired new men to keep the lottery running.[152]

The remarkable resilience of jueteng after sustained attempts at suppression illustrates the fate of the larger U.S. campaign against personal vice. At its start in 1907, the colonial executive charged the municipal police with antigambling enforcement. Five years later, when their failure was clear, the regime transferred the task to constabulary, which soon found it, too, was incapable of enforcing moral reform.[153] Criminalization of gambling forced it farther underground, increasing opportunities for corruption. Similarly, the ban on opium encouraged smuggling, and the Manila police shared in the profits. While collaboration between the U.S. regime and Filipino politicians had aided pacification, colonial officials clearly found victory in the realm of personal behavior more elusive.

Conclusion

In the aftermath of the Cavite controversy, the constabulary and Filipino nationalists reached an entente that shaped the direction of Philippine politics for another decade. When the Americans conceded legislative power in 1907, Filipino politicians used their social leverage to demobilize peasant revolts and shift the political debate in more moderate directions. For the colonial regime these concessions to Filipino leaders were necessary to defuse the Cavite crisis, stamp out messianic revolts, and burnish a tarnished legitimacy. From a Filipino perspective cooperation was a small price for strides toward the ultimate goal of national independence, an outcome that would depend, they felt, on moral regeneration through prohibition of personal vices that had troubled the country for decades. Within months these mutual concessions shifted the overall tenor of colonial relations from confrontation to collaboration, particularly between constabulary officers and Filipino politicians.

The complexities entailed in this shift from dominance to mutual dependence are well illustrated by the changing relationship between Manuel Quezon and Col. James Harbord. When they first met in 1905 Colonel Harbord was a rising colonial and Quezon a local lawyer with a checkered past and limited prospects. Over the next three years the colonel helped launch Quezon's political career by backing him, against formidable odds, in two provincial elections while deflecting scandals that threatened his ruin.[154] Only eight years later the two were peers, swapping career-saving favors. In 1913 Quezon, then the Philippines' resident commissioner in Washington, helped Harbord win command of the constabulary while Harbord used his position to help Quezon evade damaging allegations of kickbacks from the sale of land to the Manila Railway.[155]

Beyond swapping political favors, there was a quality of mutual affection in their correspondence. In late 1914 Harbord, now back in the U.S. Army at a dusty California outpost, wrote praising Quezon's recent essay on the constabulary, saying, "If we were up at Baler in dear old Tayabas I should say 'Good speech, boy!'" Two years later Quezon wrote back, acknowledging "how much good has been done to the Islands by the Constabulary" and expressing "friendly affection for some of these officers."[156]

Simple colonial dominance thus gave way to a complex hierarchy. When his former PC patrons Harbord and Bandholtz returned to the U.S. Army, Quezon cultivated more junior American and Filipino clients in the constabulary, taking care to balance these short-term alliances with his long-term plan to convert the colonial force into a Philippine national army.[157] As a part of this new political balance, the U.S. regime began training Filipinos for constabulary commands. In 1907, the same year it launched the National Assembly, the colonial government graduated two Filipinos from a short training course in Manila and then moved this fledgling Constabulary School to permanent quarters in Baguio City. There substantial numbers of Filipino cadets underwent six months of rigorous training.[158]

Radical nationalists remained outside this cozy collaboration. Denied access to elective office by their nationalist activities, radical leaders created an alternative political space by mobilizing Manila's masses with rallies, strikes, and mutual aid societies. To curtail this agitation the constabulary launched a covert campaign to break the militant movement. In its initial effort, from 1902 to 1907, the PC had worked openly to control a new generation of Filipino politicians, advancing some and attacking others. In its second phase, from 1907 to 1914, the constabulary, now restrained by Filipino legislative authority, launched discrete covert operations to demobilize Manila's masses and demoralize their leaders. In these difficult, delicate maneuvers, it intended not simply to damage individual reputations but to discredit the core ideals that had inspired two generations of nationalist struggle and six years of revolution. As we will see in the next chapter, this demanding task would require unconventional policing and covert operations that strained even the constabulary's exceptional resources.

First Company, Philippines Constabulary, Pampanga Province, 1908. (Library of Congress)

U.S. Army officers and surrendered Filipino commanders, Lucena, Tayabas Province, July 2, 1901. Front row, left to right, Capt. Milton F. Davis, Colonel Castillo, Capt. Harry H. Bandholtz, Major Nadres. Second row, left to right, unidentified, Captain Miller, Captain Price, and Major Alfonso. (Box 6, H. H. Bandholtz Papers, Bentley Historical Library, University of Michigan)

Ilocano policemen of Bangued, Abra Province, circa 1910. (Field Museum of Natural History, no. CSA24613)

Muslim soldiers, Fifty-second Company Philippine Scouts, organized by orders of Gen. John Pershing, Mindanao, Philippines, 1909. (Library of Congress)

343 LIZZIE MYERS,
Alias "Mary Sad and Queen Liz,"
Shoplifter.

SIDNEY LASALLE
344 Alias "Lord Beresford,"
Forger and Swindler.

346 CHAS. BALLENTINE,
Alias "Ernest Allaine Cheiriton,"
Forger and Swindler.

THOS. E. HARDMAN,
347 Badger and Swindler.

Byrnes, Thomas. *Professional Criminals of America.* New York: G.W. Dillingham, 1895.,

Charles Ballentine, forger and swindler, alias "Captain Edgar G. Bellairs," the Associated Press Manila correspondent in 1901–2. (Thomas Byrnes, *Professional Criminals of America*, New York, 1895)

Fernando Ma. Guerrero, editor of the newspaper *El Renacimiento*, during his 1905 crusade against the Philippines Constabulary's forced relocation of farmers into concentration camps (*campo de reconcentracion*) to pacify the town of Bacoor, Cavite Province. (*Lipag Kalabaw*, July 27, 1907)

Dionisio Sigobela (center, with chains on his ankles), the messianic leader known as "Papa Isio," and his aides after their surrender, provincial prison, Bacolod, Negros Occidental, 1907. (Box 7, H. H. Bandholtz Papers, Bentley Historical Library, University of Michigan)

From 1907 to 1916, the Nacionalista Party leader Manuel Quezon (above) fought for Filipino self-rule against Republican imperialists led by colonial Interior Secretary Dean C. Worcester (top), shown reading an editorial in the nationalist newspaper *El Renacimiento* branding him a “bird of prey.” (*Lipag Kalabaw*, June 6, 1908; *Lipag Kalabaw*, November 21, 1908)

Fourth Mountain Company, Philippines Constabulary, at presentation of the Col. Wallace Taylor Cup for marksmanship, Kiangan, Ifugao Sub-province, 1911. Front row, Lt. Owen Tomlinson (left) and Lt. Maximo Meimban (right). (Box 2, Owen Tomlinson Papers, Bentley Historical Library, University of Michigan)

In the rugged Ifugao district of Mountain Province, constabulary officers such as Lt. Eugene H. Kolb (left) led local recruits like these noncommissioned officers of the Fourth Mountain Company (below) in suppressing head-taking vendettas, circa 1913. (Box 2, Owen Tomlinson Papers, Bentley Historical Library, University of Michigan)

Mobilization of Kalinga policemen like these from Lubuangan (top) was central to the pacification strategy of Interior Secretary Dean C. Worcester (above, center), shown with Governor Blas Villamor (third from right) and four Kalinga chiefs, including Bakidan (far left) at Pinukpuk, Kalinga Sub-province, January 1905. Note the curved blade of the axe at right for head-taking. (U.S. National Archives; 5-a-10 Worcester Collection, by permission of the University of Michigan Museum of Anthropology)

Photographed at a *cañao* peace ritual in the Ifugao highlands circa 1916, Lt. William E. Dosser served the Philippines Constabulary for thirty years, rising to commander for northern Luzon and concurrent governor of Mountain Province before retiring in 1939. (Tiffany Bernard Williams Photograph Collection, Special Collections Library, University of Michigan)

By 1908 a private U.S. transit monopoly, the Manila Electric Railroad & Light Co. (Meralco), operated a citywide network of electrical trams like this one (above) on the Escolta in downtown Manila. Fares were so high that a satiric Filipino weekly caricatured the company (top) as a bloated American tycoon labeled "E.R.R. & L. Co." who hauls away bags of money as he drags a poor Filipino vomiting coins. (Library of Congress; *Lipag Kalabaw*, October 21, 1908)

Despite prohibition of opium in 1908, Chinese smuggling and official collusion in the Customs House (top) gave Manila ample supplies for illicit smoking dens like this one (above) on Malinta Street, Manila, in 1924. (*Philippines Free Press*, January 11, 1919; Library of Congress)

W. Cameron Forbes (right) and Gen. Leonard Wood (left) on a study mission investigating Philippine corruption, Cavite Province, 1921, just before Wood became governor general. (MS Am 1192.12, W. Cameron Forbes Papers, by permission of the Houghton Library, Harvard University)

In the midst of a political crisis over police graft, Detective Ray Conley thumbs his nose at Interior Secretary Jose Laurel, who has accused Conley of taking bribes from illegal gambling. (*El Debate*, April 20, 1923)

As the Philippine National Bank collapses from corruption, merchant Vicente Madrigal backhands stolen pesos to Assembly Speaker Sergio Osmeña while financier Ramon Fernandez bribes Senate President Manuel Quezon. (*Bag-ong Kusog*, March 7, 1924)

In 1941–42 Japanese American writer Mary Oyama Mittwer (top) worked as Agent B-31 reporting about alleged Japanese espionage in Los Angeles to Gen. Ralph Van Deman (above), shown in 1919 when he was chief of U.S. counterintelligence at the Versailles peace conference, Paris. (Bancroft Library, University of California; U.S. Military History Institute)

5

Constabulary Covert Operations

IN JULY 1907, Manila was stunned by news of a spectacular upset in the elections for the first Philippine Assembly. After years of harassment by the courts and constabulary, Filipino nationalists had captured a clear majority of seats, reducing the once dominant collaborators of the Federalista Party to an impotent minority. But one victory stood out as a sign of deeper changes yet to come. Only a year after the nationalist newspaper *El Renacimiento* had faced criminal charges for criticizing the constabulary, its crusading editor, Fernando Guerrero, had won an Assembly seat from Manila. Elated by his election, nationalists staged an emotional victory parade through the city's streets on August 11. They waved the red banner of the Katipunan, the secret society that had led the revolution against Spain. They ripped American flags from public buildings. They shouted "Fuera los Americanos!" "Americans Out!"—a demand that Manila's colonial rulers were determined to defeat.

Two weeks later, on August 23, the city's archcolonial police chief, John Harding, outlawed the Katipunan flag and sent officers across the capital to seize any on display. That night, in a last imperial hurrah, Manila's American colony massed to "Rally Around the Flag." Over three thousand angry Americans filled the Grand Opera House to hear speakers thunder threats of retaliation for any future denigration of the Stars and Stripes. The veterans' leader, Maj. W. H. Bishop, insisted that these islands, "purchased with the blood of American soldiers," should forever "remain the territory of the United States." Fearing mob violence, the U.S. colonial executive quickly strengthened the Sedition Law and, with some reluctance, enacted a Flag Law banning display of the Katipunan banner. The *Manila Times* cheered this tough response, asking whether the natives "take their medicine like men or . . . play the child and sulk?"[1]

As this furor over flags indicates, the U.S. decision to share power with the Filipino elite through elections was a tectonic change, disrupting a delicate colonial balance and starting a process that would lead, step-by-step, to full independence. Yet the 1907 election was also a flash point, sparking nationalist sentiment long suppressed under U.S. rule. Pushed slowly to the political margins, Filipino radicals had retreated from party politics and were creating an alternative political space of public meetings and street rallies. As the city's moderate, educated elites dominated electoral politics after 1907, these radicals gained a new following by mobilizing the city's working class with a rhetoric of unbending nationalism and social justice. Instead of trying to influence colonial policy, these militants organized both mass meetings to protest the arrival of American capital and labor unions to mount strikes against U.S. corporations. When police repression and PC penetration ended these walkouts, activist leaders formed mutual aid societies for the city's workers, creating a new constituency for radical agitation. At the extremist fringe of these movements, many radicals advocated an alliance with Japan as an alternative imperial protector and exemplar.

With each turn in this radical Filipino mobilization, the constabulary adjusted its tactics to defeat the militants, defend the moderate center, and secure the place of the U.S. regime as the islands' unchallenged ruler. The threat of scandal, so effective in controlling the actions of educated political moderates, had little impact on those outside the main arena of colonial politics. While conventional American and Filipino careerists stocked up on scurrilous intelligence to protect their reputations or destroy rivals, groups at the extremities—from Japanese agents to Filipino radicals and Chinese opium traders—played by a different set of rules. It was the constabulary's duty to neutralize all these volatile forces, an end it achieved by taking the manipulation of information to new extremes.

After five years of fighting rural revolts from 1902 to 1907, the constabulary adapted both its officer corps and order-of-battle for political operations to contain strikes, street rallies, and mass meetings. Instead of deploying rifle companies against armed peasants, the constabulary used its Information Division for intensified surveillance of Manila's militants. In this difficult political transition, the constabulary applied its coercive powers for the steady demoralization and destruction of groups that threatened the colonial order. It was discreet in its treatment of the Philippine Assembly even when assertive nationalists won election. But radical or noncooperating leaders who operated outside the bounds of electoral politics through union organizing or street rallies were subjected to surveillance, infiltration, and ultimately arrest and prison. By penetrating these radical organizations, the constabulary sought to destroy them from within through psychological profiling, disinformation, black propaganda, and entrapment. Most important, the U.S. regime strove to corrode the tenuous bonds of trust that held the upper echelons of these groups together, depriving them of effective leadership. In sum, after 1907 the constabulary's main mission shifted from counterinsurgency to psychological and information warfare. Under the pressure of this strategy, the Filipino radical movement would soon implode amid suspicion and betrayal.

Shadow Masters

The success of these covert operations was the product of an eight-year collaboration between two unconventional officers: Gen. Harry Bandholtz, chief of the constabulary, and Lt. Col. Rafael Crame, superintendent of its Information Division. Although raised in societies separated by nine thousand miles, their backgrounds and personalities were surprisingly similar, indicating that a certain character was best suited to life in society's shadows. Both men achieved distinction in the service of their respective nations, Bandholtz as founder of the U.S. Army's Military Police, or MPs, and Crame as the first Filipino chief of constabulary. Both are honored as martial paragons, Crame by the national police headquarters in Manila that bears his name and Bandholtz by a heroic bronze statue before the U.S. Embassy in Budapest.[2] They shared an aloof personality and caustic intelligence that in regular military service might have barred their rise to command. But under the peculiar circumstances of colonial policing these were attributes ideal, even imperative, for success.

Their biographies, like their personalities, are somewhat similar. As a Spanish mestizo and son of a lieutenant in the Spanish colonial artillery, Rafael Crame straddled Manila's main racial divide. He was immersed in yet apart from Filipino society, allowing him vast local knowledge and the liberty to use it for foreign rule. Born in 1863 in the small town of Malabon near Manila, he attended the elite Ateneo de Manila College and the local Spanish Military Academy before finishing his education at Manila's Spanish Infantry School in 1881. A year later he won a post in the internal revenue service by examination and rose rapidly to deputy collector. When the revolution erupted in August 1896, he took a two-year leave to fight the rebels as a soldier in the Filipino-Spanish Volunteer Battalion, winning promotion to lieutenant. After Spain's defeat in August 1898, Crame rallied to his former enemies in the Philippine revolutionary army for several months before switching sides again to join the U.S. Army's new Manila Police, quickly advancing to captain. After losing his rank in the reorganization of 1902, he transferred to the constabulary as a third lieutenant and rose inside its Information Division for the next fifteen years until his promotion to chief in 1917, a post he would hold until his death ten years later. At the close of his career, Crame, puffing his massive chest and flexing his firm biceps, would tell visitors how as a young man he "had a competition in physical endurance once with Dr. Dominador Gomez, . . . one of the strongest Filipinos," and years later one of his chief antagonists in the ranks of Filipino radicals. During his fifteen years in secret police work, Crame proved both brilliant and relentless, deploying his secret agents strategically, analyzing their reports with acute insight, and pursuing radical nationalists until he had destroyed their movement and killed their leaders. For over twelve years he tracked ex-general Mariano Noriel with the ruthlessness of a Filipino Javert, the merciless inspector in *Les Miserables,* twisting truth and law from inside the bowels of the secret service until the old general swung from the gallows of Bilibid Prison—the only execution of an educated Filipino in forty years of U.S. rule.[3]

Harry Hill Bandholtz shared similarly mixed parentage and ambiguous relations with his own society, an alienation that may have led him to find his real calling in the netherworld of colonial policing. Born in Constantine, Michigan, a small town near Chicago, in 1864, just fourteen months after Crame, Bandholtz was the child of working-class parents who could give him little more than the most basic of American birthrights. Three years earlier his mother, Elizabeth Hill, the daughter of an Irish-English mason, had married a German immigrant twice her age and settled down in this modest midwestern village. After graduating from high school in 1881, the year Crame finished infantry school in Manila, Bandholtz worked as a clerk in Chicago before winning admission to West Point by examination. Although he started at the top of his class, he developed an eye ailment and graduated with an undistinguished record in 1890, relegating him to the infantry. But the Spanish-American War rescued this lowly first lieutenant from drilling undergraduates at the Michigan Agricultural College and sent him to Cuba where he quickly won a brevet promotion to major and a silver star for gallantry near San Juan Hill. In Cuba as well, Bandholtz also found his real vocation, civil affairs, while supervising elections in Sagua la Grande. Arriving at Manila in 1900, he rose rapidly through the colonial service over the next thirteen years in civil missions that combined intelligence and politics: the mass surrender of revolutionaries on Marinduque Island in 1900, pacification of rebel-infested Tayabas Province a year later, and the elimination, by capture and assassination, of Cavite's rebel leaders in 1906–7. These successes and his refined political sensibilities won him an appointment as chief of the constabulary in June 1907 with the brevet rank of brigadier general.[4]

In assembling and assaying a daunting mass of raw intelligence, Bandholtz brought to his police work uncommon talents evident even in his choice of pastimes. Throughout his decades of military service, he was, in his words, an "ardent collector of all kinds of curios"—stamps, weapons, hats, and photographs—pursuing every object with a hunter's intensity and cataloging each with a curator's care. At the Saint Louis World's Fair of 1904, his collection of 213 pieces of Philippine memorabilia covered the entire wall of a major hall. His holdings included the original dagger that Andres Bonifacio had used to initiate revolutionaries into the Katipunan, an iconic object he later offered to Sen. Manuel Quezon as a token of their long friendship.[5]

The detachment and dark intrigues that served Bandholtz so well in police work also spilled into his private life, chilling even the most intimate of relationships. Ambition for promotion drove him to join every possible Manila organization: the Republican Party, Veterans Army, Masons, Knight's Templar, Bamboo Oasis, and Army-Navy Club. But he remained a loner, calculating in his friendships and unperturbed by their betrayal whether by his own son Cleveland, who had followed him to West Point, or his constabulary subordinate James Harbord, who rose far beyond him. At the close of his military career in the early 1920s, Bandholtz filled his army personnel file with documents to prevent his only son from "besmirching" his name and incarcerated his wife of thirty-two years in a Michigan mental hospital.[6] With the same scurrilous tactics he once used against Filipino radicals, Bandholtz later filed for divorce by detailing her fantasies of his fornication with the "wife of a prominent official" on the forward deck of a coast guard cutter.[7] While his predecessor, Henry Allen, retired to be considered for a vice presidential nomination and his successor, Harbord, chaired the Radio Corporation of America, Bandholtz returned to his native Michigan village and spent his final days there counting his savings, a tidy $101,000, and cataloging his thousands of curios.[8]

Though aloof from other American officers, Bandholtz could perform with an intuitive brilliance in foreign cultures. "Bandholtz certainly has more gift than any of us for handling the Filipino people," wrote Colonel Harbord in 1907.[9] In explosive situations Bandholtz never failed to grasp the political jugular and could restore order by sheer force of personality. Acting on his own, he contained a potentially violent demonstration by forty thousand Manila workers in 1911. Eight years later, alone and armed only with a swagger stick, he repulsed truckloads of Rumanian troops bent on plundering Budapest's National Museum. In 1921 he broke an armed uprising by eighteen thousand West Virginia coal miners with a snap of his fingers and without firing a shot.[10] The detached observation and deft manipulations that defined his personality, though hardly appealing, would prove useful in a colonial police whose work entailed betrayal, deception, disinformation, and, on occasion, assassination.

There were, however, some significant differences in the abilities of these two shadow masters. If we compare their intelligence reports, Bandholtz, though encyclopedic in his grasp of Filipino political connections, was a bit flat, often missing the critical cultural nuance. As constabulary chief in 1907, he could sweep across Luzon at dictation speed, enumerating the kinship, character, and allegiances for almost every provincial governor, calling Pangasinan's Artacho "energetic," Nueva Ecija's Gabaldon "very weak," and Cavite's Leonardo Osorio "a puppet in the hands of Dominador Gomez." But Crame's 1909 survey of elected officials demonstrates an even greater depth of local knowledge and, most important, an uncanny insight into individual character akin to what decades later would be called psychological profiling.[11] Bandholtz had a superior military education and a broader political vision, but Crame was clearly the intellectual force and social fulcrum for the constabulary's success as a secret police force, a talent that Bandholtz acknowledged by deferring to his subordinate's judgment on sensitive matters.[12]

Covert Tradecraft

Under the leadership of Bandholtz and Crame, the constabulary's Information Division devised a covert tradecraft that included surveillance and infiltration for intelligence collection, in-depth analysis of incoming data, and manipulation of target groups by means of black propaganda, psychological warfare, and agent provocateurs. Through this distinctively colonial experience, the Information Division developed an expertise unrivaled by any comparable U.S. agency.

In the seven years of its most intensive political warfare, 1907–14, the foundation for the constabulary's covert operations was the daily, shoe leather surveillance of suspected radicals by hundreds of Filipino agents—or, to be precise, 118 of these "operators" in 1904, the last year this figure was released.[13] Known only by code names or numbers, they were the full-time foot soldiers in the constabulary's secret war, moving daily through Manila's radical meetings and detailing every contact in thousands of regular reports.

Through judicious recruitment, the Information Division won some invaluable Filipino agents whose revolutionary background and paradoxical commitment to the nationalist cause gave them access to the leading Filipino militants. At the high tide of Japanese espionage in 1908–9, for example, Agent 11, known as "Justo Sagasa," showed a consistent ability to extract information from both the radical leader Felipe Buencamino Sr. and his Japanese contact, Capt. J. Ihara, a member of Japan's General Staff then working undercover as a student at Buencamino's Manila college. Although Agent 11's true identity is still concealed, he was, like others in the secret service, a former revolutionary respected by his comrades.[14] Similarly, Agent 6, known as "Mariano Nicolas," was an early member of the Katipunan and a former general in Aguinaldo's army. Indicative of both his access and his motivation for espionage, this agent's report of January 1911 charged that Manila's leading radicals—Felipe Buencamino, Ramon Diokno, Isabelo de los Reyes, and Bishop Gregorio Aglipay—had "signed a contract with Japan to cede the Philippine Customs to the latter for thirty years upon emancipation of the Philippines by aid of Japan." Expressing his deep concern over the possible success of this scheme, Agent 6 added that "as an ex-general of the revolution of 1896 and a practical expert, I want the independence of the Philippines at a day when the people are united and not in these years of division, egoism and regionalism, because civil war is inevitable."[15] When circumstances demanded it, the constabulary played on more venal instincts to recruit agents in Manila's netherworld of spies, radicals, and racketeers. In December 1909, for example, Agent 22 reported that a spy named Istellas was bragging at a local cockpit about working for Colonel Crame, saying, "Look, friend, I never lack money for expenses and clothes."[16]

Colonel Crame was also skilled at turning enemy agents into double agents. In December 1909, Agent 22 reported that a radical had recruited a PC officer to foment mutiny. The colonel soon identified this would-be mutineer as Sgt. Blas Baglagon and summoned him from Cavite with his commander, Col. Thomas I. Mair. Confronted with the agent's report, the sergeant confessed to joining "the revolution they are planning under the direction of Ishikawa, Trias, and Sandiko," adding that they were "waiting for arms from Japan." Instead of arresting the sergeant, Crame "gave him instructions to continue working with the conspiracy until he had concrete knowledge of all the plans of the revolutionists."[17]

Though lacking formal instruction in covert tradecraft, these Filipino agents were resourceful operatives, improvising to create a repertoire of surveillance techniques. In their rounds of Manila by foot, horse cart, tram, and train, full-time agents attended radical meetings in streets, empty lots, or theaters, taking extensive notes on the endless debates. At a December 1909 gathering of some 150 workers at Barrio Mangahan in Paco district, Agent 2 monitored discussions of a possible war between Japan and America to identify enemy sympathizers. At the opposite end of the social scale, he attended a meeting at the Manila Opera House in May 1910 called to protest the sale of Church lands to American trusts, listening closely as the editor of the daily *La Vanguardia* warned that "the day will come when we shall be like watchdogs tied to our master's table."[18] Covert infiltration by even the most experienced agents often risked exposure. As PC operations intensified, prominent Filipino radicals fielded their own men for counterintelligence. After one of Felipe Buencamino's spies followed Agent 11 to Colonel Crame's office in March 1910, this operative was suddenly shut out of radical circles, rendering his future reports almost useless.[19]

Intelligence Analysis

With its network of several hundred active Filipino agents, the constabulary's Information Division collected masses of political data through intensive surveillance of individuals, infiltration of radical groups, and careful monitoring of press and public discourse. All this intelligence flowed into its Manila headquarters where it was translated, typed, and filed. Using numbering systems similar to those devised by Melvil Dewey and Charles A. Cutter in the 1870s, each document in this torrent of information was coded by topic and sequence to juxtapose related reports for individual character studies, order-of-battle rosters, and longitudinal surveys of entire movements, creating a colonial frame for analysis and action.

This system reduced each detailed report, which often ran to ten or twelve typed pages, to a single "smart number." Thus, a letter from Agent 30 dated January 15, 1911, became simply report "No. A14/0223." Data was then cross-referenced in name and topical files to allow a quick response to queries prompted by subsequent reports. When a letter denouncing Colonel Crame, signed "Luis David," reached PC headquarters in May 1911, a check of the surname David found the Christian names "Agapito, Antonio, Bernardo, Felix, Guillermo, Hermogenes, Honorio, Juan and Leoncio." Through steps not explained this led to the identification of the author as "Luis David living at Angeles, Pampanga, who has been regarded as pro-Japanese."[20]

At the operational level, this information facilitated arrests of subversives, the amassing of evidence for trial, dissemination of disinformation, and psychological warfare to foster suspicions among targeted groups. At its peak after 1910, the Information Division fused close political analysis and nuanced character study to produce biographies of prominent radicals. More broadly, constabulary officers could weave diverse information retrieved from files spanning many years into a sociological study of the culture and politics of major movements.[21]

During his decade commanding the Information Division (1907–17), Rafael Crame refined these longitudinal studies to counter Japanese espionage and later used them, with considerable effect, in his covert campaign against Filipino radicals. Drawing on these files and reports, Crame's staff compiled order-of-battle rosters for Filipinos in the pro-Japan movement, identifying ten legislators, notably the future statesmen Rafael Palma and Jayme de Veyra, and fourteen newspapermen, including the entire staff of the nationalist newspaper *El Renacimiento*, as "agents of the Japanese government."[22]

Driven by this threat, Colonel Crame himself profiled the Filipino legislators elected in 1909, drawing data from the division files on family background, social networks, and personal vices to produce some insightful character studies. In sum, Crame's reports, like Goya's Spanish caricatures in *Los Caprichos*, were brutally frank portraits of the stunted personalities and blighted lives found in the shadows of empire. With withering prose, Colonel Crame portrayed Laguna's governor elect, Domingo Ordoveza, as a diffident child of colonial wealth who had returned from studies overseas with a pastiche of social superficialities instead of skills or principles. "When he came from America, he had imitated American customs," reads a passage that shows how deeply surveillance had reached into private social space, "thereby disgusting his family, for he began to discharge the servants, saying that in America rich people had no servants but did their own work, and he wished to imitate them." With sharp sensitivity to his country's political culture, Crame portrayed the representative elect for Rizal Province, Jose Lino Luna, as a wastrel with no political qualifications save one. "His public life has been in the cockpits," the colonel explained. "He has no moral influence over the masses and his triumph in the election is due to the support of his cockfighting friends who gave him great help."[23]

As its antiradical campaign expanded, the Information Division drew on this rich intelligence to profile the man it considered the greatest threat to colonial order, the irrepressible rebel, General Artemio Ricarte. In contrast to later, less sympathetic accounts, Colonel Crame's thirty-page biography of the general portrays him as a dreamer whose quixotic quest to repeat the Katipunan's mass uprising and rewind history's clock damned him to a life of prison, poverty, and perpetual failure. After several years leading the revolution's underground inside U.S.-occupied Manila, Ricarte was captured in 1900 and exiled to Guam with other "irreconcilables." Despite three years' imprisonment on that isolated island, he refused to take an oath of loyalty to America and was deported to Hong Kong where he tried in vain to revive the Katipunan. In December 1903 Ricarte slipped back into Manila on a steamer for a desperate second attempt at revolution. During his weeks of moving about Manila meeting secretly with former comrades, the radical playwright Aurelio Tolentino asked how they would fight without guns. "In the same way as against Spain in 1896," Ricarte replied, "namely, with daggers and bamboo pikes." But his plans for an uprising by "Constabulary inspectors who had belonged to the revolution" imploded in a premature mutiny, relegating Ricarte to cutting stone in a Mariveles quarry and an eventual six-year sentence in solitary confinement at Bilibid Prison. Judging from the PC reports Crame cited in his case file, Ricarte's every step in this six-month journey to defeat was the subject of detailed reports from either PC surveillance or comrades who had betrayed him.[24]

Counterespionage

After taking command of the Information Division in late 1906, Colonel Crame's covert operations moved through two distinct phases, starting with an obsessive counterespionage effort against the threat of Japanese aggression and then shifting to a successful campaign against Filipino radicals. In his initial, rather lonely crusade against Japanese conquest, Crame seemed to slip into that hall of mental mirrors common to counterintelligence, mistaking rumors for reality and fitting fragments of data into a distorted mosaic of threat.

After its defeat of Russia in 1905, Japan became, in American eyes, a rival for control of the Philippines. Two years later the islands were, in the words of PC chief Bandholtz, "simply slopping over with Japanese spies." The aim of such espionage was not, he said, invasion but "to incite the Filipinos to frequent uprisings . . . in the hopes . . . that our government would be willing to get rid of the islands at any price."[25] Half a world away inside the White House President Theodore Roosevelt shared a similar sense of Japanese threat. In 1907 he ordered the

Military Information Division to submit "weekly memoranda concerning the activities and apparent intentions of the Japanese all over the world." Reportedly "convinced that Japan was preparing a hostile move against the United States," the president, mindful of recent tensions with Tokyo over Japanese immigration, ordered the Atlantic Fleet to cross the Pacific in a show of force, producing the famed circumnavigation of the globe by America's "Great White Fleet."[26]

That dramatic demonstration of naval power was more show than substance, however, and it could not mask the reality of America's retreat from the western Pacific. Fueling a growing Filipino sense that U.S. influence was fading, Roosevelt's successor, President William H. Taft, pulled the main U.S. Navy forces back to Pearl Harbor in late 1909 and ended construction of naval fortifications at both Corregidor and Subic Bay in the Philippines. In the words of one PC secret agent, this news "sounded like a bomb in all social circles."[27] Communicating a sense of vulnerability at this edge of empire, Governor-General W. Cameron Forbes warned the War Department that "it is the policy of Japan to cultivate throughout the islands a pro-Japanese feeling and an anti-American one at the same time they are mapping and surveying . . . the roads and ports." He urged that "we should take certain precautionary measures . . . of creating among the Filipinos a public opinion distrustful of Japan."[28]

Such pronouncements were informed in part by constabulary intelligence. In his first report on this looming danger dated December 1906, Colonel Crame warned that after its victory over Russia Japan had committed itself to "the complete expulsion of the Caucasian races" from Asia and that the United States was now "its only serious obstacle." In the event of war, Tokyo would strike first at Hawaii and then occupy the Philippines, a move that would be supported by a Filipino "uprising in favor of the Japanese intervention." To this latter end Japan was working through Filipino agents to compile "a set of maps on a much larger scale . . . than exist anywhere else."[29]

If Crame sounded the warning, then starting in late 1909 his secret agents supplied ample details for his vision of a complex conspiracy. To arm the secret Filipino army that would rise in support of Japan, Vicente Lucban, an ex-general famed for slaughtering U.S. troops at Balangiga, Samar, had reportedly left for Japan to purchase ten thousand rifles while his confederates moved through the city's slums seeking recruits for a mass slaughter of American colonials.[30] Among the many reports about arms smuggling, the constabulary attached the most credibility to those involving ex-general Licerio Geronimo, who was despised by American colonials for killing their hero, General Henry Lawton. To unmask his activities the Information Division periodically dispatched secret agents to investigate the arms warehouses he was reportedly building on Polillo Island off Luzon's remote Pacific coast.[31]

In a desperate counterattack, the U.S. colonial regime used its intelligence services to mount a clandestine propaganda and surveillance effort. Writing "for the eye of the honorable secretary of war only" in October 1909, Governor-General Forbes reported that Japan was engaged in "a systematic effort . . . particularly through the extremely hostile newspaper 'El Renacimiento,' to injure American prestige, stir up race feeling, and create dissatisfaction with the government." To check this campaign, Forbes urged, in the strongest terms, the launching of a comprehensive anti-Japanese propaganda campaign "to create a terror of Japan by giving a list of fancied horrors" leading to the conclusion "that the existence of the Filipino as a separate race would be endangered or its extinction absolutely certain" under Japanese rule. This information would be disseminated covertly among Filipinos via political parties, public meetings, and the press. To this end the government's undercover agents should attend "every secret meeting, supplied with facts and arguments ready-made to give a good logical case against Japanese occupation."[32]

In the meantime, the constabulary scored some surprising successes, notably the capture of a suspected Japanese asset, the messianic leader Felipe Salvador. Alone among Luzon's peasant rebels, Salvador had eluded the Americans for over a decade, defeating even the most extreme attempts to extract intelligence from his followers.[33] After years of inactivity, in early 1910 constabulary agents reported that Salvador had returned from Japan to mount a propaganda campaign on the slopes of his sacred Mount Arayat, fanning fears of an "approaching war between America and Japan." In reality this rumor was one of several PC penetration efforts that finally led to Salvador's capture in July. After the courts sentenced him to death, the U.S. regime carried out the execution in 1912 before the mayors of the Central Luzon municipalities where he had been most active, demoralizing peasant radicals and stilling messianic revolts in that region for the next quarter century.[34]

As the constabulary surveiled its agents, Japan's Manila consulate reacted by first conducting counterintelligence to identify personnel in the PC Information Division and then withdrawing most of its operatives.[35] In April 1910, when two Japanese were jailed for attempting to buy the plans of Manila Bay's fortifications from a soldier in the U.S. Army Corps of Engineers, the consulate quickly agreed to voluntary deportation.[36] After three years of aggressive counterespionage and some success, the constabulary's initial, inflated fears of a Japanese-sponsored conspiracy thus declined and its Information Division turned to a more substantial target: Filipino nationalism.

Surveilling Radical Nationalists

As this sense of foreign threat receded in 1909–10, the Information Division shifted its gaze inward. Its agents slowly infiltrated Filipino nationalist circles so deeply that they were able to provide the constabulary with both accurate intelligence and considerable control over the movement. Gradually, the constabulary moved beyond mere surveillance to covert penetration, both damaging the radical movement and embroiling the division in political intrigues.

Colonel Crame's agents were few and his funds limited, but through painstaking analysis he identified the radical movement's weakest points and deployed his resources strategically to exploit them. Whether by accident or design, the colonel ignored the movement's institutional foundations of press, parties, and unions that so obsessed his American superiors. Instead he attacked the less visible, more vulnerable intangibles that were its real strength. Lacking a unifying organization like the original Katipunan, Manila's militant nationalist movement comprised a loose, three-tiered structure: a network of a dozen leaders, a hundred-plus mid-level cadres, and a floating mass of workers. To mobilize this amorphous movement, radical leaders relied on loose personal networks as they moved about Manila in street-corner rallies, meetings in private homes, and chance encounters on streets, trams, and trains. Their ultimate strength, as Crame understood, lay in the slender threads of shared values, language, and aspirations whose sum was trust. Attacking each element strategically, the police and PC monitored countless meetings within the nationalist networks in Manila and its surrounding provinces. At radical street rallies constabulary agents and allies rose from the crowd to deliver seemingly spontaneous rebuttals, articulating a counterpropaganda that contested the movement's ideological appeal. Simultaneously, secret agents infiltrated the militants' leadership, fomenting suspicion and division. As fear and recrimination spread throughout the nationalist network, trust, its essential social cement, eroded.

In this final, critical phase of the antiradical campaign, the constabulary owed much of its successful infiltration to Filipino agents with credibility and contacts. In this effort Bandholtz and Crame formed tactical alliances with four famed nationalists who served the constabulary as unpaid voluntary agents: Eulogio Reyes Carrillo, a Makati planter and well-known activist; Aurelio Tolentino, a famed radical dramatist; Santiago Alvarez, a former revolutionary general; and Manuel Quezon, the senior Nacionalista legislator and a rising political star. Drawing on their oratorical skills and local connections, they acted as de facto spokesmen for U.S.-Filipino collaboration. At times they went a step further, providing key intelligence that aided the constabulary's efforts to neutralize radical movements. Some, like Quezon, no doubt tried to manipulate the U.S. security apparatus to serve their vision of Filipino aspirations, but others, like Tolentino, seemed to have been broken by the pressure of police surveillance to serve colonial ends. With the help of these agents, and lesser contributions by several hundred more, the constabulary succeeded in demoralizing and dividing the radical nationalist movement between 1907 and 1912. By discrediting the leaders and disbanding their militant organizations, the constabulary in effect cleared the colony's narrow democratic space for political moderates willing to collaborate with colonial rule.

In November 1909 Carrillo set off on a personal mission to infiltrate pro-Japanese circles, producing useful intelligence that he detailed in a seven-page report to the U.S. governor-general. At Hong Kong, Carrillo had a hostile meeting with Vicente Sotto, an exiled radical second only to General Ricarte in the pro-Japan conspiracy. When Carrillo said the Filipinos "should declare themselves completely neutral" in any war between America and Japan, Sotto dismissed this visitor as "a spy of the American government." Privately, however, Sotto was eager to swap intelligence for a pardon from rape charges that were keeping him in exile and offered documents about radicals' secret negotiations with the Japanese to smuggle seventy thousand rifles into the Philippines. In concluding his report to the U.S. governor-general, Carrillo recommended an aggressive campaign to counter the radicals' pro-Japanese propaganda.[37]

Quezon's relationship with the constabulary was more complex. As noted earlier, during the first decade of his political career he had been an undercover operative for the colonial police and relied on its commanders to suppress scandals that could have destroyed his reputation. In the early 1920s, General Crame claimed that Quezon had once been his "private spy . . . used in all sorts of cases in the early days of the Constabulary." The quotation apparently refers to 1902–3, when Crame was still a junior lieutenant in the Information Division and Quezon a "penniless" student and neophyte lawyer. These were years of nationalist ferment when the constabulary was using numerous Filipino spies to monitor radical groups. Amidst this antiradical campaign in May 1903, the Manila Police raided a theater during the final scene of the incendiary play *Kahapon, Ngayon, at Bukas* (Yesterday, Today, Tomorrow). As the Filipino flag rose triumphantly to cheers from the audience, burly American officers burst in, threw one actor off the stage, and arrested its author, Aurelio Tolentino. In the famed "subversive drama" case that followed, the young attorney Quezon defended the playwright against felony charges. Even though his client was sentenced to a stiff prison term, Quezon's lead role in his defense no doubt facilitated contacts among Manila radicals that were useful to the constabulary. If Crame was correct, then Quezon, playing the colonial game with consummate skill, won nationalist credentials by defending radical leaders and colonial patronage by spying on them. Later, when he was chief of the constabulary, Crame could say of Quezon to powerful Americans, "I know him from top to bottom and he never will dare to attack me."[38]

Even after the legislature sent Quezon to Washington as its resident commissioner in 1909, he still worked closely with the constabulary, using his radical access to gather intelligence and preempt uprisings that might have complicated his negotiations with the U.S. Congress over independence. "The Manila conspirators are endeavoring to land arms over on the contra costa [east coast]," PC General Bandholtz wrote Quezon in December as he traveled to Washington. Bandholtz asked his protégé to write "your parientes in Baler and Casiguran and some of your friends in Mauban and Infanta" to keep aloof from "any so-called 'japanofilo' revolutionists or conspirators." Reminding Quezon of his protection and patronage, the chief added, "We want you to make good, to make good emphatically and there is no living Filipino who can benefit his people more than Manuel L. Quezon."[39]

Whether visiting Manila or passing through Hong Kong, Quezon met regularly with radicals to discourage their plots and gather intelligence. In October 1911, after years of fund-raising, the radicals planned to unveil a statue of Andres Bonifacio at Balintawak near Manila while mobilizing a crowd of forty thousand revolutionary veterans armed with fighting bolos, the symbolic weapon of the 1896 revolution. On a home visit from Washington, Quezon feared that fiery rhetoric and fighting bolos were a volatile combination that could mean bloodshed of tragic proportions. "Quezon inside of 48 hours also got next to the Ricarte conspiracy and verified everything that we had," General Bandholtz wrote his army colleagues, and then "came to my house one night in much concern having acquired information almost identical with our own." To avoid shooting "several hundred poor ignorant taos [peasants]," Bandholtz dispatched Colonel Crame to warn the rally's organizers that "we would see to it that the ones first hurt would be the chairmen of the committees." Finding themselves in the constabulary's sights, the radicals ordered that workers attend without their bolos.[40]

The constabulary also made good use of Quezon's access to General Ricarte himself, the last active revolutionary. During this same voyage of October 1911, Quezon, on an apparent mission to plant disinformation, met Ricarte at Hong Kong to warn that his top Manila leaders were plotting with the constabulary to stage a sham uprising that would justify mass arrests of his followers.[41] A year later, in December 1912, Agent 27 reported that Quezon had again met Ricarte in Hong Kong, urging him to delay the revolt and promising that should "peaceful measures in America fail" to win independence "the two will come to the Philippines together and begin the revolution."[42]

At the close of the Taft era, W. Cameron Forbes, who had supervised the constabulary for a decade as police secretary and governor-general, called Quezon "the most responsive little organism to outside influences that I know." Explaining why a short leash was needed to keep him in line, the governor-general added, "I have likened Quezon to a wonderfully trained hunting dog run wild. If the hunter is skilled . . . Quezon will become a sheep dog, rounding up the sheep and bringing them in admirably. But alone or in bad company, he goes wrong and ends up killing lambs and devastating hen yards."[43]

If Quezon was the constabulary's guide through the thickets of elite politics, then Aurelio Tolentino was its ideological gladiator in Manila's crowded slums. As a dedicated revolutionary and radical dramatist, Tolentino's name is synonymous, even today, with unbowed resistance to American rule.[44] But confidential PC reports reveal that by 1908 a decade of ceaseless PC pressure had transformed him from nationalist icon into colonial agent.

For over a decade, from the founding of the Katipunan in 1892 through the launching of the radical Partido Nacionalista in 1901, Tolentino had been at the storm center of revolutionary struggle. Two years later he won lasting fame after his arrest and trial for presenting the incendiary drama *Kahapon, Ngayon, at Bukas* at a time when colonial repression made the stage the only free democratic space. He then joined an abortive uprising led by General Ricarte and was again arrested in the constabulary's round-up of the conspirators. In February 1907, after an extended public campaign, Tolentino was released on a "strict parole" that required him to report monthly to Colonel Crame. Under the colonel's close supervision Tolentino resumed work as a dramatist but now submitted his scripts to the Manila Police for strict censorship that moderated his radical politics. In striking contrast to his early anti-imperialist works, his 1908 drama *Luwalhati* featured a crudely metaphoric marriage between the Philippines and America. For a full five years, until his executive pardon in 1912, Tolentino faced the threat of summary incarceration as he moved about the city producing plays and participating in political debate, circumstances that gave the constabulary an extraordinarily valuable asset.[45]

Tolentino first proved his usefulness to the police during a sudden wave of labor militancy that swept Manila in early 1909. Responding to an influx of U.S. capital after the Payne-Aldrich Tariff opened the American market to Philippine imports, militant nationalists, now marginalized in the electoral arena, shifted tactics by mobilizing workers for a renewed attack on colonial rule. Under the fiery leadership of Dr. Dominador Gomez, the Union Obrera Democratica launched strikes against American firms that dominated key sectors of the city's economy: first a successful six-day strike by fourteen hundred seamen against the port's shipping companies in January; next an abortive action by stevedores in the import-export houses in February; and, most important, a bitter monthlong walkout in March by motormen and conductors of the city's streetcar monopoly, the Manila Electric Railroad and Light Company (Meralco).[46]

When Meralco rejected the union demands, Filipino workers struck against a corporation that symbolized American colonial capital more than any other. In a massive deployment, police patrolled the yards and rode each tram with riot guns, allowing American employees to keep the streetcars running. After five days at the brink of defeat, the union suddenly shifted tactics and inspired a surge of mass support with wall posters and newspaper advertisements calling on patriotic Filipinos to boycott the trams and ride *carromatas,* the city's omnipresent horse cabs.[47] Now facing both strike and boycott, the colonial government mobilized 140 city police to ride streetcars and 730 constabulary to patrol suburban lines, an overwhelming show of force that allowed the trams to run unimpeded.[48] As the strike emptied the streetcars for a second week, the U.S. regime, reaching the limits of physical coercion, used court orders and covert operations to decapitate the movement. In mid-March the government jailed Dr. Gomez for four months on the charge that he had used "threats" in an earlier strike.[49] When he later applied for a pardon, the governor-general, in a deft use of scandalous data from constabulary files, refused, claiming that the doctor had "fleeced a . . . friend out of ₱30,000 in a sure thing gambling game" and used his medical license for "trafficking in opium . . . among his fellow countrymen."[50]

As parallel strikes spread to the Manila Railway, the El Oriente cigar factory, and the Luzon Sugar Refinery in May, the union executive decided to renew its boycott of Meralco's streetcars and chose Aurelio Tolentino as director general of the planned strike. At this sensitive juncture, Colonel Harbord, then deputy PC chief, passed a warning through Agent 16 that Tolentino would "suffer a loss of prestige" as a powerless figurehead in a potentially violent strike. The colonel also met personally with the union president, Antonio Montenegro, urging him to resign rather than lead a strike. At a mass meeting that night, Tolentino publicly refused the post of strike leader, an example followed by a dozen subsequent nominees. Adding to the demoralization, Montenegro resigned as union president. These visible losses left the union "pretty badly disorganized." When the union executive launched its strike on May 29, the usually sympathetic *El Renacimiento* accused "these good-for-nothing Messiahs" of "shameless charlatanism," a harbinger of the strike's imminent collapse.[51]

Apart from his role in curbing the union movement, Tolentino, once famed for his fiery anti-American scripts, now appeared at countless public meetings before hundreds, sometimes thousands of workers in the city's slums to challenge the ideological hegemony of radical nationalism.[52] In this age when an orator's words were a powerful force for working-class mobilization, few could equal Tolentino's mastery of Tagalog rhetoric and powers of persuasion. At a Nacionalista Party rally on Tondo's Calle Moriones in June 1910, other speakers damned the United States for enslaving the Filipinos while Tolentino praised U.S. rule as "a model of colonial governments, the worthy production of a people who had freed slaves." This government, he said in words recorded separately by the three PC secret agents present, was composed of "illustrious persons, both Americans and Filipinos," who had "passed laws with masterly wisdom" while showing respect for "political, social and religious liberty." Attacking the rally's radical speakers as "false and thieves," Tolentino insisted that "impatience for national independence should cease" since "many prominent Americans are laboring day and night to grant Filipinos what is theirs."[53] At a street rally in Manila's Trozo district in April 1913, he braved the crowd's anger to predict that the American Democratic Party would honor its commitment to "grant the Filipinos independence." Should the Americans betray this promise, then, he said, "all the Filipinos ought to arm themselves and spill their blood for the liberty of the Philippines."[54]

With his forceful personality, Colonel Crame seems to have been the key to Tolentino's compliance, winning his loyalty even while serving as his parole officer.

"I know Colonel Crame," Tolentino told a fellow radical in 1910, in words recorded by another secret agent present, "he is a good friend and as a patriotic Filipino he is one of the few good ones we have here." What then, his comrade asked, should we do about the "imminent perils" that threatened the nation's future? "All we Filipinos ought to take the side of the American government," Tolentino replied, and realize that "the tomb of our political future is prepared in the abyss of Japanese expansion."[55]

Yet in assaying the impact of police repression on such a dedicated nationalist we must take care to place any apparent inconsistencies in context. In his change from nationalist rebel to colonial agent between 1905 and 1909, Tolentino maintained his political loyalties, moving in tandem with his allies at the head of the rising Nacionalista Party, who were shifting from confrontation to collaboration with the colonial regime. In 1903–4, when Tolentino had staged his famed seditious plays and taken up arms in the hills, his nationalist allies were struggling against a U.S. regime still reluctant to share power. After 1907, when he was pardoned and emerged from prison to speak in support of U.S. rule, his Nacionalista comrades had captured the new Assembly and were cooperating with the American governor-general in drafting budgets and distributing patronage. For this dedicated nationalist, like his less idealistic political associates, police repression and political reform were intertwined in an effective colonial strategy.

In his continuing campaign against the radicals, Colonel Crame used another of his key agents, Santiago Alvarez, a former revolutionary general and famed nationalist, to split the militant Dimas Alang society, whose sudden popularity among Manila's workers had made it a serious security threat. This organization had been formed in 1910 by the radical Patricio Belen as a mutual aid society to assist Manila's working class with illnesses and burials. As Dimas Alang's membership spread through the city like wildfire, Colonel Crame's concern grew, and in June 1912 he backed ex-general Alvarez in forming a rival group, the Makabuhay society. With a skillful use of agent provocateur tactics, this constabulary-controlled society was incendiary, even revolutionary in its rhetoric, an apparent effort to draw dangerous militants from the more moderate Dimas Alang to engage in violence that would lead to their arrest, thereby eliminating them and defusing their mutual aid movement. Fighting soon started between the two societies, damaging Dimas Alang. To preempt discovery of his PC ties, Alvarez admitted "his connection with the secret service" to some members, claiming that it would further their revolutionary cause by allowing recruitment of "a large number of Constabulary soldiers . . . to strike down the tyrants."[56]

In the midst of this bitter infighting, rumors of an armed revolt swept Manila, forcing constabulary countermeasures. Just before midnight on August 24, two informants called at Colonel Crame's house to warn that the radical Felipe Buencamino was spreading news that "the members of the Dimas-Alang Association were going to rise" at Balintawak two days later, the anniversary of the 1896 revolution. The next day, August 25, the colonel moved ceaselessly about Manila, trying to block the impending revolt by confronting key actors such as Buencamino, who denied any role and pointed an accusing finger at Archbishop Aglipay. When August 26 passed without incident, Crame concluded that the PC operations had "a good effect on the conspirators."[57]

In the aftermath of August 26, the rivalry between the two societies escalated. In mid-September Dimas Alang was, Agent 6 reported, "scaring the people" with the charge that Alvarez was "a secret agent of the government" who was betraying his own Makabuhay members to the police.[58] Despite these swirling charges, the Makabuhay pressed its fight against Dimas Alang until December 19 when the *Manila Daily Bulletin* delivered a deathblow. In a sensational front-page story, the paper charged that Colonel Crame had infiltrated both societies with spies such as Alvarez and used them to incite an unsuccessful uprising by Dimas Alang on August 26. In the exposé's aftermath, Alvarez resigned and Makabuhay's members, nervous about possible arrest, dissolved their chapters to join Dimas Alang.[59] Hastily Colonel Crame also cut his ties to Alvarez.[60]

Troubled by the *Bulletin*'s report, the Assembly moved quickly to authorize a special investigation into the allegations that General Alvarez, working as a constabulary spy, had fomented the attempted August uprising. Rising to speak for the motion, Representative Pedro Guevara, a former constabulary officer, denounced the abortive revolt in three nearby provinces as "foolishness . . . because they understand that the [U.S.] Democratic Party, as soon as it assumes the administration, will comply with its promises, without the need to resort to violent measures." Since this uprising was, he added, a "plot aiming to . . . instill the impression that this is a people prone to disorder, a chaotic people, a people incapable of assuming responsibilities that come with self government," these events threatened the nation's cherished goal of independence. Broadly and boldly framed, the Assembly's final motion formed a committee armed with full subpoena powers to investigate these charges that Alvarez was "a secret service agent of the insular police, that he instigated the ignorant people of Bulacan, Rizal, and Cavite to rise in armed revolt." Approved unanimously, this measure launched the legislature's first inquiry into the nation's security services, producing a final report that cast strong suspicions on Alvarez and the constabulary.[61]

In Colonel Crame's partisan view, the legislative inquiry was a "flat failure" since at least two of the three investigators were affiliated with the Dimas Alang. Although the committee's final report "whitewashed" this radical society and blamed Makabuhay for the intramural violence against Dimas Alang, it did not, he said, determine whether Alvarez was in fact "a secret agent of the Constabulary." Rejecting the legislature's criticism of this covert operation, PC chief Bandholtz described Dimas Alang as "most detrimental to the interests of the Filipino people" and branded its leaders opportunistic plotters.[62]

Radical Implosion

Despite occasional reversals, the cumulative weight of constabulary espionage from 1909 to 1914, in combination with U.S. political concessions, marginalized the militant nationalist movement. As the Information Division elaborated its deep penetration and agent provocateur tactics, radical leaders grew angry, lashing out in impotent outbursts before turning inward for bitter recriminations. In this crippling climate, Manila's radical movement imploded through betrayals both imagined and real.

At the first signs of surveillance, radical leaders were brashly, even naïvely confident. "I do not believe that there can be a single traitor among us," Isabelo de los Reyes, the leader of the militant Union Obrera, told a closed meeting of trusted radicals, including a PC spy who took down his every word. "Up to the present the agents of the government have accomplished nothing in their investigations. . . . They succeed in learning that arms have been landed but cannot learn where they are hidden . . . since we have well paid employees to warn us, among the very secret police themselves."[63] Similar defiance rang through the Opera House in early 1911 when the Filipino Carnival was banned by the Municipal Board for competing with the American-controlled Manila Carnival. "I must remind you that for about one month, I have been watched by secret agents," said the vice chair of the Filipino Carnival Committee, Doña Constancia Poblete, in a defiant voice noted by the PC spy present. "But . . . if it is necessary to lose my life for our country, I would do it gladly."[64]

Gradually radical leaders began to accuse their comrades of espionage, often on groundless suspicions. One Sunday morning in July 1910, Manila's leading pro-Japan agitator, Jose Ramos Ishikawa, became "greatly excited, cursing his friends, whom he called traitors," and ordering his servants to bar them from his household. According to Agent 27, who had a spy inside the household, Ishikawa "said he had learned that Dr. Bonifacio Arevalo and Vicente Lukban had played the traitor to him and were acting as secret police for Col. Crame." In a report to his chief, Crame explained that Arevalo and Lukban were not his agents and had recently accompanied Ishikawa on a propaganda mission to Japan. But they had also called at his constabulary office to "learn what they were suspected of . . . and this, doubtless, was enough to make them suspicious to their accomplice."[65]

While Colonel Crame played on such suspicions, General Ricarte's revolutionary coterie was drawn into a maze of mirrors. After his second deportation to Hong Kong in 1910, Ricarte found himself in a "demimonde" inhabited by radical Filipino exiles such as Vicente Sotto, the aforementioned fugitive from rape charges in Cebu, and Japanese spies such as Usa Onkihiko, the proprietor of a local brothel. When exiles appointed him head of their Revolutionary Council, Ricarte summoned three Manila loyalists, including his trusted representative Ignacio Velasco, and instructed them to "collect war funds" by selling made-up military ranks with ornate certificates ordered from a Hong Kong printer. In a revealing coincidence, constabulary Agent 26, who was also a trusted Ricarte aide, came to Hong Kong in March 1911 with a Manila delegation for meetings at the general's Lamma Island headquarters. After an exchange of warm greetings among old comrades, Ricarte walked the party, including the PC secret agent, into the nearby hills to discuss their military plans for Manila, explaining that he did not trust his secretary Agueda Esteban, a lifelong revolutionary who would soon become his wife. In the midst of this plotting, the Revolutionary Council collapsed in an ugly public feud in which Ricarte accused Sotto of cowardice and Sotto charged Ricarte with exploitation. Reflecting the pathology of exile politics, Ricarte convened his Philippine Revolutionary government of three members to expel the other two, Sotto and Tomas Umali.[66]

As Ricarte retreated into a fog of suspicion, Resident Commissioner Quezon called at Hong Kong in October 1911 with a serious warning, duly recorded by Agent 26, that may well have been constabulary disinformation. The Revolutionary Council's top Manila leader, Licerio Geronimo, was, Quezon charged, "in combination with the General of Constabulary [Bandholtz] and Colonel Rafael Crame to start a sham battle in the city so that the Government will have a right to arrest . . . persons . . . attached to Ricarte." Without questioning this improbable scenario, Ricarte appointed his most trusted comrade, Velasco, as Manila intelligence chief and ordered him to block these betrayals. In effect, Ricarte had ordered Velasco, a traitor who was probably PC Agent 26, to spy on Geronimo, an ex-general of the revolution whose loyalty was still firm.[67]

Over the next two years, 1913–14, as the U.S. Congress debated major reforms for the Philippines, times were changing but General Ricarte was not, holding fast to the old revolutionary vision of an armed uprising. In February 1913, the constabulary scored a major coup against Ricarte when its agents in Japan learned that he was plotting to steal plans for fortifications on Corregidor Island, the U.S. Army bastion that guarded the entrance to Manila Bay. After one of Colonel Crame's agents intercepted two professional tracings "enroute to Ricarte in Hong Kong," Chief Bandholtz ordered his senior secret agent, Edwin C. Bopp, to raid the home of one Jose Gansiko, a draftsman for the U.S. Army Corps of Engineers and "chief of staff of one of Ricarte's insurrecto zones." There constables caught him "actually at work tracing . . . fields of fire of Carabao, El Fraile and Caballo Islands." Even after arresting Gansiko for espionage, the PC preferred to press lesser charges instead of "giving away our whole scheme of secret service as far as watching the Ricarte movement is concerned."[68]

By early 1914 President Wilson's election had robbed General Ricarte of elite support, reducing his following, in Crame's words, to "a class wholly without education or intelligence."[69] Growing desperate by year's end, Ricarte planned a bold, two-stage uprising to capture Manila, starting with attacks to secure arms from local police stations and culminating in a massive assault on Fort McKinley, the U.S. Army post just outside the capital. Although this revolt would be easily crushed, the colony's security services were compromised by political intrigues. In his memoirs Governor-General Francis Burton Harrison, a liberal Democrat, charged that arch-imperialists within the army's Philippine command were mounting an agent provocateur operation "to stir up an 'insurrection,'" fomenting spectacular bloodshed to show that the Filipinos were unready for the autonomy offered in the Jones bill then before the U.S. Congress. Indeed, the army's local Military Intelligence Division had infiltrated the rebels' meetings with two Filipino scouts sergeants who now "promised them arms if they would rise up." Since the initiative for the revolt came, the governor-general said, from this "secret organization in the Scouts," the constabulary's intelligence chief, Colonel Crame, suddenly finding his usually informed sources uniformed, was "puzzled and nervous because of his inability to trace these rumors to their source."[70] Alone among these security services, the Manila Police, under the leadership of Chief George Seaver, monitored Ricarte's preparations carefully and countered them effectively.

According to a detailed report by the Manila Police, Ricarte had prepared this revolt for the past two years, sending couriers from Hong Kong to appoint officers for his revolutionary army and dividing the archipelago into military zones. After printing his revolutionary constitution, the general dispatched bulk shipments of the document, which the Manila Police intercepted. Nonetheless, on October 14 the constabulary attempted to take full control of the investigation and instructed the police to cease all activities, an order they quietly ignored. At this point "certain spies or agents" of the U.S. Army's Military Information Division, Harrison claimed, convinced Ricarte's plotters that "the Scout and Constabulary organizations would mutiny," inspiring the masses in the Manila zones "to start the revolution."[71]

On December 23, police and PC spies inside the revolutionary underground warned of an impending revolt, putting the capital on a full security alert. By the time the rebels massed on Christmas Eve, Manila Police were ready. At 7:30 p.m., a cook named "Captain" Eduardo Adajar and two hundred of his "army corps" assembled at the Botanical Gardens for an attack on the constabulary's Cuartel de España barracks inside the old walled city of Intramuros. If the rebels advanced, PC troops were waiting with machine guns and primed for slaughter. Within thirty minutes, however, armed police squads swarmed the gardens, firing three warning shots in the air, scattering the rebels, and arresting twenty who were carrying daggers and Katipunan insignia. By dawn the uprising was over with minimal bloodshed. In just a few days, the Manila Police had arrested most of the revolutionary officers and scattered their remaining followers.[72]

With General Ricarte now discredited and his forces disbanded, U.S. officials required only his arrest. At their urging British authorities expelled him from Hong Kong (where he was a legal resident) into Chinese territory (where he could be arrested). In March 1915, Colonel Crame's chief agent, Lt. Edwin Bopp, trailed the general on a ship steaming north to Shanghai, the start of a fruitless four-month pursuit. With a proper warrant from a U.S. exterritorial court in China, Agent Bopp finally made the arrest and boarded a ship bound for Manila with his prisoner in tow. But Ricarte escaped during a stop at Hong Kong and fled back up the China coast with the hapless Bopp again in pursuit all the way to Shanghai. There, with the help of Japanese agents, Ricarte eluded the PC lieutenant and escaped on a steamer bound for Japan, where he would live for the next thirty-five years as the proprietor of a Yokohama noodle shop.[73] Although Bopp's attempt to capture Ricarte had failed in the most obvious sense, after fourteen years of ceaseless surveillance the constabulary's Information Division had finally succeeded in destroying the radical nationalist movement and driving the country's last active revolutionary into retirement.

Chinese Deportation

The U.S. regime was not alone in manipulating information to achieve its political ends. Even as the constabulary refined its methods to defeat Japanese agents and Filipino radicals, Manila's less visible community of Chinese vice merchants exploited the colonial regime's repression to secure its dominion over the city's illicit gambling and opium trafficking. In August 1909 Governor-General Forbes, skirting the law in the name of security, ordered the midnight deportation of twelve Chinese who were allegedly members of the notorious "Highbinder Tong," a decision of dubious legality that the press challenged from day one, creating what Forbes himself called "one of the most violent causes célèbres in the history of the Islands."[74] While the colonial government depicted the deportees as lethal Chinese criminals who could plunge Manila into dreaded tong warfare, most of the press portrayed them as respectable merchants who had been branded criminals, secretly and falsely, by their rivals in Manila's Chinese community.

For several years Manila's Chinese Chamber of Commerce had complained of extortion by criminal gangs, or tongs, particularly the recently arrived Gee Hock Tong, a criminal brotherhood of clannish Teochow (Chiu Chau) speaking immigrants from the Chinese treaty port of Swatow (Shantou). In May 1908 the Manila Police reported the tong killing of a prominent Chinese in Tondo and an attack on the Soler Street home of a wealthy merchant by eight "highbinders" armed with knives, crimes that soon led to convictions for six members of this notorious Gee Hock Tong, including the "terror of Chinatown," Luis Sane. But in a murky political move two years later the wealthy Hokkien merchants of the Chinese chamber, locked in a bitter commercial competition with the rising Fooking Merchants Association, apparently decided to effect their rivals' deportation by branding them, falsely, as clandestine tong criminals. In April 1910 the Chinese chamber's legal counsel, A. Zarate Sycip, met with PC chief Bandholtz to urge raids on the Ban Siong Tong, which he described as a criminal society that concealed its lurid crimes behind a legitimate front. To assist in these arrests, Sycip provided the constabulary with an interpreter and identified Agapito Uy Tongco as the leader of this Ban Siong criminal gang. But he did not mention that these supposed criminals were actually respectable members of the Fookien Merchants Association, which was headed by the same Agapito Uy Tongco.[75] Without consulting Forbes, who was away, two of his executive aides, mindful of the bloody Chinatown "tong wars" that had wracked San Francisco in 1886 and Boston in 1903, moved quickly to make the mass arrests.[76]

Over the next few months, the Chinese Chamber of Commerce worked with Peking's consulate and the colonial executive to arrange the deportations. Backed by the city's established Chinese merchants, the chamber collected ten thousand pesos and compiled a list of twenty-seven alleged tong criminals, including one of those Sycip had fingered earlier, Agapito Uy Tongco. On August 20 the captain of the steamer *Yuensang* delayed lifting anchor until midnight, allowing Manila detectives to sweep Chinatown just as nightfall covered their movements. Over the next five hours police broke into private homes without warrants or court orders, arresting eight Chinese merchants from the legitimate Ban Siong Society and four actual criminals from the Gee Hok Tong, acting solely on secret intelligence obtained from their enemies in the Chinese chamber.[77]

As the detectives were sweeping the streets, a reporter named James A. Guild at the *Cablenews-American,* still an aggressive newspaper, got an inside tip that "something was doing in Chinatown." According to a confidential report by PC Agent 30, Guild rushed to Binondo and soon found "a number of Chinese were being rounded up by police." That night a police detective tipped another reporter, Frank W. Holland, "to go to the new docks and keep his eyes open." Hiding behind a post at the Malecon landing, Holland watched as paddy wagons pulled up in the darkness and a dozen Chinese were loaded onto a steam launch for deportation to Amoy on China's southern coast. When Police Chief Harding and Secret Service Chief Trowbridge drove up in a *carromata,* the reporter stepped out of the darkness to ask, "What's the story, Chief?"[78]

When this scoop hit the streets, the *Cablenews-American* transformed a secret operation into a public scandal. Beneath the banner headline "Twenty Chinese Deported Untried," the paper charged that most were "men of good character" victimized by baseless accusations from enemies in the Chinese community. The next day the paper condemned this "official kidnapping" as a "despotic act," asking, "Do not the police and secret service know that Government has been made the tool of . . . the adherents of one tong to wreak vengeance on the members of another tong?" Unlike the police, the paper's editor, Frederick O'Brien, seemed to be aware that Agapito Uy Tongco's arriviste Fooking Merchants Association had been engaged in a bitter competition with the long-established merchants of the Chinese Chamber of Commerce for political leadership in Chinatown. Indeed, the supposedly criminal Ban Siong Tong was simply another name for the legitimate Fooking Merchants Association. Casting further doubts on their criminality, the *Cablenews-American* reported that the deported Ban Siong/Fooking Merchants members had been police informants in a recent anti-opium campaign while their rivals in the Chinese Chamber had controlled the city's opium traffic since the beginning of U.S. rule.[79]

The story became a sensation that divided the capital. "The manner of arresting and deporting twenty Chinamen may be contrary to our ideas of justice and the rights of the individual," Commissioner Newton W. Gilbert told the *Manila Times,* "but I hope we may never see the day that Manila is at the mercy of Chinese secret societies as is San Francisco today." Predictably, Chief Harding dismissed the deportees as the city's "worst element."[80]

When Governor-General Forbes returned to Manila a few days later he found little support, legal or factual, for deportations conducted in his name but without his knowledge. To help Forbes justify these actions retrospectively, Chief Harding forwarded police records for the twelve deported Chinese. The four Gee Hock Tong deportees had long criminal records, including tong boss Francisco Co Tiao Cha, who had four arrests for gambling and opium trafficking. Nine of his Gee Hock followers had Bertillon photos in the Manila Police "rogues' gallery," including Chua Lui, "alias Luis Sane," who was an opium den operator and gambler. By contrast, police records for the Ban Siong society's deportees consisted of a single, identical sentence typed into each file, reading, "Companion of Agapito Uy Tongco in his raids and assaults on respectable Chinese." Although he was supposed to be a tong boss leading a crime wave, police could only describe Agapito Uy Tongco as "the subject of numerous complaints from responsible Chinese merchants," who were, of course, his commercial rivals in the Chinese Chamber of Commerce. In forwarding these police files to Washington, even Forbes had to admit that they looked "as if they were prepared more for action already taken than as an impartial statement without any axe to grind." Indeed, the police had bundled the legitimate Ban Siong merchants together with hardened Gee Hock criminals, decorating the mix with some paperwork to make a plausible package for deportation.[81]

In March 1910 six of the deported Chinese returned to Manila, reviving the controversy. As soon as they stepped off the ship their attorneys were ready with a habeas corpus petition and quickly won an injunction from a liberal Manila judge, A. S. Crossfield.[82] With Washington's support fading and opposition among Manileños rising, Governor-General Forbes decided, as he told his diary, to toss "a bombshell into their camp by getting the Legislature to pass a law authorizing and ratifying the whole transaction." In the closing minutes of the session at 4:00 a.m. on April 19, the Assembly passed Act No. 1986, declaring the governor-general's deportations "legal." In a confidential letter to the secretary of war, Forbes attributed the bill's passage to the influence of Speaker Sergio Osmeña, calling him "a very good friend and cordial co-worker." Three years later, in May 1913, the U.S. Supreme Court ruled that the legislature's eleventh-hour motion had made Forbes's original deportation of the dozen Chinese legal.[83] After years of "constant abuse from some of the native papers in regard to this deportation matter," Forbes now planned to celebrate his legal victory by starting deportation proceedings against "two or three of the most vicious Chinamen," who, he said, "have sent me a letter threatening my life."[84] But just two months later Forbes was "fired" as governor-general, ending his anticrime crusade in Chinatown.[85] Most important from a police perspective, this scandal showed that Manila's elite Chinese, with skills honed under an autocratic Manchu state, fed chiefs Harding and Bandholtz just the right information to transform otherwise respectable merchants into dangerous criminals and eliminate their commercial rivals. Apparently unaware of the bruising infighting inside Chinatown, the Manila Police had played into the hands of the Chinese chamber by allowing its vice merchants to consolidate their control of the city's lucrative opium traffic.

Colonel Crame's Triumph

If it took ignorance of local context and neglect of due process to deport a handful of Chinese, only a mastery of information warfare could ensure the miscarriage of justice that would soon crown the career of Rafael Crame. Drawing on covert tradecraft refined inside the PC's Information Division, Crame maneuvered the courts and constabulary into executing a prominent Filipino nationalist, the ex-general Mariano Noriel. For eleven years Crame, like the consummate colonial Javert he had become, tracked Noriel tirelessly through revolution, revolts, and radical plots to finally catch his quarry in a murderous local love triangle. Through his long years of service in the shadows of the colonial state, Crame had risen from a lowly PC lieutenant bested by Noriel in multiple court cases back in 1903 to a colonel of intelligence who could, through adroit management of information, finally put the noose around Noriel's neck in 1915. Through this murky triumph, Crame demonstrated his dominion over the covert netherworld and his worthiness in colonial eyes for an unprecedented promotion. Two years later, when Noriel swung, Crame became the first Filipino chief of the constabulary.

This cause célèbre began, unremarkably, one night in May 1909 when assailants broke into the home of a wealthy farmer named Gregorio Magtibay at Bacoor, Cavite, just south of Manila. After fatally stabbing him, the anonymous killers fled into the darkness. Within weeks what first seemed a routine robbery became tangled in a decade-long blood feud between the town's rival political bosses: ex-general Noriel and his bitter enemy Gregorio de Guia. With the help of Luis Landas, the town mayor and Noriel's godson, the constabulary investigated and gathered what at first seemed convincing evidence against the alleged mastermind, de Guia, and his supposed henchman, Gregorio Buendia, a scouts soldier known for killing the famed rebel Felizardo. At court hearings that dragged on until March 1910, the prosecution witnesses built what appeared to be a credible case against the two accused.[86]

Just three months later, however, de Guia won a new trial when a key witness retracted his testimony, claiming he had testified falsely "from fear of Lieutenant [Eleuterio] Kalaw of the Constabulary."[87] This reversal was apparently the work of two scouts captains close to the accused, notably Frank L. Pyle of the Army's MID, who scored an early coup in this case by jailing one of Noriel's key henchman, a jueteng collector named Roman Malabanan, on trumped-up vagrancy charges. By October the captains advised PC headquarters that Lieutenant Kalaw had been guilty of "dubious judgment" and five of the prosecution witnesses had been "paid by Mariano Noriel."[88]

At this sensitive juncture in January 1911, PC Chief Bandholtz dispatched Crame to Cavite on a mission to exonerate the two accused, de Guia and Buendia, who had acted as their confidential agents five years before in killing Felizardo. At a personal level Crame was pursuing his own vendetta, one dating back to 1903 when, as a lieutenant leading a PC intelligence team in Cavite, he had made three unsuccessful attempts to prosecute Noriel for his role in the province's insurgency.[89] This Cavite campaign had inspired *El Renacimiento's* allegations of abuse in 1905, which led to the constabulary's libel charges against the paper with Crame as the star prosecution witness. When the court dismissed his evidence and exonerated the accused editors, Crame was embarrassed, even humiliated. Clearly, the colonel had ample reason for revenge.

Drawing on his many years of experience in Cavite, Crame now concocted a new theory to crack this murder case. In his view Noriel had engineered both the crime and the frame-up, first killing his local rival and then fabricating evidence to implicate his blood enemy de Guia. The aim of Noriel's faction was, the colonel said, "to avenge the death of [the bandit] Felizardo." From his earlier espionage in Cavite, the colonel regarded Noriel as "unscrupulous and brutal" for, among other crimes, executing the revolution's leader Andres Bonifacio in 1897. Maneuvering skillfully through the town's convoluted factional feuds, tight kinship ties, and torrid love affairs, Crame effected a stunning reversal in this complex case. First, he extracted sworn retractions from the eight prosecution witnesses against his secret agents, de Guia and Buendia, winning dismissal of all murder charges against them. Then he produced seventeen new witnesses to indict Noriel, his henchman Roman Malabanan, and their ally ex-mayor Luis Landas.[90]

After the local magistrate recused himself, Manila assigned a special judge, Isidro Paredes, who soon won colonial plaudits by puncturing Noriel's elaborate alibis with probing questions. But once again Colonel Crame's extrajudicial maneuvers were critical. The prosecution's star witness, Alfonso Cuenca, appeared six times for testimony that the court deemed credible even though he was still working as Crame's paid PC agent. When the trial judge asked him how he knew "all with reference to the life of the accused," Cuenca told the court: "Why should I not do so, being ordered to spy on him by the Government of the United States of America?" Pressed to elaborate, Cuenca said that he had been on the PC payroll since 1909, operating so secretly that not even his wife knew. Even more remarkably, Colonel Crame was employing de Guia, Noriel's blood enemy, as a confidential agent to investigate both the accused's culpability in this killing and his ongoing acts of subversion.[91]

The two scouts officers were also experienced investigators. In March 1912, for example, Captain Edson I. Small filed a detailed report arguing that the accused had ample motives. Ex-mayor Landas had long coveted the victim's wife and took her as his mistress after the murder. And Noriel had a history of rising tensions with the victim that culminated in an altercation at Bacoor's cockpit. Just two days before the murder, the victim Magtibay had exploded when Noriel refused to settle a cockfighting bet and, before hundreds of spectators, threw a bleeding rooster in his face. Humiliated, Noriel had stormed out, threatening "I will cut your horns for you."[92]

At every echelon of the U.S. regime, American colonials felt that Colonel Crame was the key to cracking this case. One of the governor-general's aides who attended every court hearing said that Crame's testimony "as to the character of Noriel and his history in Bacoor was very valuable." Above all, the colonel's "influence was, as always, quite extraordinary in getting witnesses to tell what they knew." He even managed to transform Agapito Boson from Noriel's former revolutionary lieutenant and "right-hand man running his jueteng games" into a witness "of great value to the prosecution." Just a few days after his testimony, Boson was attacked in the local cockpit by four defense witnesses and would have died had not one of Crame's secret service men suddenly stepped from the crowd to deftly catch the hand wielding a foot-long fan knife.[93]

In June 1912 Judge Paredes sentenced Noriel to die on the gallows in a fifty-page decision that was soon affirmed by the Philippine Supreme Court, which praised the prosecution's "voluminous and minute" evidence. But two years later when the lower court fixed the execution date for January 12, 1915, Manila's political elite suddenly rallied to save one of its own. House Speaker Sergio Osmeña pleaded with Governor-General F. B. Harrison, a liberal Democrat sympathetic to Filipino aspirations, for a stay of execution. Though "amazed beyond expression at the character of the men . . . and the anxiety they displayed," the governor-general rejected their appeals.[94] While strongly liberal on many issues, Harrison was still a colonial governor commanding a security apparatus synonymous with his authority.[95]

With Malacañang Palace cold to their pleas, Filipino leaders shifted their efforts to the White House. Osmeña cabled the Philippine resident commissioner, Manuel Quezon, that Noriel had been convicted only "after great activity . . . by military constabulary officers before special judge," adding that the Filipino public "believes scout soldier Buendia was the crime's author and his absolution, irregularly secured, was followed by [U.S.] federal secret service activity and prosecution of Noriel." As the January 12 execution date neared, Quezon lobbied furiously, apparently convinced that these covert intrigues had convicted an innocent man. In desperation on the eve of the execution, Quezon called at the White House to plead for a stay.[96] Almost immediately President Woodrow Wilson cabled the governor-general ordering that "execution Noriel be suspended until case can be investigated." Harrison replied with his resignation, insisting that Noriel was "not deserving of any clemency."[97] Within twenty-four hours the president retreated and Quezon did the same, cabling Osmeña that "Philippine cause is supreme and Harrison fidelity to it demands we should not embarrass him further."[98]

The day before Noriel's execution, delegations of tobacco workers, revolutionary veterans, and many others crowded into the governor-general's Ayuntamiento office with hundreds of petitions for clemency. That night his attorneys called at the homes of two Supreme Court justices with affidavits from prosecution witnesses retracting their testimony. Finding this new evidence compelling, the justices granted a final hearing for nine the next morning, ample time before an execution scheduled for noon. But that same night the prison authorities had secretly moved the hanging forward six hours. At sunrise on January 27, 1915, guards at Manila's Bilibid Prison marched Noriel and his two alleged henchmen to the scaffold and pulled the trap door at exactly 6:30 a.m. Outraged at the deceptions used to conceal the true hour of the execution, Noriel's gadfly American attorney, Amzi B. Kelly, fired off an accusatory open letter to the governor-general that was published in the *Manila Times*.[99]

Kelly, a colorful figure known for his quixotic attacks on the colonial regime, now launched a doomed crusade for Noriel's posthumous vindication. On the execution's first anniversary, he published a book that was bitterly critical of Colonel Crame, the Cavite judge, and the Philippine Supreme Court. To ensure maximum publicity, Kelly mailed copies to the U.S. Senate marked "Exhibit A" in a formal complaint against five Philippine justices for "criminally careless neglect of duty." Within weeks the Philippine Supreme Court ordered him disbarred, jailed for six months, and fined five hundred dollars for his book's libelous accusations. Released after just twenty-one days in response to public pressure, Kelly fought on for another five years, using his Democratic Party ties to lobby Washington untiringly but unsuccessfully for Noriel's exoneration. Four years later, in a desperate bid for readmission to the bar, Kelly dropped his accusations, met Crame as a conciliatory gesture, and tried to launch Governor-General Harrison's campaign for the Democratic presidential nomination. But the local Supreme Court still refused to readmit him to the bar.[100]

Not content with this vindication, Crame published his own seventy-page refutation of Kelly's *j'accuse*, portraying himself as an impartial policeman who had done "nothing that was a deviation from the line of my duties." Yet there is good reason to regard the colonel's pamphlet as disinformation. In his point-by-point rebuttal of Kelly's charges, he insisted, for example, that Noriel's local rival de Guia "was at no time in the service of the Constabulary" even though that same de Guia had been sending Crame secret reports, quoted above, for nearly a decade.[101]

In retrospect, Crame's triumph was nothing less than remarkable. Over tremendous opposition he had maneuvered to effect the hanging of a former general of the revolution, the only educated Filipino executed in forty years of U.S. colonial rule. So agile were his manipulations of witnesses that his seamless evidence convinced the trial court, Philippine Supreme Court, and governor-general. Working silently behind the scenes, his moves remained invisible to both Noriel's impassioned Filipino defenders and the American president, who was forced to retract his stay of execution.[102] This hard-won victory marked Crame as a master of intrigue and information, an officer amply qualified for Governor-General Harrison's appointment, just two years after Noriel's execution, as the first Filipino chief of the constabulary.

Conclusion

The constabulary's covert campaign against Filipino radicals explains a central, if understated, problem in modern Philippine history: the reasons for the rapid decline of militant nationalism after 1907. How was an ideology powerful enough to inspire Asia's first national revolution supplanted only a decade later by machine electoral politics that offered little to the masses or the middle class? Several scholars have traced the rise of elite parties while others have explored the persistence of nationalism among the masses, but none has satisfactorily explained this sudden shift from ideological mobilization to conservative patronage politics.[103] In retrospect, the constabulary's role in demoralizing the radicals by means of surveillance while protecting elected politicians from scandal seems to have been a determining factor in this demobilization.

Over time this colonial surveillance discredited the radical nationalist movement, whose coin was ideology and idealism, leaving elite politics in the hands of a conservative electoral elite whose métier was material gain through patronage politics. As they were forced from the electoral arena after 1907, the radical nationalists shifted their efforts from elite agitation to mass mobilization, organizing rallies, trade unions, and working-class brotherhoods. Although the colonial police could contain or crush the most visible manifestations of this mobilization—the nationalist church, general strikes, and mass organizations—it could not control the deeper discontent and impassioned ideals that fueled this social conflict. Mass movements maintained a certain autonomy that allowed them to move in increasingly radical directions, from tenancy strikes in the 1920s and urban unions in the 1930s to armed revolt in the 1940s.

Apart from its obvious influence on the emerging state apparatus, the constabulary played a subtle yet seminal role in setting the Philippines' larger political direction. Through its covert operations it shaped the character of the country's politics, first by influencing key social institutions such as church and legislature, next by selecting the country's new political elite, and finally by moderating its mass political culture. In its first years under Governor Taft, the colonial state focused on controlling leaders of the press, parties, and church and only later turned its attention, somewhat less successfully, to the masses, their labor unions, and mutual-aid societies. By the time the U.S. colonial regime conceded Filipinos full legislative autonomy in 1916, it had left its imprint on the key institutions that would serve as a template for social change for decades to come: the press, the church, political parties, labor unions, and fraternal organizations.

By the time Filipinos gained this legislative power, three of their leaders had risen through careers shaped in good measure by constabulary espionage. The president of the Philippine Senate, Manuel Quezon, had served for years as a constabulary intelligence asset and had been protected from disgrace during the early, critical phase of his career. House Speaker Sergio Osmeña had avoided a crippling scandal because the constabulary overlooked his wife's opium smuggling. And the first Filipino chief of constabulary, General Rafael Crame, had spent most of his service in the Information Division, rising to command of the national police through covert operations rather than combat.

By contrast, radicals who challenged American authority—labor leader Dr. Dominador Gomez and playwright Aurelio Tolentino—faced constant surveillance and endless prosecutions that first broke and then reformed them as agents of the colonial state. By advancing the moderates and checking the radicals, the imperial information regime subtly, almost invisibly, kept Filipino political development within colonial bounds. Through its use of information warfare, the colonial government simultaneously selected new leaders and influenced civil institutions, thereby shaping the country's political culture. The shift from revolutionary nationalism to patronage politics in the first decade of U.S. rule was not simply a natural response to its "policy of attraction"; it was influenced by secret police manipulation of sensitive information for effects ranging from disinformation to demoralization. Radical Filipino ideals did not die of natural political causes; they were poisoned by the colonial secret police.

The success of colonial policing in this new, American-made arena of national politics stands in striking contrast to its mixed results in two regions of forbidding cultural complexity: remote tribal territories and Manila's working-class slums. In the capital the Manila Police had to maneuver amid entrenched vice trades, impassioned nationalism, and an aggressive local press. In the tribal zone the constabulary was caught between colonial policy and local cultures in ways that compromised its larger mission. As we will see in later chapters, in both arenas the police became embroiled in petty, parochial conflicts that reverberated upward through their hierarchies until they produced major political crises for the U.S. colonial regime.

6

Policing the Tribal Zone

SOMETIME IN 1908 Captain Harold Elarth was leading a patrol of ten Filipino constabulary soldiers into the mountains of Mindanao Island to investigate rumors of a revolt by local Muslims, the "warlike" Moros. Suddenly his soldiers ran headlong into "a thousand tribesmen, armed and ready for action." Without warning, three "frenzied fanatics" broke from the crowd and attacked, screaming death as their followers unleashed a shower of spears. "Elarth dropped the first two Moros with skull shots from his pistol," reads one celebratory account, "but there was no time to stop the third, who was armed with a spear." The captain was doomed. But his loyal Filipino subaltern, Sergeant Alvarez, "leaped forward to take the spear in his chest." Leaving behind eight "bodies bristling with spears," the captain and his two surviving men fled back to the safety of their fortified post.[1]

Forty years later, Elarth, then a retired PC colonel living in Los Angeles, reflected on these experiences. "By fair dealing, unusual sagacity and confirmed courage," he said, young American officers "pacified and controlled tribes that for 300 years had continuously warred with the Spaniards." These young lieutenants, he explained, commanded deep loyalty from their Filipino troops: "Such is the psychology of the Malay . . . that his adoration is reserved solely for his own officer . . . and for him if need be, he would gladly give his very life."[2]

Setting aside this imperial sentimentality, the Philippines Constabulary played a critical role in the tribal zone. Some of its American officers did indeed have adventures not unlike those recounted by the old colonel. In contrast to the political constraints on policing the Christian lowlands, direct U.S. rule over the pagan north and Muslim south invested the constabulary with broad authority, at times even a de facto autonomy in minority areas. In the Philippine Organic Act of 1902, the U.S. Congress provided for a future Philippine Assembly to train Filipinos in self-government but denied it the right to legislate for the country's Muslim and minority areas.[3] For Americans who served in these remote regions, the constabulary was, in the words of one officer, the government's "strong right arm" and "index finger."[4] In the Moro Province, which covered the Muslim areas of western Mindanao and the adjacent Sulu Archipelago, U.S. military governors used the constabulary for patrols and pacification in vast regions otherwise beyond Manila's reach, empowering even the most junior officers and enmeshing them in complex relations with local sultans and *datus*. In the remote tribal highlands of central Mindanao and northern Luzon, PC officers often embodied the colonial state, whether as company commanders or civil lieutenant governors.

This expanded authority embroiled constabulary officers in endless political intrigues. In tribal territories far from Manila, PC officers were enmeshed in an ill-defined joint rule by the constabulary and the Bureau of Non-Christian Tribes, a unit of the colonial Interior Department that served as the regime's all-powerful agency for minority areas. From this administrative ambiguity, tensions between PC lieutenants and the bureau's lieutenant governors reverberated upward from countryside to capital, culminating in a personal vendetta between their respective leaders, Interior Secretary Dean Worcester and the constabulary's Chief Harry Bandholtz. In 1912–13, as Republican imperialism gave way to Democratic reforms, their personal clashes became political since PC commanders favored the rapid Filipinization of government, which Worcester bitterly opposed.

In the midst of this delicate transition, Worcester, playing to America's long struggle over the abolition of slavery, seized on charges that elite Filipinos were engaging in enslavement of their non-Christian brethren. Using this tenuous claim as a pretext for slowing Filipino progress to self-rule, he joined his imperialist allies in maneuvers intended to extend their reach into minority areas rich in agricultural and commercial potential. With consummate skill these colonials exploited the very tribes they pretended to liberate and translated their public offices into private wealth. This enterprise not only set them on a collision course with the constabulary but also bucked a broader trend toward Philippine independence. Though seemingly remote, these tribal territories were thus central to the U.S. imperial enterprise. Shaping and shaped by imperial politics along the Manila-Washington axis, they served as both the backdrop for individual rivalries and a battleground for colonial policy.

Moro Province

In the southern Philippines, the Moro Province became the exoticized setting for America's greatest colonial saga. While indirect rule in the Christian lowlands was complexly antiheroic, the Moro Province had all the ingredients for a classic colonial script: unexplored jungles, pirate-infested coral seas, tribal populations, and, above all, bloody combat against Muslim "fanatics." Two of the greatest U.S.

military heroes of this imperial age, Leonard Wood and John J. Pershing, served as governors of the Moro Province, leading mass slaughters of Muslim rebels that added to their allure in the eyes of the American public. In reportage, fiction, and later films, colonial writers celebrated the constabulary's American officers as agents of civilization. "The Moros are incredible," read a popular book published in 1938. "No word picture could paint . . . the ferocity and inherent fighting ability of these Mohammedans of the southern Philippines."[5] Using similarly hyperbolic language, Col. James Harbord, the first PC chief for Mindanao, noted that his work with the Moros was done "on the frontier of savage treachery."[6]

In pacifying these southern islands, the U.S. military operated in several distinct theaters, each with a cultural diversity that offered complex challenges. By the time American troops arrived in 1899, the region was divided, by history and geography, into three broad zones: a "Moroland" of Muslim sultanates in the Sulu Archipelago and western Mindanao, a Christian Filipino swath of Cebuano-speaking migrants along Mindanao's northern coast, and a vast interior of dense forests and scattered tribal villages. Among the region's half a million people, some three hundred thousand were Muslims, with the balance divided evenly between Christian townsmen and pagan tribes.[7]

While admitting the need for Filipino self-government in the Christian areas, most civil and military colonials saw Mindanao's lightly populated lands as a new American frontier and scorned the local Muslim elites as corrupt, divided, and easily manipulated. In early 1902 Gen. George W. Davis reported that the island's west coast was "inhabited exclusively by Moros whose principal industry is the slave trade" and predicted, with stunning inaccuracy, that they would "not give us any serious trouble."[8] In a similar vein the colonial vice governor, Luke E. Wright, urged that this "great island . . . be thrown open to American enterprise." The local Moro leaders, known as *datus,* were "mutually distrustful and jealous of each other," and their "absurd" claims to the island's vast lands "could doubtless be bought from them for a song . . . if they were given a small pension and used as puppets in governing their people."[9]

From the outset, however, these same Muslim leaders proved capable of determined resistance. When the Moro chiefs of Lake Lanao spurned American authority in early 1903, Capt. John J. Pershing marched around its shores attacking their formidable earthen forts, called *cotas,* and slaughtering the defenders with artillery bombardments. For his victories Pershing was celebrated as a military genius and three years later catapulted over 862 more senior officers from captain to brigadier general.[10]

In July 1903 the full force of the U.S. empire arrived when Gen. Leonard Wood landed at Zamboanga with broad authority as both the first civil governor of the new Moro Province and the military commander of Mindanao's 4,500 troops. As America's most celebrated proconsul, Wood was more than equal to the task of subduing the region's Muslim population. For the past twenty years he had won renown as a highly decorated veteran of the campaign against Geronimo's Apaches, leader of the Rough Riders in the Spanish-American War, and the governor-general of Cuba who conquered yellow fever. Applying the sum of this experience to Muslim Mindanao, General Wood quickly organized five district governments, each with municipalities and tribal wards. Working alongside Col. James Harbord, he formed local constabulary units to supervise their administration. By 1904 the constabulary had 350 troops and 17 officers, mostly Americans, who were filling civil roles as deputy district governors and judges in tribal courts.[11]

During his three years as governor, Wood's command fought over a hundred battles against Mindanao's Moros, with the general himself often leading his men in these brutal engagements.[12] But even the bloodiest of the Mindanao campaigns were overshadowed by the fighting on Jolo Island, which culminated in the massacre of some six hundred to three thousand Muslims. After Wood abrogated the 1899 Bates Treaty, which had conceded autonomy to the sultan of Sulu, and then extended the *cedula* (head tax) to the region in early 1905, opposition to U.S. rule rose sharply among local *datu* chieftains. In March 1906 several thousand Muslims withdrew to the extinct Bud Dajo volcano, which rises 2,100 feet above Jolo Island at the heart of the Sulu Archipelago, building *cota* fortifications on its steep slopes and digging breastworks along the crater's rim. During two days of fighting in this "battle in the clouds," eight hundred U.S. troops, American infantry and local constabulary troops, fought their way up the slopes. The hero of Bud Dajo, Col. John R. White, recalled leading his constables in a rush on the Moro defenses at the peak that left "the slope below us . . . carpeted with dead and dying Constabulary and regulars." In taking the last *cota,* U.S. forces, as one veteran recalled, "turned that machine gun on them and they'd stand there, the Moros would, and just look like dominoes falling." This slaughter left "over six hundred Moro men, women, and children . . . killed while resisting to the last." Almost immediately General Wood, who commanded the entire operation, cabled Washington that the killing of women and children was unavoidable since "the Moros one and all were fighting not only as enemies but as religious fanatics."[13] The *Washington Post* and some in Congress condemned Wood for the slaughter, but Republicans defended their proconsul. "It was no more possible to avoid killing women and children here," said Interior Secretary Worcester, "than it was to avoid killing them in the Wounded Knee fight in the United States." President Roosevelt hailed Wood for a "brilliant feat of arms wherein you . . . so well upheld the honor of the American flag."[14]

As governor of Moro Province from 1909 to 1913, General Pershing continued Wood's reliance on military force to contain Muslim resistance. "During the slow process of evolution leading up to civilization," he wrote in 1910, "the Moros must be kept in check by the actual application of force or by the moral effect of its presence." In support of this policy, Pershing expanded the constabulary to eighteen companies, using them for both policing and administration. In September 1911, after two years of Muslim recalcitrance, Governor Pershing decided that it was "time to teach the Moros the meaning of government" by decreeing it unlawful "for any person within the Moro Province to acquire . . . any rifle, musket, carbine, shotgun, revolver, pistol . . . or to carry . . . any bowie knife, dirk, dagger, kris, campilan, spear or other deadly cutting or thrusting weapon." The policy aroused strong resistance among these independent warrior peoples. When several *datus* led six thousand Muslim fighters to the ridges of Bud Bagsak, a mountain on Jolo Island, in early 1913, General Pershing's forces unleashed salvos against massed rebels in five days of fighting that left an estimated four hundred to two thousand dead, ending organized resistance to U.S. rule.[15] Summarizing his four years in Mindanao, Pershing stated bluntly: "As soon as a Moro is dispossessed of his firearms he becomes a peaceable Moro."[16]

With the Moro Province subdued, the governor-general and the army negotiated its transfer to civil administration. Eager to eliminate the cost of remote garrisons, the Philippine Division also pressed for the replacement of its regular units with five new constabulary companies backed by twenty scouts companies. During this transition from military rule, the new civil government invested PC officers with "dual positions" as district governors, justices of the peace, and health officers. Among the fifteen governors assigned to three Muslim subprovinces between 1913 and 1930, seven would be PC officers and five would be Americans.[17]

Worcester's Tribal Empire

In other minority areas, particularly northern Luzon and central Mindanao, the civil government exercised a direct but more ambiguous authority through its Bureau of Non-Christian Tribes. Instead of the clear military hierarchy of Moro Province, constabulary officers seconded to the bureau's territories served under civil governors who could order patrols or pacification campaigns, producing both convoluted politics and frequent conflicts. This hybrid structure was the creation of the colony's interior secretary, Dean C. Worcester, who turned his bureau's loose supervision of minorities into a bureaucratic empire that ruled nearly a million people, over 12 percent of the Filipino population.[18]

In his first years on the Philippine Commission, 1900–1902, Worcester established a half dozen minority provinces under his personal control. In 1905 he won passage of the Special Provincial Government Act, extending the executive's direct rule over minority areas and expanding the powers of his governors, symbolized by the gold-headed cane each carried. In August 1907, determined to elude the authority of the incoming Filipino legislature, he expanded his tribal empire by carving Agusan Province out of central Mindanao, thereby removing the island's resource-rich interior from Filipino oversight. In a similar move a year later, he doubled the expanse of the Luzon highlands under his direct control with the creation of the sprawling Mountain Province. By 1908 Worcester's domain had grown so large that he could proclaim himself "the ruler of all non-Christians" before the hundreds of "leaping and shouting savages" assembled for his annual inspection tours.[19]

In both public appearances and private letters, Worcester played to the imperial romance of the white explorer venturing alone into wild tribal territories. In a 1906 letter to Secretary of War William Howard Taft, Worcester described an epic trek across northern Luzon's rugged Cordillera range. After leaving behind native bearers who "were afraid to accompany me," he reached "the head waters of the Abulug River," there discovering "the presence in this hitherto unknown river valley of some twenty thousand rather warlike . . . people, very few of whom had ever seen a white man."[20] Reflecting the admiration Worcester's heroics aroused in this imperial age, in 1907 Taft congratulated him on the establishment of his tribal subprovinces under American governors and condemned Filipinos for the "mistreatment or utter neglect with which they visit the Non-Christians."[21]

In removing these special provinces from the Philippine Assembly's ambit, Worcester was, with the support of his colonial superiors, fighting a determined but doomed rearguard action against the political drive for Filipino self-rule. Apart from angering the legislature, Worcester's insistence on absolute autonomy over his tribal domain also produced periodic conflicts with the constabulary. Whenever the colonial executive created one of his special provinces, Worcester appointed experienced constabulary officers as governor and lieutenant governors while insisting on their authority over all PC troops in the territory. By carving his provinces out of areas where the constabulary was already in control, Worcester was seeking not just to second PC officers but to subordinate them.[22]

Indicative of their central role in U.S. rule, the scouts and constabulary conducted the first explorations of central Mindanao, charting the forested fastness of this island of thirty-six thousand square miles for empire's future exploitation. In early 1902 Lt. R. O. Van Horn led eleven Philippine Scouts on a 290-mile exploratory expedition across the island's northern tier, starting from the west coast and paddling eastward for six days up the great Pulangi River into the uncharted interior. Continuing on foot, the party finally reached the Mailag Valley, which the lieutenant described as "30 miles long and 8 miles wide, good rich soil covered with short grass, well watered; would support a population of 100,000." From there the party moved northward to the vast "open table land" of the Bukidnon Plateau, hiking for three days through "grass knee deep" that stretched to the horizon before descending to the town of Cagayan de Oro on Mindanao's north coast.[23]

Two years later, in May 1904, PC colonel James Harbord led a similar mapping expedition into Mindanao's northeastern forests on the opposite side of the island. After landing at Bagañga Bay on the east coast, the party marched due west for nine days through forty miles of "damp, dark forests untouched by men," encountering the "extremely timid" Mandaya pagans who lived in bamboo huts “raised high on poles.” After reaching the headwaters of the Agusan River, Harbord’s party floated downstream toward the coast, passing villages of Manobo tribesmen who “cultivated the soil more extensively” than the Mandaya but were still, in Harbord’s view, “an inferior race.” In his final report the colonel called the Agusan Basin “the largest and most productive virgin area now left in the islands,” predicting that “this magnificent stream” would in time “float to the sea some of the richest forest products and best timber in the Philippines.” But for now there was “no protection for these people against the wild tribes and agriculture worthy of the name will not begin in this splendid valley until some is afforded.”[24]

To pacify northern Mindanao, the constabulary pushed into the interior, patrolling the Bukidnon Plateau and establishing a post at Talacogon forty-five miles up the Agusan River for the “freeing of slaves and apprehension of outlaws.”[25] Apart from unsubdued tribes, the PC also met resistance from members of the Filipino political elite of Misamis Province who, as hemp brokers operating from the coastal town of Cagayan de Oro, exploited the inland farming villages in ways that fostered instability. During a 1904 inspection, Governor-General Luke Wright noted that “poor and ignorant men have been loaned small sums of money and then required to work indefinitely to pay it in hemp . . . for the practical enslavement of the man.”[26] Though order improved by 1906, the constabulary still regarded Misamis Province as “the one festering sore in the fifth district,” and their supervisor, Secretary of Police W. Cameron Forbes, branded the province’s elite “the most turbulent and troublesome of any in the Islands, next to the Moros.” Most of the trouble could be traced, PC officers said, to Cagayan de Oro’s corrupt “ring,” or political machine, whose machinations assured that “slavery continued, and poor and mountain people imposed upon in a most shameful manner.”[27]

To this delicate colonial balance the Philippine Commission added Dean Worcester by merging the Bukidnon Plateau with the Agusan River basin to create the Special Province of Agusan in 1907. For the colonial executive this new province represented, in principle, an effort to protect the pagan tribes, the forty thousand Manobos along the river and the forty-five thousand Bukidnon on the plateau, from commercial exploitation by Filipino merchants in coastal towns such as Cagayan de Oro.[28] For Worcester, with all his avarice and ambition, this was a heaven-sent opportunity to exploit the economic potential discovered during the constabulary’s explorations several years earlier.

To lead his new tribal province Worcester selected three talented officials: Frederick Johnson, an active-duty constabulary captain, as Agusan’s governor; Frederick W. Lewis, a former colonial official and experienced cattleman, as lieutenant governor of Bukidnon Subprovince; and, Manuel Fortich, an educated Filipino from Cebu City and former PC lieutenant, as the assistant governor for western Bukidnon.[29] Of these three Assistant Governor Fortich, combining the

Cebuano elite's finesse with the constabulary's raw force, achieved what Worcester called "extraordinary success in influencing wild men to come in from the hills and establish model villages."[30]

Despite Worcester's celebratory claims, his civil officials required constabulary firepower to subdue this remote region, a dependence that fostered political infighting from the very start. Reacting to colonial encroachment, a warrior known as Tawidi led the Manobo tribes along the Agusan River in open revolt, murdering a Bureau of Science researcher in May 1907 before retreating deep into the rugged highlands. By 1911 Manobo raiding in the mountain range between the Bukidnon Plateau and Agusan River had become serious, and Governor Lewis urged that an additional PC company be assigned to the river valley and sixty more constables to the Bukidnon Plateau.[31] In November Tawidi led 150 men into southern Bukidnon, killing eighteen villagers, and Manuel Fortich, now the lieutenant governor of Bukidnon, pleaded for more constabulary, a request denied by Chief Bandholtz on the grounds of limited funding.[32]

Outraged, Secretary Worcester fired off a letter to the governor-general, calling the situation in Agusan "intolerable" and condemning Chief Bandholtz's "vacillating attitude." Unless troops were sent soon, he warned, "the towns which we have established at such pains will be deserted and people will take to the hills." He asked that "the Director of Constabulary be compelled to deal effectively with this situation" or provide funds direct to Agusan so "that the province be allowed to police itself."[33]

As he usually did, Governor Forbes sided with Worcester and dispatched a company of scouts for sustained operations against Tawidi. After six months of "incessant campaigning in constant pursuit of the outlaws," Tawidi's men were so hard-pressed by constabulary patrols that they could not plant crops and the Manobo villagers that the PC had press-ganged as guides and bearers "became very weary of it all." By 1913 local leaders negotiated Tawidi's surrender to the constabulary and some four hundred of his Manobo followers settled in Bukidnon. As Worcester reported in his usual triumphal tone, at one Manobo village "in the very heart of Mindanao" these once ferocious warriors were now "cutting the grass on their town plaza with a lawnmower."[34]

Although Worcester trumpeted Bukidnon's pacification as civilization's triumph, he was playing a long colonial hand that complicated, and ultimately compromised, the constabulary's mission.[35] In 1910 the colony's chronic beef shortage and Bukidnon's unique grassland ecology converged to foster, in Worcester's methodical mind, visions of a private empire in this "ideal cattle region." The barriers to his cattle kingdom on the Bukidnon Plateau were many: legal limits on land sales to Americans, untested cattle breeds, local instability, and competition for these virgin lands from settlers, American and Filipino. In his last years of colonial service, Worcester would use his office to overcome each of these obstacles. He skirted the landownership issue by leasing rather than purchasing pastures, encouraged research into disease-resistant breeds, drove off rival Americans who threatened his domain, and, most important, barred Filipino competitors from operating on the plateau.[36]

Range War

During his six-year rule over Agusan Province, Secretary Worcester was relentless in driving rivals off the Bukidnon Plateau. From 1907 on, he worked through his local appointees to sever Bukidnon's long-established trade links with Filipino merchants in the coastal towns of Misamis Province, particularly Cagayan de Oro, playing on the colonial regime's concern about the exploitative relationship between these savvy merchants and the illiterate tribal pagans in the interior.[37] To end this exploitation his lieutenant governor, Frederick Lewis, enticed the tribes into new villages by hosting elaborate fiestas with brass bands and showering them with pennies, beads, combs, and mirrors. As the Bukidnon moved down from the hills into his settlements, he opened four government stores to cut their commercial ties to the coast and called village assemblies to attack Cagayan's hegemony.[38]

Within months the Cagayan elite maneuvered to file charges against Lieutenant Governor Lewis for his alleged "habit of raping women at the point of a six shooter." But Worcester soon quashed these intrigues by assembling the Misamis governor and his coterie, warning them that, "I should personally interest myself in . . . the arrest and trial of those who were continuing seditious secret agitation."[39] Two years later he reported that through his efforts the Bukidnon tribes were "cut off from Misamis," ending the "rapacity" that had allowed them to be "robbed of their coffee cacao, hemp, and gutta percha."[40]

Ironically, the chief barrier to Worcester's dominion over the Bukidnon Plateau was not this Filipino merchant community but a small American colony located deep in the island's interior. In 1905 a retired U.S. Army captain, Eugene Barton, had led four American pioneers into the great Mailag Valley where the headwaters of the Pulangi River spilled down from the Bukidnon Plateau. At the outset the Barton plantation made "fair profits" by trading for forest products with Manobo tribesman and farming with tribal tenants. With colonial representatives far away on the coast, the Barton group exercised considerable local authority.[41]

At first Worcester and his men treated the Barton party as allies in the administration of the new province. But in mid-1910 relations suddenly soured, locals said, because Governor Lewis "wanted an interest" in Captain Barton's farm and his brother, Richard Barton, had hired away "Lewis's mistress" Dominga as his laundry woman. Adding to these local tensions, both Barton and Lewis used the police to press-gang hundreds of tribesmen into their road crews, working them hard for starvation wages. The workers "disliked them both and feared them both, not knowing what would happen if they were disobeyed."[42]

These simmering tensions erupted on August 5, 1910, when Lieutenant Governor Lewis rode into the Mailag Valley with an exploratory party headed by Maj. Elvin R. Heiberg, governor of Cotabato, and Capt. M. H. Signor of the U.S. Navy. When Lewis asked for bearers, Eugene Barton exploded in anger, accusing him of taking the plantation's tenants for his road crews and declaring that "he would not stand for it any longer." That night Captain Signor made some astral calculations, determining that the Eighth Parallel, the official provincial boundary, was three miles north of the Barton farm. In effect, the whole Mailag Valley was in General Pershing's Moro Province not Lewis's Bukidnon Subprovince, a discovery that, if true, would release Lewis from the responsibility of defending the farm from attack.[43]

Although Major Heiberg cautioned that these calculations were unofficial, Lewis quickly declared the farm beyond his boundaries and commenced a three-month war on the Bartons. He fired Richard Barton as road foreman, canceled construction, and withdrew constabulary protection from the Mailag Valley. With the constabulary gone, Lewis and Fortich signaled to the Manobo tribes, directly or indirectly, that the Barton farm was open for retribution.[44]

On October 25 some three hundred Manobo tribesmen armed with spears and angry over unpaid government wages raided the unprotected Barton homestead, ransacking the premises and feasting on stolen pigs. During five hours in the farmyard, their leader Banao, a Manobo warrior famed for eating the liver of a local policeman and his ability to "catch bullets in his shirt," vacillated dangerously. After dancing toward the house, spear forward to signal war, he announced that he "wanted a white woman." Although accepting a servant as surrogate, he still insisted that Mrs. Barton kneel before him and swear she would not call the constabulary. Throughout this long morning, Mrs. Barton, her brother-in-law Richard, and their servant were confined inside an outbuilding, saved only by the presence of a sympathetic local chief, Manliguayan, and their own firearms.[45]

That afternoon Assistant Governor Fortich and Lt. Dorr H. Malone arrived at the farm with a detachment of eleven constables who fired on the fleeing marauders, killing ten and wounding many more. Although Mrs. Barton named several raiders, Lieutenant Governor Lewis and his constabulary unit claimed that it was impossible to track them through the mountains. Just five days later, however, Lt. Col. John White, the hero of the Bud Dajo battle, rode to Mailag from the coast, crossed the river alone and, within hours apprehended Banao himself lying wounded and bleeding in the bush. Concluding that Lewis was "headstrong and violent" and Fortich "even more violent and unbalanced than Lewis," White declared that Barton was "entitled to protection . . . and not to be hounded out of the country by all the forces of the government as will be the case if Lewis and Fortich are left alone."[46]

With order restored, charges and countercharges flew. In January 1911, Governor-General Forbes ordered a government attorney, Fisher H. Nesmith, to investigate Lewis. Just as Worcester kept files on Cagayan's *caciques,* so the *cacique* ex-governor of Misamis, Manuel Corrales, "brought out two notebooks" during an interview at Cagayan de Oro that recorded "every time a native came down from the interior . . . who had a *reclama* [complaint] against . . . any Americans in Bukidnon." After taking evidence from all parties, Nesmith compiled a damning report, describing Lewis as "intensely pugnacious" and his administration "dictatorial in the extreme." The investigator urged that, given his "violent and suspicious" nature, Lewis be transferred out of Bukidnon.[47]

On his return from another bureaucratic battle in Washington, Worcester replied to this report with a ninety-two-page rebuttal that turned the tables on his critics. With his usual mastery of derogatory information, he tarred Eugene Barton as a corrupt official who had resigned as treasurer of Misamis Province "under a cloud" and then fled into the interior where he "was selling vino to the Bukidnon people in violation of the law."[48] He mocked Captain Signor as "a naval officer with a peculiar mania for fixing the 8th parallel." Sadly, the secretary concluded, the investigator Nesmith was "a young man fresh from law school" ignorant of "the bitter hostility of certain of the Filipinos of Misamis toward the work being carried out in Bukidnon under my direction." In closing Worcester insisted "it will be little short of a real calamity if Lieutenant-Governor Lewis doesn't return to Bukidnon." The secretary praised Fortich as an official who "has long been feared and hated by evil-doers, many of whom he has himself killed." In the end Governor-General Forbes, deeply committed to Worcester's civilizing mission, backed the interior secretary against his constabulary critics.[49]

Worcester's control over Bukidnon was soon complete. In July 1911, just three weeks after this rebuttal, Worcester took Governor-General Forbes along on his annual inspection tour. The two rode together through the Mailag Valley, finally cleared of the Bartons and their farm, daydreaming about retiring from government to these "alluring" grasslands for the life of a cattle rancher. Not only did Forbes exonerate the accused officials, but he soon promoted both—Lewis to governor of Agusan Province and Fortich to lieutenant governor of Bukidnon. Forbes also extended Bukidnon's boundary south to incorporate the Mailag district, thus adding this valley's virgin grasslands to Worcester's domain.[50]

With his power over the province consolidated, Worcester moved quickly to transform this great plateau into a cattle kingdom. He barred Christian Filipinos from settling in Bukidnon, saying they had "absolutely no equitable claim to the territory of . . . the wild hill tribes."[51] In March 1913, though still the interior secretary, Worcester became vice president of the American-Philippine Company and hired former governor Lewis as his assistant to "take over the work of starting up the cattle proposition." Concealing his role through intermediaries, Worcester used his official position to negotiate low-cost grazing leases for the ten thousand hectares that became his Diklum Ranch northwest of Malaybalay. After the Republican defeat in the 1912 U.S. elections forced him to retire a few months later, he began stocking the ranch with disease-resistant Nellore cattle bought from government experimental farms at a steep discount. For another herd of twenty-five hundred head, he leased an additional seven thousand hectares to create the Nellore Ranch in the Mailag Valley, the old Barton territory. Although Worcester was now out of office, in 1914 Fortich was appointed governor of Bukidnon and served him faithfully for the next seven years, building his own herd of six thousand head on grasslands leased from the government.[52]

But Worcester and Fortich, ignoring the legislature's growing influence, finally overplayed their hand. In 1921 Governor Fortich decided to sell the province's experimental ranch and advised Worcester to purchase its seventeen hundred Nellore cattle "before the Manila caciques bought them," something the American did for the bargain price of forty-three thousand pesos. This insider deal outraged Senator Quezon, who called a special legislative session to denounce Fortich as an "Americanista" and force his resignation. The legislature also reduced the province's size substantially by lopping off all the territory north of the Tagoloan River, producing a sudden depopulation of the model settlements, the so-called sanitary villages, that had once been the hallmark of Worcester's tribal domain.[53]

Though his political regime was finally defeated, Worcester's economic imprint on Bukidnon's landscape persisted for another twenty years. In his decade-long campaign to keep this range open for cattle, he fought hard to block Filipino migration into Bukidnon where there were three hundred thousand hectares of unsettled land.[54] With Worcester intimidating any official who dared to advocate homesteading, the plateau's grasslands were carved into large corporate ranches for the balance of the colonial era. The once independent Bukidnon tribesmen, the very wards Worcester would save from Cagayan's caciques, were reduced to hired hands, mere "*muchachos*" working for wages, debt bonded to the ranchers, and denied upward mobility as landowning farmers.[55] The prosperity of this one American imperialist came at the high cost, for his ranches alone, of family farms for some twenty-five thousand poor, just as his larger policy for the Bukidnon Plateau denied prime agricultural property to some four hundred thousand land-hungry Filipinos.

Highland Head-Hunting

In northern Luzon's rugged Cordillera range, the constabulary faced the daunting mission of eliminating tribal warfare while mired in even more contentious civil-military wrangling. Inside boundaries 150 miles long and 50 miles wide, the region's Mountain Province had rugged topography and a diverse tribal population of 140,000, which made it a unique challenge for colonial policing.[56] With ridges rising to four thousand feet and peaks well above eight thousand, the Cordillera was etched with deep ravines, raging rivers, and steep rice terraces that had largely defied Spanish colonial conquest for three centuries. In these impenetrable mountains, unsubdued tribes such as the Bontoc, Ifugao, and Kalinga practiced ritual head-taking and endemic warfare with spear and shield. From the outset the U.S. regime treated this region as a tribal zone and divided its districts along ethnic lines. Reinforcing these linguistic boundaries, the constabulary recruited its companies locally, requiring American officers to command, for example, Ifugao constables in Ifugao or Bontocs in Bontoc.[57]

Along the Cordillera, which had been lately and only lightly incorporated into the Spanish state, the success of U.S. rule rested largely on the skills of young constabulary officers. In contrast to their policy of strict law enforcement in the lowlands, American officers regarded the highlanders as "martial tribes" with backward yet complex cultures whose transformation required a subtle manipulation. To check endemic conflict, PC officers compromised with these warrior cultures in ways that reinforced their martial attributes. The Americans ruled through powerful *bacanang* leaders who had won high status in battle, punished whole villages for ritual head-taking with "punitive expeditions" rather than individual arrests, and accepted "customary law as the law of the land."[58] Despite the difficulties of this mission, the PC often posted just a single company, with one American lieutenant and twenty to forty native constables, to police tribal territories with up to twenty thousand warriors scattered across rugged, unmapped terrain.[59] In their seven-year pacification of this remote highland frontier, from 1902 to 1908, young American PC lieutenants were plunged into tribal warfare that tested their character, exercising more personal power than their brother officers did anywhere else in the archipelago.

As its posts and patrols spread slowly up the Cordillera mountain range, the constabulary became a surrogate state, building roads, administering remote districts, mediating disputes, and ending the head-taking vendetta that had long isolated villages from neighbors and the entire region from the lowlands. Such warfare and its head-hunting traditions, the constabulary soon found, was not mere banditry but was central to spirit rituals celebrated by "dancing with shield and spear . . . the old men . . . taunting the young men with tales of great valor." Suppression of such religious practices would require a judicious mix of policing and politics that, civil officials and PC commanders agreed, was best done by the constabulary.[60]

In its first year, 1901–2, the constabulary advanced into the more accessible southern mountains around Baguio and Benguet as the vanguard of the civil regime and then moved due north up the Cordillera into the Bontoc tribal villages. At first contact the constabulary described the mountaineers, called Igorots, as "clear-eyed, muscular and deep chested, honest and heathen, timid in manner but courageous in fact." Physically they formed "the best military material on Luzon" and caused no trouble "except for their head-hunting forays, which persuasion could stop." Although the first posts were manned with lowland Ilocanos, in December 1902 constabulary headquarters ordered that highland companies recruit Igorot tribal constables.[61]

Through exploration and analysis, the civil government knitted these constabulary operations into a comprehensive pacification policy for the Cordillera. In late 1902 Dr. David P. Barrows, the chief of the Bureau of Non-Christian Tribes, led two anthropologists and twenty PC constables on an expedition that hiked northeast from Baguio until it reached the Ifugao rice terraces where it found both devastation and deep-seated resistance. After the sudden Spanish withdrawal in 1898, Barrows reported, "head hunting has burst out again in its most brutal form." Reflecting on this highland zone back in Manila, Barrows concluded that militarized Spanish presence had represented a welcome alternative to tribal "anarchy." By building eleven military settlements with barracks, chapels, and convents and then knitting them together with a network of highland horse trails, the Spanish had introduced order, Christianity, and coffee cultivation. Although this work was "utterly swept away in a brief period of four years" during the Philippine Revolution, Barrows recommended that the U.S. regime could use a similar paramilitary scheme to relieve this race "from the fury of its own savagery."[62]

Simultaneously, Governor L. E. Bennett of Nueva Vizcaya, another of Worcester's tribal domains, proposed posting 120 constabulary soldiers in four permanent garrisons across the nearby Ifugao highlands until roads and schools could follow. By recruiting Ifugao to fill the lower ranks, they would, he believed, be "forced into contact with the outside world . . . [and] they will gradually abandon their barbarous customs."[63] Consequently, in April 1903 Capt. Lewis Patstone and thirty constabulary soldiers marched into the Ifugao hills to locate a future garrison at Kiangan and "make peace negotiations with the Ifugao Igorrotes." In December his deputy, Lt. Levi Case, returned to establish a permanent post at Kiangan, the first of four he opened. Over the next two years the lieutenant extended his influence across central Ifugao through a mix of deft politics and punitive expeditions, leaving pigs slaughtered and houses in flames. After Lieutenant Case took a medical leave in 1906, the legendary Lt. Jefferson Davis Gallman, a nephew of his Confederate namesake, used a successful mix of force and suasion to impose colonial order on the forty thousand residents of central Ifugao with a force that never exceeded two officers and sixty men. When a local leader at Cambulo greeted the arrival of Gallman's troops with a defiant war cry, the lieutenant fired a single shot across a canyon, hitting him in the forehead—a blatant violation of U.S. law that awed local warriors. By the time the Ifugao area was merged into the new Mountain Province in 1908, Gallman's tactics had reportedly won him the respect of its tribes and appointment as the subprovince's first lieutenant governor.[64] After establishing an administrative grid and enumerating the population in each hamlet or *rancheria,* Gallman, in his civil capacity, regularly press-ganged twenty thousand laborers to blast a network of horse and hiking trails through these rugged mountains. Yet he also used his influence for development, mobilizing, for example, 496 men for up to 120 days of labor on a six-kilometer irrigation canal across the Lagawe Plateau, opening the area for cultivation and rewarding his workers with the land.[65]

Despite occasional defeats, the constabulary quickly interpolated itself among tribal societies along the Cordillera, both mediating and manipulating their vendetta for pacification with minimal force. Rather than arresting warriors for killings or head-taking done under customary practice, until 1909 the constabulary mobilized tribal armies for "punitive expeditions against the guilty community as a whole."[66] In March 1904, for example, Lt. Harry E. Miller marched east from Bontoc with twenty tribal constables to arrest five Ifugao tribesmen who were guilty of taking several heads from local Bontocs. After crossing the steep Polis range, which separated the Bontoc and Ifugao zones, the column reached the Ifugao village of Guines where the lieutenant conferred with the chiefs. Suddenly, some seven hundred warriors from Balangao village arrived to save their constabulary allies from, they said, certain slaughter. Chanting war songs, they attacked the two thousand Guines fighters massed on the terraces. Along these two ragged lines of combatants, ringing with shouts and chants, "the fighting was in the form of duels, two and two fighting," with warriors thrusting spears until one went down and the victor was "allowed to finish killing him." Outnumbered, the constables and Balangao men retreated along the trail under sniper fire, returning to Bontoc to complete what was a model mission for the constabulary. By manipulating ethnic conflicts, this lieutenant had amplified a twenty-man patrol into a tribal army of seven hundred, allowing him to extend his authority into a hostile district.[67] To minimize the need for these punitive expeditions, starting in 1903 constabulary officers also tried to arrange peace pacts between traditional enemies throughout the Cordillera.[68]

With the Ifugao and Bontoc-Igorots largely subdued by 1904, the constabulary completed its northern advance along the Cordillera by subduing the Kalingas, the most aggressive of highland warriors, through punitive expeditions intended to restrain their attacks on other villages, which were often marked by head-taking and wholesale massacres.[69] After opening its first post at Lubuagan at the heart of Kalinga in 1904 and another farther north at Babalasan, the constabulary applied paramilitary methods developed earlier in Bontoc and Ifugao, supervising road construction, patrolling aggressively, and, most important, negotiating peace pacts.[70]

After just five years of determined operations, the constabulary had laid down a coercive network across the Cordillera, posting companies strategically and patrolling aggressively to eliminate resistance. After PC telegraph lines reached Bontoc in late 1903 and its posts expanded during the next year into the violent eastern ranges of Kalinga and Ifugao, the constabulary had an effective infrastructure of control and head-taking soon declined sharply, particularly among the Bontocs. "The stimulating touch of American civilization," the PC district chief said of the highlander, "has increased his wants and sharpened his wits and aroused his genius."[71]

Instead of expanding the constabulary's authority, as some of its officers proposed, the colonial executive consolidated Secretary Worcester's control over the entire Cordillera by creating, in 1908, a unified Mountain Province with seven subprovinces, one for each major ethnic group. In effect this nominal administrative change had some profound implications, removing this vast territory from oversight by the new Philippine Assembly and incorporating it into Worcester's expanding tribal empire. To better exercise his new powers, Worcester recruited several PC officers as lieutenant governors for his new territory's subprovinces.[72]

At first Worcester seemed somewhat flexible in his use of power, seeking allies among the Assembly and constabulary to resolve serious difficulties in his new territory. In March 1909, for example, Worcester's tribal domain was shaken when Ilongot tribesmen in northeastern Luzon murdered Dr. William Jones, an anthropologist from Chicago's Field Museum. As the constabulary unleashed its usual punitive campaign against the six thousand Ilongot who remained unsubdued in the rugged headwaters of the Cagayan River, Lt. Wilfrid Turnbull swept through the hills burning crops and houses, bringing the Ilongot to "the verge of starvation," and inducing villages implicated in the killing to deliver eleven severed heads as tribute. In August, however, Worcester took a conciliatory approach by traveling to Baler on Luzon's Pacific coast "to be present at an assembly of Ilongots brought together through the influence of Señor Manuel Quezon." Quezon was part Ilongot, unbeknownst to Worcester, and willing therefore to put aside his personal antipathy toward an American he disdained as an arch-imperialist. During his "very interesting interview with these people," Worcester promised both "a special effort to see that they . . . were protected from abuses" and "swift and severe punishment" for any future raids. As the Spanish had done before him, Worcester then made Baler the headquarters for his mission to the Ilongot by opening a government store, special provincial office, PC post, and horse trail.[73] Within a few years Lieutenant Turnbull was back in Baler at a permanent constabulary post no longer burning tribal villages but instead building a new life for Ilongots in ways Quezon and Worcester had envisioned, a rare instance of cooperation between antagonists that had, in effect, completed the constabulary's pacification of Luzon's tribal highlands.[74]

Over the longer term, however, a collision between the constabulary's old autonomy and Worcester's new civil authority produced serious, sustained conflict. Within months the PC chief complained that this new structure of minority provinces was suffering from "faulty administration" since a lieutenant governor "can do nothing except thru the Constabulary," and he was, of course, a civil official outside the police hierarchy.[75] In 1909, for example, the governor of the Mountain Province, William F. Pack, wrote PC chief Bandholtz to protest the "incompetency" of a senior inspector "you have forced upon me against my wishes and against my protest." In a mocking reply, the chief addressed Pack, a former protégé, as the "Ex-Lieutenant of the Celebrated Centerville Warriors . . . And Now Governor and 'cacique-en-jefe' of the Mountain (without 'Dew') Province." In a wry reference to Worcester's lieutenant governors, Bandholtz swore that he would move mountains to give "the Mountain Province 20,000 Constabulary angels who should 'kow-tow' three times per cubic 'minute' to their Lieutenant-Excellencies."[76]

Hearts of Darkness

To break the constabulary's autonomy inside his Mountain Province, Secretary Worcester maneuvered tirelessly to subordinate the PC's lieutenants to his own lieutenant governors, the aforementioned "Lieutenant-Excellencies." Under this new regime, some of his American governors would become entangled in local and colonial politics that compromised their self-styled civilizing mission. Others went beyond these bounds to discover a heart of darkness.

A few of these accidental colonials adapted well to the complex demands of highland service, notably the incoming lieutenant governor of Ifugao, Owen Tomlinson. Fleeing small-town Indiana, he lied about his age to join the U.S. Army as a private, arrived in the islands in 1899 at the height of the Philippine-American War, and later was commissioned a third lieutenant in the constabulary.[77] After some uneventful years patrolling the central plain just north of Manila, in 1909 he transferred to the Fourth Mountain Company at Banaue in the Ifugao highlands, a colonial frontier where an ambitious officer could make his reputation. In this awe-inspiring terrain of earthen rice terraces that scaled steep mountain slopes, Tomlinson proved a natural colonial, rising to captain of constabulary and serving as lieutenant governor of the Ifugao Subprovince from 1913 to 1915. With Manila a month away by mail, he learned the local language and became a one-man regime, building schools, developing agriculture, tracking outlaws, and enforcing the ban on head-hunting.[78] Such success was due in part to his Filipino subaltern, Lt. Maximo Meimban, who had an encyclopedic knowledge of every Ifugao tribal leader and an uncanny ability to spin out long lists detailing every aspect of Ifugao's administration.[79] In 1918, after twenty years in the islands, Major Tomlinson returned home with a government pension and a final fitness rating as "a most deserving and worthy officer."[80] Although he would later complain "I wasted the most valuable years of my life" in the constabulary, he rose to become superintendent of Mount Rainier National Park and returned to Ifugao in the early 1950s for a series of emotional reunions.[81]

Further north in the Kalinga Subprovince, the civilian lieutenant governor, Walter F. Hale, responded very differently to the extraordinary authority he enjoyed under Worcester's tribal regime, becoming capricious and at times cruel.

Despite the existence of PC posts and regular patrols, these Kalinga villages had persisted in ritual head-taking.[82] In 1908 the constabulary called the forty-four heads taken in the Cordillera, nearly half by Kalingas, "the principal stain of crime on our Philippine record for the year."[83] Secretary Worcester was similarly dissatisfied with the PC's performance and invested Hale, who he described as a "man with chilled-steel nerve," with broad powers to subdue this "fine lot of head-hunting savages."[84]

Raised on a ranch in the American West where he became "a dead shot with a revolver from any position," Hale fought with the Nebraska volunteers in 1898 and later prospected for gold in the Cordillera. An American colleague described him as a man with a "fiery temper" and the build of "a large stocky gorilla" who "could outhike and outfight the bravest and strongest warriors." More savage than the supposed savages, Hale appropriated Kalinga culture to pacify the Kalingas, soon becoming the unchallenged warrior-chief of this violent land, barring his tribal charges from contacting the constabulary and thus denying them information needed for effective policing. With unchecked power and in clear defiance of the law, he doubled the road labor requirement for all Kalinga males to twenty days per year, allowing him to extend the highland trail network with unequalled speed, pleasing Worcester.[85]

Known universally as "Sapao" for having once led Bontoc warriors in a raid on an Ifugao village of that name, Hale expanded on that tactic by organizing a Kalinga police force under his personal command. Learning of the power of local leaders called *pangat* (conflict mediators), he appointed them *presidentes* of local police, in effect using their cultural authority for war instead of peace. When a Kalinga district rebelled, the lieutenant governor would assemble hundreds of warriors from rival villages and lead them on punitive raids with fire and spear.[86] "I would rather have fifteen picked natives in the capacity of Deputy Sheriffs working under our direction than all the Constabulary military officers stationed in Kalinga," Hale told the PC district commander.[87]

In January 1911 Hale's destructive attack on the unsubdued Bacari and Guinabual districts finally drew attention to his violent methods. A year earlier he had led his police into the Bacari area to arrest three men for taking the head of a Lubo man named Lissuag. Local warriors had thrown spears and set *suga* (stake traps) on the trails, forcing Hale to retreat empty-handed. This area had long been notorious, in colonial eyes, for its determined resistance. Local warriors had slaughtered a Guardia Civil unit in 1883–84 and attacked a constabulary patrol in 1903, taking two soldiers' heads. Now advised that Bacari and its neighbors had amassed two hundred warriors and one hundred guns to launch an open revolt, Hale wrote the governor of the Mountain Province proposing a pincer attack in which Bontoc's constabulary would march north while his Kalinga police and constabulary moved south.[88] In response, Governor Pack issued orders to Bontoc's lieutenant governor, J. C. Early, to march into Bacari with sixteen constables under Lt. Charles Penningroth ready "to kill, wound, and disperse."[89] The governor also instructed Hale to lead fifteen constables under Capt. W. D. Harris south "for the purpose of demonstrating to the natives . . . that our Government is in force in their district." In both sets of orders, Governor Pack gave his subordinates identical instructions about relations with their constabulary escorts indicative of a problematic, overlapping authority between PC commanders and the lieutenant governors.[90]

Two weeks later with the mission completed, Lieutenant Penningroth telegrammed a routine after-action report to the PC's northern Luzon headquarters, sparking a bitter battle in the ongoing bureaucratic war between Worcester and the constabulary. According to this report, Penningroth had marched north into the rebel zone with twenty-two men on January 14 and there encountered Hale with six hundred Kalinga "*polistas*" from Lubuagan and Balbalasan. Operating as a punitive force, the Kalinga police had slaughtered village pigs for food, scattered their entrails across the trail, and "torn down houses to provide materials for the erection of their camp." Over the next two days, the lieutenant found that "many of the houses in the district had already been set on fire" by the Kalinga police and heard reports that they would soon begin killing any locals they encountered. On January 20 the lieutenant crossed paths with a "long column" that turned out to be "Lt. Gov. Hale with soldiers and several hundred Kalingas carrying loot."[91] The Northern District Constabulary chief, Col. Wallace Taylor, reprimanded Hale, reminding him that "the use of savage war parties against others is not approved" and refusing to supply his PC troops for any future expeditions of this nature.[92]

In response to this stinging rebuke Hale telegrammed the provincial governor at Bontoc on January 30, defending his actions and belittling his chief critics, Lieutenant Penningroth and Lieutenant Governor Early, as "two very small boys, rather than two full grown men holding responsible positions in the Mountain Province." Hale admitted ordering his Kalinga volunteers "to kill pigs, dogs, bring in *palay* [rice], and destroy all shacks," but he insisted that the operation had taught Bacari and nearby districts "a very practical lesson."[93]

The constabulary was unconvinced. "It may be that higher authorities will consider the means were justified by the results," wrote Colonel Taylor, "but . . . I will refuse to furnish escorts to Lieutenant-Governors who take with them hordes of warriors for the purpose of devastating the country." When these papers reached PC headquarters in Manila, Chief Bandholtz wrote the governor-general on February 3, suggesting that "expeditions . . . composed of mixed forces and controlled by mixed leadership are faulty in their organization." He also asked for advice about whether to affirm the colonel's decision to deny troops to Worcester's officials for future punitive expeditions.[94]

Instead of a prompt reply to a routine query that was referred, in due course, to his Interior Department, Secretary Worcester spent the next eight months assembling his case, determined not merely to defeat his enemies but destroy them. Riding into Kalinga for a firsthand investigation, Worcester listened and his stenographer recorded while Lieutenant Governor Hale dictated his version of events to the assembled Bacari rebels. "You would not do what was right," Hale told them. "You would not even have a talk. . . . We burned your houses, or shacks, because you insisted on fighting me." Then Worcester spoke, warning the Bacari warriors to fear his power. "We could bring ten thousand men up here," he told them. "We have got guns that shoot from here clear over to where you live and they make such a noise . . . that you would think the whole world was blowing up." When he finished this thundering oration, one of the chastened chiefs replied, "We are afraid to do any more fighting."[95]

On October 5 Worcester finally sent Governor-General Forbes a thirteen-page memo backed with a thick dossier of nine attached documents. The secretary argued that the constabulary's original reports on the Bacari operation "constitute . . . an insidious attack by the Director of Constabulary [Bandholtz] on Lieutenant-Governor Hale." Moreover, his lieutenant governor's tally of 262 guns captured in Kalinga during the past three years was more than the constabulary had taken in the past decade. Admittedly, some of Hale's Kalingas took the jaw of one or two rebels killed in the fighting, a regrettable "manifestation of the bloodlust which still continues in the hearts of these people." But this savagery was matched, nay exceeded, by the constabulary's tribal soldiers, who shot "a poor Kalinga woman and child . . . full of buckshot at very short range" and then borrowed a Kalinga head ax to hack away her jaw, a trophy prized in their vendetta culture. Finally Worcester, playing a purloined PC document as a trump card, sought to discredit a key witness in the dispute by charging that Lieutenant Penningroth himself "had but a few days before stood calmly by . . . while his Igorot Constabulary hacked off with bayonets the head of a man whom they killed."[96]

From his private archive of damaging documents, all numbered and cross-referenced, Worcester had plucked Penningroth's report of an unrelated patrol a full year earlier in which he had pursued four warriors guilty of head-taking in the Mambucayan area. After the men threw spears and the constables fired, killing one, a Bontoc soldier, in the lieutenant's words, "did a very repulsive thing, in that he cut off the dead man's head." Penningroth reprimanded this otherwise loyal constable for "a grave impropriety in a peace officer." But the soldier replied defiantly that "it was Igorot custom," though he apparently relented and left the head. The lieutenant, deeply upset but "not knowing how the dead had been treated in similar situations," simply reported the dereliction to a senior inspector.[97]

The outcome of Worcester's protean effort was less than he might have hoped. By the time his memo hit the governor-general's desk in January 1912, Forbes was already besieged by allegations of Manila police corruption and needed closure rather than controversy from these distant highlands. In letters to his warring subordinates, he advised Chief Bandholtz that Hale's expedition had been soundly organized, at most a mild rebuke for the constabulary. He told Worcester that Hale's conduct had been "more or less admirable," at best faint praise. But he also affirmed Colonel Taylor's ban on constabulary troops "leading hordes of spearmen into fights," stating flatly that "the Government must certainly be against turning bands of savages loose against each other." To placate Worcester, the governor-general closed by saying, "Penningroth has been let out of the service."[98] But, as the ever watchful Worcester soon learned, this sop was a lie and his quarry Penningroth had escaped by resigning months before, returning to the United States for law school with full pension and an exemplary fitness rating from Colonel Taylor. Worcester was outraged and determined to have his revenge.[99]

Imperial Transition

Conflicts in remote tribal territories between constabulary lieutenants and civil lieutenant governors ramified through their respective hierarchies to Manila, fueling public controversy and stoking personal animosities. Through a mix of bureaucratic in-fighting and public debate, Worcester's special provinces became a flash point for political conflict during the larger colonial transition to greater Filipino autonomy. Worcester himself drew withering attacks from Manila's nationalist press, which mocked the interior secretary in cartoons and editorials. In October 1908 the satirical weekly *Lipag Kalabaw* published a cartoon showing Worcester as the biblical King Belshazzar asking the meaning of the phrase "Mene, Mene, Tekel, Parsin." In reply an oracle labeled "Opinión Pública" says, "It means, Oh powerful King of Amburayan, Bukidnon and Benguet, that you ought to resign as soon as the sun rises." Almost simultaneously the nationalist newspaper *El Renacimiento* published an editorial titled "Aves de Rapiña" (Birds of Prey) accusing Worcester of "ascending the mountains of Benguet to classify and measure the skulls of the Igorrote and . . . civilize them, and to espy in flight, with the eye of the bird of prey, where are the large deposits of gold." Two years later, while battling the Filipino bid for independence, Worcester sued *El Renacimiento* for libel. The colonial courts bankrupted the paper by awarding him an unprecedented sixty thousand pesos in damages. With his usual vindictiveness, Worcester appeared at the auction of the publishers' assets in January 1910 where he outbid them for the copyright to the paper's name and for their own homes.[100]

That October, during an infamous public address at the Manila Young Men's Christian Association (YMCA), Worcester invoked his experience in Bukidnon to charge that minorities "were being cruelly exploited by Filipinos." He disparaged the courage of the Filipinos, adding that "six Moros with barongs" could take any "civilized town" in the islands. Outraged, municipal councils across the archipelago passed motions demanding his dismissal. The Philippine Assembly went on strike for twenty-six days to force his resignation, only resuming sessions in February 1911 to pass a unanimous censure motion that its resident commissioner in Washington, Manuel Quezon, delivered to the War Department.[101]

Again Worcester went on the offensive. He began by attacking the constabulary command, starting in September 1910 with a formal complaint against a PC inspector on Mindoro Island for failing to enforce street-cleaning regulations. When Chief Bandholtz seemed unconcerned about the unsightly litter, Worcester complained to his colonial superior, the secretary of commerce and police, that the general's reply was "very offensive to me." In a perfunctory apology, Bandholtz expressed "great mortification" for failing to realize "my ambition to have the Constabulary 'play the game' in the non-Christian provinces."[102]

In early 1912 these disputes led Worcester to conclude, in his Manichean manner, that Chief Bandholtz was an enemy who must be destroyed. Consequently, when Bandholtz left for the United States to lobby for a promotion to the Bureau of Insular Affairs, Worcester wrote a personal letter to President Taft warning that the appointment "would be a serious misfortune for these Islands."[103] In support of these claims, Worcester added a fourteen-page catalog of complaints against constabulary officers, focusing on conflicts in Bukidnon and Kalinga and blaming Bandholtz for them all.[104] When Bandholtz was passed over for promotion, Worcester "seemed elated," bragging publicly to his provincial officials that he had blocked the appointment.[105]

As the Democrats headed for victory in the U.S. presidential elections of November 1912, the personal and political merged as Woodrow Wilson's candidacy brought the promise of systematic reforms. During the campaign's closing months, Manila colonials felt certain that Wilson would appoint more Democrats to the Philippine Commission and would almost certainly remove Worcester, by now the personification of Republican imperialism. When the election returns reached Manila, Nacionalista Party activists began agitating, in the words of one PC secret agent, for a "complete change in the present administration when the Democrats come into power." Throughout this election year and its aftermath, Republicans responded with propaganda that the Filipino practice of slavery made them unfit for self-rule. Governor-General Forbes first raised the issue in an address at Harvard that June, arguing that the Philippine Assembly's failure to pass a law "prohibiting slavery and involuntary servitude" meant that premature independence would bring oligarchic rule and "oppress the masses." After his defeat in November, President Taft joined Forbes in a determined campaign to slow independence, using Worcester's controversial research about slavery as its centerpiece.[106]

Personal disputes in Manila thus coincided with the political transition in Washington, both intensifying local vendettas and elevating them to a higher political plane with important implications for the Philippines' future. Worcester fought hard for the retention of the islands as U.S. territory while Bandholtz aligned himself with nationalists such as Manuel Quezon who were working for eventual independence. In the months before the Democratic broom finally swept him from office, Worcester mobilized his allies in a systematic hunt for two kinds of derogatory information: public allegations about slaving by members of the Filipino elite and personal scandals involving Quezon, their most visible leader. Since Quezon was then resident commissioner in Washington and Worcester planned to use slavery charges as anti-Filipino propaganda before Congress, the secretary utilized both forms of muckraking throughout the yearlong transition from Republican rule in Manila.

In contrast to his public bombast over slavery, Worcester conducted a simultaneous search for dirt on Quezon quietly and concealed the findings in his private files. In January 1913 PC lieutenant Wilfrid Turnbull wrote Worcester from Baler, Tayabas, Quezon's hometown, with news of the secret investigation he had conducted at the secretary's behest. Defying superior officers protective of Quezon, the lieutenant had found that after a legal marriage during the revolution Quezon and one Maria Cajacob had reportedly lived "as man and wife" at Baler for several months. Some years later his wife Maria, now separated but not divorced from Quezon, learned that he planned to marry again in Cebu. At this sensitive moment, the estranged wife Maria "wrote to the Cebu girl informing of his previous marriage to her," precipitating a sudden end of Quezon's engagement to the sister-in-law of Cebu governor Sergio Osmeña. Now, six years after this incident, Lieutenant Turnbull promised to obtain the full story from one of Quezon's hometown enemies, a Spanish mestizo.[107] While Worcester continued to amass evidence for his exposé of Filipino slavery, his private secretary pressed Turnbull to inquire into "slave-holdings by Mr. Quezon." The officer replied dutifully, promising results.[108]

To assist Worcester's hunt for smut, Austin Craig, a history professor and Forbes protégé, wrote from Tokyo in April 1913 with a tantalizing lead. On his return to Manila, the professor offered to help by "going to Tayabas to look up a story about Quezon's relations with his sister, said to have resulted in a nephew-son," an old rumor that had been the subject of a detailed intelligence report submitted to then PC chief Henry Allen several years earlier. Although he was a biographer of the revolutionary hero Jose Rizal and a supporter of Filipino aspirations, Craig was implicated in the colonial information regime by his appointment at the state university.[109] Moreover, in October Worcester acquired copies of papers from a 1904 Mindoro rape case against Quezon certified by the original government investigator, attorney Hartford Beaumont, who had taken the official papers along with him when he left government employ.[110]

Though salacious, even scandalous, these sexual derelictions remained secondary to charges of graft that Quezon and his PC protectors struggled to suppress. Professor Craig supplied Worcester with a letter by an American teacher charging that Quezon, working with a Tayabas attorney, Tomas Umali, had pocketed 50 to

75 percent of the payments the Manila Railroad had made for rights-of-way to their clients, a group of local landowners. When these clients filed fraud charges, Quezon persuaded his partner to assume the burden of guilt with the assurance that his case could be fixed on appeal to the Supreme Court, a risible strategy that resulted in Umali's conviction and flight to Macao.[111] A year later the insular auditor found that the "right-of-way syndicate of Tayabas" had paid six hundred thousand pesos, five times the market rate, to purchase 240 hectares of land for 30 kilometers of railroad.[112] While Bandholtz and Harbord suppressed these scandals, Worcester filed the damning documents in his private archive, ready for retrieval and release, which may explain Quezon's otherwise puzzling avoidance of any showdown with Worcester in later years.

Meanwhile, to demonstrate that the Filipino elite was unfit for self-government, Worcester, assisted by "three or four Constabulary officers" in Manila and others in his tribal domain, spent six months combing "court, police and constabulary records" for information on anything that could be construed, or misconstrued, as slavery or bondage. While providing information due Worcester as a senior official, the constabulary tried to check his partisan use of it. Prior to printing this official report on *Slavery and Peonage in the Philippine Islands,* Chief Bandholtz criticized its final draft as "unnecessarily insulting to the members of the Assembly." When it was published unaltered in July 1913 for distribution in both America and the Philippines, the report enumerated, by misrepresenting both evidence and context, the hundreds of pagan tribesmen allegedly enslaved by Christian Filipinos. By then, Worcester's ill-fated attempt to stay on as a special commissioner for the non-Christians under the new Wilson administration had failed and he submitted his resignation on June 30.[113] Released just days after his resignation, Worcester's sensational charge of widespread slavery launched a new phase in his colonial career as a professional propagandist struggling to slow any move toward Philippine independence by the U.S. Congress.

During his retirement banquet at the Manila Hotel in October 1913, Worcester told four hundred American well-wishers that the incoming Democratic governor-general's pro-Filipino policy would soon produce "a plethoric crop of new, interesting, and important data." Calling on the Republican crowd to send him "real, hard, incontrovertible facts," the raw material for political scandal, Worcester announced that his new mailing address would be 30 Church Street, New York, where his business would be to "bring home to the people of the United States the truth about the Philippines." In effect, he was appealing to fellow colonials to continue the flow of damning information that his resignation would soon deny him.[114]

After his arrival at Manila that same month, the new governor-general, Francis B. Harrison, advised Washington that the slavery question was "politically the most important matter" he faced, complicated by widespread skepticism "as to the sincerity of Secretary Worcester in this matter." Further investigation convinced

Harrison that *peonage* was a more accurate term for Philippine conditions and Worcester's campaign had not been "conducted in good faith." To defuse this political bomb, the governor worked with the Assembly from the moment he arrived in October 1913 to pass a law outlawing slavery. Then in a concerted effort, the Assembly formed five subcommittees that fanned out across the archipelago in November and December to investigate every instance of slavery alleged in Worcester's report. The legislators later compiled their findings in a three-hundred-page study concluding that slavery did not exist in the Philippines in any of its "forms and manifestations." In a dramatic endorsement of this report, the governor-general's office sent all surviving copies of Worcester's slavery report to the Manila Ice Plant for incineration. Undeterred by fact or logic, Worcester himself returned to the United States in November to launch a sustained campaign portraying the Filipino elite as slavers unworthy of self-rule, thus playing, skillfully but unsuccessfully, on the sensitivity of this issue in post–Civil War America.[115]

For the next two years Worcester crisscrossed the United States with moving pictures, lantern slides, and lectures displaying these tribal wards and arguing for a "steady hand" to restrain their dormant "blood-lust." Warning that "the Filipinos would adopt toward such hostile primitive peoples the policy of extermination," he argued passionately for the colony's permanent retention to prevent this "crime against civilization." His arguments fed live ammunition to Republican legislators fighting the Jones bill, with its promise of greater Filipino self-rule, during its fitful passage through the U.S. Congress from 1913 to 1916. This retentionist propaganda was, of course, a direct challenge to Quezon, who was championing the bill's passage as the Philippine resident commissioner in Washington.[116] As duty required, Quezon criticized Worcester's slavery report for portraying Filipinos as "savages and absolutely incapable of self-government." But Quezon did not strike back with his characteristic vehemence either in Washington or as president of the Philippine Senate four years later. After Worcester warned Congress in 1915 that the Jones bill would allow Filipinos to enslave tribal minorities, Quezon testified before the same committee without challenging these offensive remarks. Instead he promised blandly that the Philippine Assembly "will take good care of those non-Christian tribes." In part to placate Republicans legislators, who cited Worcester's doubts about Filipino fitness for self-rule, Quezon and his Democratic allies had to dilute the Jones bill's original promise of a date certain for independence to a vague rhetorical commitment. Armed with dirt on Quezon and other Filipino legislators, Worcester thus excoriated the Filipino elite with racist attacks and then returned to the Philippines to wheel and deal with near impunity, amassing a private fortune through cattle and coconut trading by the time he died at Manila in 1924. Through it all this arch-imperialist and his vulnerable enterprises were spared any attempt at retaliation by Quezon and his powerful Nacionalista Party allies.[117]

Changing Security Services

President Wilson's inauguration in early 1913 ended the tenure of Chief Bandholtz and Secretary Worcester, sparking long-term changes in both the constabulary and tribal territory. After twelve years as interior secretary, Worcester's resignation in September 1913 represented the end of an era for his department's tribal wards. His loyal, long-serving minions also resigned, notably Mountain Province governor William F. Pack and Ifugao lieutenant governor Jefferson D. Gallman.[118]

In Kalinga, Lieutenant Governor Hale tried to stay on but could not survive without Worcester's protection. Within months, the constabulary, citing Hale's inability to work with its officers, threatened to withdraw from Kalinga unless he was dismissed.[119] For another year Worcester's Democratic successor, Interior Secretary Winifred Denison, investigated complaints that Hale had "monopolized the rice trade" through his private store at the Kalinga capital of Lubuagan. "Up here I am God," he once told a Filipino trader. "You do what I tell you." In June 1915 Hale, threatened with dismissal and loss of his pension, resigned and was forcibly expelled from the province by armed constabulary soldiers.[120]

Some PC officers less wedded to Worcester's regime survived this transition. After joining the force as a second lieutenant in 1908, William E. Dosser spent twenty years among the Ifugao, mastering their complex language and leading patrols against headhunters. In the last six years of direct U.S. rule, 1929 to 1935, Dosser served concurrently as governor of the Mountain Province and constabulary commander for northern Luzon, a powerful combination that he abused to amass a vast cattle herd in Ifugao and gold-mining claims in Bontoc tribal territory. Resolved to stay beyond the end of colonial rule, he built a five-bedroom bungalow in Baguio City with his Filipina wife and financed his daughter's campaign for local carnival queen. When the Commonwealth finally Filipinized the constabulary in 1939, Colonel Dosser resigned his commission and retired to his mansion.[121]

Across the whole of Mountain Province, Secretary Denison abolished the system of tribal rule introduced by the constabulary and perfected by Worcester. Instead of collective retribution and punitive expeditions for head-taking, individual offenders would henceforth be tried and sentenced "in the same manner as in the lowlands." Along the central Cordillera, Denison reversed Worcester's policy of tolerating low-level tribal warfare by banning spear carrying except for hunting with a signed permit. Instead of governing through a personal bond between PC officers and tribal chiefs, this Democratic appointee organized regular municipal governments with voting in open-air assemblies.[122]

Through these measures direct U.S. rule over the minority regions was coming to an end. During his seven years as governor-general, President Wilson's liberal appointee, Francis Burton Harrison, systematically demolished Worcester's tribal empire, breaking down the administrative barriers that had made minorities wards of American power. In February 1920 the Philippine legislature abolished the separate administration for Mindanao and Sulu, dividing the region into seven regular provinces under the Interior Department, now headed by a Filipino cabinet secretary.[123] In July Harrison signed a decree investing local officials in the Mountain Province with a political autonomy comparable to that enjoyed by their peers in lowland provinces.[124]

The national police marked a comparable milestone when Chief Bandholtz's returned to the United States in July 1913, after eleven years with the constabulary and six years in command. From the start of civil government in 1901, the U.S. Army had controlled the colony's security forces, the scouts, directly as a regular unit and the constabulary indirectly through the detail of regular army officers. Buried in the U.S. Army Appropriation Bill of August 1912, the so-called Manchu Law restricted the future service of regular officers with the constabulary, requiring Chief Bandholtz to return home in July 1913 for reassignment and Col. James A. Harbord to follow after just six months as his successor.[125] With the end of their tours, Washington began to relinquish control of the constabulary, phasing out these army assignments and letting it become an insular police force subject to Manila's exclusive control.[126]

By the time Chief Bandholtz stepped down, the constabulary had accomplished its primary missions of breaking armed resistance and recovering the firearms scattered by the sudden collapse of the Spanish state in 1898.[127] In thousands of small engagements, the constabulary had killed 4,862 "outlaws," captured 11,977 more, and seized 7,424 loose firearms. The force itself lost 50 officers and 1,160 soldiers.[128] Through relentless searching and rigid licensing, by 1913 the constabulary had succeeded in restoring the state's monopoly on violence and removing the weapons that were its subversion.[129] In Ilocos Norte Province, for example, the PC approved only twenty-four firearm licenses between 1901 and 1919, little more than one gun per year. As regulations gradually loosened, the number of licenses nationwide doubled every decade from 6,959 in 1910 to 47,933 in 1932, producing a low ratio of one firearm per sixty-three adult males—still far below the ratio of one per fifteen at the start of martial law rule in 1972.[130]

Even the U.S. Army, initially hostile to the constabulary, now regarded it as indispensable for the maintenance of internal order and decided to preserve it as a distinct force apart from the scouts regulars and municipal police. While the scouts would be regrouped into regular regiments for external defense, they were not suited for policing and the municipal police were deemed "utterly incapable" of maintaining order. Therefore, concluded the army's chief of staff in 1911, "under no circumstance should the Insular Government lose the constabulary."[131]

Although the constabulary survived, its relationship with the colonial regime underwent some significant changes. Indeed, the coincidence of Colonel Harbord's departure and Governor-General Harrison's arrival in late 1913 allowed Quezon his first chance to influence the constabulary's choice of a chief. Only a decade after he had served as a spy for a lowly PC lieutenant, Quezon, now the Philippine resident commissioner in Washington, lobbied effectively to select the force's commander, telegramming Governor-General Harrison in July 1914 to urge the appointment of Col. Herman Hall, an army regular who was serving as the governor-general's aide.[132] Quezon was adamant in his opposition to the promotion of Col. Wallace Taylor, a career constabulary officer who had come to the islands fifteen years before with the Nebraska volunteers. After filing his official objections with the War Department, Quezon issued a public call for the appointment of a regular army officer who could keep the constabulary "free of local politics" and prepare it for later conversion "into the army of the Philippine Islands." With peace now won, the presence of a "large police force equipped with rifles," he said, was an "act of offense against the Filipino people" only warranted if the PC were trained to become "the nucleus of a future army of the Philippines." These views prevailed, and Washington appointed Herman Hall as the next PC chief and the last U.S. Army officer to hold this command.[133]

Under Governor-General Harrison as well, war and colonial policy combined to produce a rapid Filipinization of the constabulary officer corps, which had remained 75 percent American under Republican rule. In 1914 Harrison promoted Rafael Crame, who had been frozen at his old rank for the past seven years, to full colonel and assistant PC chief. Hailing this landmark appointment, the nationalist paper *La Vanguardia* reported that Crame was well known for advocating "Filipinization of the corps, and Filipino officers in the institution justly consider him as their father," a sentiment shown when subordinates presented him with a golden insignia of his new rank.[134]

Slowly the Constabulary School at Baguio began to attract educated, elite Filipinos. As early as 1906, Chief Allen had expressed a strong interest in recruiting Filipinos who were returning from U.S. universities, feeling that they "should make good officers." In 1910, however, the school still had just ten Filipinos among a class of fifty-three trainee officers.[135] By 1915, Governor Harrison's third year, Filipinization was being pursued "with increasing vigor," producing a class of thirty-four Filipinos and just fourteen Americans.[136] Among the constabulary's seventy-eight officer recruits in 1915, the number of Americans dropped to only fifteen and the overall number of Filipino officers doubled to 240, bringing them to approximate parity with Americans for the first time in the constabulary's history.[137] After its inauguration in 1916, the bicameral Philippine legislature voted funds to expand the small service school at Baguio into the Philippines Constabulary Academy, making it "a sort of West Point for the training of officers for the armies of the independent republic."[138]

World War I accelerated the Filipinization of the force. When the United States entered war in 1917, Americans still held 154 of the constabulary's 241 commissions. By war's end just eighteen months later, only 21 American officers remained among 348 PC officers. Pushed out of the constabulary by a sharp salary cut and pulled into the U.S. Army by rapid mobilization, some 125 American officers resigned from the constabulary during the war. As Americans decamped, the colonial government commissioned Filipino lieutenants from the new constabulary academy, promoted veteran Filipino officers, and in 1917 appointed Colonel Crame the first Filipino chief and indeed, the only Filipino to head any of the colony's security services until the end of U.S. rule.[139] During his decade in command, Crame, a third-generation veteran of the Spanish colonial army and now a general, transformed the constabulary into a largely Filipino force with a standard of service that satisfied his colonial mentors.[140]

Conclusion

Far from the centers of power, U.S. officials on the Philippine tribal frontiers enjoyed exceptional authority over the land and its inhabitants with ample opportunity for abuse. Men such as Walter Hale could fancy themselves demigods in a blank spot of the globe inhabited only by "savages." In reality their isolation was less complete and their dominion less secure than they imagined. Though accessible only by narrow horse trails and winding rivers, these remote provinces on Luzon and Mindanao were in fact connected to Manila and Washington through personnel networks and bureaucratic hierarchies, civil and military, Filipino and American. Even on these distant frontiers U.S. colonials were subject to both personal rivalries and colonial politics that reached far beyond their own limited compass. For a decade Dean Worcester could justify his methods as necessary to advance civilization for tribal headhunters and protect ignorant savages from Filipino exploitation. Adept at the manipulation of information, he sought to disarm his critics by amassing an archive of damning personal data and rallying public support through a propaganda broadside that denigrated the Filipino capacity for self-government in official reports, popular books, silent movies, and popular magazines such as *National Geographic*. In the end, his authoritarian tribal regime was checked by the deeper currents of partisan politics and the larger movement toward Philippine independence. As he fought the force of history's tide with the colonial information controls he had helped create, Worcester survived as the artifact of an age past, ignored by Americans and despised by Filipinos as a symbol of empire's excess.

The constabulary, by contrast, gained steady support in part through its efforts to forge a close alliance with Filipino elites. Despite constant fiscal pressures, the colonial regime maintained sufficient funding for a large, efficient constabulary. In 1920 the Philippines had one constabulary soldier for every 1,440 residents, about midpoint in the British India's police ratio of 1:1,021 in Punjab and 1:1,695 in Madras. At the close of U.S. rule in the early 1930s, the constabulary fielded six thousand troops scattered in 160 detachments with forty-five men each, serving as a reserve for a municipal police force that still totaled only

8,700.[141] Not only was the constabulary effective in enforcing colonial order, but it had also become an efficient national police force. In the early 1930s it won convictions for about 70 percent of its criminal arrests before Filipino judges, a high percentage compared to the average for metropolitan U.S. police of 50 percent.[142]

Excoriated by Filipino nationalists in 1905 for its brutal campaign in Cavite, by 1920 the constabulary was generally admired for its discipline. Through its efficiency and overall integrity, it had become, in the words of its former chief, Gen. James Harbord, "the only visible symbol of government to the people whose knowledge of the lawmaking and other branches of government is shadowy and intangible."[143] As Gen. Cicero Campos noted in his postwar study of the country's police, by 1940 the constabulary had "won the esteem and respect of the public."[144]

By design and default, the constabulary was now integrated into the Philippine state and would survive until the close of the twentieth century under five successive regimes. While the constabulary remained a symbol of colonial integrity, the Manila Police, as we will see in succeeding chapters, became mired in a morass of corruption that produced two political scandals within a decade, including one that grew into the most serious legitimation crisis in U.S. colonial history.

7

American Police in Manila

In November 1911, Manila's assistant chief of police, Capt. John F. Green, seemed exhausted. Looking "like a ghost," he collapsed into a chair before the crusading editor of the *Philippines Free Press,* R. McCulloch Dick. "I'm not feeling very well and I shouldn't be surprised if I passed in my checks almost any time," Green said. "Before I go, however, I should like to . . . place some documents in your hands." Breaking the silence that had long shielded the city's corrupt police, Green handed over sworn affidavits from rogue officers and some of their many victims. In the weeks that followed, the *Free Press* published "the story of Captain John F. Green and his heroic struggle . . . against one of the worst gangs of wolves that . . . ever fastened their fangs in the vitals of a city." Although the captain soon "left these shores a human wreck, discouraged, despondent, despairing," the *Free Press* would fight on in its crusade "to clean up this gang of thugs and scoundrels and give the people of Manila a clean city government."[1]

For two years this exposé sparked official investigations, police intrigues, and press controversy that eventually swept away the city's entire police command. In the end, Captain Green died, discredited and demoralized, in a Chicago hospital. The deputy chief of detectives committed suicide. The chief, police commissioner, and chief of detectives were all forced to resign. Yet, even as the police command changed, the city's gambling dives, opium dens, and brothels survived through a resilient symbiosis of systemic corruption and syndicated vice. Charged with duties that immersed them in the city's vice economy, Manila police officers regularly accepted bribes for protecting activities criminalized under the colony's rigid vice laws. In a city fueled by patronage politics, moreover, colonial officials responsible for police resisted reforms and shielded themselves and their protégés from public exposure. And at the highest strata of colonial society, senior officials forged alliances with American financiers in subtle forms of graft more lucrative in their rewards and farther reaching in their ramifications.

While conceding authority over municipal police to Filipino mayors, American officials maintained tight control over Manila's Metropolitan force. Right to the end of U.S. rule, Manila's police remained, like the constabulary, a symbol of colonial authority and thus a potential source of political controversy. Yet the Metropolitans were even more visibly, symbolically American. While the constabulary had a classic imperial profile of expatriate officers and native troops, Manila's Metropolitans also had hundreds of Americans serving as ordinary beat cops and detectives who remained an active presence on city streets for nearly twenty years. Moreover, command of the Manila Police remained resolutely colonial. Although the U.S. regime selected Filipinos as city mayor and councilor right from the start of civil rule in 1901, it also appointed an unbroken succession of eight Americans as Manila's police chief from 1901 to 1935 and a string of seven more as chief of its secret service from 1899 to 1932.[2] Americans thus played a uniquely important role in the Manila Police—both its modernization and systemic corruption—lending an obvious political import to its periodic scandals.

Manila Americans

Manila represented a unique challenge for colonial policing. Unlike other imperial capitals where Europeans lived apart in secure, well-guarded cantonments, American homes and businesses were scattered across the city.[3] Security for this expatriate community, both colonial officials and private citizens, thus meant the imposition of order on a difficult geography overlaid by an unplanned urban sprawl that had long outgrown its limited infrastructure. Sited in a swampy delta where the Pasig River pours into a vast, open bay, Manila was, at the start of U.S. rule in 1898, a nascent metropolis of a quarter million people split by this wide, winding river into two very different cities. Along its south bank a stolid Spanish colonial capital rose behind stone battlements. Within these massive walls, a mile long and half a mile wide, the old city of Intramuros was laid out on a grid of paved boulevards and lined with forty stone buildings, including the Manila Cathedral, which had served for three centuries as the seats of Spanish secular and religious power—a classic colonial cantonment that the Americans would soon abandon. Just beyond these battlements, scattered among the rice paddies, lay five still distinct villages that would soon be engulfed by the city, both grand colonial buildings and a tidy grid of streets named for states such as Kansas or Nebraska and lined with comfortable American-owned bungalows.

Along the Pasig's north bank, Manila had spread out in recent decades to cover a muddy estuary of swamps and streams with an urban maze that reached upriver for two miles beyond Binondo's Chinatown and then northward for another mile into Tondo's slums. In these marshy lowlands a dozen sinuous creeks and angular canals twisted the urban network into a labyrinth of narrow, bustling streets without sewers, sanitary services, or public transport. In contrast to the stone buildings, wide boulevards, and light population of just 11,000 in Intramuros, these northern districts packed 158,000 people into flammable wooden and bamboo structures that were frequently swept by fire, flood, and plague.[4] Yet it was amid this sprawl that American businesses opened smart new shops on the Escolta, the city's main commercial street, and, after 1912, built massive bank buildings along the Muelle de la Industria.

To assure the health and safety of the rapidly growing American community, U.S. colonial authorities created three overlapping regimes—sanitary, fire, and police—which ruled the metropolis through a mix of raw coercion and enforced compliance. In this distinctive urban context Manila's police became the most resolutely colonial of America's security forces, deploying patrolmen to control personal vice and detectives to check political subversion. These hundreds of American policemen were also the bedrock of a large, politically powerful expatriate community. While historians have focused almost exclusively on Filipino nationalists, colonial politics was in fact a dialectic of conflict and collaboration that made these Manila Americans key actors in the first, formative decade of U.S. rule.

Manila's American community was a fusion of colonial tycoons and petty civil servants with aspirations ranging from the altruistic to the mercenary. At the apex were the managers of major contractors such as Atlantic, Gulf & Pacific and the leading merchant houses. At the base were the uniformed ranks in the precincts, barracks, and fire stations. With arms, wealth, and connections, the Manila Americans, who numbered 8,600 in a city of 244,000 in 1901, exercised power through a patronage politics that became a major barrier to Filipino progress.[5] In late 1903 Governor William H. Taft dismissed the expatriates who fought his Filipinization program as "that class of Americans . . . who left their country for their country's good."[6] A year later the Episcopal missionary, Bishop Charles H. Brent, admitted the general "worthlessness of the Americans here," many of them little better than the "human bird of prey."[7] Although many of the colony's missionaries and teachers may have been selfless, some American merchants cut corners for the quick kill that would send them home wealthy nabobs.[8]

Reinforced by the tight social networks typical of expatriate communities in this imperial age, commerce and politics intertwined, giving the Manila Americans a formidable solidarity. Under imperialist presidents McKinley through Taft, many senior colonials came to the islands through Republican patronage networks in powerhouse states such as Ohio, Michigan, and Massachusetts. Consequently, the city's Republican Party served as an efficient political machine, pushing its allies up the ranks of the insular civil service and on to higher posts in the Caribbean or Washington, DC. During the 1904 presidential elections,

Manila Americans formed a local Republican committee and sent six delegates to the party's nominating convention at Chicago.[9] Four years later, when a colonial endorsement for Taft could help him win the Republican presidential nomination, the chief of constabulary, Harry Bandholtz, stacked the party's Philippine caucus with law enforcement personnel devoted to their former governor-general.[10] After Taft's election in 1908, these Manila loyalists were rewarded with patronage promotions, including N. W. Gilbert to the Philippine Commission, H. B. McCoy as collector of customs, and G. R. Colton as governor of Puerto Rico.[11]

To speed his own rise from a lowly army lieutenant in 1901 to a constabulary general just six years later, Bandholtz joined a dozen of the fraternal clubs central to the life of the American colony. As a director of the University Club, he rubbed elbows with the capital's top officials: the governor-general, the vice governor, and city police commissioner.[12] As both grand master of the Far Eastern Commandery, Knights Templar and high serif of the Bamboo Oasis, a branch of the Masonic Mystic Shriners, Bandholtz lorded over his real life superiors in the colony's justice system: the secretary of police, a justice of the Supreme Court, and Manila's district judge.[13] As vice chairman of the Veterans' Army of the Philippines, he also befriended the many former soldiers who dominated the American colony.[14] Through such endless socializing, senior officials solidified the personal relationships that facilitated a shared colonial agenda.

For the first fifteen years of U.S. rule, long after elected Filipinos governed most municipalities, Americans still ran Manila. They controlled the city government as councilors, civil servants, and public works contractors.[15] They dominated its public life through the church, the annual carnival, and civic associations. "The policemen, firemen, sanitation men, . . . the veterinarians, and even the bill collectors and street car conductors were all Americans recruited from among the soldiers," a prominent nationalist recalled of these years, noting that their treatment of the Filipinos was "one of the roughest."[16] These colonials firmly believed, as United Spanish War Veterans said in a 1908 resolution, that since "the precious blood of American soldiers, of our dearly-beloved comrades has been shed . . . the Philippine Islands are and should ever remain United States territory."[17]

American dominion over Manila was the product of careful planning. In the transition from military rule in 1901, the Philippine Commission, the colony's executive body, adopted a charter giving the city an appointed mayor, a municipal board dominated by executive appointees, and five departments. As in Washington, DC, these departments, which included police and fire, were subject to direct oversight by the central government.[18] In a quiet ceremony at noon on August 7, 1901, the U.S. Army's provost marshal general, in the presence of Governor William Howard Taft and General Adna Chaffee, transferred Manila to an appointive Municipal Board headed by a Filipino mayor, Arsenio Cruz Herrera.

Although he was the city's *presidente* (mayor) in name, Cruz Herrera, an attorney and prominent nationalist, was overshadowed by the board's influential Manila Americans.[19]

Epitomizing this colonial mix of service and self-interest, the city councilor Percy McDonnell came to Manila as a reporter in 1898 and stayed to serve on its Municipal Board for twelve years with what he viewed as industry, integrity, and self-sacrifice. Simultaneously, he also held secret shares in the Manila Electric Railroad and Light Company (Meralco), a consortium led by the Detroit traction tycoon Charles M. Swift. Throughout his long colonial career, McDonnell was a vigorous supporter of streetcar fares set so high that most of Manila's poor walked and of electricity charges that were double those in major U.S. cities. As chairman of Manila's police committee, he collaborated closely with Meralco's general manager, his housemate Richard T. Laffin, in crushing any union activity. Moving in the city's best circles, McDonnell parlayed these social contacts into polo with Governor-General W. Cameron Forbes, globetrotting with Secretary of War Taft, and a luncheon at the White House with President Theodore Roosevelt.[20]

Another pillar of the Manila American community, customs chief Henry B. McCoy, shared McDonnell's ambition and avarice. As colonel of the Colorado volunteers, McCoy had won lasting fame among Manila Americans by hoisting the first U.S. flag above Manila's battlements in the fighting of 1898. Appointed deputy collector of customs in 1901, McCoy rose, through intrigue and patronage, to become collector eight years later. When the Republicans triumphed in the 1920 U.S. elections, he again won a prime colonial post as manager of the Manila Railroad and was riding high until he was felled by a fatal heart attack following a scandal over embezzled bank deposits. Ignoring his malfeasance, the *Manila Bulletin,* mouthpiece of the American colony, lauded his generosity to the Methodist Church and hailed him as "one of the best known Americans in the Philippine Islands."[21]

A favorite of the American colony was the city's long-serving police chief, John Harding, who had landed in the islands with the Thirty-fifth Volunteer Infantry and then transferred to the Manila Police in 1900, quickly rising to assistant chief. When he was promoted to chief two years later, the *Manila American* acclaimed his choice with the celebratory headline "Manila Public Is Relieved, Appointment Deservedly Popular."[22] Yet in confidential correspondence Governor-General Forbes described Harding, as "rather wild in [his] early days out here" with a "sufficiently hot temper so that . . . he did things . . . for which I personally could have nearly removed him."[23] And, as we will see, Forbes's successor later found other, far more serious grounds for Harding's removal.

Although it was a new frontier for American imperialists, Manila was also home to Filipino nationalists whose roots ran deep. With its militant workers, educated middle class, and wealthy elite, the city had served for almost a half century as the locus of the Filipino nationalist struggle.[24] For these educated, engaged Manileños, colonialism was a daily reality of American police patrolling their streets, American fire brigades charging by with clanging bells, and U.S. corporate names marking every major street. In their campaign for Filipinization of the colonial government, Filipino politicians were not just espousing an abstraction; they were fighting an entrenched American colony, a Republican patronage machine, and pervasive police surveillance.

Manila Metropolitans

At multiple levels, the Manila Police was the embodiment of this American colonial presence. Only days before the inauguration of the city's civil government in July 1901, the Philippine Commission issued a police pay scale, marked by racial inequality and steep hierarchy, ranging from $900 for an American first-class patrolman all the way down to $180 for a Filipino third-class patrolman.[25] Over the next five months, Manila's new government slowly merged 300 first-class American patrolmen, 360 Filipino third-class patrolmen, and 24 secret service detectives into a nominally unified Metropolitan Police force.[26] Through this process, Manila gained a truly colonial police insulated from citizen oversight, organized on racial lines, and invested with sweeping powers.

Ending the libertine aura that made Manila a wide-open city for carousing soldiers, the Philippine Commission also drafted a city charter that directed the police to "suppress houses of ill fame" and "prohibit the printing, sale or exhibition of immoral pictures, books, or publications of any description." Under this charter, the U.S. civil governor appointed both the Municipal Board and the police chief; and the Municipal Board in turn supervised the chief, "who shall have charge of the department of police and everything pertaining thereto."[27]

During its first decade the colonial regime expanded its extensive police powers. In some eighteen decisions, the Philippine Supreme Court endorsed this broad authority and restrained police actions only in the most egregious cases. In 1901 and 1903, for example, the court ruled that officers who wounded or killed suspects in the line of duty were exempt from criminal liability (*U.S. v. Bertucio* and *U.S. v. Magtibay*); five years later it affirmed an officer's right, under English and American common law, of summary arrest for crimes committed in his presence (*U.S. v. Vallejo*). Simultaneously, the Municipal Board extended police regulation of public morals to include gambling, pool halls, opium dens, and any "indecent or obscene" display.[28] In sum the Metropolitan Police were charged with suppressing any action that challenged U.S. authority—curbing criminality that threatened American expatriates and extirpating vice that belied colonial claims of moral uplift.

By 1905 a trimmed-down, superficially integrated force of 720 police, 320 Americans and 400 Filipinos, had divided Manila into six precincts, four for the crowded native quarters north of the Pasig River and two for the colonial enclaves along its south bank. Reflecting the colony's subtle racial segregation, Americans outnumbered native officers in expatriate districts (Intramuros, Santa Cruz, Binondo, Sampaloc, and Malate) but were absent from the impoverished Filipino quarters (Tondo and Paco). In Precinct 1, which covered majestic Intramuros, the main station on Calle Real was staffed by Capt. George Seaver and 62 American officers while the native substation a few blocks away at Calle del Cabildo was manned by Lt. Felix Cortey and 37 Filipino patrolmen. In Precinct 5, located in Tondo's crowded slum of bamboo huts, Capt. Jose de Crame, a Spanish Filipino mestizo, had a force of 112 Filipino police and no Americans.[29]

Despite fiscal pressures, the colonial regime maintained a large, well-equipped metropolitan force to protect the capital and its American colony. In 1926, for example, the city's ratio of one policeman per 400 residents was double Bombay's 1:972 and comparable to New York's at 1:400 and London's at 1:375. Six years later, Manila's ratio rose to 1:355, nearly three times the ratio of 1:912 at the end of Spanish rule in 1896. Moreover, Manila spent nearly 16 percent of its budget on police, double the figure for any other Philippine municipality.[30] Amid Manila's widespread poverty, such a large metropolitan force skewed resources toward the capital's wealthiest districts and denied the city sufficient funds for schools, clinics, sewage, or roads.

The colonial character of the force was evident in its arbitrary, often harsh treatment of ordinary Filipinos. From the start, restraining police abuse by training Manila police in the "rights of private citizens was a work of great magnitude" since the Americans were conditioned by years of military service and the Filipinos, in the commission's words, were "thoroughly and totally ignorant of the American ideas of right and liberty."[31] In 1902 the city's police chief, tired of the law's limitations in controlling vagrants and petty thieves, recommended that "a proper administration of the rattan [cane] would be far more effective and expedient."[32]

Within the Manila Police, the secret service detectives quickly developed the most serious problems of morale and discipline. In his 1905 annual report, for example, Chief Charles Trowbridge praised his force as a "conscientious lot of men," but rued the "stigma that has unfortunately been placed upon the name of the native detective, or '*secreta*.'" In fact, it was the American detectives, if the Manila press is to be believed, who merited such stigma. In 1901 the city's chief detective, who was slated for promotion to chief of police, left the islands after his conviction for whipping a suspected subversive. Similarly, Detective Charles H. Horn, responding to a theft complaint from the Grand Hotel at Intramuros in 1904, took three "muchachos" to the Parian station for questioning. There, one of the victims recalled, the officer "took me by the throat and choked me asking me why I did not tell the truth. He then put his revolver into my face and told me he would kill me if I did not tell him about the robbery." After a perfunctory investigation, Chief Harding dismissed these allegations as a "false charge."[33]

Vice Syndicates

Though Manila was saturated with patrolmen at a density six times Washington's, the colonial force still strained to enforce the regime's prohibitions on personal vice. In his 1902 report Governor Taft reported that it was impossible, in a city where gambling "is so much a vice," to prevent "corruption from affecting the police in some degree."[34] Paradoxically, these colonial prohibitions on gambling, opium, and prostitution contributed to the growth of the very vices they were supposed to suppress. With the bulk of this morals enforcement on its beat, Manila's police mounted recurring vice campaigns for over thirty years and made thousands of arrests with little impact on the illicit economy.[35] In 1903 police chief John Harding called gambling "one of the most persistent, law-defying evils" and made 3,604 arrests for this single offense, 21 percent of the city's total.[36] Despite this assault, the city's major vice trades continued unabated.

Alcohol regulation was the first and arguably the most successful of America's antivice crusades. In the first two years of U.S. occupation, Manila was a wide-open leave town with unrestricted alcohol sales at 224 saloons and four thousand "native wine" shops. After the military closed liquor outlets, reducing the number of wine shops to 408, the new Philippine Commission imposed further restrictions, including barring saloons from the city's main streets, raising license fees to a hefty twelve hundred pesos for a first-class bar, and prohibiting the sale of "native wines" to U.S. soldiers.[37]

Other attempts at vice suppression had a contradictory impact. In contrast to a qualified tolerance of gambling and prostitution, the colonial government launched an agressive attempt at total drug prohibition in 1908. Between the occasional constabulary crackdowns, Manila police were responsible for daily enforcement of city bans on the possession and sale of opium, providing ample opportunity for bribes from the city's Chinese.[38] Although drug use among Filipinos almost disappeared, opium smoking remained entrenched in Chinatown.

The colonial regime's ambiguous attitude toward prostitution made it a staple of the metropolitan vice economy. As soon as American soldiers and sailors marched into Manila, a "flood of cosmopolitan harlotry" followed from ports around the Pacific. To check the spread of "runaway venereal infection," in November 1898 the military's Board of Health started subjecting "known prostitutes to certified examination and confinement" at San Lazaro Hospital. The board chair, Dr. Frank Bourns, who doubled as an intelligence operative, introduced the idea of brothel registration and police inspection that soon grew into a file card system with identification numbers and photographs for checking any prostitute "at a glance." Two years later the military government, concerned about drunken debauchery downtown, used special liquor licenses to concentrate brothels in the nearby Sampaloc district where many of its soldiers were already quartered. In January 1901 Governor Taft concurred with the army's tolerant policy, deeming the system a "military necessity . . . better than futile attempt at total suppression in Oriental city of 300,000, producing greater evil." By 1904 the sum of these decisions had fostered the Gardenia red light district in Sampaloc with fifty-seven houses occupied by some 350 women—210 Japanese, 90 Filipinas, and the balance largely American. All were now required to register directly with the chief of police, allowing him access to a rich fund of incriminating information. The civil government also authorized dance halls, a distinctly American addition to Manila's nightlife, where Filipina *bailarinas* often practiced a coy prostitution by escorting customers to nearby lodging houses. Concerned that these clubs "pervert the morals of many young men" and cause "the ruin of many girls," the Filipino public pressed the Municipal Board to curtail their hours in 1908 and then ban them altogether. In response, many simply moved to the suburbs, notably the famed Santa Ana Cabaret, which opened just outside the city limits in 1911.[39]

The Gardenia brothel area soon became one of the world's largest red-light districts. At its peak in 1915 it had nearly a hundred houses filling a full city block in Sampaloc's Tuason-Legarda Estate, with every occupant licensed by the police and inspected by the Bureau of Health. According to the national artist Nick Joaquin, the district had a four-tiered price structure, from white women in three plush houses at "five pesos a throw" down to small clubs with swinging doors and Japanese occupants for two pesos. The first blow to the top category of untrammeled vice came from Governor-General W. Cameron Forbes who, acting on the belief that white prostitutes diminished the dignity of his race, expelled all American women from the quarter by June 1912. Then in 1918, as the local U.S. military command urged moral rectitude for war mobilization, Mayor Justo Lukban closed the entire district in a burst of outrage, surrounding Gardenia with police and shipping 181 women to far-off Davao on two coast guard cutters. Just two years later, however, prostitution reappeared under de facto police protection. Instead of a hundred houses inside Gardenia and fifty more outside, the city now had over six hundred small brothels, unregulated and under the informal control of the corrupt police.[40]

By the 1920s suburban cabarets had superseded the city's brothels, lending a certain legitimacy to this illicit enterprise. Inside the sprawling Santa Ana Cabaret in Makati, the Lerma Cabaret in Maypajo, and the San Juan Cabaret in suburban San Juan, Manila's top orchestras played as *bailarinas* fox-trotted across vast hardwood floors for customers who paid by the dance. Both the Santa Ana and Lerma cabarets remained racially segregated, with an invisible barrier across the dance floor, until one memorable night when Senator Quezon and Governor-General Harrison waltzed their partners across the line, erasing it forever. With the cabaret now accepted and the problem masked, prostitution remained a low Manila police priority for the remainder of U.S. rule, accounting for only a fraction of the arrests made for gambling.[41]

Of Manila's three major vice trades, gambling was the most persistent and corrupting. Despite colonial prohibitions, the police found that Manila's population, Chinese and Filipino alike, remained "addicted to gambling" and were willing to defy the law.[42] This vice was so deeply embedded in the city's popular culture that it soon produced the "first serious case" of police corruption. In 1906 Capt. Jack Dawson, commander of Precinct 3 in Santa Cruz, was "charged with accepting bribes to permit gambling in his precinct" and providing protection for two jueteng games. Although the captain was dismissed from the service after an internal hearing before police commissioner Percy McDonnell, he was acquitted on criminal charges in a dramatic trial. After testifying about her bribes to the captain, the defense asked Señora del Rosario, described by the *Manila American* as a "buxom dame," if she could identify Captain Dawson. Confidently, the witness walked down a line of fifteen Americans and tapped patrolman John Leach on the shoulder with her folded fan, destroying with a flick of the wrist both her credibility and the prosecution's case. A week later, before a court crowded with spectators, Judge Manuel Araullo exonerated Dawson and reprimanded Chief Harding for allowing the accused a chance to flee the islands before charges were filed, prompting the *Cablenews* to call for police reforms.[43]

The Dawson case reflected the government's reluctance to investigate American police officers. In an October 1903 session of the Philippine Commission, James Smith complained that "75% and even 90% of the American policemen" had Filipina mistresses (*queridas*) who expected "protection for their relatives," degrading both justice and morality. Luke Wright, the secretary of commerce and police, argued that checking such natural "sensual relations" would require "a system of espionage . . . more objectionable than the evils you seek to extirpate."[44]

Just three years later, however, the colonial executive enacted laws whose sum was a de facto gambling ban in Manila. In 1906 the Philippine Commission outlawed lotteries and restricted horse racing to holidays. A year later it passed Act No. 1757 prohibiting any game for money that "depends chiefly upon chance," including monte, jueteng, and lotteries.[45] Nonetheless, the problem persisted. For the next thirty years gambling accounted for the largest share of the city's total arrests, constant at 24 percent from 1903 to 1907, surging to 41 percent by 1925, and dropping to 16 percent in 1931.[46] As Manila grew into a midsized metropolis, poorly paid constables were supposed to arrest influential social superiors or powerful syndicate bosses but instead opted for a well-paid symbiosis with syndicated vice. One veteran police observer, Maj. Emanuel Bajá, estimated in 1933 that "the opium, gambling, and firearm laws" accounted for over 95 percent of "all recorded cases of corruption in our police system."[47]

Captain Green's Crusade

Only a decade after its founding as an exemplary force, Manila's police succumbed to systemic graft, producing an extreme venality by both Filipino and American detectives. In effect the police had become a partner in crime, accepting bribes to protect opium dens, brothels, and gambling joints. Presiding over this miasma, Chief Harding made no move to check the corruption and instead played on it to increase his informal power. With his social contacts reaching from Gardenia's brothels to the Manila Polo Club, the chief had amassed, after a decade in command, an unequalled fund of incriminating information and commensurate political influence. By 1911 the bribery had become so blatant that a few police reformers allied themselves with the press in a public campaign to cleanse the force, sparking sensational headlines and a major political scandal whose resolution would hinge on the control of information.

The controversy began when Chief Harding took a year's home leave in July 1910, elevating his long-serving deputy, Capt. John Fulton Green, to acting chief. Within two months Captain Green, an officer of proven integrity, had found that police in Paco's Precinct 6 were gambling and Precinct 2 in Binondo's Chinatown "was running wide open and . . . plain clothes men were being paid to permit this." Determined to clean up the force and then cleanse the city, he recruited a former subordinate, patrolman Saturnino Pabalate, to set up a gambling raid on the Paco station, netting two civilians, six patrolmen, and a secret service officer.[48]

At this juncture a simple police matter became ensnared in political infighting. Instead of tough treatment for erring officers, police commissioner Percy McDonnell maneuvered for their exoneration, pressing Chief Green "to agree . . . to a fine of ten days' pay in lieu of discharge" for patrolman Simplicio Espiritu, his former servant. Failing to dissuade Green, he then persuaded the Municipal Board to withhold the chief's damning report when the case file, which recommended dismissal, was forwarded to the governor-general.[49] Further frustrating Green's attempt at reform, McDonnell lobbied hard for an executive order reducing the dismissals to fines and won the backing of two allies who were also the governor-general's trusted aides: his private secretary, Edward "Peter" Bowditch Jr.; and his assistant executive secretary, Thomas Carey Welch. Even though, in Green's view, Governor-General Forbes had "intended to sustain the sentence of dismissal," he unwittingly signed this unprecedented order for fines in lieu of discharge when it crossed his desk in a welter of official communications. To cap his underhanded victory, McDonnell chastised Captain Green for presuming to see the governor on his own, threatening him with possible dismissal for insubordination.[50] Nonetheless, the captain continued his investigations, gradually accumulating enough evidence for additional charges against seven Filipino policemen and an American officer for taking bribes from gambling clubs and opium dens.[51]

After his return to Manila in August 1911, Chief Harding informed Green that he would block any further prosecutions of corrupt police.[52] Then, in what Green called the "final sickening culmination" of this episode, the courts ruled that the seven accused Filipino policemen had taken "presents" not "bribes" and could only be suspended from office.[53]

Thus it was in early November 1911, on the eve of his departure for Persia to join its imperial Gendarmerie, that a visibly exhausted Captain Green came to the Escolta, the city's bustling rialto, for a meeting with the editor of the *Philippines Free Press,* R. McCulloch Dick. During their three-hour interview, recorded by a stenographer, the captain detailed the bureaucratic maneuvers that had frustrated his attack on police malfeasance. Then, just days before his departure, in a last-ditch effort to prod the government into action, the captain informed Vice Governor Newton Gilbert about his meeting with Dick. Suddenly, after months of inaction, Governor-General Forbes ordered his top legal officer, Solicitor General George R. Harvey, to conduct a full investigation, producing two months of closed-door hearings that seemed to fuel rather than quiet public concerns.[54]

On November 25, the *Free Press* launched an exposé of police corruption with a front-page cartoon of Green bent low beneath the burdens of "Government Indifference" and "Corruption." In its lead editorial, the magazine trumpeted "the story of Captain John F. Green and his heroic struggle on behalf of . . . the good name of the American government in these islands" against a "gang of wolves" in police clothing.[55] Almost immediately the city prosecutor filed criminal charges against the magazine for libeling McDonnell, Chief Trowbridge, and Chief Harding. But Governor Forbes repudiated the prosecutor's action in a public statement affirming the right of the press to investigate the government.[56]

Over the next two months the *Free Press* played political poker with Governor Forbes, laying down its affidavits like face cards in seven-card draw. After publishing Captain Green's damning interview on November 25, the magazine followed with patrolman Jackson S. Townsend's charges that secret service detectives John Walczykowski and Eugenio Samio were taking weekly payments to warn a "large gambling house on Calle Salazar" about impending police raids. Their superior, secret service chief Trowbridge, dismissed these allegations as "a damned lie."[57]

Within days the *Free Press* published a detailed exposé of skullduggery by Detective Samio, Trowbridge's "right hand man." Calling him "a grafter of the grafters, a crook of the crooks," the magazine described a system of kickbacks that earned Samio one to two thousand pesos monthly. Whenever Chief Trowbridge ordered a gambling raid, Samio would send one of his "spies" to tip off any house on his payroll. If opium raids netted some drugs, Samio would keep them for resale or plant them in Chinese homes to extort bribes of up to eight hundred pesos. His crew collected regular "tribute" from several dance halls, and the detective himself had procured young women for two brothels in Sampaloc. Apart from regular graft, Samio was a suspect in some of the city's ugliest crimes: the murder of a police captain, "the burying alive of a Chinaman," and a fatal shooting during a Pandacan gambling raid.[58]

Adding lurid substance to its allegations, the *Free Press* published an affidavit from one of Samio's victims, a teenage girl named Aquilina Tobias. In 1904, then a thirteen-year-old of chubby, childlike appearance, Aquilina was working as "a dancing girl" in a club on Calle Paz when she caught the detective's eye. After abducting her on a city street, Samio slept with her for two weeks at the home of his mistress, Berta, who "was also the madame in a house of prostitution." One day, Aquilina reported, Berta "told me there were others [who] wanted to enjoy me," slapped her across the face, and sent her under guard to "the house of a Chino who lives in Plaza Santa Cruz." After months of bringing home fifteen to twenty pesos nightly for the detective, the girl fled with a trusted member of Samio's household, Gregorio Buencamino. She lived happily with him for two weeks until Samio arrested her for being "a clandestine prostitute" and dragged the couple before Chief Trowbridge who "bullied and browbeat" them with threats of jail.[59] In his own affidavit Buencamino swore that he had worked in "the capacity of spy" for Samio since 1906, making regular collections from the gambling houses and opium dens under the detective's protection.[60]

While the government wavered in pursuing these charges, the *Free Press* hammered away with editorials and investigations. In early January 1912 it reported that patrolman Otto F. Lauser, a cavalry veteran from North Dakota, had abducted a thirteen-year-old girl and raped her at gunpoint.[61] With a zeal that risked almost certain reprisal, the magazine also charged that Chief Harding was able to influence American officials because he held information about their sexual indiscretions in the city's brothels and cabarets.[62]

Olympian Governor

At this delicate juncture requiring strong leadership, Governor-General Forbes seemed incapable of comprehending the gritty reality of Manila's street life. As a grandson of the philosopher Ralph Waldo Emerson and son of the Boston banker who founded Bell Telephone, Forbes had been cosseted from birth in New England's exclusive private schools, society clubs, and summer resorts. As the colony's secretary of commerce and police from 1904 to 1909, Forbes, in the view of the PC chief, had focused on "the most minor details of Constabulary work" about which he had "little or no knowledge." And as governor-general after 1909, Forbes showed a boyish enthusiasm for games such as polo and ruled with a hobbyist's view of colonialism as a succession of grand projects, letting the Manila Police, their corruption, and the current controversy spin out of control.[63]

In a January 1912 diary entry about this "rather ugly investigation," Forbes still seemed blithely ignorant of his staff's intrigues. Reflecting on the "worst charge against me . . . of being deceived by my subordinates," he wondered why aides had ignored his clear directive to start an administrative inquiry into police graft. "This was one of the few cases where Bowditch slipped up badly," Forbes said of his friend and personal secretary. Why this singular error, particularly over such a sensitive matter involving police commissioner Percy McDonnell? In that same journal entry, Forbes unwittingly answered his own question in a paragraph about procuring polo ponies for sale to his Manila teammates, noting that "McDonnell . . . has bought one . . . ; and Bowditch three." Clearly, Bowditch had not just "slipped up." He had defied the governor-general to protect police commissioner McDonnell, his partner on the polo teams that swept Manila's first seasons in 1910 and 1911, beating Hong Kong's British squad. Elsewhere in his diaries Forbes recalled affections formed on the Harvard gridiron back in 1898 that may have blinded him to these maneuvers. "I had coached Peter [Bowditch] at football," he wrote, "and learned to love him and admire him there."[64]

Slow to grasp the extent of police problems, Forbes allowed the controversy to grow into a serious political crisis. Angrily, he told his diary, the *Free Press* was a "nasty, inimical little sheet . . . glorying in its feast of carrion, and lapping and guzzling, and . . . charging common, general corruption where only lesser corruption exists."[65] Writing the War Department in mid-January, he admitted that the press had found some "instances of wrongdoing" but believed with a determined obtuseness that the affair would soon prove "to be a good deal of a fizzle."[66]

As the scandal entered its third month, Manila grew increasingly restive. Americans and Filipinos whom the *Free Press* described as "men of standing and influence" were calling for a "mass meeting" to protest official inaction. The newspaper *La Democracia,* organ of the moderate Progresista Party, insisted that "the Governor General, without contemplation or circumspection, immediately order Chief Harding's suspension." At this sensitive moment a Manila judge, Manuel Araullo, wrote the governor complaining that thieves had committed eighteen burglaries in elite households over the past twelve months with apparent impunity, charges that Chief Harding dismissed publicly as "all bosh."[67]

With the scandal now threatening his government's legitimacy, Governor Forbes finally issued a press release promising to "clean up the situation," adding that he had "directed Solicitor General Harvey to make a thorough investigation." On the recommendation of the lead investigators, Harvey and Col. Rafael Crame, the police suspended five more Manila patrolmen, bringing the total under investigation to twenty-four, including over half the detective force. In one case, the city courts sentenced patrolman Lauser to fourteen years' imprisonment for rape, but he escaped punishment by marrying his victim before a Manila judge.[68]

Within a week rising public outrage forced Governor Forbes into a more direct involvement. Even the cautious *Manila Times,* while condemning the "clamor for heads," now called on Chief Harding to step down, saying "there are too many ugly rumors afloat in Manila to justify his occupying today the post of chief of police."[69] To placate the public, on January 16 the governor ordered PC chief Bandholtz to join Solicitor Harvey in chairing the special investigation. The governor also telephoned secret service chief Trowbridge to urge his resignation and summoned Percy McDonnell for "a severe talking to," indicating that his tenure as police commissioner was by no means secure.[70]

Under such pressure the police finally cracked. Chief Harding announced that Trowbridge had requested temporary leave since he was "threatened [with] nervous collapse due to the strain which he has endured." A week later on January 24, Trowbridge's deputy, Carl Hard, shot himself in the head with his service revolver; *La Democracia* reported that "the charges launched against him had a disastrous effect." Outraged, the American community bombarded the *Free Press* with death threats, and two upstanding colonials assaulted its editor.[71]

Chief Harding, who had ruled this miasma for nearly a decade, would not be moved. The *Free Press* claimed that Forbes had telephoned him to ask for his voluntary resignation but Harding replied that he would "have a statement to make to the press" if forced to resign, an implicit threat that reportedly silenced the governor-general. In trying to explain how this subordinate could defy his superior, the magazine claimed that the chief "knows too much" about "officials in this government . . . who have been guilty of indiscretions that might drive some of them to suicide if they ever came out."[72] His knowledge of these indiscretions guaranteed, the magazine predicted, that the official investigation would end in a "whitewash."[73]

As Filipino leaders chafed at government inaction, their resident commissioner in Washington, Manuel Quezon, lobbied the chair of the House Committee on Insular Affairs, Representative William A. Jones (Democrat, Virginia), to investigate the scandal.[74] Leading Filipinos were demanding police reform.[75] In Manila the Teatro de la Comedia staged a popular Tagalog melodrama, "El Capitan Green: El Crimen," which celebrated the heroic officer's struggle against Detective Samio.[76] Clearly this controversy demanded a credible resolution.

Politics of Police Review

After eighteen months' work amassing a paper mountain of evidence, the official inquiry into the Manila police produced two reports that recommended major reforms. On February 2, 1912, Solicitor General Harvey, representing the investigators, sent Forbes a preliminary finding that both Harding and Trowbridge, though "not guilty of crookedness," should be removed for inefficiency. He further urged that all four secret services operating in the capital should be merged into the constabulary.[77]

Two weeks later Harvey and Col. James Harbord, substituting for PC chief Bandholtz, delivered a final report sharply critical of police performance. Despite numerous obstructions from the government, the investigation had determined that many detectives, particularly in the Tondo and Meisic precincts, had been guilty of a "systematic failure to enforce the laws against gambling and opium smoking" and had "profited regularly by granting immunity to such violators of the law." The disciplinary machinery of the police appeared to be "a farce," and the secret service operated with "quasi independence" from the police chief. Investigators traced these problems to the force's leadership. Commissioner McDonnell was, the report said, "inefficient to a point of justifying a complete loss of public confidence." Though not personally tainted, Chief Harding was responsible for the way "secret service and plain clothes men systematically grafted on gambling games and opium joints." Assistant Executive Secretary Welch was an "officious meddler" who had "hindered the effort made by Captain Green to clean up the police force." Chief Trowbridge was a "weak man," and under his leadership there had "reigned a revel of graft and crime" in the city's secret service. All four, the investigators urged, should be forced to resign immediately.[78]

When the court cases and official reports landed on his desk, Governor-General Forbes was away on sick leave. Acting governor Newton Gilbert took what seemed to be decisive action, ordering both Harding and Trowbridge to respond to the findings of "inefficiency." He also formed a special administrative tribunal, composed of two executive office employees, Ernest F. Du Fresne and John P. Weissenhagen, to hear charges against five American and eleven Filipino police officers. In effect this tribunal became an ad hoc review of the solicitor general's inquiry, providing the acting governor with an opportunity to whitewash his findings.[79] After the solicitor general had spent eighteen months uncovering systemic police corruption, the tribunal took just weeks to exonerate eleven of the sixteen accused policemen and overturn the findings of "inefficiency" on the part of Harding and Trowbridge.[80]

In early May, just six weeks after the solicitor general's damning report, Acting Governor-General Gilbert terminated the official inquiry and returned all the Americans to duty: Chief Harding, Chief Trowbridge, Secretary Welch, two precinct captains, and assorted police officers. In defense of this sweeping exoneration, the governor-general stated that almost everyone had been found innocent by either the courts or his tribunal. Only five low-ranking patrolmen found guilty of what Gilbert termed "petty graft" were punished in any way.[81]

The governor-general's action caused an instant press sensation. On May 4, the *Manila Times* filled its front page with dignified photos of the exonerated officials beneath a banner headline "McDonnell, Trowbridge and Harding Will Be Continued in Office."[82] The Filipino newspapers were outraged. Speaking with the voice of "more than a hundred publications in the whole archipelago," *La Vanguardia* condemned this "attempt at purification of police rottenness." In a confidential report, acting PC chief Harbord stated that "Filipinos almost to a unit condemn this exoneration and believe strongly in the inefficiency of these officials," a belief shared by a "majority of the American residents."[83]

The stunning reversal was a tribute to the talents of Chief Harding and Commissioner McDonnell in manipulating information. Only days after their exoneration, the constabulary's top secret agent, Edwin C. Bopp, submitted a confidential report to Chief Bandholtz detailing the public moves and private scheming they had used to escape punishment. On April 27, Bopp learned that McDonnell had offered one P. J. Fitzsimmons, recently arrived from Persia, a post as the city's disbursement officer if he would state that Captain Green, the source of the original corruption charges, "was crazy all the time he was enroute to and at Persia." Just nine days later, on the front page of the *Manila Times,* McDonnell published an attack on Green backed by a letter from Fitzsimmons claiming that Green had been "mentally unbalanced . . . as a result of sickness contracted by him in the Philippines." Buried inside the same edition at the bottom of page six was a brief notice that this same Fitzsimmons had just been appointed disbursement officer.[84]

Maneuvering behind the scenes, Chief Harding proved a particularly bruising infighter. On a Sunday morning, April 28, Harding convened a secret meeting at City Hall to block the proposed merger of his police secret service with the constabulary attended by McDonnell, Trowbridge, local attorney Antonius J. Burke, and magazine editor William Crozier. The group, according to Agent Bopp's "informant," agreed that Burke would file an immediate injunction if there were any move to merge the two forces.[85] In these intricate maneuvers, Chief Harding was armed with the most sensitive form of incriminating information. Through his "underground control of the women in the red-light district," Bopp reported, "Harding has it on a good many people in town for indiscretions committed." With such information, the chief had "from time to time attacked the character and integrity of every government official whom he has taken a dislike to."[86] Whether as coincidence or consequence, on May 8 Attorney General Ignacio Villamor, after consulting with Acting Governor Gilbert and Police Secretary Charles Elliott, ruled that transferring the secret service to the constabulary violated Manila's charter and required enabling legislation, thus blocking the governor's only concession to public opinion.[87]

In the inquiry's aftermath PC agent Bopp warned that Chief Harding was both "vicious and vindictive" and planned to "hound every man who had participated in any way with the investigation." Relations between the constabulary and city police were, Bopp said, "strained almost to the breaking point." The police chief has, he warned PC chief Bandholtz, "threatened to get you and Colonel Harbord openly."[88]

The first target of Chief Harding's vendetta was the crusading editor of the *Philippines Free Press,* R. McCulloch Dick. In April 1912 the city prosecutor revived criminal charges against him for libeling Harding, and Harding himself made the arrest.[89] Eight months later Dick's defense suffered a crippling blow with news from Chicago of Captain Green's death at just forty-three from an intestinal ailment. After learning that Green's sworn affidavit was no longer admissible, Dick settled the libel charges by paying a ₱250 fine and apologizing to the police.[90]

In launching its campaign against police graft in 1911, the *Free Press* had speculated that this scandal would "bring this administration tumbling down in one wild welter of destruction and ruin," sweeping away "all the bureau chiefs, several members of the commission, and possibly even the governor general himself."[91] Yet just five months later the accused police were back in office and their accuser, editor R. McCulloch Dick, was railroaded through the courts with no public protest.

With the prospect of a Democrat in the White House and an imminent purge of the Republican coterie in Manila, Filipino politicians held their fire and focused on lobbying Washington's Democrats for more fundamental reforms. Writing from Washington in May 1912, just as the police scandal was fading, resident commissioner Manuel Quezon predicted that "the present administration will surely fall, and naturally there will be a complete change of personnel on the [Philippine] Commission."[92] Indeed, in the long buildup to these presidential elections, scandals high and low, at home and abroad, reached a crescendo as political players tried to influence the outcome and then continued for months after Woodrow Wilson's victory ruptured fifteen years of Republican rule in Manila.

Colonial Scandals

Throughout 1910–12, a succession of Manila scandals threatened to converge with their Washington counterparts to form a perfect political storm that would sweep President Taft from office. Knowing that his defeat would end their colonial careers, loyal Republican protégés in Manila maneuvered desperately to quash any scandal while his Democratic opponents and their Filipino allies dug for dirt. In these volatile months an American reporter, working secretly for the PC as Agent 30, met regularly with William H. Clarke, the colony's aggrieved chief auditor who was maneuvering desperately to tar Taft's protégé, Governor-General Forbes, with graft charges over the construction of a costly colonial hill station at Baguio. Though ignored by historians, this breach between the governor and his auditor was, in Forbes's own view, the most serious crisis in his ten-year colonial career.

From 1902 to 1906, as the Kennon Road zigzagged upward through a rocky ravine to a mile-high meadow at Baguio, construction costs had soared to an astronomical ₱4.1 million, even more than those for Manila's massive new port. Designed by famed architect Daniel K. Burnham, Baguio was built as a colonial hill station to provide Americans with relief from Manila's tropical heat. As this new city of mansions, cottages, and a country club rose around an artificial lake at an additional cost of ₱762,000, American colonials colluded to drain the bottomless budget with graft and generous salaries. Then, in the largest of many storms that damaged the ill-designed highway, a powerful typhoon dumped eighty-eight inches of rain down that ravine in July 1911, a world record that washed away road, bridges, and budget. Watching the endless corruption and cost overruns, Filipino politicians railed against an imperial indulgence that was robbing poor Filipino communities of roads and schools. In testimony before the U.S. Congress, resident commissioner Quezon cited "unanimous opposition" to the Kennon Road among Filipinos, saying it was "a great injustice" to spend so lavishly on a highway to a colonial hill station instead of on public works with "immediate benefit to the people."[93]

After years of waste, Filipino anger over Baguio's costs exploded in 1910, catalyzed by a major scandal over minor graft by American employees. After reviewing evidence collected by a regional auditor, the government prosecutor, L. M. Southworth, concluded that Baguio procurements had been marked by "criminal neglect, the falsification of public documents, and the malversation of public property." In short, ample grounds for criminal charges against two midlevel colonial officials. At first Governor Forbes was convinced that "certain men of poor antecedents" had "committed some very ugly graft," but he then tried to quiet the scandal by dispatching his loyal aide, Thomas Cary Welch, who smeared that regional auditor by repeating gossip about his gambling habits. The insular auditor Clarke protested this persecution of his subordinate and barred the release of documents to the colonial executive.[94]

Backed by the War Department, the governor suspended Clarke for insubordination, citing constabulary reports that his Baguio investigation was "improper, amounting almost to persecution."[95] After sailing to Washington in March to fight unsuccessfully for his reinstatement, Clarke, now the former auditor, returned to Manila in July 1911 defeated but not disarmed. To provide the Democratic Party with "good campaign material" for the impending 1912 elections, Clarke told PC Agent 30 that he had been "entrusted by [Representative John] Martin with the gathering of data . . . to discredit officials of this government." To publicize issues such as the Baguio road fiasco, Clarke was courting the local press with some success, particularly *La Vanguardia*, the nationalist successor to *El Renacimiento*, and forwarding its critical coverage to Representative Martin for circulation among the opposition Democrats in Washington.[96] Though Clarke often seemed inept in his media manipulations, Governor Forbes was listening carefully through his PC agents and maneuvering hard to neutralize this threat.[97]

Among the many controversies surrounding Governor Forbes, it was allegations of graft in the sale of the friar lands, the large estates near Manila purchased from the Catholic church, that resonated most deeply with American domestic scandals to attract the attention of Democrats in Washington. At the outset of U.S. rule, Congress had capped land sales to corporations at twenty-five hundred acres, seeking to preempt the formation of colonial plantations that might tie the Philippines permanently to the United States. In a parallel move aimed at promoting land sales to ordinary Filipino farmers, the colonial regime had later purchased vast friar estates from the Vatican for some $7 million. In 1909 the tycoon Horace Havemeyer of the American Sugar Refining Corporation, the fifth-largest U.S. corporation with 98 percent of the nation's sugar-refining capacity, had circumvented Congress's limitations with the help of Dean Worcester by purchasing the fifty-six-thousand-acre San Jose friar estate on Mindoro Island. When rumors of such collusion reached Congress in early 1910, Democrats linked this colonial controversy to a series of domestic scandals that had made Havemeyer's "Sugar Trust" an icon of corporate corruption in the age of muckraking journalism. Launching his party's attack from the House floor in April 1910, Representative John A. Martin (Democrat, Colorado) denounced the sale of the San Jose estate to American Sugar, charging the company with trying "to secure a monopoly on free trade . . . between the United States and the Philippine Islands."[98] Broadening this accusation into a full-blown assault on the ruling Republicans, Representative Henry T. Rainey (Democrat, Illinois) followed Martin to deliver a detailed indictment of what he called "the most corrupt and rotten trust ever created by the protective tariff system," charging that American Sugar had "through its almost absolute . . . control of the Republican Party . . . been able to shape tariff schedules . . . to steal indirectly from the people."[99]

Turning to domestic events, Representative Rainey accused the White House of aiding the Sugar Trust's desperate efforts to evade justice in two recent domestic scandals. From 1897 to 1907 American Sugar had bribed revenue officers on the Brooklyn docks, rigging the scales in a bold scheme to short-weight all sugar imports and thus reduce its tariff payments—a cause célèbre that had already produced a fine of $2.1 million, a purge of the corrupt New York Customs House, and indictments that reached from the waterfront to Wall Street boardrooms. Investigated simultaneously for the fraudulent elimination of a competitor, the Pennsylvania Sugar Refinery, the trust retained the influential New York law firm of Strong and Cadwalader, whose senior partner Henry W. Taft, the president's brother, negotiated a settlement with Washington that shrank a liability of $30 million to just $2 million. Through the law firm's former partner, George W. Wickersham, now the U.S. attorney general, American Sugar had also reduced a fine of $150 million in the Brooklyn customs case to a mere $2 million. These ties were, Rainey charged, integral to a nexus of crooked connections within "the sugar-trust-owned, sugar-trust-controlled Republican New York County central committee." This cabal had engineered the recent election of President Taft, the same president who was now protecting American Sugar by warning the House of Representatives that an investigation might "prove an embarrassment."[100]

Next, Representative William A. Cullop (Democrat, Indiana) rose to deliver a blistering indictment that tied this corrupt New York–Washington nexus to the Philippines. He charged that Attorney General Wickersham had approved the Sugar Trust's purchase of the San Jose estate, which he described as "55,000 acres of the best of the sugar lands contained in the friar possessions, as rich and productive for sugar production as there is in the world, for the paltry sum of $6 per acre . . . about one-twelfth of their actual value." Although the Republican majority blocked a congressional investigation, the House approved a motion asking that the president inform it of "what facts, if any, make inexpedient a thorough examination . . . of the frauds in the customs service."[101] In effect, the House compromised by shifting its inquiry's focus from the Sugar Trust's sensitive domestic machinations to its role in the Philippines.

Desperate for damage control, President Taft delivered a formal statement to Congress on the New York customs fraud and in June 1910 dispatched his secretary of war, Jacob M. Dickinson, to Manila for a five-week investigation of the friar land sales. Predictably, the secretary soon found senior colonial officials innocent of these "charges of official misconduct of the most serious character."[102] Not satisfied with this apparent whitewash, Democrats on the House Insular Committee pressed successfully for hearings with full subpoena powers. In these December sessions the committee summoned officials from Manila and discovered widespread cronyism in land leases and mining rights among senior Republican colonials, most notably Solicitor General George R. Harvey, lands chief Charles H. Sleeper, and customs collector Henry B. McCoy. But in its final report the committee's Republican majority found that all these transactions, even those involving the Sugar Trust, had been "fairly and honestly conducted" and praised these Republican officials as "able, earnest, patriotic men."[103]

As the U.S. Congress convened in early 1911 with its new Democratic majority, Manuel Quezon, still in Washington as resident commissioner, wrote General Bandholtz that "the friar lands inquiry coupled with Clarke's trouble on the eve of Democratic House" would bring Philippine affairs before Congress "very conspicuously" in the months leading up to the 1912 presidential election.[104] Indeed, these accusatory hearings added to President Taft's image as a tool of the trusts, tarring his administration with the taint of corruption and contributing to the defeat of his bid for reelection. Meanwhile, back in the Philippines Governor-General Forbes was struggling to weather the political transition in Washington, fighting scandal with scandal in an ill-fated attempt to escape the partisan tide that was sweeping his fellow Republicans into retirement.

Only days after the November 1912 election, the *Manila Times* carried news of the Democratic victory with the banner headline, "Wilson Will Make Clean Sweep in Philippines." Clearly, the colony's entrenched Republican regime was on its way out. Colonial careers that had carried many Manila Americans from youth to middle age now hung in the balance.[105] In the midst of this historic transition, simmering rivalries among senior colonials erupted in open conflict, drawing the unresolved Manila police scandal into a larger political process.

At the political apex, Governor-General Forbes was soon locked in a bitter dispute with Representative Jones, the Democratic chair of the powerful Insular Affairs Committee, which had oversight responsibility for America's entire island empire. In January 1913 Jones denounced Forbes on the floor of the House, blasting his construction of the costly Kennon Road to Baguio as a "reckless extravagance" and lodging even "graver charges" against him for protecting the "powerful triumvirate" of police officials after they had been found guilty of "grafting" in an official investigation. Pressed to defend these criticisms, Jones cited Charles Elliott, the former secretary for commerce and police, who had recently resigned to protest "the infernal outrage" of the way Forbes "has interfered often in the administration of justice to favor personal or political friends."[106]

As befitting a public career that had started with command of the colonial police, Governor-General Forbes spent his last months before retirement in September 1913 amassing sensitive information, copying documents for deposit with his Boston attorneys, and firing off confidential letters loaded with scurrilous gossip about his enemies. In confidential letters to now ex-president Taft, he called Charles Elliot a "skunk" and L. M. Southworth a "scalawag" who had once loaned Judge James M. Liddell money and then won an unseemly number of cases in his court, collusion that had led to the judge's forced resignation back in 1907.[107] In an apparent bid to retain his post by slandering possible successors, Forbes damned George Curry, a former Rough Rider and Manila's first police chief, as a "spendthrift and a bankrupt." Another name being bruited about for governor-general, his longtime rival W. Morgan Shuster, was "a socialist at heart, a man utterly without conviction or morals."[108]

After President Wilson replaced him with a Democratic appointee in September 1913, Forbes returned to his native Boston where he strained, no longer privy to police files, to gather damaging information for Republican allies. In a long letter to Taft's former secretary of war, Henry L. Stimson, Forbes charged Democrats with injecting "party politics into the management of the Islands" and replacing veteran officials of proven ability with their inexperienced partisans. The net result of these "violent changes" was, he claimed, a government "largely paralyzed."[109]

Secret Service Showdown

Farther down the colonial hierarchy, bitter infighting between the Metropolitan Police and Philippine Constabulary resumed in the weeks surrounding President Wilson's election. While Chief Harding joined Secretary Worcester's rearguard struggle to retain the islands as U.S. territory, the constabulary's Col. Rafael Crame sided with Filipinization and ultimately Philippine independence. The sheer force of regime change soon drew the rivalry between the two security forces into a political maelstrom. During six weeks of high-stakes, rapid-fire reprisals, Manila's secret services marshaled confidential files and secret agents for an intense bureaucratic battle, momentarily dropping their veil of secrecy to expose the suppleness of their information controls—voracious in the collection yet strategic in the dissemination of data selected, timed, and directed to destroy their target.

In late 1912 Chief Harding began hitting back at Colonel Crame who just six months before had been the lead investigator in that police inquiry that had nearly ended his career with a finding of "inefficiency." Striking the first blow in early November, the chief attacked the colonel's ally, police captain Jose de Crame of the Paco precinct. Angry at de Crame for testifying at the corruption inquiry, Harding retaliated by demanding the captain's resignation for failure to report the theft of bail bonds by his desk sergeant. When Captain de Crame refused, the police filed full-blown administrative charges for this minor offense and Harding's ally in the executive bureau, John P. Weissenhagen, launched an aggressive investigation. But Colonel Crame discredited the police witnesses by citing the details of similar derelictions committed by other officers, offenses that Chief Harding himself had covered up. Even though Weissenhagen's report recommended Captain de Crame's dismissal, the governor-general, citing his "valuable and excellent services," transferred him to the customs' secret service branch at the same rank.[110]

In the next round Colonel Crame fought back by investigating Chief Harding's ally, police commissioner Percy McDonnell, focusing on his compromised relationship with Meralco, the city's mass transit monopoly controlled by the Detroit traction tycoon Charles M. Swift. At the summit of colonial politics beyond public view and police surveillance, Swift had been sedulous in his courtship of Taft, a good friend from their days as young lawyers litigating what Taft called "the street railway cases in Detroit." As governor-general Taft had eased Swift's bid for the Manila street-rail franchise, and as secretary of war he promoted colonial corporation laws that would minimize regulation of Meralco, just two of what Swift called, in a letter to Taft, "the many obligations due to you from investors in the Philippine Islands."[111] As Taft's appointee on Manila's Municipal Board in 1903, McDonnell maneuvered to award Meralco a fifty-year streetcar concession with low fees, generous rights-of-way, and high fares; then, as chair of the Municipal Board's police committee, he deployed officers armed with riot guns to break strikes against the street railway.[112]

Throughout the colonial transition brought on by the 1912 presidential elections, the constabulary gathered dirt on McDonnell from disparate sources. For months Crame's top agent, Edwin C. Bopp, had been observing "a shady side to the deals," collecting detailed documents on McDonnell's questionable transactions.[113] By penetrating confidential corporate files in New York and Manila,

Agent Bopp reported in May that one of Meralco's owners, the J. G. White Company, had paid McDonnell and others twenty-five thousand dollars in cash "for their assistance in the street-car franchises." With this bribe McDonnell had purchased Meralco shares "and received three times as much stock as was actually paid for." One of Bopp's sources known to the constabulary as Agent 30 reported that an influential Manila merchant had seen "the list of stockholders" at the office of Meralco's local attorney. That document showed a substantial seventy-three thousand dollars' worth of stock in McDonnell's name along with a note reading, "To be turned over to him when he leaves the government service."[114] When similarly damning information about McDonnell's usurious loans surfaced from unknown sources, the governor-general demanded his resignation, thus terminating one of the most sordid of colonial careers.[115]

McDonnell fought back by buying sufficient shares in the influential *Cablenews-American* to become its chief editor and then using the paper to exact revenge. In July 1913 PC Agent 49 reported that McDonnell had given "strict orders" that all mention of Chief Bandholtz in the paper must be "detrimental." A few months later the paper attacked moves to retain his successor, Colonel Harbord, as PC chief, a blatant bias that attracted wry commentary in rival Manila newspapers.[116]

In the final round of this bare-knuckle bout, Chief Harding began maneuvering, only days after McDonnell's resignation, to even the score against Colonel Crame. Around midnight on December 9, Captain Jose de Crame called at the colonel's home to warn that Chief Harding was accumulating evidence to accuse him of fomenting an armed uprising by the radical working-class society Dimas Alang. Indeed, there had been an abortive revolt by elements of this organization three months before on the night of August 26. But Colonel Crame had in fact been concerned about the group's radicalism and infiltrated its ranks with his spies to preempt any violence. He had also deployed ex-general Santiago Alvarez in a covert operation to weaken Dimas Alang by organizing the rival Makabuhay society, producing a divisive clash between the two groups.[117]

Just ten days later, the police captain's warning proved prescient. In a sensational front-page story on December 19, the *Daily Bulletin* reported that Colonel Crame had used his spies inside these working-class societies to promote an armed uprising the previous August on the outskirts of Manila. Within forty-eight hours Colonel Crame's agents inside the newspaper confirmed that Chief Harding was in fact the source for these damaging allegations.[118] At first the colonel insisted that "Harding will only succeed in making himself [look] ridiculous" by circulating such nonsense. But the police chief would remain veiled behind his anonymity as a news source while Crame was subjected to hostile headlines and protracted legislative hearings, barely escaping a humiliating dismissal.[119]

While McDonnell had been forced to resign, chiefs Harding and Trowbridge clung to office like barnacles on the ship of state. But in March 1913 Trowbridge finally quit after fourteen years in command of the city's secret service, sailing home for a minor patronage post in the U.S. Interior Department.[120] In its only attempt at police reform, the Forbes administration then appointed a famed investigator, John W. Green (no relation to former chief John F. Green), as Trowbridge's successor to clean up the city's troubled secret service. After serving five years in the Manila Police as a specialist in criminal identification, he had returned to North America as chief detective for the Mexican Central Railway and a U.S. customs agent investigating Sugar Trust bribery on the New York docks. Now, in April 1913, as Green neared the islands aboard the SS *Manchuria* with his American wife and two young daughters, the *Manila Times* carried the news on page one, telling its readers that an officer who could bust the American Sugar Trust would surely clean up Manila's detective branch.[121] Chief Bandholtz reported wryly that with the news of Green's appointment "the local police got busy and located his Filipina wife or *querida* in order to have a grip on him as soon as he arrived."[122]

Consequently, in his first years as secret service chief Green concentrated on the noncontroversial forensic innovations that were his forte, creating a card-file identification system that soon reached two hundred thousand entries and introducing the Henry fingerprinting method.[123] Yet even as the police command changed and its methods were modernized, the underlying system of syndicated vice and police corruption survived. Although he was an investigator with ample skills to attack these rackets, Green would wait until 1919, a full six years after his arrival, before daring an assault on the city's vice trades.[124]

Governor Harrison's Purge

Even though his closest allies had been dismissed and disgraced, Chief Harding was so influential that he was not removed until Governor-General Francis Burton Harrison, President Wilson's new representative and a former New York City congressman, finally reached Manila in late 1913. Only three hours after the new governor walked down the gangplank to a cheering Filipino crowd on October 6, Thomas Cary Welch, the executive secretary complicit in the exoneration of corrupt police, was sacked. To make his message clear, the governor quickly purged all senior officers identified with the 1912 police scandal.[125]

"While disposed upon my arrival to treat the police question with a good deal of leniency because of my recognition of the supreme difficulty of policing a great city," Governor Harrison wrote Washington a month after landing at Manila, "I soon found that the conditions here were intolerable." An official inquiry, he said, had urged dismissal of senior police, but a later "whitewash made by two inferior administrative officials exonerated the three men." Most important, the governor learned from a Supreme Court justice that Chief Harding had engaged in "what amounted to blackmail . . . not for money, but in order to retain the old crowd in power." In his opinion, "Chief of Police Harding would have done better in the city of Baghdad in the middle ages than in Manila today." In his place the governor appointed Capt. George Seaver, "who is a scrupulously honest and decent man," a move the U.S. secretary of war endorsed as "necessary to the restoration of confidence in the Department."[126] By the time his shake-up ended, Governor Harrison had removed all the principals in the 1912 police scandal.[127]

The police purge also launched Governor Harrison's aggressive Filipinization of the civil service, sweeping away the residue of the colony's entrenched Republican regime. In his first months the governor forcibly retired some two hundred Americans, including the head of the Bureau of Lands, Charles H. Sleeper, and the powerful customs chief, Henry B. McCoy.[128] Determined to recover their influence, the Republicans fought Filipinization with intrigue and information. Leading American merchants along the Escolta sent stories of Filipino incompetence to U.S. newspapers.[129] As criticism began circulating, the governor-general used the PC's secret service to track this "misinformation" to a single "cell" inside ex-chief Harding's business office that included Sleeper, McCoy, and McDonnell, now editor of the *Cablenews-American*. Indeed, McDonnell, concealing his espionage as press inquiries, was sending "strictly confidential" cables to New York with details of the governor's dismissals for that most vociferous critic of Filipinization, Dean Worcester, who was gathering information about maladministration, adultery, and graft under Governor-General Harrison.[130]

Toughened by his years with New York's venal Tammany machine, Harrison fought back, warning his opponents that unless the criticism stopped they "would be made to suffer."[131] To court support from powerful American colonials, the governor-general countered their criticisms by easing these ex-police out of Manila, sending Harding to Panama and McDonnell to Europe. Just four days after firing Chief Harding, the governor-general cabled Washington to recommend him for a federal clerkship to please "a considerable portion of the better element in the American community here."[132] McDonnell's trip was a study tour for the Philippine chapter of the American Red Cross, a sinecure that soon ended when the State Department withdrew his passport permanently for "certain unneutral activities."[133] Through this mix of carrot and stick, local opposition to Governor Harrison slowly faded, and by late 1915 even the *Manila Times*, the voice of the American community, had moderated its opposition to his reforms.[134]

But the purge still rankled sufficiently within the American culture of patronage to spark a bitter partisan debate between ex-president Taft and President Wilson's secretary of war, Lindley M. Garrison, in late 1915. With confidential documents that Worcester purloined through McDonnell and like loyalists in Manila, Taft launched a front-page attack on the Democrats in the *New York Times*, charging that Governor-General Harrison had "discharged, at once, upon his arrival, McCoy, collector of customs; Sleeper, Director of Public Lands; . . . Harding, Chief of the Manila Police; [Mark] Scott, captain of police." In reply the secretary of war insisted that Harding and Scott had been dismissed for their "undesirability." Taft thundered back, condemning the "partisanship of a Democrat . . . forcing resignations of competent . . . American civil servants for the purpose of giving patronage to Mr. Quezon and his group of Filipino politicians."[135]

Governor Harrison had ample information to counter these criticisms should they gain political traction. After Taft's opening salvo in September, Manila's long-serving Internal Revenue chief James J. Rafferty, a Democrat despised by Taft, detailed the derelictions of his Republican enemies in a memo to the governor-general, documenting how Henry McCoy's career was the sum of its corruptions. So great was his power that since the time of Governor Forbes "no man dared to raise his voice against McCoy and the band of legalized brigands of which he was the notable chief."[136]

Manila Police Reforms

Only months after his arrival in late 1913, Governor Harrison resolved the heated controversy over the Manila Police by dismissing the controversial American commanders and promoting structural reforms. Although the process was less direct and dramatic, this Manila Police crisis had thus been resolved, like the Cavite constabulary controversy six years before, by placating public opinion with a rhetoric of reform and gradual Filipinization, all while keeping command of security forces firmly under American control.

Although Governor Harrison had removed shady Americans from the Manila police and promoted a number of Filipinos in the constabulary, like most colonials he was generally conservative in his handling of the Manila force, passing over a well-qualified Filipino, assistant chief Gregorio Alcid, to appoint a succession of American chiefs: George H. Seaver (1913–18), a veteran officer who supported reforms during the 1912 scandal; Anton Hohmann (1918–20), who rose from beat cop to precinct captain through sixteen years' service; and Edwin C. Bopp (1920–21), a ten-year veteran of the PC Information Division.[137] Once Chief Harding and his coterie had been ousted, Harrison exempted Manila's police from further retirements, saying in May 1914, "I am opposed to the elimination of a single American policeman or a reduction of the salary of a single American policeman." Harrison's Filipinization effort succeeded almost by accident after the U.S. entry into World War I in 1917 produced an exodus of Americans from the civil service, raising the number of Filipinos on the Manila force from 64 percent in 1911 to 93 percent in 1921.[138] But reflecting Manila's unique role as the colonial capital and home of the expatriate community, Americans would remain in command of the Metropolitan Police until the end of direct U.S. rule in 1935.[139]

In the later years of his administration, 1916–21, Harrison struggled with this ambivalent transfer of power to Filipinos by creating an elected Municipal Board for Manila while retaining control over the city's police, a contradiction that emerged with spectacular force during several strikes against Meralco in 1919. After the company's streetcar motormen walked out briefly in early March, the city's Nacionalista Party mayor, Justo Lukban, quietly hired a number of dismissed strikers as third-class patrolmen, stirring controversy.[140] When Meralco's workers struck again in late May, the police force was in disarray under its acting Filipino chief, Gregorio Alcid, who lacked a mandate for reform. Led by the radical Congreso Obrero union under Crisanto Evangelista, some six hundred workers launched a militant strike at Meralco on May 23, beating tram operators and stoning police in four incidents that the American press played up with banner headlines.[141]

While Mayor Lukban flailed about trying to recruit more police and requisition revolvers, the acting governor-general, Charles Yeater, ordered his constabulary into the city. Only thirty-six hours after the strike began, some three hundred soldiers armed with repeating rifles and fixed bayonets were riding the streetcars, an action criticized by both the mayor and his police chief as an overreaction to, and even an attempt to provoke, the generally peaceful strikers. As the strike entered its fourth and then fifth week with soldiers still riding the cars, the situation became dangerously polarized, with workers growing more militant, the government unsympathetic, and the company intransigent.[142]

Frustrated over their failure to penetrate the constabulary cordon, the strikers turned to terror, attempting to derail moving cars and on June 21 trying to bomb a Meralco tram, the first such incident in Philippine history. As car 108 turned into Plaza Goiti, a striking Meralco mechanic named Bernardino Manabat lit a fuse protruding from a parcel and thirty seconds later jumped from the tram. The conductor, catching the scent of gunpowder, tossed the bomb into the street where it exploded, killing a thirteen-year-old newsboy and injuring eight pedestrians. As the bomber fled through Santa Cruz church and up Calle Bustos, Detective Fermin Yadan followed, finally cornering him at gunpoint inside the Cine Ideal movie theater. After nineteen hours of interrogation by subordinates, secret service chief John W. Green took over for a low-key conversation in Tagalog, asking how the suspect might feel had his own boy been maimed by the explosion. Weeping, the bomber signed a confession implicating Domingo Simeon, the secretary of the Congreso Obrero. Within hours the police arrested Simeon for murder and union leader Crisanto Evangelista for sedition. As their heavily publicized trial proceeded, support for the strike ebbed until Meralco could announce, in mid-July, that operations were back to normal.[143] Although military protection had proved effective, this unprecedented constabulary deployment inside the city left simmering tensions within Manila's police that would soon explode.

Manila Massacre

In late 1920, just eighteen months after the Meralco strike, a spectacular conflict erupted along the fault lines in Philippine policing, turning a minor incident into a bloody shootout between the constabulary's Santa Lucia Barracks and the nearby Luneta police station. Around midnight on December 13, three PC constables confronted police patrolman Artemo Mojica at gunpoint, accusing him of raping the wife of a fellow trooper. Instead of investigating the rape, the police arrested the PC soldiers. The next day in front of Berry's Barbershop on Calle Real in the walled city of Intramuros, Patrolman Mojica gunned down a PC private, and policemen armed with riot guns swept the streets to arrest eight more PC constables. Inside the constabulary barracks, rumors spread that police headquarters had issued orders to shoot "any contabularyman they met on the streets."[144]

Just twenty-five hours later, seventy-seven PC constables loaded their rifles and jumped the barracks wall to hunt down city policemen, who were armed only with .32 caliber pistols. Advancing in skirmish formation, some forty constables lined the Sunken Gardens just outside the city walls and on command unleashed a fusillade at the Luneta police station, killing a patrolman and wounding several civilians. A smaller detachment occupied Calle Real in the heart of Intramuros, firing a volley into a streetcar and killing a passenger. Outside the nearby Corregidor Hotel, six constables fired on patrolman James W. Driskill, who backed through the swinging doors, pistol blazing, to fall dead on the barroom floor. When police reinforcements arrived from the Meisic precinct station, the mutineers raked the patrol wagon with lethal fire, killing two officers and fatally wounding Capt. William E. Wichmann. In the midst of this mayhem, Chief Crame arrived, bellowing, "You fools, what are you doing?" When one soldier dared to raise his rifle, the chief shouted back, "Put down that gun. I am the chief of Constabulary. Stand to attention!" Meekly, the troops marched back to the barracks, leaving the city streets stained with the blood of four wounded and eleven dead, including six patrolmen.[145]

Manila was stunned. The city prosecutor filed murder charges against the seventy-seven constables. The constabulary trucked the accused to Bilibid Prison under heavy guard. The governor-general closed Santa Lucia Barracks and ordered all constables out of the city. The legislature voted unanimously for a special investigation. Then, at 4:00 p.m. on December 22, the entire city stopped. For thirty seconds nothing moved. Thousands lined the street in silence as a solemn cortège started up Rizal Avenue toward Cementerio del Norte. The procession included police platoons, a constabulary band, city officials, and six horse-drawn hearses for the fallen officers.[146]

While the city mourned its murdered officers, the press was sharply critical of the police department, almost blaming it for the shooting. "Once the pride of Manila," said the *Philippines Free Press,* "today the police force of this metropolis, if not its shame, certainly evokes no respect." The nationalist *Independent* put it bluntly, adding that: "Among all classes of people, the belief is current that a mongrel dog is a better protection for the home than the whole police force." By contrast, the paper insisted, the constabulary "has such a brilliant history as the right arm of a just, orderly, and progressive government that its defects and shortcomings cannot efface or effectively blot."[147]

On the governor's orders secretary of justice Quintin Paredes conducted an internal investigation that traced the shooting incident to deeper problems within the colonial police. The constabulary, for its part, seemed to resent an informal arrangement, dating from its founding in 1901, that barred it from making arrests inside Manila, and some city policemen still harbored a "wish to take revenge" for the constabulary's role in the 1912 corruption investigation. Just a year before the shooting these tensions had flared during the Meralco strike. Compounding the "jealousies between the two organizations," many policemen were former Meralco workers "who sympathized with the strike." In the twenty-four hours before the shooting, Paredes found, the two responsible American commanders had been woefully deficient in their duties. After the patrolman Mojica shot a constabulary soldier, Chief Bopp had returned his revolver and restored him to duty. Despite obvious signs of violence, the constabulary barracks commander, Capt. Herbert C. Page, had failed to post adequate sentries and during the shooting did nothing to restrain his troops.[148]

In two separate trials all the accused were convicted and sentenced by the Philippine Supreme Court to penalties of life for the sixty-six privates and death for the eleven noncommissioned officers. Feeling that their commanders were to blame, Governor-General Leonard Wood, Harrison's successor, convened a pardon board that in March 1922 reduced these penalties to seventeen years and life, respectively, effectively closing the case.[149] Despite strong criticism, reform of the Manila Police was limited to Chief Bopp's resignation, leaving deeper problems uncorrected.

At this low ebb the governor-general passed over acting police chief Gregorio Alcid, a Filipino veteran with twenty-two years service, to appoint John W. Green, a respected police reformer.[150] For the next seven years Chief Green devoted himself to the modernization of the force, assisted by a senior staff that would remain largely American. Most visibly, he created a traffic division with ninety-seven officers to untangle the city's snarl of ten thousand autos and six thousand horse carts. To raise standards he introduced in-service training to give every officer four hours of weekly instruction in "the law relating to arrests, search warrants, evidence, essentials of crimes, . . . discipline, and deportment." To check the "steady deterioration of the Police force," he established a police academy, making Manila's the first force in the Philippines with mandatory training for all personnel.[151]

Although not all of his recommendations were implemented, Chief Green won a marked expansion of the force to eight hundred officers by 1924. "From being one of the worst policed cities in the world," the *Chamber of Commerce Journal* said in 1929, "Manila has become one of the best."[152] At end of U.S. rule, the leading Filipino police expert, Maj. Emanuel Bajá, concluded that Manila had "the best organized, best trained, and so far the most efficient police department in the Philippines." By then the force had a record 957 officers deployed in two precincts and several specialist squads: the secret service, vice, and traffic. But some things had not changed. Although the governor-general now consulted the city's Filipino mayor on police matters, he still selected the police chief from a small pool of senior Americans, just as he had done at the start of the U.S. regime in 1901.[153]

Conclusion

In comparing political controversies across the span of a century, 1905 to 2005, a central question emerges: why did this massive police scandal in 1912 have such a modest political impact? The answer, in a word, is timing. With only ten months left in office before the November 1912 presidential elections, the Forbes administration struggled, successfully, to contain the situation by protecting Chief Harding while placating the public with reprimands of his Filipino subordinates. Instead of mobilizing press and public to challenge the governor-general as they had so successfully done back in 1905 and would again in 1923, Quezon and his Nacionalista Party decided to bide their time, confident that a new Democratic administration in Washington would bring sweeping changes in policy and personnel to Manila. If, as Jürgen Habermas reminds us, each crisis of legitimacy is best resolved by a widening of political participation, then the Filipinos realized, correctly, that they could best achieve this result in Washington rather than Manila.

As the ambit of Filipino participation widened, the colony's security services, the Philippines Constabulary and the Manila Police, experienced major changes in both mission and personnel. When the Republican Party's "days of empire" ended in 1913, both services continued their ongoing accommodation with the rising Filipino elite. These changes had begun, of course, in the aftermath of the 1905 Cavite controversy, but Republican imperialists, notably Forbes and Worcester, fought a rearguard action to preserve their control over the security services. With the Democratic victory in the 1912 presidential elections and the subsequent purge of Republican imperialists in Manila, these two forces moved rapidly from colonial repression to law enforcement and somewhat less rapidly from American to Filipino officers. In both cases these moves served to legitimate police authority.

This larger political transition also brought a relaxation of covert operations by both the constabulary and the city police. With the end of the Republican regime and the collapse of the radical nationalist movement, the extremes of colonial politics faded, drawing debate toward the political center and ending systematic surveillance of both American and Filipino extremists. Although domestic espionage subsided after 1914, the system, with its fusion of information and coercion, survived as a permanent feature of the Philippine state, ready for use in any future political crisis. Even in the latter years of colonial rule, American governors still controlled the colony's security services, the constabulary and Metropolitan Police. These both remained a possible source of high political scandal—a potential that would be fully realized in the spectacular Conley case of 1923.

8

The Conley Case

ON THE NIGHT OF JULY 17, 1923, Senator Manuel Quezon led five Filipino cabinet secretaries, all attired in formal dress, up the grand staircase into Malacañang Palace for a historic confrontation. Waiting for him at the head of the stairs was Governor-General Leonard Wood, splendidly outfitted in his full-dress U.S. Army uniform. Somewhat nervously, Senator Quezon read aloud his group's letter announcing their resignation en masse to protest the governor's control over even the "smallest detail" of government. "This policy recently culminated in an unfortunate incident which shocked public opinion in this country," Quezon said, "when you . . . reinstated a member of the secret service of the City who had been legally suspended from office." In turn Wood dismissed these charges as "unsupported by evidence and unworthy of the attention of serious minded men." After accepting their resignations, the governor placed U.S. combat forces in the Philippines on full alert. Throughout this high political drama, nobody mentioned the name of the secret service officer in question. For he was, as all Manila already knew, Detective Ray Conley, the catalyst for the most protracted political crisis in forty years of U.S. colonial rule.[1]

This controversy had started quietly six months before when Manila's Mayor Ramon Fernandez recommended that Detective Conley, then head of the police vice squad, be dismissed for allegedly taking bribes from gambling joints. When Governor-General Wood rejected this recommendation after months of wrangling, Quezon denounced the unpopular decision and rode the tide of public opinion to become his country's preeminent political leader. Over the next four years Quezon used this issue to challenge the governor-general's authority while Wood countered the attacks by circulating compromising information, collected through the colonial police, about his political enemies. By symbolizing the American regime's selective enforcement of its own laws, the Conley case would ignite the passions of the Filipino nationalist press, assure the ascendancy of the Nacionalista Party, and prepare the electorate for major political change.[2]

The conflict arose primarily from the ambiguity of Conley's role as an American policeman enforcing vice laws on prominent Filipinos. By the early 1920s the Manila's Police was still serving as both the moral guardian and mailed fist of alien rule, contradictory roles that were resolved pragmatically, on the street, by corruption that turned police officers into informal protectors of illegal gaming and other crimes. In a colonial context this resolution was politically volatile, stirring the indignation of Filipino politicians and journalists whose reportage aroused an electorate increasingly intolerant of American hypocrisy. While the conflict did not seriously threaten U.S. rule, it was a serious challenge to the terms of that dominion. If we strip away the hyperheated rhetoric on both sides, this controversy was the final showdown between rearguard Republican attempts to slow Filipino progress toward self-rule and a liberal Democratic policy of Filipinization to prepare the islands for full independence.

In considering the Conley case, historians have usually focused on the high-stakes political confrontation between an American governor and a Filipino senator. But in retrospect this great scandal, reflecting the power of Manila's low life to shape high politics, began and ended with the city police.[3] Just as constabulary brutality in Cavite had sparked a legitimation crisis in 1905, so Manila police corruption precipitated this even larger crisis in 1923.

Republican Restoration

The Conley case gained its tempestuous force from an ongoing struggle between the Filipino legislature and American executive during the long transition to national independence. Under President Woodrow Wilson's liberal policy, Washington had promoted Filipino self-rule by appointing a sympathetic governor-general, Francis Burton Harrison, in 1913 and three years later granting Filipinos full legislative powers under the Jones Act. Beginning with a preamble that for the first time promised eventual independence, this de facto colonial constitution abolished the old Philippine Commission, created the bicameral Philippine Assembly, and delineated the broad powers of the U.S. governor-general. But Harrison's personal failings as an administrator and moral exemplar tainted his legacy and jeopardized these political gains.

When Republicans won back the White House in 1920, they set about reclaiming their lost Philippine colony, exposing the malfeasance of the Harrison regime, discrediting its innovations, and reinvigorating executive authority in the hands of an assertive governor-general. After several years of simmering quietly in Manila, scandal, visible and vociferous, once again became central to the struggle over the Philippines' future. As in past colonial crises, rivalries intensified, gossip flew, dossiers opened, betrayals abounded, and reputations were ruined.

Among his first executive acts, incoming President Warren G. Harding dispatched special investigators to Manila to probe the gross mismanagement that had pushed the Philippine government to the brink of collapse. Led by two veteran imperialists, ex-governor W. Cameron Forbes and Gen. Leonard Wood, the mission was charged with exploring Democratic excesses and recommending reforms. When they sailed for Manila in April 1921, Forbes, a proper Boston Brahmin and former governor-general, came armed with deep colonial knowledge of native derelictions. "Quezon was very anxious about the kind of reception I would give him," he told his private diary, because he "happened to know that I had complete knowledge of his disloyalties and rascalities. I do not think he knew that I had in my safe a complete copy of his police record. It was lurid enough and he must have known I was pretty well informed on it. He was not quite sure of the use I would make of it."[4]

Well prepared as he was, Forbes soon found Quezon his equal in this colonial contest. At their meeting in July the Filipino senator surprised Forbes by handing over full payment for a long-forgotten debt of ₱3,050. Then, speaking with a frankness Forbes found "disarming," Quezon referred to an unnamed American justice, saying, "I am not a clean man myself, but I want the judges of the Supreme Court to be clean men." As their conversation closed Quezon executed a brilliant move in the contest over information by destroying Forbes's friendship with the Philippine resident commissioner in Washington, Jaime de Veyra, and his wife, Sofia Reyes de Veyra. Pulling out a sheaf of his own cables to and from this power couple, Quezon showed Forbes a telegram from the commissioner announcing, "I have done everything possible to eliminate Forbes" from consideration as governor-general. Recalling how he had once loaned Mrs. de Veyra a thousand dollars to save her father's house from foreclosure, a deflated Forbes was devastated by this "bit of treachery on the part of one whom I had befriended."[5]

But if Forbes proved an easy mark Quezon soon found a worthier opponent in General Wood, the living embodiment of empire. Although slope shouldered and average height, Wood had developed a powerful build in military campaigns that conquered the American Southwest, pursuing Geronimo's Apaches across New Mexico into Mexico for nearly two years. Through all that hard riding Wood won the Medal of Honor and became such a hero that Theodore Roosevelt followed him to Cuba with the Rough Riders and to fame in the charge up San Juan Hill. After ousting the incumbent military governor in Havana through media manipulations in late 1899, Wood enjoyed good press as the island's governor-general by paying some American reporters and intimidating others critical of his rule. With the press muzzled he grew suspiciously close to a Spanish syndicate that was promoting Cuba's most lucrative gambling franchise, the Havana jai alai fronton, and thereby gained the connections to win big in betting that sometimes reached fifty thousand dollars on a single match. Adding substance to such suspicions, Wood had banned all competing forms of gambling but then brokered a ten-year contract for the jai alai, accepting a five thousand dollar Tiffany silver tea service as a gratuity from the Spanish syndicate. When Wood returned to Washington in 1902, the Senate soon launched an inquiry into the seamy side his Cuban service. But close friendship with President Roosevelt bought him a face-saving political exile to the southern Philippines as governor of the Moro Province. There empire eventually cleansed his reputation through bloody campaigns against Muslim warriors, sending him home a hero to become commander of the U.S. Army and, in 1920, a contender for the Republican presidential nomination, which he narrowly lost to Harding.[6]

As a veteran imperialist Wood returned to Manila in 1921 with his sensors tuned for scurrilous gossip, recording each anecdote in a private diary that reveals, in some three thousand typed pages, the dynamics of colonial scandal. In his detailed entries about graft, concubinage, and double-dealing, Wood was assiduous in documenting the demerits of his American adversaries, particularly his former rival for command of U.S. forces during the world war, Gen. John J. Pershing. After meeting the governor of Zamboanga, Pershing's former headquarters, Wood noted that the general had "lived for a long time with a girl named Joaquina Ignacio, by whom he had a daughter." Pershing's mistress had received "a very considerable sum of money . . . when she signed a declaration before a Justice of the Peace that Pershing was not the father."[7] As if storing ammunition for some future battle, Wood noted that "she is a girl of whom I have a photograph, a striking likeness of her father."[8]

To fulfill his mission from President Harding, Wood devoted particular attention to rumors of philandering by the outgoing Democratic governor-general, Francis Burton Harrison, whose indiscretions, many believed, had made him susceptible to Filipino pressure for political concessions. An American businessman, Mr. E. Womek, said that Harrison's "tendency to follow up young girls" had led people to regard him as a "pervert" and "spoke of certain pictures taken by concealed cameras showing he was very much one."[9] Other sources reported that a constabulary colonel, James F. Quinn, angry at his wife's affair with the governor-general, had telephoned the state university's engineering dean, Clarence G. Wrentmore, at 2:00 a.m. to report that the dean's underage daughter Elizabeth was at a roadhouse with the governor. The excited father "armed himself with a revolver, . . . forced his way into the Malacañan and extracted a written promise from Burton to marry the girl." To avoid a scandal, Mrs. Wrentmore sailed home to enroll the daughter at the University of California. The governor followed in May 1919, married Elizabeth, and brought her back to Manila where their child was born in Malacañang Palace.[10] The sum of these reports led Wood to conclude that the Filipino politicians had "gradually woven an entangling net about the Governor General and greatly hampered him in the exercise of his powers under the Jones bill."[11]

Through its close investigation of the governor's domestic entanglements and affairs of state, the Wood-Forbes mission subtly merged this overall sense of Harrison's personal failings into a partisan indictment of his policies.[12] Above all the mission's final report detailed unchecked graft in government enterprises such as the newly established Philippine National Bank (PNB), a quasi-governmental agency that dispensed loans liberally to new government corporations and neophyte Filipino entrepreneurs. After noting that auditors estimated the bank's losses at $23 million through violations "of every principle which prudence, intelligence, or even honesty, dictates," the mission recommended that the government should "get out and keep out of such business."[13]

As subsequent investigations would soon discover, the financial crisis was even more serious than the Wood-Forbes mission had imagined. To expand their Nacionalista Party's patronage, Senate president Quezon and House Speaker Sergio Osmeña had, with Governor-General Harrison's support, appointed cronies to corporate and regulatory boards that voted massive loans for their own sugar mills, copra factories, and hemp trading. Under the presidency of Venancio Concepcion, an Osmeña protégé, the PNB dispensed substantial, poorly secured loans to Nacionalista Party loyalists.[14] In a clear example of crony capitalism, Quezon, working through Governor Harrison, appointed the well-connected mestizo merchant Ramon Fernandez to the PNB board in 1916. Three years later Fernandez and another PNB director, Vicente Madrigal, voted themselves interest-free personal loans for an ill-fated attempt to corner Manila's hemp supply. The market collapsed, leaving the bank with fifty-three thousand worthless bales of hemp and ₱2.2 million in bad loans that the PNB directors illegally wiped from the books. In 1920 Quezon cashed in this political debt by calling on Fernandez to finance his party's newspaper, the *Philippines Herald,* and serve a term as mayor of Manila.[15] Matching Quezon's cronyism with his own, Governor Harrison later elevated his personal stenographer to the bank's presidency and appointed his brother Archibald to its board.[16] By the time Concepcion resigned from the PNB in 1920, the bank had suffered losses of ₱75 million, the equivalent of a year of Philippine tax revenues, and the country was close to fiscal collapse.[17] To correct this lack of oversight, the Wood-Forbes mission recommended strengthening the powers of the governor-general.[18]

By his mission's end in August 1921, Wood was so troubled by these threats to American colonial progress that he accepted President Harding's nomination as governor-general. Angered by the rapid Filipinization under Harrison, the Manila American community had lobbied hard to convince the White House that there was a "serious situation" requiring Wood's firm leadership. "Strongly recommend immediate appointment General Wood," the American Chamber of Commerce cabled the president in July 1921, adding: "Urgently needed reassert sovereignty of United States, regain financial stability."[19] Wood thus took office determined to recover the colonial executive's full prerogatives and use them to liquidate government corporations, restore fiscal responsibility, and promote American investment. This reactionary agenda soon sparked a battle with Senate president Quezon, who was determined to defend the power-sharing arrangement he had won from Governor Harrison.[20]

During a five-year political standoff, Governor-General Wood was advantaged by one key perquisite of his new office: unchecked executive control over the Manila Metropolitan Police and Philippines Constabulary. Through these two key allies he gained access to incriminating information, holding and releasing damaging gossip with imperious finesse. His choice for Manila's police chief, John W. Green, was a veteran of the city's secret service who had acquired a feel for the city's mean streets.[21] His constabulary chief, Gen. Rafael Crame, was a seasoned intelligence operative who had served in its Information Division for fifteen years, directing the subtle strategy that had demoralized the radical nationalist movement.[22] Shielded from police surveillance by his appointees, Wood was in a position to withstand the most serious crisis of legitimacy to face the U.S. regime since the Cavite controversy of 1905.

Conley of the Vice Squad

The progenitor of this political crisis was Detective Ray Conley, an accidental colonialist transformed by his badge into a powerful player in the scandals swirling about Governor-General Wood. Arriving in the islands as an eighteen-year-old soldier from Hicksville, Ohio, Conley joined the Manila police in 1912 and remained an ordinary patrolman for the next five years. Then, in 1917, the secret service chief, John W. Green, adopted him as his confidential agent in Manila's netherworld of vice and crime.[23] If contemporaries regarded Chief Green as admirable and Conley as despicable, they failed to understand that this shadowy detective was a necessary adjunct to the chief's celebrated efficiency. With raw cunning, fluent Tagalog, and de facto control over the city's vice trades, Conley was a formidable force in Manila's underworld, arresting prominent Filipinos for gambling and protecting powerful Americans from sexual scandal. In this world of imperial intrigue, he tipped the colonial political balance decisively and was thus a worthy target for Filipino nationalists.

Conley's mastery over the Manila netherworld may have assuaged Chief Green's fears of scandal over an earlier liaison with a Filipina mistress and overcome his aversion to attacking the city's vice economy. Whatever their precise dynamic, the two forged a deep, lasting bond and unleashed a devastating assault on illegal gaming, which had swelled to "grave proportions" by the end of Governor Harrison's tolerant term.[24] In 1919–20, Green, then head of the secret service, picked Conley to lead his vice squads against the city's private Filipino clubs and political clubhouses, which, he insisted, "were really gambling houses." In rapid succession Conley's squad crashed through the doors of the Nacionalista Club, Club Democrata, Club Libertad, Club Alegre, Club Obreros, Club Amistad, and the Fajardo Club, rounding up both ordinary dealers and influential patrons. When Green was appointed Manila's police chief in March 1922, he picked Conley to lead his gambling and opium squads in a renewed attack on the city's vice trades.[25]

For the next twelve months Detective Conley became Chief Green's battering ram in an assault on Manila's vice. Through a series of sensational raids in mid-1922, Conley's squads closed eighteen opium dens and fourteen gambling joints that were "running almost openly." The chief reported that in a raid on the Club Nacionalista Conley arrested "a large number of prominent persons including . . . attorneys, physicians, property owners and, of course, members of both political parties." Jubilant over this restoration of public morality, the city's press celebrated Conley as the police department's "best raider of gambling clubs."[26]

These successes stirred deep hostility among members of the city's gambling syndicate, which launched a sustained counterattack. To get rid of Conley the syndicate hired a well-known local lawyer, Ramon Sotelo, to press charges against him for concubinage. Although this attorney spent a year trying to destroy the detective, his case collapsed when Conley's legal Filipina wife, Primitiva Dumasig, refused the gamblers' money to testify against him. Prosecutors failed to puncture his claim that an alleged second wife, an American named Grace, was simply his housekeeper. At the trial a bank clerk called by the prosecution admitted that a syndicate boss, Aniceto Cardeñas, had offered him a thousand pesos to testify against the detective, saying that "he and other gamblers wanted Conley out of the way."[27] Both the police chief and the governor-general agreed that the detective had been falsely accused "in revenge for his efficient services against organized vice in Manila."[28]

Back on duty, Conley again made life difficult for the gambling syndicate, leading his squad on a renewed round of 275 raids that virtually closed Manila's main gaming clubs between December 1922 and March 1923. Most notably, in December Conley crossed the city limits into San Juan del Monte to hit an elite club run by a former legislator, Jose L. Luna y Rufino, arresting "37 prominent persons." From his street sources Chief Green learned that "members of the Manila underworld," angered by this raid, had decided to involve politicians in a scheme to demonstrate that "Manila was really dirty from a police point of view," thereby tarring Conley with the brush of corruption.[29]

The efforts of the city's gambling interests to eliminate Conley would gain momentum only when they converged with more powerful forces. Just a month after the San Juan raid, the detective tangled with a figure whose close political connection to Quezon and personal ties to Manila's Spanish mestizo corporate elite made him a formidable enemy. On January 2, 1923, a Chinatown merchant named Lao Teng complained to Detective Conley that the "Mayor's spies," a crew of former police officers carrying official badges, were, in Chief Green's words, "extorting money from him under the threat of planting morphine in his premises and bringing the Mayor of the City of Manila to raid." Lending force to this threat, Mayor Fernandez himself had reportedly visited this Chinese victim in the company of the spies. Hitting hard against the mayor, Conley and his vice squad arrested three of these former officers "in the act of receiving money from the Chinese." Mayor Fernandez posted their bail immediately. When the Chinese merchant refused to withdraw his complaint, the city engineer sent men to demolish his house on Calle Ongpin and throw his personal effects into the slime of a nearby canal.[30]

Just a few weeks later Mayor Fernandez launched an elaborate scheme to implicate Conley in the act of taking bribes from "the gambling lords of the city." On February 24, the mayor asked the city secretary, Rosauro Almario, to contact his nephew, a well-known gambler named Eduardo Cardeñas. At their meeting the next day, the gambler reportedly told the mayor that he was bribing Conley to protect his club and would be making another payment within the next twenty-four hours.[31] With this enticing inside information, the mayor briefed Interior Secretary Jose Laurel, a young Filipino graduate of the Yale Law School only recently appointed to this senior cabinet post. On March 1, Mayor Fernandez summoned Cardeñas to Secretary Laurel's office in the Ayuntamiento building inside Intramuros. While the two senior officials listened on a specially wired extension, the gambler Cardeñas phoned Detective Conley to arrange payment of one thousand pesos in "hush money."[32] After Cardeñas dialed Manila 5180, Secretary Laurel monitored the bilingual telephone conversation and took verbatim notes:[33]

> CARDEÑAS: Is this 5180?
> WOMAN'S VOICE: Yes.
> CARDEÑAS: May I speak with Mr. Ray [Conley]?
> WOMAN: He is sleeping. Who is speaking please?
> CARDEÑAS: Cardeñas.
> WOMAN: All right, wait.
> CARDEÑAS: *Ang kuarta'y nakobra ko na.* [I have the money.]
> CONLEY: *Huwag kang maingay sa telefono.* [Do not speak about it on the telephone.]
> CARDEÑAS: *Ano ang gusto mo? Daldalhin ko sa ba diyan*? [What do you want? Should I bring it there?]
> CONLEY: *Oo, a las dos.* [Yes, at two o'clock.]
> CARDEÑAS: *Saan?* [Where?]
> CONLEY: *Sa oficina.* [At the office.]

After the call ended, the mayor's secretary, Almario, sent another of his nephews, secret service agent Prudencio Lumanlan, to observe the payoff at the nearby Luneta police station. According to the agent's version of events, at 2:00 p.m. he watched Conley approach Cardeñas outside the station, accept a roll of hundred-peso bills, and slip them into his pocket.[34]

With this evidence in hand, Mayor Fernandez urged the detective's immediate suspension. Secretary Laurel, now fully convinced that Conley was "a crook," issued the official order. When these two officials pressed for an internal dismissal hearing, Governor Wood, feeling that they were "plainly prejudiced," refused. Instead he opted for a criminal trial in Manila's Court of First Instance.[35]

The Conley Controversy

In referring the case to a criminal court, Governor Wood's goal was to offer the detective a hearing before an unbiased audience. Yet the move to a public forum exposed Conley to criticism from another powerful actor in colonial politics, the press. Conley's suspension was headline news. English-language newspapers such as the *Manila Times* that catered to an American audience hailed him as "the terror of gamblers in the city" and blasted Secretary Laurel's decision to suspend him.[36] Filipino and Spanish dailies such as *La Vanguardia* were more critical, admitting that Conley was "a champion of the city's morality" but noting that over four hundred citizens arrested in his raids had complained of "bad treatment" by the police. In recent months, the press implied, there had been growing signs of corruption in Conley's activities. The notorious mansion-sized club known as "El Monte Carlo Chino" was reportedly paying the police five thousand pesos monthly to operate with "impunity" as a "veritable temple of orgies and bacchanals" with opium smoking and *panchong,* a domino-like gambling game.[37]

Only a week after Conley's suspension, Manila's prosecutor, Fiscal Revilla, indicted him for accepting ₱7,200 in bribes from Eduardo Cardeñas and Eduardo Ramirez, described as gamblers who maintained "in the city of Manila . . . houses where *monte* and other games of chance were played."[38] Manila's polarized reactions to Conley's prosecution reflected a racial divide that had deepened during the recent political struggle over the Filipinization of government service. From the trial's first day in mid-April, reporters pounded out detailed accounts for front-page stories that appealed to the biases of their separate American and Filipino audiences. Looking back on the proceedings decades later, Laurel felt that by raising charges of "American immunity to the penal laws of the Islands" the trial had quickly lost "its criminal aspect and assumed the character of a huge and complicated political issue." Indeed, the Conley case had struck a nerve. Touching on visceral questions of racial equality before the law, the trial became both a battleground for colonial antagonists and a rallying point for Filipino aspirations.[39]

Judge Carlos A. Imperial opened the proceedings by dismissing the charges against Cardeñas, the self-styled illegal gambler, who immediately became a key prosecution witness. In his testimony Cardeñas recalled that after meeting Conley during a gambling raid the previous February he had agreed to pay the detective a thousand pesos monthly to protect his club at 312 Calle Azcarraga. To ensure secrecy Conley created a code of "secret signs" for their telephone conversations and set up night drops through a Chinese in Binondo.[40] In recounting that now famous phone call to Conley, Cardeñas insisted that he knew the officer's voice well since they had regular phone contact, often in code, about the delivery of bribes.[41] Before an "immense crowd" that filled the court, Mayor Fernandez testified that he had learned of Conley's graft through gambling contacts, and Laurel followed him on the stand to corroborate the story of the phone call and payoff.[42] In similar testimony the mayor's secretary, Almario, testified about recruiting his nephew Cardeñas to make the payoff to Conley, who was being watched by his other nephew, the secret service agent Lumanlan.[43]

To counter this evidence the defense challenged the integrity of the prosecution's case. Appearing for Conley, Chief Green praised him as an "efficient" officer who had never been the subject of bribery allegations. When the prosecutor asked, during cross-examination, about the charge of concubinage, the chief replied that he had not suspended Conley because he "had been informed that the complainant had been paid by the gamblers . . . to get Conley out of the way." With unintended irony, Green added that even if the charges happened to be true "he did not regard it immoral for a man to have a mistress," a practice he felt was in keeping with "local custom."[44] In another blow to the prosecution, the gambler charged with providing the bribe, Eduardo Ramirez, denied giving any money to Cardeñas.[45]

Taking the stand in his own defense, Conley claimed that there was an "organized gambling ring in Manila" headed by one Eleuterio Naboa that controlled all the witnesses appearing against him. Almario was Naboa's *compadre,* or ritual confrere, and the prosecution's key witnesses, Cardeñas and Lumanlan, were Almario's relatives. "While I am in one of the gambling squads," Conley claimed, "it is impossible for Almario to give protection to gambling houses."[46] With key elements of its case collapsing, the prosecution attacked the detective's character in an unrelenting cross-examination about his false statements of marriage to one Grace Jackson Conley when in fact his prior marriage to a Filipina remained valid.[47]

On May 19, after seventeen days of trial, Judge Imperial issued a convoluted twenty-page decision that both exonerated Conley and cast doubts on his integrity. Most important, the judge found that Secretary Laurel's testimony about the phone conversation was inconclusive since there was no certainty that the voice he had heard was Conley's. After ruling, in effect, that the sworn testimony of two prominent Filipino politicians was not credible, the judge stretched his syntax to soften the blow, saying that the prosecution had "not failed to produce . . . indications and suspicions more or less remote and possible that the accused could have been actually guilty [and] . . . his integrity was not as it should have been." Nonetheless, the judge found "a reasonable doubt . . . in favor of the accused."[48] The local American press was uniformly critical of the judge's decision, particularly his grammatical gymnastics intended to placate both sides of the city's racial divide.[49]

While the case moved from cause célèbre to political crisis, the situation on the streets was unchanged. In mid-May, as the judge was drafting his decision, Chief Green filed corruption charges against two American veterans, the chief of the secret service and the new head of his gambling and opium squad.[50] On May 25, only days after Judge Imperial's decision, the Gambling Squad, now led by Detective Jackson F. Townsend, raided the Parliamentary Club on Calle Arzobispo, next door to the National Assembly, battering down the doors to nab twenty-nine gamblers, including the club's owner, Representative Jose Ma. Veloso. As the legislator bit and kicked his arresting officer, reinforcements arrived from the Luneta police station to subdue the unruly crowd. At his trial four days later, the legislator accused the officer of demanding a thousand-peso bribe. But the judge was unconvinced and sentenced Veloso to sixty days in jail for "maintaining a gambling house," a decision ultimately affirmed by the Supreme Court.[51]

Dueling Narratives

With the court's equivocations satisfying no one, the Conley case remained unresolved, inviting further investigations. Denied the criminal conviction they felt he deserved, his accusers pressed on outside the judicial system, first launching a formal administrative inquiry and then appealing to the court of public opinion. Their accusations thus shifted emphasis from gambling and drugs to an adulterous relationship with his American housekeeper, a personal scandal that could discredit the detective among both Americans and Filipinos.

Convinced of the officer's guilt and yet rebuked by the court's rejection of his testimony, Interior Secretary Laurel persisted in his own investigation. At this opportune moment a former clerk in the Manila police department, James P. Watson, made a formal statement that "Conley was a friend to prostitutes and gave them protection."[52] Armed with information that supported his view of the detective's libertinism, on May 25 Laurel ordered Mayor Fernandez to dismiss him. Although the evidence against him was "not sufficient under the rigid rules . . . to convict him," Laurel claimed that Conley's "open concubinage" established him as "a man of immoral habits," ample grounds under civil service regulations for immediate termination.[53]

As tensions rose, both sides armed themselves with scandal. At a conference with Laurel and Mayor Fernandez on May 26, Governor Wood threatened that if they insisted on an administrative investigation of Conley he "would take it up himself and investigate the whole city from top to bottom," a step that he hoped "would not be necessary."[54] Undeterred, Laurel and Fernandez continued to demand an internal inquiry, but Wood regarded the two as biased and instead appointed a special review board. During its two days of hearings, this board was charged with determining whether the detective was guilty of (1) running a boardinghouse "without the required permission," (2) living "under scandalous circumstances" with a woman not his wife, (3) making false statements on civil service forms that "his wife is one Grace Connolly," and (4) extending "favors to gamblers for money consideration."[55] Even though the board's preliminary report found Conley's continued service inadvisable, Wood maintained his belief that the mayor and interior secretary were engaged in "a deliberate persecution" and ordered Laurel to reinstate Conley. Almost immediately Laurel replied that he was resigning since he could not "conscientiously continue" in service with such a "dishonest" subordinate as Conley. Rather than carry out this order for Conley's reinstatement, Mayor Fernandez also resigned. With the intervening officials now removed, the governor himself ordered Conley's return to duty.[56]

On July 16 the review board met with the governor to recommend Conley's dismissal for the most credible of the charges against him, keeping a mistress. If Conley's behavior were condoned, the board argued, then "no action could be taken against any other official who might make false official statements or who might live in open immorality." By implication this was a critical blow to the legitimacy of the U.S. regime, which depended on the reputations of individual Americans. In the end even Wood conceded this point, concluding that "the argument is a good one." At the same time, however, the delicate political situation required some circumspection. In view of Conley's "extraordinarily efficient service," the board recommended that he be allowed to retire in good standing. On cue Chief Green arrived at the palace with Conley's formal request for retirement, which was immediately accepted. After five months of litigation and a day back on duty, Conley was now homeward bound with his record restored, his pension intact, his passage paid, and the governor's glowing reference in hand. In his diary Wood defended this leniency, saying that "the only serious thing against Conley is that he has been living with a woman whom he recognized as his common-law wife for a number of years."[57]

But Conley's case would not be so easily laid to rest. The next afternoon, July 17, after all these deals were done, politics stoked its dying embers into a colonial firestorm. Senator Quezon, "hand shaking, face rather pale," called on the governor to charge that, as Wood put it, "I had overridden the Secretaries, violated the law, and generally run wild in the Departments." When Quezon grew "insistent and impertinent," Wood angrily dismissed the "absurdity and falsity of his statements." Then, on the historic evening described at the beginning of this chapter, the senator returned with almost all the members of the cabinet and Council of State who resigned en masse to protest the governor's defense of Conley as a violation of "the sacred pledge . . . of the United States to guarantee to the Filipino people . . . the greatest possible measure of self-government, pending the recognition of their independence." Warned of Quezon's move by his son and aide, Lt. Osborne Wood, the governor responded to the resignations with a prepared statement damning their actions as tantamount to "rebellion against the authority of the United States."[58]

Within hours *El Debate* led the Filipino press in attacking Wood. On the morning after the mass resignation, the columnist Vicente Hilario explicitly tied Wood's leniency to the larger question of U.S. legitimacy, charging that the governor had "tarnished America's hitherto brilliant escutcheon in these Islands." *El Debate* also made one last attempt to keep the discussion of Conley's corruption alive. On July 21, just five days after Conley retired, the paper hit the streets with an accusatory headline, "Gan Yong, Arrested, Denounces Conley," above a sensational story that a PC captain by the name of Silvino Gallardo had arrested this "famous Chinese trafficker," recently returned from China, in a raid on a Malabon lumberyard. In an exclusive interview inside the constabulary lockup, the Chinese criminal told *El Debate* he had paid Conley five hundred pesos monthly for nearly four years to protect his gambling and opium dens in Binondo's Chinatown. This criminal said that Conley had also planted morphine on Chinese, who were forced to pay up to fifteen hundred pesos to escape prosecution. "Conley not only sold me cocaine," said Gan Yong, but "he also sold it to other Chinese in small packets and also sold morphine powder." When his "friend" Conley doubled the price of his protection to a thousand pesos in 1921 and Gan Yong could not pay, Conley turned into an "evil traitor" who arrested him on drug charges that led to his deportation to China. For days the paper kept the story alive by chronicling Gan Yong's appearance before the special review board.[59]

At first glance the Gan Yong story seems to spring from a string of coincidences that can only be considered remarkable. First, a drug dealer from Conley's dirty past suddenly reappears from far-off China. Then, in a stunning bit of police work, a constabulary captain plucks this particular Chinese from hiding inside the maze of a suburban lumberyard. Next, an intrepid reporter somehow strides past police guards to secure an extended interview with a hardened Chinese criminal who suddenly decides to make a clean breast of his crimes and confesses to felonious drug dealing. Finally, a major newspaper splashes the entire story across page one.

On closer examination these coincidences bear the fingerprints of Quezon's nimble hand. *El Debate* was owned by ex-mayor Fernandez, Quezon's close ally.[60] Most tellingly, Gan Yong's arresting officer, Captain Gallardo, was a crooked constable climbing the police hierarchy by doing confidential political work for Quezon.[61] This timely exposé reveals Quezon as a master of police and scandal and a worthy challenger to General Wood, who was, of course, a progenitor of this political tactic. With these adversaries so evenly matched, theirs would be a duel to the political death with their weapon of choice, sexual scandal.

As the Conley case spun into a bitter confrontation, both sides of the Filipino and American colonial divide constructed moral narratives that demonized their antagonists. Filipinos condemned Conley as a bent cop who took bribes from illegal gamblers. With equal vehemence Americans branded Filipino politicians as immoral for protecting the city's gambling lords. At the height of the crisis Chief

Green compiled two detailed reports arguing for Conley's exoneration and casting doubt on his accusers. In a thirteen-page "Confidential Memorandum" of July 24, the chief charged Mayor Fernandez and his secretary Almario with dubious motives in pursuing "frivolous" complaints against a detective who was "feared by gamblers generally throughout Manila." Conley's raids on the city's illegal clubs had forced the gambling syndicate to mount a sustained campaign against him, culminating in what the chief believed was an elaborate frame up by Almario.[62]

Having identified a motive for the conspiracy in the first memo, Chief Green proceeded in the second to detail its execution, an opportunity created, he argued, by the incompetence of Secretary Laurel. In a detailed, ten-page review of the case, the chief noted that Laurel had no way of knowing whether the voice on the phone was Conley's, the two key prosecution witnesses were both nephews of the mayor's corrupt secretary, and witnesses at the Luneta police station did not place the detective there during the supposed payoff. But most important, Laurel, after painstakingly writing down "the numbers of the bills to be given to Conley," failed to take the "simple, obvious and logical step" of catching him with the marked money. Without this evidence the case against Conley was, the chief said, "pitifully weak," and the entire affair bore "all the earmarks, from beginning to end, of a deliberate frame up." Sadly, the chief continued, Laurel himself was also the unwitting dupe of "gamblers, opium dealers, and others." In Chief Green's telling, Conley was an officer of unimpeachable integrity struggling heroically against powerful enemies, a hagiography that Wood accepted uncritically and forwarded to Washington with his endorsement.[63]

To Filipino politicians, by contrast, Conley was a threatening figure whose mastery of Manila's underworld of drugs, gambling, and prostitution gave him almost unchecked power, in this colonial context, to punish or protect almost at will. Even the powerful Senator Quezon had to tread lightly around him since he was, recalled Fernandez, "somewhat afraid that his friends might be implicated" in illegal gambling.[64] With Philippine independence on the horizon, an ordinary American detective was still rounding up prominent Filipino physicians and politicians for processing through the courts with petty thieves and prostitutes, raising questions about Filipino fitness for self-rule and stirring indignation among their political leaders.

In his official biography, published decades later, Secretary Laurel would describe Conley as "an able and relentless detective" who had succumbed to "the temptation of easy money," first taking a cut to overlook a consignment of opium and then demanding "higher fees, thereby losing caution" until the "underworld squealed on him."[65] Taking a darker view, Mayor Fernandez depicted Conley as the source of a moral stain that tainted all he touched. Some forty years after the incident, Fernandez, then in his eighties, told an American historian that "there was some talk that Osborne [Wood, the governor's son] was being supplied by Conley" with women for "his possible affairs."[66] Whether or not this accusation was true, the rumor would surely have heightened the significance of Conley as an iconic figure, a vivid symbol of the double standard so deeply embedded in the enforcement of colonial laws against personal vice. Unsparing in his raids on reputed gambling houses frequented by elite Filipinos, the crusading detective was, it seems, discreetly procuring prostitutes for a well-placed American official and in the process depriving Filipinos of damaging information that could have restored some balance to the colonial politics of scandal.

Governor Wood was an elder statesman who since his jai alai days in Havana had learned to temper his avarice with a discretion that protected his reputation. Assigned to Manila as the governor's aide-de-camp, Lt. Osborne Wood seemed at first glance every inch his father's son, a rising young officer who had married a genteel American woman in a grand Malacañang Palace wedding. But the young lieutenant soon proved an unstable personality, a compulsive risk taker, a bon vivant, a bad boy rebelling against his father's austere army lifestyle, in short, a headline waiting to happen.[67]

His father's diary shows that young Osborne had succumbed to Manila's temptations during his three years in the colony. At his father's direction this young lieutenant had investigated the illicit opium traffic, an introduction to the city's sordid side. He frequented the city's cabarets, ill-concealed fronts for prostitution. But most important, Wood's diaries reveal that young Osborne had somehow saved, on a lieutenant's annual income of just $2,000, an inexplicable $490,000 in his Manila bank accounts—the equivalent of 245 years of lieutenant's pay or thirty years of his father's $18,000 salary as governor-general.[68]

The Profligate Son

His lavish lifestyle—a Packard limousine worth $5,500, steamer trunks holding forty-nine custom-tailored suits, a $5,000 donation to a favorite charity—soon made Lt. Osborne Wood the source of a Gatsby-like mystery that became one of the great financial scandals of the Roaring Twenties. In November 1923, just months after Conley left Manila, the *New York Times* Washington correspondent Richard V. Oulahan heard rumors, possibly from constabulary sources, that the lieutenant had transferred a remarkable $3 million from Manila to New York, suggesting graft on a grand scale.[69]

Following this lead from Washington to Manila, Oulahan interviewed the young lieutenant in Malacañang Palace with the governor-general at his side. Grasping the import of the questioning, Osborne assured the reporter that "none of these transactions had anything to do with Philippine enterprises." Rather, he had come by the money honestly, first profiting from local dollar-to-peso speculation and then parlaying those gains into a fortune worth $800,000 on the New York Stock Exchange. Turning to his son in the reporter's presence, Governor Wood ordered, "I want nothing concealed." So instructed, Osborne escorted the reporter to the Hong Kong and Shanghai Bank where clerks confirmed the transfers but not their amounts.[70]

Back in New York the *New York Times* carried the story under the front-page headline "Lieut. O. C. Wood, At 26, Makes $800,000 Dealing in Wall St. from Far Off Manila." But a team of *Times* financial reporters found that Osborne's story did not add up. To buy the thirty-five thousand shares of stock in his portfolio, worth $2.6 million at the market's peak, the lieutenant would have needed about $100,000 on deposit with a New York brokerage, a bankroll beyond the reach of his lieutenant's salary or any possible peso-dollar speculation. Currency traders confirmed that the Philippine peso had been moving in a narrow range, allowing at best only modest profits. But most important, the cash flow was moving the wrong way across the Pacific. Starting in late 1922 young Wood had made money transfers from Manila to a New York account with balances fluctuating between $150,000 and $250,000, providing ample funds to cover his Wall Street brokerage deposit. Market experts, the *Times* reported, "cannot understand why large sums should be coming from Manila for deposit here if the young man's winnings in the stock market were large." A Wisconsin congressman, James A. Frear, suggested a source for these funds by demanding an investigation of those who "have profited . . . through the holding or selling of stocks or bonds of companies . . . having affiliations in the Philippine Islands." As these stories broke on the front page of the *Times,* Republican legislators called for a "sweeping investigation." The secretary of war branded the lieutenant "imprudent." President Calvin Coolidge received a full report.[71]

Condemning the young officer as "amazingly dull or inconceivably reckless," the *Times* editorialized that "he must have known with what keen eyes the Filipino enemies of General Wood would watch the steps of Lieutenant Wood," making him the possible "means of bringing scandal upon the entire American Administration in the Philippines." Since the lieutenant's explanations had aroused "almost universal skepticism," the *Times* demanded that he "produce his books showing . . . every transfer of funds from New York and Manila."[72]

Just a few weeks after the *Times* exposé, Osborne, now called "the man whom Wall Street will talk about for a century," fled Manila for the baccarat tables of Europe, dogged by reporters who trailed him on his five-year road to ruin. In France looking dapper in a wire photo captioned "the Army's financial genius," he won big at Monte Carlo before he lost it all, some $200,000, at the Circle Haussman casino in Paris. "Rue Michodiere is harder to beat than Wall Street," Osborne told the *Times* ruefully before he had a last drink with a former Ziegfeld Follies girl, Florence Martin, at a Latin Quarter club, passed bad checks at Biarritz for $1,750, and crossed into Spain where he caught a steamer for Tampa. There his wife's private detective caught him in a local hotel with an Atlanta "sporting woman" named "Miss Essington," grounds for a scandalous divorce that stripped him of his family and children. After losing more money in another spree of Wall Street speculation and Broadway nightlife, he passed bad checks for $3,400 in Palm Beach and fled to Havana where his father, using old contacts, had him confined to a mental hospital. In 1928 the *Times* caught up with Osborne Wood, no longer the beneficiary of his father's protection, swinging a pick as a hard-rock miner in Pecos, New Mexico, for two dollars a day.[73]

As he rode this colonial curve upward to power, wealth, and sexual license and then down to disgrace, divorce, and penury, Osborne's half-million dollars in corrupt bank deposits were concealed from Quezon, the local press, and the *New York Times* and revealed to history only through a brief entry in his father's voluminous diary. Still, as the memories of Mayor Fernandez attest, there was "some talk" about his affairs. That this talk and the telltale signs of Osborne's decadence, his low-life affairs and high-life expenditures, did not come to the attention of the scandal-hungry Manila press is testimony to Governor Wood's control over information and the police through powerful officers such as Chief Green and Detective Conley. There was no hint of the Osborne scandal in Manila's papers before it broke ten thousand miles away on the front page of the *New York Times.* Even then the report came not from a Manila correspondent but from a Washington reporter with access to constabulary sources who may have leaked this sensitive information beyond the reach of Governor Wood's retribution.

Throughout this long scandal Detective Conley would come to symbolize for Filipinos the ugly underside of empire. Under Governor Wood's rule, the Conley case seemed to be a clear instance of colonial hypocrisy with the police punishing prominent Filipinos for a simple game of cards while powerful Americans had license to indulge in sexual debauchery and financial profligacy. It is not surprising that fighting such a sinister figure transformed a tawdry scandal into a nationalist crusade, Mayor Fernandez from an aloof mestizo financier into a populist Senate candidate, and Quezon from a party politician into his nation's preeminent leader.

Special Election

The midnight resignations of July 17, 1923, precipitated a political crisis of unprecedented gravity that Senator Quezon would play brilliantly for partisan advantage. For months before the controversy began Quezon had been locked in a bitter battle with Sergio Osmeña for control of the ruling Nacionalista Party, now split by bitter infighting. After months of legislative wrangling, Quezon's faction was threatened with the loss of its Senate majority when the Assembly voted to send his ally, Senator Pedro Guevara, to Washington as resident commissioner, forcing a special election. Since Guevara represented Manila, where the opposition Democratas were strong, Quezon desperately needed an issue that would rally voters. In the Conley affair he found not just an issue but a moral crusade that could unite his divided party and make him its unchallenged leader.[74]

After denouncing Wood's orders for a military alert and denying "any revolt against the sovereignty of the United States," Quezon turned to winning legislative control by forging an all-party nationalist coalition over the Conley case that would back the candidacy of his ally, ex-mayor Fernandez.[75] In a campaign that was "a veritable carnival with bands, parades, and huge rallies," the rhetoric was, in the words of Quezon aide T. M. Kalaw, "cruel and without precedent." Quezon's Colectivista-Nacionalista coalition portrayed Fernandez's candidacy as a revolt against Governor Wood's "khaki cabinet" of military autocrats. The opposition Democrata Party's campaign chief, Claro M. Recto, attacked the corruption of Quezon and his ruling Nacionalista coalition, citing a succession of financial scandals that had brought the National Bank and government corporations to the brink of bankruptcy. As emotions rose to a fever pitch, writers cranked out press broadsides, the best orators barnstormed, and everyone—Quezon, Osmeña, and Wood—suffered savage personal attacks.[76]

The campaign turned on concealing and revealing scandal, with the Nacionalistas trumpeting the Conley case, the Democratas countering with the National Bank fraud, and the Manila Americans scrambling to conceal corporate embezzlement.[77] As emotions rose to an electoral crescendo, the American colony was shocked to discover massive bank fraud by one of its pillars, Charles H. Sleeper, a founder of the Polo Club, an elder of Union Church, and former director of the Bureau of Lands. After Governor-General Harrison's purge of Republican officials back in 1913, Sleeper and the former customs chief Henry B. McCoy had launched the Manila Building and Loan Society, trading on their reputations to attract Filipino depositors. With the same ethics that had marked his government service, Sleeper embezzled funds to cover bad mining investments and auditors eventually found ₱143,000 missing from the bank's accounts. American business leaders met secretly to cover the losses with their own funds and help him slip quietly out of the country to avoid a scandalous prosecution.[78] However, Wood realized that he could not protect another loyal colonial just four days before the special election, and he dispatched the police chief "to inform Captain Sleeper that he should not leave until his accounts had been investigated." Wood also ordered the government auditor "to make an immediate and thorough investigation" of the bank's books." Such blatant fraud by influential Americans could easily have become another Conley case, producing a dangerous concatenation of colonial scandal. This time Wood quieted the potential controversy by ordering an aggressive investigation that felled McCoy with a fatal heart attack and soon sent Sleeper to the San Ramon prison colony for two years.[79]

When voters finally went to the polls for the special election on October 2, 1923, the Conley case trumped the Philippine National Bank scandal to score a major upset for ex-mayor Fernandez, who garnered 55,773 votes against the opposition's 40,152.[80] The American analyst Joseph Hayden concluded that "had the autonomy-independence issue not been injected into the campaign, the Democratas would have carried the district."[81] Looking back on this election thirty-two years later, the opposition leader Claro Recto described it as "disastrous and catastrophic" for his Democrata Party. Anti-Americanism was "so popular," he said, that people ignored the Nacionalista Party's decade of "corrupt administration" and passed over a candidate with "a high reputation for intellectual capacity and integrity."[82]

Four days later the legislature's official opening made the historic Ayuntamiento another battleground in this colonial warfare. At 11:30 a.m., Quezon, who had "aged ten years in the past few days," led the senators into the grand marble hall while newly elected Senator Ramon Fernandez was greeted with a thunderous ovation. Eight minutes later Governor Wood entered and read a formal message to a "profound silence." Both houses then adopted Senator Osmeña's resolution supporting the mass cabinet resignation, condemning Wood, and calling for his replacement by a Filipino governor-general.[83]

Two months later Speaker Manuel Roxas visited Washington to petition for Wood's recall and push Quezon's plan for greater Filipino autonomy. But President Coolidge stated that "no plan would be acceptable to the American people . . . that did not carry the approval of the Governor General."[84] With Washington's unqualified support, Wood was free to use his broad executive powers to pummel Quezon. In the legislative sessions of 1925–26 and 1926–27, Wood slapped vetoes on sixty-eight bills, over a third of all those put forward by Quezon's party. In retaliation Quezon used his working majority to block all of the governor's appointments for the tribal territories.[85] Stalemated in the formal legislative-executive arena, the war between Wood and Quezon shifted to less formal battlegrounds.

Wood and Quezon at War

Paralleling this legislative warfare, Quezon and Wood were also engaged in a subterranean battle over scandal. At the height of the Conley crisis in July 1923, when Wood appointed a leading Democrata, Eulogio "Amang" Rodriguez, as the new mayor of Manila to replace Ramon Fernandez, Nacionalista threats were so intense that the appointee's wife became "ill in bed."[86] Within weeks Quezon had denounced the mayor as an "ex convict," and on August 21 he cabled Washington alleging that Rodriguez "had served a year in prison for abduction," a compound crime involving kidnapping and rape. The very next day Mayor Rodriguez rushed into Wood's office carrying "a copy of Quezon's criminal record in Mindoro, where he was administratively tried on charges . . . of rape." Coolly, Wood replied that he "had a copy of this correspondence sent me many years ago by prominent officers of the Constabulary" but had no plans to use it now.[87]

As Senator Quezon and Mayor Rodriguez engaged in mutual slander, the chief of constabulary, Rafael Crame, called on the governor-general. The chief claimed that "he had nothing to fear from Quezon; that he knew his history from youth up." At first Crame said that the senator had been his servant, his "muchacho." But then the chief corrected himself, explaining that Quezon had once been his "private spy; that he had him used in all sorts of cases in the early days of the Constabulary." With Quezon so compromised, Crame now assured the governor, "I know him from top to bottom and he never will dare to attack me."[88] A year later in mid-1924, when "Quezon . . . threatened him for being too compliant with the wishes of the Governor-General," Chief Crame replied to his face, with uncommon boldness, "that I would get him and destroy him unless he behaves properly toward me and toward the Constabulary."[89]

In these vicious intrigues, each turning on the judicious release of damaging information, the Filipinos effectively neutralized each other, leaving Wood to seem a statesman above scandal. Both Filipino partisans, Quezon and Rodriguez, showed phenomenal skill in their ability to reach back decades into closed court records and pluck out just the right documents to charge each other with the same ugly sexual crime. But Wood, through his control over the colonial police, trumped them both with his detailed knowledge of their transgressions.

Armed with executive and police powers, Wood battled Quezon for nearly four years following the Conley crisis, slowly beating him back within the acceptable bounds of colonial politics. Backed by Washington and the Filipino opposition, Wood scored a succession of bare-knuckle bureaucratic victories that checked each of Quezon's legislative moves, slowly shifting their struggle into the judicial arena. In forming his new cabinet in January 1924, for example, Wood drew on suggestions from both ex-general Emilio Aguinaldo, a Quezon rival, and the opposition Democratas for some distinguished appointments, notably, Felipe Agoncillo, the revolutionary republic's senior diplomat, as secretary of interior and Miguel Romualdez, a respected attorney, as mayor of Manila.[90]

In this reconstituted cabinet Wood worked amicably with senior figures such as Agoncillo, but he relied on police surveillance to monitor his younger, more ambitious secretaries. Concerned that Justice Secretary Luis Torres was partisan in demanding the dismissal of a Manila councilor, Wood told him "every time you come out of Quezon's house I get detailed information about it." When Torres asked if he had lost the governor's confidence, Wood, apparently empowered by such surveillance, snapped, "No; the moment you lose my confidence you lose your job."[91]

Board of Control

Slowly this ongoing power struggle shifted from the legislature to the Board of Control, a joint legislative-executive body that Wood's predecessor, Harrison, had created to manage the many government corporations launched under his rule: sugar *centrals,* National Coal, Cebu Portland Cement, the Philippine National Bank, the Manila Railway, and many more. Convinced that their massive losses were the product of insider trading, Governor-General Wood had assumed office determined to arrange a quick sale of these state corporations. But both their American managers and Filipino politicians blocked his moves, resistance Wood attributed to a popular sentiment that "their sale or transfer would result in taking something away from the Filipino people, a certain denationalizaton as it were."[92] The Board of Control, consisting of just three members, the heads of the two legislative houses and himself, thus became a political wrestling ring, with Governor Wood pitted against the legislative tag team of Senate president Quezon and House Speaker Manuel Roxas. In August, after wrangling over the sale of the landmark Manila Hotel to American investors, Wood asked if nationalist politics would similarly cloud their future deliberations. With disarming frankness, Quezon and Roxas admitted "that they had been compelled to make radical statements to maintain their hold on the people."[93]

As tensions waxed and waned over the next two years, the Board of Control, stymied by nationalist opposition to the privatization of flagship firms, failed to propose any reforms for these bankrupt corporations. In late 1925 Wood negotiated the sale of the Philippine National Bank to Boston investors, but the board's working majority, Roxas and Quezon, balked. A year later the governor arranged the sale of Cebu Portland Cement, but the board again blocked the deal and Quezon called a press conference to taunt the governor-general over his defeat.[94] Finally, in November 1926, the U.S. attorney general decided that the board was "a nullity, illegally constituted." Immediately Wood, savoring his hard-won victory, issued Executive Order 37 abolishing the Board of Control and assuming its functions.[95]

At this sensitive juncture Wood's control over the police and scandal gave him a decisive victory. Only a month after Washington's ruling, Quezon and Roxas defied the governor's authority by convening a meeting of the National Coal Company to select its new board of directors.[96] Wood countered by removing them both from the board, assuming sole authority over all government corporations, and filing a case in the Philippine Supreme Court in which both sides, for different reasons, were confident of the outcome. With the nine-man court balanced informally but carefully to give American justices a one-vote majority, Quezon had reason, in a case of such clear national interest, to count on the votes of the four Filipino justices and a deciding vote from George Malcolm, a young Wilson appointee known as a strong advocate of Philippine independence. Quezon, praising "how deeply you sympathize with this aspiration of the Filipino people," had asked Justice Malcolm back in August 1920 to take on the "exceedingly important" task of drafting "a proposed constitution for the future Philippine Republic." More recently the two had celebrated their "pact of friendship" at a public banquet. But the governor-general had leverage that went beyond merit, politics, or personal loyalty. For five years he had accumulated political debts by playing upon the foibles of the American justices: E. Finley Johnson's vain hopes for the chief justiceship, Charles A. Johns's sycophancy, and George Malcolm's scandalous private life. To cultivate a possible majority, Wood courted a Filipino justice, Norberto Romualdez, the elder brother of the Miguel Romualdez he had recently appointed as mayor of Manila.[97]

In early 1927 the Philippine Supreme Court heard oral arguments in the Board of Control case, docketed as *Government of the Philippine Islands v. Milton E. Springer et al.* In his memoirs, Justice Malcolm called this case "the most sensational to be brought before the courts during the entire history of the Government of the Philippine Islands," explaining: "On one side was an American Governor-General seeking to restore the powers of his office under the Organic Act; on the other side were the Filipino President of the Senate and the Filipino Speaker of the House seeking to consolidate the powers of self-government." When it became his duty to write the majority opinion, Malcolm took great pains to assure readers of his Olympian objectivity. "Feeling ran so high," he said in painfully contorted syntax, "that I conducted my study of the case and the preparation of an opinion written in longhand in the seclusion of my study of my home." Despite the high stakes, Malcolm insisted, "I had to forget the personal equation entirely, for both General Wood and President Quezon happened to be my intimate friends."[98]

Governor Wood was "intimate" with Justice Malcolm but not in the way the justice implied. From the time Malcolm had joined the court in 1917 as a very young, very liberal Wilson appointee, Justice E. Finley Johnson, an older Republican workhorse, perhaps forgetting earlier rumors of his own "improper relations" with a stenographer, had long been vocal in his outrage at his younger colleague's libertine lifestyle, particularly his long-standing concubinage with a "native woman." During Wood's 1921 investigative tour, Johnson had told him that Malcolm "was living with a native woman, by whom he had children." In February 1926, just a year before the National Coal case, Johnson filed a morals charge against Malcolm, which, if successful, would have meant his dismissal and disgrace. Apparently supporting Johnson's view, Wood ordered Chief Green's detectives to investigate. Their report on Malcolm, duly delivered to Johnson, documented the sordid details of "his visiting this woman's house at night" and his illegitimate children, "one of whom is supposed to be alive in one of the convents here."[99]

In early 1926 Justice Johnson, armed with this damaging police dossier, steamed across the Pacific bound for Washington to press President Coolidge, another stern moralist, for Malcolm's dismissal. But at this strategic moment Governor Wood interceded unexpectedly by telegramming the White House, first on March 18 about his decision to refer this morals case to the justices for review and then, ten days later, about their report, "which is strongly commendatory of Justice Malcolm's efficiency." The next day, in a crude move, the governor showed Malcolm this second cable, which was marked "Strictly Confidential." The justice, in Wood's words, seemed "very well satisfied in that he had been given a square deal."[100] In sum, by ordering the police to collect derogatory information about Malcolm's private life and then intervening to block his certain dismissal on charges of immorality, Wood bent the young justice to his will.

In April 1927, just 364 days after Wood had saved him from public disgrace, Justice Malcolm, writing for the majority, handed down a decision that surprised observers and stunned Quezon. Setting aside his years of liberalism, Malcolm affirmed the prerogatives of the colonial governor. In this six-to-three decision for Wood, the four conservative American justices were joined by both the liberal Malcolm and, somewhat more surprisingly, his Filipino colleague Norberto Romualdez, whose brother Wood had appointed mayor of Manila. In addition to the lopsided vote, Malcolm's strong endorsement of the governor's position represented a stinging rebuke to Quezon's nationalist crusade. Noting that the parties wished to provide a definitive ruling in a case that had been "bitterly fought," Malcolm, writing for the majority, decided that the U.S. Congress "never intended that the Governor-General should be saddled with the responsibility of . . . executing the laws but shorn of the power to do so." He therefore ousted Quezon's appointees to National Coal's board and found that the law allowing such appointments was "unconstitutional and void."[101]

By ruling so unambiguously for Wood, Justice Malcolm effectively declared him the victor in the four-year war with Quezon that had started with the Conley controversy. With blazing headlines the *Manila Times* called the court's decision "a vindication . . . of the governor general" and "the worst beating the Filipino participation in the government ever had."[102] A year later the U.S. Supreme Court reviewed this decision and ruled seven to two on similar grounds in favor of Wood.[103] In his dissent from the majority ruling, however, the longtime liberal on the U.S. court, Justice Oliver Wendell Holmes, wrote, with Justice Louis Brandeis concurring, that the Philippine corporations at issue "are no part of the executive functions of the Government but rather fall into the indiscriminate residue of matters within legislative control," a position strikingly similar to that of the Filipino minority in the Philippine Supreme Court's original decision.[104]

In retrospect, Malcolm's strong defense of executive authority and narrow reading of the statute were at variance with his core judicial philosophy, which could, under other circumstances, have led him to rule against the governor-general. Indeed, after the Philippine Congress voted unanimously to award Malcolm honorary Philippine citizenship in 1955, Filipino legal scholars surveyed his three thousand decisions over eighteen years to find a "liberal tendency" that, in the spirit of Justice Holmes's dictum, "conceived the rule of law in man's social life as essentially dynamic and fluid." In a similar vein a leading legal scholar more recently wrote that Justice Malcolm's "tendency in most of his decisions to escape from the rigid confines of statute and case books" had made him, for Filipino lawyers, "a symbol of progressive judicial thought." From both text and context, it thus seems unlikely that a liberal jurist like Malcolm would have ruled so narrowly or backed the executive so strongly had he not been blackmailed by the threat of sexual scandal.[105]

After this string of victories Governor Wood pressed ahead with plans for privatization of the government corporations, seeking total victory in his war with Quezon. But in August 1927, just four months after the Supreme Court decision, he died unexpectedly on a Boston operating table during what should have been routine surgery.[106]

Following the pattern of Philippine legitimation crises, the breach between Filipino leaders and the U.S. regime was not healed until Governor-General Wood's death allowed Washington to change the offending colonial personnel and broaden, yet again, Filipino political participation. Right after Wood's death Senator Quezon led a delegation to Washington. After surveying the field, he began lobbying for the appointment of Henry L. Stimson, who he had known as secretary of war under President Taft. Arriving at Manila in March 1928, Governor-General Stimson proceeded cautiously and consulted Filipino legislators in selecting his cabinet. At an August meeting with leading Filipino legislators, Stimson accepted Quezon's suggestion to revive the legislative-executive body called the Council of State, which had empowered Filipinos under Governor Harrison, and went further than his predecessor by making it "broader in composition." In effect Quezon was arguing for the development of a cooperative cabinet government, and Stimson agreed, although he reserved, at the risk of offending "Filipino susceptibilities," ultimate American authority over finance, public health, and law enforcement. By sharing executive power with elected Filipino legislators, Stimson ushered in an "era of good feeling" that largely restored the legitimacy of American colonial authority.[107]

Conclusion

On the surface the Conley case seems to be a minor matter, at worst another instance of the countless bribes that Manila's gamblers paid to police for protection. But this petty police scandal engaged larger questions, ultimately challenging the legitimacy of the colonial state. By exempting an American police detective from what many Filipinos saw as deserved punishment, the U.S. regime subverted its own claims to an impartial justice that had justified its rule. Even though Governor Wood won this battle through a mix of executive power and political manipulation, his intervention cost him, like Governor Luke Wright two decades earlier, a loss of moral authority so profound that he could no longer command the compliance of many senior Filipino politicians. Although Wood won every battle in the four years of political warfare with Quezon, in the end the colonial regime struggled to regain its credibility. Following the pattern of past Philippine legitimation crises, the breach between the dominant Nacionalista Party and the U.S. regime was not healed until Governor Wood's death removed him from office, allowing a change in administration and a broadening of Filipino political participation to include a significant share of executive authority.

The Conley case and its electoral aftermath demonstrated the uniquely emotive impact of police scandals in rousing the Filipino electorate. In retrospect, the special Senate election of 1923 tested the comparative political potency of different sorts of scandal: petty police graft versus grand financial fraud. To capture a Senate seat in an opposition bailiwick, the Nacionalista Party picked a candidate famous for resigning in protest over the corruption of an American police officer. The opposition Democratas tried to tar the ruling Nacionalista Party with responsibility for financial fraud that had brought the economy to the brink of collapse. But not even these serious transgressions could challenge the powerful symbolism of the Conley case. By running against Governor Wood and his compromised supervision of the police, the Nacionalistas found an unassailable cause—resonant in its overtones of nationalism and undertones of justice—that aroused the electorate and carried their party to a resounding victory.[108]

The Conley controversy also marked the beginning of a long political transition from direct U.S. colonial rule to the arm's length oversight of the later Philippine Commonwealth. Although Americans would command both the Philippine Constabulary and the Metropolitan Police for another decade, they became more circumspect in their enforcement of politically sensitive areas such as gambling. Recognizing the growing power of Filipino politicians, PC headquarters now deferred to their personnel recommendations whenever possible and distanced itself from unpopular antigambling operations. By the mid-1920s, local law enforcement would become the autonomous province of Filipino politicians. Simultaneously, the country's rising national leader, Senator Quezon, began to treat the constabulary not as the root and branch of colonial power but as the seed of a future national army that he hoped to command as president of an independent Philippines. Yet as president of the Philippine Commonwealth after 1935 Quezon would quickly discover that the transformation of this colonial security apparatus, so deeply engrained in the colonial state he had inherited, would be one of the most challenging problems of his administration.

Amid all these changes the underlying patterns that had made police and scandal central to colonial politics for two decades persisted, becoming with each passing year a defining feature of an emerging Philippine state. These clandestine methods of political surveillance and covert penetration were also repatriated to Washington, where, as we will see in the next chapter, they laid the foundation for the federal government's first internal security apparatus.

9

President Wilson's Surveillance State

IN JULY 1971 the *New York Times* published a curious story, buried inside on page five, about "a private dossier on alleged Communists . . . kept for 23 years by a retired army colonel and his wife." Recently, the story continued, the Pentagon had sent this dossier to the Senate Internal Security Subcommittee, famed for its witch-hunting pursuit of American communists.[1] The army had investigated before it shipped the papers to the Senate, finding that this was not just a dossier but a massive private archive with thousands of classified documents compiled by a long-forgotten army general, Ralph Van Deman, dead now for nearly twenty years. After reviewing files full of classified reports from the army, navy, and FBI, this military investigator had remarked that "the extent, detail and quality of the information obtained by Van Deman" was "remarkable." But he warned that "the question of the Army's relationship to Van Deman could also prove embarrassing."[2]

In this era of anti-Vietnam protests when concern over civil liberties was strong, the *New York Times* followed up with an investigative report, finding that "not much is known about General Van Deman himself." After some service as an army surgeon, he "went into intelligence in the Philippines" and later became "head of military intelligence in Washington from May 1917, to June 1918." During his year in command, said the *Times,* "he was instrumental in organizing volunteer civilian sleuths, such as the American Protective League [APL], that kept watch for signs of disloyalty." After retiring to California in 1929, he spent the next quarter century amassing what the *Times* called "a secret collection of reports on 125,000 allegedly subversive persons."[3] In a later editorial the *Times* damned these files as a repository of "anti-labor, anti-Semitic, and anti-civil rights bias" and demanded that they be "destroyed."[4]

But the general's ghost could not be exorcised by burning a few bundles of paper. For Van Deman's influence was embedded deep inside the institutional architecture of the U.S. internal security apparatus that he was instrumental in building during World War I. Now, in the midst of another war with rampant domestic surveillance, the Congress, press, and public had finally seen the shadow, though not yet the substance, of this long-dead general's ambiguous legacy for American society.

During the social ferment that surrounded World War I, a mix of emergency legislation and extralegal enforcement removed the restraints of courts and Constitution that had protected Americans from surveillance and secret police for over a century. With the fear of spies and subversion everywhere, police methods that had been tested and perfected in the colonial Philippines migrated homeward to provide both precedents and personnel for the establishment of a U.S. internal security apparatus. Transformed by colonial warfare from a conventional army careerist into "the father of U.S. military intelligence," Van Deman applied his experience of empire to establish the army's Military Intelligence Division (MID) in 1917 as a comprehensive espionage and counterespionage agency.[5] After years of pacifying an overseas empire where race was the frame for perception and action, colonial veterans came home to turn the same lens on America, seeing its ethnic communities not as fellow citizens but as internal colonies requiring coercive controls. Within twelve months of introducing stringent security measures, President Wilson's wartime America circa 1918 came to bear a marked resemblance to Governor Taft's colonial Philippines circa 1901. Both had similar arrays of legislation that limited civil liberties and secret services that engaged in arbitrary arrests, rigid censorship, mass surveillance, covert penetration, and black operations. Although it was established as a seemingly transitory wartime measure, this domestic security apparatus would persist for the next half century as a defining feature of American political life.

In the years surrounding World War I, the social strain of military mobilization and demobilization produced an eruption of class and racial conflicts that made this period one of the most volatile and violent in U.S. history, leaving a lasting imprint on the character of the American state. In a coincidence that transformed these local conflicts into a larger social confrontation, this radical ferment came at a time when Washington was adopting powerful instruments, many of them forged at the periphery of empire, for actively shaping American society: immigration controls, intelligence testing, drug prohibition, mandatory public health measures, and internal security. At the war's outset, moreover, the contradiction between the country's far-flung global empire and its poor military preparedness produced a sense of urgency in Washington that soon reverberated across the country as hysteria and xenophobia. Indeed, the United States was going to war with Germany at a time when its largest ethnic group, German Americans, was only partially assimilated and harbored deep cultural and linguistic loyalties to the old country that was now considered a security threat. Just four years before the war a full 10 percent of the U.S. population had claimed German as their *first* language.[6] In the midst of the mobilization for war,

Washington coped with these myriad contradictions by establishing a powerful intelligence service.

In building a U.S. intelligence capacity, empire's stamp on the nascent national security apparatus was both broad and deep, from data management to larger design. In both colonial Manila and wartime Washington, counterintelligence was characterized by similarities large and small. The reduction of voluminous amounts of information to a single card for every subject. Recruitment of civilian auxiliaries whose identities were concealed by numbered codes. Covert operational procedures for surveillance and infiltration. An ethnic or racial template for the perception of threat. Mass relocation of suspect populations. The systematic use of scandal as political disinformation. And, above all, a sense of omnipotence over peoples deemed alien and therefore lesser. Just as the Philippines Constabulary had destroyed reputations through revelations of sexual or financial irregularities in occupied Manila, so the U.S. internal security apparatus would attack suspected subversives not by formal prosecution but by a similar social ostracism exercised through public listing or "blacklisting." Not only did Van Deman's civilian apparatus later identify Hollywood communists for blacklisting during the 1940s, but some sources argue his network also played a key role in the political rise of Richard Nixon, providing his early congressional campaigns with confidential intelligence to red-bait liberal opponents.

In this process of imperial mimesis, a state such as the United States that creates a colony with circumscribed civil liberties and pervasive policing soon shows many of those same coercive features in its own society. As the metropole's internal security apparatus starts to resemble the imperial, so its domestic politics begin to exhibit many attributes of the colonial.

Although American intelligence officers serving overseas practiced a clandestine tradecraft similar to that of their European allies, U.S. domestic security emerged from the world war as a distinctive public-private or state-society collaboration. Just as the Philippines Constabulary relied on hundreds of Filipino operatives, so the wartime Military Intelligence Division amplified its reach through the three hundred thousand citizen spies of the American Protective League. Established in 1917–18, this alliance of state security and civilian adjuncts continued, under different names, for the next fifty years as a sub rosa matrix that honeycombed American society with active informers, secretive civilian organizations, and government security agencies, federal and local. In each succeeding global crisis, this covert nexus expanded its domestic operations, producing new contraventions of civil liberties, from the systemic surveillance of German Americans during World War I through the secret blacklisting of suspected communists during the cold war. Police worldwide had long relied on low-life informers known by derogatory terms such as "snitch" or "phizz gig." Secret services in Europe and Japan had paid individual spies, informers, and agent provocateurs for the better part of a century. But U.S. internal security was now developing a unique profile as an institutional fusion of federal agencies and civilian organizations, investing this distinctive nexus with both the social force of a mass movement and the institutional resilience of a state agency—attributes that would define its operations for the next half century.

This clandestine apparatus and its anonymous apparatchiks provide an invisible thread of continuity that ties together the draconian security of World War I, the postwar repression of militant labor, Japanese American internment during World War II, and the anticommunist hysteria of the 1950s. Although American historians have often treated each episode as specific to a short-lived period, throughout this entire half century the same state-civil nexus emerged to shape events, sometimes by empowering civilian adjuncts, sometimes by enfolding these networks into an expanded system of state security.[7] Not only did U.S. colonial policing foster formidable security services within the Philippine polity, but it also played a seminal role in the formation of the U.S. national security apparatus, lending a larger significance to this fragment of America's history.

Wartime Security Services

World War I transformed the U.S. state through the mobilization of a four-million-man army, massive industrial procurements, and the creation of an Argus-eyed internal security apparatus. After a century without any significant federal policing, wartime Washington quickly built an interlocking counterintelligence complex armed with expansive legal powers. During just nineteen months of war, the fledgling Bureau of Investigation (BI, later the FBI) grew from three hundred "amateurish" employees with "no counterintelligence experience" into a "major investigative agency" of fifteen hundred. The Office of Naval Intelligence (ONI) expanded from "a tiny, insignificant organization" into an aggressive agency with three hundred officers. The army's Military Intelligence Division swelled from just one officer—the imperial veteran Van Deman—to seventeen hundred employees backed by 350,000 badge-carrying civilian agents.[8] Among all these agencies, the MID, with its comprehensive doctrines and global reach, would prove the most seminal in the formation of a U.S. national security state. By 1918 it had grown "to surpass the size and efficiency of ONI," once the nation's leading intelligence agency.[9] Through the sum of these experiences, Washington emerged from the war with a covert capacity incorporated in its military bureaucracy.

In prewar decades the federal government had limited intelligence, less operational capacity, and no covert capability. Indeed, before the founding of the Bureau of Investigation in 1908 Washington had no domestic security agency worthy of the name, leaving policing to the cities and surveillance to private agencies such as the Pinkertons. A decade later, on the eve of world war, the bureau was still what one sympathetic chronicler called "a small and inept force of 219 agents."[10] During the Philippine-American War of 1898–1902, the army had formed its first field intelligence unit, the Division of Military Information, whose commander, Van Deman, created a comprehensive intelligence capacity that proved sweeping in its data collection and deft in its application. To crush the revolutionary underground concealed within Filipino society, he compiled intelligence on the entire native elite, reduced all data to a single, synoptic "descriptive card" for each subject, and disseminated timely tactical intelligence to combat units via telegraph. After armed conflict gave way to long-term pacification, these operations became a massive counterintelligence effort against both Filipino subversives and Japanese imperial spies.

Instead of building on this Philippine experience, the War Department initially moved in the opposite direction, first downgrading and later closing its intelligence service. Operating from Manila in the aftermath of the Philippine War, Van Deman led a secretive, six-month mapping mission to China in 1906, shadowed by Japanese spies and learning firsthand the global game of espionage. A year later, back in Washington as head of the Map Section inside the small Military Information Division (MID), Van Deman presided over a similar effort in Latin America that sent a young Lt. Joseph Stillwell on a reconnaissance to Guatemala. In 1908, however, the army abolished MID, causing what Van Deman called "an immediate cessation of all military information work" in the United States. Although military intelligence disappeared from Washington, Van Deman used the Philippine unit, the army's only surviving intelligence operation, for another mapping mission to China in 1911, again trailed by Japanese spies.[11]

Returning to Washington in 1915, Major Van Deman was assigned to the War College where he found himself "the only officer . . . who had had any training or experience in what we now designate as military intelligence."[12] Determined to correct this oversight, Van Deman forged an alliance with the War College chief, Gen. Joseph E. Kuhn, and the two worked tirelessly in the year before America entered the world war, "making an extensive study of military intelligence reports from abroad" and winning a million-dollar War Department appropriation for "Contingencies—Military Information Section, General Staff." After the declaration of war in April 1917, however, the army's chief of staff, Hugh Scott, proved ignorant, like many officers of his generation, "about the vital importance of an intelligence service" and gave Van Deman "strict orders" to abandon his efforts. Through discrete maneuvers, the major brought his detailed plans directly to Secretary of War Newton Baker, who on May 11 ordered the formation of a Military Intelligence Section under Van Deman's command. Drawing on his Philippine experience and a borrowed British organizational chart, within weeks Van Deman had established a complete design for the first U.S. internal security agency. Based on his years of colonial espionage, the major framed a template that divided intelligence work into two basic operations, espionage and counterespionage. In a bold, defining feature of his plan, this new military unit would coordinate Washington's diffuse intelligence effort, centralizing information from all federal agencies, much as he had once done in Manila, and serving as the sole contact with foreign secret services. For his first recruit the major selected Capt. Alexander B. Coxe, a veteran of the Philippine campaign and his former MID comrade during a "confidential mission to China." With Coxe now serving as MID's all-powerful secretary, this core of two recruited a cadre of six regular officers and a larger pool of talented civilians with specialized linguistic and analytical skills. When a lowly State Department code clerk named Herbert O. Yardley dropped by to suggest the need to monitor enemy communications, the major commissioned him a first lieutenant with command of his Codes and Ciphers Unit. "Van Deman's heavily lined faced reminded me of Lincoln's," said Yardley of their first meeting. "He appeared old and terribly tired, but when he turned his deep eyes toward me I sensed his power."[13]

While Van Deman developed counterintelligence for domestic security, another Philippine veteran, Col. Dennis E. Nolan, created a parallel field intelligence capacity inside the American Expeditionary Forces (AEF) fighting on the western front in France. For four years before the war, 1907 to 1911, Nolan had been detailed to the Philippines Constabulary, first as its inspector and later as director for the tempestuous Southern Luzon district, positions that immersed him in colonial policing and its intelligence operations. In selecting officers for the European campaign, the AEF commander John Pershing, who had spent much of his prewar career pacifying the southern Philippines, favored fellow colonial veterans for key commands, particularly in areas of innovation such as intelligence, logistics, and policing. In the first months of war, Pershing's chief of staff, Maj. James Harbord, who knew Nolan from their shared service in the Philippines Constabulary, summoned him for an after-dark meeting at the AEF's Washington headquarters, announcing that he had been selected "to head the Intelligence Section of the General Staff."[14] After Pershing's staff crossed the Atlantic in June 1917 aboard the SS *Baltic,* Major Nolan plunged into the task of mastering combat intelligence, "a line of work in which Americans were less experienced than in any other war activity." After observing French and British procedures, Nolan drew up regulations for a comprehensive service that would collect combat intelligence about the enemy, disseminate topographic information, and engage in counterintelligence through the Corps of Intelligence Police, a new unit organized by Van Deman in Washington that later became the U.S. Counter Intelligence Corps. Under Nolan's plan, approved by General Pershing, intelligence and security units, all identified by the staffing denomination "2," were integrated into every echelon, from a battalion S-2 with twenty-eight men to a G-2 at divisional headquarters and the Intelligence Section at general headquarters with eleven officers and 332 soldiers.[15]

In the parallel area of military policing, Gen. Harry Bandholtz became the AEF's provost marshal general and was deemed by headquarters "specially fitted for the duty, having long been Chief of the Philippines Constabulary."[16] At the close of the war, General Harbord would also select Bandholtz, his former superior in the Philippines Constabulary, to form a new army security service, the Military Police, or MPs, charged with managing the chaos of occupation and demobilization. Drawing on what he called his "long experience in command of the Philippine Constabulary," Bandholtz quickly built the MPs, following their formation in October 1918, into a corps of 31,627 men stationed in 476 cities and towns across five nations—France, Italy, Belgium, Luxemburg, and the German Rhineland. To overcome a haphazard selection, Bandholtz established a specialist service school at Autun, France, that trained over four thousand officers and men in the last months of war. A surprisingly large number of former constabulary officers played formative roles in training this new service, ending early complaints of indifference, disrespect, or even "brutality" and establishing a record of respect for military regulations and "kindness . . . to the native inhabitants." Veteran PC colonel John R. White commanded the MP training school in France with a rank of lieutenant colonel and was later promoted to deputy provost marshal of the AEF.[17] The former chief of Manila's secret service, John W. Green, served as a captain in the Twentieth Division under Col. Louis P. Van Schaick, a former officer in the Philippine Scouts, also training these MPs for their European duty.[18]

With all of the combat intelligence work done on the front lines in France, Van Deman's Washington headquarters concentrated on counterintelligence, a mission quite similar to his earlier Philippine efforts.[19] At the microlevel of data management, his earlier "descriptive card of inhabitants," which reduced all the data about each Filipino subject to a single sheet, was replicated in MID's similarly compact "suspect list" for domestic subversives. By the war's end this list, Van Deman said, "consisted of many hundreds of thousands of cards."[20] Using an imperial lens for perception of threat, MID refracted the American people through a prism of difference, seeing certain ethnic communities almost as domestic colonies. In Van Deman's view Irish Americans, German Americans, "Hindus," and "Negroes" were all dangerously susceptible to enemy propaganda and required constant surveillance. As one U.S. historian put it, Van Deman seemed to be driven by "the fear that the people of the United States could not be trusted and therefore should be controlled."[21] Most important, Van Deman adapted the colonial constabulary's reliance on native agents for surveillance of these ethnic Americans.

As Major Van Deman was building his repressive machinery, the legislative and executive branches were collaborating to create an overarching legal framework for its activation. In the declaration of war against Germany on April 6, Congress had already authorized telephone and telegraph censorship, and just three weeks later the president issued an executive order assuming this authority. In quick succession Congress expanded these controls with passage of the Espionage Act in June, allowing the arrest of anyone who interfered with the war effort; the Trading with the Enemy Act in October, permitting the president to censor subversive literature and monitor the mail; and the expansive Sedition Act in May 1918, stiffening penalties for dissent. These laws allowed the president to censor the mails, suppress print media, monitor suspected subversives, and prosecute dissidents, whether antiwar activists such as the socialist Eugene V. Debs or labor militants such as "Big Bill" Haywood.[22]

Van Deman reached high to coordinate counterintelligence, besting a rival bid by the Treasury's secret service and by early 1918 making his MID the "clearinghouse" for all information from the war, navy, and justice departments. Ambitious and visionary, he pushed hard within the army's general staff to make MID a full division and win himself a star in the bargain. Yet he also overreached with an abortive attempt to supersede the Bureau of Investigation and centralize all counterintelligence under his command. Hostile toward Van Deman because of his incessant intrigues, the army chief of staff cut short his command after only a year and sent him off to Europe in June 1918 on a vague, make-work study mission, delaying his promotion to general for another decade.[23] Only weeks after his departure, an army reorganization elevated military intelligence to one of four "separate and coordinate" divisions of the general staff, winning a star for Van Deman's successor.[24]

After six months on this career-stopping study mission, Van Deman's appointment to replace Nolan as head of AEF intelligence was preempted by the armistice, and instead he became chief of Allied counterintelligence at the Paris peace talks. In this modest capacity he remained overseas for another ten months, coordinating a network of spies that monitored the postwar tumult in Central Europe, providing security for the U.S. delegation at Versailles, and developing "an abiding distrust of Bolshevism."[25] As he wrapped up the affairs of the AEF intelligence division in June 1919, Van Deman was characteristically concerned about the fate of his trademark suspect cards, which were rich in unique data about "undesirables." He urged the retention of these records by the Paris military attaché but lost out to Nolan, who favored their transfer to MID in Washington.[26]

American Protective League

From the first weeks of the war in April 1917, Washington focused its security agencies on controlling what MID called "the manifold domestic problems arising from . . . our mixed population," specifically the large German American community, elements of which had been vocal in their support of the kaiser right up to the eve of America's entry into the war. The threat of German American disloyalty and German imperial espionage created, in the view of Van Deman and colleagues at the Justice Department, an urgent need for vigilance against spies and subversion. Even though an extensive wartime study found that German intelligence did not have a significant spy network in the United States, Van Deman somehow concluded that the Germans must be using itinerant traveling agents, making the threat omnipresent.[27] Of equal concern, mass hysteria over the possibility of subversion inspired vigilantes across America. When the Justice Department urged citizens to "report disloyal acts," the number of complaints soon reached fifteen hundred a day, mostly, said the attorney general, from "hysterical women and . . . men, some doubtless actuated by malice and ill will, and the vast majority utterly worthless."[28] Patriots also formed "dozens of organizations . . . devoted to running down of spies," something Major Van Deman called "an extremely dangerous development." Yet, with MID requiring millions of man hours for its burgeoning domestic security operations, he also saw potential in these groups, feeling that a national organization of civilian spies "might be of great value to the government."[29]

The most promising of these groups, the American Protective League, had been formed in the first weeks of war when a Chicago businessman, Albert M. Briggs, convinced the Bureau of Investigation's regional supervisor to collaborate with a citizen surveillance network. For the first nine months of the war, the APL's executive operated out of Chicago under a so-called War Board with representatives from nine agencies including the Bureau of Investigation and MID—the latter represented by Maj. Thomas B. Crockett, the APL's assistant chief, now commissioned into the army.[30] After conducting "a very careful investigation" of this and other civilian organizations, Major Van Deman summoned the APL's leader to offer him both a commission and a mission on the assurance that his members would be willing "to do absolutely nothing except what they were requested to do by the Military Intelligence Branch." Through what the army's chief of staff described as an "arrangement with the Justice Department," the APL was now placed "at the disposal of M.I.D." After moving its headquarters to Washington in November, the APL reformed its executive to include just two government representatives, a lieutenant and captain from MID assigned to monitor the league's counterintelligence mission. Working closely with BI director Bruce Bielaski, Van Deman presided over the APL's transformation into a civilian counterintelligence auxiliary. It deployed over 350,000 volunteer agents in 1,400 local units who, working like constabulary spies in colonial Manila, amassed over a million pages of surveillance reports on German Americans. In just fourteen months, the league would conduct a total of three million wartime investigations for the government, including 440,000 cases of suspected subversion for MID.[31]

In their joint counterintelligence effort, the Justice Department was more mindful of civil liberties while MID sanctioned illegal methods in its unremitting pursuit of results. Government agencies would sometimes check the APL when it encroached on their jurisdictions, but the league's broad mandate allowed ample opportunity for what the U.S. Senate later called "zealous antics . . . trampling personnel sanctities, privacy, and civil liberties." Most fundamentally, by investing the APL with semiofficial status and formal missions, both War and Justice legitimated the league's role, giving it a broad compass within this new covert realm. In his annual report to Congress for 1917, Attorney General Thomas W. Gregory described the league as "a most important auxiliary and reserve force for the Bureau of Investigation."[32] At the White House President Wilson was wary of building a permanent security bureaucracy—"the danger of creating too much machinery"—and supported a civilian auxiliary force. He encouraged corporations to lend employees for the league's work but drew the line at providing any White House endorsement of its fund-raising efforts.[33] In the first months of the war, Treasury Secretary William McAdoo, determined to protect his Secret Service, denounced the APL as irresponsible and inefficient, but the president sided with the attorney general and the league survived.[34]

In a war in which ethnicity was the touchstone of loyalty, the APL quickly took shape as a xenophobe's ideal: all male, all white, predominately Protestant, with deep anti-German antipathies and strong undertones of anti-Catholic, anti-Semitic biases. After its national headquarters was moved to Washington, DC, in November 1917, its leaders lived and worked together around the clock inside a genteel townhouse for the next fourteen months, lodge brothers on a secret mission to save America.[35] When the New York City branch tried to enlist a female member in March 1918, the Washington rectory replied sternly that it was "strongly against enrolling women."[36] When Jerome Regensburg, a manufacturer with three thousand employees in his Tampa cigar factory, applied for membership in that city's APL, his application was frozen because he was "of the Jewish faith."[37] Similarly, an effective leader of the League's New York City chapter was forced out amid a drumbeat of invective over his German ancestry.[38] As a consequence of its hostility to Irish Catholics, the APL found itself a full year into the war without a Massachusetts chapter, even though its leadership considered the "situation in Boston . . . very serious."[39]

To build a rank and file with real operational capacity, the APL relied heavily on street savvy individuals with access to information, often private eyes of dubious reputation. When the William J. Burns Detective Agency of Los Angeles wrote MID about "running into considerable information of interest," Van Deman was keen to receive "whatever information your good patriotism would prompt you in sending."[40] Such an eclectic appetite for intelligence produced seamy alliances with local gumshoes such as "Captain" Foster of Buffalo, described by a War Department official who knew him well as "a shyster of the first water."[41] The APL headquarters itself complained about "a perfect deluge of people in here every day who think that they are born sleuths . . . , whereas . . . they are all about 100% rotten."[42]

The APL recruited its local leaders through elite networks, usually favoring bankers or corporate officers. In August 1917 a Brooklyn resident's uncorroborated endorsement of his brother-in-law, the treasurer of the Portsmouth Savings Bank who had reported "instances of pro-German attitude," earned this captain of industry an invitation to head the APL's New Hampshire chapter.[43] A similar strategy employed by MID was exemplified that December when two coal mine fires raised suspicions of arson and prompted Van Deman to write the Pennsylvania State Police recommending a mine owner's son as the ideal man to form "an information organization."[44] Even in areas without labor problems, Van Deman frequently appointed corporate officers as his "confidential" agents.[45]

Backed by MID, the league was intervening in social conflicts on the side of capital and opposing collective action by unions or socialists. This corporate bias became clear in August 1918 when the International Association of Machinists, the "aristocrats of organized labor," forwarded a complaint from its Milwaukee chapter that the local APL chief was threatening loyal unionists "with induction immediately into the military forces, if they show any dissatisfactions with conditions in the shop" and warning any aliens who tried to change jobs that "they would be interned." In response the attorney general informed the APL headquarters of its "suspicion that your Milwaukee office interferes . . . in the interests of the employer."[46]

Despite complaints about the league's violation of civil liberties, the attorney general and his BI director invested the group with a semiofficial status, approving badges stamped with an expansive motto that read "Auxiliary to the U.S. Department of Justice."[47] The APL also won the ultimate federal perquisite when the U.S. Postal Service awarded league headquarters "the franking privilege" of free mail.[48]

To a surprising degree, the APL took charge of most of the government's routine security operations. At the war's peak the APL's various security investigations represented 75 to 80 percent of the Justice Department's workload in midwestern areas such as Chicago or Cleveland and 50 percent in New York City.[49] Moving beyond mere paperwork, in January 1918 the attorney general asked that the APL assign one of its members to each of the 4,700 draft boards nationwide with the authority to arrest anyone who failed to appear.[50] With deserters numbering fifty thousand and draft evaders three hundred thousand by early 1918, thousands of APL agents in cities across America periodically pinned on their badges for "slacker raids," which targeted the many aliens and recent immigrants avoiding conscription.[51] The Justice Department's authorization for the APL to "take" and "hold" suspected slackers until these individuals could prove their registration for the draft was clearly illegal, a presumption of guilt with the burden of proof upon the accused. Nonetheless, when a citizen who had been detained without probable cause during a raid in Lansing, Michigan, sued for five thousand dollars in damages, the Justice Department ordered the U.S. attorney to appear for the local APL's chief as if he were a government employee.[52] With Justice endorsing extralegal operations, the APL's slacker raids soon degenerated into outright abuse and racketeering, particularly after April 1918 when the attorney general authorized bounties of fifty dollars for every arrest.[53]

Yet both the Justice Department and its BI also adopted a certain circumspection toward the APL, resisting the organization's pressure for affirmation of its official status. When the U.S. attorney at Nashville asked to make five APL members federal deputy marshals so they would be "clothed with some authority as a protection in their work," the Justice Department refused, saying that past appointments had "led to complications."[54]

Throughout the war, the APL pressed hard for limitations on civil liberties. In April 1918, for example, the Saint Louis chapter urged passage of extreme amendments to the Espionage Act that would allow detention without habeas corpus and heavy penalties for "disloyal utterances." A few days later when a mob of three hundred men lynched a suspected subversive in Collinsville, Illinois, the Saint Louis chapter fired off smug letters saying that the government's failure to suppress "pro-German utterances" had prompted these communities to "take the law into their own hands." This view was seconded by the town's mayor, an APL member, and the local jury, which later found the mob's leaders not guilty of murder.[55] Although its official letterhead read "Operating under the Direction of the United States Department of Justice," the APL systematically denied due process through its first principle of never allowing the accused to confront the accuser.[56] Consequently, some Justice Department employees resisted Washington's pressure to collaborate with the group, notably the U.S. attorney in Cleveland, who questioned the attorney general in January 1918 about the APL's "proper function" and insisted that all official inquiries should be conducted by "some other branch of the government service."[57] Indeed, after months of heavy-handed raids by the league and the police "red squad," Cleveland's Socialist Party complained to Washington that the "coarse language and rough tactics" were nothing less than a "Reign of Terrorism." In stern letters to the APL, the Justice Department stated that these raids had entailed "a great deal of brutality" and represented an "unconstitutional infringement of the rights of public assemblage and free speech."[58]

Manhattan Misadventure

Among all the APL chapters, New York City's was both the most promising and problematic, suggesting some of the pitfalls inherent in outsourcing state surveillance to a loosely regulated band of vigilantes. As the site of the country's largest German American community and busiest port of embarkation for the European war, New York held an unequalled strategic significance.[59] During its sixteen months of operation, the APL's amateurism was thrown into sharp relief by the city's sophistication, producing a succession of misadventures that involved break-ins by uncontrolled strong-arm squads, false reports intended to cripple commercial rivals, and tens of thousands of illegal arrests.

Within the vast New York area and its myriad security challenges, there was no individual or agency concerned with correcting the APL's endless problems. Its New York chapter had generally close relations with MID and Justice, but these offices used the organization as an adjunct when needed and otherwise ignored it. In March 1918 APL leaders reported that there was "no one ranking officer in command of all the intelligence branches of the Army in New York."[60] Selected by Van Deman as his chief agent for New York, Maj. Nicholas Biddle was a former deputy police commissioner who recruited twenty-three members of the city's bomb squad, New York's original antisubversion unit, diverting the main MID office and its 160 employees from war work into ordinary criminal investigations and antiradical repression.[61] Complicating matters further, the league had cool relations with the Office of Naval Intelligence despite the navy's multifaceted security concerns among the sixteen thousand employees at the Brooklyn Navy Yard. When ordered to offer their services to the navy in May 1918, the APL's local leaders met two commanders at the navy yard who mockingly suggested that the league might be able to help with the "great many cases" they were currently giving to "the Boy Scouts."[62]

In its first months the league's New York chapter had expanded too rapidly, attracting a range of irresponsible freelance agents. In these early days, an influential operative named George Lester, vice president of the Fleischmann Company in suburban Peekskill, had formed a "private free lance intelligence bureau" of "ex-policemen" who were "very apt to resort to strong-arm methods in investigating cases of very high-class people in New York, doing such little things as breaking in doors in people's apartments." When the city's APL chief, E. H. Rushmore, tried to cleanse his ranks in mid-1918, headquarters in Washington counseled him to overlook the "objectionable members of Lester's squad" and focus instead on retaining both Lester and his company president, Julius Fleischmann, "because of their rather powerful positions."[63] In February 1918 the APL's office in Washington authorized a Manhattan wheeler-dealer, Col. Fred Feigl, to open his own office at a Times Square hotel and lead squads totaling some two hundred men "on a small military basis."[64]

In the hands of these amateur gumshoes, even routine investigations could produce embarrassing incidents. The New York APL's thousands of background checks of civilian employees bound for France met angry resistance from Red Cross nurses. In January 1918, Chief Rushmore complained to headquarters that the Red Cross personnel director, a Miss Draper, had allowed a rejected nurse applicant to see the accusations against her, prompting a reply from the APL directorate that this was "a very serious mistake on the part of the Red Cross." As the APL continued to find Red Cross applicants unfit, the redoubtable Miss Draper and her New York colleagues offered "considerable criticism," charging that one league investigator had "demanded $100 from a Red Cross applicant."[65]

More sophisticated investigations were even less satisfactory. In May 1918 the APL got wind of a possible German spy when one Miss Mae Dougherty of 480 Central Park West phoned in a tip about a man she had been dating for six weeks. The suspect was "Francis Turno, 17 W. 58th Street . . . [who] looks like a German but claims to be Polish, and says that he is in the service of the United States." The APL assigned the case to Henri C. Harnickell, Esq., a Broadway lawyer, who marched into the Beaux Arts Café with a stock-broker sidekick, "both . . . very much intoxicated," flashed their APL badges, and loudly denounced the suspect as "a dirty Hun." They then prowled the Ritz-Carleton Hotel seeking to confirm the suspect's story with the city's ONI chief. Through this public spectacle, the navy complained, the APL's "drunken members exposed one of the very valuable, covered operatives of the Naval Intelligence." Harnickell responded that he had "worked very hard on this case for over a week and that it had many suspicious sides to it," but he was now satisfied that the suspect's "Government position clears up the matter entirely in his favor."[66]

Not only did the APL's amateurism compromise real intelligence work, but its cloak of secrecy allowed league members to harass commercial rivals with baseless accusations. Assigned to investigate accusations of disloyalty against Frederick W. Sells of Diehl Manufacturing in Elisabethport, New Jersey, the APL's New York office reported signs of subversion. Significantly, the League's investigator, W. D. Lindsay, was also an executive at Western Electric, a direct competitor of the target firm. After an extensive, time-consuming investigation found the accusation to be palpably false, the BI's Newark agent concluded that the only real crime was "the matter of Mr. Lindsay's motives." Consequently, APL Washington asked its New York office to determine whether Lindsay might be guilty of trying to "cripple a competitor." After a cursory review of the case, New York insisted that Lindsay gave his information to the BI "entirely with a spirit of patriotism" and was "one of our best men" through whose efforts "two men in the Electrical Industry were interned last week."[67]

Although the APL could handle routine complaints about pro-German loyalties at, say, a Lenox Avenue bowling alley, its operatives and their MID handlers proved inept when confronted with a complex case of possible German espionage.[68] In November 1917 the president of the New York Electric Society lodged a vague charge with the APL's Manhattan office that Dr. Karl Georg Frank was, "without doubt, active in the interests of Germany," sparking a major investigation. As every government agent knew, Dr. Frank was the former manager of the Telefunken-Siemens transatlantic wireless station at Sayville, Long Island, which had been seized in 1915 on the president's orders to prevent possible transmission of coded messages to German submarines cruising in the North Atlantic.[69] Ratcheting up the pressure in February 1918, MID "raided and smashed in" the Broadway offices of Frank's longtime associate Richard Pfund. Without any real evidence, Van Deman wrote BI director Bielaski, asserting that Frank was dangerous enough for "revocation of his citizenship and subsequent internment."[70] The War Department soon terminated these inconclusive inquiries, allowing Frank to emerge from the war as a founder of the patriotic Steuben Society of America in May 1919.[71]

After fourteen months of such fiascoes, the New York APL outdid itself with a series of spectacular slacker raids in September 1918. For over a year the city had been a "slacker haven" where deserters and draft dodgers faced less chance of arrest than in any other major metropolitan area in America. With U.S. forces in France desperately short of manpower and pressures from Washington mounting, the city's BI superintendent and APL chief Rushmore launched the nation's largest raids. At 6:30 a.m. on September 3, APL agents led thousands of soldiers and sailors in blockading subway entrances across the city, demanding draft registration cards and detaining some twenty to forty thousand residents the first day alone. By day three criticism was rising. The local U.S. attorney asserted that the APL men were making thousands of arrests "without authority," prompting the *New York World* to denounce this "Amateur Prussianism in New York." Highlighting this amateurism, among the 60,187 suspects detained during the three-day sweep only 199 were in any way draft dodgers. A week later Attorney General Gregory, under pressure from the president and treasury secretary, released a report stating that "contrary to law, certain members of . . . this Department . . . used . . . members of the American Protective League . . . in making arrests." This public censure dealt a crippling blow to the league's New York division. With the APL now shorn of its aura as an official law enforcement agency, both private and public organizations stopped cooperating with its investigations. Members began to resign. Chief Rushmore demanded that the attorney general affirm the APL's status as an official "auxiliary." But Gregory responded, as did BI Director Bielaski, with stern orders that the league could not arrest or "hold" anyone. In the end Rushmore told the Justice Department that his men would accept no further assignments. Although the APL mounted slacker raids elsewhere in America during the two months before the armistice, the war was over for the league's New York division.[72]

These controversies doomed the league to extinction. Its leadership wanted to continue their surveillance efforts in peacetime, but Attorney General Gregory, aware of the potential for abuse from thousands of agents holding secret, sensitive information about their fellow citizens, was determined that the organization would disappear. At the end of 1918, one of the APL's key backers, BI Director Bielaski, resigned partly from pressure over the slacker raids. On February 1, 1919, the APL itself was formally dissolved with a banquet at the Hotel Astor in New York City. All members were ordered to turn in their official-looking badges, and chapters were urged to forward their files. Many ignored the directives, leaving the fundamentals in place for a later revival.[73]

Mobilized in the heat of war, the APL's swarm of volunteers seemed almost a parody of the tight clandestine networks at Van Deman's disposal when he pioneered the collection of intelligence to pacify the Philippines. In pursuit of his mission to serve the state, he would draw on the resources available in each successive setting. In Manila circa 1901 the contest over empire versus nation produced covert warfare conducted with consummate skill on both sides of the imperial divide, forcing him to recruit several hundred Filipino agents whose contacts allowed them access to radical circles. In wartime America, Van Deman and his handful of skilled officers mobilized an abundance of ordinary Americans ignited by hysteria and indifferent to the rights of their immigrant neighbors. Once they were persuaded that war justified the suspension of constitutionally guaranteed freedoms, Americans unwittingly sanctioned the formation of the very "machinery" of state security that President Wilson had feared. Through both official policies and ad hoc practices, the APL gave the government the domestic equivalent of plausible deniability by engaging in illegality that could be disavowed. Most important, it was the first in a succession of civilian auxiliaries loosely allied with state security that would engage in similarly questionable practices for the next half century.

Wartime Vigilance

Although it was more professional than its APL auxiliaries, MID itself pursued a wartime mission that suffered from a similar combination of class bias and ethnic anxiety. With the league investing millions of man-hours in routine security work, MID was free to deploy its officers for covert counterintelligence against radical unions and socialist parties, using the full panoply of legal and extralegal tactics the army had developed in the colonial Philippines. From the MID's inception Van Deman viewed radical unions, particularly the International Workers of the World (IWW), the famed socialist union known as the Wobblies, as a serious security threat. To justify a sustained campaign, in June 1917 Van Deman reported that the IWW's "strong opposition to the war" threatened the army's strategic copper production from western mines and warned that its organizing activities in the California oil fields would bring "acts of sabotage leading to the curtailment of supplies." Consequently, he conceded wide autonomy for action to his western regional command, which operated from a sprawling San Francisco headquarters that supervised thirty-seven local offices.[74] In this war on the radical left, MID's regional offices allied themselves with plant security forces and recruited hundreds of agents from private detective agencies already expert at union infiltration.[75]

Apart from obvious concerns about German American loyalties, African Americans were another prime source of MID's ethnic anxieties. Wartime conscription was color-blind, and some four hundred thousand African Americans were a substantial share of the four million men mobilized, rupturing rigid Jim Crow segregation to produce both white repression and black resistance. Incidents such as the white race riots at East Saint Louis in July 1917, which left at least forty blacks dead, as well as the execution of thirteen black soldiers for rebelling against racist treatment in Houston in August, provided ample cause for African

American discontent. Within weeks of forming MID, Major Van Deman concluded, without any evidence, that "Negro subversion" stoked by German agents represented a serious security threat. To counteract the threat he recruited a skilled African American agent, Maj. Walter Loving, a Philippines Constabulary officer on home leave. For the next two years Loving served as Van Deman's top agent, moving continuously about the country to counter incidents that might provoke Negro subversion while also pressing the government to restrain the lynchings that reached a hundred by the end of war. When the Justice Department failed to mute the outraged tone of the *Chicago Defender,* a pioneering black newspaper, Loving warned its editor that there could be personal consequences, eliciting a more patriotic posture. But when the journal *Crisis,* published by the National Association for the Advancement of Colored People (NAACP), attacked the way a white commander had denigrated black officers in the Ninety-second Division, the famed "Buffalo Soldiers," Loving recommended that this commander be court-martialed. As a long-term corrective he also urged the commissioning of more black officers. Maj. Joel E. Spingarn, a MID counterintelligence officer who also served as the NAACP's white chairman, was assigned to monitor his own organization, scoring a propaganda coup in June 1918 when he worked with the editor of *Crisis,* W. E. B. DuBois, to convene a patriotic conference of black newspaper editors. Although MID monitored racial conflicts closely, in the end white racism and black resentment were too complex and too deeply rooted in American society for any covert intervention. Acting on all this intelligence, MID's commanders urged "a square deal for the negro" in both the army and the wider society. But their recommendations had no effect on either military or government policy.[76]

While monitoring African Americans, MID was also actively combating the militant organizing efforts of the IWW. From the first months of war, the union proved a disruptive force in the West, conducting mining strikes in the Southwest, militant actions on the San Francisco waterfront, and aggressive organizing in the docks, forests, and mines of the Pacific Northwest. In contrast to the eastern states, where Justice Department supervision restrained the APL's recourse to physical force, in the West military intelligence joined violent vigilante groups in a bid to crush the union.

In the first months of the war, employers and citizen groups across the West struck at the IWW in a desperate effort to contain worker discontent. To quash union agitation in the Pacific Northwest, local and federal officials mobilized the Minute Men, which soon attracted twelve thousand members, and the Legion of Loyal Loggers and Lumbermen, which the army organized as a closed-shop company union of thirty-five thousand men to secure spruce timber for aircraft production. Workers who refused to join were beaten, blacklisted, and drafted into the army. In South Dakota the APL worked with a group called the Home Guards to force unionists from the Aberdeen wheat fields, prompting a U.S. attorney to praise the group as "the Ku Klux Klan of the Prairies." Similarly, in the mining district of Bisbee, Arizona, the Citizens' Protective League led mobs in packing some twelve hundred suspected IWW members into boxcars and sending them, without food or water, into the New Mexico desert. After the governors of eight western states pressed Washington to "put all IWW's in concentration camps," President Wilson endorsed a "secret investigation" of the union by the Justice Department. Simultaneously, MID's Western Department, with Van Deman's approval, organized the Volunteer Intelligence Corps, which recruited a thousand "patriots" by April 1918 as part of an abortive plan to supplant the BI as the lead agency in domestic security operations.[77]

With its sprawling port facilities and surrounding forests, Seattle was a magnet for radical labor and a major battleground for MID. The region's internal security agencies—BI, MID, and ONI—joined forces for a multifaceted attack on the IWW's influence in the city with an innovative range of repressive tactics: the posting of army sentries along the waterfront, censorship of the mail, deportation of "undesirables," "indiscriminate arrests" of waterfront unionists by ONI, and the "discharge of certain undesirables from the . . . ship yards." Political intervention led to the replacement of Seattle's police chief with one who was "a very able and patriotic officer" and to the defeat in the March 1918 elections of a pro-union mayor, Hiram C. Gill, who was discredited by an earlier indictment for taking bribes from bootleggers.[78] Adding to these pressures on the union, the local Military Police commander, Colonel M. E. Saville, mobilized a forceful civil-military attack, prosecuting "seven disloyal I.W.W.'s," organizing "a Counter-Espionage system among the spruce workers," and "smashing the political vice ring in Seattle" by barring Camp Lewis soldiers from the city's bars and brothels.[79]

Moving beyond the legal to the extralegal, MID's Seattle office continued the repression with "actions" that closed union halls, tar-and-feathered union members, intercepted mail, and conducted an undercover campaign to infiltrate the IWW's clandestine structure of coded membership and cellular networks. On May 2 the Seattle police, as MID reported approvingly, dealt a decisive blow by raiding the IWW headquarters, rounding up 213 members, and ringing the building with patrols to prevent access.[80]

With Seattle's union leaders driven underground and their members "milling about without direction," MID shifted its attention to the Northwest's other flashpoint at Butte, Montana, where its agents applied extreme methods to defeat an entrenched IWW chapter in the region's copper mines, then the world's largest.[81] In June 1918 MID's Lt. Col. F. G. Knabenshue, known as "an officer in whom Colonel Van Deman had a great deal of confidence," wrote Washington requesting removal of the federal judge George M. Borquin for his impartiality and for "not permitting war hysteria influence to enter [the] judicial chamber." He also asked for a denial of reappointment for U.S. attorney Burton K. Wheeler, whose refusal to indict IWW leaders had branded him a "war program obstructor." Even though MID's new chief, Lt. Col. Marlborough Churchill, pressed the issue hard, the Justice Department did not cooperate, replying that Wheeler, who later became a distinguished U.S. senator, was fulfilling his legal responsibilities.[82]

So stymied, MID turned to disinformation and psychological warfare, prompting some objections from the Justice Department.[83] In this clandestine campaign, agent provocateur operations proved the most effective. In late August MID and its APL allies arrested twenty-seven so-called I.W.W. agitators without cause and placed thirty-two more "under surveillance." Simultaneously, MID worked with Anaconda Copper's company detectives, infiltrating the union to provoke anger and militant action against the company. When a strike began on September 13, MID led regular troops, commanded by a young Maj. Omar Bradley, in an illegal raid on the printing shop of the striking Metal Mine Workers Union—the first of many sweeps that filled the local jails.[84] As the strike continued, U.S. attorney Wheeler telegrammed Washington complaining about the "many arrests made by soldiers in Butte. Prisoners brutally treated and held without warrant or hearing." When pressed to answer for its actions, MID dismissed such criticism as "malicious propaganda."[85]

Within weeks the strike collapsed, and in late September a Butte grand jury indicted twenty-four "leaders and radicals, agitators," including all of the IWW's local leaders. Although the government had forced Judge Borquin's transfer and U.S. Attorney Wheeler's resignation, MID reported that the union's attorney was mounting a disturbingly effective defense. Backed by the public "statements of Mr. Wheeler" and some sleuthing by the Thiel Detective Agency, the union's lawyers were alleging that a Pinkerton private eye employed by Anaconda Copper had worked undercover as a "stool pigeon" to foment the IWW strike. To counter this revelation, the local MID officer, Capt. J. H. Dengel, was working with the new U.S. attorney to suggest a "secret indictment" of the union leaders that would overcome these allegations and assure convictions. He was also using "undercover operatives" to split the Butte union into rival factions, hoping to cause the union local's complete "disintegration."[86] By September news of the indiscriminate and illegal arrests reached the Justice Department, sparking blistering criticism from Attorney General Gregory and forcing MID to promise restraint in future civil operations.[87]

After the IWW was effectively paralyzed in Butte, MID shifted its attention back to Seattle, intent on breaking the union inside its red bastion. In October 1918 it scored an unexpected coup when Seattle police received an anonymous 4:00 a.m. phone call about a medical emergency that sent them rushing to a local hotel. There they found Mrs. C. E. Collier, the wife of the IWW's attorney, "in bed, nude, with a man other than her husband." After demanding to speak with MID's agent, Capt. J. H. Dengel, Mrs. Collier offered to provide "complete details of her husband's I.W.W. activities and turn over all the documents and data she could obtain" on the condition that "her reputation would be protected." As a down payment on this deal, she "gave information regarding the threatened strike of shipyard workers in Seattle," intelligence deemed so significant that it was "immediately transmitted to the Director of Military Intelligence in Washington."[88] In a parallel review of its intelligence on the union, MID produced a report that reveals efficient mail intercepts in the Northwest, another avenue of penetration.[89] When the war ended in November 1918, MID had good reason to believe that it had restrained the IWW, at least for the time being.[90]

Red Scare

At the end of World War I, there was a nationwide eruption of labor discontent and racial conflict, almost as if wartime emergency controls had momentarily suppressed a rising social ferment. In the months after the armistice, America was roiled by waterfront strikes in New York and Seattle, race riots in Chicago and Washington, militant actions among Montana's copper miners, anarchist bombings in eight American cities, and a miners' revolt in the West Virginia coal fields, the latter arguably the most serious armed violence that the United States experienced in twentieth century. In September 1919, 365,000 steel workers went on strike, and two months later 400,000 coal miners walked out. Attorney General A. Mitchell Palmer told Congress that "a wave of radicalism appears to have swept over the country."[91] After a turbulent year of such militant actions, Washington reassembled the wartime alliance of state security and civilian auxiliaries for a counterattack that mixed mass arrests and mob violence. Starting with the so-called Palmer raids of November 1919, this crackdown continued at fever pitch for six months before subsiding into routinized repression for another three years. Thus, in the midst of the army's postwar demobilization, its military intelligence unit moved in the opposite direction, reactivating wartime assets and creating new civilian adjuncts to take the place of the now dissolved APL. Encouraged by growing congressional support for internal security, senior army commanders made further use of civil control methods, many of them learned in the colonial Philippines. The triumph of the Bolsheviks in Russia added a sinister aura to these postwar outbreaks of domestic unrest. Van Deman and the intelligence community focused on this emerging alien threat, not just socialism but now communism as well.

In January 1919, only three months after the armistice, a major maritime strike by fifteen thousand workers crippled New York Harbor. When the workers won many of their demands, MID ordered its New York office to compile lists of "reds" active in the city's waterfront agitation and to identify the aliens among them for immediate deportation.[92] Labor agitation in Seattle also intensified in the aftermath of war. To check the "menace" of this "extremely dangerous movement," the local MID officer recommended reactivating wartime vigilante groups. Indicative of the heavy covert surveillance, this same officer, Capt. F. W.

Wilson, submitted summaries of twenty-five letters from IWW leaders intercepted in just one week. He also passed along a warning from an operative "working under cover in the Wobbley district" that "these Bolsheviki," imitating current trends in Russia and Germany, "plan to have an organized army of returned soldiers in their midst who, in case of a strike, would combat the government forces and enable the strikers to seize factories."[93] Within days, a strike by twenty-five thousand shipbuilders spread along the entire Seattle waterfront.[94] Ten days into the waterfront shutdown, the War Trade Board expressed concern about an impending general strike "of practically all the unions in Seattle," reporting that "men of property here" feared the possibility of bloody riots and recommending that "strict censorship of all passenger mail be resumed."[95] Indeed, on February 6 the unions voted "almost unanimously" for a general strike, America's first, sending seventy-five thousand workers into the streets and prompting MID's Seattle office to wire Washington with an urgent plea that it jail the union leaders for "inciting revolution." In an inflammatory evocation of recent events in Russia, the telegram was rich in images that made Seattle seem a reprise of the recent revolution in Saint Petersburg: "Red banners being worn by strikers. . . . Radicals copy bolsheviki movement Russia. . . . Advocating taking over local industries."[96] Within forty-eight hours, army troops armed with fixed bayonets and machine guns marched into Seattle and a train departed carrying forty IWW "agitators" to New York for deportation. These actions ended the strike within a day.[97]

Just four months later, in July 1919, violent race riots erupted, plunging Washington, DC, into four nights of shootings that left six dead and then sweeping the South Side of Chicago with violence so extreme that military intelligence branded it a "Race War." Predictably, the MID's wartime liaison with the APL, Major Crockett, spiced his report of heavy casualties with the claim that "radicals [were] reported to be urging negroes to further violence."[98] To quell these three days of racial violence in Chicago, which left thirty-eighty dead and five hundred injured, the army dispatched 4,600 troops to join the city police in occupying a riot-torn swath from the South Side to the Loop.[99] In the riot's aftermath MID's chief Churchill circulated a report by his leading expert on "Negro subversion," Major Loving, who noted that since 1915 "young Negroes of high intellectual attainments . . . boldly took up the torch of Socialism." The spark for this sudden fire of socialist enthusiasm was the "Negro soldier returning from France full of bitter resentment" only to find that "prejudice flourished as never before" after "southern white men announced the organization of a second Ku Klux Klan with the avowed object of intimidating the returning colored soldiers." But now "the Negro has been taught to fight." So during the Chicago riots, when a truck loaded with fifteen white men "turned up State Street at 30th and began shooting right and left into the crowd of Negroes on the sidewalks," within a distance of six blocks "every man in it had been killed or wounded, the Negroes capturing the truck and taking the arms of the invaders." When he resigned from MID to return to Manila, Major Loving nominated a successor to monitor Harlem, which he called "the fountain head of all radical propaganda among Negroes." But Chief Churchill advised his counterintelligence staff that "investigations in negro subversion" should be transferred to the Justice Department, closing this chapter in military intelligence.[100]

As bolshevism swept Europe and postwar America proved restive, Washington gathered its forces for a protracted battle against domestic subversion, once again perceived through a prism of race tinted by imperial hues. Writing from Europe, Van Deman had already warned General Churchill at MID of "a world-wide social and political revolution" enveloping the continent that would soon threaten America. In October 1919 an Army War College conference on domestic security described the United States as an "Anglo-Saxon nation" facing the specter of revolt by ethnic radicals, making it imperative to implement "War Plan White," a color-coded strategic scenario that the War Plans Division had prepared in the event of a Russian-style revolution by an estimated 1.5 million American radicals. Making the racial prism explicit, another War Department report stated that the greatest threats were Pan-Latinism, Pan-orientalism, and bolshevism, which had "an intimate connection of the Jews and Jewry." On October 30, a MID colonel advised Churchill that from an intelligence perspective the nation was in "practically a state of war." In a parallel shift at Justice that started in March 1919, a coterie of anticommunist hardliners took command: a new attorney general, A. Mitchell Palmer; BI director William J. Flynn; and the head of the BI's new Radical Division, J. Edgar Hoover.[101] In major cities such as New York, Chicago, and Los Angeles, influential business leaders also pressed state and local governments for aggressive action to crush the socialist threat, sometimes funding private anti-red agencies for direct action.[102]

In this changed climate MID and the Justice Department revived their network of civilian adjuncts, activating the APL and organizing returning white war veterans into the American Legion for both systematic surveillance and vigilante violence against the left. Throughout 1919 MID promoted the American Legion as its main civilian adjunct, lobbying its leadership for an antiradical commitment and encouraging its initial growth to a membership of 120,000 in thirty-one states.[103] In October, moreover, MID's Maj. Thomas Crockett, one of the APL's civilian founders, informed General Churchill that "the old American Protective League of Chicago has been reorganized . . . under the name of the Patriotic American League" and had recently assisted the army in nearby Gary, Indiana, during that city's steel strike.[104] Beyond these two stalwarts, MID encouraged multiple military networks for domestic surveillance, including, at Van Deman's suggestion, an organization of MID's own veterans and regular monitoring by army recruiters who should, MID ordered, submit weekly reports on "the numerical strength of the extreme radical or 'Red' element in your district."[105]

From November 1919 to January 1920, the nation's internal security agencies, BI and MID, unleashed their civilian adjuncts for three months of aggressive action against the left known as the "red scare" or the "Palmer raids." From MID's regional office in Chicago, Major Crockett oversaw the American Legion's attacks on socialists across the Midwest. The Chicago post announced a plan for "some night riding or what is known as 'Ku Klux' work . . . destroying stores that sell radical literature." The legion's Milwaukee post raided the local IWW offices, confiscating their literature. In Cincinnati eight hundred legionnaires ransacked radical offices, burning hundreds of pounds of socialist texts.[106] In the Pacific Northwest, the legion launched a "war of extermination against members of the I.W.W." that, in the view of one historian, "practically destroyed the Wobblies" in that region. During these months of red scare, veterans' posts in cities such as San Diego and Stockton harassed union leaders with violence that swept along the West Coast, culminating in an armed legion attack on the IWW hall at Centralia, Washington. At the urging of the local Lumbermen's Association, the town's legion post decided to "burn 'em out" as a way to celebrate Armistice Day 1919. But the unionists fought back, killing four of the attacking legionnaires. That night the veterans evened the score by publicly torturing, mutilating, and lynching an IWW member.[107]

During this winter of repression, the red hysteria drew federal agencies, state governments, and local vigilantes into a combined assault on the radical left. At the instigation of New York City's social elite, who assembled at the Union League Club, the state government in Albany formed the Joint Legislative Committee to Investigate Seditious Activities. Under the leadership of state senator Clayton R. Lusk, this committee used APL members, state troopers, and private detectives to conduct months of raids that culminated in a November sweep of seventy-three radical offices in New York City. The raiders beat suspects at gunpoint, seized tons of office papers, arrested over a thousand supposed subversives, and uncovered what the *New York Times* condemned as a sinister "plot against America." The driving force in New York's effort was two MID veterans who drafted the Union League's report on bolshevism and directed Lusk's operations as his special counsel, infusing their investigations with MID's illegal methods for break-ins, mail intercepts, secret interrogations, and violent raids. Nationwide, this repression reached a peak on January 2, 1920, when the BI's J. Edgar Hoover mobilized local police and civilian auxiliaries for raids in thirty-three cities that resulted in the arrest of four thousand suspected radicals.[108]

Slowly public hysteria gave way to a sober realization that the raids had been excessive. Desperate to stoke the fears that had made him a front-runner for the Democratic presidential nomination to succeed Wilson, Attorney General Palmer announced in April 1920 that the nation faced an immediate red "revolution" on May Day, just weeks away. When that day passed uneventfully, a newspaper chorus of "universal laughter" mocked Palmer's timorous appearance surrounded by guards, dooming his candidacy and discrediting his campaign of repression. On May 20 New York governor Al Smith vetoed a package of harsh antiradical legislation called the Lusk laws, insisting that the state should "not attempt to suppress by law those who do not agree with us." In the waning weeks of President Wilson's administration, the future attorney general Harlan Fiske Stone advised a U.S. Senate committee investigating Palmer's raids that they were an "abuse of power" that had produced "intolerable injustice and cruelty to individuals."[109]

Armed Uprising

Complementing its postwar undercover operations, the army also dispatched infantry to quell domestic disturbances, whether race riots in Chicago or strikes across America, allowing its Philippine veterans another chance to apply their colonial expertise. After the nation's largest steel strike in decades erupted at Gary, Indiana, in September 1919, Gen. Leonard Wood, the veteran colonial officer, led fifteen thousand troops into the city to impose a "modified martial law," supported by APL men who swept up suspected radicals for interrogation by MID officers.[110]

In this same tumultuous period, Gen. Harry Bandholtz, the former chief of the Philippines Constabulary, used psychological methods developed during his years combating Filipino radicals to quash a militant miners' revolt in West Virginia. After a massive increase in membership during the wartime coal boom, the United Mine Workers (UMW) tried to consolidate its gains by launching a nationwide strike in November 1919. Although mines were shut down in fourteen states, the strike collapsed under a combination of federal pressure and a flood of coal from the nonunion fields in southern West Virginia, a strategic oversight the UMW leadership was now determined to correct. Throughout 1920 armed miners in Mingo and Logan counties squared off against West Virginia state deputies and Baldwin-Felts detectives, producing a dramatic shootout in the streets of Matewan in May. There local miners led by Sheriff Sid Hatfield, a descendant of the clan that had fought the famous Hatfield-McCoy feud, shot and killed seven security men. In November the army dispatched a fresh battalion under Col. Herman Hall, a long-serving veteran of the Philippines Constabulary, who facilitated a fragile truce during his short occupation of Mingo County.[111]

In early 1921 the conflict was renewed when anti-union Republicans took office in Charleston and Washington. In May the recently inaugurated governor Ephraim F. Morgan, a close ally of the mine owners, declared a state of "insurrection and riot" and sent sixty state constables into Mingo County to seize the miners' weapons, producing the famed "Three Days Battle" along the Tug River that left four dead. On August 1, Baldwin-Felts detectives gunned down Matewan's Sheriff Hatfield as he entered a county courthouse unarmed, a brutal murder that outraged unionists. In protest nine days later, the UMW's "General" Bill Blizzard massed five thousand armed miners and began advancing on Logan, their ranks swelled by fifteen thousand supporters during the march.[112]

At 3:05 a.m. on August 26, as some eighteen thousand armed miners seemed destined for a bloody shootout with the Logan County deputies, General Bandholtz, accompanied by a single aide, stepped off the train at the Charleston depot, initiating an intervention by two former constabulary chiefs that would soon defuse this social conflict. Unimpressed by the governor's demand for federal troops, Bandholtz met privately with the UMW's two state leaders. "These are your people. I am going to give you a chance to save them, and if you cannot turn them back, we are going to snuff them out like that," the general said, reaching out to snap his fingers right under the nose of union president Frank Keeney, a charismatic local leader whose fiery words had sparked the armed march.[113] Keeney capitulated, promising that "he would act immediately by . . . using his influence to have the persons involved discontinue their march"—much as Filipino nationalists had aborted an armed demonstration at Manila in 1911 when confronted by Bandholtz.[114] To lend substance to his threats, the general telegrammed the army's deputy chief of staff, his old constabulary comrade James G. Harbord, asking for immediate mobilization of troops armed with artillery, machine guns, and poison gas. As the UMW leaders read Bandholtz's ultimatum at mass meetings, the miners, realizing they risked confronting the full force of the U.S. Army, agreed to disperse.[115] After less than two days in the state, Bandholtz boarded a train back to Washington.[116]

Within hours, however, a posse of sheriff's deputies and state police renewed the conflict when they attempted a midnight arrest of union marchers, sparking a shootout that left two miners dead. After the unionists massed to resume their march and some three thousand anti-union "militiamen" occupied blocking positions atop Blair Mountain, both sides began blasting away with rifles, firing over a million bullets. On August 29, Governor Morgan appealed to Washington for army troops to stop this "Bolshevist" uprising. Within a day, President Warren G. Harding issued a "cease and desist proclamation."[117]

By the time General Bandholtz arrived back in Charleston at noon on September 1, there were some ten thousand armed men on the firing lines along Blair Mountain. State militia held the ridge behind concrete bunkers backed by machine guns, while some 7,500 miners probed these defenses along a line of attack that stretched, the newspapers said, for twenty-five miles. Instead of obeying the president's dispersal order, the miners, fearful of being gunned down by the Baldwin-Felts guards, replied, "You send in the troops to protect us and . . . we will gladly surrender to you." Bandholtz, with the full support of the UMW's national leadership, telegrammed General Harbord asking for the immediate dispatch of federal forces. With 2,100 well-armed infantry and aircraft commanded by Gen. Billy Mitchell flying reconnaissance, Bandholtz arrayed his troops at the base of Blair Mountain for a pincer's envelopment on September 3. But just as his troops were poised to engage with lethal effect, the general ordered a sudden cease-fire. For the next four days, without firing a shot, his troops demobilized some 5,400 miners, confiscated 278 firearms, and sent everyone home. Sixteen men died in the five-day Battle of Blair Mountain, but none were shot by army troops.[118] Once he had defused the situation by ordering the "insurgents . . . returned peaceably to their homes" without any arrests, Bandholtz advised the governor that "State peace officers will now be able without difficulty to serve process" against the strikers. Accordingly, state and federal courts soon filed murder and treason charges against some six hundred miners, including the UMW leaders Blizzard and Kenney, whose trials dragged on for three years.[119]

By employing the same subtle strategies he had practiced in the Philippines, Bandholtz had scored an otherwise elusive victory for the mine owners, avoiding the heroic violence that would have given the union new martyrs and stripping the strikers of the arms they needed to resist Baldwin-Felts detectives. Unlike Governor Morgan and like-minded conservatives, Bandholtz had the advantage of colonial experience, which taught him that the threat of armed force was far more intimidating than its application. Exhausted by the eighteen-month struggle, the union's West Virginia membership fell from fifty thousand miners in 1921 to only six hundred a decade later, a decline "just short of a deathblow."[120]

Father of the Blacklist

In the aftermath of the November 1918 armistice, America's four-million-strong wartime army quickly demobilized and within six months the number of military intelligence officers dropped from a peak of 1,700 to only 230.[121] When President Wilson left office in 1921, the incoming Republicans began winding down his aggressive internal security operations. In July 1921 Congress finally declared World War I over and the military returned to peacetime status, reducing the intelligence command to colonel grade. As MID slashed staff to just twenty-four officers and demolished its once formidable records system, the army decided it should "drop out Negative Intelligence activities and all counterintelligence be entrusted to DJ [Department of Justice] in case of war." By 1924 both War and Justice had curtailed most internal security operations, with BI's force of special agents sliced in half and its records closed to the patriotic groups that once had open access. That May, Attorney General Harlan Fiske Stone, worried that "a secret police may become a menace to free government," announced that "the Bureau of Investigation is not concerned with political or other opinions of individuals." Its acting director, J. Edgar Hoover, generally complied with this directive, although he continued to accept "passive" intelligence from civilian adjuncts. In well-publicized hearings that same year Congress investigated Justice's role in the red scare, finding that the department had leaked "secret" security reports to voluntary groups such as the APL, adding fuel to the firestorm of public hysteria. In an act symbolic of the government's retreat from surveillance, Secretary of War Henry Stimson closed MID's cipher section in 1929, saying famously, "Gentlemen do not read each other's mail."[122]

After the war Van Deman's career followed this downward trend, denying him any major intelligence mission. Returning from the Paris peace conference in mid-1919, Colonel Van Deman found his successor firmly ensconced and MID shedding officers fast, relegating him to a brief posting as General Churchill's deputy before the army shipped him off to the Philippines. In 1921, writing from Manila where he now commanded an infantry division, Van Deman confessed to his old comrade Dennis Nolan a sense of boredom with "living in a cantonment" and a deep regret that "there is, of course, no chance" that he could ever again do "the thing that I feel that I can do—Intelligence." Not even his later promotion to general and award of the coveted second star as major general seemed to salve this sense of frustration.[123]

In one of history's accidents, however, General Van Deman's retirement in 1929 soon invested him with a final, far-reaching intelligence mission through the convergence of two countervailing trends: Washington's sharp reduction in internal security and a deepening economic depression that fueled both communism at home and fascism abroad. On the eve of a second world war in 1938, the FBI had just two agents on communist detail across America and army counterintelligence employed only three officers and eighteen agents worldwide. In Washington itself, the entire Military Intelligence Division had only twenty officers and a meager budget of $125,000.[124]

Van Deman's penultimate posting as commander of Fort Rosecrans in San Diego led him to retire there at a time when California was becoming a veritable nation within the nation through industrial innovation in aeronautics and cultural creativity in cinema. Moreover, in this Depression decade of nationwide social conflict "the furor was fiercest in California." According to historian Ellen Schrecker, San Francisco's three-month maritime strike in 1934 "plunged the West Coast into a state of virtual class warfare." In this climate, a dynamic branch of the Communist Party expanded rapidly across California, creating a new center of radical activism outside the old battlegrounds of New York or Chicago and thus opening a void in the nation's counterintelligence that Van Deman was poised to fill. By the time he started his anticommunist archive in 1932, Sacramento's Bureau of Identification, along with other state and local agencies, had moved beyond routine criminal work to focus on antisubversion activities, compiling, for example, a detailed ten-page report for the governor on "Communism in California."[125] The sum of all these trends would soon invest the general's regional role with national import.

But Van Deman had not just chosen California. He had chosen Southern California during interwar decades when the state's politics were defined by a tectonic divide between radical, union-shop San Francisco and reactionary, open-shop Los Angeles. During the red scare of 1919, Southern California's corporate leaders had created militant anticommunist groups and pressed their local police to form antisubversion squads that were soon notorious for attacking dissenters with arbitrary arrests and brutal beatings. Exemplifying this anticommunist zeal, San Diego's unit, responding to a state inquiry in 1935, listed the city's 38 party leaders, 102 leaflets distributed, and 179 speakers heard during the past three years. With a similar thoroughness, the Los Angeles "red squad," led by the notorious Capt. William "Red" Hynes, quickly tallied the names of 36,725 local communist supporters and a radical press with a combined circulation of 24,900.[126] Just as the Philippines transformed Van Deman from military careerist into a master spy, so Southern California changed his modest retirement plans from topographical mapping to anticommunist agitation.

From his comfortable home at 3141 Curlew Street in San Diego, Van Deman and his wife, childless and increasingly friendless, worked tirelessly for nearly a quarter century. Their incessant typing, filing, and cross-referencing animated an elaborate information exchange among members of the state's public-private security network: army and navy intelligence, police red squads, and civilian groups across California. Though long retired from government service, the general continued to receive classified reports from federal, state, and local agencies. Van Deman's private archive swelled over time to a quarter million files on suspected subversives by the time of his death in 1952. But following his trademark method in Manila and Washington, this mass of documentation was reduced to a single card for each suspect. His modest bungalow thus became a veritable search engine for intelligence professionals struggling to lift the mask of aliases that the Communist Party had donned since the red-scare round-up of 1919–20. Apart from the raw documents, the general maintained a reference library of rare communist publications and an archive of identification photos. Beyond typing and filing, Van Deman's web also included operatives inside the state's ethnic communities, an undercover agent in the aircraft industry, assets with access to Hollywood's leftist circles, private eyes in the hire of anticommunist groups, and citizen sleuths across the state—all with their names carefully concealed by a numbered code system that the army and FBI would struggle to decipher after his death.[127]

Though Van Deman remains an obscure figure, specialists have noted his central role in the anticommunist movement. The army analyst who assessed his files in 1971 wrote years later, as a distinguished historian, that Van Deman, absent any "federal agency fighting the radicals," built an influential information clearinghouse that "left the other patriotic groups in the dust." With funds from the FBI and army, he "ruled a large and sophisticated spy network."[128] A leading lawyer with the American Civil Liberties Union called the general "one of the giants of anti-communism, a super-hawk, . . . a phobic nativist red hunter" whose "undercover network penetrated not only the Communist Party but a whole spectrum of liberal targets, including religious, civil rights, and labor organizations."[129] Through his single-minded focus, unequalled experience, and ceaseless efforts, Van Deman became the spider at the center of a spreading web of domestic surveillance.[130]

While catholic in his distaste for extremism in any form, Van Deman's experience watching bolshevism spread across postwar Europe in 1919 had left him obsessed with the threat of communism. Convinced that the army's consignment of counterintelligence to the FBI was a serious mistake, he prodded the War Department with periodic reminders, writing in 1933 that "G2 should take more aggressive attitude toward subversive activities" and again in 1935 to advise that ONI is "much concerned re. subversive elements making . . . headway in infiltrating into airplane factories in So. California."[131] Under the gathering clouds of World War II, he would also monitor the state's Italian American and Japanese American communities carefully, helping the army revitalize its counterintelligence capacity while holding fast to his abiding preoccupation with the communist threat. If his army service in World War I had earned him the informal title "father of U.S. military intelligence," his private sleuthing in retirement should earn him another: "father of the American blacklist."[132]

In setting paradigms for detecting domestic disloyalty, Van Deman persisted in his earlier imperial mode, seeing subversion in terms of both radical ideology and alien ethnicity. Revolutionary ideals, whether Philippine nationalism or American communism, remained the ultimate threat. Yet in his view the means for the dissemination of these dangerous ideas was often ethnic. During the decade before Pearl Harbor, Van Deman, as he refracted threats through this prism of race, was particularly concerned with Japanese espionage in Southern California and northern Mexico, producing reports whose sum gave an unsettling sense that imperial Japan's intelligence was probing America's weakest frontier, its undefended southwestern border.[133]

Reflecting his overarching concern with communism, however, Van Deman soon shifted his focus from external to internal threats. In early 1932 he began assembling his anticommunist archive with its very first document, an unsourced report dated January 27, duly marked "R-1" and detailing the activities of one Richard Walker, a Hollywood chauffeur described as affiliated with a "suspected anarchist" and "boastful of his association . . . with notable Germans, especially cinema actors."[134] Once the general began probing for communism in deeply conservative San Diego, an amazing array of unsolicited information began arriving in his Curlew Street mailbox. Indicative of his enormous authority among local anticommunists, when he telephoned a San Diego police lieutenant in January 1932 to suggest the "attendance of a plain clothesman" at a local communist gathering, headquarters immediately dispatched Agent SD-2. Showing the general's uncanny timing and impeccable sources, this operative's report revealed that the meeting had been called "for the purpose of organizing a communist party in San Diego" and was attended by eighty "poor people, seemingly lower order of intelligence." San Diego's red squad forwarded these documents to the general, who marked them R-2a and R-2b before tucking them into his infant archive.[135]

Other documents soon followed from residents of Southern California ready to enlist in the general's campaign against communism. The sergeant at arms at San Diego City Hall wrote complaining about one Harvey C. Norsworthy, who should, for no particular reason, "be investigated regarding Communistic Party." A local private eye, Larry E. Belger, forwarded a blank membership card for the Cannery and Agricultural Workers Industrial Union, suspiciously leftist in its demands. The San Diego county clerk supplied the names of residents who had posted bond for arrested communists. A Los Angeles chiropractor, Charles Hoffmann, reported that Rev. Edwin P. Ryland of the city's Congregational Church was "the #1 Soviet propagandist in the State."[136]

By the late 1930s Van Deman's incoming reports passed the two-thousand mark and his files grew to forty thousand oversized four-by-six inch cards, thus achieving the critical mass necessary to make his archive an intelligence asset. Essential to its quality were regular reports from undercover agents, sometimes in the employ of the police or private security firms, sometimes working directly for the general. In July 1937, for example, Agent A-42 attended a meeting of "the newly formed San Diego branch of the American League against War and Fascism . . . at the residence of Mrs. Emily Hillkowitz, 136 Redwood Street," adding that the "the writer has been angling for six months for an invitation to the Hillkowitz domicile." He now used that access to discover "an excellent library on Communism," but lacked the time to locate the suspected "short wave sending outfit and ascertain its wave length."[137]

Among his many informed sources, the Better America Federation, funded by major Los Angeles corporations, sent the retired general reports from its undercover operatives and data from the files that filled its sprawling downtown office suite.[138] Van Deman also worked closely with the Civic Council of Defense, Inc., which infiltrated every leftist meeting in Long Beach, a city that served as a commercial port and navy base for Los Angeles.[139] In 1938, for example, its undercover operative monitored a local rally for striking Ford auto workers and reported on a speech by Assemblyman Sam Yorty, later the three-term mayor of Los Angeles. Yorty preached socialism, saying that "the large fortunes such as Ford's were not made by Ford, but by his workers" and calling for "government ownership of railroads."[140]

Another strand in Van Deman's spreading net was military intelligence. Agents for both the navy's ONI and the army's G-2, its overall intelligence branch, ignored security procedures and sent him classified documents through the mail. In June 1937, for example, the army's San Francisco office sent the general sensitive operational intelligence about a Soviet agent, Leon Gershevich, describing him as "Asst Chief OGPU [Joint State Political Directorate] Seattle. . . . Official courier between NYC & Seattle. . . . Member of Russian CP [Communist Party],

Comm. Intern. Com." Indeed, to speed the routing of secret documents to Van Deman this army office made up a special rubber stamp marked "VanD."[141] With similar generosity ONI forwarded "confidential" intelligence about the international movements of communist agents.[142] In return Van Deman sent G-2 San Francisco "comprehensive information" about the formation of the left-leaning American Friends of the Chinese People. Promptly, G-2's Lt. Col. H. R. Oldfield replied with intelligence about the Japanese National Salvation Association, whose leader was "Karl Hama (real name Kamamoto Hanna and alias Ken, Uchida and Goso Yoneda)."[143] From his cross-referenced files, the general already knew, via an ONI report received two weeks earlier, that Karl Hama was a Japanese, "5 feet 7 inches tall, light in color for one of his race," who edited San Francisco's Japanese-language communist paper, *Rodo Shimbun,* and was living with communist "Elaine Black as man and wife," the same Elaine Black who, Van Deman would learn six weeks later, had been an impassioned speaker before striking Salinas lettuce workers.[144]

Dress Rehearsal for Blacklisting

By the mid-1930s leftist influence in the film industry was emerging as one of the chief targets of Van Deman's anticommunist network. In a bid to influence this powerful "weapon of mass culture," the party's New York headquarters sent its top cultural "commissar," V. J. Jerome, out west to organize a Hollywood branch in 1936, starting with his fellow writers. Within a few years script writers represented about half of the three hundred party members in Hollywood, and communists made up a quarter of the active membership in the Screen Writers Guild.[145] In 1936 the general typed a card for Ring Lardner Jr., a talented writer at Metro-Goldwyn-Mayer Studios and future Oscar winner, that read, "Subject reported by good authority to be a *rabid Communist* and reported to be recruiting members for the YOUNG COMMUNIST LEAGUE in Los Angeles." The source for this report was "Commandant, Third Naval District, New York," an indication of the general's spreading net.[146]

Showing the party's increasing sensitivity to surveillance, an undercover agent, writing from a Watts mail drop, attended an August meeting of "Hollywood Unit, J-8, the Communist Party, at 1325 N. McCadden Place, Hollywood," with "surnames banned" so he could only identify five individuals, including the "wife of a screen writer."[147] A month later another agent working undercover as a "unit organizer" for the party reported that its "Hollywood sub-section" had already recruited an impressive 450 members. When a strike swept the Salinas lettuce fields, this agent reported fiery speeches by "Elaine Black, well known Communist agitator," and financial support from "a group of Hollywood Motion Pictures Actors, who are known to be sympathetic towards the Party," including James Cagney, Melvyn Douglas, Robert Montgomery, Gary Cooper, and Boris

Karloff. Two months later this same operative monitored a Los Angeles stage production of Sinclair Lewis's *It Can't Happen Here,* which, like all the plays produced as part of the Federal Theater Project, reportedly reflected "the strong Communist leadership in the theater group."[148]

As the shadow world of covert operations fused with movieland fantasy, federal operatives became entangled in an eerie case that seemed, in both its political intrigues and personal betrayals, a full dress rehearsal for the postwar blacklisting that would divide Hollywood so bitterly. The story began in December 1937 when the Beverly Hills police arrested a communist organizer, Arthur Kent, and his wife for burglary. Facing serious prison time for both himself and his wife, Kent gave the police a signed affidavit with a dramatic account of his communist career that read like a film noir screenplay, a document that soon found its way into Van Deman's files.

After majoring in music at Yale College during the 1920s, Kent wound up in San Francisco where he joined the party in 1931 and operated a swanky restaurant for four years before quitting for full-time work as a communist organizer. His duties for the party in this period included building an organization of progressive Democrats that put seventeen candidates in the state assembly, Sam Yorty of Los Angeles included. After steady communist gains that culminated in San Francisco's famed general strike of 1934, crisis swept the party ranks on August 11, 1936, when the "chain-draped body" of Raoul Lewis Cherbourg, a seaman who had recently broken with the comrades, was pulled from San Francisco Bay. At the news, said Kent, leaders of the communist "strong arm squad" that operated on the city's waterfront became "very panicky" and sought legal advice "to help out with the alibis." A year later at the 1937 annual convention of the Congress of Industrial Organizations (CIO) in Portland, Oregon, the president of the leftist Longshoremen's Union, Harry Bridges, was taped in his hotel room talking about communist control over his union—a serious indiscretion that could facilitate deportation back to his native Australia. This tape was particularly troubling, said Kent, since it "showed that Bridges had been having a sex party with somebody named Norma, wife of one of the [union] delegates," creating the threat of a damaging scandal among his union's rank and file.[149]

At this low ebb in the party's fortunes, Arthur Kent became an expropriator. Learning that he had spoken to Portland police about the hotel room tape, the leadership suspended Kent and assigned him "to raise funds, so as to show I was going forward with the Party." Apparently focusing on the wealthy West Los Angeles area, the party set up a special "apparatus" under Dr. Inez Decker and Sam Cherniak, head of the local Communist Party Finance Committee, to raise "money for the reserve fund." Working exclusively in his assigned territory of Beverly Hills, Kent committed about twenty robberies from "fashionable film colony homes" between July and November 1937, breaking windows for entry, cleaning out valuables, fencing the goods, and paying off the party. Communist leaders evidently reveled in this racket, for Kent claimed he once witnessed a "loud argument" at the Los Angeles home of Dr. Inez Decker and her husband George Shoaf about dividing up "three magnificent fur coats" stolen by other party expropriators.[150]

For five months, the robberies went off without a hitch. In late November, however, the movie comedian G. P. Huntley surprised the burglar at his home on North Maple Drive and jotted down the license plate number as Kent drove off, a clue that eventually led Beverly Hills police to the suspect in Ojai and then to a cottage in Carpinteria filled with stolen goods worth fifty thousand dollars. At his court appearance Kent, nattily dressed in Ivy League fashions, made a preliminary confession, calling his robberies a "compulsory social tax on the rich to benefit the Communist Party" and claiming that he had donated 90 percent of the proceeds to the comrades. In a public statement, the party's District 13 insisted it had ousted the Kents five months earlier "on charges of being unreliable adventurers." After the prosecutor agreed to dismiss the charges against his wife, Kent dictated a twelve-page affidavit to a police stenographer loaded with damning allegations, launching the next phase of his checkered career as a professional stool pigeon.[151]

After his affidavit received extensive coverage in both the *San Francisco Examiner* and the *Los Angeles Times,* Arthur Kent disappeared into the county jail for nine months until the Republican right made his charges a cause célèbre in the 1938 state elections. On November 3, just five days before the balloting, the newly established House Special Committee to Investigate Un-American Activities (HUAC), chaired by Representative Martin Dies, Jr., released Kent's claims that communists were running a "campaign to control California" through the Democratic gubernatorial slate. According to his affidavit, during the state legislature's 1937 session five Democratic members of the state assembly who "were all members of the Communist party," Jack B. Tenney and Sam Yorty included, had assigned all the leftist bills they wanted passed to a knowing ally, state Senator Culbert L. Olson—now the Democratic candidate for governor. On election eve the lead editorial in the *Los Angeles Times* denounced the "Communist-supported, CIO-supported Culbert Olson" as the man who would "throw open the schoolhouses to Communist meetings." Such media sensationalism had been critical to Republican Frank Merriam's defeat of Upton Sinclair's populist candidacy during the last elections in 1934. This time, however, Kent's red-baiting failed to boost Governor Merriam's reelection bid and he lost decisively to Olson, even in traditionally conservative Los Angeles County.[152]

When news of Kent's arrest and affidavit first grabbed headlines, Van Deman's apparatus bounced messages back and forth in an attempt to detect the real identities of the communists he mentioned. In such painstaking analysis, when large errors sprang from minute details, Van Deman's role moved beyond mere collecting to active collaboration. Within days of the arrest the general was corresponding with army G-2 in San Francisco to clear up confusion over the many aliases of

"Arthur Kent @ Arthur Scott @ James Allen." After reviewing the eight sources cited on its central index card for "SCOTT, Arthur, alias Margolis," G-2 advised the general that its error in failing to establish that Arthur Kent and Scott were "identical" arose from a red herring report that "Scott" was the "sweetie of Norma Pettrae; his real name Margules." This incorrect entry "should have referred to Benjamin Margolis," the left-wing Los Angeles attorney, as Norma's paramour. The general, of course, had not made this mistake.[153]

As for Kent's claim that he was working for "Cherniak, the head of the Communist Party Finance Committee," G-2 noted, in response to Van Deman's suggestions, that "The Sam Chernyok (Sta. Barbara) you mentioned appears identical with Sam Cherniak (@Sol Woloch)." Army intelligence appended a summary of his file illustrating the depth and diversity of its sources for tracking party members: "Long Beach 11909 (1932: Crim.Sydnicalism). H-dk ch.curly; E-dk.blue; 2–144; A-32 (1932); former manager Coop. Restaurant, Boyle Heights . . . Photo on page 6, Westn. Worker 12–27–37 as manager of Sta. Barbara circulation drive."[154]

With those key figures identified, G-2's Lieutenant Colonel Oldfield wrote Van Deman that the George H. Shoaf mentioned in Kent's fur coat story was an alias for V. J. Jerome, an editor of *The Communist,* who had been working in Hollywood since November 1936 "under Party directives and assigned duty of educating movie colony along party political lines. Reported as common-law (?) husband of Dr. Inez C. Decker, and living at 764 No. Hoover St., Los Angeles."[155] Indicating the depth of this cover, the Better America Federation forwarded two studies showing the lineage of these parallel identities—one for "George H. Shoaf," who appeared in eleven press articles from 1926 to 1937 as a West Coast socialist turned communist, and another for "V. J. Jerome," who showed up in a dozen articles from 1932 to 1938 as a communist active in both New York and California.[156] Clearly, Communist Party aliases were elaborate, making Van Deman's archive a valuable finding-aid for effective counterintelligence.

World War II

As war engulfed China and Europe in the late 1930s, military intelligence again expanded, lending credence to General Van Deman's earlier complaints about the army's abandonment of its once formidable counterintelligence function. In 1935 he wrote the chief of G-2 in Washington offering him his "rather extensive records covering both organizations and personnel throughout the country." A year later Chief of Staff Malin Craig, concerned about the communist role in the 1934 San Francisco strike, began a long-term renewal of army intelligence. With General Craig's support, the new G-2 chief developed plans to control civil disturbances across the country, quietly resuming antisubversion work under the army's earlier "War Plan White."[157]

In this process of intelligence rearmament, the diffuse domestic surveillance—divided among federal, state, and private sources—proved resilient. To compensate for meager interwar intelligence collection, Oldfield, the chief of G-2 San Francisco, wrote Van Deman in January 1938 about plans "to expand our subversive data base here" by sending staff to collect information "directly" from the only sources he deemed reliable: "from Clarence Morrill's files" in the state Bureau of Criminal Identification at Sacramento; from "Chet Flint in Alameda," who "maintained voluminous files" for the county's district attorney; from the "FBI here"; and finally from Van Deman himself.[158] To refresh the depleted federal data, Van Deman also advised G-2 in Washington that the "excellent records of the Better America Federation [in Los Angeles]... should be taken over by the FBI."[159]

At this high tide of New Deal liberalism, the political climate was not sympathetic to red-baiting, and the anticommunist network moved cautiously. In Washington the Senate Civil Liberties Committee, led by Wisconsin's Robert La Follette Jr., was wrapping up a four-year investigation of corporate union busting by a secret army of "3,871 industrial spies" whose methods ranged from the illegal to the brutal.[160] Similar pressures led to the dissolution of the Los Angeles red squad in 1938 after several of its top officers were convicted of trying to bomb a private eye in a bizarre corruption-driven vendetta that repulsed the public. Even HUAC's first anticommunist hearings in 1938 seemed inept, endorsing Arthur Kent's dubious allegations and charging that Hollywood's darling child star Shirley Temple was a communist dupe. But committee chair Martin Dies kept hammering away with accusations of fifth-column treason inside the ranks of the Roosevelt administration until the White House was forced to accept him, in late 1940, as "an authorized co-worker" in the FBI's "anti-subversive campaign."[161]

As war grew imminent, Van Deman played a central role in negotiating the "Delimitations Agreement" between the army and FBI that conceded the bureau complete control over domestic counterintelligence. Finding the army unresponsive to his insistent suggestions, Van Deman had begun courting J. Edgar Hoover in 1937, writing the FBI director regularly to offer his files and urging him to take charge of the "counter-espionage work." Hoover admitted some months later that "no plans have been formulated," and, over the next year, sent senior agents from Los Angeles for briefings and a close review of the general's files. Meanwhile, Van Deman's former deputy at MID, Alexander Coxe, was corresponding with the army's G-2, Gen. Sherman Miles, warning that any future relationship with "civilian spy hunting organizations such as 'The American Protective League'" would prove "very dangerous." Meanwhile, with the president's support Hoover won the lion's share of expanded counterintelligence funds in 1938. Two years later he was given responsibility for all "foreign intelligence work in the Western Hemisphere," prompting him to request another five hundred agents for these missions. When Hoover convened a "highly confidential" National

Intelligence Conference in May 1940, General Miles invited Van Deman and Coxe to attend as his advisers. Both were impressed with the "thoroughness, magnitude, and soundness" of the FBI's plan to control all "allegations of espionage, sabotage, and such related matters." Van Deman also accompanied General Miles to a follow-up meeting with Hoover to finalize "a complete agreement on the delineation of responsibility," which was signed by President Franklin Roosevelt two days later. A revised counterintelligence compact in February 1942 invested the FBI with "investigation of all activities coming under the categories of espionage, subversion, and sabotage," while wartime exigencies soon added "black bag" break-ins, warrantless wiretaps, and surreptitious mail opening to the bureau's de facto powers. The FBI also enforced the Alien Registration Act of 1940, known as the Smith Act, making it a felony to advocate "overthrowing . . . the government of the United States." So armed, the bureau compiled a "Security Index" of suspects to be rounded up in any emergency; and, along with military intelligence, mobilized over three hundred thousand informers to secure defense plants against wartime threats that ultimately proved "negligible."[162]

These events, particularly the May 1940 summit, integrated Van Deman into the revitalized counterintelligence community. He was recognized as a confidential source in the FBI's "Special Service Contact Program," and soon sent J. Edgar Hoover an elaborate plan for surveillance to "guard against expert sabotage activities in munitions plants, aircraft plants, etc." In December, FBI headquarters issued "special instructions" for a San Diego agent to "devote himself exclusively to the task of reviewing General Van Deman's files and extracting all information of value to the Bureau." Three years later the liaison officer between the FBI and G-2, Col. Leslie R. Forney, assigned two full-time clerks to his San Diego archive, paid from the "army's confidential fund." When a rival intelligence agency, the Office of Strategic Services, offered Van Deman a senior position on the West Coast, the old general spurned the overture after learning that OSS did not share intelligence with the FBI. Through these contacts, Hoover soon came to consider Van Deman "as a warm friend."[163] This unique quasi-official status, moreover, allowed the general to insert unverified civilian suspicions into government files and later disseminate military intelligence to civilian activists—making him a catalyst for the renewed public-private alliance that would animate the postwar anticommunist movement.

Even as its operations expanded on the eve of war, army intelligence continued to filter its reports through the ethnic prism adopted at its founding in 1917. Although G-2 was constrained by its ingrained imperial mind-set, in this sense Van Deman was the analytical superior of his successors, an empiricist who could learn from new information.[164] While serving as an adviser to the War Department from 1941 to 1946, for which he later received the Legion of Merit, Van Deman spent the war in San Diego presiding over an ever-increasing exchange of information via his private-public network.[165] Living amid the cultural diversity of Southern California rather than the insularity of official Washington, the general not only drew data from his ethnic informants, but he seemed to learn from them, moving beyond his agency's Anglo template for American nationhood. While G-2 would favor forced internment for ethnic Americans of Axis ancestry at the beginning of the war, the general would now reject the military's equation of ethnicity with threat. Whether motivated by empathy or pragmatism, he would oppose individual relocation orders for agents affiliated with his Italian American net and argue strongly against the mass incarceration of Japanese Americans.

Among Van Deman's many numbered agents, the former California state welfare commissioner Dr. Frank Gigliotti, known to the general's archive as operative A-70, provided both exceptional information about Italian espionage and empathy toward Italian Americans. During the Sons of Italy national conference at Philadelphia in November 1940, Gigliotti lobbied hard to defeat a candidate with "very definite Pro-Fascist leanings" and to assure the adoption of a "Pro-American program."[166] Over the next three months, A-70 submitted seven detailed reports to Van Deman listing dozens of Italian Americans of dubious loyalty, including Professor Paolo Valenti of Washington University in Saint Louis, who taught "the grandeur of Fascism"; Mrs. Prisca Marino, president of the Circolo Recreativo Italiano in San Diego, who was a "most ardent exponent of the Fascist ideal"; and Nino Calabro, the Italian consular attaché in Pittsburgh, who possibly held "a confidential position in the Italian secret police."[167]

When the outbreak of war threatened Italian Americans with restrictive curfews and forced removal from their homes, Agent A-70 submitted moving testimonials of community loyalty in lieu of finger-pointing lists. Only weeks after Pearl Harbor, he sent a secret report, stamped with an authoritative "Confidential," with the information that San Diego's Italian American fishermen had "purchased between fifty and sixty thousand dollars worth of [U.S.] Defense Bonds."[168] As wartime security tightened in September 1942, A-70 sent Van Deman another confidential report objecting to the forced removal of Mrs. Julia Besozzi, his "look out" inside the Italian consulate in San Francisco since 1937. He reminded the general that Besozzi had proven herself "thoroughly reliable and loyal," reporting on the consulate's efforts to collect funds for "propaganda purposes" through the Sons of Italy and fingering fascist spies. Forced separation "from her home and family" would, the agent said, be "a great miscarriage of justice." Just two days later Van Deman wrote his contact at G-2 San Diego opposing her relocation since the intelligence she had passed "through Dr. Gigliotti has made possible the unearthing of several subversive Italian agents in this country."[169]

When Washington's concerns about Italian American loyalties eased in late 1942, Agent A-70 wrote both the FBI and the general to say that after searching ceaselessly "for anything" suspicious in San Diego he could only report the "splendid spirit that prevails throughout the entire community." With the nation's internal security now assured, Agent A-70 resigned as an FBI informant effective December 1 and shifted his efforts to foreign espionage. In this new role Dr. Gigliotti sent Van Deman a strategic analysis for a future Allied invasion of southern Italy keyed to detailed maps that he had "placed at the disposal of the Office of Strategic Services," the government's new overseas intelligence agency.[170] As an extraordinarily skilled operative, A-70 stayed the hand of state security by naming dozens of Italian Americans as spies while also assuring the apparatus of his community's loyalty, a success that stands in striking contrast to the performance of a Japanese American agent known as B-31.

The U.S. Army's Western Division, G-2 included, became deeply concerned in December 1941 about the security threat posed by Japanese Americans from their proximity to Los Angeles defense factories, their possible collaboration with Tokyo's espionage in California and northern Mexico, and their supposedly divided loyalties. In this critical period, Van Deman's role seems contradictory. He sent an endless stream of raw reports portraying Japanese Americans as a serious security risk, yet he advised the president against using extreme measures to contain that same threat.

As war approached the general's network circulated warnings about Japanese spies. In June 1940, for example, Agent A-42 reported that Japanese homes in San Diego "exhibit an unusual number of high aerials," indicating the possible possession of "short wave receiving sets." In the immediate aftermath of the December 1941 attack on Pearl Harbor, Van Deman's network generated a torrent of intelligence that seemed to show active Japanese imperial espionage with agents and radio transmitters embedded inside the Japanese American community.[171]

Among the many reports about the Japanese threat, none was as inflammatory as those the general received from Agent B-31 of Los Angeles. Ironically, this agent was a respected Japanese American writer, Mary Oyama, who was well placed for espionage inside her community as a founder of the League of Nisei Artists and Writers. Under her pen name "Dear Deirdre," she was also a well-known advice and "gossip" columnist for Japanese newspapers in Los Angeles and San Francisco. In her first report for the general just thirteen days after the attack on Pearl Harbor, she cited "rumors . . . of some strange doings" to finger the Satsuma Nursery and Florist in Glendale, owned by Paul S. Mayemura. The business was really a "German-Japanese Post Office . . . receiving packets of mail . . . with the names of German agents on them." Then these letters were, she claimed, altered with the correct address for forwarding to enemy spies "without suspicion." Raising the specter of thousands of disloyal Japanese Americans, Agent B-31 also reported that an association on Sutter Street, San Francisco, was issuing lavishly lithographed certificates for the Japanese Military Servicemen's League (Zaibei Heimusha Kai), an organization of U.S. residents still committed to serving in the emperor's army. In her next "Confidential Report" of January 1942, she was even more ominous, warning that a hotel at 312 Ord Street in Los Angeles—"connected with Japanese gambling interests in . . . Los Angeles"—had a basement that was visited by suspicious Japanese at night and was thus a secret safe house "used by various agents to make reports and get orders for the next assignment." This last report was so serious that Van Deman forwarded two copies to the FBI.[172]

In a cruel twist of fate, her reports stopped abruptly when Mary Oyama, no longer Agent B-31 but just another Nisei, was forcibly relocated to a Japanese American internment camp at Heart Mountain, Wyoming, before being allowed to resettle in Denver. There she later wrote for the popular press, criticizing Caucasian "misconceptions concerning the Japanese in this country," misconceptions that she had helped foster with her fanciful fabrications as Agent B-31.[173] In contrast to Van Deman's later efforts to spare his Italian American operative from forced relocation, there is no evidence that he tried to save B-31 from being swept up in these mass arrests.

Van Deman himself repeatedly wrote the region's internal security offices—FBI, G-2, and ONI—about the threat from Japanese agents just across the border in Baja California, Mexico.[174] Yet as a professional analyst he also noted signs of a deeper Japanese American loyalty, as in October 1940 when he sent G-2 Washington reports about a community meeting in the Imperial Valley to "affirm allegiance to the U.S. Constitution."[175] In mid-February 1942 Van Deman became concerned over press reports about a congressional delegation on the West Coast that intended "to recommend the removal of all persons—citizens and aliens alike—from certain areas designated as 'strategic.'" Indignant at the proposed relocation of Japanese Americans, he wrote an impassioned "Memorandum for the President" and sent it, via wartime intelligence chief William Donovan, directly to Franklin Roosevelt, damning this idea as "the craziest proposition I have heard of yet." Besides ignoring "the fact that all three of the investigative agencies designated by the President have been intensively investigating people on this coast for over a year," the plan made "no provision for the gathering of information concerning the loyalty of all of these removed people." Nor did it comprehend the havoc mass removal would wreak "with the manufacture of airplanes and other similar defense material." In sum, the general said, "this is an entirely unbaked and illy considered proposition . . . morally certain to throw into the arms of the Axis powers numbers of the second generation Japanese."[176] Yet the dichotomy that Van Deman presented to the president between responsible security agencies and rabble-rousing politicians was false. As he should have known from documents dropped at his home, both G-2 and ONI were drawing data from the intelligence flow to conclude, like this congressional delegation, that forced removal was the sole solution to the perceived Japanese American threat.[177]

The army's G-2 was reporting that Japanese Americans were a serious security risk that defied conventional in situ surveillance. On January 6, 1942, the army's Counter Intelligence Branch in Washington completed a staff study on "Japanese Population Areas in the Southern California Sector," finding that there were thirty-seven thousand Japanese around Los Angeles living "in close proximity to vital defense industries, communications, and military installations where constant surveillance of their activities is difficult," even "impossible under present circumstances." From MID headquarters in the War Department, this grave warning was disseminated down the intelligence chain of command to the Army's IX Corps, which covered the entire West, thence to the Southern California Sector's G-2, and finally to the San Diego Subsector's S-2.[178]

Framed by MID's racial paradigm for the perception of threat, the jump from such alarmist intelligence, some of it generated by Van Deman's own network, to extreme action was a short one. On February 19, 1942, President Roosevelt signed Executive Order 9066, allowing military commanders to designate "exclusion zones." On March 2, the army's IX Corps commander, Gen. John L. DeWitt, issued Public Proclamation No. 1 ordering all persons of Japanese descent excluded from the Pacific coast. Starting on March 27, the army moved with particular severity against the Los Angeles Japanese, sweeping twenty thousand at bayonet point into horse stalls and makeshift barracks at the Santa Anita Racetrack, among them citizen-spy Mary Oyama, the erstwhile Agent B-31.[179] Although Van Deman had counseled against internment, the intelligence he was disseminating conveyed an impression of Japanese American espionage so omnipresent as to require nothing less than the wholesale confinement of an entire ethnic group. Even as the army was preparing to round up Japanese Americans, Van Deman's network continued to generate intelligence underscoring this threat.[180]

Under the pressures of war, the general's West Coast net also expanded to full national coverage. Starting in December 1941, for example, a new agent sent a series of reports, first on the German American Centrale of Youngstown, Ohio, whose seven listed leaders were "known Nazies" and an "outfit of sex perverts," next on several instances of alleged "Negro sabotage financed by German groups" along the East Coast, and finally on the Negro Victory Rally at Harlem's Golden Gate Ballroom, described as a "scheme to get the Negro race closer to the Communists." Van Deman forwarded all this information to his usual security correspondents: the FBI, MID, ONI, the Eleventh Naval District, and the Better America Federation.[181]

By mid-1942, with putative ethnic threats contained and his wartime counterintelligence work largely done, Van Deman, now in his eighties and helped by two assistants, returned to his core work on California's communists, refining the index card system central to his method.[182] A series of cards typed in July 1942 shows a wide-ranging search for communist influence among California's intellectuals, including Victor Tasche, "Secretary-Treasurer of the American Newspaper Guild in 1940 . . . Communistic"; Dr. Paul S. Taylor, "professor of Economics at UC . . . presented economic surveys before La Follette Committee in 1939"; and Prof. Lewis Terman, Stanford University, "called on Atty. Gen. Robert Jackson to investigate violations of Constitution by Dies [HUAC] Committee." At the bottom of each card was an annotation listing sources that, in the case of Professor Terman, the famed creator of intelligence quotient (IQ) testing, read "DIO (2); MIS [Military Intelligence Service] (2); FBI/LA (1); File (1)."[183]

The extant cards from the Van Deman archive reveal an intensified interest in the Communist Party's infiltration of Hollywood, an effort that showed his system at its most nimble and toxic. A July 1942 card on the wartime "Hollywood Writers Mobilization" summarized its activities as "a series of forums . . . with Erskine Caldwell Communistic writer recently returned from Russia" organized by a committee that included "Darr Smith (CP suspect)," the latter a Los Angeles film critic later blacklisted.[184] The archive's index cast its net wide, catching even aspiring writers like Daniel Lewis James, also later blacklisted, who was carded as "a screen writer . . . writing a musical comedy which he hopes to produce in New York City," and married to Mrs. Lilith James, "Organizer, Branch H, Northwest Section, Los Angeles Country Communist Party."[185] In pursuit of every possible Hollywood communist, the general compiled cards on a motion picture publicist, a freelance musician, a Fox Studios electrical operator, and the character actor Alvin Hammer, describing him as holding "CPA Membership Card #46956."[186] Within just a few years, Van Deman's careful compilation of this intelligence would bear fruit in the California legislature's attack on communism in Hollywood whose significance has long been overshadowed by Washington's heavily publicized HUAC hearings.

Hollywood Blacklist

In the aftermath of World War II, the nation's public-private security apparatus again expanded to create the anticommunist movement later identified with Senator Joseph McCarthy. According to a standard history of this period, the "network that helped shape the anticommunist crusade" included "labor leaders, journalists, priests, bureaucrats, ex-Communists, and ordinary private citizens." Significantly, this new coalition, far broader and more sophisticated than its predecessor in 1919, drew its strength from an informal alliance between the FBI and civic groups such as the American Legion, the Catholic Church, and a network of some seventy-five civilian "experts" in communist subversion. In this context, Van Deman's intelligence files, which had long focused on Hollywood, emerged as a valuable cache of information for the movie industry exposés that became "a major turning point in the consolidation of the machinery of McCarthyism," sparking a nationwide purge of suspected subversives in all walks of American life.[187]

In this contentious postwar period, Van Deman worked closely with Richard E. Combs, a Visalia attorney and the long-serving chief counsel to the California Committee on Un-American Activities whose investigations of Hollywood played a central, unappreciated role in the national anticommunist movement.[188] Both before and during the war, Washington's House Committee on Un-American Activities (HUAC) remained focused on New York, the traditional center of American radicalism. The committee's early investigations of Hollywood in 1938–39 had proven inept, and its coverage of both California and the film industry in its 1944 master index of communist front groups was sparse, an oversight that the state legislature tried to correct. During its most militant years, 1941 to 1949, Sacramento's Committee on Un-American Activities was chaired by state senator Jack B. Tenney, a Los Angeles musician and songwriter ("Mexicali Rose") who had entered the assembly in 1936 along with his left-wing Democratic ally Sam Yorty. Just three years later, however, Tenney turned hard right, embittered at being mocked as a "red-baiter" and "rotund" when the communists ousted him from his well-paid presidency of Local 47 of the American Federation of Musicians. During the war Tenney's committee, using Walt Disney's angry denunciations of "Communistic agitation" in his studio as its springboard, conducted four aggressive hearings into Hollywood radicalism.[189] With Moscow and Washington allied against Hitler during the war, Tenney's charges of communist influence in the film colony, on the UCLA campus, and in his old musicians' union aroused little public interest. By war's end Hollywood's leftists had dismissed the senator as a buffoon: flabby, drunken, inarticulate, shamelessly self-aggrandizing, and aggressively anti-Semitic.[190]

After the war, however, the political climate grew conservative and Republicans made major gains in the 1946 elections, creating ideal conditions for Senator Tenney's doggedly persistent investigations. In these theatrical hearings the senator played the anticommunist attack-dog, bullying witnesses and twisting facts to make baseless accusations. His chief counsel, Richard Combs, was the respected expert on communism who used archival data for both poignant questions and quick compilation of the committee's fourteen thousand data cards on suspected traitors. "It was the duty of Dick Combs," Tenney later recalled, "to conduct and supervise all investigations." Describing his chief counsel as a "good trial lawyer" with a "smooth, clever method of examination and . . . [a] suave manner," Tenney delegated the details to Combs, handed him stacks of fifty or sixty blank signed subpoenas, and sat back as he "produced witnesses who could and did testify to things that amazed the members of the committee."[191] A less sympathetic source, a former ACLU leader, described Combs as a "legendary" figure "venerated in political intelligence . . . circles" who during his twenty years with the committee "orchestrated a network of informers . . . , investigators, and contacts cloaked in secrecy."[192] In effect the senator's wholesale delegation of his subpoena powers to his counsel, and Combs's reliance on Van Deman for advice about their use, invested the old general with surrogate state power. Simultaneously, Van Deman's contact with Combs served as a conduit that allowed the U.S. intelligence community to leak damning but unconfirmed information about suspected subversives from classified files into the committee's public hearings.

In retrospect, there seems to have been a seamless interleaving of Van Deman's files and the data that Combs deployed in his role as chief inquisitor in committee hearings. Writing the general in May 1947, for example, Combs reported that a black bag operation had secured "a list of the State Communist Party functionaries" from "one of the Alameda Country comrades (without his knowledge or consent, of course.)" After checking the list of fifteen officials and twenty-one front organizations against his indexed card file, Van Deman forwarded the document to the region's internal security agencies—Military Intelligence Los Angeles, FBI San Diego, the Eleventh Naval District, the Sixth U.S. Army Presidio, and the California National Guard—advising them that "since this list was obtained in an extremely confidential manner, it should be handled with care."[193] A year later, when Combs won an additional appointment as chief counsel for the joint California-Washington Legislative Committee on Un-American Activities, he assured Van Deman that he would find time amid the crush of administrative work to assure delivery of the "Washington Committee's Reports" to the general's growing archive.[194]

Consequently, there was often a close correspondence between Van Deman's private files and the committee's published hearings. In its *Third Report* for 1947, for example, the California Committee on Un-American Activities charged that "Communist steering committees" had launched "a two-pronged agitational drive" by forming a front group called the Progressive Citizens of America. In summarizing this group's inaugural meeting at the Embassy Auditorium in downtown Los Angeles on February 11, 1947, the committee report stated that "nearly all the organizers of the Progressive Citizens . . . have been affiliated with Communist Party activities," including Lena Horne, Gene Kelly, Thomas Mann, Frederic March, Dr. Linus Pauling, Paul Robeson, Gregory Peck, and Edward G. Robinson.[195] On February 13, just two days after the event, Van Deman had received a strikingly similar typed report, still raw with personal invective, from Agent B-51, his undercover Hollywood operative. The agent described the same packed meeting, whose speakers included the song-and-dance star Gene Kelly and famed chemist Linus Pauling. As he exited this gathering of what he called the Los Angeles "swimming pool intelligentsia" and took a leaflet from a "one world" group headed by ex-congressman Jerry Voorhis, the operative fumed, closing his report to the general with a call for an "organized movement started in the press or in public hearings to expose this group . . . to the people of California."[196]

Such a movement had already started as a Sacramento-Washington pincer attack on movieland communism. Even before the end of the war Senator Tenney had announced, in July 1945, that he would assist the forthcoming Hollywood hearings before HUAC in Washington by sharing "the great volumes of information from our investigations which have shown widespread Marxism in the film colony." Indeed, the California committee had held two hearings on Hollywood in 1946, which focused on its bête noir, the Screen Writers Guild, and accused the group, in its *Third Report* of March 1947, of advocating a "plan for 'thought control'" initiated by "Comrade" Dalton Trumbo, a prominent screenwriter. With its aggressive probing of communist influence, the *Third Report* also served as the first Hollywood blacklist. For example, the veteran actress Anne Revere, though recently awarded an Oscar for her role in the film *National Velvet,* stopped getting calls after this report listed her as a stockholder in a "pro-Soviet, red-slanted" Los Angeles radio station and a director of the Progressive Citizens of America, which the report branded as "a new and broader Communist front for the entire United States." After months of correspondence and collaboration, Senator Tenney himself testified before HUAC in March 1947, submitting 372 pages of data to prepare the groundwork for Washington's highly publicized Hollywood hearings six months later. Insisting that there is "a time when tolerance becomes treason," Tenney warned that American communists were "the greatest fifth column, the greatest group of traitors, assassins, terrorists, that the world has ever seen, and America will collapse like an eggshell unless we start . . . exposing them." In a hint of things to come, Tenney used his testimony to include Frank Sinatra "in a class with John Garfield and Charlie Chaplin as movie colony figures giving aid and comfort to the communists."[197]

In these same March 1947 hearings, FBI director J. Edgar Hoover fired a sensational first shot in this war on silver-screen subversion. Armed with intelligence that some eighty American communists were in fact Soviet spies, Hoover was determined to succeed where he had failed back in 1919 by smashing the party. "The American Communists launched a furtive attack on Hollywood in 1935," Hoover told HUAC, "by the issuance of a directive calling for a concentration in Hollywood." After the director explained the many methods of communist infiltration, Representative Richard Nixon—a freshman California congressman elected by red-baiting the liberal incumbent, Jerry Voorhis—asked if there was "any one area in which the Communists are more . . . more deeply entrenched than any other." Above all, Hoover replied, Congress should concern itself with "those fields which mold public opinion and in which the Communists have been successful in effecting infiltration, such as the radio, the motion pictures."[198] This seemingly scripted dialogue indicates two defining attributes of the anticommunist movement: first, a well-publicized attack on subversive influence in Hollywood that sparked public outrage, even hysteria, over alien manipulation of an iconic American institution; and, second, an emerging political alliance between federal security agencies and California's anticommunists. From San Diego General Van Deman hailed Hoover's attack on the "Red menace," asserting that his testimony "has aroused the citizens of this country as no other one speech on any subject has done in my remembrance." As the FBI's anticommunist campaign intensified, the general advised Hoover that "we are really in the beginning of the third world war" whose object was nothing less than "the determined attempt of the Soviet Union to take over the United States."[199]

Reflecting Hollywood's new role as the nation's political battleground, California's anti-red apparatus redoubled its surveillance. The film colony's leaders fought back, producing a historic confrontation. In May 1947 Van Deman's Agent B-51 reported on a Hollywood rally for a liberal third-party presidential aspirant, Henry Wallace, sponsored by the Progressive Citizens of America, which filled Gilmore Stadium with a crowd of twenty-five thousand. As he seated himself in the bleachers among "the riff-raff from the cesspools of Europe and scum of the Seven Seas," this tough sleuth B-51 listened unimpressed while Linus Pauling, a future Nobel Prize winner, "rambled along for a while on a speech . . . written for him by some left-winger." Then came leading lady Katherine Hepburn, who swept across the stage, resplendent in a red gown, to rip the un-American committees in Congress and the California legislature as nothing other than un-American. She spoke with such grace that even this witch-hunting operative was star-stuck, admitting that her speech was "really a master piece." After hearing the thundering applause for Henry Wallace, B-51 concluded that "the left-wing groups are again on the march." In a personal letter to the general, he expressed the fear "that we are entering a very serious period in our history" for in Los Angeles "the Communists and 'fellow travelers' . . . are more outspoken and more vicious."[200] Indeed, trumpeting this massive turnout, the group reprinted Hepburn's speech as a pamphlet with her defiant words on the cover: "I speak because I am an American and as an American I shall always resist any attempt at the abridgement of freedom."[201]

Six months after J. Edgar Hoover's warning about movieland communism, HUAC reconvened in October 1947 to force actors, directors, and writers to supply the names of Hollywood's hidden communists under oath. When ten screenwriters, the legendary "Hollywood Ten" led by Dalton Trumbo and Ring Lardner Jr., refused to answer questions about their membership in the Screen Writers' Guild, Congress indicted them. The studios, acting as the Motion Picture Association, formally banned them from the industry, launching the first full Hollywood blacklist. In the decade following these hearings, the public-private security nexus reached the apex of its influence, with the FBI monitoring suspected subversives and voluntary organizations such as Van Deman's network denouncing them. In 1947 as well, a group of former internal security operatives—a retired army intelligence major and three former FBI agents—launched the influential newsletter *Counter Attack,* which drew on official and unofficial sources to name names and to advise subscribers: "Whenever you hear a party-liner on radio . . . protest to station, network, producer & sponsor." These accusations often generated threats of movie or media boycotts by the American Legion and allied anticommunist groups, compelling the studios to self-censor.[202]

Beyond the high drama in Washington, Van Deman's network continued to attack the Communist Party on the West Coast, paying particular attention to the film industry. As denunciations intensified following the blacklisting of the

Hollywood Ten, Van Deman advised counsel Combs about every detail of the California committee's upcoming hearings into communist front groups. Above all he used his encyclopedic knowledge of the party to guarantee that the committee's subpoenas could be served, an effort now complicated, he said, by the disappearance of San Diego's "reds," who had gone deep "underground as far as they can dig."[203] More broadly, Van Deman's archive served as a source for informal, possibly illegal security checks for state and local employment, vetting, for example, all applicants for teaching posts in the San Diego schools.[204]

In June 1949 the California Un-American Activities Committee moved beyond its colorless probe of communist organizations by issuing a 709-page report that condemned hundreds of liberal luminaries and Hollywood stars as "red appeasers," including, Pearl S. Buck, Charlie Chaplin, Maurice Chevalier, Helen Gahagan Douglas, Lena Horne, John Garfield, Dashiell Hammet, Lillian Hellman, Katherine Hepburn, Danny Kaye, Ring Lardner Jr., Dorothy Parker, Gregory Peck, Edward G. Robinson, Artie Shaw, Orson Welles, and even Frank Sinatra. To warn the "people of California" about a "Fifth Column of thousands of potential traitors" loyal to the "murderously aggressive . . . force of World Communism," Senator Tenney's *Fifth Report* contained forty-eight pages of carefully cross-referenced lists publicly identifying 4,307 individuals as affiliates of communist front groups. Setting a new, ultimately unsurpassed standard for anticommunist denunciations, Tenney's list was so long, so detailed, so far beyond anything *Counter Attack* or HUAC had released to date that it seemed to bear the mark of the voluminous data in Van Deman's secret archive.[205]

At the national level, FBI Director Hoover pressed for prosecution of the Communist Party under the Smith Act—producing a spectacular New York show trial that convicted eleven leaders in late 1949, crippled the party as a political force, and inspired further indictments of its second-tier leadership. Then in June 1950, *Counter Attack* published a sensational pamphlet, *Red Channels,* drawing primarily on reports by HUAC and the California committee to list 151 entertainment professionals affiliated with subversive front groups. Beyond merely naming names, the pamphlet claimed the party had dominated Hollywood since 1938 through a powerful propaganda machine that boosted its sympathizers "from humble beginnings in Communist-dominated night clubs . . . to stardom."[206] That November at the Globe Theater in downtown Los Angeles, the general's Hollywood operative, B-51, monitored a meeting of the Arts, Sciences and Professions Council, observing a speech by film noir actor Dick Powell, who attacked "the great damage the book 'Red Channels' was doing to the movie . . . and television industry." The actor criticized the three former FBI men who were using the *Counter Attack* newsletter to "operate a blacklist" that had ruined great actors such as Frederick March.[207] At the council's next meeting, Agent B-51 amplified his monitoring with the assistance of "two different agents" and appended a complete list of the group's forty-two directors, including former California attorney general Robert Kenny and longtime surveillance subject Ben Margolis.[208] Indicating the Arts Council's status as a top target for the right, just two months later Van Deman received another report from his counterintelligence contact at the California National Guard, Lt. Col. Frank Forward, with a copy of the ballot for the council's board of directors.[209]

The Arts Council's next meeting, in April 1951, came in the midst of HUAC's second and most successful round of Hollywood investigations, lending a poignant tone to these proceedings. With fifteen hundred people filling the Embassy Auditorium in downtown Los Angeles, the gathering began in darkness as an announcer read the names of twenty-five organizations blacklisted by state and federal agencies. When the lights went up, actress Gale Sondergaard strode across the stage to castigate "Larry Parks for being a stool pigeon," a reference to this actor's performance before HUAC weeping and pleading to be spared the agony of betraying his Hollywood friends. Assessing this meeting for Van Deman's network, Agent B-2 dismissed the large crowd as "typical Boyle Heights and Hollywood Jewish reds." Although the council was much diminished and now had only "the 2nd and 3rd string with a few stars scattered in among them," it must be stopped, Agent B-2 urged, "just as the others were stopped by publication of their names and their records."[210]

For the next four weeks the Los Angeles press was filled almost daily with reports of actors, directors, and writers appearing before HUAC in Washington. Some, like the writer Richard J. Collins, denounced their colleagues as communists. Some, like the gossip columnist Hedda Hopper, rattled off names. Others, like screen actor John Garfield, insisted "I am no Pink. I am no fellow traveler." A dwindling few, like the actor Alvin Hammer, a subject of Van Deman's card system, refused to name names. But all of them, either by official sanction or private censure, were damaged and sometimes destroyed. By 1957 the Communist Party was broken as a political force, reduced from a dynamic movement with seventy-five thousand members in 1947 to an "inbred, isolated sect" of only three thousand a decade later.[211]

Yet even at the peak of its power in the early 1950s, this anticommunist coalition, consumed by its own accusatory frenzy, self-destructed. In Washington HUAC suffered a heavy blow when the chairman of its Hollywood hearings, Rep. J. Parnell Thomas, was forced to resign from Congress in 1950 to enter federal prison on a corruption conviction. Four years later Sen. Joseph McCarthy's overblown accusations against the U.S. Army led to his censure by the Senate. One of the ex-communists who had given such convincing testimony before HUAC and the Smith Act trials, Harvey Matusow, published a book, *False Witness*, admitting that many of his accusations were knowing lies. Then, in 1957, the U.S. Supreme Court overturned the Smith Act convictions of second-tier communist leaders, blocking further prosecutions and restraining the zeal of FBI director Hoover.[212]

In California the anticommunist implosion was even more dramatic. In releasing his committee's fifth report in 1949, blacklisting some four thousand alleged subversives, Senator Tenney had overplayed his hand. First, he stuffed legislators' mailboxes with an inflammatory issue of the newsletter *Alert* by the anticommunist zealot Edward Gibbons, denouncing communist sympathies among a dozen state legislators and leading officials, notably District Attorney Edmund "Pat" Brown. Tenney then hired this same fanatic to write much of the accusatory fifth report, prompting a longtime ally Sam Yorty to engineer his ouster as chair of the California Committee on Un-American Activities. These reverses and a later defeat in the Republican primary for Congress in 1952 crystallized Tenney's growing sense that "organized Jewry was now openly hostile to me." After an intensive study led him to conclude that "loyalty to one's . . . country . . . could not exist in the Jewish mind," Tenney was drawn into a deeply spiritual alliance with America's leading anti-Semite, the Rev. Gerald L. K. Smith. In 1945–46 the reverend's stormy arrival in Los Angeles at the head of his Christian Nationalist Crusade had won him a rabid following among the county's conservatives and, ironically, condemnation by Tenney's committee as a "rabble-inciting crusader . . . stirring up hatred and antagonism toward the Jewish citizens of America." But seven years later in 1952, a warm meeting at Tenney's Hollywood home revealed Reverend Smith as a "virile and vigorous" visionary who wisely "opposed the mongrelization of blacks and whites." Proudly, Tenney accepted the vice presidential nomination of the reverend's Christian Nationalist Party at its Los Angeles convention. The ticket, headed by a sphinx-like Gen. Douglas MacArthur, who neither accepted nor rejected the nomination, won just eighteen hundred votes nationwide out of the sixty million cast for president in 1952. Two years later he launched a reelection campaign for state senate under the slogan "The Jews Won't Take Jack Tenney." But he suffered a career-ending defeat in the Republican primary to Mrs. Mildred Younger, a former fashion model best known as the GOP "glamour girl."[213]

With their crusade against "organized Jewry" routed in Los Angeles, these anti-Semitic activists were slowly pushed off the national stage. Jack Tenney traded his comfortable Hollywood home for life as a city attorney in Cabazon, California, a dusty high-desert town with a few hundred residents huddled around a seedy poker palace. Gerald Smith moved headquarters from his lavish Victorian home in Glendale, Los Angeles, to Eureka Springs, Arkansas, a faded resort town of fourteen hundred. There he opened a Christian theme park beneath a concrete statue he commissioned, "The Christ of the Ozarks," striking for both its soaring height of sixty-seven feet and its stunted composition. In 1968 Smith began drawing audiences of three or four thousand nightly to his Grand Passion Play, a spectacle with two hundred actors on a four-hundred-foot stage, which he proclaimed "the only presentation of this kind in the world that has not diluted its content to flatter the Christ-hating Jews." Forty years later it remains the largest pageant in America, playing to packed audiences nightly.[214]

Even after the mass anticommunist movement imploded in the mid-1950s, federal antisubversion efforts persisted for another twenty years. Reflecting the resilience of the state-civilian security alliance, the FBI and military intelligence institutionalized the movement's intensity and illegal methods. From 1955 to 1978, the FBI conducted 930,000 surveillance cases, indicating a vigilant internal security. In this same period, the bureau operated its Counterintelligence Program, which transformed many of the extralegal methods first used ad hoc against the Communist Party into a covert doctrine. According to the bureau's official history, it "responded to the threat of subversion with Counterintelligence Programs (COINTELPRO) first against the Communist Party (1956), later against other violent/subversive groups like the Black Panthers and the Ku Klux Klan (1960's) . . . at times, effectively stepping out of its proper role as a law enforcement agency."[215] More bluntly, an assistant to the FBI director, William C. Sullivan, called this operation "a rough, tough, dirty business. . . . No holds were barred." In assessing the 2,370 counterintelligence actions taken under this program during its fifteen-year history, the U.S. Senate's Church Committee called them a "sophisticated vigilante operation" involving techniques that "would be intolerable in a democratic society even if all of the targets had been involved in violent activity."[216]

After the Communist Party dwindled to insignificance by the late 1950s, COINTELPRO focused, during the 1960s, on a succession of putative security threats: the white supremacist Ku Klux Klan, the black civil rights movement, and the antiwar New Left. In its civil rights operations the bureau aimed at preventing the rise of a "messiah" who could "unify and electrify" the movement, specifically targeting Dr. Martin Luther King Jr., Stokely Carmichael, and Elijah Muhammad for disinformation campaigns to discredit them among the "responsible" white and black communities. In its attack on the New Left, the bureau attempted to "expose, disrupt, and otherwise neutralize" the movement's leaders, using a range of extralegal tactics to explore "every avenue of possible embarrassment"—an effort supported by parallel army and CIA programs to investigate, infiltrate, and discredit the Vietnam antiwar movement.[217] In each successive step from the Klan to the civil rights movement and the New Left, a Senate investigation reported, "the use of dangerous, degrading, or blatantly unconstitutional techniques" seemed to have become "less restrained with each subsequent program."[218]

In its effort to destroy the antiwar and civil rights movements, the bureau's methods, according to a later Senate report, included "secret surveillance of citizens . . . through secret informants, . . . wiretaps, microphone 'bugs,' surreptitious mail opening, and break-ins." Field agents also engaged in operations using "unsavory and vicious tactics . . . including anonymous attempts to break up marriages, disrupt meetings, ostracize persons from their professions, and provoke target groups into rivalries that might result in deaths." In fact this reliance on questionable methods became the dominant feature of FBI internal security operations. From 1960 to 1974 it conducted over half a million separate investigations of "subversive" suspects, yet a Senate committee noted that "not a single individual or group has been prosecuted since 1957 under laws which prohibit planning or advocating action to overthrow the government." By contrast the FBI succeeded in discrediting civil rights leaders "by disseminating derogatory information to the press" and demoralizing New Left leaders by circulating disinformation within their ranks. In sum, the Senate concluded, these FBI operations ran "grave risks of undermining the democratic process."[219] Though the Church committee traced these abuses to domestic roots, this counterintelligence effort seems, in its reliance on penetration and disinformation instead of legal prosecution, strikingly similar to tactics the constabulary had used against Filipino nationalists after 1901 and techniques Van Deman introduced into U.S. Military Intelligence in 1917.

The Ever-Lasting Archive

On January 22, 1952, General Van Deman, then eighty-six, died quietly at his home in San Diego. The house was filled with the confidential reports he had so carefully collected, carded, and filed for the past quarter century. In its obituary, the *San Diego Union* wrote that "his knowledge of Red activities in the subversive line probably was not exceeded by any other American," implying that this information had been extinguished along with its creator. That was not to be.[220]

Seven years earlier when Van Deman's health had begun to fail, the army and FBI engaged in extended negotiations over the disposition of his files. As the lead counterespionage agency, the bureau was the logical repository. But at least three careful FBI surveys found that his eighty-five thousand oversized cards did not fit into their standard files and recommended letting the army take control. "I think it is something we should now stay out of," J. Edgar Hoover wrote in the margin of one such memo in late 1945. "What the Army does should be *immaterial* to us." Yet the deep affection the FBI director and his men felt for this titan of counterintelligence blocked implementation of their decision. For nearly a decade, field agents had called on the general almost weekly building a relationship that was "very cordial, friendly, and intimate." As Van Deman's health faded through flu, enlarged prostate, and a serious fracture, Hoover himself sent warm notes expressing "my sincere wish for your speedy recuperation." Concerned that his files must "fall into the right hands," Van Deman hinted obliquely to Hoover in October 1951 that he wanted the bureau to take possession. Within hours, San Diego's senior agent was at the Van Demans' door, reporting that the old general "feels very strongly about his work, which he sincerely loves," and any suggestion of disinterest in the archive "would most certainly leave him heart-broken, disillusioned, and possibly hasten his death." The FBI man suggested to the general's senior aide, Colonel Forney, now retired, that he might continue the work, but the latter replied that he did not "have sufficient prestige among Army authorities in Washington."[221]

Ultimately, however, security trumped sentiment and the FBI gradually gave way. By March 1951, the army's Counter Intelligence Corps (CIC) had developed detailed plans to protect the archive, approved at the highest level by Maj. Gen. Alexander R. Bolling, chief of military intelligence. Thus, only sixty-one minutes after Van Deman died at 8:35 a.m, on January 22, 1952, an FBI teletype transmitted the news to Hoover in Washington, and General Bolling soon called to assure him the files were being secured. As the general spoke, the 115th CIC detachment moved into Van Deman's house to spend the next nine days sorting and packing. The secret archive, with classified documents and coded name cards for some 250,000 suspected subversives, was quietly split, with the bulk, estimated at ninety linear feet, taken by the army and used in federal security operations until 1968. The smaller share passed to the general's aides at his San Diego archive.[222] Once known to only a few, these secret files would now be known to even fewer.

The American public first learned of Van Deman's bequest to the nation a decade later in 1962 when a bitter partisan battle erupted in California over control of the smaller San Diego archive. In February the adjutant general of the California Highway Patrol, acting on orders from Gov. Edmund G. Brown's Democratic administration, conducted a midnight raid and removed twelve filing cabinets from San Diego's National Guard armory, where Van Deman's papers had been housed since his death. The files were then trucked five hundred miles north to Sacramento and stored at the Highway Patrol headquarters. "We had information there had been leaks from the files," the patrol's adjutant general told the *Los Angeles Times*, adding, "It had been alleged that these files were being used by unauthorized persons for purposes not in the best interests of the state." Later California government officials admitted that San Diego's state senator, Democratic leader Hugo Fisher, had complained about the right wing's use of this sensitive information. Outraged, the archive's curator, retired National Guard general George Fisher (no relation to the senator), claimed that the files were private property. At Van Deman's death in 1952, one of his close associates, Lt. Col. Frank Forward, had formed the San Diego Research Library as "an independent anti-Communist organization" and moved the files into the local National Guard armory. The records grew to fill twelve filing cabinets with information on some two hundred thousand individuals and had been used to screen employees, General Fisher claimed, by every state administration for the past ten years. Calling himself "an anti-Communist fighter," Fisher growled, "It's only Democrats who are worried about this." In its rebuttal to this blast from the right, the state insisted that Forward, as chief of counterintelligence for the California National Guard reserve, had maintained the files in an official capacity that ended with his retirement the previous December. Since the guard had now eliminated its "counter-intelligence capacity," the Highway Patrol's adjutant general had quite properly confiscated these official records. As the case became a cause célèbre among San Diego's right wing, General Fisher filed a lawsuit demanding the return of all the files. In July the parties settled out of court and Sacramento trucked the files back to San Diego.[223]

The next chapter in this story came ten years later when the federal portion of Van Deman's documents finally surfaced. In July 1971 the *New York Times* reported that the Pentagon had recently transferred the files to Sen. James O. Eastland for use by his Internal Security Subcommittee, the Senate's counterpart to HUAC. When Sen. Sam Ervin, an outspoken civil libertarian, asked the Pentagon for an explanation, its general counsel, J. Fred Buzhardt, explained that the defense secretary had recently ordered that they "will not collect or store information on people not affiliated with the Department of Defense." This transfer, the counsel said, seemed the best way to purge these personal records.[224]

Prior to shipping the files to the Senate, the army had investigated Van Deman's archive, concluding that "the most striking feature of the files" was his ability to collect classified information from the army, navy, and FBI, producing a wealth of detailed intelligence that was nothing less than "remarkable." On his death, the Sixth Army in San Francisco had kept his papers at the Presidio until 1968 when they were shipped to Fort Holabird, Maryland, home of the army's Counter Intelligence Corps. There they were integrated into the U.S. Army Investigative Records for the next three years, until public controversy over government surveillance of anti-Vietnam protesters prompted their transfer to the Senate Internal Security Subcommittee in 1971. "They were examined," said Senator Eastland, "and found pertinent and germaine [*sic*] to the subcommittee's purpose." In evaluating Van Deman's papers prior to the transfer, this anonymous assessor warned that "there may be some embarrassment to the Army because of the information contained on labor and civil rights movements."[225]

But this story had even more secrets to tell. Intrigued by the controversy, a *New York Times* reporter, Richard Halloran, called the FBI to confirm a tip that Van Deman's files "contained confidential reports" from both the bureau and military intelligence. The FBI issued a detailed denial, and Hoover himself remarked that the "N.Y. Times will characteristically distort the true facts." Despite the denial, Halloran pressed on to investigate the hidden political history of this private archive, finding that it may have played a significant, subterranean role in postwar California politics. Documents revealed that the general had "provided information in the 1930s and 1940s" to both HUAC under Rep. Martin Dies Jr. and the California Committee on Un-American Activities under state senator Jack Tenney. Interviewed by the *Times*, California Democrats charged that Richard Nixon's right-wing supporters had used sensitive information from the archive for the red-baiting that helped him unseat liberal U.S. representative Jerry

Voorhis in 1946 and defeat actress Helen Gahagan Douglas for the U.S. Senate in 1950. Indeed, Hugo Fisher, the former state senator for San Diego and now a Superior Court judge, recalled that "material from the files appeared in the so called 'pink sheets' distributed at rallies for Nixon and other Republicans in the 1950 campaign," an allegation aides in the Nixon White House waved away as no longer "pertinent." Other sources told the *Times* that "information from the Van Deman files went to the late senator Joseph R. McCarthy for his use against those he called Communists," a charge the senator's former aides could not confirm.[226] Two weeks after this report appeared, a *Times* editorial branded Van Deman's archive "politico-military poison." Condemning his files as "political paranoia, assembled with the inexcusable complicity of official military and civilian intelligence agencies," all of them should, the paper said, "be destroyed."[227] As their relevance diminished with time, the Senate transferred the general's files to the U.S. National Archives, where researchers gained limited access to them in the 1980s and unrestricted use only recently, making the writing of this chapter possible.[228]

At the same time the last vestige of Van Deman's legacy was being extinguished in Sacramento. After Senator Tenney's ouster from the California Un-American Activities Committee in 1949, his conservative successor chaired hearings for another twenty years until its long-serving counsel, the general's ally Richard Combs, retired in 1970. Only a year later the committee's death was foretold when the state Senate's president pro tem, James Mills, found that its twenty thousand card files contained dossiers on dozens of legislators, including himself. "I knew that if the committee saw fit to treat me as a possible subversive," he explained, "they could do the same to anyone." The California Senate dissolved the committee in March 1971 and sealed its records.[229]

But the general's legacy was not limited to a few perishable files. It lay deep within the architecture of the U.S. internal security apparatus that he had helped create, from the details of its filing system to the larger design of an imperious surveillance over American society. Fifty years after Van Deman had made the APL a civilian auxiliary to his newly established Military Intelligence Division, the illiberal influence of this state-civil security alliance was now all too apparent.

Conclusion

As illustrated by this half-century history of U.S. surveillance, the pacification of the Philippines served as both blueprint and bellwether for Washington's nascent national security state. In its search for security in the midst of revolution, the U.S. colonial regime at Manila drew untested technologies from the United States, perfected their practice, and then transmitted these refined repressive mechanisms back to the metropole, contributing to the formation of a federal internal security apparatus. Yet the expansion of this nexus in the years surrounding World War I also introduced a recurring tension between an eighteenth-century constitution and a twentieth-century capacity for mass surveillance that has persisted to the present. As the American state incorporated advanced information systems through this imperial dialectic, it cultivated a repressive capability manifest in the periodic political crises so central to many major events in U.S. political history during the past century: the red scare, the anti-Japanese hysteria, the McCarthy era, the anti-Vietnam protests, and, as will be discussed in the final chapter, illegal electronic surveillance since September 2001.

More broadly, colonial rule had a profound influence on metropolitan society, introducing an imperial mentality of coercive governance into U.S. domestic politics. Inspired by an expansive sense of dominion over colonized peoples abroad, Americans would apply similarly coercive methods to the reformation of their own society, acculturating immigrants, barring aliens, rehabilitating addicts, imposing public health measures, and policing suspected subversives. In the realm of internal security, this illiberal legacy of empire so evident inside the United States would prove, as we will see in part two, even more enduring in the postcolonial Philippines.

Part Two

Philippine National Police

A U.S. trooper stands guard outside the provincial capitol of Jolo in southern Philippines, a stronghold of the Abu Sayyaf terrorist group, during the visit of U.S. Ambassador Kristie Kenney on March 27, 2007. (Associated Press, Bullit Marquez)

10

President Quezon's Commonwealth

On November 15, 1935, the U.S. secretary of war stood before a half-million Filipinos massed in Manila's morning heat to inaugurate the Commonwealth of the Philippines. After four centuries of colonial rule, this autonomous government would control the country's internal affairs while Washington directed its foreign relations for ten more years until full independence. After the secretary of war's speech, "a thrill of expectancy, electric in its intensity, now swept through the vast audience" as the Commonwealth's president-elect, Manuel Quezon, rose from his seat. After his oath, nineteen guns roared, two short of the twenty-one for the head of a sovereign state.[1]

"From the grandstand," Quezon wrote in his memoirs, "I went through streets crowded with people acclaiming their first President, on to the Palace of Malacañang which had been the seat of power of foreign rulers for many decades past. I stepped out of the presidential car and walked over the marble floor of the entrance hall, and up the wide stairway." As he walked Quezon fell into a reverie of historic events played out in these grand halls. Here Spanish governor-generals had ruled the islands harshly, one spurning a mother who climbed these same stairs on her knees to beg for the life of her son, the national martyr Jose Rizal. Here back in 1901 the president of the defeated revolutionary republic, Gen. Emilio Aguinaldo, had sworn loyalty to America before a U.S. military governor. Abruptly, an aide interrupted Quezon's ruminations. The chief of the Philippines Constabulary, "whom I had summoned to my first official conference," was waiting.[2]

Why was President Quezon's first official act a closed-door meeting with the chief of the constabulary? Ever since he had defeated that same General Aguinaldo in the presidential elections two months before, Quezon had been living in "hourly, momentary terror of assassination" by the general's partisans. To avert what seemed certain death, the president-elect had surrounded himself with constabulary security and relied on its agents to supply him with detailed intelligence about his rival's maneuvers.[3]

As this anecdote indicates, the Philippines Constabulary was to play a critical role in the new Commonwealth, serving President Quezon as it had once served U.S. colonial governors. Whether Spanish, American, or Filipino, any executive who tried to rule this vast, disparate archipelago from Malacañang Palace would need a strong national police to reach remote islands and suppress any threats of revolt. Beginning with William Howard Taft, each U.S. governor-general had exercised control through the interweaving of law, police, and information. As the direct heir to this institutional legacy, Quezon, like his predecessors and successors, would reach reflexively for the constabulary as the strong arm of executive authority.

Since this was a negotiated transition without a revolutionary rupture, the new Commonwealth president inherited fully intact the formidable police powers of the colonial governors. In fact the new president's authority was even greater. Under U.S. rule, the governor-general's police powers had been checked by political concessions that gave local politicians command of municipal police and Filipino legislators fiscal control over the constabulary. Without a firm constitutional grounding, however, this de facto separation of police powers evaporated with the Commonwealth's inauguration in 1935. As Filipinos drafted and Americans approved a new constitution in 1934–35, both sides failed to recognize this fundamental flaw and incorporate some postcolonial checks on the executive's police powers. In the years that followed, this structural weakness embedded in the Philippine polity widened slowly to create serious, ultimately fatal fissures within the postwar Republic.

Further complicating these years of transition, the colonial regime had bequeathed to the Commonwealth its code of rigid laws against opium, prostitution, and gambling, activities whose very illegality enmeshed them in electoral politics. Politicians financed their campaigns by operating or protecting these enterprises. Local police often turned a blind eye to blatant violations in exchange for cash or political backing. In this ambiguous context the constabulary often represented the best opportunity for effective local law enforcement. While by no means immune to political influence, constabulary troops, particularly those transferred from other provinces, were usually in a better position to resist local pressures that compromised municipal police and thwarted efforts at prosecution.[4]

With independence on the horizon, Quezon would, as the founder of the future Philippine Republic, turn to the constabulary, the visible symbol of the state in the countryside, for essential elements of internal security and external defense. Indeed, at this crucial juncture the PC would soon find itself too much in demand, pulled simultaneously in competing, almost contradictory directions. Drafted to form the core of a new national army, it struggled at the same time to fulfill its customary role as a national police force. With the constabulary stretched beyond its limits, the tight nexus of local politics, police, and crime enjoyed a resurgence that would ultimately challenge the Philippines' capacity to re-create itself as a stable postcolonial nation unified by the rule of law.

Constabulary and Gambling

In the years leading up to independence, the transition from colonial to national police was greatly complicated by the integration of illegal gambling into Philippine party politics. As the costs of campaigning grew, politicians increasingly turned to illegal gambling for a steady stream of revenue. After Filipinos won full legislative powers under the Jones Act of 1916, machine politics had developed rapidly in the provinces, transforming elections from a genteel avocation into a crass operation dependent on professional political activists, or *liders,* whose demands drove up the cost of campaigning.[5] By the early 1930s on the eve of the Commonwealth, this cash-hungry system had fostered a symbiosis among police corruption, political patronage, and illegal gambling, particularly that distinctively Filipino lottery called jueteng.[6]

The crusading *Philippines Free Press* published an exposé in 1930 showing how jueteng had grown into a sophisticated racket through its unique probabilities and their interface with Filipino culture. With a one-peso bet on two combinations among just thirty-seven numbers, gamblers could win up to a thousand pesos. "The drawing power of jueteng," the magazine reported, "lies in the fact that the players believe that the proprietor's stakes are extremely high, say from ₱5,000 to ₱10,000, while the betters themselves may risk as little as one centavo." The local jueteng operator (*banquero*), usually "one of the town's foremost citizens," employed twenty to fifty collectors (*cobradores*) who circulated through streets and laneways taking countless *centavo* bets totaling some twenty pesos daily. At the close of their daily rounds, these collectors delivered their betting sheets for the nightly draw. Just as the "professional card sharker instinctively draws the desired card from the pack," so the jueteng operator, after a quick scrutiny of the tally sheets, often picked the two numbers with the lowest payout. Beyond the seductive lure of easy gains, a woman gambler, reflecting jueteng's immersion in the mystical dimension of Filipino daily life, told the *Free Press* that she, like many, drew on dreams to pick her numbers. "Once I dreamt of a person being stabbed to death by a man who afterwards stabbed himself," the woman said. "The dream was so clear . . . that the next morning when the collector came I bet on 22–29." Asked why she chose those numbers, the woman replied as if the logic were self-evident: "It is simple. A big knife was used in the stabbing which literally translated means 29, a term given to a twenty-nine inch knife . . . [and] there were two persons killed."[7] While players were mostly poor, the lottery's very illegality, the *Free Press* found, restricted its operation to the wealthy or well-connected who could protect its visible operations from the police.[8] Whether politicians actively participated or just provided protection, jueteng usually proliferated in the months before elections as political machines hemorrhaged cash to encourage a high voter turnout.[9]

Emperor of Iloilo City

In the last years of U.S. rule, this synergy of provincial politics, police corruption, and illegal gambling led to a succession of scandals. But few could equal the spectacular, yearlong controversy that erupted in Iloilo, then the country's second largest city.

In June 1929 two rising young media magnates, Eugenio and Fernando Lopez, launched their first newspaper, the Spanish-language *El Tiempo,* with a crusade against urban vice, branding the city's leading Chinese gambler, Luis "Sualoy" Sane, as the "Emperor of jueteng." Within months every edition printed the illegal lottery's winning number in a boldface box on page one, an implicit accusation of political protection and police malfeasance.[10] By October *El Tiempo* began to charge that Governor Mariano Arroyo and his allies, Iloilo City's police chief Marcelo Buenaflor and his brother Representative Tomas Buenaflor, were protecting illegal gambling through "corruption and bribes."[11]

The main object of this attack, the Arroyo family, had enjoyed a meteoric political rise since 1916 when Mariano's brother, Jose Ma. Pidal Arroyo, ran for the legislature from Iloilo's second district, launching a political career that soon made him first vice president of the ruling Nacionalista Party.[12] After he became a senator and his party's regional leader, Jose Arroyo discovered the political power of illegal gambling when the "banker" Luis Sane, already known in Manila as the "terror of Chinatown," arrived in Iloilo to become, as Arroyo put it, the "impresario of a game called jueteng."[13] In a letter to his leader, Quezon, Senator Arroyo warned of the political threat posed by the opposition's protection of Sane and his lucrative racket: "This Sualoy [Sane] is . . . secretly paying a thousand pesos a month to the current Municipal Mayor of Iloilo, who is a Democrata," an arrangement that gave their rival "a gold mine while our own candidates have empty pockets."[14]

After the senator's sudden death in March 1927, his brother, Dr. Mariano Arroyo, then director of Saint Paul's Hospital in Iloilo, assumed the leadership of the local Nacionalista Party and was elected provincial governor in October 1928.[15] To finance his political career without Manila's backing, Governor Arroyo abandoned his brother's distance from the racket and began taking bribes from Sane's jueteng syndicate, exposing himself to political attack.[16]

In October 1929 the local constabulary commander, Capt. Ramon Gaviola, responded to rising public pressure by raiding a gambling and opium den on Iznart Street, arresting fifteen Chinese smokers and two lottery runners (*cobradores*). With a brazenness that hinted at protection, the "emperor" quickly posted bail for the runners and sent them home in his flashy automobile.[17] When the city's press bannered these arrests, Governor Arroyo flatly denied the lottery's existence.[18] In its response, *El Tiempo* hinted at bribery, asking, "What mysterious hold has the 'Jueteng Boss' over some of our officials that he seems immune?"[19]

At this sensitive juncture the gambling syndicate miscalculated by trying to crush the controversy with violence. On October 10, the paper's editor, Jose Magalona, was entering the Wing Kee Restaurant in downtown Iloilo when he was attacked and badly beaten by a notorious local thug named Luis "Toldo" Elipio.[20] "Jueteng alone is responsible for this brutal aggression," *El Tiempo* thundered in a declaration of war on the governor.[21]

Through its moral crusade, *El Tiempo*'s publisher, Eugenio Lopez, skillfully courted support from the antipodes of colonial society. By charging corruption Lopez assured the intervention of the U.S. colonial executive, which had long been opposed to illegal gambling. Moreover, by bundling personal vice, Chinese criminality, and political corruption in a single scandal, the paper stirred strong popular emotions. As the news spread through the vernacular press, particularly in the respected *Makinaugalingon,* the city's poor workers responded with letters to the editor expressing outrage at this tax on the poor. "Arrest and imprison the operators for at least one month, but on each Sunday afternoon march them around every turn in the road so we can scream at them," raged one Ramon Quimsing, who signed himself "a poor man from Molo."[22]

The strong public response soon forced the constabulary to crack down more firmly. Constabulary lieutenant Gregorio Balbuena launched a lightning raid, crashing through a concealed entrance at 75 Iznart Street to catch the emperor himself "red handed" with gambling paraphernalia. In June 1930 Iloilo's Court of First Instance sentenced Sane to five months in prison and a fine of five hundred pesos. Significantly, all involved in this prosecution, from arresting officer Balbuena to the provincial *fiscal* and presiding judge, were outsiders only recently assigned to Iloilo and thus untainted by the emperor's generosity.[23]

Two months later, controversy flared anew when *El Tiempo* published a confidential constabulary report that underscored the ties between electoral politics and gambling. This sensational document cited Chief Marcelo Buenaflor's admission that he had conspired with Governor Arroyo in the operation of an illegal *monte* card game to fund their faction's campaign in the 1931 elections.[24] Within days the governor retaliated by filing a criminal libel case against *El Tiempo*'s entire staff, including its publisher, Eugenio Lopez.[25] With exceptional speed, the Justice Department dispatched a distinguished Manila judge, Manuel V. Moran, who found that the governor had in fact been attempting to amass one hundred thousand pesos to cover anticipated election expenses. "Governor Arroyo and Representative [Tomas] Buenaflor operated a gambling den . . . from March 3rd to April 13th, 1929, and," the judge wrote, "Governor Arroyo received ₱1,000 per month as his share of the gambling proceeds."[26]

In the subsequent administrative hearings initiated by *El Tiempo,* Governor Arroyo fared even worse before another special investigator, Judge Marceliano R. Montemayor.[27] Attorney Pio Sian Melliza recalled how Governor Arroyo had resisted his efforts to distance their party from jueteng. "*Compadre,*" the governor had said to Melliza, "why are you so determined to get rid of jueteng gambling? Isn't it clear to you that most of the jueteng runners and sellers are our own political *liders*? . . . Apart from the money they are giving us for election expenses, they can hurt us in this election because there are many of these jueteng runners in this province."[28]

In his report to the U.S. governor-general, Judge Montemayor found Governor Arroyo guilty of grave dereliction, stating that jueteng "had been played rather scandalously in the city of Iloilo and . . . the respondent . . . knowingly tolerated it so as not incur the displeasure and animosity of friends and political leaders." Citing the court's decision in the earlier libel case, Montemayor also found that the governor had received bribes of a thousand pesos per month from *monte* gambling.[29] In response to these findings, the governor-general suspended Chief Buenaflor and dismissed Governor Arroyo.[30] With the Arroyo family's aspirations to provincial dominance destroyed, they virtually disappeared from politics until, through the mysteries of mutual attraction, Senator Arroyo's grandson married President Diosdado Macapagal's daughter in 1968, making her the bearer of the family name as Gloria Macapagal Arroyo, later president of the Philippines.[31]

This high-stakes Iloilo scandal provides a rare insight into the underside of prewar Philippine politics. The governor's target of one hundred thousand pesos in illicit revenues indicates, for the first time, the outsized expense of these early elections and gambling's role in meeting the otherwise unsustainable costs. Of equal import this incident also shows that the period's dominant national leader, Senator Quezon, kept a judicious distance from a scandal that tarred all who touched it. Even though the controversy represented a devastating blow to his party in the country's second-largest city, Quezon remained aloof and ignored increasingly desperate communications from Governor Arroyo.[32] With the Senate president uninvolved, the governor-general impartial, and the constabulary largely apolitical, this spectacular instance of police corruption lacked the national linkages that would have sparked a legitimation crisis for the colony's leading political party.

Jueteng in Pampanga

In Iloilo City the dispatch of constabulary officers had cut through the symbiosis among illicit gambling, cash-hungry politics, and compromised policing. While municipal police had capitulated to local pressures, PC officers from the outside were in a better position to resist these dynamics, making arrests and pursuing prosecutions. But a similar scandal in the town of Masantol, Pampanga, illustrates that there were limits to what even an efficient constabulary could accomplish against the country's entrenched gambling culture.

After Masantol residents complained that their municipal secretary, Alejandro Bamba, was running an illegal jueteng lottery, the PC's provincial commander, Maj. Paciano Tangco, ordered a routine raid. On March 3, 1933, Lt. Lauro Dizon swept the town with troops from the Sixty-first PC Company, apprehending several suspects with incriminating gambling paraphernalia. Arriving at the town hall to book these suspects, the lieutenant suddenly found himself confronted by a violent mob and telephoned his provincial commander for support. With Pampanga's governor in tow, Major Tangco rushed to Masantol to find the telephone line cut, the constabulary car's tires slashed, one of his officers badly beaten, and his troopers surrounded by an angry mob that filled the municipal hall. Instead of jailing the suspects, local officials, led by Secretary Bamba, demanded their release. Through the governor's intervention, the town police finally agreed to accept custody of the suspects, defusing a dangerous situation.

Despite bitter local opposition, Major Tangco continued his pressure on the province's jueteng syndicates in the months that followed. Tangco wrote Governor Pablo Angeles in December about the "widespread and scandalous gambling situation in the province," requesting "appropriate action." Instead, the province's dominant Nacionalista faction—led by Governor Angeles and former interior secretary Honorio Ventura—urged the constabulary to drop the charges against Secretary Bamba, a local *lider* whose support the governor considered crucial to his reelection. Meanwhile, the new PC chief, Gen. George Bowers, pressed Major Tangco to accept a transfer to far-off Sulu under generous terms. Within three weeks Lieutenant Dizon was transferred and Tangco soon followed, producing what the major called a "complete change of officers . . . in a determined effort to block the prosecution" just two days before Bamba's gambling trial. Although these transfers failed to achieve that immediate end—Pampanga's courts found Bamba guilty—they did demonstrate the governor's "power and political strength before the masses, especially in protecting the gambling element."[33] So successful was this strategy that Angeles won reelection.

Three months later, after elections were over and General Bowers had retired, Senator Quezon wrote the new chief of constabulary, a Filipino officer named Basilio Valdes, arguing that Major Tango's transfer to Sulu had been politically motivated and asking for his return to Pampanga. Under such pressure the chief eventually ordered Tangco back to the province. Unsubdued, the province's political boss, Honorio Ventura, assured his supporters that the major would "not remain long in Pampanga" because "the present Chief of Constabulary owed him many favors."[34] Although justice was done in this case, if only momentarily, its complexity suggests the increasing connections among provincial politics, jueteng gambling, and police graft. Once again Senator Quezon, as his nation's future leader, had demonstrated an uncommon circumspection toward both the constabulary and jueteng.

Manila Vice

While antigambling enforcement in the provinces was often compromised by an alliance among politicians, police, and racketeers, these challenges were amplified in Manila by the growth of fluid criminal syndicates within a resilient vice economy and protection that reached from the streets to the secretary of the interior. As the emerging Philippine state struggled to cope with this colonial legacy of problematic vice laws, the constabulary launched a wave of crackdowns and the legislature offered a legal alternative to gambling by establishing a charity sweepstakes. Throughout these years, however, the vice trades would continue to flourish, resisting both hard and soft responses.

At the close of direct U.S. rule, Manila's police were caught on the cusp of this political transition, while simultaneously suffering budgetary restraints during the Great Depression that barred the recruitment of new patrolmen. As the city's population tripled to 620,000 during the three decades of U.S. rule, Manila grew large enough to sustain a thriving vice economy. By the early 1930s opium, illegal gambling, and prostitution, all suppressed during the previous decade, suddenly revived. Compounding the problem, inner-city criminals developed a formidable syndication that challenged the capacities of the Metropolitan Police.

Despite years of Filipinization in many areas, the U.S. colonial executive seemed reluctant to appoint Manila's first Filipino chief of police when John W. Green retired in 1929. For nearly a year, while the U.S. regime agonized over conceding such power to a Filipino, Assistant Chief Gregorio M. Alcid served as acting chief and seemed determined to prove himself worthy by raiding the city's vice dives and purging crooked cops.[35]

Alcid's best efforts had little impact. The notorious opium "dictator" Benito Rivera Yap, sentenced to a year's imprisonment, delegated his traffic to his lieutenants and fled to China while free on appeal. Syndicate leader Ang Kim Suy got off with a mere fine, a recommendation made by PC chief Charles E. Nathorst and accepted by Interior Secretary Honario Ventura.[36] In a further attempt to break what he termed Manila's "police-criminal combine," Chief Alcid launched internal investigations, the first in nearly twenty years, and identified twenty-nine tainted policemen. Although most were soon removed from the service, two senior American officers implicated "in certain anomalies" resisted, complaining to Governor-General Dwight Davis that the acting chief's charges were racially motivated. In the end Davis, citing Manila's "metropolitan population," passed over Alcid for permanent chief and appointed a colonial veteran, Columbus E. Piatt, whose long service in the traffic division soon proved ill-suited to the surge of criminal gangs and syndicated vice.[37]

By 1930 Manila's Filipino districts were disturbed by street gangs fighting turf wars over the city's cabarets and residents feared their violent rampages. To cope with the city's rising number of "unsolved and apparently unsolvable crimes," in early 1932 the colonial regime appointed Col. Juan Dominguez, the former head of the PC's Intelligence Division, as the first Filipino chief of Manila's secret service detectives. To strengthen enforcement the colonial executive's capital reorganization committee added one hundred officers in 1934, raising Manila's police-citizen ratio to 1:407, far denser than the national average of 1:1,525.[38]

In their efforts to tackle gambling, the police faced the same political barriers to effective enforcement in both capital and countryside. Although they had raided Manila's largest *monte* syndicate, known jocularly as the Partida Mayor (Party in Power), in 1928, the *Tribune* reported just three years later that the syndicate was running several games openly. Police knew the location of these houses, but the operators were tipped off and the premises were almost always empty when officers broke through the door. When one of these raids was finally successful, the result was a minor scandal. In 1932 a veteran American patrolman, Jackson F. Townsend, raided the elite Carambola Club on orders from Chief Piatt, apprehending seven leading Filipino officials in the middle of a high-stakes *monte* game, including Commerce Undersecretary Cipriano Unson, Director of Lands Serafin Hilado, Representative Enrique Magalona, and Capiz governor Rafael Acuña. After months of political intrigue, the judge issued a convoluted, ninety-five-page decision dismissing all charges against these illustrious gamblers and discouraging further raids.[39]

Weak enforcement also plagued the suburbs. Since 1918, when the city closed down the Gardenia red light district, prostitution and commercial vice spread steadily through roadhouses at the city's suburban fringe, fostering a vice zone of roadside brothels and gambling joints with tough gangsters and compromised local governments. To the north in Caloocan, La Loma district had a cluster of gang-infested cabarets that made it Manila's "Hell's Kitchen." To the east the twisting streets of San Juan concealed a half-dozen illegal casinos. In the southeast along the Pasay-McKinley Road, the notorious Culi-Culi brothel district serviced the nearby military barracks. In the south brothels dotted Baclaran and lined F. B. Harrison Street from Pasay to the Manila boundary. Periodic police campaigns, one in 1925 and another in 1931, could not break this nexus among the vice syndicates, crooked police, and local politics.[40]

By 1928 suburban corruption had become so serious that the constabulary took control of the police in nine towns ringing Manila. After investigators discovered an integration of vice and local politics in eleven more towns, the governor-general suspended six municipal presidents and eight police chiefs.

The constabulary soon found that Malabon's president, Teofilo Santos, headed the local jueteng ring. "The municipality of Makati," reported investigator Dr. Rufino Luna, "is characterized by an abundance of houses of prostitution and by all forms of gambling." Although Dr. Luna recommended long suspensions for corrupt officials in all eleven towns investigated, Interior Secretary Ventura, citing the "proximity" of the upcoming legislative elections, reduced the penalty to forty days. Two years later the *Free Press* conducted a midnight probe "into the heart of Manila's vice-ridden suburbs" and found fifty-three roadhouses operating openly in seven municipalities. At the Oriental Cabaret reporters watched while the madame bargained down her payments to two Parañaque policemen from thirty-five to twenty-five pesos. Apart from such blatant bribes, suburban towns tolerated the roadhouses because they accounted for nearly a quarter of their municipal tax revenues.[41] Just south of Manila, Laguna Province matched the capital's mix of politics and illegal gambling in ways that defeated the constabulary's four-year campaign against its local jueteng syndicates. The largest of these rackets was headed by a woman identified in the press only as "the Señora" but widely known to be the wife of the governor, Juan Cailles.[42]

In the last months of direct colonial rule, the legislature had tried to contain jueteng and its graft by establishing a legal lottery called the Philippine Charity Sweepstakes. Seeking to placate both ends of the moral spectrum, the state lottery linked the drawings to horse races and dedicated the proceeds to charity. After the first sweepstakes winners were drawn in early 1934, the press polled the country's moral leaders and discovered strong opposition. "Lotteries are a crime," proclaimed Archbishop Gregorio Aglipay of the Independent Church, insisting they would teach young people "the gambling habit" and turn them into "criminals."[43] By the time of the fourth draw in September 1935, however, the press had lost interest in the moral question and began enthusiastic reporting on the winners, portraying them as worthy members of the middle class. Coverage in the *Free Press,* for example, featured the third-prize winner, Dr. Antonio Ejercito, an uncle of the future president Joseph Estrada, describing him as a "very religious man." Although enriched by a hefty cash prize of ₱19,500, readers learned, Dr. Ejercito had not succumbed to the lure of easy money and left for work at the Bureau of Health at his usual time of 8:00 a.m. sharp.[44]

Despite its nationwide sales, the sweepstakes could not displace local jueteng syndicates. With infrequent draws, expensive tickets, and low incentives for vendors, it failed to challenge jueteng's appeal for ordinary Filipinos. In May 1935, for example, *Philippines Herald* reporters learned that the illegal lottery was thriving in the provinces ringing Manila. Revisiting Laguna, where the *Free Press* had exposed the señora's syndicate two years before, the reporter Hernando J. Abaya found that "the wife of a ranking government official" he coyly called the "*generala*" operated a lottery in the province's second district that grossed seven thousand pesos daily and garnered a million in profits every year. In Laguna's largest towns, Abaya reported, jueteng supervisors called *cabos* circulated through the neighborhoods brazenly shouting out winning numbers.[45] In its lead editorial, the *Herald* thundered against the "jueteng cancer," charging, quite accurately, that any official not blind or deaf knew "jueteng is firmly rooted in the Tagalog provinces of Luzon today."[46]

Politics of Transition

While the constabulary rarely succumbed to the pressures that compromised local law enforcement, it proved vulnerable to political influence at the national level. Long deployed as the strong arm of the U.S. governor-general, the constabulary attached itself, during the transition to the autonomous Commonwealth, to the front-runner in the race for the presidency well before the outcome of the 1935 elections. By offering Senate president Quezon both political intelligence and physical protection, constabulary commanders laid the groundwork for a close relationship with the new Philippine executive and created the potential for arbitrary, even abusive authority.

During his long tenure as the country's leading legislator, Senator Quezon had worked tirelessly to exercise some influence over the constabulary's officer corps, advancing Filipino clients in the middle ranks and courting senior American staff officers. In his first years as Senate president after 1916, Quezon's authority over the constabulary had been limited to petty patronage.[47] Gradually, however, by approving legislation for promotions and pay, he won the loyalty of the officer corps. In 1924, for example, PC chief Rafael Crame wrote Quezon to plead for passage of a constabulary pension bill, saying that "the members of the corps consider you their Savior and chosen Champion."[48]

When PC chief Nathorst finally stepped down in late 1932, Quezon struggled unsuccessfully to influence the selection of his successor. Angry at not being consulted, he wrote the governor-general in February 1933 to protest the appointment of Col. George Bowers—a distinguished officer whom Quezon had long considered a political enemy.[49] "I have told you," he wrote, "that Col. Bowers was not very rigid in the persecution of gambling houses when some prominent politician was connected to it." He also complained that the constabulary under General Nathorst and Interior Secretary Ventura had been "subject to political influences and has lost greatly in discipline and efficiency." As the Senate leader charged with confirming these appointments, Quezon insisted that he was "entitled to be heard."[50]

While the advent of the Commonwealth brought the Nacionalista Party to the gates of Malacañang Palace, ambitious constabulary officers sought Quezon's patronage. Few could surpass Maj. Silvino Gallardo's assiduous, even shameless courtship. For some years before the 1935 presidential elections, the major had attempted to ingratiate himself with the senator, first to advance and later to revive his career. In 1929 his ambitions had suffered a near fatal blow after he was removed as head of customs' secret service for permitting the importation of illegal gaming cards and smoking opium.[51] Now in the months leading up to the 1935 election, the major served as Quezon's informal campaign manager in vote-rich Iloilo Province where he was PC provincial commander.[52] Three days before the September balloting, the major promised Quezon "the biggest majority ever registered in the history of th[is] region."[53] As predicted, Quezon won a substantial majority in a province that had long been an opposition bastion.[54] Throughout these elections Gallardo had compromised his standing as an impartial defender of public order by providing Quezon's faction with valuable electoral services that included tracking polls, internal party investigations, and physical security. Nor was he alone. A month before the elections, PC headquarters filed its own report to Quezon on "political undercurrents" with data culled from units conducting similarly partisan operations across the archipelago.[55]

In the 1935 presidential campaign Quezon also turned to the constabulary for personal security, public order, and covert controls. After the Commonwealth presidential campaign began in June, ex-general Emilio Aguinaldo, the candidate for the National Socialist Party, soon realized he would be crushed by Quezon's formidable machine and reacted angrily, publicly charging fraud and privately threatening murder. Just days before the voting on September 15, the Quezon-controlled *Philippines Herald* denounced Aguinaldo and the other leading opposition candidate, Bishop Gregorio Aglipay, declaring that "their very breaths smell of assassination." When Quezon won a crushing 69 percent of the vote against Aguinaldo's 17 percent and Aglipay's 14 percent, the general attacked his rival's "abuse of power" and refused to concede.[56]

In the election's bitter aftermath, the rising tensions between Quezon and Aguinaldo threatened assassination, armed uprising, or both. In a confidential report to its superintendent, the constabulary's Intelligence Division described the "high tension" at a September 21 meeting of the general's Nationalist Socialist Party in Manila, with speakers "lambasting the entire government machinery in having coordinated smoothly to defeat GEA [General Emilio Aguinaldo]." When Aguinaldo spoke, claiming that the government had stolen fifty thousand votes from his final tally, the "irresponsible elements present . . . murmured, 'Ayan ang mabuti, revolucion na!' [That's good, it's time for revolution!]"[57]

Just two days later the constabulary's confidential Agent 110 called on the deputy intelligence chief, Capt. Jose P. Guido, to warn of a possible assassination attempt against Quezon. After asking for the strictest secrecy to protect his identity, the agent reported that "it is General Aguinaldo's plan to have President Quezon and Senator Osmeña assassinated in order that another election would be held."[58] A week later the constabulary's Cavite commander reached a similar conclusion during an otherwise "cordial" visit to General Aguinaldo at his home in Kawit. Speaking with great indignation, the general had dismissed the elections as "dirty and highly corrupted" because the entire government machinery had "campaigned openly and scandalously for the candidacy of President Quezon." Now, he said, "the only way to free the government of undesirable officials and save the people from suffering, hardships, and miseries is to put down President Quezon." By the end of this visit, the captain said of the general, "I could infer or read that he is nursing a sinister or evil design to assassinate President Quezon."[59]

The main threat came from the hundreds, sometimes thousands of General Aguinaldo's supporters, many members of his Veteranos de la Revolucion, who met nightly in the yard of his Kawit mansion just south of Manila. Addressing five hundred supporters who gathered there on October 1, the speakers were particularly incendiary according to constabulary spies. "I will prove to you that President Quezon is the most pernicious man in the Philippines," proclaimed Porfirio de Juan. The next speaker, Dominador Poblete, was even more visceral, speaking openly of scandal mentioned only sotto voce in Manila. "Quezon is a living Judas," he said, "You know Judas cohabited with his mother but President Quezon has a child with his god-daughter that Miss Philippines from Tayabas. We should get rid of persons like Quezon who is the enemy of our independence." When Poblete asked what should be done, the crowd shouted with one voice, "Mag revolution na" [It's time to rebel].[60] At another meeting a prominent Aguinaldo follower swore to kill Quezon and asked the crowd, "Who else will volunteer to give his life away if I fail?" According to a PC spy, over five hundred volunteered to a roar of approval. Although the general disavowed these death threats, he moved ahead with plans to mobilize fifty thousand followers to protest Quezon's inauguration on November 15.[61]

Under constant threat of assassination, president-elect Quezon surrounded himself day and night with constabulary security. His limousine moved in an armed cavalcade. The palace grounds swarmed with guards. He slept aboard the presidential yacht anchored in Manila Bay. To quiet the violent bombast at Aguinaldo's house, the constabulary occupied the general's hometown, checking buses for guns and taking the names of those who attended the nightly meetings. In late October, just three weeks before his inauguration, Quezon pleaded with Governor-General Frank Murphy for a U.S. Army attack on Aguinaldo's home. The governor, surprised by this suggestion from such an ardent nationalist, replied that it was "unthinkable that a single Filipino should be killed by an American soldier." As inauguration day approached, Governor Murphy met privately with Aguinaldo and, through a mix of blunt threats and Irish charm, persuaded him not to disrupt the proceedings.[62]

At the broadest level the 1935 presidential election was the fulfillment of the colonial constabulary's political mission. In its first, formative decade, 1901 to 1911, the constabulary's Information Division had shaped the direction of Filipino politics, discrediting radical nationalists such as Archbishop Aglipay and advancing more pliable, younger leaders such as its secret operative Manuel Quezon. In a striking case of historical symmetry, these former antagonists within the constabulary's worldview became principals in a political showdown over the country's future direction thirty years later. Personified by the candidacies of General Aguinaldo and Archbishop Aglipay, the opposition represented the militant nationalism of the 1896 revolution, the very ideals the old constabulary had worked so diligently to destroy. The winning coalition candidates, Senate president Quezon and former Speaker Sergio Osmeña, were former constabulary protégés who represented the patronage politics that the U.S. regime had struggled so hard to build. With these first presidential elections of 1935 the constabulary's greatest political task was complete. The electorate had repudiated the radical nationalism that had inspired the revolution and embraced an inherently conservative patronage politics, with lasting consequences for the country's future.

After a peaceful inauguration, President Quezon assumed a statesmanlike posture toward the constabulary, but could not escape the executive's habit of using this force as the strong arm of central authority. Instead of trying to influence promotions and postings as part of the anticolonial struggle, Quezon, as the new commander in chief, took steps to restrain the clientelist politics he had once played. In January 1936 he declared that it was his "fixed policy not to permit the retention of Constabulary officers in the same province for too long a time especially when they have relatives in that province." The rigid application of this policy, Quezon hoped, would disabuse "our masses [who] still have the idea . . . kinship is a consideration which influences public officials in their official acts."[63]

But partisan loyalty still had its rewards. Only weeks after taking office, President Quezon ordered that all constabulary promotions below the rank of colonel should follow "strict seniority" and merit. Chief Basilio Valdes scrutinized the PC roster and found three officers unworthy of promotion to lieutenant colonel, including Quezon's old protégé Major Gallardo whose 1930 customs case had "soiled to a great extent the good name of the Constabulary."[64] Gallardo somehow survived and later won both promotion to lieutenant colonel and a posting as regional commander for the Visayas with his headquarters at Cebu City, coincidentally the home of Quezon's intraparty rival, Vice President Osmeña.[65] The contradiction between the constabulary's role as an apolitical national police force and its partisan uses as the strong arm of executive authority would deepen as the attenuation of colonial authority left this unsheathed sword in the hands of successive Philippine presidents.

State Police

Under U.S. rule the constabulary had distinguished itself among the colony's security services as an efficient arm of colonial authority that was relatively resistant to local corruption. Consequently, as early as 1914 Quezon had advocated the eventual conversion of the constabulary to a Philippine national army.[66] Twenty years later, when he was in a position to implement this proposal, he found ready support for his plan. With the PC compelled to shift its limited resources from law enforcement to national defense, the result was a political vacuum that another police force could not fill.

With the Commonwealth on the horizon in 1934, planning for the constabulary's future role in national defense added an urgent, undeniable issue that mitigated but did not eliminate severe budgetary pressures. Both the governor-general and the legislature agreed that the force should expand to become the foundation for a national army. To ease the transition to Filipino governance, in April Governor Murphy appointed two Filipinos to lead the constabulary, replacing General Bowers with Colonel Valdes as PC chief and Col. Charles Livingston with Col. Guillermo Francisco as chief of staff. At about the same time, debates over defense policy in the constitutional convention produced a consensus that the constabulary should serve as the basis for both the national army and a new state police, lending a certain ambiguity, if not confusion, to the nascent government's defense policy.[67]

In July 1934, elected delegates assembled at Manila to draft a new constitution for both the Commonwealth and the future Philippine Republic that defined the character of the Philippine presidency and its relation to the country's security services, particularly the constabulary. Lifted almost verbatim from the Jones Act of 1916, Article VII of the new charter created an empowered executive, not found in the U.S. Constitution, by providing: "In case of invasion, insurrection, or rebellion, or imminent danger thereof, when the public safety requires it, he [the president] may suspend the privileges of the writ of habeas corpus, or place the Philippines or any part thereof under martial law."[68] Moreover, the new executive assumed the colonial governor's authority as commander in chief of the security forces, both the constabulary, with its broad police powers, and any new external defense force.[69]

With independence just ten years away, national defense became the most critical issue facing the Commonwealth. After his inauguration in 1935, President Quezon was faced with the problem of building a national army from the boots up. In December he signed Commonwealth Act No. 1, known as the National Defense Act, making mobilization his top priority and committing a quarter of his budget to the development of a national army that would have ten thousand regular soldiers and four hundred thousand reserves by the time independence was granted in 1945. Three weeks later, under Executive Order 11, he integrated the constabulary into the army.[70] For the next two years the constabulary would be the new army's First Regular Division under an old PC veteran, Gen. Jose de los Reyes.[71]

Once mobilization began, the Philippine Army found that formation of an officer corps was its most intractable problem. The new force drew its candidates from diverse sources: the few Filipino graduates of West Point, who were mostly serving in the Philippine Scouts; the larger number of college reservists; and, most important, constabulary veterans. About 80 percent of the officers in the First Regular Division were reservists who rotated through for a few months to learn leadership, largely from constabulary veterans, before moving on to staff basic-training centers in the provinces.[72] Constabulary veterans assumed key commands in the new army, including its chief of staff, Maj. General Paulino Santos; the deputy chief of staff, Brig. Gen. Basilio Valdes; and its commanding officer, Brig. Gen. Guillermo Francisco. Clearly, at multiple levels the constabulary was the "foundation" of the country's new military forces.[73]

Incorporation of the constabulary into the army solved the problem of national defense, but it created another in the realm of law enforcement. Internal order, a major preoccupation of the colonial state, was relegated to a secondary role under the Commonwealth. Building upon just eighty-seven hundred municipal police and five thousand constabulary, this transitional regime had limited resources with which to provide both external defense and internal order, placing enormous pressure on its finite coercive capacities.[74] In constructing a new state, the president was forced to experiment with police reforms, balancing partisan and national interest to produce one lasting innovation and one dismal failure.

The creation of a nonpartisan, professional investigative agency was Quezon's greatest success in the realm of policing. In November 1936 the legislature passed Commonwealth Act. No. 181 forming a new Division of Investigation (DI) inside the Justice Department. With the assistance of two U.S. advisers—Capt. Thomas Dunn of the New York City Police and Flaviano Guerrero, the only Filipino in the FBI—the new agency was organized as a national crime detection unit. With three thousand applicants for forty-eight posts, the new division set high standards, a law degree and rigorous examinations, to form a staff of forensic experts and skilled investigators. During the difficult years of postwar reconstruction, these specialists would rebuild their agency as the National Bureau of Investigation (NBI), again infusing it with high professional standards.[75]

By contrast, Quezon's attempt to form a unified state police force produced the only major political defeat of his presidency. After the constabulary became "the nucleus of the Philippine Army" in January 1936, for the next ten months the country's internal order was left in the hands of hundreds of ill-trained municipal police forces. In October the legislature passed Commonwealth Act No. 88 integrating all city, municipal, and provincial police into a new State Police under the Department of Interior. As one press account put it, the legislation aimed to end the practice of municipal mayors treating the police "like a muchacho" and instead create "a force of 12,000 men under one command." Through the efforts of the commissioner of public safety, Quezon loyalist Leon Guinto, all municipal police were soon brought under civil service regulations and a centralized budget.[76]

Although the scheme was, in the words of the political scientist Joseph Hayden, "well conceived, well planned, and ideally headed," it collapsed in just eighteen months. Indeed, the new national force died so quickly that Lt. Col.

Emmanuel Bajá, the country's leading police expert, dismissed it as "the wild dream of creating an efficient State Police out of the ruins and debris of the admittedly inefficient town policemen."[77] By late 1937 the State Police officers, recruited largely from troubled municipal police forces, were proving inadequate, and the constabulary was forced by painful degrees to once again devote the bulk of its resources to law enforcement rather than defense.[78] In effect Quezon's first attempt at balancing external defense and internal security had produced an unworkable compromise, neither fully releasing the constabulary from its new role in national defense nor fully restoring it to its former role in law enforcement.

In a second attempt at major reform, President Quezon changed tack and made the constabulary the core of a radically reconstituted national police that incorporated and subordinated municipal forces.[79] In June 1938, only two years after founding the State Police, the legislature passed Commonwealth Act No. 343 partially detaching the constabulary from the army and reestablishing it as the constitutionally mandated "national police force." While the legislature's act placed the constabulary at the beck and call of local police, Quezon issued Executive Order 153, attempting to reverse that relationship and instead place local police under constabulary supervision. This directive also made "the Chief of Constabulary . . . directly responsible to the President for the execution of all police duties." Through this political legerdemain, Quezon effectively redoubled his authority over the police, sparking a storm of opposition from municipal officials. Two months later the provincial governors "were loud in their protest" against the president's order and sent him a detailed memo objecting to executive control of municipal police as an infringement on local autonomy.[80]

Within months Quezon bowed to these protests. Under Executive Order 175 of November 11, 1938, the president took a first step, stating that governors would be "directly responsible for the efficient functioning . . . of police within their respective provinces" and mayors were "charged with direct responsibility for the efficient operation of the local police force." A month later he retreated further and suddenly transferred "all the powers and duties reserved to the president" for police supervision to his interior secretary, ending, after just four months, what the press called his "direct control of the local police forces."[81] In his state of the nation address a few weeks later, Quezon attempted to explain his recent actions, saying that law enforcement was "not properly a military responsibility," but "the necessity for using the Constabulary . . . as the nucleus out of which to establish the Army's foundation" had created the need for a "temporary consolidation." Consequently, in January 1939 he transferred the constabulary back to the Department of Interior and in November placed the now separate army under his newly formed Defense Department. Despite this administrative division, Quezon also ordered that constabulary officers would "retain their identities and legal rights" as army officers.[82] By late 1938 the constabulary was once more the national police, restored to its old strength of 350 officers and 4,500 men, and again charged, this time by Interior Secretary Rafael Alunan, with "avoiding all political entanglements" and eradicating gambling, "especially jueteng."[83]

By reestablishing the constabulary as a national police force, the president had, in a rare diminution of his powers, conceded mayoral control over municipal police checked only by loose constabulary supervision. Through all these fitful changes local police under the Commonwealth once again became creatures of the town mayors, just as they had been under U.S. colonial rule.[84] Although Quezon had lost control over municipal police, he retained his hold on the constabulary and soon found a new way to control some local police through the creation of chartered cities. Under Commonwealth legislation, the president could establish new cities by decree and appoint their mayors, who, in turn, supervised their local police. In effect the president extended direct executive control to newly chartered cities that now sprouted like weeds across the archipelago, including Baguio, Tagaytay, Cebu, Iloilo, Bacolod, Davao, and his new national capital, Quezon City. By the late 1930s the police chiefs in many of these cities were active-duty constabulary officers who answered directly to Quezon as their commander in chief.[85]

Throughout these years of politicking over the constabulary, Quezon also maintained his executive control over Manila's police, long a bastion of colonial power. After an unbroken succession of seven American chiefs that ended with Columbus E. Piatt's retirement in early 1936, Quezon made a political statement by appointing Manila's first Filipino chief of police. But in a partisan move the president passed over long-serving assistant chief Gregorio Alcid, a respected professional, for Antonio C. Torres, a sometime city councilor and Manila socialite who was married to the president's former fiancée. The son of a Supreme Court justice, Torres had learned his police skills as a spy for Col. Henry McCoy in the bitter customs intrigues of 1907–9. After marrying Corazon Chiong Veloso of Cebu in 1916, Torres used her brother-in-law, Speaker Sergio Osmeña, to win a succession of minor patronage posts. As Manila's police chief for five years under the Commonwealth, 1936–41, his action against vice was restrained by kinship ties, through his wife, to several of the city's leading gamblers—a source of periodic press scandals that did not lessen the protection he provided his lowlife relations.[86]

Under the Commonwealth as well, Manila's mayor Juan Posadas, another Quezon loyalist, appointed about a thousand "special agents" to report on criminals and maintain order. Using the threat of radical protests as a pretext, the mayor began appointing "special detectives" to gather "advanced confidential and valuable information." The Commonwealth's public safety commissioner, Leon Guinto, found these special agents, who were armed with revolvers and free from regulations, "repugnant." Finally, the president intervened, issuing Executive Order 175 of 1938, which required presidential approval for the appointment of the "special agents," a solution that further strengthened executive control over Manila's force.[87]

Quezon's Vice Crusade

Under this politicized police leadership, Manila's illegal gaming clubs revived, becoming a new source of political controversy. Just as jueteng catered to the rural masses, so these clandestine casinos met the capital's demand for a high-roller lifestyle. Filipino operators, long restrained by American-led police raids, flourished under the Commonwealth's more permissive rule, opening some thirty to forty illegal clubs. As word spread on the international gaming circuit that Manila was wide open, shadowy foreign operators arrived to set up ritzy clubs with Filipino silent partners. In 1938 the American gangster Ted Lewin, a veteran of mob-run gambling cruises off the California coast, opened a small casino inside the Alcazar Club downtown on Avenida-Rizal. With well-connected Filipino partners, he operated undisturbed by the police until the outbreak of war.[88]

In response to this upsurge in racketeering, President Quezon, like his American predecessors, insisted on strict enforcement of the country's harsh vice laws. Although he would soften the colonial laws slightly through selective decriminalization, his tactics were essentially the same and his solutions equally unsuccessful. Predictably, the president's campaign met strong resistance from local politicians along Manila's suburban fringe. In San Juan, for example, the constabulary ordered the mayor to stop posting police officers to protect the town's five illegal casinos, which were hidden behind the high walls of palatial homes—including the most notorious club operated by ex-senator Jose Ma. Veloso.

But it was Laguna Province just south of Manila that became the main battleground for Quezon's crusade. Calling on the National Assembly to impose tougher penalties in September 1937, the president condemned jueteng as a "criminal racketeering business" that victimized the poor.[89] Simultaneously, State Police commissioner Leon Guinto told the province's police chiefs that 90 percent of their men were on syndicate payrolls.[90] When Calamba's police chief proved reluctant to act, Inspector Ramon Mijares swooped down on the town with raids marked by "midnight chases, police sirens screeching, shots in the dark, and fist fights." After a month of police pressure, however, the largest lottery in the capital, Santa Cruz, run by the governor's wife, was still active and Calamba soon had at least three jueteng draws back in action. Even after a two-year campaign marked by the arrest of two town councilors who ran local lotteries, suspension of three municipal police chiefs, and wholesale police transfers, the racket was still flourishing.[91]

The Commonwealth's later campaign against Manila's vice syndicates suffered a similar fate. In February 1939 Interior Secretary Rafael Alunan issued "a declaration of war" against Manila's "commercialized gambling." This fight soon foundered on the ubiquitous gaming culture and the concomitant corruption that had frustrated earlier efforts. In June Manila's new two-fisted tabloid, *The News Behind the News*, launched volume one, number one with the sensational front-page headline "Swanky Gambling Dens Unmolested!" Beneath this bold print, the owner of the Exclusive Club on T. Pinpin Street in Binondo, recently padlocked on orders from Mayor Posadas, charged that the antigambling drive had become a pretext for police shakedowns. "From 30 to 40 clubs in the city are not molested," the Exclusive's proprietor Marciano Almario wrote the interior secretary. "The members of this police unit and the mayor's agents are . . . insatiable parasites. They go from one club to another exacting bribes from gamekeepers."[92]

This tangle of graft finally ensnared two prominent figures in a sordid tabloid scandal. In early April the Manila Police raided an illegal card game at the Great Eastern Hotel, arresting its promoters, Joe and Nick Osmeña, wastrel sons of the Commonwealth vice president Sergio Osmeña. Ten days later city councilor Hermenegildo Atienza accused the authorities of "cowardice and partiality" for failing to charge the Osmeña boys since their uncle was Manila's police chief, Antonio C. Torres. When the police finally filed charges, the Great Eastern's manager, an American named Thomas J. Mildren, tried to fix the case by paying two room boys, the only eye witnesses, fifty pesos each for their silence.[93] With its usual Manichean script, the press portrayed the youthful Councilor Atienza as a lone crusader battling powerful criminal forces.

Within days the story became more complex when hotel manager Mildren, under a "veiled threat" from the police, called Joe Osmeña to a house in Pasay for a private meeting. While the two discussed their gambling deals, four witnesses listened through hidden microphones: Police Chief Torres, Maj. Jose Guido of the PC's Intelligence Division, and two DI technicians operating a Dictagraph tape recorder. Apparently unaware that anyone was listening, Mildren tried to calm Joe Osmeña's anger at Atienza, explaining that the councilor was central to their plans for a "string of roadhouses or nightclubs outside the city limits." To expand his current operations, Mildren said he had collected twelve hundred pesos from six club owners as a payoff for Atienza and other councilors if they agreed to vote for extended club hours.[94]

When this transcript made page one in mid-May, its impact was surprisingly muted. The man who would be casino king, Thomas Mildren, sailed for Australia that same day, reportedly fearing "serious harm" from Chief Torres. In a detailed letter to the mayor dated June 3, also released to the press, the chief used Mildren's bribe allegations to smear his accuser, Councilor Atienza. The press, immediately convinced of Atienza's corruption, now delighted in exposing his scandals, producing a blaze of negative publicity that later prompted his dismissal by the president. Meanwhile, the vice president's boulevardier son Joe Osmeña soon racked up three more arrests.[95] Like Osborne Wood, son of the former governor-general Leonard Wood, this young man created scandals faster than his well-connected relatives could silence them.

Confronted with this metropolitan miasma, President Quezon began looking to selective legalization of gambling as the solution. Rather than raid Manila's illegal clubs and round up their elite clientele, his government began licensing jai alai as a legal alternative. With President Quezon's support, the Games and Amusement Board granted a twenty-five-year license to the Jai Alai Corporation, which was controlled by several of his close cronies led by financier Vicente Madrigal. In September 1940 Basque players called *pelotaris* began nightly competitions in the city's stylish art-deco fronton, attracting well-heeled gamblers to the courtside seats and society's elite to the swanky Sky Room for dinner, drinks, and dancing. The corporation took a hefty 14 percent share of all pari-mutuel bets, but the game's society clientele were indifferent gamblers and the stock price sank. The corporation was struggling to turn a profit when the Japanese army marched into Manila just a few weeks later. In November 1942 the fronton reopened on orders from the Japanese military and for the first time became profitable by serving a mass clientele. With war and runaway inflation fueling a frenzy of black market speculation, the games were packed with rough crowds of laborers, clerks, and buy-sell traders who had no other outlet for their gaming passions.[96]

The Commonwealth's parallel attempt to break the nexus between Manila's corrupt police and the city's vice syndicates suffered a similarly dismal fate. Concerned over reports of bribery, the head of the new State Police, Leon Guinto, formed a three-man committee in September 1937 to review the records of every Manila policeman. After a nine-month investigation the committee recommended dismissal of nearly 20 percent, or 178 out of 900 city police. Despite public pressure for a purge, political patrons blocked any action until President Quezon appointed his party's regional boss, Eulogio Rodriguez, as mayor of Manila three years later. Within six months of taking office in January 1940, the new mayor had fired seven secret service detectives and suspended eighteen policemen, including two lieutenants. Calling police morals "scandalous," the mayor said many were led into corruption to support their *queridas* (mistresses) and promised that seventy more would eventually be dismissed. In a particularly blatant example, the Civil Service Appeals Board sacked a Manila patrolman, Cecilio Magbual, after evidence surfaced that he had accompanied the "recognized kingpin of the Pasay underworld," Frank S. Montgomery, to the Malayan Bar, one of this district's many brothels.[97] On the eve of war in November 1941, the press would still be describing the Manila police as "inefficient" and "inept," with a poor crime-solving record and a feeble street presence.[98]

Manila's police ended the Commonwealth era compromised, politicized, and inefficient, a problematic legacy for the future republic. Despite the disruption of the Japanese occupation and American invasion during World War II, these underlying patterns seem to have persisted into the postwar era. After the battles of liberation in January 1945 left much of Manila in ruins, the U.S. Army's provost marshal—first under its interim chief, Col. J. P. Holland, and then under his Filipino deputy, Col. Angel M. Tuason—reorganized the force, rebuilt its infrastructure, and founded the Manila Police Training School and the Merit and Trial

Board. But the resumption of civilian rule in June 1946 brought Chief Tuason's resignation and "the return of politics."[99]

Like the American governors before him, President Quezon, finding police power a necessary adjunct to central authority, personally supervised the Manila Police and used the constabulary to control the countryside. But effective control of local police eluded him, just as it had his American predecessors. In the capital the metropolitan force was entangled in the city's netherworld of crime and corruption; and in the countryside municipal police remained hirelings of town mayors. By the time war came in late 1941, Quezon had in effect retained the police structure inherited from a century of colonial rule, leaving ingrained institutional problems for his postwar successors. The country's gambling culture defied Quezon as well, surviving to become the financial foundation of the country's costly postwar elections.

Conclusion

When President Quezon entered Malacañang Palace after his historic inauguration in November 1935, the separation of police powers between the colonial executive and Filipino legislature faded with his every step up the grand ceremonial staircase. Since the National Assembly's opening in 1907, the informal division of authority between legislature and executive had checked politicization of the constabulary. Now the inauguration of a Filipino president had eliminated this ad hoc division and created the potential for serious abuse. As a visionary statesman, President Quezon momentarily restrained this potential for partisan policing and used his authority to build a national army. Insulated from political pressures by the pressing imperatives of national defense, the constabulary remained generally nonpartisan under his short-lived Commonwealth.

As a politician, however, Quezon was ultimately forced to leave local police under the control of municipal officials and abandon his efforts to cut the cord between illegal gambling and provincial politics. His attempt to centralize the constabulary and the many municipal forces as a unified State Police met a storm of opposition from powerful local politicians. Similarly, his ambitious crusade against illegal gambling soon foundered on the reefs of urban vice and provincial politics. When it came to policing, not even Quezon, the most gifted politician of his generation, could resolve the contradiction embedded within the U.S. colonial state between local autonomy and an empowered executive. Toward the end of the Commonwealth period, Joseph Hayden, the leading U.S. specialist on Philippine politics, described municipal police as the "political henchmen" of local officials who served as "the instruments of oppression rather than agents of the law."[100] Through the sum of Quezon's failings in the arena of law enforcement, provincial politics remained grounded in a compromising matrix of illegal gambling and police complicity.

While all his major law enforcement efforts failed, Quezon's attempt to centralize police was another step in the accretion of executive authority. Once World War II ended and the country became independent, the constabulary would report to a Filipino president who was both commander in chief and head of a national political machine that rested on provincial brokers and bosses. In this disparate archipelago with its decentralized governance, the centrifugal force of local politics, pulling remote provinces out of Manila's orbit, would incline postwar presidents to restrain the constabulary, giving local bosses a monopoly over the armed force in their localities. Under the postwar Philippine Republic, these contradictory pulls between capital and province, or impartiality and partisanship, would create pressures for misuse of the constabulary, soon producing another string of scandals.

Unchecked by constitutional restraints, the executive's exercise of police power was limited only by the character, ambitions, and abilities of individual presidents. Under a leader of Quezon's uncommon political acumen, the constabulary's sword would remain sheathed. Over the longer term, however, the end of the colonial separation of powers and the creation of a powerful presidency left a problematic legacy for his political heirs. In an independent Republic that would be ruled by men and women rather than laws, few would prove Quezon's equal as a statesman. Several would succumb to partisan use, and even abuse, of the constabulary, creating a succession of postwar legitimation crises.

11

Philippine Republic

By 7:00 p.m. on a moist, monsoon night in August 1971, every square inch of Manila's Plaza Miranda, from Quiapo Church to Mercury Drug, was packed with a partisan crowd. For two hours senatorial candidates from the opposition Liberal Party slammed President Ferdinand Marcos's corruption and incompetence. As emotions peaked and a fireworks display erupted above the church spires at 9:00 p.m., two fragmentation grenades rolled across the stage. Shrapnel ripped through the tightly packed crowd, killing nine and wounding a hundred more, including four of the opposition's senate slate. As a local columnist later recalled, "something else had died there" that night amid the bleeding bodies at the symbolic heart of Philippine democracy, "the last shred of decency in politics, the thing that had allowed the nation to survive the killing and the stealing."[1]

Indeed, the Plaza Miranda bombing heralded a time of terror that prepared the country's citizens for martial law and delivered the fatal blow to a fragile Philippine democracy. Between March and August 1972, twenty more bombs exploded across Manila, most of them planted by Marcos's own military to provide a pretext for strongman rule.[2] In declaring martial law that September, the president would ask the Filipino people to trade their democracy for stability. By their silence and compliance, the majority would tacitly accept his Faustian bargain. While these bombings no doubt set the political stage for Marcos's declaration of martial law, broader political conditions that enabled his seizure of power were decades in the making.

The Philippines had won its independence in 1946 under challenging circumstances. At the outset of World War II, the invading Japanese had swept the archipelago, defeating the country's fledgling army and imposing a harsh occupation that soon inspired armed resistance by a quarter million Filipino guerrillas. In the battles of liberation at the end of the war in 1944–45, the U.S. Army returned to the islands, destroying cities with massive bombardments and scattering nearly a million infantry weapons—breaking the state's monopoly on the means of coercion. Although the new Republic had recovered several hundred thousand firearms by 1950, officials still estimated that four hundred thousand more were "loose in irresponsible hands," a floating arsenal that armed peasant guerrillas, provincial warlords, and street thugs. The prewar constabulary, traumatized by its defeat at the start of the war and tainted by its role as a police for the Japanese occupation, could not be readily reconstituted, weakening the new state's coercive capacities.[3] At the national, provincial, and municipal levels, the Republic failed to reestablish its monopoly on physical force. Over its brief, quarter-century lifespan, this struggling democracy would suffer iconic incidents of armed violence that weakened its legitimacy.[4]

With little time and even less revenue to respond to these challenges, the newly independent Philippine state defaulted to the three-tiered policing system left by a century of colonial rule: the Metropolitan Police for the capital; a thousand separate forces in the municipalities; and a national paramilitary police, the Philippines Constabulary, for the provinces. To reinforce this tripartite structure, the Republic revived the Commonwealth's National Bureau of Investigation in 1947 to serve as a central detective agency that grew by 1964 to some twelve hundred personnel.[5]

Among these four police forces, the constabulary, once the legitimating symbol of the U.S. colonial state, would prove the most problematic. Starting in the late 1940s, the PC lost its hard-won reputation for self-restraint and reduced the Republic's esteem in the eyes of rural Filipinos. In the mid-1960s the constabulary would also establish itself, for the first time since the 1920s, as a visible presence in the capital where its new Metropolitan Command, or Metrocom, was charged with crowd control. With training from U.S. police advisers, Metrocom would field helmeted riot troopers who bloodied student demonstrators, further degrading the Republic's legitimacy in the eyes of the urban middle class.

Despite these tumultuous changes, the postwar Republic still featured many of the same actors who had been so prominent in the prewar Commonwealth: powerful American officials, Filipino presidents, provincial politicians, criminals, the press, and the police. But now their status changed slightly yet significantly. The once-powerful American governor-general had been replaced by a U.S. ambassador, who now played a less visible though still influential advisory role. American armed forces remained at Clark Field and Subic Bay, but their presence was now graced by bilateral treaties, military aid, and advisers. Postwar Philippine presidents, in exchange for local support, allowed provincial politicians to handpick the constabulary officers assigned to their areas, with disastrous results. The newspapers that once served as the sole voice of opposition, the proverbial fourth estate, were now joined by radio and television reporters. By 1971 opium was out and heroin was in. Illicit gambling grew as illegal casinos joined the jueteng lottery. In short, it was a different political milieu, one that now included a significant new force for change in the form of a growing body of student activists—a product of the postwar boom in higher education.

Perhaps most important, the sense of boundless optimism that had greeted the Commonwealth's inaugural in 1935 had given way, in the years after independence in 1946, to a succession of crises, moving the nation slowly from desperation to despair. After a century of contact with the state mediated largely by its uniformed constables, many ordinary Filipinos still equated government legitimacy with police efficiency. But by the 1960s crime seemed to be rampant and police unequal to the task. As the constabulary increasingly succumbed to corruption, the countryside was left under the control of local politicians and their private armies. In Manila, now a metropolis of two million, murder and robbery rose to unprecedented levels. In the decades before Marcos's ascent in the mid-1960s, there was a de facto decentralization of police power as the centrifugal force of electoral politics pulled local police, provincial constabulary, and private armies away from Manila's control. Playing on an upsurge of urban crime, Ferdinand Marcos launched a new metropolitan police force in 1966 that laid the foundations for his later declaration of martial law. Whipsawed between warlord brutality in the countryside and criminal disorder in the capital, the Republic's legitimacy withered in the eyes of its citizens. Finally, in 1971–72, a rash of mysterious bombings capped what seemed a collapse of public order. On the crest of this last wave of chaos, Marcos would lead the country toward martial law, suspending the country's brief experiment with democracy.

Postwar Constabulary

From the first days of independence in July 1946, violence strained the capacities of the new Philippine state. In the chaotic aftermath of World War II, a major peasant rebellion in Central Luzon threatened the Republic's survival and forced a reorganization of its armed forces, leaving the once proud constabulary constrained and compromised. In 1947 the Communist Party launched a revolution with fifteen thousand well-armed Hukbalahap, or Huk, peasant guerrillas, their combat skills honed by three years of guerrilla warfare against the Japanese occupation during World War II. In a region that had long suffered rising agricultural tenancy, landlord usury, and government neglect, the Huk fighters were the armed extension of the militant unions and radical parties that had advocated land reform. These partisans and their political program commanded wide support among Central Luzon's 2.5 million impoverished peasants. The combination of this strong mass base and a substantial armed force made the Huk squadrons a formidable enemy for the new nation's demoralized armed forces.

To pacify this peasant revolt, the government initially relied on the Military Police Command (MPC), formed as an ad hoc auxiliary of the U.S. Army in the war's final months and later expanded to a force of twenty-three thousand men after the Philippine Army assumed control in mid-1945.[6] As a poorly trained, militarized police force, the MPC responded to peasant dissidence with nothing short of brutality. In January 1948, therefore, President Manuel Roxas abolished the MPC and, to continue counterguerrilla operations, revived the prewar Philippines Constabulary as a national police force of twenty thousand men under the secretary of interior.[7]

But this revived constabulary had lost the legendary discipline of prewar decades. With many officers hardened by conventional and guerrilla combat during World War II, the new constabulary's elite units soon became notorious for the slaughter of suspected dissidents. In the Huk heartland of Central Luzon, the PC's Nenita Unit under Lt. Col. Napoleon Valeriano entered suspected Huk barrios with Thompson submachine guns blazing. When Huk guerrillas employed ambushes, Nenita troopers retaliated with massacres in nearby villages, stacking corpses along the highways beneath warning placards. These overtly violent tactics proved counterproductive.[8] Even Colonel Valeriano later admitted that "the Constabulary had actually, though of course indirectly, helped the Huk's cause."[9] One U.S. Army staff study concluded that constabulary "standards of leadership and conduct were considerably below . . . prewar performance" and that many troops had inflicted "terror and oppression on the people of Central Luzon."[10]

Complicating Manila's response to this crisis, Washington no longer viewed the Philippines in colonial terms as its own sovereign territory to be defended at all costs. It was now but a single state among dozens in a larger system of global defense. In an assessment for the State Department dated August 1948, famed cold war strategist George Kennan included the Philippines on a short list of strategic allies—the North Atlantic nations, the Mediterranean, the Middle East, and Japan—that the U.S. "cannot permit . . . to fall into hands hostile to us." Thus, the "maintenance of political regimes in those areas . . . favorable to the continued power . . . of our nation" was, Kennan said, "an irreducible minimum of national security."[11] In pursuit of this global strategy Washington concluded two bilateral treaties with Manila in 1947—the Military Assistance Agreement and the Military Bases Agreement—that granted twenty-three installations under a ninety-nine-year lease with unrestricted use for offensive operations. Two of these, Clark Field and Subic Bay, soon became the largest overseas U.S. bases anywhere in the world. To provide a home port for the Seventh Fleet at Subic Bay, Navy Seabees moved mountains and filled swamps at a cost of a hundred million dollars to build a wharf for the largest aircraft carriers, runways for a busy naval air station, and three dry docks for a ship repair facility that employed fifteen thousand Filipino workers. As home to the Thirteenth Air Force, Clark Field had capacity for two hundred fighters and a bombing range bigger than the District of Columbia. In effect, the Philippines became the anchor for a defensive perimeter running along the Pacific Rim from Japan to Australia. Washington reciprocated by providing Manila with $704 million in military equipment and training between 1946 and 1971. Although these treaties effectively swapped Philippine bases for promises of American aid, by 1948 Washington faced more immediate communist challenges in Europe and deferred Manila's request for a mere $9 million in military assistance for a full year—until communist forces captured China and brought the cold war to Asia.[12]

A few months later in March 1950, the Huk command decided the Philippines was in a "revolutionary situation" and launched a major offensive, scoring stunning successes. In August the guerillas repeated the feat, this time hitting eleven towns across Central Luzon and hauling off 140,000 rounds of ammunition from a military depot near Manila—thus threatening yet another Asian nation with communist conquest. Shaken by the loss of China and near defeat in Korea, official Washington moved, step-by-step, toward a consensus that the Philippines must be defended. In a report to the Pentagon, the Joint U.S. Military Advisory Group (JUSMAG) in Manila warned gravely that the situation was "definitely out of hand." The Joint Chiefs of Staff, in turn, agreed that the Philippines were "an essential part of the Asian offshore island chain of bases" whose loss would represent a major strategic blow. Consequently, the U.S. defense secretary advised President Truman that "the strategic importance of the Philippines is not open to question," adding that the Huk guerrillas might win without "immediate constructive steps toward stability, probably requiring U.S. assistance."[13]

In November 1950 the U.S. National Security Council (NSC) made a formal decision to defend the Philippines and to support "a Philippine military capable of restoring and maintaining internal security." The NSC was confident that military assistance would "eliminate the Huks as a serious threat within one year." But Washington was pessimistic about its ability to promote long-term social change. The country's government was, the NSC said, controlled by a small elite "representing the wealthy propertied class who . . . have failed to appreciate the need for reform." Thus, the postwar economy has "deteriorated to a grave degree," with "inefficient production," "misdirected investment," and growing social "inequalities" marked by rising "incomes of the large landowners" and little effort "to better the position of farm workers and tenants." The "extreme sensitivity of Philippine officials . . . on the question of their national sovereignty" made encouragement of social reforms "a most difficult and delicate problem." At the broadest level, therefore, this military decision to defend the Philippines, under terms codified in NSC Memorandum 84/2, integrated the country into the U.S. defensive perimeter for the next forty years, authorizing a long-term infusion of military aid that would reinvigorate the coercive capacities of the Philippine state and its ruling oligarchy.[14]

Through this close cooperation between Washington and Manila, the military situation in Central Luzon soon changed. To end the abuses and assure U.S. aid, President Elpidio Quirino limited the constabulary to "purely police duties" and reintegrated it into the military in March 1950, thereby forming a central command under the Armed Forces of the Philippines (AFP).[15] At the height of the Huk crisis in August, the president also appointed Ramon Magsaysay, a former congressman and wartime anti-Japanese guerrilla commander, his secretary of national defense. As a politician of exceptional energy and charisma, Magsaysay worked with American advisers to radically restructure the AFP and develop an innovative doctrine for counterguerrilla warfare.[16]

At the strategic level Magsaysay gave the army primary responsibility for the Huk campaign. As the military's main striking force, the army soon expanded, through a sudden infusion of U.S. military equipment, to form twenty-six battalion combat teams or BCTs. Detached from the control of the divisional superstructure, each BCT could operate autonomously for months at a time, pursuing the enemy across the countryside without a pause for fuel, food, or firepower. To prevent guerrilla squads from ambushing these battalions, the AFP formed the Scout Rangers, company-sized mobile units of well-trained commandos. Under Magsaysay's dynamic leadership, competent officers took command, military pay improved, new battalions were formed, and morale rose.[17]

Working closely with Magsaysay, two key U.S. advisers created a complementary array of novel counterinsurgency tactics. The CIA's Maj. Edward Lansdale—a former San Francisco advertising executive later famed for his fictional portrayals in two classics of cold war cinema, *The Quiet American* and *The Ugly American*—was a master practitioner of psychological warfare. The lesser-known member of the team was Col. Charles Bohannan, a former ethnographer at the Smithsonian Institution and a specialist in Navajo folklore who applied the study of culture, particularly folk superstitions, to the war on this peasant guerrilla army.[18] Through the complex interaction of these three—Lansdale, Bohannan, and Magsaysay—the AFP achieved a major conceptual breakthrough in counterinsurgency, moving beyond earlier doctrines reliant upon applications of overwhelming military force.

With a playful, sometimes macabre amorality, Lansdale's team, comprised largely of talented Filipinos, soon broke Huk morale through innovative tactics—deep penetration agents, political propaganda, and disinformation—that played on peasant superstitions. Under Jose Crisol, a militant anticommunist ideologue and Lansdale's "psywar" protégé, the military's Civil Affairs Office mounted a massive propaganda effort, producing two million leaflets over two years with technical support from the U.S. Information Service (USIS) and logistical planning from JUSMAG. At an operational level Lansdale's tactics involved a creative commingling of intelligence operations and psychological warfare that subordinated firepower to political goals. "Conventional military men think of combat psywar almost exclusively in terms of leaflets or broadcasts appealing to the enemy to surrender," wrote Lansdale in his memoirs. "Early on, I realized that psywar had a wider potential than that. . . . When I introduced the practical joke aspect of psywar to the Philippine Army, it stimulated some imaginative operations that were remarkably effective."[19]

If a guerrilla entered their sights, the AFP often rejected the conventional alternatives of kill or capture, opting instead for summary execution to make him appear the victim of the feared *vampira* (vampires), thus encouraging desertions by his superstitious comrades. "When a Huk patrol came along the trail," Lansdale recalled, "the ambushers silently snatched the last man of the patrol, their move unseen in the dark night. They punctured his neck with two holes, vampire-fashion, held the body up by the heels, drained it of blood, and put the corpse back on the trail. . . . When daylight came, the whole Huk squadron moved out of the vicinity."[20] When found in the city, a clandestine cadre would be confronted with an evil eye painted on his wall or a black spot in his daily newspaper, a frightening experience that encouraged disappearance or defection.[21] Lansdale's team also used order-of-battle intelligence to fly over Huk squadrons calling out the names of supposed traitors in their ranks and prompting demoralizing internal recriminations. After the aircraft flew off, Lansdale recalled, this "mention of a mysterious 'friend' in their ranks had aroused the Huk's darkest suspicions of one another. Three of them were singled out and executed on the spot."[22] While the application of conventional force could often strengthen the morale of a guerrilla army, these unconventional tactics injected a pervasive psychological corrosion that gradually destroyed the insurgency from within.

Instead of deploying troops to engage the entire Huk force, AFP intelligence adopted "hunter/killer" tactics to locate and eliminate the top leadership. With well-publicized cash rewards appealing to the material side of Filipino culture, the army accumulated intelligence to pinpoint top cadres for elimination. Similarly, the AFP found that guerrillas often made the best counterguerrillas for these operations. On Panay Island, for example, a Military Intelligence Service (MIS) team used surrendered guerrillas to infiltrate the Huk's Regional Command Number Six. Following a brief shoot out inside a bamboo hut, the undercover team emerged covered in blood from the point-blank slaughter of some fifteen top cadre, breaking this Huk regional command.[23] After fourteen months of operations that combined BCT combat with psychological warfare, the once formidable Huks, in Lansdale's estimation, "had lost the initiative and were on the run."[24] While JUSMAG advisers assisted in the application of conventional counterinsurgency doctrines, Lansdale's CIA team developed new psychological and deep penetration tactics that would remain integral to AFP counterinsurgency doctrine for decades to come.

More broadly, this U.S.-Philippine security alliance was the first among many mutual defense accords worldwide that would become the hallmark of

Washington's anticommunist posture during the cold war. By 1954, U.S. forces had girded the globe with seven mutual-defense treaties, thirty-three military aid agreements, and three hundred overseas military bases backed by 2.5 million troops. Complementing the formal alliance, the CIA would remain a presence in Philippine security operations for the next forty years, engaging in constant monitoring and periodic covert operations to protect the massive U.S. military bases. The sum of these interventions was a template for the postwar projection of American power around the globe through bases, treaties, military aid, and covert operations. Of equal import, this close alliance made the Philippines a postcolonial laboratory for the creation of new counterinsurgency doctrines, first against peasant guerrillas in the 1950s and later against urban demonstrators in 1960s. Indeed, when the U.S. National Security Council developed a global counterguerrilla doctrine in 1962, it would cite, as its sole example, "Magsaysay's strategy of combining the use of force with reform measures" as a promising "model of countering insurgency." A quarter century later when the army was revising this doctrine with second-generation tactics in 1987, its chief historian called the Huk campaign a "remarkable achievement" that "provides contemporary planners with insights and observations that remain . . . valid today."[25]

Provincial Warlords

As the Huk revolt retreated, political violence in the countryside presented fresh challenges to the new Republic's monopoly on legitimate force. Before World War II the constabulary had enforced strict gun controls that denied everyone, politicians included, access to firearms. After the war, however, provincial bosses obtained arms on the black market and formed private armies. To check the constabulary and allow their goons free rein during elections, these nascent warlords pressured Malacañang Palace to restrain its PC commanders. Since local leaders could deliver blocs of votes whose sum was often the margin of victory, presidential candidates had to court these provincial warlords and incur compromising political debts.

Only three years after independence, the 1949 presidential elections marked the first appearance of armed conflict as a defining feature of the country's politics. In the year preceding this campaign, Governor Rafael Lacson of Negros Occidental had formed one of the first of these private armies and used it on election day to deliver a winning margin for the incumbent, President Quirino. If genius is the discovery of the obvious, then Lacson showed uncommon insight by divining the Philippine polity's central flaw and playing on it to win a de facto political autonomy from the new state, freeing him to unleash armed terror against his political enemies that soon became a national scandal.

Born into a wealthy sugar plantation family in Negros Occidental, Lacson, like his distinguished ancestors, played the politics of his day with the weapons available to suppress working-class dissidence and best peer rivals.[26] By 1948, Governor Lacson had all three iconic elements of postwar Philippine politics: "guns, goons, and gold." On the pretext of blocking communist infiltration, he formed what he called his Special Police (SP), which soon expanded into a force of 130 SPs and 59 provincial guards. To fund this ad hoc force, he drew on diverse sources: municipal taxes, formal provincial appropriations, and pork barrel proceeds from the Presidential Action Commission on Social Amelioration (PACSA).[27] All the soldiers in Lacson's private army were in some way agents of the state.

A small force of 190 men could not have been effective had it faced serious opposition from any of three potential rivals: the municipal police, the sugar mill security forces, or the constabulary. With a mix of political maneuvering and brute force, the governor subjugated each in succession. In the 1947 local elections, he had won de facto control of municipal police by manipulating the mayoral elections. Two years later, after terrorizing the rival political faction which owned the province's sugar mills, he raided several factory compounds and confiscated their arms, effectively neutralizing most of this industrial security force.[28]

But to maintain his local monopoly on armed force, Governor Lacson required, above all else, the acquiescence of the national government and the neutralization of its constabulary. During the first two years of his terror, the local PC command had opposed the governor's excesses, producing a succession of dramatic clashes. During the closing weeks of the presidential campaign in October 1949, members of Lacson's SP arrested twenty members of the PC's elite Nenita unit at the hacienda of an opposition senatorial candidate. They brutally tortured these troopers and their captain before locking them in the provincial prison for the next three years on spurious charges of possessing illegal firearms.[29]

These incidents epitomized the widespread violence that made the 1949 presidential elections, in the view of foreign and Filipino observers, "a national disgrace" and "the most fraudulent and violent in democratic history."[30] From the outset the campaign was a tight contest between the unpopular incumbent, Elpidio Quirino, and the wartime president, Jose P. Laurel, who still commanded a strong following. In eight key provinces across the country, armed goons harassed the opposition's political rallies. So intense was the intimidation in the provinces of Lanao and Lacson's Negros Occidental that in the weeks before election day the Commission on Elections recommended suspension of voting and imposition of constabulary control, suggestions President Quirino ignored. Among the 3.7 million votes cast nationwide, some 40 percent of Quirino's 485,000 majority came from Negros Occidental (200,000) and another 28 percent from Lanao (140,000). Although Quirino won only 51 percent of the ballots cast nationwide, Lacson delivered an incredible 92 percent of his province's vote for the president, producing the winning majority. In a subsequent investigation, the

House Electoral Tribunal found evidence of systematic terrorism in Negros Occidental and voided the results in two of its congressional districts.[31]

After single-handedly assuring President Quirino's election, Lacson could have asked him for almost anything—vast timber concessions, lucrative import licenses, or a national radio network. Instead the governor demanded a small but strategic favor: veto power over the posting of junior constabulary officers to his province. Only seven months after the elections, the governor wrote to remind the president about the terms of their agreement. "It will be recalled that in one of our conferences in Malacañan wherein [the PC Chief] General Alberto Ramos was present," Lacson said in a tone devoid of any deference, "it was then and there agreed that the officers and men who have long been assigned to this province, namely Capt. Marcial Enriquez, . . . should not be taken out . . . and that the officers and men who came in the batch with Lt. Col. Antonio Sabarre should be transferred." Over the next two months, Lacson wrote repeatedly to insist upon the retention of Captain Enriquez and eight of his loyal troopers, lowly corporals and privates.[32]

Through this blatant politicization, the local constabulary command soon backed the governor's bid to take full control of the otherwise autonomous municipal police.[33] In its formal "Plan to Check the Spread of Subversive Activities," the Negros constabulary required that "the supervision of all police agencies will be undertaken by the Provincial Governor with the [PC] Provincial Commander assisting him" and authorized formation of neighborhood vigilante groups under local police chiefs "directly responsible to the Provincial Governor."[34] Under such pressure the Provincial Board voted to merge all municipal police forces into a unified provincial command under Lacson's direct authority.[35]

With the constabulary now firmly under his control, the governor grew even more violent. In February 1950 his SP arrested a prominent opposition politician, Inocencio Ferrer, beat him badly, and buried his still breathing body in a shallow grave on Lacson's own plantation.[36] After the elections Lacson used violence to break the autonomy of any remaining industrial security units allied with the province's rival political faction.[37] He also took control of the labor movement by forcing its leaders into local unions controlled by his municipal mayors.[38]

At the start of the 1951 local and legislative campaigns, Defense Secretary Ramon Magsaysay, mindful of his responsibility for public order, dispatched two hundred Marines and nine hundred cadets from the Reserve Officers' Training Corps (ROTC) to prevent another round of electoral terror in Negros Occidental.[39] Despite their presence investigators later found fifty-one instances of intimidation by the Special Police: beatings, random gunfire, and, most disturbingly, the murder of Moises Padilla, the candidate for mayor in the town of Magallon.[40] Taking Padilla's candidacy as a personal affront, Governor Lacson had insisted the constabulary absent itself from Magallon during the elections, and the provincial commander, his protégé Captain Enriquez, obligingly complied. Two days before the voting, Lacson denounced Padilla as a communist at a public rally in Magallon and on election day, November 13, ordered his arrest. For the next three days the SP tortured Padilla publicly on the plazas of four nearby municipalities. On November 16 the Special Police shot him fourteen times before dumping his body in a shed near the town of La Castellana, making no attempt to conceal the crime.[41]

This time the governor had gone too far. The next day Secretary Magsaysay flew to Negros accompanied by the publisher of the *Manila Times,* Joaquin Roces, and his star reporter, Benigno "Ninoy" Aquino Jr. Arriving at Magallon after dark, Magsaysay climbed the stairs to a wake where Padilla's body lay facedown, stripped to expose the bullet holes and wounds of torture, the stigmata of his political martyrdom. The victim's mother threw herself at Magasysay's feet, wailing, "My son is dead! My son is dead!" When local doctors refused to perform an autopsy, Magsaysay flew the body back to Manila for a military funeral with full honors. At each step in this political Calvary, Roces clicked his camera and Aquino jotted down quotes, producing a sensational story for the front page of the *Manila Times* that stirred public condemnation. Despite the outpouring of anger, President Quirino seemed reluctant to suspend Governor Lacson. "Mr. President," Magsaysay advised, "the people are so outraged by the death of Moises Padilla that they are ready to stone Malacañang Palace." After an embarrassing delay, government prosecutors filed murder charges against Lacson and the president finally suspended him.[42]

At Lacson' s trial, a close associate of the martyred Padilla testified to the central role that Captain Enriquez had played in the governor's reign of terror. Asked why he did not complain to the constabulary, the witness replied, "The law was being handled and exercised by the SPs in their hands alone." Asked if the constabulary had refused to enforce the law, the witnesses stated, "Yes, in all instances, the Provincial Commander never pays attention . . . [to] any complaint of aggrieved persons . . . during the time of Captain Enriquez."[43]

The realization that the president had compromised the constabulary, a force synonymous with the state's integrity, dismayed the Filipino public. Two years later running as the opposition's candidate in the 1953 presidential elections, Magsaysay brought rallies to an emotional peak by reaching out as if bearing a corpse and saying, "I held in my arms the bleeding symbol of democracy: the body of Moises Padilla."[44] Throughout the campaign Colonel Lansdale's psywar team was disbursing a million-dollar CIA fund, generating favorable publicity in the Manila press, and forming support organizations headed by members of his old team, notably, the Magsaysay-for-President Movement under Jose Crisol and the National Movement for Free Elections under Jaime Ferrer. Although President Quirino exposed Lansdale as a CIA agent, forcing JUSMAG to expel him from its Quezon City compound, nothing could stop the Magsaysay juggernaut. A few days before the elections, a U.S. Navy aircraft carrier with a destroyer escort entered Manila Bay, signaling Washington's willingness to intervene.[45] Only weeks before the election, Lansdale advised the U.S. ambassador that a Quirino victory would be countered by "a Magsaysay-inspired *coup d'état*" involving the "cream of combat commanders of the AFP."[46]

After Magsaysay triumphed in the November balloting, the courts suddenly accelerated the Lacson case. In August 1954 the governor was sentenced to death for the murder of Moises Padilla, a penalty later reduced to life imprisonment.[47] In retrospect, President Quirino's tolerance of partisan violence had created a crisis of legitimacy for the older generation of machine politicians. Under Quezon's prewar system, the Nacionalista Party had been a closed coalition of municipal and national elites that awarded office to political professionals like Quirino, excluding the small middle class, urban workers, and the country's peasant majority. Now this tide of political terror, symbolized by the murder of Padilla, had exhausted the legitimacy of Quirino's cohort and its elitist politics. Thus, Magsaysay's victory not only healed this breach with the voters but opened national politics to the middle class and the peasantry, effectively broadening what Jürgen Habermas called the "scope for participation."[48] In the view of one veteran observer, Magsaysay's victory "broke election campaign patterns" by taking his candidacy beyond the town plazas controlled by local elites directly to the rural barrios. President Magsaysay, a former bus mechanic, recruited middle-class technocrats and military officers and worked through them to extend government services to the countryside, including schools, public health measures, and rural roads. Throughout his long years of leadership as defense secretary and president, however, there was one major government program that he did not deliver—land reform. Although Magsaysay won passage of the Land Reform Act in 1955, he then faced determined opposition from local elites and allowed it to "wither and die" from want of implementation.[49] This critical failing left the underlying social inequality, the root cause of the country's endemic violence, unchanged, and meant that much of his political legacy was one of transitory, essentially palliative political gestures.

Despite Magsaysay's vigorous military reforms, the politicization of the constabulary that had fostered the provincial warlords continued and the potential for political intimidation remained. During the 1960s many provinces would witness a resurgence of Lacson's trademark fusion of public office and private militia. Over time this unregulated devolution of police powers to local politicians, highlighted by periodic terror, would delegitimate the Republic and its democracy in the eyes of many citizens.

Politics of Crime

Within a decade, the strategy pioneered by President Quirino—restraining the constabulary in provinces controlled by political allies—would again create a crisis of order during the administration of President Diosdado Macapagal (1962–65). As early as 1955, moreover, the first postwar survey of Philippine policing had found severe structural deficiencies. Over 85 percent of the country's 13,100 municipal police had "no training whatsoever." The local mayor "completely dominates" appointments. Promotions were "rewards for political servitude." Salaries were way below minimum wage creating "the obvious necessity of income from other sources." And the utter lack of equipment for transportation and communication "appalled" the researcher. Unchecked by effective law enforcement, the reign of ruthless provincial warlords, the emergence of massive smuggling, and rising urban crime would erode public confidence in the capacity of the Republic to maintain stability. For the first time in the country's history, public order rather than specific scandals became an issue powerful enough to delegitimate both leaders and their administrations.[50]

By the time President Macapagal took office in 1962, Manila had grown far beyond its prewar boundaries to engulf thirteen adjacent towns and its population increased fourfold to 2.4 million.[51] As the number of unemployed shot up, "crimes against persons" kept pace, rising 27 percent in 1966 alone.[52] The capital's visibility made its problems impossible to ignore. According to a senior Filipino police official, Manila is "the principal display window of our country," and major crimes in the capital "are given undue publicity."[53] Indeed, in the early 1960s several well-publicized crimes in and around the capital increased public anxiety nationwide. At nearby Caloocan City in 1963, the mayor's son was arrested for leading the "Big Four" gang, which terrorized merchants with robbery and protection rackets. In August 1964, a gang armed with carbines shot up the Manila Opera House "gangland style," sparking an investigation that found the entire entertainment industry to be "under gangster control." At Quezon City in 1965, two policemen attempted to rape a college professor in her own car. According to the NBI, overall crime in Manila had jumped 44 percent in 1964 alone.[54]

Responding to this crisis, Mayor Antonio Villegas cooperated with the Office of Public Safety (OPS), a division of the U.S. Agency for International Development (USAID), in launching a major survey of Manila's crime problem. Headed by Frank Walton, a former deputy Los Angeles police chief, this advisory mission found that crime in Manila was surging while law enforcement was collapsing. In only seven years robberies had risen by 100 percent, homicide by 150 percent, and auto theft by 300 percent. These problems were compounded by widespread corruption. Since their salaries did not meet minimal living standards, Manila policemen closed the gap with "payoffs for permitting illegal operations . . . and participation as members of criminal gangs." Police equipment was antiquated and badly maintained. Sprawling across a 155-square-mile metropolitan area with three million people, patrolmen were forced to communicate via commercial long-distance telephones, which were "frequently out of order."[55]

These problems, which were often economic in origin, were unquestionably political in their ramifications. Following the capital's liberation from Japanese occupation in February 1945, the U.S. Army's provost marshal had become Manila's police chief. After independence in 1946, Malacañang Palace reclaimed the right to appoint the city's police chief and maintained that power even after Manila's mayoralty became an elective office in January 1952. For the next sixteen years Malacañang favored military officers who were responsive to presidential authority.[56] Since the executive was responsible for law enforcement in both Manila and adjacent Quezon City, now the country's official capital, the political fortunes of the presidency were tied to the quality of policing in this troubled metropolis.

While citizens had long expected corruption from local police, the constabulary suffered a succession of scandals in the 1960s that diminished its aura as a symbol of state authority, dealing a critical blow to President Macapagal's re-election campaign in 1965. High import duties on American cigarettes, known as "blue seals" for the distinctive U.S. tax stamp on each pack, created a strong incentive for smuggling. As this racket grew from the mid-1950s onward, politicians and the media charged the constabulary with collusion. During Macapagal's four-year term (1961–65), the Philippine Navy's seizures increased twelvefold from 153,000 cartons to 1.8 million. In 1964 an estimated 1,253 ships from North Borneo landed illegal cigarettes across the archipelago at Basilan, Negros Occidental, Cebu, Batangas, and especially Cavite.[57] Some constabulary personnel were implicated in these operations. An investigation by the Armed Forces indicated that the country had some sixteen hundred "suspected smugglers," including fifty constabulary officers and fourteen provincial commanders.[58]

Rising crime became a key issue in the 1965 presidential elections. In his campaign as the opposition's candidate, Senator Ferdinand Marcos attacked the incumbent Macapagal, accusing him of complicity in the rampant smuggling. In the opening rounds Marcos charged the administration with failing to stop the illicit importation of 3.5 billion cigarettes a year, which cost the country ₱315 million in taxes.[59] As the debate descended into partisan mudslinging, Marcos gave Macapagal a list of forty-eight senior officials linked to the smugglers and accused him of "protecting the persons mentioned in the list."[60] So armed, Marcos barnstormed the countryside under an anticorruption banner, stigmatizing the Macapagal administration and ultimately capturing the presidency.

Marcos and Crime

After campaigning against his predecessor's security policies, President Marcos was inaugurated with a law and order mandate. "When I assumed office in 1966," he said in his state of the nation address two years later, "smuggling, criminality, and other forms of lawlessness were rampant, sapping our national will and capacity to progress." Acting as his own defense secretary for thirteen months, Marcos ordered a massive constabulary shake-up on the pretext of purging officers tainted by smuggling, with every change calculated, as one study later showed, "to increase the AFP's responsiveness to the new President."[61] During his first term (1965–69), he created an array of agencies that amplified his coercive powers: the Peace and Order Coordinating Council; the National Police Commission (Napolcom); President's Agency for the Reform of Government Operations (PARGO); Anti-Smuggling Action Center (ASAC); and, most important, the PC's new antiriot force, the Metropolitan Command (Metrocom). Although most of these agencies soon faded, Metrocom would grow into a powerful civil control squadron that covered all of Metro Manila.[62] From within this strike force, Marcos would, as a martial law dictator after 1972, form an elite antisubversion squad, the Metrocom Intelligence Service Group (MISG), that used torture and extrajudicial killings to spread state terror. More than any other Philippine president, Marcos would transform the character of the country's police, receiving key assistance in these efforts from the U.S. government.

When Marcos came to power, a marked decline in police performance lent credibility to his call for reform. In April 1965 the Philippine Civil Service Commission found that only 30 percent of municipal police officers were civil service eligible; police laws were "conflicting, confusing, and antiquated"; and no agency was responsible for "the professional growth of the local police service."[63] Two years later an NBI investigation found that some forty-eight policemen were implicated in major crimes every month.[64] A major study by the U.S. Office of Public Safety confirmed these findings. After its director Byron Engle met Marcos at Malacañang Palace in April 1966, OPS contracted a team of American experts led by Frank Walton, the author of an earlier report on Manila's police, to conduct a nationwide, three-month survey.[65] "In all enforcement agencies, the Philippines Constabulary, National Bureau of Investigation, and the local police," Walton's team reported, "performance is substandard; training is inadequate; political interference is common; inspection procedures are non-existent or unsatisfactory; morale is low."[66] In the two years since his last survey of the city, "venality, corruption, and law enforcement inefficiency" had grown worse. In 1965 alone robbery was up 10 percent and murder up 12 percent.[67]

Although police performance declined further during his first term, in his second (1969–72) Marcos was masterful in playing the spreading chaos to partisan advantage. He diverted anger over lawlessness to delegitimate the Republic instead of his own administration, thus building mass support for the declaration of martial law. And by using public concern over crime to place metropolitan police under his control, he accumulated sufficient powers for the imposition of authoritarian rule.

As it turned out, Washington, working through its Office of Public Safety, furnished assistance that proved instrumental to Marcos's use of police for repression. Established in 1962 by President John F. Kennedy to improve security among third world allies, OPS grew in just six years into a global counterinsurgency effort with an annual budget of $35 million and a staff of over four hundred American advisers.[68] Though housed in USAID, a division of the State Department, the program's long-serving head was Byron Engle, a career CIA employee.[69] Reflecting his own background as a Kansas City policeman who joined the agency, OPS became a Janus-faced organization. To fulfill USAID's mission of improving police performance, its training staff was recruited from American police departments and worked on such routine matters as traffic management, fingerprinting, and communications. In pursuit of his office's covert anticommunist mission, Engle also recruited CIA personnel to improve police counterinsurgency capabilities with extralegal methods.[70]

In support of the ostensible reforms undertaken by President Marcos, from 1969 to 1973 OPS would spend $5 million to install fifty-five provincial communications networks; send 284 Filipino officers to the United States for advanced training; establish ten regional centers to train 23,902 police, about 60 percent of the nation's total; and build an integrated communications grid and an antiriot squad of two thousand well-trained PC troopers ready for instantaneous dispatch to quell any demonstration or protest in Manila. The $2.4 million that OPS budgeted for the Philippines in the mid-1960s paled before the $71 million for Thailand, but Manila's volatile street demonstrations were an important test of its success in "transforming the police into a major . . . instrument" for counterinsurgency.[71] Though masked by a rhetoric of technical reform, the OPS program forged nothing less than an infrastructure primed for political repression. By its creation of centralized communications, a metropolitan police command, and computerized data banks, U.S. aid helped Marcos to tame Manila. Over the longer term, these innovations overrode the capital's diffuse police authority and the countryside's disparate geography whose combination had long militated against any attempt at authoritarian rule.

From a historical perspective, OPS training represented another infusion of U.S. aid and advisers to reinvigorate the country's waning coercive capacities. By breaching the barrier that had restricted the constabulary's uniformed operations inside Manila for half a century and facilitating executive control over the capital's police, this U.S. program had a significant impact not only on Philippine policing but also on Washington's own capacity for global influence. Apart from curbing nationalist demonstrators demanding the ouster of U.S. military bases, this substantial aid effort gave OPS the experience in urban counterinsurgency it later used to check the worldwide surge in radical student activism that made the 1960s such a tempestuous decade. Across the globe a large postwar generation was staging student protests that shook state power—from Berkeley to Berlin, from Seoul to Jakarta—making urban crowd control by police antiriot squads a new front in cold war containment.[72]

Behind its benign developmental façade, OPS may have also recruited some of these Filipino officers as CIA assets or trained them in torture. Elsewhere in Asia and Latin America the CIA used OPS to insert its agents in key cities and recruit local police for training at a clandestine center in Washington, DC, the blandly named International Police Services, which operated behind the public cover of the International Police Academy (IPA). Indeed, congressional investigators later found, by reading theses of the academy's graduates, clear evidence of torture training. "In summary," wrote Luu Van Huu of the South Vietnam Police on lessons learned at the IPA, "we have 4 sorts of torture; use of force as such; threats; physical suffering, imposed indirectly; and mental or psychological torture."[73] Between 1962 and 1972 OPS trained an estimated eighty-five senior Filipino officers in interrogation techniques at the IPA in Washington, DC.[74] In the last years of Marcos's dictatorship, elite military units would employ psychological methods strikingly similar to those found in CIA training manuals to torture an estimated thirty-five thousand political dissidents. Thus it is possible that OPS transmitted CIA torture techniques later used by Marcos's martial law interrogators.[75]

At a minimum, the OPS program inadvertently helped Marcos lay the security infrastructure for a later declaration of martial law. By investing Philippine police with the means to dominate civil society through information systems and crowd control, OPS provided Marcos with the essentials for authoritarian rule. Soaring crime rates fed public fears that the police had lost control of the capital, providing ample pretext for expanded executive authority. As the Philippine Congress was debating the first of Marcos's police reform bills in 1966, a fifteen-man gang killed three police officers during a bank holdup near Manila. Simultaneously, a seven-man gang armed with submachine guns robbed a business in Makati and shot its way through a police cordon to escape.[76] Even as Congress legislated and Marcos implemented, Metro Manila's share of the country's crime doubled from about 25 percent in 1969—with an appalling 2,508 homicides, 7,784 robberies, and 434 rapes—to 57 percent just two years later.[77]

A study by the Rand Corporation in 1968–69 found that Filipinos viewed their country "as a violent society beset by murder, robbery, and theft." Yet closer examination of the "prevalence of crime" found that there were revealing regional variations in both actual crime and public perception. In a January 1969 survey, those outside the capital reported little personal threat and ranked crime low while Manila respondents rated criminality as the nation's number-one problem and expressed strong fears of both robbery and murder. The survey also found that the Philippines had the world's highest murder rate, with 35 homicides per 100,000 population in 1965 and a sharp increase to 42 only two years later—compared to just 25 murders for Colombia, a nation then wracked by a wave of political killings known as *La Violencia*. Yet the murder rate for individual Philippine provinces ranged widely from a low of 7 per 100,000 to a high of 120, with a countrywide spike during elections.[78] In effect, public perception, or misperception, of a national crime wave sprang from comparatively few localities, particularly Manila.

By the late 1960s illegal casinos operating openly in the capital reinforced the public's sense of a society in freefall. In buildings lining Dewey Boulevard along Manila Bay, bright signs flashed names synonymous with police corruption: Stardust, Oceans 11, D'Wave, Ambassador, El Mundo, and Bayside. From just three backroom casinos in the late 1930s, illegal gambling had grown into a neon strip of twenty-two major cabarets with a nightly glitz of flashy cars and elegant patrons. Instead of his seedy downtown club of prewar years, the American mobster Ted Lewin, a "King Rat" figure who had grown fat by blackmarket trading inside wartime Japanese internment camps, now operated his swanky Club Cairo with fourteen tables for roulette, dice, and blackjack. One CIA agent recalled Lewin as "a man who wove his way daily through the network of payoffs and chicanery" with a casino clientele that included "the high officials of the administration." Protected by steel doors and "grease money," each casino had up to sixty gaming tables and featured top acts to attract the city's social elite. Although the casinos were illegal, their doings were reported daily in the social pages of the Manila press as socialites reveled in a walk on the wild side on their way to "private clubs like Teddy Lewin's . . . for a spot of gambling." The owners were often wealthy capitalists, but for the most part the operators were tough gangsters who executed erring dealers or paraded their bloodied faces along the Dewey strip to warn others.[79] All these indices, statistical and symbolic, gave the president a strong mandate for radical reforms.

By means of adroit legislative maneuver, Marcos amplified his control over Manila's police. Although he had delegated appointment of the city's police chief to the mayor in 1967, Marcos negated this concession by creating the Metropolitan Police organization, or Metropol, to coordinate policing among the four cities and nine municipalities of metropolitan Manila. To make Metropol's control a reality, OPS began building "a metropolitan communications network," which created the "first completely integrated system in the country." By early 1971, Metropol had a twenty-four-hour communications capacity covering the four provinces, 113 municipalities, and six million people within a forty-mile radius of Manila.[80] With additional OPS funding and technical support, the NBI also developed an efficient fingerprint unit for rapid transmission of criminal prints to the entire Metropol area.[81]

Starting in mid-1967, Marcos worked with both U.S. military and police advisers to establish the PC Metrocom as a modern crowd control unit, giving the constabulary "police jurisdiction over the Greater Manila Area" for the first time. By then Manila's own force was crippled by a lack of funds. With only one poorly paid officer for every three thousand residents and just fourteen actual working police cars, the force was woefully inadequate for a metropolis with eight hundred thousand vehicles. With generous aid from OPS, Metrocom, by contrast, quickly developed a "modern police telecommunications . . . and computerized record system" and trained 2,325 Filipino police in crowd control techniques.[82] Within his regional Metropol command, the president could now dispatch the Metrocom's 2,000 mobile troopers anywhere in metropolitan Manila, overwhelming local police who had a total of only 2,800 officers dispersed across this same region.[83]

Rising Resistance

The president's heavy-handed tactics did not pass unnoticed. As student protests intensified after U.S. president Lyndon Johnson's 1967 visit to Manila, Marcos used his new police command to harass demonstrations, launching years of chaos that would give both the Manila police and Metrocom a well-earned reputation for brutality.[84] Amid this collapse of public order, the 1969 presidential elections saw an exceptional surge in violence and blatant vote buying. Although Marcos won a second term, his legitimacy suffered as a result of this tawdry campaign, sparking an eruption of student demonstrations and plunging the Republic into a downward spiral of disorder.

Until these overt displays of repression and resistance, opposition to President Marcos and his security preparations had been muted. While expanding formal police controls in the capital, Marcos had also been building an informal parallel command for sensitive, top secret missions. In the last year of his first term, one of these, Operation Merdeka, exploded into a bitter controversy over the president's plans for the conquest of Sabah, a Malaysian state adjacent to the southern Philippines. The operation began secretly in 1967 when Marcos authorized Maj. Eduardo Martelino, a dashing pilot, to begin covert penetration of Sabah with trained commandos. In the president's plan these infiltrators would destabilize the Malaysian state with sabotage, allowing easy conquest of a territory that many Filipinos felt was rightfully theirs. "We would demolish their communications equipment, burn them, plant dynamite, and simultaneously explode them," one of these commandoes later recalled. In the operation's first phase, Martelino entered Sabah three times, infiltrating an advance party of some seventeen agents. After basic training for some two hundred local recruits at a clandestine camp in Sulu in late 1967, Martelino shipped about 180 men north to Corregidor Island near Manila for more specialized skills.[85]

On that island at the mouth of Manila Bay, things started to go very wrong. While their commanders bunked at the air-conditioned Bay View Hotel in downtown Manila, Muslim trainees on Corregidor were fed miserable rations and went for weeks without pay. After three months of such harsh conditions, these angry recruits threatened a mutiny unless they were paid immediately. Faced with public exposure of the secret mission, the officers quickly disarmed the trainees and began shipping them back to Sulu. On March 18, 1968, twelve recruits left the camp at 2:00 a.m. and vanished, never to be found. Two hours later a second batch of twelve recruits was driven to an airstrip where constabulary rangers opened fire with automatic weapons, killing all but one who jumped into the sea.[86]

After fishermen pulled the surviving recruit, a Sulu native named Jibin Arula, from Manila Bay, they delivered him to opposition politicians. In the legislative inquiry that followed, Sen. Benigno Aquino charged that Operation Merdeka was a cover for the formation of a "secret strike force under the President's personal command, to form the shock troops of his cherished garrison state."[87] Despite these setbacks in both the legal and extralegal realms, by the end of his first term Marcos had acquired ample police controls over the capital and retained a residual covert capacity inside the military. His second term would stretch these capabilities to the limit.

Within just months, revelations about this murderous covert operation segued into a presidential campaign rife with goons and gold. During his 1969 reelection effort President Marcos stumped vigorously, reaching even remote villages to personally place a check for two thousand pesos in the hands of each barrio captain, obligating them, in the country's political culture, to use every possible means to deliver a winning margin. This strategy cost Marcos a hefty $50 million, far more than the $34 million Richard Nixon had spent to win the U.S. presidency in 1968.[88] In the aftermath of this spendthrift campaign, the Philippine peso lost half its value, government services were slashed, and the economy contracted.[89]

The 1969 campaign also produced incidents of political terror of the sort not seen since the 1951 elections. With the constabulary now under the command of Marcos loyalist Vicente Raval, the PC's Special Forces orchestrated violence in four swing provinces that left forty-six dead.[90] In its ruling on these violations, the Supreme Court was particularly critical of what it called the "rape of democracy in Batanes," a remote island where the Special Forces allowed motorcycle-riding goons dubbed the "Suzuki boys" to coerce a winning margin in the congressional race for a close Marcos ally.[91] Bolstered by force and fraud, Marcos scored a crushing victory, winning 74 percent of the presidential vote, eight-six of one hundred House seats, and eleven of twelve Senate seats.[92]

In the aftermath of these elections, a provincial warlord in Ilocos Sur pursued a political vendetta against local enemies, producing an incident iconic for both its brutality and its executive complicity. Since this troubled province was adjacent to Marcos's own Ilocos Norte and its warlord was his ally, the president was clearly implicated in these events. As Marcos rose through the Senate to the presidency, his close friend Congressman Floro Crisologo had tightened his grip over Ilocos Sur—building a private army of three hundred men, a monopoly on the province's electoral offices, and a vice grip on its main cash crop, tobacco. To ensure payment of an informal tax to his political machine, Crisologo's private army maintained a "tobacco blockade" on the national highway, stopping every southbound truck to check for "tax" receipts. The constabulary could have easily swept away the Crisologo roadblock were it not for the reputed intervention of General Fabian Crisologo Ver, chief of presidential security and the congressman's relative.[93]

In mid-September 1969, the Crisologo goons gunned down a former Bantay municipal mayor, and a month later prosecutors indicted the congressman's son, Vicente Crisologo, for ordering the crime.[94] In the election's aftermath political reprisals continued in Bantay as the Crisologos retaliated against two villages, Ora Este and Ora Centro, for supporting the opposition's candidates. In May 1970 Vicente Crisologo led a hundred armed men into these villages and burned both to the ground. In the confusion an elderly woman was caught in the flames and perished. During the attack residents pleaded with the provincial PC commander, but he "ignored . . . appeals to stop the arson." In its front-page coverage, the Manila press carried moving photos of survivors sorting through the ashes of their devastated homes.[95]

Outraged by such a blatant display of warlord power, forty-two civic, religious, and youth organizations formed Operation Bantay to demand an impartial investigation of the incident.[96] Despite his alliance with Congressman Crisologo, President Marcos ordered charges filed against his son Vicente for arson.[97] Such unrestrained brutality by private police, apparently operating with the president's tacit approval, challenged the Republic's legitimacy among both student activists and Manila's middle class.

Only five months after the Bantay burning, Ilocos Sur offered a chilling coda to this political violence. Angry over his unsatisfactory share of the spoils from the president's victory, Congressman Crisologo, according one Marcos aide, stormed into the palace where he "berated both Marcos and Ver for grabbing the lion's share of the proceeds of the tobacco monopoly" and "threatened to expose the entire operation." Just a few weeks later, in October 1970, Crisologo knelt during Sunday Mass at Vigan's baroque cathedral. As he bent forward in prayer, two unidentified men emerged from a confessional booth, shot him point-blank in the back of the head, and then disappeared out of the cathedral door.[98]

While electoral violence exemplified by the Crisologos escalated across the countryside, a chaotic mix of crime and protest engulfed the capital, gradually taking a form that gave it political import. For the first time since the colonial era, the crowd, this time in the form of student activists, emerged as an independent political force, challenging the Republic with a stinging critique and symbolic mass. After a century as home to small elite colleges, Manila had experienced a postwar boom in middle-class education that created a critical mass of students. As enrollments nationwide soared from 22,000 in 1938 to 601,000 in 1971, nearly half a million college students crowded into the dozen campuses that formed a "university belt" around Malacañang Palace.[99]

The full force of this demographic change was not felt until the weeks following the November 1969 elections when the National Union of Students in the

Philippines (NUSP) led Manila's campuses in protests against electoral fraud. As these demonstrations gathered force in the first three months of 1970, a period of protest known as the "First Quarter Storm," Marcos deployed his Metrocom riot police, attacking the marchers with violence that further delegitimated his government in their eyes.[100]

This cycle of repression and resistance began in December 1969 when "truncheon swinging" police beat students protesting the arrival of U.S. vice president Spiro Agnew for Marcos's inauguration.[101] Only four weeks later, on January 26, 1970, Marcos and first lady Imelda emerged from Congress after his state of the nation address to find themselves caught in an angry crowd of fifty thousand student demonstrators. "In full view of the television cameras," wrote the reporter Jose Lacaba, "the agents of the law beat the hell out of anyone who fell into their hands." In the push and shove of rival phalanxes, demonstrators linked arms to parade before the police with a mocking chant that Lacaba felt was symptomatic of a "loss of respect for the law" and the reputation of the police as "corrupt, venal, brutal, vicious."

> Police, police with uncircumcised penis!
> Police, money grubber!
> He even has a shield, as if going to war!
> Keep running, your potbelly might shrink!
> Maybe you'll rape, when you already have five wives!
> Let me take you on, bare fists!

Four days later, when police again attacked demonstrators outside Malacañang Palace, the students fought back, ramming the gates with a fire truck and storming the palace grounds. In their counterattack the police pursued demonstrators into boardinghouses and dormitories, shooting and beating all they could catch.[102] From police sources OPS reported 4 dead, 293 arrested, and "scores injured."[103] In the aftermath of this bloody clash, the journalist Lacaba sensed that a "spirit was abroad that night, and the streets spoke of it in whispers: *the revolution has arrived*."[104]

In the pageantry of protest that followed, the police and their brutality soon came to symbolize the state. As riots continued for another two months, the death toll among student demonstrators rose to nineteen. In an incident that typified the capriciousness of police brutality, a Quezon City traffic patrol opened fire while passing a student barricade, leaving one demonstrator dead. "If after giving the demonstrators a warning to stop, they continue to attack," the PC chief told his Metrocom troopers, "then let us give it to them."[105] In its cables to Washington, OPS reported that "police in a number of incidents still used excessive force in effecting arrests," producing "extensive criticism" in the press and a public climate of "mass hysteria."[106] Reacting to the heavy-handed policing, many protests, recalled the writer Petronilo Daroy, "took the form of public indignation against the men in uniform." Thus, Manila's police now symbolized the illegitimacy not only of the Marcos administration but of the Republic itself, convincing many in this activist generation "of the need to take up arms."[107]

Although Marcos focused on the demonstrators, ordinary citizens were probably even more concerned with the collapse of public order. Throughout 1971 Manila suffered an outbreak of forty-seven major fires in just five weeks, a surge in "carnapping" with over forty incidents per month, prison riots at Muntinglupa that left seventeen dead, and bloody gang wars in the Tondo slums. Instead of responding to this crisis, the city's police seemed mired in scandal. A drumbeat of headlines announced the murder of Cavite's police chief by political rivals, involvement of the Makati police in "hijacking and liquidation jobs," and the injury of five Quezon City policemen in a "full scale battle" with constabulary over smuggled goods. Lending substance to these incidents, over 20 percent of Manila's police officers and 50 percent of Quezon City's were facing disciplinary charges.[108] Testifying before Congress, constabulary chief Eduardo Garcia and police chief Francisco Villa admitted that fifty-five recent casino raids had failed to produce even a single conviction.[109] Aware of the political implications of this disorder, Executive Secretary Alejandro Melchor Jr. advised USAID that "it is absolutely essential that the local policemen be upgraded since this would be the only way the image of the government would be able to be changed."[110]

The middle and upper classes were particularly concerned over the sudden spread of heroin abuse among their children, fears confirmed by official estimates of some 150,000 drug users nationwide.[111] After a decade relatively free of drugs during the 1950s, with arrests averaging only fifty to sixty annually, Manila became the site of three small Chinese laboratories in the early 1960s, each transforming smuggled morphine base into granular no. 3 heroin. By 1971 a Chinese restaurateur named Lim Seng was producing over one hundred kilograms of powdery, white no. 4 heroin every month at laboratories concealed in rented mansions around Manila and protected by bribes made to congressmen, customs inspectors, and the police.[112]

Although he exported over 90 percent of his output to the American West Coast, Lim Seng's local sales were sufficient to fuel a spreading heroin epidemic among Manila's youth. Since only middle- and upper-class students had the cash for such a costly addiction, a moral panic spread among the city's elite. In early 1972 Marcos responded by drafting stronger narcotics laws and forming the Constabulary Anti-Narcotics Unit (CANU). Only weeks later CANU got its first break in the battle against Lim Seng's syndicate when an operative arrested two American military veterans boarding a flight to Okinawa with six ounces of no. 4 heroin.[113] Following leads from this arrest, constabulary agents soon identified all the members of the syndicate and its laboratory locations. But PC investigators were hesitant, they later admitted, to apply for a search warrant since corrupt court officials might warn Lim Seng of the raids.[114] Desperate for order, some affluent Makati families formed a "secret organization called KAP (Kill A Pusher)" to assassinate suspected heroin dealers.[115]

Capping these years of rising crime and violence, Manila suffered a wave of terror bombings in the months before martial rule. After the first attack at Plaza Miranda in August 1971, most Filipinos blamed Marcos. The president accused the communists and suspended the writ of habeas corpus to check subversion. Three months later the midterm elections—fueled by warlord gunplay in many provinces and Muslim-Christian conflict in Mindanao—became "the most violent in Philippine history."[116]

In these November elections the tide of bribery and bloodshed crested as the palace released an unprecedented one million pesos in pork barrel for each congressman and killings climbed to a historic high of 223. In Cotabato armed partisans of the Mindanao Independence Movement were fighting an ongoing war with a Christian settler militia called the *Ilagas* (Rats). In nearby Lanao del Norte the Muslim warlord Ali Dimaporo, a Marcos ally, battled Christian gangs allied with the opposition political party.[117] "Philippine democracy was digging its own grave," observed the historian Resil Mojares. "Successive elections . . . created ever widening circles of political revulsion and cynicism in Philippine society."[118] After a brief hiatus for the November balloting, the bombings resumed.

Between March and August of 1972 a climate of fear seized the capital as some twenty bombs erupted across Manila, rocking the telephone exchange on August 15 and blowing up a water main four days later. In September six more bombs blasted Quezon City Hall and caused forty-two casualties in a crowded department store. Again the president blamed the communists, particularly Maoists in the fledgling New People's Army. Then, on September 22, mysterious gunmen ambushed Defense Secretary Juan Ponce Enrile's security cavalcade near Wack-Wack Golf Club, raking his car with automatic gunfire. Reacting to this attack on a senior cabinet officer, Marcos declared martial law at 9:00 p.m., promising to put an end to the crime and chaos.

While the communists had probably ordered the Plaza Miranda bombing, reliable sources indicate that Marcos may have orchestrated most of the others, fomenting disorder to build public support for the ultimate guarantor of social order, authoritarian rule. From fragmentary evidence it seems that Marcos worked through General Ver to carry out a destabilization operation similar to his earlier, abortive plans for the conquest of Sabah. In the midst of these bombings, Senator Aquino released a copy of Marcos's secret orders "to sow violence and terror in order to lay the groundwork for the imposition of Martial Law."[119]

Although Aquino's accusation at first seemed partisan and histrionic, subsequent events lent weight to his words. Fourteen years later, when Marcos fell from power, people began talking. A senior officer revealed that a close relative, Gen. Ramon Cannu, one of General Ver's deputies in the Presidential Security Unit, had "organized some of the bombings that were done to convince people that there was a crisis and democracy was not working." In a stunning revelation Defense Secretary Enrile confessed to staging his own assassination attempt to provide Marcos with a final pretext for the declaration of martial law.[120] By then this final act was almost superfluous, for Philippine democracy had already been discredited by the long years of crime, corruption, violence, and disorder.

Conclusion

In the years leading up to martial law, electoral violence in the countryside and rising crime in the capital converged to make the Republic seem incapable of ensuring order. Indeed, the statistical indices of disorder were stark. In 1971 the constabulary estimated that there were half a million "loose firearms" in the Philippines, one hundred thousand more than in 1950 in the aftermath of a world war.[121] Looking back on these years, one police expert, Cicero Campos, claims that "the state of corruption, hooliganism and gangsterism had become so pervading that it was seriously affecting every aspect of Philippine political and social life."[122] Not surprisingly, the initial public response to martial law was, in the words of the political scientist David Wurfel, "relief at the end of crime and violence."[123] Martial law meant the death of Philippine democracy, but by 1972 a quarter century of violence had so eroded the Republic's legitimacy that few among the masses or middle class mourned its passing.

12

Martial Law Terror

In the fourth month of President Ferdinand Marcos's martial law rule, two constabulary troopers marched a middle-aged Chinese merchant across a Manila parade ground. As they tied him to a stake, Lim Seng joked with the soldiers, still confident that he could buy his way out. Only when they fixed the blindfold to his face did the realization strike home. Lim Seng, Manila's top heroin trafficker, was still straining against the thick ropes lashed across his torso when the first volley struck.[1] Graphic footage of this execution, played and replayed in movie theaters across the Philippines, sent a signal that the president's firm hand had restored public order and saved the nation's youth from the scourge of drug addiction.

Law and order were central to the legitimation of Marcos's authoritarian regime, which he grandly christened "the New Society." In the first years after he declared martial law in 1972, his restoration of security won him wide public support and a tenuous political legitimacy, particularly in Manila, where crime and chaos had been most acute under the Republic. During the first years of authoritarian rule, Marcos, then in his prime, proved to be an iron-fisted commander in chief who could control his repressive forces. With characteristic cunning, he divided military authority among trusted subordinates and then played one against the other.[2] To fulfill his mandate for order, Marcos centralized police power, merging the hundreds of municipal forces into an Integrated National Police under constabulary control. Although Marcos's motives were suspect, this new structure represented the first serious attempt in over a century to upgrade the quality of local law enforcement and proved a useful innovation that survived his later fall from power.

Over the longer term, however, the regime's reliance on this police power for covert control harbored a fatal contradiction. Along with his imposition of order Marcos created constabulary antisubversion squads, arming them with both formal decrees and informal impunity to suppress pro-democracy dissidents. After five years of "constitutional authoritarianism," Marcos's security squads shifted from formal mass arrests to extrajudicial operations. As his regime's celebrated "discipline" degenerated into systematic state terror and conspicuous corruption, citizens sensed the failure of their Faustian bargain with dictatorship, swapping democracy for stability, and slowly withdrew their support. Marcos's legitimacy faded, opposition grew, and in the end his massive police and military apparatus retreated before a million outraged citizens massed on Manila's streets. Law and order were central to the regime's early acceptance, but this legitimacy was undermined over time by the same police apparatus that had been used to impose order. In both its rise and demise, Marcos's authoritarian regime thus rested to a surprising degree on the quality of its policing.

In this sense the image of Lim Seng's on-camera execution was an illusion, another act in the dictator's brilliant use of political theater to mask the contradiction between the image and the reality of martial rule. Lim Seng would become the only criminal legally executed in the fourteen years of martial law. But there would be thousands of extrajudicial killings of labor leaders, student activists, and ordinary citizens, their bodies mangled by torture and dumped for display to induce terror. This practice was so disturbing to the country's collective consciousness that the Filipino-English dialect coined the neologism *salvaging* to capture its aura of terror.[3] Tens of thousands more were arrested and abused, arousing both domestic opposition and international opprobrium.

From declaration to decline, Marcos's martial law regime would also feel the subtle force of Washington's influence. In planning his demolition of democracy, Marcos consulted the American ambassador who, concerned by the rising opposition to the U.S. bases, lent tacit support. Several years later President Carter, though troubled by Marcos's abuses, was forced to set aside his human rights concerns to preserve the military bases at Clark Field and Subic Bay. When a democratic opposition challenged Marcos in 1986, the waning of the cold war in Asia had already reduced the strategic value of those bases, allowing the Reagan administration to withdraw support and encourage Marcos's flight into exile. Throughout the fourteen years of dictatorship, however, Washington ignored the regime's repression and backed Marcos with military aid and diplomatic support. By allowing the bases to shape bilateral relations, Washington once again found, as it had during the 1950s, that its military and economic aid was diverted to shore up a small Philippine oligarchy against the democratic aspirations of the masses and middle class.

Police Power

In the first years of the dictatorship, Marcos consolidated his control over the police by degrees in both capital and countryside, slowly transforming their institutional character. The 1973 Constitution, adopted shortly after the imposition of martial law, allowed such centralization in a clause providing that "the state shall establish and maintain an integrated national police." At first Marcos moved cautiously, increasing Manila's force to 3,200 men while leaving real power in the hands of his executive antiriot force, the constabulary's Metropolitan Command (Metrocom). Then in March 1974 he issued Presidential Decree (PD) 421, merging all police in the thirteen municipalities and four cities of Metro Manila into a new Metropolitan Police Force (Metropol) under Metrocom's commander. Once the Manila police force, the most resistant to centralization, was firmly under constabulary control, Marcos proceeded by stages, under PD 421, toward a consolidation of the country's 1,673 autonomous local forces into the Integrated National Police (INP). By 1975 the president had expanded his internal security forces, police and constabulary, to eighty-four thousand officers for a police-citizen ratio of 1:492—nearly double the density at the beginning of martial law only three years before.[4] Finally, under PD 765 of August 1975 Marcos completed this centralization by placing the INP under the Philippines Constabulary (PC) and thereby creating a unified, militarized national police, the PC-INP. By the time formal integration was complete in January 1976, the constabulary, commanded by his loyal cousin, Gen. Fidel Ramos, dominated the new force and its civilian officers were effectively "militarized."[5]

Yet this rapid consolidation could not overcome decades of bureaucratic inertia and remained at best incomplete. Under an awkward civil-military diarchy, the Armed Forces of the Philippines (AFP) directed all police operations while their routine administration remained with the constabulary. The result was, as PC veteran Rod Gutang put it, the forced marriage of "two organically distinct organizations (one civilian, one military) operating as one—the PC composed of 42,000 Constabulary officers and the INP comprising about 65,000 policemen." Although constabulary officers imposed a militarized command over local units, the old municipal police still remained civilians and were not subject to the Articles of War or military courts.[6]

Marcos's police reforms would leave a contradictory legacy of lasting institutional change and embedded corruption. With the creation of the PC-INP in 1975, the Philippines gained a single national police force for the first time in the country's history. Problems that had dogged the municipal police for decades—local politics, low qualifications, and poor training—could now, in theory, be corrected. Moreover, the formation of elite antisubversion units in the capital and regional constabulary commands in the provinces created a tremendous concentration of police power, curtailing many of the country's crime syndicates. The sweeping confiscation of private arms at the start of martial law ended warlord violence, and the Metrocom Intelligence Service Group solved several kidnappings of wealthy Chinese.[7] On the debit side of this political ledger, martial rule removed legal restraints and allowed the internal security agencies, constabulary and local police, to practice both routine human rights violations and systemic corruption.

In the first months of martial rule, Marcos also manipulated the symbols of order to create an appearance of resolute law enforcement. The military quickly disbanded 145 private armies, two for each of country's sixty-seven provinces, and confiscated 523,616 firearms, one for every fifteen adult males. To expunge the culture of violence, military censors blacked out firearms in the hands of movie poster gunmen.[8] In every city constabulary officers enforced a midnight curfew, locking up late-night revelers and forcing them to clean the streets at dawn. With great drama the constabulary closed the Dewey Boulevard casinos and eliminated notorious criminals such as Lim Seng. Indeed, the suppression of illicit drug trafficking constituted martial rule's greatest success, arguably the only facet of Marcos's law enforcement not compromised by countervailing interests. For several years before martial law, the growing incidence of heroin addiction among the Filipino student population, though minimal by international standards, had become a matter of grave public concern among the city's middle and upper classes. Just days after Marcos declared martial law in September 1972, the Constabulary Anti-Narcotics Unit launched a series of raids that netted Lim Seng, two of his laboratories, and over fifty kilograms of recently processed no. 4 heroin.[9] By 1974 a survey found that heroin use had virtually disappeared among students, and within a few more years Marcos's suppression reduced the number of drug users to only 12,000 from a peak of 150,000 in 1970.[10] Many of his other reforms were, however, double-edged. The confiscation of firearms together with the regime's systematic liquidation of the old warlords' loyal hit men both restored public order and left Marcos with an unchecked monopoly on armed force.

Despite this early rigor, crime rebounded in the latter years of Marcos's rule. At the beginning of martial law in 1972, violent crimes dropped from 3.0 per hundred thousand to 1.5, remaining low until 1977. But then they began a steady rise to over 7.2 by 1983, more than double the rate before martial law. In the last five years of the Marcos regime, the police-population ratio dropped steadily—down to 1:1,120 by 1985—while serious crime continued to rise.[11]

In another effort to burnish his law and order image during the first months of martial rule, Marcos also imposed a strict antigambling policy, enforcing a moral order that would appeal to the Catholic middle class. In Manila Marcos padlocked the illegal Roxas Boulevard casinos, and in Cebu City, the country's second metropolis, he closed the local jai alai fronton and turned it into an interrogation center, winning wide support from Cebuano elites.[12]

Not only did the casino closure lend credence to his claims of reform, but many of the old operators were protégés of the American gangster Ted Lewin, a sometime ally of Marcos's blood rival, Vice President Fernando Lopez. Adding a personal edge to this political conflict, the president's brother-in-law, Benjamin "Kokoy" Romualdez, had long hungered, as Marcos's media czar put it, to "avenge himself on Lewin's hirelings who threw him out of the Lewin-run supper club along Roxas Boulevard because he could not settle his gambling debts."[13] When martial law was declared, Kokoy, in another account, raided Club Cairo with a military intelligence squad and "watched while they beat Lewin's club operators."[14] While closing the illegal casinos had been good politics for the Marcos regime, many reopened within two years under informal police protection.[15]

After four years of martial rule, Marcos was confident enough to offend what his media adviser called "the finer sensibilities of the religious" by legalizing gambling. To carry out this major social reform, under Presidential Decree 1067-A of January 1977 Marcos established the Philippine Amusement and Gaming Corporation (Pagcor) to "operate clubs and casinos." In deference to the country's deep moral opposition to legal gambling, the president directed that half the gross earnings be spent on "priority infrastructure and socio-civic projects." Under a string of authoritarian decrees, he then allowed this quasi-governmental corporation to issue casino contracts while exempting it from regular government audits, customs duties, and taxes.[16]

As often happened under Marcos's New Society, a seemingly innovative reform created an opening for old-style crony corruption. In the regime's informal division of spoils, first lady Imelda Marcos's younger sister, Alita Romualdez Martel, had moved first, maneuvering for a share in the venerable Madrigal jai alai concern but settling for a second fronton to anchor her Century Park Sheraton Hotel. Then in 1975 the first lady's younger brother, Alfredo "Bejo" Romualdez, appropriated the Taft Avenue jai alai fronton from the Madrigals, now denied the license they had held for thirty-five years, and then boosted its profitability by opening off-fronton betting stations in slums across Manila.[17]

These jai alai intrigues soon paled before high-stakes corruption involving casinos. Through formal contracts and informal deals, casino profits were eventually divided among Marcos crony Roberto Benedicto, the first lady's Romualdez relatives, and the Macao gambling boss Stanley Ho. In December 1975, well before Marcos formally legalized gambling, Bejo Romualdez opened a casino on a small ship, the M/S *Philippine Tourist,* which was anchored, almost tentatively, in Manila Bay. A year later when Marcos formed Pagcor as a quasi-governmental corporation, its employees issued casino contracts to three Bejo-controlled front companies that would extract an estimated $200 million from legal gambling over the next decade. With casinos now fully legalized, a larger ship, the M/S *Philippine Tourist II,* dropped anchor in Manila Bay. At a grand opening of the floating casino's high-roller gaming tables, Imelda Marcos threw the first dice while President Marcos, Stanley Ho, and the Italian film star Gina Lollobrigida posed approvingly for the cameras. Within months, however, Imelda, in her capacity as the governor of Metro Manila, unexpectedly denounced gambling as an "undesirable vice"—a contradictory stance that made no sense until it became apparent that she was simply blocking licenses for competing casinos in new luxury hotels and thus preserving her family's lucrative monopoly.[18] After three years of operations, the radical, middle-class Light-a-Fire movement made its own moral statement by bombing the floating casino. The ship burned spectacularly and then keeled over, its rusting hulk visible for months to passing motorists.[19]

Instead of shutting down, casino operations expanded for the next seven years, becoming the regime's most lucrative enterprise. Bejo Romualdez shifted his single casino first to the Philippine Village Hotel and later in 1983 to a lavish new building nearby with 142 gaming tables. By the time Marcos lost power in 1986, Bejo's companies were operating ten casinos in cities across the Philippines. There were no restraints on skimming. After averaging only ₱210 million under the Romualdez reign, Pagcor's annual revenues jumped to ₱2 billion in 1987, its first full year *after* Marcos—a sudden tenfold increase in tax revenues amidst a deep recession that can only be explained by massive graft under his regime.[20]

Just as the first family monopolized high-roller casino gambling, so their police commanders syndicated the illegal, penny-ante jueteng lottery that thrived in the country's slums. With the relentless centralization of police power, senior constabulary officers protected regional vice syndicates that soon superseded the long-established local crime bosses. The bandits, outlaws, pirates, rebels, and gunmen—all celebrated in the heroic scripts of local cultures—now gave way to entrepreneurs in vice and violence protected by the national police. Instead of a few bribes to the town mayor and his police chief, the new syndicates made substantial payments to "the many military and police intelligence units which proliferated, all of them wanting a cut."[21] Moreover, the balance between police and syndicates shifted, with PC commanders rising from mere protectors to principals and the once powerful vice lords reduced to bagmen for the military.[22]

Under martial law, a new model crime boss emerged, exemplified by the career of drug kingpin "Don Pepe" Oyson. Born in 1934 at Binondo, the heart of Manila's Chinatown, Jose Oyson became a college basketball star in the 1950s, making connections through the sidelines gambling milieu to become a small-time smuggler around Manila Bay. Slowly, he established himself as a local crime boss in Manila's southern suburban sprawl. In the early 1980s, however, Oyson's fortunes changed dramatically when one of his Chinese partners allied with Marcos's security chief, General Fabian Ver, in a currency smuggling racket. Under the general's protection, petty smuggler Jose soon became the crime boss "Don Pepe" with a Roxas Boulevard nightclub, a large Manila cockpit, and impunity to smuggle. Most importantly, he took control of the illegal importation of methamphetamine hydrochloride (*shabu*), a drug whose energy surge appealed to an expanding clientele among Manila's nocturnal working class—taxi drivers, casino workers, and nightclub hostesses. In 1984, when a provincial newspaper dared to expose his drug smuggling and police protection, Don Pepe's men simply dumped the offending journalist's charred remains into the sea off Cavite.[23] Clearly, a decade of martial rule had not eradicated the vice rackets but instead fostered a more sophisticated syndication complete with national police protection.

State Terror

As martial rule continued, systemic police corruption was matched by rising human rights abuse. Initially, Marcos's military had relied on the legal formalities of arrest and detention to suppress dissent. In issuing Proclamation 1081 to declare martial law in September 1972, Marcos had invoked Article VII of the 1935 Constitution providing that the president "in case of invasion, insurrection, or rebellion . . . may suspend the privileges of the writ of habeas corpus, or place the Philippines . . . under martial law." In his next paragraph Marcos issued a sweeping order that all suspects arrested for crimes against public order "be kept under detention until otherwise ordered released by me."[24] In the weeks following this declaration, the regime rounded up some fifty thousand alleged subversives. Although the number of those officially detained fell to six thousand by May 1975, the police continued to make arrests without warrants. Armed with a blanket Arrest Search and Seizure Order (ASSO) or Presidential Commitment Order (PCO), they routinely confined suspects in extralegal "safe houses" for "tactical interrogations."[25]

During the last years of Marcos's rule, the police grew increasingly brutal, making torture and salvaging standard procedure against both political dissidents and petty criminals. Recent graduates of the Philippine Military Academy (PMA) who joined the constabulary were socialized into a permissive ethos of torture, corruption, and impunity. With unchecked legal authority, limitless funds, and immersion in both psychological and physical torture, a cohort of privileged police commanders formed in the upper ranks of the elite PC antisubversion squads, the Metrocom Intelligence Service Group (MISG) and Fifth Constabulary Security Unit (CSU). Over time martial law transformed these top police into an empowered elite engaged in systemic human rights abuses and syndicated gambling, drugs, or smuggling. Under Marcos military murder was the apex of a pyramid of terror with 3,257 killed, an estimated 35,000 tortured, and some 70,000 arrested. To subdue the population with terror, some 2,520 victims, an overwhelming 77 percent of Filipinos who died, were salvaged, that is, tortured and killed with the scarred remains dumped for display.[26]

Initially Marcos seemed insensitive to foreign accusations of human rights abuse and allowed his military commanders wide latitude in their pursuit of communist insurgents. Just as courtiers jostled for power in the first years of martial rule, so rival security units competed in the hunt for top communists. Under the chief of staff, Gen. Romeo Espino, the Intelligence Service Armed Forces of the Philippines (ISAFP) centralized military intelligence collection and operated against suspected communists through the Military Intelligence Group (MIG). As the president's cousin and chief protector, Gen. Fabian Ver commanded both the Presidential Security Unit, the palace's praetorian guard, and the National Intelligence and Security Authority (NISA). To defend himself against his blood rival Ver, Defense Minister Juan Ponce Enrile created the National Defense Intelligence Office and hunted subversives through his ministry's Security Unit. And, as chief of constabulary Gen. Fidel Ramos, a more distant Marcos cousin, commanded the most notorious antisubversion units, the Fifth CSU and MISG.[27]

By 1975, however, increasing human rights abuses began to attract criticism from both Amnesty International and Washington, creating serious political problems for the regime. In its first report on the Philippines, dated December 1975, Amnesty International devoted nine pages to the Fifth CSU's "systematic and severe torture." Women were being intimidated with "threats of sexual assault," and victims were subjected to "prolonged beatings with fists, kicks and karate blows, beatings with . . . rifle butts, heavy wooden clubs and family-sized soft drink bottles . . . , the pounding of heads against walls, [and] the burning of genitals and pubic hair with the flame of a cigarette lighter." In one example of unconventional psychological techniques, Mrs. Jean Cacayorin-Tayag was "kept sleepless for eight days and nights, made to stand naked for several hours before a full-blast air conditioner and was slapped hard."[28] Amnesty International found "convincing evidence" that torture was "widespread." Of 107 prisoners interviewed, 71 claimed that they had been abused, leading the organization to conclude that "torture was used freely and with extreme cruelty, often over long periods." In particular, Amnesty found that Marcos's suspension of habeas corpus had removed judicial oversight, allowing "a pattern of torture during the period of interrogation immediately following arrest." In a passage that angered Marcos, the rights group reported that in the three years since the suspension of habeas corpus the Philippines had been "transformed from a country with a remarkable constitutional tradition to a system where star chamber methods have been used on so wide a scale as to literally torture evidence into existence."[29] Only a few months after the report was released, U.S. president Jimmy Carter announced his policy of promoting human rights worldwide, adding pressure on Marcos to relax the level of visible repression.[30]

Marcos deflected these pressures by proclaiming the restoration of civil rights and privately pressing Washington to relent by vaguely threatening to abrogate the U.S. military bases agreement. But along with his relaxation of formal repression he intensified covert security operations, in reality producing more torture and extrajudicial executions. In October 1976 he announced that some 2,700 military personnel had been disciplined "for maltreating prisoners held under martial law."[31] To add credibility to these claims of reform, he confessed at the World Peace through Law Conference in Manila in 1977 that "there have been, to our lasting regret, a number of violations of the rights of detainees."[32] The president soon emptied his prisons, reducing the number of detainees from 6,000 in 1975 to only 563 two years later, just as Carter was launching his global human rights campaign.[33] As a part of this image building, the notorious Fifth CSU was renamed Regional Security Unit-4 (RSU-4), and its most brutal interrogator, Capt. Rodolfo Aguinaldo, known for what human rights groups called "his legendary maniacal torture sessions," disappeared inside the regime's gulag.[34] After Marcos agreed in late 1978 to extend the lease on the U.S. bases in exchange for $500 million in aid, the Carter administration began defending the regime's human rights record in the American press. "We had to choose between using our bilateral relationship for human rights objectives and using it first for putting our military facilities on a stable basis," explained the State Department official Richard Holbrooke.[35] In sum, the Philippines provided the ultimate test of Carter's human rights initiative, exposing the contradiction between American ideals and realpolitik of U.S. power that inclined his policy first to compromise and ultimately to failure.

Instead of ending human rights violations, these pressures drove the abuse underground, out of the courts and prisons into a netherworld of safe houses and special security squads. As Marcos courted Washington's support by formally restoring democratic trappings in stages between 1978 and 1981, his secret security operations intensified. In January 1981 he issued Proclamation 2045 ending martial rule. In June he ran for president in an elaborately staged electoral charade. In July he inaugurated his nominally democratic New Republic before a bevy of international observers, including U.S. vice president George H. W. Bush, who famously toasted Marcos's "adherence to democratic principles." But the same proclamation that ended martial law also allowed the suspension of habeas corpus in subversion cases, a proviso that made his restoration of democracy little more than a sham.[36]

To bridge the gap between the rhetoric of legality and the reality of repression, Marcos's antisubversion units operated at night, spreading terror through arrests, salvaging, and torture. The number of salvagings alone rose from only 3 in 1975 to 538 in 1984, a level sufficient to sustain a climate of terror.[37] Since only 5 of 123 military personnel charged with human rights abuses in 1985 were convicted, the Marcos gulag enjoyed a de facto immunity. In the capital, with only four thousand police for six million residents, the metro government deputized hundreds of "secret marshals" to shoot petty criminals on sight, producing over thirty fatalities during the program's first month, May 1985. In the countryside, the constabulary tried to check communist insurgency by arming 110,000 local militia as of 1982, flooding Mindanao with Civilian Home Defense Forces that soon degenerated into what their chief later called "private armies . . . for the personal aggrandizement of the local warlord."[38]

In this twilight between dictatorship and democracy, the constabulary's MISG became the regime's chief instrument for spreading state terror to stifle growing opposition. During the twelve years that he led the MISG (1974–86), Col. Rolando Abadilla, in the words of his obituary, "towered over other heavies in that closed, tight-knit, psychotic club of martial-law enforcers."[39] With his allure of unchecked power, Abadilla recruited bright, young Philippine Military Academy graduates and transformed them into brutal operatives, each of whom later achieved his own notoriety: Reynaldo Berroya (class of 1969), Panfilo Lacson (1971), and Rodolfo Aguinaldo (1972).[40] Under Abadilla and his Deputy Commander Lacson, the MISG emerged as the most ruthless of the regime's antisubversion units during the last six years of martial rule.[41] Abadilla and Aguinaldo cultivated a lethal aura; both were gunned down in precision communist assassinations years after the dictator's fall. Berroya and Lacson were the faceless bureaucrats of state terror; they survived to rise unchecked in the post-Marcos period.

When Marcos tried to cleanse his human rights image, the regime filed two well-publicized torture lawsuits against MISG officers, giving the unit a certain notoriety. In July 1977, just before the World Peace through Law Conference in Manila, the military court-martialed lieutenants Edward Matillano and Prudencio Regis for the torture of Mrs. Trinidad Herrera, the leader of the Zone One Tondo Organization (ZOTO) whose slum work had made her "an internationally-known figure." After her arrest that May, she told U.S. Embassy officers that "after being stripped naked, she was forced to wind an electrode wire around her nipple." Once the publicity faded, both officers were found not guilty. A year later the military charged three MISG lieutenants with the torture of Mrs. Melvin Cayabyab, then two months pregnant, who alleged that "she had been beaten, sexually molested, given electric shocks through wires placed on her thumbs and threatened with rape and application of electric shocks to her vagina and nipples." Although the court sentenced the officers to prison terms and discharge from the service, within a year two of them were back on duty at MISG.[42]

As the regime liberalized after 1978, Marcos nonetheless became increasingly reliant on the MISG and its loyal commander, Colonel Abadilla, to maintain the climate of terror. Abadilla seemed to revel in his reputation, telling a reporter who asked about torture after Marcos's fall, "With crime groups, I had to be violent with them. Meet force with force. The MISG had to be feared."[43] The human rights group Task Force Detainees (TFD) collected detailed documentation about MISG's growing brutality, estimating that twenty-seven of the thirty-eight suspects the unit arrested between 1979 and 1984 experienced physical or psychological torture. Nine of these cases involved extensive electric shocks, indicating that this technique had become a standard procedure.[44] While MISG's interrogators were dispassionate and usually anonymous thanks to their careful use of blindfolds, the Fifth CSU's interrogators practiced a highly personalized, often psychopathic torture that imprinted their names in victims' memories.

In this transition to more aggressive antisubversion operations, U.S. counterinsurgency training may have played a seminal role. By the late 1970s both the

MISG and Fifth CSU (now RSU-4) were employing psychological torture techniques, exemplified by the sleep and temperature modification earlier used on Jean Cacayorin-Tayag, which were quite similar to those utilized by CIA-trained units in Latin America. These parallels in psychological methods by militaries on opposite sides of the Pacific, joined only by a common American alliance, is a telling indication that connections between the agency and the Philippine police may have continued after the U.S. Office of Public Safety quit Manila in 1975. Indeed, just three years later a human rights newsletter reported that MISG's Colonel Abadilla was studying at Fort Leavenworth in Kansas. A year after that another group claimed that Major Aguinaldo was scheduled to go to the United States "for additional training under the Central Intelligence Agency."[45] During the 1950s the agency had developed an innovative method of mental torture that combined sensory deprivation and self-inflicted pain. For the next thirty years, the CIA disseminated these techniques among anticommunist security agencies throughout the third world, first through the Office of Public Safety (1962–75) and after the abolition of OPS through U.S. Army training programs. From the 1960s to the 1980s, army intelligence distributed interrogation training manuals to Latin American militaries that taught interrogation procedures, aimed at breaking the victim's "capacity to resist."[46] Were these Filipino officers, like their Latin American counterparts, given secret training in either tactical interrogation or torture? Since the two key commanders have been assassinated, Abadilla in 1996 and Aguinaldo in 2001, definitive answers must await the future release of classified U.S. documents.

Despite their frequent recourse to brutality, Marcos's internal security services, particularly the constabulary's antisubversion units, engaged in systematic torture that was often more psychological than physical. Indeed, some officers became innovative practitioners of this approach, using a variant that seemed to have been lifted from CIA interrogation manuals. As they probed human consciousness through thousands of torture sessions, these Filipino interrogators carried the CIA's psychological paradigm into its ultimate dimension, combining an expansive theatricality with lurid physical brutality to induce terror not just among their many victims but in the entire society. If, as often happened, these interrogations ended with a victim's death, the perpetrators discarded the mangled corpse in a public place, a roadside or busy intersection, to be seen by passersby. Every road or plaza—indeed, all public space—thus became a proscenium of psychological terror. Seeing the stigmata on the victim's body, or simply hearing of them, Filipinos could read in an instant the entire transcript of torture inside the regime's safe house. The continued suspension of habeas corpus abrogated due process and allowed the military to operate with a "de facto or de jure immunity" to civil prosecution, producing what Amnesty International called, five months after Marcos proclaimed his nominally democratic New Society in 1981, "gross and systematic violations of human rights."[47]

Aberca versus Ver

In the sunset of dictatorship, there was a quiet but historic struggle between Marcos's security services and a small group of human rights lawyers. While military units such as MISG made terror and torture instruments of state power, human rights advocates such as the Free Legal Assistance Group (FLAG) petitioned the courts for writs of habeas corpus, pressing the judiciary to assert its authority over the executive and its military. As the Marcos regime's economic performance declined, public opposition revived and the dictator's nominal reforms did little to still this dissent, making terror and torture his ultimate weapons.[48]

During the first nine years of martial rule, a supine Supreme Court had validated the authority of Marcos's military tribunals and dismissed a succession of habeas corpus petitions. But as Marcos moved to restore the semblance of democracy throughout 1981, the court issued a series of rulings on detention cases that represented the first stirrings of judicial assertiveness. In its decision in *Jose Ma. Sison v. Hon. Juan Ponce Enrile* in January, the court dismissed a petition for habeas corpus by ten detainees on the grounds that it was rendered "moot and academic" by news of the president's plan to lift martial law.[49] In November, however, when the court dismissed another habeas corpus petition by the same detainees, a dissenting justice challenged Marcos's security forces. "With the official lifting of martial law," wrote Associate Justice Claudio Teehankee in a dissent to *Bernabe Buscayno v. Military Commissions,* "there is no longer any justification for continuing to subject petitioners-civilians to trial by military commissions. . . . Since we are not enemy occupied territory nor are we under military government, the military tribunals cannot try and exercise jurisdiction over civilians for civil offenses."[50]

Trying to thread the eye of this legal needle, human rights lawyers challenged Marcos's security state by pressing, in suit after suit, for the restoration of habeas corpus that was nothing less than a struggle against the country's long colonial history. Although the U.S. regime had introduced the principle of judicial review in 1901–2, the Philippine Supreme Court was reluctant to challenge the American governor-general's extensive powers. When drafting the 1935 Constitution for their new republic, Filipino delegates had followed colonial models, particularly the Jones Act of 1916, to create a powerful executive exempt from judicial review or legislative restraint. In drawing up the bill of rights, constitutional delegates specified that the writ of habeas corpus "shall not be suspended except in cases of invasion, insurrection, or rebellion," but then they gave the president wide latitude to waive it "in case of invasion, insurrection, or rebellion, *or imminent danger thereof.*"[51] In his 1973 Constitution, promulgated after the imposition of martial law, Marcos combined these two passages into a sweeping clause providing that habeas corpus "shall not be suspended except in cases of invasion, insurrection, rebellion, or imminent danger thereof, when the public safety requires it."[52] Within the country's conservative legal tradition, this circumscribed right of habeas corpus was nonetheless, as Justice Teehankee noted in 1981, the one opening that allowed judicial review of a powerful executive. In their efforts to reestablish the rule of law under Marcos, human rights lawyers thus faced a succession of daunting hurdles: weak precedents, a timid judiciary, an empowered executive, and an unrestrained military.

These activist attorneys soon collided with Marcos's military in a major legal battle over Operation Crosswind, which had swept up suspected subversives throughout Manila in early 1982. The subsequent human rights litigation is noteworthy for both the revealing documentation about Marcos's security operations in lower court proceedings and a landmark decision issued on appeal to the Philippine Supreme Court. Moreover, this case, *Aberca v. Ver,* would become the only formal test of Marcos's powers of summary arrest to come before a Philippine court, the country's slender substitute for the formal truth commissions found in other postauthoritarian nations.

In the first months of Marcos's New Republic in 1981, General Ver had fused elements from the regime's disparate antisubversive forces—ISAFP, MIG-15, MIG-4, MISG, and the Naval Intelligence Service Group—into Task Force Makabansa. Somewhat later Ver, as armed forces chief of staff, ordered Operation Crosswind to "conduct pre-emptive strikes against known communist-terrorist [CT] underground houses in view of increasing reports about CT plans to sow disturbances in Metro Manila." Thus, on February 25, 1982, the MISG team raided "one of the UG [underground] houses located at Gen. Luis St., Novaliches, Quezon City," where officers seized documents that led to four more raids against alleged underground houses, netting twenty-three "CT suspects." All those arrested were supposedly communists, either top leaders or ordinary cadres.[53]

In their affidavits twenty of these detainees described interrogations with sophisticated torture techniques, indicating a ruthlessly efficient security network at the peak of its powers. Since a multiunit task force had carried out these raids, most victims experienced an initial tactical interview at the MISG offices at Camp Crame or the MIG-15 headquarters at nearby Camp Bago Bantay before moving to a succession of detention centers for more protracted interrogation, often by composite teams. Of the twenty victims who complained of abuse, half reported physical and mental torture at MISG. All units seemed to reserve psychological methods for educated suspects and used physical torture on peasants or workers. At MISG headquarters, for example, Alex Marcelino, a twenty-eight-year-old student at the elite University of the Philippines (UP), suffered sleep deprivation and was "exposed to torture sessions" but was spared beatings or electric shocks.[54]

By contrast MISG's deputy commander, Lt. Col. Panfilo "Ping" Lacson, reportedly subjected one suspect, Marco Palo, a property manager from Angeles City, to four torture sessions with both mental and physical methods. "His captors pummeled him with kicks," reads a legal summary of the abuse, "and banged his head several times against the concrete wall, clapped his ears simultaneously, and strangled him. He was also hit in the midsection and kicked every time he would try to stand. For about two hours, he was subject to electric shocks. As a result, he had to be hospitalized for 23 days."[55] In his later testimony Palo stated that, after the electric shocks had been applied to the upper body at MISG, he was transferred to the Naval Intelligence and Security Force (NISF) building in Fort Bonifacio where he was "blindfolded continuously for three nights and four days; . . . mauled and beaten; . . . [and] choked with a rounded rattan stick" while "constantly threatened that he would be killed if he failed to cooperate." Palo proved to be a careful observer of his tormentors and later matched the timbre of their voices to the names he heard while blindfolded to identify Lieutenant Colonel Lacson and Maj. Rodolfo Aguinaldo at MISG, as well as Lt. Pedro Tangco and Aguinaldo again at NISF.[56]

Similarly, MISG interrogated Noel Etabag, a thirty-three-year-old peasant activist and former fine arts student at the University of the Philippines, with a mix of beatings and electric shocks. "I was being electrocuted for every question asked and accusation hurled," he recalled. "I kept crying out in excruciating pain. But this man kept the electrodes in prolonged contact with my body for the length of time that it took me to answer a question." After a night of such torture at MISG, Etabag was driven to MIG-15 headquarters in Camp Bago Bantay for two weeks of interrogations interspersed with beatings. When he pleaded with Col. Galileo Kinantar of MIG-15 to "respect my person and my rights," there was a brief pause before the questions resumed, now punctuated by a rising tempo of beatings to the head until he finally signed a confession of communist activities.[57]

As these interrogations began, human rights lawyers mobilized by the Free Legal Assistance Group rushed to military camps across Manila in a desperate bid to stop the torture. At 5:00 a.m. on February 27, only fifteen hours after the first raid, FLAG's head, ex-senator Jose W. Diokno, phoned one of his young associates, Arno Sanidad, and dispatched him to MISG headquarters at Camp Crame as the attorney for four detainees. Arriving at 7:00 a.m., Sanidad joined two other lawyers in hours of pleading for an audience with the unit's commander, Colonel Abadilla. When they finally gained access, the colonel dismissed requests to see their clients, saying that "he had no personnel to administer the visits." As reports of additional arrests reached FLAG offices throughout the day, more attorneys rushed from camp to camp searching for their clients before they disappeared into the gulag of safe houses. All were denied both access and information.[58]

Undeterred, these attorneys launched a sustained attack on Marcos's security apparatus. On March 3, only days after the first raids, lawyers for seventeen of the detainees petitioned the Supreme Court for a writ of habeas corpus, challenging the military's use of Marcos's Proclamation 2045.[59] In reply Marcos's solicitor general, Estelito Mendoza, claimed that the suspects had been arrested by Task Force Makabansa under a presidential order validated by Proclamation 2045 that allowed the suspension of habeas corpus in cases of subversion. The solicitor general claimed that the detainee in question, Alex Jazmines, was head of the "major arm of the CPP [Communist Party of the Philippines] engaged in the . . . supply of arms . . . of the New People's Army" and the rest were "communist terrorists and members of the NPA out to cause civil disturbances in Metro Manila." Since "premature communication between the detainees and third parties could result in the escape of others in the subversive movement," the solicitor general asked that the writ of habeas corpus be denied.[60] The next day the Supreme Court, in a cautious decision, decided that the detainees "may confer with counsel and may be visited by immediate relatives . . . with due regard to security measures."[61]

On March 10 the Supreme Court, in a historic assertion of its authority, finally issued a writ of habeas corpus, allowing detainees to be visited by family members, attorneys, and private physicians.[62] Although the military resisted complying fully with the court, the writ had a striking impact on its treatment of the detainees. Soon after habeas corpus was issued, the military confirmed the names of those arrested, and in FLAG's view "the tortures applied on them stopped."[63] The day the court issued the writ the two MISG officers who had been identified by victims signed sworn statements denying any involvement in torture. In his affidavit Lieutenant Colonel Lacson claimed that on February 27, the date of the alleged torture of Marco Palo, he had "begged off earlier not to join the simultaneous raids" and was absent from Camp Crame. On the other days cited in FLAG's complaints, Lacson insisted that he had "not in any single occasion met nor seen the person of Marco Palo."[64] On March 10 as well, Master Sergeant Bienvenido Balaba swore a similar affidavit claiming he had met Marco Palo in his capacity as "the official photographer of the MISG, PC Metrocom," but denying that he had electrocuted him for "one to two hours."[65] As attorneys pressed the Supreme Court for transfers to more formal detention at Bicutan, interrogators tried to silence their victims with threats. At MISG Col. Saturnino Dumlao told detainee Joseph Olayer that he would be transferred to an open detention center if he would "forget" the beatings and "charge it to experience."[66] Similarly, detainee Danilo de la Fuente was "forced to sign a 'waiver' on tactical interrogation" at MIG-15, effectively denying that he had been tortured.[67]

The next day Diokno filed an urgent motion on behalf of Alex Marcelino, stating that the detainee had told his mother during a prison visit that the military had tried to force his confession by subjecting him to four days of sleep deprivation and electric shocks at a safe house. In his complaint Diokno asked that Marcelino be treated by a private physician and transferred to another camp.[68] Two days later at 8:20 p.m. one of Diokno's allies, the distinguished physician Dr. Mita Pardo de Tavera, arrived at the V. Luna military hospital carrying a Supreme Court resolution ordering medical care for Marco Palo. For the next two hours she moved up the chain of command from sergeant to colonel but was forced to leave without seeing her patient.[69]

To resolve the question of torture, which military doctors adamantly denied, the Supreme Court took the unprecedented step of ordering a court-supervised medical examination. On March 13, a medical team led by Dr. Carmen Valero, head of the Supreme Court's own medical services, examined several detainees at V. Luna Hospital. They found that Marco Palo, in particular, showed signs of serious injuries, with "multiple punctate scars in pairs with dried scabs along the two arms of Mr. Palo, similar to those found on plaintiff Noel Etabag." There were similar scars on Palo's "legs as well as his thighs and buttocks," a "healing abrasion" on his lower chest, and below that "a 2 inch linear scar."[70]

This impartial medical examination, which provided unassailable physical evidence, laid the foundations for a landmark human rights case against the Marcos regime. Eight months later, on February 25, 1983, FLAG's lawyers filed a civil suit, *Aberca v. Ver,* on behalf of the torture victims against Marcos's most feared security officers: Chief of Staff Fabian Ver, MIG-15 commander Col. Galileo Kinantar, MISG chief Col. Rolando Abadilla, MISG deputy commander Lt. Col. Panfilo Lacson, and the notorious torturer Maj. Rodolfo Aguinaldo. Led by a team of prominent attorneys—Jose Diokno, Rene Saguisag, Joker Arroyo, and Alexander Padilla—FLAG sought ₱3 million in moral and compensatory damages. Although the paucity of the damages seemed to mock the gravity of the offense, their claim was limited by the civil code's requirement that plaintiffs deposit a percentage of damages sought as bond. The fledgling anti-Marcos movement had no funding, so a young FLAG attorney, Arno Sanidad, collected lunch money from students at the University of the Philippines and Ateneo de Manila University to post bond for the detainees.[71]

Since this was a civil suit for monetary damages and not a criminal action, FLAG's lawyers devoted much of their complaint to establishing the actual harm their plaintiffs had suffered from incarceration and torture. As the primary cause of action, the lawyers alleged that their twenty clients "were subjected to . . . intense and unceasing interrogations . . . with the use of physical and psychological torture"; then, in nine gruesome pages, they summarized the damage done to each.[72]

As expected, a human rights case against Marcos's military did not prosper before his courts. In the government reply to FLAG's complaint, Solicitor General Mendoza alleged that the president's suspension of habeas corpus had denied the plaintiffs a "judicial inquiry into . . . their detention." He also argued that the military defendants were "immune from liability for acts done in performance of their official duties." After months of legal sparring, Judge Willelmo C. Fortun of Quezon City's Regional Trial Court ruled in November, accepting the solicitor general's argument "lock, stock, and barrel" and dismissing the plaintiffs' case on the grounds that suspension of habeas corpus barred any inquiry into security operations. Judge Fortun found that the plaintiffs had presented evidence of actual crimes against only the lowest-ranking accused, Major Aguinaldo and Sergeant

Balaba, and thus had "no cause of action" against superior officers, who were not liable for the actions of their subordinates. On September 21 the regional court issued a final order dismissing the charges against most defendants, leaving only Aguinaldo and Balaba to face a future trial. After this string of defeats FLAG petitioned the Supreme Court in March 1985 for a new trial. The military defendants filed comments in November, but the plaintiffs' lawyers delayed their reply until after Marcos fled into exile the following February.[73]

Two years later, in April 1988, the Supreme Court issued its decision in *Aberca v. Ver,* condemning the lower court rulings and offering a searching critique, avoided by its predecessors, of the damage the now exiled dictator had done to Philippine democracy. "In times of great upheaval or of social and political stress," the court wrote in this landmark ruling, "certain basic rights and liberties are immutable and cannot be sacrificed to the transient needs or imperious demands of the ruling power. The rule of law must prevail, or else liberty will perish." From this position the court ruled that the lifting of habeas corpus "does not render valid an otherwise illegal arrest" but simply suspends the right to a speedy court-ordered release. In a ringing affirmation of human rights, the court concluded, "In the battle of competing ideologies, the struggle for the mind is just as vital as the struggle of arms. The linchpin in that psychological struggle is faith in the rule of law."

On the specific points of law, the Supreme Court also addressed what it called "the crucial issue" in the plaintiffs' petition, asking, "May a superior officer . . . be answerable for damages, jointly and severally with his subordinates, to the person whose constitutional rights . . . have been violated?" Citing Article 32 of the Civil Code, the court ruled that both a subordinate who "directly" violated an individual's rights and a superior officer only "indirectly" responsible were equally liable for damages. Adding force to that argument, a new constitution adopted in 1987 held superiors explicitly responsible for violations of "constitutionally protected rights" by a subordinate. Branding the lower court's dismissal of the charges against the plaintiffs "a grave abuse on the part of respondent judge," the Supreme Court set aside its finding that superior officers could not be held responsible for their subordinates' actions and ordered a new trial for General Ver, Colonel Abadilla, Lieutenant Colonel Lacson, and all the other defendants.[74] Although the lower courts would deliberate and delay for another fifteen years without a resolution, through this landmark case the Supreme Court had broken with an entrenched tradition of judicial conservatism dating back to its founding in 1901. By granting the plaintiffs a writ of habeas corpus in 1982 and then speaking with clarity on constitutional issues raised by the case six years later, it seemed to announce that its historic deference to executive authority had ended and in the aftermath of Marcos's dictatorship the justices would be vigorous in their defense of individual rights against the powers of the presidency.

Loss of Legitimacy

Although terror initially intimidated the opposition, over time it also eroded Marcos's legitimacy, inspiring mass resistance to his rule. After more than a decade of dictatorship, the forces of repression and resistance collided over the brutal, point-blank assassination of opposition leader Benigno "Ninoy" Aquino at Manila International Airport in August 1983. As several million people lined Manila's streets to view his funeral cortege, the killing galvanized the middle class and business elite, breaking the regime's climate of fear and focusing the anger over salvaging on a single case too visible and blatant to be ignored. In effect Marcos's own security apparatus had become the locus of a violence so extreme that, in combination with the corruption crippling the economy, it subverted the underlying logic of authoritarian rule. As Mark Thompson later explained, "Marcos' 'politics of plunder' and arbitrary repression alienated so many segments of Philippine society that he could hardly find a place in it if he stepped down."[75]

In the three years of demonstrations that followed Ninoy's murder, the opposition—through pin prick attacks by its "mosquito press" and constant rallies by the "parliament of the streets"—formed an alternative communications network to reach a consensus that Marcos had lost legitimacy. When he announced "snap elections" in November 1985, Ninoy's widow, Corazon "Cory" Aquino, became the candidate of a unified opposition and aroused an outpouring of popular support as she barnstormed across the country. Although she drew vast crowds and may well have won a majority of the votes actually cast on election day, February 7, 1986, Cory gradually fell behind in the weeks of fraudulent ballot counting that followed. But credible charges of massive cheating soon denied Marcos an electoral mandate, and his attempt to ram ratification of the results through the legislature created a profound crisis of legitimacy.

At this impasse the anti-Marcos opposition rediscovered the crowd and gave it a renewed political meaning. Throughout three years of marches and rallies, Filipinos of both the working and middle classes had learned to mobilize outside the conventional media through pamphlets, posters, faxes, and phone trees. When military rebels mutinied only two weeks after the February elections, more than a million demonstrators massed on the eight-lane highway called Epifanio de los Santos Avenue, or EDSA. At first they came simply to save the rebel soldiers from Marcos's tanks. Over the span of three days and nights on the streets, however, they decided they were there for regime change.[76]

During this mass urban uprising, now called People Power I, sovereignty shifted from the palace and legislature to the people assembled on the streets. Suddenly and mysteriously, legitimacy ceased being a spectral constitutional abstraction and became embodied in the million-plus people who massed on EDSA to form an ad hoc popular assembly. By their sheer numbers and silent witness, they stripped Marcos of his mandate and invested it in his successor.

In the fleeting days of this mass uprising, the symbol and substance of politics merged. Though still a neophyte politician, Corazon Aquino understood the political import of her every action. Returning to Manila from the safety of a southern nunnery, she joined the crowd on the streets as they anointed her with their shouts. Though relentlessly ambitious, the leaders of the military revolt, Defense Minister Ponce Enrile and constabulary chief Ramos, knew from the tenor of these shouts that their coup had failed and the people were investing Aquino with the mantle of legitimacy. In a last bid for a share of power, Enrile and his colonels urged her to accept inauguration inside their rebel military cantonment. Aquino was wary of the symbolism inherent in their insistence. Instead she took her oath before a civilian crowd at the Club Filipino, the symbolic home of Filipino party politics, just a few blocks from the crowds on EDSA, who rejoiced at the news and chanted their confirmation.

Conclusion

In its soaring drama, people power had discovered a bloodless way to oust an entrenched dictator and legitimize a new democracy, inspiring similar demonstrations worldwide from Beijing to Berlin. But it could not solve the most problematic legacy of Marcos's rule, the persistence of his internal security apparatus. Fourteen years of dictatorship had left a lasting imprint on the country's police and constabulary. As Marcos had intended, the creation of a national police force eliminated the plurality of overlapping jurisdictions and their inherent check on central power. In a parallel move the PC-INP did not eliminate crime but only changed its character. Visible violations such as robbery or drug dealing, so disruptive of public order, had declined. But centralization fostered police corruption, which in turn encouraged a the syndication of less visible victimless crimes such as jueteng gambling, drug trafficking, and illegal logging. Moreover, martial rule itself transformed elite constabulary units such as the MISG and Fifth CSU into instruments of state terror, creating a cadre of lethal officers who survived Marcos's downfall and flight.

At a broader, analytical level, the centrality of the constabulary to martial rule illustrates the problematic legacy of U.S. imperial policing for the independent Philippines. Viewed historically, Marcos was trying to re-create a constabulary on the colonial model of total information control. Armed with legal powers akin to an American governor-general, Marcos used the constabulary as a surrogate state apparatus for both routine administration and covert operations. Just as the U.S. colonial regime had once used the PC's Information Division as its political police force, so Marcos relied on the constabulary's antisubversion squads to monitor rumors, surveil dissidents, and censor media. Less visibly, Marcos, like his colonial predecessors, invested these units with the formal and informal authority to conduct penetration, disinformation, and extrajudicial operations. Among these many analogies, there was, however, one key difference. The American colonial government, as an alien regime sensitive to its legitimacy in the eyes of the Filipino people, periodically checked and corrected its excesses. But Marcos showed no restraint and ratcheted up repression until it forced a mass uprising against his rule.

Marcos's police reforms thus left an ambiguous legacy. On the positive side, they created a national police structure that engaged the poverty of local law enforcement for the first time in a century. But they also expanded covert operations and fostered a generation of empowered police commanders who would, through their spectacular violence and corruption, compromise these same reforms and complicate the country's transition to democracy.

U.S. Marine Corps Machine Gun Squad leader Corporal James T. McCormick directs practice fire by Lance Corporal Robert G. Trudette, USMC, and Philippine Marine Private Felix Nabre during SEATO exercises, Mindoro Island, Philippines, March 1962. (U.S. Navy)

On June 21, 1948, President Elpidio Quirino (top, right) met Huk rebel chief Luis Taruc (center) at Malacañang Palace to announce amnesty for the communist guerrillas, producing a brief ceasefire before the start of a six-year insurgency. Desperate for U.S. aid to defeat this peasant revolution, Quirino (above, right) visited Washington, DC, in August 1951 where he met Secretary of State Dean Acheson (above, left) to sign the U.S.-Philippine Mutual Defense Treaty. (U.S. Information Service)

After defeating the Huk insurgency as defense secretary, Ramon Magsaysay was elected president in 1953. Here he reviews the troops at a military parade, circa 1957.

At the height of the anti-Huk campaign in November 1951, Maj. Jose Crisol, chief of the Civil Affairs Office, Department of National Defense, speaks on a national radio network delivering anticommunist propaganda designed by CIA operative Edward Lansdale.

Aircraft carrier USS *Kearsarge* at Subic Bay, Philippines, the largest U.S. overseas naval base during the Cold War, circa 1960. (U.S. Navy)

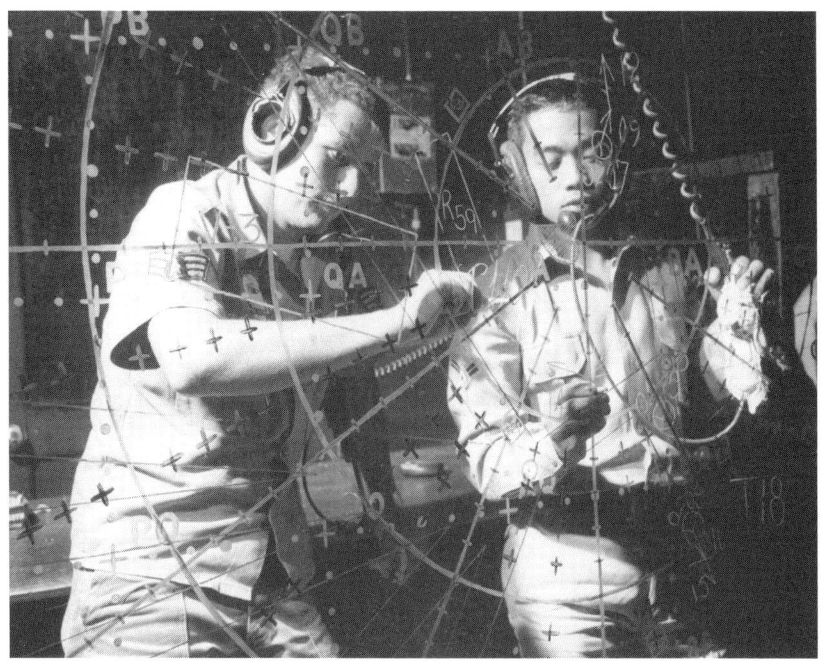

American and Philippine Air Force air traffic controllers plot flight patterns during a joint training exercise at Clark Field, the U.S. Air Force base in the Philippines, August 1962. (U.S. Air Force)

Using vintage American military equipment provided under the U.S. Military Assistance Agreement, the Philippine Army conducts training exercises in the hills of Luzon Island, August 1965.

Student leader Edgar Jopson speaks to demonstrators protesting the burning of a village in Bantay, Ilocos Sur Province, by a warlord's private army, Plaza Miranda, Quiapo, Manila, July 1970.

To contain student demonstrations, Joseph Estrada, mayor of San Juan, Metro Manila, reviews his new riot police, armed and trained with funds from the U.S. Office of Public Safety, August 1971.

Manila's chief of police, Gen. Ricardo Papa, gives orders to a detachment of the Philippine Constabulary's Metropolitan Command (Metrocom) troopers, a force funded by U.S. aid, February 1968.

President Ferdinand Marcos (left) decorates Philippine Constabulary officers, including (from left to right) PC chief Gen. Vicente Raval, intelligence chief Col. Wilfredo Encarnacion, and intelligence officer Capt. Protacio Laroya, Camp Crame, Quezon City, August 1968.

Armed with rifles and riot shields, the Philippine Constabulary's Metrocom (top) prepares to stop a student protest rally, Manila. As thirty thousand marchers approach the presidential palace in September 1984, Metrocom troopers (above) equipped with shields and armored water cannon mass at Mendiola Bridge to stop the march. (UPI, Willie Vicoy)

The League of Filipino Students rallies at the U.S. Embassy to protest the deaths of four fellow students from a brutal form of torture and murder called "salvaging" during the last, lethal years of the Marcos regime, Manila, April 1984. (Andy Hernandez)

President Ferdinand Marcos (left) reviews troops with Armed Forces chief of staff Fabian Ver (center) and Defense Minister Juan Ponce Enrile (right), 1981.

Representative Jose Cojuangco, the power behind the presidency of his sister Corazon Aquino, holding a fighting cock at his private cockpit, Hacienda Luisita, Tarlac Province, January 1988. (Philippine Daily Inquirer)

Rolando Abadilla (left), the former chief of the Philippine Constabulary's elite anti-subversion squad, appears with his defense attorney, Antonio Coronel (right), at his trial for the 1983 assassination of Benigno "Ninoy" Aquino, Manila, January 1988. (Philippine Daily Inquirer)

Senator Joseph Estrada and Representative Nikki Coseteng (left) appear at the July 1989 premier of their feature film *Sa Kuko ng Agila* (In the Eagle's Claws), which depicts Filipino struggles against the presence of the U.S. Navy base at Subic Bay. On April 25, 2001, three months after his forced resignation, former president Joseph Estrada (below) is photographed by Philippine National Police during his arrest on plunder charges. (Philippine Daily Inquirer; Associated Press)

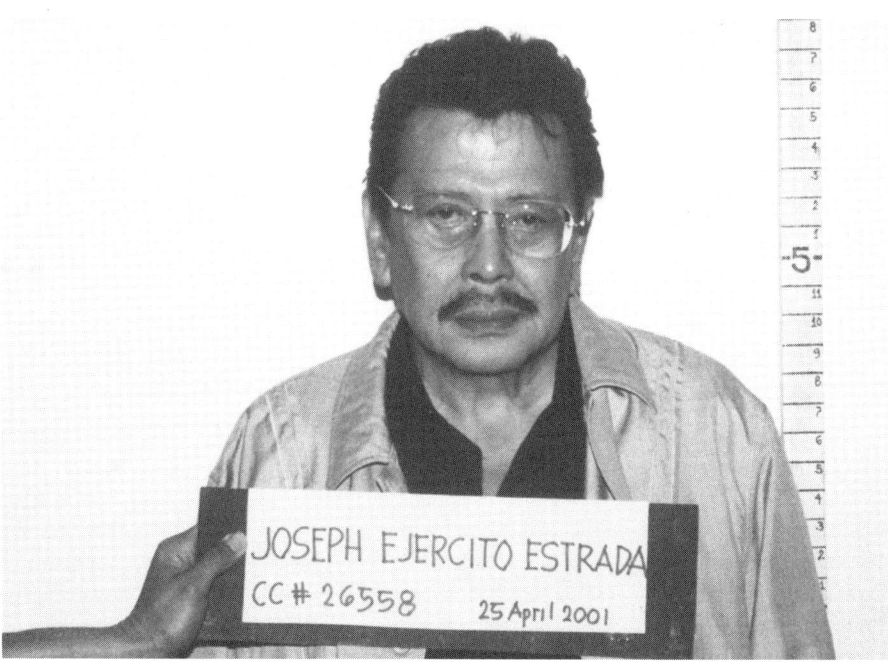

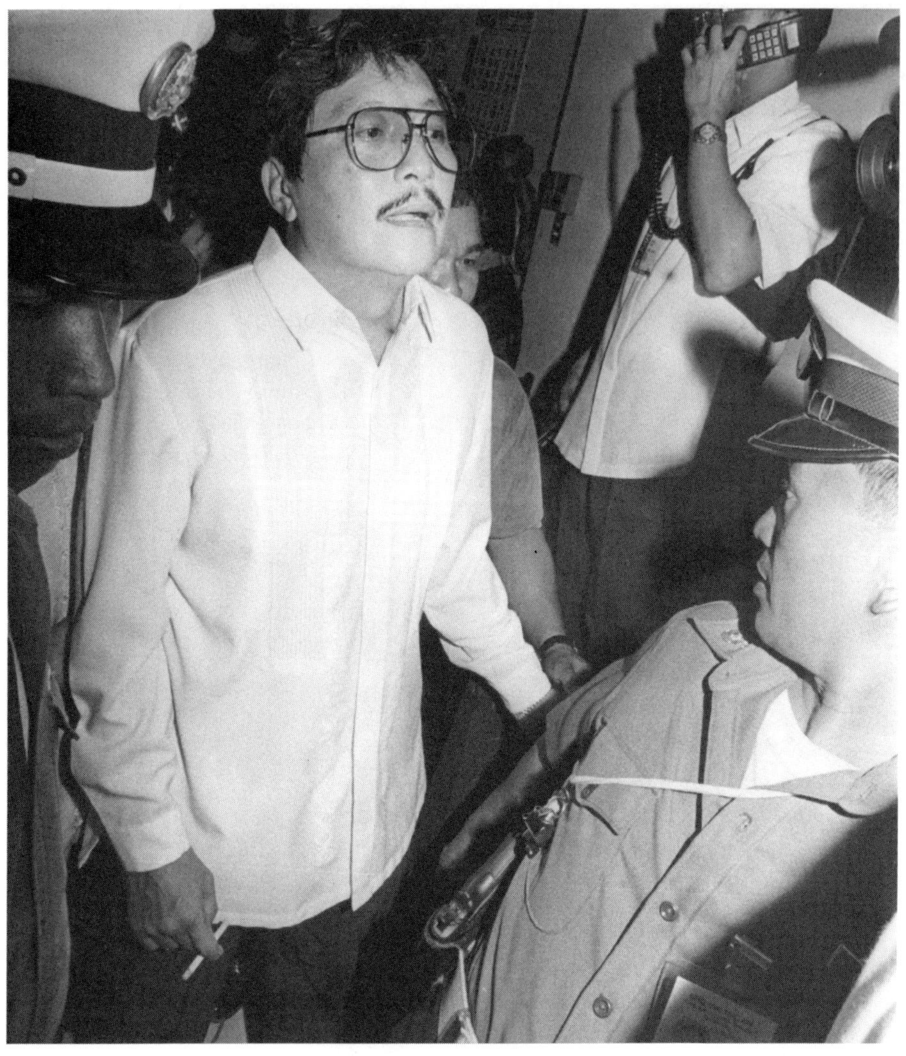

Police Superintendant Reynaldo Berroya during his 1993 trial for allegedly kidnapping Taiwanese businessman Chou Cheung Yih (alias "Jack Chou") and collecting a ransom of ₱10 million. (Philippine Daily Inquirer)

Facing page: Bodies of three of the eleven members of the Kuratong Baleleng bank robbery gang (top, right) executed point-blank by police on Commonwealth Avenue, Quezon City, May 19, 1995. After dismissal of charges for his alleged role in this massacre, former police chief Panfilo Lacson (bottom, center) joined the race against President Gloria Macapagal Arroyo (bottom, right) and opposition candidate Fernando Poe, Jr. (bottom, left), shown shaking hands at San Augustin Church, Manila, on the eve of the May 2004 presidential elections. (Philippine Daily Inquirer; Associated Press, Aaron Favila)

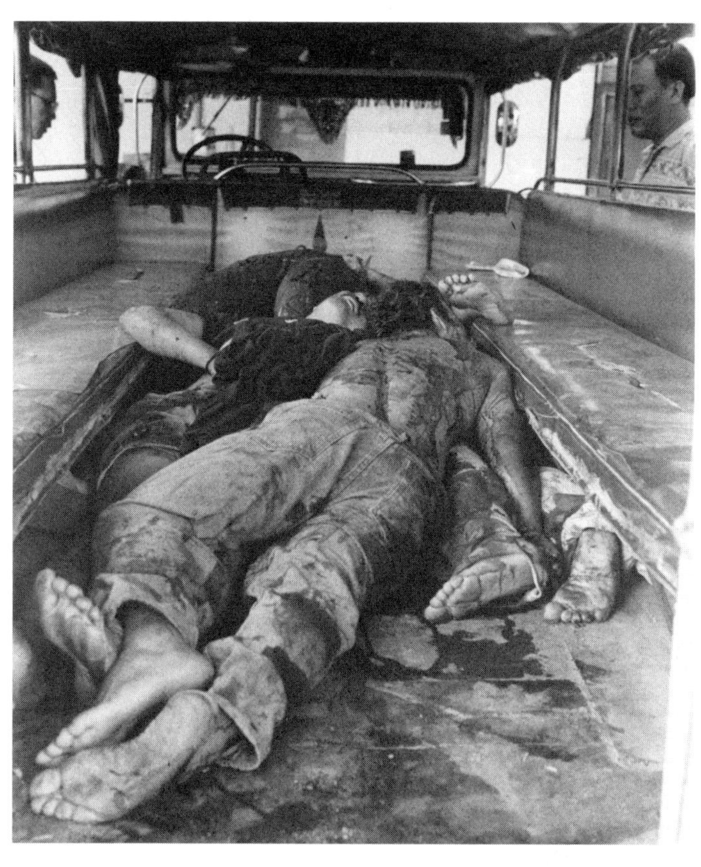

A U.S. trooper stands guard as Filipino schoolchildren wave small Philippine and American flags during the closing ceremonies of U.S.-Philippine military exercises, Indanan municipality, Jolo Province, southern Philippines, March 3, 2007. (Associated Press, Aaron Favila)

Soldier of the Moro National Liberation Front at prayer, Jolo Island, southern Philippines, circa 1988. (Philippine Daily Inquirer)

Facing page: Guerrilla fighters of the Moro National Liberation Front display their weapons, including AK-47 assault rifles and a Soviet B-40 anti-tank rocket, Jolo Island, southern Philippines, February 1988. (Agence France Press, Romeo Gacad)

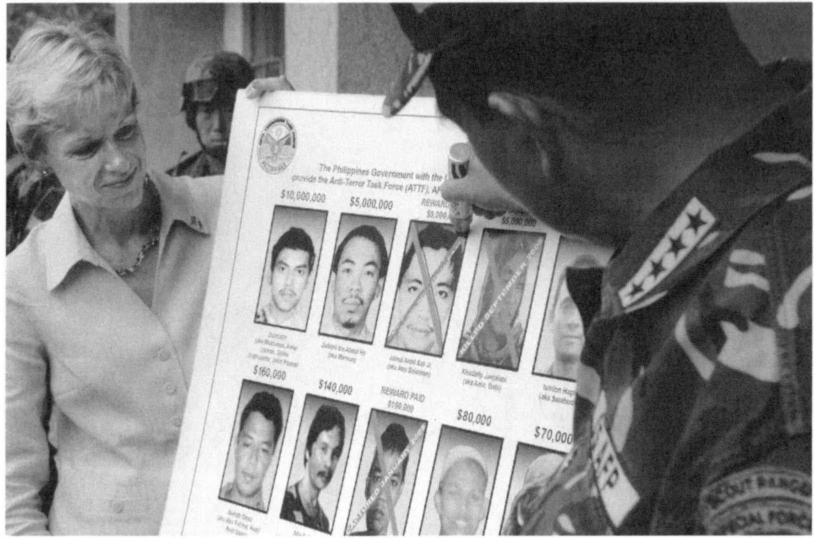

Armed Forces chief Gen. Hermogenes Esperon Jr. crosses off the name of the Philippine government's number three most wanted terrorist, Abu Solaiman, as U.S. Ambassador Kristie Kenney looks on during a "Rewards for Justice" ceremony, Jolo Island, southern Philippines, June 7, 2007. (Associated Press/U.S. Navy, Troy Latham)

While the U.S. embassy focused on the antiterror campaign in the Muslim south, the Philippine military engaged in extrajudicial killings of over seven hundred social activists elsewhere, including the husband and son of Elizabeth Calubad, who commemorates their disappearance at a memorial for the victims, University of the Philippines, Quezon City, September 15, 2006. (Associated Press, Pat Roque)

13

Unsheathing the Sword

In January 1987 some fifteen thousand peasants paraded peacefully before Malacañang Palace, carrying banners and placards calling for President Corazon Aquino to grant them land reform. Suddenly, without any apparent provocation, a ragged line of riot police and marines began firing into the crowd with M-16 rifles. After fifteen minutes of cascading gunshots, bodies lay bleeding on the pavement, seventeen of them dead and sixty-two seriously wounded. President Aquino did not apologize. Nor did she discipline her top police commanders, Gen. Alfredo Lim and Gen. Ramon Montaño. When communist negotiators walked out of ongoing peace talks to protest what they called the "Mendiola massacre," the president "unsheathed the sword of war" and spent the rest of her term trying to crush their guerrilla forces with both conventional and covert operations.[1]

More than any other incident this slaughter illustrates the Aquino administration's reliance on repression rather than social reform to maintain order during a difficult democratic transition. After the fall of the Marcos dictatorship in 1986, the economy struggled under a massive debt from Marcos's "crony capitalism." With stagnant growth and rising political conflict, the fragile, newly restored democracy was soon shaken by crime, coups, and revolution. From the left, the communist New People's Army intensified guerrilla warfare after its leaders quit the peace talks. From the right, nine attempted coups shook the Aquino administration between 1986 and 1990, with one coming perilously close to capturing the palace. As the coups subsided, criminal gangs began hitting banks and kidnapping wealthy Chinese with military precision. Illegal gambling syndicates, restrained under Marcos's martial rule, revived to operate openly by bribing police and politicians.

Although she took office committed to restoring democracy, President Aquino devoted much of her term (1986–92) to preserving and even perfecting the police apparatus introduced under U.S. colonial rule and refined under Marcos's authoritarian regime. She dismantled many aspects of his powerful executive, restoring the bicameral legislature and decentralizing some departments. But she also moved in the opposite direction by expanding the executive's police powers, transforming Marcos's PC-INP into her Philippine National Police and fully centralizing internal security for the first time in over a century. Although they avoided using Marcos's notorious antisubversion squads, her police commanders employed a mix of militia, vigilantes, and "intelligence projects" whose violent excesses were both condoned and denied. Of equal import, her administration became the first to forge a direct link with provincial gambling syndicates, appropriating a share of illicit profits from jueteng lotteries to finance election campaigns and covert operations—a well-kept secret whose full implications for national politics would surface with dramatic effect a decade later. Ironically, it was Aquino's restored democracy, despite all its idealism and avowed integrity, that first combined illegal gambling and presidential power.

In coping with the legitimation crisis that roiled the democratic transition, President Aquino refused to expand "the scope of participation" and instead relied on the powerful security services for repression. Like her predecessors Roxas and Marcos, Aquino would use the state's internal security forces to crush dissent, exempting her from any need for concession or compromise with the poor and middle class. After a decade of Marcos's economic profligacy, the country had ten million homeless, 80 percent of urban households below the poverty line, and 40 percent of workers unemployed—ample fuel for social ferment that Aquino, in the manner of her class, chose to ignore. "The answer to the terrorism of the left and the right is not social and economic reforms," she told graduating military cadets in March 1987, "but police and military action." After abandoning peace talks with the New People's Army, her administration first tried to defeat the insurgency with military force. When conventional tactics failed, she sanctioned secret operations and vigilante violence. To counter Mindanao's Muslim revolt, she used a similar combination of negotiation and coercion, first signing a four-year cease-fire but then turning to military operations when the conflict persisted.[2] In this turn to repression, Aquino enjoyed the full backing of U.S. military advisers, who were rearmed, in the post-Vietnam era, with a new counterinsurgency doctrine called low-intensity conflict (LIC) that they were eager to test under actual combat conditions. During this period of democratic transition when social reform became possible for the first time in a generation, Washington again lent its power to suppressing the signs of social unrest, redoubling the state's repressive capacity and reinforcing its ruling oligarchy.

Although her methods eventually stopped the spread of communist insurgency, Aquino's use of extralegal coercion unleashed a maelstrom of violence, damaging her legitimacy and leaving a problematic legacy. Her compromises over both counterinsurgency and conventional law enforcement fostered a climate of illegality and violence that belied much of the regime's initial promise and contributed to lasting problems of public order.

Compounding the chaos, Manila in the 1990s was, like Shanghai in the 1930s, a free port for criminal rackets, corrupt police, and covert operations. With the end of authoritarian rule, a resurgence of drug dealing, heroin smuggling, and illegal gambling fostered a thriving criminal milieu. The collapse of the Marcos regime released his police into this underworld. The NPA infiltrated its urban partisans into the capital for assassination and expropriation. Manila's Muslim enclave became a refuge for international Islamic terrorist networks. Australian "crims," Hong Kong triad members, and Japanese *yakuza* crowded waterside dives to deal drugs and traffic in women. Foreign espionage agencies trolled the city's shadows, adding to its intrigues. Just as Manila had once been an ad hoc laboratory for colonial policing, so this more recent commingling of the criminal and clandestine fostered a postauthoritarian florescence of its covert netherworld.

Police Reform

After the torture and terror of the Marcos dictatorship, police reforms ranked high on President Aquino's democratic agenda. Although she devolved much of his centralized executive authority back to the legislature and local governments, Aquino refused to return to the scandal-ridden local police of the 1960s. Her new 1987 Constitution enshrined Marcos's unitary national police in the country's fundamental law by providing under Article XVI that: "The State shall establish and maintain one police force which shall be national in scope and civilian in character." In effect, this clause, echoing the 1935 Constitution's provision for Quezon's ill-fated State Police, mandated a single national police force separate from the Armed Forces of the Philippines (AFP) and controlled by civil authorities.[3]

Once the constitution was ratified in early 1987, the Philippine Congress plunged into nearly four years of bitter debate about the shape of the new national police. Over the heated opposition of constabulary officers, who clung to their military status and civil immunity, legislators slowly hammered out Republic Act 6975 of 1990, which merged the constabulary and the many municipal forces into a unified Philippine National Police (PNP), now a civilian service under the Department of Interior and Local Government (DILG). The law barred any active member of the armed forces from serving in the PNP and invested the police with primary responsibility for internal security, including counterinsurgency. In December 1990 President Aquino signed the legislation into law, thereby creating a single, unified national police for the first time in the country's history.[4] In the last two years of her administration, the PNP dramatically increased the number of its officers from 55,000 in 1990 to 101,000 in 1992, almost doubling the density of the police-to-population ratio from 1:1,127 to 1:643.[5]

In applying this law during the last eighteen months of her term, President Aquino relied on a number of Marcos's martial law instruments, most notably his National Police Commission (Napolcom). In two years of preparation for this legislation, Napolcom had mounted an intense effort to upgrade the country's police by weeding out undesirables and holding exams for both entry and promotion. Only 22 percent passed the national exam, a rigorous selection unimaginable for municipal police in the 1920s or even the 1950s. Of equal importance Napolcom heard over a thousand cases brought against officers on charges that ranged from murder to "tong collection," dismissing 184 police officers and suspending 434 more. But, like the military, the police proved, in the words of a New York advocacy group, "unwilling to take serious action against human rights offenders in its ranks . . . for even the most serious violations."[6]

There was also a more immediate political logic driving this process. Though mandated by the 1987 Constitution, the creation of an independent police force gained momentum after a serious coup attempt in 1989. Seeing military rebels come so perilously close to capturing the palace convinced the Aquino administration of the need for a civilian counterforce. Indeed, in this coup's aftermath the government armed the constabulary with light antitank weapons, U.S.-manufactured missiles capable of knocking out the army's tanks in any future coup. Under the 1990 police legislation, moreover, the 43,000 constabulary soldiers and 54,000 police were to be fused into a single force with a projected strength of 120,000, almost equal to that of the armed forces and sufficient, in theory, to counter a future coup.[7] In sum, the Aquino administration returned the military to the barracks but left the national police immersed in both pacification and politics, making the PNP the locus of martial law's most lasting and unfortunate legacies.

Counterterror

Under both the constabulary and the succeeding National Police, counterinsurgency sparked a controversy that would prove damaging to Aquino's restored democracy. In practice, her elegant rhetoric about unsheathing "the sword of war" meant unleashing murderous vigilantes, civilian militias, and covert operations. In adopting this strategy, the president followed the advice of her top security officer, Gen. Fidel Ramos, thereby perpetuating many martial law policies that Ramos himself had crafted as Marcos's internal security chief. To combat a resurgence of NPA guerrilla activity, Ramos, first as AFP chief of staff (1986–88) and then as defense secretary (1988–91), continued martial law's reliance on civilian militias for rural pacification. Instead of Marcos's paramilitary forces, Ramos mobilized so-called vigilantes—a mix of criminal gangs, fanatical cults, and ex-communist guerrillas—to attack suspected subversives. During her six-year term, some twenty-five international fact-finding missions delivered decidedly negative reports about the country's worsening human rights record.[8]

Both the communist insurgency and Aquino's counterinsurgency strategy were largely a legacy of the Marcos dictatorship. As the economy imploded in

Marcos's last years, the communist NPA grew to twenty-four thousand guerrillas with a mass base of nearly two million supporters, making many rural areas virtual liberated zones.[9] Instead of conventional counterinsurgency, Marcos's military had relied increasingly on special intelligence operations. Using hunter-killer tactics developed in the anti-Huk campaign of the 1950s, intelligence units successfully targeted individual communist leaders.[10] Even more effectively, the military developed the novel psychological technique of using deep penetration agents (DPAs). As the NPA spread into the sprawling suburbs of Davao City during the early 1980s, military intelligence units seeded DPAs, or "zombies," inside communist recruitment zones.[11] Whether such infiltration constituted a real threat or was inflated by AFP disinformation, the NPA overreacted by slaughtering "hundreds" of its own members in a futile search for these elusive military moles. By the time the cycle of accusations and executions was exhausted, the NPA's once promising Davao front had collapsed and hundreds of dedicated cadres had become anticommunist vigilantes.[12] Elsewhere in the Philippines the NPA's search for zombies did similar damage, notably in southern Luzon where ex-guerrillas later helped the military exhume forty-eight bodies of comrades executed on the suspicion they were DPAs.[13]

After the collapse of the Marcos regime in 1986, the Philippine military's rediscovery of more conventional pacification methods coincided with codification of a special warfare doctrine by its main ally. In July 1986 the U.S. Army's Command and General Staff College published its *Field Circular: Low Intensity Conflict* with a detailed explanation of the new tactics that the Philippine military embraced with apparent enthusiasm. While conventional military science applies maximum firepower against an enemy, LIC "is often characterized by constraints on the weaponry . . . and the level of violence" since counterinsurgency is above all "the art and science of developing . . . political, economic, psychological and military powers of a government."[14] At the core of the formal LIC doctrine was a combination of social reform and unconventional military procedures, fusing appropriate force with "psychological operations."[15] Without "unduly disrupting the cultural system," the host government should "broaden the bases of political power through education and health programs."[16] Beyond such psywar and civic action, the *Field Circular* also advocated "eliminating or neutralizing the insurgent leadership"—words that repressive third world militaries could readily construe as a recommendation for selective assassination.[17]

Only months after the doctrine's release, President Reagan reportedly signed a "finding" that authorized a two-year, $10 million CIA counterinsurgency effort in the Philippines. Reflecting the administration's reliance on privatized covert operations, the Philippines, like El Salvador and Nicaragua, suddenly experienced a proliferation of Christian anticommunist propaganda and paramilitary death squads. Throughout 1987, Filipino anticommunist activists received a remarkable array of foreign visitors: Gen. John Singlaub (ret.), a former CIA officer who now headed the U.S. chapter of the World Anti-Communist League (WACL); Dr. John Whitehall, a representative of the Christian Anti-Communist Crusade; and agents of the Reverend Sun Myung Moon's anticommunist CAUSA. During his visit to Manila, General Singlaub, earlier identified with death squad activity in South Vietnam and Central America, met CIA station chief Norbert Garrett, AFP chief of staff Fidel Ramos, and Gen. Luis Villareal, head of both the National Intelligence Coordinating Agency and WACL's Philippine chapter. Their recommendations found a receptive audience in Aquino's government, particularly from Interior Secretary Jaime Ferrer, who had used CIA funds to organize election monitors in the 1950s and was now promoting armed vigilantes.[18] The Reagan administration also showed strong "animosity toward the liberal approach" to land reform, allying with conservatives in the Aquino cabinet to block any serious land redistribution.[19]

In this same volatile period, Col. James N. Rowe, commander of the green beret training program at Fort Bragg, North Carolina, arrived in Manila to head the army detachment within the Joint U.S. Military Advisory Group. As a veteran of U.S. Army Special Forces operations in Vietnam, where he was famed for escaping after five years in a Vietcong prison camp, Rowe was uniquely qualified to revitalize the country's counterinsurgency after a decade of decline under Marcos. Indeed, the posting of this top special warfare expert—who was intense, disciplined, and militantly anticommunist—was a strong sign of Washington's renewed interest in the Philippines. During his year in Manila in 1988–89, Rowe, according to the *Manila Times*, "worked closely with the CIA and was involved in a program to penetrate the NPA and the Communist Party of the Philippines which were both undergoing massive ideological upheavals that resulted in bloody purges."[20] A Filipino security specialist described him as "clandestinely involved in the organization of anti-communist death squads like Alsa Masa and vigilante groups patterned after 'Operation Phoenix' in Vietnam which had the objective of eliminating legal and semi-legal mass activists."[21]

As the Philippine military prepared for an assault on the communist underground, these American specialists and their LIC doctrine seem to have encouraged the AFP's rediscovery of counterinsurgency. Often operating on remote fronts in the Visayas and Mindanao, local military commanders also improvised, devising ad hoc tactics by drawing on AFP counterguerrilla doctrines dating back to the Huk campaign. Through the mobilization of militia, ex-guerrillas, and religious cult members, provincial PC commanders unleashed a counterterror campaign against the NPA that fostered a macabre civil war in both urban slums and remote villages.[22]

Initially wary of Aquino's promises of reform, local elites resolved their political differences with the new administration during the 1987 legislative elections and began to support its pacification effort. Significantly, this alliance of local elites and regional AFP and PC commanders produced a combination of accurate information and unrestrained repression far more effective than Marcos's centralized campaign. Through the sum of these efforts—central and local, Filipino and foreign—over a hundred anticommunist vigilante groups were formed across the Philippines in 1986–87, including urban groups such as Alsa Masa in Davao and rural messianic cults such as Tatad, famously photographed in 1987 carrying severed heads. Unable to engage the NPA guerrilla units in armed combat, the vigilantes usually found their victims in legal, cause-oriented organizations such as Task Force Detainees (TFD), human rights groups, and labor unions, notably the National Federation of Sugar Workers (NFSW) and the Kilusang Mayo Uno (KMU, May Day Movement).[23] Within a year, this local patchwork of conventional combat forces and citizen militias had been stitched together into an effective counterinsurgency strategy.

Broad Front Strategy

While this merger of military and militia operations seemed chaotic at the local level, the Philippine military command developed special warfare doctrine that knitted these strands into a coherent strategy. Starting in late 1987 Gen. Ramon Montaño, a Ramos loyalist later promoted to command the constabulary, drew up the "AFP Broad Front Strategy" based on a amalgam of the new U.S. doctrine of LIC and the AFP's own counterinsurgency experience. Pointing to the dismal results of the military's conventional operations in early 1987, Montaño targeted the "mass base support system" that "gives the CPP/NPA force maximum freedom of movement and limits severely government initiatives."[24] Instead of pursuing NPA regulars, Montaño proposed breaking the army's battalions into small Special Operations Groups (SOGs) to occupy communist-controlled villages. As these squads built mass support, the government would translate this loyalty into local Peace and Order Councils to "root out and isolate the insurgent underground," thus defeating "the NPA strategy of encircling the cities from the countryside."[25]

On the surface this formal explanation of the SOGs (later SOTs, Special Operations Teams) echoed the new U.S. doctrine of low-intensity conflict. Examined closely, however, Montaño's rhetoric seemed to mask both extralegal action and a serious tactical flaw. Once the military's SOTs weakened the NPA mass base by their presence and built support for the government, they would, in Montaño's scheme, have to withdraw. At this point the void would be filled by municipal police who could arrest and prosecute any surviving insurgents. But the NPA could return to an area after the SOT pulled out, overwhelming local police with firepower and quickly rebuilding their mass base. Since the AFP lacked sufficient forces to occupy all the communist-controlled villages, the military would have to "neutralize" dedicated NPA supporters or see its program collapse into a costly failure.

The solution apparently lay in tactics developed beyond the bounds of such formal strategy documents. Confidentially, senior AFP commanders admitted that their program had a third, sub rosa phase. After reducing the NPA mass base and building their own, each SOT would use a combination of intelligence, torture, and interrogation to identify NPA supporters for extrajudicial elimination, much as the LIC *Field Circular* had implied. After testing the program in northern Mindanao in late 1987 and Bikol in early 1988, AFP commanders began deploying SOTs in target areas across the archipelago. From the outset there were indications that the special teams were targeting legal cause-oriented groups for neutralization. In his strategy document, for example, PC General Montaño wrote about the threat of "clandestine infiltration of media, the government bureaucracy and some human rights organizations by leftist propagandists," adding that another communist "master stroke was the infiltration of clergy with Marxist ideologues."[26] Similarly, his Negros Occidental commander, Lt. Col. Miguel Coronel, launched a propaganda campaign in mid-1987 that identified the Basic Christian Communities, NFSW, and TFD as communist fronts.[27] As the AFP applied this strategy nationwide in late 1987, militias and vigilantes began summary executions of suspected communist supporters with tacit government support. Leftist groups that had been the core of the anti-Marcos movement were now branded subversive and marked for elimination, a political volte-face that weakened support for the new democratic order.

Total War

After declaring "total war" on the communists in February 1987, President Aquino marshaled her armed forces for a counterinsurgency campaign that combined covert and conventional warfare. "Fight with every assurance," the president told her military a year later, "that I will stand by you, share the blame, defend your actions, mourn the losses, and enjoy the final victory that I am certain will be yours."[28] Aquino's six-year war on the communists involved a three-tiered strategy with conventional military operations to clear NPA guerrillas from their liberated zones, local militia to secure these areas against further infiltration, and a secret, sustained counterterror operation against legal leftist groups. In this lethal warfare there were three main targets: Muslim separatists; rightist military plotters; and the communist NPA, both its rural rebels and urban partisans.

The campaign soon raised human rights violations to new heights. In key battlegrounds such as the islands of Negros and Mindanao, conventional military operations involved forced massive population relocations called "hamletting." When the AFP swept the six towns of southern Negros with Oplan Thunderbolt in April 1989, helicopter gunships blasted the hills while infantry soldiers searched villages, forcing some thirty-five thousand residents to flee. Over a thousand similar incursions between 1986 and 1991 generated over 1.2 million refugees nationwide, with most concentrated in Mindanao.[29] Although the military sweeps produced protests and negative media coverage, over the long term these operations were effective in reducing mass support for the communist guerrillas. At the end of her term in 1992, President Aquino claimed that her military operations had cut the number of NPA guerrillas by half to 13,000 and the number of communist-controlled barrios by 70 percent from 8,496 to 2,819.[30]

To fight this dirty war in city and country, the constabulary used battle-hardened combatants, both AFP veterans and ex-NPA guerrillas, to form militias for conventional counterinsurgency and extralegal operations. After abolishing the Integrated Civilian Home Defense Force (ICHDF), notorious for its atrocities under Marcos, Aquino issued a midnight decree just ten days later, Executive Order 264 of July 25, 1987, forming an almost identical force called the Citizens Armed Force Geographical Unit (CAFGU). Organized in units of eighty-eight "volunteers" and thirteen military regulars, the CAFGU forces, with generous funding of ₱578 million, grew to eighty-nine thousand militia members nationwide in 1992 and soon accounted for 70 percent of the armed encounters with the NPA in Mindanao. The CAFGU was also responsible, from 1988 to 1992, for some 3,146 human rights violations involving torture, rape, murder, and massacre.[31]

Military support for the vigilantes seemed to encourage their violence against civil groups deemed communist fronts. While most CAFGU were uniformed units subject to some military control, the vigilantes were religious cults and anti-communist groups inclined to extreme violence. Within months after Marcos's fall, regional constabulary commanders, following the broad outlines of General Montaño's plan, began arming folk Christian cults and ex-communists for an unrestrained war on NPA guerrillas and their legal activist organizations, which General Ramos branded communist fronts.[32]

The first vigilantes appeared in Davao City in southern Mindanao where Lt. Col. Franco M. Calida, the PC Metropolitan District commander (Metrodiscom), recruited NPA defectors, called "returnees," to form the group Alsa Masa. By the time Calida took command in July 1986, three years of the NPA's murderous urban warfare in Davao City's sprawling Agdao slum, along with its bloody purge of suspected infiltrators, had produced a small counterguerrilla street gang that became the core of Alsa Masa. "The infiltration ignited a purge within their ranks," the colonel recalled. "The NPAs killed left and right and even their own comrades did not like it." With the support of a Davao planter named Jesus "Chito" Ayala, a key presidential adviser, the colonel distributed arms to transform this small gang into a large militia. On the streets of this sprawling city of a million people, armed Alsa Masa patrols engaged in executions and collected "contributions" from Chinese merchants. Over the airwaves, their voice, Jun Porras Pala, broadcast with a .357 magnum handgun strapped to his hip, warning, "We will exhibit your head in the plaza. . . . Damn you, your brains will be scattered in the streets." Adding substance to these threats, the colonel decorated his parade ground with eighty-seven skeletons, each bearing the name of a murdered communist cadre. Ignoring these excesses, President Aquino, speaking before thousands in Davao City in October 1987, hailed Alsa Masa as the "model in the battle against . . . Communist insurgency."[33]

A second anticommunist front soon emerged in Negros Occidental, a central Philippine province with large sugar plantations and impoverished workers. Playing on the province's deep class divide, the local NPA command had developed a formidable force by early 1987 with 134,000 organized workers, 8,200 guerrilla fighters, and 764 "revolutionary barrios." To counter this threat, PC colonel Miguel Coronel allied himself with local planters to form some 32 vigilante groups, including the PC Forward Command, which was responsible for a string of executions. With General Montaño's backing and ₱20 million from local planters, the PC Forward Command grew rapidly into a force of 1,600 men operating out of fifty-two remote bases in northern Negros. The colonel also conducted indoctrination seminars for some 350,000 participants. And, in a complementary effort, his headquarters branded thirty-five Catholic priests out of the one hundred in the diocese as communists, prompting death threats against several and a grenade attack on Bishop Antonio Y. Fortich by a shadowy vigilante group called the Kristiano Kontra Komunismo (KKK). With the support of such groups, the province's constabulary had killed 236 guerrillas and captured 186 firearms by 1989, effectively defeating the communist threat in Negros Occidental.[34]

Struggling to check communist advances in other critical areas, the constabulary headquarters also turned to veterans of Marcos's antisubversion units, the Metrocom Intelligence Service Group (MISG) and Fifth Constabulary Security Unit (CSU), ignoring the taint of torture allegations. At Cebu City in the central Philippines, PC Metrodiscom's Panfilo "Ping" Lacson, the MISG deputy commander under Marcos, now led an elite unit allegedly responsible for the assassination of labor activists.[35] In Cagayan Province at Luzon's northern tip, the PC's provincial commander, Rodolfo Aguinaldo, the former head of Marcos's Fifth CSU, formed a militia of fourteen hundred troops. Using psychological warfare he convinced communist cadres that he had infiltrated their ranks with "deep penetration agents" and then watched with mute delight while the NPA slaughtered loyal cadres in pursuit of the nonexistent traitors.[36]

By late 1987 there were an estimated two hundred vigilante groups operating nationwide under a form of loose military control that allowed a proliferation of extrajudicial killings.[37] After two years of rising violence, the Philippine Senate issued a report in April 1988 deploring the "countless violations of human rights attributed to some vigilante groups." In response to the Senate's demand for their dissolution, the Aquino administration and its military allies mounted a vigorous and ultimately successful defense. Branding the attacks on Alsa Masa communist propaganda, General Montaño insisted that their "human rights record is better than some armed forces units."[38]

The human toll of these operations was high. President Aquino's six-year term produced 2,696 dead from salvaging, military massacre, or disappearance, a figure comparable to the 3,257 killed during Marcos's fourteen-year dictatorship.[39] Beyond these troubling statistical indices of rising violence, the constabulary's pacification campaign perpetuated the extrajudicial killings and aura of terror once characteristic of Marcos's rule.

Intelligence Projects

Apart from the many militia and vigilante groups, the military also mounted a smaller number of secret "intelligence projects" whose cohorts quickly degenerated into criminal gangs. Instead of mobilizing militia in particularly difficult areas, the military created countergroups with license to contest the rebel zone by any means necessary, be it murder, robbery, massacre, or mayhem. In both Manila and Mindanao these groups formed around leaders whose charisma and criminality inspired extreme violence against local Islamic or communist rebels. The Kuratong Baleleng Group began as an anticommunist militia in northern Mindanao but soon morphed into Manila's most lethal bank robbery crew. Similarly, the notorious Red Scorpion Group started as a military operation intended to penetrate the NPA's urban terror groups but quickly became the country's top kidnapping gang. Above all the Abu Sayyaf militia was launched as a Muslim counterforce but grew into a kidnapping gang that would be hunted by Filipino forces and U.S. military advisers on Basilan Island after September 2001.[40] In each case military handlers tolerated this devolution into criminality in exchange for a share of the income from robbery and ransom that totaled well over ₱200 million for all three groups.

Kuratong Baleleng first appeared at Osamiz City in northern Mindanao where the military transformed a local gang into an anticommunist counterforce. In early 1987 the patriarch of a criminal clan, the convicted killer Octavio Parojinog, formed a small militia with a relative, Ernesto Acapulco, a former member of Marcos's Presidential Security Command. With automatic weapons from the military, Parojinog recruited some sixty "hoodlums, robbers, car thieves and the like" and launched a reign of terror around Osamiz City, salvaging five NPA suspects, harassing human rights workers, threatening local media, and collecting protection money from Chinese merchants. In October a local congressman, Aquilino Pimentel, complained formally about the group's human rights abuses. General Ramos promised action, forcing the militia to relocate to Pagadian, Zamboanga. Prospering in the midst of all the violence in northern Mindanao, Parojinog allied himself with the local Tad-tad religious cult to harass church groups that were picketing illegal logging.[41] After a few years of such counterterror operations, the Kuratong Baleleng began using its arms and military protection to become the country's most notorious bank robbers.

In Manila constabulary intelligence used similar methods against the NPA's urban terror squads. Starting in 1984 the NPA's urban partisans, the Alex Boncayao Brigade (ABB), formed assassination cells in the metropolis and by early 1987 had one hundred urban guerrillas, called "sparrows," responsible for some thirty killings. Although their numbers were small, they instilled fear by hitting prominent targets who had "blood debts against the people," most notably Manila's northern police commander Tomas Karingal in May 1984, local government secretary Jaime Ferrer in August 1987, and the American adviser Col. James Rowe in April 1989.[42] As the ABB expanded to eighty-nine killings in 1989 and eighty more in the first half of 1990, the constabulary and military countered by recruiting some disgruntled "sparrows" as an urban counterforce. One of these, the head of an NPA assassination squad named Alfredo De Leon, secretly cooperated in a covert operation that netted many of his fellow ABB terrorists and much of the NPA general staff in 1991–92. About this time De Leon, now condemned by his comrades for "finance opportunism," broke with the party and, through clandestine military support, formed the Red Scorpion Group. As a psywar gambit intended to tar the communists and win increased funding, the military itself, the *Philippine Daily Inquirer* claimed, manufactured an image for De Leon as "public enemy number one." Other sources reported that the constabulary's special operations unit, led by the famed intelligence officer Rodolfo "Boogie" Mendoza, was responsible for "formation of the dreaded Red Scorpion kidnap gang." By early 1993, the Red Scorpions had racked up twenty-four kidnappings and netted a remarkable ₱98 million in ransoms.[43]

In the Muslim areas of Mindanao and Sulu, the military applied these clandestine methods with even more dubious results. The focus of these operations was two separatist movements: the Moro National Liberation Front (MNLF), now allied with the NPA for joint terror operations; and the Moro Islamic Liberation Front (MILF), a new force that was growing rapidly through its call for a separate Islamic state. During the 1990s the MILF expanded into a force of fifteen thousand armed fighters trained at thirteen major camps by Filipino veterans of the Soviet-Afghan war. To contain this separatist threat, sometime in 1991 the military reportedly encouraged formation of a breakaway Muslim group, the Abu Sayyaf, which, said one veteran intelligence agent, "created an internal conflict within the MNLF."[44]

Within months of its founding, Abu Sayyaf had 120 fighters, an arsenal of automatic weapons, and a liberated zone on impoverished Basilan Island. Though far smaller than the established rebel groups, Abu Sayyaf's fusion of cash, firepower, and extreme violence soon made it a major Muslim force. Through its leaders, the charismatic Abdurajak Janjalani and the shadowy Edwin Angeles, a military agent who had infiltrated communist groups in Manila during the 1980s, the group was in regular contact with Osama bin Laden's brother-in-law, Jamal Mohammad Khalifa, who was then active in Zamboanga City as a

Muslim philanthropist. Providing another al-Qaeda link, Pakistani terrorist Ramzi Yousef, later notorious for the 1993 World Trade Center bombing, came to Basilan in 1991 to train Abu Sayyaf's first fighters in the use of explosives. Through Edwin Angeles, Abu Sayyaf also forged close ties to the Philippine Marines on Basilan and the military's Southern Command in Zamboanga City, contacts that brought crates of infantry weapons to its camp. Apart from using Abu Sayyaf as a wedge to weaken the MNLF on Basilan, the marines reportedly formed an informal "partnership" to exploit the island's forests through lucrative illegal logging.[45]

So armed, Janjalani proclaimed a violent jihad against Christians by bombing a Protestant mission at Zamboanga in 1991. With spectacular violence that raised its profile in the Muslim movement, the group bombed Davao Cathedral in 1993, kidnapped four Spanish clergymen in 1994, and ravaged the town of Ipil, Zamboanga, in 1995, leaving fifty-three civilians and soldiers dead. Under Angeles, Abu Sayyaf was responsible for 102 terrorist incidents and collected ₱20 million from kidnapping alone between 1991 and 1995. By the time Angeles surfaced and mysteriously surrendered to Sulu's governor in February 1994, this mix of cash and crime had led intelligence chief Gen. Benjamin Libarnes to brand him "a crazy guy who deals only for the sake of money."[46] In retrospect, the costs of this intelligence project seem high and the tangible gains against the Muslim insurgency surprisingly few.

Although insurgency declined sharply by the time President Aquino left office in 1992, her success came at a heavy price: arming of local militia as counterterror squads; creation of a criminal netherworld; and promotion of ruthless police commanders, many of them Marcos era torturers.[47] Indeed, much of the violent crime that would trouble the Philippines during the rest of the decade was a legacy of Aquino's wayward "intelligence projects." Martial law methods of torture, penetration, and assassination were now effectively institutionalized within police and military intelligence units.

Drug Trafficking and Gambling

Aquino's juxtaposition of institutional reform and extralegal controls contributed to a surge in criminality. Stripped of both the rewards and the restraints of authoritarian rule, senior constabulary officers sanctioned criminal enterprises. Across Luzon, jueteng syndicates operated with police and political protection and thus grew to an unprecedented size. In metropolitan Manila powerful robbery gangs began hitting banks with military precision, and dozens of professional kidnapping gangs, several linked to senior constabulary officers, victimized wealthy Chinese. The PC Narcotics Command was implicated in a corrupt nexus of criminal syndicates trafficking in the increasingly popular drug *shabu* (methamphetamine hydrochloride).

Formation of the Philippine National Police and the subsequent doubling of the police force did, however, prove effective in controlling routine criminality such as robbery and rape, starting a steady, substantial drop in index crimes from 143 per 100,000 population in 1990 to just 88 four years later.[48] Yet these reforms could not restrain the surge in violent robberies and kidnappings, creating a disturbing aura of public disorder. Apart from problems of corruption and competence, the police lacked an adequate penal system for due process. Although the country had 167,000 reported felonies in 1983, there were only 15,000 prisoners in custody.[49] This disconcerting gap between crime and punishment may have contributed to Manila police reliance on summary, extrajudicial punishments such as station house beatings, executions, and corrupt alliances with criminal informants, controlling rather than prosecuting criminals.

As rising amphetamine use fueled public anxieties, President Aquino promoted her handpicked commander for the Western Police District, the ambitious Manila cop Gen. Alfredo Lim, to lead the National Bureau of Investigation in a crackdown on crime. Among his more celebrated targets was the city's top drug lord, Jose "Don Pepe" Oyson. After arrest by Lim's agents at a billiards tournament in March 1990, he was fatally shot during the drive to NBI headquarters, a catalyst for his syndicate's collapse under intense police pressure.[50]

The death of Don Pepe was but one incident in a violent struggle for control over the lucrative drug trade between the NBI and the constabulary's Narcotics Command. In July 1990, only four months after Don Pepe's execution, a dramatic shootout in the Makati financial district provided evidence of constabulary corruption. After two months' surveillance of Manila drug dealers, the U.S. Drug Enforcement Administration (DEA) contacted NBI chief Lim to arrange the joint buy-and-bust sting dubbed Operation King Cobra. On July 3 a DEA undercover agent named Philip Needham arrived from Bangkok. Posing as a Colombian dealer he met the Manila socialite and sometime drug broker Estella R. Arrastia at the Westin Plaza Hotel to negotiate for ten kilograms of heroin. While the NBI's hidden cameras rolled, Arrastia introduced the agent to a connection named "Rolly," who was, it turned out, Col. Rolando Q. de Guzman (PMA '61), the deputy chief of Manila's Northern Command and a former covert operative for Marcos. As Needham handed over the cash inside a Makati parking ramp and walked away with the heroin, fourteen NBI agents backed by Lim loyalists from the Western Police District moved in for the arrest. In the shootout that followed, two corrupt constabulary officers and a civilian agent died from bullets fired at close range. Ignoring the dubious circumstances, PC headquarters proclaimed the innocence of its fallen officers and buried them with full military honors. Chief Lim shot back that "their hands were caught inside the cookie jar," producing a volatile interservice rupture that was only stilled through presidential intervention. In its defense the U.S. Embassy released DEA reports that established a key point lost in the debate: senior members of the Philippine police were principals in the country's drug trade.[51]

While drugs remained the province of the corrupt police, legal and illegal gambling became the prime source of funding for political campaigns under President Aquino. To reduce corruption in the legal gaming industry, the Aquino administration attacked the gambling empire of Marcos's brother-in-law and purged his racketeers who were still running the Philippine Amusement and Gaming Corporation (Pagcor), resulting in an immediate tenfold increase in its annual income.[52] But Aquino compromised these reforms by awarding her allies lucrative "rents" from gaming contracts.[53] Confronted with a succession of military coups, the Aquino administration also forged the executive's first explicit alliance with regional jueteng bosses, swapping kickbacks for an executive protection that raised the income and influence of this illicit lottery to unprecedented levels. Political complicity in illegal gambling was blatant, and senior police officials were allied almost openly with syndicate bosses. These secret ties escaped the notice of press and public until scandals years later produced retrospective revelations.

Three years after her term ended, President Aquino's antigambling enforcer, Potenciano "Chito" Roque, appeared before Congress to confess his past corruption as an act of penance.[54] Appointed to head the Task Force Anti-Gambling (TFAG) during Aquino's first weeks in office, Roque made it an executive tool for taxing the jueteng racket, setting a "target monthly collection" of one million pesos from each illegal syndicate. Between June 1986 and October 1989, Roque and his four TFAG bagmen collected ₱43 million from the top twenty-five jueteng bosses.[55] When Pampanga's leading jueteng promoter, Rodolfo "Bong" Pineda, wanted to extend his operations into neighboring Nueva Ecija Province in late 1988, he met with Roque and handed over his first monthly payment of a hundred thousand pesos, thus assuring himself police protection.[56] By late 1987 the system was operating smoothly, with jueteng bosses paying Roque "religiously." If any fell behind, he recalled, "I would order . . . the jueteng operators' joints raided even if the payment was only delayed for two or three days."[57] Jueteng, said one police superintendent, had been "consolidated into one big nationwide operation" coordinated from a penthouse suite at the Silahis International Hotel in downtown Manila.[58]

Although Roque's confession revealed a great deal about the collection of this illegal income, the disbursement of these funds was still shrouded in secrecy. Roque claimed that much of the money was used for countercoup activities, but he refused to name the top politician running this racket.[59] The first hint of this mystery man's identity was revealed during these same 1995 congressional hearings when the former governor of Sorsogon, Bonifacio Gillego, described how a "powerful congressman from Central Luzon at that time" had intervened to protect jueteng in his province.[60]

This political charade continued for another five years until the name of this shadowy "congressman from Central Luzon" was finally revealed during another jueteng controversy. In October 2000, a veteran Tarlac politician told the press that during Aquino's presidency her brother, Congressman Jose "Peping" Cojuangco, had dominated the province's jueteng racket and collected a "management fee" from illegal operators in the surrounding Central Luzon region. Like the political bosses of past generations, Peping allegedly used jueteng to finance the family's political machine and shared its income with followers. During his term as municipal councilor from 1989 to 1992, this source, Gelacio Manalang, admitted receiving monthly payments of five thousand pesos from Peping's operation and used the funds to meet the welfare needs of poor constituents.[61] As a leading Tarlac politician, Peping had won election to the House in 1987 and became president of the administration's political machine, the Pilipino Democratic Party–Lakas ng Bayan (PDP-Laban). And as a longtime cockfighter, he had the connections within the gambling world to extract funding for this loyal bloc of legislators. He also used the money to arm the administration's countercoup force, the famed Yellow Army, paying Israeli mercenaries to train its civilian volunteers on the family's Tarlac plantation, Hacienda Luisita.[62] Apart from appearances during coups, the Yellow Army also provided close-in security for the first family and served as a deterrent to direct attacks on the palace.

Ironically, the proliferation of jueteng under Aquino stoked popular pressure for reform, providing the administration with another means of milking the racket. In 1988 the Philippine Charity Sweepstakes launched the country's first new legal lottery in over half a century, the Small Town Lottery, with the stated aim of undercutting the illegal jueteng business. Supervising the new game's introduction was sweepstakes' chair Fernando Carrascoso Jr., one of Peping's most trusted Tarlac followers, who granted franchises to ten corporations that were largely fronts for the jueteng bosses who were already paying kickbacks to Roque's TFAG. In striking contrast to the integrity of Pagcor's reformed casino operations, the Small Town Lottery was soon riven with corruption, including rigged draws to minimize payouts, kickbacks to the police, and direct payments to local officials. Under these franchise agreements, about 30 percent of the lottery's revenues, nearly ₱18 billion in its first year, were divided between the police and local government officials. Moreover, the lottery's ten franchise holders earned ₱3.6 billion, providing them with ample capital to expand their illegal operations. After corruption scandals forced the lottery's suspension in 1989, illegal jueteng again expanded to fill the void, by this time well rationalized, better capitalized, and more popular than ever. According to senior police officials, Congressman Peping Cojuangco dominated both lotteries, allowing him to shift seamlessly to illegal jueteng after the Small Town Lottery was suspended and thus avoid disrupting the illicit funding that supported his political machine.[63]

Through this commingling of legal and illegal gaming, jueteng bosses achieved unprecedented wealth and influence. Though born a poor peasant, Pampanga's jueteng boss, Bong Pineda, rose from a lowly syndicate bagman throughout the Marcos years to become the country's top jueteng operator under Aquino by paying ₱90 million a month to her brother Peping Cojuangco. According to police sources, such influence allowed Pineda to arrange the transfer or dismissal of over a hundred officers who dared to interfere with his operations between 1980 and 1995.[64]

In the closing months of her administration, President Aquino intervened personally to correct this dismal situation by ordering some last-hour reforms. Even these efforts were soon compromised by corruption, which was by now endemic. In 1991 NBI director Alfredo Lim, acting on the president's direct orders, raided leading jueteng operators, including Bong Pineda of Pampanga. But all charges were later dismissed.[65] In January 1992 Aquino replaced Roque's discredited TFAG with a new, untainted enforcement unit headed by Alberto "Ambet" Antonio under the Games and Amusements Board. But instead of attacking "bookie joints and other illegal forms of organized gambling" as ordered, Antonio soon allied himself with Luzon's leading jueteng bosses and used these underworld contacts to establish his own syndicate.[66] By 1995 congressional investigators would estimate jueteng collections at a hefty ₱18 billion annually and the bribes paid to police and politicians at ₱6 billion.[67] After five years of executive protection, jueteng syndicates had become so wealthy, powerful, and entrenched that they could now survive both a congressional probe and a frontal assault by the office of the president.

Conclusion

President Aquino's law enforcement record left a mingled legacy. Crippled from the outset by coups and economic crises, her government failed to curb the eruption of criminality that came with the end of Marcos's authoritarian rule. Moreover, her policy of arming anticommunist militias spawned several notorious gangs whose spectacular violence contributed to an atmosphere of disorder.

Under Aquino's anticommunist campaign, U.S. military aid again played a catalytic role in Philippine politics, providing aid and advisers to revitalize a security system that had withered in Marcos's last years. Amidst the euphoria of the 1986 "people power revolution" rich in the possibilities of change, Washington provided President Aquino, a prominent oligarch, with the military aid and diplomatic backing for raw repression, not only checking communist guerrillas but also stifling the legal struggle for land redistribution. Nor was this the first time the U.S. mission had made this political miscalculation. Just as it had done during the Huk revolt of the 1950s, Washington provided military aid in the late 1980s but failed to promote structural change, crushing the manifestations of social unrest without addressing their root causes. Within a decade, these conflicts, suppressed but not addressed, would again erupt to prompt yet another American intervention, extending this Sisyphean cycle of repression and revolt into a sixth decade.

Viewed across the arc of a century, Aquino's internal security policy was but a phase, albeit an important one, in a historical dynamic that deepened the influence of police within the Philippine polity. When she broke with popular forces and rejected their bid to broaden democratic participation in the aftermath of dictatorship, she did so with the knowledge, shared by the country's elite, that the constabulary had the overt and covert resources to constrain lower-class dissent. Her option for repression rather than reform was thus presaged by the presence of powerful security forces within the state bureaucracy—units, personnel, precedents, and policies that dated back to 1901. Similarly, her administration's ability to tap illegal gambling for black funding rested on legal prohibitions, introduced under U.S. rule in 1908, that are necessary preconditions for any vice economy.

In this time of crisis Aquino also presided over covert innovations that went far beyond her formal role in creating the Philippine National Police. The constabulary's penetration operations used agent provocateur tactics that were similar to those Colonel Crame had once deployed to split Dimas-Alang in 1912. But these efforts went much further by forming clandestine countergroups to contest the dissident netherworld with unrestrained violence. Even though the illegal gambling industry had developed as a response to colonial prohibitions circa 1908, her administration was the first to impose central controls over its illicit profits, forging direct sub rosa ties between the state and criminal syndicates.

Caught in its own contradictions, Aquino's administration failed to suppress the most spectacular crimes, suffered a progressive loss of popular support, and left a problematic political legacy. At an institutional level, she abolished the most abusive of Marcos's antisubversion units and succeeded, where Quezon had failed, in establishing a national police capable in theory of curbing local excesses and improving law enforcement. But from a broader historical perspective, centralized police power, introduced by Marcos and perfected by Aquino, allowed their successors both a covert capacity in the capital and control over criminal syndicates across the archipelago. As the vice sector expanded under a restored democracy, the empowered police became increasingly autonomous, gaining sufficient influence and income from corruption and expanded intelligence funding to emerge as a new power center in the country's politics. Over the longer term, Aquino's creation of the centralized PNP thus added yet another layer to the extraordinary police powers of the Philippine executive, amplifying the potential for abuse.

The semiformal symbiosis of national police, politicians, and jueteng fostered under Aquino's administration would persist long after she left office. From the estimated gross of ₱18 billion in 1988, her second year in office, the proceeds from jueteng doubled to ₱37 billion in 2000. Her successor Fidel Ramos would try, with limited success, to break this alliance between police and underworld. By purging senior police officials, exposing corruption in Congress, and prosecuting jueteng bosses, President Ramos would attack the entrenched syndicates, reducing their reach but ultimately failing to weaken their underlying resilience.

14

Ramos's Supercops

JUST BEFORE DAWN ON MAY 19, 1995, a cavalcade of thirty-five vehicles stopped near a flyover on Commonwealth Avenue in Quezon City, the nation's capital. Fifty muscular men got out, all armed with pistols and rifles. Several stepped into the street to stop the early morning traffic of buses, taxis, and cars. The remainder formed a ragged circle around two Mitsubishi L-300 passenger vans and on command fired erratically, bullets puncturing the thin steel of the sliding doors. Their magazines emptied, these on-duty police officers opened the vans to strip handcuffs from eleven bleeding bodies inside. From his high perch behind the wheel, the driver of a bus halted by the police was stunned. Immobilized, almost paralyzed, this involuntary witness seemed frozen until shouts and threats from the officers snapped his stupor and the traffic started moving.

Business done, the cavalcade returned to Philippine National Police headquarters where the operation's commanders reported a dangerous shootout against desperate criminals. Newspaper headlines screamed "Cops Gun Down 11 Bank Robbers." The national police chief hailed the blow against Manila's rampant crime. President Fidel Ramos praised the "successful operation," which had been made possible by "effective intelligence" from his elite police units. Even as witnesses came forward to charge that this had been a cold-blooded execution, Ramos backed his police commanders, frustrating any attempt to prosecute them for the murder of these eleven suspects.[1] This tidy yet unconvincing story soon collapsed, and competing versions of "the Kuratong Baleleng massacre" would be debated, often at the highest levels, for another decade.

If there is any deeper significance to this slaughter, then the Ramos administration seems to represent the culmination of the covert police capacity introduced by Spain, refined by American governors, and used repeatedly by Filipino presidents in times of crisis. Even more than its predecessors the Ramos administration was shaped by the culture of internal security. As President Marcos's martial law constabulary chief, Ramos had made the country's police the steel in authoritarian rule. As defense secretary under President Aquino he had merged over a thousand municipal forces with the constabulary to form the Philippine National Police. Through this slow accretion of police power, Ramos acquired the skills, military coterie, and mass following that would elevate him to the presidency in 1992. With the capital still wracked by the lurid violence of a troubled democratic transition, Ramos attracted a winning plurality because he alone could contain coup threats and crime waves even though much of the disorder was caused by his former subordinates in the Marcos military.

To his credit, President Ramos introduced important reforms that imposed professionalism on a police force that had resisted change for nearly a half century. During his six-year term as president, the budget for policing services more than doubled, mostly for increased staff and better salaries. Ramos also presided over a massive purge of the PNP that saw its chief relieved, sixty-eight generals and colonels retired, and ten thousand uniformed officers criminally charged, though only two thousand were eventually dismissed. Under the National Police Commission merit exams were required from recruitment to promotion, and new, community-based boards encouraged citizens to lodge complaints against erring officers.[2] Through these efforts, security for the ordinary Filipino would improve perceptibly during Ramos's tenure. Major crimes dropped by 44 percent from 67,354 to 37,305, and offenses against persons fell by 31 percent from 36,667 to 25,127.[3] Celebrated by laudatory media coverage, Ramos's elite anticrime squads battled the kidnappers and bank robbers who afflicted the country's economic elite. Simultaneously, police action against drug trafficking rooted in city slums increased sharply from 1,663 raids in 1990 to 5,122 three years later.[4] In sum Ramos's reforms slowly erased the PNP's public image as "a corrupt and incompetent organization" and raised its approval rating from 17 percent in 1993 to 69 percent in 1998.[5] Through its aggressive policing, the Ramos administration enjoyed popular support from a Filipino public yearning for the restoration of order.

With the end of the cold war and the close of the U.S. bases, moreover, Ramos sought to resolve the country's long-running insurgencies with negotiation rather than repression. In 1992 he repealed the Anti-Subversion Law that had outlawed the Communist Party and three years later created the party-list system of sectoral representation to channel activist energies into electoral politics. Without the support of U.S. military aid or the pressure of its global strategic priorities for the first time in forty years, his administration pursued successful peace talks with a surprising range of insurgents—communist, Muslim, and right-wing military.[6]

On closer examination, however, many of Ramos's reforms proved to be both partisan and partial: partisan because he exempted his loyalists and partial because he failed to address the most troubling legacies of the Marcos and Aquino governments. In 1997, the last full year of the Ramos presidency, police actions accounted for 1,074 of the nation's human rights violations compared to just eighty-one for the Armed Forces of the Philippines.[7] Marcos era torturers whom Ramos had protected as President Aquino's security chief now rose to senior police echelons, becoming leaders of his administration's anticrime agenda. With the apparent backing of Ramos and his vice president, Joseph "Erap" Estrada, many police officers routinely scorned due process, instead attacking crime with torture, execution, and "salvaging." Apart from their dubious contributions to law enforcement, these same methods often served venal ends, eliminating rivals and witnesses to corruption.

Much of this extrajudicial force was unleashed on formidable criminal syndicates, which, ironically, traced their origins to misguided security efforts by the Aquino administration. The Red Scorpion Group had started as an "intelligence project" by the Philippine military to counter urban guerrilla warfare but quickly degenerated into Manila's deadliest kidnapping gang, targeting wealthy Chinese. The Kuratong Baleleng Group was likewise launched as an anticommunist militia by the military before becoming notorious for its bank robberies. And Abu Sayyaf, a breakaway Muslim faction that the military formed to weaken Islamic separatist movements, soon morphed into a mercenary kidnapping ring in Mindanao feared by Filipinos and foreigners alike. Each of these syndicates represented nothing less than the failure of conventional security and the state's consequent attempt to restore order by penetrating insurgents' ranks and contesting their control over this clandestine social space. As Aquino's wayward intelligence projects merged with the Marcos era "MISG boys," criminals and crime fighters became virtually indistinguishable, blurring the boundary between police power and the vice economy until it seemed infinitely permeable. As the prime beneficiary of this process, Vice President Estrada would play both sides, winning popularity with the public through his tough stance on crime while boosting the budget for his upcoming presidential campaign with funds extracted from vice syndicates.

Presidential Anti-Crime Commission

In mid-1992 President Ramos took office in the midst of a major crime wave. In slums across the archipelago, methamphetamine abuse, driven by a low-cost version of the drug called *shabu*, continued its inexorable spread. A proliferation of terror incidents and kidnappings in Muslim Mindanao added to the aura of lawlessness. Above all, a sudden surge in bank robberies and kidnappings traumatized the capital and demoralized its business community. According to PNP figures, reported kidnappings nationwide rose from 25 in 1991 to a peak of 179 in 1996.[8] The victimization of Filipino Chinese gave these abductions a racial dimension, and Manila's 500,000-strong Chinese community demanded action.[9] In response Ramos announced the formation of the Presidential Anti-Crime Commission (PACC) headed by Vice President Estrada, who was, through a quirk in the constitution, the candidate of a rival party and a tenuous ally at best.[10]

At a press conference called to accept this appointment, Estrada, a tough-guy movie actor, explained that his years as mayor of San Juan had prepared him for the position. "I policed police," he intoned. "I patrolled the streets." Indeed, one veteran police reporter recalled that Mayor Estrada would line up erring patrolmen in front of city hall and "urinate on each one of them." Secretary of Justice Franklin Drilon recoiled at the news of Estrada's appointment and attempted to curtail his authority by reducing the PACC to a mere "policy making and monitoring body." But the vice president threatened to resign the post unless he was given real police status to pursue criminals. "If the need arises, I will arrest them personally or shoot them personally," he explained. Through such tough talk, which was enormously popular with the public, Estrada extracted expansive powers from the administration, including the authority to investigate, prosecute, and report directly to the president. To operationalize this authority, he won the assignment of forty-four police officers and a substantial budget for his new PACC. "Now that I have accepted the job," he announced with dramatic flair, "I'll spare no one. There would be no sacred cows."[11]

After assuming direct command of the PACC, Estrada formed two elite task forces, Lawin (Eagle) and Habagat (Wind). To staff these squads, Estrada, himself an unrepentant Marcos loyalist, turned to constabulary veterans of the Marcos era unit notorious for torture, the Metrocom Intelligence Service Group (MISG), and appointed its former commander, Col. Rolando Abadilla, as the senior adviser to his PACC.[12] Within this tight network of "MISG boys" two exceptional personalities, Reynaldo Berroya and Panfilo "Ping" Lacson, pursued careers that represented a new dimension in Philippine policing. Their strategic role astride the interstice between palace and underworld won them exceptional influence. Their personal intrigues would shape the direction of national politics.

Within this cohort of elite investigators, Berroya was a few years older than most and remained something of a conventional careerist. After graduating from the Philippine Military Academy in 1969, he rose quickly to become deputy chief of the MISG and played a leading role in the mass arrests that accompanied martial law in 1972. After the 1986 EDSA revolution, he joined the rebels of the Reform the Armed Forces Movement (RAM), participated in their abortive August 1987 coup against President Aquino as a local leader in Central Luzon, and was later sentenced to eight years' hard labor. When Aquino issued an amnesty in early 1992, he transferred to the new PNP and became operations chief of Task Force Gemini, the administration's elite anticrime unit. After President Ramos formed the PACC, Berroya won command of its new Task Force Lawin through his intimacy with the vice president.[13]

By contrast, Ping Lacson seemed transformed by his service in Marcos's elite antisubversion squad. At the PMA he was, according to his superior, Berroya, "known for revolutionizing hazing" of new cadets by introducing "electrocution of the genitalia and pinching a plebe's Adam's apple with pliers." Assigned to the MISG after graduation in 1971, Lacson rose quickly to deputy commander under Colonel Abadilla, winning both commendation and condemnation. In 1982 the constabulary named this young lieutenant colonel "Metrocom officer of the year."[14] That same year the Free Legal Assistance Group named him in a civil suit against Task Force Makabansa, *Aberca vs. Ver,* alleging that he had been responsible for the brutal torture of twenty prisoners by "kicking, punching, beating, boxing, slapping . . . strangulation, stepping on genitals or on the chest . . . electrocution and other similar cruel and inhuman acts."[15]

During Marcos's final months in office, Colonel Lacson and his MISG chief Abadilla remained loyal to the doomed dictator and did not share in the promotions that followed his fall. Even in this climate of democratic reform, however, Lacson somehow emerged from fifteen years' service in a unit notorious for torture with the skills and connections that soon allowed him to resume his rise. According to Berroya, his mentor and later enemy, Lacson exploited his next post as head of the PC's carnapping task force to engage "in the importation of luxury vehicles which were stolen in the United States." Appointed PC provincial commander of Isabela two years later, he allegedly allied with the warlord governor Faustino Dy to kidnap and kill a Chinese businessman, extract fees from illegal loggers, and collect millions as "co-administrator of a province-wide centralized 'jueteng' operation."[16]

As police chief for Cebu City from 1989 to 1992, Lacson formed the Special Police Action Team, known locally as the "Lacson boys," who were believed responsible for salvaging union activists. In one of the most controversial cases, the labor leader Jimmy Badayos disappeared after being picked up by a squad under Lt. Michael Ray Aquino, a young PMA graduate who was fast becoming Lacson's most trusted man. In 1991 two robbers, Amado Galan and Angelo Lawas, were found handcuffed and shot dead at close range after their arrest by fourteen of these "Lacson Boys."[17] Later, as provincial director in Laguna, Lacson reportedly formed a close alliance with gambling boss and Calauan Mayor Antonio Sanchez, who allegedly paid him ₱1.25 million a month to harass rival jueteng operators.[18]

When Vice President Estrada appointed Senior Superintendent Berroya to command Task Force Lawin in 1992, Berroya recommended his old comrade Lacson to head the new unit's other elite squad, Habagat.[19] As President Ramos's top crime fighters, these so-called MISG boys became a new breed of police that the Manila press soon branded "supercops."[20] With the public clamoring for action against crime, the legislature and executive agreed to empower these officers with seemingly limitless resources: advanced weaponry, electronic surveillance, vast discretionary funds, universal jurisdiction, and freedom from meaningful oversight. Their operations soon produced a lurid spectacle of lethal violence, blazing headlines, and seamy scandals. They tapped the phones of senators and generals. They flew 747s like patrolmen rode motorcycles. Their secret meetings were in Hong Kong and San Francisco, not Quiapo or Quezon City. Their cut from crime ran into the millions of pesos, far beyond the fifty peso bill needed to placate ordinary patrolmen. Instead of slapping recalcitrant suspects in the precinct stations, they tortured them for weeks in secret safe houses before shooting them point-blank dead. By the end of President Ramos's term, these police commanders, no longer mere servants of the state, would accumulate all the requisites for political influence at its highest levels. They had loyal followers, powerful patrons, expensive equipment, great wealth, and, most important, sensitive information.

With ample funds and political backing, the PACC's elite strike forces, Lawin and Habagat, countered violence with violence in ways that for many ordinary citizens often seemed necessary to bring the crisis under control. Within three years Estrada would claim that fifty-three kidnapping cases had been solved. His approval ratings soon soared to 75 percent, making him the country's most popular public figure. Yet behind every headline hailing a heroic shootout, a crime solved, or kidnappers captured there was a secret, sordid backstory that the public seemingly knew it did not want to know. Although President Ramos's crackdown on kidnapping was ultimately successful, the mobilization of these elite PNP operational units, armed with authority approaching impunity, created a climate conducive to police abuse, corruption, and criminal collusion. During its first three years of operation, the PACC was responsible for forty killings that one investigator for the National Bureau of Investigation (NBI) called "rub-outs, not shoot-outs." By 1995 the Commission on Human Rights, trial courts, and the House Committee on Good Government would complain that PACC operations were showing a "disturbing pattern of perjury . . . , planting and mishandling of evidence, arrests and searches without warrants, and other violations of human rights."[21] Sharp though these criticisms were, they missed the most serious aspect of the PACC's operations; senior officers, freed from routine oversight, were using their special powers to protect criminal gangs engaged in kidnapping, robbery, and drug trafficking.

In September 1992 the PACC scored celebratory headlines when its officers gunned down five Taiwanese drug traffickers at a Makati townhouse after a high-speed car chase. With pulp-fiction copy and gritty crime-scene graphics, the *Philippine Daily Inquirer* carried the story on page one with a photograph of Estrada examining "packets of shabu found inside the car of suspected drug traffickers." Another photo showed Superintendent Berroya bending over a pool of blood "looking at the bodies of two suspects." Reporting the PACC version almost verbatim, the paper quoted Superintendent Lacson saying that the suspects "ran up the apartment, all the while shooting at us." After autopsies on the five suspects, however, the NBI's chief medico-legal officer reported that "all of them had sustained gunshot wounds in their heads"—incredible dead-eye accuracy in the midst of a running shoot-out.[22]

Writing from prison five years later, Senior Superintendent Berroya admitted that the operation was in fact a staged rub-out. The night before the shooting, he said, he was dining with the vice president at the Sheraton Hotel when Rolando Abadilla, then a PACC consultant, "whispered to me that there was an upcoming operation that Erap had cleared." When Estrada and Berroya rushed to the scene, the signs of staging were obvious. The five corpses were "systematically sprawled in the stairway," and the gang's late-model cars, supposedly targets in a running gun battle, had no bullet holes. When Berroya asked about the inconsistency, Lacson replied brazenly, "Sir, I still plan to use those cars." From a police operative and a widow of one of these Chinese victims, Berroya later learned that Lacson's men had arrested the Taiwanese three days earlier and beat them until they opened their bank accounts. After Lacson and his men collected ₱10 million in drug money and fifty kilos of *shabu,* the "five were killed in Makati in what was made to appear as a 'shoot out.'"[23]

Other operations soon raised public doubts about the efficacy of PACC's violent methods. Under Berroya's own command, Task Force Lawin killed twelve suspected criminals in five months, notably, the controversial 1992 shooting of two Pasay City policemen, Elmer and Joeffrey Pueda, reportedly drug protectors, who were gunned down at close range in another apparent rub-out.[24] Only three weeks after the Pueda shooting, some twenty members of Task Force Habagat broke into the home of an innocent overseas contract worker in Tanauan, Batangas, while searching for a suspected kidnapper. Without pausing to check his identity, the police raiders dragged the victim, Wilfredo Aala, into the yard and shot him fatally while his family looked on. In hearings before the House Committee on Good Government, Representative Teodulfo Natividad, formerly chief of the National Police Commission, denounced the PACC's procedures as "outrageous" and criticized Lacson, saying, "I don't know if this is your method in the old MISG, but we are no longer under martial law."[25] Neighbors staged an indignation rally, and Congress recommended Lacson's indictment. But Vice President Estrada, according to Berroya, later quieted the controversy down with a private payment of half a million pesos to the victim's family.[26] Despite these excesses, the PACC's carefully publicized successes against crime syndicates still won wide public support for its commander, Vice President Estrada.

Red Scorpion Gang

In its crusade against crime, the PACC's most impressive score came when Task Force Habagat liquidated the notorious Red Scorpion Group, Manila's leading kidnapping gang. This victory more than any other burnished Vice President Estrada's image as a crime fighter, contributing to the success of his later presidential campaign. The Red Scorpion Group was the largest of several gangs involved in a rash of kidnapping, much of it directed at affluent members of the Manila Chinese community.[27] At the peak of this crime wave, Lloyd's of London ranked the Philippines as the world's fourth most dangerous kidnapping site. *Fortune* magazine called the country "the kidnap capital of Asia."[28] After long suffering their second-class status in silence, the Manila Chinese found these kidnappings intolerable and demanded action with loud, public protests.[29]

Led by Alfredo De Leon, the former head of a New People's Army (NPA) assassination unit, the Red Scorpions were responsible for twenty-four lucrative kidnappings throughout Metro Manila.[30] The PACC hit back with extralegal tactics. In November 1992, right after Vice President Estrada issued a public promise to get the gang, De Leon's father complained that PACC officers had picked up two female relatives without warrants.[31] According to a later affidavit by a PACC officer, Superintendent Lacson had ordered the interrogation of the missing women, the gang leader's sister and niece, to learn about his movements. For several days in November the women, bound and blindfolded, were questioned by Lacson's aide, Senior Inspector Michael Ray Aquino, in a Pasay motel. Later they were taken to Antipolo for interrogation by Lacson himself and finally to Imus, Cavite, where they were strangled to death. In the words of a police eyewitness, Aquino gave the order for torture, saying, "Make the girls confess by any means because that is the order of Ace [Lacson] and to meet the deadline promised by Vice Erap [Estrada] to the public and the media."[32]

Acting on intelligence extracted from the victims, Task Force Habagat launched successful raids in January 1993, killing six and capturing nine of the Red Scorpions. Police officers told reporters that all those killed had been involved in the earlier assassination of a U.S. military adviser, Col. James Rowe. The gang's bloody end came on February 17 when Lacson led Task Force Habagat in a raid on Calumpit, Bulacan, which netted "public enemy no. 1," Alfredo De Leon, the Red Scorpion himself. According to the PACC press release, Senior Inspector Cezar Mancao broke into a remote Bulacan bungalow at dawn, surprising De Leon. The gang leader jumped out of a window and fled on foot. But Mancao pursued his quarry, catching him at a creek and "felling him with a volley."[33] The killing was a major coup for the PACC and, in one media analysis, "helped build its image as the most efficient crime-busting unit of the country."[34]

Only days after De Leon's death, however, the press offered a more ambiguous picture of this win in the war on crime. In a front-page story, the *Philippine Daily Inquirer* reported that De Leon had been a military asset and his kidnappings were protected by his handler, a senior intelligence officer. De Leon had started his unconventional career as a student activist in the late 1970s, became a labor organizer for the Communist Party, and joined its Alex Boncayao Brigade as an armed city partisan in 1986. Through years of bank robberies and kidnappings for the party, a number of these urban guerrillas had descended slowly into simple gangsterism, most famously De Leon himself. After secretly recruiting him, the military used him for a number of successful operations against the NPA's urban underground. But somewhere the military's "noble project" went wrong. When he broke with the party in 1991 over accusations of "finance opportunism," the military created his Red Scorpion Group as a kidnapping gang, partly to share in the ransom and partly as a psywar tactic to discredit the communists. Arrested in October 1991, De Leon somehow walked out of military detention to launch a new wave of kidnappings that doubled his notoriety. The gang's military handler reportedly took a cut from these ransoms but eventually "terminated" De Leon because, in the words of one military source, "he simply knew too much."[35] In response to this press coverage, Estrada denounced the media for "grossly misleading the public on the actual facts of the encounter."[36]

Following its successes against the Red Scorpions, the PACC suffered a bitter rupture between its top commanders. In May 1993 Superintendent Lacson coyly told the press that a new gang "protected by soldiers" had kidnapped an unnamed Taiwanese businessman, later identified as Chou Chung Yih or Jack Chou, and released him for a ransom of ₱10 million. Three months later, Vice President Estrada identified the masterminds behind this kidnapping as the PACC's own Superintendent Berroya and Gen. Dictador Alqueza, the former chief of the PNP's Narcotics Command. With the dramatic flair that made him the darling of the masses, Estrada handcuffed Berroya, his own compadre, before the television cameras. After their arraignment in November, prosecutors told the press that the ransom had been banked in Hong Kong where these two kidnappers used the cash to purchase amphetamines for resale in Manila.[37]

The trial was a media sensation. General Alqueza made few statements and was eventually exonerated in a lower court. But Berroya had scores to settle and proved to be a redoubtable antagonist. The day after Estrada implicated him in the crime, Berroya issued a press statement charging that Lacson's Task Force Habagat had a "propensity for misusing the powers and resources attached to the office . . . to promote personal ends." In a later prison interview conducted while awaiting trial, he claimed that Lacson had framed him for the Jack Chou kidnapping and referred to Estrada as a "drunken pig." Such confrontation may have contributed to his ultimate conviction. Despite his many denials, a Makati court found Berroya guilty in 1995 and sentenced him to four years' imprisonment.[38]

While Berroya served his time inside Muntinglupa Prison, Ping Lacson continued his ascent. His Task Force Habagat racked up success after success against Manila's most ruthless kidnappers, winning praise from the city's press. Typical of this celebratory coverage, the *Inquirer* carried a front-page story in December 1993 under the banner headline "Colonel, Trader Held for Kidnap." A photo showed Lacson delivering a massive stack of bills—₱1.2 million in ransom money—and two manacled kidnappers to Vice President Estrada while Interior Secretary Rafael Alunan III looked on approvingly.[39]

Kuratong Baleleng Massacre

In this spreading post-Marcos crime wave, bank robbery became, like kidnapping, a scourge that mocked the new democratic regime's capacity to maintain order. Starting in 1987 bank robberies increased rapidly, peaking in 1990 and producing a spectacle of criminal violence. In these three years robbery gangs escaped with a remarkable total of ₱416 million, making crime the country's fastest-growing industry. Not only were the robberies unprecedented in their frequency and violence, but the police and military were implicated at multiple levels.[40]

The Kuratong Baleleng Group won nationwide notoriety for its steely violence. From its birth in 1986 to its bloody death a decade later, the fortunes of the gang were intertwined with those of its military and police protectors. In the eruption of insurgency that followed Marcos's fall, the Kuratong Baleleng first appeared as a militia at Osamiz City in northern Mindanao where they waged a brutal two-year campaign against local communists marked by murder, terror, and salvaging.[41] The gang then shed its military guise and reorganized itself solely as a robbery syndicate, starting with a two-million-peso heist at the Solid Bank in Tangub City in 1988. Drawing on their military training, the gang's ex-soldiers used commando-style assault tactics, cutting down bank security in a blaze of gunfire, cleaning out the vault in five minutes, and then, with blocking forces positioned at key intersections, retreating at high speed through traffic choke points.

After its patriarch, Octavio Parojinog, was gunned down by agents of the 466th PC Company, the gang grew more violent and less cautious. One of Parojinog's sons, Reynaldo, worked the Visayan Islands, racking up a string of successful robberies until his surrender to the Intelligence Service Armed Forces of the Philippines (ISAFP) at Osamiz City in March 1994. His brother Renato also had a remarkable run of bank and armored car heists in Metro Manila until his capture at a Marikina safe house in late 1993. Another crew under their cousin Carmelito Calasan focused on banks in Mindanao and then shifted to kidnapping. Sometime in 1990–91, Calasan recruited Corporal Wilson Soronda, then serving with the 44th Infantry Battalion in Butuan City, who took command after Calasan died in a Cebu shootout with the PACC in January 1994.[42] In the first four months of 1995, Soronda led his Kuratongs, many of them veterans of the 44th Infantry Battalion, in twelve bank and payroll robberies that perfected his signature "shock" assault and netted him ₱70 million in cash.[43]

At the peak of its success, the Kuratong Baleleng scored a record haul that proved to be its undoing. On May 3, 1995, Soronda's crew ambushed an armored car en route to Manila's Ninoy Aquino International Airport (NAIA) and escaped with over $2 million in U.S. currency. Two weeks later banner headlines in the *Inquirer* reported, "Cops Gun Down 11 Bank Robbers: Slain Men Opened Fire, Says Erap." Speaking to reporters, PACC chief Estrada claimed, "We tried to stop them, but they fired their guns and there was no other way but to fire back." In a statement from the palace, President Ramos proclaimed, "We credit this successful operation to the effective intelligence network, set up by . . . Task Force Habagat."[44]

Within twenty-four hours the four strike force commanders submitted a detailed, thirteen-page report describing the operation as a major victory against organized crime. According to their version, a road watch near the gang's Parañaque safe house spotted two Mitsubishi L-300 vans and followed them north up EDSA to Quezon City. As the vans rounded Quezon Circle and headed up Commonwealth Avenue, the lead police squad ordered one van to stop. But "the suspects fired at them prompting the law enforcers to return fire." A second police team, led by Inspector Michael Ray Aquino, tried to block the other van, "but they were met with volleys of fire." In the shootout that followed, the police killed all eleven suspects and recovered four M-16 rifles, ₱392,000 in cash, and "a sketch plan of the $2 million NAIA robbery." About six hours later, at 10:30 a.m., Task Force Habagat officers arrested gang leader Wilson Soronda and persuaded him to lead them to his safe house in Pasig City where "there was a grappling of the firearm . . . which resulted in Soronda's instantaneous death." In their report the commanders—Romeo Acop, Jewel Canson, Francisco Zubia, and Panfilo Lacson—claimed that these shootouts would "reverse the bank robbery picture in the Metropolis and normalize the business and economic environment."[45]

This tale of police heroism soon collapsed. Only three days later an officer involved in the operation, Senior Police Officer 2 Eduardo de los Reyes, told a radio station that the eleven dead gang members had been salvaged. In sworn testimony before the Senate Human Rights Committee, he later stated that he had witnessed the arrest of several suspects and saw policemen removing two cardboard boxes from the gang's Parañaque safe house under the supervision of senior officers Ping Lacson, Romeo Acop, and Jewel Canson. After a stop for interrogation at the PNP headquarters at Camp Crame, the police loaded the handcuffed suspects into a van and drove to the Commonwealth Avenue flyover. Sometime after 3:00 a.m., they "fired at the van using handguns and automatic weapons." When the firing stopped de los Reyes photographed the inside of the van, finding that "the slain persons were all handcuffed with their hands behind their backs." In his Senate testimony, which was broadcast live by radio and television to an audience of millions, he told the legislators, "My conscience would not let me rest."[46] Another participant in the police operation, SPO2 officer Corazon de la Cruz, corroborated his story, as did six civilian eyewitnesses to the shooting.[47]

Vice President Estrada attacked the credibility of these witnesses and defended his squad's circumvention of due process. "These kinds of people don't deserve sympathy because they are ruthless. They kill without impunity [*sic*]," he told the Associated Press in his famously broken English. "It's just right that they were exterminated."[48]

In its own official "after action report" signed by the four police commanders, the task force did not list any expended shells from the gang's van, a clear indication that the deceased had not fired.[49] Six days after the shooting the gang leader's sister, Gemma Soronda Siplon, who had been arrested with him at his Parañaque safe house, was found in Biñan, Laguna, naked, strangled, stabbed twice near the heart, and shot in the forehead and chest.[50] In its autopsy reports, the PNP crime laboratory found that the eleven victims had no gunpowder burns, indicating that they had not fired. All had gunshot wounds to the head, several at point-blank range.[51] In its final report the Senate committee investigating the massacre concluded that the eleven victims were "defenseless" and "were killed in cold blood."[52]

Other, less formal reports suggested that the police not only killed the presumed criminals on the spot but did so for personal profit. As the competition between police and military intelligence grew bitter, both sides leaked incriminating reports to the press, soon making it clear that the gang had been protected by the PACC, military intelligence, or both. On June 14 the PACC released a "confession" by gang leader Soronda, taped just hours before his death, stating that he had shared the $1.8 million from the armored car heist with unnamed military protectors inside the ISAFP.[53] Firing back, the ISAFP leaked a statement by a captured gang member charging that Lacson's PACC protégé, Michael Ray Aquino, had been involved in kidnapping. The ISAFP claimed further that the PACC had recovered $1.8 million from the armored car heist when they arrested the Kuratong gang members and later "secretly deposited the money in a Hong Kong bank."[54] From his prison cell Rey Berroya later wrote a detailed analysis tracing Vice President Estrada's alleged ties to bank robbers and kidnappers. Estrada was, Berroya argued, using command of the PACC to prepare for his upcoming presidential campaign, collecting funds from drug lords and building a covert capacity through alliances with senior police officials.[55]

While these intelligence intramurals continued, twenty-six agents of the NBI completed a careful investigation of the Kuratong case, producing a thirty-seven-page report that was nothing less than an anatomy of mass murder. Drawing on careful forensics and eyewitness statements, the NBI concluded that the killings were "pure and simple summary executions."[56]

This report and later eyewitness testimony offer the most reliable account of what happened that night on Commonwealth Avenue. At 9:30 on the morning of May 17, 1995, Kuratong leader Wilson Soronda landed at North Harbor on a ship from Dipolog and was driven to his Parañaque safe house. At about 10:30 p.m., he loaded an attaché case containing U.S. $2 million and ₱250,000 into the trunk of a new gray Honda Civic and drove to a hotel for the night.[57] An hour later the PNP's Special Action Force (SAF) smashed through the gate of the gang's compound in a V-150 light tank and apprehended eight male suspects without resistance, "lining them up side-by-side prostrate on the floor inside the house."[58] After pistol-whipping the handcuffed suspects about the face, senior PNP investigators, led by Chief Superintendent Lacson and his protégé Senior Inspector Glenn Dumlao, found three duffle bags with about ₱15 million in cash and Japanese yen. With the tactical interrogation done, the police loaded the suspects into the gang's two vans and drove north to police headquarters at Camp Crame.[59] About the same time a PACC squad picked up two more Kuratong members and the gang leader's sister, Gemma Soronda Siplon, at a safe house in Alabang. These suspects, too, were brought to Camp Crame for further interrogation.[60]

Sometime after midnight senior superintendents Zubia and Lacson called their officers into conference at Camp Crame. According to a police officer present, these two ordered their officers "to take the prisoners to Commonwealth Avenue at the bottom of the flyover and there shoot them and make it look like they died in an encounter."[61] At about 4:00 a.m., the police, led by Chief Inspector Michael Ray Aquino, loaded the eleven suspects into the vans and headed north.[62] At the bottom of the flyover the cavalcade pulled over and the police secured the crime scene by stopping an early morning bus to prevent any eyewitnesses. With traffic blocked an officer, in the words of the NBI report, "casually alighted from the front seat, opened the sliding door of the van and fired successive shots towards each of the passengers in the van." Then four police "opened fire at the L-300 van" while the second van was "fired upon by several persons with automatic rifles."[63] One witness, police agent Mario Enad, admitted removing the handcuffs from two bloody corpses while Chief Inspector Cezar Mancao's men removed the rest.[64] For three full minutes after the firing stopped, the bus driver sat in shock until police ordered him to move on.[65] With the stage now set, Lacson drove up in his van, neatly attired for his crime-scene press interview about the desperate "shoot out" with a ruthless criminal gang.[66] The NBI later conducted paraffin tests on all the victims, concluding that none had fired a weapon and several had been shot "at a distance of not more than two (2) feet which certainly belie the shoot out claim."[67]

While her friends and relatives were being butchered, Gemma Soronda Siplon, the gang leader's sister, watched from inside Inspector Aquino's vehicle. Sometime later that day her body was dumped at Biñan, Laguna, in the NBI's stark words, "naked except for a piece of panty that she wore, with two (2) stab wounds on her chest." Just two hours after the shooting, on the other side of Manila, Kuratong leader Wilson Soronda, accompanied by his teenage niece Jane Gomez and her friend Jinky Pait, knocked at the door of Gemma Soronda's Alabang apartment. When the door opened PACC agents waiting inside arrested them all. After a few questions the officers opened the trunk of Soronda's car and found the attaché case. Following a later tactical interrogation at Camp Crame, Jane Gomez was blindfolded and driven to a safe house in Antipolo where she was "made to bare while PACC agents touched her breasts." At 5:00 p.m. she was released near Makati with her friend. That night PACC agents dumped Wilson Soronda's body inside a Pasig apartment, fired two shots, and claimed that the gang leader had died struggling over a weapon.[68] In its final report to the Senate on July 25, the NBI concluded that "the killing of the Kuratong Baleleng gang members is clearly the product of a grand conspiracy among the participating commands of the Anti-Bank Robbery Intelligence Task Group" and recommended that "all officers and men who participated therein should be held criminally liable for the killing."[69]

In the ensuing controversy the four police generals, including Ping Lacson, resigned their posts and the government launched a full investigation.[70] By September, President Ramos had stripped the PACC of its powers and the PNP formed Task Force Dragon to supplant Lacson's now discredited Task Force Habagat.[71]

Despite strong evidence of their guilt, the four police generals played on connections accumulated from years of sensitive operations to avoid a trial. While postponements, reviews, and dismissals pushed the trial date over the horizon, the prosecution's case weakened.[72] In February 1996, the government's review panel voted three to two to upgrade the legal liability of Lacson. But Ombudsman Aniano Desierto overruled his own panel and decided to downgrade Lacson from a principal to a mere accessory after the fact, a ruling that would reduce the gravity of the case and allow its transfer to an ordinary regional trial court with crowded dockets and snail's-pace proceedings.[73]

After a year of procedural delays, the prosecution's five key witnesses announced their withdrawal from the case to protest the ombudsman's whitewash, saying, in the words of eyewitness de los Reyes, "we cannot participate in this mockery of justice any longer." Their attorneys cited "the fear of reprisal, knowing that the accused in this case are . . . powerful top brass of the PNP." In 1997 eyewitness de los Reyes fled to Canada, and in the months that followed four of the five witnesses retracted their allegations after visits from the accused. With its key witnesses now compromised, the PNP dropped its administrative review in December 1998 and the Regional Trial Court dismissed the criminal charges four months later.[74]

Only weeks after the case collapsed, another killing exposed the alliances that made the supercops such a formidable political force. In June 1996 six NPA "sparrow" hit men approached a car driven by Col. Rolando Abadilla, the former chief of Marcos's notorious MISG, and fired a fatal burst of gunfire through the window.[75] At Abadilla's burial with full military honors, a half-dozen of his old MISG boys, now senior police officers, turned up in full-dress uniform to promise revenge. In an emotional eulogy Chief Superintendent Lacson, Abadilla's former MISG deputy, announced "I vow to get your killers all the way up." Hovering discreetly at the edge of the crowd, reporters spotted President Ramos, Abadilla's former PC chief, who had protected him from human rights charges and promoted his MISG boys to command the anticrime campaign.[76] With the president's patronage, these supercops had dominated Manila's criminal milieu and would soon emerge from the next elections in 1998 to win even greater power under his successor.

Abu Sayyaf

After the elimination of the Red Scorpions and Kuratong Baleleng, the armed Islamic group Abu Sayyaf was the last of President Aquino's covert groups to trouble public order. With a drumbeat of terror bombings and kidnappings in the early 1990s, Abu Sayyaf gained an importance that overshadowed its modest force of 650 fighters, less than 10 percent of the Muslim rebels in the southern Philippines. In January 1995 Manila police discovered a local al-Qaeda cell closely connected to Abu Sayyaf that was plotting to assassinate the Pope and blow up eleven transpacific aircraft. Three months later Abu Sayyaf shocked the nation when it attacked the market town of Ipil, Zamboanga, killing fifty-three residents and taking thirty hostages.[77]

Under pressure to penetrate radical Muslim networks, in 1995 the PNP Intelligence Command recruited Edwin Angeles, the veteran agent who had helped found Abu Sayyaf four years earlier. Armed with guns, safe houses, and a monthly stipend of twenty thousand pesos, Angeles worked with the PNP throughout 1995, identifying suspected foreign terrorists in Manila and instigating police raids into the capital's dense Muslim districts. In 1996 he began acting as an intermediary to negotiate the surrender of Abu Sayyaf's charismatic commander, Abdurajak Janjalani. Over the next two years, Angeles formed his own rebel band to operate near Zamboanga and engaged in often byzantine negotiations with PNP intelligence and the AFP's Southern Command headquarters, trying to sell Janjalani's surrender to the highest bidder. Finally, in December 1998, police killed Janjalani in a shootout at Lamitan on Basilan Island. A month later, amid rumors that Angeles had set up the killing, an Abu Sayyaf member shot this longtime police agent in the head as he emerged from a mosque at nearby Isabela on Basilan, eliminating the last of the group's original leaders.[78]

But with arms, cash, and a mass base on Basilan Island, Abu Sayyaf survived. The leadership passed to a second tier steeped in its mix of violence and criminality. With the elimination of its ideological founders, it split into five groups and turned from political terrorism to cash-driven kidnappings. The main faction on Basilan, led by Khadaffy Janjalani, the founder's younger brother, maintained the al-Qaeda link, training its fighters in Afghanistan and receiving Arab visitors with both funds and advice. On Sulu the faction led by Ghalib Andang, known as Commander Robot, won international notoriety in April 2000 by kidnapping ten Europeans from the Sipadan resort in nearby Malaysian waters and collecting a ransom of $10 million. In May 2001 the Basilan group tried to match this coup by zipping across the Sulu Sea in speedboats to raid the luxury Dos Palmas resort on

Palawan Island, taking twenty hostages, including three Americans, among them Gracia and Martin Burnham. After twelve hundred U.S. troops arrived to lead combat training exercises on Basilan, Filipino rangers ambushed an Abu Sayyaf party in June 2002, killing Martin Burnham but freeing his wife.[79]

Instead of defeating the larger Moro Islamic Liberation Front, the Philippine military's tactics had backfired, compounding the problem. Its attempt at using Abu Sayyaf for penetration and division had amplified the Muslim insurgency, transforming a minor rebel faction into a major terrorist group that would trouble the nation for years to come.

Presidential Elections

With their covert connections and sensitive information, the leading supercops, Reynaldo Berroya and Ping Lacson, became major players in the May 1998 presidential elections. In a sordid campaign in which scandal trumped issues, the outgoing Ramos administration bent the law in a determined but doomed effort to defeat the candidacy of its vice president and rival Joseph Estrada. Although Ramos had stripped Estrada of his PACC command, Lacson mobilized his personal network within the police force to gather incriminating information on the administration's presidential slate. Five months before election day, the Supreme Court, acting on a motion by Ramos's solicitor general, Silvestre Bello III, overturned Reynaldo Berroya's kidnapping conviction and freed him from the national penitentiary. As the opposition's leading candidate, Estrada described the sudden release as part of "a hidden agenda to destroy my credibility."[80] Through such intrigues the supercops would play key roles on both sides of the partisan divide during this heated campaign.

The tenor of the 1998 campaign was set in its first weeks when the *Inquirer* published sensational front-page photos of candidate Estrada gambling with stacks of half-million peso chips at Manila's Heritage Hotel casino. Although Estrada explained that the security tape was eighteen months old and claimed the money was a gift from a club owner, critics cited his high-stakes gambling habit repeatedly during the campaign.[81]

In mid-March, with voting just eight weeks away, Berroya made headlines by charging that in 1992 then vice president-elect Estrada had ordered him to assassinate president-elect Ramos as the ballot counting was drawing to a close. Although the accusation had an inherent logic since Ramos's death would have made Estrada president, there was no corroboration. Berroya also charged that Estrada had used his command of the PACC to extract ₱500 million from criminal syndicates. When these headlines faded, military intelligence leaked a report to the press that detailed Estrada's alleged role in the arrest, torture, and strangulation of the two female relatives of Red Scorpion leader Alfredo De Leon, charges that Berroya confirmed in his own statements to the press. After publishing the stories on page one, the *Inquirer* editorialized that such allegations showed Estrada's "unworthiness for the presidency."[82]

Only days before the May elections, another elite PNP unit, Task Force Amihan, acting on orders from Justice Secretary Silvestre Bello, raided the offices of a secret PNP phone-tapping operation inside Camp Crame called Special Project Alpha—headed by Ping Lacson. There the government raiders found "bugging devices allegedly used to tap the telephones of administration candidates." After reviewing the tapes, Senior Superintendent Eduardo S. Matillano, the head of Task Force Amihan and a Berroya protégé, reported that Lacson's men were "illegally using PNP facilities and equipment in conducting partisan political activities."[83] In the end Lacson's covert operations and Berroya's public allegations neutralized each other, allowing Joseph Estrada to hold his pose as a two-fisted crime fighter and harvest the votes of loyal Filipino movie fans, capturing the Philippine presidency by an unprecedented margin.

Conclusion

Apart from the vivid violence, Philippine policing in the 1990s exhibited some striking parallels with colonial practices during the first years of U.S. rule. Amid the postrevolutionary conflicts of 1901, the colonial constabulary had won expansive authority to restore order, much as the PNP did in the postauthoritarian chaos of 1991. Just as Chief Harding had used incriminating information from the Manila's brothels to hold on to his office for over a decade, so the PNP's Rey Berroya deployed political intelligence to revive a ruined career. The old constabulary's Information Division had opened personal mail and corporate files to shape the direction of early Philippine politics; now the PNP's Ping Lacson tapped government telephones to influence the outcome of the 1998 presidential election.

Yet there were also important differences. In 1907 the secret service of the Customs House had anticipated audio and video surveillance by hiding spies in the ceiling and closet of an office for countless hours to surveil just one senior official; in 1998 a PNP task force could scan hundreds of phone calls simultaneously with a single electronic eavesdropping machine. Technology had greatly expanded state surveillance in the intervening century. But on balance the structural relations among police, crime, and covert operations had remained constant.

Indeed, the police powers embedded in the state under U.S. rule reemerged during 1990s as the democratic regime struggled to contain crime, coups, revolts, and revolution, giving the new PNP capacities comparable to those of the colonial PC. Moreover, by creating a pervasive internal security apparatus, the U.S. regime had forged a new path to power, a new cursus honorum, taken by President

Ramos and attempted by a string of unsuccessful presidential candidates—Alfredo Lim, Renato de Villa, and more recently Panfilo Lacson. In their quest for the nation's highest office, these police careerists carried the illiberal values and extralegal methods of their secret services into the presidential arena, linking the covert netherworld ever more closely to the Philippine executive.

More immediately, President Ramos's reforms cut graft inside PNP headquarters but failed to check corruption between regional police directors and gambling syndicates. As the palace pressed the PNP command to purge these "scalawags," both press and legislature focused on jueteng gambling for the first time in nearly twenty years, discovering that this back-alley lottery had become a vast industry sustained by systemic police corruption.[84] Arguing that legalization was the only long-term solution, the Ramos administration revived jai alai in 1995 and, through the Philippine Charity Sweepstakes Office (PCSO), introduced a new on-line Lotto a year later to compete with the illegal jueteng lottery, grossing an impressive ₱1.5 billion in its first year of operation. But Lotto simply added to the gambler's choices and failed, through its uncompetitive odds and poor marketing, to undercut jueteng's phenomenal popularity with the poor.[85]

As part of Ramos's campaign against illegal gambling, the NBI conducted its own inquiry into jueteng, recommending in 1995 that corruption charges be brought against seven syndicate bosses, notably Rodolfo "Bong" Pineda of Pampanga.[86] At first such police pressure seemed to restrain jueteng operations. But instead of eliminating the racket, PNP operations simply shifted control down the criminal hierarchy by breaking the near monopoly on police protection that regional bosses such as Pineda had earlier enjoyed under President Aquino. In Pineda's home province of Pampanga, for example, independent municipal syndicates emerged briefly while he was preoccupied with fighting bribery charges before the courts.[87] Then, as the presidential campaign got under way in early 1997, PNP intelligence reported that the racket was reviving "to raise campaign funds for candidates seeking the presidency and other national positions in 1998." Despite these pending criminal charges, Pineda was soon operating "full blast" through local operators acting as "dummies."[88] As Ramos's term entered its last months in mid-1998, Pineda finally extricated himself from the gambling charges and forged close ties to his successor, Joseph Estrada. After the new administration took office, Pineda was once again running Central Luzon's jueteng racket from behind the twenty-foot walls of his fortress home in Lubao, Pampanga.[89]

Through his purge of corrupt police and parallel pressure on illegal gambling, President Ramos had reduced jueteng by the end of his term. Watching this spectacle of compromise and corruption, Senator Juan Flavier expressed concern that campaign contributions from jueteng bosses would soon dominate elections, warning, with remarkable prescience, "If nothing is done, we may have a president who is indebted to gambling lords."[90] Indeed, as we shall see in the next chapter, after the 1998 elections the new president Joseph Estrada would expand upon Aquino's alliance with the underworld, producing a proliferation of gambling and precipitating one of the most severe legitimation crises in the country's history.

15

Estrada's Racketeering

ON JANUARY 19, 2001, the presidency of Joseph Estrada was in its last desperate hours. For the past four months, a provincial governor had plunged the nation into crisis by repeatedly accusing the president of taking bribes from illegal jueteng gambling. After Estrada's impeachment trial before the Senate produced damning evidence but collapsed on a technicality, tens of thousands of angry middle-class Manileños massed on the EDSA highway for four days of demonstrations known as People Power II. On the final day, the crowd grew to a quarter million, and the tide turned decisively against the president. That afternoon a phalanx of military commanders appeared on EDSA to announce their support for this "people power revolution." By 5:00 p.m., all the senior police officials in Manila had joined the military mutiny save one. Returning to National Police headquarters from the palace, Director Panfilo "Ping" Lacson walked into an office occupied by rebel police officers. Within minutes, Lacson telephoned the president, saying, "I am sorry but we will have to withdraw support from you." In desperation Estrada asked, "Can the police fight the Army?" Lacson replied, "Sir, definitely not." At that moment President Joseph Estrada fell from power.[1]

This bizarre conversation was a fitting close to an unconventional political career. More than any other issue, law enforcement was central to the rise of Joseph "Erap" Estrada from tough-guy actor to president of the Philippines. Unlike leaders past who had risen from province to palace, Estrada served his political apprenticeship as mayor in a metropolis that fused state power, police corruption, and commercial vice. As vice president under Fidel Ramos, Estrada headed an organized crime task force, leading the police in a bloody campaign against robbery and kidnapping gangs. Citing this success, Estrada campaigned for the presidency on a populist platform in 1998, deftly combining his law-and-order record with promises to uplift the poor, a full third of the population. He won with 40 percent of the vote in a field of eleven candidates, nearly double the percentage of his predecessor, President Ramos. But along with this mandate Estrada brought personal baggage into the palace. Through his immersion in Manila politics, he had forged alliances with both corrupt police and crime bosses. As an actor who had played Manila toughs in nearly a hundred films, he attracted a presidential entourage that included what one cabinet officer called "underworld characters," killers, kidnappers, and confidence men. And with four households and eleven children by six different women, he was under enormous pressure to provide far beyond his meager presidential salary.[2]

At multiple levels Estrada's presidency seemed the culmination of historical forces that had been gathering for over a century. His use of the police for covert operations relied on both U.S. colonial procedures and Ferdinand Marcos's coterie of loyal police commanders. During his first two years in office, Estrada emerged unscathed from a string of some twenty financial, administrative, and personal scandals. At the start of his third year, however, allegations that he had used the police to protect jueteng gambling, a game entwined with Philippine elections for decades, sparked a serious crisis that was his undoing.

But to dismiss Estrada as merely venal or corrupt obscures the synthesis of syndicated vice and presidential power that prevailed in the decade before his election. With each administration since 1986, the Philippine presidency had been shaped by a deepening nexus of police, crime, and covert action. By the time Estrada took office in 1998, the police were mediating two criminal networks essential to presidential power: illegal jueteng gambling in the countryside and illicit drug imports from Chinese circuits in the capital. In less than twenty years the system of extralegal controls over the vice rackets had become so embedded in Philippine politics that its mastery became a necessary adjunct to presidential power.

Yet there was also change. As president, both Corazon Aquino and Fidel Ramos had been surrounded by aides and allies who used proximity for financial gain, although their complex schemes usually shielded the executive from any charges of personal complicity. Estrada, by contrast, seemed boldly, almost defiantly blatant in his corruption. Instead of a few arm's length transactions at the end of his term, he was tainted from the very outset by hands-on scams that spanned the economic spectrum, from favoritism in financial regulation all the way to cash kickbacks from illegal gambling. Not surprisingly, his maneuvers provoked growing opposition from Manila business executives hurt by financial fraud and provincial politicians threatened with the loss of illicit gambling income. Ultimately, Estrada's corruption incited a determined middle-class mobilization, making the crowd once again a political force to challenge the executive nexus of police, crime, and covert operations. In this reprise of history known as EDSA II or People Power II, advances in information technology such as e-mail, cell phones, and instant messaging would have revolutionary consequences for the country's politics.

At a more mundane level, crime again grew under Estrada's watch into a serious public concern, subtly eroding his support among both poor and middle class. Despite a tough-on-crime image, his administration witnessed a revival of jueteng and an epidemic of illicit drugs. These "victimless" crimes did not produce the acute political crisis that President Ramos had earlier faced over the spectacular violence of robbery and kidnapping. Nonetheless, the steady, invisible spread of these illicit networks aroused an undercurrent of public concern, sapping Estrada's legitimacy and contributing to the eventual eruption of protest demonstrations that would force him from the palace.

Drug Epidemic

The proliferation of drug abuse was a silent crisis for both Estrada's presidency and Philippine society. In marked contrast to the public acceptance of jueteng, the rapid spread of methamphetamine hydrochloride, known as *shabu,* aroused deep concern. Unlike the kidnappings and armed robberies directed at wealthy businessmen, the distribution of cut-price *shabu* was concentrated in Manila's slums where the typical drug user was a twenty-seven-year-old unemployed male with a limited high school education.[3] In January 1999 Estrada declared drugs "public enemy number one" and ordered "seek-and-destroy" operations against *shabu* syndicates. That June he promised to eradicate drug trafficking within six months. The Catholic Bishops' Conference offered its full support for the president's drug war, urging him to punish police who were "under suspicion themselves of drug dealing." Indicative of the problem's scope, the head of drug enforcement for the Philippine National Police (PNP), Jewel Canson, reported that 14 percent of the nation's hamlets, a total of 6,020 *barangays,* were "seriously affected by drugs."[4]

In mid-1999 a survey found that 68 percent of Metro Manila residents regarded the drug problem as "serious or very serious."[5] Statistics confirmed these public fears. Estimates of methamphetamine abusers had doubled from 900,000 in 1995 to 1.7 million four years later. If these figures were accurate, then amphetamine users were more than 2 percent of the country's population, one of the world's highest rates for any illicit drug.[6] Under presidential pressure to take action, drug arrests doubled between 1998 and 1999, court cases rose from 12,089 to 22,287, and drug seizures increased from ₱1.1 billion to ₱2.7 billion.[7]

There was also a qualitative shift toward more sophisticated syndicate operations. During the first decade of amphetamine abuse in the 1980s, drugs were usually imported from Hong Kong or Taiwan and local labs were small ventures. Now, by contrast, the country's illicit infrastructure was achieving self-sufficiency. In 1996 the National Bureau of Investigation raided the country's "biggest clandestine *shabu* laboratory" near Manila, seizing 114 kilograms of finished drugs valued at ₱159 million. Significantly, the two principals arrested were both identified as "Chinese," reflecting the ethnic circuits that controlled the smuggling of precursor chemicals.[8] A year later police broke nine Filipino syndicates in Metro Manila that were, rather typically, distributing modest lots of one to three kilograms worth about ₱1 million per kilo.[9] Over the next three years NBI reports confirmed this ethnic segregation: Filipino dealers were usually limited to one-kilo lots, Chinese syndicates dominated both bulk imports and local manufacturing, and their ad hoc alliance produced steady supplies of low-cost drugs.[10]

International agencies offered an even darker view of the country's drug problem. In 2001 the United Nations identified the Philippines and Thailand as the two Southeast Asian nations suffering from serious amphetamine abuse.[11] That same year the U.S. State Department reported that the $78 million in PNP drug seizures was but a fraction of the $1.2 billion worth of *shabu* smuggled from southeastern China every year, supplying 1.8 million drug users who spent $5 billion annually, the equivalent of 8 percent of the country's gross national product and five times the gross revenue from jueteng.[12] But before the full political impact of this drug epidemic could be felt during President Estrada's term, a major scandal over illegal gambling would sweep him from office.

Jueteng Industry

Estrada's use of executive power to expropriate jueteng's profits was unprecedented. Throughout much of the twentieth century, this illegal lottery had funded provincial politics, with local syndicates paying kickbacks to municipal mayors, police commanders, and in some cases to governors and congressmen. For over half a century, however, the country's chief executive had remained aloof from these local rackets. But the centralized police command forged by Ferdinand Marcos had created a potential for executive corruption that was soon manifested in the first post-authoritarian administration. Even though the succeeding government tapped jueteng for operational funds, its leader, Corazon Aquino, had kept the corruption at a discrete distance. After his inauguration in 1998, however, Estrada would use this police power to take direct control of a diffuse nexus of provincial politics and extralegal gambling, creating conflicts with those who had the greatest stake in the status quo. At an ideological level Estrada's attempt to commandeer this illicit industry challenged middle-class values, national aspirations, and the Catholic Church. At a material level his takeover threatened powerful provincial syndicates and their local political patrons. In sum the sheer scale of the industry and the depth of its political connections made this a bold, even foolhardy move with wide-ranging ramifications.

By the late 1990s gambling, legal and illicit, had grown into one of the country's largest industries. The nation's second-largest source of tax revenue came from a cluster of state gaming agencies: the Philippine Charity Sweepstakes Office (PCSO), the Philippine Amusement and Gaming Corporation (Pagcor), the

Games and Amusement Board, the Racing Commission, and the Gamefowl Commission. Among these five, only Pagcor had the authority to subcontract gambling operations, making it the most likely source of lucrative rents for presidential cronies.[13] By the end of the decade illegal lotteries formed another branch of this large, lucrative industry with powerful syndicates, billion-dollar revenues, and an invisible legion of four hundred thousand workers.[14]

Instead of the local operators of pre-martial-law days, powerful regional syndicates now controlled jueteng through a few major financiers, notably, Luis "Chavit" Singson in the Ilocos region and Rodolfo "Bong" Pineda in Central Luzon. In the Visayas and Mindanao nearly forty syndicates involved in another type of illicit lottery called *masiao* divided a daily gross of ₱34.5 million.[15] The annual turnover from all these illegal lotteries in Luzon and the Visayas was a billion U.S. dollars, a vast sum for an impoverished nation. These enormous revenues, fiscal and criminal, created a tempting target for a consolidation that could yield unprecedented wealth. Soon after Estrada took office, the head of the Securities and Exchange Commission discovered that the president, despite his folksy college dropout demeanor, was a wily wheeler-dealer who had "grandiose plans" to "lord over the casinos and other gaming operations in the country"—abolishing Pagcor and privatizing its operations in partnership with foreign investors, either Macao casino czar Stanley Ho or the Las Vegas-based Cesar's Palace. These same crony corporations could also launch legal lotteries that would, through police pressure on the jueteng bosses, capture illegal betting, thereby controlling all Philippine gambling from penny lotteries to high-roller roulette.[16]

If successful, Estrada's scheme for centralizing jueteng profits would have destroyed the financial foundation of a patronage system that had, for nearly a century, provided local politicians with the currency of electoral success—jobs, campaign funds, precinct workers, and political intelligence. Just as jueteng *cobradores* (runners) circulated daily through sprawling slums to collect the small bets that aggregated into the syndicates' billion-peso profits, so during election campaigns they moved through the same numberless squatters' shacks mobilizing otherwise forgotten voters. On election day itself the *cobradores*, with their exceptional memories for faces and numbers, made superb precinct scrutinizers, checking that voters had turned out to cast their ballots as promised.[17]

Although jueteng was rampant, both the Catholic Church and the middle classes remained strongly opposed to all forms of gambling, legal or illegal, and were soon outraged by Estrada's liberal policy. During his first weeks in office he announced plans to legalize both jai alai, which President Aquino had banned back in 1986, and jueteng. "Let us be realistic," he said. "If we legalized Lotto, why not jueteng?"[18] However logical, the president's statement prompted declarations of moral outrage from the press and the pulpit. For nearly a century middle-class reformers had focused on gambling as a social cancer that impoverished ordinary

Filipinos and slowed the nation's progress. A spokesman for the Catholic Bishops' Conference argued from a theological perspective that legalizing jueteng would discourage hard work and nurture an immoral "*suwerte* mentality—an inclination to seek a better life through fate and luck." Instead of legalization, the bishops said, "the administration should try to wipe it out or at least try to stop its proliferation."[19]

Bowing to the pressure of this moral protest, President Estrada retreated just two days after his announcement, saying, "gambling is not my priority."[20] But he did not give up on the idea of capturing a share of the profits of this lucrative industry for government revenues and, ultimately, corporate gains. Without the shield of legality, he would now pursue the same end through covert means, risking exposure and the consequent loss of legitimacy.

Jueteng Monopoly

To centralize control over the diffuse jueteng industry, President Estrada adopted a two-phase strategy. During his first two years in office, he moved cautiously, first extracting a modest executive surcharge from jueteng operators that aroused little opposition. In July 2000 he went much further, attempting to impose controls that threatened the very survival of local syndicates and the political machines dependent on their largesse. Had Estrada played patron by redistributing jueteng payoffs among local politicians, his bold move might well have succeeded. Or had he forced a reallocation among existing syndicates he could have amplified his power over local officials. Instead he used police power to appropriate gambling profits for his own mansions and mistresses at the expense of entrenched local interests. By privatizing the illicit profits that had sustained provincial political machines for almost a century, he violated the norms of both public probity and outlaw ethics. In the end, his avarice would incite a revolt among Luzon's syndicate bosses.

In the effort to control jueteng, Estrada enjoyed critical support from his hand-picked police chief, Panfilo "Ping" Lacson. Apart from a certain camaraderie, their collaboration was based on deep bonds of mutual indebtedness. Immediately after his inauguration in July 1998, the president appointed Lacson, who was still under indictment for the Kuratong Baleleng mass murder, head of the newly formed Presidential Anti-Organized Crime Task Force (PAOCTF). Through the president's patronage, Lacson thus evaded prosecution for these human rights violations and resumed his rise to command of the PNP.[21]

There was, however, one obstacle that blocked Lacson's ambition—the incumbent PNP director Roberto Lastimoso. Through a disinformation campaign, Lacson maneuvered to succeed his chief, producing a sordid police scandal that filled the front pages of the Manila papers.[22] The story broke on April 26, 1999, when the *Philippine Daily Inquirer* reported that two police intelligence officers had accused PNP director Lastimoso of pressuring them to release a major drug dealer after his arrest with two kilos of *shabu*.[23] Subsequent media investigations found that the evidence against Lastimoso had originated inside a tight coterie of Lacson loyalists that included those same two sources in police intelligence.[24] Offering a somber assessment of the scandal, the National Intelligence Coordinating Agency (NICA) provided Congress with a detailed seven-page report tracing this feud to a struggle between rival drug lords. "Everybody who is anybody in the Lastimoso-Lacson tussle," NICA reported, "in one way or another, is involved in illegal activities."[25] Putting an end to the controversy, a Senate blue ribbon committee dismissed all the evidence against Lastimoso, saying that its sole source was "a faction of the national police headed by Lacson" and was thus "so biased as to be incredible."[26] Nonetheless, Lastimoso would remain on permanent leave long after the controversy had faded while the president soon restored Lacson to command of the powerful PAOCTF.

Just six months later, in November 1999, the president, citing Lacson's "sterling" record, skipped over more senior officers to appoint him director of the PNP.[27] When angry senators promised close scrutiny of Lacson's outstanding criminal charges, Estrada exempted him from confirmation hearings. Defying the critics, he then promoted Lacson further by adding a third and fourth star to his general's rank.[28] In only sixteen months Lacson had gone from criminal suspect to command of the national police, a position of exceptional power.

From the outset Lacson cultivated a tough, take-charge manner that appealed to press and public. As the PNP director he favored a flamboyantly violent rhetoric, once pointing to shade trees lining the road to his home and saying, "If God really wants to make me happy, I would like to see notorious criminals and police scalawags hanged on those trees."[29] After just two months in command, his approval ratings rose from a weak 29 to a solid 49 percent.[30] With the public applauding his action agenda, he launched a police purge that, apart from removing a few rogues, provided him with a pretext to promote allies and punish rivals. Only three days after he assumed command, seven senior officers, all personal enemies, were pushed into retirement or remote postings, notably, Reynaldo Berroya, his old nemesis, and Rodolfo Garcia, who had implicated him in the salvaging of two women during the Red Scorpion investigation.[31] Over the next year Lacson would further tighten his control over the police hierarchy by picking his own military academy classmates for the top PNP posts: six of eleven staff directorates, four of eleven elite operational units, and six of sixteen regional commands.[32] With these loyalists in place, by mid-2000 Lacson had made the PNP a pliable instrument for Estrada's plan to bring jueteng under executive control.

This transition within the vice economy began amicably enough, with cautious hopes on both sides for the mutual benefits of close collaboration. Only weeks after his inauguration in July 1998, the president summoned a rogue's gallery of gamblers to his private residence at Polk Street in the Manila suburb of

San Juan: *masiao* operator Charlie "Atong" Ang, Central Luzon jueteng boss Rodolfo "Bong" Pineda, and northern Luzon jueteng promoter Luis "Chavit" Singson, who was also the governor of Ilocos Sur. At this secret summit the president decided that his gambling buddy Charlie Ang would "set up the network" of regional racketeers and jueteng boss Bong Pineda would deliver the president's 3 percent cut to Chavit so it would not be "obvious."[33] When Charlie Ang lost Estrada's confidence by skimming executive kickbacks from a tobacco tax scam several months later, Estrada replaced him with Chavit Singson, who worked effectively with Luzon's "gambling lords" for the next two years, assigning each a fixed territory to avoid conflict and collecting the president's cut. Every month from November 1998 to August 2000, these underworld operators paid Chavit the president's share, which totaled some ₱35 million. And every two weeks Chavit made regular cash deliveries to the president. During these fifteen months Chavit collected a total of ₱545.2 million—₱414.3 million paid directly to Estrada, ₱123 million invested for him in the Fontana Casino at Clark Field, and the balance doled out to presidential kin.[34] The syndicate operated as a loose three-tiered structure. Estrada at the apex controlled the police, Chavit and Bong Pineda divided Luzon's prime jueteng regions between them, and a dozen provincial-level gambling lords operated the local lotteries.

After months of smooth operation under Chavit, the syndicate succumbed to pressure from internal rivalries and market forces. Estrada' s simultaneous expansion of legal gambling and syndication of its illegal counterpart introduced growing political instability, even volatility, into the gaming market, which gave rival courtiers a point of attack against Chavit. The administration's unprecedented expansion of gambling also generated public demands for reform. The palace countered with a campaign of further legalization as the cure for corruption, creating a political opening in which cronies could advance legal schemes that would allow them leverage over the still illegal jueteng. With the president's backing, his allies used the two state gaming agencies—Pagcor and PCSO—as vehicles for competing schemes to wrest control of illicit gambling from Chavit's group of jueteng bosses.

The first sign of the intrigue came in February 2000 at a secret government gambling summit to discuss the legalization of jueteng.[35] As word of the proposal leaked to Congress and beyond, Estrada retreated and this gambit died quietly.[36] Over time, however, news of this summit stirred deeper political currents. As the Estrada administration entered its second year, middle-class activists grew concerned about the cumulative epidemic of legal and illegal gambling. Both old and new forms of legalized gaming were spreading through aggressive marketing, including 11 casinos for high rollers, 120 off-track betting venues, 300 off-fronton jai alai stations, 1,400 Sunday cockpits for the masses, thousands of small shops selling Instant Bingo tickets, and a nationwide network of On-Line Bingo arcades in shopping malls across the archipelago. Pagcor's gross revenues shot up from ₱2 billion in 1987 to ₱12.4 billion in 1999, and there was a surge of illegal betting on the various numbers rackets: jueteng, "last two" *masiao,* and ball alai.[37] On the eve of Estrada's first state of the nation address in July 1999, Cardinal Jaime Sin prayed openly that the president would reconsider his promotion of legal gambling.[38]

Playing on rising opposition to jueteng, Estrada's closest allies renewed their pressure for legal alternatives. Appealing to the president's avarice, rival supplicants promised him even an greater income, each tugging at personal ties to promote his own scheme as the most lucrative lottery. Charlie Ang promoted a jueteng look-alike branded "Bingo 2-Ball," legalized by a Pagcor license, that promised Estrada ₱70 million a day. Dante Tan, a wealthy Chinese Filipino businessman and an early backer of Estrada's election campaign, favored a licensed on-line lottery called "Quick Pick Bingo." At a televised launch of the latter game in June 1999, the president appeared at a Manila shopping mall as the "Guest of Honor" to play the first bingo for Dante Tan's BW Resources Corporation—sending the company's stock price soaring and starting a series of financial frauds that would, within four months, bring the Philippine stock exchange to the brink of collapse.[39] Despite some significant differences in scale and financial details, these rival schemes shared a similar architecture: introduction of a legal lottery that mimed jueteng, franchises for the old "jueteng lords," and a parallel police crackdown on criminal operations to capture the market for the new scheme.

The odd man out in these fast-money maneuvers was Chavit Singson, who fought a rearguard action in defense of the old jueteng racket. He first sensed trouble, he said, at the president's birthday celebration on April 19, 2000, when Estrada asked, referring to the gambling lord Bong Pineda, "Is there anything for me?" Chavit explained that he already "had been collecting from him [Pineda] every month." To that the president replied, "When I was Vice President, I was given something during my birthday."[40] In his later testimony Chavit would attribute the president's birthday sulk to the intrigues of rival cronies. "Mr. Charlie 'Atong' Ang was bent on reclaiming his closeness to President Estrada," he recalled.[41] "They conspired against me. They said that I was pocketing from ₱5 million to ₱7 million [a month]. That's not true. There is an auditor. Erap leaves nothing to chance."[42]

To prepare the ground for an executive takeover of jueteng via quasi-legalization, PNP director Lacson had persuaded his Luzon police commanders to sign a "covenant on [a] no-take policy" in February 2000, swearing off payments from underworld operators.[43] Indicative of the intensity of these operations, the police made fifteen thousand gambling raids in the first half of 2000, arresting 19,568 bettors and operators.[44] In the midst of this general sweep, police pressure on Governor Chavit Singson's northern Luzon network was particularly intense. Within a week of the raids in June, Lacson purged twenty-four top police officials from Chavit's territory, citing bribes ranging up to ₱22 million for each, and replaced these cashiered officers with his own loyalists.[45] Raising the pressure further, Gen. Jose Calimlim, a former chief of palace security who was close to the president, led his Task Force Aduana in a raid on Narvacan, Ilocos Sur, seizing four hundred smuggled motorcycles. When an angry Chavit phoned the palace, the president sided with his favorite general and then failed to appear as godfather for the wedding of the governor's daughter—clear signs of a breach.[46]

In the weeks following these raids, continuing PNP operations in Central Luzon rounded up more than a thousand of Bong Pineda's jueteng collectors and confiscated some ₱1.2 million in bets, prompting the regional commander, Lacson loyalist Roberto Calinisan, to announce that jueteng had been "completely stopped."[47] But in Chavit's view the PNP, acting on the president's orders, was playing politics, unleashing "an all-out-war with jueteng because they wanted Bingo 2-Ball to be stronger and the collection centralized."[48]

In June 2000 Pagcor skirted its own regulations to issue a license for Charlie Ang's Bingo 2-Ball because, as its chair Alice Reyes explained, "it had the endorsement of the Office of the President." Through similar pressures in July, the Philippine National Bank gave Dante Tan's BW Resources, a crony firm at the center of a recent stock scandal, an enormous loan of ₱600 million ($12 million) to launch the new game—even though it had no collateral or capacity to repay. With the corporate pieces now in place, the president summoned his jueteng syndicate—Dante Tan, Charlie Ang, Bong Pineda, and Chavit Singson—to his lavish "Boracay" mansion in New Manila for several meetings about a "plan to centralize the collection of jueteng." At one of these syndicate sit downs the president said he would order Director Lacson "to crack down on jueteng operations in preparation for the launching of Bingo 2-Ball." Despite tensions just below the surface, relations were still amicable and the principals seemed content with their share of the new lottery.[49]

In early September Pagcor director Jose E. Rodriguez III announced the launch of Bingo 2-Ball, saying, "For most Filipinos, jueteng is not evil, it is a way of life. What makes it bad are the bribes."[50] Indeed, when Pagcor launched the new game on September 18, PNP chief Lacson ordered his police commanders to "stop illegal gambling, including jueteng," or face dismissal.[51] Ignoring the public's objections to this expansion of legal gaming, Pagcor's publicist hailed the raids as "a blitzkrieg move" against jueteng.[52]

Setting aside its usual propriety, Pagcor hired palace crony and crime boss Charlie Ang as its official Bingo 2-Ball "consultant." Not only did the government gaming board pay him an exorbitant fee of five hundred thousand pesos (eleven thousand dollars) per day, but it gave him unchecked authority over the new lottery, making it, in effect, a legal front for reorganization of the old jueteng racket. Armed with this broad authority, Ang dictated the terms for the new Bingo 2-Ball franchises: 2 percent for the PNP, 13 percent for *cobradores*, 23 percent for Pagcor, and a hefty 62 percent for his own contractors. Significantly, it was Ang, not Pagcor, who awarded the local franchises, and he did it in ways designed to destroy his rivals among Luzon's reigning jueteng lords, Chavit Singson and Bong Pineda. To ensure police cooperation with his scheme, Ang descended, deus ex machina, in a private helicopter into Central Luzon police headquarters at Camp Olivas with Pagcor's Jose Rodriguez in tow. There the alleged kidnapper and gambling racketeer lectured PNP commanders on the new gaming system and gave them copies of his official Pagcor contracts for Bingo 2-Ball.[53]

Adding insult to injury, Charlie Ang awarded the bingo contract for the Ilocos region to Eric Singson, Governor Chavit Singson's distant cousin, "mortal enemy," and rival gubernatorial candidate. "I made it known to the President," Chavit recalled, "that I felt bad when Atong Ang gave franchises for the Bingo 2-Ball to my political rivals. I told them to stop the Bingo 2-Ball operation or I would expose them." As a seasoned political brawler, Chavit was trying for a knockout blow by charging the president with personal involvement in jueteng in ways that would destroy his legitimacy within the country's political culture.[54]

Warlord's Revenge

In retrospect the notion that Manila high rollers Atong Ang and Erap Estrada could trash-talk provincial boss Chavit Singson must rank as one of the great miscalculations of Philippine political history. Throughout September 2000 Chavit pleaded with the president through intermediaries to remove the legal lottery from his province. But the message came back from Estrada, "I have nothing to do with Bingo 2-Ball. It's with Pagcor." Chavit, a straight-shooting Ilocano warlord, was outraged by this city-slick dissimulation. "What does he mean he has nothing to do with it when he was the one who assigned Ang to be the collector for Bingo 2-Ball?" Chavit recalled angrily. "The money . . . will go directly to the president. The police, the military and local officials will be bypassed. Corruption has been centralized."[55]

At 8:00 p.m. on October 3, Chavit spoke by phone with presidential adviser Mark Jimenez from Manila's Holiday Inn, again pressing his demands. The adviser replied that at that very moment he was in the middle of a palace meeting about the Bingo issue with Executive Secretary Ronaldo Zamora, PNP director Ping Lacson, and the president himself. An hour later Jimenez called back to advise Chavit of their decision: Bingo 2-Ball would stay in Ilocos Sur and Chavit should keep his mouth shut. Just two hours later the Ilocos governor drove out of the hotel parking lot into the darkened streets of downtown Manila. Suddenly three police cars blocked his vehicle. Twelve officers surrounded his car, M-16 rifles at the ready, demanding he get out. And the reason? An unlicensed blinker on the roof of his car. As a sharpshooter who had left a dozen dead in political gun fights and escaped, by his own count, six attempted assassinations, Chavit had good survival reflexes.[56] From inside his armored Suburban he spotted the designated shooter, a motorcycle cop who was gripping an M-16 rifle tensely, ready to fire as soon as the door opened, prompting a fusillade from the other officers. Confirming Chavit's suspicions, the head of the NBI, Gen. Reynaldo Wycoco, later noted that the commander of these traffic police, Gen. Renato M. Paredes, was Lacson's PMA classmate, adding that his men were primed to fire on any pretext.[57] "They wanted to kill me for a traffic violation," Singson told the press. "I was lucky I was in a bullet proof vehicle." With his cell phone Chavit called the nearby Holiday Inn to summon his loyal Ilocano mayors, who soon arrived with their armed bodyguards, ending what Chavit called "an apparent assassination attempt."[58]

The bungled hit launched Chavit Singson on a political vendetta. The next day, October 4, he told ABS-CBN television that the police had attempted his "liquidation" to silence any revelations about jueteng kickbacks to the palace crony Charlie Ang. But Chavit added, with mysterious vagueness, that an unnamed "Malacañang official" had taken the biggest bribes, worth some ₱33 million monthly.[59] On October 5 PNP director Lacson dismissed Chavit's allegations as "absurd and ridiculous," insisting that the police had stopped him for running a red light "and nothing more."[60] Two days later President Estrada tried to still the controversy by ordering a blanket suspension of Bingo 2-Ball and an intensified police crackdown on jueteng.[61] For five days Chavit did not mention Estrada's name, apparently waiting for some word, some concession from the palace.

Just after sundown on October 8, Chavit called at Villa San Miguel, the residence of Manila's archbishop, desperate for the moral support only Cardinal Sin could provide. "I need your help," Chavit told the cardinal. "My life is in danger." After detailing his payments to the president from graft and jueteng, the governor turned over the incriminating documents for safekeeping. In one of those ironies that abound in Philippine politics, the country's most notorious warlord had won the support of its moral leader.[62]

The next day Chavit Singson broke with the president. Speaking at a crowded press conference at Club Filipino in San Juan, Chavit called President Estrada "the biggest jueteng lord in the country." With a convincing directness, the Ilocano governor detailed their partnership in crime, stating that he had personally paid the president kickbacks totaling ₱130 million from a tobacco tax scam and ₱545 million from jueteng payoffs.[63]

These disclosures precipitated a major political crisis that would force President Estrada from the palace within four months. Angered by Chavit's allegations, the anti-Estrada movement coalesced around middle-class reformers, church moralists, and entrenched provincial politicians. Ironically, after surviving high-flying financial scandals that nearly destroyed the country's stock market, Estrada would be forced from office by graft from a slum lottery that took bets in pocket change. This explosive imbalance between cause and effect reflects the wide ramifications of illegal gambling within the country's political culture and the sensitivity of this postcolonial society to the symbolic role of policing. In the months of maneuvering that followed Chavit's charges, the country's three elective branches would lose legitimacy as they failed to meet public demands for impartiality and integrity. In the end it was only the appointive and extraconstitutional sectors that maintained a capacity for independent action: the Supreme Court, the armed forces, the press, and the middle classes assembled as "people power."

The day after his historic press conference Chavit testified before the House Committee on Public Order and Security, saying, "I came here personally to accuse the lord of all jueteng lords, no less than the President of the Republic of the Philippines, Joseph Ejercito Estrada." Appearing before the Senate on October 11, he provided copies of his ledger detailing jueteng bribes and kickbacks. The veracity of these records was soon established when two senators and a former presidential press secretary admitted that they had received the payments noted next to their names.[64]

In his subsequent press statements Chavit positioned himself at the intersection of several arenas of legitimacy. At the outset he launched his exposé as a confessed criminal. Within hours he shifted to a higher moral plane when asked to justify his actions. "We cannot go on like this," he said. "How can our country ever progress?"[65] For the next four months, he balanced these two spheres, the criminal and ideological, in ways that made him seem a convincing witness to the president's corruption.

Ironically, Chavit's notoriety was the source of his credibility. After thirty years as the ultimate survivor in the incestuous violence of Ilocos Sur's politics, he had become the very personification of a provincial warlord.[66] He might gun down rivals, skim off revenues, and cheat in elections like the warlord he was, but there was a consistency, even an integrity, to his accusations. At first editors at the anti-Estrada *Philippine Daily Inquirer* expressed a visceral revulsion ("we nearly threw up") at the idea of Chavit as the nation's moral guardian. But a telephone poll by the ABS-CBN network after his historic press conference found that a resounding 67 percent believed his charges against the president to be true.[67]

While Chavit was testifying before the Senate, Cardinal Sin released a statement, drafted after careful reflection by his diocesan clergy, that would ensure morality a prominent place in the national debate. "In the light of all the scandals that have besmirched the image of the presidency in the last two years," the cardinal said, calling on the president to resign, "we stand by our conviction that he has lost the moral ascendancy to govern."[68] In the weeks that followed, Estrada would use the full powers of his office—patronage, populism, and parliamentary maneuvering—in a desperate bid to evade the inescapable logic of the cardinal's command.

Meanwhile, Chavit continued to deal out revelations with the finesse of a cardsharp while Estrada's entourage scrambled to deny them. At a public forum on October 18, the governor charged that Estrada, in a bid to exonerate PNP director Lacson for the 1995 Kuratong Baleleng massacre, had ordered police to murder two women witnesses and then bribed others to recant. Four days later

Chavit released an affidavit by a former member of the PACC's Task Force Habagat, Patrolman Ramon Ocampo, alleging that Lacson and Estrada had ordered the murder of two other women linked to the Red Scorpion gang in 1992.[69] Confirming his claims, Mrs. Yolanda Ricaforte, the woman Chavit had fingered as the president's jueteng "accountant," told the Senate that she had withdrawn ₱200 million in April from the governor's accounts and delivered the checks to the president's personal attorney, Edward S. Serapio.[70]

In the midst of the debate over the missing millions, the Philippine Center for Investigative Journalism found the destination of all this graft. In an irrefutable report carried by the city's leading papers, the center showed how presidential attorney Serapio had formed front corporations to purchase five mansions for Estrada worth over a billion pesos. The most luxurious, a home for presidential mistress Laarni Enriquez, sprawled over twenty-three thousand square feet in the exclusive Wack Wack Subdivision with three saunas, a full-sized gym, a mini-theater, and a beauty parlor. A second report enumerated eighteen mansions worth ₱2.2 billion ($44 million). In demonstrating a connection between the president's illicit income and his conspicuous consumption, these reports lent credibility to Chavit's charges. More important, this story reduced the vast sums and complex transactions to the simple verities of scandal—sex and money—that ordinary voters could readily understand.[71]

With the public now convinced of Chavit's credibility and Erap's venality, only signs of real repentance could have slowed the momentum toward impeachment. Instead, speaking with his usual bluntness, Estrada dismissed the charges as lies.[72] At an emotional rally attended by one hundred thousand people before the EDSA shrine of Our Lady on November 4, Cardinal Sin commented wryly that "the immorality of the president seems to have worsened after his assumption of the highest office."[73] A week later Estrada's supporters countered with a million-strong prayer rally in Rizal Park led by the charismatic preacher Mike Velarde, a strong showing of public support that the palace hailed as a sign of legitimacy.[74]

At this sensitive juncture Vice President Gloria Arroyo, Estrada's legal successor, aroused little enthusiasm when she publicly broke with the administration. At first she seemed irredeemably tainted by her ties to gambling boss Bong Pineda, who had reportedly financed her 1998 campaign, earning her the coffee shop sobriquet *anak ng jueteng* (child of jueteng). Only a week after Chavit's exposé, Arroyo had returned from Rome to maneuver cautiously for a place in the opposition. At a news conference before a crowd of three thousand, she rebutted administration charges of closeness to Bong Pineda, saying, "I do not associate with any gambling lord or drug lord."[75] But questions persisted.[76]

A diverse coalition now formed to force Estrada from office, eroding the president's once crushing majority in the House. On November 2, Deputy Majority Leader Neptali Gonzales Jr. declared that the president had "crossed the line which the people, recognizing the frailties of men, generously tolerate." Two weeks later, on November 13, Speaker Manuel Villar, defecting to the opposition, opened the House session with a long prayer that segued seamlessly, without an "amen," into an impeachment petition. Before the pro-Estrada majority woke from its prayerful torpor, Speaker Villar had sent the petition to the Senate with the names of eleven House prosecutors. In the midst of the pandemonium, the majority exploded in outrage. But it was too late. President Estrada had been impeached.[77]

With this rising tempo of public protests, the composition of the crowds broadened and the moral rhetoric deepened. In the nationwide "Welga ng Mamamayan" [People's Strike] on November 14, the Makati Business Club, the radical Kilusang Mayo Uno, and the moderate Trade Union Congress of the Philippines joined forces for a militant strike that pulled jeepney minibuses off the streets and stockbrokers from the trading floor.[78] In announcing a nationwide Catholic mobilization a week later, the Luzon Social Action Network distilled what was by then an evolving constitutional theory within this parliament of the streets. "If the legitimate government acts according to its capability and morality," the group argued, "that government is to be followed and respected. But if it contradicts morality, it defies God's will, thus it has lost its authority to be believed."[79]

Of equal import the military began to signal its oblique support for the opposition. On November 21, a group of "Concerned Senior Officers," all retired, placed a full-page ad in the *Inquirer* calling on "comrades-in-arms . . . to take the necessary action to assist the President to realize . . . the noble and heroic act of voluntary resignation." The lead signatory was Gen. Fortunato Abat, a former defense secretary with a strong following among active-duty officers.[80] The president, failing to understand the strong ties that bound all Philippine Military Academy alumni, dismissed the letter as the grumbling of elderly "has beens."[81] General Abat went further. In a speech to the People's Consultative Assembly just three days before the impeachment trial, he urged the armed forces to withdraw "military support from the President," arguing that such military intervention would be constitutional.[82]

Mass action and media stories lifted the climate of fear Estrada had fostered through his alliance with Lacson's police, releasing a torrent of damning revelations. In the weeks between the House impeachment and Senate trial, the Manila press began publishing exposés of Lacson's corruption. On November 20 a pseudonymous Chinese Filipino dubbed "Rosebud," who claimed to be a former PACC agent, told reporters that the president had sanctioned drug dealing and recounted, with an insider's authority, how Lacson's PAOCTF had murdered six Chinese dealers. In response, Director Lacson identified "Rosebud" as Mary Ong and conceded that she had been a police informant. But he dismissed her allegations as a ploy by disgruntled former officers led by his blood enemy Reynaldo Berroya. Though publicly dismissive of his "nemesis," privately Lacson told his trusted aide Michael Ray Aquino that "It's time for you to shoot Bero"—orders that would soon be preempted by a more pressing target.[83]

Angered by Lacson's attack, Mary Ong sought Cardinal Sin's protection for an open press conference. Speaking in a room crowded with reporters and cameras, she confirmed her identity and showed passports of the Chinese victims to document their deaths. Jettisoning months of its timid palace coverage, the *Inquirer* published a detailed account of Ong's accusations with a photo showing this dignified accuser holding authoritative-looking documents.[84] Ten days later, on the eve of Estrada's impeachment, she released an affidavit identifying the officers involved in these murders as members of Director Lacson's police coterie.[85]

As the impeachment trial neared, the palace blundered again by murdering a critic who had damaging information about the president's ties to the now notorious BW Resources Corporation. On November 25 two young women called a press conference at their home to announce the disappearance of their father, Salvador "Bubby" Dacer, a publicist in the eye of every political storm, whose recent representation of BW's president, Dante Tan, made him privy to the secrets of this shadowy company that concealed major share holdings for the president. Dacer's daughters said that he had last called the day before at 10:15 a.m. from his white Toyota Revo while en route to a meeting with former President Ramos at the Manila Hotel.[86] In a city with a nose for scandal's faintest scent, the disappearance of the capital's most influential image maker aroused fear and fascination. The Manila press filled its columns with stories implicating the palace in a possible rub-out.[87]

On the day of his disappearance Dacer had in fact been driving to meet Ramos and assist in the publicity for the anti-Estrada generals. Unbeknownst to Dacer and his family, the publicist had offended the president and Lacson's elite PAOCTF had been tracking him for a month, waiting for.an opportune time to move in for the kill. When Dacer failed to appear as scheduled, Ramos faxed an alarm to PNP director Lacson. At a press conference three days later, November 27, Ramos said he was "keenly aware of possible foul play" and called on the president to launch an all-out investigation. In a transparent political pantomime, Estrada gave Lacson forty-eight hours to find the missing publicist, and the PNP director assigned the case to a PAOCTF task force headed by his protégé, Senior Superintendent Cezar Mancao. According to Mancao's later affidavit, "Lacson instructed me to head the investigation of the incident . . . to control the situation by covering up the involvement of PAOCTF personnel."[88] Within twenty-four hours two street vendors told the *Inquirer* that they had been working at a busy intersection when five heavily armed men in a Mitsubishi Galant pulled alongside Dacer's white Toyota van. Four men, one in a police uniform and armed with an M-16, climbed into the Toyota and drove away with a man they identified as Dacer. At 9:00 p.m. residents of a mountain village south of Manila heard an explosion and found the missing Toyota, without Dacer, at the bottom of a deep ravine.[89]

Almost immediately text messages began circulating throughout the city, charging Ping Lacson's PAOCTF with the crime. "Intelligence report," read one such message, "PAOCTF have had Dacer's body since Saturday [November 25]. didn't xpect the xtent of media covrage. dey hav 'sanitzd' evidnce. waiting 4 'ryt tym' 2 release it." Mancao called the *Inquirer* to insist, "We don't have Dacer's body. . . . Lacson is not involved."[90] Lacson himself expressed "outrage" at such allegations.[91]

As protest demonstrations intensified in the weeks before the impeachment trial, Lacson placed his police on red alert, saying, "We will not allow anarchy to rule in this country."[92] When the trial drew near, both sides backed away from street confrontations in a shared respect for the legitimacy of the constitutional process. After weeks of marches, meetings, and rallies, the city's millions withdrew to their televisions for five weeks of live broadcasts. From its opening gavel, the impeachment trial moved beyond Congress, in the words of columnist Conrado de Quiros, "to the fields and furrows, the alley and gutters, the streets and dirt roads of this magic-realist country."[93]

Trial by Television

The impeachment of President Joseph Estrada was a remarkable event, a fitting close to a century of tumultuous change. While millions watched the live broadcasts, twenty-two senators formed the jury and eleven House prosecutors presented thirty witnesses to establish the president's guilt on four charges: (1) bribery for accepting kickbacks from jueteng gambling lords (2) corruption for taking tobacco tax kickbacks from Governor Chavit Singson (3) betrayal of public trust by interfering in the investigation of stock fraud by BW Resources, and (4) violation of the Constitution by using fifty-two luxury vehicles seized by customs.[94] In effect, the "high crimes" debated in this, the Philippines' first impeachment, involved an illegal lottery that collected coins from the country's slums.

On December 7, 2000, just two months after Chavit Singson's accusations, the Senate opened the impeachment trial, sitting as robed jurors while the eleven House prosecutors presented their case. From day one the trial was a duel between two law school classmates and longtime enemies, Representative Joker Arroyo, a human-rights attorney who had fought the Marcos dictatorship, and Estelito Mendoza, Marcos's former solicitor general and now Manila's highest paid corporate lawyer. The prosecutors, led by Joker Arroyo, presented witnesses who spoke convincingly to establish a paper trail of corrupt transactions from jueteng lords and dummy bank accounts to the mansions built for the president's mistresses. In the course of the trial the prosecution would uncover bank accounts worth ₱10 billion ($200 million), economic plunder by any standard.[95] During their days on the stand, prosecution witnesses would face death threats, fostering a climate of fear that gave the trial the aura of a mafia prosecution rather than a presidential impeachment. Press reports about the missing palace insider Bubby Dacer, believed to have been kidnapped to silence his damaging revelations, ran like a dark undercurrent. Bloody terrorist bombings at the midpoint of the trial added to the atmosphere of threat.

Throughout this courtroom drama, a combination of legal, financial, and moral questions gained a clarity that held the national audience spellbound through hours of bilingual legalese about mazelike financial maneuvers. During the trial's twenty-three days, 88 percent of Manila's population would spend up to six hours a day watching the live broadcasts, following a political morality play that brought the abstraction of legitimacy home to every citizen.[96] By the time the president's lawyers aborted the hearings with a procedural maneuver on day twenty-three, his administration had lost its mandate.

Although much of the trial was taken up with dull procedural maneuvers, the prosecution captured the nation's attention on the first day and held it by introducing compelling testimony during about half of the subsequent sessions. Day one opened with giant pictures of luxury mansions flashing across a video screen until the frames slowed to focus on the signature of "Jose Velarde" on a check for ₱142 million and then on the signature of "Joseph E. Estrada" on a ₱500 bill. "You need not be an expert to see the similarity," announced the lead prosecutor, Representative Joker Arroyo. This check, he alleged, had passed through the account of presidential crony Jose "Sel" Yulo and thence to a front company held by the president's lawyer, Edward Serapio, who used these funds to buy land for the outlandish Boracay mansion then being built for one of the president's mistresses. These funds, Arroyo said, came from ₱130 million in tobacco tax kickbacks the president had taken from Governor Chavit Singson. In an equally dramatic opening statement, prosecutor Sergio Apostol called the president "the lord of all gambling lords" and charged that a "criminal syndicate directed by the highest office of the land . . . threatens to rule us."[97]

On the second day, the prosecution began to track the money trail by calling Governor Singson's secretary, Emma Lim. After days of nervous weeping beforehand, she was the picture of perfect calm while she testified about jueteng collections for the president's syndicate.[98] In breath-taking testimony on day three she recalled being ushered into the palace where she delivered ₱5 million in jueteng bribes to the president's secretary while Estrada chatted on the phone nearby. She corroborated her testimony with the deposit slips for ₱10 million in jueteng payoffs. Defense attorney Mendoza then launched a condescending cross-examination, firing off two hundred questions in two hours. Looking him straight in the eye, Lim used Mendoza's questions to buttress her testimony and quietly corrected his flawed Filipino usage, replying coolly to one of his endless questions, "Hindi kinakain ang iced tea" (One does not eat iced tea). As she stepped down, smiling prosecutors shook her hand warmly.[99]

Outside the courtroom the administration also suffered a succession of reverses. Head prosecutor Sergio Apostol announced that only hours before her stunning testimony Emma Lim had received a threatening phone call warning,

"Be careful. You and your family will die."[100] In another unexpected blow the Manila press carried a report from the German magazine *Der Spiegel* that the president and his adviser Robert Aventajado had recently skimmed off half the twenty-million-peso ransom paid to Abu Sayyaf for the release of foreign hostages. When President Estrada announced that he would file a libel suit, the German ambassador defended *Der Spiegel* as "credible, famous, and reliable."[101]

In the next three hearings the prosecution tried to track the paper trail of grease money from jueteng syndicates to the president. After resisting the prosecution's demands for details of the "Jose Velarde" account, the Equitable PCI Bank delivered, at the close of day four, two sealed envelopes to the presiding judge, Chief Justice Hilarion Davide, with an abject apology from the bank's president.[102]

On day five Chavit Singson presented the history of the president's jueteng syndicate, telling his story in clear, unadorned Filipino that the ordinary viewers could readily understand. Through this and related testimony, the prosecution established a paper trail of dirty money from the jueteng syndicates through Chavit to the palace. On day eight the first vice president of Equitable PCI Bank, Annie Ngo, testified that the president's accountant, Yolanda Ricaforte, had deposited ₱200 million in six bank branches in "a classic case of money laundering."[103]

Just two days before the court opened the first of the famed sealed envelopes from Equitable Bank, businessman Jaime Dichaves, the president's "close friend," came forward to claim the Equitable account and its funds as his own. Although his only official post was head of the Palace Golf Club, Dichaves was a member of Estrada's hard-drinking "midnight cabinet" and had used his connections to take control of the Pagcor franchise for jai alai gambling.[104] Thus, by the time the first sealed envelope was opened on December 20, day ten of the trial, the impact was anticlimactic. The envelope did show, as everyone suspected, deposits of ₱142 million in the "Jose Velarde" account. But, thanks to the Dichaves testimony, the evidence was now inconclusive.[105]

Outside the Senate the administration's use of gangland tactics to stifle opponents produced more negative headlines. On December 18 the *Inquirer* reported that the PAOCTF, still under Director Ping Lacson's personal command, had placed a hundred telephone taps on senators, witnesses, opposition leaders, and military intelligence officers during the impeachment trial.[106] Asked about the PAOCTF's Special Directorate X (SDX) for illegal surveillance, Lacson insisted that there was "no such thing as SDX." Citing a well-placed police source, however, the *Inquirer* reported that SDX had been formed on October 8, the day after Chavit Singson's historic press conference. The paper drew upon an internal police document to add that SDX was "highly compartmentalized . . . known only to a few trusted PAOCTF officers," and its operations were concealed inside a private security company owned by one of Lacson's relatives. The same source claimed that SDX had sixteen sophisticated "intercept scanners" for digital cellular phones.[107]

The impeachment suddenly stalled while the court probed incidents of police surveillance that seemed to threaten its integrity, plunging the proceedings into a mind maze of covert maneuvers. On day nine the court summoned *Inquirer* reporters, who presented phone records showing over a hundred targets under electronic surveillance, including the entire impeachment court except for the five senator-jurors loyal to the president. In his testimony PNP director Lacson admitted that the police were monitoring criminals, with proper warrants of course. But he insisted that negotiations with the German firm Rohde and Schwarz for sophisticated units capable of monitoring cell phones had not been completed. The press challenged his assurances, reporting claims by police sources that PAOCTF had in fact purchased the equipment secretly with unaudited intelligence funds.[108]

In the trial's last hearing before a long Christmas break, the senior vice president of Equitable-PCI Bank, Clarissa Ocampo, testified about meeting the president at the palace on February 4, 2000, to transfer funds. Impeccably groomed and looking coolly professional, Ocampo stated that she had sat at the president's left side "about a foot away" as he signed "Jose Velarde" on documents for a five-hundred-million-peso investment drawn from an Equitable account in the name of the Wellex Group, a company owned by a presidential crony. "When he signed Jose Velarde," Ocampo said, "I just couldn't believe it. He did not sign his real name, so I decided not to authenticate the signature." In an apparent reference to that second, still-sealed envelope, Ocampo added that the president also kept a hidden account in her bank under the Velarde name. Since Ocampo was one of the very few who could link President Estrada to his Jose Velarde persona, she was, she said, "very, very scared." To spare her from harm the court had docketed her as an unscheduled witness and, with the defense unprepared, she delivered her damaging statement uninterrupted and unchallenged.[109]

At Christmas parties in homes, clubs, and offices across the nation, Filipinos clustered around the television for the live broadcast and were captivated by Clarissa Ocampo's testimony.[110] With the trial suspended for the holidays, many would speculate about the contents of the second mysterious envelope.

When the impeachment trial resumed on January 2, 2001, the prosecution returned with new evidence that would shatter the president's defense over the next eight days. Playing to their strength, prosecutors opened with additional testimony by Clarissa Ocampo. Speaking with the same quiet conviction, she exposed a last-hour attempt by the president's lawyers to conceal his Equitable Bank accounts.[111] Next came the prosecution's other star witness, Governor Singson, who used six hours of intense cross-examination to expand convincingly on the key points of his own testimony.[112]

After countless hours of dull testimony, court and spectators came alive again when Estrada's former finance secretary, Edgardo Espiritu, took the stand for two days of damaging testimony about the BW stock scandal. Voice quavering and face twitching with conflicted emotions, Espiritu stunned the court when he stated that Estrada was the real owner of BW Resources, the company at the center of a massive fraud that had nearly destroyed the nation's financial markets. When the BW stock price reached dangerous heights in October 1999, exchange officials had pressed Secretary Espiritu for government intervention to pull the market back from the brink of collapse. Although the secretary pleaded that "something must be done," the president refused to take action to prevent the possible collapse of the stock exchange. Concluding his testimony, Espiritu elaborated on his reasons for resigning from the cabinet by citing the "deplorable" presence of drug traffickers and commercial smugglers at palace social functions. One of the Senate judges, intruding into this examination, asked the witness to name the smugglers. Espiritu demurred, saying, "We know that many have died for doing that."[113]

After twenty-two days of gavel-to-gavel impeachment telecasts, Estrada's high approval ratings had plunged. One survey found that nearly 100 percent of middle-class respondents believed the president was guilty as charged. An overwhelming 71 percent of those surveyed said that they would join anti-Estrada rallies if the Senate voted to acquit him.[114]

Yet the president's slender Senate majority held firm. No matter how dramatic the evidence, no matter how moving the witnesses, acquittal seemed likely, sparking a nationwide debate over what should be done. The Makati Business Club, stung by the stock market's 30 percent drop since the trial's start, warned that an "indecisive acquittal" could prove disastrous, resulting in capital flight, a collapse in the peso's value, and rising unemployment.[115] A columnist for the *Inquirer*, Conrado de Quiros, stated that "if Erap were acquitted, people power will follow as naturally as sun does at the end of night. It's already there . . . in the protest in the streets, in homes and office, in cyberspace."[116]

The denouement came at the close of the trial's twenty-third day, Tuesday, January 16, 2001. After weeks of procrastinating over that second letter from Equitable Bank, the prosecution finally demanded that it be introduced into evidence. In an impassioned speech House prosecutor Joker Arroyo charged that the sealed envelope would reveal Estrada's "mother account," worth ₱3.3 billion ($66 million), all of it kickbacks from palace cronies. Charging that the president had "prostituted and bastardized the banking system," the prosecutor pleaded with the judges to open the envelope. Defense attorney Mendoza objected, insisting that those deposits had not been mentioned in the original articles of impeachment.

After further, uninspired debate, the Senate voted eleven to ten along partisan lines to reject the prosecution's plea to open the second envelope. When the tally was announced, pro-Estrada senators cheered. To a burst of applause from the gallery, Senate president Aquilino Pimentel Jr. announced, "I realized that the nays have it and therefore I resign my presidency of the Senate."[117] All eleven House prosecutors followed suit, saying the Senate had "lost the moral authority to render judgment." Prosecutor Oscar Moreno told the press, "The forum is now in the streets, no longer in the Senate halls."[118]

With that vote middle-class Manila erupted in outrage. Retired general Fortunato Abat urged the armed forces to advise the president to resign.[119] Cardinal Sin and former president Corazon Aquino called for "people power" protests. Noise barrages broke out spontaneously across the capital. Cell phones sang with text messages. E-mail flew through cyberspace.[120] Within hours Manila resounded in spontaneous protests. Some forty thousand protestors mounted an all-night rally before the bronze statue of Our Lady towering above the EDSA highway.[121] "Across the sea of human faces," wrote columnist de Quiros, "luminescent in the light thrown by their mobile phones, while they 'texted' the world to come to where they were, emotions ran riot, sadness, exultation and resolve chasing each other like light and shadow on the face of the earth."[122]

People Power II

In refusing to open that second envelope, the president's Senate supporters had blundered. On a Tuesday the president's iron-clad Senate majority had mocked the opposition's impotence. But by Saturday anti-Estrada demonstrators would force the president from the palace. Between these two events came the drama of People Power II, a phenomenon that derived its energy from a fusion of new information technologies—cellular telephones and instant text messaging—that elevated ordinary people from spectators to actors in this political drama.

With the trial stripped of its credibility by the Senate vote, sovereignty shifted to the streets where the language of legitimacy was no longer political or constitutional but resolutely moral. As students and faculty across Manila quit classrooms to become a crowd, their military and religious elders filled the press with validating moral proclamations.[123] That same day the PMA's class of 1962, now retired, placed a full-page advertisement in the *Inquirer* calling on their active-duty comrades to take appropriate action.[124]

The spontaneous Tuesday night crowd of forty thousand grew steadily over the next twenty-four hours. "Stay here until evil is conquered by good. Stay here until corruption is overcome by integrity," Cardinal Sin told the people who filled highway and overpasses to form a nimbus of crowd and concrete above the giant statue of Our Lady. Beneath this monument to the original people power phenomenon of 1986, Corazon Aquino prayed for "more people who will gather at EDSA in coming days." Arriving from Hong Kong, former president Ramos walked ten kilometers up EDSA to join the crowd, calling on his supporters to follow.[125] Instead of the loose, spontaneous movement of 1986, these demonstrators came in tightly organized "civil society" groups, a veritable "third force in social, political, and economic affairs."[126] As the demonstrations entered their third day on January 18, the crowd grew to 250,000. More than ten thousand clerical workers and executives formed a human chain that afternoon. Adding a powerful, populist touch, the Filipino film superstar Nora Aunor, the president's former mistress, appeared at EDSA to call for his ouster and charge that he had once beat her "black and blue."[127]

Despite their public support for the president, Defense Secretary Orlando Mercado, along with many of his military commanders, was wavering.[128] Many in the crowd at the EDSA shrine seemed aware that they were playing to a military audience. Among the millions of text messages crisscrossing the skies above Manila on day three, one exchange among activists at about 2:15 p.m. read "Military nids 2 C 1 million critical mas n EDSA 2moro, Jan. 19, 2 make decision against Erap. Pls. join, pa on."[129]

On January 19, the fourth day of demonstrations, the tide turned against the president. Arriving at 9:30 a.m. for a cabinet meeting, Defense Secretary Mercado observed the president in deep "denial," preparing for a final stand by ordering combat forces into Manila.[130] But the president had already lost control of his military. At 10:30 across town inside AFP headquarters, Chief of Staff Angelo Reyes and his subordinates agreed that their "one constitutional option" amid the gathering chaos was to withdraw support from the president. "Gentlemen," the general told his staff, "I'm sure you all know we've just committed mutiny." In unison they replied, "Yes, sir." An hour later General Reyes met with Vice President Gloria Arroyo at a military safe house just minutes from the EDSA shrine and its crowd. After stating that the armed forces would support her as president, General Reyes added, "We are only asking for two things, Ma'am: Good governance and a dignified exit for President Estrada." She agreed. At 12:20 p.m., the general called the president on his cell phone "to inform him of my decision" and spent "an agonizing 45 minutes," tracing circles on the lawn while Estrada tried to dissuade him. Three hours later General Reyes and his service chiefs appeared at EDSA to announce their mutiny to the public.[131]

In the midst of a final wave of defections, PNP director general Ping Lacson was "the last senior security officer" at the president's side. Indeed, he may have been the last senior officer loyal to the president inside his own police command. For nearly a year the PNP hierarchy had slipped slowly from Lacson's grasp. Within minutes of General Reyes's appearance at EDSA, Manila's five district police commanders defied Director Lacson to break openly with the president. Inside PNP headquarters at Camp Crame, the dissident general Leandro Mendoza ordered tight security to bar entry by any police loyal to Estrada. His rebel officers marched into the camp's PAOCTF building with guns bristling and came close to a shootout with Lacson loyalists, who, finding themselves outnumbered, quickly capitulated.[132] Returning to Camp Crame from the palace at 5:30 p.m., Lacson walked into an office occupied by rebel police officers who were ready to arrest him if he resisted. Within minutes Lacson dialed the president, informing him regretfully that the PNP would have to withdraw its support and rebuffing a last-ditch suggestion by Estrada that the police should attack the army.[133]

As dawn broke over the city on the final day, January 20, a Supreme Court justice called Cardinal Sin to say that the chief justice, Hilario Davide Jr., was willing to swear in Vice President Arroyo. Although initially reluctant to break off negotiations with the palace, after speaking with an insistent Cardinal Sin at 9:45 a.m. the vice president agreed to take the presidential oath that day. At 10:00 a.m., she phoned the court to invite the chief justice to swear her in at noon. While waiting for her to fax a written request, all the justices then in Manila met with Davide and voted twelve to two to support his decision, thereby exercising their discretionary powers to oust a president who had lost his moral mandate.

Around noon Cardinal Sin appeared at EDSA for an inaugural invocation laden with sacral significance. "You watched over us in our fight for the truth to prevail and for morality to win," the cardinal intoned heavenward. "Just like at EDSA in 1986, You walked with us and cared for us and took us in Your mantle of protection." Then at 12:20 Chief Justice Davide administered the oath of office to President Gloria Macapagal Arroyo before a crowd of a quarter million. Overhead two F-5 fighters flew low over EDSA while four MG-520 attack helicopters hovered protectively over the anti-Estrada demonstrators now assembled outside the palace gates.[134]

At 2:20, ex-president Estrada—accompanied by his legal wife, their three children, and a son by "ex-starlet Guia Gomez"—finally left the palace.[135] Eight hours later PNP director Ping Lacson called on President Arroyo to offer his courtesy resignation. Amid countless competing priorities, the new administration moved quickly against his police apparatus, the coercive core of the outgoing administration. Within days the new PNP director, Leandro Mendoza, ousted six Lacson allies from top PNP posts. Police and palace joined forces to demolish Lacson's covert apparatus, the Presidential Anti-Organized Crime Task Force. While the new administration seized ₱100 million from secret accounts, the police moved to secure the sophisticated phone-tapping equipment held by elite squads. But in the chaos of transition the PNP reported that Lacson loyalists Michael Ray Aquino and Cezar Mancao had smuggled four digital intercept scanners out of Camp Crame, two of them capable of tapping 170 lines simultaneously. Only hours after the new president took her oath, they were monitoring her private conversations.[136]

As subsequent investigations uncovered PAOCTF criminality, opinion turned sharply against this elite police unit, which had once enjoyed strong public support. The PNP fired seven hundred officers who were believed to be "very loyal" to Lacson. The bureaucratic coup de grâce came in a confidential report to the president. "The modus operandi" of PAOCTF, the report revealed, "was for these people to contact different personalities in the underworld and let each organize a holdup/kidnap for ransom group. . . . Once a group gains notoriety through its exploits, it is now subjected for [*sic*] neutralization." In this final phase the criminal gang is interrogated "to determine where their loot is hidden" and then massacred while the media reports another heroic police victory against desperadoes.[137] On April 17 President Arroyo abolished the PAOCTF. In a blunt editorial the *Inquirer* said that Lacson's task force had "quickly evolved into the biggest, best organized and most ruthless criminal syndicate to operate in this country."[138] With the dismissal of Lacson and his loyalists, the key element in Estrada's power was neutralized, at least for the moment.

Conclusion

In the aftermath of Estrada's ouster in January 2001, there was a revealing debate over the legitimacy of President Arroyo's ascent to power and, more broadly, the role of the crowd in the Philippine constitutional order. With the memory of the 1986 people power movement against Marcos still strong, many nonpartisan Filipino leaders accepted the role of the crowd as legitimate, even constitutionally mandated. To those who said the military's actions had established "a very dangerous precedent where the military can . . . decide who sits" in the palace, Gen. Angelo Reyes replied that his commanders "did not initiate this, the people initiated this." The armed forces, he argued, "could not prop up a discredited regime indefinitely."[139] But the international press, which had celebrated the 1986 people power revolution, was now sharply critical of its second coming as People Power II, questioning the legality of ousting an elected president who still enjoyed considerable popular support. A *New York Times* correspondent, Seth Mydans, wrote that people power "was used not to restore democracy but, momentarily, to supplant it." He quoted American commentators who called the event "a defeat for due process" and even "mob rule."[140]

In their criticism of the Filipino crowd, these American observers were echoing unexamined assumptions embedded within a shared constitutional tradition. The authors of the U.S. Constitution, reflecting the eighteenth century's abhorrence of the mob, had designed an elaborate system of checks and balances to protect the government from direct popular rule. "In all very numerous assemblies, of whatever character composed," wrote James Madison in the *Federalist Papers,* "passion never fails to wrest the scepter from reason. Had every Athenian citizen been a Socrates, every Athenian assembly would still have been a mob."[141]

In its original 1935 Constitution, the Philippine Republic had adopted the American separation of powers in ways that strengthened an already powerful imperial executive. As colonial-era justice George Malcolm pointed out, the Philippine president was granted "vast and unusual powers" with the authority to suspend habeas corpus and impose martial law. The Philippine Supreme Court remained, in the view of a leading Filipino legal scholar, the weakest of the three branches and had, by the sum of its decisions in the U.S. colonial period, "abdicated its right to subject official actions . . . to judicial review," thus paving the way "for the emergence of a constitutional dictatorship."[142] Rather than strengthening the judiciary or modifying the powers of the executive, the revised Philippine Constitution of 1987, written in the aftermath of the first people power movement, had departed still further from its American antecedents by seeking a counterweight to executive power in the form of popular participation. Under Article II, section 23, the state is required to "encourage non-governmental, community-based, or sectoral organizations that promote the welfare of the nation." More important, the charter mandates under Article VI, section 32, that the people can, by a petition of 10 percent of registered voters, "directly propose and enact laws or approve or reject any act or law or part thereof passed by Congress."[143] In the first provision the Constitution invested civil organizations with a quasi-official status. In the second it sanctioned the people as a third, albeit informal, legislative chamber with the right to override all legislation passed by the lower and upper houses.

By its composition and comportment, the crowd at People Power II seemed to belie the charge of mob rule. If a mob is a formless mass swept along in a frenzy to a violent climax that slakes its collective passions, then the million people assembled on EDSA were something else. Many came in groups—religious, university, residential, professional, or sectoral—that in other contexts would be called civil society. Some were wealthy. Many were poor. But at its core the crowd was drawn from Manila's educated middle-class, the foundation of a functioning democracy in most societies. When the Senate's refusal to open the second envelope brought many into the streets on the night of January 16, 2001, the demonstrators were a disciplined crowd for the next four days, listening to speeches and forming a consensus by "texting" each other in Filipino-English shorthand.

The phenomenal proliferation of cell phones in the fifteen years since the first people power movement changed the character of the crowd, extending both its range and its depth. By late 1999 Filipinos were sending and receiving eighteen million text messages daily, the world's highest level after Japan. During the five days of People Power II, the country set new records with two hundred million messages flowing through just one company, Smart. Through constant cellular texting, the size of the crowd reached far beyond those actually on the streets. Moreover, the constant stream of messages allowed a lateral dialogue within the crowd, transforming demonstrators from passive observers into active participants, interpreting and shaping events as they transpired. Listening to speakers while exchanging opinions through a written medium in real time, these demonstrators had a critical distance that precluded any surge in group emotions, any surrender of individual will to collective passions. Through the density and simultaneity of these communications, this mobilization moved beyond conventional denominations of "mob" or "crowd" to become a facsimile for civil society.[144]

From a historical perspective the introduction of cell phones and text messaging thus represents a populist technological check on the state's accretion of power through information technologies that in the twentieth century had tipped the balance of power in the favor of the prevailing regime. Just as America's analogue information revolution at the end of the nineteenth century invested the state with a technological capacity for mass surveillance, so this second revolution in digital communications a century later has had the reverse effect—countering the state's control over information, decentralizing data access, and creating an independent means of popular mobilization.

Yet even within the Philippines some expressed concern that the crowd could easily become a hooting throng. "Rights in a democracy are not decided by the mob whose judgment is dictated by rage and not by reason," cautioned the justices of the Supreme Court as they remanded Estrada to a lower court for trial on corruption charges. Writing as "an elder to the youth," Justice Jose C. Vitug observed that "two non-violent civilian uprisings" in a short span forced him to ask, "Where does one draw the line between the rule of law and the role of the mob, or between 'People Power' and 'Anarchy'?" If the justification for Arroyo's presidency lay solely with the crowd at EDSA, "then it does rest on loose and shifting sands and might tragically open a Pandora's box more potent than the malaise it seeks to address." There were, this justice warned with uncommon prescience, "innate perils of people power." These perils would be revealed just three months later when a very different crowd assembled at the same EDSA shrine to protest Estrada's incarceration in a violent reprise that billed itself as People Power III.[145]

16

Extrajudicial Executions

On June 27, 2005, President Gloria Arroyo appeared on national television for an unprecedented act of political contrition. After pummeling her for months with accusations of electoral fraud, the opposition had finally proved its case by releasing the sensational "Hello, Garci" tapes with the president's own gravelly voice ordering a corrupt election commissioner to manufacture a million-vote margin in the 2004 election. To still the demands for her impeachment, Arroyo now admitted that she had spoken to the commissioner. "My intent was not to influence the outcome of the election," she insisted before softening her tone. "I recognize that making any such call was a lapse in judgment. I am sorry."[1]

While that apology may have saved the president from impeachment, it could not quiet the accusations against her husband, Miguel "Mike" Arroyo. Allegations that the "first gentleman" had collected bribes from illegal jueteng syndicates to fund his wife's presidential campaign had plunged the country yet again into a protracted crisis of rumored coups, mass demonstrations, and attempted impeachment. At first he denied the charges. But an opposition senator exposed secret bank accounts under the pseudonym "Pidal," coincidentally and convincingly the middle name of Mike Arroyo's grandfather. Only two days after this historic apology, the president felt compelled to announce that her husband would be going abroad for an indefinite period of political exile.[2]

At first glance this seemingly ephemeral scandal, one of dozens that fill Manila's front pages in any given month, could be dismissed as routine, even inconsequential. But these events gain greater significance when we recall that only a year before a similar controversy over jueteng bribery had inspired People Power II. These four days of demonstrations had forced Arroyo's predecessor, Joseph Estrada, out of the palace and into prison—a similarity suggesting that criminality has been woven deep into the fabric of Philippine politics.

At a more immediate level, however, this "Hello Garci" controversy had its origins in a political vendetta between President Arroyo and her chief political rival, Senator Panfilo "Ping" Lacson. Only weeks after taking her oath of office in 2001, President Arroyo used state security to charge Senator Lacson with illegal wiretapping and mass murder arising from his earlier tenure as director of the Philippine National Police (PNP). First as a senator and later as a presidential candidate, Lacson fought back with scandal by targeting the president's husband. At a broader level, this juncture of scandal and secret service operations in 2005 would produce a volatile legitimation crisis reminiscent of similar controversies surrounding U.S. colonial policing circa 1905, raising intriguing questions about the persistence of these political patterns over the span of a century.

Adding another thread to this skein of historical continuity, the Philippine-American security alliance, frayed by the closure of U.S. military bases in the 1990s, was repaired in the aftermath of the September 2001 terror attacks. During a decade without significant U.S. aid (1992–2001), Manila had failed to fund its military, leaving the country defenseless against Chinese incursions in the South China Sea and forcing it to favor negotiations over combat in dealing with insurgency. After 9/11, however, President Arroyo was the first Asian leader to enlist in America's Coalition of the Willing, and Washington reciprocated by making the Philippines its "second front" in the global war on terror. This foreign policy initiative had profound domestic ramifications in the Philippines. The millions in military aid and thousands of American troops that followed over the next eight years served to shore up Arroyo's shaky administration, checking Islamic rebels in the south, strengthening her ties to the armed forces, and assuring U.S. diplomatic support against her domestic rivals.[3]

From a historical perspective, this renewed military alliance represented another in Washington's periodic postcolonial infusions of aid and advisers to revitalize the coercive capacity of the Philippine state. As in past U.S. interventions, the ruling Filipino oligarchy deftly manipulated this alliance to extend armed violence beyond the designated targets, whether communist guerrillas or Islamic terrorists. With their acute sensitivity to the nuances of American policy honed by a century of close interactions, Filipino leaders quickly divined the inner logic of Washington's war on terror and played on it to turn the alliance to partisan advantage, unleashing deadly force that stifled social change. Once again the Philippines, in diverting Washington's global policy to advance a local agenda, served as a bellwether for similar contradictions that would soon appear among other American allies in the war on terror such as Afghanistan, Georgia, Iraq, Israel, and Pakistan.

People Power III

After her inauguration during a mass uprising that was forcing her predecessor from power, President Arroyo's government suffered an underlying sense of insecurity that inclined her toward repression, both legal and extralegal. Only a week after ex-president Estrada's ouster in January 2001, a survey found that 70 percent of Manila residents approved of mass demonstrations as a means of changing government.[4] Although Estrada had lost legitimacy, it was not yet clear whether Arroyo had won it, an ambiguity that would soon allow another protest march on the palace dubbed People Power III.

Rather than courting support with political concessions or populist gestures to broaden her base, Arroyo, like Cory Aquino after Marcos's fall, relied on coercion to contain any challenges. To highlight her predecessor's lack of legitimacy and affirm her own, Arroyo devoted the first hundred days of her presidency to gathering evidence against ex-president Estrada for the theft of ₱15 billion and prosecuting former PNP director Ping Lacson for the kidnapping and murder of seven Filipino Chinese.[5] Her political strategy soon won constitutional support when the Supreme Court ruled unanimously that Estrada enjoyed no residual immunity from criminal prosecution.[6]

Far more quickly than anyone could have imagined, however, President Arroyo's coercive tactics stirred a violent backlash. When the courts ordered Estrada's indictment on plunder charges in late April, the palace dispatched a force of three hundred policemen, backed by heavily armed marines, to push through the crowd of supporters outside his home. In an excess of zeal, police then booked the ex-president like a common criminal, producing mug shots of a sad-eyed Estrada that were leaked to the press, arousing a rush of pity among his poor followers.[7] Almost immediately Estrada's loyal party leaders mounted a round-the-clock protest vigil at the EDSA highway shrine to the original people power revolution, attracting throngs that soon numbered some two hundred thousand. In contrast to the polite, middle-class crowds that had massed against Estrada back in January, these demonstrators poured out of the city's slums, both ordinary workers motivated by political loyalty and street toughs attracted by drugs and cash.[8]

Even though the throngs paralyzed city traffic for five days, the police adopted a posture of "maximum tolerance" and kept their antiriot squads at a discreet distance. To defuse the situation, the PNP moved Estrada from an austere concrete jail cell to comfortable quarters at a military base outside the city. Inside the palace the administration scrambled to assure the unity of the armed forces and move an anticoup force of two thousand troops into the city.[9]

On the fifth and final night of this rally, the crowd peaked at one hundred thousand and opposition leaders stoked their emotions for a violent midnight crescendo. While speakers called for an attack on the palace, Estrada's loyal police commanders mobilized an ad hoc strike force of several hundred soldiers led by a onetime coup leader, Gregorio "Gringo" Honasan; some five hundred police officers still loyal to ex-director Lacson; and several police squads that were absent without leave.[10] After hours of incendiary speeches, some fifty thousand of Estrada's hard-core supporters set out on a ten-kilometer march to Malacañang Palace shortly after midnight. Two hours later the crowd swept past the last, lightly guarded barricades, breached the palace's security perimeter, and massed outside Malacañang's Gate 7 just before dawn.

It was a desperate moment. Surprised by the scale and speed of the attack, security forces were thin and no senior officer was on duty to coordinate the palace's defense. As the mob surged forward, palace guards fought back, firing live ammunition and killing two. For the next six hours the crowd, largely young males whose bodies were etched with slum-gang tattoos and fueled by methamphetamines, charged the gates with stones, clubs, and handmade shotguns. At 10:30 a.m., the police, at last reinforced by infantry, formed a phalanx of riot shields and advanced in a hail of tear gas, water jets, and warning shots. Slowly the demonstrators retreated from the palace precincts, throwing rocks and burning cars before dispersing. In the chaos 4 were killed, 113 injured, and 103 arrested.[11]

In the midst of this fighting, President Arroyo declared a "state of rebellion" in Metro Manila. Acting on intelligence, she authorized warrantless arrests for a dozen of the uprising's leaders, including Senator Juan Ponce Enrile, Senator Gringo Honasan, and Ping Lacson's police coterie. According to her intelligence, Honasan and Lacson had planned the attack by recruiting dissident policemen and soldiers. Simultaneously, Manila politicians loyal to Estrada had mobilized legions of "hoodlums and criminals" from the city's drug-infested slums. All this activity was financed, said a PNP intelligence report, by the billion-peso "power grab kitty" of eighteen Chinese Filipino allies of Estrada and Lacson who were "suspected of involvement in drug dealing smuggling, and jai alai operations."[12] If this repetition of history lacked the ingredients for either tragedy or farce, then People Power III resembled a political pantomime showing the covert netherworld's influence on Philippine politics.

To track down the plotters President Arroyo turned to another master of Manila's netherworld, PNP senior superintendent Reynaldo Berroya, a bitter Lacson rival. Within hours and without hesitation, Berroya led a police detachment to arrest Senator Enrile, once Marcos's powerful defense minister. Several of Lacson's loyalists among rebel PNP officers soon surrendered, but others went into hiding, notably, Michael Ray Aquino, Cezar Mancao, and Lacson himself. At the same time, the director of the National Bureau of Investigation, Reynaldo Wycoco, revived his probe into the kidnapping and murder of two Chinese by Lacson's former anticrime squad, the PAOCTF, telling the press that one of its commanders, Michael Ray Aquino, had collected the ransom for a third kidnap victim.[13]

With the approach of the 2001 midterm elections on May 14, President Arroyo soon faced strong pressure for a reconciliation sufficient to allow a credible campaign. On May 4 she visited Estrada's detention center outside Manila, where there were polite words on both sides. A week later she granted safe conduct passes to the two senate candidates implicated in the uprising, Gringo Honasan and Ping Lacson, who immediately emerged from hiding to appear at an opposition election rally.[14]

Secret Service Showdown

This tense truce masked a bitter struggle inside the police force that would shape the nation's political future more profoundly than even these congressional elections. After winning a Senate seat in May 2001 and becoming the opposition's main leader, Ping Lacson launched a sustained attack on the president, accusing her of corruption and collusion with illegal gambling syndicates. To slow his rise the president set a supercop to catch a supercop, investing Lacson's blood enemy Rey Berroya with special powers and direct access to her office.[15] Within three months this campaign culminated in a high-stakes showdown between Senator Lacson and the administration's top operatives: the street-tough Berroya, who headed PNP intelligence; the taciturn professional Wycoco, who led the National Bureau of Investigation; and the idealistic ex-communist Victor Corpus, who commanded the Intelligence Service Armed Forces of the Philippines (ISAFP). In their pursuit of Ping Lacson, these operatives used a shotgun approach, blasting away with a full magazine of explosive charges. By the end of this three-year battle, Lacson would best them all, countering their criminal charges with his media countercharges.

At first this rivalry revolved around allegations about illicit drugs instead of illegal gambling. After a decade of rising amphetamine abuse in the country's slums, the drug traffic had finally gained sufficient influence inside the PNP to erupt from Manila's back alleys onto the front pages of the nation's newspapers. Instead of jueteng's established ethos of bribes and politicians, the traffic in the cheap methamphetamines called *shabu* brought new, disconcerting dimensions to Manila's daily life: ravaged addicts, cold-blooded murders, and mangled bodies. Instead of taking a cut from the old jueteng lottery, Lacson's protégés in the PAOCTF police squad had allegedly focused on the more lucrative drug traffic, maximizing profits by kidnapping overseas Chinese suppliers, draining their bank accounts, and dumping their bodies. Alone among Arroyo's three top cops, Col. Victor Corpus grasped the implications of this shift from jueteng to *shabu*, warning that this new vice might make the nation "a narco-state like Colombia."[16]

As he joined the pursuit of Senator Lacson, Colonel Corpus soon showed the limitations of his aggressive tactics, lunging too quickly for a death blow that left his flanks exposed. In early April 2001, Corpus, as chief of military intelligence, told the press that Lacson's PAOCTF had run a kidnapping syndicate with ruthless efficiency. "The modus operandi," he explained, "was to chop the bodies to pieces, burn them and crush the remains into powder so that in the event of a trial, the prosecution would find it very hard to establish a corpus delecti." Almost immediately, however, Corpus's main source of information, Senior Inspector Medel Pone, a supposed member of this macabre police cleanup crew, called a press conference to deny the entire story, claiming that Corpus had forced him to name Lacson. Branding this sudden reversal as "a set up," Mary "Rosebud" Ong, the former undercover operative who had first fingered Lacson's men back in 2000 for murdering six Chinese drug dealers, reemerged to charge that Lacson's group was behind these recent maneuvers, adding that Pone himself had been involved in the strangulation of a drug lord named Calvin Wong.[17]

While Corpus's idealism inclined him toward haste, Wycoco's caution, the trademark of his steady rise within the police force, and Berroya's cunning, honed by decades in Manila's netherworld, proved more effective. With little media fanfare these two intelligence chiefs cooperated quietly to solve the unsettling disappearance of the publicist Salvador "Bubby" Dacer. With strong forensic evidence, the NBI soon filed criminal charges against seven PAOCTF officers who were subordinates of Lacson's loyal PNP protégé, Senior Superintendent Mancao. Moreover, a dawn raid on March 28 arrested two farmers at Indang, Cavite, who admitted to watching as three PAOCTF officers strangled Dacer and his driver with an electrical cord and then burned their bodies on a gasoline-drenched pyre. Confronted with this eyewitness evidence, four of the arrested officers soon cracked, claiming that President Estrada had ordered Dacer's killing through PNP superintendent Glenn Dumlao, a stunning revelation slammed across the city's front pages under headlines reading "Erap Named Brains in Dacer Murders." In a press interview NBI director Wycoco said the "large-scale involvement" of three disparate PAOCTF units raised questions about Dacer's death that only Lacson could answer. Angrily, Lacson shot back, saying that the Arroyo administration had "found a natural Goebbels in Wycoco."[18]

After the PAOCTF commanders were indicted for Dacer's murder, Rey Berroya, now promoted to head PNP intelligence, moved to round up the accused. On June 4 his men snatched the most senior of them, Superintendent Dumlao, from Manila's Victory Liner bus terminal. Just eight days later Dumlao wrote out a confession, stating that as PAOCTF's deputy operations chief he had interrogated Dacer right after his kidnapping at the direction of Lacson's lieutenants Cezar Mancao and Michael Ray Aquino, adding that their every move was reported to Lacson himself. Within weeks these two Lacson protégés slipped through Mactan International Airport on fake passports and disappeared into the United States. Meanwhile Ping Lacson dismissed Dumlao's affidavit as a fraud written by "the PNP Intelligence Group under Col. Reynaldo Berroya."[19]

Throughout June and July 2001, this sub rosa clash shifted to the press as Colonel Corpus began feeding information to a two-fisted crime reporter, Ramon Tulfo, an honorary member of the colonel's 1967 Military Academy class. In a blistering "Open Letter to Ping Lacson" published in Manila's leading daily, the columnist denounced Senator Lacson as a "monster" guilty of countless crimes, including salvaging criminals, torturing suspects, executing the Kuratong Baleleng gang, murdering Bubby Dacer, and bumping off a martial law detainee so he could marry the current "Mrs. Panfilo Lacson." Again Lacson shot back, saying "I smell the handiwork of Berroya" and insisting that all of Tulfo's charges were lifted from his rival's 1998 "white paper" which had been posted anonymously on the Internet.[20] In seven more columns Tulfo added to his catalog of the senator's alleged crimes. He accused Lacson of tossing two women related to the Red Scorpion boss out of a helicopter into Manila Bay, murdering the boyfriend of a runway model he fancied, and executing two girls, one just seven, after they witnessed a PAOCTF rub-out. Moving from blood to money, Tulfo claimed in his July 28 column that Lacson had played "Mr. Clean" by forgoing the usual jueteng bribes and instead secretly recycling seized methamphetamines back to the streets. In his penultimate blast on July 31, Tulfo claimed that the senator had laundered money from "kidnappings for ransom and drug trafficking" via U.S. bank accounts, an accusation substantiated, Tulfo said, by the seizure of $8 million from Lacson's officers on the Canadian-U.S. border.[21]

The day after Tulfo's last column, Colonel Corpus released an intelligence report charging that Senator Lacson and ex-president Estrada had laundered $728 million from drug trafficking and kidnapping ransom through foreign banks, assertions that stunned the nation and held television audiences spellbound for weeks. The colonel claimed that a special PNP-AFP intelligence team assisted by American customs officials had found seven U.S. bank accounts belonging to Lacson and his wife with total deposits of $211 million. Although Lacson dismissed the charges as "stupid," the government's Senate majority announced a blue-ribbon investigation, setting the stage for a spectacular secret service showdown.[22] When the Senate inquiry began in mid-August, Colonel Corpus proved to be a problematic witness, impressing viewers with his sincerity but confusing them with his tendency to make unsubstantiated accusations. Ultimately, the NBI, through its liaison with the FBI, was able to confirm just $1.2 million in Senator Lacson's American accounts, a far cry from Corpus's initial claims.[23]

As his intelligence confreres testified at the Senate's televised hearings, Senior Superintendent Berroya trolled the shadows looking for more scandals about his nemesis Ping Lacson. In August Berroya's PNP intelligence operatives caught several ex-PAOCTF officers as they tried to sell cell phone surveillance equipment stolen from the police. During an interview with the author at a hotel coffee shop on August 20, Berroya was repeatedly interrupted by cell phone calls from his officers wrapping up this sting operation. Suddenly he snapped to seated attention for an incoming call, speaking in crisp, deferential tones: "Yes, ma'am, we got it all. . . . Yes, ma'am, the equipment could triangulate to locate cell phones. . . . Thank you, ma'am." After he put down his phone, I asked the reason for this personal call from President Arroyo. "They were about to buy new equipment," he replied, "so this crazy guy Lacson was selling the old stuff on the black market for ₱24 million to all takers. We posed as buyers and made the sting."[24] The next day, with the PNP director at his side, Berroya met the Manila press to present two seized electronic eavesdropping units that were originally purchased for Lacson from Germany for ₱30 million and used by his aide Michael Ray Aquino to monitor President Estrada's enemies during his impeachment trial. Providing some corroboration for these charges, Berroya added, "While Lacson's men tried to clean up the files and delete the evidence, we found a way of retrieving them from the hard disk."[25]

In a second round of Senate hearings in September, Senator Lacson's ally Chief Superintendent Reynaldo Acop, former head of the PNP Narcotics Group, gave aggressive testimony that tried to "completely demolish" allegations by his former agent Mary Ong. But when the senators grilled him about a government check for two million pesos that Acop had sent her in 1998, he virtually admitted, as the *Inquirer* observed, that "he had embezzled public funds." Just a few days later a former civilian agent in Acop's old command, Remus Garganera, testified that narcotics officers under Superintendent Francisco Villaroman, a Lacson protégé, had made three hundred thousand pesos a day in drug sales during 1998, passing the money up the line to Superintendent John Campos and then to Acop himself. On the last day of the inquiry, Mary Ong linked officers Acop, Villaroman, and Campos to the murder of several Hong Kong drug traffickers, submitting a letter from the Chinese Embassy that linked them to the killings, charges the committee found credible.[26]

Instead of appearing to rebut these charges, in October 2001 Senator Lacson used his chamber's customary "privilege speech" to deliver a one-hour, uninterrupted address accusing First Gentleman Mike Arroyo of diverting Charity Sweepstakes funds to electioneering. Suddenly, this brilliant use of scandal put the administration on the defensive. A month later, on November 13, Lacson cited PNP intelligence reports to charge NBI director Wycoco and other top police officials with splitting annual "jueteng payola" of ₱16.5 billion from illegal gambling syndicates. President Arroyo, he noted pointedly, had failed to end this corruption. Heading the senator's list of the illegal gambling kingpins was the Pampanga jueteng boss Rodolfo "Bong" Pineda, the purported financier of the president's election campaigns.[27]

As the Senate wound up these hearings to write a report that would not appear for years, the Arroyo administration shifted the focus of its get-Lacson effort to the Kuratong Baleleng massacre, making this cold case central to the nation's politics. Investigators turned up four new eyewitnesses who claimed that one police commander had tried to spare the prisoners, but Lacson had "insisted on their elimination." In early July an activist attorney, Arno Sanidad, released an affidavit from police officer Noel Seno admitting that he had participated in the slaughter and had seen Lacson at the scene. But in late August, just as the government was moving to arrest Lacson, the Court of Appeals issued a permanent injunction against any further prosecution of this case, explaining that the grace period since an earlier dismissal of the murder charges had elapsed.[28]

President Arroyo's two-year pursuit of Lacson through her three intelligence chiefs had produced decidedly mixed results. On the debit side Colonel Corpus's headline-grabbing accusations of hundred-million-dollar deposits were not corroborated, blunting the impact of Senate inquiries into Lacson's alleged kidnapping and drug dealing. On the credit side Corpus seized a cache of C-4 explosives in January 2002 that Lacson's coterie of former police officers reportedly planned to use in "destabilization efforts."[29] Berroya had captured the eavesdropping equipment that confirmed Lacson's surveillance of senior politicians, but he had failed to link Lacson definitively to the web of crime and corruption that entangled his PNP protégés. Most important, NBI director Wycoco had pursued the Dacer murder deep into the senator's entourage, getting so close that two prime suspects, both police generals and Lacson intimates, had fled to America. But in the end Lacson bested them all through media manipulation and legal maneuvering while also establishing himself as a viable presidential candidate.

Presidential Election, 2004

During the years leading up to the 2004 elections, Senator Lacson struggled to avoid being tried for the Kuratong massacre while positioning himself for a run as President Arroyo's chief challenger. When the Supreme Court finally ruled in April 2003 that Lacson should stand trial for this mass murder, he suddenly declared his candidacy in the middle of a speech at an obscure provincial college. As the tempo of corruption charge and murder countercharge escalated, pro-administration legislators released their long-overdue final report on Lacson's alleged drug dealing, finding him "criminally liable."[30] In a rebuttal delivered on the Senate floor, Lacson dismissed the report as "political" and claimed that he possessed documents showing that his chief accuser, General Corpus "was reporting to First Gentleman Mike Arroyo in the latter's office at the LTA Building in Makati City and even received a substantial amount of money."[31]

On August 18, 2003, Senator Lacson scored a decisive blow against President Arroyo in another series of hard-hitting privilege speeches, charging that the first gentleman, as the president's "partner in everything," had headed a corrupt coterie that diverted over ₱270 million of her campaign contributions into private accounts and then used the funds to bribe his accusers: General Corpus, columnist Ramon Tulfo, and former police agent Mary Ong. Unlike the administration's unsubstantiated assertions about him, Lacson had a sheaf of bank documents showing that ₱36.6 million had been deposited in accounts under the name Jose Pidal, a fictional persona whose mailing address was in the same Makati building occupied by Mike Arroyo. The first gentleman dismissed this accusation, saying, "I don't know any Pidal." But Lacson struck back with a second in this series of speeches, disclosing a dozen bank accounts in the name of Jose Pidal with deposits totaling ₱260 million. Then, in a revelation that discredited Mike Arroyo, the ABS-CBN television network revealed that his great-grandmother was one Maria Pidal, an uncommon surname that had not appeared on the Philippine census rolls for over fifty years. To defuse this explosive revelation, the first gentleman's younger brother, Representative Ignacio Arroyo Jr., claimed unconvincingly, "I am actually Jose Pidal."[32] In a third privilege speech on October 13, Senator Lacson landed yet another blow, accusing the first gentleman of diverting Charity Sweepstakes "money for the poor" to President Arroyo's 2004 reelection campaign. Within weeks a Quezon City trial court with an Estrada appointee on the bench found "no probable cause" in the Kuratong massacre charges against Lacson, closing the books, at least for this political season, on the tangled murder case.[33] Reportedly "seething" over Lacson's personal attacks on her husband, the president rescinded a promise to retire at the end of her current term. On October 7 she announced her candidacy for reelection.[34]

At the approach of the final filing date for all candidates on December 15, 2003, crime-story sensations were momentarily swept away by the high drama of the 2004 presidential campaign. For the next five months the Filipino public was transfixed by the opposition soap opera as the matinee idol Fernando Poe Jr. and Senator Lacson flirted but failed to consummate an alliance, dooming themselves to defeat by splitting the anti-Arroyo vote. Barnstorming the country with clenched fist raised to symbolize his crackdown on crime, Lacson ran for president on his police record. "When I was the Philippine National Police chief," he told crowds at his campaign's launch in February 2004, "our countrymen felt safe." Asked on the stump how many he had killed, Lacson replied with his usual bravado, "I've lost count." But when pressed about reports that he had tortured prisoners as an MISG officer under martial law, he blamed his blood enemy, saying, "That wasn't me. That was Berroya." Just eight weeks before the elections, however, the solicitor general again petitioned the Supreme Court to allow the Kuratong massacre charges against Lacson to proceed, prompting negative press coverage. That controversy tarnished Lacson's luster, and he finished a distant third with a dismal 8 percent of the vote, well behind a victorious President Arroyo. Even so, issues of order and justice resonate so deeply with ordinary Filipino voters that Lacson's showing marked him as an influential political leader and future power broker.[35]

Politics by Scandal

In the aftermath of the 2004 campaign, President Arroyo issued the victor's usual call for national unity. But the opposition, now led by Senator Lacson, replied with a sustained attack on her legitimacy. First he impugned her integrity by circulating damaging accusations about fund-raising. Next he challenged the validity of her electoral mandate. Finally he convened Senate hearings that tarred the first family with the brush of jueteng corruption.

In this new round of recriminations, Lacson used his access to classified intelligence files from the PNP and FBI for critical information that severely damaged President Arroyo's aura of authority. From January to August 2005, a Filipino American FBI agent named Leandro Aragoncillo stole over a hundred classified reports about the Philippines from the bureau's computers in New Jersey and passed them to Lacson's former PNP aide, Michael Ray Aquino, who had fled to America to avoid trial for murder. After Aragoncillo invoked his FBI status to intervene in Aquino's deportation proceedings, an alert Immigration official became suspicious and notified the bureau, which quickly discovered the document theft and arrested the two Filipinos in October. According to U.S. prosecutors, the fugitive Filipino officer had forwarded the stolen intelligence reports to five opposition leaders in Manila, one of whom they identified publicly as "Senator #1 who . . . was formerly head of the Philippines National Police" and privately as "Senator Lacson." As part of his plea bargain, Aragoncillo admitted telling Lacson that the "the information he was transferring would be useful in . . . their attempts to destabilize and overthrow the president . . . of the Philippines."[36]

In May 2005, as his attack on Arroyo was reaching its peak, Senator Lacson announced legislative hearings into illegal jueteng gambling, claiming credible sources would present "very explosive testimony" proving that people in "high places" were on the take. Through the senator's good offices, the *Philippine Daily Inquirer* interviewed three of these witnesses, all of whom "claimed to have given or collected protection money" for the president's husband, Mike Arroyo, and her son, Representative Juan Miguel "Mikey" Arroyo. In a sworn affidavit, a syndicate bagman from Central Luzon charged that twenty-four jueteng operators had paid ₱1.93 million monthly to top PNP officials whose appointments had been "made by Mike Arroyo." Within hours the president ordered officials to investigate these charges against her son and husband.[37]

The administration tried to fight back by branding Senator Lacson's brother "a known bagman of the Cavite governor." But the controversy soon focused on the best-known secret in Philippine politics, the president's close ties to the country's top jueteng racketeer, Bong Pineda—a relationship that reached all the way back to their roots in the same small town, Lubao, Pampanga. When Arroyo first ran for the Senate in 1995 and then the vice presidency three years later, Pineda bankrolled her successful campaigns. Complementing this close political alliance, Arroyo developed a personal friendship with Pineda's wife, Lubao mayor Lilia Pineda, and stood as godmother at their son's baptism. In an interview with *Asiaweek,* Arroyo confirmed the ritual relationship but insisted that it was a traditional tie with no political significance. Yet in the first months of her administration Bong Pineda, according to journalist Sheila Coronel, was "able to expand and consolidate illegal gambling operations," taking control of all the Central Luzon lotteries and earning an unprecedented ₱2 billion annually.[38]

On June 7, 2005, this simmering scandal erupted into a full-blown crisis when the opposition released a recording of a phone call the president had made during ballot counting after the 2004 elections. As media played and replayed the infamous "Hello, Garci" tape, millions of Filipinos heard their president's inimitable voice pressing Virgilio "Garci" Garcillano, election commissioner and veteran vote fixer, to deliver a convincing margin, asking, "So I will still lead by one million overall?" During the next forty-eight hours the crisis deepened as Samuel Ong, the NBI's former deputy director, released three hours of tapes, recorded by military intelligence, that further implicated the palace in election rigging. Evidently concerned about the loyalty of her aides, the president had authorized military wiretaps of palace communications, producing an electronic sweep that had captured her own conversations and created the leaked tapes. In this same two-day period, the Senate's ongoing jueteng investigation produced banner headlines as a syndicate insider, Sandra Cam, testified about making million-peso jueteng payoffs to the president's husband, son, and brother-in-law.[39]

On June 27, in a desperate effort to defuse the scandal, the president made that unprecedented act of contrition on national television, admitting she had spoken with the elections commissioner and announcing two days later that she was sending her husband into exile to allow an unhindered inquiry into his reputed corruption.[40] In effect, President Arroyo had confessed to the lesser crime within the country's political culture, vote rigging, but denied any involvement in jueteng corruption, perhaps sensing that any admission of a direct tie to this illegal lottery could prove politically fatal.

As her cabinet resigned en masse and the opposition announced impeachment proceedings, Arroyo's government teetered at the brink of collapse. But then ex-president Fidel V. Ramos and House Speaker Jose de Venecia, Jr. played savior, announcing their support and slowing the momentum toward impeachment.[41] Frustrated, opposition leaders continued to hammer at Arroyo's mandate by linking her to both illegal fund-raising and electoral fraud. With heavy media coverage, the ongoing Senate hearings into jueteng featured insiders who testified about a corrupt nexus of police and politics that led directly to the first family. At public sessions in August 2005, a political operative, Michaelangelo Zulce, testified that he had witnessed the wife of Luzon's jueteng boss, Lilia Pineda, distributing envelopes containing thirty thousand pesos each to twenty-seven Mindanao election officials at Arroyo's home during the 2004 campaign.[42] As the president's approval ratings plummeted, 53 percent of those polled in Metro Manila said the president should resign while 80 percent said she should be impeached.[43]

All this criticism culminated on February 24, 2006, when the opposition tried to force the president from office in an abortive reprise of people power. At the outset, Gen. Danilo Lim maneuvered to mobilize military forces for a coup while a broad coalition of demonstrators massed on the EDSA highway, calling for Arroyo to step down. Instead the president hit back hard and fast. After issuing Proclamation 1017 under the Constitution's broad executive authority, she assumed emergency powers to block what she called a "concerted and systematic conspiracy" of the left and right. Simultaneously, her security forces swept the masses from EDSA and rounded up the leftist leaders believed to be responsible.[44] The next day the palace ordered the police, under Proclamation 1017, to occupy the offices of the *Daily Tribune,* a newspaper known for its critical coverage, and told other media organizations that this action should serve as a warning that reckless reporting might aid the rebels.[45]

Through this redoubled repression President Arroyo crushed every attempt to force her from power by military coup or people power. Over the next two years, the opposition defaulted to scandal as its primary weapon, crowding Manila's front pages with an endless succession of seamy allegations about Arroyo. In August 2007 "the ZTE scandal" over reported kickbacks from a Chinese firm, Zhong Xing Telecommunications Equipment, for construction of the national broadband network became, through televised Senate investigations, a political telenovella that aroused public fascination. During a privilege speech on September 11, Senator Lacson somehow produced, magician-like, the carefully concealed contract to charge that massive bribes had won this Chinese corporation the $329 million project—once again using sensitive information to damage President Arroyo. By the time its yearlong run on Manila's front pages was over, this scandal had produced the dramatic kidnapping of a key witness, the resignation of Arroyo's corrupt election commissioner, and the defeat of her ally, House Speaker Jose de Venecia, after an unprecedented five terms.[46]

By November 2008, however, the Arroyo administration had rebounded, reviving the Dacer murder case to derail the candidacy of its nemesis Ping Lacson in the upcoming 2010 presidential elections. From a U.S. prison facility at Fort Lauderdale in February 2009, the fugitive PNP officer Cezar Mancao swore that he witnessed his former director Ping Lacson ordering the assassination of publicist Bubby Dacer back in 2000. While Manila moved to extradite Mancao and another fugitive PNP officer, Glenn Dumlao, as witnesses against Lacson, the senator himself dismissed the allegations, claiming the government had offered corrupting inducements. With affidavits from two eyewitnesses who could implicate him directly in the Dacer killing, Senator Lacson was again on the defensive in his decade-long vendetta with the Arroyos.[47]

President Arroyo thus survived this endless political crisis punctuated by impeachment, scandal, and coup attempts. Nonetheless, ongoing protest demonstrations threatened to erupt into a mass mobilization at any moment, a possible People Power IV that could force her from the palace. In the midst of this tense political standoff, the president used the renewed U.S. security alliance to partisan advantage, courting allies within the military and unleashing a clandestine assassination campaign against her left-wing opponents.

War on Terror

Throughout these years of political instability, Washington's global war on terrorism provided Arroyo's administration with an infusion of military aid, revitalizing the state's security apparatus and providing her with diplomatic support in the face of both international criticism and domestic opposition. After the terrorist attacks of September 2001, Arroyo was, as noted above, the first Asian leader to promise President Bush unqualified support. Three months later a state visit to Washington, timed for the fiftieth anniversary of the U.S.-Philippines Mutual Defense Treaty, revived an alliance that had been dead for a decade. After the closure of U.S. military bases in 1992, the Philippines had found its defenses unequal to either restraining China in the South China Sea or repressing the long-running communist and Islamic insurgencies at home. Now President Bush offered Arroyo generous military assistance to fight Islamic terrorists "in any way she suggests." Emerging from this round of Washington meetings on military aid, a smiling Arroyo told reporters that she was at "$4 Billion and counting." At the visit's close, a joint Bush-Arroyo statement announced that the two nations would "maintain a robust defense partnership into the 21st century."[48]

In the next few months, Washington transformed this rhetoric into military reality by making the Philippines its "second front" in the war on terrorism. In the five years following the closure of American bases, U.S. military aid had averaged only $1.6 million per annum, putting Manila at the bottom of Washington's gift list. Now military aid increased to $19 million, a down payment on a projected $4.6 billion that would rearm the Philippine military with mortars, sniper rifles, night-vision goggles, thirty UH-1H helicopters, and a Cyclone-class patrol craft. While the full package would not be delivered before Bush left office, development assistance for Muslim Mindanao still topped $260 million for 2002–6 and actual military aid reached $520 million over the next seven years (2002–9).[49]

Starting in January 2002, the U.S. Defense Department sent 1,200 troops to the southern Philippines, including 190 special operations forces who would train the Philippine military in counterterrorism techniques and six hundred conventional troops to stiffen its fight against the Abu Sayyaf terrorist group on Basilan Island. By the time the initial deployment ended in July, a combined operation by the CIA, U.S. Navy SEALs, and Philippine Marines had recovered a kidnapped American missionary and, after months of careful targeting, killed the top Abu Sayyaf leader. With a CIA aircraft circling overhead for real-time video surveillance in the dark, Philippine Marines carried out a complex high seas ambush in June 2002, killing the leader Aldam Tilao (a.k.a. "Abu Sabaya") in a burst of bullets that cut his body in half. Significantly, this was perhaps the first successful assassination of a major target in the war on terror, foreshadowing the tactics the agency would use five years later with such lethal effect in Iraq. But these successes had still failed to eliminate the terrorist group, requiring continued operations that would keep some three hundred to five hundred special operation forces in Mindanao for the next seven years. In November 2002 the two nations, building on a Visiting Forces Agreement signed a few years before, concluded a Mutual Logistics Support Agreement that allowed the U.S. military to pre-position operational equipment in the Philippines.[50]

Over the next two years, Washington provided Arroyo the substance of military aid and the symbolism of a close alliance, ensuring her political survival until she could win a popular mandate in the 2004 presidential election. But these close ties soon aroused strong criticism in both countries. In Manila leftist demonstrators charged that the cycling of U.S. combat forces through the southern Philippines was an infringement of the nation's sovereignty. In February 2003, as the Pentagon readied seventeen hundred combat troops to pursue Abu Sayyaf through the jungles of Jolo Island, the *Washington Post* criticized this "potentially treacherous campaign" in a lead editorial, warning, "U.S. troops have already fought Muslim guerrillas on this ground, a century ago. The result was a bloody quagmire and damaging accusations of brutality." Amid complaints that foreign combat operations on Philippine soil would violate the country's Constitution, Manila downgraded the mission to a modest training exercise.[51] Undeterred, the two leaders exchanged lavish state visits in 2003. During Arroyo's trip to Washington in May, she was showered with over $100 million worth of military equipment. At Manila in October, Bush upped the ante to half a billion dollars in total aid and a commitment to upgrade the Armed Forces of the Philippines.[52]

In the first two years of this renewed alliance, the operations on Basilan Island were troubled by local and international problems. Instead of joining an ongoing Filipino campaign, the U.S. forces arrived to find a long history of government neglect and a "lack of military initiative" that made the island ideal for "the genesis of new terrorist and criminal organizations." Within months Abu Sayyaf militants would retaliate against these combined operations through terror bombings and a bloody ambush of AFP forces on nearby Jolo Island that ended with the beheading of captured soldiers.[53] After a decade of ruptured military relations and rising nationalist sensibilities, the U.S. Special Forces troops were restricted to operations at the battalion and company levels with their Filipino counterparts, limiting their utility. Moreover, intelligence gathered by U.S. P-3 Orion aircraft and Predator drones was not shared fully with forces on the ground, rendering much of it useless. Since the government was negotiating with a nearby Muslim rebel movement, the Moro Islamic Liberation Front (MILF), the Philippine-American forces were denied access to its areas of influence, creating de facto sanctuaries for Abu Sayyaf. As these and other problems were slowly resolved, the combined operations forced the terrorist group off Basilan by 2004 "because of combat losses and loss of bases and popular support." But with aid from both the

MILF and Jemmah Islamiyah (JI), Abu Sayyaf soon found new base areas on Jolo and Tawi Tawi islands farther west along the Sulu Archipelago.[54]

At first the U.S. aid seemed to have little discernible impact on the Philippine armed forces. An abortive coup in July 2003 by three hundred troops protesting corruption among the top generals indicated a deep "institutional rot" inside the military that could not be corrected by merely increasing foreign aid. Indeed, in November the press leaked a U.S. Pacific Command study finding a disproportionate presence within the Philippine military of self-styled "special ops" units with a troubling inclination toward "mystique, unconventionality, and loose discipline." The detonation of a terrorist bomb aboard a Super Ferry crossing Manila Bay in early 2004, sinking the ship and killing over a hundred passengers, indicated that the initial successes against Abu Sayyaf were far from complete.[55]

Over time, the criticism ebbed and the Philippine operation settled into a steady flow of military aid and the permanent presence of U.S. advisers throughout the country's Muslim region in western Mindanao and the nearby Sulu Archipelago.[56] Based at Camp Navarro in Zamboanga City, the logistical hub of the Muslim south, the Joint Special Operations Task-Force-Philippines (JSOTF-P) fielded between 160 and 450 U.S. special operations forces that ranged across the whole of the southern Philippines to engage in training, intelligence gathering, logistics support, psychological operations, drone surveillance, and combat advising. Starting in 2002, moreover, the U.S. military maintained a larger, "semicontinuous" military presence in the country by staging some twenty-four joint exercises annually involving up to six thousand American troops. The aid program also provided advanced training to 846 Filipino officers, built a deepwater port and modern airport in southern Mindanao, and dotted this vast, impoverished island with development projects.[57]

After five years of steady investment, U.S. military aid finally began to show results in the battle against Abu Sayyaf. In a bloody firefight in September 2006, Philippine marines patrolling Jolo Island fatally wounded the group's charismatic leader, Khadaffy Janjalani. Just four months later Philippine special forces, with intelligence from U.S. special forces, killed his presumed successor, Abu Solaiman, who was wanted for kidnapping three Americans, one of whom he had capriciously beheaded. Instead of leaving night and the jungle to the insurgents, Filipino elite units were now operating round the clock in operations that a senior U.S. adviser called "much more disciplined, much more precise." Throughout 2007 the Philippine military eliminated 144 Abu Sayyaf fighters in fifty-three bloody encounters, reducing the group's membership by 16 percent to just 379 survivors. Yet this war was far from won. Abu Sayyaf was soon back on Basilan Island, where it killed fourteen Philippine marines in June and inflicted twenty-nine casualties during an ambush of government forces in December.[58]

Gradually, it became apparent that these short-term tactical operations reflected a broad strategic shift in U.S. defense policy from fixed bases to a diffuse global response. During the forty years of the cold war, Washington had ringed the Sino-Soviet bloc with massive military bastions from Ramstein, Germany, to Subic Bay, Philippines, each bristling with strategic armadas of air and sea power for retaliatory nuclear strikes across the iron curtain. To cover the whole globe in the post-cold-war world, the Pentagon began shifting to a more agile stance with just a few main operating bases linked to a dispersed network of floating "lily pads," small forward operating sites with skeletal U.S. staff and pre-positioned heavy weapons that could support sudden strikes against rogue actors anywhere on five continents. As Defense Secretary Donald Rumsfeld explained in 2005, the Pentagon would "improve its global force posture to increase strategic responsiveness while decreasing its overseas footprint." The Visiting Forces Agreement with the Philippines was just one of ninety similar agreements worldwide. The Mutual Logistics Support treaty was one of seventy-six concluded with allied nations. The twenty-four combined exercises with the AFP were but a fraction of the 1,700 that the U.S. Pacific Command conducted annually. By 2004 Washington had assigned 300,000 service personnel to 130 countries where they staffed 725 military bases, more than double the 300 foreign installations in 1954 at the peak of the cold war. Yet even after the closure of Subic Bay and Clark Field in 1992, the Philippines remained a uniquely important strategic asset. Since U.S. defense planning in the Asia-Pacific area was focused ultimately on a calibrated "coercive engagement" or "hedged" containment of China's growing military, these islands retained their strategic significance. They remained the sole location with the requisite mix of geography and goodwill to allow semipermanent American bases for ready force projection against countries in Southeast Asia and the South China Sea.[59]

When the Bush era ended in late 2008, American conservatives once again turned to the Philippines for strategic models to pursue their war on terror. In the aftermath of the September 2001 attacks, the Republican right had misconstrued a successful Philippine police operation against an al-Qaeda bomb plot as justification for the CIA's use of torture in its global counterterror operations. A conservative commentator, Max Boot, toured the southern Philippines to report in the January 2009 issue of the right-wing *Weekly Standard* that this "tiny success story in Southeast Asia . . . may offer a more apt template than either Iraq or Afghanistan for fighting extremists in many corners of the world." Through a mix of civic and military operations, he said, this "counterinsurgency campaign has been enjoying impressive success," with extremist forces decimated, terror bombings curtailed, and the Philippine military on a clear path to victory. All this had been achieved, Boot claimed, with a very modest expenditure of U.S. blood and treasure. The sum of such success created what Gen. Salvatore Cambria, chief of U.S. Special Operations for the Pacific, called a promising "model" for future U.S. counterterror operations. Indeed, echoing this "population centric" approach, the new commander for Afghanistan, Gen. Stanley A. McChrystal, told the Senate in June 2009 that a "military-centric strategy will not succeed." Instead he advocated "a holistic counterinsurgency campaign" with an "integrated civil-military plan" that would, above all, "protect the population and set conditions for governance and economic advancement." Within a month, his command sent the Marines into Helmand Province to wrest villages from Taliban control, with the aim of "improving their lives" and without the destructive U.S. aerial bombardment that had long alienated Afghanis.[60]

Extrajudicial Killings

The gains against Islamic terrorists in the southern Philippines came at a disconcerting cost that few U.S. policy makers, liberal or conservative, seemed inclined to contemplate. With Washington providing diplomatic support and the material means for close ties to her own military, President Arroyo countered dissent with an extreme form of executive repression: rigid information controls, constraints on civil liberties, aggressive policing, and covert assassinations. To restrain the large, left-wing demonstrations that were challenging her authority, in September 2005 she issued orders for a Calibrated Preemptive Response, a policy of "no permit, no rally," prompting her justice secretary to prohibit marches without proper permits and the National Police to promise strict enforcement. In effect, this policy put the president on a collision course with the country's activist nongovernmental organizations (NGOs), arguably the most elaborate citizens' network anywhere in the developing world.[61] Her administration also began to back away from negotiations with the armed left that had produced a Comprehensive Agreement on Respect for Human Rights in 1998 and a commitment to start joint monitoring of the accord by the government and communist guerrillas in 2004. With ever-increasing military aid from Washington, the Arroyo administration was instead amassing ample funds, firepower, and diplomatic support for a violent resolution of this long-running conflict.[62]

Operating in secrecy, President Arroyo's security services escalated their terror campaign against members of leftist parties active in the opposition movement, focusing on the heartland of rural activism, Central Luzon. In September 2005 the administration assigned Gen. Jovito Palparan Jr. to command the region's infantry division even though he had gained notoriety after two activists were murdered on Mindoro Island while investigating extrajudicial killings by his old brigade. Within weeks of his transfer, a dozen members of the leftist Bayan Muna party were gunned down by masked assassins. A liquidation campaign raged across Central Luzon for a full year, hunting down environmentalists, community organizers, journalists, pastors, and land reform advocates. According to the leftist human rights group Karapatan, there were 136 cases of serious human rights violations in this region during the general's eleven-month tenure. Adding to the climate of fear, Palparan made flamboyant statements announcing that "the killing of activists are [*sic*] necessary."[63]

Throughout 2006 this lethal strategy was matched by legal moves intended to stiffen counterinsurgency operations. In January the president formed the Interagency Legal Action Group to coordinate an "end-game strategy" against the armed left, targeting so-called communist front organizations engaged in development, media, and religious work. Six months later Arroyo announced an "all-out war" against the communists and allocated a billion pesos ($20 million) to fund joint AFP-PNP operations against key NPA zones for the next two years. In a clear signal to the military, Arroyo used this announcement to brand the legal "opposition left" as communist allies and blast them for using the human rights issue to "demonize our administration" before the international community. "It's a booster to our efforts," General Palparan said of the president's call for victory. "We're going all-out now." In a series of executive decrees, Arroyo also declared a nationwide "state of emergency" to "prevent and suppress all forms of lawless violence."[64] In December she approved Operation Bantay Laya II, which her administration described as a "three-year master plan for the defeat of the New People's Army, the destruction of the Abu Sayyaf and JI [Jemmah Islamiyah], and the containment of the secessionist Moro Islamic Liberation Front."[65] Under the umbrella of an operation that bundled communist and terrorist targets, the military mobilized some fifty vigilante groups nationwide with the aim of cleansing half the NPA guerrilla zones during 2007.[66] Over time this fusion of vigilante violence and military murder started to resemble the low-intensity conflict doctrine that U.S. military advisers had introduced to counter communist guerrillas in the late 1980s.

As the terror spread across Central Luzon, a chorus of criticism arose from the press and public in Manila, prompting official inquiries. In May 2006 the PNP reported that, among the 122 known killings of leftist activists since 2001, only eighteen court cases had been filed, leaving 85 percent "under investigation."[67] According to an official inquiry headed by Supreme Court Justice Jose A. Melo, the victims were usually "gunned down by two or more masked or hooded assailants, oftentimes riding motorcycles." Melo concluded that "there is certainly evidence pointing the finger of suspicion at some elements . . . in the armed forces, in particular General Palparan, as responsible for an undetermined number of killings."[68] Apparently perpetrated by both police and military, the killings rivaled the worst excesses of the Marcos regime, with estimates for the five years of Arroyo's presidency ranging from the military's figure of 115 deaths to a count of 724 by the human rights group Karapatan.[69] Although President Arroyo condemned these assassinations in her July 2006 state of the nation address, she also hailed General Palparan's efforts to free Central Luzon from the "long night of terror." In a powerfully symbolic act, she also appointed him to her national security council.[70]

Several international investigations confirmed Justice Melo's grim findings. In August 2006 Amnesty International reported that in the five years since Arroyo assumed office there had been 244 political killings, which "constitute a pattern of politically targeted extrajudicial executions . . . within the . . . continuing counter-insurgency campaign." It also found that her government had "an implicit policy of toleration of such political killings."[71] In February 2007, the United Nations (UN) special rapporteur for human rights, Prof. Philip Alston, reported that the government's decision to "eliminate organizations" that supported the NPA guerrillas had "spilled over into decisions to extrajudicially execute those who cannot be reached by [the] legal process."[72] As evidence for these claims, Alston cited a recent AFP "order of battle" analysis that listed "hundreds of groups and individuals who have been classified, on the basis of intelligence, as members of organizations which the military deems 'illegitimate.'"[73] In his final report, the UN representative added that these killings had "eliminated civil society leaders, including human rights defenders, trade unionists and land reform advocates, intimidated a vast number of civil society actors, and narrowed the country's political discourse." At the broadest level Arroyo's show of force had negated President Ramos's earlier attempt at conflict resolution, akin to the Belfast peace process, which had encouraged armed groups "to enter mainstream politics and to see that path as their best option."[74] In June 2007 Human Rights Watch, based in New York, sent its own investigators to the Philippines. After a careful review, they concluded that the killings were "intended to eliminate suspected supporters of the NPA . . . and to intimidate those who work for progressive causes." Although the victims were "individually targeted for killing," the armed forces had "failed to hold any of its members accountable for these unlawful killings, including superior officers who ordered, encouraged, or permitted them."[75]

Amid criticism that might have otherwise delegitmated her administration, Arroyo's close alliance with President Bush provided needed political cover. With an otherwise inexplicable arrogance, the Arroyo administration derided the damning UN report. Justice Secretary Raul Gonzalez mocked the special rapporteur as "a muchacho" (houseboy) who had been "brainwashed" by leftists. Defense Secretary Hermogenes Ebdane dismissed him as "blind, mute, and deaf." Within months Washington's assessment would soften the blow from the UN criticism. "During the year," the U.S. State Department reported in March 2007, "there were a number of arbitrary, unlawful, and extrajudicial killings apparently by elements of the security services and of political killings, including killings of journalists, by a variety of actors." Not only did the last phrase blur the Arroyo administration's responsibility for the assassinations, but Washington then added an exculpatory statement, without convincing evidence, that the killings had persisted "despite intensified government efforts during the year to investigate and prosecute these cases."[76] A year later, while the assassinations continued, the State Department commended Manila for taking "steps to invigorate the investigation and prosecution of cases of . . . extrajudicial killings," producing "a significant decrease in the number of killings." When the Philippines defended its record before the UN Human Rights Council in Geneva that same month, claiming that it was conducting aggressive investigations of the killings, Human Rights Watch called the proceedings "window dressing," adding that "with inconclusive investigations, implausible suspects, and no convictions, impunity prevails." Unchecked by this international pressure, the killings continued, drawing media attention again in early 2009 when a *New York Times* stringer found his name on a military intelligence "hit list" in Mindanao and an American health worker was abducted by soldiers in Central Luzon.[77]

All the exculpatory State Department statements ignored the evidence, cited in these four independent investigations, that the Arroyo administration was responsible for the assassinations, thus providing de facto diplomatic cover for its campaign of extrajudicial killings. Although U.S. military operations were limited to Mindanao, American aid had expanded the AFP's overall operational capacity and strengthened its support for Arroyo, thereby forging a well-primed weapon for the palace. So armed, Arroyo had little incentive to pursue a negotiated settlement to the country's deep-seated social conflicts. With Manila's recourse to extreme force paralleling the Washington's covert assassination campaign in Iraq, the Bush administration was evidently not inclined to fault its Southeast Asian ally on this sensitive point. Possibly adding to this reticence, all the heavily publicized successes by combined operations in Mindanao had involved ambush assassinations of top Abu Sayyaf leaders. Indeed, the June 2002 killing of "Abu Sabaya"—through a seamless integration of CIA aerial drones with U.S. and local special operations forces—may well have forged a template for the covert assassination campaign unleashed five years later in Iraq and Afghanistan. Instead of criticism or condemnation, the Bush administration thus adopted an ambiguous stance that effectively condoned Arroyo's policy of state terror.

In 2009, as Washington expanded its war on terror in Afghanistan, conservatives and liberals alike seemed oblivious to the way allies from the Horn of Africa to the islands of Southeast Asia had used the U.S. imprimatur to mask corruption, repression, and double-dealing for the previous seven years. Like other seemingly loyal leaders such as Hamid Karzai in Afghanistan, Nuri Kamal al-Maliki in Iraq, and Gen. Pervez Musharraf in Pakistan, President Arroyo proved deft at diverting Washington's global design to local advantage in ways that directly contradict or even subvert its democratic aims. Karzai presided over the world's most corrupt government, abandoning the Afghan countryside to brutal warlords, Taliban terrorists, and opium fields that have, since 2004, produced about 90 percent of the world's illicit heroin. Maliki used police death squads and political corruption to build a nascent Iraqi autocracy, employing, said the *New York Times*, "many of the same tools of power as the predecessor he hated so much, Saddam Hussein." Musharraf placated Muslim militants by allowing

Pakistan's tribal territories to become a refuge for al-Qaeda terrorists and Taliban guerrillas fighting coalition forces in Afghanistan. Arroyo unleashed military death squads for a lethal assault on the legal Philippine left. Added up, it was a dismal record for Washington's four closest allies in the global war on terror.[78]

More broadly, this endless war on a spectral, stateless enemy has done serious damage to the international rule of law. After three years of hearings with evidence from forty nations, including the Philippines, the International Commission of Jurists reported in February 2009 that sub rosa intelligence warfare against terrorists was threatening human rights on a global scale. "We have been shocked by the extent of the damage done over the past seven years by excessive or abusive counter-terrorism measures in a wide range of countries around the world," said the chair of the inquiry, the former chief justice of South Africa, Arthur Chaskalson. "The result is a serious threat to the integrity of the international human rights legal framework." In a passage that resonates with events in the Philippines, the report states that "intelligence agencies around the world have acquired new resources and new powers allowing for increased surveillance, . . . arrest, detention, and interrogation." The result has been a dangerous "accretion of power by the executive" with little legislative or judicial scrutiny. In equally resonant words, these eminent jurists also noted how "regimes with deplorable human rights records have referred to counter-terror practices of countries like the U.S. to justify their own abusive policies." Even though these jurists documented many serious transgressions—"including torture, enforced disappearances, secret and arbitrary detentions, and unfair trials"—few nations could match the Philippine fusion of legal constraints and extrajudicial killings by state security forces.[79] Once again this close American ally has provided a poignant example of the worldwide impact of Washington's security policies.

Conclusion

As her six-year term lurched toward its end in 2010, the Arroyo administration seemed locked in political paralysis between media scandal and police surveillance. Faced with the choice between repression and reform amid a crisis of legitimacy, President Arroyo, like her predecessors Marcos and Aquino, relied on the executive's expansive police powers to suppress dissent and engage in extrajudicial killings. In effect, this stance has spurned the sort of inclusive reforms used effectively by Governor-General Henry Stimson, the archetypal Washington wise man, during the 1920s or by President Ramon Magsaysay, the celebrated Filipino populist, in the 1950s.

Resonances between President Arroyo's reaction to public criticism in 2005 and Governor-General Taft's a century earlier indicate strong underlying continuities in the character of the Philippine state. In designing a modern bureaucratic apparatus in 1901–2, Taft built an information regime that imposed legal limits on free discourse. He also created a secret police force for extralegal action against his state's enemies using surveillance, penetration, and, when needed, assassination. As an appointed colonial governor, Taft exercised police power without restraint and embedded these controls deep within a nascent Philippine executive branch. Facing harsh criticism a century later, President Arroyo activated the same special powers to constrain free speech by officials, press, and public while unleashing covert operations against her left-wing critics. As an elected president instead of a foreign governor, however, Arroyo had to impose these restrictions temporarily and deploy her extrajudicial policing covertly.

Yet Arroyo, like Marcos, not only exploited these executive powers; she elaborated them beyond anything Taft might have imagined. While Taft and his colonial successors prosecuted a few editors and assassinated some armed rebels, Arroyo sent armed police to occupy newspaper offices and presided over a paramilitary force that gunned down seven hundred prominent political activists in brazen daylight assassinations. That this state had such an ingrained inclination to abuse executive policing powers not once but four times in the same half century under presidents Roxas, Marcos, Aquino, and Arroyo, raises serious questions about the quality of the executive's broad policing powers in the country's two democratic constitutions of 1935 and 1987. This coercive capacity was fashioned under colonial rule, legitimated by the country's later constitutions, and reinforced by popular demands for public order in the face of rising criminality. But in the half century since independence in 1946, the Philippine executive's reliance on coercion rather than negotiation has also been encouraged by periodic infusions of U.S. aid and advisers, contributing ever more efficient means of armed suppression, from the CIA's counterinsurgency operations in the 1950s through U.S. counterterrorism training since 2002.

For the past half century, Washington has found it far easier to revitalize Philippine security forces than to reform the country's underlying social inequality. By comparison with coalition operations in Afghanistan and Iraq, the U.S. program in Muslim Mindanao since 2002 on the surface seems a judicious balance of civic action and military aid. But it has contributed, in the context of this complex postcolonial relationship, to a form of nationwide political repression that allows a close American ally like Arroyo to hold power in defiance of democratic pressures and encourages the Filipino oligarchy to postpone needed social reforms. In drafting its Memorandum 84/2 in late 1950, the U.S. National Security Council predicted, with uncanny accuracy, that crushing the communist insurgency would be easily done but convincing the Filipino oligarchy to embrace social reform could prove difficult. With each U.S. intervention over the next sixty years, this contradiction has assumed a Sisyphean character, as one insurgency after another has been defeated. But the underlying social inequality has deepened, sparking another insurgency and yet another U.S. intervention.

17

Crucibles of Counterinsurgency

For over a century the United States and the Philippines have collided, on their separate historical trajectories, in ways that have proven transformative for both nations. Through a prolonged pacification after 1898, the U.S. Army plunged into a crucible of counterinsurgency, forging a security apparatus that helped form the Philippine polity and transform the American state. After swiftly occupying Manila, the army found itself mired in a difficult, decade-long pacification campaign. Armed with cutting-edge technology from its antecedent information revolution, America's colonial regime created the most modern police and intelligence units found anywhere under the U.S. flag. This imperial panopticon slowly suffocated the Filipino revolutionary movement with a combination of firepower, surveillance, and incriminating information.

But the impact of colonial pacification was not contained at this remote periphery of American power. Migrating homeward through both personnel and policies, these innovations in colonial policing helped form a new federal security system during World War I. Once established under the pressures of wartime mobilization, a distinctively American system of public and private surveillance persisted in various forms for the next fifty years as an omnipresent, sub rosa matrix that honeycombed U.S. society with active informers, secretive civilian organizations, and government counterintelligence agencies. In each succeeding global crisis, this covert nexus expanded its domestic operations, producing new contraventions of civil liberties from the harassment of labor activists and ethnic communities during World War I through the secret blacklisting of suspected communists during the cold war. Just as Spain had developed the world's most advanced sixteenth-century state through its conquest of the Americas, so the United States realized the coercive potential of its new information technologies from its colonization of the Philippines. Empire, any empire, makes the state more self-consciously scientific in the application of its power.

Although born of empire, these processes of mutual transformation continued well after U.S. colonial rule came to a close in 1946 and America ascended to world power. For the next half-century, Washington would intervene in the Philippines almost every decade, using the country as an ad hoc laboratory for counterinsurgency. During the cold war, as Philippine security forces suffered an inexorable postcolonial decline, Washington sent periodic infusions of aid and advisers to retrain members of the local police and military for a shared mission against communism, thereby rearming Manila for repression. Although this alliance with the Philippines attenuated during the 1990s, the relationship resumed with stunning vigor in the aftermath of the September 2001 terrorist attacks. As millions of dollars in U.S. military aid flowed to the Philippines, Manila was emboldened to abandon ongoing negotiations and resolve long-running communist and Islamic insurgencies by the raw power of military pacification and covert assassination. In trying to create a democracy in the Philippines, the United States has thus unleashed profoundly undemocratic forces evident today. More broadly, this campaign against radical Islam has served as another crucible of counterinsurgency, forging security innovations that are still, at this writing, heading home to circumscribe civil liberties inside the United States.

Throughout this century of shared history, the cross-fertilization of security practices between these two nations has been close and constant. Empire has been a reciprocal process, shaping state formation in Manila and Washington while moving both nations into a mutually implicated, postcolonial world. Viewed through the prism of the Philippines, America's rise to global power has fostered countervailing forces that threaten progress toward democracy in both nations: powerful state security, pervasive surveillance, and an empowered executive inclined to use both.

Impact on America

At multiple levels the experience of empire circa 1898 has left a lasting imprint on the American state. As the U.S. Army plunged into the conquest of the Philippines, a group of northern intellectuals known as the anti-imperialists became deeply concerned about the costs of empire. Carl Shurz, a former U.S. senator and famed social reformer, warned that American democracy could not "play the king over subject populations without creating in itself ways of thinking and habits of action most dangerous to its own vitality." Similarly, the eminent Yale sociologist William Graham Sumner stated that "the inevitable effect of imperialism on democracy" was to "lessen liberty and require discipline. It will . . . necessitate stronger and more elaborate governmental machinery"—particularly "militarism," which, he said, is a "system" that will slowly change America's economic priorities and constitutional protections. In an imagined retrospective about the ultimate consequences of these trends, Mark Twain wrote that "lust for conquest" had destroyed "the Great Republic," since "trampling upon the helpless abroad had taught her, by a natural process, to endure with apathy the like at home." But the impact of empire was less direct and much longer in gestation than these critics could have imagined. The costs for American democracy did not become evident until the anti-imperialist movement itself had joined America's long line of lost causes. Instead of ex-colonial officers returning home with "their new-found taste for ruling with whip and gun" as Shurz had feared, the army itself became a vehicle for the long-term institutional change that Sumner had predicted, carrying myriad lessons from conquests past into the political present and beyond.[1]

Indeed, there was a certain synergy between the U.S. military and the Philippine Islands, with army conquering colony and colonization changing army. In the half century between the Civil War and World War I, the pacification of the Philippines after 1898 was the U.S. Army's largest campaign, lasting nearly a decade and combining both conventional and counterguerrilla warfare. With its resources strained to the limit, the military was forced to adopt novel missions, expanding its institutional capacity, discarding a nineteenth-century paradigm of land warfare, and training a new generation of American officers in the craft of intelligence.

As these colonial lessons came home during World War I, they provided both personnel and precedents for the formation of U.S. military intelligence. After a decade without any intelligence service, the army quickly developed an elaborate domestic counterintelligence capacity with pervasive surveillance that persisted fitfully for the next half century. Miming an imperial mindset that saw humanity as a hierarchy of higher and "lesser breeds," this domestic espionage targeted America's immigrant communities as an alien presence requiring close supervision to avert subversion. In the frenzy of wartime mobilization, this internal security mission developed as a unique alliance between federal agencies and civilian patriotic organizations, giving this apparatus both the continuity of a state bureaucracy and the force of a social movement. From the red scare of the early 1920s through the anticommunist purges of the 1950s, the FBI, army, and affiliated civilian watchdog groups maintained a vigorous, sometimes zealous pursuit of domestic subversives. After the anticommunist movement faded in the mid-1950s, the FBI then institutionalized these extreme, extralegal methods under its Counterintelligence Program (COINTELPRO), thus showing the suppleness of this state-civilian security nexus. From 1956 to 1971 this FBI program skirted the law by using undercover operatives, disinformation, break-ins, and warrantless wiretaps, first against the Communist Party in the 1950s and later against both the civil rights and antiwar movements in the 1960s.

From its peak of power in the mid-1950s, the internal security network lost influence steadily over the next twenty years through its rhetorical excesses and congressional exposés of its extralegal operations. The Senate's censure of Joseph

McCarthy and the public reaction against the endless accusations further eroded the anticommunist movement's mass support. During the ferment of the 1960s, moreover, the FBI's attack on the civil rights movement was quickly neutralized by the stature of black leaders such as Martin Luther King Jr. and the movement's string of legal and legislative victories. In this same turbulent decade, as the large, restive "baby boom" generation came of age untainted by socialist stigma, the internal security apparatus lost its intimidating aura. When the House Un-American Activities Committee subpoenaed Berkeley campus radicals for interrogation before Congress, they mocked the proceedings, dispelling the climate of fear. During the mid-1970s the Senate's revelations about illegal CIA and FBI penetration of civil society discredited the entire internal security effort, forcing the bureau to curtail COINTELPRO, the agency to open its secret dossiers, and army intelligence to cleanse its domestic files. In 1973, when the Nixon White House compiled its famed "enemies list"—including such eminent Americans as Harvard president Derek Bok, football quarterback Joe Namath, Broadway leading lady Carol Channing, and Hollywood star Steve McQueen—the country recoiled in a collective shudder at this eerie evocation of the blacklisting synonymous with the president's early political career as an anticommunist inquisitor.[2]

Thirty years later as Washington waged its war on terror, lessons learned at the edge of American power once again percolated homeward through the capillaries of empire to circumscribe the country's civil liberties. In the aftermath of the September 2001 attacks, the White House made repeated, almost reflexive attempts to revive this distinctive state-civil alliance for antisubversive surveillance. "If people see anything suspicious, utility workers, you ought to report it," said President George W. Bush in his April 2002 call for nationwide citizen vigilance.[3] Within weeks his Justice Department launched Operation TIPS (Terrorism Information and Prevention System), announcing on its Web site in May 2002 that a "pilot program" would commence in August with "millions of American truckers, letter carriers, train conductors, ship captains, utility employees and others" spying on their fellow citizens, much as the American Protective League had done during World War I. As envisioned inside the Justice Department, these watchers would monitor both workplace and neighborhood, submitting reports of possible terrorist activity that would circulate rapidly on FBI, CIA, and military computers, a latter-day reprise of the civilian auxiliaries that had spied on fellow citizens for a half century after World War I. Yet this time such efforts aroused surprisingly strong resistance. Even before this test run, there was vocal opposition from congressmen, civil libertarians, and the press, the latter often citing past excesses such as the American Protective League's wartime surveillance and the "McCarthyite witch hunts of the cold war." These protests forced the Justice Department to scale the program back before it quietly died along with the president's plan for a massive, nationwide expansion of Neighborhood Watch.[4]

In a digital iteration of the same effort, Admiral John Poindexter, working inside the Pentagon, began developing a Total Information Awareness program to prevent terrorism by compiling a "detailed electronic dossier on millions of Americans." Again the nation recoiled, Congress banned the program, and the admiral was forced to resign.[5] Clearly, public opinion had turned against the idea that Americans should spy on their neighbors.

By this time, however, the CIA, FBI, and the National Security Agency (NSA) had developed an efficient electronic capacity to monitor citizens without civilian adjuncts, rendering these retreats an ambiguous political victory for civil liberties. In January 2002 Congress erased the bright line that had long barred the CIA from domestic spying, granting the agency power to access U.S. financial records and audit electronic communications routed through the country.[6] Not satisfied with these expanded powers, sometime in 2002 President Bush ordered the NSA to commence covert monitoring of private communications, without the requisite warrants, through the nation's telephone companies and financial transactions through the international bank clearinghouse called SWIFT (Society for Worldwide Interbank Financial Telecommunication). Even though press revelations in 2005 about these activities eventually encouraged some sharp criticism, Congress capitulated by passing a new law in August 2007 that legalized this illegal executive program. A year later legislators granted the phone companies immunity from civil suits brought by aggrieved citizens. Even after Congress set wide parameters for future intercepts in 2008 legislation, the NSA engaged in systematic "overcollection" of electronic communications among American citizens. Such excess was in fact intentional, driven by a secret NSA database called Pinwale that has allowed analysts, since 2005, to routinely scan countless "millions" of domestic electronic communications.[7]

Starting in 2004, moreover, the FBI launched the Investigative Data Warehouse, a "centralized repository for counterterrorism," that swelled in two years to 659 million records—including intelligence reports, social security files, drivers' licenses, and private financial information—accessible to thirteen thousand analysts who were making a million queries monthly. By 2009, when digital rights advocates sued for a public listing of the data sucked into the FBI's top-secret system, the database had grown to over a billion documents without any protection for privacy. Shifting from defense to offense, the Obama administration announced plans in May 2009 to establish a new cybercommand, within both the Pentagon and NSA, that would effectively militarize cyberspace, attacking enemy computers and repelling hostile counterattacks on U.S. networks—with scant respect for what one general called "sovereignty in the cyberdomain." Despite the president's assurance that operations "will not—I repeat—will not include monitoring private sector networks or Internet traffic," the Pentagon's former top cyberwarrior conceded that such intrusion was almost inevitable. After a careful review of this electronic surveillance and internet data mining, the inspectors general of five federal agencies reported in July that, despite Bush's claim that these programs had "helped prevent attacks," they could not find any such "specific instances" and concluded they "generally played a limited role in the FBI's overall counterterrorism efforts."[8]

This clandestine eavesdropping was soon matched by the Bush administration's effort to build public support for its war on terror by manipulating both foreign and domestic media through overt information management and covert disinformation. While the black propaganda effort was first reported in 2004 and remained shadowy, the Pentagon office for public diplomacy opened in 2007 and operated for about two years until army field commanders complained about its "blatant propaganda" and an internal review found violations of government "guidelines for accuracy and transparency."[9]

Although the American people would not actively spy on their neighbors, many seemed willing to sacrifice personal freedom in the interest of homeland security. Amidst the pressures of war, this wavering public commitment to civil liberties gave elected officials sufficient latitude to pursue an aggressive program of electronic eavesdropping. Showing bipartisan support for such measures, in April 2007 Representative Jane Harman (Democrat, California) introduced the Violent Radicalization and Homegrown Terrorism Prevention Act. In a bid to legalize the Bush administration's warrantless intercepts, Harman proposed a powerful national commission, a standing star chamber, to "combat the threat posed by homegrown terrorists based and operating within the United States." This commission would maintain constant surveillance of the Internet, which, the bill claimed, "has aided . . . [the] homegrown terrorism process in the United States by providing access to broad and constant streams of terrorist-related propaganda to United States citizens." In the post-9/11 climate of fear, this bill passed the House with an overwhelming 404 to 6 vote before stalling, and then dying, in a Senate more mindful of civil liberties.[10]

Only weeks after a new Democratic administration took office in early 2009, Rep. Harman herself became the subject of a cautionary tale about the consequences of this expanding electronic surveillance. According to information leaked to the Washington insider journal *Congressional Quarterly,* an NSA wiretap had overheard Harman speaking with an Israeli agent in early 2005, offering to press the Justice Department for reduced charges in the case of two pro-Israel lobbyists accused of espionage. In exchange, the Israeli agent offered to help Harman win the chair of the House Intelligence Committee by threatening Democratic leader Nancy Pelosi with the loss of funding from a major campaign donor. As Harman put down the phone, she said, "This conversation doesn't exist." But an NSA transcript of her every word soon crossed the desk of CIA director Porter Goss, prompting an FBI investigation of Harman that was aborted when White House counsel Antonio Gonzales intervened. The *New York Times* was about to publish its sensational story of the NSA's warrantless wiretaps, and the Bush administration desperately needed Harman, an advocate of strict security, for damage control among her fellow Democrats. In this commingling of intrigue and irony, an influential legislator's defense of the NSA's illegal wiretapping exempted her from prosecution for a security breach discovered by another NSA wiretap—raising the question of how many incriminating conversations like hers had been similarly recorded. Eavesdropping could thus enmesh official Washington in a web of political compromise that restrained legislative efforts to check this spreading executive surveillance.[11]

Adding to these pressures on Constitutional protections, a prolonged pacification campaign overseas once again pushed the U.S. military to its limits, producing innovations in surveillance that could be applied inside America. After six years of a failing counterinsurgency effort in the Middle East, the Pentagon integrated aerial surveillance and infantry operations to produce instant field intelligence. In July 2008 the Pentagon proposed an expenditure of $1.2 billion for a fleet of fifty light aircraft loaded with advanced electronics to loiter over battlefields in Afghanistan and Iraq, "providing the ability to bring full motion video and electronic eavesdropping to the troops." By late 2008 night flights over Afghanistan from the deck of the USS *Theodore Roosevelt* were sending American ground forces real-time images of Taliban targets as small as "three warm bodies" huddled behind a wall. In Iraq, specialist infantry units were infusing similar aerial surveillance data into ongoing civil control operations. As these specialist air wings and ground forces rotate home to America, this advanced eavesdropping capacity can be deployed to counter any domestic civil disturbance. Indeed, the army's Northern Command announced in September 2008 that one of the Third Division's brigades in Iraq would be reassigned inside the United States as a consequent management response force (CMRF) to help the civilian authorities with "civil unrest and crowd control." According to Col. Roger Cloutier, his battalion's tactics include "a new modular package of . . . non-lethal weapons designed to subdue unruly or dangerous individuals"—including Taser guns, roadblock equipment, shields and batons, beanbag bullets, and improved interservice communications. At the first full CMRF mission readiness exercise that same month, the army's chief of staff Gen. George Casey flew to Fort Stewart, Georgia, to observe 250 officers from all services prepare for future coordination with the FBI, the Federal Emergency Management Agency, and local authorities in the event of a domestic terrorist threat. Within weeks the American Civil Liberties Union filed an expedited freedom of information request for details of the deployment, arguing that it is "imperative that the American people know the truth about this new and unprecedented intrusion of the military in domestic affairs."[12]

In another parallel between colonial past and imperial present, the war on terror also brought the torture issue home to America. During the Philippine pacification in 1901 and the war on terror since 2001, U.S. forces responded to a critical lack of field intelligence by resorting to the same form of torture, called "water cure" then and "water boarding" now. In both cases, press exposés became the catalyst for a public debate about the damage this foreign adventure might do to American democracy, whether by degrading the rule of law at home or by damaging its reputation abroad. There are, however, some significant differences in these two cases. Back in 1901, abuse of Filipinos by U.S. Army forces half a world away from home seemed an important moral issue that was still somehow far removed from American political life. "The American public," editorialized the *New York World* in 1902, "sips its coffee and reads of its soldiers administering the 'water cure' to rebels; of how the water . . . is forced down the throats of the patients until their bodies become distended to the point of bursting . . . The American public takes another sip of its coffee and remarks, 'how very unpleasant!'"[13] A century later revelations about torture in Iraq and Guantanamo had a much more direct domestic impact, bringing the issue home almost immediately and immersing official Washington in legal complexities from which there is no easy exit.

Throughout the forty years of the cold war, the United States had pursued a contradictory policy toward torture. At home, American officials were eloquent advocates for human rights before the U.S. Congress and the UN General Assembly. Abroad, CIA operatives trained third world allies in advanced interrogation techniques, outsourcing torture to allied security agencies and housing detainees in foreign facilities. After September 2001, however, the Bush administration resolved this contradiction between America's antitorture principles and clandestine practices by legalizing these extralegal techniques. In an unprecedented step, the president allowed the CIA to hold detainees in its own network of secret prisons from Thailand to Poland and authorized agents to use "enhanced" interrogation techniques. As counterinsurgency operations in Afghanistan and Iraq swept up thousands of suspected terrorists, the U.S. military opened its own prisons at Abu Ghraib near Baghdad, Bagram outside Kabul, and the U.S. Navy base at Guantanamo Bay, Cuba. Within two years, each of these facilities yielded reports or photographs showing undeniable human rights abuse, damaging America's international standing. After regular inspections of Guantanamo, the International Red Cross reported that the psychological techniques used on detainees "cannot be considered other than an intentional system of cruel, unusual and degrading treatment and a form of torture." When the Supreme Court challenged the administration's contention that Guantanamo was beyond the writ of U.S. law and international treaties, the Bush White House reacted by enacting the Military Commissions Act 2006—legalizing endless detention at Guantanamo, granting the CIA immunity for past abuse, and authorizing the president to order interrogation techniques tantamount to torture.[14]

After his inauguration in January 2009, President Barack Obama tried to break with this troubled past by rescinding Bush's authorization for the CIA to torture and closing its secret prisons. But the legacy of this latest iteration of imperial mimesis has continued, entangling the new administration in a skein of institutional continuity. "Our government does not torture," Obama had promised during the 2008 presidential campaign. "That will be my position as president. That includes, by the way, renditions. We don't farm out torture. We don't subcontract torture."[15]

Despite this unequivocal opposition to rendition, President Obama's Justice Department quickly invoked the Bush administration's use of sovereign immunity to block detainees from legal redress after their rendition to foreign nations for torture. In another case, the administration argued for denial of habeas corpus to detainees held for years without charges at the U.S. air base in Bagram, Afghanistan. At his confirmation hearings, the incoming CIA director, Leon Panetta, insisted on his agency's prerogative to engage in the rendition of detainees to third countries where they will very likely be at risk of abuse. Moreover, the U.S. legal system had no clear means of adjudicating the fate of dozens of top al-Qaeda captives whose torture has tainted all lawful evidence against them. The Obama administration was thus faced with the unpalatable alternatives of endless incarceration without trial or the admission, for the first time in two centuries, of tortured testimony before U.S. courts. Confronted with this difficult choice, President Obama reversed his oft-repeated criticism of the Bush administration's military commissions and announced, in May 2009, that continuing these controversial Guantanamo tribunals would be "the best way to protect our country, while upholding our deeply held values." As he struggled to extricate himself from what he called the "mess" left by Bush's "misguided experiment," Obama suggested that the best disposition for some cases might be "prolonged detention" without trial—an almost unprecedented legal step. In another breathtaking reversal that same month, the president rescinded his promise to release photos of detainee abuse in Iraq and Afghanistan, repeating Bush's discredited argument that these crimes had been "carried out in the past by a small number of individuals." After a half-century of the CIA's indirect involvement in torture on far-off covert battlegrounds, this practice has been domesticated, under the pressures of the war on terror, to become a formal weapon in the arsenal of American power—degrading the nation's reputation worldwide, embroiling the United States in divisive human rights litigation for years to come, and demanding a disposition of Guantanamo detainees that would in some way damage the rule of law. In sum, Obama's stance toward NSA surveillance, CIA rendition, and military detention echoed the expanded executive powers championed by the Bush administration. According to Prof. Jack Balkin of Yale Law School, this bipartisan affirmation would "reverberate for generations," making these policies "entrenched features of government."[16]

In two counterinsurgency campaigns separated by a century, lessons learned at the edge of empire later compromised civil liberties back home. America's experience of colonial policing in the Philippines after 1901, repatriated during World War I, would remain deeply inscribed in the nation's politics for the next half century, fostering an empowered internal security apparatus capable of egregious excess. At the outset of the global war on terror in 2001, memories of the cold war witch-hunt discouraged the use of formal censorship or civilian vigilantes. But sophisticated security methods, developed for counterinsurgency overseas, eventually came home to jeopardize the constitutional freedoms of U.S. citizens. With surprising speed, presidential power grew to permit unchecked electronic surveillance, endless detention of terror suspects, and inhumane interrogation. Somewhat more slowly, innovative techniques of biometric identification, aerial surveillance, and civil control refined abroad in Afghanistan and Iraq were domesticated to create the potential for even more intrusive state infringement of individual liberties. Both then and now, however, surprisingly few Americans seemed aware of the toll that empire was exacting from their civil liberties.

Philippine Praxis

In the Philippines the global war on terror involved legal restraints and extralegal violence that bear the imprint of American influence exercised over the span of a century. Indeed, the patterns of police control formed in the first years of U.S. colonial rule after 1898 would continue for decades, both political surveillance and the prohibition of personal vice.

In establishing the Philippines Constabulary and its Information Division in 1901, the U.S. colonial regime combined formal police powers with an informal use of information for sub rosa control, embedding a powerful police apparatus within the Philippine executive branch that would remain an instrument of its authority throughout the twentieth century. Moreover, by criminalizing gambling, opium, and prostitution, American colonials unwittingly created a thriving underground economy that compromised those whose duty it was to contain it. When combined with police control over information, these prohibitions against personal vice effectively oiled the machinery of corruption and scandal, creating a system of political controls that revealed itself with stunning clarity in both the Manila police scandal of 1912 and the Conley crisis of 1923.

A century later, from 1995 to 2005, Panfilo Lacson's network of PAOCTF police veterans played a role comparable to the colonial constabulary's Information Division in the first years of American rule. They commanded an elite unit within the larger police force that served as a fecund incubator of scandal, exercising an invisible influence suddenly evident in President Estrada's jueteng controversy of 2001 and President Arroyo's "Hello, Garci" crisis of 2005. Beyond an ironic circularity from colonial to postcolonial practices, these parallels show that, under both colony and republic, secret services and their netherworld nexus of intelligence and illicit income had emerged from society's shadows to become a significant force in Philippine political life.

In this same century, the vice trades have expanded exponentially, particularly in the realm of illicit drugs. After independence in 1946 breached the bilateral isolation of colonial rule, the Philippines was once again open to unfiltered contacts with the vast Chinese cultural imperium looming to the northwest. At first influence was limited to Taiwan and the overseas Chinese diaspora. But South China's capitalist transformation after the cold war opened the Philippines to Chinese crime syndicates and their chief export, methamphetamines. During the 1990s the Chinese presence suddenly became an omnipresent feature of Manila's crime scene through kidnappings, community protests, drug dealing, and gangland killings. The scale of this change is evident in the striking contrast between "Emperor" Sualoy's thousand-peso bribes to municipal officials in the 1920s and the billions of pesos in the South China drug circuits of the late 1990s. Reflecting the transformative impact of globalization, Senator Lacson, if his detractors and supporters are to be believed, was elevated by the same transnational circuits, first emerging as Manila's top cop through his subordinates' control of overseas Chinese traffickers, then serving as the local Chinese community's protector in the face of countless kidnappings, and later drawing campaign funds from Manila Chinese to challenge an established Filipino political dynasty, the Arroyos. By 2007, moreover, China's role had moved beyond contraband smuggling to the acquisition of major development contracts through the likes of the LTZ digital technology corporation, producing more conventional controversies over kickbacks in the government's tender process.

As guardians of Manila's burgeoning criminal netherworld, the police forces have experienced a parallel expansion in the scale of their corruption and the scope of their power. Although members of Iloilo's municipal police took small bribes to protect the city's jueteng racket in 1930, the national police, then called the Philippines Constabulary, was still free from systemic corruption and thus symbolized the legitimacy of the colonial state. After its formation in the early 1990s, the command echelons of the new national police, the PNP, soon showed a systemic corruption as the protector of regional jueteng syndicates and principals in the nation's drug traffic.

Manila's crime and corruption also increased significantly during the twentieth century, moving by degrees from precinct-level protection of gambling and prostitution in 1911 to command-echelon syndication of drug trafficking and kidnapping in 2001. Instead of Chief Harding's control of brothels and police commissioner Percy McDonnell's streetcar bribes, contemporary supercops have been implicated in a seamy mix of international drug deals, political intrigues, kidnapping, torture, and executions. Reflecting its role as a quasi-autonomous power center within the Philippine state, the national police has produced candidates for every presidential election over the past twenty years. In 2004 Senator Lacson led a law and order campaign that combined PNP veterans as staffers, police intelligence used to create scandal, and possible funding from illicit sources, arousing enough popular support to split the opposition and position himself as a potential power broker in the 2010 elections and beyond.

A comparison of scandals throughout the twentieth century reveals both continuity and change, indicating the covert netherworld's recurring role in Philippine politics. First there are some strong continuities, highlighted by juxtaposing two jueteng scandals across the span of three generations in a single elite family. In 1930 a newspaper in Iloilo City accused the province's governor, Mariano Arroyo, of funding his reelection campaign through a local jueteng syndicate, an exposé that destroyed his local political machine. Three generations later in 2005, First Gentleman Mike Arroyo, the grandson of Governor Arroyo's brother, was accused of funding his wife's presidential reelection with bribes from national jueteng syndicates, precipitating a crisis that nearly destroyed her presidency. In their reach for political power, two generations of the same elite family, separated by seven decades of turbulent change, tried to milk the same gambling racket for illegal campaign finance. Despite the many social changes that separate the two scandals, both arose from the same underlying cause, an unrelenting escalation in campaign costs that has strained society's resources to the breaking point.

Next there are some troubling changes. If we juxtapose Senator Manuel Quezon's careful distancing from the jueteng scandal in 1930 with the calculated, even cynical complicity of President Arroyo's husband, son, and brother-in-law some seventy-five years later, it is easy to see that over time the country's political culture has relaxed the ethical constraints on public officials, extending vice and corruption into the country's highest echelons. At the dawn of the twenty-first century, diverse members of the Filipino political elite, whether the arriviste Joseph Estrada or the aristocratic Arroyo family, seemed to share a willingness to take bribes from gambling racketeers. Paralleling this extension of jueteng's influence from provincial to national politics, the scale of the racket's profits and political payoffs expanded ten-fold, when adjusted for inflation, from Governor Arroyo's goal of ₱100,000 ($50,000) in illegal campaign collections in 1930 to Mike Arroyo's political slush fund of ₱260 million ($4.7 million) in 2005. Indeed, jueteng's passage from provincial to national influence reveals much about the changing character of Philippine politics, particularly the shift from tight rural patronage networks to impersonal urban electoral mobilizations fueled with cash and celebrity.

Turning this analytic microscope into a telescope, we can attempt to glimpse the future. The four-year confrontation between President Arroyo and Senator Lacson may be a bellwether of changes in the country's informal political economy with some potentially profound implications for the Philippines. If, as their critics have alleged, Lacson loyalists inside the PNP had ties to overseas Chinese drug syndicates and Arroyo's campaigns were financed by jueteng bosses, then illicit drugs may be replacing illegal gambling as the dominant form of campaign finance. Although it has been illegal for nearly a century, jueteng still enjoys a certain legitimacy within the moral economy of Filipino popular culture. Its massive cash transactions are conducted without violence, and its political bribes fund both electoral campaigns and local welfare payments. More important, jueteng binds the potentially disaffected mass of the urban poor to the Philippine polity. Daily dreams of jueteng jackpots provide hope in the midst of squatter desperation. On election day every two years, the slum networks of jueteng collectors mobilize their poor clients for political participation, lending an air of legitimacy to an otherwise inequitable and unsustainable social contract. By contrast, drug use is universally condemned, its traffic is marked by violence, and its bribes, lacking the compensatory value of good works, seem to encourage asocial, individual acquisition.

If these subterranean rackets do have the power to shape the political superstructure, then drug trafficking's displacement of jueteng as the defining force in the country's covert netherworld might introduce lurid violence, self-aggrandizing corruption, police brutality, and a host of irredeemably amoral actors. Changes in the vice trades may yet shape the country's moral economy, superseding an illegal lottery that fosters, through ballots and dreams, social bonds across the class divide. In its place a violent, demoralized drug milieu is forming that offers neither political participation nor the shared hope for a better future.

At the risk of overburdening a single election, the 2004 presidential campaign may represent a turning point in which established oligarchic families like the Arroyos were displaced by a new kind of national politician. If the provincial politicians of the postwar Republic relied on the famed "three Gs" of guns, goons, and gold, then we can describe the new forces that emerged after the end of the Marcos dictatorship in 1986 as the "three Cs" of celebrity, criminality, and Chinese. Just as movie and basketball stars have played on their celebrity to win seats in the Philippine Senate, once the chamber of aristocratic statesmen, so Ping Lacson's presidential campaign allegedly fused criminality and overseas Chinese influence to challenge an incumbent president with an established profile of educational achievement, aristocratic lineage, and jueteng finance. If this electoral cameo is indicative of larger trends, then landed rural patrons with their armed peasant militias, agricultural profits, family prestige, and illegal gambling networks are giving way to a new kind of urban politician supported by slum gangs, Chinese capital, mass media advertising, and illicit drug profits. Further changes in the netherworld of police and criminality may yet play a central, even catalytic role in the country's future political direction.

Beyond the electoral arena, Philippine society has slowly been polarized between a wealthy oligarchy and an impoverished mass, allowing the country's security forces exceptional influence as enforcers of order within an otherwise unstable polity. Through their fusion of legitimate force and corrupt control over the illicit economy, the national police has evolved into an almost autonomous locus of power within the Philippine state.

As police brutality and venality have been routinized to become an adjunct of presidential power, the crowd has emerged as a new element to challenge this political entente. Indeed, the three people power uprisings since 1986 have prompted a protracted debate over the deeper meaning of the crowd's role in Philippine democracy. In assessing the role of direct action in Philippine politics, we need to distinguish between the crowd of one hundred thousand urban poor that rallied on EDSA for the ousted president Joseph Estrada and the mob of fifty thousand that later attacked his successor inside the palace. In this latter, very violent mobilization, the ex-president's loyal mayors, military strategists, and rogue police officials played a key role, marshaling drug gangs from the slums and pumping them with alcohol and methamphetamines until they were ready to rumble at the palace gates. In this third reprise of people power, history provided elements of both tragedy and farce. Yet we cannot ignore certain parallels at the constitutional level between the well-mannered, middle-class crowd of People Power II and slum mobs of People Power III. "If you keep calling the mob into the streets and glorifying that as 'People Power,'" wrote the conservative columnist Max Soliven, "the time will come when the mob comes even if you don't call for it."[17] From the other side of the political spectrum, the liberal columnist Armando Doronila sadly agreed, noting that people power has "brought Philippine democracy to the edge of mob rule, even if exercised in the name of social change."[18]

The Philippines is indeed at such an impasse, with an entrenched elite, impoverished masses, and now, after the sordid spectacle of People Power III, a demobilized, increasingly disenfranchised middle-class—its numbers depleted as some eight million educated Filipinos have emigrated to form one of the world's largest diasporas.[19] With an empowered police force defending the state and its inequitable social contract by legal and extralegal means, there was no clear, constitutional path forward, no way to extricate the nation from this political stalemate. At society's base in urban slums and peasant villages, the country's prospects seemed even more dismal. As poor squatters slip from jueteng's daily dreams into *shabu*'s drug-induced stupor, society might move collectively from an illegal lottery that has long promoted political solidarity to an illicit drug traffic that can, by demoralizing the polity and delegitimating its political elite, rend the social fabric. In another generation or two the middle-class diaspora might repatriate its overseas earnings and exceptional talents to rebuild the vital center of Philippine politics, breaking this political paralysis and moving the nation forward. But for the foreseeable future there appears to be nothing on the horizon that can end this cycle of social polarization and political stagnation.

This scenario presents a troubling prospect and is a depressing note on which to close a lengthy book and a lifetime's study of Philippine national history. But the confluence of syndicate crime, police corruption, and political collusion—all set in a context of political gridlock among established elites, an exiled middle class, and miserable masses—seems so deeply ingrained that speculation about a more positive outcome, at least for the medium term, would seem to be false optimism.

In this sense U.S. colonial nation building has left a political legacy far more contradictory than the creation of what President George W. Bush once called "the first democratic nation in Asia."[20] Simply put, there is a dark underside to America's formation of this model Asian democracy marked by recourse to legal restraints on press freedom and reliance on secret police for extralegal operations, whether mass arrests, clandestine manipulations, or selective assassinations. If we probe beneath the surface of politics, U.S. colonial policy, by its prohibition of personal vice and its creation of powerful police, inadvertently fostered a netherworld of syndicate crime and corrupt state security whose symbiosis has integrated illegality into the Philippine polity far more fully than anyone could have imagined. The thirty-two hundred extrajudicial killings under President Marcos and seven hundred more under Arroyo make a mockery of claims to exemplary nation building in the Philippines. To return to the analogy between colonial pacification of the Philippines and the occupation of Iraq first broached in this book's prologue, the U.S. experience in Manila seems to have been a harbinger of a troubling long-term American legacy in Baghdad rather than historical evidence for the unalloyed Iraqi triumph that President Bush once imagined.

Global Change

Although changes in policing have reverberated deeply within both Philippine and American societies, it is their sum, their intertwining into a global order, that strains our comprehension and leads us, albeit tentatively, to some somber reflections.

Most immediately, we are confronted with the way that the covert action arms of these two sovereign states arrived with an eerie simultaneity at systematic assassination as their ultimate weapon in the global war on terror. In the Philippines the Arroyo administration, unable to suppress the communist and Islamic insurgencies, unleashed a clandestine military operation to assassinate over seven hundred social activists merely suspected of subversion. In Iraq the CIA, unable to curtail a terror campaign by Muslim militants, undertook the systematic assassination of innumerable al-Qaeda radicals and wavering tribal moderates, sweeping through Baghdad nightly and ranging, with U.S. special operations forces and CIA Predator drones, into Syria and Pakistan with fatal effect.[21]

If we place these recent developments in historical perspective, a steely hegemonic logic emerges to explain why these two states arrived at assassination separately yet simultaneously. In its drive for omniscience and even omnipotence over the Philippines, the U.S. colonial information regime applied a realpolitik rationality to accomplish its ends by any means necessary, whether repression, disinformation, or assassination. Although heir to this apparatus, the postcolonial Philippines also developed a weak bureaucracy and fluid society, allowing political resistance that its state security could not contain through standard surveillance, hence the recourse to assassination. Similarly, in Iraq the United States found itself mired in a pacification campaign with a collapsed state and fragmented society that defied conventional counterinsurgency. At opposite poles of power within the same imperium, the Philippine and American clandestine services seem to be driven by a similarly relentless logic to resort to the same lethal tactics. And in each case the covert nature of the mission furnished the requisite opportunity for unchecked experimentation.

At a broader level, the intertwined histories of the two nations reveal much about the costs and character of Washington's global hegemony. Since the 1950s, American analysts have usually separated overt aid, developmental and military, from covert operations, ignoring or minimizing the CIA's role in the conduct of U.S. foreign policy. From a local Filipino perspective, these two aspects appear fused in a unitary application of American power whose impact was both more and less than it might seem.

This situation is not unique to the Philippines. America's allies have long been able to dissimulate and divert, twisting Washington's global agenda to suit their own, often narrow self-interests. Yet in the context of global hegemony Washington's influence also exceeds the raw tangibles of development dollars or military firepower. In impoverished developing societies even the comparatively small exercise of U.S. power often has an outsized impact in the context of sparse local resources and a weak state apparatus. As befits the world's preeminent power, Washington's priorities can also have a potent demonstration effect, serving as models for local political elites trying to gauge global trends or placate a powerful ally. For client states trying to divine Washington's intent, the multiplicity of U.S. programs often sends contradictory signals, with USAID promoting development, USIS advocating democracy, DOD privileging the military, and CIA pressing for suppression of dissent. Yet on balance the sheer preponderance of military aid and covert pressure has tilted the American presence toward coercion, sacrificing social change to reinforce political stability.

Thailand's recent history offers parallel insights into the local impact of America's half century of global hegemony. At the start of the cold war in 1950, Washington allied itself with Bangkok as a frontline state in the containment of Chinese communism. Pursuing a dual-track policy, Washington committed ninety-seven U.S. advisers and $44 million per annum to building a Thai army of sixty thousand while two hundred CIA operatives forged a close alliance with the national police. In the first decade of this close alliance, the CIA collaborated with Thai leaders to build the national police into a formidable anticommunist force, creating a Border Patrol Police (BPP) of 4,200 officers and a Police Aerial

Reconnaissance Unit of four hundred commandos while expanding the regular territorial units.[22] As the Vietnam War escalated during the mid-1960s, American advisers worked with their Thai counterparts to launch an aggressive counterinsurgency campaign, expending $63 million, almost half of all U.S. aid to Thailand, to expand the police from fifty-one thousand to seventy-four thousand officers armed with M-16 rifles and an armada of thirty-seven helicopters. Throughout these decades of changing policies and shifting politics, American advisers and Thai autocrats converged in their commitment to building a powerful police force that was mobile, lethal, and amplified with civilian auxiliaries.[23]

As its operational capacity grew steadily across the span of generations, the Thai national police became a vehicle for carrying the accrued influence of myriad U.S. aid programs past into the political present. When democratic forces mounted a challenge to military rule between 1973 and 1976, Thailand's autocrats deployed the police to act as a counterforce. At the beginning of the democracy movement in October 1973, the police opened fire on student demonstrators, killing sixty-five. But the army and monarchy soon sensed the depth of mass support and retreated. Three years later, however, these police units and their civilian adjuncts attacked the campus of Thammasat University, the heart of the pro-democracy movement. After a fusillade of machine gun and rocket fire, BPP officers armed with M-16 rifles led thousands of civilian auxiliaries, including the Red Gaurs and Village Scouts, in storming the campus to beat and lynch students in a spectacle of violence that left at least forty-six dead and stilled the democratic movement for a decade. As Thomas Lobe concludes, a quarter century of U.S. aid to the Thai police "created the preconditions, the infrastructure, the readiness for a more coercive, repressive, and vehemently anti-communist set of political-military leaders" in an application of American power that "once again, subverted all middle ground."[24] Thus, at a rare moment of possible change in both Thailand and the Philippines, a ruling oligarchy closely allied with the United States unleashed a deadly police apparatus, the product of U.S. aid, to close off a democratic opening, whether by shooting Thai student demonstrators in October 1976 or massacring Filipino peasant marchers before Malacañang Palace in January 1987.

This political dynamic has long been evident in the Philippines. For well over a hundred years, a transnational alliance of U.S. and Filipino forces has provided security at the price of compromising human rights and slowing social progress. Throughout the twentieth century, U.S.-trained police officers and military troops defended the ruling oligarchy and served as a vector of institutional continuity, carrying the legacy of countless security operations from the colonial past into the postcolonial present. Whenever this brittle polity and its established elites have faced a serious challenge from the social margins, U.S. intervention has stiffened the Philippine security forces, preventing both political compromise and social change. During the early 1950s, a counterinsurgency campaign organized by the CIA and U.S. military advisers broke the Huk agrarian revolt through a close coordination of military operations and psychological warfare. In Washington's view, this signal success blocked a communist challenge to strategic U.S. bases and served as an exemplar for counterguerrilla operations during the cold war. From the Philippine perspective, however, American intervention tipped the local balance, defeating peasant rebels with sheer force of arms, thereby preempting any serious attempt at land reform that was, in retrospect, essential to the country's long-term social progress, economic growth, and political stability. Similarly, the infusion of U.S. aid and military advisers under the war on terror allowed the Arroyo administration to curtail negotiations and crush social activists through aggressive policing and covert assassinations. In his report on Arroyo's extrajudicial killings in 2007, the United Nations' rapporteur for human rights, Philip Alston, observed that such repression precluded a resolution akin to Northern Ireland's negotiated peace settlement and silenced an entire sector of Filipino social activists who were offering alternatives to armed violence.[25] After each U.S. intervention since 1948, Philippine paramilitary operations have thus suppressed the surface resistance without resolving deeper social problems.

The full implications of the American alliance for the Philippines can best be understood through a brief exercise in counterfactual history. From 1896 to 1902 the Philippines plunged into seven years of armed revolution that, through its fusion of nationalist ambitions and lower-class aspirations, manifested a potential for countless outcomes—from a reactionary oligarchic regime to a progressive social democracy. At the midpoint of this social upheaval, the U.S. Army intervened with a four-year pacification campaign that broke the revolutionary forces. This was followed by thirty years of colonial rule that achieved a stable political settlement through power sharing with a narrow political elite. Whenever this political pact was challenged by peasant revolts in the countryside and working-class resistance in the capital, the colonial regime deployed its police apparatus to curb both. Absent such efficient suppression, a sustained resistance might have forced American colonials and their Filipino allies to accept a more inclusive social settlement and invest in education or economic opportunities for the peasantry as well as emerging urban elites. Assessing the impact of the French secret police, the Sûreté, on Vietnam in this same period, Norwegian scholar Stein Tønnesson reached some parallel conclusions about the legacy of colonial policing that resonate with the Philippines. "The Sûreté's use of agents and informers throughout Vietnam created an incriminatory atmosphere which destroyed attempts to establish a civil society," creating a repressive political climate that is still "felt in Vietnam even today." Similarly, the historian Merle Ricklefs argues that Dutch colonial controls bequeathed the Indonesian Republic the "traditions, assumptions, and legal structure of a police state."[26]

The half century that followed Philippine independence in 1946 witnessed more missed opportunities for a peaceful resolution of this widening social inequality. Without U.S. interventions almost every decade to rearm the country's security forces, one can imagine a weak Philippine state reaching a negotiated settlement with the Huk guerrillas in the 1950s or the New People's Army in the 1980s. Such negotiations might have brought land redistribution and the development of prosperous owner-farmers as the foundation for a stable middle-class democracy, perhaps obviating the need for more long years of this never-ending counterinsurgency.

During the past forty years as well, each infusion of U.S. military aid has rearmed Manila for a renewed war on the Islamic secessionist struggle that has simmered in the southern islands since the early 1970s. Peace talks with Muslim rebels seemed to advance when U.S. aid reached a low ebb in the mid-1990s and to retreat when American assistance expanded after 2001. While Manila battled Muslim rebels, Northern Ireland achieved peace, South Africa abolished apartheid, Muslim secessionists in Aceh reached a modus vivendi with Jakarta, Bosnia settled a murderous sectarian war, and the cold war ended without conflagration. By contrast, the Philippines is still roiled by bloody insurgencies that show no signs of resolution. This half century of armed violence is a vivid manifestation of an inequitable society, polarized between a rich oligarchy and poor majority, that can only be maintained through sophisticated security operations whose high costs have been met through the Philippine-American security alliance.

Nor has the ambiguous impact of American power been limited to Southeast Asia. Throughout the cold war, Washington was antagonistic to social reformers such as Jacobo Arbenz in Guatemala and Salvador Allende in Chile. The CIA's support for Ramon Magsaysay, a moderate Filipino populist, was an exceptional embrace of social reform during a period when the agency promoted authoritarian military regimes on five continents. Yet even in the Philippines the American mission sacrificed land reform as the price of the oligarchy's support for the presence of U.S. military bases.[27] Generally, Washington found its closest allies throughout the third world among autocrats such as Marcos, Mobutu, Somoza, Suharto, and the shah of Iran.

In the aftermath of the cold war, the Clinton administration tried to transcend the nation-state, with its entanglements of democracy and development, and advance a new world order of multilateral governance and multinational corporations. With the advent of the war on terror, however, Washington has once again allied itself with conservative client states across Asia and the Middle East, pressing for decisive action against terrorists and ignoring the regimes' corruption and oppression. While President Bush chatted weekly via videoconference with President Hamid Karzai, illicit opium and Taliban insurgency spread unchecked across Afghanistan.[28] While Bush and Arroyo toasted the success of their combined antiterror operations against Muslim militants in the southern Philippines, Filipino military assassins were targeting social activists across the archipelago. Admittedly, the U.S. counterterror operations in

Mindanao tried to balance military aid with social development; yet the sheer power of the American alliance in a poor society with weak institutions induced a shift toward repression and reaction. Again and again, America has supported allies who have not only crushed communist and terrorist enemies but also distorted local political dynamics, slowing social change and political progress. Whether inherent or incidental to the exercise of American power, such social retrogression has often followed U.S. unilateral intervention and bilateral alliances across the span of five continents and as many decades.

If the twentieth century witnessed a U.S. imperium that grew from a slender string of island colonies into a global hegemony, with intervention abroad matched by repression at home, then the question remains whether the twenty-first century will see continuity or change, a stiffening or a softening of this global order and its impact on America. Those mindful of these trends would be well advised to watch the Philippines and other arenas of U.S. intervention, whether in Asia, Latin America, or the Middle East. Although seemingly remote from America, these overseas occupations may again serve as a bellwether of changing U.S. global power and its domestic consequences.

While such future directions remain uncertain, the lessons of the past seem clear. In both the colonial Philippines and contemporary Iraq, the United States possessed such an overwhelming superiority of force that armed resistance would, with sufficient time, almost certainly be defeated. Yet this local opposition was so determined and the pacification so protracted that American forces were pushed beyond the bounds of law and military capability, forcing the creation of new forms of surveillance and lethal force. In this amplification of state power, such counterinsurgency campaigns have left lasting scars on both conquerors and conquered, damaging democracy abroad and curtailing civil liberties at home. Living under foreign military occupation—with its arbitrary incarceration, pervasive policing, and autocratic administration—has traumatized these subject societies, impeding the formation of the vibrant civil society critical to a functioning democracy. Importing these same advanced security technologies into the United States has introduced corresponding transgressions of law and constitution that might take decades to repair. Each intervention abroad in defense of this expanding imperium seems to rebound back into America as a new round of domestic repression, reinforced by innovative security techniques and ideological imperatives from the overseas mission. In this process of imperial mimesis, a state, like the United States, that rules a foreign territory through political repression and pervasive policing soon finds many of those same coercive methods moving homeward to degrade its own democracy.

Such are the costs of empire.

Notes

Abbreviations

ARDC	*Annual Report of the Director of Constabulary*
ARWD	*Annual Report of the War Department*
BCF	Beyer Collection of Filipiniana, Tozzer Library, Harvard University
BIA	Bureau of Insular Affairs Library, Record Group 350, National Archives and Records Administration
CA	*Cablenews-American*
CHB	Charles Henry Brent Papers, Manuscript Division, U.S. Library of Congress
CN	*Cablenews*
DCW	Dean C. Worcester Papers, Harlan Hatcher Library, University of Michigan
DOJ	Department of Justice, Record Group 60, National Archives and Records Administration
ER	*El Renacimiento*
FBH	Francis Burton Harrison Papers, Manuscript Division, U.S. Library of Congress
FBIVD	Subject: Van Deman, Ralph Henry, Files 65-37516, 94-37515, Federal Bureau of Investigation, Washington, DC
GGPI	*Annual Report of the Governor General of the Philippine Islands*
HCP	Henry C. Corbin Papers, Manuscript Division, U.S. Library of Congress
HHB	Harry H. Bandholtz Papers, Michigan Historical Collections
HR	U.S. House of Representatives
HTA	Henry T. Allen Papers, Manuscript Division, U.S. Library of Congress
KR	*Khaki and Red*
LAT	*Los Angeles Times*
LD	*La Democracia*
LV	*La Vanguardia*
LWP	Leonard Wood Papers, Manuscript Division, U.S. Library of Congress
MA	*Manila American*
MB	*Manila Daily Bulletin, Manila Bulletin, Bulletin Today*
MC	*Manila Chronicle*
MCN	*Manila Cablenews*
MID	Military Intelligence Division, Correspondence 1917–1941, Record Group 165, National Archives and Records Administration
MLQ	Manuel L. Quezon Papers, Philippine National Library

MLQMI Manuel L. Quezon Papers, Bentley Historical Library, University of Michigan
MT *Manila Times*
NARA National Archives and Records Administration
NYT *New York Times*
OROECSP *Official Roster of Officers and Employees in the Civil Service of the Philippines*
OT Owen Tomlinson Papers, Bentley Historical Library, University of Michigan
PDI *Philippine Daily Inquirer*
PFP *Philippines Free Press*
PI Philippine Islands
PNA Philippine National Archives
PS *Philippine Star*
PSC *Reports of Cases Determined in the Supreme Court of the Philippines Islands*
RG Record Group
RPC *Annual Report of the Philippine Commission*
RVD Ralph Van Deman Papers, Records of the U.S. Senate Internal Security Subcommittee, Record Group 46, National Archives and Records Administration
RTC Regional Trial Court, Branch 107, Quezon City
SEN U.S. Senate
USAID U.S. Agency for International Development, National Security Archive, Washington, DC
WCF W. Cameron Forbes Papers, Houghton Library, Harvard University
WD U.S. War Department
WDAR *War Department Annual Reports*
WHT William Howard Taft Papers, Manuscript Division, U.S. Library of Congress

Prologue. Analogies of Empire

1. *NYT*, 10/19/2003.

2. President George W. Bush, "Remarks by the President to the Philippine Congress," Office of the Press Secretary, The White House, 18 October 2003, http://whitehouse.gov/news/releases/2003/10/print/20031018-12.html, accessed October 21, 2004.

3. Michael Isikoff and David Corn, *Hubris: The Inside Story of Spin, Scandal, and the Selling of the Iraq War* (New York, 2006), 411, 418; Frank Hindman Golay, *Face of Empire: United States–Philippine Relations, 1898–1946* (Quezon City, 1997), 17–45.

4. Max Boot, *The Savage Wars of Peace: Small Wars and the Rise of American Power* (New York, 2002), 125; Stanley Karnow, *In Our Image: America's Empire in the Philippines* (New York, 1989), 194; Brian McAllister Linn, *The Philippine War, 1899–1902* (Lawrence, 2000), 325; Glenn May, "Why the United States Won the Philippine-American War, 1899–1902," *Pacific Historical Review* 52, no. 4 (1983): 375; Matthew Smallman-Raynor and Andrew D. Cliff, "The Philippines Insurrection and the 1902–4 Cholera Epidemic," part 1: "Epidemiological Diffusion Processes in War," *Journal of Historical Geography* 24, no. 1 (1998): 70; *Washington Post*, 10/29/2004; *NYT*, 10/11/2006. In a count of individual Iraqi civilian deaths, the United Nations reported a total of 34,452 during 2006, lending credence to estimates in excess of 100,000 killed during six years of U.S. occupation. See *NYT*, 1/17/2007. Similarly, the Internet database "Iraq Body Count" made 16,587 database entries to produce an estimate of Iraqi civilian casualties in the range of 88,952 to 97,094 by November 2008. See "Iraq Body Count," http://www.iraqbodycount.org/database/, accessed November 17, 2008. The higher figure of 601,000 violent Iraqi deaths between March 2003 and September 2006 was the result of an epidemiological survey conducted by researchers from the Johns Hopkins School of Public Health. See Gilbert Burnham, Shannon Doocy, Elizabeth Dzeng, Riyadh Lafta, and Les Roberts, "The Human Cost of the War in Iraq: A Mortality Study, 2002–2006," *Lancet* 368, no. 9545 (October 11, 2006): 1421–28; and *Washington Post*, 10/11/2006.

5. Golay, *Face of Empire*, 9–10; Brian McAllister Linn, *The Guardians of Empire: The U.S. Army in the Pacific* (Chapel Hill, 1997), 14.

6. Linn, *The Philippine War*, 223, 253, 322; Seymour M. Hersh, *Chain of Command: The Road from 9/11 to Abu Ghraib* (New York, 2004), 1–72; Alfred W. McCoy, *A Question of Torture: CIA Interrogation, from the Cold War to the War on Terror* (New York, 2006), 115, 121, 124.

7. *NYT*, 5/14/2003, 5/19/2003, 5/25/2003, 6/1/2003, 6/30/2003, 4/21/2004, 4/23/2004, 5/3/2004, 10/21/2004, 11/3/2005, 11/6/2005, 10/17/2006; Rajiv Chandrasekaran, *Imperial Life in the Emerald City: Inside Iraq's Green Zone* (New York, 2006), 161–66, 262–64; Thomas Ricks, *Fiasco: The American Military Adventure in Iraq* (New York, 2006), 69–75.

8. *NYT*, 10/17/2006.

9. Adrian Buzo, *The Making of Modern Korea* (New York, 2002), 18; Peter Duus, *The Abacus and the Sword: The Japanese Penetration of Korea, 1895–1910* (Berkeley, 1995), 223–24; Thant Myint-U, *The Making of Modern Burma* (Cambridge, 2001), 193–99.

10. *NYT*, 8/24/2008, 8/28/2008, 9/2/2008, 9/4/2008, 9/9/2008, 9/15/2008, 4/12/2009, 4/16/2009.

11. *NYT*, 5/21/2006, 7/24/2006, 10/18/2006, 11/12/2006, 11/19/2006, 11/26/2006, 12/4/2006, 12/11/2006.

12. *NYT*, 4/4/2007; *Washington Post*, 12/1/2007; Robert Parry, "Mobile Labs Target Iraqis for Death," Consortiumnews.com, December 13, 2007, http://www.consortiumnews.com/Print/2007/121307.html, accessed March 5, 2008.

13. Bob Woodward, *The War Within: A Secret White House History, 2006–2008* (New York, 2008), 380; CNN [Cable News Network], September 9, 2008, http://www.cnn.com/2008/WORLD/meast/09/09/iraq.secret/, accessed October 4, 2008.

14. *NYT*, 11/10/2008, 4/16/2009.

15. *NYT*, 11/26/2006, 2/9/2007.

16. *NYT*, 11/23/2008.

17. After searching the massive records of the otherwise meticulous Dutch colonial state in Indonesia, one researcher was forced to conclude that "political intelligence will largely remain shrouded in mystery for lack of written sources." Harry A. Poeze, "Political Intelligence in the Netherlands Indies," in Robert Cribb, ed., *The Late Colonial State in Indonesia: Political and Economic Foundations of the Netherlands Indies, 1880–1942* (Leiden, 1994), 230. See also Philip J. Ethington, "Vigilantes and Police: The Creation of a Professional Police Bureaucracy in San Francisco," *Journal of Social History* 21, no. 2 (1987): 197–98, 220; David H. Bayley, "The Police and Political Development in Europe," in Charles Tilly, ed., *The Formation of National States in Europe* (Princeton, 1975), 350–53.

18. David M. Anderson and David Killingray, "Consent, Coercion, and Colonial Control: Policing the Empire, 1830–1940," in David M. Anderson and David Killingray, eds., *Policing the Empire: Government, Authority, and Control, 1830–1940* (Manchester, 1991), 1–2.

19. Itty Abraham, "Illegal but Licit," *IIAS Newsletter* 42 (2006): 1, 4; William van Schendel and Itty Abraham, eds., *Illicit Flows and Criminal Things: States, Borders, and the Other Side of Globalization* (Bloomington, 2005), 1–15.

Chapter 1. Capillaries of Empire

1. James A. LeRoy, *The Americans in the Philippines: A History of the Conquest and First Years of Occupation*, vol. 1 (Boston, 1914), 156–71, 238–48.

2. HR, *ARWD 1898, Report of the Major-General Commanding the Army*, 44–45; HR, *ARWD 1901, Report of the Lieutenant-General Commanding the Army*, part 5, 78–79, 86–88, 103–11; Emanuel A. Bajá, *Philippine Police System and Its Problems* (Manila, 1933), 253–54; WD, *RPC 1902*, part 1, 105–7; LeRoy, *The Americans in the Philippines*, vol. 2, 20.

3. *PDI*, 5/1/2001, 5/2/2001, 5/4/2001, 5/5/2001, 5/6/2001, 5/8/2001, 5/9/2001; *PS*, 5/2/2001, 5/10/2001.

4. Several authors have used the term *surveillance state* to describe the combination of restricted civil liberties, state security, and citizen vigilantism that appeared in the United States during World War I and its immediate aftermath. To describe a parallel trend toward systematic surveillance in Europe during the war, Peter Holquist uses the term *national security state*. See Paul L.

Murphy, *World War I and the Origin of Civil Liberties in the United States* (New York, 1979), chap. 4; Richard Polenberg, *Fighting Faiths: The Abrams Case, the Supreme Court, and Free Speech* (New York, 1987), chap. 5; and Peter Holquist, "'Information Is the Alpha and Omega of Our Work': Bolshevik Surveillance in Its Pan-European Context," *Journal of Modern History* 69, no. 3 (1997), 426–50.

5. Martin Thomas, *Empires of Intelligence: Security Services and Colonial Disorder after 1914* (Berkeley, 2008), 1–4, 25–28, 33–36, 215–19, 294, 302–3; C. A. Bayly, *Empire and Information: Intelligence Gathering and Social Communication in India, 1780–1870* (New York, 1996), 3–6, 364–67; David Arnold, *Police Power and Colonial Rule: Madras, 1859–1947* (Delhi, 1986), 13, 27–35, 72–78, 116–31, 185–99, 230–36; Peter Robb, "The Ordering of Rural India: The Policing of Nineteenth-Century Bengal and Bihar," in David M. Anderson and David Killingray, eds., *Policing the Empire: Government, Authority, and Control, 1830–1940* (Manchester, 1991), 126–47; Harry A. Poeze, "Political Intelligence in the Netherlands Indies," in Robert Cribb, ed., *The Late Colonial State in Indonesia: Political and Economic Foundations of the Netherlands Indies, 1880–1942* (Leiden, 1994), 229–42; Robert J. Goldstein, *Political Repression in Nineteenth-Century Europe* (London, 1983), 69–72; Shawn Frederick McHale, *Print and Power: Confucianism, Communism, and Buddhism in the Making of Modern Vietnam* (Honolulu, 2004), 39–60; Clifford Rosenberg, *Policing Paris: The Origins of Modern Immigration Control between the Wars* (Ithaca, 2006), 40–45; Holquist, "Information Is the Alpha and Omega of Our Work," 415–26; Sidney Monas, *The Third Section: Police and Society in Russia under Nicholas I* (Cambridge, 1961), 20–21, 35, 62–65, 288–94. Reflecting the spottiness of French surveillance, the Carnet B list of subversives from 1886 to 1940 contained only 2,481 names at its peak and proved "unhelpful, unnecessary, or irrelevant in the major domestic crises." Donald N. Baker, "The Surveillance of Subversion in Interwar France: The Carnet B in the Seine, 1922–1940," *French Historical Studies* 10, no. 3 (1978): 486–516; Allan Mitchell, "The Xenophobic Style: French Counterespionage and the Emergence of the Dreyfus Affair," *Journal of Modern History* 52, no. 3 (1980): 414–25.

6. For example, Joan Jensen's superb history of U.S. intelligence concludes with the enticing remark that "the first systematic army surveillance system in the Philippines did spread . . . throughout the country in 1917." But her chapter on the Philippines focuses on Washington policy debates instead of intelligence operations, eschewing any specifics about personnel or policies repatriated from the Philippines. See Joan M. Jensen, *Army Surveillance in America, 1775–1980* (New Haven, 1991), 88–108.

7. H. H. Gerth and C. Wright Mills, eds., *From Max Weber: Essays in Sociology* (New York, 1946), 77–78.

8. E. P. Thompson, "Patrician Society, Plebian Culture," *Journal of Social History* 7, no. 4 (1974): 389–90; Michel Foucault, *Discipline and Punish: The Birth of the Prison* (New York 1979), 49.

9. Benedict R. O'G. Anderson, "Introduction," in Benedict R. O'G. Anderson, ed., *Violence and the State in Suharto's Indonesia* (Ithaca, 2001), 10.

10. James C. Scott, *Seeing Like a State: How Certain Schemes to Improve the Human Condition Have Failed* (New Haven, 1998), 1–3, 11–22, 24, 29–33, 44–45, 59–61, 64–72, 373.

11. Zoe Laidlaw, *Colonial Connections, 1815–45: Patronage, the Information Revolution, and Colonial Government* (Manchester, 2005), 170–95.

12. G. Tilghman Richards, *The History and Development of Typewriters* (London, 1964), 23–25; Lewis Coe, *The Telegraph: A History of Morse's Invention and Its Predecessors in the United States* (Jefferson, 1993), 89.

13. Coe, *The Telegraph*, 38–42, 86–87, 97–104; Richard A. Schwarzlose, *The Nation's Newsbrokers*, vol. 2: *The Rush to Institution from 1865 to 1920* (Evanston, 1990), 4–6, 10–11, 111–17; "Telegraphy," in *McGraw-Hill Encyclopedia of Science and Technology*, vol. 13 (New York, 1997), 421–25; Menahem Blondheim, *News over the Wires: The Telegraph and the Flow of Public Information in America, 1844–1897* (Cambridge, 1994), 169–95; Robert Luther Thompson, *Wiring a Continent: The History of the Telegraph Industry in the United States, 1832–1866* (Princeton, 1947), 427–39.

14. Armand Mattelart, *Mapping World Communication: War, Progress, Culture* (Minneapolis, 1994), 12–17.

15. Joel D. Howell, *Technology in the Hospital: Transforming Patient Care in the Early Twentieth Century* (Baltimore, 1995), 33–34, 40–42; Charles J. Austin, *Information Systems for Health Services Administration* (Ann Arbor, 1992), 13–21; F. H. Wines, "The Census of 1900," *National Geographic*, January 1900, 34–36; Friedrich W. Kistermann, "Hollerith Punched Card System Development (1905–1913)," *IEEE Annals of the History of Computing* 27, no. 1 (2005): 56–66; Emerson W. Pugh, *Building IBM: Shaping an Industry and Its Technology* (Cambridge, 1995), 1–36; "The Electric Tabulating Machine Applied to Cost Accounting," *American Machinist*, August 16, 1902, 1073–75; S. G. Koon, "Cost Accounting by Machines," *American Machinist*, March 26, 1914, 533–36; Douglas W. Jones, "Punched Cards: A Brief Illustrated Technical History," http://www.cs.uiowa.edu/˜jones/cards.history.html, accessed May 19, 2005; Mark Howells, "High Tech in the 90s: The 1890 Census," http://www.oz.net/~markhow/writing/holl.html, accessed March 14, 2007.

16. Helmut Gernsheim and Alison Gernsheim, *The History of Photography from the Camera Obscura to the Beginning of the Modern Era* (New York, 1969), 403–9.

17. Wayne A. Wiegand, *Irrepressible Reformer: A Biography of Melvil Dewey* (Chicago, 1996), 14–24; Wayne A. Wiegand and Donald G. Davis Jr., *Encyclopedia of Library History* (New York, 1994), 147–50; John Comaromi and M. Satija, *Dewey Decimal Classification: History and Current Status* (New York, 1988), 4–9; Leo E. LaMontagne, *American Library Classification with Special Reference to the Library of Congress* (Hamden, 1961), 52–60, 63–99, 179–233.

18. Elizabeth Bethel, "The Military Information Division: Origin of the Intelligence Division," *Military Affairs* 11, no. 1 (spring 1947): 17–24.

19. Henry L. Minton, *Lewis M. Terman: Pioneer in Psychological Testing* (New York, 1988), 46–54, 64–74; James Reed, "Robert M. Yerkes and the Mental Testing Movement," in Michael M. Sokal, *Psychological Testing and American Society, 1890–1930* (New Brunswick, 1987), 84–85; Stephen Jay Gould, *The Mismeasure of Man* (New York, 1996), 186–87, 209–13, 260–63.

20. Theodore Roosevelt, *An Autobiography* (New York, 1920), 168–69, 173, 175–76, 180–81, 190–91, 196–97; Francis V. Greene, *The Present Condition of the Police Force by Police Commissioner Greene* (New York, 1903), 3–8.

21. Alphonse Bertillon, *Alphonse Bertillon's Instructions for Taking Descriptions for the Identification of Criminals and Others by the Means of Anthrometric Indications* (New York, 1977), 6, 17, 91–94; Frank Morn, *"The Eye That Never Sleeps": A History of the Pinkerton National Detective Agency* (Bloomington, 1982), 124–27; E. R. Henry, *Classification and Uses of Fingerprints* (London, 1900), 61; Henry T. F. Rhodes, *Alphonse Bertillon: Father of Scientific Detection* (London, 1956), 71–109; Jürgen Thorwald, *The Century of the Detective* (New York, 1965), 20–26.

22. Donald C. Dilworth, ed., *Identification Wanted: Development of the American Criminal Identification Systems, 1893–1943* (Gaithersburg, 1977), 1–3, 6–8, 60–68, 78–79, 82–83, 103–6, 131, 161–66; Henry, *Classification and Uses of Fingerprints*, 4–7, 61–69; Bertillon, *Alphonse Bertillon's Instructions*, 10–12; *Police Chiefs News Letter* 2, no. 3 (March 1934): 2; *Police Chiefs News Letter* 3, no. 7 (July 1936): 2; Polenberg, *Fighting Faiths*, 165.

23. Robert "Buzz" Hill, "Retina Identification," in Anil Jain, Rudd Bolle, and Sharath Pankati, eds., *Biometrics: Personal Identification in a Networked Society* (Boston, 1999), 123–41; *NYT*, 4/4/2007.

24. Gamewell Fire Alarm Telegraph Co., *Emergency Signaling* (New York, 1916), chaps. 2–7; William Maver Jr., *American Telegraphy and Encyclopedia of the Telegraph: Systems, Apparatus, Operation* (New York, 1903), 440–53; Paul Ditzel, *Fire Alarm!* (New Albany, 1990), 5, 16–28, 40–42; William Werner, *History of the Boston Fire Department and Boston Fire Alarm System* (Boston, 1974), 177–84.

25. Gamewell Fire Alarm Telegraph Co., *Emergency Signaling*, chap. 8; Maver, *American Telegraphy and Encyclopedia of the Telegraph*, 472–93.

26. *NYT*, 8/10/1890, 1/30/1892, 12/8/1895, 4/8/1896, 7/31/1896, 8/25/1896, 3/5/1898, 11/4/1900, 5/9/1901, 5/28/1901; *Times* (London), 8/19/1912; Ditzel, *Fire Alarm!* 26–27.

27. Robert W. Little Jr., *York City Fire Department, York, Pennsylvania* (York, 1976), 83; Richard Heath, *Mill City Firefighters: The First Hundred Years, 1879–1979* (Minneapolis, 1981), 32, 45, 69–71; Ditzel, *Fire Alarm!* 27; U.S. Bureau of the Census, *Abstract of the Twelfth Census of the United States, 1900* (Washington, DC, 1904), 421–22.

28. Ben B. Fischer, *Okhrana: The Paris Operations of the Russian Imperial Police* (Washington, DC, 1997), 6–18.

29. Stephen Skowronek, *Building a New American State: The Expansion of National Administrative Capacities, 1877–1920* (Cambridge, 1982), 8–18, 39–46.

30. In the twenty-five years since Skowronek's seminal work appeared, scholars have challenged his thesis about the patchwork nature of U.S. state formation but, like him, they have generally ignored the critical role of police, military intelligence, and national security in this process. See ibid., 100; Daniel Carpenter, "The Multiple and Material Legacies of Stephen Skowronek," *Social Science History* 27, no. 3 (2003): 465–74; and Richard R. John, "Ruling Passions: Political Economy in Nineteenth-Century America," *Journal of Public Policy* 18, no. 1 (2006): 1–20.

31. Sidney L. Harring, *Policing a Class Society: The Experience of American Cities, 1865–1915* (New Brunswick, 1983), 30–41, 49–60, 239–46; Robert M. Fogelson, *Big-City Police* (Cambridge, 1977), 1–66; Marilynn Johnson, *Street Justice: A History of Police Violence in New York City* (Boston, 2003), 41–56; *NYT*, 12/27/1894, 12/28/1894, 3/26/1917; Egon Bittner, "The Rise and Fall of the Thin Blue Line," *Reviews in American History* 6, no. 3 (1979): 421–28; Eric H. Monkkonen, *Police in Urban America, 1860–1920* (Cambridge, 1981), 30–64; Erick H. Monkkonen, "From Cop History to Social History," *Journal of Social History* 15, no. 4 (1982): 575–85; Erick H. Monkkonen, "History of Urban Police," *Crime and Justice* 14 (1992): 547–53; Peter Balda, "The Corrupting of New York City," *American Heritage* 38, no. 1 (1986): 81–96; Roger Lane, "Urban Police and Crime in Nineteenth-Century America," *Crime and Justice* 2 (1980): 1–43; Roger Lane, "Urban Police and Crime in Nineteenth-Century America," *Crime and Justice* 15 (1992): 1–50; Philip J. Ethington, "Vigilantes and Police: The Creation of a Professional Police Bureaucracy in San Francisco," *Journal of Social History* 21, no. 2 (1987): 197–220; Gerda W. Ray, "From Cossack to Trooper: Manliness, Police Reform, and the State," *Journal of Social History* 28, no. 3 (1995): 565–73; William A. Geller and Norval Morris, "Relations between Federal and Local Police," *Crime and Justice* 15 (1992): 241–42, 280–87.

32. David H. Bayley, "The Police and Political Development in Europe," in Charles Tilly, ed., *The Formation of National States in Europe* (Princeton, 1975), 353–75; Raymond Fosdick, *European Police Systems* (New York, 1915), 315–85; Fischer, *Okhrana*, 1–28; Rita T. Kronenbitter, "The Illustrious Career of Arkadiy Harting," in Fischer, *Okhrana*, 71–86.

33. Heath Twichell Jr., *Allen: The Biography of an Army Officer, 1859–1930* (New Brunswick, 1974), 66–68, 76–86; H. T. Allen, *The Military System of Sweden* (Washington, DC, 1896), 11, 18, 59–76.

34. WD, Military Information Division, *Notes and Statistics of Organization, Armament, and Military Progress in American and European Armies* (Washington, DC, 1896), 91–112 (see pages 101–2 for intelligence); Arthur L. Wagner, "The Autumn Maneuvers of 1895 in Europe," in *Miscellaneous Papers* (Washington, DC, 1896), 147–61; Marc B. Powe, *The Emergence of the War Department Intelligence Agency, 1885–1918* (Manhattan, 1975), 28–32. For a similar oversight, with a single paragraph devoted to field intelligence in 143 pages, see WD, Military Information Division, *The Autumn Maneuvers of 1896* (Washington, DC, 1897), 124–25. For the paucity of information on intelligence in the MID library, see WD, Military Information Division, *Sources of Information on Military Professional Subjects* (Washington, DC, 1896), 3–109.

35. Arthur L. Wagner, *The Service of Security and Information* (Kansas City, 1903), 16–17, 54–98, 123–29, 180–93.

36. Sidney Howard, *The Labor Spy* (New York, 1924), 17; Morn, "*The Eye That Never Sleeps*," 169; Ethan A. Nadelmann, *Cops across Borders: The Internationalization of U.S. Criminal Law Enforcement* (University Park, 1993), 46–55; *Annual Report of the Secretary of the Treasury on the State of the Finances for the Fiscal Year Ended June 30, 1902* (Washington, DC, 1902), 51–52.

37. In 1865, the Secret Service was established within the Treasury Department, and in 1883 it became a distinct division with thirty-two operatives. After the assassination of President McKinley in 1901, Congress invested it with "the protection of the person of the President of the United States." See Department of Treasury, United States Secret Service, *Excerpts from the History of the United States Secret Service, 1865–1975* (Washington, DC, 1978), 8–17; *Annual Report of the Secretary of the Treasury on the State of the Finances for the Year 1884* (Washington, DC, 1884), 61–67; *Annual*

Report of the Secretary of the Treasury on the State of the Finances for the Fiscal Year Ended June 30, 1901 (Washington, DC, 1901), 65.

38. SEN, Select Committee to Study Governmental Operations with Respect to Intelligence Activities, 94th Congress, 2d Session, *Supplementary Reports on Intelligence Activities* (Washington, DC, 1976), 73–74, 94–95.

39. Elizabeth Bethel, "The Military Information Division: Origin of the Intelligence Division," *Military Affairs* 11, no. 1 (1947): 17–24; Twichell, *Allen*, 117–46; Marc B. Powe, "American Military Intelligence Comes of Age: A Sketch of a Man and His Times," *Military Review* 40, no. 12 (1975): 17–21.

40. Richard Brown, "General Emory Upton: The Army's Mahan," *Military Affairs* 17, no. 3 (1953): 128–31; Philip C. Jessup, *Elihu Root*, vol. 1 (Boston, 1938), 329–45.

41. Brian McAllister Linn, *The Philippine War: 1899–1902* (Lawrence, 2000), 127, 191; Brian McAllister Linn, "Intelligence and Low-Intensity Conflict in the Philippine War, 1899–1902," *Intelligence and National Security* 6, no. 1 (1991): 90–96. The senior intelligence officer was Col. Arthur L. Wagner, former head of the Military Intelligence Division. See SEN, 57th Congress, 1st Session, doc. no. 331, part 3, *Affairs in the Philippine Islands: Hearings before the Committee on the Philippines of the United States Senate* (Washington, DC, 1902), 2850–51.

42. Linn, "Intelligence and Low-Intensity Conflict in the Philippine War, 1899–1902," 100–104, 107–9; Ralph E. Weber, ed., *The Final Memoranda: Major General Ralph H. Van Deman, USA Ret., 1865–1952, Father of U.S. Military Intelligence* (Wilmington, 1988), 7–9.

43. Frank Hindman Golay, *Face of Empire: United States–Philippine Relations, 1898–1946* (Quezon City, 1997), 75; Daniel F. Doeppers, "Manila's Imperial Makeover: Health, Security, and Symbolism," in Alfred W. McCoy and Francisco A. Scarano, eds., *Colonial Crucible: Empire in the Making of the Modern American State* (Madison, 2009), 489–92.

44. *KR*, 9/1927, 5–9, 9/1932, 12; *PFP*, 5/11/1918, 3.

45. Greene, *The Present Condition of the Police Force*, 3–8.

46. Eliodoro Robles, *The Philippines in the Nineteenth Century* (Quezon City, 1969), 35–43; Reglamento para establecer la comisión de policía, ordenada, con acuerdo de la Real Audiencia de las Islas Filipinas, por su presidente el Excmo, Señor D. Mariano Ricafort, Gobernador y Capitán General, Superintendente General Subdelegado de Real Hacienda de las mismas, Sampaloc, 1826, Archivo General de Indias: Filipinas 515, Archivo de Indias (Seville).

47. Cicero C. Campos, "The Role of Police in the Philippines: A Case Study from the Third World," PhD diss., Michigan State University, 1983, 124–25; Ruby R. Paredes, "The Partido Federal, 1900–1907: Political Collaboration in Colonial Manila," PhD diss., University of Michigan, 1990, 51–56.

48. SEN, *RPC 1901*, vol. 4, 33–35; Campos, "The Role of Police in the Philippines," 124–25; Paredes, "The Partido Federal," 51–56; Robles, *The Philippines in the 19th Century*, 193–95; El informe sobre reforma del Reglamento de la Guardia Civil Veterana, Manila, July 1880, Guardia Civil (1880–1894), SDS 14220, PNA.

49. Extracto del Orden del Cuerpo del día 29 de diciembre de 1894, December 1894 to September 1895, Guardia Civil, 1875–1898, SDS 14217, S518–636, PNA.

50. Greg Bankoff, *Crime, Society, and the State in the Nineteenth-Century Philippines* (Quezon City, 1996), 136.

51. SEN, *RPC 1901*, vol. 4, 33–35; HR, *ARWD 1901, Report of the Lieutenant-General Commanding the Army*, part 2, 265; Miguel Berriz, *Diccionario de la Administración Pública, Anuario de 1888*, vol. 2 (Manila, 1888), 998–1000.

52. Sub-inspección de telegráfos, Real Orden, January 10, 1887, Guardia Civil, 1886–1887 (1872–1892), SDS 14212 S196–207, PNA.

53. Cárcel Bilibit, map no. 112–21, 1866, Inspeccion Gral. Obras Públicas, PNA; Bankoff, *Crime, Society, and the State*, 159; Dirección General de Administración Civil, Sección de Gobernación, Negociado de establecimientos penales, Sobre Establecimientos Penales, March 29, 1883, Guardia Civil, 1880–1894 (1883–1889), SDS 14220, S548–587, PNA.

54. Bankoff, *Crime, Society and the State*, 12, 137–38, 156.

55. Inventario de Libros del Laboratorio Médico Legal de Manila, November 1, 1898, Laboratorio Médico Legal de Manila, Inspección General de Beneficiencia y Sanidad, part 2, bundle 3, SDS 12646; Dirección General de Administración Civil de las Islas Filipinas, letter, July 31, 1894, S375–382; Letter from M. Ga. del Rey, December 31, 1894, 433–437, Laboratorio Médico-Legal de Manila, part II, SDS 12646; Reglas con arreglo a las cuales deben remitirse las sustancias u objetos para su análisis al laboratorio Médico-Legal, Manila, November 5, 1894, S420–421, Laboratorio Médico-Legal de Manila, part II, SDS 12646; Letter from Audiencia Criminal de Manila, Laboratorio Médico Legal de Manila, Inspección General de Beneficiencia, August 22, 1895, part 2, SDS 12646, PNA.

56. Relación de los individuos que radican en la expresada provincia [Pampanga] y que figuran en el cuadro de sospechosos como filibusteros y desafectos a la autoridad, San Fernando, March 10, 1889, Guardia Civil (1860–1897) (1898 B-1898 A), SDS 14197, S47–47b, PNA.

57. *Gaceta de Manila,* August 20, 1895.

58. SEN, *RPC 1901,* vol. 4, 33.

59. HR, *ARWD 1901, Report of the Lieutenant-General Commanding the Army,* part 5, 130.

60. Copia del expediente relativo a los servicios prestados por el Juez de la 1a Instancia de Cavite con motivo de la insurrección de la provincia de Cavite, n.d., National Commission on Culture and the Arts, Manila.

61. Inspector Jefe, Cuerpo de Vigilancia de Manila, September 1896, National Commission on Culture and the Arts, Manila; Informe del Cuerpo de Vigilancia, September 30, 1896, Sediciones y Rebeliones, 1884–1897, SDS 10559, PNA.

62. Letter from Inspector Jefe to Gobernador Civil de Manila, July 23, 1898, Cuerpo de Vigilancia, Rollo 1, Legajo 1, SDS 12230-G, 1869–1898, PNA.

63. Informe, Agente 2a Clase Gregorio Enriquez, February 15, 1897, Cuerpo de Vigilancia, Rollo 1, Legajo 1, SDS 12230-E, 1876–1898, PNA.

64. Theodore Grossman, "The Guardia Civil and Its Influence on Philippine Society," *Archiviana,* December 1972, 4–7.

65. Frederic H. Sawyer, *The Inhabitants of the Philippines* (London, 1900), 28–29.

66. Dean C. Worcester, *The Philippines Past and Present* (New York, 1930), 308–9.

67. Jose Rizal, *Noli Me Tangere* (Makati, 1996), 430–37.

68. Carlos Quirino, *The Young Aguinaldo: From Kawit to Biyak-na-Bato* (Manila, 1969), 85–91.

69. Bankoff, *Crime, Society, and the State,* 136.

70. David Barrows, "The Governor-General of the Philippines under Spain and the United States," in H. Morse Stephens and Herbert E. Bolton, eds., *The Pacific Ocean in History* (New York, 1917), 253, 265.

71. David M. Anderson and David Killingray, "Consent, Coercion, and Colonial Control: Policing the Empire, 1830–1940," in Anderson and Killingray, *Policing the Empire,* 1–2.

72. John McCracken, "Coercion and Control in Nyasaland: Aspects of the History of a Colonial Police Force," *Journal of African History* 27 (1986): 127–48; Harold Tollefson, *Policing Islam: The British Occupation of Egypt and the Anglo-Egyptian Struggle over Control of the Police, 1882–1914* (Westport, 1999), xi–xiv, 1–21, 84–109, 180–93; Bayly, *Empire and Information,* 1–9, 365–76.

73. Thomas, *Empires of Intelligence,* 47–48.

74. Stanley H. Palmer, *Police and Protest in England and Ireland, 1780–1850* (New York, 1988), 24; M. Brogden, "An Act to Colonise the Internal Lands of the Island: Empire and the Origins of the Professional Police," *International Journal of the Sociology of Law* 15 (1987): 179–208.

75. David M. Anderson and David Killingray, "An Orderly Retreat? Policing the End of Empire," in David M. Anderson and David Killingray, eds., *Policing and Decolonisation: Politics, Nationalism, and the Police, 1917–65* (Manchester, 1992), 1–2; David Arnold, "Police Power and the Demise of British Rule in India, 1930–47," in Anderson and Killingray, *Policing and Decolonisation,* 43–58; David Arnold, "The Armed Police and Colonial Rule in South India, 1914–17," *Modern Asian Studies* 11, no. 1 (1977): 101–25; Richard Rathbone, "Political Intelligence and Policing in Ghana in the late 1940s and 1950s," in Anderson and Killingray, *Policing and Decolonisation,* 84–104; David

Throup, "Crime, Politics, and the Police in Colonial Kenya, 1939–63," in Anderson and Killingray, *Policing and Decolonisation,* 127–57.

76. Glenn A. May, *Social Engineering in the Philippines: The Aims, Execution, and Impact of American Colonial Policy, 1900–1913* (Westport, 1980), xv–xvii, 50–55, 97–105; Linn, *The Philippine War,* 202–3; Howell, *Technology in the Hospital,* 49–50.

77. In using the term *panopticon,* I reference both Michel Foucault and Manila's main prison, which was built in the 1860s as an "*edificio panóptico,*" thus investing the term with specific meanings beyond its usual provenance. See Foucault, *Discipline and Punish.*

78. *PFP,* 4/21/1928, 4, 6; 12/1/1928, 6, 8.

79. May, *Social Engineering in the Philippines,* xv–xvi.

80. Golay, *Face of Empire,* 70–89.

81. Weber, *The Final Memoranda,* 7–23; Michael E. Bigelow, "The First Steps: Battalion S2s in World War I," *Military Intelligence* (January–March 1992): 26–28; Linn, "Intelligence and Low-Intensity Conflict in the Philippine War," 108–9.

82. Walter Robb, "Chief of Police Green: Remarks on Career," *American Chamber of Commerce Journal,* January 1929, 7; U.S. Department of the Army, *U.S. Army Register for 1910* (Washington, DC, 1909), 319.

83. David M. Kennedy, *Over Here: The First World War and American Society* (Oxford, 1980), 26–27, 84–86; Christopher Capozzola, "The Only Badge Needed is Your Patriotic Fervor: Vigilance, Coercion, and the Law in World War I America," *Journal of American History* 88, no. 4 (2002): 1354–62.

84. Charles Burke Elliott, *The Philippines to the End of the Commission Government* (Indianapolis, 1917), 168–83; Henry Parker Willis, *Our Philippine Problem: A Study of American Colonial Policy* (New York, 1905), 118–19, 146–47, 159–65; J. Michael Sproule, *Propaganda and Democracy: The American Experience of Media and Mass Persuasion* (Cambridge, 1997), 14; Emerson Hough, *The Web* (Chicago, 1919), 13, 34, 46–50, 52, 89. The estimate that the American Protective League and allied groups compiled a million pages of surveillance reports is based on research into those papers at the U.S. National Archives from 2001 to 2007. Judging from the League's three million investigations, this estimate is conservative.

85. Frank J. Donner, *The Age of Surveillance: The Aims and Methods of America's Political Intelligence System* (New York, 1980), 293.

86. Thomas, *Empires of Intelligence,* 18, 27, 56–57, 296–97.

87. Alfred W. McCoy, Francisco A. Scarano, and Courtney Johnson, "On the Tropic of Cancer: Transitions and Transformations in the U.S. Imperial State," in McCoy and Scarano, *Colonial Crucible,* 14–17; Victor Heiser, *An American Doctor's Odyssey: Adventures in Forty-five Countries* (New York, 1936), 116; Barbara Gutmann Rosenkrantz, *Public Health and the State: Changing Views in Massachusetts, 1842–1936* (Cambridge, 1972), 128–45; Warwick Anderson, *Colonial Pathologies: American Tropical Medicine, Race, and Hygiene in the Philippines* (Durham, 2006).

88. Stuart Creighton Miller, *"Benevolent Assimilation": The American Conquest of the Philippines, 1899–1903* (New Haven, 1982), 2–8; Peter Stanley, *A Nation in the Making: The Philippines and the United States, 1899–1921* (Cambridge, 1974), 268–72; Theodore Friend, *Between Two Empires: The Ordeal of the Philippines, 1929–1946* (New Haven, 1965), 266–67; May, *Social Engineering in the Philippines,* xv–xvii.

89. Bartholomew H. Sparrow, *The Insular Cases and the Emergence of American Empire* (Lawrence, 2006), 58–64, 160–61, 221–28.

90. Reynaldo C. Ileto, *Knowing America's Colony: A Hundred Years from the Philippine War* (Honolulu, 1999), 19–41, 56; Raymond Schwab, *The Oriental Renaissance: Europe's Rediscovery of India and the East, 1680–1880* (New York, 1984), 51–128, 289–336; Edward W. Said, *Orientalism* (New York, 1994), 49–110, 149–65.

91. For liberals who use the imperial frame for analysis of U.S. power, see Chalmers Johnson, *The Sorrows of Empire: Militarism, Secrecy, and the End of the Republic* (New York, 2004); Michael Ignatieff, "The Burden," *New York Times Magazine,* January 5, 2003, 22–23; Paul Kennedy, "The

Eagle Has Landed," *Financial Times* (London), 2/2/2002, 1. For conservatives, see Max Boot, "American Imperialism? No Need to Run Away from Label," *USA Today*, 5/6/2003; Eliot A. Cohen, "History and the Hyperpower," *Foreign Affairs* 83, no. 4 (July/August 2004): 49–63; Niall Ferguson, *Colossus: The Price of America's Empire* (New York, 2004), 14–15; Charles S. Maier, *Among Empires: American Ascendancy and Its Predecessors* (Cambridge, 2006), 14–15, 20–21, 32–33.

92. Ian Tyrrell, "Empire in American History," in McCoy and Scarano, *Colonial Crucible*, 541–56.

93. Lewis E. Gleeck Jr., *The Manila Americans (1901–1964)* (Manila, 1977), 13–16; J. A. Mangan, *The Games Ethic and Imperialism: Aspects of the Diffusion of an Ideal* (New York, 1986), 79, 86–90; May, *Social Engineering in the Philippines*, 85.

94. Thomas, *Empires of Intelligence*, 62–64; Letter from W. C. Rivers to Harry H. Bandholtz, November 15, 1907, Reel 2, HHB.

95. Mangan, *The Games Ethic and Imperialism*, 71–100, 130–31; J. A. Mangan, *Athleticism in the Victorian and Edwardian Public School: The Emergence and Consolidation of an Educational Ideology* (Cambridge, 1981), 122–40; Thomas, *Empires of Intelligence*, 51–52. Of the 362 members of the Sudan Political Service from 1899 to 1952 whose secondary schools were known, nearly 92 percent graduated from elite "public schools." Among the 265 members whose university records were found, 67 had degrees in classics (Latin or Greek) versus 6 with degrees in anthropology. See Mangan, *The Games Ethic and Imperialism*, 79, 87–90.

96. Bernard S. Cohn, *Colonialism and Its Forms of Knowledge* (Princeton, 1996), 4–5.

97. Thomas, *Empires of Intelligence*, 49–52.

98. W. Cameron Forbes, Journals, vol. 2, August 21, 1906, WCF; Lewis E. Gleeck Jr., *The American Governors-General and High Commissioners in the Philippines: Proconsuls, Nation-Builders, and Politicians* (Quezon City, 1986), 88–89.

99. Emma H. Blair and James A. Robertson, eds., *The Philippine Islands, 1493–1898*, vol. 52 (Cleveland, 1907); Gloria Cano, "Blair and Robertson's *The Philippine Islands, 1493–1898:* Scholarship or Imperialist Propaganda?" *Philippine Studies* 56, no. 1 (2008): 4–36.

100. See McCoy, Scarano, and Johnson, "On the Tropic of Cancer," 24–26.

101. Tony Ballantyne, "Empire, Knowledge, and Culture: From Proto-Globalization to Modern Globalization," in A. G. Hopkins, ed., *Globalization in World History* (London, 2002), 130–36; Leopoldo Y. Yabes, "Observations on Some Aspects of Philippine Scholarship and H. Otley Beyer," in Mario D. Zamora, ed., *Studies in Philippine Anthropology (In Honor of H. Otley Beyer)* (Quezon City, 1967), 54–56; A. L. Kroeber, "Roy Franklin Barton, 1883–1947," *American Anthropologist* 51, no. 1 (1949): 91–95; Donna J. Amoroso, "Inheriting the 'Moro Problem': Muslim Authority and Colonial Rule in British Malaya and the Philippines," in Julian Go and Anne L. Foster, eds., *The American Colonial State in the Philippines: Global Perspectives* (Durham, 2003), 137–38; Cesar Abid Majul, "Introduction," in Najeeb M. Saleeby, *The History of Sulu* (Manila, 1963), ix–xiv; Peter Gordon Gowing, *Mandate in Moroland: The American Government of Muslim Filipinos 1899–1920* (Quezon City, 1977), 68–69, 112, 122, 135, 152–53, 166, 183, 336.

102. Jose Algue, S.J., and Jose Clos, S.J., *El Archipiélago Filipino: Colección de Datos Geográficos, Estadisticos, Cronológicos y Científicos, Relativos al Mismo Entrescados de Anteriores u Obtenidos con la Propria Observación y Estudio* (Washington, DC, 1900); E. Arsenio Manuel, *Dictionary of Philippine Biography*, vol. 2 (Quezon City, 1970), 14–21.

103. H. N. Whitford, *A Preliminary Check List of the Principal Commercial Timbers of the Philippine Islands* (Manila, 1907); G. E. Nesom and Herbert S. Walker, *Handbook on the Sugar Industry of the Philippine Islands* (Manila, 1912); WD, Bureau of Insular Affairs, *A Pronouncing Gazetteer and Geographical Dictionary of the Philippine Islands, United States of America, with Maps, Charts, and Illustrations* (Washington, DC, 1902).

104. Joseph Ralston Hayden, *The Philippines: A Study in National Development* (New York, 1955), 542–43, 642–43; Lewis E. Gleeck Jr., *American Institutions in the Philippines, 1898–1941* (Manila, 1976), 150–54.

105. William J. Robbins, *Elmer Drew Merrill, 1876–1956: A Biographical Memoir* (Washington, DC, 1958), 273–333; Rodney J. Sullivan, *Exemplar of Americanism: The Philippine Career of Dean C. Worcester* (Ann Arbor, 1991), 13–30.

106. Scott, *Seeing Like a State*, 2–3, 65–71.

107. See, for example, Ferguson, *Colussus*, 205–11.

108. Johnson, *The Sorrows of Empire*, 151–86; *NYT*, 1/20/1991, 12/24/2001, 10/5/2007, 2/15/2009; Bill Stamets, "Anthropologists at War," *In These Times*, June 19, 2008, http://www.Inthesetimes.com/main/print/3749, accessed February 8, 2009; David Vine, "Enabling the Kill Chain," *Chronicle of Higher Education*, November 30, 2007, http://chronicle.com/free/v54/i14/14b00901.htm?utm_source=cr&utm_medium=en, accessed February 10, 2009.

109. For some sources on scandal, see John H. Summers, "What Happened to Sex Scandals? Politics and Peccadilloes, Johnson to Kennedy," *Journal of American History* 87, no. 3 (2000): 825–54; and Alex Hall, *Scandal, Sensation, and Social Democracy: The SPD Press and Wilhelmine German, 1890–1914* (Cambridge, 1977), 10–11, 27–29, 100–103, 143–87. For analysis of scandal in modern democracies, see Andrei S. Markovits and Mark Silverstein, *The Politics of Scandal: Power and Process in Liberal Democracies* (New York, 1988), 1–12; and John B. Thompson, *Political Scandal: Power and Visibility in the Media Age* (Cambridge, 2000), 6–7.

110. Robert Baer, *See No Evil: The True Story of a Ground Soldier in the CIA's War on Terrorism* (New York, 2002), 33; Lt. Col. Lucien Conein, former CIA operative in Saigon, interview with the author, McLean, Virginia, June 18, 1971.

111. *NYT*, 6/26/1997; United Nations International Drug Control Programme, *World Drug Report* (Oxford, 1997), 31–32, 124; United Nations Office for Drug Control and Crime Prevention, *World Drug Report 2000* (Oxford, 2000), 70.

112. E. H. Norman, "The Genyosha: A Study in the Origins of Japanese Imperialism," in Jon Livingston, Joe Moore, and Felicia Oldfather, eds., *The Japan Reader I* (New York, 1978), 355–67; Maruyama Masao, *Thought and Behaviour in Modern Japanese Politics* (London, 1963), 84–131; Tim Lindsey, "Law, Violence, and Corruption in the Preman State" (Melbourne: Conference on Government of the Shadows, August 10–12, 2006).

113. Theodore Friend, *The Blue-Eyed Enemy: Japan against the West in Java and Luzon, 1942–1945* (Princeton, 1988), 34–48.

114. John T. Sidel, *Capital, Coercion, and Crime: Bossism in the Philippines* (Stanford, 1999), 146–47.

115. Eva-Lotta Hedman and John T. Sidel, *Philippine Politics and Society in the Twentieth Century* (New York, 2000), 108, 172–73.

116. John T. Sidel, "Filipino Gangsters in Film, Legend, and History: Two Biographical Case Studies from Cebu," in Alfred W. McCoy, ed., *Lives at the Margin: Biography of Filipinos Obscure, Ordinary, and Heroic* (Quezon City, 2000), 149–80.

117. Gerth and Mills, *From Max Weber*, 82–83.

118. Ray Bonner, *Waltzing with a Dictator: The Marcoses and the Making of American Policy* (New York, 1987), 76–77; Conrado de Quiros, *Dead Aim: How Marcos Ambushed Philippine Democracy* (Pasig City, 1997), 65–66, 221.

119. For various press reports on the gross revenues from jueteng, see *MB*, 9/18/2000; *PDI*, 3/22/2000, 10/6/2000, 10/9/2000; and Wilfredo R. Reotutar, *So The People May Know All about the Gambling Menace in the Philippines* (Quezon City, 1999), 113–17. On jueteng's popularity, see Social Weather Stations, SWS Media Release, December 8, 1999, "Moral Attitudes against Gambling Hardly Affect Gambling Behavior: SWS Survey," http://www.sws.org.ph/pr120899.htm, accessed June 5, 2001. For sources on employment in jueteng, see *MB*, 9/18/2000, 10/11/2000, 11/21/2000; and *PDI*, 10/6/2000. For sources on gross sales of illicit drugs, see U.S. Department of State, Bureau of International Narcotics and Law Enforcement Affairs, *International Narcotics Control Strategy Report 2001*, Philippines, http://www.state.gov/g/inl/rls/nrcrpt/2001/rpt/8483.html, accessed March 28, 2002. In 2000 the U.S.$6 billion gross for gambling and drugs was equivalent to ₱300 billion or 46 percent of ₱651 billion in total Philippine government expenditures for that year. For budgetary statistics, see Republic of the Philippines, National Statistical Coordination Board, *2000 Philippine Statistical Yearbook* (Manila, 2000), tables 15.2, 15.4, 15.5. For employment in the Philippine electronics industry, see Steven C. McKay, "Securing Commitment in an Insecure World: Power and the Social Regulation of Labor in the Philippine Electronics Industry," PhD diss., University of

Wisconsin–Madison, 2001, chap. 2, fig. 8; and Steven C. McKay, *Satanic Mills or Silicon Islands? The Politics of High-Tech Production in the Philippines* (Ithaca, 2006), 46–47.

120. *PDI*, 10/18/2007; Paul D. Hutchcroft, "The Arroyo Imbroglio in the Philippines," *Journal of Democracy* 19, no. 1 (2008): 151.

121. *PDI*, 11/10/1995.

122. David H. Bayley, "The Police and Political Change in Comparative Perspective," *Law and Society Review* 6, no. 1 (August 1971): 7.

123. John Kleinig, *The Ethics of Policing* (Cambridge, 1996), 13, 18, 27–28.

124. *Congressional Record: Containing the Proceedings and Debates of the Sixty-second Congress, Third Session*, vol. 49 (Washington, DC, 1913), 3102.

125. Bajá, *Philippine Police System and Its Problems*, 279.

126. Campos, "The Role of Police in the Philippines," 30–32, 264, 322–24.

127. Ibid., 346.

128. Jürgen Habermas, *Legitimation Crisis* (Boston, 1975), 69, 73, 95–96; David Held, "Crisis Tendencies, Legitimation, and the State," in John B. Thompson and David Held, eds., *Habermas: Critical Debates* (Cambridge, 1982), 183–84.

129. Teodoro Agoncillo, *Revolt of the Masses* (Quezon City, 1956); Reynaldo C. Ileto, *Pasyon and Revolution: Popular Movements in the Philippines, 1840–1910* (Manila, 1979).

130. Amy Blitz, *The Contested State: American Foreign Policy and Regime Change in the Philippines* (Lanham, MD, 2000), 81–156; Alex B. Brillantes, *1898–1992: The Philippine Presidency* (Quezon City, 1994), 116–28, 222–27.

Chapter 2. Colonial Coercion

1. *MT*, 4/28/1903, 4/30/1903.

2. Lewis E. Gleeck Jr., *The Manila Americans (1901–1964)* (Manila, 1977), 13–16.

3. David G. Nitafan and Mario Guarina III, "The American Regime (1898–1946)," in Philippine Judiciary Foundation, *The History of the Philippine Judiciary* (Manila, 1998), 283, 306.

4. WD, *RPC 1903*, part 1, 637–41; Paul Ditzel, *Fire Alarm!* (New Albany, 1990), 27–37, 74–81.

5. HR, *ARWD 1903*, vol. 3, 201–4; HR, *ARWD 1902*, vol. 9, *Report of the Lieutenant-General Commanding the Army and Department Commanders*, 201.

6. David P. Barrows, *A History of the Philippines* (Indianapolis, 1905), 314–15; Conrado Benitez, *History of the Philippines: Economic, Social, Political* (Boston, 1940), 410–17; Glenn Anthony May, *Social Engineering in the Philippines: The Aims, Execution, and Impact of American Colonial Policy, 1900–1913* (Westport, 1980), 123–26; Glenn Anthony May, *Battle for Batangas: A Philippine Province at War* (New Haven, 1991), 26–27, 60–61, 201–7, 262–67; Ken De Bevoise, *Agents of Apocalypse: Epidemic Disease in the Colonial Philippines* (Princeton, 1995), 142–90; Teodoro A. Agoncillo and Oscar M. Alfonso, *History of the Filipino People* (Quezon City, 1971), 433–34.

7. Greg Bankoff, *Crime, Society, and the State in the Nineteenth Century Philippines* (Quezon City, 1996), 13–38, 121–23, 147–51, 167.

8. PI, Bureau of Civil Service, *OROECSP 1903*, 16–19, 28–34, 40–50, 104, 117.

9. WD, *RPC 1903*, part 3, 49; HR, *ARWD 1903*, vol. 3, 206.

10. SEN, *RPC 1900*, vol. 1, 245–46; George Y. Coats, "The Philippine Constabulary, 1901–1917," PhD diss., Ohio State University, 1968, 25; HR, *ARWD 1901*, *Report of the Lieutenant-General Commanding the Army*, part 2, 244.

11. HR, *ARWD 1901*, *Report of the Lieutenant-General Commanding the Army*, part 2, 98–99, 102–3; Letter from Adna R. Chaffee March 17, 1902, Box 1, File: Chaffee, Adna R., Jan–Mar 1902, HCP.

12. PI, *ARDC 1908*, 17–18.

13. Ignacio Villamor, *Criminality in the Philippine Islands* (Manila, 1909), 15, 31.

14. HR, *GGPI 1923*, 92–93, 98; HR, *GGPI 1924*, 63–64.

15. Bankoff, *Crime, Society, and the State*, 137–38.

16. Villamor, *Criminality in the Philippine Islands*, 12, 38, 42–43, 88–90.

17. HR, *ARWD 1901, Report of the Lieutenant-General Commanding the Army,* part 2, 264.

18. Brian McAllister Linn, *The Philippine War, 1899–1902* (Lawrence, 2000), 15, 23.

19. James A. LeRoy, *The Americans in the Philippines: A History of the Conquest and First Years of Occupation, with an Introductory Account of the Spanish Rule,* vol. 1 (Boston, 1914), 232–47; Charles Burke Elliott, *The Philippines to the End of the Military Régime: America Overseas* (Indianapolis, 1916), 318, 425.

20. HR, *ARWD 1898, Report of the Major-General Commanding the Army,* 44–45; HR, *ARWD 1901, Report of the Lieutenant-General Commanding the Army,* part 5, 78–79, 103–7; LeRoy, *The Americans in the Philippines,* vol. 1, 238–48.

21. Emanuel A. Bajá, *Philippine Police System and Its Problems* (Manila, 1933), 253–54; WD, *RPC 1902,* part 1, 105–7; HR, *ARWD 1898, Report of the Major-General Commanding the Army,* 44–45; HR, *ARWD 1901, Report of the Lieutenant-General Commanding the Army,* part 5, 78–79, 86–88, 103–5, 109–111; LeRoy, *The Americans in the Philippines,* vol. 1, 248, 260.

22. HR, *ARWD 1901, Report of the Lieutenant-General Commanding the Army,* part 5, 82–84, 89, 100–101; HR, *ARWD 1901, Report of the Major-General Commanding the Army,* part 2, 33; Headquarters, Department of the Pacific and Eighth Army Corps, *Index to General Orders and Circulars Issued from Headquarters, Department of the Pacific and Eighth Army Corps, and Office of the U.S. Military Governor in the Philippine Islands* (1899), circular no. 4.

23. HR, *ARWD 1901, Report of the Lieutenant-General Commanding the Army,* part 2, 264.

24. Stuart Creighton Miller, *"Benevolent Assimilation": The American Conquest of the Philippines, 1899–1903* (New Haven, 1982), 46–47; Linn, *The Philippine War,* 13, 29, 91, 198–99; Elliott, *The Philippines to the End of the Military Régime,* 480–81.

25. LeRoy, *The Americans in the Philippines,* vol. 1, 248; HR, *ARWD 1899, Report of the Major-General Commanding the Army,* part 2, 102, 276.

26. HR, *ARWD 1899, Report of the Major-General Commanding the Army,* part 2, 12–13, 32–33, 297–98.

27. Ibid., 152, 264–67, 271–72; Elliott, *The Philippines to the End of the Military Régime,* 431; E. Arsenio Manuel, *Dictionary of Philippine Biography,* vol. 2 (Quezon City, 1970), 108–11.

28. HR, *ARWD 1899, Report of the Major-General Commanding the Army,* part 2, 36–37, 143–44.

29. Ibid., 52–54.

30. HR, *ARWD 1901, Report of the Lieutenant-General Commanding the Army,* part 2, 468–69.

31. HR, *ARWD 1899, Report of the Major-General Commanding the Army,* part 2, 44–45, 93, 256; HR, *ARWD 1901, Report of the Lieutenant-General Commanding the Army,* part 2, 224–25.

32. John R. M. Taylor, *The Philippine Insurrection against the United States: A Compilation of Documents with Notes and Introduction* (Pasay City, 1971), vol. 2, 142–45, vol. 3, 306–7, 332–34, 378–79, 570, 626–27, 636–37; Hector Villarroel, *Eminent Filipinos* (Manila, 1965), 250.

33. LeRoy, *The Americans in the Philippines,* vol. 1, 293, 352–53.

34. Taylor, *The Philippine Insurrection against the United States,* vol. 2, 158–59; HR, *ARWD 1899, Report of the Major-General Commanding the Army,* part 2, 70–71.

35. LeRoy, *The Americans in the Philippines,* vol. 1, 399–404.

36. Elliott, *The Philippines to the End of the Military Régime,* 446–47; HR, *ARWD 1899, Report of the Major-General Commanding the Army,* part 2, 77–79; Linn, *The Philippine War,* 36.

37. Taylor, *The Philippine Insurrection against the United States,* vol. 2, 155–56, vol. 3, 479–84.

38. HR, *ARWD 1899, Report of the Major-General Commanding the Army,* part 2, 93, 96–97, 100–101, 205–7; Linn, *The Philippine War,* 52; LeRoy, *The Americans in the Philippines,* vol. 2, 8–9.

39. LeRoy, *The Americans in the Philippines,* vol. 2, 26–28; Pascual Casimiro, "Reseña de la Vida Revolucionara," in E. Arsenio Manuel, *Dictionary of Philippine Biography,* vol. 1 (Quezon City, 1955), 123–24; Taylor, *The Philippine Insurrection against the United States,* vol. 2, 203–4; HR, *ARWD 1899, Report of the Major-General Commanding the Army,* part 2, 426, 499–500.

40. HR, *ARWD 1899, Report of the Major-General Commanding the Army,* part 2, 143–47; SEN, *RPC 1900,* vol. 1, 122–25.

41. HR, *ARWD 1901, Report of the Lieutenant-General Commanding the Army in Four Parts,* part 2, 246–47.

42. HR, *ARWD 1900, Report of the Military Governor of the Philippine Islands on Civil Affairs,* 282–83.

43. HR, *ARWD 1901, Report of the Lieutenant-General Commanding the Army,* part 5, 98–99.

44. Ibid., 81–83.

45. HR, *ARWD 1901, Report of the Lieutenant-General Commanding the Army in Four Parts,* part 2, 250–52.

46. *MT,* 5/6/12; HR, *ARWD 1898, Report of the Major-General Commanding the Army,* 119; HR, *ARWD 1899, Report of the Major-General Commanding the Army,* part 2, 144, 261–62.

47. HR, *ARWD 1899, Report of the Major-General Commanding the Army,* part 2, 143–45; HR, *ARWD 1901, Report of the Lieutenant-General Commanding the Army,* part 5, 80–81.

48. HR, *ARWD 1900, Report of the Military Governor of the Philippine Islands on Civil Affairs,* 308–9; HR, *ARWD 1900, Report of the Lieutenant-General Commanding the Army,* part 3, 192–95.

49. HR, *ARWD 1900, Report of the Military Governor of the Philippine Islands on Civil Affairs,* 308–11.

50. D. R. Williams, *The Odyssey of the Philippine Commission* (Chicago, 1913), 50–51.

51. Manuel Luis Quezon, *The Good Fight* (New York, 1946), 90.

52. HR, *ARWD 1901, Report of the Lieutenant-General Commanding the Army,* part 5, 84–85.

53. Ibid., part 2, 92.

54. Elliott, *The Philippines to the End of the Military Régime,* 512–13; Linn, *The Philippine War,* 214.

55. HR, *ARWD 1901, Report of the Lieutenant-General Commanding the Army,* part 2, 436–39, part 5, 85–86, 124–26.

56. Ibid., part 2, 467.

57. HR, *ARWD 1901, Public Laws and Resolutions Passed by the Philippine Commission,* 118.

58. Edgar G. Bellairs, *As It Is in the Philippines* (New York, 1902), 64–66; letter from George Curry to W. H. Taft, August 13, 1900, Reel 31, WHT.

59. HR, *ARWD 1901, Report of the Lieutenant-General Commanding the Army,* part 2, 436–37.

60. Bajá, *Philippine Police System and Its Problems,* 253–54; WD, *RPC 1902,* part 1, 105–7; HR, *ARWD 1901, Report of the Lieutenant-General Commanding the Army,* part 2, 134.

61. HR, *ARWD 1901, Report of the Lieutenant-General Commanding the Army,* part 5, 100–101, 127–31.

62. Ibid., 100–101, 127–31, 143–44, part 2, 491–504.

63. Ibid., part 5, 131–65; Joseph Ralston Hayden, *The Philippines: A Study in National Development* (New York, 1955), 98–304.

64. Emanuel A. Bajá, *Philippine Police System and Its Problems,* book 2: *Police of the Commonwealth* (Manila, 1939), 170–71, 253–54; WD, *RPC 1902,* part 1, 105–19; WD, *RPC 1904,* part 1, 192–93; HR, *ARWD 1902,* vol. 11: *Acts of the Philippine Commission,* 45–47.

65. Bajá, *Police of the Commonwealth,* 170–71, 253–54; WD, *RPC 1902,* part 1, 115; Third Annual Report, Philippine Commission, Year Ending October 1, 1902, Exhibit E: Municipal Board, City of Manila, 91/9/89, A-185, vol. 904, BIA.

66. Bajá, *Philippine Police System and Its Problems,* book 2: *Police of the Commonwealth,* 170–71, 253–54; WD, *RPC 1902,* part 1, 105–19; WD, *RPC 1904,* part 1, 192–93; HR, *ARWD 1902,* vol. 11: *Acts of the Philippine Commission,* 45–47.

67. *Graphic,* June 2, 1928, 17–18. To determine the promotion rate by 1911, we enumerated the number of policemen in the 1902 cohort who had received a promotion by 1911. To determine the 1921 promotion rate, we counted the number of policemen on the roster in 1911 who had been promoted by 1921. PI, Bureau of Civil Service, *OROECSP 1902, OROECSP 1905, OROECSP 1911, OROECSP 1916, OROECSP 1921, OROECSP 1926, OROECSP 1931, OROECSP 1935.*

68. *MT,* 1/23/1908.

69. *MT,* 1/25/1908.

70. PI, Bureau of Civil Service, *OROECSP 1911, OROECSP 1916, OROECSP 1921.*

71. WD, *RPC 1902,* part 1, 105–19; Exhibit E: Department of Police, Central Office, Manila, July 1, 1903, B1313, vol. 911, BIA.

72. WD, *RPC 1903,* 618–20.

73. WD, *RPC 1902,* 105–19; Exhibit E: Municipal Board, City of Manila, 91/9/89, 1902, A-183, vol. 904; Exhibit E: Department of Police, Central Office, Manila, July 1, 1903, B1323, vol. 911; City of Manila, Department of Police, Central Office, July 12, 1905, Philippine Commission Report 1905, vol. 1, part 2, GP1397, vol. 932, BIA; *KR,* 9/1927, 5–8, 9/1932, 12; Alphonse Bertillon, *Alphonse Bertillon's Instructions for Taking Descriptions for the Identification of Criminals and Others by the Means of Anthrometric Indications* (New York, 1977), 5–10, 17–21, 49–52, 93–94; Donald C. Dilworth, ed., *Identification Wanted: Development of the American Criminal Identification Systems, 1893–1943* (Gaithersburg, 1977), 2–3, 12, 22–28, 82; Henry T. F. Rhodes, *Alphonse Bertillon: Father of Scientific Detection* (London, 1956), 71–129.

74. City of Manila, 1909 Annual Report for the Police Department, Philippine Commission Report 1909, vol. 1, 285, vol. 955, BIA.

75. *KR,* 9/1927, 5–8, 9/1932, 12; *PFP,* 5/11/1918, 3.

76. Walter Robb, "Chief of Police Green: Remarks on Career," *American Chamber of Commerce Journal* (Manila), January 1929, 6–7; *PFP,* 2/28/1925, 4; letter from Jose Gil to Secretary to the Governor-General, August 2, 1929, Personal Name Information Files: John W. Green, Box 249, Entry 21, BIA.

77. WD, *RPC 1903,* 622–26.

78. City of Manila, Department of Police, Central Office July 12, 1905, Philippine Commission Report 1905, vol. 1, part 2, GP1397, vol. 932, BIA.

79. WD, *RPC 1903,* 618–20.

80. HR, *ARWD 1900, Report of the Lieutenant-General Commanding the Army,* part 3, 140.

81. Linn, *The Philippine War,* 129–30, 204; HR, *ARWD 1899, Report of the Major-General Commanding the Army,* part 2, 144–45; Headquarters, Department of the Pacific and Eighth Army Corps, *Index to General Orders* (1899), General Order 43.

82. HR, 56th Congress, 1st Session, doc. no. 659, *Municipal Government in the Philippine Islands* (Washington, DC, 1900), 1–15.

83. HR, *ARWD 1901, Public Laws and Resolutions Passed by the Philippine Commission,* 95; HR, *ARWD 1901, Report of the Lieutenant-General Commanding the Army,* part 2, 243–45.

84. HR, *ARWD 1901, Public Laws and Resolutions Passed by the Philippine Commission,* 144–47.

85. Ibid., 369–72.

86. WD, *RPC 1903,* part 3, 74; WD, *RPC 1904,* part 3, 24, 42; WD, *RPC 1905,* part 3, 32–33, 61, 74–81; WD, *RPC 1907,* part 2, 299; Report of the Trip of the Civil Governor through the Southern Islands, November 12, 1904, to December 8, 1904, 14–17, Carl Remington Papers, Rare Book and Manuscript Library, Columbia University.

87. WD, *RPC 1908,* part 2, 331–32, 372–73.

88. Brian McAllister Linn, "Intelligence and Low-Intensity Conflict in the Philippine War, 1899–1902," *Intelligence and National Security* 6, no. 1 (1991): 91–96.

89. John Moran Gates, *Schoolbooks and Krags: The United States Army in the Philippines, 1898–1902* (Westport, 1973), 194–200, 206–10; Elizabeth Bethel, "The Military Information Division: Origin of the Intelligence Division," *Military Affairs* 11, no. 1 (spring 1947): 20–22; HR, *ARWD 1901, Report of the Lieutenant-General Commanding the Army,* part 2, 131–33.

90. Joan M. Jensen, *Army Surveillance in America, 1775–1980* (New Haven, 1991), 112; Marc B. Powe, "American Military Intelligence Comes of Age," *Military Review* 40, no. 12 (1975): 18–21; Kenneth Campbell, "Major General Ralph H. Van Deman: Father of Modern American Military Intelligence," *American Intelligence Journal* 8 (summer 1987): 13; Michael E. Bigelow, "Van Deman," *Military Intelligence* 16, no. 4 (1990): 38.

91. Ralph E. Weber, ed., *The Final Memoranda: Major General Ralph H. Van Deman, USA Ret., 1865–1952, Father of U.S. Military Intelligence* (Wilmington, 1988), 7–8; Linn, "Intelligence and Low-Intensity Conflict in the Philippine War," 100–108; Brian McAllister Linn, *The U.S. Army and Counterinsurgency in the Philippine War, 1899–1902* (Chapel Hill, 1989), 155–56.

92. Thomas H. Barry, Brigadier General U.S. Volunteers, Chief of Staff, to the Commanding General, Department of Northern Luzon, March 11, 1901, Entry 4337, RG 395, NARA.

93. Information, taken from Descriptive Cards of Inhabitants, Concerning Insurgents Etc., Book I, March 31, 1901, Entry 2244 (1); Headquarters Division of the Philippines, General Orders No. 294, September 28, 1901, Entry 3399, RG 395, NARA.

94. Captain R. H. Van Deman, To: Lieut. Leon L. Roach, Intelligence Office, Pila, Laguna, February 20, 1902, Entry 4755, RG 395, NARA.

95. Weber, *The Final Memoranda,* 7–8.

96. Descriptive Card of Inhabitants, Juanito Reyes, May 1, 1901, Entry 4337, RG 395, NARA.

97. Captain R. H. Van Deman, For the information of the Division Commander, October 30, 1901, Philippine Insurgent Records, Special Documents, Publication 254, Microreel 80, Folder 1303, NARA.

98. Captain R. H. Van Deman, For the information of the Division Commander, November 3, 1901, Philippine Insurgent Records, Special Documents, Publication 254, Microreel 80, Folder 1303, NARA.

99. Captain W. W. Wotherspoon, To: The Adjutant General, Third Separate Brigade, February 6, 1902, Entry 2354 (2), RG 395, NARA.

100. Captain J. Morrison, To: The Adjutant General, Third Separate Brigade, November 27, 1901, Entry 2354 (2), RG 395, NARA.

101. Linn, *The Philippine War,* 285–97.

102. Samuel S. Sumner, To: Adjt Gnrl., Dept. Southern Luzon, August 2, 1901, Entry 5101, RG 395, NARA.

103. Samuel S. Sumner, To: Adjutant General, Department of Southern Luzon, Manila, September 28, 1901, Entry 2349, RG 395, NARA.

104. Linn, "Intelligence and Low-Intensity Conflict in the Philippine War," 102–4.

105. Captain R. H. Van Deman, To: Commanding General, 3rd Separate Brigade, November 8, 1901, Entry 2354, RG 395, NARA.

106. Capt. VanDieman [*sic*], To: Intelligence Officer, Pila, Laguna, 4:40 p.m., n.d., Entry 4755, RG 395, NARA.

107. Capt. R. Van Deman, December 16, 1901, Entry 4755, RG 395, NARA.

108. Letter from Adna Chaffee, January 10, 1902, Folder 4, Box 1; letter from Adna Chaffee, November 5, 1901, Folder 3, Box 1; letter from Adna Chaffee, December 9, 1901, Folder 3, Box 1; letter from J. F. Bell to General Chaffee, Box 1, Folder 5, HCP; Linn, *The Philippine War,* 285–321; Linn, *The U.S. Army and Counterinsurgency in the Philippine War,* 152–61; Glenn Anthony May, "The Zones of Batangas," *Philippine Studies* 29 (1981): 89–103; May, *Battle for Batangas,* 262–67.

109. Weber, *The Final Memoranda,* 8–18; Gates, *Schoolbooks and Krags,* 250–51; Linn, "Intelligence and Low-Intensity Conflict in the Philippine War," 104–5; Captain R. H. Van Deman, For the information of the Division Commander, December 9, 1901, Philippine Insurgent Records, Special Documents, Publication 254, Microreel 80, Folder 1303, NARA.

110. Chas. R. Trowbridge, To: George Curry, Chief of Police, and Capt. R. H. Van Deman, January 3, 1902; W. Haskell, Descriptive Card of Inhabitants, Bito (Vito) Belarmino, February 26, 1902; R. H. Van Deman, To: Intelligence Office, Camalig, Albay, December 12, 1901, Entry 3399, RG 395, NARA; Norman G. Owen, *The Bikol Blend: Bikolanos and Their History* (Quezon City, 1999), 139–62.

111. Cicero C. Campos, "The Role of Police in the Philippines: A Case Study from the Third World," PhD diss., Michigan State University, 1983, 132.

112. *MT,* 12/24/1903.

113. HR, *ARWD 1901, Public Laws and Resolutions Passed by the Philippine Commission,* 369–71, 699–700.

114. J. T. Moore, ed., *Tennessee: The Volunteer State, 1769–1923,* vol. 2 (Chicago, 1923), 5–9; Dumas Malone, ed., *Dictionary of American Biography,* vol. 10 (New York, 1936), 561; *The National Cyclopedia of American Biography Being the History of the United States as Illustrated in the Lives of the Founders, Builders and Defenders of the Republic, and of the Men and Women Who Are Doing the Work and Molding the Thought of the Present Time,* vol. 26 (New York, 1937), 94–95.

115. Coats, "The Philippine Constabulary, 1901–1917," 4; Campos, "The Role of Police in the Philippines," 133.

116. Edward M. Coffman, "The Philippine Scouts, 1899–1942: A Historical Vignette," in *Acta No. 3: Teheran 6/16 VII 1976* (Bucharest, 1978), 73; HR, *ARWD 1902*, vol. 9, 203–4; HR, *ARWD 1906*, vol. 3, 237–38; HR, *WDAR 1909*, vol. 3, 170–73; HR, *WDAR 1910*, vol. 3, 194–95.

117. Letter to Carpenter, May 22, 1905, Reel 1, HHB.

118. Bajá, *Police of the Commonwealth*, 45; WD, *RPC 1904*, part 3, 18–20; WD, *RPC 1903*, part 3, 25–26; *Army and Navy Journal*, July 15, 1905; Letter to General Allen, May 6, 1904, Reel 1; letter to Colonel W. C. Taylor, December 2, 1914, Reel 10, HHB.

119. Chief of Staff, U.S. Army, "The Proposed Amalgamation of Scouts and Constabulary," February 18, 1911, Reel 4, HHB.

120. Letter from Elihu Root to Brigadier General Adna R. Chaffee, February 26, 1901, Box 1, File: Chaffee, Adna R., Jan–Oct 1901, HCP.

121. Letter from Adna R. Chaffee, September 30, 1901, Box 1, File: Chaffee, Adna R., Jan–Oct 1901, HCP.

122. Letter from Adna R. Chaffee, October 25, 1901, Box 1, File: Chaffee, Adna R., Nov–Dec 1901, HCP.

123. Mrs. William Howard Taft, *Recollections of Full Years* (New York, 1914), 218–21; Gleeck, *The Manila Americans*, 37–38.

124. Letter to General William Crozier, February 5, 1902, Box 7, File: 1902 Jan–Mar, HTA; letter from Luke E. Wright to William H. Taft, January 30, 1902, Reel 34; letter from Wm. H. Taft to Judge Harlan, October 21, 1901, Reel 33, WHT.

125. Heath Twichell Jr., *Allen: The Biography of an Army Officer, 1859–1930* (New Brunswick, 1974), 124–25; letter to William H. Taft, March 28, 1902, Box 7, File: 1902 Jan–Mar, HTA.

126. Letter from Clarence Edwards to Major Henry T. Allen, April 26, 1902, Box 7, File: 1902 Apr–June, HTA; Twichell, *Allen*, 124–25.

127. Letter from Luke E. Wright to William H. Taft, January 13, 1902, Reel 34; Wm. H. Taft to Judge Harlan, October 21, 1901, Reel 33, WHT; HR, *ARWD 1902*, vol. 11: *Acts of the Philippine Commission*, 36; HR, *ARWD 1901, Public Laws and Resolutions Passed by the Philippine Commission*, 425, 523–27.

128. Letter from Luke E. Wright to William H. Taft, January 13, 1902, Reel 34, WHT.

129. Letter to Colonel Clarence Edwards, January 31, 1903, Box 7, File: 1903 Jan–Mar; letter from Acting Executive Secretary to Henry T. Allen, February 12, 1903, Box 8, File: 1902; W. H. Taft, A Proclamation, January 30, 1903, Box 8, File: 1903 Jan–Mar, HTA; letter to the Secretary of War, April 4, 1913, Confidential Letter Box, vol. 2, WCF.

130. See, for example, C. W. Rosenstock, *Rosenstock's Manila City Directory, January February March 1905* (Manila, 1905), 309; and letter to Colonel W. C. Taylor, December 2, 1914, Reel 10, HHB.

131. HR, *ARWD 1903*, vol. 3, 144–45.

132. Ibid., vol. 5, 33–34.

133. Letter from General Geo. W. Davis, November 22, 1901, Box 1, File: Chaffee, Adna R., Apr–June 1902, HCP.

134. Letter from General Adna R. Chaffee, June 9, 1902, File: Chaffee, Adna R., Apr–June 1902, HCP.

135. Letter to Major General Henry C. Corbin, Box 8, File: 1903 Jan–Mar, HTA.

136. Emphasis in the original, where these offensive words were underlined. Letter to W. H. Taft, October 17, 1904, Box 8, File: 1904 Sept–Oct, HTA.

137. Letter to Captain W. C. Rivers, May 27, 1904, Reel 1; Subject: A New Military Policy for the United States in the Philippines, June 22, 1911, Reel 4, HHB.

138. Moore, *Tennessee*, 5–9; *The National Cyclopedia of American Biography*, 94–95; Lewis E. Gleeck Jr., *The American Governors-General and High Commissioners in the Philippines: Proconsuls, Nation-Builders, and Politicians* (Quezon City, 1986), 33–35.

139. WD, *RPC 1903*, part 3, 4.

140. Frank Lawrence Jenista, *The White Apos: American Governors on the Cordillera Central* (Quezon City, 1987), 198; PI, Bureau of Civil Service, *OROECSP 1911,* 21–24.

141. W. Cameron Forbes, *The Philippine Islands* (Cambridge, 1945), 110–11; Rodney J. Sullivan, *Exemplar of Americanism: The Philippine Career of Dean C. Worcester* (Ann Arbor, 1991), 148–49; Dean C. Worcester, *The Philippines Past and Present* (New York, 1930), 314–15.

142. See, for example, Second-Lieutenant M. Meimban, PC, "Biographical Sketches of Subprovince of Ifugao," Personal of Capt. O. A. Tomlinson, Senior Inspector of Ifugao, Mt. P., n.d., OT; and letter from 3rd Lieut., J. V. Agdamag, to Station Commander, Natonin, Mt. Prov., January 23, 1911, Book No. 1, DCW.

143. Twichell, *Allen,* 4–6, 19, 24, 26, 36–59, 65–67, 75–84, 86, 290; Robert Lee Bullard, *Fighting Generals: Illustrated Biographical Sketches of Seven Major Generals in World War I* (Ann Arbor, 1944), 87–90.

144. Twichell, *Allen,* 103; letter to Wm. H. Taft, January 16, 1902, Box 7, File: 1902 Jan–Mar, HTA; *MT,* 4/8/1902, 4/9/1902, 4/20/1902, 4/26/1902.

145. Letter from Senator Albert J. Beveridge to Major Henry T. Allen, March 19, 1902, Box 7, File: 1902 Jan–Mar; letter to Albert J. Beveridge, May 3, 1902, Box 7, File: 1902 Apr–June, HTA.

146. Letter to Colonel Clarence R. Edwards, January 31, 1903, Box 7, File: 1903 Jan–Mar, HTA.

147. Letter to Colonel John A. Johnston, January 21, 1902, Box 7, File: 1902 Jan–Mar, HTA; letter from Henry T. Allen to Wm. H. Taft, June 13, 1904, Reel 44, WHT.

148. Henry T. Allen, "Notes on the Extreme Orient," May 1904, Box 8, File: 1904, HTA.

149. *Lexington Herald,* 3/24/1906; speech by Henry T. Allen, Box 9, File: 1906, HTA.

150. *NYT,* 4/11/1902.

151. Letter to Colonel Clarence R. Edwards, April 8, 1902, Box 7, File: 1902 Apr–June; letter to General J. Franklin Bell, April 10, 1902, Box 7, File: 1902 Apr–June; letter from Clarence Edwards to Major Henry T. Allen, August 25, 1902, Box 7, File: 1902 July–Oct, HTA.

152. Letter to Luke E. Wright, November 19, 1902, Box 7, File: 1902 Nov–Dec, HTA.

153. Letter to Colonel Arthur Murray, January 31, 1903, Box 8, File: 1903 Jan–Mar, HTA.

154. Twichell, *Allen,* 106–7, 111; letter from Luke E. Wright to William H. Taft, January 13, 1902, Reel 34, WHT.

155. WD, *RPC 1903,* part 3, 3–4; Captain Alfonso A. Calderon and Marciano C. Sicat, eds., *Golden Book Philippine Constabulary* (Manila, 1951), 26, 73; Lewis L. Gould, *The Presidency of William McKinley* (Lawrence, 1980), 157–58.

156. PI, Bureau of Civil Service, *OROECSP 1902, OROECSP 1904, OROECSP 1905, OROECSP 1911, OROECSP 1916, OROECSP 1921, OROECSP 1926, OROECSP 1931, OROECSP 1935.*

157. Coats, "The Philippine Constabulary, 1901–1917," 9–12; Registry Committee, Association of General and Flag Officers, *General and Flag Officers of the Philippines (1896–1983)* (Quezon City, 1983), 15; *KR,* 8/1936, 12–14; Adjutant General's Office, *Official Army Register* (Washington, DC, 1924), 676–77; George W. Cullen, *Biographical Register of the Officers and Graduates of the U.S. Military Academy at West Point, N.Y.,* vol. 3 (Boston, 1891), 69, 335, 361, 397, 410, 413, 415.

158. *KR,* 9/1932, 25–27, 10/1932, 9–11, 35–37, 5/1938, 2–4, 16; letter from J. G. Harbord, April 4, 1919, WCF; Radio Corporation of America, *The First 25 Years of RCA: A Quarter-Century of Radio Progress* (New York, 1944), 12, 16, 55, 72; Robert Sobel, *RCA* (New York, 1986), 51–58, 154–55.

159. Bellairs, *As It Is in the Philippines,* 229–30, 237–38.

160. Letter to Colonel John A. Johnston, January 21, 1902, Box 7, File: 1902 Jan–Mar, HTA; *KR,* 7/1939, 5.

161. Lewis E. Gleeck Jr., *Laguna in American Times: Coconuts and Revolucionarios* (Manila, 1981), 121–22; Feliciano Gomez, Sexta Legislatura Filipina, *Directorio Oficial de la Camara de Representantes* (Manila, 1923), 167–70.

162. Jenista, *The White Apos,* 64–65, 69, 74, 195, 280–81; PI, Bureau of Civil Service, *OROECSP 1918, OROECSP 1919, OROECSP 1920.*

163. *KR,* 12/1932, 6.

164. WD, *RPC 1905,* part 3, 60.

165. WD, *RPC 1904*, part 3, 3.

166. *KR*, 8/1935, 17.

167. R. A. Duckworth-Ford, Memoranda, February 4, 1909, Reel 2; letter to Lieut. R. A. Duckworth-Ford, n.d., Reel 5; letter to Mark L. Hersey, August 6, 1909, Reel 3, HHB.

168. *KR*, 7/1931, 113–31, 3/1935, 15; Association of General and Flag Officers, *General and Flag Officers of the Philippines*, 201, 414. Out of fifty-nine lieutenants, seven were an exception to the rule since they rose from the ranks to win commissions.

169. *KR*, 7/1931, 27, 56, 11/1931, 18–25, 9/1934, 16; *PFP*, 3/12/1927, 14, 8/6/1932, 30.

170. Albert J. Reiss Jr., *The Police and the Public* (New Haven, 1971), 186–87.

Chapter 3. Surveillance and Scandal

1. *Evening Post*, 4/3/1903; *MT*, 7/3/1902.

2. One historical account stated, incorrectly, that the Associated Press correspondent Charles Ballantine (actually Ballentine) wrote a book that "was so bloodthirsty that he published it under a *nom de plume* [Edgar Bellairs]." Stuart Creighton Miller, *"Benevolent Assimilation": The American Conquest of the Philippines, 1899–1903* (New Haven, 1982), 210–11.

3. Hermann Hagedorn, *Leonard Wood: A Biography*, vol. 1 (New York, 1931), 409–10.

4. David Barrows, "The Governor-General of the Philippines under Spain and the United States," in H. Morse Stephens and Herbert E. Bolton, eds., *The Pacific Ocean in History* (New York, 1917), 255–65.

5. United States, *Debate in the Senate of the United States, February 6, 1902, on the Philippine Treason Law* (Washington, DC, 1902), 8; Alejandro M. Fernandez, *International Law in Philippine Relations, 1898–1946* (Quezon City, 1971), 91; letter from W. H. Taft to C. H. Brent, January 3, 1922, Reel 237, WHT; Abbott Lawrence Lowell, "The Status of Our New Possessions: A Third View," *Harvard Law Review* 13, no. 3 (November 1899): 155–76.

6. Julian Go and Anne L. Foster, eds., *The American Colonial State in the Philippines: Global Perspectives* (Durham, 2003); Elleke Boehmer, *Empire, the National, and the Postcolonial, 1890–1920: Resistance in Interaction* (Oxford, 2002); Pedro A. Cabán, *Constructing a Colonial People: Puerto Rico and the United States, 1898–1932* (Boulder, 1999).

7. Letter from J. Luna to Henry T. Allen, January 24, 1907, Reel 63, WHT; Headquarters Second District Philippine Constabulary, July 8, 1904, Reel 1, HHB; letter from George McVey Hally, May 25, 1905, Reel 1, HHB; letter to George McVey Hally, June 6, 1905, Reel 1, HHB.

8. Henry F. Pringle, *The Life and Times of William Howard Taft*, vol. 1 (New York, 1939), 38–41, 51, 59–62, 66–67, 138, 150, 268–69; Hebert S. Duffy, *William Howard Taft* (New York, 1930), 176–77, 204–5; Herbert Croly, *Marcus Alonzo Hanna: His Life and Work* (New York, 1912), 136–37; Joseph Benson Foraker, *Notes of a Busy Life* (Cincinnati, 1916), vol. 1, 87, 123, 383–84, vol. 2, 214–16, 236–40; Zane L. Miller, "Boss Cox's Cincinnati," *Journal of American History* 54, no. 4 (March 1968): 823–38; Zane L. Miller, *Boss Cox's Cincinnati: Urban Politics in the Progressive Era* (Chicago, 1968), 77–79, 91–92, 189, 199–200, 206–9; Allen Johnson and Dumas Malone, eds., *Dictionary of American Biography*, vol. 4 (New York, 1930), 473–74; Charles Frederic Goss, *Cincinnati: The Queen City, 1788–1912*, vol. 1 (Chicago, 1912), 266–76; Lincoln Steffens, *The Struggle for Self-Government* (New York, 1906), 170–78, 198–200; *Congressional Record: Containing the Proceedings and Debates of the Sixty-first Congress, Second Session*, vol. 45 (Washington, DC, 1910), 4704; letter from Luke E. Wright to W. H. Taft, September 16, 1908, Reel 94, WHT; letter to Senator J. B. Foraker, June 19, 1908, Reel 605, WHT; letters from J. B. Foraker, April 2, 1882, and July 7, 1882, Reel 29, April 3, 1888, January 31, 1890, Reel 30, WHT; letter from J. B. Foraker to the president, September 23, 1889, Reel 30, WHT; letters from M. Hanna to William H. Taft, July 5, 1901, September 24, 1901, Reel 33, February 8, 1902, Reel 34, February 18, 1902, Reel 35, May 19, 1903, Reel 39, WHT; letters from William H. Taft to M. A. Hanna, January 6, 1902, Reel 34, February 14, 1902, Reel 35, May 14, 1902, Reel 36, September 14, 1903, Reel 40, WHT.

9. Letters from William H. Taft to Dean C. Worcester, December 26, 1913, December 27, 1913, Reel 522, September 10, 1921, Reel 233, WHT.

10. Dumas Malone, ed., *Dictionary of American Biography,* vol. 18 (New York, 1936), 266–72.

11. Letter from Wm. H. Taft to Judge Harlan, October 21, 1901, Reel 33, WHT.

12. HR, *ARWD 1902,* vol. 11: *Acts of the Philippine Commission,* 39–41, 51–54; United States Philippine Commission, Minutes of Proceedings, November 2, 1901, November 4, 1901.

13. David G. Nitafan and Mario Guarina III, "The American Regime (1898–1946)," in Philippine Judiciary Foundation, *The History of the Philippine Judiciary* (Manila, 1999), 274–76, 286–87, 310–11, 326–29, 336–37, 339–40; Brian McAllister Linn, *The Guardians of Empire: The U.S. Army in the Pacific* (Chapel Hill, 1997), 24; James H. Blount, *The American Occupation of the Philippines* (New York, 1913), 443–44; HR, *ARWD 1902,* vol. 8, 396–98; WD, *Acts of the Philippine Commission,* vol. 8 (Washington, DC, 1904), 215, 536–39; *Felix Barcelon v. David J. Baker, Jr.,* Philippine Supreme Court (Manila), G.R. no. 2808, September 30, 1905, http://www.lawphil.net/judjuris/juri1905/sep1905/gr_2808_1905.html, accessed October 1, 2008.

14. Mrs. William Howard Taft, *Recollections of Full Years* (New York, 1914), 218–21; Edgar G. Bellairs, *As It Is in the Philippines* (New York, 1902), 191–93, 241–43; Linn, *The Guardians of Empire,* 24.

15. Letter from William H. Taft to Senator J. B. Foraker, September 7, 1903, Reel 40; letter from Senator J. B. Foraker to William H. Taft, October 19, 1903, Reel 41, WHT.

16. Dean C. Worcester, *The Philippines Past and Present* (New York, 1930), 11, 27, 75–77, 266–68; Rodney J. Sullivan, *Exemplar of Americanism: The Philippine Career of Dean C. Worcester* (Ann Arbor, 1991), 13, 19–20, 27–28, 79.

17. Peter W. Stanley, "'The Voice of Worcester Is the Voice of God': How One American Found Fulfillment in the Philippines," in Peter W. Stanley, ed., *Reappraising an Empire: New Perspectives on Philippine-American History* (Cambridge, 1984), 135–36.

18. Teodoro M. Kalaw, *Aide-de-Camp to Freedom* (Manila, 1965), 69–76.

19. Stanley, "The Voice of Worcester Is the Voice of God," 129–30.

20. Personal and Police History of Deputies to First Filipino Assembly, 1–15, vol. 1, DCW.

21. Records of Certain Members of the Philippine Assembly, 36, vol. 1, DCW; Asemblea Filipina, *Directorio Oficial: Segunda Legislatura Filipina* (Manila, 1912), 54–55.

22. Letter from Secretary of Interior to Governor-General, January 31, 1912, no. 21274–15, DCW; letter from Dr. John R. McDill to President of the United States, May 27, 1912, no. 15711–16, DCW; Secretary of Interior, Report, November 10, 1911, no. 21274–16, DCW; Bureau of Insular Affairs, General Records, General Classified Files 1898–1945, NARA; Report to the Honorable Vice Governor from Secretary of Interior, November 10, 1911, 11, 48–54, 61–65, 73–83, 93–95, 100–104, 112–13, 117–20, 122–23, 158–60, vol. 20, DCW; letter to Dean C. Worcester, November 17, 1910, Confidential Letter Box, vol. 1, WCF; *American Journal of Public Health* 6, no. 6 (June 1916): 615.

23. Ignacio Villamor, *Criminality in the Philippine Islands* (Manila, 1909), 13–14.

24. Hagedorn, *Leonard Wood,* vol. 2, 446–47.

25. Letter to Captain Julius C. Buttner, September 11, 1907; letter from Captain Julius C. Buttner, September 14, 1907, Reel 2, HHB.

26. Letter to Manuel L. Quezon, February 21, 1906, Reel 1, HHB.

27. Letter from Manuel Quezon to Colonel H. H. Bandholtz, August 23, 1906, Reel 1, HHB.

28. Letter to the Special Mission, August 4, 1921, Box One, Folio: Papers concerning Wood-Forbes Mission to the Philippine Islands, 1921–1922, DCW.

29. Frank Hindman Golay, *Face of Empire: United States-Philippine Relations, 1898–1946* (Quezon City, 1997), 95–96; memo prepared by Secretary of War, May 1914, Box 42, FBH.

30. Letter to Luke E. Wright, December 23, 1902, Box 7, File: 1902 Nov–Dec, HTA; *MT,* 5/2/1902; PI, Bureau of Civil Service, *OROECSP 1902.*

31. Letter to Major-General Leonard Wood, May 12, 1910, Reel 3, HHB; letter from Captain E. M. Joss to Genl. H. H. Bandholtz, May 27, 1910, Reel 7, HHB; letter to Captain E. M. Jose, June 23, 1910, Reel 3, HHB; United States, Department of the Army, *U.S. Army Register for 1909* (Washington, DC, 1908), 388.

32. Villamor, *Criminality in the Philippine Islands,* 12, 38, 42–43, 88–90.

33. Henry Parker Willis, *Our Philippine Problem: A Study of American Colonial Policy* (New York, 1905), iv, 118–19, 146–47, 159–62, 165; Peter W. Stanley, *A Nation in the Making: The Philippines and the United States, 1899–1921* (Cambridge, 1974), 236–40; *MT,* 2/26/1906.

34. Letter to Colonel Clarence R. Edwards, April 8, 1902, Box 7, File: 1902 Apr–June, HTA.

35. Letter from Adna Chaffee, November 5, 1901, Folder 3, Box 1, HCP; letter to the President, November 7, 1901, Box 7, HTA.

36. Letter to General Henry C. Corbin, February 1, 1902; letter to General William Crozier, February 5, 1902, Box 7, File: 1902 Jan–Mar, HTA.

37. WD, *Report of the United States Philippine Commission to the Secretary of War for the Period from December 1, 1900 to October 15, 1901* (Washington, DC, 1902), 386; WD, *RPC 1902*, part 1, 220–23.

38. WD, *RPC 1904*, part 3, 3, 28.

39. WD, *RPC 1905*, part 3, 142.

40. WD, *RPC 1902*, part 1, 205–10.

41. Michael Cullinane, "*Ilustrado* Politics: The Response of the Filipino Educated Elite to American Colonial Rule, 1898–1907," PhD diss., University of Michigan, 1989, 81–94.

42. Ibid., 134–40; letter from Luke E. Wright to Governor Taft, December 26, 1902, Reel 37, WHT.

43. Cullinane, "*Ilustrado* Politics," 112–14, 120–28.

44. Pascual Poblete, March 7, 1902, Box 7, File: 1902 Jan–Mar, HTA.

45. Cullinane, "*Ilustrado* Politics," 120–25; HR, *ARWD 1902*, vol. 11: *Acts of the Philippine Commission*, 51–54.

46. Mary Dorita Clifford, "Iglesia Filipina Independiente: The Revolutionary Church," in Gerald H. Anderson, ed., *Studies in Philippine Church History* (Ithaca, 1969), 234–45; Captain Winfield S. Grove, To: Brig. Gen. Henry T. Allen, 1903??, Box 8, File: 1903 Nov–Dec, HTA; Pedro S. Achutegui, S.J., and Miguel A. Bernad, S.J., *Religious Revolution in the Philippines*, vol. 1: *1860–1940* (Quezon City, 1961), 206–8.

47. Captain Winfield S. Grove, To: Brig. Gen. Henry T. Allen, 1903, Box 8, File: 1903 Nov–Dec, HTA.

48. Ibid. A comparison between this report and a well-documented history of the IFI indicates a number of errors in the PC biography. For example, Aglipay was ordained in 1889, not 1899; Bishop Hevia was beaten by his revolutionary jailers, not Aglipay, who was generally protective of Spanish priests and nuns; and there is no record of anything approaching a lethal three hundred lashes. See Achutegui and Bernad, *Religious Revolution in the Philippines*, vol. 1, 17, 67–75.

49. Letter from Brent to Dr. Tuttle, May 2, 1904, File: Jan–June 1904, CHB; letter from Brent to Bishop Hall, May 5, 1904, File: Jan–June 1904, CHB; Private Addendum to "Report on Religious Conditions in the Philippine Islands," File: July–December 1904, Box 6, CHB; Achutegui and Bernad, *Religious Revolution in the Philippines*, vol. 1, 389–91; Kenton J. Clymer, *Protestant Missionaries in the Philippines, 1898–1916: An Inquiry into the American Colonial Mentality* (Urbana, 1986), 121–22; notes of interview between Bishop Brent and Aglipay, June 13, 1904, File: Jan–June 1904, Box 6, CHB.

50. Charles H. Brent, "Religious Conditions in the Philippine Islands," File: July to December 1904, Box 6, CHB; Second Annual Report of the Bishop of the Missionary District of the Philippine Islands, attached to a letter from C. H. Brent to My Dear Secretary, October 17, 1904, Reel 46, WHT.

51. Letter from Daniel Tuttle to Bishop Brent, August 16, 1904, July to December 1904, Box 6, CHB; letter from C. H. Brent to E. F. Baldwin, July 24, 1903, Reel 40, WHT.

52. C. H. Brent to General Allen, July 11, 1904, Box 8, File: 1904 June–Aug, HTA; C. H. Brent to Gen. Henry T. Allen, October 12, 1904, Box 8, File: 1904 Sept–Oct, HTA. Letter from Henry T. Allen to C. H. Brent, July 12, 1904, CHB; letter from Brent to Gen. Henry T. Allen, October 12, 1904, File: July to December 1904, Box 6, CHB. In an otherwise excellent account, Clymer minimizes the significance of this constabulary report in changing Bishop Brent's attitude toward Aglipay from "mildly skeptical" to outright hostile. Clymer, *Protestant Missionaries in the Philippines*, 122.

53. Charles H. Brent, Private Addendum to Report on Religious Conditions in the Philippine Islands (For Bishops Only), Box 6, CHB; Achutegui and Bernad, *Religious Revolution in the Philippines*, vol. 1, 388–90; Clymer, *Protestant Missionaries in the Philippines*, 120–22.

54. Clifford, "Iglesia Filipina Independiente," 245–48; Achutegui and Bernad, *Religious Revolution in the Philippines*, vol. 1, 340–48.

55. Letter to William H. Taft, July 23, 1906, Box 9, File: 1906 June–Sept, HTA.

56. Letter from Gregorio Aglipay, November 29, 1905, Box 8, File: 1905 Sept–Dec, HTA.

57. Family History of M.Q. [ca. 1900], Box 7, File: 1900 Oct, HTA. Although the document only gives the author's name as "Captain Pyle, P.S.," U.S. Army records show that a Frank L. Pyle joined the Philippine Scouts as a second lieutenant on June 27, 1902, while retaining the permanent rank of sergeant in Troop D, U.S. First Cavalry. See Military Secretary's Office, *Official Army Register for 1905* (Washington, DC, 1904), 359; and letter from Hartford Beaumont to Honorable Henry C. Ide, December 7, 1904, Book 21:II, DCW.

58. Letter from J. G. Harbord to Bandholtz, March 13, 1907, Reel 1, HHB.

59. Cullinane, "*Ilustrado* Politics," 388, 408–13, 482–83.

60. The Local Spanish and Native Press, January 10, 1902, Box 1, File: Chaffee, Adna R., Nov–Dec 1901, HCP.

61. Lewis E. Gleeck Jr., *The Manila Americans (1901–1964)* (Manila, 1977), 41–43.

62. *Miau,* 7/20/1902, 11.

63. Arthur F. Odlin, "Sentence of the Court," *United States and Benito Legarda vs. Vicente Garcia Valdes*, Central File 14959–2, BIA; *MT,* 9/28/1901, 10/10/1901, 10/15/1901; Ruby R. Paredes, "The Partido Federal, 1900–1907: Political Collaboration in Colonial Manila," PhD diss., University of Michigan, 1990, 320–23; *Miau,* 7/20/1902, 10–13, 6/10/1902, 3–4.

The tensions within the Tuason family arose from the 1794 will of its founder who assigned much of his estate to a *mayorazgo,* a perpetual trust to be administered by means of male primogeniture. After the untimely death of the male Tuason heir in 1874, control of the *mayorazgo* passed jointly to his widow Teresa and his younger brother Gonzalo Tuason y Patiño. In March 1875, just thirteen months after her husband's death, Teresa forfeited her privileges under the will by marrying her husband's third cousin and manager of his estate, Benito Legarda y Tuason (1853–1915). But just three years later in 1878, the death of her minor son Jose Victoriano, heir to the *mayorazgo,* produced another reversal of fortune, investing Teresa with full control over the family's vast fortune. Soon after his wife Teresa's death in 1890, Legarda tried to marry his twenty-four-year-old stepdaughter, Teresa Eriberta Tuason. Meanwhile, Vicente G. Valdez had married Maria Soterrañea Tuason, Teresa Eriberta's sister, and had two children with her: Antonio Tuason (1893–1937); and Angel M. "Bobby" Tuason (1899–1948), who appears in a later chapter as Manila's postwar police chief. Reflecting the bitterness of a breach between Vicente Valdez and Maria Soterrañea, their children, though born in wedlock, discarded their father's surname and adopted their mother's. Whether from personal choice or to avoid the taint of scandal, the unfortunate Teresa Eriberta never married and lived out her life as a humorless governess to two generations of the extended family's children. Meanwhile, the legal wrangling between the family's main line, which controlled the estate, and the dispossessed cousins continued until 1927 when the Philippine Supreme Court ruled that Teresa and her husband Benito Legarda had violated the trust by expropriating proceeds due these cousins.

For a sanitized account of the Tuason-Legarda family history, see Benito J. Legarda Jr., *After the Galleons: Foreign Trade, Economic Change, and Entrepreneurship in the Nineteenth-Century Philippines* (Quezon City, 1999), 210, 230–31, 278, 315–17, 329–32. For hagiographic accounts, see Luciano R. Santiago, "Lola Teresa (1841–1890): Her Life and Times," 1–14; "Don Severo Tuason," 37–38; Wito Tuason Quimson, "The Post Don Severo Tuason," 39–43; Benito Legarda Jr., "The First Legarda," 55; "A Guardian for the Minor Children of Teresa de la Paz," 58; Howard A. Huberty, "The Valdes Connection," 109–14; "The Family Tree of Doña Teresa de la Paz," all in Descendants of Teresa de la Paz, *Teresa de la Paz and Her Two Husbands: A Gathering of Four Families* (Manila, 1996). For the full story of the "fraud" that dispossessed the secondary Tuason lineages, see Antonio Ma. Barretto et al. v. Augusto H. Tuason et al., no. 23923, March 23, 1926, in *Reports of Cases Determined in the Supreme Court of the Philippine Islands from March 2, 1929, to October 5, 1927* (Manila, 1929), 888–971. Other sources include *MT,* 5/13/1902; and E. Arsenio Manuel, *Dictionary of Philippine Biography,* vol. 1 (Quezon City, 1955), 292, 328, 395.

64. Letters from Luke E. Wright to William H. Taft, January 13, 1902, January 30, 1902, Reel 34, February 28, 1902, Reel 35, WHT.

65. United States v. Fred L. Dorr et al., no. 1051, May 19, 1903, *PSC 2/21/1903–11/30/1903,* 332–35.

66. Bellairs, *As It Is in the Philippines,* 45–46; letter from Luke E. Wright to William H. Taft, April 19, 1902, Reel 36, WHT.

67. *Manila Freedom,* 4/10/1902, 4/11/1902; Bellairs, *As It Is in the Philippines,* 45–46; letters from Luke E. Wright to William H. Taft, April 19, 1902, May 8, 1902, Reel 36, WHT.

68. *MT,* 3/25/1902, 4/15/1902, 4/16/1902.

69. Letter to Melville E. Stone, January 14, 1903, Reel 38, WHT.

70. *Manila Freedom,* 4/16/1902; *MT,* 8/4/1904; letters from Luke E. Wright to William H. Taft, April 19, 1902, May 8, 1902, Reel 36, WHT.

71. Letter from Benito Legarda to William H. Taft, May 15, 1902, Reel 36, WHT; *MT,* 5/13/1902.

72. Letter from William H. Taft to Benito Legarda, June 22, 1902, Reel 36, WHT; letter to Luke E. Wright, June 22, 1902, Reel 36, WHT; letter from Arthur F. Odlin to Secretary Taft, February 8, 1904, Reel 42, WHT; *Witton's Manila and Philippines Directory, 1904* (Manila, 1905), 740; Bellairs, *As It Is in the Philippines,* 79–80.

73. Lewis E. Gleeck Jr., *The American Governors-General and High Commissioners in the Philippines: Proconsuls, Nation-Builders, and Politicians* (Quezon City, 1986), 29–30; Gleeck, *The Manila Americans,* 42–43; *MT,* 4/11/1902, 7/27/1904, 8/4/1904, 8/6/1904; United States v. Fred L. Dorr et al., no. 1048, May 16, 1903, *PSC 2/21/03–11/30/03,* 269–93; Dorr v. United States, no. 583, May 31, 1904, *United States Reports,* vol. 195: *Cases Adjudged in the Supreme Court at October Term 1903 and October Term 1904* (New York, 1905), 269–93; Bellairs, *As It Is in the Philippines,* 22, 45–47; letter from Wright to Taft, May 8, 1902, Reel 36, WHT; United States v. Fred L. Dorr et al., no. 1051, May 19, 1903, *PSC 2/21/1903–11/30/1903,* 332–43; Benito Legarda y Tuason v. Vicente Garcia Valdez, no. 513, December 19, 1902, *PSC 8/8/01–2/20/03,* 562–66; Trinidad H. Pardo de Tavera v. Vicente Garcia Valdez, no. 922, November 8, 1902, *PSC 8/8/01–2/20/03,* 468–71.

74. *MT,* 12/19/1903, 12/20/1903, 12/22/1903, 12/23/1903, 12/24/1903, 1/2/1904, 1/27/1904, 3/17/1905; Tomasa Fidelino v. Benito Legarda, no. 1770, March 16, 1905, *PSC 14/22/04–9/7/05,* 285–88; Paredes, "The Partido Federal," 323–27.

75. *MT,* 12/24/1903, 1/27/1904.

76. Letter from Senator Albert J. Beveridge to Henry T. Allen, January 25, 1902, Box 7, File: 1902 Jan–Mar, HTA; letter to General Henry C. Corbin, February 1, 1902, Box 7, File: 1902 Jan–Mar, HTA; letter from Luke E. Wright to William H. Taft, January 30, 1902, Reel 34, WHT; letter from General Adna Chaffee, June 9, 1902, Folder 5, Box 1, HCP; *NYT,* 1/22/1902, 1/23/1902; *MA,* 1/26/1902, 1/29/1902.

77. Letters from Luke E. Wright to William H. Taft, January 13, 1902, January 30, 1902, Reel 34, February 28, 1902, Reel 35, WHT.

78. *MA,* 1/26/1902; letter to Governor, January 27, 1902, Box 7, File: 1902 Jan–Feb, HTA; letter to William H. Taft, January 31, 1902, Box 7, File: 1902 Jan–Mar, HTA.

79. Letter from E. G. Bellairs to Wm. Taft, October 5, 1901 Reel 33, WHT; letter from W.H.T. to Captain E. G. Bellairs, October 19, 1901, Reel 33, WHT; letter to Governor, January 27, 1902, Box 7, File: 1902 Jan–Feb, HTA; letter to William H. Taft, January 31, 1902, Box 7, File: 1902 Jan–Mar, HTA.

80. Letters from Luke E. Wright to William H. Taft, January 30, 1902, February 13, 1902, Reel 34, February 15, 1902, March 6, 1902, Reel 35, WHT.

81. Letter to General J. Franklin Bell, n.d. 1902, Box 7, File: 1902 Apr–June, HTA; letter from Luke E. Wright to William H. Taft, March 29, 1902, Reel 35, WHT.

82. Letter to J. B. Bishop, January 24, 1903, Reel 38, WHT; letter from Melville E. Stone, May 3, 1902, Reel 36, WHT; letter to Melville E. Stone, May 5, 1902, Reel 36, WHT; letter from Melville E. Stone, July 22, 1903, Reel 40, WHT; letter from Luke E. Wright, March 29, 1902, Reel 35, WHT; letters to Luke E. Wright, April 11, 1902, April 22, 1902, Reel 36, WHT; Frank S. Cairns, Headquarters Philippine Constabulary, January 13, 1903, Box 8, File: 1903 Jan–Mar, HTA.

83. Bellairs, *As It Is in the Philippines,* vi, 15–17, 21, 47–52, 243–45, 255.

84. Frank S. Cairns, Headquarters Philippine Constabulary, January 13, 1903, Box 8, File: 1903 Jan–Mar, HTA; SEN, 58th Congress, 2d Session, Executive C [Confidential], *Nomination of Leonard Wood to Be Major-General. Hearings before the Committee on Military Affairs concerning the*

Nomination of Brig. Gen. Leonard Wood to Be a Major-General, United States Army (Washington, DC, 1904), 111. On the title page of *As It Is in the Philippines,* Bellairs is described as "Correspondent of the Associated Press, Cuba, 1898–1900; China, 1900–1901; Philippines, 1901–1902."

85. Letter to J. B. Bishop, January 24 1903, Reel 38, WHT; letter to Revered Doctor Lyman A. Abbott, January 24, 1903, Reel 38, WHT; letter to Wm. M. Laffan, January 26, 1903, Reel 38, WHT; Gleeck, *The American Governors-General,* 29–30, 376; John W. Leonard, ed., *Who's Who in America: A Biographical Dictionary of Notable Living Men and Women of the United States, 1903–1905* (Chicago, 1905), 862; Hagedorn, *Leonard Wood,* vol. 1, 409–17.

86. *Sun* (New York), 4/2/1903; letter from Luke E. Wright to William H. Taft, November 28, 1902, Reel 37, WHT.

87. *Sun,* 4/3/1903; Richard A. Schwarzlose, *The Nation's Newsbrokers,* vol. 2: *The Rush to Institution from 1865 to 1920* (Evanston, 1990), 152, 171, 185; Thomas Byrnes, *Professional Criminals of America* (New York, 1895), 220–21. Although Byrnes describes Ballentine/Cheiriton as a Cheltenham alumnus, the college has no record of anyone by that name. The college did have several students named Bellairs between 1850 and the 1890s, a coincidence that increases the possibility that Ballentine/Cheiriton had some contact with it. E-mail correspondence with Christine Leighton, College Archivist, Cheltenham College, February 11, 2005.

88. *Evening Post,* 4/3/1903. Although they had separate managements, the two papers cooperated closely in this period, notably during an 1899 newspaper strike when *Evening Post* presses printed the *Sun.* See James Melvin Lee, *History of American Journalism* (Boston, 1917), 368–69, 374, 385–86.

89. Letter from William H. Taft to Colonel Clarence R. Edwards, June 5, 1903, Reel 39, WHT; SEN, 58th Congress, 2d Session, Executive C, *Nomination of Leonard Wood to Be Major-General,* 490; Melville E. Stone, *Fifty Years a Journalist* (Garden City, 1921), 232.

90. Malone, *Dictionary of American Biography,* vol. 8, 226–27; Croly, *Marcus Alonzo Hanna,* 259–63, 297–99; Margaret Leech, *In the Days of McKinley* (New York, 1959), 86–87, 138–39; Lewis L. Gould, *The Presidency of William McKinley* (Lawrence, 1980), 51–54, 167–68.

After obscurity as a U.S. Secret Service agent (1874–83), a banker in Hamilton, Ohio, an Ohio senator (1888–89), and fourth assistant U.S. postmaster general (1891–93, 1897–98), Rathbone won notoriety during bitterly contested balloting in the Ohio legislature for the state's second U.S. Senate seat. The legislature deadlocked on January 12, 1898, in a close vote for Marcus A. Hanna or his rival, forcing a special joint session that elected Hanna by three votes. Only a day later the Ohio Senate authorized a special committee to investigate "the charge of attempted bribery of John C. Otis, a member of the house of representatives." In April the committee's majority concluded that Rathbone was one of "the authorized agents and representatives of Marcus A. Hanna [who] attempted to bribe John C. Otis . . . to vote for him for United States Senator." Despite the controversy, Hanna retained his Senate seat and rewarded Rathbone with the appointment as postmaster general in Cuba. For details, see "Rathbone, Estes George," in *The National Cyclopedia of American Biography,* vol. 7 (New York, 1897), 56; *Journal of the House of Representatives of the State of Ohio for the Regular Session of the Seventy-third General Assembly Commencing Monday, January 3rd, 1898,* vol. 93 (Norwalk, Ohio, 1898), 34–42; Leech, *In the Days of McKinley,* 72, 100–101; Croly, *Marcus Alonzo Hanna,* 260; *NYT,* 5/15/1900, 2/16/1904; Steffens, *The Struggle for Self-Government,* 171, 180–81; SEN, Committee on Privileges and Elections, 55th Congress, 3d Session, Report 1859, *Election of Hon. M.A. Hanna* (Washington, DC, 1899), i–xi, 2–12, 193; *Cleveland Plain Dealer,* 2/18/1897, 2/19/1897, 2/26/1899; Elliot Howard Gilkey, *The Ohio Hundred Year Book* (Columbus, 1901), 298.

91. Croly, *Marcus Alonzo Hanna,* 136–38, 254–55, 294; *NYT,* 11/13/1903; Charles Frederic Goss, *Cincinnati: The Queen City, 1788–1912,* vol. 4 (Chicago, 1912), 817–18; Hagedorn, *Leonard Wood,* vol. 1, 401–15, vol. 2, 30–31; Marcus A. Hanna, "William McKinley as I Knew Him," *National Magazine,* January 1902, 405–10. For a vivid description of the long rivalry between Foraker and Hanna, see Leech, *In the Days of McKinley,* 40–41, 50–51, 63–65, 99–103, 414–15, 425–26.

92. *NYT,* 1/11/1899, 1/19/1900, 3/10/1900, 5/15/1900, 7/26/1900, 3/25/1902, 6/21/1903, 12/8/1903; Henry Harrison Lewis, "General Wood at Santiago: Americanizing a Cuban City," *McClure's,* March 1899, 460–69; Ray Stannard Baker, "General Leonard Wood: A Character Sketch," *McClure's,*

February 1900, 368–79; J. E. Runcie, "American Misgovernment of Cuba," *North American Review* 170 (February 1900): 284–94; Theodore Roosevelt, "General Leonard Wood: A Model American Administrator," *Outlook*, January 7, 1899, 20–23; George Kennan, "Friction in Cuba," *Outlook*, March 25, 1899, 675–68; Joseph B. Bishop, "Our Work as a Civilizer," *International Quarterly* 6 (September-December 1902, December–March 1903): 201–5; SEN, 59th Congress, 1st Session, *Senate Documents*, vol. 8 (Washington, DC, 1906), 129–133, 218–19, 223–24; SEN, 58th Congress, 2d Session, Executive No. 2, *Nomination of Leonard Wood* (Washington, DC, 1904), 3–6; SEN, 58th Congress, 2d Session, Executive No. 1, *Confirmation of Leonard Wood* (Washington, DC, 1904), 55–73; SEN, 58th Congress, 2d Session, Executive C, *Nomination of Leonard Wood to Be Major-General*, 192, 399–402, 818–20; Lewis L. Gould, *The Presidency of William McKinley* (Lawrence, 1980), 193–94; Leech, *In the Days of McKinley*, 374–75, 392–93.

93. *MA*, 4/24/1903; *MT*, 4/28/1903; *NYT*, 7/26/1900, 3/25/1902, 11/13/1903, 11/21/1903, 11/25/1903, 12/1/1903, 12/4/1903, 12/8/1903, 12/11/1903, 12/15/1903; SEN, 59th Congress, 1st Session, *Senate Documents*, vol. 8, 129–33, 218–19, 223–24; SEN, 58th Congress, 2d Session, Executive C, *Nomination of Leonard Wood to Be Major-General*, 399–411, 608–9, 618–19, 627–29; SEN, 58th Congress, 2d Session, Executive No. 2, *Nomination of Leonard Wood*, 21–24; Stone, *Fifty Years a Journalist*, 230–32.

94. SEN, 58th Congress, 2d Session, Executive C, *Nomination of Leonard Wood to Be Major-General*, 403–11. In 1902 the Associated Press was located in the Western Union Building at 193 Broadway while the Pinkerton offices were at 57 Broadway, both in lower Manhattan. See *NYT*, 4/6/1914; *Trow's Business Directory of Greater New York*, vol. 5 (New York, 1902), 404; and Stone, *Fifty Years a Journalist*, 230–32.

95. *NYT*, 2/16/1904, 2/18/1904, 3/19/1904; Foraker, *Notes of a Busy Life*, vol. 2, 414–16; Malone, *Dictionary of American Biography*, vol. 20, 467–69; Hagedorn, *Leonard Wood*, vol. 2, 22–24, 30–36.

96. Hagedorn, *Leonard Wood*, vol. 1, 404–9; Jack McCallum, *Leonard Wood: Rough Rider, Surgeon, Architect of American Imperialism* (New York, 2006), 207–11, 235–37; Mark Twain, "Major General Wood, M.D.," in Jim Zwick, ed., *Mark Twain's Weapons of Satire: Anti-Imperialist Writings on the Philippine-American War* (Syracuse, 1992), 154–55.

97. *MT*, 4/12/1902.

98. Letter from Frank Cairns to William H. Taft, August 9, 1906, Reel 59; letter from William H. Taft to F. S. Cairns, August 13, 1906, Reel 59; letter from F. S. Cairns to Ralph O. Sheward, August 31, 1906, Reel 79, WHT.

99. Letter from F. S. Cairns, June 28, 1906, Reel 58, WHT; *New York Daily News*, 6/8/1906, 6/11/1906, 6/12/1906.

100. Letter from F. S. Cairns, October 12, 1906, Reel 61, WHT.

101. Letter from F. S. Cairns, August 23, 1906, Reel 60, WHT.

102. W. Cameron Forbes, Journals, vol. 1, June 27, 1905, vol. 3, April 20, 1909, WCF; letter from James J. Rafferty, September 9, 1915, Box 40, File: McCoy Case, *U.S. vs. Henry B. McCoy*, FBH; Bellairs, *As It Is in the Philippines*, 54–55; letter from H. B. McCoy, April 30, 1904, Reel 43, WHT; letter from W. Morgan Shuster to Henry C. Ide, October 25, 1903, Reel 41, WHT.

103. W. Cameron Forbes, Journals, Volume 3, April 20, 1909, WCF; letter from F. S. Cairns to William H. Taft, April 16, 1908, Reel 79, WHT; letter from Secret Service Agent, Customs, to the Chief Secret Service, June 12, 1907, Reel 79, WHT; statement of F. S. Cairns, Manila, January 24, 1908, Reel 79, WHT; *United States v. Henry B. McCoy*, case no. 3594, Court of First Instance, Manila, Box 40, File: McCoy Case, U.S. vs. Henry B. McCoy, FBH; *MT*, 12/13/1907, 3/19/1908.

104. *MT*, 12/12/1907, 12/16/1907, 1/15/1908, 2/8/1908, 2/10/1908, 3/17/1908, 3/18/1908, 3/19/1908, 4/2/1908, 4/3/1908, 4/4/1908; *United States v. Henry B. McCoy*, case no. 3594, Court of First Instance, Manila, Box 40, File: McCoy Case, U.S. vs. Henry B. McCoy, FBH; letter from James J. Rafferty, September 9, 1915, Box 40, File: McCoy Case, U.S. vs. Henry B. McCoy, FBH; W. Cameron Forbes, Journals, vol. 3, April 20, 1909, WCF.

105. *MT*, 10/25/1909, 11/2/1909.

106. Letter from J. G. Harbord to Gen. H. T. Allen, December 31, 1907, Box 9, File: 1907 July–Dec, HTA; letter from Harry Bandholtz to General Henry T. Allen, May 24, 1907, Reel 68, WHT; Cullinane, "*Ilustrado* Politics," 418–19; Gleeck, *The American Governors-General*, 98–109, 116–17.

107. *PFP*, 1/16/1909, 8; Sullivan, *Exemplar of Americanism*, 237; Gleeck, *The American Governors-General*, 107–10; letter from William H. Taft to Dean C. Worcester, December 27, 1913, Reel 522, WHT.

108. Letter from Wm. H. Taft to W. Morgan Shuster, February 16, 1911, Box 1, W. Morgan Shuster Papers, Manuscript Division, U.S. Library of Congress; *NYT*, 2/11/1911, 4/16/1911; K. S. Maclachlan, "Economic Development, 1921–1979," in Peter Avery, G. R. C. Hambly, and C. P. Melville, eds., *The Cambridge History of Iran: From Nadir Shah to the Islamic Republic*, vol. 7 (Cambridge, 1991), 609; W. Morgan Shuster, *The Strangling of Persia: A Personal Narrative* (New York, 1912), 6–10.

109. *CA*, 10/08/1911; *NYT*, 7/31/1911, 8/20/1911, 11/26/1911, 11/29/1911, 12/1/1911, 12/21/1911, 12/23/1911; *Times* (London), 1/10/1912, 1/15/1912, 1/27/1912, 1/30/1912, 1/31/1912; *Independent*, November 23, 1911, 1153–55; Elisha Douglass, "Anglo-Russian Friction, 1907–1911, and the Morgan Shuster Affair" (ms, June 1947), 6–18, 38–40, 42–46, 52–55, Box 1, W. Morgan Shuster Papers; Shuster, *The Strangling of Persia*, xviii–lii, 69–70, 190–91, 226–30, 282–318, 358–66, 372, 392–93; letter from F. S. Cairns to W. H. Taft, August 9, 1911, Reel 424, WHT.

110. *CA*, 10/08/1911; *NYT*, 1/1/1912, 1/12/1912, 1/19/1912, 1/30/1912, 2/23/1912, 2/25/1912, 2/27/1912, 3/1/1912, 3/2/1912, 7/7/1912; *Times* (London), 10/18/1911, 11/10/1911, 11/11/1911, 11/18/1911, 11/29/1911, 11/30/1911, 12/4/1911, 1/10/1912, 1/15/1912, 1/27/1912, 1/30/1912, 1/31/1912; letter from F. S. Cairns to W. H. Taft, August 9, 1911, Reel 424, WHT; Gleeck, *The American Governors-General*, 127–33; Shuster, *The Strangling of Persia*, 223–25, 319–25.

111. See, for example, letter from William H. Taft to Right Rev. C. H. Brent, October 13, 1904, Reel 483; letter from C. H. Brent to My Dear Secretary, October 17, 1904, Reel 46; letter from C. H. Brent to W. H. Taft, October 31, 1904, Reel 46; letter from Wm. H. Taft to the Right Rev. C. H. Brent, May 20, 1905, Reel 485, WHT.

112. W. Cameron Forbes, Journals, vol. 2, October 3, 1907, vol. 4, March 3, 1911, WCF; Gleeck, *The Manila Americans*, 43.

Chapter 4. Paramilitary Pacification

1. Journal of Gen. Allen, Feb 10, 1905–April 26, 1905, 22–24, Box 1, File: 1905 Feb–April, HTA.

2. WD, *RPC 1903*, part 3, 11–12, 34–37; WD, *RPC 1904*, part 3, 34–38, 47–48; WD, *RPC 1905*, part 3, 3, 141; WD, *RPC 1908*, part 2, 379–82; *Army and Navy Journal* (New York), July 15, 1905; Edgar G. Bellairs, *As It Is in the Philippines* (New York, 1902), 234; letter from M. Davis to General Harry H. Bandholtz, October 24, 1907, Reel 2, HHB.

3. Henry Parker Willis, *Our Philippine Problem: A Study of American Colonial Policy* (New York, 1905), 130–34.

4. SEN, 56th Congress, 1st Session, Document No. 138, *Report of the Philippine Commission to the President, January 31, 1900*, vol. 1 (Washington, DC, 1900), 67–69.

5. WD, *RPC 1904*, part 3, 28.

6. WD, *RPC 1903*, part 3, 146.

7. WD, *RPC 1904*, part 3, 28, 74, 101–8; Artemio Ricarte, *Memoirs of General Artemio Ricarte* (Manila, 1992), 122–30; David R. Sturtevant, *Popular Uprisings in the Philippines, 1840–1940* (Ithaca, 1976), 199.

8. Michael Cullinane, "*Ilustrado* Politics: The Response of the Filipino Educated Elite to American Colonial Rule, 1898–1907," PhD diss, University of Michigan, 1989, 123–28, 170–73, 487–88; HR, *ARWD 1903*, vol. 5: *RPC*, 36–37; George A. Malcolm, *American Colonial Careerist: Half a Century of Official Life and Personal Experience in the Philippines and Puerto Rico* (Boston, 1957), 180, 223.

9. Letter to A. C. Carson, April 18, 1907, Reel 2, HHB.

10. Dagohob was the illegitimate son of a Spanish friar from Masbate. He came to Samar as secretary to a Filipino peace negotiator in 1902, just as the revolutionary forces under General Vicente Lukban were collapsing. WD, *RPC 1905*, part 3, 4–5, 28–31, 84, 89–90; letter to W. Cameron Forbes, March 5, 1905, Box 8, File: 1905 Jan–Apr, HTA; letter to Governor, May 25, 1905, Box 8, File: 1905 May–Aug, HTA; *MCN*, 12/24/1904; letter from Henry T. Allen to W. H. Taft, June 30, 1905, Reel 51, WHT.

11. *MCN*, 12/14/1904, 12/24/1904; *MT*, 12/20/1904, 12/24/1904, 12/27/1904; letter from Henry T. Allen to W. H. Taft, June 30, 1905, Reel 51, WHT.

12. *MT*, 2/4/1905; letter from Gurney to Governor-General Francis B. Harrison, n.d., Box 39, File: Traps etc. used by the Pulajans, FBH.

13. Letter from Henry T. Allen to W. H. Taft, June 30, 1905, Reel 51, WHT.

14. Letter to Colonel Arthur Murray, February 1, 1902, Box 7, File: 1902 Jan–Mar; letter to W. Cameron Forbes, March 5, 1905, Box 8, File: 1905 Jan–Apr, HTA.

15. Journal of Gen. Allen, February 10, 1905 –April 26, 1905, 29 –32, 38, Box 1, File: 1905 Feb–April, HTA.

16. Letter to W. Cameron Forbes, March 5, 1905; letter to Luke E. Wright, March 5, 1905, Box 8, File: 1905 Jan–Apr, HTA.

17. Letter to Luke E. Wright, March 11, 1905, Box 8, File: 1905 Jan–Apr, HTA.

18. Journal of Gen. Allen, February 10, 1905 –April 26, 1905, 22–24, Box 1, File: 1905 Feb–April, HTA; *MT*, 3/1/1905, 3/3/1905, 3/4/1905, 3/16/1905; Stanley Portal Hyatt, *The Diary of a Soldier of Fortune: His Experiences as Engineer* (London, 1910), 306 –56.

19. WD, *RPC 1905*, part 3, 4 –5, 28 –31, 91–92; *MT*, 4/1/1905.

20. Telegram from Wright to Allen, Constabulary Catbalogan, May 23, 1905, Box 8, File: 1905 May–Aug, HTA.

21. Telegram from Scott, Colonel, to General Allen, Tacloban Leyte, May 24, 1905, Box 8, File: 1905 May–Aug; letter from Frank A. Prescott to General Henry T. Allen, May 15, 1905, Box 8, File: 1905 May–Aug, HTA.

22. Letter to Governor, May 25, 1905, Box 8, File: 1905 May–Aug, HTA.

23. *Annual Report of Major General Henry C. Corbin, Adjutant General Commanding the Philippine Divisions for Fiscal Year 1905* (Manila, 1905), 41–45, Box 2, File: Adjutant General, Reports 1898 –1906, HCP; *MA*, 6/11/1905; *MT*, 1/4/1905, 5/23/1905; Heath Twichell Jr., *Allen: The Biography of an Army Officer, 1859–1930* (New Brunswick, 1974), 140–41; Brian McAllister Linn, *The Guardians of Empire: The U.S. Army in the Pacific* (Chapel Hill, 1997), 43.

24. *Army and Navy Journal*, June 10, 1905; letter to Wm. H. Taft, December 29, 1906, Box 9, File: 1906 Oct–Dec, HTA.

25. Hyatt, *The Diary of a Soldier of Fortune*, 348 –56.

26. Letter from Theodore Schwan, February 16, 1900, Box 2, File: Schwan, Theodore, 1899 – 1902, HCP.

27. Letter to the President, November 7, 1901, Box 7, File: 1901 June–Dec, HTA.

28. Letter from Adna R. Chaffee, March 22, 1902, Box 1, File: Chaffee, Adna R., Jan–Mar 1902, HCP.

29. To extract intelligence from reluctant Filipino civilians, American soldiers used the "water cure"—a form of torture done by forcing water into victim's lungs, thus inducing a sense of drowning, and then pounding on his stomach until he regurgitated the water. Despite some differences in detail, the water cure is quite similar to the contemporary CIA interrogation technique called "water boarding." Letter from Adna R. Chaffee, February 28, 1902, Box 1, File: Chaffee, Adna R., Jan–Mar 1902, HCP; letters from Luke E. Wright to William H. Taft, February 13, 1902, Reel 34, February 13, 1902, February 21, 1902, March 29, 1902, Reel 35, April 11, 1902, April 19, 1902, Reel 36, WHT; *NYT*, 4/11/1902; *MT*, 5/15/1902; Twichell, *Allen*, 144.

30. Major Emanuel A. Bajá, *Philippine Police System and Its Problems* (Manila, 1933), 127–30, 395 –96, 399 –403; Brian McAllister Linn, *The Philippine War, 1899–1902* (Lawrence, 2000), 300–305; WD, *Acts of the Philippine Commission [Acts Nos. 425–949, inclusive]*, vol. 8 (Washington, DC, 1904), 363 –68.

31. Linn, *The Philippine War*, 300–305; letter to J. Franklin Bell, April 25, 1902, Box 7, File: 1902 Apr–June, HTA; HR, *ARWD 1905*, vol. 7: *RPC*, part 3, 6 –7; *MCN*, 12/10/1904; Reynaldo Clemeña Ileto, *Pasyon and Revolution: Popular Movements in the Philippines, 1840–1910* (Quezon City, 1979), 237 –44.

32. Letter to Governor, May 13, 1904, Box 8, File: 1904 Mar–May, HTA.

33. George D. Long, To: Executive Inspector, Philippine Constabulary, June 30, 1912, Reel 5, HHB; WD, *RPC 1904*, part 3, 69.

34. WD, *RPC 1904*, part 3, 68–71.

35. *MCN*, 10/14/1904.

36. HR, *ARWD 1905*, vol. 7: *RPC*, part 3, 6–7; George Y. Coats, "The Philippine Constabulary, 1901–1917," PhD diss., Ohio State University, 1968, 173; Lewis E. Gleeck Jr., *The American Governors-General and High Commissioners in the Philippines: Proconsuls, Nation-Builders, and Politicians* (Quezon City, 1986), 48–49; *MT*, 1/9/1905, 1/25/1905.

37. Letter to Wm. H. Taft, March 11, 1905, Box 8, File: 1905 Jan–Apr, HTA.

38. Coats, "The Philippine Constabulary," 168–71; HR, *ARWD 1905*, vol. 12: *RPC*, 7–8; WD, *RPC 1905*, part 3, 130–31; *MCN*, 2/1/1905.

39. WD, *RPC 1905*, part 3, 128–30.

40. Coats, "The Philippine Constabulary," 170–75; HR, *ARWD 1905*, vol. 7: *RPC*, 7–9; WD, *RPC 1905*, part 3, 54.

41. James H. Blount, *The American Occupation of the Philippines* (New York, 1913), 508–14; Peter W. Stanley, *A Nation in the Making: The Philippines and the United States, 1899–1921* (Cambridge, 1974), 122–23; Coats, "The Philippine Constabulary," 178–81; *MCN*, 3/3/1905.

42. W. Cameron Forbes, Journals, vol. 1, August 22, 1904, January 24, 1905, WCF.

43. Gleeck, *The American Governors-General*, 48–49.

44. W. Cameron Forbes, Journals, vol. 1, April 18, 1905, WCF; *MT*, 4/11/1905; *MCN*, 3/3/1905; Ruby R. Paredes, "The Partido Federal, 1900–1907: Political Collaboration in Colonial Manila," PhD diss., University of Michigan, 1989, 360–61.

45. Coats, "The Philippine Constabulary," 181–84; WD, *RPC 1906*, part 2, 200, 225, 240; WD, *RPC 1907*, part 2, 291–92.

46. WD, *RPC 1905*, part 3, 132–33.

47. Memorandum for Colonel Bandholtz, n.d., Reel 1; Record of Harry Hill Bandholtz, n.d., Reel 7; letter to Brigadier-General Henry T. Allen, December 14, 1905, Reel 1; letter to Colonel J. G. Harbord, December 25, 1905, Reel 1, HHB.

48. 1st Lieut. R. Crame, August 1, 1904, Reel 8, HHB; R. H. Van Deman, To: Intelligence Officer, Pila, Laguna, December 23, 1901, December 26, 1901, Entry 4755, RG 395, NARA.

49. *MT*, 9/18/1905, 3/2/1906; *ER*, 10/27/1906.

50. Superintendent, Information Division, Memorandum for Acting Director, July 2, 1912, Reel 8, HHB; letter to Acting Director, Bureau of Constabulary, March 7, 1906, Reel 7, HHB; *MT*, 3/2/1906; *MCN*, 3/3/1906; *ER*, 3/10/1906; W. Cameron Forbes, Journals, vol. 1, March 7, 1906, WCF; Letter to A. C. Carson, April 18, 1907, Reel 2, HHB.

51. Coats, "The Philippine Constabulary," 185–87; *MT*, 4/5/1906, 4/27/1906.

52. Letter to Colonel J. G. Harbord, July 28, 1906, Reel 1, HHB; letter to Colonel J. G. Harbord, September 27, 1906, Reel 1, HHB; letter to A. C. Carson, April 18, 1907, Reel 2, HHB; Coats, "The Philippine Constabulary," 187–88; U.S. vs. Macario Sakay, no. 3621, July 26, 1907, *Philippine Reports*, vol. 8 (Manila, 1908), 254–63; *MA*, 11/20/1906, 11/21/1906; *MT*, 6/18/1906, 7/14/1906, 7/25/1906, 9/10/1908; *CN*, 7/14/1906, 7/22/1906, 11/20/1906, 12/22/1906.

53. W. Cameron Forbes, Journals, vol. 1, April 12, 1905, April 13, 1905, WCF.

54. Ibid., April 13, 1905, WCF.

55. Lewis E. Gleeck Jr., *The Manila Americans (1901–1964)* (Manila, 1977), 25–26, 64–65; Cullinane, "*Ilustrado* Politics," 154–62.

56. Paredes, "The Partido Federal," 358–64, 366–67.

57. Ibid., 361–62.

58. *ER*, 1/16/1905, 1/23/1905, 3/6/1905; *MCN*, 1/19/1905, 2/28/1905.

59. *ER*, 5/11/1905.

60. *ER*, 6/7/1905; *MT*, 6/13/1905; *MA*, 6/24/1905.

61. *MT*, 6/9/1905, 6/13/1905; Teodoro M. Kalaw, *Aide-de-Camp to Freedom* (Manila, 1965), 44–45.

62. *MT*, 6/23/1905; Cullinane, "*Ilustrado* Politics," 203–4; WD, *RPC 1905*, part 3, 133.

63. Letter to General W. H. Carter, June 22, 1905, Box 8, File: 1905 May–Aug, HTA.

64. *ER*, 7/24/1905, 8/7/1905; *CN*, 7/27/1905, 7/28/1905, 7/30/1905; *MT*, 7/8/1905, 8/3/1905.

65. *CN*, 9/3/1905.

66. *MT*, 9/22/1905, 9/23/1905, 9/29/1905; *CN*, 9/23/1905; *ER*, 9/30/1905.

67. E. Arsenio Manuel, *Dictionary of Philippine Biography,* vol. 1 (Quezon City, 1955), 141–42; letter from W. Morgan Shuster to William H. Taft, August 30, 1905, Reel 52, WHT; Paredes, "The Partido Federal," 427–29; Rodney J. Sullivan, *Exemplar of Americanism: The Philippine Career of Dean C. Worcester* (Ann Arbor, 1991), 137–38; *MT,* 6/3/1905.

68. Letters from Henry T. Allen to W. H. Taft, June 30, 1905, Reel 51, November 20, 1905, Reel 53, WHT.

69. WD, *RPC 1906,* part 2, 234–35; letter from Henry T. Allen to Chief of Fifth Constabulary District, September 1, 1905, Reel 52, WHT; *CN,* 7/25/1905, 10/1/1905.

70. WD, *RPC 1906.* part 2, 198, 204, 245; Annual Report of the Director of Constabulary for the Fiscal Year Ending June 30, 1909, Philippine Commission Reports 1909, vol. 3, 1470, vol. 957, BIA; HR, *ARWD 1906,* vol. 3, 209; *CN,* 10/1/1905; *ER,* 11/9/1905, 11/17/1905; *MT,* 1/5/1906.

71. WD, *RPC 1905,* part 3, 31, 64; *MT,* 8/18/1905; *ER,* 8/21/1905, 9/11/1905.

72. WD, *RPC 1906,* part 2, 203.

73. WD, *RPC 1907,* part 2, 338–39; PI, *ARDC 1909,* 15; PI, *ARDC 1910,* 14.

74. Cullinane, "*Ilustrado* Politics," 203–5; Paredes, "The Partido Federal," 435; *MT,* 1/20/1906, 2/4/1906, 3/15/1907; *CN,* 10/1/1905, 2/25/1906, 2/26/1906, 2/27/1907; *ER,* 2/27/1906; W. Cameron Forbes, Journals, vol. 4, March 5, 1911, WCF; letter from L. R. Wiffley to Henry T. Allen, March 16, 1906, Reel 156, Reel 522, WHT; *MT,* 6/8/1921.

75. Gleeck, *The American Governors-General,* 53–55, 62; letter from William H. Taft to Dean C. Worcester, December 27, 1913, Reel 522, WHT.

76. Gleeck, *The American Governors-General,* 84; W. Cameron Forbes, Journals, vol. 2, October 28, 1906, WCF; WD, *RPC 1907,* part 2, 267, 291; *CN,* 2/4/1906; *MT,* 10/27/1906; *ER,* 10/27/1906; *MA,* 10/28/1906, 10/30/1906; letter to Colonel D. J. Baker, Jr., November 8, 1906, Reel 1, HHB; letter from D. J. Baker, Jr. to Bandholtz, February 6, 1907, HHB; letter to Captain D. J. Baker, Jr., March 22, 1907, Reel 1, HHB; letter from Wm H. Taft to Gen. Henry T. Allen, November 21, 1906, Box 9, File: 1906 Oct–Dec, HTA.

77. Letter from Henry T. Allen to Wm. H. Taft, December 29, 1906, Box 9, File: 1906 Oct–Dec; letter from Henry T. Allen to Governor, February 20, 1906, Box 9, File: 1906 Jan–May; letter from W. Cameron Forbes to General Henry T. Allen, April 2, 1907, Box 9, File: 1907 April–June, HTA.

78. Stanley, *A Nation in the Making,* 122–23.

79. *MA,* 10/27/1906.

80. Letter from D. J. Baker, Jr., August 6, 1907, Reel 2, HHB.

81. Letter from W. Cameron Forbes to General H. H. Bandholtz, July 6 1907, Reel 7, HHB.

82. Letter to Captain Julius C. Buttner, September 11, 1907, Reel 2, HHB.

83. Letter to Lieut. R. A. Duckworth-Ford, n.d., Reel 5, HHB.

84. James F. Smith to Brigadier General H. H. Bandholtz, November 17, 1907, Box No. 59, Series 7, MLQ.

85. WD, *RPC 1907,* part 2, 267.

86. H. H. Bandholtz, To: The Adjutant, Lucena, December 14, 1901, Entry 2354 (2), RG 395, NARA.

87. Michael Cullinane, "The Politics of Collaboration in Tayabas Province: The Early Political Career of Manuel Luis Quezon, 1903–1906," in Peter W. Stanley, ed., *Reappraising an Empire: New Perspectives on Philippine-American History* (Cambridge, 1984), 69–81.

88. WD, *RPC 1903,* part 3, 38, 100–101; WD, *RPC 1904,* part 3, 88; telegram from Bandholtz to Executive Secretary, August 18, 1902, Reel 7, HHB; telegram from Bandholtz to Executive Secretary, September 3, 1902, Reel 7, HHB; letter to Executive Secretary, January 15, 1903, Reel 1, HHB.

89. WD, *RPC 1903,* part 3, 138–39; WD, *RPC 1904,* part 3, 82–85.

90. Manuel Luis Quezon, *The Good Fight* (New York, 1946), 86–89, 105; letter from H. H. Bandholtz to William H. Taft, August 6, 1908, Reel 90, WHT.

91. Carlos Quirino, *Quezon: Paladin of Philippine Freedom* (Manila, 1971), 65–70; Quezon, *The Good Fight,* 101–2; *MT,* 7/28/1904.

92. Letter from Manuel L. Quezon, November 20, 1907, Reel 8; letter from D. J. Baker, Jr. to Bandholtz, February 6, 1907, Reel 1; letter from J. G. Harbord to Gen. H. H. Bandholtz, April 29, 1907, Reel 2; Confidential Memorandum for General Carter, August 30, 1909, Reel 3; letter to J. G.

Harbord, September 14, 1909, Reel 3; letter from Henry T. Allen to Brig. G. H. H. Bandholtz, December 23, 1909, Reel 3; letter to Gervasio Unson, June 25, 1910, Reel 3; W. H. Simpson, Receipt, October 4 1905, Reel 10; Memorandum Relative to Proposition to Purchase Polillo Claims, n.d., Reel 10; letter to M. F. Lowenstein, December 10, 1909, Reel 10; extract from the Report of M. E. Randolf Hix, Coal Expert of the Philippine Government, with Reference to the Coal Measures on the Island of Polillo, I, n.d., Reel 10, HHB.

93. Letter from Chas. H. Crooks to Col. Bandholtz, January 31, 1907, Reel 1; letter from H. H. Bandholtz to Charles H. Crooks, February 7, 1907, Reel 1; letter from G. Unson to Col. H. H. Bandholtz, February 13, 1907, Reel 1; letter from G. Unson to Charles H. Crooks, February 13, 1907, Reel 1; letter from H. H. Bandholtz to Mrs. Gertrude B. McCabe, May 18, 1914, Reel 8; letter from Manuel [Quezon] to General Bandholtz, May 16, 1914, Reel 8, HHB.

94. Letter from Harry Bandholtz to Henry T. Allen, May 16, 1907, Reel 68, WHT; Cullinane, "*Ilustrado* Politics," 495–501.

95. Letter from J. G. Harbord to General Henry T. Allen, June 10, 1908, Box 9, File: 1908 May–June, HTA.

96. Letter to President William H. Taft, November 13, 1909, Confidential Letter Box, vol. 1, WCF; Cullinane, "*Ilustrado* Politics," 500–501.

97. Letter to C. R. Edwards, May 17, 1909, Reel 3, HHB.

98. WD, *RPC 1906*, part 2, 226; WD, *RPC 1907*, part 2, 270, 292, 302; *MT*, 7/17/1906.

99. WD, *RPC 1907*, part 2, 270, 292, 302; letter from J. G. Harbord to Bandholtz, April 24, 1907, Reel 2, HHB.

100. WD, *RPC 1905*, part 3, 88–89; WD, *RPC 1906*, part 2, 252; WD, *RPC 1907*, part 2, 293; *MT*, 7/24/1906, 8/1/1906.

101. WD, *RPC 1907*, part 2, 294–95, 310–11; WD, *RPC 1908*, part 2, 402–3; *El Tiempo*, 8/8/1907; Evelyn Tan Cullamar, *Babaylanism in Negros: 1896–1907* (Quezon City, 1986), 65.

102. WD, *RPC 1905*, part 3, 92–93.

103. WD, *RPC 1906*, part 2, 260–61.

104. WD, *RPC 1907*, part 2, 308–9.

105. Letter to Dr. J. Paul Goode, November 22, 1911, Reel 4; letter from J. G. Harbord to Bandholtz, September 4, 1907, Reel 2, HHB.

106. Letter to Captain D. J. Baker, Jr., October 6, 1907, Reel 2, HHB.

107. Charles H. Brent, "Religious Conditions in the Philippine Islands," File: July to December 1904, Box 6, CHB.

108. Ricardo Zarco, "The Philippine Chinese and Opium Addiction," in Alfonso Felix Jr., ed., *The Chinese in the Philippines*, vol. 2 (Manila, 1969), 100–101; HR, *ARWD 1903*, vol. 6, 96; Andrew R. Wilson, *Ambition and Identity: Chinese Merchant Elites in Colonial Manila, 1880–1916* (Honolulu, 2004), 195–96; Emma H. Blair and James A. Robertson, eds., *The Philippine Islands, 1493–1898*, vol. 52 (Cleveland, 1907), 318; Fedor Jagor, *Reisen in den Philippinen* (Berlin, 1873), 309–10.

109. International Opium Commission, *Report of the International Opium Commission, Shanghai, China, February 1 to February 26, 1909* (Shanghai, 1909), vol. 2, 21–26; Wilson, *Ambition and Identity*, 195–96; Anne L. Foster, "Models for Governing: Opium and Colonial Policies in Southeast Asia, 1898–1910," in Julian Go and Anne L. Foster, eds., *The American Colonial State in the Philippines: Global Perspectives* (Durham, 2003), 97–101; HR, *ARWD 1903*, vol. 5, 63; HR, *ARWD 1903*, vol. 6, 96; HR, *ARWD 1906*, vol. 7: *RPC*, part 1, 60; W. Morgan Shuster, Administrative Circular No. 129, December 13, 1902, BIA no. 1023–4, Entry 5, BIA; letter from Homer Stuntz to Dr. Wilbur F. Crafts, May 2, 1903, BIA no. 1023–17, Entry 5, BIA; letter from Homer Stuntz to William H. Taft, May 29, 1903, BIA no. 1023–81, Entry 5, BIA; cable from Taft to Secretary of War, June 9, 1903, BIA no. 1023–25, Entry 5, BIA.

110. HR, *ARWD 1906*, vol. 7: *RPC*, part 1, 60; Secretary of War to President, March 9, 1906, BIA no. 1023–141, Entry 5, BIA.

111. HR, *ARWD 1904*, vol. 12: *RPC*, part 2, 16, 142; HR, *ARWD 1905*, vol. 11: *RPC*, part 2, 86–87; HR, *ARWD 1906*, vol. 9: *RPC*, part 3, 99; HR, *WDAR 1909*, vol. 7: *The Philippine Commission*, 178; Wilson, *Ambition and Identity*, 155, 195–96; Foster, "Models for Governing," 99–101; letter from P. G. McDonnell to Civil Governor, July 11, 1903, BIA no. 1023–84, Entry 5, BIA.

112. Letter from Charles H. Brent to William H. Taft, February 6, 1904, File: Jan–June 1904, Box 6, CHB; letter from C. H. Brent to My Dear Governor, July 24, 1903, Reel 40; October 16, 1903, Reel 41, WHT.

113. WD, *RPC 1903*, part 3, 58–59; Edward Champe Carter, José Albert, and Charles Henry Brent, *Report of the Committee Appointed by the Philippine Commission to Investigate the Use of Opium and the Traffic Therein* (Washington, DC, 1905), 43, 47–49, 129–50, 155–57, 168–69; *NYT*, 9/22/1904; cable from Secretary of War to Wright, January 8, 1905, BIA no. 1023/111, Entry 5, BIA.

114. *MT*, 3/2/1905, 3/2/1908; *NYT*, 3/12/1911; International Opium Commission, *Report*, vol. 2, 21–26; David Musto, *The American Disease: Origins of Narcotic Control* (New Haven, 1973), 25–28; Gary Reid and Genevieve Costigan, *Revisiting the 'Hidden Epidemic': A Situation Assessment of Drug Use in Asia in the Context of HIV/AIDS* (Fairfield, 2002), 170; HR, 59th Congress, 2d Session, *House Documents in 112 Volumes*, vol. 11 (Washington, DC, 1907), 188–96; Philippine Commission, *Public Laws Passed by the Philippine Commission during the Period September 1, 1906 to October 15, 1907, Comprising Acts Nos. 1537 to 1800, Inclusive*, vol. 6 (Manila, 1908), 406–16; HR, *ARWD 1906*, vol. 9: *RPC*, part 3, 98–100; HR, *ARWD 1906*, vol. 7: *RPC*, part 1, 60–62; Zarco, "The Philippine Chinese and Opium Addiction," 102–7; HR, *WDAR 1908*, vol. 8: *The Philippine Commission*, part 2, 6; Ellis Cromwell, "Comment on Enforcement of the New Opium Law, Act 1761," January 28, 1908, BIA no. 1023/64, Entry 5, BIA.

115. Victor Heiser, *An American Doctor's Odyssey: Adventures in Forty-five Countries* (New York, 1936), 167–70; Ignacio Villamor, *Criminality in the Philippine Islands: 1903–1908* (Manila, 1909), 79, 81–82; *MB*, Chinese Supplement, February 21, 1923; Kenton J. Clymer, *Protestant Missionaries in the Philippines, 1898–1916: An Inquiry into the American Colonial Mentality* (Urbana, 1986), 52; Zarco, "The Philippine Chinese and Opium Addiction," 102–3; HR, *WDAR 1907*, vol. 7: *The Philippine Commission*, vol. 2, 18, 83; HR, *WDAR 1908*, vol. 8: *The Philippine Commission*, part 2, 25–27, 108–11, 756–57; HR, *WDAR 1909*, vol. 7: *The Philippine Commission*, 102, 178–79; letter from John W. Green to Secretary to the Governor General, June 5, 1926, BIA no. 1023/272-B, BIA; letter from Rev. Hobart E. Studley to John S. Hord, January 1, 1908, BIA no. 1023/160, BIA.

116. International Opium Commission, *Report*, vol. 2, 22–26; Foster, "Models for Governing," 111–12.

117. William T. Nolting, "Memorandum Showing Results Obtained in Enforcement of Laws Aimed at the Total Suppression of the Opium Habit in the Philippine Islands," n.d., BIA no. 1023/192, BIA.

118. *CA*, 4/13/1910, 4/14/1910.

119. *CA*, 1/13/1911, 1/19/1911.

120. John H. Osmeña, interview with Michael Cullinane, Cebu City, March 23, 1974; Cebu Protocolos, Document 128, July 26, 1893, 1406, 694–97, PNA; Cebu Protocolos, Document 266, September 21, 1893, 1406, 848–61, PNA; Resil B. Mojares, *The Man Who Would Be President: Sergio Osmeña and Philippine Politics* (Cebu, 1986), 7–8.

121. WD, *GGPI 1919*, 25–26.

122. Letter from Leonard Wood, February 9, 1922, WCF; *MB*, 2/14/1921 (Chinese Supplement), 2/21/1923; letter from John W. Green to Secretary to the Governor General, June 5, 1926, BIA 1023/272-B, BIA; letter from Rafael Crame to Secretary of Justice, June 24, 1921, BIA 1023/238-C, BIA.

123. HR, *GGPI 1925*, 266, 273; letter from V. Aldanese to Secretary of Finance, June 7, 1926, BIA 1023/272-B, BIA; letter from A. Parker Hitchens to Richard Ely, June 15, 1926, BIA 1023/272-C, BIA.

124. Villamor, *Criminality in the Philippine Islands*, 42; Greg Bankoff, *Crime, Society, and the State in the Nineteenth Century Philippines* (Manila, 1996), 27, 46, 51–55.

125. Villamor, *Criminality in the Philippine Islands*, 42; Bankoff, *Crime, Society, and the State*, 27, 46, 51–55.

126. *El Comercio*, 3/12/1896, 3/13/1896, 3/14/1896, 3/15/1896; Wito Tuason Quimson, "The Post Don Severo Tuason," in *Teresa de la Paz and Her Two Husbands: A Gathering of Four Families* (Manila, 1996), 40.

127. Victor Buencamino, *Memoirs of Victor Buencamino* (Mandaluyong, 1977), 6–23.

128. *MT*, 8/21/1899.

129. Filomeno V. Aguilar Jr., *Clash of Spirits: The History of Power and Sugar Planter Hegemony on a Visayan Island* (Honolulu, 1998), 192.

130. Frank Hindman Golay, *Face of Empire: United States-Philippine Relations, 1898–1946* (Quezon City, 1997), 96; HR, *ARWD 1903*, vol. 8: *Acts of the Philippine Commission*, 90, 384–85.

131. Gleeck, *The American Governors-General*, 78–79.

132. Jose Rizal, *Noli Me Tangere* (Makati, 1996), 406–8.

133. Clymer, *Protestant Missionaries in the Philippines*, 77.

134. Dean C. Worcester, *The Philippines Past and Present* (New York, 1930), 535.

135. George A. Malcolm, *The Commonwealth of the Philippines* (New York, 1936), 31.

136. WD, *RPC 1903*, part 3, 54, 58, 136; WD, *RPC 1904*, part 3, 68; WD, *RPC 1905*, part 3, 74–75; WD, *RPC 1906*, part 2, 272, 281; Memoranda for Colonel Harbord, n.d., File 1, Reel 2, HHB; letter from J. G. Harbord to Gen. H. H. Bandholtz, May 4, 1907, Reel 2, HHB.

137. *ER*, 4/7/1906, 4/17/1906; *MT*, 7/25/1906.

138. *MA*, 3/18/1906, 3/25/1906; Clymer, *Protestant Missionaries in the Philippines*, 167–69; *MT*, 5/12/1906, 6/16/1906; letter from Percy G. McDonnell to William H. Taft, August 3, 1906, Reel 59, WHT.

139. HR, *ARWD 1906*, vol. 10, 306, 363; Clymer, *Protestant Missionaries in the Philippines*, 168–69.

140. Villamor, *Criminality in the Philippine Islands*, 14, 73–74, 90.

141. HR, *WDAR 1907*, vol. 10, 440–43.

142. Agent 2, Confidential Report, March 29, 1910; Agent 6, Confidential Report, August 27, 1912, Reel 8, HHB.

143. United States vs. Prudencio Salaveria, no. 13678, November 12, 1918, *PSC 11/6/18–8/14/19*, vol. 39, 102–20; George A. Malcolm, *The Revised Ordinances of the City of Manila* (Manila, 1917), 320–22; George A. Malcolm, *The Revised Ordinances of the City of Manila* (Manila, 1927), 36–37; *PFP*, 8/30/1919, 4.

144. *MT*, 2/20/1908, 2/21/08, 2/22/1908, 2/24/1908; Clymer, *Protestant Missionaries in the Philippines*, 170.

145. Serafin E. Macaraig, *Community Problems: An Elementary Study of Philippine Social Conditions* (Manila, 1933), 188–95.

146. Camilo Osias, *The Filipino Way of Life: The Pluralized Philosophy* (Boston, 1940), 137–38.

147. Bajá, *Philippine Police System and Its Problems*, 367–68; WD, *GGPI 1919*, 41, 45; HR, *GGPI 1925*, 267, 273.

148. Agent 2, Confidential Report, April 29, 1910; Agent (-.), Confidential Report, May 27, 1910; M. Nicolas, Confidential Report, August 16, 1910; Superintendent, Memorandum for the Director, September 18, 1911; Agent 11, Confidential Report, January 22, 1912, Reel 8, HHB.

149. *PDI*, 10/6/2000.

150. Bajá, *Philippine Police System and Its Problems*, 349–54.

151. Ibid., 356, 369–71.

152. Ibid., 353–56, 372–74, 423–25, 428–29, 432–33, 467–68.

153. Ibid., 346–47; Aguilar, *Clash of Spirits*, 192–93; HR, *WDAR 1907*, vol. 10: *Acts of the Philippine Commission*, 440–43.

154. Cullinane, "The Politics of Collaboration in Tayabas Province," 59–84.

155. Letter from James A. Harbord to Manuel L. Quezon, July 14, 1913, File: Constabulary, Box 59, MLQ; letter from James A. Harbord to Manuel L. Quezon, November 28, 1913, File: Constabulary, Box 59, Series 7, MLQ; letter from Manuel Quezon to Honorable James L. Slayden, November 4, 1912, Book no. 1, DCW; letter from Manuel Quezon to Marlin E. Olmsted, December 3, 1912, Book no. 1, DCW.

156. Letter from James G. Harbord to Manuel L. Quezon, December 3, 1914, File: Constabulary, Box 59; letter from Manuel L. Quezon to Col. James G. Harbord, May 11, 1916, File: Constabulary, Series 7, Box 59, MLQ.

157. Letter from Manuel L. Quezon to Governor General Francis Burton Harrison, n.d. ca. 1914, File: Constabulary, Box 59, Series 7, MLQ.

158. Cadet Corps, *The Academy Scribe* (Manila, 1988), 19–23, 526.

Chapter 5. Constabulary Covert Operations

1. Letter to Captain Ralph Van Deman, General Staff, U.S.A., August 21, 1907, Reel 2, HHB; letter from J. G. Harbord to Bandholtz, August 26, 1907, Reel 2, HHB; letter to Major Henry T. Allen, September 11, 1907, Reel 2, HHB; *MT,* 8/21/1907, 8/22/1907, 8/23/1907, 8/24/1907, 8/26/1907, 10/19/1907; *ER,* 8/20/1907; *MA,* 8/23/1907, 8/24/1907; Lewis E. Gleeck Jr., *The Manila Americans (1901–1964)* (Manila, 1977), 57–58; HR, *WDAR 1907,* vol. 10: *Acts of the Philippine Commission,* 305–6; W. Cameron Forbes, Journals, vol. 2, August 23, 1907, WCF.

2. The statue to Bandholtz was erected at Budapest to honor him for preventing the looting of the National Museum by Rumanian troops at the end of World War I. American Hungarian People's Voice, "Monument Erected in Budapest, Hungary to the Perennial Memory of Major General Harry Hill Bandholtz, United States Army," Reel 7, HHB.

3. Registry Committee, Association of General and Flag Officers, *General and Flag Officers of the Philippines (1896–1983)* (Quezon City, 1983), 106; Jaime J. Bugarin, "Six Decades of Noble Soldiering," in Philippine Constabulary, *1960 Yearbook, Philippine Constabulary* (Manila, 1960), 20–21; Hector K. Villarroel, *Eminent Filipinos* (Quezon City, 1965), 82; E. Arsenio Manuel, *Dictionary of Philippine Biography,* vol. 1 (Quezon City, 1955), 136–38; Superintendent Information Division, Memorandum for the Director, November 8, 1909, Reel 8, HHB; *CA,* 11/1/1906; *PFP,* 1/12/1924; Colonel C. E. Nathorst, General Orders No. 1, January 3, 1927, Personal Name Information Files: Rafael Crame, Entry 21, BIA.

4. Letter to Colonel M. L. Hersey, April 1, 1913, Reel 5; Memorandum [Genealogy], August 12, 1912, Reel 7; Record of Harry Hill Bandholtz, Reel 7; Record of Harry Hill Bandholtz, U.S. Army, Reel 7; Record of Major General Harry Hill Bandholtz, United States Army, Reel 7, HHB.

5. Letter from American Museum of Natural History, To: Colonel Bandholtz, January 5, 1906, Reel 7; H. H. Bandholtz to M. L. Quezon, August 4, 1922, Reel 8, HHB.

6. Letter from Harry H. Bandholtz, To: John White, June 23, 1914, Reel 7; letter from Dr. Herman Ostrander, Kalamazoo State Hospital, To: Brig. Gen. H. H. Bandholtz, July 20, 1921, Reel 9; Memorandum, n.d., Reel 9; Harry to Hattie, April 6, 1925, Reel 7, HHB.

7. *Harry H. Bandholtz, plaintiff, vs. May C. Bandholtz, defendant,* Circuit Court for the County of St. Joseph, In Chancery, November 21, 1921, Reel 9, HHB.

8. Estimated Assets, March 25, 1922, H. H. Bandholtz U.S. Army, 185, Reel 8, HHB; Heath Twichell Jr., *Allen: The Biography of an Army Officer, 1859–1930* (New Brunswick, 1974), 259–62.

9. Letter from J. G. Harbord, July 9, 1907, Box 9, File: 1907 July–Dec, HTA.

10. Letter to Leonard Wood, October 30, 1911, Reel 8, HHB; letter to Colonel W. C. Rivers, October 17, 1911, Reel 4, HHB; Memorandum: Concerning Mission of Brigadier General H. H. Bandholtz to West Virginia for the Period August 25th to August 28th, 1921, Inclusive, August 29, 1921, Reel 9, HHB; *Truth White Pidgeon* (Michigan, n.d.); *Uj Nemzedé* (Budapest), January 29, 1920; "Monument Erected in Budapest, Hungary to the Perennial Memory of Major General Harry Hill Bandholtz," Reel 7, HHB.

11. Memoranda for Colonel Harbord, October 27, 1905, Reel 1; letter to A. C. Carson, April 18, 1907, Reel 2; Superintendent Information Division, Memorandum for the Director, November 8, 1909, Reel 8, HHB.

12. Letter from Maj. Gen. H. H. Bandholtz (ret.) to General Rafael Crame, October 2, 1924, Reel 7, HHB.

13. WD, *RPC 1904,* part 3, 3, 28.

14. R. Crame, Memorandum for the Director, August 6, 1908, Reel 8; Eleven, Report, August 24, 1909, Reel 8, HHB.

15. M. Nicolas, November 17, 1910; M. Nicolas, January 30, 1911, Reel 8, HHB.

16. Agent 22, Report, December 28, 1909, Reel 8, HHB.

17. Twenty-Two, June 4, 1910; Agent 22, Report, December 28, 1909; Superintendent Information Division, Memorandum for the Director, February 27, 1910, Reel 8, HHB.

18. Agent 2, Report, December 6, 1909; Agent (.), May 26, 1910, Reel 8, HHB. One document in the Bandholtz papers has a handwritten note identifying Agent (.) as Agent 2. See Agent 2, March 29, 1910, Reel 8, HHB.

19. Agent 11, March 1, 1910, Reel 8, HHB.

20. Agent 30, Subject: F. W. Holland, January 15, 1911, No. A14/0223; Director, Confidential Memorandum for the Secretary of Commerce and Police, May 27, 1911, Reel 4, HHB.

21. For a good example of this type of analysis, see Artemio Ricarte, *Memoirs of General Artemio Ricarte* (Manila, 1992), app. N, 157–216. The section on ex-general Mariano Noriel (193–95) indicates that Rafael Crame probably wrote this report.

22. R. Crame, Preface, "Compilation of Papers on Japanese Propagandism, vol. 2, October 19, 1907, to October 31, 1909"; "Report on the Principal Leaders and Agents of the Japanese Government Residing in the City of Manila," n.d., Reel 8, HHB.

23. Superintendent Information Division, Memorandum for the Director, November 8, 1909, Reel 8, HHB; Asemblea Filipina, *Directorio Oficial: Segunda Legislatura Filipina* (Manila, 1912), 51–52, 85.

24. Superintendent Information Division PC, Memorandum for the Director, February 28, 1911, Reel 8, HHB; David R. Sturtevant, *Popular Uprisings in the Philippines, 1840–1940* (Ithaca, 1976), 199.

25. Letter to Captain Ralph Van Deman, General Staff, U.S.A., August 21, 1907, Reel 2, HHB.

26. "Memoirs of Major General R. H. Van Deman" (San Diego, April 1949), 20–22, Special Collections, Georgetown University Library; H. W. Brands, *TR: The Last Romantic* (New York, 1997), 605–13.

27. Agent 16, Report, November 18, 1909, Reel 8, HHB; Lewis E. Gleeck Jr., *The American Half-Century (1898–1946)* (Quezon City, 1998), 132–33; Brian McAllister Linn, *Guardians of Empire: The U.S. Army and the Pacific, 1902–1940* (Chapel Hill, 1997), 84–92.

28. Letters to Jacob M. Dickinson, September 18, 1909, October 11, 1909, Confidential Letter Box, vol. 1, WCF.

29. Major R. Crame, Memorandum for the Director of Constabulary, August 29, 1907, Reel 8, HHB; letter from Henry T. Allen to William H. Taft, December 17, 1906, Reel 62, WHT.

30. Report, September 19, 1909; Report, October 21, 1909; Superintendent Information Division, Memorandum for the Director, November 20, 1909; Agent 22, May 11, 1910, Reel 8, HHB.

31. Agent 2, Report, December 23, 1909; Charles C. Smith to Colonel T. Mair, December 18, 1909; anonymous letter, January 24, 1910, Reel 8, HHB.

32. Letter to Jacob M. Dickinson, October 11, 1909, Confidential Letter Box, vol. 1, WCF.

33. Memorandum for Colonel Bandholtz, n.d., Reel 1, HHB; Ignacio Villamor, *Criminality in the Philippine Islands: 1903–1908* (Manila, 1909), 51–53; *KR*, 7/1931, 41–42.

34. Agent 2, March 12, 1910; Agent 2, March 22, 1910, Reel 8, HHB; Agent 2, April 24, 1910, Reel 8, HHB; Superintendent Information Division, Memorandum for the Director, August 25, 1910, Reel 8, HHB; Sturtevant, *Popular Uprisings in the Philippines*, 132–38; letter from Edward Bowditch to Governor Forbes, May 9, 1912, Box One, Correspondence: Bowditch, Ed., WCF.

35. Agent 11, Report, October 10, 1910, Reel 8; memorandum, March 12, 1910, Reel 8; letter to Major General Leonard Wood, January 20, 1913, Reel 5; Agent 16, March 11, 1910, Reel 8, HHB.

36. *MT*, 4/5/1910.

37. Letter from Eulogio Reyes Carrillo, January 19, 1910; Superintendent Information Division PC, Memorandum for the Director, February 28, 1911, 19, Reel 8, HHB.

38. Leonard Wood, "Diaries, 1921–27," August 15, 1923, LWP; Manuel Luis Quezon, *The Good Fight* (New York, 1946), 83–86; Sol H. Gwekoh, *Manuel Quezon: His Life and Career* (Manila, 1948), 43; Arthur Stanley Riggs, *The Filipino Drama [1905]* (Manila, 1981), xv–xvi, 277–81; E. Arsenio Manuel, *Dictionary of Philippine Biography*, vol. 2 (Quezon City, 1970), 376–78, 432; Michael Cullinane, "*Ilustrado* Politics: The Response of the Filipino Educated Elite to American Colonial Rule, 1898–1907," PhD diss., University of Michigan, 1989, 173–85.

39. Letter from H. H. Bandholtz to Manuel L. Quezon, December 19, 1909, Reel 47, MLQMI.

40. Letter to Leonard Wood, October 30, 1911, Reel 8; letter to Colonel W. C. Rivers, October 17, 1911, Reel 4, HHB.

41. Agent 26, November 4, 1911, Reel 8, HHB.

42. Superintendent, Information Division, Confidential Memorandum for the Director, Philippine Constabulary, December 27, 1912, Reel 8, HHB.

43. Letter to Right Reverend C. H. Brent, July 21, 1913, Confidential Letter Box, vol. 2, WCF.

44. Teodoro A. Agoncillo and Oscar M. Alfonso, *History of the Filipino People* (Quezon City, 1971), 306–7.

45. Riggs, *The Filipino Drama,* xv–xvi, 277–81; Manuel, *Dictionary of Philippine Biography,* vol. 2, 379–83; Cullinane, "*Ilustrado* Politics," 179–82; Thomas C. Hernandez, *The Emergence of Modern Drama in the Philippines (1898–1912)* (Honolulu, 1976), 121–32; letter from Aurelio Tolentino to Col. Rafael Crame, January 4, 1911, Reel 8, HHB.

46. *MT,* 1/22/1909, 1/27/1909, 1/28/1909, 2/19/1909, 2/22/1909, 2/23/1909, 2/24/1909, 3/3/1909.

47. *MT,* 3/3/1909, 3/4/1909, 3/6/1909, 3/8/1909, 3/13/1909; *LD,* 1/26/1909, 1/28/1909, 3/5/1909, 3/9/1909; *PFP,* 11/7/1908, 9–11, 3/6/1909, 1; letters from Percy G. McDonnell to William H. Taft, May 27, 1905, Reel 50, July 15, 1905, Reel 52, WHT.

48. City of Manila, 1909 Annual Report for the Police Department, Philippine Commission Report 1909, vol. 1, 290–94, vol. 955; Annual Report of the Director of Constabulary for the Fiscal Year Ending June 30, 1909, Philippine Commission Reports 1909, vol. 3, 1475, vol. 957, BIA.

49. *MT,* 2/25/1909, 3/10/1909, 3/11/1909, 3/12/1909, 3/13/1909, 3/15/1909; *LD,* 2/27/1909, 3/2/1909, 3/9/1909; *PFP,* 3/13/1909, 4, 11; letter to General C. R. Edwards, March 2, 1909, Reel 2, HHB.

50. *LD,* 3/9/1910, 3/10/1909, 3/12/1909, 3/16/1909, 3/18/1909, 3/22/1909, 3/26/1909, 3/27/1909; *MT,* 3/20/1909, 4/26/1909, 5/13/1909; Personal and Police History of Deputies to First Filipino Assembly, 8, vol. 1, DCW; Leonard Wood, "Diaries, 1921–27," July 27, 1924, LWP.

51. Letter from J. G. Harbord to General H. H. Bandholtz, May 28, 1909, Reel 8, HHB; *LD,* 3/13/1909; *MT,* 4/27/1909, 4/28/1909, 5/11/1909, 5/25/1909, 5/27/1909, 5/28/1909, 5/29/1909, 6/2/1909, 6/4/1909.

52. Agent (.), May 18, 1910, Reel 8, HHB.

53. Agent 16, June 13, 1910; Agent 11, June 13, 1910; Agent 37, June 13, 1910, Reel 8, HHB.

54. Agent 16, July 13, 1910; Superintendent Information Division, Confidential Memorandum for the Director, April 21, 1913, Reel 8, HHB.

55. Report, January 28, 1910, Reel 8, HHB.

56. Ricarte, *Memoirs of General Artemio Ricarte,* app. N, 209–12; Superintendent, Memorandum for the Director, November 15, 1910, Reel 8, HHB; letter from Aurelio Tolentino to Col. Rafael Crame, January 4, 1911, Reel 8, HHB; Agent 11, September 22, 1911, Reel 8, HHB.

57. Superintendent, Confidential Memorandum for the Acting Director, August 26, 1912, Reel 8, HHB; Superintendent, Confidential Memorandum for the Acting Director, August 30, 1912, Reel 8, HHB; letter from Edward Bowditch to Governor Forbes, August 30, 1912, Box One, Correspondence: Bowditch, Ed., WCF.

58. Agent 6, September 16, 1912, Reel 8, HHB.

59. Agent 6, October 30, 1912, Reel 8, HHB; Agent 6, November 15, 1912, Reel 8, HHB; Superintendent, Information Division, Confidential Memorandum for the Director, December 19, 1912, Reel 8, HHB; Superintendent, Information Division, Confidential Memorandum for the Director, December 20, 1912, Reel 8, HHB; Ricarte, *Memoirs of General Artemio Ricarte,* app. N, 211.

60. Ricarte, *Memoirs of General Artemio Ricarte,* app. N, 211; Agent 6, January 24, 1913, Reel 8, HHB.

61. *MT,* 12/20/1912; *LD,* 12/20/1912; *CA,* 12/20/1912; *Diario de Sesiones de la Asemblea Filipina,* Session 57, December 21, 1912, 341–43, Session 85, February 3, 1913, 630–31.

62. Ricarte, *Memoirs of General Artemio Ricarte,* app. N, 211; Report to the Secretary of Commerce and Police, June 30, 1913, Philippine Commission Report, vol. 3, 2572–73, vol. 973, BIA.

63. Agent (-.), October 10, 1910, Reel 8, HHB.

64. Agent (.), February 13, 1911, Reel 8, HHB.

65. Superintendent, Information Division, Memorandum for the Director, July 6, 1910; Superintendent, Information Division, Memorandum for the Director, November 20, 1909, Reel 8, HHB.

66. *PFP,* 1/9/1915, 12–13; *El Ideal,* 5/17/1915; Personal Name Information Files: Artemio Ricarte, Box 145, Entry 21, BIA; Sturtevant, *Popular Uprisings in the Philippines,* 200; Agent 26, March 13, 1911, Reel 8, HHB; Agent 26, March 16, 1912, Reel 8, HHB; Lilia Quindoza Santiago, *Tales of Courage and Compassion: Stories of Women in the Philippine Revolution* (Manila, 1997), 61–64.

67. Agent 26, November 4, 1911, Reel 8, HHB. Of the three Manila loyalists who visited Ricarte in Hong Kong in March 1911, only Velasco is identified in multiple sources as a possible PC spy. See Agent 6, September 18, 1912, Reel 8, HHB; *PFP,* 1/8/1915; *El Ideal,* 5/17/1915; and Personal Name Information Files: Artemio Ricarte, Box 145, Entry 21, BIA.

68. Letter to Major General Leonard Wood, January 20, 1913, Reel 5, HHB; letter to Major General Leonard Wood, February 3, 1913, Reel 5, HHB; letter to General Frank McIntyre, February 20, 1913, Reel 5, HHB; letter to Major General Leonard Wood, February 21 1913, Reel 5, HHB; *MT,* 2/15/1913.

69. Ricarte, *Memoirs of General Artemio Ricarte,* app. N, 159.

70. Francis Burton Harrison, *The Corner-Stone of Philippine Independence: A Narrative of Seven Years* (New York, 1922), 150–52.

71. Memorandum for Honorable Manuel Quezon, September 10, 1915, Box 40, File: Report Sept. 10, 1915, of Chief of Police Seaver on Christmas Eve 1914 "Uprising," FBH; Semi-annual Report of the Chief, Philippine Constabulary for the Period July 1 to Dec. 31, 1913, Philippine Commission Report 1914, vol. 4, 182–83, vol. 980, BIA.

72. Ricarte, *Memoirs of General Artemio Ricarte,* app. N, 157–70; Sturtevant, *Popular Uprisings in the Philippines,* 201–2, 216; Memorandum for Honorable Manuel Quezon, September 10, 1915, Box 40, File: Report Sept. 10, 1915, of Chief of Police Seaver on Christmas Eve 1914 "Uprising," FBH.

73. Letter from Henry Breckinridge to Secretary of State, March 24, 1915; Telegram from W. J. Bryan to Secretary of War, March 24, 1915; *LD,* 4/14/1915; *Taliba,* 6/25/1915; Personal Name Information Files: Artemio Ricarte, Box 145, Entry 21, BIA; Sturtevant, *Popular Uprisings in the Philippines,* 202–3; *LD,* 4/8/1915; *MT,* 8/6/1915.

74. W. Cameron Forbes, Journals, vol. 3, September 4, 1909, WCF.

75. Those in the Ban Siong group identified as tong leaders included its president, Agapito Uy Tongco, secretary Dy To, and directors Pua Kang-O and Go Hun. Letter from A. Zarate Sycip, To: General H. H. Bandholtz, April 3, 1909, Reel 2, HHB; *CA,* 5/8/1908, 8/1/1908; Andrew R. Wilson, *Ambition and Identity: Chinese Merchant Elites in Colonial Manila, 1880–1916* (Honolulu, 2004), 169, 198, 200.

76. Wilson, *Ambition and Identity,* 188–92, 200–201; W. Cameron Forbes, Journals, vol. 3, September 4, 1909, WCF.

77. *MT,* 8/21/1909, 8/23/1909, 3/29/1910, 4/2/1910.

78. Agent 30, no. A14/0223, January 15, 1911, Reel 7, HHB. The agent identified the reporter only as "Guild," but the name of one James A. Guild appears on the Civil Service roster of 1907 as a "Constabulary inspector." He was not listed in 1908, so it is possible that he transferred to a non-Civil Service post as a revenue inspector. See PI, Bureau of Civil Service, *OROECSP 1907,* 25.

79. *CA,* 11/13/1907, 8/21/1909, 8/22/1909, 8/24/1909; *MT,* 3/30/1910; Wilson, *Ambition and Identity,* 155, 199–201, 204–7. For example, Benito Sy Cong Beng, a wealthy import-export merchant, served as president of the Chinese Chamber of Commerce from 1907 to 1911 and 1913 to 1916. See Wong Kwok-Chu, *The Chinese in the Philippine Economy, 1898–1941* (Manila, 1999), 40, 43–44.

80. *MT,* 8/21/1909, 8/23/1909; *CA,* 8/22/1909; Wilson, *Ambition and Identity,* 203.

81. Letter from W. Cameron Forbes to Jacob M. Dickinson, September 13, 1909, BIA no. 370–232, BIA; cablegram from Forbes to Secretary of War, September 14, 1909, BIA no. 370–227, BIA; letter from J. Harding to Executive Secretary, September 4, 1909, BIA no. 370–234, Entry 5, BIA.

82. *MT,* 3/29/1910, 3/30/1910, 4/9/1910; cable from Forbes to Secretary of War, April 1, 1910, BIA no. 370–239, Entry 5, BIA; cable from Dickinson to Forbes, April 1, 1910, BIA no. 370–239, Entry 5, BIA; letter from law officer to chief of bureau, March 31, 1910, BIA no. 370–238, Entry 5, BIA; letter from Forbes to Jacob M. Dickinson, June 8, 1910, BIA no. 370–256, Entry 5, BIA.

83. Wilson, *Ambition and Identity,* 211–12; Tiaco v. Forbes, nos. 254, 255, 256, *United States Reports,* vol. 228: *Cases Adjudged in the Supreme Court at October Term, 1912* (New York, 1913), 549–58.

84. Letter to Lindley M. Garrison, June 2, 1913, Confidential Letter Box, vol. 2, WCF.

85. Letter to Professor Henry J. Ford, September 1, 1913, Confidential Letter Box, vol. 2, WCF.

86. Amzi B. Kelly, *The Killing of General Noriel* (Manila, 1987), 12–110.

87. Ibid., 112, 115–17.

88. Rafael Crame, *Contestación a los Cargos de que se Imputan al Colonel Rafael Crame en El Libro Titulado: "Mariano Noriel Innocent" Escrito por El Abogado Amzi B. Kelly* (Manila, 1916), 4–5, 23, 41–42; United States vs. Amzi B. Kelly, No. 12109, December 1, 1916, *PSC 9/23/16–12/22/16*, 512–13, 525.

89. Superintendent, Information Division, Memorandum for Acting Director, July 2, 1912; 1st Lieut. R. Crame, August 1, 1904; Report, October 19, 1909; R. M. Crame, Memorandum for the Director, May 22, 1911, Reel 8, HHB.

90. Superintendent, Information Division, Memorandum for Acting Director, July 2, 1912, Reel 8, HHB; 1st Lieut. R. Crame, August 1, 1904, Reel 8, HHB; Report, October 19, 1909, Reel 8, HHB; R. M. Crame, Memorandum for the Director, May 22, 1911, Reel 8, HHB; H. G. Upham, Confidential Memorandum for District Director, June 23, 1911, Reel 8, HHB; H. G. Upham, Confidential Memorandum for District Director, July 6, 1911, Reel 8, HHB; Teodoro A. Agoncillo, *The Revolt of the Masses: The Story of Bonifacio and the Katipunan* (Quezon City, 1956), 265–75, 302–5; Kelly, *The Killing of General Noriel*, 157–68, 223; Crame, *Contestación a los Cargos*, 48–49.

91. Superintendent, Information Division, Memorandum for Acting Director, July 2, 1912, Reel 8, HHB; R. M. Crame, Memorandum for the Director, May 22, 1911, Reel 8, HHB; Kelly, *The Killing of General Noriel*, 140–42; United States vs. Amzi B. Kelly, No. 12109, *Reports of Cases*, 550–52; letter from Hugh Minturn to W. Cameron Forbes, July 2, 1912, Box 1, Correspondence: Bowditch, Ed., WCF.

92. Crame, *Contestación a los Cargos*, 29–32, 35; *PFP*, 1/16/1915, 11; *MT*, 3/24/1914; letter from Hugh Minturn to Governor Forbes, July 2, 1912, Box 1, Correspondence: Bowditch, Ed., WCF.

93. Letter from Hugh Minturn to Governor Forbes, July 2, 1912, Box 1, Correspondence: Bowditch, Ed., WCF; letter from Edward Bowditch to W. Cameron Forbes, May 9, 1912, Box 1, Correspondence: Bowditch, Ed., WCF; Kelly, *The Killing of General Noriel*, xi, 218.

94. *PFP*, 1/16/1915, 11; *MT*, 6/24/1912, 6/28/1912, 3/24/1914; United States vs. Amzi B. Kelly, No. 12109, *Reports of Cases*, 572; Gleeck, *The American Half-Century*, 197–98; Teodoro M. Kalaw, *Aide-de-Camp to Freedom* (Manila, 1965), 109–111; Kelly, *The Killing of General Noriel*, 5–6; letter from Rafael Palma to Governor-General Francis Burton Harrison, January 5, 1915, in Amzi B. Kelly, *A Petition for Redress of Grievances to the Hon. Manuel L. Quezon* (n.p., n.d.), 10–12; letter from Hugh Minturn to W. Cameron Forbes, July 2, 1912, Box 1, Correspondence: Bowditch, Ed., WCF.

95. Memorandum for the Secretary of War, August 17, 1915, File 2, Entry 48, RG 350, NARA.

96. Cable from Osmeña to Quezon, January 7, 1915, Reel 50, MLQMI; Cable from Osmeña to Quezon, January 10, 1915, Reel 50, MLQMI; cable from Osmeña to Quezon, January 12, 1915, Reel 50, MLQMI; letter from Manuel Quezon to My Dear General [Frank McIntyre], January 5, 1915, Reel 50, MLQMI; cable from Quezon to Harrison, January 10, 1915 File 4, Entry 48, RG 350, NARA; cable from Quezon to Harrison, January 11, 1915 File 4, Entry 48, RG 350, NARA; letter from War Department to Francis Burton Harrison, January 19, 1915, File 4, Entry 48, RG 350, NARA.

97. Cable from Quezon to Harrison, January 11, 1915; cable from Garrison to Harrison, January 11, 1915; cable from Harrison to Secwar, January 12, 1915; cable from Woodrow Wilson to Harrison, January 12, 1915; cable from Harrison to Secwar, January 13, 1915, Box 39, File: Noriel Case 1915, FBH.

98. Cable from Quezon to Osmeña, January 13, 1915, Reel 50, MLQMI.

99. *MT*, 1/26/1915, 1/27/1915, 1/28/1915; *PFP*, 2/6/1915, 12.

100. Lewis E. Gleeck Jr., *Nueva Ecija in American Times: Homesteaders, Hacenderos, and Politicos* (Manila, 1981), 15–16; Kelly, *The Killing of General Noriel*, xii–xiii; *NYT*, 2/18/1916; letter from Amzi Kelly to Thomas R. Marshall, February 8, 1916, File 3, Entry 48, RG 350, NARA; *Amzi B. Kelly vs. Sherman Morehead and Others*, January 27, 1916, File 3, Entry 48, RG 350, NARA; *Consolidacion Nacional*, 2/16/1916, File 3, Entry 48, RG 350, NARA; letter from acting executive secretary to chief, BIA, February 18, 1916, File 3, Entry 48, RG 350, NARA; letter from S. Ferguson to George E. Anderson, February 17, 1916, File 3, Entry 48, RG 350, NARA; letter from Amzi Kelly to Newton D. Baker, April 29, 1916, File 3, Entry 48, RG 350, NARA; letter from Mrs. Amzi B. Kelly to president of the United States, June 9, 1918, File 4, Entry 48, RG 350, NARA; letter from Mrs. Angel B. Kelly to Señor Quezon, August 15, 1917, Reel 49, MLQMI; letter from Amzi B. Kelly to Francis Burton Harrison, December 5, 1918, Reel 49, MLQMI; letter from Amzi Kelly to Manuel L. Quezon, March 9, 1920, Reel 49, MLQMI; letter from Amzi Kelly to Manuel L. Quezon, April 16, 1920, Reel 9, MLQMI.

101. Crame, *Contestación a los Cargos,* 19, 22, 38–39, 62–63, 68–69.

102. For praise of Crame see Harrison, *The Corner-Stone of Philippine Independence,* 151.

103. See, for example, Cullinane, "*Ilustrado* Politics"; Peter W. Stanley, *A Nation in the Making: The Philippines and the United States, 1899–1921* (Cambridge, 1974), chaps. 5, 6; and Reynaldo C. Ileto, "Orators and the Crowd: Philippine Independence Politics, 1910–1914," in Peter W. Stanley, ed., *Reappraising an Empire: New Perspectives on Philippine-American History* (Cambridge, 1984), 85–113.

Chapter 6. Policing the Tribal Zone

1. Vic Hurley, *Jungle Patrol: The Story of the Philippine Constabulary* (New York, 1938), 298–99.

2. Harold Hanne Elarth, *The Story of the Philippine Constabulary* (Los Angeles, 1949), 14–15.

3. W. Cameron Forbes, *The Philippine Islands* (Cambridge, 1945), 260.

4. Letter from Senior Inspector R.A.D. Ford, to Lieutenant O. A. Tomlinson, August 17, 1909, OT.

5. Hurley, *Jungle Patrol,* 310.

6. WD, *RPC 1905,* part 3, 125.

7. Peter Gordon Gowing, *Mandate in Moroland: The American Government of Muslim Filipinos, 1899–1920* (Quezon City, 1977), 243.

8. Letter from Geo. W. Davis to Luke E. Wright, January 7, 1902, Reel 34, WHT.

9. Letter from Luke E. Wright to William H. Taft, January 13, 1902, Reel 34, February 13, 1902, Reel 35, WHT.

10. Gowing, *Mandate in Moroland,* 37–41, 88–94.

11. Forbes, *The Philippine Islands* (1945 ed.), 279; Gowing, *Mandate in Moroland,* 101, 108–9, 112–17, 149–50.

12. Gowing, *Mandate in Moroland,* 151–54.

13. Message from the President of the United States Transmitting an Account of the Engagement on Mount Dajo between United States Forces and a Band of Moros, HR, 59th Congress, 1st Session, Document no. 622, *House Documents, vol. 49* (Washington, DC, 1906), 1–2; Brian McAllister Linn, *The Guardians of Empire: The U.S. Army in the Pacific* (Chapel Hill, 1997), 38–39.

14. Gowing, *Mandate in Moroland,* 160–64; Rodney J. Sullivan, *Exemplar of Americanism: The Philippine Career of Dean C. Worcester* (Ann Arbor, 1991), 149; Forbes, *The Philippine Islands* (1945 ed.), 283–84; John R. White, *Bullets and Bolos: Fifteen Years in the Philippine Islands* (New York, 1928), 310–12.

15. Gowing, *Mandate in Moroland,* 230–42, 260; *KR,* 7/1931, 192.

16. Letter from Brigadier General John J. Pershing, To: The Commanding General, Philippine Department, November 1, 1913, Box 41, File: Moros, Reorganizations and Concentrations of Troops Nov–Dec 1913, FBH; *MT,* 10/3/1911, 10/14/1911.

17. Letter from Brigadier General John J. Pershing, To: The Commanding General, Philippine Department, November 1, 1913, FBH; letter from Brig. Gen. John J. Pershing, To: The Commanding General, Philippine Department, July 20, 1913, FBH; letter from John J. Pershing to Governor-General Francis Burton Harrison, November 3, 1913, FBH; letter from J. F. Bell to Governor-General Francis Burton Harrison, FBH; Cablegram from Harrison to Secwar, November 25, 1913, Box 41, File: Moros, Reorganizations and Concentrations of Troops Nov–Dec 1913, FBH; Philippine Constabulary Report, January 19, 1916, Philippine Commission Report 1915, vol. 3, 1705, vol. 987, BIA; *PFP,* 1/24/1931, 10, 58.

18. HR, 62d Congress, 2d Session, *Limit of Indebtedness of the Philippine Government: Hearings before the Committee on Insular Affairs* (Washington, DC, 1912), 98; Charles H. Brent, "Religious Conditions in the Philippine Islands," File: July to December 1904, Box 6, CHB.

19. Sullivan, *Exemplar of Americanism,* 142–43, 150–52; Dean C. Worcester, *The Philippines Past and Present* (New York, 1930), 442–43, 478–79, 508; Forbes, *The Philippine Islands* (1945 ed.), 262–63; Dean C. Worcester, *The Philippines Past and Present,* vol. 2 (New York, 1914), 544; HR, *ARWD 1905,* vol. 15: *Acts of the Philippine Commission,* 167–69; Annual Report of the Secretary of the

Interior for the Fiscal Year Ended June 30, 1912, Philippine Commission Report 1912, vol. 2, 1005, vol. 968, BIA.

20. Letter from Dean C. Worcester to William H. Taft, November 23, 1906, Reel 61, January 27, 1908, Reel 74, WHT.

21. Letter from William H. Taft to Dean C. Worcester, November 30, 1906, Reel 71, WHT.

22. HR, *ARWD 1905*, vol. 14: *Acts of the Philippine Commission*, 165–85.

23. Lieutenant R. O. Van Horn, "Exploring Expedition Cotabato to Cagayan, Mindanao," March 18, 1902, in HR, *ARWD 1902*, vol. 9, 585–92; Ronald K. Edgerton, "Frontier Society on the Bukidnon Plateau, 1870–1941," in Alfred W. McCoy and Edilberto C. de Jesus, eds., *Philippine Social History: Global Trade and Local Transformations* (Quezon City, 1982), 362.

24. Letter from J. G. Harbord to Adjutant General, Philippine Constabulary, June 3, 1904, Book no. 2, DCW.

25. WD, *RPC 1902*, part 1, 215; WD, *RPC 1903*, part 3, 116; WD, *RPC 1905*, part 3, 36, 120, 122; letter from Geo. W. Davis, November 22, 1901, Box 1, File: Chaffee, Adna R., Nov–Dec 1901, HCP; letter from Adna R. Chaffee, February 28, 1902, Box 1, File: Chaffee, Adna R., Jan–Mar 1902, HCP; Annual Report of the Governor of the Province of Misamis for the Year 1902, Philippine Commission Report 1903, vol. 4, B1980–81, 1987–88, vol. 912, BIA.

26. Report of the Trip of the Civil Governor through the Southern Islands, November 12, 1904, to December 8, 1904, 184, Carl Remington Papers, Rare Book and Manuscript Library, Columbia University.

27. WD, *RPC 1906*, part 2, 306–7, 310; W. Cameron Forbes, Journals, vol. 2, October 2, 1907, WCF.

28. Forbes, *The Philippine Islands* (1945 ed.), 269–71; Report of the Provincial Government of Agusan, July 31, 1913, Philippine Commission Report 1913, vol. 1, 574–75, vol. 971, BIA.

29. Worcester, *The Philippines Past and Present* (1930 ed.), 71, 478–79, 483, 487; Edgerton, "Frontier Society on the Bukidnon Plateau," 370–71; Evidence Taken by Mr. Nesmith, 15, Book no. 21-II, DCW; Narciso Pimentel, *Directorio Oficial de la Asemblea Nacional* (Manila, 1938), 142–43.

30. Sullivan, *Exemplar of Americanism*, 217; Edgerton, "Frontier Society on the Bukidnon Plateau," 370.

31. WD, *RPC 1908*, 422–23; letter from Frederick Lewis, Governor, Agusan, to Director, District of Mindanao, October 12, 1911, DCW; letter from Acting Lieutenant-Governor Manuel Fortich to the Secretary of Interior, November 10, 1911, Book no. 4, DCW.

32. Letter from Acting Lieutenant-Governor Manuel Fortich to the Secretary of Interior, November 10, 1911; letter from Director H. H. Bandholtz to Secretary of Commerce and Police, November 22, 1911, Book no. 4, DCW.

33. Letter from Secretary of Interior Dean C. Worcester to the Governor-General, December 21, 1911, Book no. 4, DCW.

34. Forbes, *The Philippine Islands* (1945 ed.), 113; WD, *RPC 1912*, 83–84; WD, *RPC 1913*, 176.

35. Worcester, *The Philippines Past and Present*, vol. 2 (1914 ed.), 609–32.

36. Sullivan, *Exemplar of Americanism*, 155, 215–16; WD, *RPC 1910*, 71.

37. Edgerton, "Frontier Society on the Bukidnon Plateau," 368–69.

38. Forbes, *The Philippine Islands* (1945 ed.), 271; Evidence Taken by Mr. Nesmith, 20, Book no. 21-II, DCW.

39. Report by the Secretary of the Interior on the Lewis-Fortich Matter, 5a–6, Book no. 21-II, DCW; WD, *RPC 1910*, 72.

40. WD, *RPC 1912*, 84–85.

41. Evidence Taken by Mr. Nesmith, 20, 47–48, Book no. 21-II, DCW.

42. Ibid., 23–25, 49–50, 101–2.

43. Ibid., 26–27; Philippine Commission, *Public Laws Passed by the Philippine Commission during the Period September 1, 1906, to October 15, 1907, Comprising Acts Nos. 1537 to 1800, Inclusive*, vol. 6 (Manila, 1908), 270.

44. Evidence Taken by Mr. Nesmith, 15, 36–37, 40–41, 43, 78–80, 115, 119, Book no. 21-II, DCW.

45. Ibid., 27–34, 39, 55, 78–80, 98–99, 153, 158; Notes of an Interview between Lieutenant-Governor Lewis and Mr. Worcester, 6–8, Book no. 21-II, DCW.

46. Evidence Taken by Mr. Nesmith, 13–14, 55–58, 76, 78–79, 82–83, 136, 155, 160, Book no. 21-II, DCW; Notes of an Interview between Lieutenant-Governor Lewis and Mr. Worcester, 12, 16, Book no. 21-II, DCW; Report by the Secretary of the Interior on the Lewis-Fortich Matter, 46, Book no. 21-II, DCW; *MT,* 12/2/1910.

47. Evidence Taken by Mr. Nesmith, 84–85, 90–91; Report by the Secretary of the Interior on the Lewis-Fortich Matter, 5a, 20, 21, 41–43, 46–47, 55–57, Book no. 21-II, DCW.

48. WD, *RPC 1910,* 82.

49. Report by the Secretary of the Interior on the Charge of Murder against Señor Fortich, 14–15, 33; Report by the Secretary of the Interior on the Lewis-Fortich Matter, 4, 16, 24, 47, 58, Book no. 21-II, DCW.

50. Worcester, *The Philippines Past and Present* (1930 ed.), 488–89; Sullivan, *Exemplar of Americanism,* 170–71; WD, *RPC 1912,* 82; WD, *RPC 1911,* 59–60; PI, *ARDC 1911,* 8.

51. WD, *RPC 1910,* 75.

52. Worcester, *The Philippines Past and Present* (1930 ed.), 488–89; Sullivan, *Exemplar of Americanism,* 155, 168–71, 194, 215–23; *CA,* 9/14/1911; Edgerton, "Frontier Society on the Bukidnon Plateau," 370, 374–76; WD, *RPC 1913,* 101–2; Pimentel, *Directorio Oficial de la Asemblea Nacional,* 142–43.

53. Sullivan, *Exemplar of Americanism,* 221–22; Pimentel, *Directorio Oficial de la Asemblea Nacional,* 142; letter to The Special Mission, August 4, 1921, Box One, Folio: Papers concerning Wood-Forbes Mission to the Philippine Islands, 1921–1922, DCW; *MT,* 6/19/1921.

54. Report of the Provincial Government of Agusan, July 31, 1913, Philippine Commission Report 1913, vol. 1, 566, vol. 971, BIA.

55. Sullivan, *Exemplar of Americanism,* 215–23; Edgerton, "Frontier Society on the Bukidnon Plateau," 374–76; WD, *GGPI 1918,* 44; Philippine Commission, *Public Laws Passed by the Philippine Legislature during the Period October 16, 1912, to October 15, 1914, Comprising Acts Nos. 2192 to 2413,* vol. 9 (Manila, 1915), 456.

56. Howard T. Fry, *A History of the Mountain Province* (Quezon City, 1983), 265.

57. Worcester, *The Philippines Past and Present* (1930 ed.), 314–15.

58. WD, *RPC 1908,* part 2, 369, 406; Fry, *A History of the Mountain Province,* 36–37; HR, *ARWD 1904,* vol. 11: *Acts of the Philippine Commission,* part 1, 526; WD, *RPC 1915,* 121–22.

59. WD, *RPC 1904,* part 3, 51–60.

60. HR, *ARWD 1904,* vol. 11: *Acts of the Philippine Commission,* part 1, 519, 525, 527; WD, *RPC 1906,* part 1, 318; WD, *RPC 1906,* part 2, 236; WD, *A Pronouncing Gazetteer and Geographical Dictionary of the Philippine Islands* (Washington, DC, 1902), 355, 590; WD, *RPC 1908,* part 2, 406–7.

61. WD, *RPC 1902,* part 1, 183, 189–90; WD, *RPC 1903,* part 3, 62.

62. Letter from Dr. David Barrows to Governor L. E. Bennett, December 5, 1902, Paper no. 97, BCF; David Prescott Barrows, A Preliminary Report of Explorations among the Tribes of the Cordillera Central of Northern Luzon, May 25, 1903, Paper no. 98, BCF; Frank Lawrence Jenista, *The White Apos: American Governors on the Cordillera Central* (Quezon City, 1987), 24–26.

63. Letter from Governor L. E. Bennett to Dr. David Barrows, October 21, 1902, Paper no. 94; letter from Governor L. E. Bennett to Dr. David Barrows, October 31, 1902, Paper no. 95; letter from Governor L. E. Bennett to Governor William H. Taft, November 4, 1902, Paper no. 96, BCF.

64. Captain Lewis Patstone, Report of an Expedition into the Igorrote District of Quiangan, Nueva Viscaya, April 1903, Paper no. 143, BCF; Levi E. Case, Folklore of the Igorrotes, 1905, Paper no. 91, BCF; Jenista, *The White Apos,* 35–37, 39–46, 50–82.

65. Jeff D. Gallman, A New List of Districts and Rancherias of the Settlement of Quiangan, Suprovince of Ifugao, Mountain Province, May 1, 1912, Paper no. 28; Lieutenant-Governor Jeff D. Gallman, Annual Report, Subprovince of Ifugao, July 20, 1910, Paper no. 29; Captain Jeff D. Gallman, Notes and Suggestions for Lt. Tomlinson with Reference to Public Works Projects for the Next Six Months, January 24, 1911, Paper no. 105; letter from Lieutenant-Governor Jeff D. Gallman to the Hon William F. Pack, January 24, 1911, Paper no. 104; Lieutenant Maximo Meimban, Servicios de Captura Facilitados por Policías y Cabecillas en el Settlement de Quiangan, January 1911, Paper no. 106; Lieutenant-Governor Jeff D. Gallman, Extracts from the Records of the Justice of the Peace

Court, Subprovince of Ifugao, Paper no. 107; Jeff D. Gallman, Letter to the Secretary of the Interior, Relating to Church Lands, November 7, 1912, Paper no. 149, BCF.

66. WD, *RPC 1915*, 121.

67. Guines is also known as Ginneh or Ginihon. See Harold C. Conklin, *Ethnographic Atlas of Ifugao* (New Haven, 1980), 47, 103, 105, 110; WD, *RPC 1904*, part 3, 51, 60, 109–11, 116–17, 119.

68. WD, *RPC 1905*, part 3, 114–15; WD, *RPC 1906*, part 2, 284–87.

69. HR, *ARWD 1905*, vol. 10: *Acts of the Philippine Commission*, part 1, 304; WD, *RPC 1906*, part 2, 288.

70. WD, *RPC 1906*, part 2, 288–89; WD, *RPC 1907*, part 2, 323–24.

71. WD, *RPC 1904*, part 3, 51, 58–60, 115–17, 119–21; WD, *RPC 1906*, part 2, 229–30, 263.

72. Sullivan, *Exemplar of Americanism*, 151–52.

73. Renato Rosaldo, *Ilongot Headhunting, 1883–1974: A Study in Society and History* (Stanford, 1980), 259–61; WD, *RPC 1909*, 131–32; Major Wilfrid Turnbull, "Among the Ilongots Twenty Years Ago," *Philippine Magazine* (Manila), November 1929, 337–38, 374–76; Manuel Luis Quezon, *The Good Fight* (New York, 1946), 4–7, 38; Carlos Quirino, *Quezon: Paladin of Philippine Freedom* (Manila, 1971), 2–5, 26; Fry, *A History of the Mountain Province*, 89–90; Sol H. Gwekoh, *Manuel Quezon: His Life and Career* (Manila, 1948), 8–10. One of Quezon's few public references to his Ilongot ancestry is found in Fry's *History of the Mountain Province*, which cites his testimony at U.S. Congress, Hearings before the House Committee on Insular Affairs, February 12, 1912, BIA. When I searched for this record at the U.S. National Archives in August 2003, the document was missing, so the citation could not be corroborated.

In response to an e-mail about Manuel L. Quezon's Ilongot ancestry, his grandson, Manuel Quezon III, replied, "We have F. B. Harrison mentioning in his diary that MLQ [Manuel L. Quezon] said he had Ilongot blood from his mother. We are still piecing together the family tree (no effort was made in the past because of all the incest and the friar), but the Ilongot blood would come from the two Molina sisters impregnated by a friar named Urbino de Esparragoza; one of the sisters was the mother of Maria Dolores Molina (mother of MLQ) and Zeneida (mother of AAQ) [Aurora Aragon Quezon]. What is known is that Lucio Quezon [MLQ's father], perhaps by virtue of his marriage to Dolores Molina [MLQ's mother], was made 'protector' or 'administrator' of the Ilongots, which MLQ in turn inherited and passed on to his elder half (or full, depends on whom you ask) brother, Teodorico Molina. . . . As a side note, my aunt Maria Aurora (Baby) had kinky chestnut hair which the family says was a sign of Ilongot blood in the family. There is a monograph published a few years back by a Dominican which I think mentions the relationship between our family and the Ilongots in Baler." E-mail communication, Manolo L. Quezon III to the author, June 23, 2003.

74. WD, *RPC 1912*, 77; WD, *RPC 1911*, 50; WD, *RPC 1913*, 93–94.

75. Memorandum, n.d., Reel 5, HHB.

76. Letters to Major H. S. Howland, November 11, 1907, November 12, 1907, Reel 2; letter from Governor Wm. Pack to General Bandholtz, November 2, 1909; letter to William F. Pack, November 11, 1909, Reel 10, HHB.

77. Letter from Captain James W. Clinton, 12th Infantry, Military Record, n.d.; Constabulary record of Captain Owen A. Tomlinson, n.d.; letter from Lieut. Colonel H. S. Foster, 12th Infantry to Chief Philippine Constabulary, July 19, 1904, OT.

78. Roy Franklin Barton, "Economic and Industrial Conditions in Ifugao," chap. 1 (1914), OT; letter from C. C. Batchelder to Captain O. A. Tomlinson, June 9, 1916, OT; Jenista, *The White Apos*, 287–88.

79. Second-Lieutenant M. Meimban, PC, "Biographical Sketches of Subprovince of Ifugao," Personal of Capt. O. A. Tomlinson, Senior Inspector of Ifugao, Mt. P., n.d., OT; letter from Capt. Jeff D. Gallman to Lt. Tomlinson, January 24, 1911, Paper no. 105, BCF; letter from Lieutenant-Governor Jeff D. Gallman to Dean C. Worcester, December 2, 1912, Paper no. 144, BCF; Historical Documents from the Subprovince of Ifugao, compiled by 2nd Lieutenant Maximo Meimban, October 10, 1911, Paper no. 89, BCF.

80. Constabulary record of Captain Owen A. Tomlinson, n.d., OT.

81. Jenista, *The White Apos*, 238–39.

82. R. F. Barton, *The Kalingas: Their Institutions and Custom Law* (Chicago, 1949), 7, 142–43, 159, 236–37.

83. WD, *RPC 1908*, 368, 406–7.

84. Worcester, *The Philippines Past and Present* (1930 ed.), 456.

85. Laurence L. Wilson, "Sapao: Walter Franklin Hale, in Memoriam," *Journal of East Asiatic Studies* 5, no. 2 (April 1956): 1–4, 9; Fry, *A History of the Mountain Province*, 44–45; Samuel E. Kane, *Life or Death in Luzon: Thirty Years of Adventure with the Philippine Highlanders* (Indianapolis, 1933), 286; HR, *ARWD 1905*, vol. 14: *Acts of the Philippine Commission*, 179.

86. Kane, *Life and Death in Luzon*, 286, 288; Barton, *The Kalingas*, 147, 220; Edward Dozier, *Mountain Arbiters: The Changing Life of a Philippine Hill People* (Tucson, 1966), 38–39; Wilson, "Sapao," 1–2; *MT*, 12/2/1910.

87. Fry, *A History of the Mountain Province*, 45.

88. Letter from W. F. Hale to Wm. F. Pack, January 6, 1911, Book no. 1, DCW.

89. Letter from Wm. F. Pack to Lieut.-Governor J. C. Early, January 7, 1911, Book no. 1, DCW.

90. Letter from Wm. F. Pack to Lieut.-Governor W. E. Hale, January 8, 1911, Book no. 1, DCW.

91. Letter from Chas. Penningroth to Adjutant, District of Northern Luzon, January 23, 1911, Book no. 1, DCW.

92. Letter from Wm. E. Moore, Adjutant, to the Senior Inspector, Mountain Province, Bontoc, January 28, 1911, Adjutant, District of Northern Luzon, January 23, 1911, Book no. 1, DCW.

93. Letter from W. F. Hale to Provincial Governor, Mountain Province, Bontoc, January 30, 1911, Book no. 1, DCW.

94. Letter from Dean C. Worcester to the Governor-General, October 6, 1911, Book no. 1, DCW.

95. Stenographer's report of interview between Lt.-Gov. Hale, Dean C. Worcester, and people of the Guinabal district, at Lubuagan, n.d., Book no. 1, DCW.

96. Letter from Dean C. Worcester to the Governor-General, October 6, 1911, Book no. 1, DCW.

97. Letter from 3rd Lieutenant Chas. Penningroth to the Adjutant, San Fernando, La Union, January 3, 1910, Book no. 1, DCW; Wilson, "Sapao," 27.

98. Letter from W. Cameron Forbes to Brigadier-General H. H. Bandholtz, January 5, 1912; letter from W. Cameron Forbes to Hon. D. C. Worcester, January 5, 1912, Book no. 1, DCW.

99. Letter from C. B. Elliott to the Secretary of the Interior, January 29, 1912, Book no. 1, DCW.

100. Sullivan, *Exemplar of Americanism*, 158–61, plate 23.

101. Ibid., 161, plate 23; letter from J. M. Dickinson to Dean C. Worcester, April 5, 1911, Reel 363, WHT.

102. Letter from Dean C. Worcester to C. B. Elliott, September 8, 1910; letter from H. H. Bandholtz to Hon. Dean C. Worcester, November 5, 1910, Book no. 1, DCW.

103. Letter from Dean C. Worcester to the President, February 14, 1912, Book no. 1, DCW.

104. Letter from Dean C. Worcester to Brigadier General Clarence R. Edwards, February 14, 1912, Book no. 1, DCW; letter from Dean C. Worcester to the President, February 14, 1912, Book no. 1, DCW; letter from Dean C. Worcester to the President, May 2, 1912, Reel 417, WHT.

105. Letter from Captain G. O. Fox to General H. H. Bandholtz, January 4, 1913, Reel 7; letter to M. L. Quezon, May 24, 1913, Reel 5, HHB.

106. Agent 11, Confidential Report, December 11, 1912, Reel 8, HHB; letter from Frank McIntyre to General H. H. Bandholtz, March 12, 1913, Reel 5, HHB; letter from Edward Bowditch to Governor Forbes, August 30, 1912, Box One, Correspondence: Bowditch, Ed., WCF; Michael Salman, *The Embarrassment of Slavery: Controversies over Bondage and Nationalism in the American Colonial Philippines* (Quezon City, 2001), 181–95.

107. Letter from Wilfrid Turnbull to the Secretary of the Interior, January 21, 1913, Book no. 21: II, DCW; letter to Manuel L. Quezon, December 14, 1906, Reel 1, HHB; letter from M. L. Quezon to Colonel Bandholtz, December 18, 1906, Reel 1, HHB; Michael Cullinane, "*Ilustrado* Politics: The Response of the Filipino Educated Elite to American Colonial Rule, 1898–1907," PhD diss., University of Michigan, 1989, 426–27; *Ang Camatuoran* (Cebu), 2/9/1907; letter from James Harbord to Manuel L. Quezon, December 16, 1911, Reel 49, MLQMI.

108. Letter from Wilfrid Turnbull to the Secretary of the Interior, August 20, 1913, Book no. 21: II, DCW.

109. Letter from Austin Craig to the Secretary of the Interior, April 28, 1913, Book no. 21:II, DCW; E. Arsenio Manuel, *Dictionary of Philippine Biography,* vol. 2 (Quezon City, 1970), 131–39.

110. Letter from Hartford Beaumont to Honorable Henry C. Ide, December 7, 1904, Book no. 21: II, DCW.

111. Letter from Austin Craig to the Secretary of the Interior, April 28, 1913, Book no. 21:II, DCW; *PFP,* 1/9/1915, 12.

112. *MT,* 11/26/1912, 12/3/1912, 12/4/1912, 12/5/1912, 12/10/1912; *CA,* 12/8/1912.

113. Sullivan, *Exemplar of Americanism,* 163–64, 171; Worcester, *The Philippines Past and Present* (1930 ed.), 59–60; H. H. Bandholtz, Confidential Memorandum for His Excellency, the Governor General, on "Report on Slavery and Peonage in the Philippines," by Dean C. Worcester, May 30, 1913, Reel 10, HHB; letter from Lieutenant-Governor Jeff D. Gallman to Dean C. Worcester, "Slave-Dealing in Ifugao," December 2, 1912, Paper no. 144, BCF.

114. *MT,* 10/14/1913; *Consolidacion Nacional,* 10/15/1913.

115. Reflecting Worcester's cavalier treatment of fact in his allegations about slavery, the BIA documented that some of his criticisms were made "without . . . any foundation whatever." (See letters from Frank McIntyre to Dean C. Worcester, March 3, 1914, March 20, 1914, March 26, 1914, April 17, 1914, and letters from Dean C. Worcester to Frank McIntrye March 5, 1914, March 21, 1914, March 28, 1914, June 14, 1914, Reel 143, WHT.) Sullivan, *Exemplar of Americanism,* 171–77; Salman, *The Embarrassment of Slavery,* 213–45; letter from WCR to Bandholtz, November 29, 1913, Reel 8, HHB; letter from Francis Burton Harrison to Secretary of War Lindley M. Garrison, December 4, 1912, Bureau of Insular Affairs, General Records, General Classified Files 1898–1945, Declassification Review Project, NND 760024, NARA; letter from Harrison to Lindley M. Garrison, October 24, 1913, Box 42, FBH.

116. Sullivan, *Exemplar of Americanism,* 161, 171–82; Worcester, *The Philippines Past and Present* (1930 ed.), 32, 61; Worcester, *The Philippines Past and Present,* vol. 2 (1914 ed.), 659, 671; HR, 61st Congress, 3d Session, Report no. 2289, *Administration of Philippine Lands, Report by the Committee on Insular Affairs of the House of Representatives of Its Investigation of the Interior Department of the Philippine Government Touching upon the Administration of Philippine Lands and All Matters of Fact and Law Pertaining Thereto, in Pursuance of House Resolution No. 795,* vol. 1 (Washington, DC, 1911), 47–97; Fry, *A History of the Mountain Province,* 89–90; letter from Manuel L Quezon to Gen. H. H. Bandholtz, February 21, 1911, Reel 4, HHB.

117. Sullivan, *Exemplar of Americanism,* 171–72, 200–207, 221–22; Salman, *The Embarrassment of Slavery,* 247–53; letter from Felipe Buencamino, Jr., to Don Manuel, October 2, 1914, Reel 57, MLQMI; letters from Dean C. Worcester to William H. Taft, January 5, 1915, January 12, 1915, January 15, 1915, Reel 147, July 29, 1921, Reel 231, September 26, 1921, Reel 234, WHT; letters from William H. Taft to Dean C. Worcester, January 6, 1915, January 13, 1915, Reel 528, September 10, 1921, Reel 233, WHT.

118. WD, *RPC 1913,* 89.

119. Jenista, *The White Apos,* 259–60.

120. Fry, *A History of the Mountain Province,* 90, 104–5; Jenista, *The White Apos,* 236, 259.

121. Jenista, *The White Apos,* 82–90, 118–20, 126–28, 130–32, 236–39; Fry, *A History of the Mountain Province* (Quezon City, 1983), 179–83; Gerard A. Finin, *The Making of the Igorot: Contours of Cordillera Consciousness* (Quezon City, 2005), 65–67; *KR,* 5/1931, 24, 7/1932, 31–34, 3/1935, 4.

122. WD, *RPC 1913,* 101; WD, *RPC 1915,* 121–22; Jenista, *The White Apos,* 194, 254.

123. Gowing, *Mandate in Moroland,* 260–61, 313.

124. Fry, *A History of the Mountain Province,* 115–17.

125. Letter from Manuel L. Quezon to General Bandholtz, May 28, 1913, Reel 8, HHB; letter from Manuel L. Quezon to General Bandholtz, August 2, 1913, Reel 8, HHB; letter to Justice A. C. Carson, February 28, 1913, Reel 5, HHB; letter to Major Herman Hall, May 16, 1913, Reel 5, HHB; *MT,* 8/29/1912.

126. Letter to Major General Leonard Wood, April 11, 1913; letter to M. L. Quezon, April 15, 1913; letter from Harbord to Major General Leonard Wood, April 18, 1913; letter from W. Cameron Forbes to the Secretary of War, April 4, 1913, Reel 5, HHB.

127. *KR,* 6/1930, 9.

128. Worcester, *The Philippines Past and Present* (1930 ed.), 321; Jaime J. Bugarin, "Six Decades of Noble Soldiering," in Philippine Constabulary, *1960 Yearbook Philippine Constabulary* (Manila, 1960), 19; Casualties in the Philippine Constabulary, vol. 11, DCW.

129. HR, *GGPI 1925*, 267; HR, *GGPI 1930*, 52–53.

130. *KR*, 6/1930, 9; Emanuel A. Bajá, *Philippine Police System and Its Problems* (Manila, 1933), 112–21. By adult the text means males between the ages of twenty and sixty-five. See Bureau of Census and Statistics, Republic of the Philippines, *Yearbook of Philippine Statistics, 1946* (Manila, 1947), 15.

131. Chief of Staff, U.S. Army, "The Proposed Amalgamation of Scouts and Constabulary," February 18, 1911, Reel 4, HHB.

132. Extract from General McIntrye's cable of July 1, 1914; Journal (Syracuse), July 1917, Personal Name Information Files: Herman Hall, Box 260, Entry 21, BIA.

133. Letter to Colonel W. C. Taylor, December 2, 1914, Reel 10, HHB; *LV*, 7/2/1914, Reel 10, HHB; Manuel L. Quezon, "The Control of the Constabulary," *The Filipino People* 2, no. 11 (July 1914), Reel 10, HHB; letter to Rudolph Forster, August 1, 1910, Reel 3, HHB.

134. *LV*, 2/16/1914; Colonel C. E. Nathorst, January 3, 1927, General Orders no. 1, Personal Name Information Files: Rafael Crame; Philippine Constabulary, General Orders no. 3, Personal Name Information Files: Herman Hall, Box 260, Entry 21, BIA.

135. Letter from H. T. Allen to William H. Taft, September 29, 1906, Reel 60, WHT; WD, *RPC 1910*, 127; WD, *RPC 1912*, 146.

136. WD, *RPC 1915*, 132. In 1911 there were 283 Americans among a total of 377 constabulary officers. See PI, Bureau of Civil Service, *OROECSP 1911*.

137. Philippine Constabulary Report, January 19, 1916, Philippine Commission Report 1915, vol. 3, 1713–14, vol. 987, BIA.

138. Charles Burke Elliott, *The Philippines to the End of the Commission Government: A Study in Tropical Democracy* (Indianapolis, 1917), 176; Jose G. Syjuco, *Military Education in the Philippines* (Quezon City, 1977), 15.

139. Captain Alfonso A. Calderon, "The Philippine Constabulary, 1901–1951: Half-Century of Service," in Capt. Alfonso A. Calderon and Marciano C. Sicat, eds., *Golden Book Philippine Constabulary* (Manila, 1951), 28–29; letter from Rafael Crame to Secretary of the Interior, July 24, 1918, File: Constabulary, Box 60, Series VII, MLQ; Registry Committee, Association of General and Flag Officers, *General and Flag Officers of the Philippines (1896–1983)* (Quezon City, 1983), 106; WD, *GGPI 1919*, 25; HR, *GGPI 1925*, 13; HR, *GGPI 1922*, 77; letter from Francis Burton Harrison to Gen. Herman Hall, May 24, 1917, Personal Name Information Files: Herman Hall, Box 260, Entry 21, BIA; Rafael Crame, Acting Chief of Constabulary, General Orders No. 18, July 5, 1917, Personal Name Information Files: Herman Hall, Box 260, Entry 21, BIA.

140. Bugarin, "Six Decades of Noble Soldiering," 20–21.

141. Calderon, "The Philippine Constabulary 1901–1951," 26; Emanuel A. Bajá, *Philippine Police System and Its Problems*, book 2: *Police of the Commonwealth* (Manila, 1939), 93–94; Bajá, *Philippine Police System and Its Problems*, 548–49, 559, 576.

142. Bajá, *Philippine Police System and Its Problems*, 416–17.

143. Cicero C. Campos, "The Role of Police in the Philippines: A Case Study from the Third World," PhD diss., Michigan State University, 1983, 147.

144. Ibid., 203–4.

Chapter 7. American Police in Manila

1. *PFP*, 11/18/1911, 1, 11/25/1911, 1–3, 1/20/1912, 7, 12.

2. Manuel Deala Paruñgao, *The Manila Police Story* (Manila, 1976), 3–4; *KR*, 9/1933, 4–6.

3. C. A. Bayly, *Empire and Information: Intelligence Gathering and Social Communication in India, 1780–1870* (New York, 1996), 338–39.

4. WD, *A Pronouncing Gazetteer and Geographical Dictionary of the Philippine Islands* (Washington, DC, 1902), 187–94; U.S. Bureau of the Census, *Census of the Philippine Islands*, vol. 2: *Population* (Manila, 1903), 130; letter from Percy G. McDonnell to Governor Wm. H. Taft, May 21, 1903, Reel 39, WHT.

5. By 1918 the number of Manila Americans had dropped to 2,900 among a city population of 285,000. PI, Census Office, *Census of the Philippine Islands*, vol. 2: *Population and Mortality* (Manila, 1921), 32, 106; WD, *A Pronouncing Gazetteer and Geographical Dictionary of the Philippine Islands*, 184.

6. James H. Blount, *The American Occupation of the Philippines, 1898–1912* (New York, 1913), 437–38; letter from Luke E. Wright to Secretary of War, June 15, 1904, Reel 44, WHT; letter from Wm. H. Taft to Judge Harlan, October 21, 1901, Reel 33, WHT.

7. Charles H. Brent, "Religious Conditions in the Philippine Islands," File: July to December 1904, Box 6, CHB; Second Annual Report of the Bishop of the Missionary District of the Philippine Islands, attached to letter from C. H. Brent to My Dear Secretary, October 17, 1904, Reel 46, WHT.

8. *PFP*, 5/21/1910, 12.

9. For evidence of colonial patronage, see letters from General John J. Pershing, April 22, 1914, January 19, 1922, WCF; Journals, Second Series, vol. 2, 323, WCF; B. F. Coyne, secretary, Convention minutes, n.d., Reel 10, HHB; Minutes of the Insular Republican Convention, March, 31, 1904, Reel 10, HHB; A. S. Crossfield, Chairman of the Convention, April 9, 1904, Reel 10, HHB.

10. Letter to Secretary of War William H. Taft, January 29, 1908, Reel 2; [1907?], n.d., Reel 10, HHB; letters from H. H. Bandholtz to William H. Taft, January 29, 1908, Reel 75, July 19, 1908, Reel 88, WHT; letter from J. G. Harbord, December 31, 1907, Box 9, File: 1907 July–Dec, HTA; *CA*, 1/19/1908.

11. Letter from J. G. Harbord to Newton W. Gilbert, February 1, 1911, Reel 7, HHB.

12. University Club of Manila, Noted: February 27, 1910, Reel 5, HHB.

13. Letter to Colonel J. G. Harbord, September 27, 1906, Reel 1; letter from Amos G. Bellis, November 11, 1907, Reel 2; letter from J. G. Harbord to General H. H. Bandholtz, March 30, 1909, Reel 2; Memorandum: The Following Constabulary Officers Belong to the Masonic Fraternity, February 5, 1911, Reel 4; Far Eastern Commandery, Knights Templar, Constitution, October 22, 1910, Reel 10; Members of Bamboo Oasis, January 29, 1908, Reel 2; Desert of Manila in the Philippine Islands Bamboo Oasis, Joyful Feat of Nezletoo'l-Hajj, October 2, 1909, Reel 10; letter from Scribbler, May 15, 1909, Reel 3, HHB.

14. Letter to J. N. Wolfson, March 23, 1909, Reel 2; letter from F. Warner Karling, January 25, 1913, Reel 5, HHB.

15. In 1908, for example, twenty-seven of the thirty-nine senior officials in Manila's government were Americans. See George A. Malcolm, *The Revised Ordinances of the City of Manila* (Manila, 1908), 3–4.

16. General Jose Alejandrino, *The Price of Freedom* (Manila, 1949), 196–200.

17. Letter from H. H. Bandholtz to William H. Taft, August 19, 1908, Reel 91, WHT.

18. For the provost marshal general's draft charter of June 13 and the Philippine Commission's final law of July 31, 1901, see HR, *ARWD 1901, Report of the Lieutenant-General Commanding the Army*, part 5, 131–65; and Joseph Ralston Hayden, *The Philippines: A Study in National Development* (New York, 1955), 298–304.

19. E. Arsenio Manuel, *Dictionary of Philippine Biography*, vol. 1 (Quezon City, 1955), 140–44; HR, *ARWD 1901, Report of the Lieutenant-General Commanding the Army*, part 5, 86–87, 165–66; Edgar G. Bellairs, *As It Is in the Philippines* (New York, 1902), 63–64.

20. *PFP*, 11/7/1908, 9–11; William J. Pomeroy, *American Neo-colonialism: Its Emergence in the Philippines and Asia* (New York, 1970), 183, 186; Arturo G. Corpuz, *The Colonial Iron Horse: Railroads and Regional Development in the Philippines, 1875–1935* (Quezon City, 1999), 53; *MT*, 3/4/1909, 3/6/1909, 3/13/1909; letter from Edwin C. Bopp to General Bandholtz, May 11, 1912, Reel 7, HHB; Agent 30, Subject: Interest of G. McDonnell in the Manila Electric Railroad and Light Company, August 28, 1912, Reel 7, HHB; letters from Percy G. McDonnell to William H. Taft, May 26, 1905, May 27, 1905, Reel 50, July 15, 1905, Reel 52, August 3, 1906, Reel 59, October 5, 1907, October 17, 1907, October 25, 1907, Reel 70, January 25, 1908, Reel 74, WHT.

21. *MB*, 10/1/1923; *El Comercio*, 11/22/1920; *CN*, 8/14/1906; letter from Frank McIntyre to Acting Secretary of War, October 1, 1923, Personal Name Information Files: Henry B. McCoy, Entry 21, BIA; Leonard Wood, "Diaries, 1921–27," September 25, 1923, September 28, 1923, LWP; letters from Henry B. McCoy to Warren G. Harding, December 28, 1920, December 29, 1920, Reel 222, WHT;

letter from Henry B. McCoy to William Howard Taft, March 23, 1921, Reel 224, WHT; W. Cameron Forbes, Journals, vol. 5, January 11, 1912, WCF.

22. *MA*, 1/1/1903.

23. Letter to Henry L. Stimson, January 17, 1912, Confidential Letter Box, vol. 1, WCF.

24. Letter from Percy G. McDonnell to William H. Taft, August 3, 1906, Reel 59, WHT.

25. HR, *ARWD 1901, Public Laws and Resolutions Passed by the Philippine Commission*, 420–21.

26. Emanuel A. Bajá, *Philippine Police System and Its Problems*, book 2: *Police of the Commonwealth* (Manila, 1939), 170–71, 253–54; WD, *RPC 1902*, part 1, 105–19; WD, *RPC 1904*, part 1, 192–93; HR, 57th Congress, 2d Session, Document no. 2, *ARWD 1902*, vol. 11: *Acts of the Philippine Commission* (Washington, DC, 1902), 45–47.

27. HR, *ARWD 1901, Report of the Lieutenant-General Commanding the Army*, part 5, 137–38, 143, 148, 150–51, 156–57.

28. George A. Malcolm, *The Revised Ordinances of the City of Manila* (Manila, 1917), 321–23, 332–34; Malcolm, *The Revised Ordinances of the City of Manila* (1908 ed.), 67, 229–32.

29. *Witton's Manila and Philippines Directory, 1904* (Manila, 1905), 281–84.

30. Emanuel A. Bajá, *Philippine Police System and Its Problems* (Manila, 1933), 254–58, 569–70, 576.

31. WD, *RPC 1902*, part 1, 107–8.

32. Ibid., 112–13.

33. City of Manila, Department of Police, Central Office July 12, 1905, Philippine Commission Report 1905, vol. 1, part 2, GP 1399, vol. 932, BIA; *MT*, 5/23/1902, 8/22/1904.

34. Bajá, *Philippine Police System and Its Problems*, 254, 270.

35. Letter from Percy G. McDonnell to William H. Taft, August 3, 1906, Reel 59, WHT.

36. Bajá, *Philippine Police System and Its Problems*, 254, 270; WD, *RPC 1903*, part 1, 621, 629–31.

37. Report of the United States Philippine Commission 1900, 52–56, BIA; HR, *ARWD 1901, Public Laws and Resolutions Passed by the Philippine Commission*, 96–101, 202–3.

38. Malcolm, *The Revised Ordinances of the City of Manila* (1917 ed.), 321–22; International Opium Commission, *Report of the International Opium Commission*, vol. 2 (Shanghai, 1909), 21–26; *PFP*, 1/4/1930, 16–17.

39. Ken De Bevoise, *Agents of Apocalypse: Epidemic Disease in the Colonial Philippines* (Princeton, 1995), 86–87; Andrew Jimenez Abalahin, "Prostitution Policy and the Project of Modernity: A Comparative Study of Colonial Indonesia and the Philippines, 1850–1940," PhD diss., Cornell University, 2003, 290–94, 323–24; Ignacio Villamor, *Criminality in the Philippine Islands* (Manila, 1909), 56, 74; Lewis E. Gleeck Jr., *The Manila Americans (1901–1964)* (Manila, 1977), 100–101, 136–37, 176–77; Luis C. Dery, "Prostitution in Colonial Manila," *Philippine Studies* 39 (1991): 481–82; WD, *RPC 1904*, 29; Henry Parker Willis, *Our Philippine Problem: A Study of American Colonial Policy* (New York, 1905), 254–61; Homer C. Stuntz, *The Philippines and the Far East* (Cincinnati, 1904), 480; Francis Burton Harrison, *The Origins of the Philippine Republic: Extracts from the Diaries and Records of Francis Burton Harrison* (Ithaca, 1974), 110; Motoe Terami-Wada, "Karayuki-san of Manila: 1890–1920," *Philippine Studies* 34 (1986): 300.

40. Bajá, *Philippine Police System and Its Problems*, 446–67; Gleeck, *The Manila Americans (1901–1964)*, 88–89; HR, *GGPI 1924*, 68–69; *MT*, 9/20/1918, 9/21/1918, 4/9/1919, 4/13/1919; *PFP*, 10/4/1919, 4, 23, 8/23/1924, 16, 5/2/1970, 4; Zacarias Villavicencio et al. vs. Justo Lukan et al., no. 14639, March 25, 1919, *PSC 6/11/18–8/14/19*, vol. 39, 780–89, 808; letter from Edward Bowditch to Governor Forbes, May 13, 1912, Box 1, Correspondence: Bowditch, Ed., WCF; Terami-Wada, "Karayuki-san of Manila," 310–12.

41. *PFP*, 5/2/1970, 4.

42. Exhibit E: Department of Police, Central Office, Manila, July 1, 1903, B1325, vol. 911, BIA; WD, *RPC 1902*, 113, 116–19.

43. Exhibit E: Department of Police, Central Office, Manila, July 1, 1903, B1325, vol. 911, BIA; WD, *RPC 1904*, 197; WD, *RPC 1905*, part 1, 569, 573; WD, *RPC 1906*, part 3, 137; letter from William H. Taft to Percy G. McDonnell, November 5, 1903, Reel 41, WHT; *PFP*, 1/20/1912, 6; *CN*, 2/14/1906, 2/25/1906; *MA*, 2/17/1906, 2/22/1906, 2/24/1906, 2/25/1906, 3/6/1906, 3/9/1906, 3/14/1906.

44. Lewis E. Gleeck Jr., *The American Governors-General and High Commissioners in the Philippines* (Quezon City, 1986), 78–79.

45. HR, *ARWD 1906*, vol. 10, 306, 363; HR, *WDAR 1907*, vol. 10, 440–43.

46. WD, *RPC 1903*, 630–31; WD, *RPC 1904*, part 1, 195–96; WD, *RPC 1905*, part 1, 570; WD, *RPC 1906*, part 3, 135; WD, *RPC 1907*, part 1, 110; HR, *GGPI 1925*, 273; HR, *GGPI 1931*, 100.

47. Bajá, *Philippine Police System and Its Problems*, 388–89.

48. *PFP*, 11/25/1911, 2–13; *CA*, 1/19/1911.

49. *PFP*, 11/25/1911, 2–13.

50. Ibid.; letter to Colonel W. C. Rivers, January 9, 1912, Reel 5, HHB.

51. *PFP*, 11/25/1911, 2–13.

52. *PFP*, 1/20/1912, 7.

53. *PFP*, 11/25/1911, 2, 1/20/1912, 2.

54. *PFP*, 11/18/1911, 1, 1/25/1911, 1–3, 1/20/1912, 7, 12; *MT*, 10/9/1911; *LD*, 12/16/1911, 12/22/1911.

55. *PFP*, 11/25/1911, 1–3.

56. *PFP*, 1/20/1912, 12.

57. *PFP*, 12/16/1911, 3.

58. *PFP*, 12/23/1911, 2, 3.

59. Ibid., 4–7.

60. Ibid., 6–7.

61. *PFP*, 1/6/1912, 1–4, 13.

62. *PFP*, 1/13/1912, 3–6, 1/20/1912, 1, 25, 12/16/1911, 2.

63. Gleeck, *The American Governors-General and High Commissioners in the Philippines*, 90–91; *Who's Who in America*, vol. 10 (Chicago, 1919), 942; letter from Henry T. Allen to William H. Taft, July 23, 1906, Reel 59, WHT.

64. W. Cameron Forbes, Journals, vol. 2, note 102, 271, vol. 5, January 11, 1912, January 27, 1912, WCF; *The Manila Polo Club, 1909–1939* (Manila, 1939), 5–11; Peter W. Stanley, *A Nation in the Making: The Philippines and the United States, 1899–1921* (Cambridge, 1974), 100–101; *NYT*, 12/13/1903.

65. W. Cameron Forbes, Journals, vol. 5, January 11, 1912, WCF.

66. Letter to Henry L. Stimson, January 17, 1912, Confidential Letter Box, vol. 1, WCF.

67. *PFP*, 1/13/1912, 3–6; *LD*, 1/22/1912; *CA*, 10/6/1911; letter from Manuel Araullo to the Governor-General, January 16, 1912, Reel 8, HHB; Justice Isagani A. Cruz and Cynthia Cruz Datu, *Res Gestae: A Brief History of the Supreme Court (from Arellano to Narvasa)* (Manila, 2000), 61–64.

68. *PFP*, 2/24/1912, 9; *MT*, 5/7/1912, 1/10/1912, 1/11/1912, 1/25/1912, 5/7/1912; Constabulary Form no. 35-A, June 2, 1932, Personal Name Information Files: Otto F. Lauser, Entry 21, BIA; *MB*, 6/24/1932.

69. *MT*, 1/22/1912.

70. *PFP*, 1/20/1912, 2–13, 5/11/1912, 4; *MT*, 1/20/1912; letter to Colonel W. C. Rivers, January 9, 1912, Reel 5, HHB; letter from Edward Bowditch to Governor Forbes, April 15, 1912, Box One, Correspondence: Bowditch, Ed., WCF.

71. *PFP*, 1/20/1912, 1, 1/27/1912, 14, 2/24/1912, 1, 2, 3/2/1912, 3; *MT*, 1/24/1912, 2/21/1912, 2/24/1912; *LD*, 1/24/1912.

72. *PFP*, 1/20/1912, 1, 25.

73. *PFP*, 12/16/1911, 2, 2/17/1912, 2.

74. *PFP*, 3/2/1912, 1; *MT*, 2/26/1912.

75. *PFP*, 2/3/1912, 12, 2/10/1912, 4.

76. *PFP*, 3/9/1912, 5.

77. Letter to the Governor General, February 2, 1912, Reel 7, HHB.

78. *PFP*, 5/11/1912, 11; *MT*, 5/6/1912.

79. *MT*, 3/21/1912, 5/6/1912, 5/9/1912, 10/29/1913; letter from Francis Burton Harrison to Secretary of War Lindley M. Garrison, December 4, 1912, BIA, General Classified Files 1898–1945, Declassification Review Project, NND 760024, NARA.

80. *MT*, 5/6/1912, 10/29/1913; letter from Francis Burton Harrison to Secretary of War Lindley M. Garrison, December 4, 1912, BIA.

81. *PFP,* 3/23/1912, 1, 5/11/1912, 4; *MT,* 3/20/1912, 5/6/1912; letter from R. M. Shearer to Luther W. Mott, March 17, 1914, Personal Name Information Files: Walter E. Wilson, Entry 21, BIA.

82. *MT,* 5/4/1912.

83. *LV,* 5/11/1912; BIA, General Classified Files 1898–1945, no. 2552, NARA; letter from Edward Bowditch to Governor Forbes, May 9, 1912, Box 1, Correspondence: Bowditch, Ed., WCF.

84. *PFP,* 5/11/1912, 1; *MT,* 5/6/1912; *CA,* 10/8/1911; *LD,* 5/11/1912; letter from Edwin C. Bopp to General Bandholtz, May 11, 1912, Reel 7, HHB.

85. Letter from Edwin C. Bopp to General Bandholtz, May 11, 1912, Reel 7, HHB; *MT,* 5/7/1912.

86. Letter from Edwin C. Bopp to General Bandholtz, May 11, 1912, Reel 7, HHB.

87. *MT,* 5/8/1912, 5/16/1912; letter from Edward Bowditch to Governor Forbes, May 9, 1912, Box One, Correspondence: Bowditch, Ed., WCF.

88. Letter from Edwin C. Bopp to General Bandholtz, May 11, 1912, Reel 7, HHB.

89. *PFP,* 4/13/1912, 4.

90. *PFP,* 2/8/1913, 6, 4/19/1913, 4; *MT,* 2/4/1913, 4/14/1913, 4/21/1913; letter from Edward Bowditch to Governor Forbes, April 15, 1912, Box One, Correspondence: Bowditch, Ed., WCF.

91. *PFP,* 12/16/1911, 2.

92. H. W. Brands, *Bound to Empire: The United States and the Philippines* (New York, 1992), 102–3.

93. HR, 62d Congress, 2d Session, *Limit of Indebtedness of the Philippine Government: Hearings before the Committee on Insular Affairs* (Washington, DC, 1912), 31–33, 56–69.

94. Letter from L. M. Southworth to Solicitor General Harvey, November 16, 1910, Box 38, File: Baguio Scandal, Southworth Letter On, FBH.

95. Ibid.; W. Cameron Forbes, Journals, vol. 4, October 31, 1910, November 1, 1910, November 14, 1910, WCF; *MT,* 11/12/1910.

96. Agent 30, August 1, 1911, August 19, 1911, August 21, 1911, September 23, 1911, Reel 7, HHB.

97. W. Cameron Forbes, Journals, vol. 2, July 24, 1907, vol. 4, August 7, 1911; letter to Brigadier General Frank McIntyre, May 5, 1913, Confidential Letter Box, vol. 2, WCF.

98. *Congressional Record: Containing the Proceedings and Debates of the Sixty-first Congress, Second Session,* vol. 45 (Washington, DC, 1910), 3784–89, 4705; Jonathan Fast and Luzviminda Francisco, "Philippine Historiography and the De-mystification of Imperialism: A Review Essay," *Journal of Contemporary Asia* 4, no. 3 (1974): 348–49; Richard Tucker, *Insatiable Appetite: The United States and the Ecological Degradation of the Tropical World* (Berkeley, 2000), 37–42, 105–10.

99. *Congressional Record: Containing the Proceedings and Debates of the Sixty-first Congress, Second Session,* vol. 45, 4689, 4695–97; *New York World,* 6/9/1909; *NYT,* 6/13/1909; J. A. Hobson, *The Fruits of American Protection: The Effects of the Dingley Tariff upon the Industries of the Country, and Especially upon the Well Being of the People* (New York, 1906), 8–11.

100. *Congressional Record: Containing the Proceedings and Debates of the Sixty-first Congress, Second Session,* vol. 45, 4698–4706; HR, 61st Congress, 2d Session, Document no. 901, *Examination of Custom House Frauds* (Washington, DC, 1910), 3–14; SEN, 55th Congress, 1st Session, Document no. 390, *Charges of Bribery and Corruption* (Washington, DC, 1897), 3–7; Frank Hindman Golay, *Face of Empire: United States–Philippine Relations, 1898–1946* (Quezon City, 1997), 134–36; Charles Burke Elliott, *The Philippines to the End of the Commission Government: A Study in Tropical Democracy* (Indianapolis, 1917), 55–57; *NYT,* 11/19/1909, 11/30/1909, 12/21/1909, 4/15/1910, 5/18/1910, 6/1/1911; Godfrey Hodgson, *The Colonel: The Life and Wars of Henry Stimson, 1867–1950* (New York, 1990), 65–67; Henry L. Stimson and McGeorge Bundy, *On Active Service in Peace and War* (New York, 1948), 10–14; Charles Norcross, "The Trail of the Hunger Tax," *Cosmopolitan* 47 (November 1909): 588–97 (continued November 1909, 712–21; December 1909, 65–73; January 1910, 192–98); Howard J. Howland, "The Case of the Seventeen Holes," *Outlook* 92 (May 1909): 25–38.

101. *Congressional Record: Containing the Proceedings and Debates of the Sixty-first Congress, Second Session,* vol. 45, 4706–10.

102. HR, 61st Congress, 3d Session, Document No. 1261, *Special Report of J. M. Dickinson Secretary of War to the President on the Philippines* (Washington, DC, 1911), 13–17; *NYT,* 5/13/1911; *MT,* 9/3/1910.

103. Golay, *Face of Empire,* 137–39; HR, 61st Congress, 3d Session, Report no. 2289, *Administration of Philippine Lands,* vol. 1 (Washington, DC, 1911), xxvii–xl, 203–4.

104. Letter from Manuel Quezon to General H. H. Bandholtz, February 25, 1911, Reel 4, HHB.

105. *MT,* 11/11/1912.

106. *Congressional Record: Containing the Proceedings and Debates of the Sixty-second Congress, Third Session,* vol. 49 (Washington, DC, 1913), 2150–51, 2154–55.

107. Letters to William H. Taft, February 11, 1913, April 4, 1913, Confidential Letter Box, vol. 2, WCF.

108. Letter to Right Reverend C. H. Brent, July 21, 1913, Confidential Letter Box, vol. 2, WCF.

109. Letter to Professor Henry L Stimson, February 9, 1914, Confidential Letter Box, vol. 2, WCF.

110. *MT,* 11/5/1912, 11/12/1912, 11/19/1912, 11/22/1912, 12/6/1912, 12/10/1912, 12/11/1912, 12/21/1912; *CA,* 12/6/1912; Superintendent, Information Division, February 4, 1913, Reel 8, HHB; *PFP,* 5/4/1912.

111. Letters from Charles M. Swift to W. H. Taft, January 24, 1903, Reel 38, April 6, 1904, Reel 43, January 7, 1905, Reel 47, February 3, 1906, Reel 55, July 20, 1906, Reel 59, November 25, 1908, Reel 110, February 19, 1916, Reel 163; letter from W. H. Taft to "My Dear Charley Swift," September 18, 1927, Reel 295, WHT.

112. McDonnell served on the Municipal Board from January 4, 1902, to December 1, 1912 (see letter from Chas. C. Walcutt Jr., November 7, 1918, Personal Name Information Files: Percy McDonnell, Entry 21, BIA). Letters from Percy G. McDonnell to William H. Taft, May 27, 1905, Reel 50, July 15, 1905, Reel 52, WHT; letter from W. H. Taft to Luke E. Wright, January 7, 1905, Reel 484, October 19, 1905, Reel 486, WHT; *PFP,* 11/7/1908, 8; Pomeroy, *American Neo-colonialism,* 183; Malcolm, *The Revised Ordinances of the City of Manila* (1908 ed.), 303–20; George A. Malcolm, *The Revised Ordinances of the City of Manila* (Manila, 1927), 446–48, 490–92, 494–95.

113. Letter from Edwin C. Bopp to General Bandholtz, May 11, 1912, Reel 7, HHB.

114. Ibid.; Agent 30, Subject: Interest of G. McDonnell in the Manila Electric Railroad and Light Company, August 28, 1912, Reel 7, HHB. For details on the corrupt influence of street rail on U.S. cities such as Milwaukee, Cleveland, and Cincinnati, see Lincoln Steffens, *The Struggle for Self-Government* (New York, 1906), 112–13, 165–66, 176–77, 189–91.

115. *MT,* 11/12/1912, 11/16/1912, 11/18/1912; *PFP,* 11/16/1912; Memorandum for Superintendent, Information Division, December 4, 1912, Reel 7, HHB.

116. Agent 30, December 24, 1912, Reel 7, HHB; Agent 49, July 3, 1913, Reel 7, HHB; *LV,* 11/5/1913, Reel 10, HHB; *LD,* November 5, 1913, Reel 10, HHB; *MT,* 11/29/1912, 11/30/1912.

117. Superintendent, Information Division, December 10, 1912, Reel 8, HHB.

118. Superintendent, Information Division, December 21, 1912, Reel 8, HHB.

119. Ibid.

120. *MT,* 1/15/1913, 3/1/1913; letter from Assistant to Chief of Bureau to Appointment Clerk, Department of Interior, November 20, 1916, Personal Name Information Files: Charles R. Trowbridge, Entry 21, BIA; letter from Appointment Clerk, Department of the Interior to Appointment Clerk, BIA, November 13, 1916, Personal Name Information Files: Charles R. Trowbridge, Entry 21, BIA.

121. *MT,* 4/19/1913; *PFP,* 5/17/1913, 4, 5/11/1918, 3; Walter Robb, "Chief of Police Green: Remarks on Career," *American Chamber of Commerce Journal,* January 1929, 7; letter from Frank McIntyre to Adjutant General, July 2, 1918, Personal Name Information Files: John W. Green, Box 249, Entry 21, BIA; letter from John W. Green to Adjutant General, July 2, 1918, Personal Name Information Files: John W. Green, Box 249, Entry 21, BIA.

122. Letter to A. C. Carson, April 11, 1913, Reel 5, HHB.

123. *KR,* 9/1927, 5–8, 9/1932, 12.

124. JWG [John W. Green], Confidential Memorandum, BIA, July 24, 1923, Personal Name Information Files: Ray Conley, Entry 21, BIA.

125. Letter from Thomas Cary Welch to William H. Taft, January 5, 1916, Reel 162, WHT.

126. Letter from Francis Burton Harrison to Secretary of War Lindley M. Garrison, December 4, 1912, BIA; memo prepared by Secretary of War, May 1914, Box 42, FBH.

127. *MT,* 10/27/1913, 10/28/1913, 10/29/1913, 11/6/1913; *PFP,* 11/1/1913, 13.

128. Lewis E. Gleeck Jr., *The American Half-Century (1898–1946)* (Quezon City, 1998), 181–83; *PFP,* 11/1/1913, 13.

129. Agent 11, November 8, 1913, Reel 8, HHB.

130. Gleeck, *The American Half-Century,* 188–89; *MB,* 2/4/1916; telegram from Dean C. Worcester to John R. Wilson, July 2, 1914, Reel 142, WHT; telegram to Dean C. Worcester, September 29, 1914, Reel 142, WHT; letter from Percy McDonnell to Dean C. Worcester, July 23, 1914, Reel 142, WHT; letter from Dean C. Worcester to J. Northcott, January 28, 1916, Reel 162, WHT; letters from J. Northcott to Dean C. Worcester, January 27, 1916, February 10, 1916, Reel 162, WHT; letter from Dean C. Worcester to W. H. Taft, February 5, 1916, Reel 162, January 8, 1916, Reel 167, WHT; letters from Heiser to Worcester, January 27, n.d. [1906], Reel 162, WHT; letter to Frank Herrier, January 28, 1916, Reel 162, WHT; letter from Lt. Whitmarsh to Worcester, January 21, 1916, Reel 162, WHT.

131. Letter from W. A. Kincaid to H. L. Higgins, December 18, 1914, BIA no. 13931-A-355-B, Entry 5, BIA; letter from T. C. Welch to W. A. Kinkaid, December 18, 1914, BIA no. 13931-A-355-C, Entry 5, BIA; Stanley, *A Nation in the Making,* 210–12.

132. Gleeck, *The American Half-Century,* 186–87; letter from Henry Breckenridge to Attorney General, October 31, 1913, Personal Name Information Files: John Harding, Entry 21, RG 350, NARA; letter from Harrison to Lindley M. Garrison, October 24, 1913, Box 42, FBH.

133. Letter from Robert Lansing to Governor General of the Philippine Islands, February 10, 1917, Personal Name Information Files: Percy McDonnell, Entry 21, BIA; letters from Percy G. McDonnell to William H. Taft, June 29, 1916, July 13, 1916, Reel 168, WHT.

134. Stanley, *A Nation in the Making,* 211–12.

135. *NYT,* 12/2/1915; letters from Dean C. Worcester to William H. Taft, December 29, 1914, Reel 146, January 5, 1915, Reel 147, January 30, 1915, Reel 148, May 19, 1915, January 28, 1916, Reel 162, WHT; letter from Dean C. Worcester to J. Northcott, January 28, 1916, Reel 162, WHT.

136. Letter from James J. Rafferty, September 9, 1915, Box 40, File: McCoy Case, *U.S. vs. Henry B. McCoy,* FBH; Gleeck, *The Manila Americans,* 303. In a letter to Worcester, Taft called Rafferty "a trimmer and a blatant office seeker." Letter from William H. Taft to Dean C. Worcester, May 29, 1915, Reel 531, WHT.

137. For details about George Seaver, see *American Chamber of Commerce Journal,* April 1938, Personal Name Information Files: George H. Seaver, Entry 21, RG 350, NARA; *MB,* 1/9/1920; *MT,* 1/9/1920; *American Chamber of Commerce Journal,* February 1930, 6; James J. Halsema, *E. J. Halsema: Colonial Engineer* (Quezon City, 1991), 136; and *KR,* 9/1933, 4–8.

138. *MT,* 5/3/1914; WD, *GGPI 1917,* 11; PI, Bureau of Civil Service, *OROECSP 1911, OROECSP 1916, OROECSP 1921.*

139. Paruñgao, *The Manila Police Story,* 3–4; *KR,* 9/1933, 4–6.

140. *MT,* 3/20/1919, 3/27/1919, 4/2/1919; Zacarias Villavicencio et al. vs. Justo Lukan et al., No. 14639, March 25, 1919; *PSC 11/6/18–8/14/19,* vol. 39, 778–812.

141. *MT,* 5/23/1919, 5/24/1919.

142. *MT,* 5/25/1919, 5/27/1919, 5/28/1919, 5/29/1919, 5/30/1919, 5/31/1919, 6/9/1919, 6/13/1919, 6/16/1919, 6/17/1919, 6/19/1919; *Weekly Times,* 6/1/1919.

143. *MT,* 6/21/1919, 6/22/1919, 6/26/19, 7/12/1919; *PFP,* 6/28/1919.

144. *MT,* 12/14/1920, 2/4/1921; *MB,* 12/15/1920.

145. *MT,* 12/16/1920, 12/18/1920, 1/3/1921, 2/4/1921; *MB,* 12/16/1920; *NYT,* 12/17/1920, 12/19/1920.

146. *MB,* 12/17/1920, 12/18/1920, 12/22/1920, 12/23/1920; *MT,* 12/17/1920, 12/19/1920, 12/22/1920, 12/23/1920.

147. *PFP,* 12/18/1920, 16; *MT,* 12/20/1920, 12/21/1920; *Independent,* 1/6/1923, 21, 1/29/1921, 3.

148. *MT,* 2/4/1921.

149. Jaime J. Bugarin, "Six Decades of Noble Soldiering," in Philippine Constabulary, *1960 Yearbook Philippine Constabulary* (Manila, 1960), 22; *NYT,* 7/2/1921; *PFP,* 3/11/1922, 13; *MT,* 1/29/1929, 11/17/1922.

150. Robb, "Chief of Police Green," 7; *PFP,* 5/11/1918, 3; *MB,* 1/9/1920; *El Ideal,* 3/9/1922; *KR,* 4/1927, 5; JWG [John W. Green], Confidential Memorandum, July 24, 1923, Personal Name Information Files: Ray Conley, Entry 21, BIA; telegram from Palma, January 24, 1919, Personal Name Information Files: John W. Green, Box 249, Entry 21, BIA; letter from Gregorio Alcid to Sadie M. Yackey, February 16, 1921, Personal Name Information Files: John W. Green, Box 249, Entry 21, BIA; letter from Jose Gil to Governor-General, August 2, 1929, Personal Name Information Files: John W. Green, Box 249, Entry 21, BIA.

151. HR, *GGPI 1922,* 82–83; HR, *GGPI 1923,* 98; *PFP,* 12/16/1922, 2, 4; Robb, "Chief of Police Green," 6–7; *KR,* 6/1927, 11, 12.

152. HR, *GGPI 1924,* 68; *MT,* 2/10/1923; Robb, "Chief of Police Green," 6.

153. Bajá, *Philippine Police System and Its Problems,* 254–58, 569–70, 576.

Chapter 8. The Conley Case

1. Teodoro M. Kalaw, *Aide-de-Camp to Freedom* (Manila, 1965), 176–78; Michael Onorato, *Leonard Wood and the Philippine Cabinet Crisis of 1923* (Marikina, 1988), 62–64; Leonard Wood, "Diaries, 1921–27," July 17, 1923, LWP.

2. George A. Malcolm, *American Colonial Careerist: Half a Century of Official Life and Personal Experience in the Philippines and Puerto Rico* (Boston, 1957), 31.

3. Joseph Ralston Hayden, *The Philippines: A Study in National Development* (New York, 1955), 339–40; Teodoro A. Agoncillo and Oscar M. Alfonso, *History of the Filipino People* (Quezon City, 1967), 368–69; Renato Constantino, *The Making of a Filipino: A Story of Philippine Colonial Politics* (Quezon City, 1969), 48–50; H. W. Brands, *Bound to Empire: The United States and the Philippines* (New York, 1992), 131–32.

4. W. Cameron Forbes, Journals, Second Series, vol. 2, 45–46, WCF.

5. Ibid., 46, 108–9.

6. For Wood's career, see *NYT,* 1/11/1899, 3/10/1900, 5/15/1900, 7/26/1900, 3/25/1902, 6/21/1903; Eric Fisher Wood, *Leonard Wood: Conservator of Americanism* (New York, 1920), 56–71; Henry Harrison Lewis, "General Wood at Santiago: Americanizing a Cuban City," *McClure's,* March 1899, 460–69; Ray Stannard Baker, "General Leonard Wood: A Character Sketch," *McClure's,* February 1900, 368–79; Major J. E. Runcie, "American Misgovernment of Cuba," *North American Review* 170 (February 1900): 284–94; Theodore Roosevelt, "General Leonard Wood: A Model American Administrator," *Outlook,* January 7, 1899, 20–23; George Kennan, "Friction in Cuba," *Outlook,* March 25, 1899, 675–68; Joseph B. Bishop, "Our Work as a Civilizer," *International Quarterly* 6 (September-December 1902, December–March 1903): 201–5; SEN, 59th Congress, 1st Session, *Senate Documents,* vol. 8 (Washington, DC, 1906), 129–33, 218–19, 223–24; SEN, 58th Congress, 2d Session, Executive 2, *Nomination of Leonard Wood* (Washington, DC, 1904), 3–5; SEN, 58th Congress, 2d Session, Executive 1, *Confirmation of Leonard Wood* (Washington, DC, 1904), 55–73; Lewis L. Gould, *The Presidency of William McKinley* (Lawrence, 1980), 193–94; and Margaret Leech, *In the Days of McKinley* (New York, 1959), 374–75, 392–93.

For the controversy surrounding Wood's Cuban record, see *MA,* 4/24/1903; *MT,* 4/28/1903; *NYT,* 3/19/1903, 11/13/1903, 11/21/1903, 11/25/1903, 11/28/1903, 12/1/1903, 12/4/1903, 12/8/1903, 1/5/1904, 3/12/1904; SEN, 59th Congress, 1st Session, *Senate Documents,* vol. 8 (Washington, DC, 1906), 129–33, 218–19, 223–24; SEN, 58th Congress, 2d Session, Executive C [Confidential], *Nomination of Leonard Wood to Be Major-General. Hearings before the Committee on Military Affairs concerning the Nomination of Brig. Gen. Leonard Wood to Be a Major-General, United States Army* (Washington, DC, 1904), 631–32, 778–80, 813–20; SEN, 58th Congress, 2d Session, Executive 3, *Nomination of Leonard Wood* (Washington, DC, 1904), 8–16, 18–24; SEN, 58th Congress, 2d Session, Executive 2, *Nomination of Leonard Wood* (Washington, DC, 1904), 6–16; and Hermann Hagedorn, *Leonard Wood: A Biography,* vol. 1 (New York, 1931), 305–6, 388–89.

7. Leonard Wood, "Diaries, 1921–27," August 17, 1921, LWP; Hagedorn, *Leonard Wood,* 222–23, 267–71.

8. Leonard Wood, "Diaries, 1921–27," August 13, 1924, LWP.

9. Ibid., May 9, 1921, May 10, 1921, June 7, 1921, June 13, 1921.

10. Ibid., June 1, 1921; James J. Halsema, *E. J. Halsema, Colonial Engineer: A Biography* (Quezon City, 1991), 156, 344–45; Lewis E. Gleeck Jr., *The American Governors-General and High Commissioners in the Philippines* (Quezon City, 1986), 160–61, 382–83; Malcolm, *American Colonial Careerist,* 30; *NYT,* 5/16/1919. The diary entry identifies the caller only as "Colonel Quinn (?)," but the constabulary roster shows only one person of that name, the assistant chief, Col. James F. Quinn. See PI, Bureau of Civil Service, *OROECSP 1917,* 20.

11. Leonard Wood, "Diaries, 1921–27," June 7, 1921, June 13, 1921, LWP.

12. Ibid., May 21, 1921, May 29, 1921, June 5, 1921.

13. HR, 67th Congress, 2d Session, House Document 325, *Report of the Special Mission to the Philippine Islands to the Secretary of War* (Washington, DC, 1922), 7–10; Frank Hindman Golay, *Face of Empire: United States–Philippine Relations, 1898–1946* (Quezon City, 1997), 231–32; W. Cameron Forbes, *The Philippine Islands,* vol. 2 (Boston, 1928), 536–44.

14. Peter W. Stanley, *A Nation in the Making: The Philippines and the United States, 1899–1921* (Cambridge, 1974), 240–46.

15. Carlos Quirino, *Philippine Tycoon: The Biography of an Industrialist* (Manila, 1987), 58–60; Katherine Mayo, *The Isles of Fear: The Truth about the Philippines* (New York, 1925), 110–11; F. C. Fisher and Michael Camus, Report Concerning Liability, Civil or Criminal, of Former Directors of the Philippine National Bank, November 28, 1923, 161–62, 186–91, 194–216, 225, 241, 244–46, 248, 250–55, File: PNB-1923 Oct.–Nov.; letter from Manuel Quezon, To: Directors, Philippine National Bank, August 23, 1923, File: PNB-1923, Box 170, MLQ.

16. Stanley, *A Nation in the Making,* 244; Lewis E. Gleeck Jr., *The Manila Americans (1901–1964)* (Manila, 1977), 109.

17. Lewis E. Gleeck Jr., *The American Half-Century (1898–1946)* (Quezon City, 1998), 262–63; Forbes, *The Philippine Islands,* vol. 2, 273; HR, *GGPI 1922,* 15.

18. W. Cameron Forbes, *The Philippine Islands* (Cambridge, 1945), 354–55.

19. Letter from Frank McIntyre, August 5, 1921; cable from McIntyre to General Wood, July 28, 1921; letter from Daniel R. Williams to president, July 18, 1921; letter from Chas. Welch, June 29, 1921; letter from James E. Watson to Warren G. Harding, July 26, 1921; letter from Wm. H. Anderson to Judge W. N. Towner, July 19, 1921, Personal Name Information File: Leonard Wood, Entry 21, BIA.

20. Forbes, *The Philippine Islands,* 345–64.

21. Halsema, *E. J. Halsema,* 136, 149, 163; JWG [John W. Green], Confidential Memorandum, July 24, 1923, Personal Name Information Files: Ray Conley, Entry 21, BIA.

22. Registry Committee, Association of General and Flag Officers, *General and Flag Officers of the Philippines (1896–1983)* (Quezon City, 1983), 106.

23. Letter from Ray Conley to Chief Bureau of Insular Affairs, July 8, 1930, Personal Name Information Files: Ray Conley, Entry 21, BIA; letter from John W. Green to Richard Ely, September 15, 1938, Personal Name Information File: John W. Green, Entry 21, BIA.

24. *Independent,* 6/9/1917, 1–2, 9/15/1917, 1–2; *PFP,* 5/5/1917, 16, 5/26/1917.

25. *LV,* 3/10/1923; *MT,* 4/28/1923; *MB,* 2/14/1921; JWG [John W. Green], Confidential Memorandum, July 24, 1923, Personal Name Information Files: Ray Conley, Entry 21, BIA; letter from Jose Gil to Ray Conley, February 26, 1921, Personal Name Information Files: Ray Conley, Entry 21, BIA.

26. *LV,* 3/10/1923; *PFP,* 9/23/1922, 33; JWG [John W. Green], Confidential Memorandum, July 24, 1923, Personal Name Information Files: Ray Conley, Entry 21, BIA.

27. *MT,* 5/3/1923; Investigation Conducted by the Manila Police Investigating Board at the Office of the Director of Civil Service, Manila, July 9, 1923, Personal Name Information Files: Ray Conley, Entry 21, BIA; JWG [John W. Green], Confidential Memorandum, July 24, 1923, Personal Name Information Files: Ray Conley, Entry 21, BIA.

28. HR, *GGPI 1923,* 37–39; Leonard Wood, "Diaries, 1921–27," July 14, 1923, LWP.

29. *MT,* 4/28/1923; JWG [John W. Green], Confidential Memorandum, July 24, 1923, Personal Name Information Files: Ray Conley, Entry 21, BIA.

30. JWG [John W. Green], Confidential Memorandum, July 24, 1923, Personal Name Information Files: Ray Conley, Entry 21, BIA. For the leadership role of Ramon J. Fernandez in San Miguel, see *Manila Times, Investors and Settlers Edition,* February 1910, 66–67; *MT,* 6/27/1912; and *Tribune,* 2/25/1931.

31. *MT,* 4/26/1923; *LV,* 4/26/1923.

32. *MT,* 4/18/1923.

33. *LV,* 4/26/1923.

34. *LV,* 4/26/1923; *MT,* 4/26/1923, 4/27/1923; *El Debate,* 4/25/1923.

35. Kalaw, *Aide-de-Camp to Freedom,* 176–78; Carlos Quirino, *The Laurel Story: The Life and Times of Dr. Jose Laurel, President of the Second Republic of the Philippines* (Manila, 1992), 32–33;

Remegio E. Agpalo, *Jose Laurel: National Leader and Political Philosopher* (Quezon City, 1992), 117–20; Secretary of Interior, Memorandum: Conley case, To Mayor Manila thru Director of Civil Service, May 25, 1923, Laurel Library; HR, *GGPI 1923*, 37–38.

36. *MT*, 3/9/1923.

37. *LV*, 3/10/1923. For *panchong*, see *Visayan Daily Star Negros Oriental*, August 20, 2008, http://www.visayandailystar.com/2008/August/20/negor2.htm, accessed March 4, 2009.

38. *PFP*, 3/17/1923; *MT*, 3/12/1923.

39. Teofilo del Castillo and José del Castillo, *The Saga of José Laurel (His Brother's Keeper)* (Manila, 1949), 76–77; Mayo, *The Isles of Fear*, 135.

40. *MT*, 4/18/1923.

41. *Independent*, 4/28/1923, 13–14, 23–25, 27–28.

42. *MT*, 4/18/1923.

43. *MT*, 4/26/1923; *LV*, 4/26/1923.

44. *MT*, 4/28/1923, 4/30/1923; *PFP*, 4/28/1923, 8, 5/5/1923, 8.

45. *MT*, 5/3/1923.

46. *PFP*, 5/5/1923, 8.

47. *Independent*, 5/12/1923, 6–8.

48. *MT*, 5/19/1923; *PFP*, 5/26/1923, 4–5.

49. *Independent*, 5/26/1923; *El Debate*, 5/20/1923; *PFP*, 5/26/1923; *MT*, 7/15/1923.

50. *MT*, 6/26/1923; *El Debate*, 6/29/1923, 7/11/1923, 8/4/1923.

51. *PFP*, 6/2/1923, 14, 7/17/1926, 36–37; *MT*, 6/26/1923; *El Debate*, 5/6/1923.

52. Statement of James Watson, April 18, 1923, Laurel Library. Several colonial registers list James P. Watson as "clerk, Police Department." See *Witton's Manila and Philippines Directory, 1904* (Manila, 1905), 820; and PI, Bureau of Civil Service, *OROECSP 1905*, 122.

53. Secretary of Interior, Memorandum: Conley case, To Mayor Manila thru Director of Civil Service, May 25, 1923, Laurel Library. The document is also published in Ricardo T. Jose, ed., *Selected Correspondence of Dr. Jose Laurel* (Manila, 1997), 20–23.

54. Leonard Wood, "Diaries, 1921–27," Memorandum of a Conference Held This Date by the Governor-General—May 26, 1923, LWP.

55. HR, *GGPI 1923*, 38–39; *Philippines Herald*, 7/17/1923; Leonard Wood, "Diaries, 1921–27," Memorandum Order—July 6, 1923, July 12, 1923, Luis Torres to the Governor General—July 12, 1923, LWP; Investigation Conducted by the Manila Police Investigating Board at the Office of the Director of Civil Service, Manila, July 9, 1923, Personal Name Information Files: Ray Conley, Entry 21, BIA.

56. Agpalo, *Jose Laurel*, 117–20; HR, *GGPI 1923*, 39; Leonard Wood, "Diaries, 1921–27," July 14, 1923, Luis Torres to the Governor General—July 14, 1923, C. W. Franks to Jose Laurel—July 14, 1923, LWP; *PFP*, 7/21/1923, 27, 30; *El Debate*, 7/15/1923.

57. HR, *GGPI 1923*, 38–39; Leonard Wood, "Diaries, 1921–27," July 16, 1923, LWP; *PFP*, 7/21/1923, 27, 30; *El Debate*, 7/17/1923; letter from Leonard Wood, To Whom It May Concern, August 31, 1923, Personal Name Information Files: Ray Conley, Entry 21, BIA; letter from Leonard Wood, To Whom It May Concern, August 30, 1923, Box 163, LWP.

58. Kalaw, *Aide-de-Camp to Freedom*, 176–78; Onorato, *Leonard Wood and the Philippine Cabinet Crisis of 1923*, 62–64; Leonard Wood, "Diaries, 1921–27," July 17, 1923, LWP.

59. *El Debate*, 7/18/1923, 7/21/1923, 7/26/1923.

60. Quirino, *Philippine Tycoon*, 59–60, 66–67.

61. Letter from Silvino Gallardo to Manuel L. Quezon, April 6, 1929, File: Constabulary, Box 61, Series 7, MLQ; Summary of All Records of Captain Silvino Gallardo (of Rizal), Headquarters Philippine Constabulary, January 6, 1936, File: Constabulary, Box 62, Series 7, MLQ.

62. JWG [John W. Green], Confidential Memorandum, July 24, 1923, Personal Name Information Files: Ray Conley, Entry 21, BIA.

63. JWG [John W. Green], Confidential Memorandum, August 1, 1923, Personal Name Information Files: Ray Conley, Entry 21, BIA.

64. Michael Onorato, interview with Don Ramon Fernandez, Manila, April 2, 1964. Dr. Onorato generously shared his notes of the interview with me.

65. Del Castillo, *The Saga of José Laurel,* 76.

66. Ibid.

67. Leonard Wood, "Diaries, 1921–27," April 2, 1922, August 19, 1922, January 20, 1923, May 7, 1923, July 11, 1923, January 9, 1924, LWP. According to General Wood, "Osborne married . . . Miss Katherine Thompson of Greenville, Delaware, a very nice girl who was at the same station with Louisita in France." Letter from Leonard Wood, April 14, 1922, WCF.

68. Leonard Wood, "Diaries, 1921–27," August 19, 1922, July 11, 1923, September 23, 1924, October 9, 1924, LWP; Adjutant General's Office, *Official Army Register, January 1, 1923* (Washington, DC, 1923), 1312–13.

69. Leonard Wood, "Diaries, 1921–27," September 28, 1923, April 1, 1925, March 1, 1926, LWP; Gleeck, *The American Half-Century,* 286. Since General Bandholtz was on an intimate first-name basis with the reporter and still corresponded with both Crame and Quezon, he could have been the conduit for this information from Manila. See letter to Herbert Swope, March 4, 1922, Reel 8, HHB.

70. *NYT,* 12/26/1923.

71. *NYT,* 12/26/1923, 12/27/1923, 12/28/1923, 12/29/1923, 1/4/1924.

72. *NYT,* 12/27/1923.

73. Leonard Wood, "Diaries, 1921–27," January 21, 1924, May 11, 1924, June 3, 1924, September 23, 1924, January 16, 1925, February 24, 1925, February 26, 1925, March 5, 1925, April 5, 1925, September 17, 1925, November 4, 1925, February 4, 1926, February 13, 1926, LWP; *NYT,* 2/3/1924, 4/13/1924, 4/20/1924, 10/28/1924, 12/20/1924, 12/23/1924, 12/28/1924, 2/21/1925, 2/24/1925, 3/30/1925, 5/13/1925, 11/21/1925, 2/14/1926, 11/27/1926, 9/15/1928.

74. Onorato, *Leonard Wood,* 55–58; Golay, *Face of Empire,* 236–37, 243–44.

75. Kalaw, *Aide-de-Camp to Freedom,* 176–82; Leonard Wood, "Diaries, 1921–27," July 17, 1923, July 19, 1923, LWP; letter from Leonard Wood, June 12, 1922, WCF; Malcolm, J., "Decision," Ramon R. Papa, Petitioner-Appellee, versus the Municipal Board of the City of Manila, Respondent-Appellant, *PSC,* G.R. No. 23892, March 23, 1925; Onorato, *Leonard Wood,* 64–65; Hayden, *The Philippines,* 339; Michael Onorato, interview with Don Ramon Fernandez, Manila, February 12, 1964.

76. Kalaw, *Aide-de-Camp to Freedom,* 181–82.

77. Leonard Wood, "Diaries, 1921–27," September 24, 1923, September 27, 1923, LWP.

78. Leonard Wood, "Diaries, 1921–27," September 25, 1923, September 28, 1923, LWP; letter from Leonard Wood to Forbes, November 16, 1923, Box 164, LWP; letter from John W. Haussermann, September 28, 1923, Box 164, LWP; Gleeck, *The Manila Americans,* 68, 105, 107, 108, 128; Forbes, *The Philippine Islands,* vol. 2, 223–24; Gleeck, *The American Half-Century,* 285–87; letter from F. R. McCoy, March 17, 1924, WCF.

79. Leonard Wood, "Diaries, 1921–27," September 28, 1923, September 29, 1923, LWP; letter from Leonard Wood to Ben F. Wright, September 28, 1923, Box 164, LWP; Gleeck, *The American Half-Century,* 285–87; letter from F. R. McCoy, March 17, 1924, WCF; letter from Leonard Wood, November 16, 1923, WCF.

80. Onorato, *Leonard Wood,* 64–66.

81. Hayden, *The Philippines,* 339.

82. Constantino, *The Making of a Filipino,* 50–51.

83. *NYT,* 10/20/1923.

84. Golay, *Face of Empire,* 249–50.

85. Ibid., 261–62.

86. Leonard Wood, "Diaries, 1921–27," July 21, 1923, August 2, 1923, LWP.

87. Ibid., August 21, 1923, August 22, 1923, LWP; Constantino, *The Making of a Filipino,* 49.

88. Leonard Wood, "Diaries, 1921–27," August 15, 1923, LWP.

89. Ibid., July 12, 1924, July 18, 1924.

90. Ibid., November 24, 1923, January 29, 1924.

91. Ibid., November 20, 1923.

92. Gleeck, *The American Half-Century,* 262–63; Golay, *Face of Empire,* 245–48; HR, *GGPI 1922,* 14, 36; letter from Leonard Wood, November 9, 1921, WCF.

93. Leonard Wood, "Diaries, 1921–27," August 14, 1923, LWP.

94. Ibid., July 21, 1925, August 15, 1925, November 3, 1925, March 3, 1926, March 5, 1926, September 15, 1926, November 10, 1926, LWP; Golay, *Face of Empire*, 264–65; HR, *GGPI 1925*, 16–17.

95. Leonard Wood, "Diaries, 1921–27," November 10, 1926, November 11, 1926, November 17, 1926, February 15–25, 1927, May 26, 1927, May 27, 1927, LWP; Halsema, *E. J. Halsema*, 154–61; Golay, *Face of Empire*, 264–66; HR, *GGPI 1926*, 15.

96. Government of the Philippine Islands vs. Milton E. Springer, Dalmacio Costas, and Anselmo Hilario, No. 26979, April 1, 1927, *PSC 3/2/27–10/5/27*, vol. 50, 270–73.

97. Leonard Wood, "Diaries, 1921–27," July 16, 1924, August 2, 1924, August 8, 1924, August 10, 1924, September 12, 1924, October 27, 1924, November 17, 1924, December 6, 1924, December 12, 1924, LWP; letter from Manuel L. Quezon to Justice Malcolm, August 25, 1920, Reel 9, MLQMI; George A. Malcolm, *The Commonwealth of the Philippines* (New York, 1936), 79–80, 182–86, 390; Malcolm, *American Colonial Careerist*, 29, 84–85, 139, 143; *MT*, 6/15/1917; Norberto Romauldez Centennial Committee, *Master of His Soul: The Life of Norberto Romauldez (1875–1941)* (Manila, 1975), 185–88, 396–97; Carmen Navarro-Pedrosa, *The Untold Story of Imelda Marcos* (Rizal, 1969), 27–37; Justice Isagani A. Cruz and Cynthia Cruz Datu, *Res Gestae: A Brief History of the Supreme Court (from Arellano to Narvasa)* (Manila, 2000), 50; Supreme Court of the Philippines, Government of the Philippine Islands vs. Springer, G.R. No. 26979, *PSC*, vol. 50, 296, 333.

98. Malcolm, *The Commonwealth of the Philippines*, 79–80; Malcolm, *American Colonial Careerist*, 31–32.

99. Leonard Wood, "Diaries, 1921–27," June 5, 1921, July 5, 1921, February 20, 1926, February 24, 1926, March 11, 1926, November 11, 1926, LWP; letter from William H. Taft to Senator J. B. Foraker, September 7, 1903, Reel 40, WHT; letter from Manuel L. Quezon to George A. Malcolm, August 25, 1920, Box 43, Reel 9, MLQMI; Malcolm, *American Colonial Careerist*, 139–40; Malcolm, *The Commonwealth of the Philippines*, 184; *National Cyclopaedia of American Biography*, vol. 49 (New York, 1966), 456–57.

100. Leonard Wood, "Diaries, 1921–27," March 18, 1926, March 25, 1926, March 26, 1926, March 28, 1926, March 29, 1926, LWP.

101. Government of the Philippine Islands vs. Springer, G.R. No. 26979, *PSC*, vol. 50, 295–96.

102. *MT*, 4/1/1927; Cruz and Cruz Datu, *Res Gestae*, 79–81.

103. Springer et al. v. Government of the Philippine Islands, Agoncillo v. Same, nos. 564, 573, May 14, 1928, *United States Reports*, vol. 277: *Cases Adjudged in the Supreme Court at October Term, 1927* (Washington, DC, 1929), 189–209.

104. In their dissent the Filipino justices argued that "the voting of the stock of the Government is a private act" and thus the role of Roxas and Quezon was "not an encroachment upon the power of supervision and control over all executive functions . . . vested in the Governor General." See Government of the Philippine Islands vs. Springer, G.R. No. 26979, *PSC*, vol. 50, 333–48. In a similar argument, U.S. Justice Holmes wrote in his dissent, with Brandeis concurring, that the "corporations concerned were private corporations" and were "no part of the executive functions of the Government." See Springer et al. v. Government of the Philippine Islands, Agoncillo v. Same, nos. 564, 573, May 14, 1928, *United States Reports*, vol. 277, 209–12.

105. Cruz and Cruz Datu, *Res Gestae*, 80–81; Vicente J. Francisco, "George A. Malcolm," *Lawyers Journal* 21, no. 10 (October 31, 1956): 469; Restituto B. Roman, "Malcolm in Public Law," *Philippine Law Journal* 25, no. 1 (March 1950): 446–55; Teodoro Padilla, "Malcolm in Private Law," *Philippine Law Journal* 25, no. 1 (March 1950): 457–76; Anna Leah Fidelis Castañeda, Memorandum: Doctrinal Analysis of the Board of Control Cases, January 8, 2005. I am indebted to Dr. Castañeda for close analysis of the legal principles in the Board of Controls cases.

106. Leonard Wood, May 26, 1927, May 27, 1927, LWP; Golay, *Face of Empire*, 271–72.

107. Kalaw, *Aide-de-Camp to Freedom*, 218–21; Michael Onorato, "The Death of Leonard Wood," *Philippine Studies* 40, no. 3 (1992): 333–47; Gleeck, *The American Governors-General*, 227–32.

108. Stanley, *A Nation in the Making*, 237–48; Dean C. Worcester, *The Philippines Past and Present* (New York, 1930), 750–51.

Chapter 9. President Wilson's Surveillance State

1. *NYT*, 7/9/1971.
2. *NYT*, 9/7/1971.
3. Ibid.
4. *NYT*, 9/20/1971.
5. Michael E. Bigelow, "Van Deman," *Military Intelligence* 16, no. 4 (1990): 40; Kenneth Campbell, "Major General Ralph H. Van Deman: Father of Modern American Military Intelligence," *American Intelligence Journal* 8 (Summer 1987): 13.
6. Christopher Capozzola, *Uncle Sam Wants You: World War I and the Making of the Modern American Citizen* (New York, 2008), 179–80.
7. For a few of the many histories that treat these periods separately, see David M. Kennedy, *Over Here: The First World War and American Society* (New York, 1980); Robert K. Murray, *The Red Scare* (Minneapolis, 1955); Greg Robinson, *By Order of the President: FDR and the Internment of Japanese Americans* (Cambridge, 2001); and Richard H. Rovere, *Senator Joe McCarthy* (Berkeley, 1959). Two works that trace a more continuous narrative thread are Geoffrey R. Stone, *Perilous Times: Free Speech in Wartime from the Sedition Act of 1798 to the War on Terrorism* (New York, 2004); and Joan M. Jensen, *Army Surveillance in America, 1775–1980* (New Haven, 1991).
8. Theodore Kornweibel Jr., *"Seeing Red": Federal Campaigns against Black Militancy, 1919–1925* (Bloomington, 1998), 7, 184; Jeffrey M. Dorwart, *Conflict of Duty: The U.S. Navy's Intelligence Dilemma, 1919–1945* (Annapolis, 1983), 7; Charles H. McCormick, *Seeing Reds: Federal Surveillance of Radicals in the Pittsburgh Mill District, 1917–1921* (Pittsburgh, 1997), 3, 12–13; Rhodri Jeffreys-Jones, *The FBI: A History* (New Haven, 2007), 65–72.
9. Jeffery M. Dorwart, *The Office of Naval Intelligence: The Birth of America's First Intelligence Agency, 1865–1918* (Annapolis, 1979), 116–20.
10. Don Whitehead, *The FBI Story* (New York, 1956), 14, quoted in SEN, Select Committee to Study Governmental Operations with Respect to Intelligence Activities, 94th Congress, 2d Session, *Supplementary Reports on Intelligence Activities,* book 6 (Washington, DC, 1976), 95.
11. "Memoirs of Major General R. H. Van Deman" (San Diego, 1949), 1–2, 15, 17–20, 26–30, Special Collections, Georgetown University Library; Marc B. Powe, "A Sketch of a Man and His Times," in Ralph E. Weber, ed., *The Final Memoranda: Major General Ralph H. Van Deman, USA Ret., 1865–1952, Father of U.S. Military Intelligence* (Wilmington, 1988), xii–xiv; Marc B. Powe, *The Emergence of the War Department Intelligence Agency, 1885–1918* (Manhattan, 1975), 48–50; Marc B. Powe, "American Military Intelligence Comes of Age: A Sketch of a Man and His Times," *Military Review* 40, no. 12 (1975): 21.
12. "Memoirs of Major General R. H. Van Deman," 28–32.
13. Powe, "A Sketch of a Man and His Times," xiv–xix; "Memoirs of Major General R. H. Van Deman," 33–39; Powe, *The Emergence of the War Department Intelligence Agency,* 88–89; David Kahn, *The Reader of Gentlemen's Mail: Herbert O. Yardley and the Birth of American Codebreaking* (New Haven, 2004), 14–21; Herbert O. Yardley, *The American Black Chamber* (Indianapolis, 1931), 33–36; Roy Talbert Jr., *Negative Intelligence: The Army and the American Left, 1917–1941* (Jackson, 1991), 20–21; Guide to the Alexander B. Coxe, Sr., Papers, 1866–1874, 1899–1964 (Manuscript Collection no. 193), Joyner Library, East Carolina University, http://digital.lib.ecu.edu/special/ead/findingaids/0193/, accessed March 9, 2009.
14. Karen Kovach, *The Life and Times of MG Dennis E. Nolan, 1872–1956: The Army's First G2* (Fort Belvoir, 1998), 18, 23–24.
15. James G. Harbord, *The American Army in France, 1917–1919* (Boston, 1936), 94–95; Michael E. Bigelow, "The First Steps: Battalion S-2s in World War I," *Military Intelligence* (January–March 1992): 26–31; Kovach, *The Life and Times of MG Dennis E. Nolan,* 25–34; Weber, *The Final Memoranda,* 33, 37.
16. Harbord, *The American Army in France,* 487–88.
17. *Washington Evening Star,* February 20, 1940, Personal Name Information Files: John R. White, Entry 21, RG 350, NARA; H. H. Bandholtz, "Provost Marshal General's Department," April

30, 1919, *United States Army in the World War 1917–1919: Reports of the Commander-in-Chief, Staff Sections and Services* (Washington, DC, 1991), 313–28; Robert Wright, Jr., *Army Lineage Series: Military Police* (Washington, DC, 1992), 8–9.

18. Walter Robb, "Chief of Police Green: Remarks on Career," *American Chamber of Commerce Journal,* January 1929, 7.

19. Bigelow, "Van Deman," 40.

20. "Memoirs of Major General R. H. Van Deman," 54–55; letter from Ralph Van Deman to General Marlborough Churchill, June 6, 1919, in Ralph Van Deman, "Memorandum," April 10, 1951, Special Collections, Georgetown University Library, 21.

21. Jensen, *Army Surveillance in America,* 166; Talbert, *Negative Intelligence,* 17–19, 113–15.

22. Colonel M. Churchill, Memorandum for the Chief of Staff, Subject: Authority for Military Censorship, August 5, 1918, Glasser File ca. 1918, Internal Disturbances, Box 6, DOJ; Clayton D. Laurie and Ronald H. Cole, *The Role of Federal Military Forces in Domestic Disorders, 1877–1945* (Washington, DC, 1997), 224–25.

23. Jensen, *Army Surveillance in America,* 166–71; Talbert, *Negative Intelligence,* 23–28, 43; Ralph Van Deman, "Memorandum," April 10, 1951, Special Collections, Georgetown University Library, 5.

24. Otto L. Nelson Jr., *National Security and the General Staff* (Washington, DC, 1946), 232–33, 264–65.

25. "Memoirs of Major General R. H. Van Deman," 10–68; Van Deman, "Memorandum," April 10, 1951, Special Collections, Georgetown University Library, 1–27; Powe, "American Military Intelligence Comes of Age," 28–29.

26. Letter from Ralph Van Deman to General Marlborough Churchill, June 6, 1919, in Ralph Van Deman, "Memorandum," April 10, 1951, Special Collections, Georgetown University Library, 21.

27. Powe, "A Sketch of a Man and His Times," xix; "Memoirs of Major General R. H. Van Deman," 50–63; Marlborough Churchill, "The Military Intelligence Division, General Staff," *Journal of the United States Artillery* 52, no. 4 (April 1920): 294; Powe, *The Emergence of the War Department Intelligence Agency,* 93–94; Jensen, *Army Surveillance in America,* 166–67.

28. Harold M. Hyman, *To Try Men's Souls: Loyalty Tests in American History* (Berkeley, 1959), 272.

29. "Memoirs of Major General R. H. Van Deman," 44, 50–55.

30. Emerson Hough, *The Web* (Chicago, 1919), 29–30; Joan Jensen, *The Price of Vigilance* (Chicago, 1968), 17–19, 52–53, 217; Historical Statement of Hinton G. Clabaugh, Division Superintendent, U.S. Bureau of Investigation, in Hough, *The Web,* 483–87.

31. Hough, *The Web,* 29–30, 34, 46, 52; "Memoirs of Major General R. H. Van Deman," 50–54; Peyton C. March, *The Nation at War* (Garden City, 1932), 228; SEN, *Supplementary Reports on Intelligence,* 102–3.

32. Jensen, *The Price of Vigilance,* 91; "Memoirs of Major General R. H. Van Deman," 50–54; March, *The Nation at War,* 228; SEN, *Supplementary Reports on Intelligence,* 105; letter from A. M. Briggs to Thos. W. Gregory, May 24, 1918, D.J. Central Files Straight Numerical Files, Box 2186, Entry 112, DOJ.

33. Jensen, *The Price of Vigilance,* 39–41; Hyman, *To Try Men's Souls,* 275, 280.

34. Hyman, *To Try Men's Souls,* 286–88.

35. Hough, *The Web,* 37, 53–54; Jensen, *The Price of Vigilance,* 87–89.

36. Letters from National Directors, American Protective League to E. H. Rushmore, March 30, 1918, April 20, 1918, Box 5, Entry 12, RG 65, NARA.

37. Letter to E. H. Rushmore, June 21, 1918, Box 5, Entry 12, RG 65, NARA.

38. New York City, n.d., Box 5, Entry 12, RG 165, NARA; letter from American Protective League to E. H. Rushmore, May 23, 1918, Box 5, Entry 12, RG 165, NARA.

39. Letter from John Lord O'Brian to Hugh Bancroft, April 10, 1918, Central Straight Numerical File, Entry 112, DOJ; letter from T. W. Gregory to Charles R. Choate, Esq., May 3, 1918, Central Straight Numerical File, Entry 112, DOJ; letter from C. D. Frey to Elting, March 6, 1918, Box 5, Entry 12, RG 65, NARA; Jensen, *The Price of Vigilance,* 126.

40. Letter from G. Pross to Colonel A. Van Dieman [*sic*], November 1, 1917; Lieutenant Colonel R. H. Van Deman to G. Pross, November 8, 1917, Box 3053, MID.

41. Letter from Edmund Leigh to Major Nicholas Biddle, November 12, 1917; letter from Nicholas Biddle to Colonel R. H. Van Deman, November 13, 1917; letter from Edward B. Cochens to Major Herbert Parsons, December 10, 1917; letter from Major Herbert Parsons to Edward B. Cochens, December 13, 1917, Box 3053, MID.

42. Letter from National Director to E. H. Rushmore, February 26, 1918, Box 5, Entry 12, RG 65.

43. Letter from Chas. Jerome Edwards to Richmond Levering, August 13, 1917, Box 5, Entry 12, RG 65; letter from general superintendent to Geo. B. Lord, August 17, 1917, Box 5, Entry 12, RG 65; letter from William E. Chilton to T. W. Gregory, December 20, 1917, D.J. Central Straight Numerical Files, Box 2186, Entry 112, DOJ.

44. Memorandum to Major Parsons, December 6, 1917; letter from Colonel R. H. Van Deman to Supt. Pennsylvania State Police, December 8, 1917; letter of John A. Reilly to Commanding Officer, Troop A, December 20, 1917, Box 3053, MID.

45. Letter from H. W. Bennett to Colonel R. H. Van Deman, January 19, 1918; letter from Wm. R. Stone to Colonel R. H. Van Deman, January 25, 1918, Box 3053, MID.

46. Hyman, *To Try Men's Souls,* 282; letter from International Association of Machinists, August 31, 1918, D.J. Central Straight Numerical Files, Box 2186, Entry 112, DOJ; letter from Samuel W. Randolph to the attorney general, September 5, 1918, D.J. Central Straight Numerical Files, Box 2186, Entry 112, DOJ; letter from John Lord O'Brian to American Protective League, September 9, 1918, D.J. Central Straight Numerical Files, Box 2186, Entry 112, DOJ.

47. Jensen, *The Price of Vigilance,* 41–53, 91, 102–3; letter from Attorney General to Victor Elting, April 8, 1918, D.J. Central Files Straight Numerical Files, Box 2186, Entry 112, DOJ; letter from A. M. Briggs to Thos. W. Gregory, May 24, 1918, D.J. Central Files Straight Numerical Files, Box 2186, Entry 112, DOJ; letter from John Lord O'Brian to American Protective League, May 27, 1918, D.J. Central Files Straight Numerical Files, Box 2186, Entry 112, DOJ.

48. Letter from E. H. Rushmore to Victor Elting, April 10, 1918; letter from American Protective League to E. H. Rushmore, May 22, 1918, Box 5, Entry 12, RG 65, NARA.

49. Hough, *The Web,* 38; letter from Bureau of Investigation, New York City to E. H. Rushmore, March 2, 1918, Box 5, Entry 12, RG 65, NARA; letter from Division Superintendent to A. M. Briggs, April 13, 1918, Box 5, Entry 12, RG 65, NARA; letter from E. H. Rushmore to Captain Charles D. Frey, April 19, 1918, Box 5, Entry 12, RG 65, NARA.

50. Letter from T. W. Gregory to A. M. Briggs, January 26, 1918; letter from Provost Marshal General to The Governor of (all States), February 7, 1918; letter from Victor Elting to T. W. Gregory, February 11, 1918, D.J. Central Straight Numerical Files, Box 2186, Entry 112, DOJ.

51. Jensen, *The Price of Vigilance,* 45–46, 189–96; letter from Isaac H. Vrooman, Jr., assistant chief Albany Division to American Protective League, September 5, 1918, Box 6, Entry 12, RG 65, NARA.

52. Jensen, *The Price of Vigilance,* 192, 214–15; letter from John Lord O'Brian to John E. Kinnane, April 5, 1918, Box 2186, Entry 112, D.J. Central Straight Numerical Files, DOJ; letter from John E. Kinnane to Attorney General, April 12, 1918, Box 2186, Entry 112, D.J. Central Straight Numerical Files, DOJ.

53. Jensen, *The Price of Vigilance,* 194–213.

54. Letter from Lee Douglas to Col. Jonas T. Amis, January 11, 1918; letter from Assistant Attorney General Saml. J. Graham to Jonas T. Amis, January 18, 1918, D.J. Central Straight Numerical Files, Box 2186, Entry 112, DOJ.

55. Letter from C. H. Walker to National Directors, American Protective League, April 3, 1918, D.J. Central Straight Numerical Files, Box 2186, Entry 112, DOJ; letter from Sterling E. Edmonds, April 5, 1918, D.J. Central Straight Numerical Files, Box 2186, Entry 112, DOJ; *Saint Louis Globe-Democrat,* 4/5/1918; *Chicago Daily Tribune,* 4/5/1918; *Edwardsville Intelligenser,* 6/18/1918.

56. Letter from National Directors to E. H. Rushmore, July 2, 1918, Box 5, Entry 12, RG 65, NARA.

57. Letter from U.S. Attorney, Northern District of Ohio to the attorney general, January 3, 1918, D.J. Central Files Straight Numerical Files, Box 2186, Entry 112, DOJ.

58. Hyman, *To Try Men's Souls,* 283; letter from Local Cleveland Socialist Party to Bliss Morton, July 9, 1918, D.J. Central Files Straight Numerical Files, Box 2186, Entry 112, DOJ; letter from John Lord O'Brian to Edwin S. Wertz, September 10, 1918, D.J. Central Files Straight Numerical Files, Box 2186, Entry 112, DOJ; letter from W. F. Bronstrup to Atty. Gen. Gregory, September 6, 1918, D.J. Central Files Straight Numerical Files, Box 2186, Entry 112, DOJ; letter from John Lord O'Brian to American Protective League, September 10, 1918, D.J. Central Files Straight Numerical Files, Box 2186, Entry 112, DOJ.

59. Hough, *The Web,* 199.

60. Letter from E. H. Rushmore to Captain Charles D. Frey, March 13 1918; letter from national directors to E. H. Rushmore, March 26, 1918, Box 5, Entry 12, RG 65, NARA.

61. Jensen, *Army Surveillance in America,* 163.

62. Letter from National Directors to E. H. Rushmore, April 3, 1918; letter from E. H. Rushmore to National Directors, May 6, 1918, Box 5, Entry 12, RG 65, NARA.

63. Letter from National Directors to E. H. Rushmore, June 13, 1918; letter from E. H. Rushmore to Captain Charles D. Frey, June 14, 1918, July 3, 1918; letter from National Directors to E. H. Rushmore, July 6, 1918, Box 5, Entry 12, RG 65, NARA.

64. *NYT,* 3/22/1919; letter from E. H. Rushmore to Victor Elting, n.d.; letter from Victor Elting to A. W. Briggs, February 25, 1918; letter from Fred Feigl, March 12, 1918; letter from E. H. Rushmore to Captain Charles D. Frey, March 13, 1918; letter from national directors to Colonel Fred Feigl, March 21, 1918; letter from national directors to E. H. Rushmore, March 21, 1918; letter from chairman to Colonel Fred Feigl, March 22, 1918; letter from Chairman to E. H. Rushmore, March 22, 1919, Box 5, Entry 12, RG 65, NARA.

65. Letter from E. H. Rushmore to Victor Elting, January 22, 1918; letter from National Director to E. H. Rushmore, January 24, 1918; letters from E. H. Rushmore to Victor Elting, January 26, 1918, January 29, 1918, February 1, 1918, February 25, 1918; letter to E. H. Rushmore, March 1, 1918; letter from E. H. Rushmore to Captain Charles D. Frey, April 3, 1918, Box 5, Entry 12, RG 65, NARA.

66. In re. Francis Turno, May 10, 1918; Memorandum for Commander Eddy, n.d.; letter from national directors to E. H. Rushmore, May 21, 1918, Box 5, Entry 12, RG 65, NARA.

67. Letter from A. B. Bielaski to Victor Elting, December 8, 1917; letters from American Protective League to E. H. Rushmore, March 7, 1918, March 26, 1918; letter from E. H. Rushmore to American Protective League, March 14, 1918, Box 5, Entry 12, RG 65, NARA.

68. Letter from national directors to E. H. Rushmore, June 29, 1918; letter from E. H. Rushmore to American Protective League, February 11, 1918, Box 5, Entry 12, RG 65, NARA.

69. A. G. Adams, In Re. Carl Georg Frank, November 5, 1917, Box 3053, MID; *NYT,* 7/2/1915, 7/9/1915, 7/10/1915.

70. Report of Agent D. J. Keleher, Subject: Dr. Karl G. Frank—Richard Pfund, June 11, 1918; Dr. Karl G. Frank, May 22, 1918; letter from Colonel R. H. Van Deman to A. Bruce Bielaski, June 1, 1918, Box 3053, MID.

71. Letter from Edmund Leigh, to Chief, Military Intelligence Branch, June 12, 1918, Box 3053, MID; Randall J. Ratje, "Remembering Our Founders and Our Past National Chairmen," *Steuben News* 79, no. 2 (March–April 2006), http://222.stuebensociety.org/News/MarApr06.htm, accessed June 18, 2008.

72. Jensen, *The Price of Vigilance,* 198–218; Hyman, *To Try Men's Souls,* 290–91; Capozzola, *Uncle Sam Wants You,* 48.

73. Hyman, *To Try Men's Souls,* 292–94; Capozzola, *Uncle Sam Wants You,* 53.

74. Jensen, *Army Surveillance in America,* 175–76; Talbert, *Negative Intelligence,* 10–19, 92–98.

75. McCormick, *Seeing Reds,* 22, 24.

76. Mark Ellis, *Race, War, and Surveillance: African Americans and the United States Government during World War I* (Bloomington, 2001), 48–73, 222; Kornweibel, *Seeing Red,* 38–39, 55–56; Talbert, *Negative Intelligence,* 113–23; J. E. Elliot, Re: National Colored Soldiers Comfort Association, January 18, 1918, January 21, 1918, Box 2962, MID; Clopton, Adjt Gen of the Army November 20, 1918, Box 6, Glasser File ca. 1918, Dept. of Justice, DOJ; letter from C. A. Hedekin to Commanding General, October 9, 1918, Box 6, Glasser File ca. 1918, Dept. of Justice, DOJ.

77. Jensen, *The Price of Vigilance,* 58–59, 61–64, 122–27; Hyman, *To Try Men's Souls,* 300–15.

78. From: Aid[e] for Information, Office of the Commandant, 15th Naval District, To: Director of Naval Intelligence, February 28, 1918, Glasser File ca. 1918, Internal Disturbances, Box 6, DOJ; William Preston Jr., *Aliens and Dissenters: Federal Suppression of Radicals, 1903–1933* (Cambridge, 1963), 152–63, 171.

79. From: Commanding Officer, 316 Trains Hdqts. & Military Police, To: Commanding General, 91st Division, March 30, 1918, Glasser File ca. 1918, Internal Disturbances, Box 6, DOJ.

80. From: Office of Military Intelligence, Seattle, To: Chief, Military Intelligence Branch, April 29, 1918, May 10, 1918, Glasser File ca. 1918, Internal Disturbances, Box 6, DOJ.

81. From: Office of Military Intelligence, Seattle, To: Chief, Military Intelligence Branch, May 10, 1918, Glasser File ca. 1918, Internal Disturbances, Box 6, DOJ.

82. Telegram from Knabenshue to Military Intelligence Branch, Washington, June 6, 1918, Glasser File ca. 1918, Internal Disturbances, Box 6, DOJ; letter from M. Churchill to A. Bruce Bielaski, June 7, 1918, Glasser File ca. 1918, Internal Disturbances, Box 6, DOJ; letter from John Lord O'Brian to Lieutenant Colonel M. Churchill, June 19, 1918, Glasser File ca. 1918, Internal Disturbances, Box 6, DOJ; Talbert, *Negative Intelligence,* 50.

83. Letter from M. Churchill, To: Intelligence Officer, Western Department, 9 July 1918, Glasser File ca. 1918, Internal Disturbances, Box 6, DOJ.

84. Letter from Colonel M. Churchill to Dr. E. M. Hopkins, August 27, 1918, Glasser File ca. 1918, Internal Disturbances, Box 6, DOJ; Jensen, *The Price of Vigilance,* 225–29, 231–32.

85. Telegram from Wheeler to the Attorney General, October 4, 1918; telegram from Byrn to Bielaski, October 4, 1918; telegram from Watkins to Military Intelligence Branch Washington, October 6, 1918, Glasser File ca. 1918, Internal Disturbances, Box 6, DOJ.

86. Letter from M. Churchill to A. Bruce Bielaski, September 26, 1918, Glasser File ca. 1918, Internal Disturbances, Box 6, DOJ; letters from Captain J. H. Dengel to Director of Military Intelligence Washington, November 8, 1918, November 19, 1918, Glasser File ca. 1918, Internal Disturbances, Box 6, DOJ; Jensen, *Army Surveillance in America,* 178.

87. Talbert, *Negative Intelligence,* 49–51.

88. Letter from J. H. Dengel to Department Intelligence Officer, October 16, 1918, Glasser File ca. 1918, Internal Disturbances, Box 6, DOJ.

89. Letter from M. Churchill to Paul Fuller, Jr., Bureau of War Trade Intelligence, November 9, 1918, Glasser File ca. 1918, Internal Disturbances, Box 6, DOJ.

90. Letter from J. H. Dengel to Director of Military Intelligence, November 19, 1918, Glasser File ca. 1918, Internal Disturbances, Box 6, DOJ.

91. Kornweibel, *Seeing Red,* 9; Richard Polenberg, *Fighting Faiths: The Abrams Case, the Supreme Court, and Free Speech* (New York, 1987), 179; Ellen Schrecker, *Many Are the Crimes: McCarthyism in America* (Boston, 1998), 55–56.

92. *NYT,* 1/21/1919, 3/6/1919, 4/16/1919, 7/13/1919, 7/24/1919; letter from David W. Swain to Director of Naval Intelligence, January 16, 1919, Glasser File ca. 1918, Internal Disturbances, Box 6, DOJ; letter from Captain F. W. Wilson to Director of Military Intelligence, January 21, 1919, Glasser File ca. 1918, Internal Disturbances, Box 6, DOJ; letter from M. Churchill to Major H. A. Strauss, October 30, 1919, Glasser File ca. 1918, Internal Disturbances, Box 6, DOJ.

93. Letters from Captain F. W. Wilson to Intelligence Officer, Western Department, November 22, 1918, December 14, 1918, Glasser File ca. 1918, Internal Disturbances, Box 6, DOJ.

94. Letters from Captain F. W. Wilson to Director of Military Intelligence, January 13, 1919, January 21, 1919, January 22, 1919, Glasser File ca. 1918, Internal Disturbances, Box 6, DOJ.

95. Letter from Representative War Trade Board to Norman Schaff, January 30, 1919, Glasser File ca. 1918, Internal Disturbances, Box 6, DOJ.

96. Telegram from Sullivan to Captain F. W. Wilson, February 6, 1919, Glasser File ca. 1918, Internal Disturbances, Box 6, DOJ.

97. *NYT,* 2/8/1919, 2/9/1919, 2/10/1919, 2/11/1919, 2/18/1919.

98. Lieut. D. C. Van Buren, July 28, 1919, July 30, 1919, Glasser File ca. 1918, Internal Disturbances, Box 6, DOJ; telegram from Crockett to Milstaff, July 29, 1919, Glasser File ca. 1918, Internal Disturbances, Box 6, DOJ; Talbert, *Negative Intelligence,* 130.

99. *NYT,* 7/30/1919; Talbert, *Negative Intelligence,* 130.

100. M. Churchill, Memorandum for the Chief of Staff, August 20, 1919, Glasser File ca. 1918, Internal Disturbances, Box 6, DOJ; Major J. E. Cutler, Memorandum for the Director of Military Intelligence, August 15, 1919, Glasser File ca. 1918, Internal Disturbances, Box 6, DOJ; Major W. H. Loving, C., To: Director of Military Intelligence, Subject: Final Report on Negro Subversion, August 6, 1919, Military Intelligence Division, War Department, RG 165, NARA; Colonel J. E. Cutler, Memorandum for General Churchill, August 8, 1919, Military Intelligence Division, War Department, RG 165, NARA; Major W. H. Loving, C., To: Director of Military Intelligence, Subject: Maintenance of Operative in New York, August 21, 1919, Military Intelligence Division, War Department, RG 165, NARA; M. Churchill, Memorandum for the Chief, Negative Branch, August 11, 1919, Document 10218-361, Military Intelligence Division, War Department, RG 165, NARA; Laurie and Cole, *The Role of Federal Military Forces in Domestic Disorders,* 300–301.

101. Jensen, *Army Surveillance in America,* 185–91; Talbert, *Negative Intelligence,* 204–5; letter from Colonel C. H. Mason to General Churchill, October 30 1919, Box 3502, MID.

102. Better America Federation, n.d., Box 69, RVD.

103. Van Deman, "Memorandum," April 10, 1951, Special Collections, Georgetown University Library, 14; Jensen, *Army Surveillance in America,* 193–94; letter from Lt. Col. Theodore K. Spencer to Acting Director of Military Intelligence, June 21, 1920, Box 2964, MID; List of Chartered Posts in the Department of Massachusetts, The American Legion, June 9, 1920, Box 2964, MID; Colonel Gordon Johnston, To: Director of Military Intelligence, February 17, 1920, Box 2964, MID; letter from Colonel Gordon Johnston to General M. Churchill, November 21, 1919, Box 2964, MID; letter of General M. Churchill to National Commander of the American Legion, December 16, 1919, Box 2964, MID; Major General W. G. Haan, Memorandum for General Churchill, November 28, 1919, Box 2964, MID.

104. Letter from Thos. B. Crockett to Brigadier-General Marlborough Churchill, October 11, 1919, Box 2964, MID; letter from Brigadier-General M. Churchill to Crockett, October 20, 1919, Box 2964, MID; Major Thomas B. Crockett, Circular No. 64, December 8, 1918, Box 3734, MID; From Colonel Gordon Johnston to Director of Military Intelligence, January 13, 1920, Box 3734, MID.

105. Colonel C. H. Mason, Memorandum for General Churchill, October 7, 1919, Box 3502, MID; M. Churchill, Memorandum for the Adjutant General, October 20, 1919, Box 3502, MID; M. Churchill, To: The Recruiting Officer, November 11, 1919, Box 3502, MID; Jensen, *Army Surveillance in America,* 202.

106. Letter from Major Thomas B. Crockett to Director Military Intelligence, December 24, 1919, Box 2964, MID; Chas. Furthmann, Report, November 21, 1919, Box 2964, MID; *Chicago Tribune,* 11/20/1919, 11/22/1919; *Herald Examiner,* 11/22/1919; *Chicago Post,* 11/19/1919.

107. William Pencak, *For God and Country: The American Legion, 1919–1941* (Boston, 1989), 149–52.

108. SEN, *Supplementary Reports on Intelligence,* 112–15; Jensen, *Army Surveillance in America,* 191–92; Don Whitehead, *The FBI Story: A Report to the People* (New York, 1956), 48–51; Todd J. Pfannestiel, *Rethinking the Red Scare: The Lusk Committee and New York's Crusade against Radicalism, 1919–1923* (New York, 2003), 19–35, 78–96; Talbert, *Negative Intelligence,* 175–81; Major W. H. Loving, C., To: Director of Military Intelligence, Subject: Final Report on Negro Subversion, August 6, 1919, Document 10218-361, Military Intelligence Division, War Department, RG 165, NARA; *NYT,* 5/3/1919, 5/7/1919, 6/13/1919, 6/19/1919, 6/20/1919, 6/22/1919, 6/26/1919, 7/13/1919, 7/16/1919, 7/21/1919, 7/22/1919, 7/27/1919, 8/16/1919, 11/8/1919, 11/9/1919, 11/10/1919, 11/11/1919, 11/19/1919; New York State Archives, "The Lusk Committee: Committee Activities," http://www.archives.nysed.gov/a/research/res_topics_bus_lusk_activities.shtml, accessed June 22, 2008.

109. Christopher M. Finan, *From the Palmer Raids to the Patriot Act: A History of the Fight for Free Speech in America* (Boston, 2007), 1–3, 35–37; Kenneth D. Ackerman, *Young J. Edgar: Hoover, the Red Scare, and the Assault on Civil Liberties* (New York, 2007), 234–35, 283–84, 322–28, 358–63.

110. *NYT,* 10/7/1919; Jensen, *Army Surveillance in America,* 187.

111. Laurie and Cole, *The Role of Federal Military Forces in Domestic Disorders,* 303–13.

112. Ibid., 313–17; *NYT,* 8/2/1921; Proclamation by the Governor, E. F. Morgan, June 27, 1921, Ephraim F. Morgan Papers, West Virginia Collection, West Virginia University.

113. H. H. Bandholtz, Memorandum, August 29, 1921, Reel 9, HHB; Minutes, Twenty-Ninth Consecutive and Fourth Biennial Convention of District No. 5, United Mine Workers of America, First Day, Pittsburg, Pa., September 6, 1921, Reel 9, HHB; Laurie and Cole, *The Role of Federal Military Forces in Domestic Disorders,* 317; David A. Corbin, "'Frank Kenney Is Our Leader and We Shall Not Be Moved': Rank-and-File Leadership in the West Virginia Coal Fields," in Gary M. Fink and Merl E. Reed, eds., *Essays in Southern Labor History* (Westport, 1976), 146–49.

114. Memo of Conference with Governor E. F. Morgan at Charleston, W.Va., August 26, 1921 (Report no. 1), Reel 9, HHB.

115. Telegrams from Bandholtz, To: Chief of Staff, August 26, 1921 (Report no. 1), August 26, 1921 (Report no. 3), Reel 9, HHB; Laurie and Cole, *The Role of Federal Military Forces in Domestic Disorders,* 317–19.

116. Telegram from Bandholtz, To: Chief of Staff, August 27, 1921 (Report no. 4); H. H. Bandholtz, Memorandum, August 29, 1921, Reel 9, HHB; Laurie and Cole, *The Role of Federal Military Forces in Domestic Disorders,* 319.

117. Laurie and Cole, *The Role of Federal Military Forces in Domestic Disorders,* 320–23; Daniel Jordan, "The Mingo War: Labor Violence in the Southern West Virginia Coal Fields, 1919–1922," in Fink and Reed, *Essays in Southern Labor History,* 112.

118. Major General J. G. Harbord, To: Brigadier General H. H. Bandholtz, August 31, 1921, Reel 9, HHB; Brig. Gen. H. H. Bandholtz, Proclamation, September 2, 1921, Reel 9, HHB; A Proclamation by the President of the United States, n.d., Reel 9, HHB; Bandholtz, Copy Telegram No. 2, To: Adjutant General, n.d.; Minutes, Twenty-Ninth Consecutive and Fourth Biennial Convention of District No. 5, United Mine Workers of America, First Day, Pittsburg, Pa., September 6, 1921, Reel 9, HHB; Brigadier General H. H. Bandholtz, To: the Adjutant General, September 12, 1921, Reel 9, HHB; Institute for the History of Technology and Industrial Anthropology, *The Battle of Blair Mountain (West Virginia): Cultural Resource Survey and Recording Project* (Morgantown, 1992), 35–50; Laurie and Cole, *The Role of Federal Military Forces in Domestic Disorders,* 320–24.

119. Jordan, "The Mingo War," 112; letters from H. H. Bandholtz to Ephraim F. Morgan, September 6, 1921, September 12, 1921, Box 9; letter from Governor to Brigadier General H. H. Bandholtz, September 8, 1921, Box 9; letter from Major General G. W. Read to Governor to Ephraim F. Morgan, October 14, 1921, Box 10, Ephraim F. Morgan Papers, West Virginia Collection, West Virginia University.

120. Laurie and Cole, *The Role of Federal Military Forces in Domestic Disorders,* 323–25; Jordan, "The Mingo War," 118–19.

121. Nelson, *National Security and the General Staff,* 264–66.

122. Jensen, *The Price of Vigilance,* 287–89; Hyman, *To Try Men's Souls,* 323–24; McCormick, *Seeing Reds,* 202; Kornweibel, *Seeing Red,* 174–75; Kahn, *The Reader of Gentlemen's Mail,* 94–103; Talbert, *Negative Intelligence,* 208–11; Ralph Van Deman, December 15, 1928, Office of Chief of Staff, Cross Reference Card, Microform 1194, RG 350, NARA; SEN, *Supplementary Reports on Intelligence,* 105–6; Regin Schmidt, *Red Scare: FBI and the Origins of Anticommunism in the United States, 1919–1943* (Copenhagen, 2000), 324–28, 368.

123. Letter from Van Deman to Nolan, May 24, 1921, Microfilm 1024, Military Intelligence Division Correspondence, 1917–41, Entry 2354, RG 165, NARA; Talbert, *Negative Intelligence,* 156, 208; *NYT,* 9/23/1927, 6/25/1929.

124. *LAT,* 9/8/1940; letter from Lieut. Colonel H. R. Oldfield, January 14, 1938 (R-2346), Box 18, RVD; SEN, *Supplementary Reports on Intelligence,* 136, 183–85.

125. Schrecker, *Many Are the Crimes,* 68; State Bureau of Identification, "Communism in California," (R-58), Box 1, RVD.

126. Report from the Police Department, City of San Diego, To State Division of Criminal Identification, as Requested by Letter Dated March 31, 1935 (R-10145), Box 76, RVD; Report by the LAPD [Los Angeles Police Department], September 9, 1936 (R-1665), Box 12, RVD; Carey

McWilliams, *Southern California Country: An Island on the Land* (New York, 1946), 273–94; Edwin Layton, "The Better America Federation: A Case Study of Superpatriotism," *Pacific Historical Review* 30, no. 2 (1961): 137–47; Frank Donner, *Protectors of Privilege: Red Squads and Police Repression in Urban America* (Berkeley, 1990), 59–63; Dorothy Ray Healy and Maurice Isserman, *California Red: A Life in the American Communist Party* (Urbana-Champaign, 1993), 40; Carl Bernstein, *Loyalties: A Son's Memoir* (New York, 1989), 70; Finan, *From the Palmer Raids to the Patriot Act,* 49; *LAT,* 5/15/1935, 2/24/1937, 12/1/1938, 12/9/1939.

127. *NYT,* 7/9/1971, 9/7/1971; Bigelow, "Van Deman," 40; Schrecker, *Many Are the Crimes,* 23; letter from SAC San Diego to Director, June 13, 1957, FBIVD.

128. Talbert, *Negative Intelligence,* 234–35.

129. Frank J. Donner, *The Age of Surveillance: The Aims and Methods of America's Political Intelligence System* (New York, 1980), 418.

130. Weber, *The Final Memoranda,* 7–23; Michael E. Bigelow, "The First Steps: Battalion S2s in World War I," *Military Intelligence* (January–March 1992): 26–28; Brian McAllister Linn, "Intelligence and Low-Intensity Conflict in the Philippine War, 1899–1902," *Intelligence and National Security* 6, no. 1 (1991): 108–9.

131. Ralph Van Deman, December 9, 1933, October 22, 1935, Office of Chief of Staff, Cross Reference Card, Microform 1194, RG 350, NARA.

132. Bigelow, "Van Deman," 38, 40; Weber, *The Final Memoranda.*

133. Ralph Van Deman, February 1, 1932, April 18, 1933, August 12, 1933, May 28, 1937, Office of Chief of Staff, Cross Reference Card, Microform 1194, RG 350, NARA.

134. A subject, one Richard W. Walker, January 27, 1932 (R-1), Box 1, RVD.

135. To Asst. Chief Patrick, January 22, 1932 (R-2a), Box 1, RVD.

136. Letter from City Hall Sergeant-At-Arms to Gen. R. H. Van Deman, August 18, 1932 (R-13), Box 1; Secy-Mgr to James K. Fisk, June 6, 1933 (R-8), Box 1; letter from Larry E. Belger to General R. H. Van Deman, September 30, 1933 (R-136), Box 1; letter from F. M. Tobin Court Clerk to Major General R. H. Van Deman, June 9, 1933 (R-83), Box 1; letter from Charles W. Hoffmann to General R. H. Van Deman, December 17, 1932 (R-23), Box 1; letter from G. W. Pardy to General Van Deman, April 16, 1934 (R-343), Box 2; letter from C. W. Hoffmann to General R. H. Van Deman, February 26, 1934 (R-2726), Box 2, RVD.

137. A-42, n.d. (R-2032), Box 15, RVD; letter from R. R. Roach to D. M. Ladd July 13, 1945, FBIVD.

138. Letter from Margaret A. Kerr to Brig. General Ralph Van Deman (R-52), Box 1, RVD; Better America Federation, n.d., Box 69, RVD; McWilliams, *Southern California Country,* 291; Layton, "The Better America Federation," 137–47.

139. League for Democracy against Nazism, September 16, 1936 (R-1667); Civic Council of Defense, "Bulletin," June–September 1936 (R-1677); from CCD, November 6, 1936 (R-1731), Box 12, RVD.

140. Mass Meeting for Ford Local 406, May 17, 1938 (R-2607), Box 20; letter from Dorothy, Civic Council of Defense, to General R. H. Van Deman, August 18, 1936 (R-1626), Box 12, RVD.

141. Letter from Lieut. Colonel H. R. Oldfield to Maj. Gen. R. H. Van Deman, June 2, 1937 (R-2006), Box 15, RVD; Talbert, *Negative Intelligence,* 249.

142. Letter from W. D. and HCD to General Van Deman, August 10, 1936 (R-1732), Box 12, RVD.

143. Letter from Lieut. Colonel H. R. Oldfield, to Major General R. H. Van Deman, August 20, 1936 (R-1634), Box 12, RVD.

144. Communist Activities, September 27, 1936 (R-1679); Re: Karl Hama, July 20, 1936 (R-1606), Box 12, RVD.

145. Victor S. Navasky, *Naming Names* (New York, 2003), 78, 240; From MAK [Margaret A. Kerr, secretary, Better America Federation], V. J. Jerome, n.d. (R-2551a), Box 20, RVD. During testimony before Congress in March 1951, Victor Jeremy Jerome admitted that he had been in Los Angeles in 1936–37 and made periodic visits thereafter. See HR, 82nd Congress, 1st Session, *Hearings before the Committee on Un-American Activities: Communist Infiltration of Hollywood,* part 1 (Washington, DC, 1951), 55–77.

146. Lardner, Ring, Jr. (R-1620), Box 12, RVD; Larry Ceplair and Steven Englund, *The Inquisition in Hollywood: Politics in the Film Community, 1930–60* (Urbana, 2003), 54–82.

147. Memorandum for H. C. Davis, August 16, 1936 (R-1629), Box 12, RVD.

148. Radical Activities Re: Aircraft Industry, September 8, 1936 (R-1649); Radical Activities Re: Aircraft Industry, September 23, 1936 (R-1676); Radical Activities Re: Aircraft Industry, November 4, 1936 (R-1727); Communist Activities, September 27, 1936 (R-1679), Box 12, RVD.

149. Exhibit C, *Ivan Francis Cox vs. The Thirteenth District of the Communist Party*, Superior Court of the State of California, No. 278084, Filed Jan. 27, 1938 (R-2416), Box 18, RVD; *San Francisco Examiner*, 1/28/1938 (R-2348), Box 18, RVD; Weekly Report of Communist Activities, Portland, Oregon, July 23, 1937 (R-2075), Box 15, RVD; Memorandum in Re: Harry Bridges Hearing, Radical Research Bureau, The American Legion, May 5, 1938 (R-2566), Box 20, RVD; *LAT*, 8/11/1939.

150. Exhibit C (R-2416); *San Francisco Examiner*, 1/28/1938 (R-2348), Box 18, RVD; *LAT*, 12/17/1937.

151. Exhibit C (R-2416), Box 18, RVD; *LAT*, 12/15/1937, 12/16/1937, 12/17/1937, 12/18/1937, 3/1/1938.

152. *San Francisco Examiner*, 1/28/1938 (R-2348), Box 18, RVD; *LAT*, 2/2/1938, 11/4/1938, 11/5/1938, 11/6/1938, 11/9/1938; Edward L. Barrett Jr., *The Tenney Committee: Legislative Investigation of Subversive Activities in California* (Ithaca, 1951), 4–6; David L. Shippers, *Jack B. Tenney: California Legislator: Oral History Transcript*, vol. 2 (Los Angeles, 1969), 524–30.

153. Memo for General Van Deman, December 29, 1937 (R-2310); Memo for Colonel Oldfield, January 5, 1938 (R-2314), Box 18, RVD. This "James Allen" alias was not the same as "James S. Allen," the alias for Communist Party official Sol Auerbach (1906–86) who reorganized the Philippine Communist Party in the late 1930s.

154. Memo for General Van Deman, 29 December 1937 (R-2310), Box 18, RVD.

155. Letter from H. R. O. to General Van Deman, n.d. (R-2558), Box 20, RVD.

156. From MAK [Margaret A. Kerr, secretary, Better America Federation], V. J. Jerome, n.d. (R-2551a); From MAK, George H. Shoaf, n.d. (R-2551b), Box 20, RVD.

157. Jensen, *Army Surveillance in America*, 205–7.

158. Letter from Lieut. Colonel H. R. Oldfield, January 14, 1938 (R-2346), Box 18, RVD; Clarence Severin, Chief Clerk in the Alameda County District Attorney's office, Interview with Miriam Feingold, "Perspectives on the Alameda County District Attorney's Office," vol. 2, 26, Earl Warren Oral History Project, Online Archive of California, California Digital Library, University of California, http://content.cdlib.org/xtf/view?docId=kt900006nw&brand=oac&doc.view=entire_text, accessed June 25, 2008.

159. Ralph Van Deman, August 28, 1940, November 10, 1940, January 17, 1941, Office of Chief of Staff, Cross Reference Card, Microform 1194, RG 350, NARA.

160. *NYT*, 9/26/1936, 2/13/1937, 2/16/1937, 5/7/1937, 7/3/1937, 12/22/1937, 12/22/1939; *LAT*, 8/11/1939.

161. *LAT*, 4/24/1935, 2/22/1938, 4/10/1938, 5/17/1938, 6/17/1938, 6/23/1938, 6/28/1938, 12/1/1938; *NYT*, 8/23/1938, 8/26/1938, 10/27/1938; Schmidt, *Red Scare*, 349–55.

162. Talbert, *Negative Intelligence*, 255–59; SEN, 94th Congress, 2d Session, *Final Report of the Select Committee to Study Governmental Operations with Respect to Intelligence Activities*, book 2 (Washington, DC, 1976), 33–38; Jeffreys-Jones, *The FBI*, 103–8, 114–19; Schmidt, *Red Scare*, 356–59; Schrecker, *Many Are the Crimes*, 106–7; letter from Ralph Van Deman to J. Edgar Hoover, October 24, 1938; letter from J. Edgar Hoover to Ralph H. Van Deman, November 4, 1938; letter from Special Agent in Charge R. B. Hood to J. Edgar Hoover, October 6, 1939; letter from J. Edgar Hoover to R. H. Van Deman, August 3, 1940, FBIVD.

163. Talbert, *Negative Intelligence*, 270–71; letter from R. H. Van Deman to J. Edgar Hoover, July 8, 1940; letter from J. Edgar Hoover to R. H. Van Deman, August 3, 1940; letter from R. R. Roach to D. M. Ladd, July 13, 1945; letter from Special Agent in Charge J. F. Santoiana to Director, October 5, 1951; letter from Murphy to Director, November 12, 1946; letter from R. B. Hood to Director, March 20, 1942, FBIVD.

164. Bigelow, "Van Deman," 40.

165. Ibid.

166. A-70, Report, Trip to Philadelphia at Meeting of Supreme Council of the Order of the Sons of Italy, December 16, 1940 (R-3921), Box 28, RVD.

167. A-70, Continuation of List of Suspects, February 7, 1941 (R-3924), Box 28; A-70, Confidential Report on Italian Organizations of San Diego, February 10, 1941 (R-3926), Box 28; A-70, Report

on Mazzini Society, February 17, 1941 (R-3927), Box 28; A-70, Report, February 17, 1941 (R-3928), Box 28; A-70, Confidential Report, Italian Affairs in San Diego, February 27, 1942 (R-5521d), Box 34; A-70 to Maj. General Ralph Van Deman, August 28, 1940 (R-3709b), Box 26, RVD.

168. A-70, Confidential Report, January 7, 1942 (R-5435g), Box 32, RVD.

169. A-70, Confidential Report, Major General Ralph Van Deman, September 30, 1942 (R-5901c), Box 38; letter from Major General R. H. Van Deman to Captain Victor I. Coppard, October 2, 1942 (R-5901d), Box 38; letter from R. H. Van Deman, CC: ONI, G-2, June 19, 1940 (R-3555), Box 26, RVD.

170. A-70, Confidential Monthly Report, December 1, 1942 (R-5992), Box 39, RVD.

171. From: A-42, To: General R. H. Van Deman, June 22, 1940 (R-3567a) Box 26, RVD.

172. From Mittwer, Confidential Japanese Notes, December 1941 (R-5420); From B-31, Confidential Japanese Notes, December 1941 (R-5408); Confidential Reports, January 1942 (R-5434), Box 32, RVD. In determining that Mary Mittwer was this agent, I noted similar serifs in the type face of the first two reports, indicating that Agent B-31 and Mittwer were the same. Next, several clues led to the conclusion that "Mittwer" was in fact Mrs. Fred Mittwer, who wrote under her maiden name, Mary Oyama: (1) the report writer's combination of Japanese-language ability and idiomatic English journalism; (2) the surname's scarcity (only five Mittwer deaths have been reported by U.S. Social Security in California during the previous sixty-two years); and (3) the reports' distinctive fund of information, which matches Mary Mittwer's personal background, specifically, her husband's career as a lithographer, her brother's work as a journalist for a Los Angeles newspaper fighting gambling in Little Tokyo, and the reports' gossip-column literary devices. See "Mrs. Fred Mittwer who writes under the name Mary Oyama," caption for photograph by Iwasaki Hikaru, 5/13/44, Bancroft Library, University of California, Berkeley, Online Archive of California, California Digital Library, University of California, http://content.cdlib.org/ark:/13030/ft0779n5zm&brand=oac/, accessed June 26, 2008; Harry K. Honda, Interview, April 1, 1998, June 17, 1999, 47–49, in, "REgenerations Oral History Project: Rebuilding Japanese American Families, Communities, and Civil Rights in the Resettlement Era, Los Angeles Region: Volume II," Online Archive of California, California Digital Library, University of California, http://content.cdlib.org/xtf/view?docId=ft358003z1&brand=oac&doc.view=entire_text, accessed June 26, 2008; Valerie Matsumoto, "Desperately Seeking 'Deirdre,'" in Linda Trinh Vo and Marian Sciachitano, eds., *Asian American Women: The Frontier Reader* (Lincoln, 2003), 56–62; and Kenny Murase, "Who's Who in the Nisei Literary World," *Current Life,* October 1940, 8.

173. "Mrs. Fred Mittwer who writes under the name Mary Oyama," caption for photograph by Iwasaki Hikaru, 5/13/44; Glenna Matthews, *The Rise of Public Woman: Woman's Power and Woman's Place in the United States, 1630–1970* (New York, 1994), 194–95.

174. Ralph H. Van Deman, January 8, 1942 (R-5438a); Ralph H. Van Deman, January 9, 1942 (R-5438b) Box 32, RVD.

175. Ralph Van Deman, October 20, 1940, Office of Chief of Staff, Cross Reference Card, Microform 1194, RG 350, NARA.

176. Memorandum for the President, William J. Donovan, February 17, 1942, No. 258, File: 16–28 February, President's Secretary's File, Box 164, Franklin Delano Roosevelt Presidential Library.

177. Gerald A. Baker, To the Secretary of State, December 30, 1941, Copy for Naval Intelligence, December 30, 1941 (R-5463b); Major Gordon D. Ingraham, To: S-2, San Diego Subsector, Subject: Transmittal of Information, January 16, 1942 (R-5455b, c, and d), Box 32, RVD.

178. Major Gordon D. Ingraham, To: S-2, San Diego Subsector, Subject: Japanese Population in the Southern California Sector, January 15, 1942 (R-5455e) Box 32, RVD.

179. "Mrs. Fred Mittwer who writes under the name Mary Oyama," caption for photograph by Iwasaki Hikaru, 5/13/44.

180. 108T, 2/24/42 (R-5520a); 112K, Re: Frank Furuya, Solana Beach, March 2, 1942 (R-5529), Box 34, RVD.

181. German-American Centrale, Youngstown, Ohio, December 21, 1941 (R-5905a), Box 38, RVD; Negro Sabotage Financed by German Groups, April 7, 1942 (R-5909b), Box 38, RVD; B-31, Negro Victory Rally, Golden Gate Ballroom, June 24, 1942 (R-5941h), Box 38, RVD; *Time,* June 1, 1942.

182. Letter from General R. H. Van Deman to R. E. Combs, August 25, 1948, Box 68, RVD.

183. Victor Tasche, 7/22/42; Dr. Paul S. Taylor, 7/22/42; Prof. Lewis Terman, 7/22/42 (R-5886-a), Box 38, RVD.

184. Card, Hollywood Writers Mobilization, 8/6/42 (R-5866d), Box 38, RVD; *Time*, September 1, 1952.

185. Card, Daniel Lewis James, Jan. 1, 1944 (R-9098), Box 39, RVD; *NYT*, 5/21/1988.

186. George H. Thomas, Jr., June 8, 1944 (R-10232e), Box 76; Cyril Towbin, March 6, 1945 (R10232f), Box 76; Sam Cloner, April 4, 1944 (R-10545), Box 78; Irving Dratler, October 31, 1944 (R-10684g), Box 79, RVD.

187. Schrecker, *Many Are the Crimes*, 42–52, 61–81, 84–85, 318–19.

188. California Legislature, *Third Report, Un-American Activities in California, 1947: Report of the Joint Fact-Finding Committee on Un-American Activities to the Fifty-Seventh California Legislature* (Sacramento, 1947), 1, 4, 23, 35, 99, 108, 169–200; Navasky, *Naming Names*, 79.

189. In the four hundred pages of the "First Section" of its six-part 1944 report, HUAC covered thirty-one organizations in New York City, with entries as long as sixteen pages, and only five organizations for all of California, most only a paragraph long. See HR, 78th Congress, 2d Session, on House Resolution 282, *Investigation of Un-American Propaganda Activities in the United States. Special Committee on Un-American Activities Committee*, appendix, part 9: *Communist Front Organizations with Special Reference to the National Citizens Political Action Committee*, first section (Washington, DC, 1944), 261–660; Ceplair and Englund, *The Inquisition in Hollywood*, 123–24, 155–59; Shippers, *Jack B. Tenney*, vol. 2, 547–48, 592–92, 601–19, 648–66, 786–87; *LAT*, 4/19/1939, 2/9/1940, 2/16/1940, 2/22/1940, 8/21/1940, 8/22/1940; and Schrecker, *Many Are the Crimes*, 91–92.

190. Nancy Lynn Schwartz, *The Hollywood Writers' Wars* (New York, 1982), 120–21, 158–62, 174–75, 196–203, 217–19.

191. Barrett, *The Tenney Committee*, 3–7, 17–20, 44–46, 197, 203–9, 211–34; Schwartz, *The Hollywood Writers' Wars*, 231–35, 240–43; Shippers, *Jack B. Tenney*, vol. 2, 870–71.

192. Donner, *Protectors of Privilege*, 63–64.

193. Letters from R. E. Combs to General R. H. Van Deman, May 6, 1947, March 9, 1948, March 17, 1948 (R-9044); R.H.V.D, Memorandum, May 13, 1947, Box 68, RVD.

194. Letter from R. E. Combs to General R. H. Van Deman, August 13, 1948, Box 68, RVD.

195. California Legislature, *Third Report, Un-American Activities in California*, 234–40.

196. Report on Meeting: Progressive Citizens of America, February 13, 1947, Box 67, RVD.

197. Barrett, *The Tenney Committee*, 30–32, 192–211; Ceplair and Englund, *The Inquisition in Hollywood*, 257–58; Stephen Vaughn, *Ronald Reagan in Hollywood: Movies and Politics* (New York, 1994), 211–12; Schwartz, *The Hollywood Writers' Wars*, 251–52, 259; California Legislature, *Third Report, Un-American Activities in California*, 179–81, 189–92, 238–40, 286–88, 369; HR, Committee on Un-American Activities, 80th Congress, 1st Session, *Investigation of Un-American Propaganda Activities in the United States* (Washington, DC, 1947), 246–52, 262–67; Shippers, *Jack B. Tenney*, vol. 3, 1344.

198. Kathryn S. Olmsted, *Red Spy Queen: A Biography of Elizabeth Bentley* (Chapel Hill, 2002), x–xi, 32–33, 36–56, 89–111; Schrecker, *Many Are the Crimes*, 170–76; Schmidt, *Red Scare*, 365–66; Richard Gid Powers, *Secrecy and Power: The Life of J. Edgar Hoover* (New York, 1987), 286–92; HR, Committee on Un-American Activities, 80th Congress, 1st Session, *Investigation of Un-American Propaganda Activities in the United States*, 37, 39, 45–47.

199. Letter from R. H. Van Deman to J. Edgar Hoover, April 15, 1947; letter from R. H. Van Deman to J. Edgar Hoover, February 21, 1951, FBIVD.

200. Report on: Meeting Sponsored by Progressive Citizens of America, May 20, 1947 (R-9091a); Dear General, May 26, 1947, Box 69, RVD.

201. Hepburn's speech was written by Dalton Trumbo, later one of the blacklisted Hollywood Ten. See Schwartz, *The Hollywood Writers' Wars*, 255–57; and "I Speak," Katherine Hepburn, July 16, 1947 (R-9103a), Box 69, RVD.

202. *Counter Attack: Facts to Combat Communism*, no. 74 (October 1948): 1–4; Thomas Doherty, *Cold War, Cool Medium: Television, McCarthyism, and American Culture* (New York,

2003), 8, 33; *Time,* June 30, 1952; Ceplair and Englund, *The Inquisition in Hollywood,* 387–88, 392–93; Schrecker, *Many Are the Crimes,* 218.

203. Letters from General R. H. Van Deman to R. E. Combs, August 19, 1948, September 3, 1948, November 9, 1948, Box 68, RVD; letter from C. E. Combs to General R. H. Van Deman, November 6, 1948, Box 68, RVD; *Counter Attack: Facts to Combat Communism,* no. 74 (October 1948): 1–4; Patrick McGilligan and Paul Buhle, *Tender Comrades: A Backstory of the Hollywood Blacklist* (New York, 1997), 185, 551–52.

204. Teletype from Santoiana to Director, January 23, 1952, FBIVD.

205. *NYT,* 6/9/1949, 6/10/1949, 9/7/1971; California Legislature, *Fifth Report of the Senate Fact-Finding Committee on Un-American Activities, 1949* (Sacramento, 1948), 411, 448–49, 488–537; McGilligan and Buhle, *Tender Comrades,* 368–69. The famous appendix 9 of HUAC's 1944 report, which included a similarly massive list of communists, was unknown to the public and restricted to a very narrow circle of government investigators as late as 1951. See Barrett, *The Tenney Committee,* 20–22.

206. *NYT,* 10/23/1949; Mari Jo Buhle, Paul Buhle, and Dan Georgakas, eds., *Encyclopedia of the American Left* (New York, 1998), 755–57; American Business Consultants, *Red Channels: The Report of Communist Influence in Radio and Television* (New York, 1951), 4, 71, 109, 123; Merle Miller, "The Judges and the Judged," in John Cogley and Merle Miller, *Blacklisting: Two Key Documents* (New York, 1971), 82; Barrett, *The Tenney Committee,* 79.

207. Meeting held at: The Globe Theater, November 11, 1950 (R-10479), Box 78, RVD.

208. Report on: Meeting of the Arts, Sciences & Professions Council Convention, December 2, 1950 (R-10482), Box 78, RVD.

209. R.H.V.D., Memorandum, February 14, 1951 (R-10558), Box 78, RVD.

210. B-2, Report on Meeting of the Arts, Sciences & Professions Council, April 6, 1951, Box 79, RVD.

211. *LAT,* 4/13/1951, 4/18/1951, 4/26/1951, 5/17/1951; *San Diego Union,* 4/24/1951; Schrecker, *Many Are the Crimes,* 19–20.

212. Schmidt, *Red Scare,* 366; Buhle, Buhle, and Georgakas, *Encyclopedia of the American Left,* 755–57; Schrecker, *Many Are the Crimes,* 46–47, 345–54; Michael J. Ybarra, *Washington Gone Crazy: Senator Pat McCarran and the Great American Communist Hunt* (Hanover, 2004), 741–42.

213. Shippers, *Jack B. Tenney,* vol. 3, 1342–43, vol. 4, 1546–54, 1567–78, 1598–617, 1634–35, 1777–79, 1799, 1806–18, 1860–957, 1969–70; California Legislature, *Third Report, Un-American Activities in California,* 48, 359–60; *LAT,* 5/4/1948, 4/9/1954, 6/6/1954; *Time,* April 12, 1954, June 21, 1954; Glen Jeansonne, *Gerald L. K. Smith: Minister of Hate* (New Haven, 1988), 162–63; Jack B. Tenney, *Zion's Fifth Column: A Tenney Report* (Tujunga, 1953), 5, 37–38; Jack B. Tenney, *Zionist Network: A Tenney Report on World Zionism* (Tujunga, 1953); Jack B. Tenney, *Zion's Trojan Horse* (Hollywood, 1954).

214. Shippers, *Jack B. Tenney,* vol. 4, 1969–70; Jeansonne, *Gerald L. K. Smith,* 99–100, 188–205; Glen Jeansonne, "Gerald L. K. Smith: From Wisconsin Roots to National Notoriety," *Wisconsin Magazine of History* 86, no. 2 (2002–3): 28.

215. Federal Bureau of Investigation, "Celebrating a Century, 1908–2008," http://www.fbi.gov/libref/factsfigure/shorthistory.htm, accessed October 29, 2008.

216. SEN, 94th Congress, 2d Session, *Final Report of the Select Committee to Study Governmental Operations with Respect to Intelligence Activities,* book 3 (Washington, DC, 1976), 3–4, 7–8.

217. Ibid., book 2, 67, 77, 86–89, 98–104.

218. Ibid., book 3, 16.

219. Ibid., book 2, 5, 15–20.

220. Powe, "American Military Intelligence Comes of Age," 29; *NYT,* 9/7/1971.

221. Letter from R. R. Roach to D. M. Ladd, July 13, 1945; letter from J. K. Mumford to D. M. Ladd, July 18, 1945; letter from J. K. Mumford to D. M. Ladd, July 19, 1945; letter from T. E. Naughten to Director, February 2, 1945; letter from Special Agent in Charge J. F. Santoiana to Director, October 5, 1951; letters from J. Edgar Hoover to Ralph Van Deman, April 2, 1947, July 10, 1947, January 19, 1949; letter from G. A. Nease to Director, March 7, 1949; letter from John Edgar Hoover to Mr.

Tolson, September 21, 1951; letter from SAC Los Angeles to Director, September 24, 1951; letter from Hoover to San Diego, October 1, 1951, FBIVD.

222. Talbert, *Negative Intelligence*, 270–71; *NYT*, 9/7/1971; letter from R. R. Roach to D. M. Ladd, July 13, 1945; letter from D. M. Ladd to E. A. Tamm, October 29, 1945; letter from Colonel F. W. Hein to Commanding Officer 115th CIC Detachment, March 8, 1951; letter from A. H. Belmont to D. M. Ladd, November 9, 1951; letter from Colonel H. S. Isaacson to Major General A. R. Bolling, November 27, 1951; letter from Director to SAC San Diego, December 11, 1951; letter from V. P. Keay to A. H. Belmont, January 22, 1952; letter from Santoiana to Director, January 22, 1952; letter from SAC San Diego to Director, February 4, 1952; letter from SAC SF to Director, n.d., FBIVD.

223. *LAT*, 2/16/1962; *NYT*, 6/21/1962, 7/28/1962; *San Diego Union*, 2/18/1962.

224. *NYT*, 7/9/1971.

225. *NYT*, 9/7/1971; Donner, *The Age of Surveillance*, 412–13.

226. *NYT*, 9/7/1971; letter from T. E. Bishop to Mr. Mohr, August 12, 1971, FBIVD.

227. *NYT*, 9/20/1971.

228. Talbert, *Negative Intelligence*, 270–71, 277.

229. Donner, *Protectors of Privilege*, 63–64; James R. Mills, "Locking up the Tenney Files," *The Nation* (New York), July 5, 1971, 10–11.

Chapter 10. President Quezon's Commonwealth

1. Carlos Quirino, *Quezon: Paladin of Philippine Freedom* (Manila, 1971), 285–87; Theodore Friend, *Between Two Empires: The Ordeal of the Philippines, 1929–1946* (New Haven, 1965), 184–86; *Blue Book of the Inauguration of the Commonwealth of the Philippines* (Manila, 1935), vi.

2. Manuel Luis Quezon, *The Good Fight* (New York, 1946), 161–63.

3. Joseph Ralston Hayden, *The Philippines: A Study in National Development* (New York, 1955), 429–30; Lewis E. Gleeck Jr., "The Putsch That Failed," *Bulletin of the American Historical Collection* 26, no. 3 (1998): 36–41; Lewis E. Gleeck Jr., *The American Half-Century (1898–1946)* (Quezon City, 1998), 377–80, 491–92.

4. Emanuel A. Bajá, *Philippine Police System and Its Problems* (Manila, 1933), 69–71, 136–40, 142–46.

5. Rafael Palma, *My Autobiography* (Manila, 1953), 60–61, 104–5.

6. John T. Sidel, *Capital, Coercion, and Crime: Bossism in the Philippines* (Stanford, 1999), 58–63.

7. *PFP*, 4/26/1930, 12–13.

8. *PFP*, 4/26/1930, 12–13, 11/4/1933, 2–3, 40.

9. *PFP*, 4/12/1930, 2, 42, 4/19/1930, 6–7.

10. *Makinaugalingon*, 9/10/1929.

11. *El Tiempo*, 10/2/1929.

12. Newspaper clipping "Ignacio Arroyo Dies of Heart Failure in Residence in Iloilo," in letter from Dr. Mariano Arroyo to Manuel Quezon, January 19, 1935, Box 65, File: Arroyo, Ignacio, MLQ; letter from Jose Ma. Arroyo to Manuel Quezon, December 27, 1924, Box 182, File: Iloilo 1921–23, MLQ; Fernando Ma. Guerrero, *Directorio Oficial del Senado de Filipinas* (Manila, 1921), 34–35; Fernando Ma. Guerrero, *Directorio Oficial del Senado y de la Camara de Representatives* (Manila, 1917), 157–58; Republic of the Philippines, Supreme Court, *Beaterio del Santisimo Rosario de Molo vs. Court of Appeals, Jose Arroyo, et al.*, G.R. No. L 44204, July 11, 1985, http://www.lawphil.net/juduris/juri1985/ju11985/gr_144204_1985.html, accessed June 6, 2006; Jet Damazo, "The Pidal Connection," *Newsbreak* (Manila), September 15, 2003; *Inquirer News Service*, August 20, 2003, http://www.inq7.net/nat/2003/aug/20/text/n at_5-1ht, accessed June 13, 2006; T. Villavert, "FG Arroyo to Continue 'Arroyo Tradition,'" PIA Information Service, "PIA Press Release 05/05/2005," http://www.pia.gov.ph/news.asp?fi=p050505.htm&no=1, accessed June 6, 2006.

13. *CA*, 8/1/1908, 8/22/1909; letter from Jose Ma. Arroyo to Manuel Quezon, January 24, 1925, Box 182, File: Iloilo 1921–23, MLQ; Bajá, *Philippine Police System and Its Problems*, 356; letter from J. Harding to Executive Secretary, September 4, 1909, No. 370–234 Entry 5, RG 350, NARA.

14. Letter from Jose Ma. Arroyo to Manuel Quezon, January 24, 1925 Box 182, File: Iloilo 1921–23, MLQ.

15. Letter from Dr. Mariano Arroyo to Senate President Manuel A. Quezon, August 15, 1927; letter from Manuel A. Quezon to Dr. Mariano Arroyo, August 23, 1927, Box 182, File: Iloilo 1926–29, MLQ.

16. Letter from Jose B. Ledesma to Manuel A. Quezon, February 23, 1929; letter from Manuel Quezon to Senator Jose B. Ledesma, May 29, 1929; letter from Dr. Mariano Arroyo to Manuel Quezon, January 5, 1929; letter from Manuel Quezon to Dr. Mariano Arroyo, January 10, 1929, Box 182, File: Iloilo 1929, MLQ.

17. *El Tiempo*, 10/5/1929.

18. Ibid.

19. *El Tiempo*, 10/7/1929.

20. *Makinaugalingon*, 10/11/1929.

21. *El Tiempo*, 10/11/1929.

22. *Makinaugalingon*, 10/11/1929, 10/22/1929, 10/29/1929, 11/1/1929.

23. *PFP*, 6/28/1930, 4, 44; *Makinaugalingon*, 6/20/1930. In October 1937 a Manila court convicted Sane for possession of false banknotes and ordered him deported to China. *El Tiempo*, 3/31/1937. But he appealed the decision to the Philippine Supreme Court and fled to China, where he died at Kinchang, Chingkang, of heart disease on August 3, 1940. *Makinaugalingon*, 8/24/1940.

24. *Makinaugalingon*, 8/6/1930.

25. *Makinaugalingon*, 8/11/1930.

26. *Makinaugalingon*, 9/22/1930.

27. *MT*, 9/27/1930.

28. *Makinaugalingon*, 9/24/1930.

29. *El Tiempo*, 11/15/1930; *Makinaugalingon*, 10/3/1930.

30. *El Tiempo*, 10/24/1930, 11/15/1930; Godofredo Grageda, "The *El Tiempo* and *Iloilo Times*," manuscript, 1976, 1–10; *Makinaugalingon*, 10/3/1930.

31. After the death of Senator Jose Ma. Pidal Arroyo on March 8, 1927, his widow, Jesusa Lacson vda. de Arroyo, moved to Negros Occidental where she raised her seven children, including her fourth son, Ignacio Lacson Arroyo (born April 25, 1917). Ignacio Arroyo married Lourdes Tuason (born August 10, 1907). Their marriage produced two sons, Jose Miguel Tuason Arroyo (born June 27, 1946) and Ignacio Tuason Arroyo Jr. (born October 24, 1950). On August 2, 1968, Jose Miguel, known as "Mike," married Gloria Macaraeg Macapagal (born April 5, 1947), the eldest child of Diosdado Macapagal, the former president of the Philippines. See Curriculum Vitae, Gloria Macapagal Arroyo, http: //www.macapagal.com/gma/bio/main/html, accessed June 6, 2006; and "The Family Tree of Doña Teresa de la Paz," in *Teresa de la Paz and Her Two Husbands: A Gathering of Four Families* (Manila, 1996).

32. Letter from Manuel Quezon to Mariano Arroyo, June 13, 1929; telegram from Buenaflor/Arroyo to Manuel Quezon, September 26, 1930, Box 65, File: Arroyo, Ignacio, MLQ.

33. Memorandum for Brigadier General Basilio J. Valdes by Major Paciano Tangco, May 30, 1934, File: Constabulary, Box 62, Series VII, MLQ.

34. Letter from Manuel Quezon to General Basilio Valdes, July 6, 1934; letter from General Basilio Valdes to Manuel L. Quezon, July 7, 1934; Memorandum from Brigadier-General Basilio J. Valdes from Major Paciano Tangco, August 14, 1934, File: Constabulary, Box 62, Series VII, MLQ.

35. *PFP*, 4/12/1941, 11; *MB*, 1/7/1930, 1/9/1930.

36. *PFP*, 4/29/1933, 8–9, 11/25/1933, 6, 36–37, 4/12/1941, 11, 1/4/1930, 16, 1/18/1930, 18, 40, 7/19/1930, 2–3, 38.

37. *PFP*, 4/12/1941, 11–12; *American Chamber of Commerce Journal*, February 1930, 6; *MT*, 12/5/1928, 1/20/1930; *MB*, 1/18/1930; *KR*, 1/1930, 3–6, 13, 9/1930, 44, 9/1933, 8.

38. Emanuel A. Bajá, *Philippine Police System and Its Problems*, book 2: *Police of the Commonwealth* (Manila, 1939), 145–46; *KR*, 10/1930, 6, 12, 10/1931, 16–17, 2/1932, 25, 9/1933, 8, 14, 15, 19, 3/1934, 16.

39. Bajá, *Philippine Police System and Its Problems*, 341–59, 378–81; *PFP*, 1/19/1929, 14, 3/5/1932, 30, 3/26/1932, 30, 1/21/1933, 2, 38, 9/1/1934, 4–5.

40. *PFP*, 10/17/1931, 4, 37, 12/2/1933, 53, 12/21/1940, 54.

41. *PFP*, 1/21/1928, 32, 1/28/1928, 32–33, 6/28/1930, 25, 27, 7/5/1930, 56; HR, *GGPI 1928*, 50.

42. *PFP*, 11/4/1933, 2–3, 40.

43. *PFP,* 2/17/1934, 4–5, 40.

44. *PFP,* 9/14/1935, 4–5, 34.

45. *Philippines Herald,* 5/22/1935, 5/23/1935.

46. *Philippines Herald,* 5/17/1935, 5/23/1935, 5/25/1935, 5/27/1935.

47. Letter from Rafael Crame to Mrs. Aurora A. Quezon, October 20, 1922; letter from Rafael Crame to Manuel L. Quezon, April 29, 1925, File: Constabulary, Box 60, Series VII, MLQ.

48. Letter from Brigadier-General Rafael Crame to Manuel L. Quezon, February 5, 1924, File: Constabulary, Box 60, Series VII, MLQ.

49. Letter from Chief of Constabulary to Jose G. Sanvictores, November 15, 1921, File: Constabulary, Box 60, Series VII, MLQ.

50. Letter from Manuel L. Quezon to Governor-General, February 22, 1933, File: Constabulary, Box 62, Series VII, MLQ.

51. Letter from Silvino Gallardo to Manuel L. Quezon, April 6, 1929, File: Constabulary, Box 61; Summary of All Records of Captain Silvino Gallardo (of Rizal), Headquarters Philippine Constabulary, January 6, 1936, File: Constabulary, Box 62, Series VII, MLQ.

52. Unsigned letter to Manuel Quezon, July 29, 1935, File: 1935 Elections July 29, Box 116, MLQ.

53. Letter from Silvino Gallardo to Manuel Quezon, September 12, 1935, File: 1935 Elections September 12, Box 122, MLQ.

54. Iloilo, Box 127, File: 1935 Election Returns Iloilo, MLQ.

55. Unsigned letter to Manuel Quezon, n.d., File: 1935 Elections August 29, Box 120, MLQ.

56. Hayden, *The Philippines,* 387–92, 409–18, 426–29; Gleeck, "The Putsch That Failed," 36.

57. Confidential Memorandum for—The Superintendent, Intelligence Division, September 21, 1935, Series IV, Box 44, MLQ.

58. Captain Jose Guido, Assistant Superintendent, Intelligence Division, Confidential Memorandum for—The Superintendent, September 23, 1935, Series IV, Box 44, MLQ.

59. Captain Severo C. Cruz, Acting Provincial Commander, Confidential Memorandum for—Adjutant-General, C., September 29, 1935, Series IV, Box 44, MLQ.

60. Memorandum for—Superintendent, Intelligence Division, C., October 1, 1935, Series IV, Box 44, MLQ.

61. Hayden, *The Philippines,* 429–30, 433–34; Gleeck, "The Putsch That Failed," 36.

62. Hayden, *The Philippines,* 429–35; Gleeck, "The Putsch That Failed," 36–41; Gleeck, *The American Half-Century,* 377–80, 491–92; letter from E. Aguinaldo to secretary of war, November 3, 1935, Reel 18, MLQMI; Major M. N. Castañeda, Memorandum for—The Chief of Constabulary, October 28, 1935, Series IV, Box 44, MLQ.

63. Dictated by the President, Malacañang Palace, January 16, 1936, File: Constabulary, Box 62, Series VII, MLQ.

64. Letter from Manuel L. Quezon to General Basilio Valdes, n.d.; letter from G. B. Francisco for the President, January 6, 1936, File: Constabulary, Box 62, Series VII, MLQ.

65. Letter from Manuel L. Quezon to General Basilio Valdes, n.d., File: Constabulary, Box 62, Series VII, MLQ; letter from G. B. Francisco for the President, January 6, 1936, File: Constabulary, Box 62, Series VII, MLQ; *KR,* 7/1939, 12.

66. Letter from Manuel L. Quezon to Governor Harrison, 1914, File: Constabulary, Box 59, Series VII, MLQ.

67. Suzanne G. Carpenter, "Toward the Development of Philippine National Security Capability, 1920–1940: With Special Reference to the Commonwealth Period," PhD diss., New York University, 1976, 123–24, 139–42, 174–75, 211–12; *KR,* 5/1934, 8.

68. David Wurfel, *Filipino Politics: Development and Decay* (Ithaca, 1988), 76–77.

69. Anna Leah Fidelis T. Castañeda, "The Origins of Philippine Judicial Review, 1900–1935," *Ateneo Law Journal* 46, no. 121 (2001): 121–70; W. Cameron Forbes, *The Philippine Islands* (Cambridge, 1945), 97–99.

70. Florencio F. Magsino and Rogelio S. Lumabas, *Men of PMA,* vol. 1 (Manila, 1978), 69–70; Robert M. Carswell, "Philippine National Defense," *Coast Artillery Journal* 84, no. 2 (March–April 1941): 122; Sergio Osmeña, *National Defense and Philippine Democracy: Address Delivered by*

Honorable Sergio Osmeña at the Commencement Exercises of the Philippine Military Academy, Baguio, March 15, 1940 (Manila, 1940), 7; Robert H. Ferrell, *The Eisenhower Diaries* (New York, 1981), 8–10. For contemporary reports of the plan, see *NYT*, 11/20/1934, 11/25/1934, 5/30/1936, 6/20/1936; and Pacual F. Jardiniano, *Police Manual on Public Accountability* (Manila, 1994), 14–15.

71. *KR*, 3/1936, 14, 7/1939, 6.

72. Ricardo Trota Jose, *The Philippine Army, 1935–1942* (Quezon City, 1992), 227; *KR*, 6/1936, 4, 9/1937, 23.

73. Jose, *The Philippine Army*, 32–34; *KR*, 5/1936, 2.

74. Bajá, *Philippine Police System and Its Problems*, book 2: *Police of the Commonwealth*, 45, 93–95.

75. Frank Walton et al., *Survey of Law Enforcement: Customs Enforcement* (Washington, DC, 1966), 97–98.

76. Cicero C. Campos, "The Role of Police in the Philippines: A Case Study from the Third World," PhD diss., Michigan State University, 1983, 166–69; Hayden, *The Philippines*, 292–94; Bajá, *Philippine Police System and Its Problems*, book 2: *Police of the Commonwealth*, 45, 189–92; *KR*, 12/1936, 14, 7/1939, 6; *PFP*, 7/31/1937, 10, 37.

77. Hayden, *The Philippines*, 294; Bajá, *Philippine Police System and Its Problems*, book 2: *Police of the Commonwealth*, 89–90.

78. Carpenter, "Toward the Development of Philippine National Security Capability," 460–61.

79. Ibid., 460–62.

80. Bajá, *Philippine Police System and Its Problems*, book 2: *Police of the Commonwealth*, 22–36, 56–66; *KR*, 6/1938, 6, 26; *PFP*, 5/14/1938, 8, 48, 7/2/1938, 50–51.

81. Bajá, *Philippine Police System and Its Problems*, book 2: *Police of the Commonwealth*, 41–43, 56–66; Hayden, *The Philippines*, 741–42; *Tribune*, 12/2/1938.

82. Carpenter, "Toward the Development of Philippine National Security Capability," 460–63, 469–72, 473–74; *KR*, 3/1939, 7, 26.

83. *KR*, 7/1939, 51–52; Hayden, *The Philippines*, 741–42; *Tribune*, 12/2/1938.

84. *PFP*, 1/2/37, 14–15, 46.

85. Bajá, *Philippine Police System and Its Problems*, book 2: *Police of the Commonwealth*, 72–74.

86. *MB*, 7/31/1977; *KR*, 5/1927, 2, 2/1935, 18, 3/1936, 25, 9/1939, 18–20; *Graphic*, March 2, 1939, 4–5. After Manuel Quezon's engagement to Corazon Chiong Veloso y Rosales in 1907 was broken off, she married Antonio Torres. *Ang Camatuoran* (Cebu), 2/3/1907; *Nueva Fuerza* (Cebu), 2/27/1916, 11/19/1916, 12/10/1916; Dr. Michael Cullinane, personal communication, April 1, 2004.

87. Bajá, *Philippine Police System and Its Problems*, book 2: *Police of the Commonwealth*, 165–73; *Graphic*, March 2, 1939, 4–5; *KR*, 8/1936, 45; *Tribune*, 9/1/1937.

88. Ivar Gica and Prudencio R. Europa, *Cash, Charity, and Controversy: The Story of the Gaming Casinos in the Philippines* (Las Piñas City, 2000), 1–3; Gavan Daws, *Prisoners of the Japanese: POWs of World War II in the Pacific* (New York, 1994), 88–89; *The News Behind the News* (Manila), June 4, 1939, July 2, 1939, July 9, 1939, July 23, 1939.

89. *Sunday Tribune*, 9/5/1937.

90. *PFP*, 9/30/1939, 52.

91. *PFP*, 10/30/1937, 4–5, 39, 9/30/1939, 52–53.

92. *The News Behind the News*, June 4, 1939, July 16, 1939.

93. Ibid.

94. Ibid.

95. *The News Behind the News*, June 4, 1939, June 11, 1939, July 16, 1939, August 6, 1939, July 28, 1940; *PFP*, 1/13/1940, 26–27; *MB*, 5/18/1939.

96. Carlos Quirino, *Philippine Tycoon: The Biography of an Industrialist* (Manila, 1987), 9–10, 16, 89–93, 97, 104–6; Gica and Europa, *Cash, Charity, and Controversy*, 1–2.

97. *PFP*, 12/21/1940, 54.

98. *PFP*, 3/27/1937, 10–11, 7/2/1938, 24–25, 9/17/1938, 1, 13, 1/13/1940, 26, 1/20/1940, 30, 6/1/1940, 4–5, 11/22/1941, 32–33.

99. Benito Legarda Jr., "Bobby Tuason in World War II," in *Teresa de la Paz and Her Two Husbands: A Gathering of Four Families*, 46–48.

100. D. Michael Schafer, *Deadly Paradigms: The Failure of U.S. Counterinsurgency Policy* (Princeton, 1988), 207.

Chapter 11. Philippine Republic

1. Jovito R. Salonga, *A Journey of Struggle and Hope: The Memoir of Jovito R. Salonga* (Quezon City, 2001), 163–64; Conrado de Quiros, *Dead Aim: How Marcos Ambushed Philippine Democracy* (Pasig City, 1997), 9–15.

2. Raymond Bonner, *Waltzing with a Dictator: The Marcoses and the Making of American Policy* (New York, 1987), 126–27.

3. George A. Malcolm, *First Malayan Republic: The Story of the Philippines* (Boston, 1951), 382–83.

4. Paul Hutchcroft, "Oligarchs and Cronies in the Philippine State: The Politics of Patrimonial Plunder," *World Politics* 43, no. 3 (April 1991): 414–50; Max Weber, *The Theory of Social and Economic Organization* (New York, 1964), 346–54.

5. Frank E. Walton, *A Survey of the Manila Police Department* (Washington, DC, 1964), 16, 17.

6. Generoso F. Rivera and Robert T. McMillan, *An Economic and Social Survey of Rural Households in Central Luzon* (Manila, 1954), iii–13; Alfonso A. Calderon, "The Philippine Constabulary, 1901–1951: Half-Century of Service," in Alfonso A. Calderon and Marciano C. Sicat, eds., *Golden Book Philippine Constabulary* (Manila, 1951), 34.

7. A. H. Peterson, G. C. Reinhardt, and E. E. Conger, eds., *Symposium on the Role of Airpower in Counterinsurgency and Unconventional Warfare: The Philippine Huk Campaign* (Santa Monica, 1963), 14–15; Calderon, "The Philippine Constabulary," 37.

8. Gen. Ramon Gelvezon, interview with the author, Manila, November 18, 1988; villagers in Barrio Isawan and Barrio Isian Kasling, Tigbauan, Iloilo Province, interviews with the author, May 1975; Brian Fegan, "The Social History of a Central Luzon Barrio," in Alfred W. McCoy and Edilberto C. de Jesus, eds., *Philippine Social History: Global Trade and Local Transformations* (Honolulu, 1982), 116–17.

9. Peterson, Reinhardt, and Conger, *Symposium on Airpower,* 17.

10. John G. Jameson Jr., *The Philippine Constabulary as a Counterinsurgency Force, 1948–1954* (Carlisle Barracks, 1971), 18–19.

11. John Lewis Gaddis, *Strategies of Containment: A Critical Appraisal of American National Security during the Cold War* (New York, 2005), 29.

12. Nick Cullather, *Illusions of Influence: The Political Economy of United States–Philippines Relations, 1942–1960* (Stanford, 1994), 79–80; Stephen Rosskamm Shalom, *The United States and the Philippines: A Study of Neocolonialism* (Philadelphia, 1981), 63–66, 109–10; Alfredo Bengzon and Raul Rodrigo, *A Matter of Honor: The Story of the 1990–91 RP-US Bases Talks* (Manila, 1997), 16–18, 41–42; Gerald R. Anderson, *Subic Bay: From Magellan to Mt. Pinatubo* (Dagupan, 1991), 76–89.

13. Cullather, *Illusions of Influence,* 80–82, 89, 132–33; Shalom, *The United States and the Philippines,* 65–66; D. Michael Schafer, *Deadly Paradigms: The Failure of U.S. Counterinsurgency Policy* (Princeton, 1988), 213–14, 219–21.

14. NSC 84/2, November 9, 1950, in U.S. Department of State, *Foreign Relations of the United States 1950,* vol. 6: *East Asia and the Pacific* (Washington, DC, 1976), 1515–20.

15. Malcolm, *First Malayan Republic,* 382–33; Jose V. Abueva, *Ramon Magsaysay: A Political Biography* (Manila, 1971), 147–48.

16. Cullather, *Illusions of Influence,* 90.

17. Alfred W. McCoy, *Closer Than Brothers: Manhood at the Philippine Military Academy* (New Haven, 1999), chapter 4.

18. Col. Charles Bohannan (ret.), interviews with the author, Manila, February 1982.

19. Shalom, *The United States and the Philippines,* 78–79; Jose M. Crisol, *The Red Lie* (Manila, 1954), 197–204; Edward G. Lansdale, *In the Midst of Wars: An American's Mission to Southeast Asia* (New York, 1972), 71–72.

20. Lansdale, *In the Midst of Wars,* 72–73.

21. Col. Charles Bohannan (ret.), interviews with the author, Manila, February 1982.

22. Lansdale, *In the Midst of Wars,* 74.

23. Members of the MIS team involved in this mission, interviews with the author, Alfredo Gloria, Manila, November 26, 1975; Pablito Gepana, Iloilo City, November 26, 1973; and Eduardo Tajanlangit, Iloilo City, November 26, 1973.

24. Edward G. Lansdale, *Lessons Learned: The Philippines, 1946–1953* (Washington, DC, 1963), 3.

25. *Chicago Daily Tribune,* 9/11/1954, 2/14/1955; HR, Committee on Armed Services, 82d Congress, 2d session, *Hearings before Committee on Armed Services of the House of Representatives on Sundry Legislation Affecting the Naval and Military Establishments 1952* (Washington, DC, 1952), 4494–97; Interdepartmental Committee, *U.S. Overseas Internal Defense Policy,* September 1962, Approved as Policy by National Security Action Memorandum 182 of August 24, 1962, drworley.org/NSPcommon/OIDP/OIDP.pdf, accessed November 30, 2008; William A. Stofft, foreword, in Lawrence M. Greenberg, *The Hukbalahap Insurrection: A Case Study of a Successful Anti-Insurgency Operation in the Philippines, 1946–1955* (Washington, DC, 1987), iii.

26. *El Tiempo* (Iloilo City), 1/28/1946.

27. Negros Occidental, Provincial Board, *Minutes,* General Fund-Chief Executive, October 6, 1950; Abueva, *Ramon Magsaysay,* 140–41.

28. *El Civismo,* 5/23/1948; *Liberator* (Iloilo City), 10/29/1949.

29. *Rafael Lacson v. Hon. Luis R. Torres,* Philippine Supreme Court, G.R. L-5543, Annex B; *PFP,* 7/12/1952.

30. Dapen Liang, *Philippine Parties and Politics: A Historical Study of National Experience in Democracy* (San Francisco, 1971), 311.

31. *PFP,* 1/27/1951; Abueva, *Ramon Magsaysay,* 140–42; Remegio E. Agpalo, *Jose Laurel: National Leader and Political Philosopher* (Quezon City, 1992), 245–47; Carl H. Landé, *Leaders, Factions, and Parties: The Structure of Philippine Politics* (New Haven, 1965), 66; John T. Sidel, *Capital, Coercion, and Crime: Bossism in the Philippines* (Stanford, 1999), 109.

32. Landé, *Leaders, Factions, and Parties,* 66; letters from Rafael Lacson to President Elpidio Quirino, July 31, 1950, August 28, 1950, September 28, 1950, Elpidio Quirino Papers, Syquia Mansion, Vigan, Ilocos Sur.

33. Negros Occidental, Provincial Board, *Minutes,* January 18, 1950, November 15, 1950.

34. *People v. Lacson,* Criminal Case 3220, Bacolod, Negros Occidental, Lt. Col. Nicolas Jabutina, n.d.

35. Negros Occidental, Provincial Board, *Minutes,* November 15, 1950.

36. *Lacson v. Torres,* G.R. L-5543, Annex B.

37. *El Civismo,* 7/23/1950, 8/20/1950.

38. *Lacson v. Torres,* G.R. L-5543, Annex B.

39. *El Civismo,* 10/7/1951, 9/11/1951.

40. *Lacson v. Torres,* G.R. L-5543, Annex A.

41. *People v. Lacson,* Criminal Case 3220.

42. *PFP,* 8/28/1954; Abueva, *Ramon Magsaysay,* 201–3; Carlos Quirino, *Magsaysay of the Philippines* (Manila, 1958), 79–80; Jesus V. Merritt, *Magsaysay: Man of the People* (Manila, 1953), 33–34; Nick Joaquin, *The Aquinos of Tarlac: An Essay on History as Three Generations* (Metro Manila, 1986), 221–23.

43. *People v. Lacson,* Criminal Case 3220, testimony of Narciso Dalumpines, November 26, 1951.

44. Abueva, *Ramon Magsaysay,* 202–3, 254–55; Quirino, *Magsaysay of the Philippines,* 116; Merritt, *Magsaysay,* 34; Joaquin, *The Aquinos of Tarlac,* 224.

45. Cullather, *Illusions of Influence,* 108–17; Shalom, *The United States and the Philippines,* 86–92.

46. *MT,* 7/11/1953, 11/4/1953; Abueva, *Ramon Magsaysay,* 221, 225; Col. Ed Lansdale of JUSMAG, "Memorandum Prepared for the Ambassador in the Philippines (Spruance)," in John Glennon, ed., *Foreign Relations of the United States, 1952–1954,* vol. 12: *East Asia and the Pacific,* part 2 (Washington, DC, 1987), 548, 551; Cullather, *Illusions of Influence,* 116, 217.

47. *PFP,* 8/28/1954. In the mid-1960s Lacson was released from prison. He returned to Negros where he retired into obscurity.

48. Jürgen Habermas, *Legitimation Crisis* (Boston, 1975), 95–96.

49. Amando Doronila, *The State, Economic Transformation, and Political Change in the Philippines, 1946–1972* (Singapore, 1992), 96–98; Francis J. Murray Jr., "Land Reform in the Philippines: An Overview," *Philippine Sociological Review* 20, nos. 1–2 (1972): 157–58; Frances Starner, *Magsaysay and the Philippine Peasantry: The Agrarian Impact on Philippine Politics, 1953–56* (Berkeley, 1961), 140–41, 184–87, 195–99.

50. Jeter L. Williamson, *A Survey of Police Services and Problems in the Philippines* (Institute of Public Administration, University of the Philippines, 1955), 17–31; Walton, *A Survey of the Manila Police Department,* 36.

51. Republic of the Philippines, Bureau of Census and Statistics, *1971 Philippine Yearbook* (Manila, 1973), 82; Aprodicio A. Laquian, *The City in Nation Building* (Manila, 1966), 47–48.

52. Frank E. Walton et al., *Survey of Philippine Law Enforcement* (Washington, DC, 1966), 38, 46.

53. Letter from Crispino M. de Castro to President Ferdinand Marcos, January 10, 1972, USAID.

54. *MT,* 7/11/1964, 7/23/1964, 7/25/1964, 7/31/1964, 4/14/1965; Franklin G. Ashburn, "A Study of Differential Role Expectation of Police Patrolmen in the Manila Police Department, Republic of the Philippines," PhD diss., Florida State University, 1966, 31–33; Laquian, *The City in Nation Building,* 67–69.

55. U.S. Agency for International Development, OPS, Manila, Airgram, May 9, 1965, USAID; Walton, *A Survey of the Manila Police Department,* 3, 8, 22, 38–39, 69, 79, 154, 165, 227–28, 242, 306–8.

56. Manuel Deala Paruñgao, *The Manila Police Story* (Manila, 1976), 8–12.

57. Frank Walton et al., *Survey of Law Enforcement: Customs Enforcement* (Washington, DC, 1966), 97, 106, 111, 129.

58. *MT,* 12/11/1963, 12/17/1965.

59. *MT,* 3/10/1964.

60. *MT,* 3/18/1964.

61. Donald L. Berlin, "Prelude to Martial Law: An Examination of pre-1972 Philippine Civil-Military Relations," PhD diss., University of South Carolina, 1982, 186–87.

62. OPS, Calvin B. Cowles, East Asia Mission Director Conference, October 21, 1968, USAID; Walton, *Survey of Philippine Law Enforcement,* 84–85.

63. Walton, *Survey of Philippine Law Enforcement,* 178–79.

64. John Sidel, "The Philippines: The Languages of Legitimation," in Muthiah Alagappa, ed., *Political Legitimacy in Southeast Asia: The Quest for Moral Authority* (Stanford, 1995), 147.

65. Walton, *Survey of Philippine Law Enforcement,* v, xvi–xvii.

66. Ibid., 1; Cicero C. Campos, "The Role of Police in the Philippines: A Case Study from the Third World," PhD diss., Michigan State University, 1983, 294, 266, 204; Cleto B. Señoren, "A Historical Perspective of the Philippine Police System," *International Police Review* 6, no. 3 (1972): 3–4.

67. Walton, *Survey of Philippine Law Enforcement,* 29, 35.

68. Michael T. Klare, *War without End: American Planning for the Next Vietnams* (New York, 1972), 245, 241, 247, 250; Thomas David Lobe, "U.S. Police Assistance for the Third World," PhD diss., University of Michigan, 1975, 82; Thomas Lobe, *United States National Security Policy and Aid to the Thailand Police* (Denver, 1977), 5.

69. A. J. Langguth, *Hidden Terrors* (New York, 1978), 47–52, 124–26, 300.

70. Lobe, "U.S. Police Assistance," 56–57, 60–61, 67; Lobe, *United States National Security Policy,* 9.

71. HR, Committee on Appropriations, 93rd Congress, 2d Session, *Foreign Assistance and Related Agencies Appropriations for 1975* (Washington, DC, 1974), 285; OPS, Philippines, Report, August 15, 1973, USAID; OPS, "U.S. Public Safety Assistance in the Country of Philippines: Fact Sheet," September 10, 1973, USAID; OPS, Monthly Report, June 9, 1971, USAID; Klare, *War without End,* 382–83; Lobe, *United States National Security Policy,* 7–8.

72. Jeremi Suri, *Power and Protest: Global Revolution and the Rise of Détente* (Cambridge, 2003), 1–2, 88–130, 164–212, 269–71.

73. U.S. General Accounting Office, *Stopping U.S. Assistance to Foreign Police and Prisons*

(Washington, DC, 1976), 14; SEN, 93rd Congress, 2d Session, *Congressional Record*, vol. 120, part 25 (Washington, DC, 1974), 33474.

74. Lobe, "U.S. Police Assistance," 56–57, 60–61, 67.

75. McCoy, *Closer Than Brothers*, chap. 6.

76. *Far Eastern Economic Review*, 7/14/1966, 59.

77. *1971 Philippine Yearbook*, 270–76; letter from Crispino M. de Castro to President Ferdinand Marcos, January 10, 1972, USAID.

78. Harvey A. Averch, F. H. Denton, and J. E. Kohler, *The Matrix of Policy in the Philippines* (Princeton, 1971), 3, 115–17, 120–21, 179–98.

79. Ivar Gica and Prudencio R. Europa, *Cash, Charity, and Controversy: The Story of the Gaming Casinos in the Philippines* (Las Piñas City, 2000), 1–8; Wilfredo R. Reotutar, *So The People May Know All about the Gambling Menace in the Philippines* (Quezon City, 1999), 54–55; Chito Madrigal-Collantes, *Picture Me* (Manila, 1997), 121; Sterling Seagrave, *The Marcos Dynasty* (New York, 1988), 329; Gavan Daws, *Prisoners of the Japanese: POWs of World War II in the Pacific* (New York, 1994), 160, 310–12; Joseph Burkholder Smith, *Portrait of a Cold Warrior* (New York, 1976), 293–94.

80. Paruñgao, *The Manila Police Story*, 11; OPS, Monthly Reports, March 12, 1969, October 10, 1969, February 12, 1971, July 15, 1971, USAID; U.S. Agency for International Development, *U.S. A.I.D. Assistance to the Philippines, 1946–1969* (Manila, 1969), 15.

81. OPS, Monthly Report, May 9, 1969, USAID.

82. Campos, "The Role of Police in the Philippines," 213–14; OPS, Monthly Reports, February 18, 1969, July 5, 1969, USAID; *Daily Mirror*, 12/16/1968.

83. OPS, Internal Security Program—FY 71, August 13, 1969, USAID; OPS, Monthly Report, March 12, 1969, USAID.

84. Petronilo Bn. Daroy, "On the Eve of Dictatorship and Revolution," in Aurora Javate-de Dios, Petronilo Bn. Daroy, and Lorna Kalaw-Tirol, eds., *Dictatorship and Revolution: Roots of People's Power* (Metro Manila, 1988), 2–8.

85. Marites Dañguilan Vitug and Glenda M. Gloria, *Under the Crescent Moon: Rebellion in Mindanao* (Quezon City, 2000), 2–12, 15.

86. *MT*, 3/21/1968; Vitug and Gloria, *Under the Crescent Moon*, 12–23.

87. *PFP*, 4/6/1968, 68.

88. Bonner, *Waltzing with a Dictator*, 76–77.

89. Mark Thompson, *The Anti-Marcos Struggle: Personalistic Rule and Democratic Transition in the Philippines* (New Haven, 1995), 34–35; Lela Garner Noble, "Politics in the Marcos Era," in John Bresnan, ed., *Crisis in the Philippines: The Marcos Era and Beyond* (Princeton, 1986), 79–80.

90. Thompson, *The Anti-Marcos Struggle*, 35–37, 192–93; Willem Wolters, *Politics, Patronage, and Class Conflict in Central Luzon* (The Hague, 1983), 166–67; de Quiros, *Dead Aim*, 46, 66–67; Seagrave, *The Marcos Dynasty*, 218–19.

91. De Quiros, *Dead Aim*, 66–67.

92. Seagrave, *The Marcos Dynasty*, 218.

93. Primitivo Mijares, *The Conjugal Dictatorship of Ferdinand and Imelda Marcos I* (San Francisco, 1976), 151; Luis "Chavit" Singson, interviews with the author, Vigan, June 1974.

94. *Daily Mirror*, 10/15/1969.

95. *MT*, 6/3/1970; *Daily Mirror*, 6/7/1972; Alan Robson, "Patrimonial Politics in the Philippine Ilocos," *Pilipinas* 38 (2002): 8–12.

96. *MT*, 6/13/1970.

97. *MT*, 6/3/1970.

98. Mijares, *The Conjugal Dictatorship of Ferdinand and Imelda Marcos I*, 151; *MT*, 10/19/1970.

99. *1971 Philippine Yearbook*, 192–93, 226–43; Republic of the Philippines, National Economic and Development Authority, *1980 Statistical Yearbook* (Manila, 1980), 606.

100. Jose F. Lacaba, *Days of Disquiet, Nights of Rage: The First Quarter Storm and Related Events* (Manila, 1982), 27–60.

101. Ibid., 13–14.

102. Bonner, *Waltzing with a Dictator*, 77–79; Resil B. Mojares, *The Man Who Would Be President:*

Serging Osmeña and Philippine Politics (Cebu, 1986), 145; Daroy, "On the Eve of Dictatorship and Revolution," 2–8; Lacaba, *Days of Disquiet,* 15–19, 69–70.

103. OPS, Monthly Reports, February 11, 1970, March 11, 1970, USAID.

104. Lacaba, *Days of Disquiet,* 19.

105. OPS, Monthly Reports, March 12, 1971, July 15, 1971, March 20, 1972, April 26, 1972, USAID.

106. OPS, Monthly Report, March 11, 1970, USAID.

107. Daroy, "On the Eve of Dictatorship and Revolution," 2–8.

108. OPS, Monthly Reports, January 14, 1971, February 12, 1971, March 12, 1971, April 7, 1971, May 17, 1971, June 9, 1971, July 15, 1971, August 16, 1971, September 15, 1971, October 8, 1971, USAID.

109. Gica and Europa, *Cash, Charity, and Controversy,* 6–10; Reotutar, *So The People May Know,* 54–55.

110. OPS, Memorandum of Conversation, Executive Secretary Melchor's views on AID's Public Safety Program, July 28, 1971, USAID.

111. Gary Reid and Genevieve Costigan, *Revisiting the 'Hidden Epidemic': A Situation Assessment of Drug Use in Asia in the context of HIV/AIDS* (Fairfield, 2002), 171.

112. Ricardo M. Zarco, "Drugs in School 1974: A Five Philippine City Study," in *Two Research Monographs on Drug Abuse in the Philippines* (Manila, 1975), 81–82; members of the Constabulary Anti-Narcotics Unit, confidential interviews with the author, Manila, November 1975. For details of Philippine heroin trafficking, see Alfred W. McCoy, *Drug Traffic: Narcotics and Organized Crime in Australia* (Sydney, 1980), 349–51.

113. Romeo J. Sanga, Dangerous Drugs Board, interview with the author, Manila, November 27, 1975; Constabulary Anti-narcotics Unit, *Third Anniversary* (Quezon City, 1975).

114. Members of the Constabulary Anti-narcotics Unit, confidential interviews with the author, Manila, November 1975.

115. OPS, Monthly Reports, January 14, 1971, February 12, 1971, March 12, 1971, April 7, 1971, May 17, 1971, June 9, 1971, July 15, 1971, August 16, 1971, September 15, 1971, October 8, 1971, USAID.

116. David Wurfel, *Filipino Politics: Development and Decay* (Ithaca, 1988), 18–19; Joaquin, *The Aquinos of Tarlac,* 355–58; de Quiros, *Dead Aim,* 309–12; Thompson, *The Anti-Marcos Struggle,* 41–43; Gregg R. Jones, *Red Revolution: Inside the Philippine Guerrilla Movement* (Boulder, 1989), 59–69; Lt. Col. Victor Corpus, interviews with the author, Quezon City, April 1, 1987, April 5, 1987.

117. Wolters, *Politics, Patronage, and Class Conflict in Central Luzon,* 166–67; Thompson, *The Anti-Marcos Struggle,* 42–43, 45–46.

118. Mojares, *The Man Who Would Be President,* 144.

119. Bonner, *Waltzing with a Dictator,* 126–27; Benigno "Ninoy" S. Aquino Jr., *A Garrison State in the Make and Other Speeches* (Manila, 1985), 345–51; Filemon C. Rodriguez, *The Marcos Regime: Rape of the Nation* (New York, 1985), 85–86; Ferdinand E. Marcos, *Notes on the New Society of the Philippines* (Manila, 1973), 2–3; Alex Bello Brillantes Jr., *Dictatorship and Martial Law: Philippine Authoritarianism in 1972* (Quezon City, 1987), 88–90.

120. *NYT,* 2/23/1986; Bonner, *Waltzing with a Dictator,* 125, 468; a member of the Philippine Military Academy, class of 1940, interview with the author, Metro Manila, August 1996. According to his biodata Ramon L. Cannu, a specialist in "countersubversion" and Marcos's bodyguard as chief of the Physical Protection Brigade in the Presidential Security Unit, was promoted to brigadier general on September 19, 1972, just two days before martial law was declared. See Registry Committee, Association of General and Flag Officers, *General and Flag Officers of the Philippines,* vol. 1: *(1986–1983)* (Manila, 1983), 89.

121. OPS, Monthly Report, June 9, 1971, USAID.

122. Campos, "The Role of the Police in the Philippines," 217.

123. Wurfel, *Filipino Politics,* 22.

Chapter 12. Martial Law Terror

1. Members of the Philippine Constabulary, confidential interview with the author, Manila, November 1975.

2. Gen. Rafael Ileto, interview with the author, Manila, July 2, 1986.

3. The term *salvaging* probably derives from Tagalog *salbahe,* meaning "wild" or "savage," which may in turn come from the Spanish *salvaje,* meaning "barbarous." In an editorial on these "summary killings," the *Philippine Daily Inquirer* (6/29/1996) commented, "[W]e call this 'salvaging,' demonstrating our talent to reinvent the English language." During Marcos's dictatorship, the military reportedly coined the term to mean "the elimination of detainees after torture instead of placing them in official detention centers." Task Force Detainees, *Political Detainees of the Philippines,* book 3 (Manila, 1978), 41–43.

4. Manuel Deala Paruñgao, *The Manila Police Story* (Manila, 1976), 11, 168–74; Cicero C. Campos, "The Role of Police in the Philippines: A Case Study from the Third World," PhD diss., Michigan State University, 1983, 206–7, 217–18, 222–23, 276; *Far Eastern Economic Review,* 10/15/1982, 86; *MB,* 7/31/1977.

5. Rod B. Gutang, *Pulisya: The Inside Story of the Demilitarization of Law Enforcement in the Philippines* (Quezon City, 1991), 9, 35–37; *MB,* 7/31/1977.

6. Gutang, *Pulisya,* 5–6, 37, 247–58.

7. *PDI,* 6/14/1996.

8. By adult males I mean those between the ages of twenty and sixty-five. See Ferdinand E. Marcos, *The Democratic Revolution in the Philippines* (Manila, 1977), 222.

9. Constabulary Anti-narcotics Unit, *First Anniversary* (Quezon City, 1973).

10. Ricardo M. Zarco, "Drugs in School, 1974: A Five Philippine City Study," in *Two Research Monographs on Drug Abuse in the Philippines* (Manila, 1975), 11–12; Dangerous Drugs Board, *Annual Report, 1974* (Manila, 1975), 18; Dangerous Drugs Board, "Seizures and Apprehensions: Aggregate Total for the Period January 30–September 1975," unpublished document; Gary Reid and Genevieve Costigan, *Revisiting the 'Hidden Epidemic': A Situation Assessment of Drug Use in Asia in the Context of HIV/AIDS* (Fairfield, 2002), 171.

11. *PC-INP General Information Handbook* (Quezon City, June 1984), 11–13; Republic of the Philippines, National Statistical Coordination Board, *2003 Philippine Statistical Yearbook* (Manila, 2004), tables 17–3, 17–5.

12. Dr. Michael Cullinane, interview with the author, Madison, Wisconsin, October 8, 2004.

13. Primitivo Mijares, *The Conjugal Dictatorship of Ferdinand and Imelda Marcos I* (San Francisco, 1976), 220; Sterling Seagrave, *The Marcos Dynasty* (New York, 1988), 328–29; Joseph Burkholder Smith, *Portrait of a Cold Warrior* (New York, 1976), 293–94.

14. Seagrave, *The Marcos Dynasty,* 329–30.

15. Wilfredo R. Reotutar, *So the People May Know All about the Gambling Menace in the Philippines* (Quezon City, 1999), 54–55.

16. Mijares, *The Conjugal Dictatorship of Ferdinand and Imelda Marcos I,* 102–3; Ivar Gica and Prudencio R. Europa, *Cash, Charity, and Controversy: The Story of the Gaming Casinos in the Philippines* (Las Piñas City, 2000), 200–14; New Pagcor, Philippine Amusement and Gaming Corporation, *1991 Annual Report* (Metro Manila, 1991), 3.

17. Mijares, *The Conjugal Dictatorship of Ferdinand and Imelda Marcos I,* 206–7; Chito Madrigal-Collantes, *Picture Me* (Manila, 1997), 144; Ricardo Manapat, *Some Are Smarter Than Others: The History of Marcos' Crony Capitalism* (New York, 1991), 399–400.

18. Manapat, *Some Are Smarter Than Others,* 128–29, 400–401; Gica, *Cash, Charity, and Controversy,* 21–22; Reotutar, *So the People May Know,* 105–6; *Far Eastern Economic Review,* 2/17/1978, 32–33; Seagrave, *The Marcos Dynasty,* 330, 333–34.

19. Aurora Javate-de Dios, Petronilo Bn. Daroy, and Lorna Kalaw-Tirol, eds., *Dictatorship and Revolution: Roots of People's Power* (Metro Manila, 1988), 72–73; Mark Thompson, *The Anti-Marcos Struggle: Personalistic Rule and Democratic Transition in the Philippines* (New Haven, 1995), 87–88; Steve Psinakis, *Two Terrorists Meet* (San Francisco, 1981), 10–11.

20. Gica and Europa, *Cash, Charity, and Controversy,* 19–26, 199–214; Reotutar, *So the People May Know,* 55–56; Manapat, *Some Are Smarter Than Others,* 128–29, 399–401; Seagrave, *The Marcos Dynasty,* 334; New Pagcor, *1991 Annual Report,* 5, 13; Philippine Amusement and Gaming Corporation, *1996 Annual Report* (Metro Manila, 1996), 6–7, 9.

21. *MT,* 12/4/1995.

22. *PDI,* 6/26/2000.

23. John Sidel, "The Usual Suspects: Nardong Putik, Don Pepe Oyson, and Robin Hood," in Vicente L. Rafael, ed., *Figures of Criminality in Indonesia, the Philippines, and Colonial Vietnam* (Ithaca, 1999), 70–90.

24. Joseph Ralston Hayden, *The Philippines: A Study in National Development* (New York, 1955), 833; Republic of the Philippines, Supreme Court, *Martial Law and the New Society in the Philippines* (Manila, 1977), 1878–79.

25. Amnesty International, *Report of an Amnesty International Mission to the Republic of the Philippines, 11–28 November 1981* (London, 1982), 1–9, 56–66.

26. *NYT,* 11/10/1986; Richard J. Kessler, *Rebellion and Repression in the Philippines* (New Haven, 1989), 137. To reach the figure of 3,257 killed under Marcos, Kessler's enumeration for 1975–85 is supplemented by adding 93 more "extrajudicial killings" in 1984 from data in Rev. La Verne D. Mercado and Sr. Mariani Dimaranan's *Philippines: Testimonies on Human Rights Violations* (Geneva, 1986), 89.

27. Amnesty International, *Report of an Amnesty International Mission to the Republic of the Philippines, 1981,* 21–22; Gemma Nemenzo Almendral, "The Fall of the Regime," in Javate-de Dios, *Dictatorship and Revolution,* 200; Rigoberto D. Tiglao, "The Consolidation of the Dictatorship," in Javate-de Dios, *Dictatorship and Revolution,* 2, 54.

28. Amnesty International, *Report of Amnesty International Mission to the Republic of the Philippines, 22 November–5 December 1975* (London, 1976), 12, 22–30.

29. Ibid., 9, 12–14, 56–57, 72–73.

30. Raymond Bonner, *Waltzing with a Dictator: The Marcoses and the Making of American Policy* (New York, 1987), 163–70.

31. Amnesty International, *Report of Amnesty International Mission to the Republic of the Philippines, 1975,* 85.

32. Task Force Detainees of the Philippines, *Pumipiglas: Political Detention and Military Atrocities in the Philippines, 1981–1982* (Quezon City, 1986), 44–45.

33. Association of Major Religious Superiors in the Philippines, *Political Detainees in the Philippines,* book 2 (Manila, 1977), 1; Amnesty International, *Human Rights Violations in the Philippines* (New York, 1982), 1.

34. Task Force Detainees, Association of Major Religious Superiors in the Philippines, *Pumipiglas: Political Detention and Military Atrocities in the Philippines* (Manila, 1980), 103–7.

35. Bonner, *Waltzing with a Dictator,* 220–23, 250–52, 278–80.

36. Emmanuel S. De Dios, "The Erosion of Dictatorship," in Javate-de Dios, *Dictatorship and Revolution,* 79–80, 473–74; Amnesty International, *Report of an Amnesty International Mission to the Republic of the Philippines, 1981,* 62; Bonner, *Waltzing with a Dictator,* 245–46; Return of the Writ and Comment on the Urgent Motion and Its Supplement, March 11, 1982, *In the Matter of the Petition for the Issuance of the Writ of Habeas Corpus for Joseph Olayer*, Republic of the Philippines, Supreme Court, G.R. 59787.

37. Mercado and Dimaranan, *Philippines,* 86; Kessler, *Rebellion and Repression in the Philippines,* 137; Ma. Serena I. Diokno, "Unity and Struggle," in Javate-de Dios, *Dictatorship and Revolution,* 147.

38. Diokno, "Unity and Struggle," 147; *MB* 5/6/1985, 5/7/1985, 5/11/1985, 5/13/1985, 5/14/1985, 5/15/1985, 5/17/1985, 5/19/1985, 5/28/1985, 6/6/1985, 6/10/1985, 6/12/1985; Jeffrey M. Riedinger, *Agrarian Reform in the Philippines: Democratic Transitions and Redistributive Reform* (Stanford, 1995), 30–31; Roger J. Bresnahan, "Interview with Cicero C. Campos, Ph.D. Chair of the National Police Commission of the Philippines," *Pilipinas* 9 (1987): 69, 76; Kessler, *Rebellion and Repression in the Philippines,* 120–21.

39. Amnesty International, *Report of an Amnesty International Mission to the Republic of the Philippines, 1981,* 21–23; *PFP,* 6/29/1996; Task Force Detainees, *Pumipiglas* (1980), 64.

40. *PDI,* 6/14/1996.

41. Senior Superintendent Reynaldo Berroya, interview with the author, Pasig City, August 20, 2001.

42. Amnesty International, *Report of an Amnesty International Mission to the Republic of the Philippines, 1981,* 86–87; Bonner, *Waltzing with a Dictator,* 191.

43. *Graphic,* July 1, 1996; *PFP,* 6/29/1996; *PDI,* 1/30/88.

44. Armando Estiller, Statement, August 3, 1980, Task Force Detainees, Quezon City.

45. "Torturer in U.S. for Training," *Tanod* (Manila) 1, no. 3 (September 1978): 3; Task Force Detainees, *Pumipiglas (*1980), 106–7.

46. Christopher Simpson, *Science of Coercion: Communication Research and Psychological Warfare, 1945–1960* (New York, 1994), 4–5, 72–73, 114–15; *Baltimore Sun,* 1/27/1997; *Washington Post,* 1/28/1997; *NYT,* 1/29/1997. For more on this point, see Alfred W. McCoy, *Closer Than Brothers: Manhood at the Philippine Military Academy* (New Haven, 1999), chap. 6; and Alfred W. McCoy, *A Question of Torture: CIA Interrogation, from the Cold War to the War on Terror* (New York, 2006), chap. 3.

47. Amnesty International, *Report of an Amnesty International Mission to the Republic of the Philippines, 1981,* 1–12, 22–23; Satur C. Ocampo, "Leaving the Pain Behind," *PST Quarterly* 1, no. 2 (July–September 1996): 13; Amnesty International, *Philippines: Unlawful Killings by Military and Paramilitary Forces* (New York, 1988), 5–6.

48. Thompson, *The Anti-Marcos Struggle,* 102–21; Diokno, "Unity and Struggle," 146–49.

49. *Jose Ma. Sison v. Hon. Juan Ponce Enrile,* January 15, 1981, Republic of the Philippines, Supreme Court, GR No. L-49579.

50. *Bernabe Buscayno v. Military Commissions,* November 19, 1981, Republic of the Philippines, Supreme Court, GR No. L-58284; Amnesty International, *Report of an Amnesty International Mission to the Republic of the Philippines, 1981,* 62–63.

51. Hayden, *The Philippines,* 824, 831–34; Anna Leah Fidelis T. Castañeda, "The Origins of Philippine Judicial Review, 1900–1935," *Ateneo Law Journal* 46, no. 121 (2001): 136–51, 167–68. I am indebted to Dr. Castañeda for her elaboration of several points that she made in her article. E-mail message dated July 28, 2002.

52. Supreme Court, *Martial Law and the New Society,* 1832.

53. Colonel Fidel C. Singson, "Presidential Order of Arrest and Detention against Felix Manuel Y, Macaraeg and Twenty Six (26) Others," February 27, 1982, Annex 1, *Rogelio Aberca, et al., Plaintiffs, versus Maj. Gen. Fabian Ver et al., Defendants,* Civil Case No. 37487, RTC.

54. Detainee Profile: Alex B. Marcelino, Task Force Detainees, Teachers Village, Quezon City.

55. Victim's Profile, Marco Palo, Task Force Detainees, Teachers Village, Quezon City; "Decision," February 19, 1993, *Aberca versus Ver,* RTC.

56. "Summary of Plaintiffs Appellees' Ex-Parte Evidence," Annex F, *Aberca versus Ver,* RTC; interviews with Marco Palo, Metro Manila, November–December 2002.

57. An Account of the Arrest and Torture of Noel Etabag, Task Force Detainees, Teachers Village, Quezon City.

58. "Summary of Plaintiffs Appellees' Ex-Parte Evidence," Annex F, *Aberca versus Ver,* RTC.

59. Petition, March 3, 1982, I*n the Matter of the Petition for the Issuance of the Writ of Habeas Corpus for Joseph Olayer et al., Petitioners, versus, General Fabian C. Ver, Major General Prospero Olivas and Colonel Rolando Abadilla, Republic of the Philippines,* Supreme Court, G.R. 59787.

60. "Return of the Writ and Comment on the Urgent Motion and its Supplement," *Olayer versus Ver.*

61. Jose W. Diokno, "Supplement to Motion to Set Conditions for Visits," March 12, 1982, *Olayer versus Ver.*

62. "Summary of Plaintiffs Appellees' Ex-Parte Evidence," Annex F, *Aberca versus Ver,* RTC.

63. "Complaint," February 23, 1983, *Aberca versus Ver,* RTC.

64. Lt Colonel Panfilo M. Lacson, "Counter Affidavit," March 10, 1982, Annex 3, *Aberca versus Ver,* RTC.

65. MSgt Bienvenido Balaba, "Counter Affidavit," March 10, 1982, Annex 4, *Aberca versus Ver,* RTC.

66. "Summary of Plaintiffs Appellees' Ex-Parte Evidence," Annex F, *Aberca versus Ver,* RTC.

67. Detainee Profile: Danilo de la Fuente; Account of the Arrest and Torture of Danilo de la Fuente, Task Force Detainees, Teachers Village, Quezon City.

68. Jose W. Diokno, "Urgent Motion in Behalf of Alex B. Marcelino," March 11, 1982, *Olayer versus Ver.*

69. Affidavit, Dr. Mita Pardo de Tavera, March 15, 1982, Annex F, *Aberca versus Ver*, RTC.

70. "Summary of Plaintiffs Appellees' Ex-Parte Evidence," Annex D, *Aberca versus Ver*, RTC.

71. "Complaint," February 23, 1983, *Aberca versus Ver*, RTC; Arno Sanidad, interview with the author, Quezon City, August 25, 2001.

72. "Complaint," February 23, 1983, *Aberca versus Ver*, RTC; Arno Sanidad, interview with the author, Quezon City, August 25, 2001.

73. Republic of the Philippines, Supreme Court, *Rogelio Aberca, et al., Plaintiffs, versus Maj. Gen. Fabian Ver et al.*, G.R. No. L-69866, April 15, 1988.

74. Ibid.

75. Thompson, *The Anti–Marcos Struggle*, 5, 120–21.

76. Ibid., 114–21, 158–62.

Chapter 13. Unsheathing the Sword

1. Rowena Carranza-Paraan, "Patterns of Human Rights Violations and Their Institutional Roots," in Bobby M. Tuazon, ed., *Pumipiglas 3: Torment and Struggle after Marcos* (Quezon City, 1993), 49–52; Jo-Ann Q. Maglipon, *The Mendiola Tragedy: A Smoldering Land* (Quezon City, 1987), i–xi.

2. Max M. de Mesa, "Human Rights and the Struggle for Peace: The Philippine Experience," in Evert de Boer Gerard Prickaerts, Huub Jaspers, and Mercedes V. Contreras, eds., *We Did Not Learn Human Rights from the Books: The Philippines and Human Rights in the Period 1986 to 1996* (Quezon City, 1996), 19–22; Ninotchka Rosca, "'Total War' in the Philippines," *The Nation*, June 19, 1989, 840.

3. Republic of the Philippines, Constitutional Commission of 1986, *The Constitution of the Republic of the Philippines* (Manila, 1986), 54.

4. Rod B. Gutang, *Pulisya: The Inside Story of the Demilitarization of Law Enforcement in the Philippines* (Quezon City, 1991), 97–98, 140–44; *PDI*, 10/30/1989, 1/3/1991; Pascual F. Jardiniano, *Police Manual on Public Accountability* (Manila, 1994), 20.

5. Republic of the Philippines, National Statistical Coordination Board, *2003 Philippine Statistical Yearbook* (Manila, 2004), table 17–5.

6. National Police Commission, *1990 Annual Report National Police Commission* (Makati, 1991), 9, 14, 20–24; Lawyers Committee on Human Rights, *Immunity: Prosecutions of Human Rights Violations in the Philippines* (New York, 1991), 5–6.

7. *Far Eastern Economic Review*, 7/27/1989, 28, 1/25/1990, 18; *Philippine Daily Globe*, 10/30/1989.

8. Maglipon, *The Mendiola Tragedy*, 60–73; Eileen C. Legaspi, "The Cory Mystique and the International Community," in Tuazon, *Pumipiglas 3*, 95–104.

9. Tuazon, *Pumipiglas 3*, 3.

10. Walden Bello, *U.S.-Sponsored Low-Intensity Conflict in the Philippines* (San Francisco, 1987), 42.

11. *Asia Week* (Hong Kong), September 13, 1985, 6.

12. Australian military attaché, interview with the author, Manila, January 9, 1988. Lawyers Committee for Human Rights, *Vigilantes in the Philippines: A Threat to Democratic Rule* (New York, 1988), 23–24; Luis Jalandoni, foreign representative of the National Democratic Front, interview with the author, Sydney, May 30, 1987.

13. David Bitel, *The Failed Promise: Human Rights in the Philippines since the Revolution of 1986: Report of a Visit* (Geneva, 1991), 113; Bello, *U.S.-Sponsored Low-Intensity Conflict in the Philippines*, 42–44.

14. U.S. Army Command and General Staff College, *Field Circular: Low Intensity Conflict* (Fort Leavenworth, 1986), v, 3–1. This copy is marked "valid until July 1989."

15. Ibid., 3–2.

16. Ibid., 3–9.

17. Ibid., 3–3.

18. *NYT,* 4/4/1987; *MT,* 2/8/2007; Alexander Cockburn, "The Cory Myth," *The Nation,* September 19, 1987, 258–59; Sara Diamond, *Spiritual Warfare: The Politics of the Christian Right* (Boston, 1989), 181–91; Isagani R. Cruz, *Once a Hunter, Always a Hunter: Jaime N. Ferrer as Public Servant* (Parañaque, 1994), 143–47; Doug Cunningham, "Singlaub Recruits His Own Army in the Philippines," *The National Reporter* (Spring 1987), 6–7; *PDI,* 2/20/1987, 2/21/1987, 2/22/1987, 2/23/1987, 2/26/1987; *Washington Post,* 2/15/1987, 2/18/1987, 2/20/1987.

19. James Putzel, *A Captive Land: The Politics of Agrarian Reform in the Philippines* (New York, 1992), 235–36, 283–304.

20. *NYT,* 4/22/1989; *MT,* 2/8/2007.

21. Roland G. Simbulan, "Covert Operations and the CIA's Hidden History in the Philippines," lecture at the University of the Philippines, Manila, August 18, 2000, http://www.derechos.org/nizkor/filipinas/doc/cia.html, accessed October 7, 2008.

22. Lawyers Committee for Human Rights, *Vigilantes in the Philippines,* ix–xvii.

23. Rosca, "'Total War' in the Philippines," 839–42; Diamond, *Spiritual Warfare,* 182; *NYT,* 11/11/1987.

24. Brigadier General Ramon E. Montaño, Acting Deputy Chief of Staff for Operations, "The AFP Broad Front Strategy against the Communist Insurgency," General Headquarters, Armed Forces of the Philippines, n.d., manuscript.

25. Ibid; *NYT,* 6/5/1988.

26. Gen. Ramon Montaño, interview with the author, Camp Aguinaldo, January 6, 1988; Montaño, "The AFP Broad Front Strategy."

27. Lt. Col. Miguel Coronel, interview with the author, Bacolod City, January 14, 1988.

28. Legaspi, "The Cory Mystique and the International Community," 110–11.

29. Carranza-Paraan, "Patterns of Human Rights Violations and Their Institutional Roots," 27–35; Tuazon, *Pumipiglas 3,* app. 2, table 2.

30. Tuazon, *Pumipiglas 3,* 3.

31. Rene V. Sarmiento, "The Post-Marcos Agenda on Human Rights," in Tuazon, *Pumipiglas 3,* 13, 25–27; Lawyers Committee for Human Rights, *Out of Control: Militia Abuses in the Philippines* (New York, 1990), 68–69.

32. Bobby Tuazon, "How Aquino's Pledge Became a Big Letdown," in Tuazon, *Pumipiglas 3,* 112–23.

33. Lawyers Committee for Human Rights, *Vigilantes in the Philippines,* xv, 23–38; Lawyers Committee for Human Rights, *Out of Control,* 29–31; 35–36; Tuazon, *Pumipiglas 3,* 15; Sheila S. Coronel, *Coups, Cults, and Cannibals: Chronicles of a Troubled Decade (1982–1992)* (Metro Manila, 1993), 134–39.

34. Lawyers Committee for Human Rights, *Vigilantes in the Philippines,* xi, 39–55, 57–107; Miguel G. Coronel, *Pro-democracy People's War* (Quezon City, 1991), 664–66, 669–70, 693, 702, 705–6, 710, 726–30, 732, 734–41.

35. "Curriculum Vitae of P/Supt Panfilo M. Lacson," File: Panfilo Lacson, Library, *PDI;* Satur C. Ocampo, "The Boys from MISG," *Philippine News and Features,* June 22, 1996; *Philippine Graphic,* July 1, 1996; *PDI,* 5/28/1995, 11/16/1999; *MT,* 11/20/1999.

36. Governor Rodolfo Aguinaldo, interview with the author, Tuguegarao, Cagayan Province, January 10, 1988; Coronel, *Coups, Cults, and Cannibals,* 209–11.

37. Lawyers Committee for Human Rights, *Vigilantes in the Philippines,* xi.

38. Ibid., 145–47; Lawyers Committee for Human Rights, *Out of Control,* 31–35.

39. Tuazon, *Pumipiglas 3,* app. 2, table 1; *NYT,* 11/10/1986. Task Force Detainees reported a lower figure of 2,833 salvaged and disappeared during the Marcos dictatorship. Bello, *U.S.-Sponsored Low-Intensity Conflict in the Philippines,* 39. Protestant church groups reported a total of 2,367 murders and disappearances from 1977 to 1984. Protestant Association for World Mission, *The Pain Will Go on Until Justice Is Done. What Can We Do to Enforce Human Rights in the Philippines? A European Initiative* (Hamburg, 1986), 23.

40. *NYT,* 1/16/2002, 2/1/2002, 6/4/2002, 6/8/2002, 6/22/2002, 9/22/2002, 1/21/2003.

41. *PDI*, 5/22/1995, 5/23/1995, 6/14/1995, 6/15/1995; Lawyers Committee for Human Rights, *Vigilantes in the Philippines*, 109–18, 130–33.

42. Ma. Ceres Doyo, *Journalist in Her Country: Articles, Essays, and Photographs, 1980–1992* (Metro Manila, 1993), 147–52; Lawyers Committee for Human Rights, *Out of Control*, 14; *NYT*, 4/22/1989.

43. *PDI*, 11/24/1992, 2/19/1993, 2/20/1993; "Kidnappings Persist: Gov't Scores Hit vs. Crime Lords," *Tulay*, March 8, 1993, 4–5; Marites Dañguilan Vitug and Glenda M. Gloria, *Under the Crescent Moon: Rebellion in Mindanao* (Quezon City, 2000), 215; Lawyers Committee for Human Rights, *Out of Control*, 12–14.

44. Vitug and Gloria, *Under the Crescent Moon*, 40–42, 106–15, 219; Angel Rabasa and Peter Chalk, *Indonesia's Transformation and the Stability of Southeast Asia* (Santa Monica, 2001), 86–88.

45. Vitug and Gloria, *Under the Crescent Moon*, 198, 207–20, 234–36, 243; Maria A. Ressa, *Seeds of Terror: An Eyewitness Account of Al-Qaeda's Newest Center of Operations in Southeast Asia* (New York, 2003), 26–29, 107–9; Dirk J. Barreveld, *Terrorism in the Philippines: The Bloody Trail of Abu Sayyaf, Bin Laden's East Asian Connection* (San Jose, 2001), 113–22, 218–19; Taha M. Basman, "MILF and Abu Sayyaf Group," in S. Yunanto, ed., *Militant Islamic Movements in Indonesia and South-East Asia* (Jakarta, 2003), 258–61.

46. Vitug and Gloria, *Under the Crescent Moon*, 213–20, 241; Jose Torres Jr., *Into the Mountain: Hostaged by the Abu Sayyaf* (Quezon City, 2001), 33–42; Barreveld, *Terrorism in the Philippines*, 123–27, 131.

47. *PDI*, 11/11/1993.

48. Republic of the Philippines, National Statistical Coordination Board, *2003 Philippine Statistical Yearbook*, table 17–3.

49. National Economic and Development Authority, *Philippine Yearbook, 1985* (Manila, 1986), 91, 97. In 1999, for example, there were 44,048 index crimes ("murder, homicide, physical injury and rape") reported, of which 96 percent were "solved," but among this possible pool of 42,286 new convicts only 3,022 actually joined the prison population. See Republic of the Philippines, National Statistical Coordination Board, *2000 Philippine Statistical Yearbook* (Manila, 2000), tables 17–1a, 17–20.

50. John Sidel, "The Usual Suspects: Nardong Putik, Don Pepe Oyson, and Robin Hood," in Vicente L. Rafael, ed., *Figures of Criminality in Indonesia, the Philippines, and Colonial Vietnam* (Ithaca, 1999), 86–87.

51. *Manila Chronicle*, 8/3/1990; *Philippine Daily Globe*, 8/5/1990; *PDI*, 8/8/1990; Doyo, *Journalist in Her Country*, 164–75.

52. *PDI*, 9/14/2000; Ivar Gica and Prudencio R. Europa, *Cash, Charity, and Controversy: The Story of the Gaming Casinos in the Philippines* (Las Piñas City, 2000), 38, 43–55, 97–98, 115–22; Wilfredo R. Reotutar, *So the People May Know All about the Gambling Menace in the Philippines* (Quezon City, 1999), 55–57; New Pagcor, Philippine Amusement and Gaming Corporation, *1991 Annual Report* (Manila, 1991), 4; Philippine Amusement and Gaming Corporation, *1996 Annual Report* (Manila, 1996), 9.

53. Reotutar, *So the People May Know*, 147–54.

54. *PS*, 12/7/1995.

55. *PDI*, 11/29/1995, 12/25/1995; *PS*, 12/29/1995.

56. *PDI*, 12/7/1995, 12/23/1995.

57. *PDI*, 12/25/1995.

58. *PDI*, 11/29/1995.

59. *PDI*, 11/29/1995, 11/30/1995, 12/22/1995.

60. Republic of the Philippines, House of Representatives, Committee on Public Order and Safety, Transcript of Hearings, October 18, 1995, VI-2 to VI-3, November 16, 1995, XVI-2 to XIII-2.

61. *PDI*, 6/18/2000, 6/26/2000, 10/20/2000.

62. *The Philippine Congress, 1987–1992* (Las Piñas, 1988), 121; Dabet Castañeda, "For Land and Wages," *Bulatlat* 4, no. 46 (December 19–25, 2004), http://www.bulatlat.com/news/4-46/4-46-land

.html, accessed April 17, 2009; Max Singer, "Cory Aquino and the Psychology of Bubbles," *The National Review,* August 14, 1987, http://www.thefreelibrary.com/Cory+Aquino+and+the+psychology+of+bubbles.-a05114780, accessed April 17, 2009.

63. Leandro Mendoza, chief of the PNP, interview with the author, Camp Crame, August 24, 2001; Gica and Europa, *Cash, Charity, and Controversy,* 107–8; Reotutar, *So the People May Know,* 59–60; former Central Luzon police chief, interview with the author, Camp Crame, August 23, 2001; Fernando Carrascoso Jr., interview with the author, Makati, August 30, 1986.

64. *PDI,* 12/7/1995, 12/23/1995, 6/18/2000, 6/26/2000, 10/20/2000.

65. *PS,* 11/24/1995.

66. *PDI,* 11/30/1995.

67. Sheila S. Coronel, "The Jueteng Republic," in Sheila S. Coronel, ed., *Investigating Estrada: Millions, Mansions, and Mistresses: A Compilation of Investigative Reports* (Quezon City, 2000), 27, 33.

Chapter 14. Ramos's Supercops

1. National Headquarters, Philippine National Police, Anti-Bank Robbery Intelligence Task Group, "Re: Neutralization of Wilson Sorronda @ Nonoy Koreano and Eleven (11) Others," May 19, 1995; Salvador R. Ranin, Regional Director, National Capitol Region, National Bureau of Investigation, "Re: Kuratong Baleleng Case," To: Director RD, NCR, Thu: DDIS, July 14, 1995; *PDI,* 5/19/1995, 6/19/1995, 7/17/1995, 7/19/1995, 7/22/1995.

2. Republic of the Philippines, House of Representatives, Committee on Public Order and Safety, Transcript of Hearings, November 16, 1995, XI-3.

3. Philippine National Police, *Annual Report, 1999* (Quezon City, 2000), 35–36.

4. Republic of the Philippines, National Statistical Coordination Board, *2003 Philippine Statistical Yearbook* (Manila, 2004), table 17–15.

5. *PDI,* 9/2/1992, 9/26/1998; Gerardo A. Sandoval and Pedro R. Laylo, "Crime Victimization in the Philippines: Demographic Patterns and Attitudinal Correlates," in *Social Weather Bulletin 93-3* (Quezon City, 1993), 5.

6. Human Rights Watch, "Scared Silent: Impunity for Extrajudicial Killings in the Philippines," part III, June 27, 2007, http://www.hrw.org/en/reports/2007/06/27/scared-silent-0, accessed February 1, 2009.

7. Human Rights Watch/Asia, *Bad Blood: Militia Abuses in Mindanao, the Philippines* (New York, 1992), 8–9; Lawyers Committee for Human Rights, *Impunity: Prosecutions of Human Rights Violations in the Philippines* (New York, 1991), 5–6, 23–28; *MT,* 12/10/1998; "Summary of Human Rights Violation Cases in the Philippines, January–December 2002," *Journal of Philippine Statistics* 54, no. 2 (2003): 116; Rod B. Gutang, *Pulisya: The Inside Story of the Demilitarization of the Law Enforcement System in the Philippines* (Quezon City, 1991), 26–28, 127–32.

8. *Today,* 12/1/1998; Caroline S. Hau, "'Who Will Save Us from the 'Law'? The Criminal State and the Illegal Alien in Post-1986 Philippines," in Vicente L. Rafael, ed., *Figures of Criminality in Indonesia, the Philippines, and Colonial Vietnam* (Ithaca, 1999), 134–36; Philippine National Police, *Annual Accomplishment Report, 1998* (Quezon City, 1998), 3–4.

9. "City Dads Act on Kidnapping Cases," *Tulay,* October 11, 1992, 5.

10. *PDI,* 6/25/1992.

11. *PDI,* 6/27/1992, 7/1/1992, 7/2/1992, 7/3/1992, 7/4/1992, 7/7/1992, 7/8/1992, 7/9/1992, 7/12/1992, 7/19/1992.

12. Joker Arroyo, "Military Justice Is No Justice at All," *PDI,* 6/20/1996; *Philippine Graphic,* July 1, 1996; *PFP,* 6/29/1996.

13. *PDI,* 3/17/1998, 3/18/1998; Colonel Reynaldo Berroya, interview with the author, Pasig City, August 20, 2001; Reynaldo Berroya, "The 'Erap' Presidency: A Chilling Scenario," November 9, 1997, manuscript.

14. "Curriculum Vitae of P/Supt Panfilo M. Lacson," File: Panfilo Lacson, Library, *PDI;* Satur C. Ocampo, "The Boys from MISG," *Philippine News and Features,* June 22, 1996; Berroya, "The 'Erap' Presidency."

15. "Appeal Brief for Defendants-Appellants Fidel B. Singson, Rolando N. Abadilla, and Panfilo Lacson," June 21, 1994, *Rogelio Aberca et al., Plaintiffs-Appellees, versus Fabian C. Ver et al., Defendants-Appellants*, CA-G.R. CV No. 37487, Court of Appeals, Republic of the Philippines; "Reply Brief for Defendants-Appellants Singson, Abadilla, and Lacson," November 23, 1994, *Aberca et al., Plaintiffs-Appellees, versus Fabian C. Ver.*

16. "Curriculum Vitae of P/Supt Panfilo M. Lacson"; Bio Data, Ping Lacson Web site, http://www.pinglacson.com.ph/Bio%20Data%20.html, accessed May 19, 2008; Berroya, "The 'Erap' Presidency."

17. "Curriculum Vitae of P/Supt Panfilo M. Lacson"; Ocampo, "The Boys from MISG"; *Philippine Graphic,* July 1, 1996; *PDI,* 5/28/1995, 11/16/1999; *MT,* 11/20/1999.

18. "Curriculum Vitae of P/Supt Panfilo M. Lacson"; Berroya, "The 'Erap' Presidency."

19. "Curriculum Vitae of P/Supt Panfilo M. Lacson" ; Ocampo, "The Boys from MISG"; *Philippine Graphic,* July 1, 1996; *PDI,* 5/28/1995, 11/16/1999; *MT,* 11/20/1999; Berroya, "The 'Erap' Presidency"; Gemma Corotan, "The Crimebusters," *Investigative Reporting,* July–September 1995, 12–14.

20. *PDI,* 7/24/1998. As chief of the Presidential Anti-Organized Crime Task Force under President Estrada in 1999 and 2000, Panfilo Lacson appropriated this term to describe his elite unit's operations. See *The Supercop: Presidential Anti-Organized Crime Task Force* (Quezon City), July 20, 2000.

21. Corotan, "The Crimebusters," 12–13.

22. *PDI,* 9/16/1992, 9/17/1992.

23. Reynaldo Berroya, "A Tale about Oink-Oink," April 14, 1997, manuscript; Berroya, "The 'Erap' Presidency."

24. *PDI,* 10/3/1992, 10/4/1992, 10/5/1992, 10/7/1992, 10/8/1992, 10/23/1992, 7/2/1993, 3/27/1998; Berroya, "A Tale about Oink-Oink."

25. *PDI,* 11/20/1992.

26. Berroya, "The 'Erap' Presidency."

27. Corotan, "The Crimebusters," 12–13; Teresita Ang "Despite the Government Assurances: No Let Up in Kidnapping," *Tulay,* January 17, 1993, 4–5.

28. *Today,* 12/1/1998; Hau, "'Who Will Save Us from the 'Law'?" 134–36; Philippine National Police, *Annual Accomplishment Report, 1998,* 3–4.

29. "City Dads Act on Kidnapping Cases," 5.

30. "Kidnappings Persist: Gov't Scores Hit vs. Crime Lords," *Tulay,* March 8, 1993, 4–5; *PDI,* 11/24/1992.

31. *PDI,* 11/21/1992, 11/22/1992, 11/24/1992.

32. *PDI,* 10/23/2000.

33. Jackie Co, T. A. See, and Liza Alcayde, "Kidnappings: Tales and Trails of Terror," *Tulay,* February 14, 1993, 6–7; "Kidnappings Persist," 4–5; *PDI,* 2/2/93, 2/18/93.

34. Corotan, "The Crimebusters," 15.

35. *PDI,* 2/19/1993, 2/20/1993.

36. *PDI,* 2/21/1993, 2/24/1993.

37. *PDI,* 5/28/1993, 8/3/1993, 8/4/1993, 11/26/1993; Ellen Tordesillas and Greg Hutchinson, *Hot Money, Warm Bodies: The Downfall of President Joseph Estrada* (Manila, 2000), 51.

38. *PDI,* 8/4/1993, 9/29/1993, 10/17/1997.

39. *PDI,* 12/24/1993.

40. *PDI,* 11/9/1993.

41. *PDI,* 5/22/1995, 5/23/1995, 6/14/1995, 6/15/1995; "Briefing Manuscript: The Kuratong Baleleng Group," April 20, 2001, htttp://www.geocities.com/pinglacson2001/pacc2.htm, accessed July 17, 2001.

42. *PDI,* 11/10/1993, 5/22/1995, 5/23/1995.

43. *PDI,* 5/23/1995; National Headquarters, Philippine National Police, Anti-Bank Robbery Intelligence Task Group, "Memorandum For—The Chairman PACC, Re: Neutralization of Wilson Sorronda @ Nonoy Koreano and Eleven (11) Others."

44. *PDI,* 5/19/1995, 6/19/1995.

45. National Headquarters, Philippine National Police, Anti-Bank Robbery Intelligence Task Group, "Re: Neutralization of Wilson Sorronda @ Nonoy Koreano and Eleven (11) Others."

46. *PDI*, 5/23/1995, 5/26/1995, 5/27/1995.

47. *PDI*, 5/31/1995, 7/20/1995; Republic of the Philippines, Department of Justice, National Bureau of Investigation, *1995 NBI Annual Report* (Manila, 1996), 14.

48. *PDI*, 5/24/1995.

49. *PDI*, 5/27/1995.

50. *PDI*, 5/27/1995, 5/30/1995, 6/6/1995, 10/19/2000.

51. *PDI*, 5/31/1995.

52. *PDI*, 6/12/1995.

53. *PDI*, 6/14/1995, 6/21/1995.

54. *PDI*, 6/17/1995, 6/21/1995.

55. Berroya, "The 'Erap' Presidency"; Corotan, "The Crimebusters,"14.

56. *PDI*, 7/17/1995, 7/19/1995, 7/22/1995; Ranin, "Re: Kuratong Baleleng Case."

57. Ranin, "Re: Kuratong Baleleng Case."

58. Affidavit, Ysmael S. Yu, March 24, 2001; Sinumpaang Salaysay, SPO2 Noel Seno y Pentinio, May 31, 2001.

59. Department of Justice, Manila, *People of the Philippines (P/Dir Gen Leandro R. Mendoza) Complainant versus P/Dir Gen Panfilo M. Lacson et al.*, Criminal Cases No. Q-99 -81679 to 89, "Resolution," June 6, 2001; Sinumpaang Salaysay, SPO1 Wilmor Medes y Belando, April 24, 2001.

60. Ranin, "Re: Kuratong Baleleng Case."

61. Sinumpaang Salaysay, Senior Inspector Abelardo Ramos, March 24, 2001.

62. Sinumpaang Salaysay, SPO2 Noel Seno y Pentinio, May 31, 2001.

63. *PDI*, 7/17/1995, 7/19/1995, 7/22/1995; Ranin, "Re: Kuratong Baleleng Case."

64. Department of Justice, *People of the Philippines versus P/Dir Gen Panfilo M. Lacson et al.*, Criminal Cases No. Q-99 -81679 to 89, "Resolution," June 6, 2001.

65. *PDI*, 7/17/1995, 7/19/1995, 7/22/1995.

66. Sinumpaang Salaysay, SPO2 Noel Seno y Pentinio, May 31, 2001.

67. Ranin, "Re: Kuratong Baleleng Case."

68. *PDI*, 7/17/1995, 7/19/1995, 7/22/1995; Ranin, "Re: Kuratong Baleleng Case."

69. *PDI*, 7/26/1995.

70. *PDI*, 6/3/1995.

71. *Business World*, 9/4/1995.

72. "Summary of What Happened to the First Kuratong Baleleng Case," Free Legal Assistance Group (FLAG), n.d.

73. Ibid.

74. Ibid.; Department of Justice, *People of the Philippines versus P/Dir Gen Panfilo M. Lacson et al.*, Criminal Cases No. Q-99 -81679 to 89, "Resolution," June 6, 2001.

75. *PFP*, 6/29/1996; Fr. Roberto Reyes, "Philippines: Christmas with a Dead Man's Watch," Asian Human Rights Commission, May 7, 2008, http://www.ahrchk.net/statements/mainfile.php/2008 statements/1510/, accessed March 27, 2009. For torture by Rolando Abadilla and the MISG, see Task Force Detainees, *Pumipiglas: Political Detention and Military Atrocities in the Philippines* (Manila, 1981), 64 -65; and Task Force Detainees of the Philippines, *Pumipiglas: Political Detention and Military Atrocities in the Philippines, 1981–1982* (Manila, 1986), 53 -64.

76. *PFP*, 6/29/96; Ocampo, "The Boys from MISG"; *Philippine Graphic*, July 1, 1996.

77. Marites Dañguilan Vitug and Glenda M. Gloria, *Under the Crescent Moon: Rebellion in Mindanao* (Quezon City, 2000), 192–95, 198, 207, 214 -15, 222–24; Maria A. Ressa, *Seeds of Terror: An Eyewitness Account of Al-Qaeda's Newest Center of Operations in Southeast Asia* (New York, 2003), 28 -38.

78. Vitug and Gloria, *Under the Crescent Moon*, 205, 214 -17; Ressa, *Seeds of Terror*, 108 -9; Dirk J. Barreveld, *Terrorism in the Philippines: The Bloody Trail of Abu Sayyaf, Bin Laden's East Asian Connection* (San Jose, 2001), 133 -35; Angel Rabasa and Peter Chalk, *Indonesia's Transformation and the Stability of Southeast Asia* (Santa Monica, 2001), 88 -89.

79. Ressa, *Seeds of Terror*, 109–23; Rabasa and Chalk, *Indonesia's Transformation and the Stability of Southeast Asia*, 89–91; *NYT*, 1/16/2002, 2/1/2002, 6/8/2002, 6/10/2002.

80. *PDI*, 12/13/1997, 12/14/1997.

81. *PDI*, 2/6/1998.

82. *PDI*, 3/17/1998, 3/18/1998, 3/22/1998, 3/24/1998, 4/15/1998; *Philippine Graphic*, April 27, 1998.

83. *PDI*, 5/6/1998, 5/7/1998, 5/8/1998, 5/11/1998; *PS*, 5/22/1999; Bio Data, Ping Lacson Web site, http://www.pinglacson.com.ph/Bio%20Data%20.html, accessed May 19, 2008.

84. *PDI*, 8/24/1992, 8/25/1992, 10/20/1992, 10/26/1992.

85. *PDI*, 9/14/2000; Wilfredo R. Reotutar, *So the People May Know All about the Gambling Menace in the Philippines* (Quezon City, 1999), 46–47.

86. *PS*, 12/10/1995, 12/12/1995; *PDI*, 2/3/1996.

87. Philippine Center for Investigative Journalism and Institute for Popular Democracy, "Illegal Gambling Has Grassroots Base," *MT*, 12/4/1995; *PDI*, 4/17/1996, 6/23/1997.

88. *PDI*, 1/24/1996, 3/1/1996, 4/27/1996, 10/2/1996, 10/6/1996, 10/20/1996, 2/10/1997.

89. *PDI*, 3/22/2000, 6/14/2000, 6/26/2000, 10/20/2000.

90. *PDI*, 2/11/1997.

Chapter 15. Estrada's Racketeering

1. *PDI*, 1/20/2001, 2/4/2001; *MB*, January 20, 2001; Ellen Tordesillas and Greg Hutchinson, *Hot Money, Warm Bodies: The Downfall of President Joseph Estrada* (Pasig City, 2000), 206–7; Amando Doronila, *The Fall of Joseph Estrada: The Inside Story* (Pasig City, 2001), 176–77.

2. *PDI*, 2/18/2001; Ramon N. Villegas, "Illusion and Discontent," in Thelma Sioson San Juan, ed., *People Power 2: Lessons and Hopes* (Quezon City, 2001), 181–85; Cynthia B. Bautista, "The Middle Classes: A Natural Constituency for Democracy," in Sioson San Juan, *People Power 2*, 190; Sheila S. Coronel and Sigfred C. Balatan, *EDSA 2: A Nation in Revolt, a Photographic Journal* (Pasig City, 2001), 10–12; Sixto K. Roxas, *Jueteng Gate: The Parable of a Nation in Crisis* (Manila, 2000), 73; Yvonne T. Chua, "The Company He Keeps," in Sheila S. Coronel, ed., *Investigating Estrada: Millions, Mansions, and Mistresses: A Compilation of Investigative Reports* (Metro Manila, 2000), 132–41; Yvonne T. Chua, Sheila S. Coronel, and Vinia M. Datinguinoo, "Estrada's Entrepreneurial Families," in Coronel, *Investigating Estrada*, 59–69; Tordesillas and Hutchinson, *Hot Money, Warm Bodies*, 138; Doronila, *The Fall of Joseph Estrada*, 5, 62–63; Jose V. Abueva, "From 'Electoral Democracy' to 'Substantive Democracy,'" in Amando Doronila and Jose V. Abueva, eds., *Between Fires: Fifteen Perspectives on the Estrada Crisis* (Pasig City, 2001), 90; Arsenio M. Balisacan, "Did the Estrada Administration Benefit the Poor?" in Doronila and Abueva, *Between Fires*, 101; Karina Constantino-David, "Surviving Erap," in Doronila and Abueva, *Between Fires*, 212.

3. Republic of the Philippines, National Statistical Coordination Board, *2003 Philippine Statistical Yearbook* (Manila, 2004), tables 17–12.

4. *MT*, 6/10/1999; *Today*, 6/5/1999, 6/6/1999; *PDI*, 6/1/1999, 6/17/1999.

5. *Today*, 6/6/1999.

6. Gary Reid and Genevieve Costigan, *Revisiting the 'Hidden Epidemic': A Situation Assessment of Drug Use in Asia in the context of HIV/AIDS* (Fairfield, 2002), 170–76.

7. Philippine National Police, *Annual Report 1999* (Quezon City, 2000), 37.

8. Republic of the Philippines, Department of Justice, National Bureau of Investigation, *1996 NBI Annual Report* (Manila, 1997), 28.

9. Republic of the Philippines, Department of Justice, National Bureau of Investigation, *1997 NBI Annual Report* (Manila, 1998), 15–46.

10. Republic of the Philippines, Department of Justice, National Bureau of Investigation, *1998 NBI Annual Report* (Manila, 1999), 5; Republic of the Philippines, Department of Justice, National Bureau of Investigation, *1999 NBI Annual Report* (Manila, 2000), 24–25; Republic of the Philippines, Department of Justice, National Bureau of Investigation, *2000 NBI Annual Report* (Manila, 2001), 13–14, 29, 39–40.

11. United Nations, International Narcotics Control Board, *Report of the International Narcotics*

Control Board for 2001 (New York, 2002), 61; Reid and Costigan, *Revisiting the 'Hidden Epidemic,'* 91, 170.

12. U.S. Department of State, Bureau of International Narcotics and Law Enforcement Affairs, *International Narcotics Control Strategy Report 2001,* Philippines, http://www.state.gov/g/inl/rls/nrcrpt/2001/rpt/8483.html, accessed March 28, 2002.

13. Wilfredo R. Reotutar, *So the People May Know All about the Gambling Menace in the Philippines* (Quezon City, 1999), 6, 110.

14. *MB,* 9/18/2000, 10/11/2000, 11/21/2000; *PDI,* 10/6/2000.

15. These figures are drawn from tables provided by Gen. Wilfredo R. Reotutar (ret.) with the operators' names removed (see Reotutar, *So the People May Know,* 53, 113–17) and identical tables that include the names in an anonymous study found in the files of the Philippine Center for Investigative Journalism, "Latest Developments on Jueteng and the Protection Rackets as of June 1, 1999."

16. For various reports on the gross revenues and operations of jueteng, see *MB,* 9/18/2000; *PDI,* 3/22/2000, 10/6/2000, 10/9/2000; Reotutar, *So the People May Know,* 113–17; and Perfecto R. Yasay, Jr., *Out of the Lion's Den: The Travails and Triumphs of a Public Servant* (Quezon City, 2005), 44–45.

17. *PS,* 12/5/1995.

18. *PDI,* 7/19/1998; Glenda Gloria, "Estrada and Associates Monopolize Gambling," Philippine Center for Investigative Journalism, 2000, http://www.pcij.org/stories/print/gambling2.html, accessed March 15, 2009.

19. *PDI,* 7/21/1998, 7/24/1998.

20. *PDI,* 7/24/1998.

21. *MT,* 11/26/1998, 4/1/1999; *PDI,* 7/9/1998, 7/24/1998, 8/25/1998, 8/29/1998, 11/27/1998, 4/1/1999; *Today,* 12/16/1998;"Summary of What Happened to the First Kuratong Baleleng Case," Free Legal Assistance Group (FLAG), n.d.; Department of Justice, *People of the Philippines versus P/Dir Gen Panfilo M. Lacson et al.*, Criminal Cases No. Q-99–81679 to 89, "Resolution," June 6, 2001.

22. *PDI,* 4/26/1999, 4/27/1999.

23. *PDI,* 4/26/1999.

24. *PDI,* 4/29/1999; *Today,* 4/29/1999; *MT,* 4/29/1999, 4/30/1999.

25. *PDI,* 5/25/1999, 5/26/1999, 5/27/1999.

26. *MT,* 5/27/1999; *PDI,* 5/27/1999.

27. *PDI,* 11/16/1999.

28. *MT,* 11/17/1999; *PDI,* 11/17/1999, 12/15/1999, 3/21/2000.

29. *PDI,* 7/27/2000.

30. *PDI,* 1/31/2000.

31. *PDI,* 11/24/1999, 1/12/2000, 1/24/2000.

32. Philippine National Police, *Annual Report, 2000* (Quezon City, 2001), 43–49; *PDI,* 12/9/1999, 12/28/1999, 1/30/2000, 10/2/2000; *Sun Star Daily* (Cebu City), 1/26/2000; *Cebu Daily News,* 1/28/2000.

33. *PDI,* 3/29/2000, 6/26/2000, 10/12/2000, 10/18/2000; Coronel, *EDSA 2,* 13.

34. *PDI,* 10/10/2000, 10/12/2000, 10/13/2000, 11/8/2000; *MB,* 10/10/2000, 10/14/2000; Tordesillas and Hutchinson, *Hot Money, Warm Bodies,* 61.

35. *PDI,* 4/5/2000, 4/7/2000.

36. *PDI,* 3/30/2000, 4/5/2000, 4/27/2000, 9/12/2000.

37. Ivar Gica and Prudencio R. Europa, *Cash, Charity, and Controversy: The Story of the Gaming Casinos in the Philippines* (Las Piñas City, 2000), 4, 34–35, 46–47, 76, 93, 171–73; Philippine Amusement and Gaming Corporation, *1999 Annual Report* (Manila, 1999), 8.

38. *MT,* 7/26/1999.

39. *PDI,* 10/13/2000; Jovito Salonga, "Foreword," in Yasay, *Out of the Lion's Den,* xv–xx.

40. Ibid.

41. *MB,* 10/10/2000.

42. *PDI,* 10/13/2000.

43. *PDI,* 2/25/2000, 6/18/2000.

44. *MB,* 10/6/2000.

45. *PDI,* 6/14/2000, 6/15/2000, 6/16/2000; *MB,* 9/27/2000; Philippine National Police, *Annual Report, 2000,* 48–49.

46. *PDI,* 10/19/2000; Tordesillas and Hutchinson, *Hot Money, Warm Bodies,* 44, 69.

47. *MB,* 9/23/2000.

48. *PDI,* 10/13/2000.

49. *PDI,* 10/15/2000; Sheila S. Coronel, "The Jueteng Republic," in Coronel, *Investigating Estrada,* 60; Doronila, *The Fall of Joseph Estrada,* 150–51.

50. *PDI,* 9/10/2000.

51. *MB,* 9/19/2000.

52. Gica and Europa, *Cash, Charity, and Controversy,* 189–90; *PDI,* 9/12/2000.

53. *PDI,* 10/6/2000; *MB,* 9/21/2000; Dirk J. Barreveld, *Erap Ousted: People Power versus Chinese Conspiracy* (Mandaue City, 2001), 150–51, 254–55, 268–69.

54. *PDI,* 10/6/2000, 10/7/2000, 10/10/2000; Tordesillas and Hutchinson, *Hot Money, Warm Bodies,* 34–35, 41.

55. *PDI,* 10/5/2000, 10/6/2000, 10/12/2000, 10/13/2000.

56. Tordesillas and Hutchinson, *Hot Money, Warm Bodies,* 41–43; Doronila, *The Fall of Joseph Estrada,* 12–13; Alan Robson, "Patrimonial Politics in the Philippine Ilocos," *Pilipinas* 38 (2002): 10.

57. Governor Luis "Chavit" Singson, interview with the author, Manila, August 23, 2001; Reynaldo Wycoco, director, National Bureau of Investigation, interview with the author, Manila, August 20, 2001.

58. *PDI,* 10/12/2000, 10/13/2000; *MB,* 10/10/2000.

59. *PDI,* 10/5/2000.

60. *MB,* 10/6/2000.

61. *MB,* 10/9/2000.

62. Peachy F. Yamsuan, "The Church: A Moral Battle," in Sioson San Juan, *People Power 2,* 42–43.

63. *PDI,* 10/10/2000; *MB,* 10/10/2000.

64. *PDI,* 10/11/2000, 10/12/2000, 10/13/2000.

65. *PDI,* 10/9/2000.

66. *PDI,* 10/6/2000, 10/9/2000, 10/22/2000, 10/24/2000.

67. *PDI,* 10/9/2000, 10/11/2000.

68. *PDI,* 10/12/2000, 10/13/2000; Yamsuan, "The Church," 42–45; Socrates B. Villegas, "A Prophetic Church," in Sioson San Juan, *People Power 2,* 199–200.

69. *PDI,* 10/13/2000, 10/19/2000, 10/23/2000.

70. *PDI,* 10/31/2000.

71. Philippine Center for Investigative Journalism, "Estrada's Fronts: Cronies and Attorneys," October 23, 2000, http://www.pcij.org.ph/stories/2000/erapwealth.html, accessed January 23, 2001; *PDI,* 10/23/2000; Sheila S. Coronel, Yvonne T. Chua, Luz Rimban, and Vinia M. Datinguinoo, "The Mansions," in Coronel, *Investigating Estrada,* 71–82.

72. *PDI,* 11/10/2000, 11/12/2000; Tordesillas and Hutchinson, *Hot Money, Warm Bodies,* 134–37.

73. *PDI,* 11/3/2000, 11/7/2000, 11/8/2000; *MB,* 11/5/2000.

74. *PDI,* 11/12/2000, 11/13/2000.

75. *PDI,* 10/18/2000; Tordesillas and Hutchinson, *Hot Money, Warm Bodies,* 34–38.

76. *PDI,* 10/31/2000.

77. *PDI,* 11/3/2000, 11/14/2000, 11/15/2000.

78. *PDI,* 11/10/2000, 11/16/2000.

79. *PDI,* 11/15/2000, 11/20/2000; *MB,* 11/22/2000.

80. *PDI,* 11/23/2000.

81. *PDI,* 11/25/2000, 11/26/2000; Tordesillas and Hutchinson, *Hot Money, Warm Bodies,* 25–28; Doronila, *The Fall of Joseph Estrada,* 188.

82. *PDI,* 12/5/2000.

83. *PDI,* 11/21/2000, 11/22/2000, 3/20/2009.

84. *PDI*, 11/25/2000.
85. *PDI*, 12/5/2000.
86. Yasay, *Out of the Lion's Den*, 77, 122–25; *PDI*, 11/26/2000, 11/27/2000.
87. *PDI*, 11/25/2000, 11/27/2000, 11/28/2000, 12/2/2000, 12/5/2000; *MB*, 11/28/2000; *PS*, 11/26/2000, 11/28/2000, 11/30/2000, 12/2/2000, 12/8/2000.
88. *PDI*, 11/27/2000, 11/28/2000; *MB*, 11/28/2000, 3/20/2009.
89. *PDI*, 11/29/2000.
90. *PDI*, 11/30/2000.
91. *PDI*, 12/1/2000.
92. *PDI*, 11/28/2000.
93. *PDI*, 11/20/2000.
94. *MB*, 12/2/2000.
95. Isagani de Castro Jr., "Congress Impeachment," in Sioson San Juan, *People Power 2*, 26; Doronila, *The Fall of Joseph Estrada*, 115.
96. Mahar Mangahas, "Metro Manilans Welcome Gloria," Social Weather Stations, February 1, 2001, pinoytok@yahoogroups.com, accessed January 14, 2007.
97. *PDI*, 12/8/2000.
98. *PDI*, 12/9/2000, 12/12/2000; *MB*, 12/9/2000; Jesselynn De La Cruz, "In the Witness Stand," in Sioson San Juan, *People Power 2*, 31–33.
99. *PDI*, 12/12/2000, 2/23/2001; De La Cruz, "In the Witness Stand," 31–32.
100. *MB*, 12/12/2000.
101. *PDI*, 12/11/2000, 12/12/2000.
102. *PDI*, 12/13/2000; *MB*, 12/13/2000.
103. *PDI*, 12/19/2000.
104. *PDI*, 12/16/2000, 1/3/2001.
105. *MB*, 12/21/2000.
106. *PDI*, 12/18/2000.
107. *PDI*, 12/19/2000.
108. *MB*, 12/21/2000, 12/22/2000; Oscar S. Valladolid and Alice Colet Valladolid, *The Impeachment of a President* (Manila, 2001), 93–94; Barreveld, *Erap Ousted*, 133–34, 141–42, 155–56, 177–78.
109. *PDI*, 12/23/2000; Valladolid, *The Impeachment of a President*, 96–97.
110. *PDI*, 12/24/2000.
111. *PDI*, 1/3/2001; *MB*, 1/3/2000.
112. *PDI*, 1/4/2001.
113. *PDI*, 1/12/2001, 1/13/2001, 1/14/2001; *MB*, 1/13/2001; Raul J. Palabrica, "The Road to Impeachment and Ouster was Short and Bumpy," in Doronila and Abueva, *Between Fires*, 235.
114. *PDI*, 1/13/2001, 1/15/2001.
115. *PDI*, 1/15/2001.
116. *PDI*, 1/16/2001.
117. *PDI*, 1/17/2001; *MB*, 1/17/2001.
118. *Straits Times* (Singapore), January 18, 2001.
119. *PDI*, 1/17/2001.
120. Ibid.
121. *NYT*, 1/18/2001.
122. *PDI*, 1/18/2001.
123. Ibid.
124. *PDI*, 1/19/2001.
125. *PDI*, 1/18/2001.
126. Roxas, *Jueteng Gate*, 97–98.
127. *PDI*, 1/19/2001; Jose Dalisay Jr., "Showtime at EDSA," in Sioson San Juan, *People Power 2*, 244–46.
128. *PDI*, 1/20/2001.
129. Text message received by the cellular phone of Teresita Maceda, University of the

Philippines–Diliman, January 18, 2001, 14:15:28. The quotation was kindly provided by Professor Maceda. See also *PDI*, 2/25/2001.

130. *PDI*, 2/25/2001; Doronila, *The Fall of Joseph Estrada*, 175, 195.

131. *PDI*, 2/4/2001, 3/23/2001, 3/24/2001; Doronila, *The Fall of Joseph Estrada*, 173.

132. *PDI*, 1/20/2001, 2/25/2001, 2/27/2001; *MB*, 1/20/01; Manny Mogato, "At 4:00 pm the President Falls," in Sioson San Juan, *People Power 2*, 56–59; Reynaldo Wycoco, director, National Bureau of Investigation, interview with the author, Manila, August 20, 2001; Tordesillas and Hutchinson, *Hot Money, Warm Bodies*, 193; Doronila, *The Fall of Joseph Estrada*, 175–79.

133. *PDI*, 1/20/2001, 2/4/2001; *MB*, 1/20/2001; Tordesillas and Hutchinson, *Hot Money, Warm Bodies*, 206–7; Doronila, *The Fall of Joseph Estrada*, 176–77.

134. *PDI*, 1/21/2001, 1/22/2001, 2/6/2001, 2/25/2001; *NYT*, 1/20/2001; Tordesillas and Hutchinson, *Hot Money, Warm Bodies*, 221–26; Doronila, *The Fall of Joseph Estrada*, 211–12.

135. *PDI*, 1/21/2001; *MB*, 1/21/2001; *NYT*, 1/20/2001.

136. *PDI*, 1/22/2001, 1/25/2001, 1/26/2001, 2/2/2001, 3/24/2001; *PS*, 3/10/2001.

137. *PDI*, 3/27/2001, 3/31/2001, 4/17/2001; *PS*, 3/30/2001, 4/16/2001.

138. *PDI*, 4/16/2001, 4/17/2001, 4/18/2001, 4/20/2001; *PS*, 4/18/2001, 4/25/2001.

139. *Far Eastern Economic Review*, 2/15/2001, http://www.feer.com/_01012_15/p023region.html, accessed January 14, 2007; *PDI*, 3/26/2001.

140. *NYT*, 2/5/2001; Michael Vatikiotis, "Estrada's Overthrow in a Regional Context," in Doronila and Abueva, *Between Fires*, 280; A. Lin Neumann, "Nothing to Cheer About: People Power 2 a Sad Commentary on the Philippines," *Time Asia*, January 29, 2001, 22.

141. Jacob E. Cooke, *The Federalist* (Middletown, 1961), 373–74.

142. George A. Malcolm, *First Malayan Republic: The Story of the Philippines* (Boston, 1951), 204–7; Anna Leah Fidelis T. Castañeda, "The Origins of Philippine Judicial Review, 1900–1935," *Ateneo Law Journal* 46, no. 121 (2001): 167–68.

143. Republic of the Philippines, Constitutional Commission of 1986, *The Constitution of the Republic of the Philippines* (Manila, 1986), 4, 16.

144. *NYT*, 7/5/2000; Bautista, "The Middle Classes," 189.

145. *Joseph E. Estrada vs. Aniano Desierto et al.*, G.R. Nos. 146710–15, *Joseph E. Estrada vs. Gloria Macapagal-Arroyo*, G.R. No. 146738, Philippine Supreme Court, Decision, March 2, 2001.

Chapter 16. Extrajudicial Executions

1. "President Gloria Macapagal-Arroyo's Statement on the Issue of the Tape Recordings," Monday, June 27, 2005, Study Room, Malacañang, http://www.op.gov.ph/speeches.asp?iid=668&iyear=2005&imonth=6, accessed April 15, 2008.

2. *PDI*, 8/19/2003, 8/20/2003, 8/27/2003.

3. *LAT*, 7/30/2002; *Newsweek*, November 18, 2002; John Gershman, "Is Southeast Asia the Second Front?" *Foreign Affairs*, July–August 2002; Walden Bello, "A 'Second Front' in the Philippines," *The Nation*, March 18, 2002; Andrew Feickert, *U.S. Military Operations in the Global War on Terrorism: Afghanistan, Africa, the Philippines, and Colombia* (Washington, DC, 2005), http://fas.org/sgp/crs/natsec/RL32758.pdf, accessed December 15, 2008, 16, 19.

4. Dr. Mahar Mangahas, "Metro Manilans Welcome Gloria," Social Weather Stations, February 1, 2001, pinoytok@yahoogroups.com, accessed January 14, 2007.

5. *PDI*, 3/9/2001, 3/20/2001, 5/10/2001; *PS*, 4/30/2001.

6. *Joseph E. Estrada v. Aniano Desierto et al.*, G.R. Nos. 146710–15, *Joseph E. Estrada v. Gloria Macapagal-Arroyo*, G.R. No. 146738, Philippine Supreme Court, March 2, 2001; *PDI*, 4/4/2001.

7. *PDI*, 4/26/2001, 5/9/2001; Amando Doronila, *The Fall of Joseph Estrada: The Inside Story* (Pasig City, 2001), 221–22.

8. *PS*, 4/28/2001; *PDI*, 4/30/2001.

9. *PDI*, 4/28/2001, 4/29/2001, 5/8/2001; *MT*, 4/29/2001; *Today*, 4/29/2001; *PS*, 4/29/2001.

10. *PDI*, 4/30/2001, 5/1/2001, 5/9/2001; *PS*, 4/30/2001, 5/1/2001, 5/2/2001, 5/6/2001; Doronila, *The Fall of Joseph Estrada*, 227–28; Randolf S. David, "Erap: A Diary of Disenchantment," in

Amando Doronila, ed., *Between Fires: Fifteen Perspectives on the Estrada Crisis* (Pasig City, 2001), 176–77.

11. *PDI*, 5/1/2001, 5/2/2001, 5/4/2001; *PS*, 5/2/2001; Doronila, *The Fall of Joseph Estrada*, 240–41, 245–46.

12. *PDI*, 5/2/2001, 5/4/2001, 5/5/2001, 5/6/2001, 5/7/2001, 5/9/2001, 5/10/2001; *PS*, 5/2/2001, 5/10/2001; Ellen Tordesillas and Greg Hutchinson, *Hot Money, Warm Bodies: The Downfall of President Joseph Estrada* (Manila, 2001), 246–47; Gen. Leandro Mendoza, interview with the author, August 24, 2001, Camp Crame.

13. *PDI*, 5/2/2001, 5/4/2001, 5/5/2001; *PS*, 5/2/2001, 5/4/2001, 5/5/2001.

14. *PS*, 5/4/2001, 5/11/2001, 5/13/2001, 5/23/2001.

15. A year later a reputable columnist described Berroya as "close to First Gentleman Mike Arroyo and the First Family." *PDI*, 7/8/2002.

16. *PDI*, 8/8/2001.

17. *PDI*, 4/3/2001.

18. *PDI*, 1/26/2001, 2/21/2001, 2/22/2001, 2/27/2001, 3/7/2001, 3/12/2001, 3/13/2001, 3/28/2001, 3/29/2001, 3/30/2001, 4/4/2001, 4/17/2001, 4/19/2001, 4/21/2001, 4/22/2001, 4/25/2001, 5/12/2001, 5/18/2001; *PS*, 3/30/2001, 3/31/2001, 4/5/2001, 4/19/2001, 5/18/2001.

19. *PDI*, 4/12/2001, 4/18/2001, 4/22/2001, 5/30/2001, 6/5/2001, 6/8/2001, 6/22/2001, 6/23/2001, 6/24/2001, 8/3/2001, 8/4/2001, 8/8/2001, 5/19/2002, 2/12/2003; *PS*, 4/15/2001, 4/18/2001, 4/19/2001, 4/21/2001.

20. *PDI*, 6/29/2001, 6/30/2001, 7/3/2001, 7/5/2001, 7/6/2001, 7/7/2001, 7/10/2001, 7/12/2001, 7/14/2001, 7/17/2001, 7/19/2001, 7/20/2001, 7/25/2001, 8/12/2001.

21. *PDI*, 7/17/2001, 7/19/2001, 7/21/2001, 7/25/2001, 7/26/2001, 7/28/2001, 7/31/2001, 8/1/2001, 8/2/2001, 8/4/2001.

22. *PDI*, 8/5/2001, 8/6/2001, 8/7/2001, 8/8/2001, 8/10/2001, 8/11/2001, 8/12/2001; *MB*, 8/7/2001.

23. *PDI*, 8/20/2001, 8/24/2001, 6/16/2002, 8/5/2003; *PFP*, 8/25/2001, 3–6.

24. Senior Superintendent Reynaldo Berroya, interview with the author, Pasig City, August 20, 2001; *PDI*, 8/22/2001.

25. *PDI*, 7/30/2001, 8/22/2001, 8/23/2001; Senior Superintendent Reynaldo Berroya, interview with the author, Pasig City, August 20, 2001. On its Internet home page, the German company in question, Rohde and Schwarz, describes itself as "an independent group of companies specializing in electronics. . . . Company headquarters are in Munich, Germany." The same home page lists the company's Manila distributor as Rohde and Schwarz (Philippines) with offices at "PBCom Tower, 23rd Floor, Unit 2301, Ayala Avenue cor. Herrera Sts., Makati City, Philippines," http://www.rsd.de/www/dev_center.nsf/Homepage, accessed June 21, 2006.

26. *PDI*, 9/26/2001, 9/27/2001, 9/30/2001, 10/2/2001, 10/6/2001, 10/23/2001, 6/7/2002.

27. *PDI*, 10/4/2001, 10/6/2001, 11/14/2001, 11/15/2001, 11/16/2001; *Filipinas*, October 2001, 39.

28. *PDI*, 7/2/2001, 8/7/2001, 2/16/2002, 3/10/2002, 4/5/2003; *PS*, 3/30/2001, 8/25/2001.

29. *PDI*, 1/2/2002, 1/4/2002, 7/27/2003, 7/28/2003, 7/30/2003, 7/31/2003, 8/2/2003, 8/5/2003, 8/12/2003, 8/17/2003, 8/21/2003.

30. *PDI*, 2/21/2002, 5/29/2002, 4/1/2003, 4/2/2003, 4/3/2003, 4/4/2003, 4/5/2003, 4/12/2003, 6/21/2003, 8/5/2003, 8/6/2003.

31. Speech of Senator Panfilo M. Lacson (On the Points Raised in Committee Report No. 237), August 4, 2003, http://www.p1.888ph/speeches/rebuttal.htm, accessed June 6, 2006.

32. *PDI*, 8/19/2003, 8/20/2003, 8/27/2003; *Time Asia*, September 15, 2003; Inquirer News Service, May 20, 2005; Miriam Grace A. Go, "Mike's Companies," *Newsbreak*, September 15, 2003; Miriam Grace A. Go, "Ping's Coup," *Newsbreak*, September 15, 2003; Miriam Grace A. Go and Jet Damazo, "Who Is Victoria Toh?" *Newsbreak*, September 15, 2003; Miriam Grace A. Go, "Shadow President?" *Newsbreak*, November 10, 2003; Panfilo M. Lacson, "The Incredible Hulk, Chapter One: Privilege Speech on the Floor of the Senate," August 18, 2003, http://www.p1.888ph/speeches/Incredible%20Hulk.htm, accessed June 6, 2006; Panfilo M. Lacson, "The Incredible Hulk, Chapter Two: Privilege Speech on the Floor of the Senate," September 1, 2003, http://www.p1.888ph/speeches/Incredible%20Hulk%202.htm, accessed June 6, 2006; Panfilo M. Lacson, "The Incredible Hulk,

Chapter Three: Privilege Speech on the Floor of the Senate," October 14, 2003, http://www.p1.888ph/speeches/Incredible%20Hulk%203.htm, accessed June 6, 2006.

33. *PDI,* 10/8/2003, 10/9/2003, 10/11/2003, 10/14/2003, 11/15/2003, 11/16/2003; Lacson, "The Incredible Hulk, Chapter Three."

34. Concepcion Paez, "Run, Gloria, Run," *Newsbreak,* November 10, 2003; Aries C. Rufo, "It's Make or Break for Ping," *Newsbreak,* November 10, 2003.

35. *PDI,* 8/7/2001, 4/24/2003, 11/16/2003, 11/22/2003, 11/27/2003, 12/3/2003, 12/5/2003, 2/11/2004, 2/22/2004, 3/5/2004, 3/9/2004, 3/10/2004, 3/13/2004, 3/14/2004, 3/17/2004, 3/23/2004, 3/24/2004, 3/25/2004, 4/1/2004, 4/18/2004, 5/1/2004, 5/2/2004, 5/7/2004, 5/10/2004, 5/12/2004, 5/14/2004, 5/20/2004, 6/7/2004, 6/22/2004.

36. *NYT,* 9/13/2005, 10/7/2005; *International Herald Tribune,* 10/7/2005; *PS,* 9/21/2005; *United States v. Leandro Aragoncillo,* Indictment, U.S. District Court for New Jersey, 2005; *United States v. Michael Ray Aquino,* Indictment, U.S. District Court for New Jersey, 2005; News Release, U.S. Attorney's Office, District of New Jersey, Leandro Aragoncillo and Michael Ray Aquino, May 4, 2006; "Espionage/Spy Case: Leandro Aragoncillo Michael Ray Aquino," and "Quotes from Aragoncillo/Aquino Case Court Records (AP, 17 January 06)," Centre for Counterintelligence and Security Studies, Alexandria, VA, http://cicentre.com/Documents/DOC_Aragaoncillo_Quotes.html, accessed October 25, 2006; *PDI,* 1/19/2006. In a phone interview, U.S. federal prosecutor Karl Buch said his staff had collected strong evidence that Aquino passed classified information purloined from FBI data banks to Senator Lacson in Manila. Lacson, in turn, distributed these documents to opposition press and politicians, generating criticism that destabilized the Arroyo administration. Karl Buch, U.S. federal prosecutor, telephone interview with the author, Madison, WI, to Newark, NJ, March 2, 2006.

37. Inquirer News Service, 5/19/2005, 5/20/2005; *Sunstar,* 5/20/2005; *PDI,* 5/21/2005, 6/14/2005.

38. *Sunstar,* 5/26/2005; Inquirer News Service, 5/20/2005; Sheila S. Coronel, "Anak ng Jueteng," *I Report* (Manila), September 2005, 2–5; Yvonne T. Chua, "Jekyll-and-Hyde Campaign," *I Report,* September 2005, 7.

39. *PDI,* 6/1/2005, 6/8/2005, 6/9/2005, 6/25/2005; *International Herald Tribune,* 6/30/2005; *NYT,* 7/22/2005; *MT,* 8/25/2005, 1/13/2006; Sheila S. Coronel, "The Unmaking of a President," *I Report,* special edition: *The Queens' Gambits* (2005), 3–6; Sheila S. Coronel, "System under Stress," *I Report,* September 2005, 20–23; Sheila S. Coronel, "Master Operator," *I Report,* special edition: *The Queens' Gambits* (2005), 18–21; "Shame and Scandal in the Family," *I Report,* special edition: *The Queens' Gambits* (2005), 28–29; "Hello, Garci? Transcript of Three-Hour Tape," *I Report,* special edition: *The Queens' Gambits* (2005), 39–51.

40. *International Herald Tribune,* 6/30/2005; Kate McGeown, "Gloria Arroyo's Toughest Week," *BBC News,* 6/30/2005, http://news.bbc.co.uk/1/hi/world/asia-pacific/4637055.stm, accessed April 19, 2008; Coronel, "The Unmaking of a President," 3–6.

41. *MT,* 8/5/2005, 8/7/2005, 8/25/2005, 1/13/2006; *Manila Standard,* 11/8/2005; Coronel, "The Unmaking of a President," 3–6; Luz Rimban, "Despite Susan, the Opposition Is Not Quite Smelling Like Roses," *I Report,* special edition: *The Queens' Gambits* (2005), 9–11; Paul D. Hutchcroft, "The Arroyo Imbroglio in the Philippines," *Journal of Democracy* 19, no. 1 (2008): 145–46.

42. Coronel, "Anak ng Jueteng"; Chua, "Jekyll-and-Hyde Campaign," 7.

43. Social Weather Station, SWS Media Release, August 6, 2005, SWS August 2–4, NCR Telephone Survey.

44. *PDI,* 2/24/2006, 2/25/2006.

45. *PDI,* 2/25/2006, 2/28/2006, 3/2/2006, 3/3/2006.

46. *PDI,* 8/1/2007, 8/28/2007, 8/31/2007, 9/17/2007, 9/25/2007, 9/30/2007, 2/5/2008, 2/7/2008, 2/10/2008, 2/11/2008, 2/12/2008, 2/13/2008, 3/3/2008, 3/10/2008, 4/21/2008; Avigail Olarte, "The Case of the 'Missing' Broadband Contract," *The Daily PCIJ,* September 11, 2007, http://www.pcij.org/blog/?p=1958, accessed April 13, 2009.

47. *PDI,* 11/21/2008, 3/20/2009, 3/23/2009, 4/7/2009.

48. Segundo E. Romero, "The Philippines in 1997: Weathering Political and Economic Turmoil," *Asian Survey* 38, no. 2 (1998): 201; Mel C. Labrador, "The Philippines in 2001: High Drama, a

New President, and Setting the Stage for Recovery," *Asian Survey* 42, no. 1 (2002), 147–48; Lesek Buksynski, "Realism, Institutionalism, and Philippine Security," *Asian Survey* 42, no. 3 (2002): 488–90; Herbert Docena, *'At the Door of All the East': The Philippines in United States Military Strategy* (Quezon City, 2007), 3.

49. Renato Cruz de Castro, "The Revitalized Philippine-U.S. Security Relations: A Ghost from the Cold War or an Alliance for the 21st Century?" *Asian Survey* 43, no. 6 (2003): 980–85; Docena, *At the Door of All the East,* 79; Herbert Docena, "U.S. Strategy in Bangsamoro," *Foreign Policy in Focus,* September 4, 2008, http://www.fpif.org/fpifxt/5503, accessed February 5, 2009; New America Foundation, "U.S. Arms Recipients, 2006/07: East Asia and the Pacific," http://www.newamerica.net/publications, accessed February 10, 2009.

50. Michael J. Montesano, "The Philippines in 2002: Playing Politics, Facing Deficits, and Embracing Uncle Sam," *Asian Survey* 43, no. 1 (2003): 161–64; Cruz de Castro, "The Revitalized Philippine-U.S. Security Relations," 980–85; Mark Bowden, "Jihadists in Paradise," *Atlantic,* March 2007, 54–75.

51. Cruz de Castro, "The Revitalized Philippine-U.S. Security Relations," 982; *Washington Post,* 2/22/2003; Michael J. Montesano, "The Philippines in 2003: Troubles, None of Them New," *Asian Survey* 44, no. 1 (2004): 99–100.

52. White House, Office of the Press Secretary, "Fact Sheet: Announcement Related to the Visit of President Arroyo," May 19, 2003, http://www.whitehouse.gov/news/releases/2003/05/20030519-2.html, accessed February 21, 2008; White House, Office of the Press Secretary, "Joint Statement between the United States of America and the Republic of the Philippines," May 19, 2003, http://www.whitehouse.gov/news/releases/2003/05/20030519-3.html, accessed September 21, 2008.

53. Cherilyn A. Walley, "Impact of the Semipermissive Environment on Force-Protection in Philippine Engagements," *Special Warfare* 17, no. 1 (September 2004): 36–41.

54. David S. Maxwell, "Operation Enduring Freedom–Philippines: What Would Sun Tzu Say?" *Military Review,* May–June 2004, 20–23; C. H. Briscoe, "Why the Philippines? ARSOF's Expanded Mission in the War on Terror," *Special Warfare* 17, no. 1 (September 2004): 2–3.

55. Cruz de Castro, "The Revitalized Philippine-U.S. Security Relations," 985; Montesano, "The Philippines in 2003," 96–97; Temario C. Rivera, "The Philippines in 2004: New Mandate, Daunting Problems," *Asian Survey* 45, no. 1 (2005): 130.

56. *Sun Star Zamboanga,* 9/24/2008, http://www.sunstar.com.ph/static/zam/2008/09/24/news/us.troops.up.for.rotation.html, accessed October 10, 2008; *MT,* 9/19/2008, http://www.manilatimes.net/national/2008/sep/19/yehey/prov/20080919pro1.html, accessed October 10, 2008.

57. Focus on the Global South, *Unconventional Warfare* (Quezon City, 2007), 6–9; Docena, *At the Door of All the East,* 52–62.

58. *International Herald Tribune,* 2/12/2007; *Stars and Stripes,* 3/10/2007; *PDI,* 12/31/2007; Max Boot and Richard Bennet, "Treading Softly in the Philippines," *Weekly Standard* 14, no. 16 (January 5, 2009), http://www.cfr.org/publication/18079/treading_softly_in_the_philippines.html, accessed January 26, 2009.

59. Chalmers Johnson, *The Sorrows of Empire: Militarism, Secrecy, and the End of the Republic* (New York, 2004), 151–85; Chalmers Johnson, "America's Empire of Bases," TomDispatch.com, January 15, 2004, http://www.tomdispatch.com/post/1181, accessed September 12, 2007; Docena, *At the Door of All the East,* 7, 22–23, 45–51, 71, 91–106; David Shambaugh, "Containment or Engagement of China? Calculating Beijing's Responses," *International Security* 21, no. 2 (1996): 182–88; Gideon Rachman, "Containing China," *Washington Quarterly* 19, no. 1 (1996): 129–40; Robert Kagan, "What China Knows That We Don't: The Case for a New Strategy of Containment," *Weekly Standard,* January 20, 1997; Jing-dong Yuan, "Friend or Foe? The Bush Administration and U.S. China Policy in Transition," *East Asian Review* 15, no. 3 (2003): 39–64.

60. Marites Dañguilan Vitug and Glenda M. Gloria, *Under the Crescent Moon: Rebellion in Mindanao* (Quezon City, 2000), 222–24, 227, 229–30, 232; Matthew Brzezinski, "Bust and Boom," *Washington Post Magazine,* December 30, 2001; *Wall Street Journal,* 10/23/2001; Steve Randall, "Pro-Pain Pundits," *Extra!* January–February 2002, http://fair.org/extra/0201/pro-pain.html, accessed

December 22, 2002; CBS Broadcasting, *60 Minutes* (Co-Host: Mike Wallace, Executive Producer: Don Hewitt), January 20, 2002; *LAT,* 11/8/2001; Alan M. Dershowitz, *Why Terrorism Works: Understanding the Threat, Responding to the Challenge* (New Haven, 2002), 136–39; Richard A. Posner, "The Best Offense," *New Republic,* September 2, 2002, 28–31; Boot and Bennet, "Treading Softly in the Philippines"; SEN, Committee on Armed Services, *Hearing to Consider the Nominations of Admiral James G. Stavridis, USN, for Reappointment to the Grade of Admiral and to be Commander, U.S. European Command and Supreme Allied Command, Europe; Lieutenant General Douglas Fraser, USAF to be General and Commander, U.S. Southern Command; and Lieutenant General Stanley A. McChrystal, USA to be General and Commander, International Security Assistance Force and Commander, U.S. Forces Afghanistan.* June 2, 2009, 10–12, http://armed-services.senate.gov/Transcripts/2009/06%20June/09-36%20-%206-2-09.pdf, accessed July 3, 2009; *NYT,* 7/3/2009.

61. *PDI,* 9/23/2005, 9/25/2005; National Council of Churches in the Philippines, *"Let the Stones Cry Out": An Ecumenical Report on Human Rights in the Philippines and a Call to Action* (Quezon City, 2007), 45–46.

62. Amnesty International, *Philippines, Political Killings, Human Rights, and the Peace Process* (London, 2006), 6–8.

63. Jose A. Melo, *Report, Independent Commission to Address Media and Activist Killings, Created under Administrative Order No. 157 (s. 2006)* (Manila, 2007), 16, 20; National Council of Churches in the Philippines, *Let the Stones Cry Out,* 44; United Nations, Human Rights Committee, 94th Session, "Views: Communication No. 1560/2007," November 11, 2008.

64. *PDI,* 9/30/2005, 6/17/2006, 6/18/2006; National Council of Churches in the Philippines, *Let the Stones Cry Out,* 43–46.

65. *Malaya,* 12/23/2006, http://www.malaya.com.ph/dec23/metro5.htm, accessed September 20, 2008.

66. National Council of Churches in the Philippines, *Let the Stones Cry Out,* 44–46; Sheila S. Coronel, "The Philippines in 2006: Democracy and its Discontents," *Asian Survey* 47, no. 1 (January–February 2007): 179.

67. Amnesty International, *Philippines, Political Killings, Human Rights, and the Peace Process,* 18.

68. Melo, *Report, Independent Commission to Address Media and Activist Killings,* 5–6, 50.

69. Ibid., 16, 20.

70. *Sun Star,* 9/20/2006; *PDI,* 7/25/2006, 9/10/2006.

71. Amnesty International, *Philippines, Political Killings, Human Rights, and the Peace Process,* 2, 17, 21.

72. "Press Statement: Professor Philip Alston, Special Rapporteur of the United Nations Human Rights Council on Extrajudicial, Summary or Arbitrary Executions," Manila, February 21, 2007.

73. "Preliminary Note on the Visit of the Special Rapporteur on Extrajudicial, Summary or Arbitrary Executions, Philip Alston, to the Philippines (12–21 February 2007)," Human Rights Council, Fourth Session, Agenda Item 2, United Nations General Assembly, March 22, 2007.

74. *PDI,* 11/28/2007.

75. Human Rights Watch, "Scared Silent: Impunity for Extrajudicial Killings in the Philippines," June 27, 2007, http://www.hrw.org/en/reports/2007/06/27/scared-silent-0, accessed February 1, 2009.

76. Human Rights Watch, "Universal Periodic Review of the Philippines: Human Rights Watch's Submission to the Human Rights Council," April 6, 2008, http://www.hrw.org/en/news/2008/04/06/universal-periodic-review-philippines, accessed January 30, 2009; U.S. Department of State, Bureau of Democracy, Human Rights, and Labor, "Philippines: Country Reports on Human Rights Practices, 2006," March 6, 2007, http://www.state.gov/g/drl/rls/hrrpt/2006/78788.htm, accessed September 20, 2008.

77. U.S. Department of State, Bureau of Democracy, Human Rights, and Labor, "Philippines: Country Reports on Human Rights Practices, 2007," March 11, 2008, http://www.state.gov/g/drl/rls/hrrpt/2007/100535.htm, accessed October 10, 2008; Human Rights Watch, "Universal Periodic Review of the Philippines: Human Rights Watch's Submission to the Human Rights Council,"

April 6, 2008; Human Rights Watch, "Philippines: Justice Absent in Killings and 'Disappearances,'" March 25, 2008, http://s.hrw.org/en/news/2008/03/25/philippines-justice-absent-killings-and-disappearances, accessed January 30, 2009; *NYT*, 5/26/2009; *Asia Sentinel*, 5/19/2009, http://www.asiasentinel.com/index.php?option=com_content&task=view&id=1879&Itemid=196, accessed May 26, 2009.

78. *NYT*, 8/31/2007, 6/28/2008, 1/2/2009, 1/26/2009, 1/28/2009, 2/8/2009, 7/1/2009.

79. International Commission of Jurists, press release, "Leading Jurists Call for Urgent Steps to Restore Human Rights in Efforts to Counter Terrorism: Prominent Judges and Lawyers Release Findings of Three-Year Investigation," Geneva, February 16, 2009; International Commission of Jurists, *Assessing Damage, Urging Action: Report of the Eminent Jurists Panel on Terrorism, Counter-terrorism, and Human Rights* (Geneva, 2009), i, 56–88, 193–99.

Chapter 17. Crucibles of Counterinsurgency

1. Robert L. Beisner, *Twelve against Empire: The Anti-Imperialists, 1898–1900* (New York, 1968), 22–23, 28–29, 32–33, 230–35; William Graham Sumner, *War and Other Essays* (New Haven, 1911), 292, 322, 326, 331–32, 347–48; Mark Twain, "Passage from 'Outlines of History' (suppressed.) Date 9th Century," in Jim Zwick, ed., *Mark Twain's Weapons of Satire: Anti-Imperialist Writings on the Philippine-American War* (Syracuse, 1992), 78–79.

2. *NYT*, 6/28/1973; *LAT*, 6/27/1973, 6/28/1973, 7/2/1973.

3. *NYT*, 4/9/2002.

4. *NYT*, 4/9/2002, 9/10/2002; Nat Hentoff, "Rescued by Dick Armey from Big Brother," *Washington Times*, 7/29/2002; *Boston Globe*, 8/10/2002; Cynthia Crossen, "Early TIPS Corps Did More Harm Than Good in Hunt for Subversives," *Wall Street Journal*, 10/2/2002; Nat Hentoff, "The Death of Operation TIPS," *Village Voice*, 12/18/2002.

5. *NYT*, 8/1/2003, 5/17/2004, 7/27/2005.

6. *NYT*, 1/20/2002; Tim Weiner, *Legacy of Ashes: The History of the CIA* (New York, 2007), 482–83.

7. *NYT*, 12/16/2005, 12/18/2005, 12/21/2005, 12/24/2005, 1/20/2006, 6/23/2006, 4/14/2007, 6/23/2006, 4/14/2007, 6/29/2007, 8/6/2007, 8/17/2007, 8/19/2007, 11/16/2007, 12/16/2007, 6/20/2008, 4/16/2009, 6/17/2009, 6/18/2009.

8. Robert M. Mueller III, Testimony "FBI Oversight," U.S. Senate Committee on the Judiciary, May 2, 2006, http://www.fas.org/irp/congress/2006_hr/050206mueller.html, accessed April 25, 2009; *Washington Post*, 8/30/2006; *Wisconsin State Journal*, 4/20/2009; *NYT*, 6/13/2009, 7/11/2009.

9. *NYT*, 8/18/2004, 12/13/2004, 4/16/2009.

10. HR, 110th Congress, 1st Session, H.R. 1955, "Violent Radicalization and Homegrown Terrorism Prevention Act of 2007," http://www.govtrack.us/congress/billtext.xpd?bill=h110-1955, accessed August 16, 2007.

11. *CQ Politics*, April 19, 2009, http://www.cqpolitics.com/wmspage.cfm?docID=hsnews000003098436&cpage=1, accessed May 4, 2009; *CQ Politics*, April 20, 2009, http://innovation.cq.com/liveonline/54/landing, accessed May 6, 2009; *NYT*, 4/21/2009, 4/23/2009, 4/24/2009, 5/2/2009.

12. *NYT*, 7/26/2008, 2/24/2009; *Army Times*, 9/8/2008, 9/30/2008; Patti Bielling, "Top Army Leader Visits Newly Assigned Consequence Management Force," United States Northern Command, September 15, 2008, http://www.northcom.mil/news/2008/091508.html, accessed December 7, 2008; American Civil Liberties Union, "ACLU Demands Information on Military Deployment within U.S. Borders," October 21, 2008, http://www.aclu.org/safefree/general/3727prs20081021.html, accessed December 7, 2008.

13. Stuart Creighton Miller, *"Benevolent Assimilation": The American Conquest of the Philippines, 1899–1903* (New Haven, 1982), 250–52.

14. See Alfred W. McCoy, *A Question of Torture: CIA Interrogation, from the Cold War to the War on Terror* (New York, 2006), chapters 1, 4, 5, afterword; *NYT*, 11/30/2004.

15. Transcript, CNN Live Event/Special, Democratic Candidates Compassion Forum, Aired April 13, 2008, 20:00 ET, http://transcripts.cnn.com/TRANSCRIPTS/0804/13/se.01.html; accessed February 25, 2009.

16. *NYT,* 1/12/2009, 1/23/2009, 2/5/2009, 2/6/2009, 2/10/2009, 2/19/2009, 2/21/2009, 5/14/2009, 5/16/2009, 5/22/2009, 5/23/2009, 7/2/2009.

17. *PS,* 5/1/2001, 5/2/2002.

18. Amando Doronila, *The Fall of Joseph Estrada: The Inside Story* (Pasig City, 2001), 254–56.

19. Lina V. Castro, "Measuring International Migration in the Philippines (with Focus on Emigration Statistics)," in *U.N. Expert Group Meeting on Measuring International Migration December 4–7, 2006, U.N. New York* (Quezon City, 2006).

20. President George W. Bush, "Remarks by the President to the Philippine Congress," Office of the Press Secretary, The White House, October 18, 2003, http://whitehouse.gov/news/releases/2003/10/print/20031018-12.html, accessed October 21, 2004.

21. Bob Woodward, *The War Within: A Secret White House History, 2006–2008* (New York, 2008), 380; *NYT,* 11/10/2008, 3/17/2009, 4/7/2009.

22. Thomas Lobe, *United States National Security Policy and Aid to the Thailand Police* (Denver, 1977), 20–25; Daniel Fineman, *A Special Relationship: The United States and Military Government in Thailand, 1947–1958* (Honolulu, 1997), 132–35, 182–83.

23. Marvin J. Jones and Philip D. Batson, *A Brief History of USOM Support to the Thai National Police Department* (Bangkok, 1969), 2–4; Lobe, *United States National Security Policy and Aid to the Thailand Police,* 48–49, 79–87, 90–93.

24. William Shawcross, "How Tyranny Returned to Thailand," *New York Review of Books* 23, no. 20 (December 9, 1976); Lobe, *United States National Security Policy and Aid to the Thailand Police,* 117–23; Katherine A. Bowie, *Rituals of National Loyalty: An Anthropology of the State and the Village Scout Movement in Thailand* (New York, 1997), 24–32.

25. *PDI,* 11/28/2007.

26. Stein Tønnesson, "Review," *Journal of Peace Research* 29, no. 3 (1992): 356; Patrice Morlat, *La Repression Coloniale au Vietnam (1908–1940)* (Paris, 1990), 185–206; M. C. Ricklefs, *A History of Modern Indonesia since c. 1200* (Stanford, 2002), 289.

27. Francis J. Murray Jr., "Land Reform in the Philippines: An Overview," *Philippine Sociological Review* 20, nos. 1–2 (1972): 157–58; Nick Cullather, *Illusions of Influence: The Political Economy of United States–Philippines Relations, 1942–1960* (Stanford, 1994), 107, 125–27.

28. *NYT,* 1/28/2009.

Index

Illustrations are indicated by *italic* page numbers.
Abbreviations used in subheadings can be found on page *xv–xviii.*

New Perspectives in Southeast Asian Studies

From Rebellion to Riots: Collective Violence on Indonesian Borneo
Jamie S. Davidson

Amazons of the Huk Rebellion: Gender, Sex, and Revolution in the Philippines
Vina A. Lanzona

Policing America's Empire: The United States, the Philippines, and the Rise of the Surveillance State
Alfred W. McCoy

An Anarchy of Families: State and Family in the Philippines
Edited by Alfred W. McCoy

Pretext for Mass Murder: The September 30th Movement and Suharto's Coup d'État in Indonesia
John Roosa

The Social World of Batavia: Europeans and Eurasians in Colonial Indonesia, second edition
Jean Gelman Taylor

Việt Nam: Borderless Histories
Edited by Nhung Tuyet Tran and Anthony Reid

Modern Noise, Fluid Genres: Popular Music in Indonesia, 1997–2001
Jeremy Wallach